# THE SHAPING OF
# THE MODERN WORLD
## 1870-1914

# THE SHAPING OF
# THE MODERN WORLD
## 1870–1914

MAURICE BRUCE

RANDOM HOUSE   NEW YORK

BdT
7.50
10-14-69 mw
3-16-65v

# CONTENTS

Chapters V, XV and XVIII have been contributed by colleagues of the author on the Staff of the University of Sheffield; V by Dr. K. H. Francis, Lecturer in French, XV and XVIII by Dr. William Carr, Lecturer in Modern History.

# MAPS

# ACKNOWLEDGMENTS

Permission to quote copyright material from the books named is gratefully acknowledged to the following publishers:

George Allen and Unwin: M. Hentze, *Pre-Fascist Italy*; S. Maccoby, *English Radicalism, 1853–1886*; W. P. Reeves, *The Long White Cloud*.

Appleton-Century-Crofts: H. U. Faulkner, *American Political and Social History*; R. J. Sontag, *Germany and England . . . 1848–94*.

Edward Arnold: E. M. Forster, *A Passage to India*.

Brown University Press: L. W. Muncy, *The Junker in the Prussian Administration under William II*.

Cambridge University Press: R. Chaplin, *Wobbly*.

The Catholic University of America Press: A. Murphy, *The Ideology of French Imperialism*.

Chatto and Windus: Clarence Day, *Life with Father*.

Collins: S. Cloete, *Turning Wheels*.

Columbia University Press: A. J. Berlau, *The German Social Democratic Party*; S. R. Tirrell, *German Agrarian Politics after Bismarck's Fall*.

Thomas Y. Crowell Company: F. R. Dulles, *Labor in America*.

E. P. Dutton and Company: S. Gompers, *Seventy Years of Life and Labor*.

Librairie Hachette: P. Renouvin, *La Question d'extrême Orient*.

Harcourt, Brace and Company: *The Autobiography of Lincoln Steffens*.

Harper and Brothers: H. U. Faulkner, *American Economic History*.

Harvard University Press: A. J. May, *The Hapsburg Monarchy*; W. R. Murphey, *Shanghai: Key to Modern China*.

vii

Henry Holt and Company: W. Johnson, *William Allen White's America*.

Houghton Mifflin Company: M. Antin, *The Promised Land*.

Alfred A. Knopf: W. Langer, *European Alliances and Alignments*; *The Diplomacy of Imperialism*.

John Lane, The Bodley Head: S. Leacock, *Sunshine Sketches of a Little Town*.

Longmans Green and Company: A. R. M. Lower, *Colony to Nation*.

Louisiana State University Press: M. R. Dearing, *Veterans in Politics*.

McGraw Hill Book Company: A. H. Hansen, *The American Economy*.

Macmillan and Company: T. A. Bailey, *The Man in the Street*; *Robert Laird Borden: His Memoirs*; N. Chaudhuri, *Autobiography of an Unknown Indian*; D. Creighton, *John A. Macdonald: The Young Politician*; M. Florinsky, *Russia, a History and an Interpretation*; O. Lattimore, *Manchuria: Cradle of Conflict*; R. I. Lovell, *The Struggle for South Africa*; Lady Minto, *India, Minto and Morley*; G. T. Robinson, *Rural Russia under the Old Régime*; E. Thompson and G. T. Garratt, *The Rise and Fulfilment of British Rule in India*; J. P. R. Wallis, *Fitz. The story of Sir Percy Fitzpatrick*; *The Autobiography of William Allen White*.

Wm. Mullar and Sons: S. F. Wright, *Hart and the Chinese Customs*.

John Murray: W. Phillips, *Ventures in Diplomacy*.

Oxford University Press, New York: S. E. Morison and H. S. Commager, *The Growth of the American Republic*; R. L. Schuyler, *The Fall of the Old Colonial System*.

University of Pennsylvania Press: A. W. Salomone, *Italian Democracy in the Making*; E. H. Zabriskie, *American Russian Rivalry in the Far East*.

Princeton University Press: W. W. Lockwood, *The Economic Development of Japan*; T. J. Pressly, *Americans Interpret their Civil War*; R. M. Robbins, *Our Landed Heritage*.

Charles Scribner's Sons: A. Nevins, *Study in Power: John D. Rockefeller*.

Martin Secker and Warburg: R. Musil, *The Man Without Qualities*.

Yale University Press and Ryerson Press, Toronto: J. B. Brebner, *North Atlantic Triangle*.

The permission of the author is also acknowledged for quotations from N. A. Pelcovits: *Old China Hands and the Foreign Office*, and of The Public Trustee and The Society of Authors for a quotation from Bernard Shaw's *John Bull's Other Island*.

A*

# PREFACE

THE Virgilian tag chosen as a motto by the University of Sheffield, *Felix qui potuit rerum cognoscere causas*, is a particularly happy one for the student of history, for it is with the causes of things that history is especially concerned: history, in short, explains events. And it is as a contribution towards an understanding of the causes of things that this book has been written. It is not intended to serve as a textbook, presenting in convenient arrangement the factual answers to examination questions. It has been written rather in the knowledge that there are many who wish to understand the great historical movements going on around them, and who would welcome some guidance as a basis for their own reading and thought. It has been written, too, in the belief that history is above all else a story, that its record should be read as a narrative, not as a series of facts conveniently listed as causes, course and consequences.

Any work of history is inevitably an essay in selection, for although the story can be picked up in the middle it has no known beginning or end. It is the task of the historian so to sift and check and select his material as to present as accurate a picture as he can of what happened, and how and why. For us today, if we are to concentrate our attention upon any part of the historical record in the hope of finding clues to the understanding of the tumult around us, there is much to be said for beginning in the years around 1870. Why that should be so will become apparent from the chapters that follow. Eighteen-seventy does, indeed, mark something of a watershed in the affairs of the world, and with due attention to some part at least of what had gone before it is possible to trace, in all parts of the globe, a coherent and developing story to the present time.

The story is, of course, a long one, and if it is to have life and interest cannot be too seriously condensed. This first volume carries it to 1914, and omits consideration of certain regions—notably the Balkans, the Near and Middle East,

Spain and Portugal and Latin America—which can be more conveniently studied in the second volume. The story, however, is one to be *read*, not to be dipped into for dates and isolated facts. Every effort has been made to produce a text which carries the reader on, while providing him with telling detail, with contemporary quotations, with sketches of the principal personages concerned, and with references to fui ther reading from which he can check the opinions expressed and form his own conclusions. Where a quotation from another writer could particularly well illuminate an event, a scene or a character, it has, with due acknowledgment, been borrowed. In this way the indispensable contribution of other historical works, of biographers, travellers, essayists, novelists and other observers of the human scene, has been closely woven into the text. The aim has been to produce a fully integrated work which shall be both reliable and readable, and which when complete will be a fully rounded whole, and a contribution to the understanding of the modern world.

The duties of a Director of Extramural Studies are not today—if, indeed, they ever were—such as to leave untapped many resources of time and energy. The book has therefore been longer in the making than it is pleasant to contemplate, and a word of special thanks is due to the publishers for their patience and consideration. The assistance of two colleagues, Dr. William Carr and Dr. K. H. Francis, without whose contribution of three important chapters the book would still have been incomplete, is also gratefully acknowledged. At the end will be found a comparative table which it is hoped will be found useful by any student of the period, and six maps have been specially—and most admirably—drawn by Mr. M. Cutler, Chief Technician of the Department of Geography in the University of Sheffield. A number of publishers have readily given permission for the quotation of material from works of which they hold the copyright: their co-operation is acknowledged in the list that precedes this Preface. Without the resources of the London Library and the ever-ready assistance of the Library of the United States Information Service in London it would have been difficult, if not impossible, to obtain many of the books needed over a period of years for the preparation of this work, and for this help, too, appreciation is expressed.

Finally, a personal note: if the book had a dedication it would be to the three men who taught me to understand history—Sir Bernard Pares, R. W. Seton-Watson and Pieter Geyl. I hope that this first volume is not altogether unworthy of their teaching and example.

*Department of Extramural Studies*
*University of Sheffield*

# I

## THE SITUATION IN 1870

THE short period of ten months between August, 1870,
and May, 1871, despite all that has happened since, must
be regarded as one of the most fateful of modern times, for
while it marks the central point of an era of significant change
throughout the world it also brought to Europe in particular
an abrupt and violent alteration in the balance of international
forces that was destined to have far-reaching consequences.
In these few short months a great country, long the acknowledged leader of the Continent, had been overthrown and
plunged into disorder, while a new and powerful State had
thrust itself into the forefront of the European system. The
record of the past is full of colourful and dramatic episodes that
mark important stages in historical development, but few
such episodes can surpass in drama and significance the
collapse of France in the late summer of 1870 at the hands of
Prussia, and the establishment a few months later of a German
Empire, based on Prussia, which arose from the wave of
patriotic emotion in Germany that followed the defeat of the
ancient foe. Yet war had been totally unexpected in the summer
of 1870. Indeed, the experienced Under-Secretary of the
British Foreign Office, Edmund Hammond, commented in
July that he had never known "so great a lull in foreign affairs",
an observation that has become historic. Two months later the
decisive battles of a great war had already been fought, and
the French Empire of Napoleon III had collapsed with the
surrender of Napoleon himself and no less than 80,000 troops
at Sedan. Within seven months, whlle the war dragged
hopelessly on, the German Empire was proclaimed, and a new
star had arisen in Europe. Rarely can so decisive a change
have come with such sudden and unexpected force. European
history was given an abrupt and startling twist, and though
many observers recognized that new influences were at work,
none could foretell the ultimate consequences. Nevertheless,

although there was nothing inevitable about the course of events, the path is clear from the triumphs of 1870 to the disasters of 1945; from William of Prussia's assumption of the German imperial crown of the "Second Reich" at Versailles on 18th January, 1871, to the ignominious end of Adolf Hitler, Leader of the "Third Reich", in his bunker at Berlin on the last day of April, 1945. Germany, and the German struggle to find a settled position in the European system and the world, dominate, as we look back, the period of three-quarters of a century which opens with the dramatic episodes of 1870-71.

## THE WAR OF 1870 AND ITS CONSEQUENCES

The background of those episodes is a complicated one, involving political and economic considerations that must be touched on in their place. Ostensibly the Franco-Prussian war of 1870 arose out of a dynastic dispute over the crown of Spain, but at bottom the quarrel was the outcome of a clash between, on the one hand, the rising power of a new Germany, conscious of its need for unity and growing in population and industrial strength, and, on the other, the decaying power of the France of Napoleon III's "Second Empire", ill-organized, out-matched, yet resolved not to surrender its leading place in Europe. In its personal aspect the quarrel was a triumph for the Prussian Minister-President, Bismarck, against Napoleon III; a triumph for the forceful, brilliant but unscrupulous Minister, supremely confident of his country's strength and of his ability to wield that strength to advantage, against the ailing and now weak-willed Emperor, exhausted by indulgence, racked with the pain of the disease that was already killing him, but clutching, to preserve his precarious throne, at any opportunity of asserting France's leadership in the face of the new forces that were arising in Europe, and which he was vainly struggling to control. It seems now a pre-ordained triumph of numbers, organization and power, but so high stood France's reputation and the appeal of the Napoleonic legend that even the best-informed of foreign observers were astounded at the speed and certainty of the result. France was confident of an altogether different outcome, and it was the folly of the French imperial government that precipitated war. But if the enemy played into his hands it was Bismarck who held the pieces: it was he who exploited the strained situation to make war certain, it was he who took advantage of the rapid succession of victories to achieve his life's aim, a Germany united around Prussia.

The significance of Bismarck's work can hardly be exaggerated: the greatness of the man and the magnitude of his achievement are almost beyond challenge. Whatever may be thought of the ultimate outcome of the achievement, there is no denying his success, the enthusiasm he inspired in his lifetime or the power and fascination that even the most sharp-eyed of foreign observers felt in him. His success placed him among the "heroes of the nations"; he became a legend long before his death. Only Napoleon I and Lenin can be ranked with him as titans who, causing immense forces to move, have shaped the world of the present day. Yet no more than they was Bismarck a worker in a political vacuum. If, like them, he rode the storms of his day, it was because he sized up the political movements of his time, realized whither they were tending, and ensured that while they maintained their direction his should be the controlling hand. If Napoleon I dominated and shaped the French Revolution and Lenin the Russian, Bismarck gave force and direction to the long-frustrated movement for unification in Germany, a movement that had been stirred into life by the French Revolution, fired to resistance by the French invasions and frustrated since by particularism and reaction. Yet by his very success Bismarck, as will be shown, liberated forces that even he could not control. He knew the value of restraint, and never, until his last years of power, allowed success to cloud his judgment. To some of those around him, and, more significantly, to those who followed him, success and power came as a heady wine. Set as she was in the very heart of Europe, able to throw her influence and her power in almost all directions, with rapid and triumphant industrial expansion to increase her wealth and strength and with growing social problems to absorb her energies, Germany needed a steady course, needed, as Bismarck realized, a long period of peace and reconstruction until her place in the European system had been firmly established. This for a time she had. But Bismarck's achievements, his means even more than his ends, had aroused suspicion in Europe, and made of Germany an unsettling rather than a pacific influence. And those who followed him rarely had a coherent policy to offer. The results were seen in 1914, when Germany failed to repeat the lightning victories of 1870, and blundered into the tragic war of attrition that drew upon her all the fear and hatred that had been piling up since Sedan. If the Empire of 1871 was Bismarck's answer to the long-standing problem of the political organization of the German people, and the answer that gave them, or most of them, the united *Reich* for which they longed, it was by no means the final answer. And for reasons with which we shall be concerned throughout this book, that final answer is still to seek: 1945 can only be understood in the context of 1871 and of the historical forces that gave to German history the particular turn that then, under Bismarck's guidance, it took.

## "THE OTHER GERMANY"

The Germany of Bismarck's earlier years was something less of a patchwork than had been the case before the Napoleonic wars, and the Vienna Settlement of 1814 had to some extent reordered the map, but it remained a singular jumble of States, the more remarkable at a time when Italy, long equally disunited, was being drawn together into a single nation under the House of Savoy. Austria was in many respects the leading German State, but although the head of the German ruling family in Vienna, the Habsburgs, bore the title of Emperor and was regarded by most Germans as in a special sense the leading prince of Germany and the heir of the medieval Empire centred on Germany, yet the Austrian Empire contained, in addition to some six million Germans, several times as many non-German peoples. Moreover, in 1867 the Habsburg Empire, on the morrow of defeat at the hands of Prussia, had been reconstituted as a Dual Monarchy, the Empire of Austria and Kingdom of Hungary. It could no longer claim to be merely a German State, with subject peoples: it had become a partnership. Henceforth, as events were to show, its interests lay much more to the south and east than to the north and west where the new Germany lay.

Austria apart, Germany in the 'sixties consisted of some twenty-five States—four kingdoms, six grand duchies, five duchies, seven principalities and three republics—varying in size from Prussia, with its population of nearly twenty-five millions, to the tiny principality of Schaumburg-Lippe, with only 32,000 inhabitants. This variety of political organization reflected the arrested development of Germany, checked for centuries by a complex of historical forces, and while among these varied states Prussia at least ranked as one of the great powers of Europe, others were so small that at times the humorous complaint had been made that if a hat blew off in one state it was whisked over the border by the wind before its owner could catch it. Yet the variety of states provided an almost equal variety of forms of political organization, from "Free Cities" like Hamburg, Bremen and Frankfurt, with their ancient trading guilds and jealously guarded rights, to powerful kingdoms still run on almost autocratic lines. There was, in fact, throughout German life a rich diversity which, though it brought political weakness, could be appreciated in almost every branch of learning and which was reflected particularly in the cultivation of the arts. Indeed, the very lack of scope for political advancement, together with the slow rate of economic development, served to encourage Germans to develop the arts as outlets for their abilities. In almost every branch of culture Germans made contributions which placed them in the very forefront of European civilization, and led to the hope that with the unification of their country a potent force for peace would arise in Europe.

Yet on the last day of the very year of victories, 1870, the Crown Prince Frederick of Prussia, son-in-law of Queen Victoria and a man of strong liberal leanings in politics, noted with despair in his diary that already in the eyes of the world Germany had ceased to be a land of artists, thinkers and poets, for "conquerors and destroyers" had taken their place. "Bismarck has made us great and strong," he wrote, "but he has robbed us of our friends, of the sympathies of the world— and of our conscience."[1] It was a prophetic judgment, and it is certainly true that after 1870 the world's attitude to Germany was increasingly coloured not so much by appreciation of her services to culture as by other and less kindly features, and it inevitably poses the question to which there can now be no answer, whether the unification of Germany could have been achieved in any other way and without war. Bismarck's latest and most profound biographer, Erich Eyck, suggests that it could have been, and this was also the view of Prince Frederick at the time. A further note in his diary records the opinion that had unity come without war "German culture, German science and German genius must have won us respect, ɪove and honour. The insolent, brutal *Junker* (Bismarck) willed it otherwise."

Forces were actually at work, as we shall see, especially in the industrial field, that must eventually have brought German unity in some form. The credit for what was done in 1870–71 —and for the manner of its doing—is essentially Bismarck's in the first place, as Prince Frederick was careful to point out. Had Bismarck failed, the "other Germany", with its more easy-going, liberal traditions, might have exercised a greater influence on the shaping of events, though whether the Free Cities and the old, princely families possessed the political sense that was demanded by nineteenth century developments is a matter for doubt. The princes, in particular, with certain exceptions, such as the liberal rulers of Württemberg and Baden, were almost entirely ineffective in matters of politics. Few of them possessed the interests and intelligence of the German Prince, Albert of Saxe-Coburg-Gotha, who was husband of Queen Victoria and father-in-law of Frederick of Prussia. Albert was fortunate, however, in being able to exercise his gifts, and his enlightened grasp of politics, in a country in a rapid state of political evolution, where his abilities had full play. England, moreover, was a country with a strong commercial and industrial class, a country where privilege, though still strong, was losing its influence, and where no military caste existed to resist change. Germany, on the other hand, as the failure of the revolutions of 1848 had shown, lacked a middle-class sufficiently large and powerful to sweep away traditional forms of government and create conditions in which an Empire fundamentally different from Bismarck's might have emerged.

## BISMARCK AND THE LIBERALS

By the 'sixties such a middle-class was developing, especially in Prussia, and Liberal elements were increasing their influence in politics. Bismarck found it necessary to make certain concessions to them as Minister-President in Prussia from 1862, Chancellor of the North German Confederation from 1867 and Imperial Chancellor from 1871. But his success in the main objects of his ambition lay in his out-manœuvring the Liberals, in securing and maintaining political control, with the support of the King and Emperor, against their opposition, in diverting them from internal reform with the bait of national unification. To achieve unification and to keep them from power he would stoop to almost any measures. For the sake of unification they were prepared, in the event, to condone almost all that he did. Such was their unhappy dilemma that, while opposed to all that he stood for in the internal affairs of the country, they could not but approve his supreme aim, the achievement of a unified Germany; could not fail to rejoice in its fulfilment. And it was the achievement of unification that at the critical moments seemed to them, as to him, the paramount consideration.

Prince Albert held, and constantly preached to his relatives in Germany, that only liberal reforms could bring the German states and peoples together. It was to Prussia that he looked for a lead, but to a reformed and liberal Prussia, taking the lead through moral influence, and not by force. Prussians, he wrote to a German friend in the summer of 1861, after the creation of the new united Italy, "are dazzled and misled by the quite exceptional case of Frederick the Great": their country must win the moral leadership of Germany by a liberal policy, and thereby draw the other states to her, even as "the liberal principles of government in Sardinia . . . made it possible for her to count upon the feeling of the inhabitants of the rest of Italy, when the great rush came".[2] Germany's "great rush" came in 1870, when Prince Albert had been nine years dead, and it was not liberalism which gave it its impetus. Yet in that same summer of 1861 Albert had seen the dangers of the course on which Prussia was set, and had criticized, in a letter to his uncle, King Leopold of the Belgians, the Prussian govern-ment which "raises money for the augmentation of the army without the knowledge of the Chambers, and in the face of all its promises to them, and which in its heart will not listen to a word on the subject of popular rights".[3] It was not until a year after this criticism was made that Bismarck came to power, but the policy which Prince Albert had criticized was the policy which Bismarck took office to defend, and which he carried to a triumphant conclusion in 1871. It was then seen that the strength of the German Liberal movement had been over-estimated, and that insufficient allowance had been made for the appeal of the one element in Germany, the power of Prussia, which, in the hands of a political master-craftsman, who well understood what he was at, and had luck on his side, proved capable of launching the "great rush" and sweeping away at a blow the obstacles to unity.

## France and German Unification

Nor, perhaps, was it fully appreciated at the time how much the unification of Italy had owed to the help of France and Prussia in the wars of 1859 and 1866. The liberal principles of the Sardinian kingdom had done much, but they could not have expelled the Austrians from North Italy: French and Prussian victories alone had succeeded in doing that. Yet even Napoleon III, with all his devotion to the idea of a united Italy, had shrunk back in alarm on realizing what potential rivalry for France he was creating. Who, it might have been asked in 1861, could be so disinterested as to lend support to the creation of a united Germany? The rise of a new State across the Rhine could not but be a matter of concern for France. Napoleon III had claimed Nice and Savoy as the price for his aid to Italy: what compensation would he seek for the rise of an even greater rival in Germany? Bismarck in 1866 drew from him the suggestion that Belgium might be the prize, and the proposal was embodied in a draft treaty prepared by Benedetti, Napoleon's Ambassador at Berlin. This revealing document Bismarck carefully preserved, only to publish it to the world in July, 1870, as a weapon of propaganda to swing opinion against France.

That France should stand idly by while a new Germany came into existence was unthinkable, but Napoleon III was out-manœuvred in his efforts both to avert and to profit by the event. Yet even had there been nothing but good will on all sides, it would have been difficult to decide on the form which a Germany unified by agreement should take. Before 1866, when Austria was pushed aside and Prussia assumed the lead, the two States were rivals, and not until the defeat of France and the final consolidation of Prussian power in 1870–71 did Francis Joseph of Austria at last abandon all hopes of resuming that leadership of Germany which for centuries had been almost a prerogative of his House. In 1862, when Bismarck first took office, the issue was by no means certain. It had long been debated in terms of a distinction between a smaller and a larger Germany, *klein-deutsch* or *gross-deutsch*, and the distinction turned upon the position of Austria. A Great-Germany, with Austria included, would have contained within its boundaries some thirty-million non-German peoples, the Magyar, Slav and other subjects of the Habsburgs. To exclude Austria, however, would be to shut out six million Germans and the leading German dynasty. The "Frankfurt Parliament" of 1849, which had grappled with the problem of German unity in the optimistic heyday of the revolution of 1848, had indeed decided for the *klein-deutsch* solution, and had offered an imperial crown to the King of Prussia, Frederick William IV. Frederick William, however, had indignantly rejected the notion of kingship by grace of the people, and the recovery of the anti-revolutionary forces in both Prussia and Austria had put an end to the wordy debates at Frankfurt. With the conservative forces regaining their confidence and restoring their military authority, and with the King of Prussia refusing the lead that was offered to him, the movement for unification had sunk back in frustration. Sir Lewis Namier has given in his study of this abortive *Revolution of the Intellectuals* an incisive summary of one view of the results of its failure:

> The year 1848 proved in Germany that union could not be achieved through discussion and by agreement; that it could be achieved by force alone; that there were not sufficient revolutionary forces in Germany to impose it from below; and that therefore, if it was to be, it had to be imposed by the Prussian army.[4]

## "Blood and Iron"

This certainly was not the conclusion of Prince Albert and other German liberals at the time. Equally certainly, however, it was the conclusion drawn by Bismarck as from Prussia he contemptuously watched the doings of 1848 and 1849. And when in 1862 he was summoned by King William of Prussia to serve as chief Minister, and to carry through, against strong opposition, and with or without the concurrence of the Chamber, a scheme for the reorganization and strengthening of the army, in a speech which became historic he deliberately and defiantly flung this conclusion at his opponents:

> The great questions of the time are not decided by speeches and majority decisions—that was the great mistake of 1848 and 1849—but by blood and iron.

The rest of his career was a gloss on this challenging statement, which shocked opinion at the time but proved prophetic. The strength of his position lay in the fact that, appointed by his sovereign, he could not be removed, while, by a legal quibble, he could raise taxes for the army without parliamentary consent. It lay, too, in his shrewd appreciation of the popular desire for German unification, inflamed by the success of Italy, and of the price that Germans were willing to pay. He realized that, while to many Germans freedom was the aim, it was above all national freedom that was sought; freedom from particularism and narrow local interests, freedom to live in a strong and united Germany, freedom from the danger of foreign interference, which had been so tragic an influence upon Germany in the past. His personal contributions to the historic process that he led to fruition were his expulsion of Austria from Germany, and his basing of the whole edifice of the Empire of 1871 upon an unreformed Prussia. He carried through a "revolution from above", forcing the rest of Germany into the Prussian mould and imposing a new pattern on its development. His system rested upon the privileged Prussian nobility of service, the *Junker* caste, to which he himself belonged, and on which the foundations of the Prussian State had been built by the Great Elector in the seventeenth century. Yet to this antique system, still firm in its opposition to popular control in any form, Bismarck harnessed the driving force of the popular feeling for German unity. The result of his work was a striking change in the very spirit in which German political life was conducted. The contrast between the Germany into which he was born and that which he left has been neatly summed up in the epigram: *Weimar or Potsdam? Goethe or*

*Bismarck? Kant or Krupp?* and President Masaryk expressed
the same notion in a pithy phrase when he wrote, "In Beethoven
I see a German genius unspoiled by Prussia".

That Bismarck took accurate measure of his countrymen is
proved by the event. Within four years of taking office in 1862,
and by means of two wars, he achieved his first aim of making
Prussia the leading State in Germany. He did it in defiance of
strong opposition from the Prussian Chamber, which vainly
resisted his costly expansion of the army. Two years after taking
office he joined Austria in an attack on Denmark, the reasons
for which do not concern us here. Two years later, in 1866,
he tried conclusions with Austria and saw her defeated in a
campaign of only seven weeks. As a result of that defeat
Austria was excluded from Germany, and Prussia became the
head of a North German Confederation, allied with the South
German States. The effect in Prussia was exactly what Bismarck
had anticipated. His triumphs were greeted with delight, and
when elections were held he won a striking majority. When it
assembled, the new Chamber at once condoned his previous
defiance of parliamentary authority. Henceforth, although
Germany continued to possess a representative assembly,
which even at times sought ineffectually to make its influence
felt, constitutional government as Britain knows it was held in
check. Bismarck had successfully flouted the principles of
parliamentary control and little could be done to offset his
influence until the Empire he had created through a succession
of victories collapsed in military defeat in 1918. His career,
even if we consider only that part of it which ended in 1866,
is a striking commentary on the adage, "Nothing succeeds like
success". He satisfied, as did Hitler after him, certain fundamental needs of the German people at a price, not perhaps
fully appreciated, which, nevertheless, they were willing to pay,
for their primary concern was rather with national unity than
with individual freedom. "The Germans," it has been truly
observed, "did not really desert liberalism: they discovered
that they had never been liberals, as the English understood
the word."[5] A well-informed contemporary observer, the
British Commercial Attaché in Berlin, James Crowe, commented, in similar terms, on the position of the German
Liberals in 1881, ten years after the establishment of the

Empire. However much they disliked Bismarck's policy in home affairs, he wrote, the Liberals were at one with him in foreign policy. Their course was clear, however, but only "if they preferred the constitutional welfare of Germany to the glory of her position among European states".[6] It was a choice in which few British liberals would have hesitated.

The last stage of Bismarck's work of unification came in 1870–71, when out of the shattering triumphs that brought France to her knees he welded the Germanic States into a united Empire. As his successes in 1866 had overcome the opposition of the Chamber, so the victories of 1870, won against the traditional enemy, largely reconciled the other States to Prussian leadership and helped to establish an Empire in which, with her King as German Emperor, Prussia played the leading part. Above all, it made possible the elevation of the King of Prussia into German Emperor almost by right of conquest, without any suggestion of the free grant of the title by the German people. The "drop of democratic oil" that had been insisted on in 1849 as the solemn bond between ruler and people was once again rejected. Bismarck so arranged matters that the unification of Germany in an Empire under the Prussian King was settled by negotiation between the States, with the German people waiting, as it were, in an ante-room while their destiny was settled. The risk that the imperial crown might be offered by the Assembly of the North German Confederation of 1867, the *Reichstag*, was skilfully avoided: in Erich Eyck's words, "the Reichstag was compelled to be satisfied with the role of the chorus in Greek tragedy".[7] And it was the overwhelming victories of 1870 alone that made this possible. Without them the process of unification must have proceeded more cold-bloodedly: agreement would, no doubt, have been achieved in time, but more concessions would have had to be made to popular control. In the event, the rulers of Prussia, with whom the critical decisions rested, showed themselves as much opposed to popular rights in 1870 as when Prince Albert had criticized them nine years earlier. The incompetence of Napoleon III, it may be said, spelt the ruin of the hopes of German liberalism, though it was long before the Liberals realized that their aims had been triumphantly frustrated: not until the 'nineties, indeed, did this finally become clear.

## ORIGINS OF THE WAR OF 1870

The war itself, which in its very outbreak took Europe by surprise, arose out of a dynastic dispute that brought to a head a struggle for power long concealed from any but the most acute observers, and was manifestly intended by both belligerents to be a test of strength. Its origins lay, first, in the political chaos of Spain. There in 1868, the irresponsible Queen Isabella II, after a quarter of a century of inefficient rule, interrupted by no less than eighteen military interventions in political life, had been overthrown by yet another rising and forced into exile. After her flight a *Cortes* (Parliament) was summoned to determine the future form of government, and a constitutional monarchy was decided on. Isabella's family, the Bourbons, having been discredited, the first candidate considered for the vacant throne was Prince Leopold of Hohenzollern-Sigmaringen, whose elder brother, Charles, had been made ruler of Rumania in 1866. Prince Leopold was a distant relative of the King of Prussia, and his father had been Prime Minister of Prussia a few years earlier. In favouring his candidature Bismarck was probably hoping either to provoke France to war or to encircle her in readiness for some later conflict. Accordingly he urged the Spanish offer upon the reluctant Leopold, pressed the Spaniards to endorse his efforts, and even endeavoured to persuade the *Cortes* to settle the whole question hurriedly, before France could intervene. He also sought to induce King William of Prussia, as head of the Hohenzollern family, to give the affair his blessing, intending thereby to involve the honour and prestige of Prussia in the matter. The French reaction was exactly what he sought. On 6th July, 1870, the French Foreign Minister, de Gramont, announced in the Chamber of Deputies that the acceptance by Prince Leopold of the Spanish crown would imperil the interests and honour of France, and that Frenchmen would do their duty in that event "without hesitation and without weakness". In a despatch a few days later to Benedetti, the French Ambassador at Berlin, he wrote:

> If the King (of Prussia) will not advise the Prince to withdraw, well, it is war forthwith, and in a few days we are on the Rhine.

It cannot be said, therefore, that Bismarck was forcing war on an unwilling France. The French Government, confident of success even in the event of war, was taking a high tone: it was their confidence in the outcome that made the Prime Minister, Ollivier, declare when war actually broke out that France had entered it "with a light heart". Moreover, many Frenchmen were anxious to check the rise of Prussia, in which they saw a potential menace to their country's position in Europe, while not a few influential members of the circle around Napoleon III undoubtedly looked to a successful war to restore the fading prestige of the dynasty. Napoleon himself had visions of an alliance with Austria that would revenge the Austrian defeat of 1866, put Prussia in her place, and restore Germany to a condition less dangerous to French interests. On the other hand, Bismarck also had war in mind: one of his chief assistants, Lothar Bucher, later described the whole affair as "a trap for Napoleon", though this may have been no more than part of the carefully created legend of Bismarck's infallibility.

The result of the French protest against Prince Leopold's candidature was that his father withdrew it. France had won a diplomatic victory, and the Paris press, which had been clamouring for war, now exulted in the triumph: "Prussia climbs down" ran one headline.

The withdrawal of Prince Leopold was a bitter blow to Bismarck. He felt, as he records in his memoirs, that his country had suffered a great humiliation, but the French obligingly played into his hands. Napoleon III and his advisers, urged on by the hysterical agitation of the Chamber and the Paris press, rashly decided to drive home their advantage and to gain a further diplomatic success which might bolster the tottering régime almost as effectively as a successful war. Benedetti was instructed to demand from King William the assurance that Leopold's candidature would never be renewed. It was a fatal blunder. The King was perfectly civil to the Ambassador when they met at Bad Ems, but he would do no more than say that the withdrawal of Leopold had his approval; and when Benedetti, acting on his instructions from Paris, pressed for a further audience, William politely declined to see him. A telegram was then sent to Bismarck from the King, reporting these developments, and it was this telegram, after skilful editing, that became the famous "Ems Telegram", of which the Chancellor was wont to boast in his later years. The message was received by Bismarck as he was dining with the Prussian military leaders, Moltke and Roon, and he at once saw in it the opportunity for which they had all been working. In its original form the telegram ran to some two hundred words and contained an account of the King's discussions with Benedetti, together with the text of his final message, refusing to take the matter further. This Bismarck reduced by about a half, the result being that the condensed text gave the impression that the French Ambassador had insulted the King, who had thereupon broken off relations. Public opinion in Prussia was already inflamed by the French attitude, and the "Ems Telegram", in its condensed form, gave the final touch. As Bismarck wrote out the new version in readiness for the Press, Roon, realizing the effect it would have, is said to have exclaimed with relish, "Our God of old still lives and will not let us perish in disgrace".

## War and Peace

But it was the French who took the first actual steps towards war, and it was not until it had become clear that the French Government, urged on by the inflamed state of feeling in Paris, was bent on war that the Prussian armies were set in motion. The Prussian preparations, however, were at once more thorough and more advanced than those of the French, and the issue was not long in doubt. War was declared on 19th July, and the first serious fighting took place on 4th August. Within a month, to the amazement of Europe, the French armies were shattered and Napoleon himself was a prisoner. The French troops fought with their usual gallantry, but they were out-generalled, ill-led and ill-equipped. The Emperor, in such distress from his internal complaint that he had to rouge his cheeks to conceal their pallor, could do nothing to arrest the collapse. In his weakness and agony he personified only too well the dying régime that crashed to ruin when he surrendered with a great army of some 80,000 men at Sedan on 2nd September. It was the end of the "Second Empire": for the seventh time during the century France had to devise a new system of government.

The Empire had gone, but France was not yet beaten. The struggle was a hopeless one, but resistance continued until

Paris fell, after a long and bitter siege, at the end of January, 1871; the last French army, frozen and starving, crossed the frontier into Switzerland a few days later. A difficult period of negotiation followed, complicated by the necessity for establishing a new government in France and by the rising of the "Commune" in Paris, of which more will have to be said in a later chapter. Finally, a treaty of peace was signed at Frankfurt on 10th May. Under its terms France lost the province of Alsace and most of Lorraine, with a total population of some 1,600,000. In addition she had to pay a war indemnity of 4,000,000,000 francs (about £200,000,000 at the rate of exchange of those days), the largest that Europe had ever known; and to this vast sum was added the cost of the Army of Occupation that Germany maintained in north-eastern France until the indemnity itself was paid off in 1873.

## ALSACE–LORRAINE

The frontier provinces of Alsace and Lorraine, though long associated with the medieval Empire in Germany, had been seized by the French during the wars of the seventeenth and eighteenth centuries. Their absorption in 1871 into the new Germany could therefore be justified as an act of sentiment and historic revenge. More significantly, it provided the Empire with a western frontier along the Vosges, to the west of the Rhine, that was more easily defensible than the river-line itself. Nevertheless, quite apart from the sullen opposition of so many of the inhabitants, transferred without even the form of consultation, the political disadvantages outweighed the strategic gains. Alsatians, many of whom were German-speaking, might in some areas, as more recent events have shown, become reconciled to German rule, but French-speaking Lorraine was by this time far more obviously a part of France. Its loss rendered any reconciliation between the new France and the new Germany wellnigh impossible. Moreover, the very security which Germany achieved left France, of necessity, an open frontier. The proclamation by which William I's acceptance of the imperial crown was made known pointed with pride to the new boundaries "which will give to the Fatherland that security against renewed French attacks which it has lacked for centuries". In so doing they weakened France's defences and compelled her to rely to an increasing extent upon military power for security no less than for the achievement of revenge. The "vicious spiral" of rival armaments was the almost inevitable outcome. In Toynbee's graphic phrase, France and Germany were as "two flagellants who had gone into a partnership to wield the lash for one another in turn",[8] the end of which was—and perhaps still is—not yet.

## BRITISH CONCERN

The terms of the settlement as a whole shocked European opinion even as they enraged Frenchmen. British opinion, in particular, was aghast at their severity, and complained that Germany was trying to cripple France permanently. The British Government had maintained an attitude of neutrality during the war, but Queen Victoria, after the first crushing victories of the Prussians, had begged King William—her daughter's father-in-law—to be magnanimous. She received only a non-committal reply. The Prime Minister, Gladstone, with his stern sense of the necessity of upholding moral principles in politics, wished to express public disapproval of the annexation of Alsace-Lorraine, which he saw, prophetically, as "the *beginning* of a new series of European complications", but was restrained by his colleagues, who realized more clearly than he did what little effect such disapproval would have. In the end he had to content himself with writing for the *Edinburgh Review* an anonymous article in which he asked the pertinent question—*can Germany afford, and does she mean, to set herself up above European opinion?* The history of the following seventy years has given him his answer, but not even Gladstone, for all his moral power, could affect the issue at the time. London was able to offer more practical help by sending £80,000 worth of supplies to the people of Paris after the siege, but in the main the British people could only stand by helplessly while the balance of power in Europe was decisively tilted towards the east.

## THE PROCLAMATION OF THE GERMAN EMPIRE AND THE ENTRY INTO PARIS

Before peace was signed, however, two striking events had taken place that were destined to influence decisively the future course of European history. The first was the proclamation of the Prussian King as German Emperor in the great Hall of Mirrors at Versailles on 18th January, 1871; the second, the formal entry of German troops into Paris itself on 1st March. As we look back, these events, dwarfed though they have been by what has come after, stand out as symbols, expressive in themselves of the historical processes of which they were the climax, and pointing the way towards much that was to follow.

That the new German Empire should have been inaugurated in the very palace of Louis XIV, the "Sun King", under whose rule, two hundred years earlier, France had reached the apogee of her power and influence, was in itself an act of grave significance. The German Empire was founded on the defeat of France, was actually proclaimed near Paris some ten days before the siege of the great city ended, and Frenchmen did not forget it. When in June, 1919, Germany, defeated and humiliated in her turn, had to sign the treaty which brought to an end the First World War, she signed it at Versailles, in that selfsame Hall of Mirrors which had witnessed the colourful scene of January, 1871. But it was for more than defeat that France then took her revenge. Defeats could be avenged, and lost provinces reconquered. What Frenchmen did not forget was the humiliation of the peace terms, and especially the condition that in return for one fortress on France's eastern frontier, Belfort, which France would otherwise have lost, a German army should be allowed to march into Paris in triumph. With bitter reluctance the condition was accepted, and on 1st March some 30,000 German troops accordingly made a triumphal entry into Paris and camped for two days in the Champs-Elysées, around the Arc de Triomphe of Napoleon I. This march into Paris was insisted on by the German army commanders, and it was intended to do more than merely to mark the great victory that had been won. Sixty-five years earlier Napoleon I had occupied Berlin after defeating the Prussian armies at Jena, and for more than two centuries France had at times made the German States feel the weight of her military power. Now was the moment for an historic revenge. The episode was symbolic, and it was met by the Parisians symbolically. The Germans entered Paris in triumph, but were greeted by a city in mourning: the streets were silent and largely deserted, shops and restaurants were closed and black crape veiled the public monuments. Paris mourned, and France mourned in the person of Paris. 150,000 Frenchmen had died, great provinces had been torn away, and the military reputation of the era of Napoleon I had passed. France had good reason to mourn. Yet the symbolic act had a significance even greater than any that could be appreciated at the time, for the German entry into Paris, in conjunction with the proclamation of the German Empire a few weeks earlier, was itself the symbol of a new era; it marked the passing of one period of European history and the opening of another, one, moreover, in which a new and harder spirit was to be abroad. Contemporaries were uneasily aware of this, and were disturbed at the untimely gesture, a reversion, despite the exemplary behaviour of the German troops, to earlier and rougher traditions. "It makes the Fatherland no safer," commented a contemporary English newspaper, "that the Uhlans have galloped down the Champs-Elysées; it heals no wounds caused by the depredations of the old Napoleonic wars."[9]

## BISMARCK AND THE LESSONS OF THE WAR

Bismarck had not approved of the march into Paris. He had opposed it, as he saw only too clearly the bitterness that such a humiliation would cause. But he was overruled. The soldiers wished to indulge their triumph and refused to read any political significance into what seemed to them a fitting, and merely military, act, "a pure matter of business", in the words of The Times special correspondent. Further, they remembered that in 1866, after their defeat of Austria in the "Seven Weeks' War", Bismarck had refused them a victorious march into Vienna. They were determined not to be foiled again, and Bismarck's opposition was therefore disregarded. Yet his judgment was sounder than theirs. He aimed at preserving Germany's conquests by reconciling her defeated enemies. Austria he soon won over, and she became a firm friend of the new German Empire, until in the end she entered upon the humble role of a "brilliant second" to William II. With France, however, Bismarck did not succeed: from the first

B

his efforts were hampered by the memory of the sufferings and humiliations of 1871. And it was one of those who had suffered in that year, the young politician, Georges Clemenceau, who led France to her revenge in 1918.

Towards the end of his life, when he had been forced out of office by the young and ambitious William II, Bismarck strove to console himself by building up the legend that he alone had been responsible for the historic events of 1870-71. The claim is exaggerated, but it remains fundamentally true. Bismarck alone knew where he was going, and though events played into his hands he at least had the skill to turn them to his purpose: in the words of one not entirely sympathetic observer, Prince Alexander of Hesse, he "managed to force luck to go the way he wished".[10] Yet as many episodes revealed, not least among them the entry into Paris, there were limits to his influence: he had let loose forces that even he lacked the power to control. He realized that his methods were questionable, as he showed when he boasted of his unscrupulous use of the "Ems Telegram", and he once confessed that "our linen was not always of the cleanest", but evil though his means often were he had the greatness to limit his ends and to be content when he had attained them. Not for him the false appearance of strength which snatches at every advantage and knows not whither it is bound. His successors were lesser men who failed to distinguish between ends and means, who did not realize that "blood and iron" was never intended by Bismarck to be a policy in itself. It seemed easy to them to use Germany's great strength to flatter her vanity, and their own, with a series of petty "triumphs" which, in the end, led to a terrible war which no one had sought. Bismarck criticized this policy in the last year of his life, when he wrote:

> Nothing could be more strongly opposed to Germany's interest than to enter upon more or less daring and adventurous enterprises, guided merely by the desire to have a finger in every pie, to flatter the vanity of the nation, or to please the ambitions of those who rule it.

He wrote with the bitterness of one who has been excluded from power: yet he wrote truly, and his criticism of the policy of William II and his advisers is a just one.

These words of Bismarck's were written in 1897, but there

were already a few shrewd observers in 1870 who could visualize only too clearly the disastrous consequences of his great achievement. Thus, the Crown Prince Frederick, whose diary has already been quoted, entered in it on that same last day of 1870 the revealing passage:

> We must prove that the power acquired is not to beget dangers but to bring with it a blessing, the blessing of peace and civilization. But how hard it will be to combat the worship of brute force and mere outward success.

## "EUROPE . . . HAS FOUND A MASTER"

How hard it would prove to be was realized by an English observer, the brilliant diplomat, Henry Bulwer, Lord Dalling and Bulwer, whose comment on the news of the French defeats in 1870 has become historic: "Europe," he said, "has lost a mistress and found a master." It was, indeed a prophetic judgment, and the phrase neatly sums up the striking change that had come upon Europe in so sudden and unexpected a form.

France, it is true, had long been a disturbing factor in European affairs. Yet, while as recently as the tumultuous years of the Revolution and the First Empire France had striven to dominate Europe, she had done it in the name of an idea that was greater than herself, and that looked to civil gains rather than to military success for its justification. Like Britain, France has achieved her most notable and enduring successes in the field of politics, in government and in the enlargement of individual freedom. Germany, however, has lacked political growth: the paralysis which followed the exhaustion of the Thirty Years' War in the seventeenth century still checked development in Bismarck's time. The German people as a whole were unified before they were politically mature: they took little part in the process of unification except as soldiers and applauding onlookers. Germany, it might be said, was *ordered* into unity. Moreover, it was unified by Prussia, the State that was most firmly wedded to out-of-date political principles. As Ernest Barker has pointed out in a revealing comment, for France and for Britain the landmarks in history have been the stages of revolution and reform—in England the "Glorious Revolution" of 1688 and the first reform bill of 1832; in France the revolution of 1789 and the institution of the Third Republic in 1871. In Prussia, however, the decisive years have been marked by changes in army organization.[11] It was the founder of modern Prussia, Frederick William, the "Great Elector", who, to centralize and defend his scattered territories after the Thirty Years' War, deprived the nobility and middle-classes of their political rights, concentrating his resources upon a powerful army, in which, by way of compensation, the noble Junkers had the monopoly of officer rank. An army which in 1640 had numbered only some 3,000 had by the time of his death in 1688 become a well-organized force of 30,000, already a factor in European politics. It was the Great Elector who created that phenomenon, that "army with a country", which was Prussia, and which, with the social system on which it rested, endured, strengthened by his successors in the eighteenth century, to be modified in the early and middle years of the nineteenth century, but to retain its essential character under the régime established by Bismarck until the Empire collapsed in 1918. The development of the Great Elector's army under King Frederick William I of Prussia (1713–40) made possible the successes of Frederick the Great (1740–86); the changes made in the years 1807–13 contributed to the defeat of Napoleon and laid the foundations for the development of Prussia during the next half-century; the further reforms carried through by Bismarck, in the face of opposition, between 1860 and 1864 prepared the way for the triumphs of 1870, while much of Bismarck's later political manœuvring turned on the voting of army credits by the Reichstag. In 1918 it was the collapse of the army which brought down the Empire, and its indifference and neutrality in the years that followed which largely contributed to the decline of the Weimar Republic of 1919–33; while Hitler's successes followed from his re-introduction of conscription, against the ban of the Treaty of Versailles, in 1935. Even after 1918 much of the essential spirit and influence of the Great Elector's creation lingered on, less diminished, ironically enough, by the Republic than by Hitler, until with Prussia itself it was swept away in the storm that burst upon Germany from the east at the end of the Second World War. Germany is unique in recent history in the vast influence her army has exercised upon the national life. It is a damning comment upon her military leaders, and the tradition they inherited, that so few of them after 1933 would challenge even Hitler's vaulting ambitions as long as their authority and aggrandizement were assured.

## THE CONSEQUENCES OF THE GERMAN VICTORY

The rapidity of Germany's rise in 1870, and the strength and character of the Prussian tradition on which the new Empire was based, radically altered not only the balance of power in Europe but almost every notion as to how power was to be exercised. The new organization in central Europe, the pivot of the Continent, looking both east and west, over-shadowed all existing states. As recently as 1866 a British diplomat, Lord Augustus Loftus, not it is true noted for his percipience, had been of the opinion that the new Germany would be no disadvantage for Britain, "for a strong Germany would look to England for moral support and would need an alliance with a great sea-power", a comforting view that was widely shared. But the speed and thoroughness of Germany's success in 1870 showed that she had little need of moral support, while within thirty years she was herself toying with the notion of becoming a great sea-power. Much of her success was due, as the French had discovered to their cost, to the thorough application of the principles of conscription, of the "nation in arms", and this, with the harsh severity of the terms imposed on the conquered people, created new standards. National power was, everywhere but in Britain, mobilized more thoroughly. Indeed, the immediate result of the successes of 1870–71 was the reorganization of the armies of Europe, for the victories of the Prussian conscript levies over the regular troops of France had astonished most observers.

Hitherto the armies of the Powers had been in the main regular formations, with long-service soldiers. The principle of conscription had been introduced by the French Revolution, as part of the citizen's duty to the State, but it had, in practice, been largely allowed to lapse in France. The Prussian army, however, had been formed of short-term conscripts since the reforms of the War of Liberation against Napoleon I. In 1870, therefore, Prussia had the advantage of numbers over France:

in spite of her smaller population she could, and did, immediately put twice the number of troops into the field. Moreover, the training and organization of those troops were far superior to those of the French. It was generally expected, however, that the gallantry and *esprit* of the French regulars, so successful, not long since, against Russia and against Austria, would outweigh these disadvantages, and their defeat came, therefore, as something of a shock. Almost immediately the armies of most of the Powers were overhauled, and conscription was widely extended. In Austria it had already become the rule as the result of the war of 1866, and France now applied it more rigorously in her reconstituted army from 1872, while Russia adopted the principle two years later. Japan, we may note in passing, also adopted conscription in 1872: it is a point of no small significance that she should first have appeared on the international scene at this moment of German triumph. Henceforth, while it was to Britain that Japan looked for guidance in naval matters, Germany was the model for her army. Among the Great Powers Britain alone, secure in her isolation behind the barrier of the sea, could safely ignore the warning that had been sounded.

The extension of conscription began the process by which Europe gradually came to appear an armed camp, and the powers of every government were immeasurably increased by its control, through military discipline, of much of its man-power, while the sense of citizenship, and therefore of national-ism, was heightened in the individual by army service. German severity, the despair and bitterness of France, a general unsettling and uncertainty in the face of the new and still unmeasured power of Germany, and, in the background the consciousness of the forces that conscription could deploy, all tended to heighten international tension. Germany held the central position, and upon her policies the peace of Europe would inevitably depend. Her policies were in Bismarck's hands, and it is a tribute to his skill and pacific purpose during the twenty years he held office after 1870 that it was not until the 'nineties that the dangers began to be apparent. Yet, as a German historian, writing in the hour of Germany's collapse in 1945, has said, the later nineteenth century had "the effect of a mounting roar of waves tumultuously beating against one another—waves which might sometime bear down all together and bring forth untold and indescribable catastrophe"[12]—as in the end, indeed, they came near to doing.

REFERENCES

1.  *The War Diary of the Emperor Frederick III*, 1870–71, trans. A. R. Allinson, p. 241.

2.  Sir Theodore Martin: *The Life of the Prince Consort*, V, p. 345.

3.  ibid., p. 344.

4.  Sir Lewis Namier: article in *The Times Literary Supplement*, 3rd January, 1948.

5.  R. J. Sontag: *Germany and England, Background of Conflict, 1848–1894*, p. 79.

6.  *Letters from the Berlin Embassy*, ed. P. Knaplund, p. 205.

7.  *Bismarck and the German Empire*, p. 180.

8.  A. J. Toynbee: *A Study of History*, II, p. 108.

9.  *Sheffield and Rotherham Independent*, 4th March, 1871.

10.  Count E. C. Corti, *The Downfall of Three Dynasties*, p. 208.

11.  Sir E. Barker: *The Development of Public Services in Western Europe, 1660–1930*, p. 48 n.

12.  A. Weber: *Farewell to European History*, p. 68.

# II

# THE SECOND GERMAN EMPIRE, 1871–1914

THE Germany that Bismarck welded into a powerful and seemingly united nation was still in 1871 in the early stages of its development as a modern state. In fact, until that January day at Versailles there had been no Germany as a political unit; as *The Times* commented on the morrow of the proclamation of the Empire, a mere "geographical expression" had become, within only a short period of years, "a new power destined to an unexampled career". The sole link uniting the Germanic peoples in the past had been the shadowy existence of the "Holy Roman Empire", an outworn survival of early medieval times which Napoleon had swept away in 1806. The dynasty of the Habsburgs, which had for some four centuries worn the imperial crown, then abandoned its wider claims and devoted its main attention to its Austrian territories. But in so far as there had ever been a Germany it had been a Germany that included Austria, and in all the attempts made from 1806 to frame a united Germany Austria had played an important, and often a leading, part. Bismarck's creation, from which Austria had been deliberately excluded, was an entirely new State. In that fact alone lies the clue to much that has happened in Central Europe since 1871.

Yet there had been other possibilities for the combining of the German states, and there were other dynasties, some, like that of the Wittelsbachs in Bavaria, considerably older than the Hohenzollerns, which, under other circumstances, might well have worn the crown of a modern German Empire. In fact, it was only with the greatest reluctance that the King of Bavaria led the princes of Germany in inviting King William of Prussia to assume the title of German Emperor. The letter in which this was done was carefully drafted by Bismarck, and Bavaria's reluctance was overcome only under great pressure, and at the price of some concessions—together, it is said, with

26

the aid of financial inducements which were distributed throughout the Bavarian Court. Even then William, to his disgust, could call himself only "German Emperor". The title of "Emperor of Germany" would have been unacceptable to the other rulers, as it would have implied the absorption of their hereditary territories by the Hohenzollerns.

The independent attitude of the German princes, which found expression in the federal constitution which was adopted for the new Empire, was reflected in the separatism of their peoples. In many parts of Germany the enthusiasm with which the achievement of unification was greeted was tempered by the unpopularity of the Prussians, and it was long before men began to think of themselves primarily as Germans rather than as Saxons, Bavarians, or Prussians: there were still many who, while they welcomed the Empire, were apprehensive of Prussian dominance. Some had already experienced it after the war of 1866, when the kingdom of Hanover and the city of Frankfurt, with others, had suffered forcible incorporation into Prussia as the price for their support of defeated Austria. The treatment of these two states long rankled, and the Hanoverians in particular formed an irreconcilable element in German political life even after 1914. Opposition was kept alive by Bismarck's treatment of the Welf (Guelph) dynasty of Hanover, descendants of King Ernest, Duke of Cumberland and uncle of Queen Victoria, who but for her sex would have inherited Hanover with Britain. When Ernest's son, the blind King George V of Hanover, went into exile after the defeat of 1866 his considerable private fortune was confiscated by the Prussian Government, and Bismarck used the income from it for so many doubtful political purposes that these *Welfen-Fonds* were popularly known as the *Reptilien-Fonds* (reptile-funds): they played their part in the last months of 1870 in overcoming Bavarian resistance to the Empire, and some had probably passed earlier into Spanish hands during the canvassing of Prince Leopold's candidature. In later years they served Bismarck's purpose by financing press campaigns. Not until after his fall was the income restored to the Guelph family, and it was only in 1913 that Guelphs and Hohenzollerns were reconciled by the marriage of Ernest Augustus, great-grandson of King Ernest, to the Emperor William II's

B*

daughter, and his acceptance of the Dukedom of Brunswick as compensation for the abandonment of his claim to Hanover.

## PROBLEMS OF THE NEW EMPIRE

But, whatever the latent opposition, in Hanover and elsewhere, Bismarck carried to a successful conclusion in 1871 the project to which he had devoted himself less than ten years before, and carried it amid almost universal acclamation. Nevertheless, it was a new state that he had created, and, despite all the strength and seeming unity that the powerful German armies provided, it possessed, as Bismarck realized, all the political weaknesses of a new state. The immediate past had been glorious and triumphant: the "unexampled career" of which *The Times* had spoken was yet to make. Unification had been achieved, but a real unity had yet to be established, and the varied elements—political, social and economic—of the new state reconciled and co-ordinated. Moreover, the Empire had to be fitted into the European system, and the fears aroused by Prussia's military triumphs had to be calmed. Bismarck saw himself after 1871 as essentially the unifier and peacemaker, preserving the peace while the diverse elements that made up the new Germany grew together into a well-founded unity. Hence his fear of a war of revenge on the part of France, of any international complication that might overstrain the delicate structure that had been so hastily thrown together. Hence, too, his fear of any social upheaval, which made of him a stern opponent of Socialism and an advocate of social policies aimed at drawing the workers from revolutionary ideas. Germany in Bismarck's view was a "satiated" power. Having gained so much, he wished to sit tight, but his protestations that Germany had no further territorial ambitions, though sincere enough, were regarded with almost as much suspicion as Hitler's at a later date. Alsace-Lorraine, Schleswig-Holstein and Prussian Poland aroused memories too recent for the protestations to be regarded as anything but hypocritical. Any upsetting of the stability of the Empire, or of the peace of Europe, would endanger these conquests, and with them not only the prestige but the very frontiers of the *Reich*. Germany's policy had, therefore, to be a conservative one: no risks could be undertaken. It had also to be based upon military strength: the army was needed to maintain unity, to defend the frontiers and to deter aggression or wars of revenge. And with the army went the social system on which it rested. The Prussian army had created the Empire, and had created it in a Prussian image. The very strength of the Empire, as it had been established, with all the hostages that had been given to fortune, depended upon the maintenance of the Prussian system. Any other pattern for Germany seemed unthinkable. The limit of the power of the system which Bismarck had created was, as he admitted in 1870, "where we no longer have Junkers to fill our commissions in the army".[1] Hence the resistance to any attempts to alter the basis of representation in the Prussian Diet, which, while founded on a wide suffrage, preserved until 1918 a three-class system which gave a preponderance of voting strength to the propertied classes. There was a further reason for conservative policies. To the east, on Germany's very frontiers and sharing with her the spoils of unhappy Poland, lay the unmeasured power of Russia, the archetype of conservatism, which had been drawn into central Europe as recently as 1849 by the 1848 revolutions. Of this vast power on Germany's eastern flank, as of the bitter enmity of France on the west, Bismarck was for ever conscious. His nightmare was that they might combine against his creation, as, in 1914, they did. He himself went far between 1870 and 1890 to placate the Tsarist Empire and to exclude it from Central European affairs.

## ECONOMIC FORCES MAKING FOR UNIFICATION

Yet for all its conservatism and political immaturity the German Empire was undergoing sweeping developments in the years after 1871. The constitutional changes, important though they were in themselves, had their counterpart in economic developments that raised Germany in a few years to the rank of one of the leading industrial powers of the world. The political revolution that brought unification was accompanied by an industrial revolution, and, as in England at an earlier period, the character of the national life was considerably modified.

Hitherto stress has been laid on the political aspects of the creation of the German Empire. But the picture would be incomplete without a survey of the economic factors that helped to make Bismarck's achievement possible and that raised Germany, within a period of half a century, so high. Without these economic factors Bismarck's task would have been far more difficult of achievement, and it was as a result of the achievement of unity that Germany underwent the further economic changes that radically transformed its appearance and organization and put into the hands of William II an instrument of wealth and power which he proved tragically incapable of handling. Political and economic developments therefore went hand in hand, and the one cannot be understood without the other.

## THE *Zollverein*

To appreciate the part played by economic affairs in the process of unification it is necessary to look back to the establishment of the *Zollverein*, the German Customs Union set up by Prussia in 1834. The *Zollverein*, which became in the end one of the means by which Prussia established her hegemony in Germany, was never intended at first to be more than a solution of the economic problems of a Germany divided into nearly forty economically independent States. In Great Britain economic unity had been established by the Act of Union between England and Scotland in 1707, and great developments in commerce and industry had thereby been rendered possible. In France the same results had followed from the sweeping-away of old barriers after the Revolution of 1789, and in both cases political unity had preceded economic. In Germany, however, the process was reversed. Germany was partially united economically long before political unity was achieved, and the *Zollverein* foreshadowed the political and military leadership established by Prussia in 1866. Yet the events of the period from 1848 to 1870 showed that economic union was not enough, in itself, to bring political unification. Some political move was essential, and it was a tragic accident of history that placed that move in the hands of the apostles of "blood and iron".

## GERMANY'S RESOURCES

By removing internal barriers to trade and manufactures the *Zollverein* gave a tremendous impetus to economic development throughout Germany, and the thirty years that followed its establishment were years of rapid expansion. But it was not the removal of trade barriers alone that made the expansion possible. Germany possessed many advantages which ensured that development when it came would be spectacular. Her natural resources were great—and became greater still after the absorption of the Lorraine mines in 1871 —and her skilled craftsmen had long been famous: Solingen on the Rhine, for instance, had been noted for fine cutlery longer than Sheffield. Moreover, there was a considerable middle-class, well educated and with a notable cultural and scientific tradition, to take the lead in economic if not in political life. In chemical research and industrial design, particularly, Germany was far ahead of England, as an official observer reported to the British Government as early as 1840. Such conditions were, as Sir John Clapham has said, "the flower of Germany's whole economic civilization and of her intellectual qualities",[2] and given economic unity, and the example of the English industrial revolution as a stimulus, progress was bound to be rapid.

## RAILWAY DEVELOPMENT

Progress first showed itself in the improvement of communications. Germany had the advantage over England that her industrial revolution did not come until the railway age. Customs union, railways, and the factory system all arrived together, to alter fundamentally within a comparatively short period the character of German economic life and the very appearance of the country in many regions. The 'forties and 'fifties were the great period of railway construction, and before the Empire was established Germany possessed one of the finest railway systems in the world, a system, moreover, that had been largely shaped to the strategic requirements of the High Command. An excellent network of strategic railways was one of the advantages possessed by the Prussian armies over the French in 1870.

## BISMARCK'S RAILWAY POLICY

In the main the German railways were not built haphazardly, as was the case with the British system. Less private capital was available for them than in Britain, and the German States therefore played an active part both in the raising of the necessary funds and in the actual planning of the lines. Nevertheless, by the time the main railway systems were complete, in 1875, the variety of controls had produced a confused picture of rates and regulations. Bismarck saw the advantages, political, economic and strategic, to be gained from the centralization and rationalization of the whole system, which would have enhanced the authority of the imperial government and brought Germany nearer to unitary control. The resistance he encountered showed, however, that there were limits to what the critics of his policies were prepared to swallow. The Liberals in Prussia were opposed to nationalized control of so important an element in the country's economic life, and among the other States Bavaria, in particular, was determined to retain her railway system in her own hands. The Chancellor could go no further than to set up in 1873 an Imperial Railway Office to co-ordinate the working of the various lines. When, however, economic developments in the late 'seventies caused him to abandon free trade and introduce a policy of protection, the case for national control became stronger, and it was further strengthened by strategic considerations—the danger of the "war on two fronts". In view of the Bavarian attitude Bismarck did not, however, move towards direct nationalization. Instead, in 1879, the very year in which his new tariff law was introduced, he inaugurated the policy of the purchase of railway systems by the *Prussian* government which, in thirty years, put the ownership and control of nearly two-thirds of the main lines of the whole Empire in Prussia's hands. By 1909 only about one-sixteenth of the total standard mileage of German railways was privately owned: the rest belonged to the larger States, and most of it to Prussia. Once again Bismarck had shown himself a master of manœuvre.

The results of this policy were far-reaching. Its strategic consequences are obvious, and, in addition, it made the railway workers a civil branch of the army, organized and disciplined on semi-military lines. Hence the complete absence of a labour movement among them until the collapse of the Empire in 1918, in marked contrast to developments in Britain and France. In economic policy, also, State ownership and control was important. The control of railway rates became part of Germany's general economic policy, and, in view of the Empire's geographical position, played no small part in her relations with her continental neighbours. In short, the railways became one of the instruments, partly political, partly economic, of the imperial Government in its efforts to strengthen its position both at home and abroad, while inside Germany control of so large a proportion of the railway system tended to increase Prussian dominance.

## GERMANY'S POPULATION—THE MOVE TO THE TOWNS

The growth of the railway system, combined with the development of industry, caused a drift in population from the countryside to the towns. In the early part of the century Germany was a region of agricultural districts and small towns, but like the rest of western Europe it saw a rapid increase of population during the century and the development of a new urban and industrial civilization. The total population in 1810 was about twenty-five millions, and by 1910, in spite of emigration, no less than sixty-five millions. France, whose population stood at rather less than forty millions in 1910, had been overtaken and passed, with a wide margin to spare, and the change reflected the alteration in the seat of power in Europe. Not until 1904 was the increase in the German birth-rate checked, a generation later than was the case with Britain, and several generations later than in France.

This great increase in population was confined to the urban areas, owing to the steady movement of people away from the countryside. In Prussia in 1816 three-quarters of the population was classed as rural, and the proportion was still as high as seventy per cent when Bismarck first took office in 1862. At that time throughout Germany only one citizen in every three lived in a town, but development was rapid after 1870. By 1900 the urban population was greater than the rural, and in 1910, when the last imperial census was taken, the situation of the 'sixties had been reversed: almost two-thirds of the population was urban. Yet the rural population had remained stable at between twenty-five and twenty-six millions during the period, and the shortage of agricultural labour made it necessary to employ every year several hundred thousand Polish seasonal workers for the harvests. Important though agriculture still was—and the army leaders valued the peasant also as soldierly material—Germany had become a great industrial nation, and the picturesque little towns of the earlier period, relics of the Middle Ages, had given place to the manufacturing centres of today.

## EMIGRATION

But for a wealth of raw materials, especially coal and iron, this great change could not have taken place, and the rapid expansion of the population, which would have occurred in any case, would have been compelled to seek relief in emigration, as it did, for instance, in Italy. Some five million emigrants left Germany, it is true, between 1845 and 1895, most of them coming from rural areas, but millions more moved into industrial towns, and after about 1895 the stream of emigration diminished. Half a million Germans had left for the United States in the two years, 1881–82, and the corresponding figure for 1891–92 was still more than a quarter of a million, but a rapid fall followed and in the last year of the century the total was only some eighteen thousand.

But for the railways, again, it would not have been possible to develop so rapidly Germany's natural resources, in their widely separated zones, or to shift vast numbers of workers from the land to the towns. The railways, the historian Treitschke claimed, broke the economic stagnation of the country.

## "THE GERMAN EMPIRE HAS BEEN BUILT... ON COAL AND IRON"

### (I) COAL

It was on the exploitation, in the first place, of Germany's resources in coal and iron that the prosperity of the Empire was built up. As Lord Keynes argued, with characteristic vigour, in 1919 in his critical analysis of the Treaty of Versailles, *The Economic Consequences of the Peace*, "The German Empire has been built more truly on coal and iron than on blood and iron".[3] Blood and iron were needed for political advancement, but the rapid progress of the Empire after 1871 was made possible by its natural resources, and led to Germany's becoming the leading industrial nation of the Continent. In the 'forties the total coal output of Prussia, which contained most of the German deposits, had been little more than three million tons a year, less than the annual consumption of London. Most of this total was produced in the Ruhr and Roer coalfields in the west, as the great Silesian field was hardly touched until later. Yet by 1871 the German output, most of it Prussian, had reached thirty million tons, and it continued to expand rapidly until in 1913, if lignite is included, it was approaching three hundred millions. British production still held the lead, but France and Belgium, which had been far ahead of Prussia in the 'forties, were well outdistanced: the Silesian coalfield alone was producing more than the whole of France.

## (2) Iron and Steel

Developments in iron and steel output were no less striking. In the 'forties ironworks on the English model were only just being introduced, and most of the work was still done by independent craftsmen. Belgium, a pioneer of industrialization on the Continent, was producing more iron than all the members of the *Zollverein*, and the famous firm of Krupp at Essen was in its modest early stages, employing only 122 men in 1846. But the development of the railways and of the Ruhr coalfield, conveniently situated for the Rhine valley ironworks, opened the way for the new industry. Belgium was soon overtaken, and in the 'sixties German production of iron drew level with that of France, and passed it. In iron output, the basis of modern industrial civilization—and of modern war—France was beaten before she met the German armies in the field in 1870, and the acquisition of Lorraine further strengthened Germany's position. In 1875 imperial Germany produced two million tons of pig-iron, against France's million-and-a-half tons.

But Britain, with her output of between six and seven million tons, still maintained a long lead, and the story of the next thirty years is the story of Germany's industrial triumph; between 1880 and 1910 Britain also was overtaken and passed. 1910 saw the production in Germany of fourteen million tons of pig-iron, and thirteen million tons of steel, against Britain's output of ten million and seven million, respectively. Germany had become the leading producer of iron and steel in Europe, and her output was surpassed in the world only by that of the U.S.A.

How was this tremendous achievement in heavy industry made possible? A wealth of natural resources, an expanding population, and rapidly improving communications all played their part, but a great deal was owed also to government policy, and to the fact that Germany had Britain's experience to draw on. As early as 1821 the Prussian Government had founded the *Gewerbe Institut* (Institute of Trades) to spread knowledge of new industrial methods and to encourage experiment, and the Institute inevitably drew heavily on British practice. Within twenty years its work, helped by the *Zollverein*, was beginning to tell, and its pupils were setting up their own undertakings. The *Zollverein* itself proved a useful instrument. Its control of tariffs over a wide area of Germany helped to protect industry as it developed, and by its very existence it encouraged the investment of capital in that improvement of communications which did so much to stir the whole country into industrial activity.

## TARIFF POLICY

The 'fifties and 'sixties saw the *Zollverein* gradually extended, until by 1871 it included the whole of imperial Germany with the exception of the old Hansa towns of Hamburg and Bremen (which finally entered it in the 'eighties). The period was one of low tariffs, though in many quarters less from a belief in free trade than from a determination to exclude Austria, which favoured a high tariff policy, from the union. Throughout Europe the 'sixties marked the peak of the free trade era. German industry, though it had benefited from moderate tariffs, was not yet sufficiently developed to demand a home market protected from foreign competition, and the Prussian Minister of Commerce, Rudolf von Delbrück, a convinced free trader, was left a free hand by Bismarck.

## LIST AND HIS INFLUENCE

Nevertheless, a strong demand for protection had already arisen, for in 1841 had appeared Friedrich List's *National*

*System of Political Economy,* a work destined to exercise on German economic development an influence as lasting as that of Adam Smith's *Wealth of Nations* in Britain. Friedrich List (1789–1846) had grown up during the period of Napoleonic domination of Germany, and the significance of the period for Germany had made a lasting impression on him. Like many other Germans he became an ardent advocate of German freedom and unity, and in the reaction that followed the fall of Napoleon he was imprisoned, and finally exiled, for his views. He emigrated to America, but later returned to Germany and in 1840 settled at Augsburg, where his *National System* was compiled.

At a time when the rapid expansion of trade and industry seemed to justify Adam Smith's views and encourage the lowering of trade barriers, List threw his influence, in the interests of Germany, against those views and urged a system of protection for her "infant industries". How, he asked, had Britain achieved her position of economic supremacy? Not in the first place by free trade, but by the Mercantilist system of State supervision of commerce that Adam Smith had attacked. Britain had grown out of this stage and, now that her industries were well established, had most to gain by commercial freedom and a general removal of trade barriers. But Germany was in an earlier stage of development, and if German industry were to flourish it must be protected: national power, not the wealth of nations, must be the aim of statesmanship:

> Power is of more importance than wealth because a nation, by means of power, is enabled not only to open up new productive resources but to maintain itself in possession of former and of recently acquired wealth, and because the reverse of power—namely, feebleness—leads to the relinquishment of all that we possess, not of acquired wealth only, but of our powers of production, of our civilization, of our freedom, nay, even of our national independence.

Although in point of time the publication of the *National System* antedates our period by thirty years, it is true to say that its full influence was hardly felt until after the founding of the Empire in 1871. List prepared the way for much later German thought, and it was to his teaching that Germans turned in the economic depression that was to cloud the middle 'seventies. Delbrück then fell from power, and the doctrines of free trade were never again officially encouraged in Germany. But List's influence continued, and one of his greatest admirers, Eugen Dühring, as a lecturer in Economics at Berlin University from 1864 to 1874 did much to popularize his doctrines by making them the basis of his own teaching. Dühring is now remembered chiefly for the attack made on him by Marx and Engels in 1877 in their last joint work *Die Umwälzung der Wissenschaft* (The Revolution in Knowledge), better known as the *Anti-Dühring*, but he exerted a considerable influence in his own day. He was strongly anti-capitalist in his views, but his socialism was of a strictly nationalist character, and he carried further List's stress on the nation as a natural entity, urging the need for a controlled national economy and associating with it virulently anti-Jewish principles. He thus provides a link between List and Nazi ideology.

When the views of eminent and original thinkers are popularized, if they are not distorted out of recognition they are usually deprived of all qualifications and subtleties and become only a travesty of their original form. Like many others who contributed to the development of Germany in the nineteenth century, among whom in fairness Bismarck must be included, List has suffered this fate, and the shape his teaching took under Nazism would almost certainly have been repudiated by its originator. List believed in parliamentary government, and in the achievement—ultimately—of some form of international union. He regarded Protection only as a temporary measure, necessary while an industrial system was being created, and he strongly opposed its extension to agriculture. This last qualification was rejected in Germany as early as 1879, when Bismarck decided to adopt a general system of tariffs, and Nazi Germany in more recent days overlooked all but the cruder aspects of his teaching. Yet in its emphasis on the necessity for State control of economic development in the interest of power the *National System* has proved a significant pointer to modern developments, even though that control has taken forms which List himself would have opposed.

## BISMARCK'S ECONOMIC POLICY

It was not until the world economic depression which began in 1873 that Bismarck concerned himself directly with economic affairs. Then by carefully prepared stages he reversed the tendency towards a liberal economic policy and established a system of protection such has had been advocated earlier by List. The protectionist measures that were eventually passed in 1879 proved then, however, to be in many respects the economic counterpart of the political constitution of the Empire as it was established in 1871. Together the two aspects of State policy set the pattern for Germany's development up to 1918, and, indeed, up to 1945. The constitution, though to some extent federal in form, centralized the new Reich under the direction of Prussia: economic policy increased the tendency to centralization and, while creating new interests of power and wealth, gave to all classes a vested interest in the success and stability of the whole structure that was the "Second Reich".

## THE CONSTITUTION OF THE EMPIRE

The key to the political constitution was to be found in the history of the Empire's creation. The first essential, in the view not only of Bismarck, not only of Prussian militarists but of many others who were mindful of events since 1848, was that unification should rest on a stable system of power. Prussia alone had proved capable of providing the power to achieve unification, and the power of Prussia rested on its army and the social system which maintained it in traditional disciplined form. The German Empire, whatever its constitutional form, was in fact, therefore, an enlarged Prussia. The Prussian King became Emperor and his Minister-President Imperial Chancellor, and the direct and wellnigh irresponsible control of the army, which King and Minister had successfully maintained against the Prussian Diet in the 'sixties, became, in practice, the standard of the Empire also. With characteristic and cynical realism Bismarck left the Prussian system intact. He was openly scornful of the three-class suffrage but was not prepared to disturb Prussia's well-organized strength. Only a great social upheaval could have brought about a change, and of that there were no signs. Wealth and class privilege retained control in Prussia and even the Liberals acquiesced in a system which had achieved so much and which, with its war-lord as Emperor, maintained the basis of the Empire's security. Yet in the constitution of the Imperial

Parliament, the Reichstag, concessions to popular forces were made. Already the principle of universal manhood suffrage had been admitted for the Reichstag of the Confederation that had been established after 1866, though the vote was given only at the age of twenty-five. Now the principle was extended to the whole Empire. Bismarck thereby associated the German people with the political direction of the Reich, but while conceding the shadow he was careful to retain the substance. The Reichstag was required to give its consent to legislation and taxation, but army affairs and foreign policy were excluded from its influence, and it had no control over ministers, who were responsible only to the Emperor. In practice the control of taxation was limited: the effective power of the purse, on which the strength of the English House of Commons had been built, was withheld to the last. It is doubtful, therefore, whether even by 1914 the Reichstag had strengthened its position in the constitution. Ministers owed it no allegiance and it lacked even a sense of corporate unity, of duty to itself such as has dignified and strengthened the English House of Commons. The parties which composed it saw themselves as separate entities rather than as parts of a greater whole, and there was little contact between them even in the Reichstag building. Membership certainly never carried the prestige that has so long attached to the position of a M.P. in Britain. Nor, in view of the limitation of its powers, did the Reichstag attract the best talent of the country. It was, in fact, as a German Socialist critic, with pardonable exaggeration, later described it, hardly more than a fig-leaf to cover the nakedness of absolutism.

Yet the creation of the Reichstag was a recognition of the popular forces which, though foiled in 1848–49, had striven for unification, and an attempt to ensure their support for the Empire. The Bismarckian creation was, therefore, a curious blend of eighteenth-century absolutism with nineteenth-century liberalism. Bismarck was never able to ignore the Reichstag, and was careful to secure majorities for his policies, often by the most unscrupulous means. Yet real power rested with the Emperor, or with the Chancellor who was directly responsible to him. While they maintained control of Prussia and its army, while by political manœuvre they could command adequate majorities in the Reichstag to approve taxation, or could raise money by other means, the system was unshakable. Despite appearances, the imperial government was responsible to no popular control. Bismarck's own opinion of parliamentary government was probably shown in the advice he claimed to have given Napoleon III in 1867. Discussing with the French Emperor the expediency of making political concessions, Bismarck had then advised him that, as long as he kept in Paris fifty thousand picked troops on whom he could rely, "he could afford the luxury of liberal institutions". It was a revealing comment, and Bismarck might be said to have carried out his own maxim in establishing the German Empire: there was never any doubt, as was shown by their loyalty until long after defeat had become a certainty in 1918, that the conscript soldiers of the Second Reich were the "picked troops" of the Bismarckian régime.

## EMPEROR AND CHANCELLOR

To the fig-leaf of the Reichstag was added in the imperial constitution the fiction of the *Bundesrath* (Federal Council), nominally the controlling organ of the whole Empire, to which each of the States of Germany sent representatives. The Council was convened annually, and was presided over by the Chancellor: laws affecting the Empire as a whole had to be passed by it, and its consent was needed for a declaration of war. Nevertheless, although the Empire had nominally been established by the rulers of the German States, the Council's influence was slight. Despite concessions to some of the States the Empire was in practice more unitary than federal in form. Bavaria, Saxony and Württemberg retained a measure of control over their railway, postal and telegraph services and over their armed forces, while Bismarck deliberately limited the Reichstag's functions by reserving *direct* taxation to the States. The Emperor, however, controlled foreign policy, commerce and internal matters affecting the Empire as a whole, while of the fifty-eight seats in the Bundesrath Prussia held seventeen, the largest single block, and more than enough, under the terms of the constitution, to wield the veto. In effect the Bismarckian Empire was, in the words of a modern German critic, "a Napoleonic creation whose prosperity depended to a very large extent upon the personality of the ruler—the

Emperor or the Imperial Chancellor"[4] Given Germany's strength and resources the Emperor was, therefore, the most powerful ruler in the world. Under William I, who had already reigned for ten years as King of Prussia when he became Emperor, the reality of power rested largely in Bismarck's hands. William I was a man of strong but simple character and moderate ability, pacific in purpose and with a high sense of duty. Under him the growing power that lay in his control never obtruded itself upon the world. Though it could never be entirely discounted, his influence, during the first seventeen years of the Empire's existence, until his death in 1888, a few weeks before his ninety-first birthday, was largely thrown behind Bismarck's experienced handling of affairs. Within two years of his death, however, his grandson, William II, determined to make the imperial authority a reality, had rid himself of Bismarck, and was seeking to surround himself with men who would take his orders. The dichotomy between the enormous power vested in the imperial office and the ability and restraint needed to exercise it then became painfully apparent. Confident of his ability to lead William I where he wished him to go, Bismarck had created a system which demanded a succession of equally able and influential chancellors. Soon after the creation of the Empire, he had said scornfully of a meeting between the three Emperors of Germany, Austria and Russia, "How little those three Potentates really knew of the arts of peace, of the wants of their subjects, or of modern legislation."[5] Bismarck had made good the deficiency as far as William I was concerned; yet while bending the Emperor to his will, he had done nothing to render impossible a reversal of rôles, the management of a Chancellor by an Emperor who, unlike Bismarck, would owe his position not to ability but to the accident of birth. He did not, in short, foresee the second William, and it was an ironical comment on his own long tenure of power that his immediate successor, Caprivi, made it clear from the first that, like the good soldier that he was, he accepted office to take, not to give, orders.

## LIMITATIONS OF THE CONSTITUTION

In view of the peculiar strategic position occupied by Prussia it is unlikely that any more liberal conception of the government of the Empire could have been introduced in a system that was based on Prussia and largely run by Prussians. Yet the issue was a serious one, not only for Germany but for Europe. A parliament that has little control over ministers or finance becomes either ineffective or irresponsible. It cannot produce an alternative government and can indulge only in sterile criticism. Despite the existence of strong parties in the Reichstag Imperial Germany suffered through the lack of an organized and experienced Opposition, and when the Empire collapsed in 1918 there were no political figures experienced in the business of responsible government to assume control. The fault was partly Bismarck's, for the Iron Chancellor had always been intolerant of criticism, and after 1871 he insisted on treating all disagreement with his policies as tantamount to treason. Under these conditions, with the ministers in no way answerable to the Reichstag, there was no scope for the development of a "loyal Opposition" such as has been the peculiar strength of the British Constitution. A fresh start had therefore to be made in 1918, and fresh habits formed, but all under the chill handicap of defeat and national humiliation. The strength and attraction of Bismarck's system lay, until its collapse, in its success: the Weimar Republic was handicapped from the start, and the growth of Nazism reflected the hankering after the certainty and security of the Second Reich.

It is not enough to lay the blame for this state of affairs upon Bismarck. Given his principles and his background it was unlikely that he would establish any system of responsible government. Yet he needed the support of the middle classes throughout Germany if the work of unification were to endure, and that support he gained through the Reichstag. Had the Liberals, the party of the middle class, set themselves resolutely to extend their influence, the system might in time have been modified in their favour, but their patriotic enthusiasm for Bismarck's achievement led them into an uncritical support not only of Bismarck but also of his successors. Their dilemma was a painful one, for in gratefully accepting Bismarck's creation they saw no alternative but to accept his policies in their entirety, "warts and all". Some there were, ever-mindful of the hopeful days of 1848, who were not deceived: President

Heuss has described one such in sketching a portrait of his grandfather, a true "man of 'forty-eight":

> For him and his fellow thinkers the Prussian minister who won war after war was not the bringer of order, but the destroyer of the federal, perhaps republican, world of German unity which they had planned. They had no respect for militarism and remained distrustful when Prussia of all States introduced the very social reforms they were demanding.[6]

Here was the "other Germany", powerless to control events, and, though impotent, unreconciled. For the rest, many had to choose, as a British observer had noted, in words quoted earlier, between the constitutional welfare of Germany and the glory of her position among European states. To many of them it must always have seemed that in fact no freedom of choice existed at all. The name of their party, National-Liberal, was, in itself, revealing: they were national in the first, and liberal only in the second, place. They proved incapable of taking action independently of the government, and therefore made possible the follies of William II and his advisers. Bismarck had taught them to look to him, and great was his fury, when, after his fall in 1890, he found the support that had for so long been his transferred without hesitation to his successor and his imperial master.

## THE CONTROL OF THE ARMY

In the later years of William II, it is true, the Reichstag became restive under the blunders of the régime, but it lacked both the will and the means to carry its disapproval into effect, and the crisis of 1914 brought a united nation into the war. Ranks were closed in the face of the war on two fronts that Bismarck had most feared. Yet the unity then achieved was but the climax of the concern with Germany's position among the nations, which had served for so long to distract attention from the constitutional development of the Empire. This concern showed itself most notably in the debates on the armed forces, which began in 1874. Already, before the war of 1870, William and Bismarck had tried to retain in the Confederation the control of the army which they had successfully maintained in Prussia since 1862. After a serious parliamentary tussle a compromise had been reached whereby the Reichstag had agreed to fix for a period of seven years the number of men called to the colours and the money needed to maintain them. The arrangement, prolonged during the war, was due for revision in 1874. The Emperor and his military advisers would have liked a permanent agreement, which would have withdrawn the army for all time from parliamentary control. Bismarck had no desire to extend the Reichstag's influence, but he was equally reluctant to see the generals too securely seated. He therefore worked for a further compromise by which the army's strength should be voted forthwith for a period of seven years, and forced this arrangement on the National-Liberals by threatening resignation or dissolution. The National-Liberal leaders, well aware of the Chancellor's popular following, thereupon yielded, but the result was an inevitable weakening of their position and a strengthening of militarism. It showed, too, that the Reichstag could be managed by appeals, or threats of appeals, over its head to the electors whom it represented. Henceforth Bismarck and his successors were able to carry their military policy. Each renewal of the seven-year law, the *Septennat*, saw a parliamentary storm, but each eventually passed: the compromise of 1874 proved in the event a surrender not only of Liberalism but of one of the means by which responsible government might in time have been introduced, had it been possible to form an Opposition sufficiently united and resolute, sufficiently alive to the internal dangers to risk a weakening of Germany's international position. There were signs of restlessness in later years—a defeat for the government over colonial policy in 1906, and in 1913 over the high-handed action of a garrison commander in Alsace, the Zabern affair, to which reference must be made later; while in 1908 William II encountered severe criticism in the matter of the *Daily Telegraph* interview. But war came before it could be seen whether these were straws in the wind of opinion, and criticism was then smothered until the latest stages of the war. After each of the crises of 1906, 1908 and 1913 opposition sank back. More typical was the almost uncritical acceptance of the Navy Laws which established Germany's naval power and in so doing roused Britain's suspicions and thereby ensured that the Balkan conflict of 1914 would become a world war. In the words of a friendly contemporary observer:

> It is not too much to say that during the years immediately preceding the war the policy of naval expansion had drawn German parties together as nothing else had succeeded in doing since the Empire was established, and that, more than any other movement, it enlisted the nation's enthusiastic and undivided attachment.[7]

There were, it is true, special reasons for this attachment. The creation of a fleet had been one of the aims of the abortive movement for unification in 1848-49, and, while the army had behind it the traditions of the component States, a navy could be regarded with pride as a truly imperial creation. Moreover, it was the obvious hall-mark of a world power, marking Germany as the equal of long-envied Britain. Nevertheless, the ready acceptance of a defensive arm, the annual cost of which rose in little more than a dozen years before 1914 from three to twenty-two million pounds, is sufficiently remarkable.

The basis of the Empire's unity and strength, in fact, was the widespread acceptance among the German people of the need for a strong system of defence, with which they had to accept—for there was as yet no alternative—the form of government and social system, both firmly based on the Prussian model, with which Bismarck had endowed them. The tragedy was that while loyally providing the means for their security the Germans made little or no effort to control the ends of policy. Bismarck was trusted, not unjustly, to preserve the nation from war: his successors blundered into war, but not until too late did they forfeit the nation's confidence.

## BISMARCK'S POSITION

Such, then, was the system which Bismarck created and with which he chose to work. He was sure of the support of Conservatives as long as he did not touch their privileges; Liberal opposition was being diverted or worn down, and, although he had been alarmed by the outbreak of the "Commune" in Paris, he had nothing to fear at first from the German working-class movement. The Socialists held only two seats (out of a total of 382) in the elections to the Reichstag in 1871 and, though they gained ten more in 1877, Socialism was still in its early stages as a political movement. Yet, almost as soon as the Empire had been established, Bismarck plunged into a bitter political struggle, and the opponent on whom he fell was the Roman Church.

## THE *Kulturkampf* AND THE CENTRE

His opposition to Roman Catholicism was based on purely political considerations. He was determined to maintain the leadership of Protestant Prussia, and to break the power of the old federal movement, which had its political centre in Vienna and drew spiritual inspiration from Rome. In other words, he was safeguarding the victory of 1866, which had excluded Austria from the Reich, by depriving of political influence those individuals and organizations which had for long been seeking to establish a German Federation under the leadership of Roman Catholic Austria. His campaign, which lasted for seven years (1871-78), is known as the *Kulturkampf*, the "fight for civilization", for the Liberals saw it as a struggle against clerical influence in which Bismarck was assured of their support. Bismarck, however, was interested less in its ideological than in its political aspects. The Roman Catholics had organized themselves on the foundation of the Empire into a party which they called the "Centre" (*Centrum*). Its main object was to resist the centralization of the Empire, and Bismarck took so strong a view of this attempt to undo his work that to the end of his days he denounced the Centre as "an enemy to the country".

That there was danger to Bismarck's conception of the Empire in the existence of this party was clear from the election results. With 58 seats in 1871 the Centre was the second strongest party in the Reichstag (second only to the National-Liberals), but within a few years it could command, with the support of other groups—notably the oppressed Poles and the deputies from Alsace-Lorraine—some 130 votes, a third of the total number in the Reichstag, and a number proportionate to the size of the Roman Catholic population of the Empire.

The struggle began with a split in the Roman Catholic Church in Germany over the proclamation of Papal Infallibility in 1870. Many Germans resisted the new teaching of the

Church, and disciplinary measures were taken by the Roman
Catholic hierarchy. When these measures were extended to
schools, the Prussian Government ordered that all school
inspectors in Prussia should be appointed by the State, and
the struggle was then joined throughout the Empire. The
"May Laws" of 1873 aimed at placing the Church practically
under State control, and two years later the Reichstag passed
legislation enforcing civil marriage. The priesthood resisted
stubbornly and were sternly punished. Two archbishops were
imprisoned, four bishops deposed, and some fifteen hundred
parish priests expelled, while heavy fines were imposed. So
far was the campaign carried, however, that Protestants began
to be alarmed, and the civil marriage law lost Bismarck much
conservative support in Prussia. The election of a new Pope,
Leo XIII, in 1878 made a change of policy possible, and the
struggle was allowed to die down. Bismarck, pondering other
policies, and anxious now for an understanding with Austria,
agreed to come to terms: the main result for the Centre was that
it became the strongest party in the Reichstag. From 1881
until 1912, when it was overtaken by the Socialists, it held
first place, and it continued to be a powerful and influential
group under the Weimar Republic.

## THE CAMPAIGN AGAINST LIBERALS AND SOCIALISTS

Bismarck had fought the Centre with the aid of the
National-Liberals, but he had no intention of making the
alliance a permanent one. The sole aim of his political manœuvres was to win as much united support for his policies in
the country as he could, and the Reichstag was no more than a
means of ensuring that support. "As long as we are expected to
rule constitutionally," he said in 1872, "we must have a
majority in order to pursue any given policy", and in this frank
statement is to be found the explanation of much of his
complicated political manœuvring. The implied threat of
unconstitutional rule and the obvious assumption that
majorities follow from policies, rather than policies from
majorities, show how far apart were German and English ideas
of parliamentary government. Bismarck was determined to
rule, and he therefore rounded next on the Liberals in order
to make it clear to them that any hopes they had of turning to

their own advantage their association with him were doomed to failure. He could do it the more easily because the bitterness that was stirred up by the *Kulturkampf* tended to weaken Liberal support.

## ANTI-SOCIALIST LAWS

But it was not only the Liberals whom Bismarck now attacked. The number of Socialist voters had risen from 124,000 in 1871 to nearly half a million in 1877. Here was a new danger to Prussian conservative and middle-class Liberal alike, and Bismarck took advantage of two attempts on the life of the Emperor in 1878 to introduce stern anti-Socialist legislation. The attacks on the Emperor were made by anarchists, and no German Socialists were implicated, but it suited Bismarck's purpose to blur the distinction between the parties of the Left, and he raised the spectre of a German "Commune" as justification for his measures. It is significant that when he heard the news of the second attempt his immediate thought was not of the wounded Emperor, to whose service he was professedly devoted, but of the opportunity he now had of striking at his opponents, both Liberals and Socialists, by dissolving the Reichstag and conducting elections in the panic emotions of the moment. The Socialist Press was immediately suppressed and Socialist associations were disbanded. When the laws were submitted to the Reichstag they were, however, rejected, as Bismarck had anticipated. He promptly called for a dissolution, and new elections were held. Many Liberal voters, alarmed at the prospect of revolution, were stampeded into support of the Conservatives, and the new Reichstag, with the Liberals reduced to two-thirds of their former strength, duly passed the anti-Socialist laws. They were renewed regularly until Bismarck's fall in 1890, and were applied with severity. That many Liberals should have lent their support to this attempt to stifle freedom of opinion is an indication of the shallowness of their creed. As with the Centre Party, however, the result of persecution was an increase in strength. The 493,000 Socialist votes of 1877 became nearly 1,500,000 by 1890, and made the Socialists the strongest party in the country, though not yet the strongest in the Reichstag. Again Bismarck had failed.

CONFOUNDING THE LIBERALS: THE NEW TARIFF
POLICY

But with the other enemy with whom he tried his strength
he succeeded. The losses of 1878 were the first blows suffered
by the Liberals, but they were not the last. With parliamentary
government the Liberals were devoted to free trade, and during
the 'sixties and early 'seventies Bismarck had followed a free-
trade policy. But the economic crisis of 1873, which followed
on the rapid industrialization of Germany and the over-hasty
absorption of the French war indemnity, brought a change of
policy. Industry began to clamour for "protection", and at the
same time agricultural interests were affected by a succession
of poor harvests and by the flow of grain from eastern Europe.
The railways were beginning to bring grain from Hungary,
Roumania and Russia; and Germany, which had been
exporting food as late as 1865, was now importing it as her
industrial population increased. Nearly a million tons of grain
were imported from Russia in 1872 and the figure was doubled
within two years. This hit the food producers of East Germany,
whether great landowners or peasant farmers, and it gave
Bismarck the opportunity of depriving the Liberals of much of
the support they had hitherto enjoyed in the countryside among
the peasantry. In 1879 a new system of protective tariffs
was introduced. A new agrarian interest was then formed, a
combination of Conservatives and ex-Liberals, and by 1890
the tariffs had been further raised until some of them were five
times the 1880 figure. The main political result was that the
old Liberal party almost ceased to exist. The party that had
held 155 seats in the Reichstag in 1874 had fewer than fifty
in 1881. Many of the party's middle-class supporters in the
towns had been scared by the Socialist bogy, and the protectionist policy had weaned away much of its rural backing.
There was no longer any danger, therefore, of a strong movement for true parliamentary government: what had not been
won over by the achievement of unification had been converted
by tariffs and the attack on the Socialists. In addition, the
Centre, though strong, had been restrained by the agreement
made in 1879 with Austria, the first step in the close association
of the two Empires that was to drag them together to their
ruin in 1918. Bismarck's parliamentary position seemed secure.

## THE RADICALS

For a time in the 'eighties, it is true, it was threatened by the formation of a new, "progressive", Liberal party, the *Deutschfreisinnige Partei* (German Radical Party), led by such notable Liberal politicians as Eugen Richter (1838–1906) and Ludwig Bamberger (1823–99), and enjoying the sympathetic interest of the Crown Prince Frederick. The elections of 1881 gave this party the largest single group in the Reichstag, but it was outmanœuvred by Bismarck, who set to work to whittle away its strength by nationalist agitation. Circumstances, as always, played into his hands. Against the Radicals he was able to exploit first a colonial dispute with Britain in 1884–85, and then, two years later, the "war scare" of 1887. The latter proved an invaluable electioneering weapon. Russian moves in the Balkans and the Boulangist agitation in France, which Bismarck magnified into the threat of a war of revenge, enabled him to raise the cry of "the *Reich* in danger" and to stampede German electors away from the progressive parties. The elections of 1887 saw the new Radical Party reduced in strength by more than two-thirds, and although it recovered to some extent in 1890 its last effective struggle was made at the election of 1893. It was squeezed out between the more conservative elements on the one side and the growing strength of Socialism on the other. 1893, it has been said, marked the end of Liberalism in German politics. Henceforth effective opposition came only from the Centre and the Socialists. But the significance of the Radical Party's rise and decline is to be seen not only in its reflection of the fortunes of German Liberalism, but in the illustration it provides of Bismarck's brilliant and skilful but utterly unscrupulous handling of political issues. The colonial differences of 1884–85 and the international tension of 1887 were exploited for party advantage to secure the defeat of a dangerous opponent, and, in particular, to ensure that on the death of the aged William I, Frederick, his successor, might not have to hand a strong Liberal party in the Reichstag opposed to the Chancellor.

## THE CASE FOR "PROTECTION"

The causes of the new protectionist policy of 1879, which struck so shrewd a blow at the Liberals, are to be found in the changing economic conditions of the 'seventies. In 1873 Delbrück, pressing his free-trade measures to their logical conclusion, began to remove the duties on imports of iron, and fixed on 1st January, 1877, as the date for the completion of the process. Manufacturing interests, shaken by the depression, agitated in the Reichstag for protection, and Bismarck saw an opportunity for further increasing his own political following. Academic arguments for and against free trade left him unmoved, but a substantial and obedient majority in the Reichstag was a potent consideration. The iron duties were removed, temporarily, but before they went Delbrück himself had resigned, ostensibly for reasons of health, and Bismarck was free to shape his economic policy by the light of the purely political considerations which alone weighed with him.

## (1) FINANCIAL CONSIDERATIONS

There were other, and equally important, reasons for a change of policy. For one thing, the imperial Government was poor, and if it were not to rely entirely on the Reichstag for supplies—and Bismarck was determined that this should not happen—it must have independent sources of income. Direct taxes would lend themselves too readily to parliamentary control, and had, in any case, been deliberately left in the control of the States. Tariffs and indirect taxation were, therefore, the obvious sources, sources, moreover, which though obvious to the politician would not be too apparent to the taxpayer. Bismarck's interest in the tariff question rested mainly on this aspect of the case. If the Government were to be financially independent, and if it were to have, in particular, the money necessary to maintain the armed forces that were to ensure the Empire's security, the control exercised by the British Parliament through the budget must be avoided.

## (2) AGRARIAN CONSIDERATIONS

With the armed forces were bound up the interests of the landowning Prussian aristocracy, the solid basis of the Empire's strength. For these Junkers, as for the landowners of Britain, the 'seventies were a period of great difficulty. Improvements in both transport and methods of production brought a steadily increasing flow of cheap food from abroad and threatened serious agricultural depression. In Britain agriculture was left to decay, and the country became dependent on imported food-stuffs, which were easily balanced by exports of manufactured goods. But Germany's position, in Bismarck's view, was less fortunate. Strategy forbade that a land power should depend on imports for its food, and the Bismarckian conception of the Empire—dependent on Prussia, and on the Junkers who provided Prussia with military and civil leadership—insisted that, even if the new class of industrial workers paid more for their bread, the economic position of the landowners, both great and small, should be maintained. "I am an Agrarian," said Bismarck, "not because I am a member of a class, but because I see in the decline of agriculture one of the greatest dangers to our permanence as a State." Dependence on foreign food, and the decline of the landed stock, both Junker and peasant, which was needed for the army, would undermine the foundations of the Empire. Britain was secure behind her sea-wall, but, as Bülow wrote later, "the German Empire, situated in the middle of Europe and insufficiently protected by Nature on its frontiers, is and must remain a military state". Therefore agriculture had to be protected by tariffs, and Germany main-tained in her position as one of the leading food-producers of Europe. When she had established her industrial supremacy, one-third of her people still lived on the land, and although she had to yield first place to Russia in cereal output she led the way in the production of potatoes and sugar-beet, a fact which assumed a new significance after 1914, when the policy of agricultural protection seemed to have justified itself.

## (3) POLITICAL CONSIDERATIONS

Yet another factor which weighed with Bismarck was the support which the Centre Party drew from the industrial but mainly Roman Catholic Rhineland. When he decided to bring the *Kulturkampf* to a close, the industrial protection which he was contemplating was a further means of ensuring the future co-operation of the Centre. Here again Bismarck was bending economic policy to the political needs of the Empire.

## "THE AGE OF STEEL"

The change of policy coincided with technical developments in the iron and steel industry that were particularly significant for Germany. The year 1870 is usually considered as marking the opening of the "Steel Age", and though the experimental work on steel was done in Britain, and Britain herself was the pioneer in steel production, in which she easily led the world in the 'seventies, by the end of the decade her own technical improvements had opened the way for the passing of her lead to Germany and the U.S.A. In particular, the invention in 1878 by the brilliant amateur, Sidney Gilchrist Thomas (1850–85), of the "basic" process of steel manufacture, coinciding as it did with the new tariff policy, did more than anything else to bring about the spectacular doubling of German steel output in the 'eighties.

## THE GERMAN STEEL INDUSTRY

The cheap production of steel on a large scale was first made possible in England by the Bessemer process in 1856, and another process, the "open hearth" of Siemens, had followed in 1867. But it was the adaptation of the Bessemer process by Thomas, working in collaboration with his cousin, the ironworks chemist, Percy Gilchrist, that was of such importance to German ironmasters. Germany's ores, especially those in which the newly conquered territory of Lorraine was rich, had a high phosphoric content that made them unsuitable for the original Bessemer process, but the new process made it possible to remove the phosphorus and therefore to employ ores hitherto regarded as of little use. England, it may be said, was the birthplace of the processes that created the "Steel Age", but it was Germany who most obviously benefited from them, and by the end of the century, in consequence, her steel production had far outstripped that of Britain, while on the eve of the 1914 war it was some ten million tons ahead. Germany was then exporting iron and steel goods to the value of £100,000,000 a year, much of the total going to Britain, where, owing to its lower cost, it was used extensively in the shipbuilding and engineering industries. Indeed, but for the Admiralty's insistence on British steel for its ships, the British navy might well have found itself using ships that were largely "made in Germany". It is typical of the changes brought about by this industrial expansion in Germany that the Krupps works, which had employed only 122 men in 1846, already had a staff of 16,000 in 1873, and by 1913 were employing a total of nearly 70,000. Thus did the new Germany take shape.

## GERMANY'S EDUCATIONAL LEAD

Thomas and Gilchrist were educated men with a sound knowledge of chemistry, and it was this knowledge that made their invention possible. Yet in this they resembled the German manufacturer of their day far more than his English counterpart. Educational standards in Germany were then, and remained, generally higher than in England, while technical education was more thoroughly developed, and organizations like the *Gewerbe Institut* served to disseminate knowledge and maintain standards. In general there was far more awareness of the need for technical knowledge and training (it is symptomatic that a scheme for training foremen was introduced as early as 1880), and though this was due in part to a recognition of the advantages derived by Britain from her long lead, it was due no less to the high level of culture in Germany and to the emphasis placed upon education. England, so long secure in her virtual monopoly, was far slower to appreciate the importance of technical education.

## SHIPBUILDING

One of the most striking manifestations of the progress of the iron and steel industry was the growth of shipbuilding and of the German mercantile marine. At the foundation of the Empire the total tonnage of the mercantile marine was about one million, of which less than a tenth represented steam tonnage. By 1880 this steam tonnage had been doubled, but in the decade that followed it rose to 724,000, and by 1914 it had reached two millions and a half. In the last years before the war Germany was turning out 400,000 tons of merchant shipping every year, even while she was building a powerful navy. The British Empire, with a total tonnage of some eleven millions, and a maximum annual output of about two millions, still held first place, but German progress had been rapid and an industry of world-wide importance had been established. Two great steamship lines, the *Hamburg-Amerika* and the *Norddeutscher Lloyd* were making regular sailings on every major shipping route of the world, and there were many smaller lines. "For the first time since the age of steam," it has been said, "there existed a merchant navy which could compare itself with that of England without appearing ridiculous"; while, still more significantly, "in point of quality comparison was far from ridiculous".[8]

## GERMANY'S EXPORT TRADE

Merchant shipping has no purpose but to carry men and goods, and it was the increase in German exports that justified the great increase of mercantile tonnage. Between 1873 and 1913 Germany's total exports increased from £125,000,000 to £500,000,000, while the share of manufactured goods in these totals rose from £45,000,000 to £320,000,000: in short, while total exports were quadrupled, manufactures increased more than sevenfold. Englishmen saw the passing of their industrial supremacy with alarm. The British "Merchandise Marks Act" of 1887, which required all manufactured imports to be marked with their country of origin, revealed, in particular, the ubiquity of the mark "made in Germany": something more than the spirit of a good jest once caused the crew of a German liner to hang the words over the bows of their ship as she steamed into Southampton Water.

## THE CREATION OF NEW INTERESTS

Tariffs and the later development of cartels hastened this impressive development, the fruit of Germany's ability, organization and resources, and created new interests in the Reich. Industrial and commercial interests made themselves felt in politics, and with the weakening of agriculture even members of the Junker class were drawn into political activity to defend their position as landowners, a situation that developed through the "Farmers' League" of the 'nineties into the shady deals of the Hindenburg régime during the period of the Weimar Republic.

## THE NEW LIBERALISM

Bismarck did not wish, after the decline of the National-Liberals, to become too much dependent on the conservative and agricultural interests. He wanted the support of the growing industrial and commercial middle class, and he therefore encouraged in the 'eighties the formation of a new National-Liberal Party. It was Liberal only in name, for it was essentially a "big business" party, and its attitude in all constitutional matters was strictly conservative: despite the continuity of name the old Liberal Party had practically ceased to exist.

## THE NEW CONSERVATISM

There were changes also in the Conservative Party in the 'eighties. A group of Conservatives, led by the Prussian Court Chaplain, Adolf Stöcker, had come together during the *Kulturkampf*, alarmed by the attacks on religion and by Bismarck's alliance with the free-thinking Liberals. This group wished to see Liberalism curbed, and adopted a Christian-Socialist programme of social reform with the object of protecting the working man against exploitation by Liberal capitalists. Such a programme, it was hoped, would check the rising tide of Socialism, and it accorded well with the Prussian tradition of government paternalism, which had been reflected earlier in the century in the abolition of serfdom and the reform of education and local government. Stöcker therefore opposed the repressive measures which Bismarck directed against the Socialists.

The 'eighties, then, saw the phenomenon of a new "Liberal" group supporting Bismarck, with a small Conservative group opposing him. To the Chancellor himself, however, the main enemy after 1879, apart from the passing challenge of the Radicals, was Socialism. In his treatment of the Socialists Bismarck proved far less sympathetic and idealistic than Stöcker's Christian-Socialists, and the difference of outlook eventually came to a head in 1890, when William II, who had imbibed Stöcker's teaching, resisted an extension of the repressive legislation. Yet for some years Bismarck sought to win over the Socialists. He hoped to check revolutionary agitation by the stern application of the law, but at the same time he wished to attach the German workmen loyally to the Empire and thereby to complete the process of building up throughout the country a wide body of support on which the imperial Government could rest secure for years to come. With this object in view he introduced his experiments in "State Socialism", and thereby unwittingly prepared the way for much social legislation in other countries.

## "STATE SOCIALISM"

Bismarck had little sympathy with the desire of the German working man to improve his conditions of life, and none at all with his political aspirations, but he wanted the working classes to be loyal to the Empire and he was fully alive to the advantages to be gained from making them more contented with their lot and grateful to the system which protected them. He hoped, in short, to buy off their support of the Socialists, and to give them a "vested interest" in the Empire. The motive was clearly revealed in the speech he made to the Reichstag when introducing an Accident Insurance Bill in 1884:

> The whole matter centres in the question, 'Is it the duty of the State, or is it not, to provide for its helpless citizens?' I maintain that it is its duty. . . . There are purposes which only the State as a whole can fulfil. . . . To these belong the help of the necessitous and the removal of those just complaints which provide Social Democracy with really effective material for agitation. This is a duty of the State, a duty which the State cannot permanently disregard.

That he did not look at the issue from the point of view of the working man—he can hardly have been expected, in any case, to do that—is clear from a passage in his Memoirs:

> I do not believe that the worker at the bottom of his heart is grateful to those who forbid him to earn money on such days and at such times as he chooses.

Yet the laws he passed made Germany in many respects a pioneer in social legislation. Compulsory insurance against sickness was introduced in 1883, accident insurance in 1884, and, five years later, old age pensions insurance, based on contributions from both employer and workman and payable at seventy.

This social legislation was, as Bismarck undoubtedly intended, a final blow to the Liberals, who were opposed to any interference by the State with economic and individual freedom. At the same time it won him support from the

Centre, which had long been advocating an extension of social services: in particular it gained him the support of the Roman Catholic trade unions. Bismarck knew what he was about when he asked the Reichstag "to heal social evils by means of legislation based on the moral foundation of Christianity".

Nor were the Conservatives overlooked. The Stöcker group remained dissatisfied, but Bismarck's emphasis on the State's duty even to its humblest citizen appealed to the Prussian tradition of government paternalism. The recognition of the supreme power and duty of the State won much conservative support. Yet the legislation, be it noted, did no more than establish an elaborate system of insurance. Bismarck would not interfere between master and man, and there was, therefore, no such thorough system of factory inspection and regulation as was being built up in Britain. Nor was there any unemployment insurance (that did not come until 1927). Nothing was done, that is to say, to upset the Conservative doctrine that an employer, whether on the land or in the factory, should be "master in his own house".

## THE SOCIALISTS AND THE EMPIRE

In its main object, that of creating a "vested interest" in the Empire, Bismarck's social legislation achieved a measure of success. The Socialists, well aware of its implications, long opposed it, and as the membership of their party continued to grow, it speedily became clear that social reform would not compensate the working classes for their lack of political influence. Nevertheless, a change took place in the attitude of the Socialists themselves to the Empire. Hitherto they had opposed its very existence, but by the end of the century many, especially among the younger leaders, had come to accept it and were seeking political control: "revisionism" rather than revolution was their aim. One cause of the change was the general popularity of the insurance legislation, and by the early years of the twentieth century many Socialists had come to regard that legislation as "foundation walls" on which even the structure they desired might be built. The mass of the German people, in fact, came to acquiesce, as Bismarck had intended that they should, in the system that so vitally affected their lives. As an historian of Social Democracy has said, in a gloss on a famous phrase by Marx, "Bismarck had succeeded in giving the workers something more valuable to lose by revolution than merely their chains."[9] The alteration in their outlook is revealed in a striking episode recounted by Sir Valentine Chirol, then Foreign Editor of *The Times*, in his memoirs. About the turn of the century he met August Bebel, the German Socialist leader, in Berlin, and together they watched on one occasion a party of soldiers marching in the street. Bebel remarked that the soldiers were all men he knew personally, men who had voted Socialist in the elections, yet he was sure that they would shoot him without hesitation if ordered to do so. "The whole nation," he added in a significant comment, "is still drunk with military glory, and there is nothing to be done until some great disaster has sobered it."[10] It is no matter for wonder, therefore, that on the outbreak of war in 1914 the 110 Socialists in the Reichstag not only voted the war credits, but allowed the Government, sheltering behind the Kaiser's famous slogan "No more parties, Germans all!" to continue unrestrained control of national affairs at the very moment when a broader association of people with Government was more than ever necessary. The wartime *Burgfrieden* silenced criticism, and, until the prospect of rapid victory had faded, guaranteed to the Government the solid backing of the nation whatever the policies it might pursue. There was not even, until 1917, a demand for a statement of war aims.

## BISMARCK'S ACHIEVEMENT, 1871–90

By his own standards, though he had many doubts, Bismarck had done his work well. He left many irreconcilable elements in a state of uneasy balance, but he had successfully resisted all attempts to place the Government under parliamentary control, and he had not been unsuccessful in reconciling the various political groupings to the existing order of things. The growing strength of Socialism filled him with alarm, and caused him, before he fell from power, to contemplate seriously a re-founding of the Empire on more autocratic lines. Apart from this internal stress, however, he always maintained that only in war would there be danger of a crack in the structure he had so laboriously built up. The Empire needed time and peace in which to establish itself firmly and create new loyalties. Peace was the best guarantee of the stability of the régime.

The German people learnt the lesson only too well. When Bismarck fell in 1890 the obedience that he had extorted was immediately rendered to William II and his nominees. "You are overthrown, Prince, with the power you created," Lord Rosebery told the fallen Chancellor, "Hoist with your own petard, as Shakespeare says."[11] And Bismarck could only reply "Quite true". Under William II this passivity, which Bismarck now belatedly deplored, continued to restrain serious opposition and rendered impossible the establishment of parliamentary control of the Government. Moreover, material progress was too rapid in the Empire for serious dissatisfaction to make itself felt.

## THE POLES IN PRUSSIA

There remains to be considered yet another aspect of Bismarck's home policy, his treatment of the Poles, who formed one of Prussia's most intractable problems. To Bismarck the Polish question was closely bound up with Prussia's security, and he therefore approached it with the ruthlessness which always marked his policy when security was at stake. "Beat down the Poles," he wrote once in a letter to his sister, "there is nothing to be done but to exterminate them. It is not the fault of the wolf that God has made him what he is, yet everyone seeks to destroy him."

The struggle with the Poles for the control of the Baltic coast-line, which flared up again in 1939, has been for centuries a consistent feature of Prussian politics. It is one aspect of the *Drang nach Osten*, the "Drive to the East", which carried German settlers across the Elbe, along the Baltic coast, where the "colony" of East Prussia was established and even into Lithuania and the other Baltic States (whence came the "Baltic barons" of German descent who for several centuries provided members of the ruling caste in Russia). Prussia is itself a frontier region of Germany: the basis of the Hohenzollern Kingdom was originally the *Mark* (frontier region: "March" in English) of Brandenburg, which, after three centuries of border warfare, was established in the twelfth century as a bulwark for the Germans against the Slavs of the east. From Brandenburg the tide of conquest and colonization swept eastwards as the Germans gained strength, but the memory of earlier struggles has never faded from their minds. Moreover, they were an outpost of Christianity, for the Slavs were heathen, and the safeguarding and extension of the frontiers of Germany was both a religious and a political duty. "The country is excellent, rich in meat, honey, poultry and flour," ran a proclamation of the year 1108, "therefore come hither, you Saxons and Franconians, men from Lorraine and from Flanders, for both can be obtained here: deeds for the salvation of your souls and settlement on best land."[12] "God has created the Germans," was the Nazi version some 830 years later, "to carry the light into the wilderness." It was a traditional notion, based on the mission of crusade and conquest that the German settlers in the East carried out in the Middle Ages.

But the frontiers were never secure. Hence Prussia's later tradition of militarism, with all the consequences which that entailed for Prussia itself, for Germany, and for the world. Between Prussians and Slavs—and particularly the Poles—there was for centuries a struggle for existence, and the fear of the Slav has remained as a potent factor in German life. Fear is mingled with a contempt for the lower standards of life of the Slav peoples, which is itself a legacy from the Baltic crusades. When Hitler spoke of the "Slav masses" the venom engendered by centuries of conflict was evident in his voice, and his references to the Russians after 1941 as "swamp dwellers" with whom the German soldier could not contend on equal terms reflected the fear aroused in Germany by the increase in power and population of the greatest of the Slav peoples. Yet in both fear and contempt he was but echoing the thousand-year-old sentiments of Germans towards their dangerous neighbours to the East.

Russia appeared late on the scene: the main conflict for a long period was between Prussia and Poland, then the leading Slav state. But Poland was crushed at the end of the eighteenth century, her territory being divided between Prussia, Austria, and Russia. The aim of Prussian policy from that time was to keep the Poles in subjection, and thereby to stabilize the eastern frontiers. By the time of the foundation of the Empire in 1871

Polish national feeling was beginning to revive, and the Polish population of the eastern provinces was increasing much more rapidly than the German. Bismarck decided on stern measures, the old policy of colonization. In 1886 an Expropriation Bill was passed by the Prussian Chamber, authorizing the Government to buy the estates of Polish landowners and lease them to German farmers, who were to be pledged to marry only German wives. By 1914 more than £50,000,000 had been spent in this way, with results that can only be called minute in proportion to the effort expended. The Poles used the purchase money in many cases to buy other estates—often from Germans—which they sub-let to Polish peasants in order to preserve the balance of the populations. They also established a co-operative land bank to help Polish peasants to buy land. In short, they frustrated Bismarck's scheme by every means in their power. The first ten years of the scheme saw as many new Polish settlements created as German, and, when the last census of the Empire was taken in 1910, in the region which after 1918 became the "Corridor" (the Polish province of *Pomorze*, which Hitler claimed in 1939) the Poles, with their higher birth-rate, still outnumbered the Germans, in spite of all the Government's efforts, by 550,000 to 430,000.

Bismarck did not stop at land purchase. He strove hard to stamp out Polish nationalism and to inculcate a spirit of devotion to Prussia. Among the methods adopted were the prohibition of Polish speech in all official matters, and the flogging of Polish schoolchildren who refused to say the Lord's Prayer in German—typical measures which failed, as they always do, to break the spirit of a people resolved to maintain their national character intact. Bismarck failed, as others had failed before him, and as the Nazis were to fail after him. "You will never realize your ambitions," he told the Poles, "except as the result of a war, disastrous to Germany, when Prussia has been smashed to pieces." He had intended to suggest the impossible, but the remark proved prophetic.

The policy of coercion and expropriation was not abandoned after Bismarck's fall. It was even intensified from 1906, when investigations showed how little had been achieved: it was then discovered that while 90,000 German farmers had been settled on Polish land, the Polish population had increased by no less than 200,000. But the characteristic reaction to this was to increase the pressure rather than to attempt conciliation, and the results were reaped in 1918. The traditional Prussian view, which has been put forward again in our own day, was expressed in the Reichstag by Dr. Sattler, leader of the National-Liberals, in 1898:

> The opposition between us Germans and you Poles is a natural necessity: it is not the result either of ill will or of the desire to harm any Polish national, but primarily the consequence of the geographical situation of the territories on which our two nations live. *We Germans cannot permit that another nation be the ruler of a territory which is at a distance of only a few hours' ride from our capital.* From this point of view you (Poles) must realize that we are compelled to eliminate this other nation ... that it is our natural obligation to seek not only to make loyal citizens of the Prussians of Polish nationality, but also to transform them into real Germans.[13]

In this speech are expressed both the Prussian creed of force and the traditional policy of the *Drang nach Osten* which for so long had sought to justify the subjection of Slav peoples in the interests of German security. The policy has led in our own day to the decisive defeat of the Germans and the loss of lands which they had conquered and settled several centuries ago. The Drive to the East has ended in a Slav Drive to the West. Only the future can show whether stability has at last been reached, after a thousand years of conflict, on the river lines of the Elbe, Oder and Vistula.

## The Fall of Bismarck

The end of Bismarck's long domination of the political scene came in the spring of 1890. William II had then been Emperor for nearly two years, and it was not likely that a young, energetic and ambitious ruler, increasingly alive to his powers and responsibilities, would accept the control of an old man who obviously regarded him as a wayward and immature pupil. And although Bismarck himself, at seventy-five, could not expect to hold office for many more years, it was only too evident that he hoped before retiring to see his son, Herbert, whom he had been training for office, installed in his place: like so many able fathers he was blind to his son's lack of distinction. It had become a question for the Emperor "whether the Bismarck dynasty or the Hohenzollern dynasty should rule", and circumstances played into William's hands. He had come under the influence of Stöcker, and, wishing to mark the beginning of his reign with the adoption of a "new course" in domestic politics, was particularly anxious to seek a reconciliation with the Socialists. Although the Reichstag election of 1887, conducted by Bismarck on virulently nationalist lines, had seen a reduction of Socialist representation, the number of Socialist votes cast had increased by more than 200,000: the combination of repression and social legislation had clearly failed to check the growth of the movement. The repressive laws were due for renewal, and Bismarck had no policy to offer but an increase in their severity. The Emperor, however, wished for concessions, and planned to call an international conference on Labour and Social Problems. Bismarck's new anti-Socialist laws were rejected by the Reichstag in January, 1890, and in the elections that followed the Socialists increased their votes from 750,000 to nearly 1,500,000.

There were other causes of disagreement, especially in the field of foreign policy, which Bismarck had skilfully manipulated for so long. The essence of his policy in eastern Europe, as is shown elsewhere, had always been to maintain a balance between Austria and Russia, and his "Reinsurance Treaty" with Russia was due for renewal in 1890. William II, however, preferred to rely on the Austrian connexion, and resented, in any case, Bismarck's habit of giving to his master only so much information on foreign affairs as he thought was good for him. William I had been content with such an arrangement, and had, indeed, marvelled at the Chancellor's skill in handling complex affairs, but the new Emperor was forming his own views, seeking new contacts and even travelling widely: in 1889, for instance, he had paid his first visit to Constantinople. But whatever the reasons for disagreement, at bottom it was simply a matter of incompatibility of rôle, of age, and of temperament. In March, 1890, under great pressure, Bismarck was compelled to resign; the pilot was dropped, the heroic age at an end. In political circles there was relief, and individuals, in the words of a later Chancellor, Prince Hohenlohe, "swelled

out like sponges placed in water"[14] at the passing of the
dominating figure. Bismarck was, indeed, hoist with his own
petard. He stood at the height of his popularity in the country,
but he had always resisted the "parliamentary" notion of a
popular appeal, and he was therefore powerless to resist the
pressure placed upon him by the imperial system which he
had done so much to create. He could only withdraw, loaded
with honours, into the grumbling retirement which endured
until his death eight years later, in 1898. A period had ended,
but had ended only with a palace revolution. The German
people had not been consulted about a change that was to bear
heavily on their future.

## The Succession to Bismarck: (1) Caprivi

Nor, of course, were they consulted about the choice of a
new Chancellor. The succession to such a man as Bismarck
holding high office of such responsibility in a period of change
and development called for a rare combination of qualities,
outstanding ability and considerable experience, together with
a personality that could make itself felt in the shadow of the
great predecessor. Apart from the encouragement given to
Herbert Bismarck, whose abilities he had over-estimated, and
who was too conscious of his position as his father's son,
Bismarck had done nothing to train up a successor, and
political conditions during his long rule had not made it easy
for men of independent views to come forward. The choice
was, therefore, no easy one. The Emperor was determined,
however, to have a loyal tool, and his choice fell on General Leo
von Caprivi (1831–99), an able soldier who had also been an
efficient naval administrator, but who lacked experience of
politics and whose chief quality was his sincerity. He modestly
maintained that he had been summoned to lead the German
people back from the mighty deeds and figures of the past to
the prose of everyday life, but he was handicapped by the
Emperor's refusal to allow Bismarck or any of his circle to
instruct him in the principles on which policy had been
conducted. Soon after Bismarck's retirement William promised
to his people, uncertain of what the future might hold, a "new
course" in imperial policy, and for his four years of office

(1890–94) Caprivi loyally endeavoured to follow his wishes. Some important measures were carried, especially in the level of tariffs, and attempts were made to devise a more liberal social policy, but it was only too soon apparent that powerful interests stood in the way of new measures, while the speedy and dramatic results that the Emperor looked for to enhance his prestige were not to be expected. In foreign affairs the new course made a particularly unfortunate start. The Foreign Office had been for several years in charge of Herbert Bismarck, whom both William and Caprivi would have been prepared to retain in office, had he not resigned with his father. His successor, Baron Marschall von Bieberstein, was, like Caprivi, an inexperienced amateur, and the control of foreign policy fell into the hands of the mysterious figure who was for the next sixteen years the *éminence grise* of the Foreign Office, Friedrich von Holstein (1837–1909), the only senior member of its staff who could carry over into the new period some knowledge of the workings of Bismarck's diplomacy. Holstein was unknown outside his office, and his secretiveness, combined with Caprivi's ignorance and the Emperor's impulsiveness, does much to explain the weaknesses of German foreign policy after 1890.

## (2) HOHENLOHE; BÜLOW; BETHMANN-HOLLWEG

Caprivi fell in 1894, and was succeeded by the aged Prince Hohenlohe, a skilled diplomat of ability, and Statthalter (Governor) of Alsace-Lorraine, who was, however, too old at seventy-five to be able to influence affairs. He retired from office in 1900, having achieved little, though maintaining, in private, that he deserved a public memorial for the things he had prevented the Emperor from doing. William then appointed in his place Bernhard von Bülow, who had succeeded Marschall at the Foreign Office in 1897, and was destined to hold the Chancellorship for nine years, the longest period of any of Bismarck's successors. Bülow was a man of brilliance and charm, cool and astute, but superficial, malicious and inordinately vain, as his four volumes of memoirs, published after his death in 1929, glaringly revealed. After the *Daily Telegraph* affair of 1908 William sought an excuse to be rid of him, and in the following year he was succeeded by Bethmann-

Hollweg, a civil servant of lofty character but of only moderate ability, who presided ineffectively over the later years of the Empire, and was eventually pushed aside in 1917 by the military leaders, Hindenburg and Ludendorff, who were by that time in practical control of affairs.

## WILLIAM II

These were the four men who were selected in turn by the Emperor to fill Bismarck's shoes: with them at the helm Germany could hardly be expected to follow a steady course. Indeed, Caprivi alone pursued a consistent policy, and he ran into such difficulties that the experiment was not repeated. The Empire after Bismarck's fall has been compared to a coach drawn by a team of horses, some old, some young, unaccustomed to working together, and with no coachman on the box. As Hohenlohe noted, as early as the summer of 1890, there was no longer "unity of will".[15] The Emperor flattered himself that he would be his own coachman, but long before 1914 it was clear that Germany lacked a controlling hand. "One of the tragedies of the situation (in 1914)," wrote Sir Horace Rumbold, who was then Counsellor at the British Embassy in Berlin (and was later to be British Ambassador, in 1928–33), "was the absence of any real statesmen in Germany capable of controlling events."[16] The Emperor himself, though well-meaning, was tragically unstable and erratic. His personality has been clearly, indeed cruelly, revealed to the world by the enormous publication of diplomatic papers bearing upon the origins of the First World War. He was by no means lacking in ability, and, when he pleased, knew well how to charm and attract. He was active and industrious, and zealous for his country's good. But he lacked penetration, and was easily swayed by events and opinions. Had he been surrounded by men of greater calibre his mental and physical exuberance might have been directed into safe channels, for he had warm human sympathies and his instincts were often sound. His presence was commanding, and he possessed considerable oratorical gifts (no less an authority than Sarah Bernhardt saw in him the makings of a great actor). But he had too great a passion for public speaking, and when on his feet would pour out his innermost thoughts without reckoning the consequences. He was capable, therefore, of *gaffes* which shocked his people and alarmed foreign opinion, his choicest efforts being due generally to the inspiration of military audiences, for he fancied himself best as the All-Highest War Lord, in spite of a nature that was not fundamentally warlike (as was shown by his mental anguish during the war). Thus, he was fond of telling recruits that "there is but one law and that is my Will. I am the instrument of the Most High." And it was he who, in one of his orations, first fixed on the Germans the name of "Huns". Addressing in characteristic style the troops who were being sent to help suppress the Boxer Rising in China in 1900 he said:

> You are about to meet a crafty, well-armed, cruel foe. Meet him and beat him! Give no quarter! Take no prisoners! Kill him when he falls into your hands! Even as a thousand years ago the Huns under their King Attila made such a name for themselves as still resounds in terror in legend and fable, so make the name of Germany resound through Chinese history a thousand years from now.

It was utterances like this, and there were many of them, that made observers both inside and outside Germany doubt his sanity. Holstein told Sir Valentine Chirol in 1908 that the Emperor "would either die in a madhouse or destroy the German Empire".[17] Certainly the intemperance of his language made him seem a constant menace to European peace.

Holstein held the flatterers at Court responsible for much of the trouble. William II was surrounded by men who flattered him to the top of his bent and concealed from him as well as they could any opinions which might be displeasing. Hence the blow to the Emperor's pride when, after one or other of his effusions, criticism at home or abroad forced itself on his attention. Then for a time he would behave with more discretion. But before long the Byzantine atmosphere of the court and the lack of sustained criticism in the Reichstag encouraged him to fresh flights.

He was justly proud of the strength, greatness and prosperity of Germany, as was the nation itself, but he did not realize, as Bismarck had done, that the foundations were still weak. He could not help seeing himself as the autocratic ruler of a firmly united Empire, and the lack of responsible government and of an influential public opinion gave him more freedom of action than he could be trusted to exercise. He longed at once to be the supreme war-lord and the emperor of peace; to mark his reign with brilliant coups, without, however, incurring the heavy cost of war; to show that the Wilhelmian era could provide striking successes no less than the Bismarckian. Hence the over-dramatized speeches and ceremonies which, as a critical member of the court circle, Count Zedlitz-Trützschler, commented, could hardly have appeared more resounding if they had indeed had major victories to celebrate.[18]

## GERMANY WITHOUT DIRECTION

Hohenlohe's comment on the lack of unity after Bismarck's fall proved prophetic. Powerful sectional interests had developed in Germany, and it proved in the end impossible to unify them except through war. The Emperor was pulled in all directions by conflicting counsels, and neither he nor his chancellors had any coherent policy to offer. The appearance of unity and stability was preserved by the highly efficient civil service and administrative machine, which kept the wheels of government running smoothly almost to the last. Germany was the most highly organized of all states, but direction was lacking. The "new course" proved in the end to be no course at all, as contemporary critics were quick to realize: as early as 1891 an anonymous satirical pamphlet appeared under the title *Was für einen Kurs haben wir?* (What sort of a course have we?)[19] The British statesman who knew Germany best, Lord Haldane, recorded after his famous mission to Berlin in 1912 that "the Emperor lived amid a sea of conflicting opinions", and quoted the opinion of a foreign diplomat:

> In this highly organized nation, when you have ascended to the very top storey you find not only confusion but chaos.[20]

A constitutional system could have survived confusion and indecision, but a system devised deliberately to place firm control in the hands of one man could only lead to disaster if instead of autocracy there was anarchy at the top. In 1917 Max Weber, the distinguished sociologist and politician, who in 1919 was to be one of the German delegates at Versailles, wrote a series of outspoken articles on "Bismarck's Legacy":

> Bismarck left behind as a political heritage a nation without any political education, far below the level which, in this respect, it had reached twenty years earlier. Above all, he left behind a nation without political will, accustomed to allow the great statesmen at its head to look after its policy for it.[21]

How this lack of political will struck one foreign observer we know, in an unusual context, from the entertaining record of a bicycling tour in Germany, *Three Men on the Bummel*, which Jerome K. Jerome wrote in 1900 as a sequel to his immortal *Three Men in a Boat*. Jerome's views are roughly contemporary with the despondent comments of Bebel to Chirol, which have been quoted earlier, and his impressions provide interesting confirmation, by an outside observer, of Bebel's intimate knowledge of the situation:

> In Germany today one hears a good deal concerning Socialism, but it is Socialism that would only be despotism under another name. Individualism makes no appeal to the German voter. He is willing, nay, anxious, to be controlled and regulated in all things.

To Jerome it seemed that Germany was run by the highly efficient police, and he could not imagine the German taking control of his own destiny. As the majority of Germans seemed well satisfied with the system, however, he did not regard this as a serious defect, so long as the Government was efficient.

> Hitherto the German has had the blessed fortune to be exceptionally well governed: if this continue, it will go well with him. When his troubles begin will be when by any chance something goes wrong with the governing machine.

## THE REIGN OF WILLIAM II

In 1890, however, the breakdown of government lay far in the future, and William II began his personal rule in unbounded confidence, with the assurance to his people, "I will lead you forward to glorious days". In view of the world tragedy of 1914, the interest of his reign has seemed since to lie mainly in the field of foreign affairs, and a tendency to concentrate on this aspect has undoubtedly been encouraged by the enormous publication of State papers bearing on the subject. Even when the Second World War started to add its own mountains of printed revelations to the pile, the published record of the origins of the 1914 war was still not complete. Yet, though it is less well documented, there is much of significance in the internal development of Germany under William II, and the events of the Weimar period and of the rise of Nazism cannot be understood without some knowledge of the shaping of internal policy in the years between the fall of Bismarck and the coming of the war.

## SECTIONAL INTERESTS

The four years of Caprivi's chancellorship were a period of moderate reform, which, though it left the Socialist movement in a stronger position, at the same time stirred up potent economic interests which for many years were to play an increasingly important part in German affairs. A number of powerful organizations now became active to defend interests and to win over public support, and, in the absence of a strong Government firmly based on a united popular opinion, these became pressure groups that found it only too easy to check Government measures that they disliked and to win Government approval for sectional interests. In the chaotic circumstances of German political life no move could be made in a liberal direction without stirring antagonisms that rendered progress impossible. Thus, Caprivi's enlightened tariff policy brought into existence a Farmers' League to agitate for higher tariffs on agricultural imports, and his relaxation of pressure upon the Poles led to the formation of an "Eastern Marches Association" which soon compelled a return to repression. Industrial cartels had already come into existence, and, though their activities were investigated, no measures were taken to check them, while an Industrialists' Association struck a bargain with the Agrarian League to maintain high tariffs. Colonial societies had already been formed, and in 1890, partly in protest against Caprivi's East African agreement with Britain, the Pan-German League was founded. Eight years later came the Navy League, which, with a membership that ultimately attained half-a-million, exercised an influence on foreign policy that was little short of disastrous. Nor were the traditional influences less strong. Caprivi realized the need to modify the illiberal

Prussian franchise, but when, in 1910, Bethmann-Hollweg eventually tried to carry a very modest reform, his measure was defeated by the Prussian Conservatives, who rejected all concessions. Most ominous of all, in the light of later developments, were the beginnings, in 1890, of anti-Semitic agitation, associated with Stöcker, among others. In the elections of 1893 no fewer than sixteen representatives pledged to anti-Jewish policies were returned to the Reichstag, and the more rabid Conservatives found anti-Semitism a useful weapon in election appeals.

Developments of this kind were by no means peculiar to Germany, but it is doubtful whether sectional interests were quite so potent an influence in any other country that claimed to be something more than an avowed autocracy, such as, for instance, was Russia. Everywhere where parliamentary institutions existed they served as an arena for conflicting interests which sought to sway public opinion, and therefore, votes, in their favour. In an autocracy the pressure was less open, and was, indeed, usually conducted behind the scenes. Germany being neither an open autocracy nor a responsible parliamentary régime suffered the worst results of both systems, and after Bismarck there was no national leader with the ability and the power to devise a policy that could be called truly national in scope.

## The "New Course" and Social Legislation

Caprivi's achievement has probably been under-estimated. He was inexperienced, but his instincts were sound, and he had the courage of his convictions, though his failure showed that something more than a direct soldierly approach and honest purpose was needed to grapple with the complexities of German politics. Compared with him, Hohenlohe, Bülow and Bethmann-Hollweg were nonentities, while Bülow, for all his shallow brilliance, was dangerous, for where he did not prefer to do nothing he was openly reactionary. After the brief liberal experiment of Caprivi, and the interlude of Hohenlohe, in fact, the régime became once again reactionary. Nevertheless, the "new course" started in high hopes. The Emperor himself was, at first, interested in social questions, and there were indications that his reign might earn the title of the "social empire".

The anti-Socialist laws were dropped, and the International Labour Conference which had been planned before Bismarck's fall was held, and was followed by ameliorative legislation. Hours of work were restricted, though mainly for the benefit of women and young people, and efforts were made to improve the inadequate inspection of factories. To mark his own concern with social problems the Emperor instituted an Order to be awarded for conspicuous social service. In 1895, after Caprivi's fall, a programme of housing reform was begun, and four years later, after a long struggle, the right of association received its first formal recognition. An Act of 1903 imposed the final restrictions on the employment of children, and the early years of the new century also saw the insurance laws improved and extended. In 1910 they were consolidated in a great Imperial Insurance Code, embodying the results of thirty years of legislation. Bismarck's prediction that his social policy would outlive his generation proved well-founded.

## The Growth of Social-Democracy; the "Erfurt Programme"

His repressive legislation did not, however, survive his fall. Its repeal led to a rapid increase in the strength of the party, for which the ground was prepared by the first party congress since the proscription, held at Erfurt in 1891. From this conference, which gave the party the name of Social-Democratic, emerged the "Erfurt Programme", a lengthy and developed statement of the party's principles and aims, which, as the charter of the largest of all Marxist parties, assumed an international significance. The document was in two parts, the first, an exposition of the principles of Marxist socialism, which while based on Marx's teaching did not, however, commit the party to all his theories; the second, a statement of practical aims for the democratization of German political and economic life. This second part gave implicit recognition to the influence of the other great pioneer of German socialism, Ferdinand Lassalle (1825–64), who had always been more prepared than Marx to make use of the machinery of the State, if it could be turned to the advantage of the workers. It implied the acceptance of the State and of the possibility of achieving fundamental economic changes through it, and therefore offered at least a potential alternative to the strict doctrines of Marxism. For some years the contrast, already apparent in the two sections of the Erfurt Programme, was veiled by the need for unity in the building up of the party and by the personalities and abilities of its leaders. Outstanding among the leaders was August Bebel (1840–1913), to whom reference has already been made, and who led the party from 1900 until his death in 1913. Bebel saw the voting strength of the party at the Reichstag elections increase from 1,427,298 in 1890 to 4,250,329 in 1912, its membership of the Reichstag rise from 35 to 110 in a total of 397. By 1912 the Social-Democrats formed the largest party in the country, numbering rather more than one-third of the voters, and holding nearly one-third of the seats in the Reichstag. With these forces behind him Bebel, it has been said, was something of a "shadow-Emperor":[22] his successor Ebert, became, indeed, the obvious choice as first President of the newly established Republic in 1919. Bebel was the last of the great personalities who had come under Marx's direct influence, and although, while he lived, unity was preserved around the Erfurt programme, his death opened the way for divisions in the party. The very size of the party, which with its four million supporters contained other than purely proletarian elements, militated against revolutionary policies. Moreover, the workers clearly had a growing stake in the stability of the Empire. The rapid expansion of industry was bringing prosperity to all classes, and the workers' interests were protected by the Insurance Code. It seemed not unreasonable to suppose that political pressure could achieve still more without going to the lengths of revolution, and there were, in any case, many who regarded the Empire with pride and were glad to serve it.

It was difficult to consider sweeping away a system which, while it could do more, nevertheless brought the German workers no little advantage. With the pattern of their minds formed by military service, which they did not unduly resent, and by training in duty to the State, they accepted the benefits that followed from an expanding economy, buttressed by the system of social insurance, and sought mainly to control the machinery of government with their own well-ordered organizations. In general a "spirit of order" was their most striking characteristic, and when in 1918 the prevailing order broke down, in the telling phrase of the Communist writer, Ernst Toller, "they found their freedom chaos".[23]

## DIVISIONS WITHIN SOCIAL-DEMOCRACY

With Bebel's death in the year before the war the latent split in the ranks of Social-Democracy came into the open, the party dividing into Radical (revolutionary), Revisionist (reformist), and Centre sections. The Revisionist leader was Eduard Bernstein (1850–1932) who, while in exile in Britain during the years of repression, had come under the influence of the Fabians, and the tendency of the party was in the reformist direction which he favoured, until, by the end of the war, Social-Democracy had, in practice, repudiated Marxism, and become a party of democratic reform similar to the Labour Party in Britain. For the succession to Bebel as leader of the party was selected Friedrich Ebert (1871–1925), a member of the moderate Centre group of the party. Pre-eminent among the Radicals were Karl Kautsky (1854–1938) and Karl Liebknecht (1871–1919): it was from this wing of the party, under Liebknecht's influence, that German Communism was to stem. In the developments within the Social-Democratic party on the morrow of Bebel's death, and in the circumstances which brought them about, are to be found, in fact, the springs of much of Germany's political shaping from 1919, but the critical division within the ranks of the party was already apparent in the Erfurt programme, if not in the earlier rivalry between Marx and Lassalle.

Moderate though its policies were to become, there were many, both in Germany and elsewhere, as is shown by numerous contemporary references (among which *Three Men on the Bummel* may be included), who were alarmed at the growth of Social-Democracy, not appreciating that a party with a membership of millions does not go in for red revolution. If Bismarck had hoped to destroy the movement by a combination of repression and social reform, William II had hoped to win it over by conciliatory measures, believing that it was "a transient phenomenon which could be exhausted by its own violence". With the expansion of the party there was, however, no sign of a conversion to "loyalty", and with his usual impulsiveness the Emperor then abandoned the attitude of sympathy. Within a few years he was urging the disaffected workers, "the fellows without a fatherland", to "shake the dust of Germany off their feet" and emigrate. As early as 1891, in an address to recruits, he had inveighed against the Socialists and warned the newly joined soldiers that they might have to shoot agitators, even if they were their own kith and kin, a characteristic remark which was not calculated to endear him to Socialist critics, but which reveals his lack of real understanding of the situation. Count Zedlitz-Trützschler, who was for some years his Controller of the Household, and therefore knew the Emperor well, complained that William never realized how much the average German had developed in education and intelligence since 1871, though it was apparent in the quality of the recruits whom he addressed.[24]

## The "New Course" and Tariffs: Agrarian Interests

The Social-Democrat attitude to the war crisis of 1914 must be analysed in its place. For the present other aspects of the "new course" must be considered. The most important development of the Caprivi period, apart from the courting of the Socialists, was the attempt to settle Germany's tariffs on a satisfactory basis. Tariffs had been increased in 1887, and the countries with which Germany was trading most extensively, Russia and Austria, had also raised their tariffs. These countries were important to Germany both as sources of food imports and as markets for manufactures, and the trade treaties with them were due for revision in 1892. Caprivi hoped to get better terms for German manufactures and aimed also, as part of the policy of winning over the workers, at lowering the price of their food by smaller import duties. Russia was now the greatest single source for wheat and rye consumed in Germany, but a series of poor harvests had raised prices, and in 1892 there were bread riots in Berlin. Caprivi realized the need for a measure of agricultural protection: "in a future war", he said prophetically, "feeding the army and the country would play a decisive rôle". His hands were tied, too, by the fact that, despite the movement of population, there had been no revision of representation in the Reichstag since 1871: the rural areas tended therefore to be over-represented, a factor of some importance if the Chancellor were to carry the Reichstag with him. Yet he understood the fundamental change that had taken place in Germany's economic life, and realized that it was now an industrial and no longer merely an agricultural country. As such it had to export its manufactures, and Caprivi hoped by reciprocal tariff arrangements to guarantee good markets for German industry abroad and to get cheaper food for the German worker. The result of his negotiations was the new tariff system of 1892, which won lowered tariffs for German manufactures abroad in return for a lowering of tariffs on food imports into Germany. This led to a violent agitation among agricultural interests, from great landowners to peasant farmers alike, which culminated in 1893 in the founding of the *Bund der Landwirte* (Farmers' League), which henceforth exercised a powerful influence in politics. The membership of the League was very wide, and, although its leaders were mainly to be found among the landowning nobility, small and medium farmers predominated in it. It could therefore muster considerable voting strength in the rural areas in elections: "next to the party of Social Democracy", commented an English observer in 1908, "no political organization in Germany is more energetic and consistent in the pursuit of class interests".[25] The League's members protested their loyalty to the Empire, but in the spirit of the old cynical Prussian tag, *Unser König absolut, wenn er unsern Willen thut* (Our King is absolute when he does what we wish), they claimed that "we support authority, but only if it is the right authority".[26] Caprivi, with his broad views and liberal measures, was suspected of not being the right authority, and agrarian opposition to him, which implied the total opposition of the influential conservative elements of Prussia, was largely responsible for his downfall in 1894. The general decline in agricultural prices which took place in these years was blamed on him, and opposition was further embittered in eastern Germany by his conciliatory attitude to the Poles. After his fall the League set itself to undo his work, and when his tariff policy came up for revision in 1902, when Bülow was Chancellor, rates were again raised. The League showed itself too powerful to be resisted by Bülow, who claimed in any case to be "an agrarian chancellor" and was essentially conservative in his approach to Germany's internal problems. To achieve its purpose the League struck a bargain with the leaders of industry. High tariffs and high prices were to be maintained inside Germany in order to make it possible to export manufactures at lower prices and thereby to offset higher foreign tariffs. The domestic market was therefore assured to the farmer, and the foreign market to the manufacturer. Whether in the long run the arrangement suited Germany's interests is another matter: after Caprivi no Chancellor tried to follow a broad national policy, which would serve something more than sectional interests.

## THE DEVELOPMENT OF INDUSTRY:
### (1) CHEMICALS

While agriculture was thus establishing for itself a powerful and privileged position, the same process was taking place in the expanding world of industry. If the earlier stages of German industrialization are associated with coal, iron and steel, it was with the chemical and electrical industries, which were soundly based on the achievements of German scientific education, that the next phase of industrial growth was concerned. In the field of chemicals the connexion between British and German developments has always been close, as the famous name of Ludwig Mond (1839–1909), the German from Cassel who laid the foundations of the later I.C.I. combine, bears witness: in chemicals as in steel it was to England that German manufacturers first looked for a lead. Like England, Germany was rich in the natural salts and other raw materials on which chemical industry is based, and the technical skill of her chemists added to the production of "heavy" chemicals, which were especially needed in agriculture, an important industry in dyes, which by 1913 were being exported to the value of nearly ten million pounds a year. Germany never equalled Britain as an exporter of chemicals, but the strategic value of her well-organized chemical industry—as of her protected agriculture—became apparent after 1914.

### (2) ELECTRICITY

It was, however, in the new field of electrical engineering that Germany made her greatest, and at the same time her most original, single contribution to modern industry. The generation of electrical power on a large scale was first rendered possible by Werner von Siemens's invention of the dynamo in 1867, and although it was in America that the possibilities of the new source of power were most quickly appreciated, Germany did not lag far behind. The German Edison Company, better known under its later title of "A.E.G." (*Allgemeine Elektrizitäts-Gesellschaft*) was established in 1883, and, with the similar group founded by Siemens, soon gained for Germany a virtual monopoly of electrical development on the Continent. By 1913 the total output of the electrical industries had reached a value of £65,000,000, against Britain's £30,000,000. Exports of electrical goods of all kinds were approaching £11,000,000 a year, and, significantly enough, cable was even being sold to Britain, the original home of the cable industry. With its rapid growth, its semi-monopolistic position and its powerful economic hold, backed by Government support, on many neighbouring States, the German electrical industry, as typified by the A.E.G., is representative of much of the Empire's industrial development. The demands for the new electrical equipment, together with a constant supply of replacements, obviously gave the A.E.G. a highly favoured position in every country where it could establish itself, but the position was strengthened, as in the case of so many industries, by the setting-up of cartels, the industrial and trading organizations which, in their varying forms, were so marked a feature of German, as also of American, economic development in these years.

## (3) CARTELS

Cartels arose as the result of a number of factors, but in the main because of the instability of German industry owing to its rapid development. The boom of the early 'seventies, encouraged by military victory and the French indemnity, led to forced growth and over-capitalization, and when expansion was checked by the depression that followed, the inevitable first result was the demand for protection against the foreigner. The tariff of 1879, however, was not high enough to give complete protection, and during the 'eighties manufacturers drew together to maintain prices both against falling prices in the world outside and against fluctuations in internal price levels. In this move they were often inspired by banking interests, which had a considerable stake in industrial development. It was, perhaps, a natural tendency in newly established industries that were compelled to face the pressure of older and more experienced competitors, but it was encouraged by the imposition of tariffs, for these, although low at first, acted as a breakwater against world price changes, and made possible the maintenance of stable conditions. By the end of the century there was hardly a single industry without its appropriate cartel, and, from the maintenance of prices, control was passing on to the regulation of output and the assignment of markets, while there was a tendency, at least in some of the heavier trades, for a change to the American (trust) type of cartel, in which unified control rather than free association was the characteristic feature. Of this latter type the A.E.G. was one of the earliest examples, and from the very nature of its business it was also one of the earliest organizations to create demand as well as supply, since the demand for the new electrical equipment had to be stimulated before orders could be expected. This had important consequences. With their monopoly of the home market secured by tariffs, and powerful organizations behind them to regulate supply and prices, the German cartels were able to enter the international market in a very advantageous position. Whatever prices were maintained at home—and prices in Germany were kept, on the whole, above the world level—the cartels were able to offer in foreign markets the prices that were most thoroughly competitive, and even, if necessary, to indulge in "dumping". It was this aspect of German business, together with the sharp practice that sometimes accompanied it, which caused irritation in free-trade Britain, and made the expansion of German trade a direct influence in international diplomacy. Moreover, the powerful position of the cartels at home enabled them to bring influence to bear upon the Government, and therefore at times to seek diplomatic support for their negotiations abroad.

For all this the German people paid in artificially high prices, as they were to pay again under the trade policy of the Third Reich after 1933, and the whole mighty and highly efficient machine came to be regarded as another aspect of

German power politics, an unintended introductory sketch, as we see it now, for the "guns before butter" technique of more recent times. To imperial Germany the process brought both guns and butter. The butter was unevenly distributed, it is true, and the German worker got far less than his share, but the nation as a whole was able to raise its standard of life very considerably, and even the workman had his simple luxuries, while it was noticed by foreign observers as a sign of the times that champagne was the most widely advertised product in the Reich. It is significant that with the development of trade and industry emigration, as has been mentioned earlier, fell away in the 'nineties. Yet, but for the blurring of the issue by war in 1914, there is little doubt that there would eventually have been a struggle between the growing forces of Socialism and the powerful interests of organized industry. This is not to suggest, as some would have us believe, that war was deliberately adopted as an outlet for internal stresses, but, given the type of organization that has been described, economic as well as political forces were directed to power as the aim of policy and eventually, therefore, to war as, in the well-known phrase, "the continuation of policy by other means". The characteristic faith of the free trader in the notion that developing trade would ensure peace was doubly disproved when the resources of the modern State were deliberately marshalled behind the merchant, and trade policy became a weapon in international politics. With the continued insistence on the need for military preparedness in Germany's weak strategic position, on which Bismarck laid such stress, it was probably inevitable that economic policy should, in this way, become the tool of considerations of power, but the process was carried through with characteristic thoroughness, and brought unwelcome results in the resentment of other countries. This was interpreted in Germany as jealousy, and after 1914, therefore, the opinion grew that jealous rivals had plotted the Empire's ruin.

## INTERNATIONAL REACTIONS TO GERMANY'S DEVELOPMENT

But it was the methods rather than the successes of Germany's expanding economy which caused resentment, and added to the international tension. Germany was not alone in seeing the development of well-organized economic and financial interests in this period, but nowhere else was the preoccupation with conceptions of power so marked, or the connexion between State policy and private interests so close. In the words of one commentator:

> The German people and their Government were trying to overcome the tardiness of their attainment of great national strength by systematic, united use of it. In this unity of interest all foreign enterprise took on a faint official tinge. The rest of the world recognized the fact, exaggerated it, and, though striving for the same purposes, resented it.[27]

In the peculiar conditions of German development, as they had been fostered by Bismarck, pressure groups had arisen and had become, in practice, almost "states within the state". The Prussian conservatives set the pattern which the Farmers' League and the cartels adopted and extended. Bismarck himself was subjected to pressure in the 'eighties by the agitation for colonial expansion, to which in the end he did to some extent yield, and it was the characteristic combination of private enterprise with State backing that created such a colonial empire as Germany came to possess. Official support, both in trade and in colonies, was often less than foreign observers suspected, but the propaganda of nationalist organizations, reinforced later by the speeches of William II, roused fears that might have been lulled by less blatant publicity. In 1901, in a speech to merchants from the old Hansa towns, the Emperor seemed to justify the worst fears of those who were watching German expansion with concern:

> As head of the Empire, I rejoice at the departure of each new Hanseate . . . who goes out to foreign parts, looking with his keen, unbiased eye for new points where we may hammer in a nail on which to hang our armour.[28]

It was such open threats of power behind even the most innocent trading activity that created resentment, and aroused hostility even when—as, for instance, in Morocco and the Persian Gulf later—the German Government actually refused a forceful backing to German traders. Fear and suspicion accounted for more opposition than did active hostility. It was

D

the organized pressure for colonial—and naval—expansion, in blind rivalry with Britain, that finally destroyed the traditional English sympathy for Germany. It was this striving for a world political position to match Germany's economic expansion that in 1914 magnified into a world war the struggle with Russia for the control of the Balkans, the latest round in the long conflict of Teuton and Slav, and thereby ensured defeat.

## THE DEMAND FOR COLONIES

The agitation for colonies was stimulated by several considerations. There was, no doubt, an element of envy of Britain's position, a sense that, as Napoleon I had said, Britain had acquired "world power on the cheap". A tendency to exaggerate the part played by colonial development in British prosperity has certainly existed into our own times, in spite of the efforts of the statisticians. A more potent factor was the loss of millions of Germans through emigration. Further, there was the memory of earlier trading and colonial activities by Germans in the seventeenth century, when Brandenburg-Prussia had for a time possessed stations in India, West Africa and the West Indies, and there was the notable record of German exploration in many parts of the world. Before they entered the Customs Union of the Reich in the 'eighties, Hamburg and Bremen had already developed trading relations with many areas that were afterwards to become German colonies, and it was largely in trading circles that the agitation for colonies was initiated. But many interested individuals were also to be found in other spheres, especially among those who were encouraging exploration, while the teaching of List, who had advocated colonial expansion, was now taking effect. Moreover, it was precisely at this time that other Powers were actively engaged in expansion. Britain had acquired a share in the control of the Suez canal in 1875, and, as Bismarck had foreseen, had been compelled by circumstances to intervene in Egypt in 1882. France, encouraged by Bismarck to seek in overseas expansion compensation for the loss of Alsace-Lorraine, had acquired Tunis in 1881, and Italy was beginning her penetration of the Red Sea littoral. The moment was ripe for a move by Germany, and many felt that the establishment of a colonial empire would set the seal on the political achievements of the Reich. Treitschke expressed this notion in the lectures he was delivering in Berlin University from 1874: "People from older States, who have been disciplined, go out and found new States ... every virile people has established colonial power".

In 1882, therefore, there was founded at Frankfurt the *Kolonialverein* (Colonial Association), followed two years later by the *Gesellschaft für Deutsche Kolonisation* (Society for German Colonization) of Berlin. This latter organization was founded by Dr. Karl Peters (1856–1918), the unsavoury adventurer who was later dismissed from the German colonial service for scandalous and brutal conduct, but was afterwards canonized by the Nazis as one of Germany's colonial heroes. Peters's organization was intended merely to raise money for the colonization of East Africa, and was therefore opposed first by the *Kolonialverein*, which had the more general object of arousing interest in colonial matters. But the two bodies fused in 1887 to become the *Deutsche Kolonialgesellschaft* (German Colonial Society), and this organization became an influential factor in the shaping of German policy. Its membership was never great, reaching some 43,000 in 1914, but through its propaganda activities, its lecture tours, exhibitions and congresses, it exerted on Government and people alike an influence out of all proportion to its size, which was strikingly revealed, for instance, in the elections of 1907. Moreover, it prepared the way for other similar bodies. Thus, in 1890 the *Alldeutscher Verband* (Pan-German League) was founded by a group which included Karl Peters and a number of industrialists, with its avowed object "to arouse patriotic self-consciousness at home . . . and, above all, to carry forward the German colonial movement to tangible results" in order to make Germany "the paramount power in world affairs". Eight years later came the Navy League, inspired by Alfred von Tirpitz (1849–1930), the naval officer and later Grand Admiral, whose influence on William II and on German policy was ultimately fatal to the Reich. Tirpitz had supporters in the highest circles, and the money for the Navy League's activities was largely supplied by Krupps, which had an obvious interest in battleship construction. Within a few years the membership of the

League had risen to more than half a million, and it proved an influential factor in the deterioration of Anglo-German relations between 1900 and 1914.

Colonial agitation, it is clear, was one of the earliest manifestations of the activities of "pressure groups" in Germany, but it cannot be said that the direct results achieved were commensurate with its efforts. Bismarck himself never favoured colonial adventures: to the end he was far more concerned with developments in Europe. Thus, in 1888 he opposed an attempt to extend German territory in East Africa with the words:

> Your map of Africa is very beautiful, but my map of Africa is in Europe. Here is Russia and here is France, and we are in the middle. That is my map of Africa.

## BISMARCK'S COLONIAL POLICY

Earlier he had declared, in the well-known phrase, that "for Germany to acquire colonies would be like the poverty-stricken Polish nobleman providing himself with silks and sables when he needed shirts". He regarded colonies as an unnecessary indulgence, which would prove costly hostages to fortune, diverting resources that were needed at home and threatening a rift between Germany and England that would play into the hands of the Reich's enemies in Europe. As late as 1881 he said that as long as he was Chancellor there would be no colonial policies. Yet within a few years he did lend his support to the colonial agitation, giving the movement its head at a moment when it was valuable to him in the working-out of his broader lines of policy. The two years, 1884–85, saw him engaged on a rapprochement with France in an attempt to lay the bogy of a war of revenge, and as Anglo-French relations were strained it suited him to stir up a dispute with Britain, partly to whip up feeling in Germany, and partly to sweeten the French at the tactical moment. There was a further motive. William I was now ageing rapidly, and his son, the Crown Prince Frederick, was well-known to be dominated by his English wife, to whom, as to his mother, the Empress Augusta, Bismarck, intolerant of any influence but his own, at no time showed either loyalty or respect. He did not wish to be confronted, on William's death, with an Anglophile Emperor liable to be subject to British influence. It therefore suited him to sharpen relations with Britain. Moreover, as was shown earlier, there was at this time a strong Radical Party, which had the Crown Prince's sympathy, and might be expected to gain in influence on his accession. The Radicals were opposed to any policy of colonial acquisitions, especially if it endangered good relations with Britain, and their opposition played into Bismarck's hands. Any weapon, in his view, was good enough to ensure that he would retain power on Frederick's accession and avoid the combination of hostile Emperor and Reichstag that would inevitably pull him down. Material for a dispute with Britain lay ready to hand in the pressure of German traders for an active policy in Africa, and German feeling was exacerbated by the clumsy handling by the British Government of Bismarck's inquiries about its views on the future of certain territories, notably in South West Africa. The British Government was careful to consult the colonial government at the Cape about a matter which manifestly affected the future of the Cape Colony, but this consultation caused delay, and the home government did not appreciate the effect its dilatoriness would have upon opinion in Germany. When the affair was finally settled, a division of hitherto unoccupied territory took place between Britain and Germany, which found itself with a colonial empire in East and West Africa and the Pacific. Having done something to placate the agitation inside Germany, and finding France unresponsive to his approaches, Bismarck then dropped the matter. New events in eastern Europe now claimed his attention, and he could no longer afford to estrange Britain, while the onset of the Crown Prince's fatal illness showed that there was little to be feared from him. Nevertheless, Bismarck had, albeit unwittingly, done enough to gain himself the title of founder of the German colonial empire. Further, he had given the "pressure groups" a taste of power, and had taught the German people in general to look to firm methods in their dealings with Britain, a lesson that was destined to have unfortunate results.

## THE GERMAN COLONIAL EMPIRE

When the colonial position was finally stabilized at the end of the century Germany possessed in West Africa

Togoland, the Cameroons and South West Africa; on the other side of the continent, German East Africa; and, in the Pacific, parts of New Guinea and Samoa, together with the Solomon, Caroline, Pelew, Marianne and Marshall Islands. There was also a naval base at Kiao-Chow in China. The total extent of territory was some 1,135,000 square miles, with a population of thirteen millions, of which, however, only 24,000 people were white, most of them being officials. Togoland alone was self-supporting, the administration of the other colonies entailing an annual deficit of many millions of marks. The capital invested in the territories represented only two per cent of Germany's overseas investments, their imports only one half of one per cent of Germany's total export of goods. In short, they were the expensive luxury that Bismarck had foretold, while their strategic significance did much to alarm opinion in England and later prevented the discussion of their return to Nazi Germany when it agitated for them. Opinion in Germany was frankly interested in the colonies for the wealth they could produce, and could not be satisfied, therefore, with the inadequate gains that had been made. Far more profitable was the peaceful penetration of Turkey by German trade, which led to the great Berlin-Baghdad railway project. Yet the acquisition of the colonial territories did flatter the national vanity. It was sincerely felt by many, even among the Social-Democrats, that the advanced civilization of Europe had an honourable mission in the more backward parts of the world, in which Germany must take her part. It was felt, too, that the Germans had shown themselves to be, in Treitschke's phrase, a "virile people", and Chancellor Bethmann-Hollweg later applied the same test to the navy when he claimed that it was necessary "for the general purposes of Germany's greatness". The same words might well have been applied to the colonies, though the navy, which cost no less than £200,000,000 between 1900 and 1914, was an even more expensive indulgence. In the event, much was sacrificed to what an embittered critic of the régime, the widowed Empress Frederick, who in colonial matters was hopelessly British in her outlook, described in 1896 as "the *vanity* of being able to say 'We have colonies' ".[29]

## A PLANLESS POLICY

A later critic, Professor Erich Brandenburg, writing after the collapse of the Empire, has exposed the fundamental weaknesses of German policy, which betrayed themselves with particular ineptitude in the search for colonies:

> Had our colonial activity been based on a well-thought-out comprehensive plan, such as a great interdependent colonial territory in Africa, we might have used our central position . . . to secure what we were striving for. . . . But there was no definite tangible goal. . . . We wished in a general sort of way not to be left out, and wherever others were getting something, to secure a bit for ourselves; and so we went on playing this sinister, double game for the sake of snatching here and there some petty colonial advantages. . . . The result was that the other powers, unable to credit such aimlessness in policy, suspected Germany of concealing deep-laid and dangerous schemes. . . . Germany's policy was looked upon as unreliable and unintelligible, whereas it was merely planless, petty and uncertain.[30]

## INDICATIONS OF STRESS:
### (1) SOUTH WEST AFRICA AND THE 1907 ELECTIONS

"Planless, petty and uncertain" much of German policy certainly was, in these as in other directions. Colonial policy had its contemporary critics, but in the main these took for granted the need for expansion and fastened on the methods adopted, which in the early days were only too often crude and brutal. It was in 1906 that a dispute over the handling of South West Africa, where the resistance of the native Herero people was being harshly suppressed, was aggravated to the level of a major political conflict, the first of three which marked the last years before the war, and indicated the stirrings of uneasiness in some political circles. In December, 1906, in a vote on military measures against the Hereros, the Government was defeated in the Reichstag by a significant combination of Centre Party and Social-Democratic votes, the first joint action by the chief critics of the régime, normally kept apart by ideological differences. Bülow was quick to seize advantage of the opportunity presented by this combination of his opponents. Since 1890 the Centre had held the largest block of seats in the Reichstag: here, it seemed, was an opportunity of striking at the party's arbitral position. Proclaiming that the imperial prerogative in military affairs had been challenged, Bülow went to the country on a nationalist and militarist platform. The elections that followed in January, 1907, in which the Colonial Society played an active part, provided a handsome majority for his *bloc* of supporters, and were celebrated by the Emperor, no less than by Bülow himself, as a triumph for the régime. But the victory was a Pyrrhic one. The Social-Democrats, it is true, lost heavily: although their votes rose by a quarter of a million from the total of the 1903 election, the percentage fell by three and they lost 38 of their 81 seats in the Reichstag. The Centre Party, however, more than maintained its position. With 105 seats, five more than in 1903, it still formed the largest single group in the Reichstag, and two years later Bülow was to feel its strength. Nevertheless, with characteristic superficiality of judgment, he was exhilarated by the result of the elections. "The soul of our people has been moved, as never since the days of Bismarck," he exultantly proclaimed, in unconscious imitation of the Emperor's extravagant style, and an admirer hailed his victory as "a Sedan on the home front".[31] The Chancellor did not, however, follow up his success. His tactics had produced a parliamentary majority such as neither of his predecessors since Bismarck had enjoyed, but he lacked the essential grasp of political strategy which might have enabled him to exploit it, as Bismarck himself would have done. Only two years later, in 1909, the Centre took its revenge by assisting at his overthrow, and when the next election was held, in 1912, the Social-Democrats more than made good their losses, gaining no fewer than 67 seats. So much for the new Sedan.

REFORMS IN COLONIAL POLICY

Only in colonial policy did Bülow make any significant changes. The Herero rising was crushed, but the criticism which had been widely expressed of the blunders that had brought it about was heeded. The colonial administration was separated from the Foreign Office, which had hitherto handled it, and was placed in charge of the banker, Dr. Bernhard von Dernburg (1865–1937) as first Colonial Secretary. Dernburg, a man of enlightened views, with a real interest in the colonies, thoroughly reformed the administration. He visited colonies, made a study of British methods, encouraged economic development and established a system of rule which by 1914 had already done much to wipe out the memory of earlier mistakes and to win over the loyalty of the native peoples.

## (2) THE *Daily Telegraph* EPISODE, 1908, AND THE FALL OF BÜLOW

While the colonial administration was being reformed, however, Bülow was blundering to his fall, and the fundamental weaknesses of the Wilhelmian Empire were being glaringly exposed. In October, 1908, occurred another revealing episode, the publication in the London *Daily Telegraph* of an interview with the Emperor, in which, in a burst of good will but with extraordinary ineptitude, William poured out his thoughts and wishes about Anglo-German relations during the past ten years. He protested his affection for Britain, claiming that he had prevented Russia and France from intervening in the Boer War, and that he had provided the plan of campaign by which the Boers had been defeated: he acknowledged that his people were hostile to Britain, but asserted that his fleet was being built for use against not Britain but Japan. This irresponsible effusion had been in Bülow's hands before publication, but he had not troubled to read it himself, possibly because he realized that, however much he might object to it, he could not, without serious unpleasantness, prevent its appearance. He had contented himself with passing it to his Foreign Office for consideration, but the well-trained officials there, equally mindful of the risks of crossing the Emperor, had handled it, in Holstein's revealing phrase, "like a hot potato",[32] and made only minor alterations. There followed a storm of criticism in Germany such as the most bitter critic of the régime could hardly have dared to hope for. Bülow had failed lamentably in his responsibility, but the criticism fell rightly upon the Emperor: all parties in the Reichstag were united against him, and he had to give assurances through the Chancellor that he would in future, "observe even in private conversation the reserve which is essential to the unity of our policy and the authority of the Crown". It was the moment, if ever there were one between 1871 and 1914, when the constitutional weaknesses

D*

of the Second Reich might have been corrected, and the
political organization of Germany brought into line with its
advanced standards of industrial and cultural development.
The Emperor's nerve collapsed under the shock of the
criticism he had to endure, and he even thought of abdicating.
Advantage might well have been taken of the situation to
establish a more responsible system, which would not have
left the German people without guidance and at the mercy of
the incompetent successors of William I and Bismarck. But
the chance was not seized; it is doubtful, indeed, whether many
realized it existed. After expressing unanimous criticism the
Reichstag made no further move, and even the Reichstag's
criticism had little effect in the country: the Emperor soon
found that he was welcomed no less warmly by the crowds
when he appeared in public, and his confidence quickly
returned. He was furious with Bülow, whom he not unreason-
ably held to have betrayed him, and in the following year,
feeling once more secure, he took advantage of a minor defeat
for the Government in the Reichstag to get rid of the Chancellor.
In his place he appointed, as evidence that no change had
taken place, the honest but mediocre Bethmann-Hollweg.
That such a man at such a time could be put in charge
of German policy was evidence of the bankruptcy of the
régime only a few years before its sternest test was to fall
upon it.

Bülow's defeat had come about as the result of an attempt
to impose a modest death-duty on landed property, which was
resisted by the Conservatives. The ruling elements in Prussia,
like their King, were not prepared to waive their traditional
privileges. Yet the Prussian elections of 1908 had shown how
completely outdated was the Prussian suffrage system, which
Bismarck had openly criticized forty years before. In those
elections the Conservatives, with 16 per cent of the votes, had
received 212 seats in the Prussian Chamber, the Socialists,
with 23 per cent, only 7 seats. A situation so anomalous, and
in such contrast to the position in the Reichstag, called for
remedy, but, as has been mentioned earlier, even the slight
measure of reform attempted by Bethmann-Hollweg in 1910
was rejected. Not until the hour of defeat in 1918 was the three-
class system of voting finally abolished.

## (3) THE ZABERN INCIDENT, 1913

That there was a serious undercurrent of concern at the Emperor's handling of affairs was apparent, however, at the Reichstag elections of 1912, when the moderate and left wing parties greatly increased their poll. In the following year they had an opportunity of showing their strength, when there occurred the notorious Zabern incident. Zabern (Saverne) was a little garrison town in Alsace, notable for its loyalty to the Empire. There in November, 1913, a dispute between civilians and young officers led to demonstrations which caused the garrison commander, Colonel von Reuter, high-handedly to place civilians under arrest. His action was sharply criticized in the Reichstag, and when the Government, resenting any attack on the army, strove to defend his conduct it found itself defeated by 293 votes to 54, with only the Conservatives behind it. But again the Reichstag was unable to follow up its victory, and ironically it was the very Chancellor, Bethmann-Hollweg, who had been most decisively defeated in the Reichstag in December, 1913, who, only eight months later, received a unanimous vote of approval on the declaration of war.

## THE UNITY OF 1914:
### (1) ITS BASIS

The Zabern incident showed that final authority in the Empire still rested with Prussia—with the army and the Prussian conservatives. What would have happened but for the coming of war it is impossible to say. If there was dissatisfaction it had not gone far, as the united outburst of loyalty in August, 1914, showed. Yet, as in Russia, the war tragically cut across a process of political evolution which, though slow, was taking place. In the event, it was not until the Prussian grip had been relaxed by military defeat in 1918 that it was possible to consider an alternative basis for German unity, and by that time there was nothing to take Prussia's place. The German people, in the words of Ernst Toller which have already been quoted, then found their freedom chaos. Everything had for so long come from above, and there was no tradition of freedom, no Magna Carta or Bill of Rights to which to appeal, no Declaration of Independence or Bastille

Day to stir the imagination. The traditions of the Empire were traditions of military triumph, and they availed little in the days of defeat.

## (2) THE SOCIAL-DEMOCRAT ATTITUDE

The unity of the nation in the final crisis that began in the summer of 1914 was a revelation of the underlying strength of the Empire, despite its many flaws. That all but the parties of the left would rally round the Emperor was a foregone conclusion, but even the Social-Democrats fell into line and voted the war credits on the fateful Fourth of August. The motives of the Social-Democrats were mixed, and an analysis of their attitude, as the representatives of a considerable section of the German people, and that the most critical of the régime, is revealing. Social-Democracy had never taken a pacifist line, especially in the matter of national defence. As far back as 1880 Bebel had written:

> In a struggle for the integrity of German soil it may be very hard for the party to help defend the infamous domestic system of the Government and the mortal enemy of the party, but the party will not rid itself of these by foreign conquerors.[33]

So now, in 1914, the party formally gave its assent in the Reichstag to the motion for the war credits, with the words:

> The horrors of hostile invasion stare us in the face. . . . It is of paramount importance to prevent this danger and to ensure the position and independence of our own land. We stand by what we have ever maintained: we will not desert our own Fatherland in the hour of peril.[34]

To the horrors of invasion was added the prospect of the incursion of the armies of the arch-enemy of all radical thought, Tsarist Russia. "Defeat would be something unthinkable," ran another party statement, "we will not have our women and children sacrificed to the bestiality of Cossacks."[35] This fear of Russia was common to all parties, and was one of the most powerful motives making for national unity, though hatred of England was to rival it after the shock of the British declaration of war. Victory, however, was regarded as certain, and opposition to the war effort, if it could ever have been contemplated, seemed, therefore, futile. To many Social-Democrats, unconscious of the fact that a victorious government is rarely generous, it seemed that through loyal service to the Empire in war the party might hope to achieve some of its aims. "It was folly to resist history for the sake of theorizing," declared the party newspaper *Neue Zeit* in 1916, "the more patriotic the working class had proved itself during the war, the easier it would be to effect its social and political demands."[36] The element of wishful thinking was not inconsiderable, but no more in Germany than elsewhere was there any realization of the magnitude of the crisis into which Europe had stumbled. The war brought an uplifting of hearts, a touch of the heroic into a materialistic civilization: long pent-up energies and ambitions were released, and many Germans, even in the party, expected it to "sweep away much that was rotten and decayed".[37] In this spirit the Social-Democrats joined with the other parties in support of the war effort, and allowed themselves, once the war credits had been voted, to be dismissed. Under the conditions of the *Burgfrieden* not only was all opposition stilled, but the Reichstag, unlike the British Parliament and the French Chamber, did not remain in session to watch the conduct of the war. All was left to the soldiers, who were above criticism: with the army the Empire had begun, with the army it was to end. After August, 1914, the Reichstag was not even a fig leaf: the absolutism of the German system, based still upon Prussian traditions, stood clearly revealed.

## CONCLUSION

It was essentially the power complex in German policy that created the situation which led to war. Britain and Germany were almost each others' best customers in 1913, and Germany, through her great import and export trade, was closely inter-locked economically with the rest of the world. The breaking of the links was almost as disastrous to Germany as it would have been to Britain had unrestricted submarine warfare succeeded in its object. The Reich's true interest, as Bismarck had always insisted after 1871, lay in the maintenance of peace. Development had come too rapidly, success had been too easy: there was no time to mitigate the stresses of hurried growth, or to build up a world position by slow and easy stages. Germany was a parvenu, and uneasily conscious of the fact:

as far back as 1880 the British Ambassador had described it as "the most sensitive nation in the world".[38] On the one hand by 1914 was a volume of international trade totalling £1,000,000,000, with foreign investments of £1,500,000,000; on the other, an army on a peace footing of 870,000, more than double the number of forty years earlier. And the last word was still with politics and the power motive.

REFERENCES

1.  E. Eyck: *Bismarck and the German Empire*, p. 151.
2.  Sir J. Clapham: *The Economic Development of France and Germany, 1815–1914*, 4th edn., p. 102.
3.  pp. 74–75.
4.  A. Rosenberg: *The Birth of the German Republic*, p. 37.
5.  *Letters from the Berlin Embassy*, ed. P. Knaplund, p. 67.
6.  T. Heuss: *Preludes to Life: Early Memoirs*, p. 18.
7.  W. H. Dawson: *The Evolution of Modern Germany*, 2nd edn. (1919), p. 336.
8.  Clapham, p. 359.
9.  A. J. Berlau: *The German Social Democratic Party, 1914–21*, p. 68.
10. Sir V. Chirol: *Fifty Years in a Changing World*, p. 274.
11. Lord Crewe: *Lord Rosebery*, II, p. 673.
12. F. L. Carsten: *The Origins of Prussia*, p. 10.
13. R. L. Buell: *Poland: Key to Europe*, p. 66.
14. Prince Hohenlohe: *Memoirs*, II, p. 416.
15. ibid.
16. Sir H. Rumbold: *The War Crisis in Berlin, 1914*, p. 342.
17. Chirol, p. 301.
18. Count R. Zedlitz-Trützschler: *Twelve Years at the Imperial German Court*, p. 104.
19. S. R. Tirrell: *German Agrarian Politics after Bismarck's Fall*, p. 108.
20. Lord Haldane: *Before the War*, pp. 91 and 71.
21. J. P. Mayer: *Max Weber and German Politics*, p. 59.
22. Rosenberg, p. 44.
23. E. Toller: *I Was a German*, p. 180.
24. Zedlitz-Trützschler, p. 51.

25.    Dawson, p. 253.

26.    L. W. Muncy: *The Junker in the Prussian Administration under William II*, p. 71.

27.    H. Feis: *Europe, The World's Banker, 1870–1914*, p. 181.

28.    E. Staley: *War and the Private Investor*, p. 45 n.

29.    *The Empress Frederick writes to Sophie*, ed. A. Gould Lee, p. 217.

30.    E. Brandenburg: *From Bismarck to the World War*, p. 206.

31.    Prince von Bülow: *Memoirs: 1903–09*, pp. 270 and 272.

32.    *The Holstein Papers:* Vol. I—*Memoirs and Political Observations*, ed. N. Rich and M. H. Fisher, p. 172.

33.    Berlau, p. 46.

34.    P. Scheidemann: *Memoirs of a Social Democrat*, I, p. 201.

35.    ibid., p. 189.

36.    Berlau, p. 75.

37.    ibid., p. 331.

38.    *Letters from the Berlin Embassy*, ed. P. Knaplund, p. 171.

# III

# CENTRAL EUROPE, 1867–1914

## GERMANS, MAGYARS AND SLAVS

### THE "EASTERN QUESTION"

GREAT though their repercussions were to prove, the first shots of the war of 1914–18, which brought down four Empires, were heard in the little Bosnian town of Sarajevo; the war began essentially as another manifestation of that "Eastern Question" which in the previous hundred years had been the cause of a dozen international crises, with five wars. The Question was that of the succession to the declining power of the Ottoman Empire, for which there were two chief rivals, the Habsburg Empire of Austria and the Romanoff of Russia, but in which, directly or indirectly, all the Powers were concerned. Austria and Russia had ambitious eyes upon the Balkans, and warily watched each other's every move there. Germany was opposed to any Russian move that might weaken Austria, and Italy to an Austrian advance along the east coast of the Adriatic, opposite her own western shores. France and Britain were concerned with the future of the Near East and of Turkey's Arab lands, and Britain, more particularly, with the Russian threat to Constantinople and the "land bridge" that stretched from the Straits to the Indian Ocean, flanking the line of communication with India. The pistol shots which killed the Archduke Francis Ferdinand and his wife, and caused Austria, in blind disregard of the fearful consequences, to attempt the subjugation of Serbia, brought Russia to Serbia's aid, Germany to Austria's and France to Russia's, while the German attempt to beat down France in a rapid campaign through Belgium drew Britain into the maelstrom. The pattern of alliances that had recently been built up as a result of Germany's rise to power therefore became involved in the older struggle to decide the fate of the Balkan lands; Eastern and Western Europe became one.

Yet the issue was only the latest of a series of crises which had created such tension that one ill-advised move, such as Austria made in attacking Serbia, was enough to upset the precarious balance of peace. And the tension existed to a critical degree both within and without the Austrian Empire, where the internal problems of a multi-national Dual Monarchy were inextricably intertwined with foreign policy, with Serbia as the focus of the hopes of discontented Slavs within the Monarchy and therefore a constant menace to its unity.

## THE CENTRAL EUROPEAN COMPLEX

One of the most complex of European problems had been for centuries the establishment of settled conditions in the centre and east of the Continent, the fluctuating frontier between the well-organized states of the west and the almost unceasing pressure of eastern peoples. Germany had long suffered from the threats of invasion from the east and southeast, and the preoccupation with those threats had played its part in delaying her development. For the Slavs and other peoples who actually inhabited the wide frontier zone the situation was still more difficult. Before they had been able to establish themselves sufficiently securely in organized states they had disappeared for the most part in the flood of the Ottoman invasions, their native dynasties and nobility, the natural leaders of the people, largely destroyed. When, as the Turks were pressed back, they began to reappear, it was as vassals of conquering Austria, or, in the eastern Balkans, as unwilling clients of the advancing power of Russia. To the north Poland alone had maintained her independence, and she had disappeared in the eighteenth century into the maws of Austria, Russia and Prussia. When, during the nineteenth century, the position came to be stabilized, the problem of the organization of a vast area remained. On what principle was Austria, in particular, to govern all the peoples gathered under the Habsburg sceptre, whether original subjects, as in German Austria, or those acquired by marriage, inheritance and conquest, such as the Czechs and Magyars, and the other varied peoples recovered from the Turks from the end of the seventeenth century onwards? The question was implicit, it may be said, from that moment in 1683 when the Turks were rolled back from the very gates of Vienna, and it became a major issue during the nineteenth century, as the rising tide of Nationalism spread through Magyars and Czechs to all the submerged peoples of the Empire.

The movements of peoples through the centuries, the invasions and reconquests and resettlements and colonization, had, however, produced such a tangle of races as no political settlement could resolve. While all were held down, whether under Turkish Sultan or under Austrian Emperor, this mattered little. As national consciousness recovered and the struggle for political freedom began, the problem of the rights of minorities, often enough of considerable size, achieved everywhere an ominous significance. President Wilson appealed in 1918 to "self-determination", a typically naïve expression of American goodwill, but had ruefully to admit that nations were coming forward which he had not known to exist. Under these complex conditions the ideal solution for central and eastern Europe after 1918 would have been a federal system, possessed of sufficient power to keep Germany and Russia, when they regained their strength, at arm's length. Never, however, was this within the bounds of possibility. Before 1914 a properly constituted Austria might have achieved it, if the Hungarians could have been persuaded to accept the Slav peoples as equals (a decisive point to which we must return). In the Habsburg Empire, indeed, the framework for such a system did exist: hence the nostalgic appeal it has had for some in the years of despair since 1938. But the necessary readjustments were never made, and the Empire collapsed in 1918 before any attempt had been made to solve its problems. Diagnoses and solutions were not lacking, but tended to cancel each other out, while every remedy proposed had to face the challenge of centrifugal tendencies and intense national rivalries. In the event, therefore, a *vis inertiae* kept the Empire in being, aided, it may be said, by a large, efficient, and highly respected bureaucracy, and it took four years of a war that saw nearly three-quarters of a million Habsburg subjects killed to break up the Empire. Well might the Emperor Francis Joseph have claimed, as he is said to have done in 1904, that "the Austro-Hungarian monarchy is no fanciful work of art, but an absolute necessity for the present existence and for the future of her peoples. It is a refuge for all those fragmentary nations of Central Europe which without a common home would have a deplorable existence, and be tossed about by all their powerful neighbours."[1] The tragedy was that for so many the common home, for all their desire to preserve it, eventually became an almost intolerable bondage. After 1683 the logic of events made of Austria no longer a German state but the successor to the fading power of Turkey, a refuge, indeed, for the disorganized peoples of central and south-eastern Europe for as long as they needed a common centre. Not until the Empire's defeat at the hands of Prussia in 1866 did this become completely apparent, but from that time the whole question of the *raison d'être* of Austria as a State was an issue of the first importance to Central Europe and, as events were to show, to the whole world.

## THE FEDERAL SOLUTION: KARL RENNER

Among those who boldly faced the problems of the Habsburg Monarchy before 1914, but who were powerless to put their ideas into practice, was the Social-Democrat, Karl Renner (1870-1950), to whom on two occasions the irony of history was to commit the care of the independent Austria which emerged from the wreckage of the Empire after the First World War. When the First Republic was established in 1918 Renner served it for two years as Chancellor: 1945 saw him once again Chancellor of the Second Republic, in which he then became President until his death in 1950. To him, in the years before the First War, it was clear that only in a federal system, which would allow free development to all its peoples, was to be found a secure future for the Empire. Without that, he argued in 1906, the Empire would be crushed between Germany and Russia.[2] It was a prescient view, unhappily justified by the event—by the German domination of Austria in 1914-18, by the Nazi occupation of 1938 and by the consequent Russian irruption of 1945. Only the weakness of both Germany and Russia after 1918 permitted the establishment of an independent Austria, and the majority of Austrians then saw a future for their country at first only in a union with Germany, which was, however, prevented by the victorious Allies. In

1945, with Germany again shattered by defeat, the threat came
from victorious Russia, and was averted only by the powerful
presence of the U.S.A. Thus was demonstrated, in even wider
scope, that inter-connexion of events on the Danube with
larger movements throughout the world which had first been
revealed in 1914. Yet the forty years since 1906 had shown only
too clearly the correctness of Renner's diagnosis of the
problems confronting the Austrian Empire. Whether, in fact,
a federal solution was ever possible is another matter: the odds,
as we shall see, were against it. That Austria's problems were
never solved reflects on the inadequacies of the Empire's rulers,
but no less on the complexity of the issues with which they
were confronted and the intractability of so many of the
peoples involved.

## THE HABSBURG EMPIRE: AUSTRIA

The Empire consisted from the late 'sixties of a wide
variety of territories and peoples, grouped around the Danube
basin and united by the single link of the Habsburg family,
which had been ruling in Vienna since the thirteenth century
and in Hungary, in practice, since the seventeenth (the greater
part of Hungary having been in Turkish hands from 1526,
when the Habsburgs succeeded the last non-German dynasty,
until 1699). In the west was Austria itself, the original Duchy
which had served the Habsburgs as a base for the territorial
aggrandizement of their House, and provided them in Vienna
with the natural centre for the domination of the central
Danube area. North of Austria was the old Czech kingdom of
Bohemia-Moravia, together with parts of the once independent
Polish kingdom: farther south, but still forming part of the
western half of the Empire, was another Slav territory,
Slovenia, a Habsburg possession since the fourteenth century
which gave access to the Adriatic. Bohemia-Moravia had been
acquired by election, like Hungary, in 1526, after King Louis
of Bohemia and Hungary had fallen on the fatal field of
Mohács. Hungary had gradually been recovered from the
Turks, though the reconquest had not been completed until
1718, but Bohemia, though never overrun by the Sultan's
armies, had in effect become a Habsburg conquest after the
rebellion of 1618 which had opened the terrible Thirty Years'

War in Germany. That the Czechs were a conquered people explains much of the bitterness which made of Bohemia a Central European Ireland and presented the Empire, as will be seen, with the almost insoluble problem of the reconciliation of Czech and German which has brought untold tragedy in our own times.

## HUNGARY

The eastern half of the Empire consisted of the kingdom of Hungary, which included the Slav territories of Croatia and Slovakia and the largely Roumanian region of Transylvania. The Magyars of Hungary were a proud people, still, unlike the Czechs, possessing much of their ancient nobility, and firmly opposed to the Habsburg notion that their liberation from Turkish rule had not restored their old and jealously guarded liberties but had merely conferred upon them a more congenial sovereign. The restoration of the independence they had lost in 1526, and of the full rights of the Crown of St. Stephen, the symbol of national unity, had long been the aim of the Magyar leaders, even as the recovery of Czech rights was the ambition of the rising generation of intellectuals and politicians in Bohemia. The Magyar leaders were, however, irrevocably opposed to any sharing of their national freedom with their subject peoples unless they would accept magyarization: from this was to stem much of the tragedy of the last years of the Empire.

## POLES AND ITALIANS

The Polish territory, Galicia, on the northern and north-eastern frontier of the Empire, has already been referred to. This had been acquired when the ancient kingdom of Poland had first been partitioned in 1772, and to retain their allegiance the Polish nobility of Galicia had long been among the more favoured of imperial subjects, to the detriment, however, of the local Polish and Ukrainian peasantry. At the other extreme of the Empire, to the south of Austria itself, were Trieste and the Trentino, the last remaining relics of the great possessions once held by the Habsburgs in North Italy, and a constant source of strained relations with the newly united Italian kingdom.

## THE COMPLEX OF PEOPLES

The very recital of these varied territories is an epitome of centuries of European history and of the fluctuating fortunes of one of the most influential of Europe's reigning families. The Habsburg symbol, the double-headed eagle, facing both west and east, was an apt one, characterizing as it did the family's interests both in Germany and western Europe and in Hungary and eastern Europe. Vienna was a German city, but the East, as Metternich had claimed, began at its gates: the nineteenth century was to see the Empire's focus of interest shifting eastwards, until in a struggle with Russia for the control of south-eastern Europe it finally perished. The Empire itself, though governed by a German family, and German in its form and official language, had long since ceased to be German in composition. The Germans were still the dominant race (though from 1867 they had to share their dominance with the Magyars) but they formed only about one-fifth of the Empire's total population. Census returns were misleading from the racial point of view, as they were taken on the basis of the language normally spoken, not of racial affinities: many Slavs, in particular, were therefore returned as Germans or Hungarians. Nevertheless, the figures of the last imperial census in 1910 provide a record of the Empire in its last stages, and reveal the variety of its composition. Returns were made separately for the western, Austrian, half (which was officially styled "the kingdoms and provinces represented in the *Reichsrat*" (Parliament), but was more conveniently referred to as "Austria"), and for Hungary. In Austria the Germans numbered in 1910 nearly ten millions, as against more than six million Czechs, five million Poles, three-and-a-half million Ruthenes (Ukrainians) and two million South Slavs: comparison with the returns of a generation earlier shows that the proportion of Germans was falling. In Hungary, where the figures were gravely distorted by the pressure of "magyarization", Magyars numbered nearly ten millions, Germans and Slovaks nearly two millions each and Roumanians three millions: the success of "magyarization" was shown by the increase in the proportion of Magyars and the relative decline of the other peoples of the kingdom. Throughout the Empire as a whole there were at this time, if we consider only the most considerable national groups, nearly twelve million Germans, nearly ten million Magyars and more than eight million Czechs and Slovaks. Of Slavs, including not only Czechs and Slovaks but Poles, Ruthenes, Croats, Serbs and Slovenes, there were in all some twenty millions, while the remaining nationalities numbered more than four millions. Until 1867 the main national conflict within the Empire was between Germans and Magyars. In that year the rights of the Magyars were at last recognized, and they were left in control of Hungary. The struggle then transferred itself in Austria to the Czechs, who in their turn sought recognition of their historic rights, and in Hungary, as the years passed, to the submerged peoples, Slovaks, Ruthenes and Roumanians, who struggled desperately for national recognition against the pressure of magyarization. Meanwhile the Germans, long in the ascendant, resented and resisted the decline in their influence. There was, therefore, hardly a single national group, except after 1867 the Magyars, which found in the Empire satisfactory scope for its development, though to the last there were few who saw their future anywhere but within the Empire's frontiers.

## THE EMPEROR FRANCIS JOSEPH

Over this conglomeration of jarring peoples presided the august figure of the Emperor Francis Joseph, twentieth of his line, who had become Emperor at the age of eighteen in 1848, when he had taken over the crown in the middle of a revolution from his semi-imbecile uncle, Ferdinand, and who was destined to live on until 1916, when his Empire was already tottering to its fall. For nearly seventy years Francis Joseph embodied in himself the unity of the Habsburg territories, until it seemed that in this dignified and gracious figure, courteous, industrious and conscientious, but at the same time reserved and aloof, was bound up the very spirit of the Empire, the very hope of its continuance. For nearly seventy years the storms of personal and political affliction beat round Francis Joseph's head— revolts and rebellions, defeats in war, the loss of inherited territories, the tragic deaths of wife, of son, of brother, and, at the end, of nephew and intended successor—until it seemed that nothing was to be spared him, and he himself complained, with characteristic restraint, that he had no luck. Yet while he lived, a legacy from an earlier period, "the last representative of the old system", as he described himself to Theodore Roosevelt in 1910, the Empire stood shaken but unbroken, though it was widely expected that it would not long survive him. Critics accused him of "seventy years of wasted opportunities", and it is true that under his rule few, if any, of his Empire's problems were solved. Indeed, it is doubtful whether he understood its problems or even appreciated that there were problems to be solved: "the great tides of life of our time", one of his ministers, Joseph Baernreither, confided to his diary in 1910, "hardly reach his ear as the most distant echo".[3] He slaved at his desk, rising before 5 a.m. to get through his audiences early, and from his desk he ordered the affairs of his vast domain. He saw to everything, it has been said, and in consequence achieved nothing. The very mass of business that he was content to grapple with allowed him no scope for wider considerations of policy: "the number of things to be handled left him no time to be Emperor".[4] To him the Empire was a great family estate, and he ruled it from his desk, as one would manage some vast and impersonal business concern. He was incapable of realizing that statesmanship entailed something more than administration, for he lacked imagination and, though not cold, rarely allowed himself the indulgence of personal feelings.

But the mistakes of Austrian policy must not be credited to Francis Joseph alone. Inadequate though he may have been to the demands made upon him, he was sustained by a high sense of duty and did not spare himself in official tasks. A long reign that began in autocracy and military rule ended with a system of government which, though not responsible in any technical sense, was—or endeavoured to be—responsive to popular forces which expressed themselves through the medium of a wide suffrage. If Parliament failed to achieve unity within itself, and in its internecine strife made itself the laughing-stock of Europe, this to Francis Joseph was no more than another instance of the ill luck that dogged him: it could hardly be laid at his door. Meanwhile, the very length of his reign, his misfortunes, his simple and dignified bearing and handsome presence and the fascination of the ancient tradition that was embodied in him, all served to create, especially among the

Germans of Austria and in his own city of Vienna, a personal respect and affection akin to that felt for Queen Victoria in Britain. The impression was general, too, that he alone held the Empire together, that with his passing it would disintegrate. What, in any case, could replace him? If the Empire failed to hold together its peoples could not but be the worst sufferers. While he lived there was at least a focus of unity, and an opportunity of devising, with however little hope of success, some means of overcoming the growing separatism of the Danube peoples. As the American Minister in Vienna shrewdly noted in 1895:

> Nothing holds Austria and Hungary together but the fear of the result of separation and the great personal influence of Francis Joseph. [5]

Even the Socialists, for all their opposition to everything that Francis Joseph stood for, based their policy upon the preservation of the Empire's unity, and sought only, as the reference to Karl Renner's views has already shown, to reshape it on federal lines, which would provide full scope for the development of each national grouping. Like their comrades in Germany, they realized the necessity for maintaining a united front, in particular against the hated reactionary power of Russia. "So long as the Russian Tsardom remained intact," wrote the Socialist leader Otto Bauer (1881–1938) after the war, "the existence of the Austro-Hungarian Empire was an historical necessity."[6] Peoples and Emperor, however, had different ends in view in seeking the preservation of the Empire. If the peoples sought security and national self-expression, Francis Joseph's object was the simple one of maintaining the Empire as a Habsburg possession. Hence his willingness to yield to the inevitable when, as with the Magyars in 1867, political forces became too strong to be resisted further. Yet his decisions were rarely final ones. No course was to him unalterable if the interests of the Monarchy seemed to demand a new line of policy. Hence his compromises, his shifts and changes of policy, his abrupt discarding of seemingly trusted ministers, whom he flung away, it was said, like "squeezed lemons". The full implications of his measures were rarely apparent to him, and it was therefore possible for him to pursue conflicting aims, or to make sudden changes of front that caused bitter criticism and shook confidence and loyalty. Nowhere was this more apparent, as will be seen, than in his dealings with the Czechs. Yet if his policies fluctuated they did so largely in response to political forces which he found it impossible to reconcile: if he lost much loyalty in Bohemia he lost it among Germans no less than among Czechs.

## THE GERMANS AND FRANCIS JOSEPH: ADOLF HITLER

By making concessions to the Czechs, indeed, he forfeited the allegiance of many Germans, as Adolf Hitler, who was born a subject of the Emperor, revealed in the record of his early years in Vienna in *Mein Kampf*. For centuries the Empire had been ruled and shaped by Germans: now the submerged nationalities were stirring and threatening the long German domination, and this at the very time when a great and purely German Empire had been created by the Hohenzollerns in the north. Many German subjects of the Habsburgs felt as Hitler did:

> I had a feeling of pride and admiration when I compared the rise of the young German Empire with the decline of the Austrian State.

## THE PROBLEM OF UNITY: NATIONALISMS IN CONFLICT

It is in the Austria of 1866–1914, in fact, that many of the roots of Nazism are to be found: Austria produced not only the leader but much of the ideology. Yet if many Germans felt that the Habsburgs had in the end betrayed them, the feeling was shared by most of the other peoples, who were ultimately driven to the conclusion that they were hardly more than pawns in the dynasty's struggle for survival. Personal rule of the type which Francis Joseph represented had long lost its historical justification, but what was to replace it? What principles, what institutions could be adapted or devised to provide a new basis for the essential unity of the Danube region? Under the pressure of growing nationalist feeling among its varied peoples Austria became, in the words used by a Transylvanian advocate of federalism, Aurel Popovici, in his book, *The United States of Great Austria* (1906), a house full of quarrelsome families. If Austria was to do justice to all her peoples the house must be modernized and divided into flats:[7]

> All the peoples concerned are at bottom devoted to the Austrian idea, for between all of them there exists an inner community of interest. . . . A great Austria which would do justice . . . to all her peoples would have a special mission beyond her own frontiers in eastern Europe, and by fulfilling it would render her own future secure.

Yet every attempt to refashion the Empire by conceding rights to the submerged peoples was faced with the determined hostility of the Germans and Magyars, who were not prepared to yield their position of dominance, justified as it was in their view by centuries of leadership. The very realization of the necessity for relaxing autocratic control raised new issues and introduced new sources of strife, bringing into the open rivalries and ambitions that had hitherto been concealed by the common subjection: in this Austria has but shared the experience of such countries as Ireland and India. The time had come for the existence of the Empire to be justified by a new declaration of its functions, but in their striving for self-expression its peoples found themselves almost irreconcilably in conflict. The Austrian novelist, Robert Musil (1880–1942) has hit off with ironical deprecation in his great novel of the last years of the Empire, *The Man without Qualities*, the nationalist disagreements that afflicted those years:[8]

> They were so violent that they several times a year caused the machinery of State to jam and come to a dead stop. But between whiles . . . everyone got on excellently with everyone else and behaved as though nothing had ever been the matter. Nor had anything real ever been the matter. It was nothing more than the fact that every human being's dislike of every other human being's attempts to get on —a dislike in which today we are all agreed—in that country crystallized earlier.

Only a unity based on consent could maintain the Empire, but the "dislike of every other human being's attempts to get on" was so strong among the Germans and Magyars in particular that strife was inevitable. It is doubtful whether even the dynasty, unless in the hands of a man of outstanding ability, could have reconciled the differences. Francis Joseph certainly made no attempt to do so. His aim was rather to keep things

going, to make piecemeal and half-hearted concessions when
there was no remedy, to keep all the nationalities, since their
demands were irreconcilable, in the words of one of his
ministers, "in a state of uniform, nicely-tempered discontent"[9]
—to muddle along, that is to say, in the true spirit of pre-war
Austrian *Schlamperei*. His nephew and heir, Francis Ferdinand,
had other views and would have sought some solution of the
problems of national rights, to which he had devoted a good
deal of attention: through his entourage he was in touch with
Popovici, whose proposals for reform influenced him. But he
lacked his uncle's extreme caution, and his violence of temper
and savage hostility to the Magyars would hardly have helped
matters. If it was his assassination in 1914 that eventually
brought the Empire down four years later, it is by no
means unlikely that a breakdown would have come had he
lived.

## THE BEGINNINGS OF CONFLICT: GERMANS AND MAGYARS

The strain had first been felt in 1848 when in an outburst of
the liberalism and nationalism that characterized that year of
revolutions, the Germans and Magyars had revolted against
autocracy and demanded a share of political power. In the main
the other peoples, apart from the Italians, remained loyal to the
dynasty at this period, and, in the true spirit of the old Habsburg principle of divide and rule, it had been with their help
that the revolt had been crushed. The resistance of the
Hungarians had been particularly bitter, and had been beaten
down in the end only with the help of Russian troops lent by
the Tsar. This cruel repression left tragic memories (revived,
alas, in 1956), but it was not long before Hungary had her
revenge. For twelve years after 1848 the young Francis Joseph
maintained a centralized dictatorship based on the army and
German officials, but the reverses he suffered from 1859 at the
hands of France and Prussia compelled him to modify the
regime. Already before 1866 he had made concessions both to
his own German subjects in Austria and to the Hungarians.
Finally, in 1867 the Empire was refounded on an entirely new
basis, the *Ausgleich* (Compromise), which lasted until 1918
and contributed in no small degree to the final breakdown of
that year.

## THE *Ausgleich* AND THE DUAL MONARCHY

The very weakness of the imperial Government after the loss of two wars within seven years compelled it to accept the Hungarian terms for a constitutional settlement, and the need for acceptance was the more pressing because during the war of 1866 Bismarck had been in touch with the Magyar leaders, inciting them to revolt and so to add to Austria's difficulties. By the terms of the settlement of 1867 Hungary gained complete equality with Austria and a "Dual Monarchy" of Austria-Hungary came into existence, with Francis Joseph as Emperor in Austria and King in Hungary. Apart from a few subjects of common interest—foreign affairs, finance and the army—each half of the dual state had complete and independent control over its own affairs. The Hungarians, therefore, won all they had fought for, and their chief concern until 1918 was to maintain the *Ausgleich* system intact.

## OTHER CLAIMS: THE "BARBARIANS"

Yet the system was doomed from the first. If the Magyars were to retain their equality with the Austrians and dominate their half of the Empire-Kingdom, they had to deny their subject peoples—Slovaks, Serbs, Croats and Roumanians—the very freedom which they themselves had wrested from the Emperor. Their policy was summed-up by one of their leaders, Count Andrássy, afterwards famous as Foreign Minister of the Dual Monarchy, when he said to the Austrian representatives during the course of the negotiations, "You look after your barbarians, and we will look after ours". To him the subject peoples, mainly peasants and farmers who for centuries had had no independent political existence, were no more than barbarians. Their own natural leaders, their native aristocracy, had long since been destroyed or absorbed into the ranks of their conquerors, and for hundreds of years they had acquiesced in their servitude. Now, however, new leaders were springing up, a small band of educated men, teachers, priests and poets, striving to create the spirit of nationhood from ancient cultures and traditions. After 1848 these men were increasingly active, and the years from 1867 to 1918 in Austria-Hungary are marked by the struggle of the "barbarians" to win national rights for themselves. These they gained when not only the system of 1867 but the very Empire itself collapsed in 1918, and they then found themselves confronted by problems of political education and of economic and social development which had hardly been foreseen in the hopeful early days of national renaissance.

## THE *Ausgleich* PERIOD AND ITS AFTERMATH
## (1) HUNGARY

The developments of the *Ausgleich* period differed considerably in the two halves of the Dual Monarchy. As a whole, Austria-Hungary consisted partly of peoples without a history, and partly of peoples over-conscious of earlier glories. The latter, the Germans and Magyars, ever mindful of past greatness and domination, had little sympathy for the peoples they had long held in subjection, and would admit their claims only if they consented to be absorbed into the "master race". To the Czech who became German, or the Slovak who magyarized himself, all paths were open: discrimination was based on language and culture, not, as with the Nazis later, on blood. But while the Germans, in their half of the Monarchy, failed to maintain their supremacy and saw the Czechs winning ever more privileged positions, in Hungary the claims of the subject peoples were successfully resisted to the last, apart from some concessions made to the Croats. The Slovaks, kinsmen and neighbours of the Czechs, suffered particularly under a régime that regarded all languages but Magyar as "barbarian". Moreover, among the Hungarians themselves political power remained the prerogative of the landowning aristocracy and gentry. As a result, Hungary was faced in 1918 with a social revolution as well as a revolt of the subject peoples. The revolution was crushed, but the social problems it sought to cure still remained and have reappeared since the final passing of the old Hungary of privilege in 1945. Further, the memory of the *Ausgleich* period left among the subject peoples who gained their freedom in 1918, the Slovaks, Croats and Roumanians, a legacy of distrust and suspicion of Hungary which made effective co-operation among the Danubian countries impossible. This played into Germany's hands, and Hitler's Reich alone gained from a situation which had its roots far back in the past.

## (2) Austria, the Czech Renaissance

Although developments in Austria were different, a situation was created there which similarly shaped the conditions of the period after 1918. The leading subject people in the western half of the Dual Monarchy were the Czechs. They had been held down under Austrian rule since 1620, but were now reviving their sense of national destiny and the memory of the great days of the independent kingdom of Bohemia in the fourteenth and fifteenth centuries. In this process of national recovery a notable part was played by František Palacký (1798–1876), whose *History of Bohemia*, published between 1836 and 1865, made him "the father of his people" and the founder of the modern Czech State. He was assisted by a group of poets and philosophers, though to the world outside the greatest figures of the Czech revival, before Masaryk, were the composers, Bedřich Smetana (1824–84) and Antonín Dvořák (1841–1904).

Dvořák and Smetana came to represent for the Czechs not only the peak of their cultural tradition, but also the assertion of national individuality against the German rule which had for centuries suppressed every expression of the national spirit. The most potent expression of the nationalist movement was to be found, however, in the gymnastic organization, *Sokol* (Falcon), which, founded by Tyrš and Fügner in 1862 as an answer to the challenge of German youth organizations, became the disciplined inspiration of Czech patriotism and fired the enthusiasm of the other Slav peoples. The aims of the Sokols were:

> By the education of body and spirit, by physical energy, by art and science, by all moral means, to revive the fatherland.

Through their emphasis on education and discipline they played a vital part in the revival of the Czech State, and it is a tribute to their activity that their movement was suppressed by the German authorities in the two world wars. Their last great demonstration in Prague before 1939, the rally in the summer of 1938, was a moving gesture of national confidence at a moment when, once again, the storms were closing in on their people. "What the Czechs are today", a leading authority has said, "they owe in very large measure to the Sokols."[10]

In the middle of this intellectual and moral ferment, from which in time the Czech State was to be born, came the *Ausgleich* and the decisive developments that flowed from it. To the Czech leaders, anxious to assert the rights of the Czechs and their brother Slavs alike, the new policy brought a dashing of hopes. In 1848 Palacký, concerned at the rise of German nationalism, with its contempt for the Slav peoples, had used the phrase, "If Austria did not exist, it would be necessary to create her, in the interests of humanity itself." But the Austria he had in mind was an Austria which would recognize the true basis of its existence in the principle of equal rights for all its peoples, and when in 1865 he realized the turn events were taking he uttered in his book, *The Idea of the Austrian State*, a prophetic warning against a merely *Dual* Empire, with a German-Magyar hegemony. "If the Slavs", he wrote, "are really to be declared a lower race . . . and fit only to be the stuff for two other people to rule", terrible consequences would follow: "we Slavs are peaceful people, but we warn you —do not sow wind lest you reap storm. . . . Is that man free to whom it is said, 'Thou shalt be free, but not as thou willst, only as I dictate to thee?' " He concluded with the memorable phrase, "Before Austria was, we were; and when Austria no longer is, we still shall be". This, rather than the dictum of 1848, represented his true attitude.

Francis Joseph made one effort to satisfy Czech claims. In 1871 he promised, actually for the third time, to be crowned King of Bohemia in Prague, as already, after the *Ausgleich*, he had been crowned King of Hungary in Budapest, and he accepted a constitution which would have made Bohemia part of a *Triple* Empire, an equal partner with Austria and Hungary. But the opposition of German-Austrians and of Hungarians was so strong that he withdrew the promise, and for the rest of his life did not waver in his acceptance of the 1867 settlement as final. For this the Czechs never forgave him. It is significant that Smetana's great nationalist opera, *Libuše*, appeared within a year of this blow to their hopes. At about the same time Palacký in his "political testament" deliberately revoked his earlier attitude to Austria. He died soon afterwards, in 1876, and with him passed the first fine flush of the Czech revival.

## Czech-German Rivalry

Nevertheless, the Czechs did not remain without rights, as did their kinsmen, the Slovaks, under Hungarian rule. For eight years they were held down while the Austrian constitutional system, established by the "December Constitution" of 1867, was managed by the centralist and nationalist German Liberals, who had stoutly resisted the concessions offered by the Emperor in 1871. The Liberals did not understand, however, that they held office only on sufferance: Francis Joseph had no intention of becoming a completely constitutional ruler. In particular he would not surrender his control of the army and foreign policy which, apart from his personal interests, he regarded as essential to the preservation of the Empire's unity. By their attempts to interfere in army affairs and by their opposition to the occupation of Bosnia-Herzegovina in 1878 (on the ground, as will be seen later, that it would further increase the Slav population of the Empire), they alienated him from them, and drove him to seek a parliamentary majority in the support of the Czechs. From 1879 the Czech representatives, abandoning their earlier attitude of abstention, played an active part in the *Reichsrat*, but the rift between them and the Germans of Austria and Bohemia steadily widened, until parliamentary government eventually became a mockery. How it struck an uninformed observer, brought up in a romantic atmosphere of German nationalism, is shown in the earlier pages of Adolf Hitler's *Mein Kampf*. The seeds of Hitler's contempt for all parliamentary systems were sown in his Vienna days, when he saw at close quarters a system which the Austrian historian and authority on Parliament, Joseph Redlich, has described in scathing terms:

> Political control passed from the leading statesmen in the contending nations and parties to the loudest-voiced and most irresponsible nationalists in the various political parties, and any sort of effective legislative activity was ruled out.[11]

Under these circumstances the ultimate control rested with the Emperor and his aristocratic advisers, and both Germans and Czechs intensified their nationalism and drew away from the dynasty. Long before 1914, while in Hungary Magyar domination remained unshaken, Austria was crumbling.

E

An Austrian writer has neatly summed up the process of disintegration that was apparent before 1914 in the phrase, "the racial shirt was closer to the heart than the imperial uniform".

## Austria's Expulsion from Germany, 1866, and its Consequences

If the events of 1866 and 1867 exercised a decisive influence upon the later development of Austria-Hungary, the Franco-Prussian War—or, rather, its rapid termination in Prussia's favour—also played a part. In 1870 Francis Joseph had not yet become reconciled to the exclusion from Germany which had been inflicted upon him by Prussia in 1866, and between that year and 1870 toyed with the idea of a war of revenge that would create a powerful union of South German States under Austrian leadership to thwart Prussia's ambitions. Only three months after the fatal defeat of Königgrätz he appointed as his Foreign Minister Bismarck's bitterest opponent, the former Saxon Premier, Count von Beust, and with his aid sought to reverse the verdict of the battle. The obvious ally was France, which had its own reasons for desiring the curtailment of Prussian power, and with Napoleon III Francis Joseph therefore had several meetings. Early in 1870 the campaign against Prussia began to be sketched, and a decisive battle which should throw Prussian influence back into North Germany was planned to take place near Leipzig. But for many reasons Francis Joseph shrank from war. Hungarian influence, now strong with the Emperor, was opposed to it, fearing that whatever the outcome it would prejudice Hungary's newly won privileges, while there was no guarantee that Italy would remain inactive in Austria's rear, and—an even more potent consideration—Russian sympathies were known to be with Prussia. Moreover, Francis Joseph realized that an unprovoked attack on Prussia in alliance with France would serve only to rally the other German States round Prussia. Hence his insistence during the course of the negotiations with France that he would go to war "only if compelled to". But the issue was resolved for him. Before an alliance could be made the war-clouds had suddenly loomed up, and France was already prostrate. Francis Joseph drew back in relief that he had not committed himself: henceforth he accepted without question the verdict of 1866.

The consequences, as they made themselves felt both in the policy of the Dual Monarchy and in the position of the Austrian Germans, now finally cut off from the main body of their kinsmen, were fraught with future dangers. The exclusion of Austria from Germany not only led to the growth of a Pan-German movement in Austria which proved to be the precursor of Nazism; it also drove the Habsburg government to take a greater interest in the affairs of the Balkans. Most of the Empire's Italian territories had already been lost, and Austria's historic rôle in Germany had been brought to a close; inevitably attention was directed to the south-east, to the Balkan regions where Turkish power was in rapid decline. But here there was no clear field for expansion, as Russia had long been casting covetous eyes on the legacy of the Sultans. And Russia, both as the leading Slav State and as the champion of Greek Orthodox Christianity, possessed a far greater power of attraction for the Balkan peoples. There followed a bitter rivalry between the two Empires, a rivalry which led ultimately to war over Serbia in 1914. In short, the victory of Prussia in 1866, with the dashing of Austria's hopes of revenge in 1870, prepared the way both for the war of 1914 and, through the agitation for the reuniting of all Germans, to the Nazi seizure of Austria and Czechoslovakia in 1938–39.

## THE RECONCILIATION WITH GERMANY

Francis Joseph's acceptance of the new situation was first marked by a reconciliation with the Germany of William I. Beust was dismissed in November, 1871, and the Hungarian Prime Minister, Count Julius Andrássy, was summoned to fill his place: he held office for eight decisive years. The move was a significant one, for Andrássy had been one of the chief architects of the *Ausgleich* system, and his policy was directed towards the maintenance of the system by the bolstering of the position of the German-Austrians, who would thus, with the Magyars, retain supremacy over the Slavs. In foreign affairs this entailed a friendly attitude to Hohenzollern Germany and a coolness towards Russia; in home affairs, the fateful breach between the Emperor and the Czechs, which has already been referred to.

## THE *Dreikaiserbund* AND BALKAN RIVALRIES

June, 1873, saw the formal establishment of the *Dreikaiser-bund*, the "Alliance of the three Emperors" of Austria, Germany, and Russia, which was intended to maintain peace and conservative principles in Europe. A further link between the three Emperors was the possession by each of them of part of the old Polish kingdom, which had been partitioned a century earlier: any quarrel between them would inevitably mean a reopening of the Polish question, as was seen after 1914. Yet, in another part of the Slav world, the Balkans, the seeds of disagreement were already sown, and Bismarck, to whom the whole "Eastern Question" was, in his own graphic phrase, "not worth the bones of a single Pomeranian Grenadier", was faced with the dangerous possibility of a rift between Austria and Russia over Balkan developments. To the end of his career he strove to avoid committing Germany to either of the protagonists, endeavouring by friendship with both to prevent their rivalry from coming to a head, but the task became increasingly difficult, especially after the death of the Tsar Alexander II in 1881. The Alliance was for Bismarck an important element in German policy, intended to gain the time for peaceful settlement which the Empire needed, but the other two partners had different views. Both Austria and Russia, Andrássy's son has written in a study of his father's policy, "were anxious to make use of the alliance for the promotion of their differing Eastern policies";[12] both, in fact, hoped through it to be able to keep a wary eye on each other's Balkan moves. Bismarck, on the other hand, had formed it "for the very purpose of eliminating the Eastern Question and isolating France". Under these circumstances the Alliance could not stand any severe test. It did not long remain unshaken.

## THE "EASTERN CRISIS" OF 1876–78

The first test came when risings against Turkish rule in Herzegovina and Bosnia in 1875 led to an attack by Serbia on Turkey. The defeat of Serbia and a further rising in Bulgaria, which led to the infamous "Bulgarian Atrocities" committed by the Turks in reprisal, brought Russia into the war in 1877, and by the beginning of 1878 Russian armies had broken their way through to Constantinople. In March peace was concluded at San Stefano, and the peace treaty, while it gave Russia important territorial gains, most disturbed European opinion by setting-up a great autonomous State of Bulgaria, which was obviously designed to be a protégé of Russia and an indirect means of expanding Russian influence deep into the Balkans.

To Austria this treaty came as a severe blow. Already in 1876, when war had first broken out in the Balkans, Francis Joseph and the Tsar had met at Reichstadt and agreed on the gains each should make in the event of a Turkish collapse. The agreement was intended to avoid a conflict of aims, and to ensure that each Power should gain *pari passu* with the other. But Russia developed other ideas when she entered the war herself, and Andrássy to his alarm found himself faced with the possibility of a great Slav state in the Balkans, backed by Russia, which would obviously exercise a dangerous attraction upon the Slavs of Austria-Hungary and threaten the whole *Ausgleich* system. As a good Magyar Andrássy was opposed to the notion of absorbing any more Slavs into Austria-Hungary, but if the integrity of Turkey could not be maintained he was prepared to annex some of its territories, though only to prevent the establishment of any large Slav state or the excessive extension of Russian influence. The Dual Monarchy, he argued, "was no aggressive State" and ought to extend its territories "only if there were no other means of defending our present possessions".[13] Circumstances might arise, however, when Austria would have to move to prevent the absorption of Bosnia and Herzegovina into an enlarged Serbia which would inevitably become the focus of the nationalist aims of the Monarchy's Slav subjects. If this were not prevented, "we should just give ourselves up and take over the rôle of Sick Man".[14] Andrássy had therefore accepted, though with some reluctance, the Reichstadt agreement, which had awarded Bosnia and Herzegovina to Austria as her share of the Turkish spoils, if they should come to be divided, and in 1878 he resisted the San Stefano treaty which by ignoring Austria's claims seemed to violate the earlier agreement.

Bismarck's rôle was now a most difficult one. He wished to play the part of an "honest broker" between Austria and Russia and avoid forfeiting the friendship of either. At the same time he realized that the Russian demands must be reduced, and he shrank from taking part in a conference which would inevitably leave Russia dissatisfied and might therefore weaken the good relations between Berlin and St. Petersburg. In other words, he was beginning to be faced with the necessity for choosing between Austria and Russia: events were running away with him, and the course was being set which was to lead, in 1914, to Germany's being disastrously tied to a reckless Austria.

## THE CONGRESS OF BERLIN, 1878—BOSNIA-HERZEGOVINA AND THE AUSTRO-GERMAN ALLIANCE, 1879

Nevertheless, it was to Bismarck that everyone turned, and it was at Berlin, and under his chairmanship, that a great European congress opened in June, 1878, to revise the San Stefano treaty. It led to a compromise solution which satisfied no one, with the significant exception of Austria, and which held within it the seeds of much future conflict. San Stefano was set aside, but Austria, whose policy had hardly been a glorious one, received the right to garrison Bosnia and Herzegovina, an obvious invitation to formal annexation (which for fear of other complications was, however, delayed until 1908). Great was the indignation in Russia when the terms of the Treaty of Berlin (July, 1878) were made known. The Tsar had secretly pledged himself to Francis Joseph not to oppose the occupation of the two provinces, but the high hopes raised by Russia's successes, and sacrifices, in the war had been dashed, and Alexander spoke bitterly of the Berlin conference as "the European coalition against Russia, under the leadership of Prince Bismarck". Russo-German relations rapidly deteriorated, and Bismarck, alarmed by the manifestations of Russian hostility, turned to Austria-Hungary for support. If a choice had to be made he could not abandon the Dual Empire to its fate: its collapse at the hands of Russia would mean a vast extension of Russian influence into Central

Europe, which could not but be dangerous to Germany. He therefore approached Andrássy, and found him more than willing to form a defensive alliance specifically aimed against Russia. William I, whose relations with the Tsar had long been very close, was more difficult to convince, but after a reluctant consent had been dragged from him a secret defensive alliance of Germany and Austria-Hungary was signed in October, 1879.

It was a significant move, and Andrássy's comment on the new alliance, in a telegram to Francis Joseph, is revealing. "Now the Monarchy's road to the East is free," he wrote. Undeterred by the general opposition among the Germans and Magyars to the addition of a million and half Slavs to the population of the Empire, he accepted the implications of the acquisition of fresh territory in the Balkans and set Austria-Hungary firmly on the road to the East. His motives are not far to seek. His initial reluctance had been overcome by the fear of the creation of a new and independent Slav State out of the ruins of the Turkish Empire, and by jealousy of Russian gains. To these factors was added the powerful consideration of the obvious delight of Francis Joseph at the acquisition of new lands which could serve as some compensation for the losses in Germany and Italy which the Habsburg territories had suffered under his rule. "It is easy to read in the Emperor's face," reported the German Ambassador at Vienna, "the satisfaction occasioned to him by the thought that the years of his reign will not be wholly lacking in triumphs. It seemed to me that the melancholy expression which so many have noted had fallen from his face when I last saw him."[15]

## AUSTRIA'S BALKAN POLICY

But there was more than Francis Joseph's dynastic pride at stake. Austria-Hungary's commerce was expanding and seeking new outlets; the Balkans, in particular, offered a convenient market for the manufactures of Austria, and Austrian railway interests were concerned with the opening of routes through the western Balkans to Salonika, the key port on the Aegean, and south-eastwards, through Bulgaria, to Constantinople itself. No pressure was to be brought to bear upon Turkey, but if Turkish control over these railways should weaken the Monarchy would ensure that they passed to her. In private conversation Andrássy was quite open as to his aims. "The acquisition of Bosnia," he said at this time, "is a police measure which we require to master frontier risings, but our aim is to bring the western half of the Balkan peninsula —I do not wish to conquer it—permanently under our influence."[16]

Here, in fact, was the obvious outlet for the imperialism which in other countries at this time was tending to the creation of colonial empires. It was genuinely felt, from this period down to 1914, that the Monarchy had a "civilizing mission" among the Balkan peoples who were now beginning to shake themselves free of the dead hand of Turkey, a mission to be carried out, less violently than in other imperialisms, by influence and commerce. The extension of influence, rather than of occupation, was a necessary consequence of the balance of forces in the Dual Monarchy, and of the need to avoid the absorption of more Slavs. It had the additional advantage that Russia would not be provoked to rivalry for the control of the Balkan region. The two Empires had long had an understanding, which had been made explicit in the Reichstadt agreement, on their parallel interests in the Balkans. Despite periods of tension in the 'seventies and 'eighties the policy of restraint was maintained, by mutual agreement, for nearly thirty years. It was only after Russia's defeat at the hands of Japan, when Austria herself began to pursue an active Balkan policy for purposes of prestige, that the long-veiled conflict that was to lead to war became apparent.

## AUSTRIA AND SERBIA

Across the most convenient line to Salonika, through Belgrade and Niš, stood the small state of Serbia, now declared finally independent of Turkey by the Treaty of Berlin, and it was with Serbia that Austro-Hungarian policy in the Balkans was to be most closely concerned for the next thirty years. The ruler of Serbia at this time was Prince Milan Obrenović, who had been elected Prince in 1868, when only thirteen, on the murder of his uncle, Prince Michael. Michael, the ablest of modern Serbia's rulers, had been murdered in one of the spasms of that deadly feud between the rival Obrenović and Karageorgević families which clouded Serbia's struggle for freedom (and culminated in 1903 in the ghastly murder of the last of the legitimate Obrenović, Milan's son, Alexander—the worthless son of a worthless father—and in the election of Peter Karageorgević as ruler). Milan was a young man of extravagant tastes, totally unfitted by temperament or training to lead his vigorous but simple people, whom he despised, at a critical stage of their history. He preferred the company he found in the gay cafés and glittering music-halls of Vienna, and though, to celebrate Serbia's complete liberation from the Turks, he proclaimed himself King in 1882, it was to Vienna that he retired only seven years later, when, tiring of his responsibilities, he abdicated at the age of thirty-four. His predecessor, Michael, before his untimely death had hoped to unite his country with Bosnia in a greater Serbia, and it was in pursuit of the policy he had laid down that Serbia went to war in 1876. Austria-Hungary, however, had suspected Michael's purpose, and had resolved to frustrate it. Hence the occupation of Bosnia and Herzegovina, which came to Serbia as a bitter blow, intensified by the manner in which the Habsburg forces crushed the opposition with which they were greeted, some two hundred thousand men being eventually engaged in what was alleged to be no more than a police operation. Henceforth Serb opinion regarded the Dual Monarchy both as the oppressor of Slav peoples and as the main obstacle to the formation of a great Slav state, an enlarged Serbia, in the western Balkans.

Nevertheless, had Serbian policy been conducted with more skill, as had been the case during the short rule of Prince Michael, relations between Serbia and the Monarchy might have been put on a sound footing. Russia's encouragement of Bulgaria in the recent conflict had also been a blow to Serb feeling, and Serbia now had no choice but to look to Vienna. In 1881, therefore, Milan concluded with Austria-Hungary a secret treaty which, in return for commercial and railway concessions, pledged Austrian support for Serbian expansion *to the south* (away, that is, from Bosnia-Herzegovina), but at the same time tied Serbia, in matters of political and economic foreign policy, to the Dual Monarchy. In this move Milan was encouraged at first by the Tsar, who, realizing that Russia had been seriously weakened by the war with Turkey, and

E*

alarmed by the indications he had received of the alliance between Germany and Austria-Hungary, was anxious to do nothing which would further estrange Francis Joseph. Milan, however, behaved with such obsequiousness to Austria-Hungary after the treaty, and made such offers of vassalage, as to cause acute embarrassment and disgust in Vienna. The sturdy independence of the Serb people was overlooked in the unbalanced fawning of its ruler, and an opinion of Serbia was formed throughout Europe which, aggravated by the events of 1903, played no small part in the general appreciation of the situation which led to 1914.

### AUSTRIA AND RUSSIA, 1881 AND 1884

The most striking result of the new line in Russian policy was seen in the secret re-establishment of the *Dreikaiserbund* in June, 1881. Three months earlier Tsar Alexander II had been murdered, but his son and successor, Alexander III, though personally hostile to Germany, was in no position yet to show his hand, and for a time, therefore, the gradually increasing tension between Russia and Austria-Hungary was again smoothed over. A year later, in May, 1882, Austria-Hungary and Italy came to terms at the instigation of Bismarck, and the Dual Alliance of 1879 was converted into a Triple Alliance. Little reliance was placed on Italy's value as an ally, but her entrance into the circle guaranteed Austria-Hungary's rear, and thus made her Balkan policy easier. In 1884 the Three Emperors' League was again renewed, but the crisis that arose in the following year, owing to the reunion of the two divided parts of Bulgaria, proved the final blow.

### THE BULGARIAN CRISIS, 1885–87, AND ITS RESULTS

The crisis which arose in 1885 from the reunion of the two separate Bulgarian provinces that had been created in 1878 is considered elsewhere. It is sufficient here to note that Russian policy had undergone a striking change in the intervening seven years. Disappointment at the independence and seeming ingratitude of the Bulgarians and their popular Prince, Alexander of Battenberg, caused the Tsar to resist the new move, and then to force Alexander to resign. The Bulgarians, with the tacit approval of Austria-Hungary, promptly elected Prince Ferdinand of Saxe-Coburg to succeed Alexander, and when Russia sought also to force him aside and to install in his place a Russian general, there was real danger of war. Tension was acute between Vienna and St. Petersburg for three years, and Bismarck was compelled to play one of the most complicated diplomatic games of his career in his efforts to preserve peace.

The crisis did not pass until 1887, but eventually Russia drew back, realizing that Ferdinand had the support of the Bulgarians and that in the event of war Germany could not be relied on to support her against Austria-Hungary. But, not unnaturally, the Three Emperors' League was allowed to lapse: the interest of two of the three Powers had become too divergent for the pretence of solidarity to be maintained. There followed, too, a decline of the influence of Russia in the Balkans, and a corresponding extension of that of Austria Hungary. Bismarck, however, did not abandon his efforts to remain on good terms with both. He secured temporary compensation for the loss of the *Dreikaiserbund* by concluding with Russia in 1887 a secret "Reinsurance Treaty"—secret even from Austria-Hungary. But when he fell in 1890 this treaty also was not renewed. The choice between Russia and Austria-Hungary, which Bismarck had for so long struggled to avoid, was now irrevocably made, and the pattern of the alliance of 1914 began to take shape. Russia and France, incompatible though they were in their internal politics, were already feeling their way towards each other, and at the end of 1893 their Dual Alliance came into existence as an answer to the alliances of 1879 and 1882. Europe had begun to split into two camps.

## ANDRÁSSY RESIGNS: CHANGES IN INTERNAL POLICY

Andrássy's tenure of office as Francis Joseph's chief adviser lasted for eight years, from 1871 to 1879: he retired as soon as the negotiations for the alliance with Germany had been completed. With his retirement came one of the abrupt changes of internal policy which were so characteristic of the Emperor. Andrássy's successes in foreign affairs had been warmly approved by Francis Joseph; indeed, over Bosnia-Herzegovina the minister had gone further in deference to his master's views than he himself had originally intended. But

Magyars and German-Austrians alike had expressed their disapproval of the forward move in the Balkans, and Francis Joseph would not countenance the implied questioning of his supreme authority in such matters. He objected the more because of the significance he personally attached to Bosnia-Herzegovina as an offset to his previous losses of territory. Furthermore, the German Liberal majority in the Austrian *Reichsrat*, upon which Andrássy had relied, had criticized army policy, which the Emperor regarded as another of his unassailable prerogatives. It was time to look elsewhere for a parliamentary majority, and he therefore turned once more to the Czechs.

There were other reasons for this step. Francis Joseph disliked the Liberal policy of the German-Austrian leaders, but he believed that whatever happened he could count on their loyalty to the dynasty, and in any case the alliance between him and William I made it impossible for them to look to the Hohenzollern Empire for support. The Slav peoples, on the other hand, had to be handled with care at a time when relations with Russia were deteriorating. The Liberals, too, like their opposite numbers in other countries at this time, were becoming the party of business and industrial interests, and had earned an unfortunate reputation in the financial crisis of 1873 and the scandals that had accompanied it. At the elections of June, 1879, they lost their majority in Austria, and two months later Francis Joseph appointed as Premier his old friend, Count Edward Taaffe (1833–95), an Austrian aristocrat of Irish descent who had no party affiliations and regarded himself above all as the "Emperor's Minister" (*Kaiserminister*).

## THE TAAFFE ERA: THE "IRON RING" AND THE CONCESSIONS TO THE CZECHS

The "Taaffe Era", as it came to be called, lasted from 1879 to 1893. In after years the period of comparative calm over which Taaffe had presided was looked back to with regret, but though the fourteen years were in the nature of a breathing-space, little was achieved, and the underlying conflict between the races of the Empire was not resolved. Lacking a solid parliamentary backing, and having been appointed, in any case, to free the Emperor from constitutional demands,

Taaffe based himself on the support of several groups, notably the Czechs and Poles, forming an "Iron Ring" as opposed to a solid parliamentary party, and, to use his own expression, "muddled along". Important concessions were, however, made to the Czechs. In 1880 it was decreed that for judicial and administrative matters in which Czechs were concerned their language should be used, and every encouragement was given to Czech education. A step of particular importance was taken in the following year, when the historic University of Prague was divided into two Universities, a Czech and a German. From the moment of its inauguration the Czech University took a leading place in the life of the nation: one of the first Professors to be appointed was a little known philosopher from Vienna University, the Moravian, Thomas Masaryk (1850–1937), who was destined to become the intellectual and moral leader of the Czech people, and after 1918 the first President of an independent Czech State.

## DEVELOPMENTS IN BOHEMIA-MORAVIA

There were at this time other developments of importance in Bohemia-Moravia. The coal and metallurgical industries were now expanding rapidly in the Czech lands, and they were becoming the industrial centre of the Empire. Especially notable were the Škoda works at Pilsen (Plzeň), famous as an armaments centre. With the development of industry came a great move of population. Changes in agricultural technique, and especially the increased growing of sugar-beet, forced many thousands of Czech peasants off the land and into industry, and the Germans of Bohemia-Moravia (later to become only too well-known under the general, and not altogether accurate, name of the *Sudetendeutsch*, which was correctly applied only to the region of the Sudeten mountains in north-east Bohemia) found themselves in a minority in what had hitherto been mainly German settlements. Thus in Pilsen the attraction of the Škoda works raised the Czech population of the town from some 4,000 to more than 40,000 between 1850 and 1890,[17] while in Prague during the same period the number of Czechs rose from 60,000 to 150,000, and the Germans fell from 73,000 to 30,000 (by 1910 the Germans numbered only 19,000 in the city's total population

of 220,000).[18] The general situation was not improved for the
Germans by the fact that their birthrate was markedly lower
than that of the Czechs. The favour shown by the Taaffe
administration to the Czechs therefore increased the German
alarm. From having been for centuries the only people to be
considered in Bohemia-Moravia they were threatened with the
position of a mere minority, the position, in fact, that they had
to accept in 1918, and which, at the instigation of Hitler, they
finally resisted. The result was a bitter and unending conflict
over schools, street names, even the signs over public lavatories;
a conflict which continued for half a century, and which has
ended only with the expulsion of most of the Bohemian
Germans since 1945 and the final triumph of the Czechs
among whom they had lived for so long. It has been well said
that popular education is the chief instigator of nationalism,
and it is certain that the German and Czech schools in Bohemia-
Moravia from the 'eighties onwards were sources both of
national inspiration and of further strife. (The effect of nationalist propaganda in the schools in another part of the Empire
in the 'nineties can be judged from the tribute paid by Hitler
in *Mein Kampf* to his teachers.) The struggle was not, however,
merely one over national traditions or the language of instruction: the struggle for education was the struggle for effective
political power. Austria was essentially a bureaucratic State,
and power resided not in parliamentary control, but in the
bureaucracy. Where in Britain the demand was for the franchise and parliamentary representation, in Austria it was for a
fair share of official posts. The way to appointments in the
State service lay through education, both in the schools and at
the Universities. Hence the struggle over educational institutions and the demand from the subject races that their children
should have the opportunity for advancement through education in their own language. In the words of one of the closest
contemporary observers of the Empire, Henry Wickham
Steed (1871–1956), *The Times* correspondent in Vienna from
1902 to 1913, "the essence of the language struggle is that
it is a struggle for bureaucratic influence":[19]

The bureaucracy feels itself to be the State; and for the public at
large it is the State. So instinctively is this truth recognised that the
'race struggle' in Austria . . . is largely a struggle for bureaucratic

appointments. Germans and Czechs have striven for years to increase on the one hand and defend on the other their patrimony of official positions.

Yet another source of conflict lay in economic and social conditions. Bohemia-Moravia developed rapidly as the industrial centre of the Empire, producing the greater part of Austria's output of coal, metals, chemicals, glass, porcelain, textiles, paper, sugar and leather and more than half of her beer.[20] (To this last item Pilsen, of course, made a notable contribution.) Before the end of the century Bohemia alone was providing a quarter of Austria's revenue.[21] Industry advanced behind tariff barriers which were the highest in Europe, apart from those of Russia, and enjoyed, through the long established Customs Union with Hungary, the advantage of what was practically the closed market of the whole Danube area. The industries were, however, largely in German hands, and where Czech businesses flourished their owners tended, as did successful business men elsewhere, to "ape their betters". This in the Bohemian context meant their absorption into the German ruling group. Thus, Emil Škoda, founder of the great armament works, though born a Czech, when he had achieved wealth and greatness came to regard himself as a German. Social stresses, the clash of German Capital with Czech Labour, therefore tended to give a sharper edge to racial disputes, especially in view of the low economic standards of Czech workers.

## CZECH NATIONALISM—THE "YOUNG CZECHS"

One significant result of the increase in education and of the development of industry, with the consequent disturbance of traditional ways of life, was the growth of extremism among Czechs and Germans alike. Hitherto the Czech national movement had been in the hands of men of moderate views, many of them of high social standing. The elections of 1889 in Bohemia, however, went in favour of the more radical "Young Czechs", and tension increased. In 1892, for instance, a Sokol delegation visited Nancy, and made it clear that they shared the French hatred of the Germans by declaring "Our enemies are yours, and yours ours", while in the following year there were anti-Habsburg riots in Prague. As the mass of the people became politically conscious the tension between the nationalities increased. The new movements can be dated from the 'eighties, and it is perhaps typical of the Dual Monarchy that the presiding political figure should then have been that of Taaffe, the apostle of "muddling along".

## THE GERMAN NATIONALIST REACTION:
### (1) THE LINZ PROGRAMME

The conflict between Czechs and Germans dominated the political scene in Austria, and as Czech national feeling increased it was met by a mounting wave of pan-Germanism that complicated all other issues. In 1882 a group of young German Nationalists drew up a statement of the German Austrian case to which was given the name of the "Linz Programme". This project advocated a closer connexion between Germany and Austria, and the abandonment of the Austrian Slavs, with the exception of the Czechs and Slovenes, to Hungary, so that in Austria itself the Germans might maintain their majority. The project was still-born, but it served to fan the flames of racial conflict, and it marked the introduction to political activity of several remarkable men. As a movement with a "popular" backing it reflected the broadening of the basis of political activity which was now taking place, and was noticeable among the Czechs, as already indicated, no less than among the Germans.

### (2) SCHÖNERER

The chief driving force behind the Linz programme was Georg von Schönerer (1842–1921), the man to whose teaching Hitler later owed so much and to whom he paid tribute as a precursor of Nazism. With him were associated, among others, Heinrich Friedjung (1851–1920), of Moravian-Jewish descent, who actually drafted the programme, and Viktor Adler (1852–1918), the brilliant Bohemian Jew who founded the Austrian Socialist Party and died soon after he had helped to establish the Austrian Republic in 1918. The unity suggested by the Linz programme did not long endure, and divergent aims soon appeared. The first rift came over Schönerer's insistence upon the inclusion in the programme of a clause aimed against the Jews, whereupon Adler, Friedjung and other Jews were forced out of the movement. Adler soon interested himself in the development of a Socialist organization among Austria's industrial workers. Friedjung, however, was typical of many Jews in his devotion to Germanism. He became one of the foremost historians of Austria, but his patriotism later caused him to blunder badly, and he achieved an unenviable notoriety through his acceptance of forged Serbian documents which led to the famous "Friedjung Trial" of 1909, of which something will be said in its place.

Schönerer was significant as an extreme product of the tensions in Austria. He was violently opposed to the Habsburgs, regarding them as traitors to German unity, and became an advocate of the unification of all Germans under the Hohenzollerns: his motto, it was said, was "There is one God, Bismarck, and Schönerer is His Prophet." In 1885 he established a German Nationalist Party, and, finding in himself a talent for mob-oratory, began to develop the ideas on the Aryan race, racial purity and anti-Semitism, which Hitler was later to propagate. "One hears talk of equality between Germans and Slavs," ran one of his characteristic pronouncements, "it is as if one compared a lion to a louse because both are animals."[22] His great opportunity came in 1897, when Count Badeni, then Premier, made a bold effort to settle the conflict between Germans and Czechs in Bohemia by putting the two languages on an equal footing and requiring that every official should know both. This measure would soon have ensured to the Czechs, with their higher birth-rate, a position of ascendancy, and it was strenuously resisted by the Germans. In Prague and Vienna Schönerer and his followers whipped-up street agitations, and there were riots which led to Badeni's fall.

After this episode Schönerer, conscious of the unacceptability of the mainly Roman Catholic Germans of Austria to the Protestant Empire of the Hohenzollerns, started a *Los von Rom* ("Away from Rome") movement to convert Roman Catholics to Protestantism and "break at last the chains that bind us to a Church that is the foe of Germanism".[23] This extravagant campaign met with no great response, and was in any case as much a movement away from the Habsburgs as from the Roman Church. Later Schönerer turned away from Christianity altogether, seeking to revive the cult of the old

German gods, and even dating his calendar from early Teutonic history. To the ferment of ideas that marked the later years of the Habsburg Empire he made a significant contribution that was destined to bear fruit in the future. Without knowledge of the "overheated climate" which made Schönerer possible, Wickham Steed has written in an account of the origins of Nazism, "neither Hitler nor Hitlerism is intelligible".[24] Even the Nazi salute and the *Heil* greeting date from these years, and the early pages of *Mein Kampf* bear all the marks of Schönerer's influence. When, for instance, Hitler accused the Habsburgs of working to make Austria a Slav State, and saw in the murder of Francis Ferdinand the avenging hand of a conveniently pro-German Deity, he was reproducing Schönerer's wild teaching, and there are many similar passages.

## (3) LUEGER

Another and more reputable figure which appeared on the Austrian political scene at this time was that of Karl Lueger (1844–1910), a founder of Austrian Christian-Socialism and afterwards a great Burgomaster of Vienna. Unlike Schönerer, Lueger was both a fervent Austrian patriot and a loyal son of the Church. Elected to the Vienna Municipal Council in 1875, in the difficult times that followed the financial crisis of 1873, he soon made his mark by his attacks on corrupt administration and by his defence of the lower middle classes against powerful capitalist interests. Ten years later he became a member of the *Reichsrat*, and in 1897, after his election had four times been rejected by the Emperor, Burgomaster of Vienna, where he reigned, it was said, as "uncrowned king" until his death in 1910. Lueger was a fine and striking figure ("Handsome Karl" to his admirers) and a powerful orator, with a popular appeal in his speeches through the use of Viennese dialect. He was anti-Socialist, anti-Capitalist, anti-Liberal, and above all—and most significantly in Vienna—anti-Jewish, and put over his views with passionate conviction. The seeds of later Fascism are to be seen in him. But he had great depths of character and a charm of manner and a sterling honesty that made him the idol of the city he served for so long. He was a demagogue, it has been said, "but a lovable one",[25] and the early pages of *Mein Kampf* reflect the admiration felt for him by the German Austrians of the lower middle class among whom Hitler was brought up. It was the violence of his views that caused Francis Joseph to refuse to accept him as Burgomaster on four occasions in 1895–96, but his outlook broadened after he had had experience of office: if he remained anti-Jewish he himself decided, as he said, who were the Jews. A devout Christian, he was equally opposed to Liberalism and to Marxism for their materialism, and his objection to Jewish influence was religious rather than racial in origin. He was above all the representative of the "little men", the middle and lower-middle classes, whom he sought to protect against the "big business" which had so powerful a hold in Vienna, and whom he hoped, with the aid of religion, to restrain from extremism and desperation. In matters affecting the nationalities of the Empire he was anti-Czech as far as Austria was concerned, but in general he was sympathetic to the Slavs, though bitterly hostile to the Magyars. To his dislike of Hungary he added a lively opposition to Hohenzollern Germany and all pan-German notions, and his party was active in resistance to the *Los von Rom* movement. His long administration of Vienna was a notable one, which saw many improvements in the city and introduced elements of municipal socialism in opposition to business interests. He was an outstanding, though violent and unintellectual, product of that reaction against the materialism of both Liberalism and Marxism which distinguished many elements in the Roman Church of the time, and turned thoughtful Roman Catholics to the application of the Church's teaching to social problems. He could hardly be classed as a leader of Christian-Socialism or Christian-Democracy, for his ideas were too inchoate, and represented rather the impulsive reations of an able mind to the uneasy conditions of his time than any reasoned body of doctrine. The origins of Austrian Christian-Socialism were, in any case, to be found elsewhere, in the press and pamphlet propaganda of the convert and social reformer, Baron Karl von Vogelsang (1818–90), and much of its following among the clergy and peasantry of rural Austria who after the war were to be the basis of the support of Seipel, Dolfuss, and Schuschnigg. Lueger's was rather the backing of the middle-class elements in the city which, in other and more difficult conditions, and lacking the steadying influence of a respected monarchy, tended to succumb to the spell of Nazism. Nevertheless, if Schönerer's ideas were a factor in the bewildered Germany of the Weimar Republic, Lueger's were not without significance in truncated Austria after 1918. He insisted, in the first place, that German Austria had a distinct mission to fulfil, and could not play its part if absorbed into the larger Reich. Events have shown that in that at least he had a case to argue.

## (4) ANTI-SEMITISM

The element which Schönerer and Lueger and others of the period had in common was anti-Semitism. The Jewish problem was an old one in Central Europe, but it was becoming more marked through the success of numerous Jewish business men and the intellectual brilliance of the Jews who played so large a part in the great Viennese Press. In the peculiar conditions of the Dual Monarchy, which, with its mixture of races, had always possessed a high proportion of Jews, many were able to climb to positions of distinction, and embittered German Austrians, who saw their world of German pre-eminence crumbling away through the steady upsurge of other races, found in the Jews an easy target.

The subject of anti-Semitism is a painful one after the horrors of the mass exterminations carried out by the Nazis, but it is an essential part of the picture of Austria before 1914 and a significant legacy from the Empire to the post-war world. The religion and customs of the Jews and their exclusiveness (as much a product of their creed as of the Gentile hostility which had long restricted them to the ghetto) have always marked them as a people apart, a dangerous position in times of stress. A gifted people, they suffer, whether in poverty or in worldly success, from the disadvantage of being conspicuous. A bad Gentile is overlooked; a bad Jew, or one who flaunts his success, is too readily apparent. Even the best might be marked as different by their outlook and ideals, for "their inspirations were mainly drawn", in the phrase of an eminent British Jew, "from the distant past and not from the present or the future".[26] Thus it was in Austria. The legal disabilities of the Jews, relics of earlier intolerance, had been removed in 1867. Hitherto they had been prohibited from owning land or from entering the civil service or the legal profession. Entry to the professions continued to be difficult even after legal equality had been achieved, and Jews therefore tended to seek careers in finance or journalism, to which they were drawn in any case by their natural adaptability and quickness of intelligence. They also became outstanding in Austria's cultural life. They congregated in the cities, the natural centres of finance, commerce and the arts, until they largely controlled the trade of Vienna, and Budapest, through their predominance in the Hungarian capital, was styled by cynics *Judapest*. Some, such as the Rothschilds, achieved almost fabulous wealth and influence as bankers and financiers; others, like Adler, turned their lively analytical minds, and their resentment of the conditions around them, to the dissemination of Socialist doctrines, combining an intellectual materialism with an emotional reaction to misery and distress that was reminiscent both of Karl Marx and of earlier prophets of the chosen race. Others, again, strove to become assimilated, claiming that they "felt like Germans": of these Friedjung was a notable example. Assimilation, however, was not always successful—or acceptable to other Germans. The designation "Germanic Germans" was actually coined by some ardent German Austrians to distinguish themselves from the assimilated "Semitic Germans", while attempts at assimilation could themselves bring at times dangerous psychological tensions, as they did, to name only one instance, in the case of the brilliant Moravian-Jewish conductor and composer, Gustav Mahler (1860–1911).[27] These, however, were the educated and cultured: there were many others less well endowed. From Galicia, for instance, which, since the Polish kings had opened their territories as a refuge in the Middle Ages, had become a "Jewish reservoir", and from other regions of Eastern Europe, a steady stream of rootless wanderers moved west, away from the poverty and insecurity and sporadic anti-Semitic outbreaks of the peasant lands. Many made their way to Britain and the United States, joining the stream of refugees from Russian persecution, but many others settled in central Austria, and especially in Vienna, where they lived in squalid, overcrowded districts, eking out a living in small businesses or on the fringes of society. Sprung from poor communities and preserving in many cases the strict costume and customs of their people, they were marked out as peculiar even in polyglot Austria, and there were not a few Austrians who refused to accept them as compatriots. Hitler has told in *Mein Kampf* of his reactions on seeing in Vienna for the first time a Galician Jew in traditional garb: "Can this be a German?" was his thought. A spontaneous repugnance was only too often stirred to hatred by the success of the newcomers as small business men who could drive a harder bargain, and demanded less of life, than the people among whom they settled. This was particularly true after the financial crisis of 1873, in which many Jews were involved, and it provided Lueger and Schönerer with much of their following. In times of failure and stress the search for a scapegoat can satisfy some deeply felt need in a society. To some extent the Jews were scapegoats of Austria's difficulties, as they were to be later, and most tragically, of the frustrations of defeated Germany.

## THE JEWISH REACTION: "ZIONISM"

Of anti-Semitism at this time it can at least be said that it was mainly confined to words, though Jewish and Gentile students sometimes came to blows. Social discrimination occurred, however, and the verbal onslaughts of the anti-Semites acquired a bitterness that was an ominous pointer to later developments. The Jewish reaction was no less significant than the spirit that provoked it. In the face of the Jewish "assimilationists", who wished only to be absorbed and to lose their identity in the mass of the German population (the "hundred-and-five-per-cent Germans", as they were sometimes called), a movement arose to stress pride in Jewish descent and even to strive for the age-old dream of a restored Jewish State. This revived "Zionism" was a product in the first place of Austrian Jewry. The name of the movement, indicative in itself of Jewish aspirations, was the invention of the Viennese Jew, Nathan Birnbaum, but the movement owed its real strength and inspiration to the Budapest-born Theodor Herzl (1860–1904), an able journalist who became literary editor of Vienna's greatest paper, the *Neue Freie Presse*. Herzl began as an assimilationist: the paper he served, though entirely in the hands of Jews, was the mouthpiece of enlightened German-Jewish opinion and for all its international reputation regarded itself as an essentially German organ. The rise of anti-Semitism caused Herzl, however, to change his views, and he began to devote himself to building up a Zionist organization in preparation for the establishment of a Jewish State. This he hoped to achieve by winning the support of the Powers, but his hopes for Turkish-controlled Palestine were soon dashed and to the concern of many of his followers he clutched at the offer of territory in Uganda which was made by a sympathetic Britain in 1903. In 1896 had appeared his celebrated book *Der Judenstaat* (The Jewish State), which gave new hope and confidence to afflicted Judaism, but it was his foundation in the following year of the Zionist Congress which marked him out as the boldest and most constructive of Jewish leaders. Thenceforth he was "the servant of the idea",[28] the idea which, through all the vicissitudes and terrors of the intervening years, led to the establishment, first of a Jewish National Home in Palestine under British auspices, and eventually, in 1948, of an Israel once again independent. Whether but for British interest, American money, the accidents of war and the desperation born of the horrors of Nazism, Herzl's dreams would have been realized on any significant scale is uncertain. Nevertheless, the origins of modern Israel are to be found in the comparatively liberal atmosphere of Habsburg Austria no less than in the ghettoes of persecuting Russia, which produced the great leader who carried Herzl's mission to success, Chaim Weizmann.

## AUSTRIA'S POLITICAL DEVELOPMENT: NEW TRENDS IN THE 'NINETIES

Taaffe's long period of rule in Austria came to an end in 1893, at a critical moment in the Empire's development, when extreme opinions were spreading and the conflict between Germans and Czechs in Bohemia was entering upon a new phase. Three years earlier, in 1890, a compromise had been reached between Czech and German claims, based upon an administrative division of Bohemia. The negotiations had been conducted on the Czech side principally by the son-in-law and successor of Palacký as national leader, Ladislav Rieger (1818–

1903), now, however, an old man leading an old party which had, indeed, come to be known as the "Old Czechs". A new and vigorous generation of "Young Czechs", more middle class and peasant in composition, was now coming forward, a generation destined to play a decisive part in the history of the Czech people, for in its ranks were to be found such leaders as Alois Rašín (1867–1923) and Karel Kramář (1860–1937), who with Masaryk were to be among the founders of the Czechoslovak Republic of 1918. The Young Czechs were determined to uphold the historic unity of Bohemia and to achieve for it autonomy under Habsburg rule, with a clear recognition of equal national rights. This, unless the Bohemian Germans were prepared to abandon their position and pretensions, was an unrealizable aim, and was to prove an obstacle to all the attempts which were to be made either to find a solution within Bohemia itself or to submerge it in one of the wider schemes for the federalization of the Empire which were to be increasingly canvassed in unofficial discussions and publications. Yet the Young Czech case was not without justification. Their attitude was becoming increasingly radical, but their notions were democratic and their social policies advanced; they did not suffer from the wild and intolerant views which were afflicting the German parties. Moreover, their very stress upon the need for autonomy was a counter to the centralization of the rising German radical groups. Yet Czech opinion was clearly hardening, and the attempted compromise of 1890 was followed by sweeping Young Czech successes in the *Reichsrat* elections of the following year: even Rieger, who had served his people so well and so long, was thrown aside. Taaffe's well-intentioned attempts to carry out the agreement led to violent scenes in Prague, and the easy-going "Taaffe era" drew to a close with police rule in the city and the trial of the revolutionary *Omladina* group for treason. Within a few years, it is true, Count Badeni's renewed efforts for a settlement led, as has already been mentioned, to equally angry German demonstrations, egged on by Schönerer and his followers, but it was clear that something more than good will and friendly gestures to either side was required. A new approach to the whole problem of the nationalities seemed to be called for, and it was to electoral reform, in particular, that many, including the Emperor himself, looked for a solution. New classes were coming forward, and, if their share of political power were increased, their influence might be thrown on the side of moderation. Further, Socialism was taking root, and the Social-Democrat Party had been founded, under Adler's influence and guidance, in 1888. If revolutionary agitation of a new kind was to be avoided, the industrial workers must be admitted to political rights: with the growing recognition of the need for social legislation, they might in any case be expected to be more concerned with the stability of government than the wealthier classes which provided the leadership of the nationalist parties. Taaffe and his Finance Minister, the able Jewish public servant, Emil Steinbach, had already carried some modest social reforms, including a system of insurance on the German model, and it was Steinbach who persuaded both Taaffe and Francis Joseph of the need for further measures. Hitherto elections to the *Reichsrat* had been conducted, under the electoral law of 1873, on the basis of social groupings, deputies being elected by the four Estates, or *curiae*, of the great landowners, the chambers of commerce, the towns and the rural areas. The property qualification in the case of the two last groups had been lowered by Taaffe in 1882, and he now proposed, in effect, the extension of the franchise for these groups on the principle of universal suffrage. It was the first step towards the measure for manhood suffrage on a new basis which was finally carried in 1907, but it met with determined opposition not only from conservative elements but from Germans who feared for their position in the face of the other nationalities (and, it may be said, from Magyars who were concerned at the example which might be set to Hungary).

FRUSTRATION AND BUREAUCRATIC GOVERNMENT, 1893–1914

Realizing that his proposals could not be carried, Taaffe decided that the time had come for him to resign. The history of the next thirteen years is largely the history of attempts to succeed where he had failed, to find a more representative basis for parliament and to bring together the Germans and Czechs. There were also problems of relations with

Hungary. The whole period from 1893 to 1914 was, however, one of failure and lost opportunities. Ministries succeeded each other in rapid succession—there were no fewer than fifteen in the twenty-one years—and were largely groupings of officials with no real parliamentary basis. The *Reichsrat* itself suffered from the uncertainties and frustrations of the period, and was discredited by obstructionism that outdid the worst efforts of the Irish at Westminster. As Taaffe had discovered to his cost, whatever was proposed was fiercely resisted from some quarter, and street agitation was quickly added on occasion to clamour in parliament. Irresponsibility could the more easily be indulged in since in the last resort government could be carried on under the emergency powers permitted by article XIV of the constitution of 1867. Governments of officials, independent of parliamentary majorities and ruling when necessary by emergency decrees, therefore seemed to provide an answer to Austria's difficulties, though repeated efforts were made to discover a remedy on more constitutional lines. As Robert Musil wrote jestingly of the situation in the last years before the war:

> There was a parliament, which made such vigorous use of its liberty that it was usually kept shut; but there was also an emergency powers act by means of which it was possible to manage without Parliament, and every time when everyone was just beginning to rejoice in absolutism, the Crown decreed that there must now again be a return to parliamentary government.[29]

Whatever his limitations, Francis Joseph had no desire to be an absolute monarch, but he felt himself to be helpless in the face of parliamentary disunity. Yet the reliance upon "official" ministers and the constant use of emergency powers served but to increase the general irresponsibility and the traditional tendency to bureaucratic rule. While constitutional forms were observed, "in point of fact", as a contemporary critic, Joseph Redlich, whose views have already been quoted, later observed, "the government was a bureaucratic absolutism", and parliament "a broken-down clock".[30] This was particularly true after the failure of Badeni's Ministry (1895–97), when as a result of the attempt to satisfy Czech claims parliamentary obstructionism reached the depths scathingly described in the comment by Redlich quoted earlier.[31] Nor was there any lasting improvement before 1914. When war came, indeed, the *Reichsrat* had been suspended for several months, and could not be recalled lest internal political strife impair the unity of the Empire in the moment of crisis. The impotence of the *Reichsrat* in the face of the situation in July, 1914, was in itself a telling comment on the whole development of Austria since 1867.

## ELECTORAL REFORM, 1907

Badeni carried in 1896 an electoral reform which created a fifth *curia* elected by manhood suffrage, but the concession was a limited one which only emphasized the incongruities of the system of voting by classes. After him the two most significant administrations were those of Dr. Ernst Körber (1900–04) and Baron Beck (1906–08), two of the outstanding Austrian statesmen of their day. Körber was a man of progressive views who sought to divert the energies dissipated on political squabbles into more constructive channels by a vigorous programme of economic development, but his health eventually broke under the strain. He endeavoured to reduce the tension in Bohemia by creating three types of administrative areas, German-speaking, Czech-speaking and mixed, but it proved impossible to agree on the last and the Czechs were as intransigent as ever against any implied threat to the unity of their country. After Körber's resignation it was clear that more sweeping changes were needed, and the example of Russia, where after the revolution of 1905 a parliamentary régime was at last introduced, made the need more urgent. Already Francis Joseph, as will be shown later, had accepted the principle of manhood suffrage in order to overcome a constitutional crisis in Hungary. Now he lent his open support for a similar move in Austria, and in 1907 Beck carried a thorough reorganization of the electoral system, which gave Austria, on paper, a wider franchise than that of Britain before 1918. The *curiae* were abolished, the vote was given to all men of twenty-four and seats in the *Reichsrat* were distributed on nationalist lines, the number of representatives of each nationality being determined by economic and historical considerations as well as by the number of voters. This meant that the Germans were over-represented, but the system was probably as fair a one as could be devised, and it produced for a time striking results. When the first election was held, in May, 1907, the extreme nationalists, as had been hoped, suffered a setback, even Schönerer losing his seat, while the great mass parties of Social-Democracy and Christian-Socialism made important gains (it may be noted, too, in passing, that four Zionists were elected).

## FRUSTRATED HOPES, 1907-14

The improvement was not, however, a lasting one. Had it been possible to carry further political changes in the direction of some form of federalism, 1907 might have opened a new era for Austria. The thoughts and hopes of the heir to the throne, the Archduke Francis Ferdinand, who understood how critical the situation was, were certainly fixed on some such move. But to many, including the Emperor himself, now in the sixtieth year of his reign, universal suffrage marked the close of a long and difficult period, rather than the opening of new opportunities. Moreover, apart from the Socialists, the German Austrians, now in a permanent minority in the *Reichsrat*, were not in any case prepared for further concessions, while the unyielding opposition of the Magyars to any suggestion of federalism was ever in the background. The German Austrians, indeed, caught nothing of any new spirit: it was typical of their attitude that after Lueger's death in 1910 they went so far in their efforts to keep Vienna itself under German control that they closed the schools which the considerable Czech colony in the imperial city had built with its own funds. As the Social-Democrat paper, the *Arbeiterzeitung*, commented some years later:

> The Germans were once in Austria those who fought for freedom, while the Slavs opposed to them the resistance of the dead mass. Today, on the contrary, all Slav nations are democratic, while the German bourgeoisie is obstinately opposed to democratic progress.[32]

Meanwhile other developments had served to inflame racial passions. In 1908 came the annexation of Bosnia and Herzegovina, which might have been used to attach the South Slavs to the Empire but proved to be no more than a flash in the pan. No less ominous were the Agram (Zagreb) and Friedjung trials of the following year, with their exposure of the Foreign Ministry's methods and of its rabid anti-Serb policy. Under the pressure of these events the Slav peoples of the Monarchy tended to come together. Masaryk, in particular, was drawn from academic life to an active part in politics, and made a new reputation by his exposure of the anti-Slav prejudices of the Foreign Ministry. The alliance of the various Slav groups that was to split the Monarchy in 1918 was already taking shape. More than this, many Czechs, realizing how closely Austria was bound to Germany, were turning to Slav Russia. Kramář was the leading spirit in this movement, which inevitably increased the tension in Bohemia, where patriotic German Austrians could not but regard pro-Russian sentiments as treason, and began to speak of Prague as the "Western Moscow". The day was not far distant, in fact, when Masaryk would be proscribed in exile, and Czech regiments at the front would desert to the Russian forces.

Renewed distrust in Bohemia and his own opposition to the annexation of Bosnia caused Beck's resignation in 1908. The first flush of optimism caused by the electoral reform had already passed, and the *Reichsrat* was slipping back into its old ways. Francis Joseph was forced to follow suit, and for the last eight years of his life again appointed officials to lead his governments. The hopefulness engendered by the active measures of 1907 and 1908 in both internal and external affairs had led nowhere. While the old Emperor lived, further change was now impossible: the Empire seemed doomed.

## DEVELOPMENTS IN HUNGARY, 1867–1914

While Francis Joseph lived, too, no change in the relations of Austria with Hungary could be contemplated. In this matter above all Francis Ferdinand, however, had other views. Violent in all his opinions, he was particularly bitter in his opposition to the Magyars, whom he regarded as interlopers in Europe and enemies of the true welfare of the Empire. But the *Ausgleich*, supported as it was by the coronation oath which he had taken as King of Hungary in 1867, was sacred in Francis Joseph's eyes: he would not risk splitting Hungary from Austria. Yet Magyar policy, as Francis Ferdinand realized, was a constant provocation to the non-German peoples of

Austria. While in the western half of the Monarchy German domination, however much the Germans might regret it, was but a faded glory of the past, in the eastern half Magyar control over the subject peoples was steadily tightening. Of this the Czechs, close kinsmen of the Slovaks of Hungary, were only too well aware. Racial problems in both halves of the Monarchy and in matters of foreign policy were, in fact, becoming one, and it was racial policy in both internal and external affairs that eventually brought the Monarchy down.

## THE ARMY CRISIS, 1902

The settlement of 1867 had done more than recognize the personal union between Austria and Hungary under the Habsburg crown. It had left internal affairs in each half of the Monarchy to the respective governments, but had recognized the unity of the joint Army and Foreign Ministry under the Emperor-King's direct control. Hence Francis Joseph's touchiness in any matters affecting these aspects of the Monarchy's life, which he regarded as vital both to his prerogative and to the unity of his dominions. In the army the obvious need for a common tongue for orders kept German as the language of command. Already in the 'nineties, however, nationalist Czech conscripts had caused trouble by insisting on answering *Zde* (Here) to the roll-call instead of the German *Hier*, and in 1902 similar difficulties arose in Hungary. In that year measures for the increase in the number of conscripts called to the colours, made necessary by the rise in population, were introduced in both Vienna and Budapest, and touched off in Hungary the fiercest political storm that the country had to face between 1867 and 1918. On the surface the point at issue was the supersession of German by Magyar as the language of command in Hungarian regiments, on which the more rabid Magyar nationalists insisted as the price of their support for a larger army. To this Francis Joseph would not agree, and after four years of political conflict he held his own. Fundamentally, however, the struggle reflected the rise of new, self-conscious elements in Hungarian political life, and their desire to achieve greater independence for their country, severing the ties with Austria until only a personal, dynastic link should remain. This it was that embittered Francis Ferdinand in the first place. He resented the concessions which the Magyars had wrung from his uncle in 1867 at the expense of the unity of the Empire, and was determined to resist any further weakening of the Monarchy's power. He realized too, that the magyarization of the subject peoples of the Hungarian kingdom was creating new difficulties and might prejudice loyalty to the crown among helpless peoples who could not get their wrongs redressed. He was making his own contacts among these peoples, encouraging them in their hopes and toying with various schemes for admitting them to equal rights and thereby increasing the attractiveness—and therefore the strength—of the Monarchy to which he hoped soon to succeed. Had he lived, his accession would almost certainly have been the occasion for a first-class political storm in Hungary from which, even without a European war, the Monarchy might not have recovered. Francis Joseph, however, had long since had his fill of Magyar opposition, and unless his own position was affected, as it was in the struggle over the army bill, he contented himself with playing in Hungarian affairs a strictly constitutional rôle.

## MAGYAR POLICY

The key to the policy of the Magyar leaders was to be found in the historic conception of a united Hungarian kingdom, which, whatever the racial origins of the seven other peoples (German, Roumanian, Slovak, Ruthene, Serb, Croat and Italian) who lived under its rule, remained—and was intended to remain—essentially a Magyar creation. "Our non-Magyar fellow citizens," said the great leader of Hungary's last years, Count Stephen Tisza, in 1910, "must first of all reconcile themselves to the fact that they here belong to a national state, which is not a conglomerate of different races, but which one nation has conquered and founded, upon which one nation has stamped the ineradicable impress of its individuality."[33] Never, indeed, until 1945, when for the second time in a hundred years Russian troops overran Hungary and the relics of the ancient kingdom were at last swept away, did the Magyars—or at least the most influential among them—cease to hold in lively recollection the conquests of Árpád and King Stephen, in the ninth and tenth centuries, as creators of a great Magyar state centred on the Danubian plain. In 1867, after centuries of division and oppression at the hands of Mongols, Turks and Germans, the freedom of a united Hungary was at last assured by the *Ausgleich*, which, as has already been shown, was founded on the acceptance of Magyar control in the eastern half of the Dual Monarchy and of German-Austrian in the west. Henceforth the Magyar aim was to keep the freedom and unity of their country unimpaired: much of what seems inexplicable or unenlightened in the policies pursued is to be understood in the light of this aim.

## THE AIMS OF DEÁK AND EÖTVÖS

To the more enlightened of the men who had regained Hungary's freedom the new régime was not intended to deny to the subject peoples their natural development. "If we wish to win over the nationalities," said Francis Deák (1803–76), the true architect of the *Ausgleich* on the Hungarian side, in a speech in 1872, "we must not seek at all costs to magyarize them: this can only happen if we create in them love and attachment for Hungarian conditions."[34] His view was endorsed by his friend and collaborator, Baron Joseph Eötvös (1813–71), who wrote, in one of the studies of the nationalities problem to which he devoted himself after the failure of the 1848 revolution, the prophetic words: "the supremacy of our nation would be the greatest calamity which could happen to it".[35]

## THE LAW OF NATIONALITIES AND ITS NON-IMPLE-MENTATION

It was largely through the influence of these men that the *Ausgleich* was followed in Hungary in 1868 by an enlightened "Law of Nationalities", which, while preserving the unity of the kingdom, with Magyar as the State language, legalized the use of other languages in local affairs, and especially in schools, while guaranteeing equal scope for official appointments to qualified non-Magyar citizens. With Eötvös, as Hungarian Minister for Education, influenced by the discussions on compulsory education then proceeding in Britain, the Law of Nationalities was followed in the same year by a "National Schools Act", which made education compulsory in the mother tongue between the ages of six and twelve, and required the erection of State schools where no church schools existed. These were admirable measures: indeed, the Law of Nationalities has been authoritatively described as "one of the best nationality laws that have ever been drafted".[36] The League of Nations Minority Treaties, more than fifty years later, drew heavily upon it. Unfortunately both laws quickly became a dead letter. Eötvös and Deák died in the 'seventies, and there were few after them to maintain their principles until the end, when in 1918 the radical Government of Count Michael Károlyi, with Oscar Jászi as Minister for Nationalities, too late endeavoured to undo the harm of fifty years and apply a liberal nationalities policy. In the meantime, in the words used in 1908 by a close observer of the pre-war scene, R. W. Seton-Watson, who travelled widely in Hungary as the "wandering Scot" (*Scotus Viator*), "the whole energy of the Magyars for a generation past has been devoted to the creation of a Magyar middle class, with which to feed officialdom and maintain the Magyar predominance",[37] and educational policy in particular was directed to this end.

## THE POLICY OF MAGYARIZATION—AND ITS JUSTIFICATION

The reasons for the intensification of Magyar nationalism and for the denial, in practice, of equal rights to the subject peoples, are not far to seek. Hungary was still dominated by the great Magyar landed families, whose wealth and power were to be steadily increased by the growing, tariff-protected, markets of Hungary and Austria: only shortly before the war the Austrian minister, Joseph Baernreither, whose penetrating judgments on the situation in the Dual Monarchy are quoted elsewhere in this study, recorded in his diary the admission by a Magyar politician that "Hungarian economic policy is really run for the benefit of some three hundred landowning families".[38] To these noble families—Esterházy, Andrássy, Apponyi, Károlyi and the like—with their offshoots and the lesser nobility, belonged almost one-third of the arable land of the kingdom: nowhere else in Europe, except in England, was the landowning interest so wealthy and so powerful. Around the great families was the considerable class of country

F

gentry, the real backbone of Magyardom, who for centuries had stubbornly resisted conquest and alien oppression. To all these landowners, small and great alike, the Magyar peasantry was of little account, the subject peasant peoples—"our barbarians", as Andrássy had called them—of even less note. The rebellion of 1848 and the triumph of 1867 had inevitably reinforced the intense national pride of the Magyars to the degree of chauvinism. Time was needed for peaceful consolidation and development. Yet in the very hour of triumph new stresses had appeared. The 1848 revolution had stirred the subject peoples, while the growth of independent states in Serbia and Roumania (finally freed from Turkish control in 1867 and 1878 respectively), and the rising hopes of autonomy among the Czechs, could not fail to inspire the nationalism of related peoples living under the Crown of St. Stephen. The danger of disruption seemed real. Yet wealth, culture and education rested largely in Magyar hands. Despite the laws of 1868 the way to advancement, as well as the way to a securely unified Hungary, seemed to Magyars, therefore, to lie through the acceptance of magyarization. Increasingly all ways were opened to those of the other nationalities who learnt to speak, behave and think as Magyars. The rest were felt to be ignorant peasants who could be ignored, or, if they were too troublesome, threatened, significantly enough, with the fate of the Red Indians in North America.[39]

## THE TISZAS AND MAGYARIZATION

There was a further reason for the intensification of the nationalist spirit. While the great landowners continued to flourish, the lesser gentry, like their counterparts in other lands, were hard hit by the importation into Europe of overseas produce—wheat from the U.S.A. and Canada, wool from Australia—which deprived them of their foreign markets. Great estates could be run on sound modern lines, but the gentry lacked capital for machinery and had to look for another livelihood. At a time when the development of government called for an increasing number of public officials, State service provided an obvious outlet, but the very expansion of the public services in the hands of Magyar officials increased the pressure for magyarization. Leading representatives of the gentry in political life were the Tiszas, father and son, Koloman (1830–1902) and Stephen (1861–1918). Koloman was Premier of Hungary from 1875 to 1890, his son from 1903 to 1905 and again from 1913 until his murder in October, 1918, on the very eve of collapse. It was under these two able, but narrow, men, in particular, that the screw was tightened on the subject peoples.

## THE INFLUENCE OF KOSSUTH

Another element in the situation was the Kossuth legend and the growth of "Kossuthism". The dynamic leader of the 1848 revolution, the best known Hungarian of his day, Louis Kossuth, was in exile abroad from 1849 until his death in 1894 at the age of ninety-two. As a radical Kossuth disapproved of Hungary's rulers after 1867: as a separatist he refused to reconcile himself to the arrangement which, however advantageous to Hungary, had left her linked to Austria and subject to the hated Habsburg. Kossuth, like the poet of the revolution, Petöfi, was by origin a Slovak, magyarized only by adoption, but he had become a fervent Magyar patriot, and with his advocacy of Hungarian separatism he combined a centralism which would have left little scope for the free development of the non-Magyar peoples. From his exile in Italy Kossuth inspired and instructed his followers, while his death in 1894, and the homecoming of his body, were made the occasion of great patriotic demonstrations. A Kossuthist independence party took shape under the leadership of his son, Francis, and tended to heighten nationalist fervour. Everything conspired, in short, to diminish the chances of the implementation of the liberal measures of 1868, even had the Magyar leaders been less self-righteously convinced of the soundness of the policies they pursued.

## EDUCATION

The measures that were actually taken forced every non-Magyar who wished to advance himself, and many others, into the Magyar mould. Elementary schooling was so controlled that by 1904, though Magyars formed less than half of the population, instruction in nine-tenths of the State schools was purely in their language, while considerable pressure was brought to bear upon church schools to increase its use. Secondary schools were almost entirely Magyar, three Slovak schools, for instance, being forcibly closed down in 1874. Well might the State schools be described, in the phrase of a Magyar publicist, as "a huge machine" for the production of good Magyars. In the courts the right to plead in the mother tongue was denied until, in the memorable phrase of Father Andrew Hlinka (1864–1938), the Slovak nationalist who was imprisoned by the Magyars and lived to play an equivocal part in the politics of the Czechoslovak Republic, "the non-Magyar peasant stood like an ox, dumb before the courts of his native land".

## ELECTIONS

Similar methods were applied in elections. A limited and complicated franchise, public voting and open pressure guaranteed Koloman Tisza and his immediate successors practically a Magyar monopoly, the other nationalities being in practice excluded, or abstaining in despair. In the words of Aurel Popovici, the Roumanian from Transylvania whose views on the need for reform have already been quoted, and whose political activities caused him to flee from Hungary to escape imprisonment, Magyar tyranny had made of Hungary "a Bastille of the nationalities".[40]

Had the Magyars been able to apply their policies centuries earlier, they might have succeeded in establishing uniformity in their country, as had been done in western Europe. Had the war not come, they might still have succeeded, though by 1914 tension was increasing, and Francis Ferdinand's attitude boded ill. Yet the nationalities were not making any considerable headway, and Baernreither's view, in June, 1914, was that the Magyar attitude was "more intransigent than ever".[41] Even as late as October, 1918, when the unhappy Emperor Charles, in a desperate attempt to stave off collapse, promised to transform Austria into a federation, the Hungarian government demanded a recognition of the integrity of Hungary, under the threat of cutting off from Austria the food supplies without which she would starve. Not until 1945, indeed, did there come a final breach with the past.

## DIVERGENT INTERESTS OF AUSTRIA AND HUNGARY

It was against this background that the question of the control of the army arose in 1902. Already problems had arisen between Austria and Hungary to encourage thoughts of separation. Under the terms of the agreement of 1867 the common tariff policy of the Dual Monarchy and the quotas to be paid by each half for joint State expenditure were to be revised every ten years. By 1897 Hungary was beginning to develop her own industries, and Austria was feeling that her share of the joint expenses, more than two-thirds, was too large. When the revision due in 1897 was undertaken, therefore, several years of protracted negotiation followed. The customs union was eventually prolonged, and the Hungarian quota slightly increased, but it was clear that as Hungary developed her natural resources she would aim at economic independence: the days when an industrialized Austria and an agricultural Hungary would supplement each other were well past. In 1902, while the negotiations were still proceeding, the new army bill was introduced, and the Kossuthists seized the opportunity to demand that Magyar should be used in the army, that the officers of Hungarian regiments should be Magyars and that the Hungarian flag should be carried by their regiments. This was essentially a matter for the Crown, but Austrians could not remain indifferent to demands which underlined the divergence of the ways of the two halves of the Monarchy. The demands did more, for the efforts of Körber, as Premier in Vienna, to represent Austria's concern for the unity of the army, drew a sharp reproof from Stephen Tisza for his interference in Hungarian affairs, and added to the difficulties which eventually caused Körber to resign.

## FRANCIS JOSEPH AND THE ARMY CRISIS

Had the Kossuthists' demands been accepted, discipline would have been affected in the Hungarian units, for the privileged Croats at least would have resisted the use of Magyar. Francis Joseph, however, had no intention of yielding. He was prepared to make some concessions, but would not compromise on the language of command. After attempts at a settlement had been frustrated by obstruction in the Hungarian Parliament, he issued an army order reaffirming the unity of his army: "uniform

and undivided as it is now, so shall my army remain". Stephen
Tisza was appointed Premier to force through a settlement,
but even the prestige of a Tisza could not break the impasse.

## STEPHEN TISZA PREMIER: HIS FAILURE AND THE FRANCHISE PROPOSALS

Tisza now as always was convinced of the need for the
Dual Monarchy. Without Austria, he realized, Hungary could
neither maintain a position as a Great Power, nor resist the
attraction of Roumania and Serbia for her subject peoples.
Though a fervent nationalist he was, therefore, opposed by
the separatists, and the two years of his first Ministry were
marked by violent scenes in Parliament. At last, in 1905,
he appealed over Parliament's head to the electorate. His confident expectations of success were, however, dashed, and he
suffered an overwhelming defeat, which indicated the temper
of the electorate. A Coalition of Kossuthists and others was
then formed, but as the language of command was one point
in its programme Francis Joseph refused to treat with it.
Following precedents in Austria under similar conditions he
appointed a government of officials to tide over the difficult
situation, but taxes and recruits were withheld and there was
defiant approval among Magyars of the conduct of the
Norwegians, who in this very year had broken away from
Sweden—an ominous example. Francis Joseph, however, was
not as powerless as King Oscar. There were in Hungary, as in
Austria, new forces that could be drawn into the political
conflict, the mass of the subject peoples and of the socially
unprivileged. The Hungarian Minister of the Interior,
Joseph Kristóffy, put forward a scheme for manhood suffrage,
with secret balloting, in order, as he said, to open Parliament
"to those who will develop their legislative activity, not in
constitutional conflicts, but in the organization of the nation's
work",[42] and Francis Joseph accepted it. The franchise was to be
restricted, it is true, to men literate in Magyar, but the move was
none the less a bold one which would have increased the electorate from nine hundred thousand to more than two millions and
a quarter (though leaving some two million still disfranchised),
and would have shaken Magyar predominance: as the dis-
coverer of a way out of the constitutional impasse Kristóffy was

promptly nicknamed "Kristóffy Columbus".[43] Francis Joseph
made his decision known, and early in 1906, by a dramatic
stroke, Parliament was dissolved, the proclamation being read
in the Parliament building by an officer escorted, in a crowning
act of royal displeasure, by a squad of *Roumanian* soldiers.

## THE CRITICAL YEAR—1906

It was a critical moment. For long the subject peoples had
been looking to the Emperor-King, who had never since 1867
offered them any encouragement, to "mount his horse", in the
spirit of old legends, and restore their rights. Now, perhaps, the
moment had come. Francis Ferdinand warmly approved, and
those with whom he was in contact looked forward hopefully.
The results, however, were what might have been expected in
the context of Hungarian politics. Hungary was not Austria,
and the Magyars had a firmer control of the country than the
Germans had of their half of the Monarchy. After considerable
manœuvring behind the scenes the Coalition parties climbed
down, accepting Francis Joseph's terms in the matter of army
control and staving off Kristóffy's sweeping measure by undertaking themselves to introduce a reform of the franchise. For
Francis Joseph this was enough. He had gained his point,
and, when the Coalition restored constitutional government,
gave him his recruits and recovered arrears of taxes, he had no
further claims to press. Kristóffy's plans were not without their
effect, for it was upon them that the electoral reform of 1907
in Austria was based, but in Hungary they were conveniently
forgotten, and little more was heard of franchise reform. The
hopes of the nationalities were dashed, and, as in Austria, the
frustration of hopes raised by plans for an extension of the
suffrage marked a turning point in the Monarchy's last years.
Increasingly the subject peoples in Hungary, despairing of
timely Habsburg assistance, looked outwards for comfort and
support. "The last milestone on the road to ruin," it has well
been said, "had been passed."[44]

## THE SOUTHERN SLAVS—CROATIA, SERBIA AND "TRI-ALISM"

If, in fact, the situation was beyond remedy after 1906, the
milestone was also one on that road to the east, which, Andrássy

had earlier boasted, had been cleared for the Monarchy by the Treaty of Berlin in 1878 and the Dual Alliance of the following year. In southern Hungary, in particular, as loyalty for the Monarchy faded, it was the example of independent Serbia that inspired the Croats and other Slav peoples of the Hungarian realm, and it was the powerful attraction exerted by Serbia that impelled the Monarchy into the final catastrophe. It is to the unsettled frontiers towards the Balkans, the relics of the long conflict with the Turks, that we must therefore turn.

The western, Dalmatian, coast of the Balkan peninsula, with the exception of Hungary's outlet to the sea at Fiume, formed part of Austria. Inland and eastwards lay Bosnia and Herzegovina, occupied by the Monarchy since 1878; further east still, and effectively cut off from the sea, was Serbia. North of Bosnia was Croatia, north of Serbia the Banat of Temesvár, both forming part of the Hungarian kingdom. Serbia's position was therefore a critical one. The Croats, though Slavs, were the one privileged non-Magyar nationality of the kingdom. They had been under Magyar rule since early in the twelfth century, but had preserved their own individuality and political rights, which they had asserted against the Magyars as recently as 1848, when, under their renowned military leader, Jellačić, they had supported Habsburg authority against the Magyar revolt, and contributed not a little to the victory of reaction. Given Francis Joseph's indifference to Slav claims, this had availed them little, and when the *Ausgleich* was framed they had been advised by the Emperor to make their own terms with the Magyars. The result was another "Compromise", the *Nagoda* of 1868, by which, without prejudice to the unity of Hungary, Croatia was permitted its own Parliament and a considerable measure of control over local affairs, with the public use of the Croat language. The arrangement was an unpopular one, however, and was carried and sustained only by political corruption and a narrowly limited franchise. Many Croats wanted complete autonomy under Habsburg rule; others had wider views and aimed at attracting Bosnians and Serbs into a South Slav (Yugoslav) partnership with themselves which might eventually act as a counterpoise to German and Magyar domination and convert the Dual Monarchy into a *Trial* system. Few were prepared to become reconciled to Magyar rule.

Among the advocates of Trialism, which later found favour with Francis Ferdinand, was the notable Roman Catholic Bishop of Djakovo, J. G. Strossmayer (1815–1905), an ardent Croat nationalist (though, as his name reveals, of German Austrian descent), who was at the same time a figure of European standing, notable for his resistance to the proclamation of Papal Infallibility in 1870 and for his correspondence with Gladstone on Balkan problems during the Eastern Crisis of the later 'seventies. Croat national development and Yugoslav unity owe much to Strossmayer. He used his great wealth and influence to encourage Croat education and culture, and founded at Zagreb (Agram) a University and, still more significantly, a Southern Slav Academy of Science and Art which had the avowed object of encouraging the intellectual development of Serbs and Bulgars no less than of the Croats themselves. Strossmayer's was a romantic outlook, and the possibility of uniting all the South Slavs was a remote one. Differences of history, of culture and of development were too great, and fostered jealousies and rivalries which, inflamed as they were in the Balkan Wars of 1912–13 and in the First World War, have embittered the relations of kindred Balkan Slavs into our own day. Before the great Bishop died, Croats, Bosnians and Serbs were beginning, it is true, to draw together, but the bonds of union were the negative ones of common opposition to the Habsburg Monarchy rather than any positive acceptance of a common policy for the future—as the tragic story of Yugoslav politics after 1918 was to reveal only too clearly.

A close association of Croats with Serbs seemed particularly unlikely. Though probably of common origin they had been divided in their Balkan homeland for more than a thousand years, and had steadily grown apart, the Croats becoming Roman Catholic and looking west for their culture and inspiration, the Serbs joining the Orthodox Church and looking to Constantinople, first as the centre of the Eastern Empire and then as the capital of their Turkish overlords. Though they had a common tongue they wrote it differently, the Serbs using the Cyrillic alphabet. On the whole the Croats enjoyed higher

F*

standards of living and of education and culture. Serbia was poorer and its people had had a hard and bitter struggle against Turkish oppression. Yet they had succeeded in creating an independent State and the achievement inevitably coloured their outlook. They tended to despise the less independent Croats, and, when ultimately united with them, to regard their country as a conquest, a mere province of an enlarged Serbia: the disastrous consequences were seen in Yugoslavia between 1941 and 1945. The elements of this situation were already present during the nineteenth century. Scattered among the Croats, and stretching eastwards from Croatia into the Banat, were considerable numbers of Serb settlers, introduced earlier by the Habsburgs, as the Turks retreated, to form a military frontier. To these Serbs, who numbered about one-quarter of Croatia's total population, the Croats, unwilling to risk any diminution of the solid unity of their country against the Magyars, denied the equal rights which they themselves wished to assert. The result was a tense situation which played into the hands of the Magyar rulers. Count Charles Khuen-Héderváry, a cousin of Koloman Tisza, who held the office of Ban (Governor) of Croatia, to which he was appointed by Tisza, from 1880 to 1903, proved himself particularly adept at encouraging the Serbs and playing them off against the Croats. Loyalty to the dynasty diminished on both sides, however, for both resented Francis Joseph's abandonment of them to the Magyars, and before the end of the "Khuen era" a rapprochement was taking place, though as late as 1902 there were anti-Serb riots in Zagreb.

## MAGYAR RULE IN CROATIA

Khuen-Héderváry was appointed Ban to deal with the strained political situation arising from Croat resentment at the occupation of Bosnia and the crushing of resistance. His régime became notorious, apart from his calculated favours to the Serbs of Croatia, for the unrelenting pressure with which he strove to create a pro-Magyar party and to diminish Croat nationalism. He did much for the economic development of the country, but corrupted a whole generation, his critics claimed, by blocking the advancement of any who asserted Croat claims. Opposed to him were such leaders as Anthony

Starčević and Joseph Frank, men of more extreme views than Strossmayer, who, despising the backward Serbs, rejected any notion of a wider union and aimed at an association only of South Slavs who were already Habsburg subjects. Their dislike of the Serbs was intensified by religious differences, and Frank, in particular, was narrowly clericalist in outlook. At the end of the century, however, new forces and personalities began to appear. After anti-Magyar riots in Zagreb in 1895, on the occasion of a visit by Francis Joseph, a number of University students, to evade the attentions of Khuen's police, withdrew to Prague, where they came under the influence of Masaryk. Their studies at Prague marked a decisive stage in the history of Yugoslav unity, and among them were three who were to play a significant part in the development of the Yugoslav idea, Stephen Radić, Svetozar Pribičević and Francis Supilo. Stephen Radić (1871–1928) after his return from Prague founded, with his brother Anthony, the Croatian Peasant Party, while Pribičević (1875–1936) became a leading figure among the Serbs of Hungary: both were later to play an important, though in the main unfortunate, part in the united Yugoslavia of the post-war years, Radić as a bitter opponent, and Pribičević as a protagonist, of Serb centralism. Supilo (1870–1917) became an able journalist, editor of the leading Croat opposition newspaper, *Novi List* (News Sheet) which to evade Khuen's severe press laws was published in Fiume. With him was soon to be associated in political developments a prominent Dalmatian Croat, Anthony Trumbić (1864–1938), notable later as Yugoslavia's representative at the Paris Peace Conference.

## The "Fiume Resolution", 1905, and its Frustration

In 1903 Francis Joseph was looking for a Premier who could overcome the constitutional crisis in Hungary, and Khuen-Hédervary's reputation for firmness in Croatia led to his transference to Budapest. All Croatia, it was said, "took a deep breath", and Hungary's crisis seemed her opportunity. Francis Joseph had recently refused to receive a deputation presenting a petition on Croat grievances, and Supilo, Trumbić and others, despairing of help from the Crown, conceived the notion of coming to terms with the Magyar Coalition, and joining with them in their opposition to Francis Joseph, in return for greater freedom for Croatia. Frank and Radić would not associate themselves with this move, Frank on account of his fanatical hatred of the Serbs, Radić because he saw, justly, that there was more to be gained for Croatia from Austria than from Hungary. Conferences of Croat representatives at Fiume and of Serbs at Zara were, however, able to reach agreement, and the "Fiume Resolution" of 1905 opened the way both for Croat-Serb co-operation and for an understanding with the Magyar Coalition soon to come into power in Budapest. Croat hopes rose, and in the elections of 1906, the first free elections in Croatia for many years, the Croat-Serb Coalition of "Resolutionists" won a majority. Disappointment was at hand, however. Within a year Francis Kossuth introduced in the Hungarian Parliament a measure which declared Magyar to be the official language on the Croatian railways, in flagrant disregard not only of the Fiume Resolution but of the terms of the *Nagoda* itself, and when the Croats resisted Baron Paul Rauch was appointed Ban in 1908 to hold the country down during the critical period of the Bosnian annexation. Rauch found it impossible, however, to revive Khuen's pro-Magyar group. The elections of 1908 gave 57 seats to the "Resolutionists", 24 to Frank's followers, 7 to the Peasant Party and none at all to the pro-Magyars. If the Fiume Resolution had done little to reconcile Slav and Magyar, it had at least set the Croats and Serbs on the path which was to lead in 1918 to the establishment of a Yugoslav State.

## The Agram and Friedjung Trials

Present and future, however, were fraught with difficulties. Rauch, deprived of parliamentary support, was able to fall back on other methods, while the Resolutionists were assailed by Frank as betrayers of purely Croat ideals: already the divisions between the Croat-Serb Coalition group and the Croat extremists, which later were to produce the sinister figure of Pavelić, the Croat quisling of 1941, were taking shape. At the height of the agitation which followed the annexation of Bosnia Rauch turned on the Coalition and arrested more than fifty Croats and Serbs on vague charges of conspiring to attach Croatia to Serbia. They were tried in Agram (Zagreb) in March, 1909, after months of imprisonment, and the conduct of the trial was so manifestly unjust that there was an outcry both in the Monarchy and throughout Europe. The sentences given were quashed on appeal, but there is little doubt that if the expected war with Serbia had broken out there would have been executions for treason on evidence which had only too obviously been fabricated as part of the Austrian Foreign Ministry's "cold war" (as it would now be called) on Serbia.

The notorious "Friedjung Trial" followed. About the time of the Agram trial, shortly before it became clear that Serbia would not refuse to recognize the annexation of Bosnia, Friedjung published in the *Neue Freie Presse* wholesale accusations against the Resolutionists, charging them with treasonable dealings with Serbia and basing his case on photographs of documents, which, though this was never acknowledged, had been supplied to him by the Foreign Ministry. Pribičević and Supilo were among those named and with the rest sued Friedjung for libel. The case came on in December, and proved a *cause célèbre*. A crushing body of evidence, which Masaryk had helped to put together, proved the documents which Friedjung had used to be forgeries, and the charges were withdrawn. It was a blow to the Rauch régime and to the Foreign Ministry, which had its real aims only too grossly exposed. Friedjung, indeed, deceived by the material which had been supplied to him, and which he handled with less than his usual technical skill, let slip out in his articles the true purpose of the whole affair:

> Should it be ordained that the Austrian arms shall thoroughly purge Belgrade of the nest of conspirators and help the healthy elements of the Serbian people to triumph, this would be a civilizing deed of great value—not merely an advantage for the Austro-Hungarian Monarchy, but also the liberation of a whole people from a company of conspirators.

The concern for the well-being of the Serbs did not conceal the sinister design. "Rarely, if ever," wrote a contemporary observer, "has so much dirty linen been washed before the Austrian public."[45] A year later Supilo was able to publish the confession of the Serb renegade, Vasić, who had actually perpetrated the forgeries at the Austro-Hungarian legation at Belgrade. The whole episode was, as Baernreither commented, "a hideous game . . . a Hungarian plot against the (Resolutionist) Coalition in Croatia".[46] It was this—and more. Magyar intrigues against the Croats and the Foreign Ministry's designs on Serbia were equally at fault. The only result was to reveal the tensions in the Monarchy and the explosive nature of the whole South Slav problem, and on the next occasion there was to be not a lawsuit but war.

## THE SOUTH SLAV REACTION—TERRORISM

Baron Rauch was replaced as Ban in 1910, but Magyar oppression continued and in 1912 the Croatian constitution was actually suspended by a new Ban, von Cuvaj. The situation was deteriorating to such a degree that hot-headed students, who in 1895 had contented themselves with a public burning of the Hungarian flag, now began to attempt political assassination, in the worst traditions of Balkan feuds. The first shot was fired, significantly enough, in Bosnia in 1910, but von Cuvaj's life was also attempted, and when a new, and more liberal, Ban, Baron Skerlecz, was appointed he was shot at and gravely wounded almost as soon as he had arrived in the country. A new and more fanatical spirit was entering into the vexed problem of the South Slavs, a spirit which was soon further inflamed by Serbian successes in the Balkan wars of 1912–13.

## THE ASSASSINATION OF FRANCIS FERDINAND

Meanwhile, in Bosnia, despite a programme of public works, little was done for the real advancement of the country, for education, for political development or for the economic betterment of the peasantry, crushed under the burden of the unreformed system of Turkish land laws. The contrast with vigorous Serbia was a telling one, and needed none of the underground agitation of which Serbia was accused to drive it home. Oppression was countered by terrorism, the first shot being fired in 1910 by the young Bosnian, Žerajić, whose dying words, "I leave it to Serbdom to avenge me", became the inspiration of the revolutionary movement *Mlada Bosna* (Young Bosnia) under the guidance of Serb nationalist organizations, and especially of the terrorist *Black Hand*. When the ultimate protest was made at Sarajevo on 28th June, 1914, it was again the hand of a Bosnian and member of *Mlada Bosna* and the *Black Hand*, Gavrilo Princip, that fired the fatal shots. Princip represented the crest of a mounting wave of South Slav resentment, but he was also continuing, desperately and fanatically, the struggle for Bosnian freedom, which had begun with the revolt against Turkey in 1875. In the words of a leading authority, "as in 1875 the initiative lay with the Bosnian rebels, fighting in the mountains, so in 1914 the initiative lay with their sons and grandsons, the revolutionary students".[47] Francis Ferdinand paid in his person for the errors and miscalculations of Austrian and Hungarian policy over several decades. His own supreme miscalculation lay in his paying an official visit to Sarajevo on St. Vitus's Day, the anniversary of the Serb defeat of Kossovo in 1389, an occasion of poignant recollection for all Serbs, and a great national festival. It was, as one historian has said, as if "a British royalty had visited Dublin on St. Patrick's Day at the height of the Troubles".[48] Trouble was to be expected, though it was the gross neglect of police precautions that turned an incident into a major disaster.

## RELATIONS WITH SERBIA

Nowhere were the Monarchy's miscalculations more marked than in its dealings with Serbia. Something has already been said of their relations in the years following the crises of the 'seventies. Under King Milan and his son, Alexander, Austro-Hungarian influence had been paramount in Serbia, but it had been agreed with Russia that nothing should be done to disturb the Balkan *status quo*. Ominous developments came with the new century, however. In 1903 there was a palace revolution in Belgrade, and the incompetent and self-indulgent King Alexander Obrenović was murdered by a group of army officers who were admitted into the royal palace by a Lieutenant Živković of the Royal Guard (who was to appear in the limelight again when as a general, a quarter of a century later, he became for a time the right hand man of the ill-fated dictatorship of King Alexander Karageorgević). In 1903, with Alexander Obrenović out of the way, Peter

Karageorgević, the heir to the century-old feud, was proclaimed king in his stead. In Vienna the news was received with cynical indifference, the prevailing view being that it mattered little who reigned in Belgrade provided that he remained on good terms with Austria-Hungary. Yet the new King Peter was not prepared to adopt the humble attitude of his immediate predecessors. Himself a man of radical views, he realized that their autocratic ways had lost them the support of the Serbs, and he resolved from the first that his policy should reflect more closely his people's wishes. In foreign affairs this undoubtedly entailed a less subservient attitude to the Dual Monarchy. His hands were soon to be strengthened by the defeat of Russia in the war with Japan, which, although for several years it reduced Russia's bargaining power, by forcing Russian attention to turn again to Europe reopened the rivalry between the two Empires in the Balkans. The truce was nearly at an end.

## Austro-Russian Relations: the Critical Year, 1906, and the Policy of Aehrenthal

From 1895 to 1906 Austro-Hungarian foreign policy was in the hands of Count Agenor Goluchowski, an easy-going Polish aristocrat who believed that the Monarchy could not stand the strain of an active foreign policy and was resolved, above all, to maintain friendly relations with Russia. Under him the policy of the preservation of the *status quo* became a matter of formal agreement, for he realized that a forward move by either would not only endanger peace but also add to the internal strains of Austria-Hungary, which already possessed more Slav subjects than she could comfortably digest. Hence, in 1903, after a revolt in Macedonia against Turkish misrule, the Mürzsteg agreement by which Austria-Hungary and Russia agreed jointly to supervise reforms in the Turkish administration. In 1906, however, Goluchowski was succeeded by Baron Alois von Aehrenthal (1854–1912), an able diplomat who had been for eight years Ambassador in St. Petersburg and might therefore have been expected to maintain easy relations with Russia. Aehrenthal's political sympathies were with the Tsarist Empire, and like his predecessor he was well aware of the weaknesses of Austria-

Hungary, but his cure for her malaise lay in an active rather than a passive policy. He hoped by some cheap but resounding success in foreign policy to restore the prestige of the Monarchy and cure internal dissensions, and material for an easy coup was ready to hand in the anomalous position of Bosnia and Herzegovina. Further, he was perturbed at the independent attitude of Serbia under Peter, and realized that, if the Monarchy were to survive unshaken, Serbia's powers of attraction to its Slav subjects must be either diminished or destroyed. This was the conclusion that had already been reached by the new chief of the General Staff, the bellicose General Francis Conrad von Hötzendorf (1852–1925), whose influence on events, both now and in 1914, was to be disastrous. The only question, in Conrad's view, was whether a union of the South Slavs would come within the Dual Monarchy at Serbia's expense, or under Serbia at the Monarchy's expense,[49] and he was determined to achieve the first.

Aehrenthal's mind was also working this way. Already economic pressure had been brought to bear upon Serbia, though with results that might have been taken as significant warnings. A "tariff war" (known, from one of Serbia's principal exports, as the "Pig War") had taken place and Serbia had won. Austria-Hungary had trusted too much in Serbia's reliance on the Monarchy as a market for her produce, and had seen with alarm that Peter had found alternative markets, while he had been able to raise money for defence purposes in France and to buy there the arms that had hitherto been obtained from Škoda. The days of the obliging Milan were obviously long past. The signs were not read aright, however, and it was decided that Serbia must be taught a lesson. In 1907, after only a year in office, Aehrenthal told Conrad that he aimed at annexing Bosnia-Herzegovina and with it parts of Serbia. He had other reasons at this time for taking a determined line. Russia had recently concluded an *Entente* with her old enemy, Britain, who had so often resisted her southwards expansion, and was therefore in a better position to pursue an active policy in the Balkans. With the *Entente*, too, Russia was less dependent on German friendship, and had more room for manœuvre, though she was still weak from the effects of war and revolution, as Aehrenthal, who had until recently lived in St. Petersburg as Ambassador, knew well. She could therefore do little yet to hamper any Austro-Hungarian move. At the same time Russia's greater freedom meant that in the event of a clash Austria-Hungary herself would be correspondingly more dependent upon Germany. In fact, Germany and Austria-Hungary were both being forced, by their own inept policies, into a position where each had no friend but the other.

## AEHRENTHAL'S COUP

In 1908 Aehrenthal felt that the moment for action had come. It was the year of Francis Joseph's Jubilee, an auspicious occasion, and in July occurred the revolution in Turkey that swept away the notorious Sultan Abdul Hamid and placed the revolutionary "Young Turks" in power. At last the fever of nationalism had touched even the Turks and it seemed that the "sick man of Europe" was to be cured of his numerous ills. Any move by the Dual Monarchy must therefore come soon. To Russia also the Turkish revolution appeared as an opportunity for strengthening her position. The Russian Foreign Minister, Izvolsky, had been appointed in the same year as Aehrenthal, and was fired with similar ambitions. His country's prestige had been brought low by the war with Japan, and he sought an occasion of reviving it. His aim was to secure for Russia the free passage of the Straits for her warships, which had always been denied to her by the other Powers. The achievement at such a moment of one of Russia's historic ambitions would do much to outweigh recent reverses. The two Foreign Ministers, both intent on measures which, they hoped, would redound to their countries' credit—and their own—saw an opportunity for striking a bargain. At a meeting at Buchlau in Moravia in September, 1908, they agreed, therefore, not to oppose each other's moves. No record was kept of their conversations, however, and as they heartily detested each other the way was open for the serious misunderstanding that soon arose. Izvolsky, whose aim was the more ambitious one and needed the more careful preparation, left the conference feeling that he had time in which to plan his own project, but in October, before he could make any move, Aehrenthal abruptly forestalled him with a proclamation, signed by Francis Joseph, of the annexation of Bosnia and Herzegovina. It was a blow for Izvolsky, for Russia and for all Slavs. Above all it was a challenge to Serbia, which at once turned to Russia for support.

## THE CRISIS OF 1908–09

The crisis that followed lasted for six months and brought Europe to the brink of war. Indeed, had Russia not been convalescing from the strain of her defeat at the hands of Japan, war would almost certainly have broken out. As it was, before the crisis finally passed Germany had to make it plain that she would support Austria-Hungary in the event of hostilities: Germany, William II proclaimed in a flamboyant speech, would support her ally "in shining armour". It was a Pyrrhic victory for Aehrenthal, for the Dual Monarchy, which he had hoped to buttress, was exposed to further strains, and Serbia and Russia, humiliated together, inevitably drew together for comfort. Russia set to work to reorganize her army, and the Balkan peoples were urged to await patiently the completion of her preparations. When Russia was ready, they were told in a secret circular sent from a Pan-Slav conference in St. Petersburg in 1909, she would "take up energetically her mission as protectress of the Slav world".[50] Even more pointed was the conclusion drawn from the affair by the Russian Ambassador in Paris:

> Russia, England and France must pay more attention than ever to action in common and at the same time must take the military measures necessary to convince their opponents that they have to deal with a political combination which knows how to ensure respect for itself and will carry through its demands.[51]

In fact, Aehrenthal's narrowly conceived attempt to enhance the standing of the Dual Monarchy had led to nothing short of a major crisis which has justly been characterized as "a grand rehearsal" for 1914.[52] Alarmed by what had happened, and by the exposure of the methods of the Foreign Ministry in the Friedjung trial which followed, Aehrenthal pursued a more cautious policy until his death in 1912, and Conrad went into retirement in the previous year, but the damage had already been done.

## THE BALKAN WARS, 1912-13

Aehrenthal died early in 1912, and in the autumn a new crisis flared up. Montenegro, Serbia, Bulgaria and Greece, united in an alliance which had been secretly encouraged by Russia, went to war with Turkey, and within a month the Turkish armies were everywhere rolled back. Before the end of November the Greeks were in Salonika and Serbia had regained "Old Serbia" (with the fatal field of Kossovo), lost to the Turks since the fourteenth century, and had pressed south-west through Albania to the Adriatic at Durazzo. It seemed that a Greater Serbia, with an outlet to the sea, was taking shape, but Austria-Hungary, astonished and concerned at the Serb victories, intervened to impose a veto. In December troops were concentrated on the frontier against Serbia and Conrad was recalled as Chief of Staff. Conrad henceforward was unwearying in his stress on the need for trying conclusions with Serbia: "we have reached the point where there is a trial of strength between the Monarchy and Serbia," he wrote to Francis Ferdinand, "it is a trial which must be seen through. . . . Serbia must be defeated in war."[53] Francis Joseph would not agree to war, however, and William II let it be known that Germany would not stand by her ally in a struggle for a few "Albanian goat-pastures". Eventually the London Conference of Ambassadors decided to establish an independent Albania, and Serbia, on Austria-Hungary's insistence, was compelled to sacrifice her outlet to the sea. Meanwhile the victors had quarrelled among themselves over the spoils, and Bulgaria had treacherously attacked her allies, who had then been joined in their counter-attack by Roumania. Peace was not finally restored until September, 1913, and it left the Dual Monarchy feeling that she had "stood on one side while the Balkan map was being remade".[54]

## BERCHTOLD AND CONRAD AND THE FINAL CRISIS

Aehrenthal's successor as Foreign Minister was Count Leopold von Berchtold (1863-1942), who like his predecessor had been Ambassador at St. Petersburg. Berchtold was not the man to withstand Conrad as Aehrenthal had done: "I will not lay myself open to the reproach levelled against Aehrenthal in 1908 that he prevented a settlement of accounts with Serbia," he wrote at the end of 1912.[55] Nevertheless he followed the lead of Francis Joseph and Germany in avoiding war in 1912–13, though at the same time he spurned Serbia's efforts to reach an understanding. Pašić, the Serbian Premier, tried through Masaryk to arrange a meeting to discuss terms, but Berchtold declined to see him. It was assumed that sooner or later Serbia must be dealt with, and both Russia's reactions to the crisis of 1908–09 and the evidence recently provided of the vitality and preparedness of Serbia were ignored. When the murder of Francis Ferdinand came the excuse it offered was only too readily seized upon. It was accepted as axiomatic, despite the revelations of the Agram and Friedjung trials, that Serbia was officially involved: "the Sarajevo crime", Berchtold later recorded in his memoirs, "was simply one of the latest examples of the work of destruction organized against us, of the sapping and mining which was to blow up the home in which we dwelt".[56] It was true, of course, that individual Serbs (some of whom had been concerned in the murder of King Alexander in 1903, and had since formed the *Black Hand* organization) were involved, and involved deeply, but there were extenuating circumstances: "the real crime for which Serbia is entitled to be indicted", it has well been said, "is her existence as a free and independent state, which became inevitably a centre of attraction for her malcontent kinsmen under foreign rule".[57]

## THE DUAL MONARCHY AND THE WAR

Yet it was widely felt in Austria-Hungary, and not merely in official circles, that Serbia must be put in her place, that if the Monarchy were not to sink into a decline she must show herself capable of vigorous action against a country which was believed to be directly responsible for the Sarajevo crime, if not actually its instigator. The annexation of Bosnia six years earlier, the first resolute step in foreign affairs taken by the Monarchy for many years, had for a time encouraged hopes that new creative policies were to be adopted, as much at home as abroad. It had soon become clear, however, that Aehrenthal had been pursuing a policy of prestige, with nothing constructive to offer. Since then the Balkan wars had served to depress still further the Monarchy's status. Great events had taken place on her doorstep in which she had had but a small part. In 1914, in consequence, the prospect of a forward policy stirred some enthusiasm, notably among the German Austrians who had suffered most from the changes in the Monarchy's fortunes and who were relieved at coming to blows with some at least among the recalcitrant Slavs. Frank's Croatian supporters also welcomed the opportunity of coming to grips with Serbia.

Elsewhere in the Monarchy there could be little enthusiasm. Hungary was reserved in her attitude for, although the Serbs were disliked, the death of the heir who was known to be anti-Magyar in outlook was not unwelcome, and there was considerable uneasiness at the prospect of absorbing still more Slavs into the Monarchy. Tisza at first opposed war, but eventually gave his agreement on condition that no Serb territory should be annexed. Loyalty to the Emperor-King and to the unity of the Monarchy in international affairs weighed with him, but his scruples were the more readily overcome when German support was assured, though it was the intervention of hated Russia which finally decided Magyar opinion.

For the Slav peoples the war was a more serious issue. Such leading men as Masaryk, Supilo, and Trumbić soon slipped out of the country into refuge abroad, where their activities were eventually to have spectacular results. But they were no more yet than a tiny minority. Meanwhile, thousands of political suspects were rounded-up by the Austrian and Hungarian governments (Pribičević, for instance, being interned, with other Hungarian Serbs, during most of the war), while at the front a certain number of soldiers, especially among the Czechs, deserted to the enemy. For the most part it was long before loyalty to the Monarchy was seriously shaken. Even had opposition not been checked by conscription and the activities of the secret police (an entertaining account of whose methods may be read in the early pages of Jaroslav Hasek's lively Czech satire, *The Good Soldier Schweik*), there were no channels through which opinion could be expressed. The Austrian *Reichsrat*, as already recorded, was closed, and the Hungarian Parliament represented little but Magyar opinion.

Whatever the divisions within the Monarchy it seemed to Francis Joseph, as to Conrad and Berchtold, therefore, that there was no way out but war. "If the Monarchy is doomed to perish," was Francis Joseph's fatalistic comment to Conrad, "let it at least perish decorously." Only in the crushing of Serbia could security be found, and if that raised other dangers, honour and prestige demanded that they should be faced unflinchingly. Had the lives of millions not been involved, it might have been regarded as an heroic, or at least a quixotic, attitude, worthy of "the last representative of the old school". A more liberal policy in Bosnia and Croatia might have remedied the situation, but would have entailed a fundamental reshaping of Magyar policy, which to the all-powerful Magyars was out of the question. In any case, the situation had probably gone too far by 1914: Berchtold hardly possessed the qualities of a statesman, but he had little enough room for manœuvre. He and Conrad bear a heavy burden of responsibility for the decision that was taken, but they accepted the risks involved, counting on the overwhelming support which Germany assured them, and reckoning that the overthrow of Serbia would be no more than a "military promenade".

## Conclusion

The situation as it finally emerged was summed-up in telling fashion by Count Ottokar Czernin, a member of Francis Ferdinand's circle who was to be Foreign Minister of the Monarchy in its last tragic phase from 1916 to 1918:

> We were bound to die. We were at liberty to choose the manner of our death, and we chose the most terrible.[58]

On that note this survey of the last half century of Central Europe under the Habsburg Monarchy may well close. It appears now a miracle that, with all its strains and divisions, the Monarchy so long survived the storms of war. Military discipline apart, it was held together in the last resort by the impossibility of devising, under the complex conditions and rivalries that have been described, another bond of union for the varied peoples who had been gathered together under the Habsburg crowns. Not until Francis Joseph was dead, Russia had collapsed in revolution, and the strain of war without victory had become unbearable, did the unity begin seriously to crumble, though even then the Magyar leaders, under Tisza, maintained their grip in Hungary almost to the last.

## REFERENCES

1. K. Tschuppik: *The Reign of the Emperor Francis Joseph*, p. 354.
2. A. G. Kogan: "The Social Democrats in the Habsburg Monarchy": *Journal of Modern History*, XXI, pp. 204 *et seq.*
3. *Fragments of a Political Diary*, p. 176.
4. Quoted from H. Münch, *Böhmische Tragödie*, in review in *Times Literary Supplement*, 20th July, 1951.
5. Quoted in A. J. May: *The Hapsburg Monarchy, 1867–1914*, p. 488.
6. *The Austrian Revolution*; English translation (1925), p. 72.
7. Quoted in May, p. 482.
8. Translated by E. Wilkins and E. Kaiser.
9. C. A. Macartney: *National States and National Minorities*, p. 145.
10. R. W. Seton-Watson: *A History of the Czechs and Slovaks*, p. 212.
11. J. Redlich: Introduction to Baernreither's *Fragments of a Political Diary*, p. xx.
12. Count J. Andrássy: *Bismarck, Andrássy and their Successors*, p. 18.
13. ibid., p. 26.
14. M. D. Stojanović: *The Great Powers and the Balkans, 1875–78*, p. 32.
15. Tschuppik, p. 248.
16. R. W. Seton-Watson: *Disraeli, Gladstone and the Eastern Question*, p. 473.
17. E. Wiskemann: *Czechs and Germans*, p. 108.
18. May, p. 204.
19. *The Hapsburg Monarchy* (1914), p. 77.
20. H. Wanklyn: *Czechoslovakia*, p. 273.
21. May, p. 202.
22. ibid., p. 211.
23. Wickham Steed: *Hitler, Whence and Whither?* p. 77.
24. ibid., p. 78.
25. Tschuppik, p. 317.
26. Viscount Samuel: *Memoirs*, p. 141.
27. See, for instance, the brief but revealing account of Mahler's origins in H. F. Redlich: *Bruckner and Mahler*, pp. 109–10.

28. Chaim Weizmann: *Trial and Error*, p. 62.
29. *The Man Without Qualities;* see note 8.
30. J. Redlich: *Emperor Francis Joseph of Austria*, pp. 453 and 448.
31. cf. p. 115.
32. *A History of the Czechs and Slovaks*, p. 241.
33. R. W. Seton-Watson: *History of the Roumanians*, p. 428.
34. R. W. Seton-Watson: *Racial Problems in Hungary* (1908), p. 163.
35. ibid., p. 162.
36. C. A. Macartney: *Hungary and Her Successors*, p. 20.
37. *Racial Problems in Hungary*, p. 210.
38. *Fragments of a Political Diary*, p. 131.
39. *History of the Roumanians*, p. 394.
40. ibid., p. 425.
41. *Fragments of a Political Diary*, p. 302.
42. *Racial Problems in Hungary*, p. 193.
43. Wickham Steed: *Through Thirty Years, 1892–1922*, I, p. 223.
44. A. J. P. Taylor: *The Habsburg Monarchy, 1815–1918*, p. 251.
45. R. W. Seton-Watson: *The Southern Slav Question* (1911), p. 284.
46. *Fragments of a Political Diary*, pp. 104 and 258.
47. R. W. Seton-Watson: "The Role of Bosnia in International Politics, 1875–1914": *Proceedings of the British Academy*, 1931, p. 367.
48. A. J. P. Taylor: *The Struggle for Mastery in Europe, 1848–1918*, p. 520, n.2.
49. *The Role of Bosnia*, p. 364.
50. B. E. Schmitt: *The Annexation of Bosnia, 1908–09*, p. 248.
51. ibid., p. 253.
52. G. P. Gooch: *History of Modern Europe, 1878–1919*, p. 426.
53. Tschuppik, pp. 436–37.
54. ibid., p. 430.
55. ibid., p. 434.
56. G. P. Gooch: *Before the War: Studies in Diplomacy*, II, p. 446.
57. *The Role of Bosnia*, p. 367.
58. Count O. Czernin: *In the World War*, p. 32.

# IV

# UNITED ITALY, 1870–1914

### Italian Unification—"Poetry" and "Prose"

IT was in 1870 that a united Kingdom of Italy with its capital in the historic city of Rome first appeared. From 1848 to 1870 had been years of struggle and unification. 1870 saw the beginnings of consolidation, the process that is still far from complete: after the poetry the prose, as Victor Emmanuel II aptly declared in his opening address to the first Parliament of United Italy. Until 1870 all energies were concentrated on the struggle to achieve unity and freedom from foreign rule. Afterwards the unity had to be made a reality, and the new kingdom set firmly on its feet. Events in our own day have shown how much of these tasks has remained unfulfilled after three-quarters of a century. Yet against the background of the more distant past the failures are less striking and can be seen in truer proportion. "The evils of modern Italy," wrote an English historian in 1911, "are the result of two thousand years' misgovernment and three hundred years of foreign domination."[1] The Italy that took Rome as its capital city in 1870 was an amalgam of seven States, with differing dialects, cultures and traditions, long subjected to foreign control, at first Spanish, then Austrian; economically weak and backward, and unable even to achieve unification by its own unaided efforts. It was dangerously easy, both for Italians and for their sympathizers in other countries, to assume that the chief purpose of the *Risorgimento*, the "resurrection" of the national spirit, was achieved when a united country had been established. It was far more difficult— and far less heroic—to weld into one prosperous, well-organized and modern State the widely differing regions of the disunited, "geographical expression" that had so long been Italy. And while there had been many elements of heroism in the twenty years' struggle of the *Risorgimento*, there was little glory in the stages by which national freedom was eventually attained.

## PROCESS OF UNIFICATION—FOREIGN PARTICIPATION

Like united Germany, united Italy grew around one of its constituent parts; the task that was performed in Germany by Prussia being undertaken in Italy by the north Italian kingdom of Piedmont-Sardinia, under the House of Savoy. But whereas Prussia attracted the other German States by her own victories in the field, and especially by the triumphant defeat of France, Piedmont-Sardinia had to rely on foreign support and could hardly have achieved her aim without the active assistance of France in 1859 and of Prussia seven years later. It was the victories of Napoleon III's armies over the Austrians in 1859 that gained Lombardy for Victor Emmanuel II (reigned 1849-1878) and inspired the wave of national feeling which in the following year brought in the States of Central Italy and, after Garibaldi's gallant exploits, the Bourbon Kingdom of Naples and Sicily. It was Prussia's victory over Austria in 1866 that added Venice, as the price of Italy's intervention against the Habsburg Empire. But, on the other hand, it was the France of Napoleon III that for four more years preserved Rome for the Pope and compelled Victor Emmanuel to establish his new capital at Florence. When in 1867 Garibaldi led a band of volunteers to Rome, in the hope of repeating the exploits achieved by "The Thousand" in Sicily and Naples seven years earlier, it was French guns that brought this last great adventure of his to an end at Mentana. Only in 1870, when the French, in the hour of defeat, withdrew their garrison from Papal territory, was the Pope left to face the new Italy alone. Rome was then occupied by Victor Emmanuel's troops, and in the following year the capital was transferred there, but here again Italy's gains were the result of foreign assistance: Prussian victories played no less significant a part in 1870 than in 1866. When, finally, the last vestiges of foreign rule in Italy were removed in 1918 by the absorption of *Italia irredenta*, the "unredeemed" territories of Trieste and the Trentino, it was once more with the help of powerful allies, while the later transitory successes of Mussolini's foreign policy were the direct result of the rise of Nazi Germany.

## THE ITALIAN PEOPLE AND THE *Risorgimento*

The Italian people themselves remained, as ever, largely aloof from the political changes that were thrust upon them. Brought up under alien systems of government, subjected to misrule and to the horrors of war in causes that touched them not at all, and sunk in poverty that little was done to alleviate, the great mass of the people in their various States had learnt through generations of suffering to regard all government as oppression, and had come to accept it with an indifference and resignation that were to prove a serious stumbling block after 1860. Centuries of alien oppression left a *damnosa hereditas* of psychological malaise which the *Risorgimento* failed to remove and which has since revealed itself only too clearly in the conditions attending both the rise and the fall of Mussolini. "No people, perhaps, have suffered through the centuries, with so much resignation, evils so grave as have the Italian people," said Giolitti in 1901, and the prevailing view among the less ardent spirits in 1860 was that "we are too old a people", that the Italians had already endured too much history even when their history as a united nation was but just beginning. In the words of a young Italian-American historian of our own day:

> A thousand years of calamities and of bad and indifferent governments had left too profound a heritage of physical and moral misery for even the combined genius of a people to undo it in a short space.[2]

## UNIFICATION WITHOUT UNITY

"The combined genius of a people": the phrase strikes at the root of one of Italy's historic difficulties, for it was precisely the sense of unity and the ability to combine that the Italians so long lacked. The foreign oppressor was hated, and at times was resisted, but there was little to draw the people together. Tradition, culture, trade, political allegiance, were all dividing, not uniting, factors. Even after the establishment of political unity, there were no common economic interests, such as there were in Germany, to underpin the political structure. No *Zollverein* could have prepared the way for unification, as it did in Germany, for there was little trade between the various States. Given the geographical conditions of Italy, and her resources, both markedly different from those of Germany, the Italian States were economically in rivalry, rather than complementary to each other.

Moreover, the movement for unification was essentially one of the educated middle class: even in the case of the romantic descent on Sicily in 1860 very few of the peasants who formed the vast majority of Italy's people were involved, as Garibaldi himself complained. The new Italy was created by a small, though active, minority, aided by foreign arms, against the dead weight of the apathy of the majority of its people, and it was long, in consequence, before the new régime was even accepted: it is doubtful whether it ever became really popular. The great mass of the people, unprepared for change and probably hostile to it, but long resigned to alien rule, acquiesced without enthusiasm in the new situation, and before long were complaining that "we were better off when we were worse off". Unification and national freedom had come on a wave of enthusiasm, in a manner totally unexpected, before the significance of what had happened had been grasped. A group of men who had been accustomed to the politics of a small kingdom suddenly found themselves responsible for a great country of twenty-five millions, with their one really able leader, Cavour, dead, and lacking any successor who could match him in the imaginative vision that was necessary to convert the politics of Piedmont into those of a united Italy. "It was an élite of moderate Liberal intellectuals," the leader of Italian Christian Democracy, Luigi Sturzo, has said, "who, having improvised the Italian nation, took on themselves the burden of creating the Italian State,"[3] and the burden, which others were unwilling to share, proved too much for them. "We have made Italy," ran the famous dictum of the novelist-politician Massino d'Azeglio (1798-1866) after the proclamation of national unity, "now we have to make the Italians." It was a task that demanded more than nationalist slogans, more than an intellectual élite, and one for which foreign help could not be expected. In fact, the real test of the *Risorgimento* was to come in the long years after 1860, and d'Azeglio was not alone in appreciating the difficulties that lay ahead, though there were few in Italy who saw as clearly as he did. Two foreign observers had their doubts. Thus Elizabeth Barrett Browning wrote of her beloved Italy:

> Can it last, this gleam?
> Can she live and be strong?
> Or is it another dream
> Like the rest we have dreamed so long?

while the death of Mazzini in 1872 drew from his friend Carlyle the comment:

> Poor Mazzini! After all, he succeeded. He died receiving the homage of the people, and seeing Italy united, with Rome for its capital. Well, one may be glad he has succeeded. We wait to see whether Italy will make anything great out of what she has got. We wait![4]

Some forty years later, G. M. Trevelyan, surveying the history of the intervening years in the last volume of his famous study of Garibaldi, commented on the "remarkable stability" of the Italian kingdom, but noted the "stagnation" of Italian political life.[5] A sympathetic observer, he had yet touched on an aspect of the life of the new State that could supply an answer to Carlyle's rhetorical question. Italy had done much—and yet had done little. Always on the fringe of the Great Powers, and unequal to the burden she felt compelled to carry in competition with them, she had neither built up her strength adequately nor founded herself firmly upon the varied peoples of the kingdom. Another close observer of the same period, Thomas Okey, was more critical: drawing attention in the twelfth volume of the *Cambridge Modern History* in 1910 to the many weaknesses of Italy, he touched on the one which above all others, perhaps, revealed the lack of confidence between people and Government:

> Italy still awaits the courageous and resolute reformer, who shall grapple with the shameless corruption which is so exhausting a drain on the national resources.

Fascism, later, was an attempt to repair the mischief, but failed, vitiated by its own inner corruption, and the true task of 1861, as d'Azeglio and Carlyle had seen it, has been handed on to the post-Fascist Republic of 1946.

## PROBLEMS OF THE NEW ITALY—NORTH AND SOUTH

The chief problems facing the Republic of today, which are magnified versions of the tasks that confronted the Kingdom in

1861, are now becoming apparent. In the first place, despite popular impressions based on misleading maps, Italy by geography, race, tradition and culture is not altogether a unity. Between North and South, in particular, are divergencies of interest and outlook that have exerted a significant influence upon events since 1860. As in Germany, unification came from the North and was therefore accepted with only qualified enthusiasm in the South. As in Germany too, the lead in the shaping of policy and the development of the national life was largely taken by the North. In the Italy of 1860, though the economic development of Piedmont was of recent growth, and owed much to the policy of Cavour and to his admiration for England, the North was on the whole more advanced than the South. Illiteracy, it is true, was rife, but while throughout the country about three-quarters of the population was illiterate, in the South the figure reached nine-tenths, while the introduction of compulsory elementary education in the 'seventies, though it was comparatively effective in the North, largely failed of its purpose in many parts of the South. At the end of the century, for instance, the percentage of illiteracy in Piedmont had dropped to seventeen, but it was still about seventy-five in the more backward regions of the South. The reason for the disparity is to be found in the economic back-wardness of the old Bourbon kingdom. In general the South has the more extreme climate, the poorer soil, the greater physical obstacles, the smaller rainfall and the greater proneness both to natural disasters (earthquakes, volcanic eruptions, and floods) and to human epidemics (especially malaria and *pellagra*). Moreover, it possesses only three-tenths of the total natural resources of a country which is notoriously poor in most raw materials. In 1860 there were very few industries, and these could not hope to survive the competition of the North except behind the protection of tariff barriers. Most of the population were poor peasants, with little or no land, often living in conditions of the greatest misery and squalor, at the mercy of great landowners and their agents. In Sicily, in particular, the system of *latifondi*, vast estates belonging to absentee landlords, both lay and ecclesiastic, was general: to the miserable poverty and backwardness of the people here must be ascribed in great part the succession of peasant risings that has lasted into our own times, together with the long tradition of brigandage and secret societies, which were here, as elsewhere, manifestations of the blind resentment against the established order of an adventurous but frustrated, people.

Again, unlike the North, the South had not felt the influence of the French Revolution, and possessed no considerable educated middle class to attempt to apply to Italian conditions the ideas which the Revolution had inspired. Yet to the men of the North, over-conscious as they were of the strain imposed upon Piedmont by the struggle with Austria, the South was a land of great potential wealth, and it was not until 1902, when the elderly Prime Minister, Zanardelli, gallantly undertook a tour of investigation, that it was realized that there was a "Southern Question" at all. By that time much damage had been done, "a bigger Ireland", as it has not unjustly been called, created. Had he lived, Cavour might have set the right course, for he had few illusions and realized the difficulty of fusing the widely different parts of Italy into a united nation: the task, in his own well-known words, was equal to "a war against Austria or a struggle against Rome". But there was none among his successors who shared his insight, and the delicate task of fusion was undertaken abruptly, without preparation, and with results that were little short of disastrous.

## Economic and Administrative Policies
### (1) The Economic Burdens

The two main blunders that arose from the fusion of North and South were made in the twin fields of economic and administrative policy. By 1860 Piedmont, under the guidance of Cavour, had become a stronghold of free trade, and had benefited, on the whole, from a policy that was inspired by Cavour's enthusiasm for England. In a few years foreign trade had been doubled, and coal imports, the basis of industrial expansion, quadrupled, while a great programme of railway construction had been undertaken. The way had been prepared, in fact, for the developments that later made the northern cities, despite Italy's lack of raw materials, important industrial centres. It was not until the twentieth century had opened that the famous F.I.A.T. works were established at Turin, but the foundations for great enterprises of this kind were laid in Cavour's time. Standards of life were low, but not so low as in the South. The great majority of the population were still peasants, but they were peasants who owned their own land, and in general the holdings were sufficiently large to support their families. The predominance of great estates, with a poor and backward class of peasant labourers, was a feature rather of the South than of the North.

In the South conditions were markedly different. There the widespread poverty of the soil, and the existence of great landed estates, especially of the *latifondi*, combined with centuries of unenlightened rule, had created a problem of peasant poverty of a type which was becoming familiar in many parts of Europe, and which, as in Ireland, there was little industrial development to relieve. Such few industries as had grown up were mainly in competition with the more efficient industries of the North. When, after the establishment of unity in 1860, economic barriers disappeared with the political frontiers, and the South was forced into the doctrinaire free-trade system of the North, these industries were crippled. Even more serious was the financial burden which the South was called on to bear. Taxes were abruptly increased in order to bring them into line with those paid in Piedmont, increases of as much as forty per cent being not uncommon. Protests were vain, as Piedmont had already assumed a heavy burden of debt during the struggle with Austria, and northern opinion grossly over-rated southern resources. In consequence the South paid considerably more than a proportionate share of the national taxation, and it was later estimated that the excess amounted to some £1,200,000 annually. Moreover, while the burden was unevenly distributed as between regions, it was also unfairly distributed between the classes: the extensive use of indirect taxation caused far too heavy a share of the load throughout the country to fall on the poor peasant. Hence the common phrase, "They have made Italy only to devour her", and the even more telling "We were better off when we were worse off", which has already been quoted. In the words of a modern Italian novelist, Ricardo Bacchelli, whose family chronicle, *The Mill on the Po*, recaptures the spirit of these harsh, formative years:

> Little people felt oppressed by the civil and military obligations incumbent upon a modern nation, which fell upon their shoulders

G

before they received any advantage from their new condition, or were even aware of its meaning. . . . The common people played no part in the events of the *Risorgimento* but they were called upon to pay its debts and did so courageously.[6]

## (2) POPULATION AND EMIGRATION

The truth was, of course, that the process of liberation and unification had seriously overstrained the limited resources of Italy. In the years after 1860 the public debt, already large, was quadrupled, and by 1876 the interest on it was absorbing no less than a third of the revenue: the new state "cost more than it produced".[7] Industrial and commercial developments brought some relief later, but many of Italy's difficulties in the past eighty years can be ascribed to the simple fact that she has lacked the resources to match her position in the world and the rapid increase in her population, which, beginning at some twenty-five millions in 1860, was approaching forty millions at the time of the First World War. The increase would have been even greater but for emigration, to which many, especially in the South, were driven by poverty. It has been estimated that between 1880 and 1913 Italy lost some fifteen millions in this way. At one time more than three-quarters of a million were leaving the country in a year: Sicily alone lost 127,000 in a single year in 1906. The scale of emigration was, as elsewhere, a measure of the national poverty, which the remittances of the emigrants did something to relieve. But even if the internal economy had been conducted with more wisdom and dis-interestedness the strain would still have been considerable. "If our Liberals had known the country better," said a future Prime Minister, Sidney Sonnino, in 1880, "perhaps they would not have found the courage to create Italy."[8] It was certainly a profound ignorance of the true situation, together with the fact that the lead in unification had come from the North, that for very many years placed an impossible burden on the South and kept it the most backward part of the country.

## (3) THE CENTRALIZATION OF GOVERNMENT

In addition to the economic there were administrative blunders. With the Piedmontese system of taxation the Piedmontese administrative machine, reasonably efficient, but narrow and pedantic, was extended to the whole country after 1860, and a rigid centralization forced on the varied regions of Italy, with their strongly marked local and individualist traditions. The results were not always necessarily disadvantageous, but the sudden imposition of the inflexible Piedmontese system caused discontent among all classes. Taxes and the administration of the Civil Service and Army were rapidly assimilated to the Piedmontese model, and the *Statuto*, the constitution granted by Charles Albert in 1848, became the basis of the whole country's government: "Italy found herself endowed with a constitution imitated from Britain and imported in a bad French translation." The constitution presupposed such a unity as Britain and France possessed, a centralized administration as effective as that of France, and a two-party system on English lines. Under Italian conditions it could work only by methods which in the end brought the whole system into disrepute and prepared the way for Fascism. When Mussolini denounced liberal and parliamentary forms of government he was denouncing some sixty years of a parliamentary régime that had been ill-suited to the needs and conditions of Italy.

In particular, the system based on the *Statuto* ignored the local roots of Italian life and the strong regional traditions of the country. For many years patriots had expected a federal system to emerge from the struggles of the *Risorgimento*, and some realized clearly wherein lay the error of Piedmontese policy. Thus, the writer and historian Ferdinando Ranalli (1813–94) demanded "a constitution of Italian character . . . a constitution which conforms to the municipal institutions of our country",[9] with a fusion of national representation and local responsibility. Ranalli realized that in so far as the control of government by Parliament in England was centralized it worked effectively owing to the two-party system, with a clearly defined Government and Opposition. Italy, however, had many parties, or, rather, she had none, for every political grouping was an association of politicians with local rather than national interests. Great national parties on English lines have never been, until recent times, a feature of Italian political life, and even today, as events since 1945 have shown, the division of interest between North and South remains strong. Hence the concessions to regionalism in the Constitution of 1946.

## (4) THE PAPACY

A further factor making for serious disunity was the stern opposition of the Roman Church, after 1870, to the new State. Rome had not been gained without a struggle, for, even after the withdrawal of the French garrison which had hitherto sustained his temporal sovereignty, Pope Pius IX had refused to yield to anything but force. On the occupation of Rome in September, 1870, he withdrew into the Vatican, refusing to acquiesce in the loss of his temporal authority or to acknowledge the new Government. Moreover, when in the following year the Law of Guarantees was passed, which assured to the Pope full liberty and authority in spiritual matters and awarded him an income equal to that provided in the last budget of Papal Rome, he ignored it, leaving the Government to honour a one-sided engagement which had been intended to reconcile Church and State. It was in any case doubtful whether a reconciliation could have been effected between Pius IX, intransigent in his opposition to liberal notions, and a State which, though loyal in the main to the Church, was imposing secular laws in matters of education and marriage, in the true spirit of nineteenth century liberal thought. Not until 1929 was a reconciliation with the Papacy finally effected. In addition to cutting himself off from Italy in this way, the Pope by the decree *non expedit* forbade Roman Catholics to take any part in national political life, though they were free to engage in local affairs. In practice the ban was not widely observed, but it remained in force until nearly forty years later, in 1905, the growth of Socialism made a relaxation seem expedient, and it added to the difficulties of the new kingdom by causing for many Italians a conflict of allegiance.

## (5) *Campanilismo*

The first problem, therefore, which confronted Italy after 1860, and still confronts the Republic today, was the lack of well-founded national unity. Another is to be found in the lack of purpose which has marked Italian political life through the intervening years. Crispi, d'Annunzio, and Mussolini all tried to create a sense of purpose, to discover the "mission" without which, it has seemed to many, a country that would be great cannot long exist, but their aims were largely irrelevant to Italy's real problems. Yet they were, however incompetently, working on the right lines, for there has been since the *Risorgimento* no party or principle to give reality to a national unity that was essentially imposed from above and had little to offer the average Italian. Such party differences as existed before 1860 were suppressed in order to maintain a united front against the common enemy, Austria, and when unity had been achieved it was discovered that the parties had nothing to disagree about. Again, the franchise was extremely limited, and voting was mainly on local issues. Because of the lack of real unity and real representative institutions, *campanilismo*— or, as it would be called in England, "parish-pump" politics— has been the predominant feature of Italian politics, which have been more often concerned with the purchase of Deputies' votes by concessions to their constituencies than with the achievement of truly national objects. Italy, it has well been said, "had a Parliament, but no parliamentarism". A super-structure of parliamentary forms on the English model had been built up, but it had no foundations in Italian soil. Successful politicians, as was shown by the careers of such men as Depretis and Giolitti, were not primarily national leaders but rather skilful manipulators of parliamentary majorities. With-out national parties and the inspirations of truly national principles the famous English dictum, "the King's Govern-ment must be carried on", becomes, as it did in Italy, a mere means of political jobbery in which the real objects of govern-ment are lost sight of in the intrigues and bribes necessary to keep a government of sorts in being: Italy, it was said, "is governed by decorations".[10] Cavour had already complained of the multitude of political interests which surrounded him that "you cannot govern on the point of a needle". This, however, was largely what was done between his death in 1861 and the advent of Mussolini in 1922. It is a sufficient comment on the system to record as one of its results that there were no less than thirty-one different Ministers of Finance in forty-three years of this period. Under these circumstances—and this is but a typical instance—G. M. Trevelyan's comment in

1911, that "nothing is more remarkable . . . than the stability of the Italian Kingdom" can be seen in its full significance.

## THE METHODS OF GOVERNMENT
### (I) THE RULE OF THE RIGHT

The lack of party principles became particularly noticeable after 1876, in what came to be called the era of *Trasformismo* (Transformism). Until 1876 power rested with the party of the Right, the heirs of Cavour, representing in the main the landed, professional and commercial classes of the North, cautious and unimaginative in policy, and lacking in able leadership since the passing of Cavour himself. To this party belongs the credit of having steered the new Italy through the difficult early years of consolidation, but the measures by which this was done brought serious consequences. The main aims of the Right in internal affairs were the establishment of uniform administration and the achievement of financial stability through a balanced budget. But the forcing of all Italy into the mould of a centralized administration intensified regional feeling, and the strain of taxation, which hit the South more than the North, embittered many who had voted for unification in the hope of better times. Finance was a fundamental problem, however, for the achievement of unity had cost more in money than in blood, and revenue in 1861 was little more than half of expenditure, while a heavy programme of spending on public services, administration and defence was unavoidable. Taxation, therefore, had to be kept high, and the burden of the "grist tax", an old duty on all milled grain, which was re-introduced in 1868, was particularly serious.[11] It was widely denounced as a "tax on hunger" and became a strong plank in the platform of the Left parties, but as an indirect tax with universal application it brought in a steady revenue, and despite much agitation was not dropped until 1880. As a result the Italians became, for some years, the most highly taxed people in Europe, but by 1876, after the most strenuous efforts, the budget was finally balanced and a surplus achieved. During this same period roads and railways were built, while a few years later the opening of the great St. Gothard tunnel through the Alps established speedy communication with Western and Central Europe, and made it possible for the trade of the

East to reach Europe via Suez and Brindisi, with a much reduced sea journey. At the same time government subsidies helped to build up a large mercantile marine, and considerable harbour works were undertaken at the ports.

## (2) DEPRETIS AND *Trasformismo*

But the strain on the country was severe, the more so because of the unfair and unequal incidence of taxation, with which no one had the courage to grapple, and the achievement of financial stability in 1876 was the signal for an attempt to change the direction of policy. In March of that year the right-wing Government of Marco Minghetti was overthrown by a revolt of his Tuscan supporters, disgruntled by the lack of consideration shown for the claims of Florence to compensation for the losses sustained when the capital had been transferred from there to Rome in 1870. The King then exercised his powers under the *Statuto* by selecting a leader from among the parties of the Left, and characteristically chose a Piedmontese, Agostino Depretis (1813–87), who as the dominant parliamentary figure of the next eleven years, and Prime Minister for most of the period, gave a sinister twist to Italian politics. As soon as he was installed in office, Depretis appealed to the country, the elections were "made" in the usual way, and a handsome Left majority was duly returned. The whole country now looked forward to a régime of prosperity and enlightened rule.

The Left, however, was very far from being a united party with a single programme. Depretis drew support from all the groups which had become hostile to the fifteen-year rule of the Right, and especially from disaffected elements in the South, but there was little to hold the groups together, and the Premier himself certainly lacked the ability to do that. On the whole the Left represented the middle, and, in so far as they were enfranchised, the urban lower, classes, but there was no profound difference of doctrine between Left and Right, while the Left "programme", which had promised such incompatibles as greater government expenditure together with lower taxation, was a collection of rousing election cries rather than a statement of practical politics. In the event, Depretis found that there was little he could do to improve on the achievements of the Right. The financial needs of the Government made it impossible to carry through any reduction of taxation, while any serious investigation of conditions in the South would have estranged northern supporters by revealing the necessity for relief there. Instead of tackling the grave problems that called for solution, Depretis contented himself with the political juggling at which, with his subtle and sceptical mind, he was a master. A great part of his following consisted of men new to politics who were mainly interested in getting concessions and assistance for their constituencies—or themselves—and without committing himself to real reforms Depretis maintained his party in office by political bribery, ensuring majorities by purchasing support. Indifferent to party labels, he rarely failed to win adequate support, and when necessary he was able to induce opponents to "transform" themselves into supporters of the Government—for a consideration. Hence the descriptive title of *trasformismo*, by which his period of rule is remembered.

A typical example of his methods was his handling of the taxes on sugar and salt. Salt, "the poor man's sugar", bore a heavy tax, and sugar a light one, and Depretis promised in an election speech to reduce the disparity between them. This he did when in power by the ingenious, but unexpected, method of increasing the sugar-tax, a measure which was threatened with strong opposition in Parliament but was carried, in the tradition of "government by decorations", by the simple device of awarding the title of *Commendatore* to sixty Deputies who voted for it. The later technique of *trasformismo*, as Depretis came to develop it, was rather more subtle. When faced with opposition, or defeated on a measure, he would "transform" a sufficient number of his opponents into supporters by whatever means were appropriate—whether by awarding office or title, by bribery, or by granting some concession to the constituencies of the Deputies concerned—and would then claim credit for having preserved the stability of his administration. He justified his policy by pointing to the difficulty of welding into an effective unity the varied groupings of the Left, and by claiming that he was in effect drawing together into a "national" party the most able men on both sides, and adapting himself to the necessity for political change. His enemies argued, however, that "transformism" represented "the renunciation of ideas, convictions and principles for petty or interested reasons", and taken together with the inertia of Depretis's later years it certainly exercised upon Italian political life a dangerously corrupting influence. In particular, it established as a normal condition of Italian politics what has been called "government by personal ascendancy", which from Depretis onwards to Mussolini came to be accepted as the only means of ensuring any stability where political principles and well-knit national parties were lacking. Steady government was impossible under these conditions, and it is no accident that from 1876 to 1922 Italy had no less than thirty-two administrations. After the strain of the First World War Fascism arose partly as a movement of protest against this system, but it is significant that Mussolini, for all his ideological posturings, remained to the last an exponent of "transformism" himself. In his opportunism and his determination to retain his personal ascendancy he proved himself a typical Italian politician of the type which Depretis, and, later, Giolitti, had made so well known.

The rule of Depretis did not pass unchallenged, for the Left was not without men of ability, containing as it did in Crispi and Zanardelli two who afterwards became Premiers of distinction, but his hold was not to be shaken for long and after each defeat he emerged stronger than ever. Those who had been at first among his leading supporters went into opposition, and attracted to themselves the more able of the younger politicians, notably Giolitti, who first entered politics in the 'eighties and was destined to become twenty years later as astute a master of political techniques as Depretis himself. But the defection of his leading followers merely set Depretis more firmly on his path, and "transformism" achieved one of its greatest successes in 1887, a few months before the death of its creator, when the powerful and able Crispi was won over. This brought a new and dominant figure on to the political scene, for Crispi succeeded Depretis and the next ten years were essentially the period of his ascendancy. But before considering Crispi's achievements, his concern with Italy's position in the world and the disaster that ruined him, it is necessary to glance at some other aspects of the period between 1870 and 1887.

G*

## FOREIGN RELATIONS: ITALY'S LIMITATIONS

Cavour's title to fame as one of the founders of Italian unity rests very largely on his success in interesting Europe in the Italian question. It was his grasp of the European situation and the skill with which he exploited the situation for his country's benefit that brought the foreign aid without which the difficulties in Italy's path could hardly have been overcome. In particular, his handling of the enigmatic figure of Napoleon III, though it brought less than had been hoped for, set in train the events that led to the establishment of the United Kingdom of Italy in 1861. But the problems of foreign politics that faced the united Italy of 1861 were no less serious than those which had had to be solved when Cavour took office ten years earlier, and were destined to become increasingly difficult. In the first place Cavour himself died before Italy's position could be consolidated, and though, before his death, he marked out the lines of future policy—for instance, in the friendly relations with Prussia that bore fruit in 1866—he left no successors who could match him in ability. And while so much had been achieved, Italian arms had not been covered with glory: 1866 brought Venice, but Europe did not soon forget the defeats of Custozza and Lissa. "Italy," Bismarck once said, "has such poor teeth, and such a large appetite." Moreover, unity had been achieved at a critical moment in European history. The "age of steel" had already begun, and the establishment of the German Empire in 1871 inaugurated a new era of power politics in which powerful armies were needed, backed by large and well-organized industrial societies. But Italy lacked the natural resources and industrial organization that were called for, and Piedmont could not breathe a new spirit into her as Prussia did into Germany. Italy became, and remained, the least of the Great Powers, unable to sustain the rôle which the recollection of imperial Rome seemed to mark out for her, but at the same time unwilling to accept the secondary place which almost every factor except the size of her population dictated. She became, in consequence, a "hanger-on" in international politics, uneasily conscious of powerful rivals and tending to be drawn into the orbit of the strongest among them, until the day when Mussolini, striving to assert her independence, paradoxically flung her into the arms of Hitler, and sank to the rôle of a *Gauleiter*.

## Relations with Austria and France

Italy's difficulties in the realm of foreign affairs after the achievement of unification can be ascribed in the first place to enmities stirred up during the national struggle for unity. Austria, it is true, rapidly became reconciled to the loss of the Italian territories of the Habsburgs, and as early as 1875, only nine years after the cession of Venice to Italy, Francis Joseph paid a state visit to Victor Emmanuel in that city. But Austria still retained in the Trentino a wedge of Italian territory of great strategic significance, while the possession of Trieste enabled her to command the northern Adriatic. While these *Terre Irredente* (unredeemed territories) lay in foreign hands, Italo-Austrian relations were bound to remain fundamentally unsound, and public opinion in Italy, still mindful of a century-and-a-half of Austrian rule, had a constant source of agitation available. At times feeling became tense, as when, in 1881, during a visit to Vienna, King Humbert donned the hated Austrian uniform on being made an honorary Colonel of the imperial army; or, when, in the following year, the fanatical Italian patriot from Trieste, Oberdan, was hanged for an attempt on the life of Francis Joseph. "Irredentism" remained a constant motif in public opinion, even when, after 1882, Italy was allied with Austria. In the end it was under the pressure of public feeling, and in order to recover the "unredeemed territories", that Italy went to war in 1915.

There were other reasons for strained relations with Austria. The Habsburg Empire, as has been explained elsewhere, was forced by the loss of its historic role in Germany and Italy to seek a fresh field of influence in the Balkans, and any extension of Austrian power down the east coast of the Adriatic was obviously a matter of concern to the new Italy. For the present she lacked the strength to play any active part in the affairs of the Balkans, but it was not in her interests to see any Great Power extending its influence there. She was, therefore, as much opposed to Russian ambitions as to Austrian, though this did not become apparent until later. Her introduction to the Balkan problem came with the Berlin Conference of 1878, which, though it saw Russian ambitions checked, at the same time set Austria on the path of expansion. From that time onwards Italy became increasingly concerned with

Balkan developments, and the lines of policy were gradually laid down which eventually led, under Fascism, to Mussolini's intrigues against Yugoslavia and his insane attack on Greece. After 1878 the main problem was to restrain Austria without provoking an open struggle, and this Italy lacked the means to achieve alone. As the least of the Powers in resources, organization, and diplomatic skill and experience, she needed allies, now no less than during the struggle for liberation. "Isolation," Sonnino wrote in 1881, "means for us annihilation." The natural ally, it might have been thought, was France, and there were many ties of interest and sympathy between the two Latin peoples. But to France, as to Austria, the rise of a united Italy was not a matter for congratulation. If Austria, as we shall see, came to resent Italy's concern with her Balkan policies, France was no less disturbed by the rise of a new Mediterranean Power, and the two countries soon found themselves in conflict over developments in North Africa. Moreover, France had rendered invaluable help to Italy in 1859, and, although this help had been paid for by the cession to France of Savoy and Nice, there was resentment among Frenchmen that Italy did nothing to assist them in their hour of defeat in 1870. Furthermore, after 1871 clerical influence was strong in France, and Italy was therefore unpopular as the country which had taken advantage of French weakness to snatch Rome from the Pope: for several years, in fact, a French naval vessel lay off Civita Vecchia in case the Pope should wish to leave Italy and seek refuge elsewhere.

## LACK OF POLICY

Italy's position was, therefore, a difficult one, and while she was hampered by her own weakness she also suffered from a lack of knowledge and skill in the men who shaped her foreign policy. It had been the hope of the idealists of the *Risorgimento* that an Italy united under Rome would give a moral lead to Europe, but the Europe into which their country had eventually to fit herself was dominated by the stern realism of Bismarck, and there was now no Cavour to direct affairs. For some years the general attitude of Italians to problems of foreign affairs was summed-up in the revealing comment of Depretis, "When I see an international question on the horizon I open my umbrella and wait till it has passed," but it was not long before a series of crises compelled the adoption of a more realistic outlook. Nevertheless, the men brought up in the romantic school of the national revival found it hard to abandon their provincial views and to devise policies that would serve their country's interests over a long period. Thus, Depretis, when asked by an Ambassador for instructions during the crisis over the union of Eastern Rumelia with Bulgaria in 1885, pathetically replied, "But I know nothing about it either. When have I ever thought about Eastern Rumelia?"; while as late as 1901 Zanardelli could excuse the appointment of an inexperienced Minister by arguing that he had been given "only the Ministry for Foreign Affairs". With such men at the head of affairs it was not to be wondered at that the magniloquent phrase of the *Risorgimento*, *Italia grande e una*, was soon scornfully degraded into a mere *Italietta*, "Little Italy", as it came to be realized how inattentive Europe was to the claims of the new State.

"THE CRIME OF BERLIN", 1878

The first blow to Italy's pride came with the Berlin Conference. Depretis had recently been replaced as Prime Minister by the honest idealist, Benedetto Cairoli, who announced his foreign policy in the words, "We shall not be clever, but we wish above all to be honest," and in loyal adherence to this admirable but artless sentiment, no attempt was made to secure any gain for Italy out of the international scramble that marked the Conference. Austria increased her influence in the Balkans by occupying Bosnia and Herzegovina, but the demand for compensation in the Trentino that might well have been made by Italy was never pressed. Indeed, it was cynically said that Count Corti, the Italian representative at the Conference, had gone with clean hands and returned with empty ones, and there was widespread resentment in Italy at this "crime of Berlin". Worse was to come, however, for only three years later, in 1881, Italy suffered a humiliation as bitter as defeat when France unexpectedly seized Tunis.

TUNIS, 1881, AND THE TRIPLE ALLIANCE, 1882

Tunis was an outlying part of Turkish territory which had long been, in fact, independent, though the Bey still owed a nominal allegiance to the Sultan. Its government was weak, and the country itself under-developed, and in view of its important strategic position at the narrow centre of the Mediterranean, flanking the French colony of Algeria, it was clearly marked out for early occupation by one of the Great Powers. Britain and France, as Mediterranean Powers, were alike concerned with its fate, and both had taken part in the development of the country and the improvement of its communications. At the Berlin Conference, in return for French acquiescence in the occupation of Cyprus, Britain had undertaken to support French interests in Tunis, and Bismarck had on several occasions encouraged France to seek in North Africa compensation for the loss of Alsace-Lorraine. Bismarck saw the advantages of diverting French attention from Europe, and he also hoped to embitter relations between France and Italy. Italy, in spite of her weakness, was of some interest to him at this time, since he was drawing closer to Austria and had just framed the Dual Alliance of 1879, aimed against Russia. If Austria were to be involved in any conflict with Russia her rear must be secured against Italy, whose "irredentism" was running high after the "crime of Berlin", and this could most easily be achieved by playing up Franco-Italian differences and forcing Italy to turn to Germany for support.

Southern Italy, because of its proximity, had long had close relations with Tunis, and many peasants, forced from Sicily by poverty, had settled in the Bey's territories: their number by 1880 had reached some twenty thousand. Italy, therefore, was also interested in Tunisian developments, and a keen rivalry had grown up between the French and Italian representatives on the spot. Italy, however, lacked the means to annex Tunis, and was not disposed, in any case, to risk a serious disagreement with France. She hoped that the *status quo* might be preserved, with Italian labour and French capital developing the country, until such time as a settlement were possible. German suggestions that a more active policy might be followed were rejected, in the knowledge that they were intended to embroil Italy with France. A situation so artificial, however, could not long endure. France was disturbed at the growing interest shown by Italy in Tunis, and realized that, whatever their present views, the Italians hoped eventually to make Tunis an extension in Africa of their united kingdom. Clumsy handling of the situation by the Italian Government served only to add to French suspicions. In 1880 an English company in Tunis offered for sale a railway which had proved unprofitable. Its value was some £20,000, but strenuous competition between French and Italian interests raised the price to more than £160,000, at which figure an Italian company, actively backed by the Government, acquired it, to the discomfiture of the French. In the following year, while King Humbert was touring Sicily, he received there not only a deputation of Italians from Tunis but also the brother of the Bey, and the French, now thoroughly roused, felt that it was time to move. Taking advantage of a frontier raid by tribesmen, they dispatched troops to Tunis, and by the Treaty of Bardo (May, 1881) formally established a protectorate over it.

The news took Italy by surprise and overthrew the Government of Cairoli, who had been naïvely insisting that the French moves had no permanent significance. The sense of national humiliation was deep, and, as Bismarck had hoped, Italy was thrown into the arms of the Dual Alliance. There was a further reason for the move. Pius IX had died in 1878, but his remains were not transferred to the final resting-place he had desired until 1881. Their removal then led to an outbreak of anti-papal agitation which seriously alarmed the new Pope, Leo XIII, and his advisers, and revealed the strength of the feeling still running in Italy. The Italian Government for its part was no less concerned at the prospect of foreign, and especially French, intervention on the Pope's behalf. With the added complication of Tunis, itself a manifestation of rival ambitions in the Mediterranean, French threats to Italy seemed real. Security seemed to lie in an understanding with the Central Powers, and through its dynasty Austria was regarded, in any case, as the leading Roman Catholic State: allied to Austria, therefore, Italy need fear no foreign intervention in support of the Pope. Bismarck himself insisted that Italy must come to terms with Austria before an alliance could be made, and a secret treaty was eventually signed at Vienna in May, 1882. By its terms Italy and Germany were alike guaranteed support against any unprovoked attack by France, while, in effect, Austria received no more than a guarantee of benevolent neutrality from her allies if she were at war with Russia. This, however, was enough for Bismarck's purpose, and on her side Italy received the implicit assurance she required. An important secret "Additional Declaration" was added to the treaty, stating that under no circumstances could it be regarded as directed against Britain: it was manifestly impossible for Italy to risk any conflict with the strongest naval power in the Mediterranean.

## SIGNIFICANCE OF THE TREATY OF VIENNA

By the Treaty of Vienna Bismarck's Dual Alliance was broadened into a Triple Alliance, and an association formed which, on paper, lasted until 1915. The Alliance was repeatedly renewed, even as late as 1912, for it suited Italy's purpose to be able, through close association with Austria, both to restrain Austria's own moves and to check Russia's advance into the Balkans. But it was never popular in Italy. Despite many differences, sympathy for France was strong, and there was at first a sound mutual interest in the active trade carried on between the two countries. Yet, as Sonnino had said, Italy could not afford to stand alone, and there was much to be gained from at least a paper accord with Austria. An alliance with France under existing conditions could only have brought the open hostility of both Austria and Germany, and even British relations with France were not good. Count Nigra, Italian Ambassador in Vienna, expressed the quandary neatly when he said that it was a case of "either the Austrian alliance with all its burdens, but with security; or fall at the feet of France". Crispi further summed up the general view in the words: "alliances may be compared to marriages: there are those of love, and those of convenience". The Triple Alliance was for Italy essentially a marriage of convenience, and never took root in popular feeling. Nevertheless, it brought some very real advantages. In the first place, though its terms were secret, it represented a formal recognition of Italy's place among the Great Powers, and might therefore be regarded as an indication of international acceptance of the *Risorgimento*, and especially of Austria's acquiescence in the loss of Habsburg territories. Further, by tacitly recognizing the occupation of Rome it left the Roman question to be dealt with by Italy as an internal, rather than an international, issue. In spite of the eventual fate of the alliance, 1882 must therefore be regarded as a significant date in the growth of the Italian nation.

## CONSEQUENCES OF THE TREATY: RELATIONS WITH FRANCE

Out of the alliance itself came two further developments of importance for Italy; one, an understanding with Britain on the Mediterranean situation, the other, a cautious agreement with Austria as to the policies to be pursued in matters affecting the Balkans and Turkey. Both had their origin in the first renewal of the Triple Alliance, which took place in 1887. The middle years of the 'eighties were almost everywhere years of stress. It has been shown elsewhere that Russia and Austria then came to the brink of war over Bulgaria, and for Britain also at this time relations with Russia were strained, partly because of the Bulgarian crisis and the suspicions it aroused about Russian policy, and partly, too, through events in Central Asia. German relations with France, which Bismarck had been endeavouring to improve, deteriorated with the appearance of Boulanger, and Franco-British tension was kept up by rivalries in Africa. For her part, Italy found her relations with France worse than they had ever been. Cavour's free-trade policy was being abandoned in order to protect the industries of North Italy, and Italian tariffs against French goods were met with restrictions on imports into France, which hit particularly hard the peasant wine-growers of the South, long dependent on the French market. Furthermore, France undoubtedly hoped by economic pressure to force Italy out of her association with Germany and Austria. A "tariff war" followed, which lasted for ten years, from 1888 to 1898, and, coinciding as it did with a period of strained relations between France and Britain, made the Triple Alliance for a time rather more of a reality. In particular, as commercial relations with France deteriorated, economic ties with Germany were strengthened. German banking interests were encouraged by their Government to lend support to Italy's strained finances, which were further weakened by the withdrawal of French credit, and German capital did much to stimulate Italian industrial development.

## The "Mediterranean Agreements"

The logical outcome of all these developments was the renewal of the Triple Alliance, when the period of five years for which it had been framed ran out in 1887. But Austria was reluctant to commit herself too deeply to Italy, in view of Franco-Italian rivalry in the Mediterranean, while Italy for her part feared that Austria's Balkan aims might involve her in war with Russia. Bismarck, who was anxious to see the Alliance renewed, with characteristic skill found a way round the difficulty. Britain, under her new Prime Minister, Lord Salisbury, was drawing nearer to Germany, owing to her difficulties with France and Russia, and Bismarck, while keeping himself in the background, helped to bring Britain and Italy together to form an agreement promising mutual support in any Mediterranean crisis (February, 1887). This relieved Austria's fears that she alone might be involved in war with France on Italy's behalf, and the Triple Alliance was duly renewed only a week later. Italy thus found her position greatly strengthened, while her own Mediterranean ambitions were recognized for the first time: the third article of the agreement with Britain specifically stated that while Italy would support Britain in Egypt, "Great Britain in her turn is disposed, in case of encroachments on the part of a third Power, to support the action of Italy at every other point whatsoever of the North African coast districts, and especially in Tripolitania and Cyrenaica". The way was pointed, in fact, for the "Tripoli War" of 1911. To this first "Mediterranean Agreement" Austria gave her adherence in March, 1887, and the arrangement was given final shape nine months later when a formal "Second Mediterranean Agreement" was framed (December, 1887).

With Austria herself Italy had a similar clarification of aims. In view of the situation in the Balkans it was established, in a separate treaty attached to the Triple Alliance, that if the two countries should find it necessary to take steps to alter the *status quo* in the Balkans, or in the Adriatic and Aegean Seas, they should agree in advance on the steps to be taken, and should each receive compensation for any gains made by the other. It was this clause, which was incorporated in the renewal of the Treaty made in 1891, 1902 and 1912, which was invoked by Italy in 1915 to excuse her abandonment of the Triple Alliance, Austria being informed then that her attack on Serbia was in itself an infringement of the agreement.

## ITALY'S COLONIAL POLICY

If 1882, therefore, saw the appearance of Italy as an equal among the Great Powers, 1887 certainly marked a further important step forward. Yet it is to be noticed that the initiative in the agreements that had been made was not taken by Italy herself. Her policy was largely dictated by her geographical and strategic position, and by the rivalries of the other Powers: now, as later, there was little independent action that she could take. Nevertheless, the 'eighties saw the first cautious steps in Italian expansion, and when Crispi took office on the death of Depretis in 1887 the time seemed ripe for the active policy that he favoured. After the crisis of 1881 there had followed the British occupation of Egypt in 1882, and, in view of the French refusal to participate, Britain had invited Italy to join with her in the settlement of the Egyptian problem. There were many in Italy who welcomed the opportunity to assert their country's position in the international sphere, but others saw in the Arab leader, Arabi Pasha, an Egyptian national hero, another Garibaldi. The Government therefore preferred to adopt a non-committal policy which it dignified by the title of "wise inertia", a phrase that excited the contempt of the Opposition parties. The opportunity was lost, but Italy was not long to remain without interests in Africa. Already in 1882 the trading post established by an Italian company at Assab on the Red Sea coast had been purchased by the Government, and after the murder of an Italian traveller and his companions in 1884 a garrison was sent to the port. From there a strip of coast, including the port of Massawa, was occupied: the foundations of the colony of Eritrea, and of Italy's colonial Empire, had been laid. In taking these steps Italy was supported by Britain, who preferred to see her rather than France in possession of Massawa, and some slight compensation for the loss of Tunis had been gained. It could hardly be foreseen that instead of consolidating her position and occupying Abyssinia, Italy would suffer serious reverses and only return to the attack, in very different circumstances, some forty years later.

Characteristically, the Italian Government, in dispatching an expedition to the Red Sea in 1885, claimed to be carrying out no more than a "prudent and modest colonial policy", and the result of the hesitancy implied in the phrase was seen two years later in the destruction of a column of Italian troops by the Abyssinians at Dogali. It was from the political crisis that followed this disaster that Crispi arose, to give to Italian politics, for the first time since Cavour's death, a spirit of energy and a sense of direction that were badly needed by the country.

## THE CRISPI ERA

Francesco Crispi (1829–1901) was an able but impulsive Sicilian, who as an ardent republican had taken a leading part in Garibaldi's descent on Sicily in 1860, and had since accepted the monarchy as the institution which divided Italians least. Bred in the school of conspiracy which had marked the earlier stages of the *Risorgimento*, he was marked above all, and in spite of many inconsistencies, as an ardent patriot, who when he took office was resolved to redress the harm that had been done to Italy, "my Italy", by twenty years of inglorious government. His motives were good and his sincerity was not to be doubted, but his emphasis on "energy" led to accusations of megalomania, and, like a later ardent but unbalanced spirit, he overreached himself and demanded of Italy more than she could perform. Yet Italian prestige undoubtedly stood higher in the 'nineties for his activities. "A day has come", he once said in Parliament, "when a man has arisen who believes Italy to be the equal of other nations, and wishes to make her words heard and respected." For all the strain he imposed on the country he did something to correct the pessimism that had been induced by years of frustration, by "transformism" and the humiliation of Tunis.

The contrast between Crispi and Depretis, both personal and political, was striking. Where Depretis had been astute, conciliatory and evasive, and had sought by every means to build himself a secure parliamentary majority, Crispi was frank and forceful, and held himself aloof from all political ties. "I am Crispi" was his invariable reply to any inquiry about his party allegiance, and the self-confidence that underlay the remark had something of a tonic effect on public opinion. Yet his aloofness had serious disadvantages. Confident as he was that he could by his leadership enhance Italy's power and prestige, he did not realize the necessity for creating a body of informed support for his views, and failed to appreciate the disparity between his grandiose aims and Italy's narrow resources. Hence the disaster in East Africa which ruined him. "You—you are too great for Italy", a critic once said to him, and his ideas were certainly in startling contrast to the limited views that had prevailed hitherto. It is a telling comment on him that the Rudini Ministry, which succeeded him after his second parliamentary defeat in January, 1891, should have adopted as its mottoes "economy" and "a stay-at-home-policy".

Yet Italy's position at the end of the "Crispi era" was, on the whole, stronger than it had been ten years earlier. The late 'eighties were a period of economic depression, rendered more difficult by the "trade war" with France, while the strain of building up a modern State apparatus continued to be severe. In particular, membership of the Triple Alliance entailed a heavy expenditure on armaments. If Italy had been regarded since 1882 as a Great Power, the liabilities involved were costly: in the ten years between 1881 and 1890 national expenditure had increased by one-third, and the deficit for Crispi's first effective year of office was little short of one hundred million lire. Yet the underlying tendency in trade and industry was towards expansion, and the 'nineties saw a marked improvement. Thus foreign trade doubled between 1890 and 1900, and had been trebled by 1910, while a series of budget surpluses began in 1897, though the national debt continued to increase owing to the policy of treating much current expenditure as capital outlay.

Crispi's entry into office coincided with the beginning of the economic struggle with France, and the fact coloured his outlook on foreign affairs. At heart, like most Italians, he was strongly inspired by French culture and the revolutionary tradition, and he once declared that a war between France and Italy would be civil war rather than a struggle between nations. But he feared the Mediterranean ambitions of France, which he regarded with a degree of suspicion that was little short of hysterical, and saw the overriding advantages of an understanding with Austria. Accordingly he supported the Triple Alliance with characteristic zeal, even while regarding it as essentially a "marriage of convenience", and he was encouraged in this course by the skilful flattery of Bismarck. He lacked the ability, however, to make his policy palatable at home, and drew serious criticism upon himself by his attempts to suppress "irredentism" in deference to the representations of Austria. He came to be associated, therefore, both with an unpopular foreign policy and with the economic depression that followed the "tariff war" with France, and his insistence on the necessity for stern taxation measures to meet budget deficits led to his fall from office in 1889 and again in 1891. Nevertheless, he grappled with internal problems as his immediate predecessors had never done. The country's financial position was improved, changes were made in the machinery of government, and the scope of local government was increased, while the public health laws and penal code were also improved. Abroad, the influence of Italy was widened by the establishment of special schools for the children of Italians settled in the ports of the Eastern Mediterranean, the East African settlements were united in a colony to which Crispi himself gave the name of Eritrea, and a further colony was established on the Somali coast (Italian Somaliland).

## INTERNAL UNREST: SICILY

It was as a result of serious disturbances in the South, however, that Crispi received his greatest opportunity. After his defeat in 1891 his government was succeeded by Rudini's, and that, a year later, by Giolitti's first administration. In the summer of 1893, while the exposure of unsavoury scandals connected with the Bank of Rome was undermining Giolitti, trouble broke out in Sicily, and in December Crispi was back in office, supported by a general view that he was the only man who could deal with the crisis.

## THE IDEOLOGY OF UNREST: ANARCHISM AND MARXISM

The situation that had arisen in Sicily was the first major manifestation of the labour unrest that was to dominate the Italian political scene until 1922 and to play an all-important part in the evolution of Fascism. The economic situation of southern Italy has already been touched on. By 1893 the difficulties had been intensified by the loss of the French market, and by the manifest indifference of all governments since the Union to the problems of the South. As early as 1867 Bakunin had found in Naples ready material for the propagation of his Anarchist brand of Socialism: significantly enough, it was his conception of a Socialism which should arise out of organization from below, in opposition to government, rather than Marx's ideal of dictatorship from above, that appealed at first to the intellectual leaders of the Italian working class. But although Anarchism remained a force in Italian left-wing politics, the influence of Marx, who had been able to expel Bakunin from the International Socialist movement in 1872, gradually became predominant, and by the 'nineties not only was the Italian Socialist movement largely Marxist, but Marx's teaching was exercising a profound influence on Italian philosophical and political thought. A young thinker, Benedetto Croce (1866–1952), then felt his mind, as he has revealed in his autobiography, "burst into flame" under the stimulus of Marxism:

> in the socialistic vision of the rebirth and redemption of mankind through labour and in labour, I seemed to breathe a new air of faith and hope.[12]

And the stimulus, the faith and hope that stirred enthusiasm, came at a time of depression and despair in intellectual circles, a time when it seemed that the high hopes of earlier years were being smothered in corrupt and ineffectual politics. As Croce has written in an analysis of the intellectual currents of these years:[13]

> Marxian Socialism came to fill the void created in Italian thought and ideals. . . . It could not give back to Italy the spirit of romanticism, idealism and the *Risorgimento*, because there is no going back into the past . . . but it did raise her from the depths into which she had sunk when the spiritual force of her heroic age had spent itself.

It was, however, the method and the approach of Marx's teaching, rather than its content, that excited this enthusiasm. The scientific approach, the attempt to reveal the underlying principles of social organization by the close study of historical phenomena and the evolution of society, the confidence that these principles could be re-shaped in the interests of greater social justice, all came as a revelation to a generation for whose idealism the narrow round of Italian political intrigue offered no outlet. It was a generation, too, that had studied its Darwin and Herbert Spencer and been influenced by the work of the great pioneer criminologist, Cesare Lombroso (1836–1909), with his emphasis on environment. It was, in short, a generation susceptible to the attractions of a gospel that sought to explain as well as to exhort. But if Marx's methods inspired enthusiasm his revolutionary conclusions were less readily accepted. Croce's own critical analysis of those doctrines "vaccinated" him—in the phrase he used later—and prepared the way for the "revisionist" attitude to Marxism that, in its advocacy of reform rather than revolution, was to influence many elements in Italian Socialism during the next twenty years, even as, at this same time, it was modifying German Social-Democracy.[14] (Indeed, both Eduard Bernstein, the German "revisionist", and Georges Sorel, the French apostle of another "revisionist" gloss on Marx, Syndicalism, came under Croce's influence.)

## THE RISE OF SOCIALISM: REFORM OR REVOLUTION?

The results for Italian Socialism of the ferment of ideas in the 'nineties were important. The movement had begun, appropriately enough, in the great industrial and commercial centre of North Italy, Milan, in 1882, with the founding of a purely workers' movement, the Italian Workers' Party. This had been followed in 1890–91 by the development of the Milanese Socialist League, a group of intellectuals led by Filippo Turati (1857–1932), a barrister whose sympathies had been aroused by his professional work on behalf of the Workers' Party. The two groups came together in 1891, and organized a joint conference at Genoa in the following year. There the Italian Socialist Party was born. First, however, the conference expelled its left wing of Anarchists, after which, with the new party established, its policy was shaped in such a way as to hold together both revolutionary and revisionist elements. The Workers' Party had already grown up in a "reformist" atmosphere, opposed to the violence of Bakunin and pledged to the amelioration of the conditions of working-class life by practical reforms. The Socialist League, though openly Marxist in its views, was studiously vague as to the means to be employed, having stated in its programme:

> Socialism considers as idle, and leaves open, the question whether the unfolding of the great ends of economic and political evolution will make necessary . . . a violent and bloody clash.[15]

The programme that emerged at Genoa, though Marxist, was largely inspired by the League and was equally non-committal. It offered only a "professional struggle" to improve conditions of work and a "wider struggle for the conquest of political power" that could come equally well by reform as by revolution. Ten years later the Socialist Deputy, Camillo Prampolini (who had moved the expulsion of the Anarchists at Genoa) neatly explained the reformist position in a speech in the Chamber:

> our revolution is inherent in the final results of the reforms we advocate, and not in the means we use to attain those reforms.[16]

This bridging of the gap between moderates and revolutionaries, between those who were content with improved conditions and those who strove for the complete overthrow of society, involved more than a mere matter of words. As the years passed, and especially as the modest reforms of the Giolitti era made themselves felt, the rift widened, until in 1912, just twenty years after the conference that had seen the expulsion of the Anarchists, it was the turn of the right, reforming, wing of the party to be expelled by a conference that was largely under the dominating influence of the fiery revolutionary, Benito Mussolini: the way was then clear for the violence of "Red Week" in 1914—and for the fateful climax in 1919-20. A real unity was never achieved by the party, which was, therefore, never able, despite its growing electoral strength, to influence events to its advantage. As in Germany, the growing strength of the Socialists caused the Government to make concessions in political and social policy, but brought political control no nearer. More seriously, the failure to present a united front after 1918, when the situation was further complicated by the emergence of Communism, directly encouraged the rise of Fascism, while dissensions after the Second World War produced a tripartite Socialism, with moderates on the one flank, Communists on the other and Pietro Nenni's "Nenni Socialists" uneasily balanced near the Communist flank. This situation has but carried into our own day the unresolved and unreconciled differences of 1892.

## CRISPI AND SOCIALISM

But it was not only the conflict of ideas within the party that made the 'nineties significant for Italian Socialism. The period was one of repression and persecution that was set off by the events in Sicily. There the first stirrings of Socialism, following on the pioneer activities of Bakunin, had led to the formation of unions (*fasci*) of peasants and workers, who, often with the help of members of the local nobility and middle classes, strove by organization to improve their lot. Clashes with landowners and police inevitably followed, and it was with this situation of social unrest that Crispi was called upon to deal when he took office for the third time in 1893. Although a Sicilian himself, and aware of the island's poverty and backwardness, he had no understanding of Socialism, however, and no sympathy with its aims. As a typical representative of the "heroic" aspect of the *Risorgimento*, he had little conception of social problems and could not sympathize with any attempt to solve them by direct action. Like most men of his age and class throughout Europe he had no notion of the changes that were taking place in political opinion, and his reputation for "energy" led him in any case to the traditional reply of force. Some forty thousand troops were sent to Sicily, and the disorders were stamped out. The process had begun that within twenty years was seriously to weaken the Italian army by using it too much as a police force to maintain internal order. Crispi was not the man to handle such a situation. Having crushed the Sicilian disturbances, which he characteristically ascribed to French intrigues, he proceeded in 1894 to move against Socialism throughout Italy, dissolving all Socialist societies and prosecuting their newspapers. Before his fall in 1896 public opinion had forced some relaxation of these measures, but Crispi's position was secure, and had it not been for his colonial adventures he might have remained in power for several more years: it was his energetic policy in East Africa that ruined him.

## CRISPI AND EAST AFRICA—ADOWA, 1896

After the defeat of Dogali opposition in Italy had for a time prevented any further moves against Abyssinia, and in his first Ministry Crispi had been able to do no more than extend Italian influence by intrigues among rival Abyssinian leaders. Particularly close relations had been developed with Menelik, King of Shoa, who in 1889, on the death of the Negus John, made himself Emperor of Abyssinia. Menelik needed foreign support while he was consolidating his position, and therefore concluded with Italy the Treaty of Uccialli (May, 1889), which recognized Italian interests in Abyssinia. He was merely playing for time, however, and was soon encouraged, both by the obvious indifference in Italy to colonial expansion and by the intrigues of the French and Russian representatives at his court, to adopt a more independent line. When Crispi took office in 1893 he felt that the time had come to assert Italy's claims, and, encouraged by some military successes against tribesmen, he resolved to force Menelik's hand. But the preparations made for campaigning in notoriously difficult country were inadequate, and the commander on the spot, like Crispi himself, was too confident of success and over-anxious for speedy results. The result was the disaster of Adowa (March, 1896), with the loss of 4,600 men. The wave of indignation that arose in Italy on the news of the defeat swept Crispi from power and into unhonoured retirement. "The most striking political personality the new Italy produced", as he has been called, had demanded too much of his country.

Disastrous colonial adventures could be wound up, and Italy speedily withdrew from Abyssinia, though she retained Eritrea and Somaliland, but Crispi's legacy in internal politics could not so easily be disposed of, and he had left no obvious successor. The next few years were to be dominated by the problems presented by the rise of Socialism. The general election of 1895 had given the Socialists twelve seats in Parliament, and with their Radical and Republican allies and their strong backing in the country they bade fair to become the only true party in Italian politics.

FURTHER UNREST—MILAN AND THE ASSASSINATION
OF KING HUMBERT

In 1897 disorders caused by economic distress had again
broken out in the South, and this time they had spread North,
reaching Milan in a wave of riots in May, 1898, and combining
there with political agitation. The Government's handling of
the situation was typical. Having done nothing to relieve the
South, it delayed action in the North until the situation was
serious, and then struck with violence. Crowds were fired on,
and the general commanding at Milan, who had given the
order to fire, was awarded a high decoration for "services to the
State". Finally the reactionary General Pelloux was made
Prime Minister with the task of restoring order, and for
two years a struggle against his authoritarian rule was carried
on in Parliament by the parties of the Left, which came together
to form an "Extreme Left" group (l'Estrema Sinistra) and
carried through a steady policy of obstructionism in the name of
constitutional government. The struggle succeeded and Pelloux
had to resign. Hardly had he left office when on 29th July,
1900, King Humbert was assassinated by an anarchist, in reprisal for the shooting at Milan. A new situation and a new King,
the young Victor Emmanuel III, suddenly confronted Italy.

A NEW PERIOD?

Whatever may be thought of his actions later, Victor
Emmanuel, despite his intellectual limitations, showed himself
in this first half of his reign to be a sensible and constitutional
ruler. Faced with a difficult choice, and with no obvious
solution to commend itself, he eventually offered the premiership to the veteran Giuseppe Zanardelli (1826–1903), who
gladly accepted the opportunity of "restoring Liberalism".
It was a significant move. Violence on both Right and Left
had been discredited, and it seemed the moment when Italian
politics might at last be stabilized, with two groups of parties
competing for power. "Two great coalitions," wrote some
close English observers in 1901, "the alliance of Socialists,
Republicans, Radicals and advanced Liberals—and the party
of authority—the capitalists, the army, the bulk of the
Clericalists—will contest the future of Italy."[17] It was an over-
simplified picture, and one that chimed too easily with

English predispositions in favour of a two-party system, but there was a general impression that, as a participant afterwards wrote, "after the failure of reaction we were at the commencement of a new historical period".[18] Much depended, however, on the Socialists, who were not prepared to go so far with bourgeois parties as to accept the responsibilities of office, and who still lacked, in any case, any considerable following in the country. Moreover, Zanardelli, man of high principles though he was, lacked the ability to create a united party behind him. Such Liberal measures as the rights of public meetings and a free press, together with reforms of the labour laws, were carried, and the encouragement thereby given led to an outburst of strikes which totalled some fourteen hundred in 1901 alone, with more than two hundred a day at one time. Tax reforms were proposed, but were defeated by a majority in a Parliament that had been created by Pelloux, and was therefore not noticeably Liberal in its composition. A divorce law could not be passed because of the opposition of the Church. Only in his policy for the South did Zanardelli meet with any success, and even there the measures of reform that he put forward were carried into effect by his successor. In 1903, worn-out, and within a few months of death, the old Liberal finally withdrew, and Italy's political development passed into what was to prove its last stage before Fascism, with the coming into power of Giolitti, now Premier for the second time, and destined to dominate the political life of the country for the next twelve years.

## The Giolitti Era

Giovanni Giolitti (1842–1928) has well been called a caricature of Cavour. Both men were parliamentarians who excelled in the handling of political situations, but where Cavour had sought to reshape Italy's political life through institutions based on English models, Giolitti never attempted more than to maintain in equilibrium the system he had inherited. Both were masters of diplomacy, but where Cavour had used his gifts in single-minded devotion to his country, Giolitti applied his undoubted abilities to the maintenance of a personal supremacy, carrying "transformism" and the management of elections to heights undreamed of by Depretis. If he had ideals, they are not easily to be discovered in the prosaic and deliberately unadorned passages of his parliamentary speeches. Like Cavour a Piedmontese, and therefore lacking many characteristics that are generally regarded as "Italian", he was opposed to ceremony and display and preferred, as a close friend has said, "the drab and severe".[19] No greater contrast to Crispi could be imagined, and it was a contrast which Giolitti took pains to emphasize. Yet by his shrewdness and by his skill in playing off one faction against another, by his cynical appraisal of men's motives, and by the corrupt electoral methods that won him the title of "the Minister of the Underworld",[20] he kept the country on an even keel during critical years, and gave scope for the great economic developments that marked the years before the war. Italy had been profoundly shaken by the events of 1898, and as the long-neglected masses of the people began to be stirred by Socialist teaching that could find no constitutional outlet, a serious threat arose to the stability of the country. Giolitti, averse to everything that savoured of excess, was at the same time not unsympathetic to the needs of the peasants and the industrial workers. By imposing no restrictions on agitation he strove to win their support for his "system", while measures such as the encouragement of co-operative enterprises, new factory legislation, the electoral reform of 1912 and the establishment of a system of national insurance in the same year, did something to meet the demands at least of the "reformists".

Yet Giolitti's aim was stability rather than social progress. "When the national institutions gather within their orbit the largest share of national interests," he wrote later in criticism of reactionary policies, "they acquire that solidity which methods of reaction and violence, instead of insuring, gravely compromise".[21] With this unimpeachable doctrine in mind Giolitti courted the Socialists, and even tried to draw them into his administrations. Yet at the same time he gratified the Right by his loyalty to the monarchy and by his seizure of Tripoli in 1911–12, while he even succeeded in winning clerical support against Socialist extremism, and thereby brought to a partial end the long *impasse* between Church and State. Had he possessed truly constructive aims he might have been able to achieve that identification of the people of Italy with the new State that had been lacking since 1860. But, though a skilful parliamentary leader, he had in him, as a contemporary Liberal critic complained, too little of the statesman: "at the best he can be said to represent the policy of pedestrian common sense, living from day to day".[22] And this was hardly the policy to remake Italy.

At the same time it must be admitted that her entry into the First World War in 1915 imposed upon Italy a strain that she was by no means adequately prepared to face. Giolitti's undramatic methods, in pointed contrast to those of Crispi, aimed at the eventual reconciliation of opposing elements in the State, but needed time for their working-out, time which they were not given. It was typical of Giolitti's cautious realism that he resisted the entry into war. United Italy needed a long period of peace and social development before the country could be regarded as fundamentally stable, and its people could begin to approach political maturity.

Yet a national aim, which might have inspired wider support for a cautious policy, seemed always to be lacking in Giolitti's declarations. With him every policy was a political manœuvre, and no overriding national object was apparent. "A majority which devotes all its activity to maintaining itself perpetually in power," said a penetrating critic in 1909, "may (by means of electoral tricks) maintain itself in power for some years, but its detachment from the country is fatal."[23] It is a measure of Giolitti's ultimate failure that few would listen to him in 1915. Despite achievements of value, he had confused the government of a great country with the manipulation of majorities. By 1915 it was felt that he had made himself in practice a dictator, reducing the whole constitutional system to an arena for the exercise of his political gymnastics.[24] As another critic complained in an outspoken attack in the Chamber in 1913:

> under a democratic banner we have imperceptibly arrived at a dictatorial régime. The Honourable Giolitti has four times conducted the elections: in 1892, in 1904, in 1909 and in 1913. In his long parliamentary career he has, moreover, nominated practically all the Senators, all the prefects and all the other high officials in the administrative, judiciary, political, and military hierarchy of our country. . . . He has done the work of drawing parties together by means of reforms and of drawing individuals together by means of personal attention.[25]

Crispi, with all his faults, had been a national figure: Giolitti remained to the end an enigma. It was widely agreed that although by his conciliatory measures he had done much to preserve the unity of Italy during years of difficulty, the methods he had employed "had killed the national soul". If he had drawn the parties together it was by adopting as much of their aims as was necessary to "transform" them into his supporters. If he had drawn individuals together by "personal attention" (a polite euphemism for the award of titles, decorations and official posts) it was to ensure their local support in elections. In his peroration the critic of 1913 had urged Giolitti not to leave in the country "a more profound and irreparable moral disorder" than he had created in Parliament. This, however, was what the Premier, with his corrupt methods, did achieve, and the results were seen in the post-war years. When, in 1920, he returned to power at the age of 78, there were not a few who felt that "after all that had occurred, after the death of 600,000 heroes at the front, Giolitti still governs Italy!",[26] and who therefore clutched desperately at the new prospects which Fascism seemed to offer.

## REFORM OF THE FRANCHISE

Giolitti was not actually in office during the whole of the period from 1903 to 1915, but he held the premiership for three terms—1903–05, 1906–09 and 1911–14—during which were held the important general elections of 1904, 1909 and 1913, which he was therefore able to "manage". Even when he was not in direct control it was usually because it suited him to stand back in order to test political feeling: his influence was constantly at work behind the scenes. On the whole the period was one of prosperity, but of increasing social tension, with a growing realization that fundamental changes were needed. The franchise had been extended as long ago as 1882 to include all men over the age of twenty-one who were literate, but the progress of education had been slow, and by 1912 only some three million men were entitled to vote. Italy was by then alone among the Powers in maintaining a narrow suffrage. Moreover, the entry of new voters upon the scene had not infused fresh vigour into the stale forms of Italian parliamentarism, as had been hoped. In 1912 Giolitti carried a new extension of the franchise, which added a further five-and-a-half million to the registers. He hoped in this way to divert the revolutionary pressure of Socialism, and to give the mass of the people an interest in the preservation of the State. His characteristic approach to the problem he later set out in his *Memoirs*:[27]

> When the masses know that they are unable to modify laws that menace their interests by means of their votes and with lawful methods, it is obvious that they will easily let themselves be persuaded that the only way to change such a state of things is by revolution. On the other hand, when the masses take their share in the country's political life, not only are they in a position to appreciate the difficulties which the State has to overcome in order to better their conditions, but they can realize the limits which the country's circumstances . . . place on the fulfilment of their demands.

As an additional precaution Giolitti undoubtedly hoped that he would be able to bring the extra millions of voters within the scope of his electoral manipulations. But the parliamentary system as Italy knew it was not sufficiently well-founded to withstand the pressure of mass parties. "Transformism" and election-making had served their purpose with a limited electorate: a new technique was required to deal with mass politics, and Giolitti lacked the necessary gifts. The scandals of the general election of 1913 which followed the 1912 reforms did much to discredit the parliamentary system, and Giolitti showed in 1920 that the new situation was beyond him. In Britain it had been possible to adapt an ancient parliamentary system to the requirements of the new social forces because the administration of the system had long inspired confidence in the country. It could hardly be claimed that the Italian system had any similar title to popular support.

## The Church and Politics

In consequence, social unrest, both before and after 1912, found its expression in extra-parliamentary agitation. The middle years of Giolitti's rule were the years of moderate, "reformist" control in the Socialist movement. They were also the years which saw the first tentative Clerical intervention in politics with the removal in 1905 of the ban on Roman Catholic participation in elections. This significant move, which was eventually to lead, in 1919, to the appearance of a

H

new force in Italian politics, the *Partito Popolare* (Christian-Democrats), was intended as a counter to the growing influence of the Socialists. The year 1903 had seen the election of a new Pope, Pius X, who adopted a more conciliatory attitude towards the State than his predecessor, Leo XIII, and although no specifically Roman Catholic party was formed until after the war, the Church became a more active influence in politics. Furthermore, on the basis of the doctrines of Leo XIII's encyclical of 1891, *Rerum Novarum*, with its encouragement of the formation of associations for the improvement of the condition of the working man 'in body, soul and property', Roman Catholic trade unions were formed, and were soon to be welded into an *Italian Labour Union*, rival to the Socialist *General Confederation of Labour*. Thus, two of the major forces of Italian politics in the future, Socialism and Christian-Democracy, were confronting each other as rivals before the reforms of 1912 made possible the formation of mass parties on the two sides. The political shape of Italy, as it appeared after the First War, and again, in 1945, after the tragic aberration of Fascism, was already being formed; the stage of the *Little World* of Guareschi's famous figure of the post-1945 era, *Don Camillo*, was already being set. As early as 1897 the Sicilian historian and politician, Gaetano Mosca (1858–1941), had spoken of "the two religions which now exercise so much influence in the western European world . . . the Catholic Church and social democracy".[28] Nowhere was the clash of these two forces, with their all-embracing demands on their followers, more open than in Italy, long masked though it was to be by the interlude of Fascism.

## The General Strike, 1904

The first steps towards the formation of a Clerical party, and the success of "reformism" within the Socialist movement, were the outcome of a decisive event of Giolitti's early years as Premier, the general strike of September, 1904, the first effective general strike ever known. For several years since the successes of 1900 the revolutionary wing of the Socialist Party had been pressing for direct action, and the outbreak of fresh disorders in the still-neglected South in the summer of 1904 led to the proclamation of a general strike from Milan. Giolitti, however, was not to be stampeded. His attitude was entirely different from that of the panic-stricken authorities of 1898, and he had already made it known. In 1901, when Minister of the Interior under Zanardelli, he had encouraged the formation of workers' unions, and had argued that "the friends of order have a duty to persuade the working class, and to persuade them with deeds, not words, that they have more to hope from the present order than from dreams of the future".[29] Now he refused to believe that the strike had arisen from "any great economic or national question" and prophesied its speedy collapse.[30] Collapse it did, after only four days, upon which Giolitti went to the country and was returned with a more conservative majority, the number of Socialist deputies being reduced from 33 to 27. Giolitti then set to work to encourage moderate counsels among his opponents. The moderate Socialists had supported the strike without enthusiasm, and were now able to take over the leadership of the party for several years. At first unity was preserved, under the device of "integralism", but at the party congress of 1908 the Syndicalists, who had been chiefly responsible for the strike, were formally expelled, and after this, although Socialists still abstained from taking office, opposition to the Government became milder. Giolitti was justified in assuming that the Socialists were undergoing "transformism", as he had long hoped: "the country has gone ahead," he said in 1911, "the Socialist party has greatly moderated its programme, Karl Marx had been relegated to the attic".[31] Events were soon to show, however, that this was wishful thinking: nothing had really been solved. Within a few months, indeed, and as a result of the outbreak of the war with Turkey, the Modena conference of the Socialist Party disavowed moderate counsels and showed that new and violent revolutionary forces were stirring, under the lead of the dominant figure of later years, Benito Mussolini, now launched on his political career. If Giolitti's mild reforms satisfied moderate Socialists, the new generation was growing up in disillusionment, and would accept no compromise.

## Economic Progress

Nevertheless, the country was going ahead, as Giolitti had claimed. Economic progress, in particular, was impressive, and seemed to justify his calm optimism. After the fall of Crispi, and with the memory of Tunis fading, negotiations had been opened with France for a conclusion of the "tariff war", and satisfactory commercial agreements had been made in 1898. A rapid development of trade followed, while in the new century industry took great steps forward. Coal imports, a significant measure of industrial expansion, rose from some four million tons in 1901 to eleven millions in 1913, while hydro-electrical plants were established in great numbers, and metallurgical, engineering and chemical industries were built up. Considerable land-reclamation projects were also undertaken. The ten years before 1915 were probably the best that modern Italy has known.

## THE NEW NATIONALISM

The steadily increasing international tension of the period continued to impose upon Italian resources the strain of heavy expenditure on defence, but from about 1905 the greater national prosperity encouraged among the intellectuals a movement of national revival that was partly inspired by the success of Japan, another newcomer on the international scene, against Russia. The most famous spokesman of this movement, which also drew inspiration from similar trends in France, was the poet Gabriele d'Annunzio (1863–1938), who set the tone with the flamboyant phrase, "Arm the prow and set sail towards the world". To the influence of d'Annunzio, of the nationalist writer, Enrico Corradini (1865–1931), and of others like them, must be ascribed much of the frustrated patriotic fervour that later became an element in Fascism. Corradini's description of war as "the supreme act of a nation" has a familiar ring from the experience of more recent times.

## THE TRIPOLI WAR, 1911–12

Giolitti was not above exploiting this new nationalist movement, and in 1911 he launched Italy into the attack on Tripoli that had been projected for nearly thirty years. Unlike Crispi, he prepared the ground carefully, ensuring in advance adequate military preparation. Characteristically, he made no secret of the fact that it was a calculated move, undertaken not from any patriotic enthusiasm but because of the advantages that the territory would bring to Italy, and of the dangers that would confront her if another Power held it. By a succession of diplomatic agreements dating back to 1887 Italy had already received from the Powers a recognition of her interest in Tripoli, but action had long been deferred. After the "Young Turk" revolution of 1908, however, it was clear that the new rulers of Turkey were reluctant to see the last remnants of Turkish rule in North Africa pass from their control, while Germany was also concerned in its fate, especially after her rebuff over Morocco in the summer of 1911. Giolitti therefore decided to move before it should be too late, and war was declared on Turkey in September, 1911. As in 1915 and, again, in 1940, the Italian Army was by no means as effectively prepared as had been hoped, and the war dragged on for a year, but the Treaty of Lausanne (October, 1912) left Italy with Tripoli and in effective occupation of the Dodecanese Islands. The gains were generally felt to be out of proportion to the effort and the losses involved, and although the war had done much to stimulate public opinion, Giolitti was not the man to give a lead to the new spirit of national pride that had been created. Above all, however, the war brought to a head the stresses within the Socialist party, and opened a new phase of violence that was to prove a decisive factor in the reaction that was later to produce Fascism.

## THE WAR AND SOCIALISM

The Socialist party in its "reformist" phase had already been described by Salvemini as "a party of Liberal action with a Socialist banner",[32] and it was precisely the party's satisfaction with Liberal reforms which, at the time of "imperialist war" in Libya, aroused the tempestuous ire of the unrepentant revolutionaries. Already the Syndicalist leader Arturo Labriola, challenging the views of Prampolini which have been quoted earlier, had denounced "reformism" and urged Socialists everywhere to renounce two illusions:

> that socialism is the result of the addition of reforms, and that these may be accomplished through parliaments.[33]

At the party congresses of 1910 and 1912 a new voice made itself heard, advancing similar views, a voice from the Romagna, traditionally the home of extreme revolutionists, the voice of Benito Mussolini. Socialism, Mussolini argued at Milan in 1910, was more than a matter of voting rights or social reforms:

> I call to the attention of those who have extolled universal suffrage that advanced nations, like Austria and Germany, have universal suffrage; and it is not yet certain that socialism can be attained through it. I call to the attention of those who have extolled social legislation that in the countries where it is most widespread, we are still very far from socialism. England is a case in point. Finally, I declare that if the Italian proletariat were no longer represented by deputies in parliament, the harm would be slight.[34]

Universal suffrage he denounced at the Reggio Emilia congress two years later as merely the oxygen pump administered to the dying parliamentary régime:[35]

> The almost universal suffrage granted by Giovanni Giolitti is an able attempt made with the aim of giving . . . another period of life to the parliamentary régime (which) is not absolutely necessary to socialism . . . but . . . is necessary to the bourgeoisie as a justification and perpetuation of its political rule.

Here is all the later Fascist scorn of parliamentarism, seen in its revolutionary socialist origins. In 1910, it is true, Mussolini failed to carry the congress with him. In 1912, however, he succeeded, and his success was critical both for the party and for Italy.

## THE RISE OF MUSSOLINI

Born in 1883, the son of an ardent fighter for Socialism, Mussolini had grown up an instinctive rebel and individualist, who to escape military service had left Italy for Switzerland, where he had engaged in revolutionary propaganda. In 1904, taking advantage of the amnesty that celebrated the birth of Crown Prince Humbert, he returned to Italy, and, after performing his military service, became teacher, journalist, and Socialist agitator, under the constant eye of the police. His disgust at the moderation of the Socialist Party, still dominated by the reformists, was expressed after the Milan congress when he wrote:

> There is here, on the stage of the political comedy of the third Italy, a big corpse: the official Socialist Party. Should it be buried?[36]

Despite his moderate educational attainments and his wide reading, Mussolini's appeal, now as always, was essentially an emotional one. "What does it matter to the proletarian to understand socialism as one understands a theorem?", he asked in 1912; "Is socialism perhaps reducible to a theorem? We want to believe in it; we must believe in it. Humanity needs a *credo*."[37] It was the emotional appeal, the challenge to moderation and reason, punched home in what Mussolini himself called a "telegraphic" style—the unchanged, staccato style of later years—that won applause from ardent, thwarted revolutionaries, and taught him his power. The Tripoli war gave him his opportunity, and the change in his fortunes from 1910 to 1912 is a measure of the impact which the war made upon the party and upon Italian politics.

The war aroused all the latent anti-militarism of the Socialists, which was felt nowhere more strongly than in Mussolini's homeland of the Romagna, where railway lines were obstructed and stations attacked to stop the passage of troop trains. For his encouragement of these outbreaks, and for his criticism of the war as a "red herring" for the Italian workers, Mussolini was sent to prison in 1911 with his friend Pietro Nenni, from whom he was later to be so widely separated in politics, and who was to pass the years of Fascism in exile. Released from prison after five months, Mussolini prepared to lead the struggle against reformism at the Reggio Emilia congress. The war provided material for the attack, and there was, in addition, the episode of March, 1912, when, after an unsuccessful attack on Victor Emmanuel's life, Socialist deputies had been associated with the Chamber's address of congratulation to the King. The episode brought to a head the growing dissatisfaction with the party's leadership. "Why be touched and weep for the King, only for the King?" Mussolini cried: the event was but "an accident of the trade of kings".[38] The result of his onslaught was a defeat for the moderates, who withdrew to form their own Reformist Socialist Party. Mussolini himself took over from them the editorship of the Socialist paper *Avanti!*, which had been established as far back as 1881 in imitation of the German Socialists' *Vörwarts*, and had been since 1892 the party's official organ. Under Mussolini's editorship its daily circulation rose from 28,000 to 94,000.

Yet in little more than two years Mussolini himself was expelled from the party—that "destroyer of men", as he came to call it[39]—and from his editorial chair, because of his propaganda on behalf of Italian intervention in the war of 1914. From its foundation the Italian Socialist Party had suffered more than most others from the uneasy amalgam of reformist and revolutionary elements. Its divagations, its expulsions, its incapability of forming and maintaining a sustained policy, were fatal to its chances of success. It was dragged constantly towards impatient action by its frustrated extremists. The traditions of an older and disunited Italy, the lack of faith in the new State, the corruption and lack of appeal of the parliamentary régime, all combined with the individualism and rebelliousness of the Italian soul to produce a situation wherein the purity of revolutionary doctrine seemed of greater importance than practical reforms. That the party should have produced Mussolini is an indication both of its strength and of its weakness: he knew well how to turn against it its own weapons, which he was able to wield with greater force. It was the Syndicalist Arturo Labriola who had seen in the Libyan war the struggle of a proletarian Italy against capitalist Europe. Mussolini was to use the case with deadly effect in later years, and his success then was typical of his distortion of Socialist opinion, the appeal of which to an emotional and frustrated people was to him a matter of personal experience.

## "RED WEEK", 1914

The last eruption of Socialism before the First World War came with the "Red Week" of June, 1914, which, beginning with an anti-militarist protest at Ancona, spread throughout the country, and led to the proclamation of the Republic in the Romagna and the hoisting of the Red Flag on the Town Hall of Bologna. Through *Avanti!* Mussolini whipped up the agitation, against the urgings of more moderate Socialists who strove to show that Socialism was not to be achieved by "outbursts of disorganized mobs".[40] The State staggered through the crisis, but already, in the elections of the previous year, Giolitti had written off the Socialists and made an electoral pact with the Roman Catholics in the person of Count Vincenzo Gentiloni, president of the *Italian Catholic Union*. The pact created for the first time a Roman Catholic group in the Chamber, the beginnings of a Christian-Democrat party. For this support Giolitti had to pay a price in restrictions on his freedom of action in matters concerned with education and divorce, but wider issues were involved. Opposition to Socialism and the new policy of the Vatican had brought not only peace but co-operation between Church and State: new forces were visibly taking shape in Italian politics.

## The Crisis of 1914

Across this developing struggle was to be drawn, however, the veil of war. Italy, so long the spectator of international events, had made her first prepared moves in 1911, selecting the declining Ottoman Empire as her victim: 1914 was to see her brought face to face with the quandary imposed by her geographical position and her historical development, the choice between the long-hated *Tedeschi* of Austria and Germany on the one side and the Mediterranean rival, France, on the other, with the necessity for maintaining good relations with the naval power of Britain to weight the balance.

Giolitti had followed the Libyan War with a renewal of the Triple Alliance in 1912. It was now a gesture of little significance, for improved relations with France and the growing tension between Britain and Germany had long since deprived the alliance of much of its original value; while the change in Austrian policy which dated from Aehrenthal's coming into office in 1906 had revived the conflict of interest between Austria and Italy which his more pacific predecessor, Goluchowski, had done much to remove. Italy's necessity for good relations with Britain, in particular, dictated an attitude of reserve, and after the establishment of the Franco-British Entente in 1904 she had adopted what Aehrenthal later called a "see-saw policy" between the rival camps. Her hesitation was in itself an acknowledgement of her weakness, but good relations with Austria were not without their value, for they made it possible to keep a wary eye on Austrian policy in the Balkans, particularly with regard to the strategically important region of Albania. The military party in Austria, however, had no illusions about Italy's real sentiments. Its leader, the Chief of Staff, Conrad, remembering the Italian defeats of

H*

earlier years, constantly spoke of making "a military promenade to Milan", confident that against Italy at least the Habsburg armies would win victories that would do something to restore the fading prestige of the Dual Empire. Already in 1906, when Italy had been struck by an eruption of Vesuvius only a year after a serious earthquake in Calabria, Conrad had seriously considered taking advantage of her difficulties, and the project was revived during the Tripoli war. Austria must decide, he wrote in 1911, "whether to take a hostile position towards Italy's aspirations in Tripoli . . . or to settle accounts with Italy after that State has become involved in Tripoli, thus frustrating for a long time to come her designs on the Italian territory of the Dual Monarchy, her plans for the mastery of the Adriatic, and her activities in the Balkans".[41] Aehrenthal's refusal to fall in with these views was among the factors which caused Conrad's resignation, but that such a project could be advanced by the Chief of Staff is a striking commentary on the bankrupt politics of the Dual Monarchy.

When the final crisis came in 1914 Italy behaved as her allies of the Triple Alliance had long since come to expect, and, though the sympathies of the majority of Italians were with France and Britain, a policy of neutrality was at first the only possible course. The country was lacking, as was said at the time, in both the material and the spiritual preparation for war, the crisis of "Red Week" was but recently over, and the Army was in no condition to engage in a major conflict. Giolitti, now out of office but characteristically preparing for his return, argued that "much may be obtained without going to war"[42], a statement that caused an outcry through its cynical suggestion that Italy should sell her neutrality to the highest bidder (the expression used, *parecchio*, which might be idiomatically translated as "quite a bit", was particularly resented). There was, however, no obvious course of action. The majority of the country probably preferred to remain out of the deadly conflict, but there were not a few who saw an opportunity for Italy at last to realize her full destiny. With past weaknesses in mind, and the tragic disunity so recently revealed, the Government tended to welcome an opportunity of strengthening both itself and Italy's standing among the nations. Yet the Foreign Minister, San Giuliano, took a narrow, but realistic, view, which he set out in a frank despatch to the Italian Ambassador in London, Imperiali, in September, 1914:[43]

> Italy's major interest, and that the one most threatened, is in the Adriatic. We have no interest in other fields of the actual conflict. . . . Our enemy is Austria-Hungary, and not Germany.

San Giuliano has been much criticized for his hesitation. He was weak and vacillating, and hampered by the mortal illness which was very soon to bring his death, but he was anxious to manœuvre his country into the best position for making real gains from the war, and differed from Giolitti in realizing that gains would come through intervention rather than through neutrality. Others moved towards similar views, and Mussolini spoke for them when he wrote of the "hard travail of the inward crisis" of those who wished "to give our contribution, however modest, to historical creation"[44]. A true revolutionary, and therefore both an opponent of the conservatism and militarism of the Central Powers and a child of the French Revolution, he soon swung away from the pacifism of the Socialist Party. His views led to his expulsion from the party and from *Avanti!* in November, 1914. He thereupon launched a new journal, *Popolo d'Italia*, under the significant motto *Qui a fer a terre* (Whoever has iron has land) (the more significant for being in French since he was probably in receipt of French funds). In this he appealed for intervention on the Allied side in the name of the future of Socialism:

> if tomorrow . . . Prussian reaction should triumph in Europe and, after the destruction of Belgium with the planned annihilation of France, should lower the level of human civilization, the deserters and apostates will be all of those who did nothing to avert the catastrophe.[45]

All over the country groups, *fasci*, sprang up to agitate for war and drew inspiration from Mussolini's writings. It was a portent of what was to come later, a first essay of the forces that were eventually to overthrow the constitutional system. Now, with the Government willing to take its chance of success, the *fasci* succeeded in driving the nation into war; succeeded where the Socialists had failed, in making Italy go where they would.

When the plunge was taken in 1915, however, none could foresee the fearful strain that war would place on the country, the humiliation of defeats, the loss of 600,000 dead, the bitter disillusionment and political strife that would follow. Italy, with her inadequate resources and her unresolved internal conflicts, flung herself cold-bloodedly into a struggle that was to tax the strongest Powers. That out of the slaughter and bitterness that followed strange political developments should arise is hardly a matter for wonder. The problems posed in 1860 were still largely unsolved, and the system established then was generally discredited. It could be counted as an achievement that united Italy still lived; whatever her weaknesses and her errors, she had by 1915 come far since 1848. Yet, as a modern commentator has written of the situation in 1915, "in spite of recent prosperity there was a case for declaring that the Piedmontese unification of Italy had failed and that therefore new methods must be tried".[46] The new methods when they were applied took strange and terrible forms, but their origins in the pre-war situation are plain to see.

### REFERENCES

1.  G. M. Trevelyan: *Garibaldi and the Making of Italy*, p. 295.
2.  A. W. Salomone: *Italian Democracy in the Making. The Political Scene in the Giolittian Era, 1900–1914*, p. 9.
3.  Quoted in M. Hentze: *Pre-Fascist Italy*, p. 341 n.
4.  Quoted in H. W. Rudman: *Italian Nationalism and English Letters*, p. 163.
5.  p. 294.
6.  p. 521.
7.  R. Bacchelli: *Nothing New Under the Sun*, p. 194.
8.  Quoted in Salomone, p. 10.
9.  W. K. Hancock: "A Lonely Patriot, Ferdinando Ranelli": *Proceedings of the British Academy*, Vol. XXVII, p. 294.
10. Bolton King and T. Okey: *Italy Today* (1901), p. 24.
11. cf. the references to this tax in Bacchelli's novels.
12. *An Autobiography*, trans. R. G. Collingwood, p. 57.
13. *A History of Italy, 1871–1915*, p. 149.
14. W. Hilton-Young: *The Italian Left*, p. 23.
15. Quoted in Hilton-Young, p. 24.

16.  Salomone, p. 48.

17.  King and Okey, p. 13.

18.  G. Giolitti: *Memoirs of My Life*, trans. E. Storer, p. 145.

19.  Giolitti, Introduction by O. Malagordi, p. 4.

20.  The title fastened on him by the historian Gaetano Salvemini.

21.  *Memoirs*, p. 139.

22.  Quoted in Hentze, p. 241.

23.  Antonio Salandra (1853–1931), quoted in Hentze, p. 301.

24.  Hentze, p. 282.

25.  Salomone, p. 113.

26.  The sentiment is suggested by H. Finer: *Mussolini's Italy*, p. 126.

27.  p. 237.

28.  Quoted in review of edition of Mosca's works in *Times Literary Supplement*, 17th March, 1950.

29.  Quoted in Salomone, p. 66.

30.  *Memoirs*, p. 175.

31.  Quoted in Salomone, p. 59.

32.  ibid., p. 46.

33.  ibid., p. 66.

34.  G. Megaro: *Mussolini in the Making*, p. 259.

35.  Quoted in Salomone, p. 77.

36.  Megaro, p. 302.

37.  ibid., p. 321.

38.  Quoted in Salomone, p. 77.

39.  ibid., p. 72.

40.  ibid., p. 61.

41.  Quoted in A. F. Pribram: *The Secret Treaties of Austria-Hungary, 1867–1914*: English edn. ed. A. C. Coolidge, Vol. II, p. 157.

42.  *Memoirs*, p. 392.

43.  Quoted by R. Pryce from Italian diplomatic papers as yet unpublished: article on "Italy and the Outbreak of the First World War" in the *Cambridge Historical Journal*, Vol. XI, No. 2 (1954), p. 225.

44.  Finer, pp. 100–101.

45.  ibid., p. 102.

46.  E. Wiskemann: *Italy*, p. 55.
     An important article on Italian parliamentary development is D. Mack Smith: "Cavour and Parliament" in the *Cambridge Historical Journal*, Vol. XIII, No. 1 (1957).

# V

# THE THIRD FRENCH REPUBLIC, 1871–1914

THE history of the first forty-four years of the Third
Republic in France is strange and complex. During this
period, between the crushing defeat of 1870 and the advent
of an even greater conflict which was to tax her resources to
the uttermost, and from which France never fully recovered,
French life and institutions as we know them today took shape.
While her achievements in the cultural and scientific fields
brought her great honour and prestige, and proved that France
was still in the forefront of European intellectual movements,
in the world of politics and economic affairs the picture is quite
different. The sharp political divisions of the eighteen-seventies
persist, though the ideologies underlying these divisions constantly evolve and develop; sensational scandals involving
prominent personalities in parliament, finance and the army
cast an unpleasant atmosphere over politics productive of
cynicism and distrust not merely among the electorate; and
although outwardly France appeared to be a rich and prosperous
land her economy was gravely threatened by the loss of
Alsace-Lorraine to Germany—two of her wealthiest provinces.
It took many years for French industry to reorganize itself
after 1870, and the characteristic problems of modern French
economy—the shortage of coal and the protection of home
industries against rapidly expanding foreign competition
were aggravated by her defeat in the Franco-Prussian war.
It is therefore not unnatural that there should be a bitter
resentment in the hearts of the majority of Frenchmen, and
particularly in the generation reaching maturity in the
'seventies, against the treatment meted out to France by the
victorious Germans; the desire for revenge became almost a
political philosophy, and many of the events of the period—
and by no means only in the diplomatic sphere—are closely
connected with this idea of *revanchisme*. But the France of 1914
differed profoundly from the France of 1870; not only had a

distinct and unmistakable pattern of political life emerged firmly based on Republican institutions, but France had also created for herself a new and permanent position among the powers of Europe to which she was entitled by virtue of her geographical position, her recently acquired greatness as a colonial power of the first magnitude, and her long tradition as the custodian of elementary human rights and privileges.

## THE DEFEAT OF 1870 AND THE SIEGE OF PARIS

The spontaneous revolution of 4th September, 1870, overthrew the régime of Napoleon III. But it simultaneously created new dangers and difficulties for a land still stunned by the catastrophe of Sedan, by entrusting the supreme power to men who, despite their patriotic fervour and passionate desire to carry on the war to the bitter end, had had very little first-hand experience of the intricacies of government. France, now without a Constitution, without calm and undivided direction, and without a large part of her military strength as the result of the battle of Sedan and the siege of Bazaine's army at Metz, had only her will to victory to spur her on. Public opinion, however, was obstinately optimistic, but it was a public which knew nothing of the incomparable superiority of German military organization and armaments; it was a public which clung to the memory of past Republican victories, Valmy and Jemappes, which pinned its faith on the already obsolete *chassepot* rifle, and which revelled too much in the psychological tonic of Revolution to face realistically the perils which such a revolution occurring at such a critical juncture must inevitably bring. Parisians, captivated by the magnificent oratory and unflagging enthusiasm of Léon Gambetta, vainly imagined that "republic" was the password to victory. By the end of September the position was already beginning to change. The rapidity of the German advance had by now brought the enemy to the gates of Paris, and the siege of this city which lasted for four months is one of the most significant events in the history of modern France, for out of it was to arise the Commune with its train of bloodshed and social disorder which was ultimately to discredit the Republic and bring down upon France the suspicion of many European powers. The sufferings of the Parisians during this hard winter under enemy bombardment and the mental and physical stresses of siege have many times been described;[1] the city's unyielding temper in the face of immense odds was universally regarded with respect and admiration. While Paris continued to resist, the organization of forces in the provinces to hold the German advance at least on the line of the Loire was in the hands of Government representatives at Tours cut off from their colleagues in the beleaguered capital and unable to act with forcefulness and urgency. In order to bring a sense of unity and direction to their efforts, Gambetta decided to make a dramatic escape from Paris by the only possible means still remaining—by balloon. This dynamic personality (this "raging madman" as Thiers was later to call him), one of the greatest but at the same time one of the most misunderstood of nineteenth-century politicians, had already before 1870 made a name for himself as a vehement critic of the imperial regime. Still in his early thirties, he had played a large part in the proclamation of the Republic and had become Minister of the Interior in the provisional government of National Defence. Gambetta's heroism and energy, however, were of little avail; the tasks of reorganizing the army and training a force strong enough to break through the German lines to the relief of Paris were too great even for him. The capitulation of Bazaine at Metz, the fall of Orléans, and the eventual collapse of Parisian resistance at the end of January, 1871, brought the military operations to an end. Nearly half the country had fallen under German occupation.

## ELECTIONS AND THE PEACE TREATY

Meanwhile those members of the Government who had remained in Paris negotiated an armistice of twenty-one days with the Germans in order that a National Assembly might be elected on 8th February. Gambetta, however, still believed that all was not irretrievably lost, and this intervention by his ministerial colleagues without his approval was, in his view, tantamount to betrayal. He resigned his office, but in the years which followed his voice was frequently heard in parliament and through his influential journal *La République Française*. Though he was no longer *persona grata* with the leading politicians of the 'seventies, he must always be considered

one of the major architects of the Republican system, but the full extent of his influence was not apparent until the next decade. Parliamentary elections were held in February, 1871, and their result showed an extraordinary change in public opinion. Instead of the large majority of Republican members which might have been expected from the nation's attitude of the previous autumn, the new Assembly showed an alignment of forces in which Monarchists and Right-wing deputies outnumbered the Republicans by about two to one. This curious landslide was the result of a universal desire for stability and peace. The Republic had not kept its promises; it had brought defeat and dissension. Many voters could remember the painful days of 1848 when the Second Republic had failed to keep social order, and it was felt that in 1871 France had no need of doctrinaire idealists who would doubt-less dissect the corpse still further in pursuance of their aims, but of an established proven way of life and government under which the nation could recoup its strength with unified direc-tion. There was, however, still no Constitution, monarchical or republican; and until one could be drawn up a provisional government must continue to wield power. The great responsibility of head of the state fell upon Thiers, an elder statesman and distinguished historian with forty years of political life behind him. He had been chief minister under Louis Philippe, he had been opposed to the declaration of war in 1870, but his patriotism was unquestionable and his experience invaluable. Furthermore he had not been a member of the government of National Defence, and was therefore regarded as being above political manœuvre and ready to place the national interest above party strife. His first task was to sue for peace terms with the Germans, and the Treaty of Frankfurt signed in May, 1871, illustrates at once the severity of the German demands and the French Government's desire to salvage what they could from the wreck. France was to pay an indemnity of five milliard francs within three years, and until payment was completed a German army of occupation was to hold certain northern and eastern departments. The loss of Alsace and Lorraine, henceforth incorporated in the German Empire, was however a far more serious blow to France even than the extortionate indemnity, since both these provinces contained agricultural land of the richest, and vast deposits of iron ore the full extent of which was not fully known at the time. Alsace, moreover, was a major textile centre, and many prosperous business concerns were transferred to Germany at a time when French economy was badly dislocated and ill-equipped to stand the loss. It was a crippling treaty, yet the Assembly had no choice but to ratify it.

## THE COMMUNE

While the negotiations for the Treaty were still going on, a fresh complication suddenly arose which threatened to complete the ruin of the nation. Paris had for long been the centre of "advanced" political thought, and particularly during the siege left-wing groups had won for themselves much influence in the city's administration. The elections of February, which had brought into being an "Assembly of country bumpkins" in which provincial and landed interests were so prominent, were greeted with alarm by the Parisian artisans. Paris too had felt slighted by the Assembly's decision to meet at Versailles, but more especially by the Government's latest decree to withhold the wages of the National Guard upon whom had fallen most of the brunt of the defence of the city against the Germans during the previous winter. The Government thus committed the capital blunder of stopping the Guards' pay but without depriving them of their weapons, which included a large number of guns subscribed for by the Parisians themselves in the emergency. The Government behaved with grave lack of tact in their handling of the crisis; it is by no means certain that the Commune was inevitable, and few politicians had taken into account the very special and irritable temper of the Parisians after their ordeal. They were proud of their feat of endurance, and felt with some justification that they merited some particular consideration; disturbed by Gambetta's resignation, they saw no one in authority to speak for their claims. Resisting the Government's demand for the handing over of the guns, they were further strengthened by the behaviour of the Government troops, who, when sent to enforce the wishes of authority, fraternized with the National Guards. Thus for the second time within three months, Paris was besieged, but on this second occasion it was a city in revolt rather than a city at war, and a prey to the unpleasant emotions of civil strife. The name "Commune" given to this episode originates from the municipal government of Paris created by the rebels; it has nothing to do with party labels or political affiliations. The *commune* is in fact the basic unit of French local government presided over by the elected *maire*. Most of the Communards were influenced to varying degrees by Socialist thought, but they were in no sense of the term Communists as we understand the word nowadays. The weakness of the Commune derives from lack of leadership; *quot homines, tot sententiae*. Having no unanimously agreed policy, the Communards sought to gain their ends by methods of terrorism. They tried to bargain with the Government by a system of hostages, which Thiers quite rightly refused to acknowledge. During the notorious Bloody Week (21st–28th May, 1871), the rebels executed the Archbishop of Paris and several other priests, some of these executions being carried out with great brutality. Public buildings with a symbolic significance were destroyed, among them the Tuileries, symbol of the monarchy, and the Hôtel de Ville, symbol of the old municipal administration. But this orgy of destruction was the work of one week only, and the persecutions have been much exaggerated: the Government forces killed far more Communards than Communards executed hostages. When, at the end of May, Paris was reoccupied by the Assembly's troops, the Commune was suppressed with a ruthlessness which muzzled the left-wing political groups for more than a decade. The National Guard was abolished, and Parisian pride was humbled. It could no longer be said that where Paris led, the rest of France would follow. Thiers had won his first major victory, but it had cost the country dear in prestige, and the memory of the Commune was never completely eradicated.

## Reconstruction: Monarchy Versus Republic

After the upheavals of nine stormy months, the stock-taking which ensued was thorough. There was a national examination of conscience, in which the Church attributed the defeat of 1870 to the spirit of irreligion abroad in the country: "*La France a péché; ses malheurs sont bien une expiation*."[2] The political climate of the 'seventies favoured the growth of religious movements; the practice of pilgrimages to shrines such as Lourdes and Paray-le-Monial was encouraged by the powerful Assumptionist order, the building of the Basilica of the Sacré-Cœur on the *butte de Montmartre* was undertaken as an act of national dedication. The Catholic press, and particularly the highly Ultramontane and anti-Liberal *L'Univers*, rapidly increased its circulation. The power of the Church was much increased by larger grants from State funds, and by giving the clergy representation on local—and national—education committees. Another sign of the times was the attention given to the reform of the army. There had been no major legislation concerning military service and organization for over half a century, and although conscription existed in theory, exemption from it could be purchased without difficulty. In Germany, conscription was universal, and the magnificent organization of the German army taught France a lesson from which she was anxious to profit immediately. France therefore must impose an even longer term of conscription than Germany, and so by the law of August, 1872, compulsory military service for all was introduced, and the purchase of exemptions became illegal. But in order to ease the financial burden of supporting a large standing army in peacetime, the annual contingent was divided into sections by the drawing of lots, whereby some conscripts served a period of up to one year, and others were obliged to serve the full term of five years. Exemptions did not, however, automatically disappear, and priests and teachers for the time being escaped military service altogether.

The Government's reconstruction programme was based upon three principles—social stability, full employment, and the liberation of French territory from the army of occupation. The last German soldier crossed the frontier in the summer of 1873; the indemnity was paid off comfortably within the time-limit imposed by the Treaty. The economic policy practised by Thiers was cautious and traditional, aimed at winning the confidence of the middle classes. By 1873, the provisional government had gone a long way towards creating a public state of mind favourable to Republican institutions. In view of the rapidly growing popularity of Republicanism (even the venerable Thiers himself had become a convert), the Royalist majority, if they were to take advantage of their superior position in Parliament, must strike before it was too late. Unfortunately the monarchists were divided in their support of two rival claimants to the throne: on the one hand, the Comte de Chambord, the descendant of the legitimate Bourbon line, grandson of Charles X, and on the other, the Comte de Paris, grandson of Louis Philippe. The supporters of neither candidate would acknowledge the authority of the other, and the royalist restoration was further complicated by the fact that Chambord would not consent to rule with the *tricolore* as the national flag of France, but only with the ancestral white flag of the Bourbons: on which subject public opinion— and especially military opinion—was extremely sensitive. A compromise seemed possible in that Chambord was childless, and his legal heir was the Comte de Paris, but no compromise was possible with the adamant Pretender on the question of the flag. He maintained obstinately that "Henri V cannot abandon the flag of Henri IV", and although an endless series of representations were made to him in exile at Frohsdorf in Austria by official delegations and private individuals, by 1873 it had become clear that his intractability had doomed the monarchist cause to failure. It was equally clear by 1873 that a restoration of the monarchy would not be as widely welcomed as in 1871; the balance of forces in the Assembly was no longer overwhelmingly in favour of such a restoration. The loss of Thiers to the Republicans, and the increasing fear in the provinces that lands might be confiscated to recompense royalist supporters, as well as the fear of greater clerical inter- ference in the State, had lost the royalists much of their support.

## THE CONSTITUTION OF 1875

Meanwhile, Thiers had been forced to resign the Presi- dency under strong pressure from the parliamentary right wing. His successor, Marshal MacMahon, of Irish descent, a devout Catholic, and with a distinguished military career behind him, was, from the Conservatives' point of view, more likely to pave the way for a return of a king than Thiers. He was sup- ported by a ministry under the Duc de Broglie, in which the influence of the old aristocracy appeared to be predominant. This phase has often been called *La République des Ducs,* as several of Broglie's colleagues in key ministries were also of ducal rank. Broglie's main concern in this government of "moral order" was to block the road to radicalism; his policy therefore was cautious and unsatisfactory to Right and Left alike. The journalist Edmond About wrote: "The Duc de Broglie strokes France, but rubs her the wrong way".[3] Even now, after the failure of monarchism, the final establishment of the Republic seemed almost as far away as ever, despite the introduction in November, 1873, of the "Septennate", by which MacMahon's tenure of the Presidency was extended to seven years. It was nevertheless obvious that France could not be governed for much longer without a definite Constitution— too much time had already been wasted by the Assembly in waiting for the monarchists to make up their minds. The fall of Broglie in May, 1874, and the increasing complexity of the political situation made it imperative that a solution to the deadlock should be found as quickly as possible. However, it was not until January of the following year that the Assembly seriously undertook the work of providing the country with a Constitution, and it is significant that the most important and fundamental clause in the Constitution, that providing for the election of a President of the Republic, was passed by a majority of only one vote. This slender majority which acknowledged the existence of the Republic rapidly grew with succeeding debates, and by 3rd February the first of the major constitutional laws was passed by the Assembly. The Constitution of 1875 is remarkable for its brevity and simplicity, yet few contemporary observers had a good word to say for it. Inevitably it bears the mark of the extraordinary circumstances which prevailed during its gestation, but none the less of all the many constitutions which France had known since 1791 this one—the most half-heartedly formulated, and at the time thought to be the least likely to survive—conferred upon France a set of institutions destined to last sixty-five years. The Constitution could be revised by a very simple procedure requiring merely an absolute majority of the votes of members of both houses meeting together, but during the entire sixty-five years of its existence, revision took place only four times, and apart from the final revision in 1940 major issues and principles were never involved.

The Constitution was essentially a compromise between republican and monarchical principles; wide appeal was made to precedent, and the whole corpus of constitutional law was remarkable for its lack of dogmatism It was a wise Constitution, nevertheless, if one accepts the principle that the object of a Constitution should be to prevent the arbitrary exercise of authority, to guarantee individual liberties, to give popular aspirations full opportunity to show themselves, and to ensure the rights of the majority while protecting the interests of minorities.[4]

## The Triumph of the Republicans

The first elections to be held under the new régime produced a Chamber and a Senate in which Republicans at last held the upper hand. It was a vote of confidence, and a vote of gratitude for the excellent work of reconstruction done by the provisional government. This Republican majority, however, placed the President—still a monarchist at heart—in a paradoxical position. Unable to find a Cabinet capable of survival, and one which would govern in accordance with his own conscience and principles, he fell back upon the clause in the constitution which enabled him to dismiss ministers and dissolve the Chamber. This crisis of 16th May, 1877, when MacMahon brought back the conservative Broglie to office against the wishes of the Chamber, was the first test of the strength of the Constitution. The 1877 elections were a resounding defeat for the President; though he had acted in accordance with his constitutional rights, no President after him dared to defy the majority party in Parliament. MacMahon continued in office, but the tension between President and Chamber was so great as to render the existence of both intolerable. The final clash came in January, 1879; the Republicans, further strengthened by their success in the recent senatorial elections, in trying to appoint their sympathizers to key administrative positions, asked MacMahon to sanction the dismissal of a number of his former colleagues in the army. His reply was typical: "You wish to dishonour me. . . . I cannot consent to strike down good officers, brave soldiers, my companions in arms. If it is a matter of satisfying party spirit, I shall not sacrifice them. I shall resign rather than consent to it. If I abandoned the army today, if I did this thing which I consider hostile to its interests and to those of the nation, I should no longer even dare to embrace my children."[5] Two days later, on January 30th, MacMahon resigned the Presidency. With his departure, the first phase, the *période héroïque* of the Republic, comes to an end.

The first nine years of the Republic brought France peace, and the rapid recovery of her economy after the war. Thiers, who died in 1877, and MacMahon had both steered the nation over the worst initial dangers, and helped regain for France some of the respect she had lost. In 1875 the country survived a serious war scare emanating from Germany, and behaved with great restraint. The issue of Monarchism versus Republicanism had been settled by democratic means, and by 1879 France found her feet firmly planted on the path of order, democracy and stability.

In the Republican victories of 1877–79, Gambetta had played a leading part, but he refused to stand as MacMahon's successor. The Assembly's choice fell upon Jules Grévy, seventy-two years of age, a Republican of long standing and bourgeois background, a man respected by all, and who, by his election, brought at last even the Presidency into the hands of the Republicans. The first two years of Grévy's administration brought a systematic consolidation of the Republican position; public works were put in hand to keep employment at a high level, an amnesty was granted to the Communards, 14th July was henceforth celebrated as the Republic's national festival, Parliament at last returned to Paris from Versailles, the famous press law of 1881 removed all restrictions on printing, publishing, retailing and placarding within the limits of the law of libel, and trade unions, which had hitherto been tolerated but not encouraged, received the Government's blessing when formed to protect the economic interests of the workers. Behind these and other reforms of the period were two great ministers—Freycinet and Jules Ferry. Ferry was a politician of extraordinary versatility, whose activities extended to education, colonial policy and foreign affairs with equal success, but not without stirring up the bitterest enmity in each of these fields. He was a man with a strong sense of duty, and as Minister of Public Instruction he aimed at making education free, compulsory and secular throughout France, an aim destined to bring him into conflict with the Church, and to fire the first shots in a battle which is still far from ended today.

## ANTI-CLERICALISM AND EDUCATIONAL REFORM

The anti-clerical tradition of the Republican party was of long standing, and an essential part of its political creed, being most strongly marked among the *petits bourgeois* and town artisans. It can be traced back to the time of the 1789 Revolution, and the close alliance of throne and altar in the early nineteenth century stimulated the Republicans' fear that unless the power of religious organizations were curbed by law—particularly in education, where the Catholic Church had almost unlimited opportunities for the fashioning of young minds, a restoration of the monarchy would ultimately and inevitably follow. But many Radicals were not atheists, and anti-clericalism as a political force should be distinguished from atheism; many of them were sincerely attached to the principle of the secular state, or *laïcité*—the idea that the State should remain strictly neutral in religious affairs—and held the view that a nation preaching the doctrine of toleration should not dispense more favours to one sect than to another. The financial drain upon the State caused by the annual *budget des cultes* (for which the State obtained nothing in return) was regarded with increasing disquiet by the Left, since it seemed to them that the Republic was subsidizing an avowedly anti-Republican body. The Communards had already in April, 1871, given expression to this tradition by decreeing the separation of Church and State, and suppressing the *budget des cultes*, a premature move for the time, but clearly indicative of the strength of anti-clericalism in the capital.

Since 1850, when the *loi Falloux* had allowed religious associations to found schools, the power of the Church had increased rapidly in the educational field, so that by about 1880 approximately one half of the school population was taught by members of the religious orders. In their desire to build a free democracy in France, the Republicans had come to look upon the monarchy and the Church as their two main enemies; having removed the one, they now sought to crush the other.

Strongly influenced by the ideas of freemasonry, which was both popular and powerful in the 'seventies and 'eighties, they believed that democracy was based on education, which should be free from religious bias. The expulsion of the religious orders, or *congrégations*, was the logical means to this end. By laws passed in 1881 and 1882, every teacher had to be certificated, and education in State schools was made free and compulsory between the ages of six and thirteen. To make it secular was more difficult; the Right-wing parties complained that by ignoring God in the schools, Ferry was creating an atheistic education based not on the traditional "instruction morale et *religieuse*" but on "instruction morale et *civique*". However, reinforced by fresh electoral successes, Ferry prohibited clerical supervision in state primary schools by law in March, 1882. These educational laws are only a part of a long series of attacks on the power of the Church continuing throughout the 'eighties, which included the expulsion of the Jesuit order (the most highly organized and influential of the teaching orders) and other unauthorized *congrégations*, the reintroduction of divorce into the Civil Code, the removal of distinctions in cemeteries, the suppression of public prayers, and in 1889 the extension of the conscription laws to seminarists. The purpose of this latter law was to stop excessive recruitment to the clergy, favoured by its exemption from military service.

## FERRY AND COLONIAL EXPANSION

In 1882, by the accidental death of Gambetta, parliamentary life lost its most colourful personality. Despite his great prestige and popularity, which would have carried him to any position in the State if he had so desired, he only once, for ten weeks (November, 1881 to January, 1882), held office as Premier. It has been said with truth that "his was the power behind the throne"; his influence can be detected everywhere in his last years. To some extent, his mantle fell upon Ferry, who shared many of Gambetta's ideas, and notably the view that colonization is a life or death question for the modern state. During the 'seventies France had shown no interest whatever in colonial expansion, partly because of the need to stabilize the home régime and restore the national economy, partly in reaction against Napoleon III's humiliating Mexican adventure. But Ferry, like Gambetta, saw that colonization was essential to increase French economic strength, that colonial markets were needed to help offset the depression of the 'seventies, and that French prestige might be restored by overseas victories while Germany blocked her ambitions in Europe. In 1881, a speaker at the Geographical Conference on Africa said:

> We seek to fix public opinion on our colonies. . . . where France, reduced in Europe by painful circumstances will find a field of indefinite development. . . . There the living forces of the nation which are beginning to find themselves compressed within the narrow limits of the Treaty of Frankfurt will be able to accomplish complete expansion.[6]

Ferry was much influenced by Leroy-Beaulieu's book, *De la colonisation chez les peuples modernes* (published in 1874), which put forward the theory that France must renounce her continental policy, since she could not hope for revenge against the growing might of Germany. She must, therefore, in order to remain a great power, turn to colonial expansion. The expression of this view at this particular time was highly satisfactory to the Germans themselves, and Bismarck, to distract French attention from the "line of the Vosges", encouraged France to intervene in Tunis where corruption and disorder were a threat to the security of Algeria. Alleging a series of frontier incidents, Ferry sent an expeditionary force to Tunis, and enforced the Treaty of Bardo (May, 1881) which opened the way for the establishment, two years later, of a French protectorate. Although France was so successful in Tunis, she was to fail in Egypt through timidity. Since 1876, France and Britain had exercised a virtual condominium in Egypt by their control of Egyptian finances, but in 1881 the nationalistic revolt of Arabi Pasha threw the entire country into a state of ferment. The Freycinet government which succeeded Gambetta's short ministry (Gambetta had been willing to co-operate with Britain in putting down the revolt by force if necessary) reversed the policy of its predecessor, knowing that French public opinion would not support new colonial ventures so soon after the Tunisian expedition, and withdrew after the Alexandria riots, leaving Britain to complete alone the pacification of Egypt, and to establish her preponderance there. Subsequent French jealousy of Britain's success in the Nile valley poisoned Franco-British relations until the settlement of 1904.

## INDO-CHINA AND THE FALL OF FERRY

Ferry encouraged expeditions in Senegal and the Niger valley, in Madagascar, and particularly the great work of Savorgnan de Brazza, who concluded treaties of friendship and protectorate with the tribes of Equatorial Africa. Ferry was also interested in the Far East, and endeavoured to strengthen the French foothold in Indo-China, which was considered in the nineteenth century as a potential outlet for the trade of central China, and even as some sort of compensation for the loss of influence in India. Having succeeded in creating a French protectorate in Annam (August, 1883), Ferry next proceeded to the acquisition of Tonkin, a much more difficult undertaking in which French troops were fighting guerrilla forces reinforced with Chinese units through fever-ridden country. Local checks to French progress were magnified into major defeats by Ferry's enemies, and all the pent-up hatred of Right and Left alike vented itself in the spring of 1885 in a violent press campaign directed against Ferry personally, who was hated by the Right for his anti-clericalism and by the Left for his conservatism and imperialism. The reverses in Tonkin, insignificant though they were, were seized upon as a perfect opportunity for overthrowing the Government. The unfortunate Premier was caricatured mercilessly and pilloried as *le Tonkinois*, and attacked for his lavish expenditure on a pointless mission. The *coup de grâce* was delivered in the Chamber by Clemenceau in his bitterest and most scornful vein. Ferry, howled down by the Deputies, and accused in Clemenceau's vitriolic speech of sacrificing national interests in Europe to featherbrained schemes wasteful of money and manpower, which had brought nothing but the humiliation of France, was forced to resign. In the streets the crowds were shouting "A bas Ferry! A l'eau Ferry! A mort le Tonkinois!"[7] He lived on another thirteen years, but his unpopularity never left him. An ungrateful public failed to see in him the creator of the new French empire.

## ECONOMIC CRISIS

The 'eighties inherited some serious problems from the previous decade. Among these was an agricultural depression rapidly approaching catastrophe by 1885. France, normally self-sufficient in wheat, had experienced bad harvests in 1878 and 1879 necessitating heavy imports; her vineyards were attacked by the phylloxera blight which in the ten years after 1875 spread to all wine-producing areas; and the emergence of America as a large-scale producer of cheap corn and meat brought an unaccustomed and upsetting element of competition into the traditional economy of France. The small landowner and cultivator, in order to meet the challenge of changing economic conditions, was obliged to expend more capital—which he could ill afford—and greater effort, bidding all the time for labour against the expanding industries of the towns which the new railways had made easily accessible. From the mid-'seventies onwards, while the total population of France steadily increased, the percentage of town dwellers likewise increased; a drift of population detrimental to agriculture was set on foot. But although industry was expanding, all was not well. France is traditionally a land of small industrial concerns, and political events in the late nineteenth century tended to keep it so. Slow to modernize methods, obliged to import raw materials on a large scale at unprofitable prices, the silk industry of the Rhône valley crippled by worm disease, suffering from the lack of an overall economic policy from the Government, French industry in the early years of the Third Republic was never an effective competitor with Britain and Germany more happily provided with ample supplies of excellent coal.[8] Working-class discontent with the Government's complacency was manifested in the increased Radical vote, and the growth of Socialism and trade unionism.

## RADICALISM AND SOCIALISM

The doctrine of the early Radicals was resumed in the *programme de Belleville*, an election manifesto of 1869, demanding universal suffrage, freedom of the press and association, separation of the Church and State, compulsory free secular education, competitive examinations with equality of opportunity for administrative posts, and greater freedom in local government. Many of these aims were realized in the early years of the Republic, but after 1880 a true Radical party began to coalesce around Clemenceau and Pelletan, co-founders of the newspaper *La Justice*, who added new ideas involving constitutional reform, particularly of the Senate, and further social reforms. The more extreme members of the group even added Socialist to their party label, thus creating a small but vocal Radical-Socialist minority in the Chamber. The modern Socialist party in France was built up on the varied doctrines of Proudhon, Blanqui, and Louis Blanc, all of whom sought justice for the proletariat but differed in their opinion of how social justice was to be achieved. The impact of Marxism, which took up many of the ideas of earlier French thinkers and gave them colour and a more logical form, was responsible for the crystallization of Socialism in France and the formation of a permanent organization. In 1880 Jules Guesde, a disciple of Marx, founded the *Parti ouvrier français*, but although Socialism henceforth became an electoral force, it was not until 1905 that a single united Socialist party emerged, and the revolutionary Marxist and Blanquist groups under Guesde and Vaillant merged with the moderate "parliamentary" Socialists under Jaurès.

## The Emergence of Boulanger

The uncertainty of the mid-'eighties was demonstrated by the 1885 elections, which increased both Right-wing and Radical representation, at the expense of the moderate Centre. Early in 1886, Freycinet, took office for the third time as Premier, and he included in his Cabinet a certain General Boulanger as Minister of War. Georges Boulanger (1837–91) came to politics after a brilliant military career in North Africa; he was a colourful personality with a flamboyant manner and distinguished appearance. A protégé of Clemenceau, he was supported by the Radicals, but this did not prevent him from having cordial relations with the monarchists as well. He lost no time in putting into effect measures which won him immediate popularity; he improved the lot of the conscript, and declared his intention to reduce the term of conscription from five years to three, abolishing all exemptions. At the great Longchamp review on 14th July, 1886, Boulanger was greeted with rapturous enthusiasm by a crowd who saw in him the saviour of the army, the personification of revenge against Germany, a hero with his battle scars, and a virile contrast to the insipid figures of contemporary politics. The famous *chansonnier* Paulus expressed the public's devotion in a song *En revenant de la revue* which became a nation-wide hit; Boulanger soon became *le général Revanche*, "General Victory":

> Regardez-le là-bas! Il nous sourit et passe:
> Il vient de délivrer la Lorraine et l'Alsace.[9]

Dangerous talk. Boulanger's popularity mounted higher in April, 1887, when German agents in Alsace imprisoned a French police commissioner, Schnaebelé, and the war of revenge appeared to be at last in sight. Although on the orders of the German Emperor Schnaebelé was released and the war scare passed, Boulanger and his flag-wagging had plainly become an embarrassment to his ministerial colleagues. In a wave of panic, the Government was overthrown, and Boulanger removed to an army command at a safe distance from Paris. His departure from the Gare de Lyon was made the occasion for a riotous demonstration by the infatuated Parisians. The Government hoped this would be the end of Boulanger. In fact, it was barely the beginning; *boulangisme* as a movement had been launched.

## THE WILSON SCANDAL: THE FAILURE OF *boulangisme*

Meanwhile, Grévy had been re-elected to the Presidency on the expiry of his seven-year term of office. But he was soon to become involved in a scandal concerning his son-in-law Daniel Wilson, who had been conducting a vast correspondence at the public expense under the Presidential seal, and was also found to have used his influence at the Elysée to obtain the Legion of Honour for his friends. Grévy, despite his disavowal of Wilson, was forced to resign, but it was no easy matter to choose a successor in view of public excitement. Ferry's candidature was scarcely to be taken seriously, but in order to exclude *le Tonkinois* the Assembly elected Sadi Carnot, the personification of bourgeois and Republican virtues, more famous for his distinguished family name than for his political abilities. The Wilson case, with its revelation of corruption in high places, produced a wave of anti-parliamentary feeling in the country, which worked to the profit of Boulanger and his ambitious friends. The country, still in chauvinistic mood, sought a leader; the monarchists and Bonapartists saw in Boulanger a man of whom they could make use to bring about a *coup d'état* and restore authoritarian government. Financed by a wealthy aristocrat, the Duchesse d'Uzès, Boulanger stood for election to the Chamber simultaneously in a number of provincial by-elections, and was triumphantly elected. The climax of his career came on 27th January, 1889, when he was also elected by a large majority to a vacant seat in Paris. Had he wished to place himself at the head of the delirious crowd of his supporters and march to the Elysée Palace, a victorious *coup d'état* would have been his that night. Hesitation to seize power illegally, the assertion of the disciplined soldier over the ambitious gambler, lost him for ever his chance of dictatorship. The Government circulated a rumour of a warrant for Boulanger's arrest, and by preparing to prosecute some of his more fanatical adherents they sought to spread confusion in the *boulangist* camp. Fearful of an imprisonment which would separate him from his mistress, he fled to Brussels, where he later, dramatic to the last, committed suicide. Even though *boulangisme* collapsed through the General's lack of moral courage at the moment of decision, the causes of the movement still survived—the lingering sense of humiliation left by the defeat of 1870, and the disillusionment provoked by the rapidly stagnating Republic with its mediocre leaders. Unquestionably the movement gave greater strength to the spirit of nationalism abroad in the country, which expressed itself in the strongly *revanchiste* and increasingly anti-republican *Ligue des Patriotes*, and in the writings of Maurice Barrès. Yet it contributed also to the final discrediting of monarchism, and although it shook the Republic to its foundations, the Republic was enabled to put its house in order and ultimately to emerge fortified.[10]

The year 1889 was a glorious one. To commemorate the centenary of the Revolution a great Exhibition of French art and industry was held in Paris on the *Champ de Mars* and in the Trocadéro gardens. The two showpieces of the Exhibition were the *Galerie des Machines* and the Eiffel Tower. The whole concept was one of great imagination which

captivated the entire nation, and stirred enthusiastic journalists to write lyrical paragraphs extolling the wonders of
science and the brilliance of French achievements.[11] Justi-
fiably. New discoveries—notably in the realm of electricity
—here displayed for the first time, opened up seemingly
endless vistas, and the bicycle with inflatable tyres heralded
a revolution in transport. Novels by Bourget, Zola, Maupassant,
Loti poured from the printing presses; poetry at the height
of the Symbolist movement still fascinated a wide public;
the Impressionist school of painters, though still banned
from the official salons, was no longer derided, and a galaxy
of distinguished composers—among them Saint-Saëns, Fauré,
d'Indy, Massenet, Franck—perpetuated the glories of French
music. The cult of Mallarmé's "dieu Richard Wagner"
was also spreading, despite the Opéra's interdict; so too,
equally significant, was the cult of Russian literature. There
was then much cause for pride and optimism in 1889, and
the Government's new conscription law of 18th July (the
*loi Freycinet*) suppressing the drawing of lots and fixing
a three-year period of service with few exemptions was
deservedly popular and well-timed. But there were signs
that the *culte de l'uniforme* was less universally celebrated
than previously. Old pacifist and humanitarian ideologies
began to reappear, chiefly among intellectuals and in University
circles, while a series of novels depicted military discipline in an
unfavourable light. Unimportant in itself at this period, the
state of mind engendered by these developments was to play
a part ten years later during the Dreyfus case.

## TARIFF REFORM

The Government next turned its attention to tariff reform.
In this branch of the national economy there was little coher-
ence; laws were very complex, and the free-trade tendencies of
the 'sixties had not been well received by either agriculture or
industry. The general fall in prices during the 'eighties,
coupled with the agricultural and industrial difficulties already
mentioned, led to complaints and demands for the protection
of home producers. A commission was set up in 1890 under the
chairmanship of Jules Méline, a keen student of economics
and a "high protectionist", but it was not until January, 1892,

I

that a final agreement on tariff reform—generally known as the "Méline Tariff"—was reached. It was decided that in future no commercial treaties should be concluded, but only revocable conventions, and that two scales—a general tariff and a minimum tariff—should be applied. The general tariff was almost prohibitive, and it was applicable in the absence of a particular convention. Even the minimum tariff was very high, particularly with regard to metallurgical, textile and pharmaceutical goods. The object of Méline's system was quite clearly to keep the internal market free for the products of French industry and agriculture, and to restrict imports as far as possible to raw materials. Within this highly protectionist framework, the colonies were included; without industries of their own, they served as little more than outlets for the produce of metropolitan France. The tariff succeeded in giving the expanding industries the protection they needed, but by raising duty on imported machinery it may have retarded modernization and further progress.[12] France, however, was merely following the majority of other European powers: Germany had had a protectionist tariff since 1879.

## THE *ralliement*

Reason and common sense having prevailed at last in the economic sphere, it is not surprising to find these virtues spreading to other aspects of the national life, and the moderating influences at work after 1890 seemed even to point to a healing of the breach between Church and State caused by the anti-clerical laws of the 'eighties. Pope Leo XIII, a man of great perception and diplomatic ability, realized that the Church must accept modern society and adapt itself to it. Although he himself had no personal sympathy with Republicanism as such, he was anxious to avoid a breach with France, and he saw that French Catholics must accept the *status quo* in their own interests—if they sought to destroy the Republic, the Republic would probably destroy them.[13] Taking advantage of the more favourable atmosphere, the Pope turned to finding means of bringing about a *ralliement* of the Catholics to the Republican system of government. In 1890, he invited Cardinal Lavigerie, Archbishop of Algiers, to make a public pronouncement on the subject; unfortunately

Lavigerie chose his moment badly—a banquet given to mostly monarchist officers of the Mediterranean fleet—and his toast to the unification of Church and Republic was received with stupefaction. Despite this unexpected setback, the Pope persevered, and in February, 1892, the Papal encyclical *Au milieu des sollicitudes* gave an *ex cathedra* invitation to French Catholics to accept Republican institutions. In an interview which the Pope gave about the same time to a journalist of *Le Petit Journal* (the granting of such an interview was itself a sensational event) he said: "Every man may keep his personal preferences; but in the realm of action, there is only the government which France has chosen for herself. The Republic is as legitimate a form of government as any other. . . ." These utterances provoked a serious split in the Catholic ranks. Catholics asked if this was a spiritual matter in which Papal Infallibility must be obeyed, or a temporal matter of allegiance outside the Pope's jurisdiction. Nevertheless it is a duty for Catholics to receive Papal directives as advice needing humble consideration, and many members of the Church did obey the call. However, broadly speaking, the monarchists remained unmoved by it, and the extreme nationalism of the Right-wing groups was suspicious of the intervention of an Italian in French domestic politics. The essential predicament for the Catholics was—how could they vote Republican and yet reconcile past Republican legislation with their consciences? The Left-wing groups likewise were suspicious, and regarded the Pope's move as an attempt to block further anti-clerical legislation by the creation of a Catholic conservative party as a bulwark against the irreligion of the Radicals. The *ralliement* then was misunderstood on all sides, and although it was a great attempt at a settlement of a long-standing problem, its political repercussions were surprisingly small.

## The Franco-Russian Alliance

Fascinating though these matters were to politicians and people alike in the early 'nineties, they were dwarfed by major developments in the field of foreign affairs. Since 1870, France had been in isolation; intensely preoccupied with working out her domestic problems, and unprepared for the day of revenge against Germany on the one hand, and on the other held in suspicion by the monarchies of Europe for her Republican institutions. The formation of the Triple Alliance between Germany, Austria and Italy in 1882, however, showed the dangers of isolation, and revived old fears of encirclement dating back to the sixteenth century. Into this orbit Britain might conceivably be drawn; there was scarcely a region in the world where French and British interests had not conflicted in the past and threatened to do so again at any time. Russia presented a problem to French statesmen of a rather different kind. Franco-Russian relations in the nineteenth century had on the whole been far from cordial, and as late as 1884 Russian diplomats were still decrying the Republic and its representatives as "rabble".[14] But Russia was for France a natural ally: both countries had common frontiers with the Triple Alliance powers, and the Alliance itself was a threat to each of them. Autocratic and "Holy" Russia, it is true, had good grounds for disliking democratic and anti-clerical France, but political necessity was drawing them together. The disappearance of Bismarck, and Germany's failure to renew the Reinsurance Treaty with Russia, made Russian diplomats wonder about Germany's future intentions. Financial necessity also contributed to the Franco-Russian *rapprochement*; Russia, needing money urgently to finance her rapidly developing industries and railways, gratefully accepted large loans from France after Germany had refused to co-operate. The French Government also courted Russian favour by arresting a group of Nihilists in Paris who were manufacturing bombs for use in Russia. The Russian Government, however, was in no hurry to cast itself into the arms of France, and it was not until diplomatic circles learned of the renewal of the Triple Alliance in May, 1891, that Giers, the Tsar's Foreign Minister, broached the subject of a Franco-Russian *entente* to Laboulaye, the French Ambassador in St. Petersburg. That Russia had taken the initiative in suggesting talks was highly gratifying to the French Government. Ribot, the then occupant of the Quai d'Orsay, immediately drew up a draft agreement for transmission to Giers. While these negotiations were in progress, a French naval squadron paid a visit to Kronstadt, where it was warmly welcomed; the Tsar was much impressed by the smartness and efficiency of what he saw. The cordiality of the Russian reception touched off a wave of enthusiasm in France for all things Russian; but as yet there was no question of an alliance, merely of an *entente*, by which the two governments agreed to consult each other on matters relevant to the preservation of peace, and on measures to be taken if either party were threatened by aggression. This vague and unsatisfactory arrangement could only be fully effective if completed by a military convention. After prolonged hesitations, the Franco-Russian Alliance in its final form embodying such a convention was signed in January, 1894; by it, France and Russia agreed to intervene on each other's behalf in the event of either being attacked by Germany, or by Austria or Italy supported by Germany. They further agreed that the treaty should remain in force as long as the Triple Alliance. Although the treaty was theoretically secret, its broad outlines were soon made known; its effect was to bring France out of her diplomatic isolation and to free her from the oppressing and strangulating sense of inferiority and insecurity which had beset her since her defeat. Nevertheless, though the treaty was welcomed almost without exception in the France of 1894, posterity has legitimately questioned the wisdom of the Alliance in dividing the continent of Europe into two armed camps. French opinion did not foresee that France would now be committed to the defence of Russian interests in the Balkans against Austria: the crisis of 1914 was still a long way off. Meanwhile visible signs of the new friendship between the two countries in the form of visits by the Tsar to Paris in 1896 and by President Faure to St. Petersburg in 1897 gave a tonic to French morale and pleasanter things to envisage than the muddy waters of domestic politics.

## THE PANAMA AFFAIR

In the mid-'nineties these waters were muddy indeed. The Wilson case had only recently shown the seamy side of politics to a scandalized public, but the unpleasant disclosures of 1887 were to pale into insignificance in comparison with the Panama Scandal. The project of cutting a canal through the isthmus of Central America was far from new: the versatile Napoleon III in his solitary confinement at Ham—long before he even became President of the Second Republic—had interested himself in the possibility of constructing such a canal in Nicaragua. But in 1880, at seventy-five years of age, the distinguished French engineer de Lesseps, the triumphant conqueror of Suez, had founded a company with a capital of three hundred million francs to start work on a canal linking the Atlantic with the Pacific at the narrowest point. Geography and climate conspired against the Company from the start, and a succession of loans, including a State-licensed lottery destined to supplement the already vanishing original capital, failed to bring in sufficient new shareholders to save the organization from ruin. At the beginning of 1889, the Company was forced to go into liquidation, by which date middle-class investment in its shares totalled some 1,335 million francs. Petitions addressed by the frightened shareholders to the Government appealing for official intervention presented politicians with a potential election issue of some gravity. Deputies, thinking primarily of the uproar in their constituencies, chose to hunt down the people responsible for the failure rather than take a long-term view of the national interest by subsidizing what might have been an extremely profitable enterprise for France. In the summer of 1892, proceedings were set on foot against the principal directors of the Company—among them de Lesseps himself and his son, together with the celebrated Eiffel, who was alleged to have demanded exorbitant fees for his work as contractor—for having obtained money under false pretences and for malversation of funds. Public indignation was already high enough, but the flames were now fanned by the appearance of a series of sensational articles in Drumont's paper *La Libre Parole* accusing members of both Houses of having taken bribes from the Company to vote one of the loans. The intermediary was stated to be a certain Jewish financier, Reinach, in association with another shady character Cornelius Herz, who with the assurance of an accomplished blackmailer had a hold over Reinach and a group of some hundred Members of Parliament. Drumont was well known as the author of a substantial work *La France Juive*, which was little more than a violent attack against the Jews, and especially against Jewish finance. These anti-Semitic tendencies were kept alive in *La Libre Parole* which reminded the public of the part the Rothschilds had played in the crash of the Union Générale

Bank, and of the dangers to the French way of life of the continued unchecked immigration into France of refugee Jews from eastern Europe. Drumont, then, as the self-appointed defender of society and yet another apostle of nationalism, felt it his duty to expose the machinations of Reinach and Herz. Reinach committed suicide, Herz fled to England; three of the directors of the Panama Company were imprisoned. Press and Parliament alike demanded the exposure of the guilty Deputies; in a stormy debate, Clemenceau, who counted Herz among the shareholders of his paper *La Justice*, was implicated. The scandal continued to rage until the spring of 1893, when the sentences on the Panama directors were quashed, and only one of the several accused Deputies was condemned. Though the affair petered out, there had been so much mud-slinging that inevitably some of it stuck. Prudently, many prominent politicians decided to lie low for a time—among them Clemenceau, defeated in the 1893 elections. The effects of the scandal were considerable, however; a wave of apprehension passed over the nation with regard to finance and big business; the anti-Semitic movement gathered strength; politicians—particularly among the centre groups most affected by the disclosures—began to lose the confidence of their electors. Yet a new generation arose upon the debris of shattered reputations, and brought to the fore men of such distinction as Poincaré, Delcassé, Millerand, Barthou, Deschanel, men who had been untainted by Panama and consequently were not suspect to the public.

## POLITICAL UNREST

The elections of 1893 showed a striking decline in conservative representation (about 100 seats instead of 210 as in 1889), and as striking an increase in the number of Radical and Socialist seats (the Socialists more than trebled their number of Deputies). These parliamentary changes reflected the *temps difficiles*, as this period is sometimes called. From March, 1890, until June, 1899, there was a succession of fourteen different Cabinets, though the ministerial personnel changed but little. This constant rise and fall of governments prevented serious and coherent legislation, and certainly no Cabinet had the courage, until the great Waldeck-Rousseua ministry (1899–1902), to tackle major social reforms. In such conditions it was natural that movements such as Socialism, which sought to sweep away the domination of the bourgeoisie, should flourish; that trade unionism, legalized only in 1884, with its endeavours to improve working conditions and to obtain fair play for the working class, should likewise develop rapidly. But it was also the age of Anarchism, with its defence of violence, extreme internationalism and aim of destroying the State in order to obtain a free association of individuals aware of their rights and duties. The Anarchists worked by methods of exhibitionism, the use of methods destined to draw public attention to itself—sabotage, desertion, bomb throwing, passive resistance. On 6th December, 1893, a bomb was thrown by an Anarchist into the Chamber of Deputies, wounding one member. This outrage led the Government to bring in a bill making the propagation of Anarchism a crime, extending the ordinary criminal law to Anarchists, and exerting stricter control over the manufacture of explosives. These are the famous *lois scélérates*, which caused such an outcry in extreme Left-wing circles. The Anarchists, however, were far from suppressed, and in June, 1894, the President of the Republic was assassinated by one of their number at Lyons. Carnot was succeeded by Casimir-Périer, a conservative, destined to occupy the Elysée for only six months.

## L'Affaire Dreyfus

On top of these disorders came the greatest and most shattering of the scandals to be disclosed during the Third Republic—the Dreyfus case, or *"the* Affair"*, as it soon came to be known. Towards the end of September, 1894, the Intelligence branch of the War Office discovered that certain important military information was leaking through to the German Embassy in Paris. A crumpled scrap of paper—the *bordereau*—retrieved from a wastepaper basket by a charwoman at the Embassy, started a train of events and crises which was to unfold with increasing complexity over a period of five years until it dominated the entire political scene and produced effects of incalculable significance. The information contained in the *bordereau* was such that it could have been given only by a highly-qualified officer of artillery. By a process of elimination, the guilt appeared to fall on Captain Alfred Dreyfus, who, as well as being disliked by many of his superiors, was doubly unfortunate—and suspect—in view of the anti-Semitic climate of the time by reason of his Jewish faith. Dreyfus's handwriting was compared with that of the *bordereau*, was pronounced identical, and Dreyfus himself was placed under arrest. The Press, seizing upon what little evidence was available, clamoured for Dreyfus's execution; the Minister of War, General Mercier, anxious to hush up the business as rapidly as possible for reasons of security and military prestige, sanctioned his trial by secret court martial. On 22nd December, by a unanimous vote, Dreyfus, as well as having to endure the bitter humiliation of military degradation, was sentenced to deportation and life-imprisonment on Devil's Island. There, under appalling conditions, an innocent man was incarcerated from March, 1895, until June, 1899. But he was not forgotten. His wife and brother determined to find evidence to prove his innocence, and they were not for long to work alone. In July, 1895, the direction of the counter-espionage department at the War Office was placed in the hands of Colonel Picquart, who, like Dreyfus, was an Alsatian, but although present at Dreyfus's trial and being in possession of the documents on the basis of which Dreyfus had been condemned, he was at this stage, like the majority of the nation, satisfied with the verdict. However, in March, 1896, a fresh discovery was made, indicating that the leakages of information were still going on, and Picquart, his curiosity aroused, seeing that the new document proceeded from the same source as the *bordereau*, studied the Dreyfus files and became convinced that Dreyfus had been condemned in error, and that the guilty party was a certain Major Esterhazy, whose military record was far from good, whose private life appeared to be one of debauchery, and who was always short of money (here was the motive lacking from the accusation of Dreyfus). The further Picquart investigated, the more the evidence seemed to point to Esterhazy. When Picquart reported his discovery to his superior officers, they were very alarmed. Rather than endure the uproar and recriminations which a second court martial would produce, they preferred to dispose of Esterhazy quietly and refrain from reopening the Dreyfus case at all. Picquart refused to connive at this piece of

I*

injustice, and, becoming an embarrassment to his superiors for his persistent and continued investigations, was sent away from Paris. Before his departure, he confided in his immediate subordinate Major Henry. But Henry, whose knowledge of the army had been differently and more painfully acquired than Picquart's, was well aware of the fact that one has nothing to gain by making oneself a nuisance to one's superiors.[15] It has, however, been pointed out in fairness to Picquart's commanding officers that his desire to reopen the Dreyfus case was only one reason—and a comparatively unimportant one—for his removal; a better view is that there was in existence no concrete evidence on which Esterhazy could be condemned, and in the meantime sufficiently incriminating evidence must be found.[16] Henry now decided that in the interests of the prestige of the intelligence branch the Dreyfus part of the affair must be kept closed, and in order to establish conclusively the guilt of Dreyfus forged a document (the *faux Henry*) which he inserted in the Dreyfus dossier.

## THE GROWTH OF "REVISIONISM"

Meanwhile Dreyfus's brother had been carrying on his investigations, and endeavoured to interest individual Members of Parliament in the possibility of revision, but with very little success. It was essential for the small band of Dreyfusists to obtain influential support, and early in 1897 they found it in Scheurer-Kestner, yet another Alsatian, and vice-president of the Senate. Public opinion, the Press and the Government, however, were interested only in heaping abuse upon the Dreyfusists (a common charge being that they were in the pay of the Jews), and wild rumours and fantastic fabrications about Dreyfus's treasonable activities were eagerly swallowed up. The Government's attitude to Dreyfus was to rest upon the principle of the *res judicata*—Dreyfus had been found guilty, and the sentence must stand in the absence of conclusive contradictory evidence. The Dreyfusists, now possessed of Picquart's suspicions of Esterhazy, felt themselves strong enough to bring a charge against Esterhazy, who in his turn was court martialled in January, 1898, and acquitted, now having taken on the halo of "martyr of the Jews". The day after the acquittal, Picquart was arrested. The work of the

Dreyfusists thus appeared to have been in vain. But fresh developments rapidly followed; on 13th January, the newspaper *L'Aurore* carried Zola's open letter to the President of the Republic under the inspired headline *J'accuse*. The intervention of Zola had the effect of transferring the affair to another plane, of raising it from the gutter-press and scandalmongers to make it a matter of concern to the intellectuals, a matter of abstract principles. Zola was not popular, his novels had had merely a *succès de scandale*, but the very stridency of his voice compelled attention. He accused the War Office of deliberately suppressing evidence proving the innocence of Dreyfus, and of having given instructions to the court martial to acquit Esterhazy. Yet by no means all the *intelligentsia* were behind Zola; although men like Anatole France, Marcel Proust, and the painter Monet signed a petition for the revision of the Dreyfus case, others, including Barrès, Degas, Brunetière, stood on the opposite side. The working class was not interested in a case the complexity of which they could not fully understand, and the parliamentary Socialists, at least in 1898, decided to keep out of a quarrel in which their enemies, the bourgeoisie, the army, and the clericals (who had come out against Dreyfus) were split into rival groups tearing themselves to pieces. These unedifying and undignified squabbles went on throughout the spring of 1898. Picquart, tried, was found guilty of infraction of discipline; Zola's long trial for slander ended with the imposition of the maximum penalty—twelve months' imprisonment and a heavy fine. However disappointing to the Dreyfusists the outcome of the Zola trial might have been, it had at least made possible certain fresh deductions, notably that at the original court martial the judges had seen documents not available to the defence, and that under the cloak of secrecy for reasons of military security much was being deliberately concealed. Private feuds, even duels, were provoked; reprisals against the Dreyfusists led to censures and dismissals. The defeat of Méline's Government in June, 1898, on a technicality paved the way for a predominantly Radical Cabinet under Brisson, in which the War Ministry was given to the popular anti-revisionist Cavaignac, who at once decided to cut through the tangled threads of the Dreyfus case by proving the guilt of both Dreyfus and Esterhazy, whom he believed to have collaborated. On 7th July Cavaignac spoke in the Chamber, asserting the guilt of Dreyfus on the basis of the *faux Henry*, and claiming that Esterhazy, as the undoubted author of the *bordereau*, had been wrongfully acquitted. The Deputies, feeling that at last everything was crystal clear, gave Cavaignac an ovation. Esterhazy was therefore again arrested, together with Picquart, who had incurred the Government's displeasure by writing an open letter to Brisson stating that Cavaignac in his speech to the Chamber had quoted documents irrelevant to Dreyfus, and that one of them appeared to be a forgery. Meanwhile, independent investigations at the War Office on the *faux Henry* showed that it was indeed quite clearly a forgery; Henry, interrogated by Cavaignac—now exasperated by the humiliating discovery that he had publicly asserted the truth of a forged document—confessed, and committed suicide in the fortress of Mont-Valérien in which he had been imprisoned. Esterhazy, dismissed from the service, fled to England; Cavaignac, still obstinately convinced of Dreyfus's guilt, resigned.

## DISORDERS IN 1899

These sensational developments at last gave the supporters of Dreyfus hope that permission to appeal for a retrial might be forthcoming, and in September Mme Dreyfus's application for revision reached the Court of Cassation. While the Court's investigations were still proceeding, the President of the Republic—Félix Faure—died suddenly in circumstances sufficiently mysterious to set on foot a new wave of scandal and rumour. Although the official version stated that Faure's death was caused by a stroke, public opinion was openly sceptical, and the readers of *La Libre Parole* were even led to suspect murder. The election of the new President, Emile Loubet, on 18th February, 1899, encouraged the Dreyfusists, since he was known to favour revision, and was not "Conservatively-minded". There was therefore great excitement early in 1899, which was intensified by a Nationalist attempt under the bitter opponent of the Dreyfusists, Déroulède, to provoke a *coup d'état* by appealing to the troops returning from Faure's state funeral. Déroulède, supported though he was by the Royalists and inspired by the tradition of Boulanger, was surprisingly acquitted by the Assize Court in May, but this news was immediately overshadowed by the decision of the Court of Cassation to quash the 1894 verdict on Dreyfus and order a fresh court martial. The fury of the anti-revisionists was unpleasantly demonstrated by a personal assault on President Loubet at the Auteuil races. The Cabinet was forced to resign on a charge of having failed to protect the President. The task of forming a new Government in this crisis, with the retrial of Dreyfus about to begin, was an unenviable one, and Poincaré having failed, Loubet summoned R. Waldeck-Rousseau (1846–1904), a prominent lawyer of unquestioned honesty and great energy, who was to give France her longest period of continuous government during the entire course of the Third Republic—thirty-five months. Since the defeat of Ferry in 1885, Waldeck had taken no active part in politics, seldom even speaking in the Senate's debates, but his high sense of duty, his impartiality and his lack of fanaticism made him an ideal choice. His Cabinet, as it will be necessary to recall later, was a galaxy of talent, yet it was only given Parliament's confidence by a majority of twenty-five votes, uncomfortably small by French standards.

## THE SECOND TRIAL AND REHABILITATION OF DREYFUS

Dreyfus, then, was fetched from Devil's Island and brought to Rennes, where his second court martial began on 7th August. Doubts have been expressed about his physical fitness to stand trial so soon; he certainly knew practically nothing of what had been going on in his absence. His two counsel disagreed on the conduct of the case; the usual wild rumours were circulated, including one that General Mercier had in his possession a copy of the *bordereau* annotated by the German Emperor, while the over-confidence of Dreyfus's friends that an acquittal was certain and the fact that by this time the whole world's interest was focused on that classroom in the Lycée de Rennes—all these things cast an entirely different atmosphere over the second trial. The same old stories were retold with embellishments, the accumulation of fact and fiction which had been amassed in the trials of Esterhazy, Zola, Picquart and in the Court of Cassation; the same old familiar figures reappeared. The hearings dragged on interminably, and it was not until 9th September that the verdict was given—guilty by a majority of five votes to two, but with extenuating circumstances. The penalty was ten years' detention. It was the generally expected verdict, at least in official circles, but it produced an upsurge of anti-French feeling in the press of western Europe. To put an end to what might easily become an everlasting series of appeals and retrials, Waldeck-Rousseau wisely persuaded President Loubet to grant Dreyfus a pardon and cancel the order for his degradation. Not until 1906 however was the Affair finally settled, when the Court of Cassation quashed the Rennes verdict, and Parliament passed bills reinstating both Dreyfus and Picquart, who were promoted in rank, Dreyfus being given, in addition, the fourth grade of the Legion of Honour.

## SIGNIFICANCE OF THE CASE

The Dreyfus case was from first to last a conflict of principles, which was made the opportunity for political intrigue. The anti-Semitic aspect has been much exaggerated; despite the ravings of Drumont, the fact that Dreyfus was a Jew had little or nothing to do with the misfortunes he underwent. The great majority of the Jewish community in France showed no inclination to spring to Dreyfus's defence. Though military justice was shown up, those officers who testified against Dreyfus honestly believed they had found a traitor, and that the interests of the Army and the State should be placed above the individual. Even Henry, it has been claimed, had his own conception of loyalty.[17] Those who emerged least creditably from the affair were the professional politicians, who until 1898–99 were satisfied that justice had been done, and after the pardon of 1899 assumed an air of virtue and wisdom after the event. "It is only by examining the case in detail," writes Guy Chapman, "that a picture emerges, not of virtue at grips with villainy, but of fallible human beings pulled this way and that by their beliefs, their loyalties, their prejudices, their ambitions, and their ignorance."[18] The eventual victory of Dreyfus's supporters had political consequences far greater than could have been foreseen by the early fighters in his cause, and much of the history of the first decade of the twentieth century is unfolded in an atmosphere of aftermath.

## WALDECK-ROUSSEAU'S CABINET

The success of Waldeck-Rousseau's ministry is due to two factors: it had a policy, and it had outstanding leadership in capable hands. The retention of Delcassé at the Quai d'Orsay, and the appointment of Caillaux at the Ministry of Finance brought into the Cabinet men of great ability and energy. Waldeck-Rousseau himself held the Ministry of the Interior, and by giving the War Office to General de Galliffet— unpopular though he was with the Left for the part he had played in the suppression of the Commune—Waldeck entrusted a key ministry to a man with sufficient authority and prestige to maintain military unity and discipline when this was most needed. But the most controversial appointment was that of the Socialist Millerand to the Ministry of Commerce: it was the first time that a Socialist had ever taken office in any Cabinet. Waldeck's aim was to create as broadly based a government as possible, and although Millerand's appoint- ment caused many Socialists to question the propriety of his accepting office in a "bourgeois" Cabinet, it did at least recog- nize the importance of the Socialist group in Parliament. A precedent was created, but it was based on the necessity of Socialist support for the reforms which Waldeck-Rousseau hoped to introduce. The orientation of government forces thus shifts Leftwards, and the policy of "*Pas d'ennemis à gauche*" was inaugurated.

Waldeck's first task was to restore order and confidence in the régime. By prosecuting Déroulède and his associates for fomenting riots and disorders in 1899 the Government showed that it intended to be firm; by passing an amnesty bill covering minor crimes connected with the Dreyfus case it showed leniency and a desire to liquidate the affair completely. The Paris Exhibition of 1900 demonstrated to the nation that after all it had much to be thankful for. Reforms in the high command and the transference of the power of promotion to the War Minister indicated the Government's intention to strengthen its political hold over the army. It was, however, in religious affairs that the Waldeck-Rousseau ministry made its strongest mark. Waldeck himself, a Republican with the Republican's characteristic secular outlook, though no adversary of the Catholic Church as a moral force, had seen with alarm the intervention of the Assumptionist order on behalf of Nationalist candidates in recent electoral campaigns. Certain sections of the Church had been closely concerned in the Dreyfus case because most of Dreyfus's adversaries had belonged to the aristocracy and army, which had long traditional connexions with Catholicism; the behaviour of these Catholics gave definite proof that Leo XIII's policy of *ralliement* had failed. In the eyes of many Republicans, the clergy had again shown their hostility to liberalism and democracy. Waldeck therefore determined to limit the power of the religious orders and submit them to Republican law. In 1900, the Government decreed the dissolution of the Assumptionists on the pretext that they had broken an article in the Penal Code which forebade associations of more than twenty people without official authorization. In the following year, the Law of Associations laid down that all religious orders must apply for authorization within three months, and although the principle of freedom to form societies was openly proclaimed, those composed of foreigners or with headquarters abroad were forbidden. In addition, all members of unauthorized congregations were prevented from joining the teaching staff of any establishment.

## RETURN OF ANTI-CLERICAL LEGISLATION

The elections of 1902 reinforced the anti-clerical majority in Parliament, and brought a much more aggressive spirit into legislation. Waldeck-Rousseau, a sick and tired man, resigned, and recommended the appointment of J. L. E. Combes as his successor—an error of judgment, since Combes was to betray Waldeck's intentions, which had been essentially moderate and cautious. By 1902 the Republican programme had changed but little, and still rested upon three fundamental points—an attack upon the religious orders or *congrégations*, educational reform, and the separation of Church and State. Although Ferry had expelled the congregations, subsequent governments had tacitly allowed them to return; the Church had been excluded from public schools, but there was no check on private education, and the idea of separation had been abandoned as impracticable. Combes, however, was a man with an *idée fixe*. Originally destined for the Church, he had taken up medicine, and later entered politics as a Radical. The extreme Catholicism of his early years veered round to an extreme anti-clericalism, and his Cabinet was supported by the Socialists and Radical-Socialists who believed that the Church, as the bulwark of capitalism, was a major obstacle preventing the establishment of true democracy. Combes began by a strict application of the law of 1901, closing all schools of congregations which did not apply for authorization. Bishops who protested against this arbitrary closure found that the Government had stopped their stipends. All further demands for authorization were refused, and the same principles were applied to the preaching as to the teaching orders. Throughout 1903 there was intense agitation in the country, with many local incidents even involving bloodshed. Members of the armed forces were forbidden to belong to religious organizations and the clergy were prevented from taking higher degrees at the universities. By October, 1903, more than ten thousand schools had been closed, but there were still about eight thousand under the control of the authorized congregations. In order, therefore, to complete the work of excluding the congregations from teaching altogether, the law of 7th July, 1904, was passed, by which all schools under the direction of religious orders must close within a period of ten years, and the teaching orders were to be dissolved. The property of these dissolved congregations was confiscated by the State and later sold to private individuals. Having thus got rid of the congregations and closed their schools, it only remained to separate Church and State, to put the State on a completely lay footing.

## BREACH WITH THE VATICAN: THE SEPARATION OF CHURCH AND STATE

The election of Pope Pius X in August, 1903, brought about an immediate change in the tone of French relations with the Vatican. Unlike the moderate and tactful Leo XIII, Pius X was intransigent and authoritarian, believing that the Church's political actions should show no consideration for the régime. A series of crises arose in 1902 and 1903 over the nomination of bishops and the wording of Papal bulls instituting the bishops nominated by the Government. It had become the practice for the Government to inform the Papal nuncio in Paris in advance of the nominees they intended to propose for vacant sees, but with the advent of Combes, the Government showed that they intended to choose their candidates without consulting Rome—a clear breach of the Concordat and a century's tradition. Deadlock was reached over a very unsuitable nomination to the bishopric of Ajaccio, and this was made worse by the development of a fresh diplomatic storm caused by the exchange of state visits between the King of Italy and President Loubet. The Papacy since 1870 had been unable to tolerate visits from the heads of Catholic states to Rome, since this implied acceptance of the Italian annexation of Rome. Although Delcassé had nothing but scorn for the fanaticism of his colleagues in religious matters, he was of the opinion that these visits were necessary to cement the Franco-Italian *entente* which he had recently engineered. As a result of the uproar in the Press and the diplomatic protests which the visits produced, the French ambassador was withdrawn from the Vatican, and in 1904 diplomatic relations between Paris and the Papal Court were finally severed after a further dispute concerning the Pope's desire to dismiss the Bishops of Laval and Dijon. By this date, the Concordat had plainly become, as a French historian has aptly said, nothing more than a *dis*cordat, but very few Catholics looked favourably upon the idea of separation; the force of tradition and the organization of family life were not easily broken, and the financial jeopardy in which the Church would be placed, standing as it did to lose an annual income of some 35 million francs from the State, could not be envisaged without grave concern. However, in 1903 the Government had set up a committee under the brilliant young Socialist lawyer Aristide Briand (1862–1932), to investigate the possibility of a separation, though before the committee was ready to report the Combes administration came under heavy fire from both Left and Right in the Chamber, the Left accusing Combes of concentrating exclusively upon religious reform at the expense of social reform, the Right seeking to precipitate a crisis immediately by forcing the Government to bring in a bill. By the beginning of 1905, Combes' parliamentary majority had dwindled almost to nothing owing to this general feeling of disgust with his obsessional policy. After his resignation the task of completing the work of separation fell to the new Minister of Public Worship, Bienvenu-Martin, although the hand of Briand is everywhere to be seen in the final settlement. Briand had no deep knowledge of the Church, but he was anxious to make the separation an act of neutrality, not an act of oppression, seeking not to destroy Catholicism but to get rid of an encumbrance upon the State. The Government, by bringing in this act, was placed in a most paradoxical position: it claimed to be legislating in the interests of the Church at a time when France was not represented at the Papal Court, and it was committing itself to the unilateral breach of a treaty, the Concordat. Nevertheless, on 9th December, 1905, Parliament passed the Law of Separation by a majority of 108 votes.

Henceforth, the Republic ceased to recognize or give salaries or subsidies to any religion, Catholic, Protestant, or Jewish. While the freedom of worship was guaranteed, the State refused to give official precedence to ecclesiastical dignitaries or to nominate bishops. Church property and revenues were to be handed over to *associations cultuelles* consisting of members chosen from among the laity of the parishes, whose duty it was to maintain religious services. This law brought up many complex legal problems beyond public comprehension, but at the same time it conferred immense benefits on both parties which were not fully realized at the time. It gave Catholics complete freedom to meet in national and regional councils, freedom of speech and writing without fear of reprisals from the Government, freedom to choose their own dignitaries; from now onwards the Vatican nominated bishops without State interference. But it was freedom at a price; the clergy lost prestige and precedence, as well as the greater part of its regular annual income. The great question was: what attitude would the Church take to this law? If Catholics refused to form the *associations*, the Church would lose to the State a vast amount of property as well as the privilege of using its buildings. Yet in condemning the *associations*, the Church accepted this risk. The *associations* were in fact never formed on this pattern, and not until 1924 did the Pope finally agree to the establishment of *associations diocésaines* with a roughly similar function. The State, however, in 1906 showed great moderation in the application of the law, and even the formality of taking inventories of Church property was carried through without serious disorders. The priest was allowed to remain unmolested in his church, and thanks largely to the diplomatic skill and legal knowledge of Briand, to whom it fell to put his own law into operation, Church assets were transferred in 1908 to ecclesiastical friendly societies and super-annuation funds in the absence of *associations*. To protect church fabrics from falling into disrepair, the Government passed a law which brought all churches built before 1800 (which were therefore presumed to have some architectural merit) under the care of the Ministry of Beaux-Arts. Church finances generally profited considerably from legacies and appeals to the wealthy, but the ultimate effect of this was merely to strengthen and confirm working-class suspicions that the Church was hand in glove with the capitalists. In prosperous dioceses such as Paris it was even possible to build several new churches between 1906 and 1914. Nevertheless, these improvements were slow to show themselves, and were by no means universal; the poverty of the parish priest, already serious enough before 1905, became extreme in many districts. The Church as a career ceased to be attractive, particularly to the lower classes who in the past had often sought social advancement through the priesthood, but although recruitment to the clergy fell off rapidly, the quality of ordinands was higher. The social composition of the clergy began to change, as more men from middle-class urban families presented themselves, men of real vocation with no thought of financial gain or social prestige.

## THE CHURCH AND SOCIAL REFORM

The late nineteenth century's increasing awareness of the "social problem" was also reflected within the Catholic Church. The modern Christian-Democrat movement was born out of the Church's work in fighting against the material and moral misery of the working classes produced by the Industrial Revolution and a *laissez-faire* economy. This work originally expressed itself in two ways; on the one hand in

*L'Oeuvre des cercles*—a paternalist organization which called upon the wealthier members of society to form associations of workers around a church—and on the other in the work of the so-called *abbés démocrates*, who, following the recommendation of Leo XIII's Encyclical *Rerum Novarum*, were inspired to carry the gospel to the workers and to mix more freely with them in their own surroundings. *L'Oeuvre des cercles* did pioneer work in study groups and in propaganda for the limitation of working hours, retirement pensions, accident insurance and privileges for expectant mothers. Yet the *cercles* failed, since employers regarded their industrial ideas as too revolutionary, and the workers themselves resented the patronage of the wealthy. The *abbés démocrates* likewise scandalized conventional Catholic opinion, and offended employers who were horrified to find priests speaking to workers of their rights and not of their duties. Both these movements, however, lacked coherent leadership, and relied upon a sentimental approach which was unsuited to the gravity of the problems. They are nevertheless important in that they sought a solution to social discontent by avoiding the provocation of class-hatred. It was not until the early twentieth century that there was any real movement by Catholic workers to form their own trade unions, and although by 1913 there was a national federation of Catholic unions, the religious basis of these groups aroused the hostility of the C.G.T., chiefly because it had the effect of breaking working-class solidarity.

The *Sillon* was a Catholic organization of a different type; conceived originally with the aim of stressing the need for a spiritual revival, it was swept away by the fervour of its leaders into the political field and the stormy scenes preceding the separation of Church and State. But its advocacy of unpopular measures—such as its defence of conscientious objection and its attacks against the repressive Tsarist régime in Russia—prevented its members from gaining parliamentary support for the social reforms in which they were most interested, and exposed the movement to the censures of the Catholic hierarchy. Despite this opposition, the *Sillon* had a considerable following, especially among the student population and bourgeois intellectuals, many of whom preferred its spirituality to the dogmatism and discipline of *L'Action française* whose recruits were also largely drawn from middle-class Catholic circles.

## THE PERSONALITY AND POLICY OF DELCASSE

While such tremendous changes were taking place in the traditional religious structure of France, equally significant developments were occurring in foreign affairs. From June, 1898, until June, 1905, the post of Foreign Minister was held by Théophile Delcassé (1852–1923), in five successive governments, and this remarkable continuity in office of a most remarkable statesman at a time of great stress consolidated France's position in Europe, and completed the work which the Franco-Russian Alliance of 1894 had begun. Delcassé was a southerner, from a small town in the foothills of the Pyrenees. He had none of the training which made the traditional diplomat; he came of a middle-class family, was a mediocre student, a poor speaker, and a man of insignificant appearance. Like many of his colleagues, he came to politics through journalism, but his early engagement on the staff of Gambetta's paper *La République Française* was the decisive act in his career. He was from the first an ardent disciple of Gambetta, many of whose ideas on foreign policy he was later to put into practice. He soon specialized in writing articles on foreign and colonial affairs, and as early as the 'eighties he showed a profound understanding of European diplomacy and the part played in it by Bismarck. He entered the Chamber in 1889 as a Radical, but he really belonged to no definite political group, a fact which ensured his subsequent availablity to any Republican ministry. His first portfolio was the Colonial Office in Dupuy's short ministry (1894–95), and it was in fact Delcassé who was responsible for the creation of a separate colonial department in premises of its own away from the Ministry of Marine where it had previously been housed. Out of his preoccupations as Colonial Minister logically arose his interest in diplomacy, but he was also much concerned with the state of the French navy. Much later in his career (1911–12) he became a very successful Minister of Marine, and his work in this capacity will be referred to in its place; meanwhile his thoughts dwelt upon the greatness of the British fleet and the advantages which the support of British sea-power would confer upon France.

His speeches in the Chamber showed a very friendly tone towards England at a time when Franco-British rivalry in Africa and Asia was at its height, but in his desire to come to an understanding with Britain based on the peaceful settlement of outstanding disputes he had no intention of allowing French interests to be overridden, and he always remembered Gambetta's remark that the English respect as allies only those who make themselves respected.

## DELCASSÉ AND ITALY

An *entente* with Britain, however, was only one of several aims which he set out to realize when he accepted Brisson's offer of the Foreign Ministry in June, 1898. His theory of diplomacy revolved around the principle of *ententes* between nations rather than fixed alliances, which he regarded as too rigid and circumscribed; nevertheless the alliance between France and Russia remained the basis of his foreign policy, and to strengthen it further in the face of German pressure was his prime ambition. He saw that Bismarck's greatest success had been the establishment of a European balance of power in which Germany occupied the most important place; around Germany European diplomacy had revolved since 1871, and to Delcassé any understanding between France and Germany based on French acceptance of the German occupation of Alsace-Lorraine was impossible. In order to weaken the power of the Triple Alliance, he set out to cultivate the friendship of Italy. Franco-Italian relations had been strained for many years; the Italians were distrustful of the French Catholic's support for the restoration of the Pope's temporal rights, and they had also never reconciled themselves to Ferry's occupation of Tunisia. The anti-French policy of Crispi had plunged Italy into an exhausting tariff war with France, and a long period of economic rivalry in the Mediterranean. Delcassé was helped in his task of bringing about a *rapprochement* with Italy by his friend and former associate on the staff of *La République Française,* Barrère, then French Ambassador at Rome. In November, 1898, a commercial treaty was signed which put an end to the tariff war, and in 1900 a secret agreement gave Italy a free hand in Tripolitania in exchange for Italian recognition of Morocco as a French sphere of influence. Two years later, when renewing her obligations under the Triple Alliance, Italy refused to participate in any aggressive moves directed against France. The Italian fleet visited Toulon in 1901, and state visits were exchanged between King Victor Emmanuel III and President Loubet, but this atmosphere of cordiality was only achieved at a price—the rupture of diplomatic relations with the Vatican. Delcassé's policy was, however, justified when, in 1914, Italy did not intervene in the war on behalf of the Central Powers.

By his skilful mediation in the Spanish-American War of 1898, Delcassé won the respect and confidence of both Spanish and United States Governments. The improvement of relations with Spain led to the conclusion of a treaty in 1902 dividing Morocco into French and Spanish spheres of influence which, however, owing to British objections, was never ratified in its original form. In 1899 Delcassé visited Russia and obtained a signed agreement extending the scope of the military convention between the two countries. From this date onwards, the French and Russian Governments consulted each other continuously; France lent Russia substantial sums of money to construct strategic railways which might hasten the mobilization of troops on her western frontier, and in 1902 the Alliance was extended to Far Eastern affairs in the event of an attack upon the integrity of China. These moves, which demonstrate the personal influence Delcassé had acquired over the Tsar, had the effect of fully transforming the 1894 Alliance, making it an effective diplomatic instrument. There now only remained for the complete attainment of Delcassé's immediate objectives the *rapprochement* with Britain, and, if possible, to induce Britain and Russia to settle their differences on the *entente* principle. Such a Triple Entente was to crown the edifice of his work, and until it was achieved he had no desire to lay down the reins of office. But when he came to the Quai d'Orsay, relations between France and Britain could scarcely have been worse, and he was immediately confronted with a major crisis which needed all his patience and tact to solve.

## FRANCO-BRITISH RIVALRY

The main cause of this friction was the "scramble for Africa", though elsewhere in the world, notably in the Far

East, French and British interests were in constant conflict. Despite the Tonkin fiasco and the general lack of public understanding at home, French colonial enterprises had expanded with great rapidity. The exploration of Indo-China under Pavie and the proclamation of the Union of Indo-China in 1887, together with a systematic pacification of the country and a spectacular improvement in its economic position, gave France a colony of immense size and strategic importance in south-east Asia, although its value was to some extent diminished by the sporadic outbreaks of terrorism. The excessively strict repressive policy of the administrators of the colony created a gulf which widened rapidly in the years after 1914.[19] In West Africa, the upper Niger basin including the important centre of Timbuktu was conquered by 1894: the Ivory Coast and Dahomey became separate colonies, which in 1899 were integrated into a single administrative area— Afrique Occidentale Française (A.O.F.), with its capital at Dakar, and comprising five colonies and an area of some four million square kilometres, but only sparsely populated and with very little economic life. Madagascar became a colony in 1896 after a prolonged and difficult period of semi-protectorate. The appointment of Joseph Galliéni (1849–1916)—one of the great French empire-builders—as governor of Madagascar brought peace and prosperity to the colony, but only after the application of ruthless measures. French Equatorial Africa (A.E.F.) did not come into being until 1910, and it remained for long the Cinderella of French colonies, having no railways, practically no roads, and very little modern equipment, but exploration of this area had been going on since the 'seventies, and its inexorable penetration eastwards towards the Upper Nile was anxiously watched by the British Government. In March, 1895, Sir Edward Grey had affirmed in the House of Commons that the British zone of influence covered the entire Nile valley, and that any French interference in that region would be considered an unfriendly act. It was naturally of the utmost importance to France that this whole matter should be brought to a head, and it was precisely to clarify the position and to obtain some sort of understanding relative to the Upper Nile that the French Government sponsored Marchand's adventurous mission by way of the Congo and Ubangi valleys to Fashoda on the Upper Nile, which he reached with his small band of troops in July, 1898. There was no territorial motive behind Marchand's expedition; he was merely "showing the flag", and the points he occupied were destined to be abandoned later as he moved on into Abyssinia. Kitchener, fresh from his victory at Omdurman at the beginning of September, though five hundred miles to the north of Marchand, was now indisputably master of the Sudan, and as he advanced to meet Marchand later in September, the full force of the crisis broke over Paris and London. Diplomacy alone could offer France any hope of a peaceful settlement to her advantage, but Britain held all the trump cards. The Quai d'Orsay had thought that by sheer force of legal argument, Britain would be bound to give way, but the British Government had no intention of making this a legal matter; Britain would take a stand on facts, that Fashoda should be occupied by British forces in the name of Egypt and by right of conquest. Britain was rigidly uncompromising, and not disposed either to argue or bargain. The situation was as serious as it was ridiculous, and both sides were by now so deeply involved that neither could withdraw without loss of prestige. The French position was particularly grave. France, split asunder by the Dreyfus controversy, had brought herself to the brink of war with the very country whose friendship she needed above all other, and for whose sake she had already made painful sacrifices in Egypt. A France whose entire system of defences was concentrated on the frontier of Alsace-Lorraine had no chance of withstanding a war with Britain in which she would almost certainly lose her newly-won African colonies. Delcassé, however, threaded his way through the maze with a clear head. By prolonging the crisis until the last minute, he succeeded in his objective of making France respected. By persuading Dupuy to withdraw Marchand from Fashoda, he had to take the unpopular step of sacrificing French pride, but in so doing he gave Britain tangible proof of his good faith, and by sending his most able diplomat Paul Cambon as ambassador to London he underlined the gesture of goodwill. But the Convention of March, 1899, by which France undertook not to acquire territory or to exert influence east of the Upper Nile valley or Britain to the west did not clear up once and for all the whole Egyptian question; it did, however, at least prevent French infiltration into the Egyptian Sudan, thus removing the most acute cause of misunderstanding between France and Britain in Africa. The only remaining sources of friction all appeared capable of a similar peaceful settlement.

## THE ENTENTE CORDIALE

There were other factors conspiring in favour of a Franco-British *entente* after the Fashoda episode. The gradual change in British policy with regard to Germany and her increasing awareness of the dangers of isolationism played into Delcassé's hands. Furthermore, Delcassé's tenure of the Quai d'Orsay was reassuring to Britain. He appeared to be the one permanent institution in the ever-changing and bewildering world of French politics. His prestige was high in England, and his frequent speeches in the Chamber favouring an Anglo-French *rapprochement* were highly praised in the British press, as well as finding a good deal of parliamentary support in his own country. From the British point of view, the advantages of a comprehensive agreement were numerous, since an *entente* with France would entail no real sacrifices; all the traditional and serious sources of dispute had been removed either by the Belgian settlement of the eighteen-thirties or by the various colonial conventions signed in the last years of the nineteenth century in which Britain had almost always got her own way. Though Britain's power and prestige were higher than ever before, this position had only been won at the price of jealousy and suspicion, as public opinion demonstrated during the South African War. And even in 1904, before the arms race had fully begun, it was apparent that Germany had taken the place of France as the main challenger of British colonial supremacy. In July, 1902, Cambon approached Lord Lansdowne with the object of holding Anglo-French conversations about the Moroccan problem, and offering the prospect of a neutralized Tangier to safeguard Gibraltar in exchange for Britain's allowing France to "influence" the southern region of Morocco outside the Spanish Zone. The anarchy in Morocco under the Sultanate of Abd-el-Aziz had led to the provocation of frontier incidents with Algeria, but apart from her desire to suppress these incidents France had need of a dependent Morocco in order to round off her North African empire, which extended from the Niger to the Mediterranean and from the Atlantic to the borders of Egypt. France also needed to act with some celerity, because other Powers were beginning to show a disturbing interest in the domestic politics of Morocco. The visits of Edward VII to Paris and of President Loubet and Delcassé to London in 1903 helped materially in the creation of a friendlier atmosphere. On 8th April, 1904, the Anglo-French conventions were signed, to which history has given the name of the Entente Cordiale—something of a misnomer, as it was merely one of several similar *ententes* which Delcassé concluded or was instrumental in bringing about. These conventions were in no sense a formal alliance, and apart from the questions of Morocco and Egypt clarified only minor issues; old sources of dispute over fishing rights off Newfoundland, spheres of influence in Siam, Madagascar and the New Hebrides were settled, and in exchange for French recognition of British preponderance in Egypt, the British Government undertook not to impede French expansion in Morocco. There is nothing in this treaty to suggest defence or attack against any Power, nothing to suggest encirclement of Germany, nothing save a desire on both sides to suppress all causes of disagreement between them. If Germany was disturbed by it, Bülow gave no sign, but the sudden acute development of the Moroccan crisis in the following year was a warning that Germany resented her exclusion from the Franco-British conversations. Relations between France and Britain were henceforth revolutionized, and by the extremely skilful mediation of Delcassé in the Dogger Bank affair the *entente* of 1904 survived its first test within a few months of its being called into existence. The way was thus opened for a similar agreement between Britain and Russia in 1907, which completed the pattern of pre-war European diplomacy: Triple Alliance was confronted by Triple Entente. But by this date Delcassé had been driven from office; his refusal in the spring of 1905 to agree to the German demand for an international conference on Morocco, after William II's sensational appearance at Tangier, brought him into conflict with his colleagues in the Cabinet, who were alarmed at Germany's menacing attitude, and who did not share his confidence that Britain would stand by France. The resignation of Delcassé in June, 1905, marks the end of a very spectacular phase in the evolution of French foreign policy, but although he was reviled in the Chamber and the Press after his fall for the dangers into which his policy had carried France—rather as Ferry had been abused earlier—no serious attempts were made to undermine it. On the other hand, his work was strengthened in the years preceding 1914, and brought to its logical conclusion.

## TRADE UNIONISM AND INDUSTRY

At home, the first decade of the twentieth century was a turbulent and disturbed period, in which the religious struggles were merely symptomatic of a profound social discontent. The lack of unity among the various Socialist groups had prevented systematic Left-wing pressure on the Government to bring in desirable reforms, and it was not until 1905 at the Paris Congress that a united Socialist party finally emerged (the *Section Française de l'Internationale Ouvrière*). In its declaration of unity, it made few concessions to the moderate parliamentary Socialists, in reaffirming its refusal to co-operate with bourgeois governments, to vote military and colonial credits, and in continuing to proclaim the need for a class war. Many of the early doctrinal squabbles had been fought out in the unions, but in France the membership of these unions was small; despite the very rapid growth between 1900 and 1911, the average union had only 200 members, and the total membership of all the unions was not much in excess of one million by 1911.[20] Federation therefore became an essential, and the grouping of the unions into two well-organized bodies —the *Fédération des Bourses du Travail* and the more revolutionary *Confédération générale du Travail* (C.G.T.)—gave labour its first nation-wide organizations. The amalgamation of these two federations in 1902 was a great step forward, and at the Amiens Congress of the C.G.T. in 1906 the future programme of the unions was revealed. While proclaiming their lack of political affiliations, they advocated the use of the general strike and similar "direct" methods to compel the Government to introduce reforms. Already something had been done to alleviate industrial unrest. Under the inspiration of Millerand, the Waldeck-Rousseau government had in 1900 introduced a Factory Act limiting the working day to ten hours, sanitary conditions in factories had been improved, and joint councils of employers and employees set up to mediate in labour disputes. But in general France was behind both Britain and Germany in legislation of this type. The year 1906 was one of major industrial disturbances, but in the great wave of strikes which spread across the country between 1906 and 1910 organized labour was never able to effect a general strike of all workers, though at various times builders, dockers, post office staffs, electricians, civil servants, workers in the food distributive trades and vine-growers were all involved.

## STRIKES AND GOVERNMENT PARALYSIS

The Radical successes in the 1906 elections brought Clemenceau to power for the first time as Premier, with an independent Socialist, Viviani, at the new Ministry of Labour. Clemenceau, now in his sixties and with his formidable reputation as a breaker of ministries, was not a man to be intimidated by strikers. Constantly attacked by Jaurès and the parliamentary Socialists, he was obliged to rely increasingly for support upon the moderates whom he had bitterly lashed in the past. He resorted to arrests, dismissals, and the severest repressive measures, even calling out troops to deal with demonstrators, yet in spite of the unpopularity which he earned by these methods, his government survived from October, 1906, till July, 1909, only being defeated on a motion of censure introduced by Delcassé criticizing the administration for its failure to put an end to the long series of naval disasters which had cost the loss of many lives and valuable ships of war. The Briand government which succeeded Clemenceau mobilized for military service the rail strikers of 1910, and was inevitably attacked on the ground that it had suppressed the strike in order that the railway companies might profit. It is interesting to see how men such as Briand, Millerand, and Clemenceau, on coming to power, moved farther and farther away from their former political allies, the heavy burden and responsibility of office causing them to adopt a more sober and realistic attitude towards the problems of the day, and to acknowledge that doctrinaire ready-made "party" solutions were not always either practicable or economic or even desirable. The only major piece of social legislation dating from this period is the introduction by Briand of a system of old-age pensions in 1910. After the fall of Briand in 1911, there was a distressing return to the old pattern of political life, and between March, 1911, and the outbreak of war there were nine successive cabinets—the shortest surviving only two days, and the longest, that of Poincaré, twelve months. "The dissolving action of a myriad groups and committees"[21] has been blamed for this ministerial instability, and it is certainly true that the great majority of the Deputies and Senators of this period were more concerned with keeping their seats than with governing the country. The excessive conservatism of the senate, a third of which was always nine years behind the times, is another reason why so many essential reforms (for example, the introduction of income tax) never reached the statute book. Clemenceau and Briand having failed by their disciplinary tactics to awaken a new sense of responsibility and urgency among the politicians, there only remained Poincaré with sufficient moral courage to attempt the task. Raymond Poincaré (1860–1934), was indeed acceptable to all parties—to the Radicals for his long support of the principle of the secular state, to the Socialists for his desire to reform electoral procedure by the introduction of proportional representation, to the Centre groups for his hostility to income tax, while since he was a Lorrainer the Nationalists were inclined to look sympathetically upon him. But he was genuinely admired for his honesty, his sound knowledge of affairs, and his industry; he had furthermore been for many years in Parliament without making personal enemies; his legal training and his reserve, his "mind of a chartered accountant" made him another Waldeck-Rousseau. His Cabinet, which included Briand, Millerand and Delcassé, was well received, and he himself also took the vital portfolio, in these crucial times, of Foreign Minister. Though his project for parliamentary reform was rejected by the Senate, his popularity remained high in the country, and on the retirement of President Fallières early in 1913 he became an obvious choice for the Presidency.

## The Problem of Conscription

The main concern of the pre-war administration in home affairs was the question of military service. The growth of anti-militarism, to which some reference has already been made, developing in reaction against *boulangisme* and the more unpleasant aspects of military organization revealed by the Dreyfus case, was encouraged by the pacifist and internationalist leanings of French Socialism, and in 1905 a law had been passed reducing the period of compulsory service from three years to two, and much reducing expenditure on the armed forces. The series of international crises and the rapid rearmament of the other European powers since that date determined the parties of the Right with the support of Poincaré to press the Government for the return of the three years' conscription law. Despite the opposition of Jaurès and the Socialists[22] who still clung to their belief that the solidarity of the working classes would prevent a conflict between France and Germany, the new law was passed in August, 1913. The elections of May, 1914, were largely fought on the merits and demerits of this act, and the Socialist and Radicals, playing upon the increased financial burdens which a longer period of conscription would force upon the taxpayer, won a resounding victory. Poincaré, well aware of the gravity of the international situation, was determined that the law must stay, and he chose as Prime Minister, Viviani, who pledged himself to retain the law at least temporarily. It is ironical that this predominantly pacifist Chamber should within two months have found itself engaged in the conduct of the First World War. In the last hours of peace Jaurès was assassinated by a Nationalist fanatic for his alleged pro-German sympathies. With the peace-loving Jaurès, idol of the Left but anathema to the Right, perished the peace of France.

## French Interest in Morocco

The Moroccan crisis of 1905 had been the first of a series of international crises recurring at regular three-yearly intervals until the outbreak of war, and punctuating the general deterioration in relations between the two main groups of European powers. Since Delcassé had come to power in 1898, relations between France and Germany had been cool and correct; Delcassé was despised and underrated by German diplomats, and German pride was wounded by his unbending attitude. He had refused to collaborate with the Germans in the Portuguese financial crisis of 1898, and over the building of the Baghdad railway; he had been suspicious of German motives during the Boer War, and during the Boxer rebellion in China. The *entente* with Italy aroused alarm and jealousy in Germany and German politicians who had predicted that France and Britain would not be able to reach an agreement in the immediate future were annoyed at having been proved wrong; it was therefore altogether natural that the German Government should seek to precipitate a crisis in Morocco which might drive from office the one man who, in every major international issue had deliberately, as it seemed to them, set out to block German expansion and restrict German interests. Though they had cause for satisfaction in seeing Delcassé disgraced, the Algeciras Conference of 1906 disappointed the Germans in that French financial control over the Moroccan Bank was strengthened and the organization of a police service in Moroccan ports was entrusted exclusively to France and Spain. But the international character of the agreement had the effect of limiting French freedom of action, and giving German diplomacy a pretext for further interventions. Growing anarchy in Morocco and an insurrection led by the Sultan's brother, Moulay Hafid, compelled France to intervene in fulfilment of her duties under the Act of Algeciras, and occupy Ujda and Casablanca. German protests that France had exceeded her treaty rights having failed, a more conciliatory attitude led to an uneasy agreement in 1909 recognizing French political preponderance in Morocco provided that Germany obtained the right to take part in the economic exploitation of the country. A fresh wave of xenophobia and riots against the Sultan broke out in 1911, and in order to protect the European residents of Fez, a French expeditionary force was sent to occupy that city and Meknès also. The German Government, again protesting that France had violated the Act of Algeciras, informed Selves, the French Foreign Minister, that a gunboat, the *Panther*, had been sent to Agadir in southern Morocco to protect German nationals and German interests threatened by the riots. It seems clear that by this action the Germans hoped to bring off a *coup* similar to the Tangier incident of 1905 which had caused

J

the fall of Delcassé, but since 1905 French public opinion had changed, and it now expected the Government to resist. The Germans made it plain that they would only give France complete freedom of action in Morocco in exchange for the whole of the French Congo. The impossibility of accepting such a bargain provoked a war scare of extreme gravity, and only the British Government's expressed intention of intervening on France's behalf caused more moderate counsels to prevail in Berlin. Prolonged Franco-German negotiations finally led to the Convention of November, 1911, by which Germany conceded France the right to establish a protectorate in Morocco in exchange for territory in Equatorial Africa, which gave the German colony of Kamerun access to the Ubangi and Congo rivers, thus driving a wedge through old-established French possessions. In Parliament, vehement attacks against the Prime Minister, Caillaux, for having sacrificed French territory to German greed, and the revelation of disagreement between Caillaux and Selves, brought down the Government. In March, 1912, by the Treaty of Fez, the French protectorate over Morocco was established, and General Lyautey became the first Resident. Louis Lyautey (1854–1934), one of the greatest soldiers and administrators of his time, with long experience of colonial service in Tonkin and Madagascar, brought methodical pacification to Morocco and a far-reaching programme of reforms and modernization.

## The Strengthening of the Triple Entente

The Moroccan crises led to a significant development of the Entente Cordiale. In 1906, Britain and France held staff conversations to study the basis of common military action. Although the two governments were in no way bound by the decisions reached, these conversations became a regular feature in times of international tension. In 1912, a comprehensive naval agreement between Britain and France enabled the French to concentrate their maritime forces in the Mediterranean while Britain could reinforce her North Sea defences by the withdrawal of part of her Mediterranean squadron. The French fleet was at this date undergoing a profound transformation. Thanks largely to Delcassé's organic naval law of March, 1912, a complete building programme on an ambitious scale was laid down, and although the full effects of this law did not have time to show themselves by 1914, naval administration and morale were much improved. Poincaré meanwhile strove incessantly to strengthen the Triple Entente; during his visit to Russia in the summer of 1912, he had frank discussions with the Tsar on the Balkan problem, and showed his desire to act in full accord with the Russian Government. Nicholas II congratulated him on the part he had played in the French national and military revival: his welcome from the Parisians on his return home demonstrated that he had become something more than head of the Government, the personification of a new temper abroad in the country. In a speech he made at Nantes in October, he declared: "We must retain all the patience, all the energy, all the pride of a race which does not desire war but which, nevertheless, does not fear it. . . . So long as there are people in the world capable of obeying a warlike ideal, those nations which are most sincerely attached to an ideal of peace are under an obligation to remain ready for any eventuality." [23] And in November, 1912, Sir Edward Grey and Paul Cambon exchanged notes by which their governments undertook to consult each other with a view to common action if peace appeared to be threatened. Though the British Government had again avoided committing itself to a definite alliance, the French were satisfied that a more formal basis had been given to relations between the two countries.

## TOWARDS WAR

President Fallières is reputed to have said on the expiry of his term of office: "I greatly fear that war will follow me at the Elysée." This remark must not be interpreted in a sense hostile to Poincaré—on the contrary, Fallières had the greatest respect for and confidence in his successor—but as a clear realization that a major conflict could not be long delayed. Poincaré and Delcassé both held this view in 1913. The system of alliances was already showing itself to be an instrument more likely to provoke war than to preserve peace, and as the Balkan crises of 1912-14 revealed, France became more and more liable to intervene in disputes which did not immediately affect her interests. But Franco-German rivalry, despite negotiation, was more bitter than ever, and France had never been willing to buy peace at the price of a definite renunciation of Alsace-Lorraine. The sultry international atmosphere at the beginning of 1914 gave the lie to the optimistic utterances of diplomats, and when on 28th June the Archduke Francis Ferdinand, heir to the Austro-Hungarian throne was assassinated at Sarajevo, a train of events was set in motion leading inevitably to war. In a crisis such as this, where the issues were of such tremendous significance for Russia, France did not wish to adopt an attitude which might risk undermining the alliance. In July, Poincaré and Viviani, while visiting St. Petersburg, reaffirmed that France would support Russia if Germany intervened in an Austro-Russian conflict. Total mobilization of the Russian forces led Germany to issue an ultimatum demanding the French Government to state what attitude it would take in the event of war between Germany and Russia. France, replying that she would act in accordance with her interests, ordered mobilization, and proclaimed a state of siege throughout the country. On the same day (1st August), Germany declared war on Russia; on the 2nd the Germans demanded a free passage for their troops through Belgium, and on 3rd August the German Government declared war on France. In 1814 and 1870, German forces had invaded France and won a rapid and complete victory; in 1914, though the invasion was on a larger scale than ever before, the temper of France was more sober and realistic, and French resistance was fortified, as it had not been before, by the assurance that she was not fighting alone. The war of 1870—classic, circumscribed, in conformity with European traditions—whose memory had for two generations haunted French minds, was no longer *The* War. In August, 1914, France was brought into a conflict of a type previously unknown, which was to overthrow the old order and inaugurate a new age, an age of confusion, anxiety and disillusionment.

## La belle époque

The Presidency of M. Fallières (1906–13) has often been called nostalgically *la belle époque*, much as the British look upon Edwardian England as a kind of Golden Age. There is much to justify this view. It was a brilliant period socially and intellectually; France had never appeared more prosperous. Good harvests, rising industrial output, the greater use of modern methods in agriculture and industry, a record level of exports and imports caused no fears for the economic state of the country. The cost of living was low, and the general standard of living had continued to rise. But already France was beginning to be troubled by a falling birth-rate consequent upon the higher standard of living, the growth of alcoholism, and the inheritance laws which provided for the equal division of a man's property among his heirs. Society, although superficially it appeared little changed by modern inventions, was in 1914 on the brink of a radical transformation. In the work of Proust we can find an extra-ordinarily vivid and complete picture of the different social classes at this time, with their rigid class-distinctions, mutual misunderstandings, and prejudices. "The bourgeois," says Proust, "built up a somewhat Hindu conception of society, and considered it as composed of closed castes in which every-body, from birth, was placed in the position which his parents occupied, and from which nothing, save the luck of an excep-tional career or an unexpected marriage, could remove you in order to attain a higher social rank." And this age belonged essentially to the bourgeois. All the great achievements in the arts, in science, in philosophy, in politics, were bourgeois achievements. Despite the great respect shown to women, this was also essentially a masculine age, and apart from Sarah Bernhardt and Marie Curie (whose reputation was in any case confined to a very small circle) few women made a lasting reputation for themselves. Family life and an inflexible code of etiquette occupied a woman's time almost to the exclusion of everything else, and there was never in France a suffragette movement comparable to that in Britain.

## THE STATE OF FRANCE IN 1914

The greatness of France before 1914 rested upon five things: her economic stability, the richness of the land, the immense capacity of her people for work, the greatness of her civil servants and administrators, and her inventiveness. Frenchmen were leading pioneers in cinematography, aviation, and the development of the automobile, three of the most revolutionary modern inventions. Paris was more than ever the cultural capital of Europe, and it never ceased to be a magnet for all aspiring artists. There were, however, certain disturbing signs which did not augur well for the future, and the most serious of these was the Government's instability which, as we have seen, hampered the work of legislation. This instability arose largely from the multiplicity of political groups in Parliament. Apart from the Socialists, who were themselves beneath a semblance of unity divided ideologically and over the question of tactics, political parties as we know them in Britain did not exist in France. France, which is fundamentally a land of individualists, was not favourable terrain for the emergence of large party organizations. Although in 1914 there were five main political groups in Parliament, there were several powerful bodies—ranging from the extreme Right-wing neo-Royalist *Action française*, the descendant of Déroulède's *Ligue des Patriotes*, under the energetic leadership of Maurras, to the Anarchists—who were not represented in the Chamber. These numerous groups merged into one another, but between Right and Left there was a sharp political division not paralleled in the Britain of 1914. The individualism of the Frenchman, and his innate dislike of officialdom and State interference in his private affairs, made the question of income tax a more than usually controversial matter, and although Viviani on the eve of war undertook to bring pressure to bear on the Senate to force the project through, it seems likely that if war had been avoided his government would have fallen, as so many others had fallen, on this very issue. French politics also suffered from a lack of real leadership. After the 1877 crisis, the Presidency of the Republic, with the single exception of Poincaré, was continuously in the hands of second-rate men. Parliament, which elected the President, was content to see it so, since a strong will and forceful personality at the Elysée might curb their own power, as MacMahon had sought to do, by a strictly literal interpretation of the President's constitutional rights. The great politicians of the age were few. Clemenceau and Briand, brilliant men who were yet to come into their own, were distrusted for their very brilliance; of those who remained, the really outstanding figures—Gambetta, Ferry, Waldeck-Rousseau, Delcassé, Jaurès—were either made the centre of violent storms of partisan feeling, or, as was the case with Waldeck-Rousseau, came to power too late to restore equilibrium.

Unfortunately, the growth of the French colonial empire was too much entangled with domestic politics. The dangers of its haphazard acquisition and the Government's lack of a coherent colonial policy were only realized between the two World Wars, when little could be done to remedy past defects. Not all the colonies were the responsibility of a single Ministry, and the Empire's extreme diversity, together with the Government's tendency to favour a policy of assimilation rather than one of local self-government, made the problems of colonial administration increasingly acute with the passage of time. The poverty of many of the colonies, too, made them an economic liability rather than an asset, and the reluctance of the majority of Frenchmen to leave their native soil to assist in the exploitation of territories overseas compelled administrators on the spot to shoulder more than their fair share of responsibility.

Between 1870 and 1914, France experienced great upheavals which, though they affected the even tenor of life and the tradition of social and economic stability but little within this period, ultimately undermined public confidence in authority, sharpened political rivalries and made the country a prey to alien ideologies. Fascism was already latent in movements such as *L'Action française*, Communism in the more extreme Left-wing groups. The diminishing influence of the Church, particularly among the working classes, despite the noble work of *L'Oeuvre des Cercles* and later of the *Sillon*, deprived society of a counterpoise. Strong though the Republic was as a form of government, and while it was still possible to speak of France, with her second largest colonial empire, as a first-class power, her declining population, her inner restlessness and her industrial inferiority to Britain and Germany did not encourage an optimistic view of the future.

## REFERENCES

1.  One of the most graphic English accounts is that given in Mrs. Belloc Lowndes's biography of her mother: *I too have lived in Arcadia.*

2.  A. Dansette: *Histoire religieuse de la France contemporaine* (Paris, 1948), Vol. I, p. 441.

3.  D. Halévy: *La République des Ducs* (Paris, 1937), p. 131.

4.  J. Chastenet: *L'Enfance de la Troisième* (Paris, 1952), p. 192.

5.  *L'Enfance de la Troisième*, p. 257.

6.  Agnes Murphy: *The Ideology of French Imperialism, 1871–81*, p. 19.

7.  J. Chastenet: *La République des Républicains* (Paris, 1954), p. 165.

8.  J. H. Clapham: *The Economic Development of France and Germany, 1815–1914*, Chs. VIII and X.

9.  *La République des Républicains*, pp. 180–87.

10.  A. Dansette: *Le Boulangisme* (Paris, 1946), pp. 371–77.

11.  *La République des Républicains*, pp. 215–19.

12.  *The Economic Development of France and Germany*, p. 265.

13.  *Histoire religieuse de la France contemporaine*, II., p. 106.

14.  *La République des Républicains*, p. 282.

15.  G. Chapman: *The Dreyfus Case*, p. 133.

16.  ibid., pp. 137–38.

17.  ibid., p. 358.

18.  ibid., p. 360.

19.  E. Tersen: *Histoire de la Colonisation* (Paris, 1950), pp. 93–94.

20.  *The Economic Development of France and Germany*, p. 273.

21.  J. P. T. Bury: *France, 1814–1940*, p. 214.

22.  M. Drachkovitch: *Les Socialismes français et allemand et le problème de la guerre* (Geneva, 1953), Ch. IV.

23.  J. Chastenet: *La France de M. Fallières* (Paris, 1950), p. 102.

# VI

# GREAT BRITAIN AND IRELAND, 1867–1914

## "A New World . . ."

IT has already been suggested, in an earlier chapter, that Englishmen in 1870 did not fail to recognize the significance of the events which in a few short months had shattered the long dominance of France and replaced it with the new and unknown power of a united Germany. When Parliament assembled after the recess, early in 1871, Disraeli expressed the prevailing disquiet in a powerful, if somewhat overdrawn, speech:

> Let me impress upon the attention of the House the character of this war between France and Germany. It is no common war. . . . This war represents the German revolution, a greater political event than the French revolution of last century. . . . Not a single principle in the management of our foreign affairs, accepted by all statesmen for guidance up to six months ago, any longer exists. There is not a diplomatic tradition which has not been swept away. You have a new world, new influences at work, new and unknown objects and dangers with which to cope. . . . The balance of power has been entirely destroyed, and the country which suffers most, and feels the effects of this great change most, is England.

How penetrating this analysis of the situation was to prove, Disraeli could hardly have conceived at the time. His object, as leader of the Opposition, was to castigate the Government for its impotence in the face of events abroad, but one sentence might be extracted from the speech to serve as a text for this study of the development of Britain between 1870 and 1914— "You have a new world, new influences at work, new and unknown objects and dangers with which to cope." The year 1870 has well been described as a "watershed" in British history:[1] within a few years it was clear that while a new world of power-politics was taking shape on the Continent, at the same time new influences were at work in Britain's political, economic and social life. New men and new measures were to become the order of the day, and the complacency and optimism which are so often regarded as characteristic of Victorian England were to be put to severe tests.

## THE VICTORIAN AGE

No period of British history, it may be said, has seen greater changes than the Victorian Age. The growth of what a leading authority on the period has called "the compact, self-centred organism of 1830" into "the loose and world embracing fabric of 1900" is no less striking than the similar and contemporary developments in Germany and the United States. Within a space of three-quarters of a century a population of some twenty-four millions had been almost doubled, to become nearly forty-two millions; a country still mainly rural in character, with agriculture its chief industry, had become the first industrial and commercial nation of the world, with competitors already surpassing it; an island Kingdom, with dependent territories that were yet hardly more than strategic points and trading posts, had grown into the centre of a vast world-wide Empire, on which, men boasted, the sun never set. Standards of life had risen, the public health improved, and the average expectation of life increased by about ten years. Education had become general, the franchise had been widely extended and an efficient system of local government had been set up. Hours of work were shorter, Trade Unions, Factory Acts, and Friendly Societies protected the worker, and Local Authorities were able to concern themselves with his housing. Apart from the distant Crimean War, and a series of colonial and imperial conflicts, Britain had been long at peace, and in the 'nineties it was still too early to foresee any impending menace. Well might it be felt that the country when it celebrated Queen Victoria's Diamond Jubilee in 1897 "had come into port after a long voyage".[2]

## NEW CONDITIONS

Nevertheless, it is, perhaps, the elements of stability and continuity that best characterize the Victorian Age in so many of its aspects. Winston Churchill who, born as he was in 1874, has some claim to be regarded as the last of the Victorians, has spoken for his contemporaries in describing the period as the

British Antonine Age. "Those who were its children", he has said, "could not understand why it had not begun earlier or why it should ever stop", and he has pointed to its "peace, prosperity and progress" as its outstanding characteristics.[3] These were without doubt the features of the period that most readily caught the attention. Yet before the end of the century all three were threatened by changing conditions throughout the world. The Boer War, on which the country was launched, with inadequate preparation, in 1899, was no more than the latest of the series of colonial wars, though the effort it called for gave it a greater significance. But already the strain of increasing international tension was being felt. Expenditure on the Services increased by about one-half during the 'nineties, and war with France, the traditional enemy, seemed dangerously near at the time of the Fashoda incident in 1898. The most disturbing portent, though few saw it at the time, was, however, the passing of the German Navy Laws in 1898 and 1900, with the attendant propaganda that was necessary to arouse the interest of the German people in naval expansion. The British Navy, supreme since 1713 and unchallenged since 1805, was again to be threatened with serious rivalry. Gladstone had finally retired from politics, at the age of eighty-four, in 1894 after a disagreement with his colleagues over the increased Naval Estimates, which he, with his characteristic concern for public economy, regarded as excessive. Yet within seven years Germany was building a powerful fleet, openly aimed against British sea-power. In the association of these two events alone, is to be seen the passing of one of the main conditions of the Victorian peace. Within a further period of seven years the traditions of a century had been reversed: understandings had been reached with France and Russia, whom the Victorians had long regarded with suspicion and hostility, and Germany was looming up as a far more formidable foe. There had clearly been a greater element of chance about the long prevalence of peace than had been realized.

## The "Watershed"

The progress and prosperity of the age were being threatened at the end of the century no less than its peace. England's long lead as "the workshop of the world" had reached its limit about 1870, when her foreign trade had been almost equal to that of France, Germany and the United States put together, and, to quote a single striking example, her output of pig-iron had actually exceeded their united total by very nearly one-fifth. Yet within thirty years in the production of most heavy goods both Germany and the United States, aided by high tariff policies, had taken the lead, and Britain had fallen to third place. Industry was continuing to expand, but the rate of growth had been halved, and German foreign trade alone had reached a total not far behind that of Britain. It is true that the general level of prosperity continued to rise, but this occurred rather more through the development of measures of social welfare than under the stimulus of the phenomenal expansion of earlier years. The confidence and optimism that had marked the Mid-Victorian period, from the time of the Great Exhibition of 1851 until the 'seventies, had long passed, and the notion of the year 1870 as a "watershed" in our history is not without contemporary warrant. Events had caused a host of assumptions to be questioned, and a great overhaul of methods and institutions was about to take place. Gladstone's first administration, formed in 1868 and carrying many notable measures before its fall in 1874, may be regarded as the opening of the new period, but the dramatic stroke which inaugurated it was the passage of Disraeli's Reform Act in 1867. From that measure can be dated the first steps towards Democracy in Britain, and it was soon followed by a number of others which pointed the way towards the "social-service State" of the twentieth century. The extension of the franchise to working men in the towns (and in 1884 to the countryside), the introduction of the secret ballot (1872), and of a national system of elementary education (1870), the Trade Union Acts of 1871 and 1875, and the reform of local government in 1888, all contributed to the developments that caused Sir William Harcourt in 1889 to coin the famous, though somewhat premature, phrase, "We are all Socialists now".

## THE SECOND REFORM ACT, 1867

The Reform Bill of 1867 was an event far more striking in its consequences than the hard-fought measure of 1832. Carried by Disraeli with the avowed intention of "dishing the

Whigs", it was a deliberate attempt to exploit for the Conservative Party the general recognition of the need for further reform of the franchise, which had been stimulated by widespread agitation and particularly by the action of the London reform mob in tearing up the railings of Hyde Park in July, 1866. Disraeli might have said of himself, as he had said twenty-two years earlier of Sir Robert Peel, that he had "caught the Whigs bathing, and walked away with their clothes". Lord John Russell (1792–1878), who, at the age of seventy-three, had succeeded Palmerston as Prime Minister, had endeavoured to carry a moderate extension of the franchise in 1866, but had been defeated, and the Tories had taken office under Lord Derby (1799–1869), with Disraeli as Chancellor of the Exchequer, but with no majority in the House. The keynote of the new Government's policy is to be found in a letter from Derby to Disraeli: a number of proposals were to be put forward, in order to "afford an opportunity for feeling the pulse of Parliament and the country". In the event, after five months of discussion, amendment and negotiation, a Bill was carried which went far beyond Russell's modest proposals, and introduced the thoroughly Radical principle of "Household Suffrage", with the vote given to ratepaying householders in the towns (an ingenious combination of Radical principle and Tory respectability) and to lodgers who paid at least £10 a year. For rural voters the extension was very much smaller, but throughout the country as a whole the number of voters rose from rather more than a million to a figure little short of two millions, and although the landowning interests was to retain its influence in the countryside until 1884, in the towns something akin to a democratic franchise had now been admitted. It was a bold move, but justified by the manifest demands of the country. In his speech on the third reading Disraeli had argued that any further delay in settling the franchise "would be fatal, not merely to the Conservative Party, but most dangerous to the country", and any partial solution would soon have called for further amendment, as, indeed, happened, when the rural franchise was brought into line in 1884. It says much for the measure that, apart from this further step, it endured until 1918, having removed at least one potential cause of revolutionary agitation.

Its Consequences

Gladstone and Disraeli were at one in accepting the Act as an essential step, though their approaches to it differed greatly. Gladstone was swayed by a realization of the justice of the working men's claims to political responsibility; Disraeli, with his more astute and empirical sense of political realities, by his recognition of the danger of delaying thorough reform and by his hope that the new voters would support the "Tory Democracy" which he had long sought to create. Others, however, regarded the measure with some trepidation. Derby himself described it as "a great experiment . . . a leap in the dark", while Carlyle denounced it as "shooting Niagara". But the changes that followed, though considerable, were not catastrophic. Inevitably, more attention had to be paid to working-class opinion, and measures of social reform acquired a new significance, though Disraeli had already struck the new note with his phrase *Sanitas santitatum, omnia sanitas*, coined in a speech at Aylesbury in 1864, in reference to the growing concern with public health and conditions of work. The full effects of this new emphasis were not felt until later, but it was already apparent in 1868, when the first General Election under the new dispensation was held, that a fresh spirit was abroad. For the first time party leaders began to appeal to the electorate in campaigns of speech-making up and down the country: platform oratory began to make itself felt not only as a means of expounding a party's policy, but also as an instrument for rousing public support for that policy among the new voters. Lord Derby complained of Gladstone's "stumping tour" in 1868, but it was the great Midlothian campaign of 1879 which first exploited to the full the possibilities of the new situation, and caused alarm in many quarters by its tacit acknowledgement that the centre of political gravity had shifted outside the walls of Parliament. Later still, Chamberlain and Lloyd George were to carry Gladstone's methods to lengths that would have appalled him, but the "stump" was an obvious result of the sudden extension of the franchise. Disraeli claimed that he had had to educate his party for their rôle in 1867, but it was now necessary to educate the widened electorate in its new responsibilities, and to submit for its consideration a programme of projected legislation. Legislation, indeed, increased steadily in quantity. The House of Commons had for long been a select club and debating chamber, where a Government, still reliant on the Sovereign's active support, depended to a large extent on the votes of individual, independent members. It now became far more a means of putting into effect policies upon which the public had already expressed an opinion through an election. Political programmes were framed, both as an expression of the popular will and as a means of attracting support for the party concerned. The party labels of Whig and Tory, which had meant little more than the "Republican" and "Democrat" of modern America, were now finally replaced by the more expressive "Liberal" and "Conservative", and party bonds were gradually tightened. Majorities, which had hitherto been small both in elections and in parliamentary divisions, now assumed more considerable proportions, and the "swing of the pendulum" made its appearance. Thus, Disraeli found his government decisively rejected by the electorate in 1868, but the pendulum swung in his favour in 1874 and back to Gladstone in 1880. Yet there was little significant change in the composition of Commons and Cabinets. The proportion of members representing the landed interest tended to fall, but not until the "Liberal landslide" of 1906 was there any considerable influx of working men into the House or any marked decline in aristocratic membership of Cabinets. Until the formation of the Labour Party, in fact, Disraeli's claim that, in introducing the reforms of 1867, "we have not done anything but strengthen the institutions of the country", would seem to have been justified.

Derby had resigned in February of 1868, handing the premiership to Disraeli, who now, at the age of sixty-two, found himself for the first time at what, in a typical mood of ironic depreciation, he called "the top of the greasy pole". Russell had already surrendered the leadership of the Liberal Party to Gladstone, and when the election took place in the autumn the Liberals returned with a majority of 112. The first administration of a new age was now formed, and the two remarkable men, Disraeli and Gladstone, were left face to face. Their bitter antagonism was to colour the whole political scene for a dozen years, and to introduce a new spirit into politics, a spirit in keeping with the conditions of the period that had now opened.

## THE "SECOND REFORM ERA"

The achievements of Gladstone's first administration have given his six years of office the title of the "Second Reform Era", in pointed comparison with the measures that were passed in the period after the Reform Act of 1832. Gladstone's first thought, when he was asked to form a government, was for Ireland, but before considering the ramifications of the great Irish problem, with which he was to be so strenuously concerned for the rest of his career, it would be well to survey the record of a Ministry that opened with high hopes but was destined to finish its course under a cloud of unpopularity.

## EDUCATION

The Education Act which was designed to supplement the work of 1867, to educate "our future masters", in the contemporary phrase, was passed in 1870 as part of a programme of reform aimed at limiting privilege and opening careers to talents. With it were associated considerable changes in the organization of the Universities, the Civil Service and the Army. It proved impossible to establish a State system of education, free of the complication of Church schools, but national elementary education, administered locally, in the main, by new "School Boards", was set up, and 1880 saw it become compulsory, while in 1891 it was made free. In the twenty years from 1870 to 1890 the school attendance rose from 1,300,000 to 4,500,000, and, while the amount of public money spent on education remained lamentably small, the way was opened for the later Acts of 1902, 1918 and 1944. In little more than ten years after 1870 a Northumberland miner could say:

> Our Elementary Schools are now turning out a class who have tasted of the tree of knowledge. This class will one day have control of the funds of our Trade and Co-operative Societies, and I have full confidence in the result.[4]

Elementary education, though little enough, was indeed fundamental to the later development of the working-class movement.

## THE BALLOT

A further significant reform was the Ballot Act. This abolished the disgraceful scenes at the hustings, which Dickens had caricatured in *Pickwick Papers*, and struck a blow at the political ascendancy of the landowning interest in the countryside, which was soon to be further weakened by the extension of the rural franchise in 1884, and, more disastrously, by the ruin which fell on English agriculture during the 'seventies. It was in Ireland, however, that the Ballot Act had its most significant results. It made possible there the free expression of opinion at the polls, and therefore the creation of the Irish Nationalist Party, opposed to the ascendancy of the Anglo-Irish landowners. The man who saw and seized the opportunity was Charles Stewart Parnell. Between his entry into the House of Commons in 1875 and his tragic collapse in 1890 he was to exercise, not only upon Irish politics but upon the career of Gladstone and the history of Great Britain an influence almost without parallel. It was the Ballot Act, in the first place, which made that influence possible.

## TRADE UNIONS

Another measure which passed through Parliament at this time, though as a Private Member's Bill and not as a part of the Government's policy, was Sir John Lubbock's Bank Holiday Act of 1871, which might be described as the first tentative introduction of the principle of "holidays with pay". Of greater significance was the Trade Union Act of the same year, which marks one of the important stages in the evolution of the Trade Union movement in the country. Since 1825 Trade Unions had been accorded a limited recognition, but their legal standing was far from clear, and in particular they lacked the power to protect their funds. Outrages among the unions in Sheffield, which had been exposed in 1866, had led to the appointment of a Royal Commission in the following year, and on the report of this Commission was based the Act of 1871, which gave the Unions for the first time adequate legal status and protection. It was accompanied, however, by a further measure, the Criminal Law Amendment Act, which made picketing, and indeed, almost all strike action, illegal. Gladstone himself took little interest in these Acts, which are, significantly, without mention in Morley's official *Life*, and appeals to him for further consideration led to no action. As a result the whole weight of the Trade Union movement was thrown against the Government in the Election of 1874, and contributed to its defeat. In the following year Richard Cross (1823–1914), Disraeli's Home Secretary, carried a further measure, the Conspiracy and Protection of Property Act, which repealed the Criminal Law Amendment Act, legalized peaceful picketing and increased the freedom of strike action, while removing from Unions the stigma of "conspiracy", provided that they did nothing which would be illegal if done by one person. In the same year the Employers and Workmen Act for the first time set masters and men on an equal footing before the law. The importance of these three Acts of 1871 and 1875 can hardly be exaggerated. Morley in his *Recollections* claims that they "averted a revolution": without them the whole history of the Labour movement might, indeed, have taken a different turn. For enduring significance, as G. M. Young has said, they stand with Chamberlain's municipal administration in Birmingham as "the doings of the mid-seventies, which in the long run mattered most". They came, moreover, at a moment when new influences were at work in the Trade Union world. The first official Trade Union Congress had been held in 1868, and the second, in the following year, set up the "Parliamentary Committee" as its standing executive for pressing its resolutions upon Parliament's attention. Several leaders of the movement had stood for Parliament in 1868, though unsuccessfully, but two were elected in 1874, and were joined by a third in 1880. The days of an independent Labour Party were not far distant, though much had to happen before such a party became possible.

## THE GOVERNMENT'S DECLINE

By 1872 Gladstone's ministry, with two more years of parliamentary life to run, was rapidly losing its hold on the country. Trade Unionists were estranged by the rebuff to their claims, Nonconformists by the concessions to the Church Schools in the Education Act, and the publicans, powerful in their influence upon public opinion, by a new Licensing Act. The Government gave the impression of having little more to offer: Disraeli compared them, in a phrase which has stuck, to "a range of exhausted volcanoes". Moreover, their handling of foreign affairs had lost them much prestige. The death of the able and experienced Foreign Secretary, Lord Clarendon, shortly before the outbreak of the Franco-Prussian war, weakened their influence in Europe, and their impotence in the face of the rising power of Germany alarmed many who recalled the days of Palmerston. Gladstone, as has already been shown, had wished to protest against the annexation of Alsace-Lorraine, but it was manifestly impossible to make more than a purely verbal protest, which would probably have served only to exacerbate the situation. The neutrality of Belgium, it is true, was safeguarded during the war by special treaties, but, on the other hand, Russia took advantage of the international disturbance to free herself from the restrictions on her naval power in the Black Sea which had been forced on her at the end of the Crimean War. Gladstone was able only to insist that the matter should be settled by a conference of the States concerned, instead of by unilateral action on Russia's part. More could hardly have been achieved without risk of conflict, but Disraeli summed-up the general feeling of the country when he said in 1874: "it would have been better for us all if there had been a little more energy in our foreign policy, and a little less in our domestic legislation." The *Alabama* award of 1872 was a further source of ill-feeling. For ten years Anglo-American relations had been embittered by the dispute over the *Alabama* privateer, which had been built on the Mersey for the Confederate States in 1862, and had done much damage to Union shipping during the Civil War. The exaggerated American claims for compensation had at last been submitted to arbitration, and when the award of £3,250,000 against Britain was announced, Gladstone accepted it. It was a wise move, but an intensely unpopular one. The final blow to the Government came, however, over Ireland, and its handling of the Irish problem during these years must now be considered as a whole.

## THE IRISH PROBLEM: GLADSTONE AND IRELAND

Nowhere, perhaps, was Gladstone's characteristic slowness to learn, and tenaciousness to hold, a lesson shown more clearly than in his attitude to Ireland. As early as 1845 he had written to his wife of "Ireland, Ireland! that cloud in the west, that coming storm", but twenty years were to pass before an Irish policy began to take shape in his mind, and a further twenty before he launched "Home Rule" at the age of seventy-six. The real tragedy of Ireland lay in the fact that in his slowness to learn he was only too typical of the majority of his countrymen where Ireland was concerned. It seems now extraordinary that a man, widely travelled in Europe, and confronted throughout his whole career by so many aspects of the Irish problem, should only once have visited the country, and then for but a few weeks in 1877. Yet in that fact again Gladstone was typical, for while Ireland was legally a part of the United Kingdom, it was for the majority of Englishmen essentially a foreign land. Disraeli never went there, and Queen Victoria, who had so great an affection for Scotland, spent only five weeks in Ireland in all the sixty-three years of her reign. Efforts were frequently made to persuade her to establish an Irish Balmoral, or at least to allow the Prince of Wales to visit the country regularly, but for a variety of reasons, though mainly from a disinclination to expose herself or her family to a risk of violence, she invariably refused to consider the suggestion. Like many people in England she did not appreciate the peculiar difficulties of Ireland, or the need for careful handling of Irish problems. More frequent royal visits would not have solved those problems, but they would at least have appealed to Irish sentiment, as the Queen's gallant visit in 1900, at the age of eighty-one, unmistakably did. Moreover, they might well have removed from Irish minds the impression, gained from painful experience since the Act of Union of 1800, that Irish interests were overlooked in far-off Westminster. Ireland suffered from being an integral part of Great Britain, and from being regarded in consequence as similar to England and Scotland—except in the intractability of her people. Yet, in fact, the differences were very great, and increased, except in Ulster, as England gradually changed from an agricultural to an industrial country. Government was carried on, however, in tragic unawareness of the true conditions, and every effort was long made to arrange Irish affairs on English principles. Gladstone criticized this tendency in 1867 when, in discussing the future of England, Scotland and Ireland, he said: "no man ought to be able to say that any of these nations is governed according to the traditions, the views or the ideas of another". But he had then been in politics for thirty-five years, and had long since won a European reputation by his active sympathy for the oppressed peoples of Europe, especially the Italians, without, however, finding it necessary to intervene in Irish affairs. Sympathy for the Italians, the Hungarians, the Poles, was widespread, but apart from the help given in the terrible time of the famine, 1845–48, little was done for the typical Irish worker, the peasant, at a time when serious attention was beginning to be given to the needs of the English working man. The reasons for the contrast are to be found partly in the fact that Ireland's problems were religious, economic and social, as well as political, and partly in the belief that any reversal of the policy of 1800 that endangered the Union might endanger with it the security of England. Ireland had long been a dangerous opening on England's flank, and the successes of other Unions in the American Civil War and the Franco-Prussian War suggested that the trend of the times was towards greater, not lesser, associations. It was this aspect of the problem, in particular, that inspired much of the later opposition to Home Rule.

## IRISH GRIEVANCES

The grievances of the Irish were at once political and religious, social and economic. The Union of 1800 was never accepted by the great majority of the people, who cherished a belief that if left to themselves they could satisfactorily solve their own problems. An ignorant and backward peasantry regarded repeal of the Union, or Home Rule, as it came to be called, as the solution of all their ills: it is significant that the movement which finally achieved independence was called *Sinn Fein* (ourselves alone). Moreover, when the Union was passed it had been accompanied by certain undertakings which were not carried out. In particular, the political rights long denied to Roman Catholics had not been restored until 1829, and then only after a long agitation by Daniel O'Connell's Catholic Association, while a further nine years of agitation had been necessary to secure the commutation of the tithes due by law from the Roman Catholic peasantry to a Protestant Established Church, heavily over-endowed, which they abhorred and ignored. Attempts to enforce the payment of tithe had been met by peasant violence and cruelty, which were further inflamed by incessant strife between peasants and landlords. Throughout most of Ireland, except in Ulster, tenants were without rights and were at the mercy of their landlords, many of whom, permanently resident in England, managed their estates through agents. Evictions were frequent, and everything conspired to keep both people and land in poverty and squalor. English land law was applied in circumstances which differed greatly from those of England itself, and, until much later in the century, the obvious solution, that of buying out the landlords and resettling the peasantry on the land as smallholders, was regarded as a dangerous attack on the principle of private property which might have unpleasant repercussions in England. Frustrated in their demand for security, and taught by experience to believe that agitation would secure their aims, the Irish plunged into a vicious circle of violence and government repression, which disgusted law-abiding opinion in England, and rendered increasingly difficult an understanding between the two peoples who had so many interests in common. When, at long last, the religious and economic problems were solved, the demand for political freedom, therefore, remained. "Our nationalism is not founded upon grievances," declared the Irish Republican Party to President Wilson in 1918, "we are opposed not to English misgovernment, but to English government in Ireland." But by then there had arisen inside Ireland itself serious differences as to the form political freedom should take, while an intense emotional nationalism had led to an assertion of national individuality that has had strange results. "The greatest curse of Ireland," an Irish writer has said, "has not been English invasions or English misgovernment; it has been the exaggeration of Irish virtues."[5] The criticism is perhaps just, but the causes of the tendency to exaggeration are not far to seek, however much may be said in extenuation of English blunders. "A conquered nation," wrote Shaw in the Preface to *John Bull's Other Island*, "is like a man with cancer; he can think of nothing else."

## Gladstone's "Mission" in Ireland

Yet it is well to remember that at a time when hardly a single voice was raised in Germany on behalf of the Poles, who were treated with a deliberate severity unknown in Ireland, a powerful public opinion was gradually built up in England in sympathy with Irish claims. Without able and influential leadership that sympathy could have availed little, and it says much for Gladstone that when he knew his power he also knew how, and where, to use it. "My mission is to pacify Ireland", he said when he realized after the election of 1868 that it would be his duty to form a government. To that mission he devoted the rest of his career, eventually splitting his party in the process and also, as events showed, seriously delaying the progress of the social reforms which were a logical consequence of the Act of 1867. For many years Irish affairs seemed to dominate British politics, and they must loom large in any account of the period between 1870 and 1914. "The Irish question," as Gladstone himself once said, "is in a category by itself." The reasons for his own absorption in it he made clear in a letter to his friend and closest political confidant, Lord Granville, in 1870:

> To this great country the state of Ireland . . . is an intolerable disgrace, and a danger so absolutely transcending all others, that I call it the only real danger of the noble Empire of the Queen.[6]

Irishmen might be indifferent to his concern with the Empire, but the memory of his struggle for Irish freedom still lingers: "he was a great man", a modern Irish historian has written, "though an Englishman".[7] To the stern patriot, mindful of bitter days still not far removed in time, there could, perhaps, be no higher praise.

In Irish as in English affairs, therefore, Gladstone's first administration marked a new point of departure. He had already decided that a new approach was called for, and with a majority based on the new popular vote it was now possible to make head against the Irish landowners in the House of Lords. Moreover, recent events, the "Fenian outrages" of 1867, had brought home to the public the immediacy of the Irish question.

## GLADSTONE'S IRISH POLICY

During the American War thousands of Irishmen had fought for the North. The end of the war in 1865 left them unsettled and without occupation, accustomed to violence and well-trained in a fierce struggle. Among them had sprung up, since 1858, a strong patriotic association, the Fenian Brotherhood, named after the *Fianna*, the armed force which had defended Ireland in legendary times. This association at the end of the war tried to stir up armed rebellion in Ireland and disturbances in England, while bands of Fenians in America made raids into Canada. In September, 1867, two Fenians who had been arrested in Manchester were rescued from a prison van and a policeman was killed. Three months later a barrel of gunpowder was exploded against the wall of Clerkenwell prison where two other Fenians were confined: twelve people were killed and more than a hundred injured. Opinion in England was shocked by these outrages into an awareness of the Irish situation, and Gladstone, alive, as he later acknowledged, to the new mood of the country, brought forward his first scheme, the disestablishment of the Irish Church. He became Prime Minister in December, 1868, and this first measure was introduced in March, 1869. After considerable opposition in the Lords it became law in July. Gladstone then turned to the land problem, to which he devoted three months' study. The result was the Land Act of 1870, which proved to be a step, though only a step, in the right direction. It was an ingenious attempt to afford some protection to tenants without at all interfering with rights of property. Arbitrary eviction was limited, and compensation for improvements effected by tenants enforced: in effect, the Act applied to other parts of the country the customary tenant-rights of Ulster. But there was no security for fair rents and fixity of tenure; this had to await the greater measure of 1881, in Gladstone's second administration. The Act of 1870 probably went as far as influential opinion in England was prepared to go at the time, but it is again indicative of English ignorance of the true situation in Ireland that the desire of the peasant to be secure in the possession of his piece of land was not better appreciated.

Before he took office Gladstone had spoken of "the upas tree of Irish woe", with its three branches, the Church, the land, and education. Two of the branches had been dealt with by 1870: the third was tackled in 1873 when he introduced a Bill for the establishment of an Irish University. But this project was foiled by sectarian strife, and actually brought about the defeat of the Government: not until 1908 was an Irish University established.

## The Irish and "Home Rule": Isaac Butt

The carrying of the Irish Church and Land Bills had imposed a tremendous strain on Gladstone, but events soon showed that they had done little to assist him in the self-imposed mission of pacifying Ireland. If English opinion was shocked by Fenian outrages, Irish feeling was no less embittered by the execution of three men for the Manchester crime, and the cry of the "Manchester Martyrs" became a nationalist slogan, raising up everywhere where there was an Irishman, it has been said, an enemy for England:[8] it was soon to be effectively used by Parnell. But before Parnell appeared, the movement which he was to lead had been initiated by another, more moderate, Irishman, Isaac Butt (1813-79), whose memory has been largely obliterated by the violence of later conflicts. Butt, like Parnell, was a Protestant: his training had been in the law, and he had first been attracted into the Nationalist Movement by the land problem. From 1865 he stood as counsel for all the Fenian prisoners, and in 1870 he decided that the time had come to organize an agitation to take advantage of the extension of the franchise and Parliament's new interest in Irish affairs. He had a great veneration for Parliament (in striking contrast to Parnell, who, master though he was of parliamentary management, despised it), and proved an able parliamentarian.

Butt's aim was to organize an Irish group within Parliament which by a moderate presentation of its case might win support for the establishment of an Irish government and parliament at Dublin for purely Irish affairs. He was, therefore, reviving the "repeal" agitation of earlier years, though he gave it a more positive character by describing his object as "Home Rule". The term, which was coined by one of his coadjutors, was first presented to the world in 1870 when a "Home Rule Association" was formed by Butt in

Dublin: it was to prove for nearly fifty years one of the main preoccupations of British politics. Butt himself was elected to Parliament in 1871, and at the election of 1874 fifty-nine Home Rulers followed him into the House. Their efforts under his moderate and constitutional leadership were to prove of little avail, however. Butt never ceased to believe in purely constitutional methods of agitation, but, as his biographer has said, "it was the fate of all Irish politicians to have to repeat the same case over and over".[9] Butt was "listened to and voted down":[10] experience was to show once more that violence, not repetition, would bring consideration. Not until the wilder spirits of the Home Rule party under Parnell had won control, and Gladstone had lent the weight of his name and following to the movement, was Home Rule taken seriously in England. The first reactions, even among those most sympathetic to the Irish case, were that so desperate a remedy as separation should not be attempted until it had been shown that Irish grievances could be removed in no other way, and this remained the attitude of the opponents of Home Rule till the last. Gladstone's policy at first, and the policy of the Conservatives in their measures of relief at the end of the century, was to "kill Home Rule by kindness". Gladstone, however, kept an open mind on the subject. He deprecated the movement, but there was in him a strong, if limited, strain of political realism and he was eventually prepared to countenance Home Rule if it could be shown to be the only means of placating Ireland, though as late as 1882 he was still reassuring the Queen as to his opposition to it.[11] Unfortunately, this attitude, at a time when a definite statement might well be expected from a political leader, exposed him to a charge of casuistry, to which, indeed, with his involved and elaborate style of speaking, he had always been liable. Moreover, when once his conscience had been aroused, he was intolerant of opposition and unsympathetic to the honest doubts of others. Hence the serious differences in his party when, "an old man in a hurry", he tried to draw it after him in support of Home Rule in 1886.

## DISRAELI'S GOVERNMENT, 1874

It has already been noted that the Irish University Bill had led to the defeat of the Government in 1873. Gladstone had resigned, but Disraeli, with a shrewd sense of the way feeling was running in the country, had refused to take office, preferring to await the outcome of the general election that was due in 1874. Gladstone had therefore returned, but the election had confirmed Disraeli's hopes, and in February he became Prime Minister, with a handsome majority in the House. Gladstone resigned, and soon announced his retirement from the leadership of his party: he was now sixty-four, and though he was still in robust health no one could have imagined that he had twenty years of strenuous political life yet before him.

## BENJAMIN DISRAELI

Benjamin Disraeli (1804–81) was at the time of the formation of his second administration in his seventieth year. His career, begun with literary successes as early as 1826, had led him into Parliament in the year of Queen Victoria's accession, 1837, but, brilliantly gifted though he was, his own predilections and the political circumstances of his time had long kept him from high office. His approach to many of the problems of the age was radical, but he was opposed to the fundamental assumptions of Liberalism, and, with his mystic reverence for traditional institutions, had conceived it to be his task to reconstruct the Tory party after Peel had split it on the issue of Free Trade in 1846. The spectacle of the "gentlemen of England", led by a romantic Jewish adventurer, remains one of the most fascinating in parliamentary history, but Disraeli's success in consolidating and inspiring a party through nearly thirty years of opposition must always stand as a remarkable tribute to his genius. Unlike Gladstone, he had had little opportunity of acquiring any skill as an administrator or legislator. His gifts lay rather in the management of men and votes, in the handling of parliamentary business, in the throwing-out of pregnant suggestions on political affairs. Of all the Prime Ministers of this country he had the keenest insight and imagination: in many respects Winston Churchill alone can be said to have resembled him. What he might have achieved had power come earlier it is impossible to say. In the event he interested himself most actively in the Near Eastern Question, which for two years, 1876–78, almost monopolized his attention. He then strove to restore that British influence in

Europe which he felt that Gladstone had flung away, and his name is associated (less happily since 1938) with the idea of "Peace with Honour", which, even at the time, *Punch*, Liberal in its leanings, dismissed with a pun on Disraeli's first name, *Si non é vero, é BEN trovato*. The effort exhausted him, and after the defeat of 1880 and his death his party was never again so brilliantly led. Justly or not, it is as a parliamentary leader, rather than as a successful Prime Minister, that he is remembered.

When his opportunity came Disraeli found himself with little more power than Gladstone to intervene effectively in Europe. The "Eastern Question" gives an unfortunate impression of having been "got up for the occasion" by another "old man in a hurry", who had to make the best he could of the material to hand. Nevertheless, whatever may be thought of his practice, Disraeli had a sound grasp of the principles of British foreign policy: he may be credited with having given the country the salutary warning that home affairs do not exist in a vacuum. Gladstone once said that the first necessity for a sound foreign policy was a sound home policy. Disraeli would have reversed the order, and was far more alive than his rival to the implications for Britain, with her imperial responsibilities, of the recent developments in Europe.

## DISRAELI AND THE NEW IMPERIALISM

To him has often been ascribed the inspiration of the new spirit of Empire which marked the last thirty years of Victoria's reign. The origins of that new spirit must be investigated in the next chapter. Here it must be sufficient to say that although Disraeli was not its creator, he was one of the first to appreciate its significance and to apply it to political issues. The notion of Empire had long been discredited, but with 1870 came an abrupt change of view. It had been assumed that all colonies would go the way of the American Colonies in the previous century, and the very word Empire had been discredited through its association with Russia and with the France of Napoleon III: 1867 had seen the establishment of the Dominion of Canada, and the Gladstone Government had contained several ministers long noted for their anti-imperialist opinions. Yet by 1875 W. E. Forster could write,

"Who talks now of casting off the colonies? What more popular cry than the preservation of our colonial empire?". Many factors contributed to the change, but an outstanding one was the creation of the new Germany, which exposed the folly of dissipating any strength which Britain might draw from her imperial position.

In a speech at the Crystal Palace in 1872 Disraeli claimed that his party had three great objects: "to maintain our institutions, to uphold the Empire, and to elevate the condition of the people". The upholding of the Empire entailed the maintenance of British influence in Europe, and the two aspects of policy were closely connected in the main episodes of Disraeli's premiership—the purchase of the Suez Canal shares (1875); the proclamation of the Queen as Empress of India (1877); the resistance to Russian pressure upon Turkey (1876–78); and the forward policies pursued both in India and in South Africa. Yet however sound his views Disraeli was less fortunate in their application. In both foreign and imperial affairs he showed an inadequate appreciation of possibilities, and the disasters of 1879 in South Africa and Afghanistan contributed seriously to the Conservative defeat in 1880. His summoning of 7,000 Indian troops to Malta in 1878 as a precaution, in view of the tension with Russia, was a typical gesture. In Britain it caused some excitement; on the Continent, owing to the size of the force, only derision. It was a precedent, and an imaginative one, but the country was not yet prepared to compete with the Continental States in military power.

## "SANITAS SANITATUM"

The new interest in imperial affairs did not cause Disraeli to overlook the "condition of England" question with which he had been so much concerned in his earlier years. The "two nations" of his novel, *Sybil* (1845), were still in his mind, and the desire to "elevate the condition of the people" was no mere form of words. The improvement effected in the legal position of Trade Unions has already been noticed. It was accompanied in the same year (1875) by the Artisans' Dwellings Act, which made it possible for Local Authorities to begin the lengthy process of slum-clearance. Nowhere was this measure welcomed more warmly than in Birmingham, where the rising Radical, Joseph Chamberlain, now Mayor, was engaged in his programme of "sagacious audacity", cleaning up a sprawling, industrial city, and revolutionizing municipal government in the process. "Thank God for the Tories" he had said when the Act passed, and the powerful speech with which he recommended his rebuilding scheme to his Council has been deservedly remembered:

> We bring up a population in the dank, dreary, filthy courts and alleys . . . we surround them with noxious influences of every kind, and place them under conditions in which the observance of even ordinary decency is impossible; and what is the result? . . . Their fault! . . . It is no more the fault of these people that they are vicious and intemperate than it is their fault that they are stunted, deformed, debilitated, and diseased.

The year 1875, "an *annus mirabilis* for useful domestic legislation,"[12] as it has justly been called, saw also the passing of a great Public Health Act, and a Friendly Societies' Act. Already, in the previous session, a Factory Act had been passed to limit the hours of work of women and children, and four years later the Home Secretary, Cross, crowned his labours with a Factory and Workshops Act, which codified, consolidated and improved existing legislation, and drew blessings from the veteran of factory reform, Lord Shaftesbury. "The Conservative party," said Alexander Macdonald, one of the two "Labour" M.P.s, in 1879, "have done more for the working classes in five years than the Liberals have in fifty." Well might Disraeli write to Lady Chesterfield that the legislation would "gain and retain for the Tories the lasting affection of the working classes".[13] He might have remembered, however, that, as he himself always insisted, there are other things than merely material interests to be considered in politics.

## THE DEPRESSION OF THE 'SEVENTIES

If in matters of social policy the Conservative government achieved some notable successes, its imperial and foreign policy exposed it to serious criticism. It suffered particularly, however, from the difficult economic circumstances of the period. Industry and trade were hard hit by a severe international depression which began in 1873, the aftermath of a long period of intense activity due to the rapid development of the United States and Germany after their victorious wars. England had benefited, for instance, from the railway boom in the United States since the Civil War: the four years 1869–72 had seen no less than 25,000 miles of line put into commission, and much of the material had come from England. But America had been especially hard hit by the depression, and British industry felt the shock. Between 1872 and 1879 exports fell from £256 millions to £181 millions. Wages fell with them, and unemployment rose from one to ten per cent in the same period: the very word "unemployment", hitherto almost unknown, passed into general speech. A short recovery was followed by a second depression in the 'eighties. In the long run, however, it was agriculture that suffered far more than industry and trade. Thirty years earlier, after the repeal of the Corn Laws, Disraeli had prophesied the ruin of British farming. It was an irony of history that made him Prime Minister at the time when that prophecy actually came to be fulfilled.

## The Decline of Agriculture

The years 1875 to 1879 were years of wet summers and poor harvests, and prices were upset by the general depression. These were passing difficulties: it was the sudden development of American competition that struck British agriculture a blow from which it has never recovered. Hitherto, although the United States had exported foodstuffs, the quantities had not been so great as to disturb Europe's economy. But now, with the opening-up of the prairies by railways, the improvement of marine engines, which drastically lowered ocean freight charges, and the development of agricultural machinery (the reaper-binder, for instance, appeared in 1873), it was possible for American grain to undercut European grain. From 1874 the U.S.A. provided more than half of the total British consumption, and within a decade the price of British home-grown wheat was almost halved. On the Continent there was a reaction in favour of protection, and American competition was checked by tariffs: 1879 was the year of the new German tariff policy. In Britain an agitation for protection began, and farmers urged "the repeal of this iniquitous free trade", but no move was made. Disraeli, whose speeches of thirty years earlier were being disinterred, could offer nothing more constructive than patience and a lowering of rents. The results were startling. Food prices fell, and continued to fall, but home production of food in ten years declined from four-fifths of the total consumption to less than half. By the time of the 1881 census one hundred thousand farm workers had been forced off the land, and a million people had emigrated. Grazing continued to flourish for a time, but in the 'eighties that also was hit by the import of frozen meat: the first load of frozen New Zealand mutton was shipped in 1882. Within the space of twenty years a whole rural civilization was well-nigh destroyed. Landowners lost much of their political influence, an event signalized by the extension of the franchise to the countryside in 1884, and England at last became essentially an industrial State.

## DISRAELI AND THE EASTERN QUESTION

It might have been expected that Disraeli's premiership would not have lacked its touches of colour, and the dramatic episodes of the purchase of the Suez Canal shares and the proclamation of the Indian Empire have been better remembered than social legislation or agricultural decay. But it is particularly with the diplomacy of the Eastern Crisis that his memory is associated, and his foremost biographer has claimed the Treaty of Berlin of 1878 as his "main international work", the test of his reputation as a European statesman.[14] With the details of the crisis, which filled the years from 1875 to 1878, we cannot be concerned in this chapter, but its effects upon British politics must be considered, and its significance in the development of British policy estimated.

## GLADSTONE'S INTERVENTION

The crisis is important, apart from its place in Disraeli's career, because it marked the first major intervention by Britain in international affairs after the decisive events of 1870. It was, therefore, something of a test of her standing under the new dispensation. It also served to bring forward Robert Cecil, Lord Salisbury (1830–1903), who became Foreign Secretary in the middle of the crisis, and was destined to dominate the later years of the century, as Prime Minister from 1885 for most of the rest of the reign. But above all, it brought Gladstone back into politics and made possible his unhappy second administration, from 1880 to 1885. Gladstone had retired from the leadership of his party in 1875, having determined to devote himself, as a "disembodied spirit", free of political cares, to religious and philosophical writing, but what Disraeli, in a happy phrase, described as his "return from Elba" soon occurred, and in 1876 he flung himself into a struggle with the Government that was to open a new aspect of his career. The occasion was provided by the outbreak of war in the Balkans, and the committing by Turkish irregular troops of the terrible "Bulgarian atrocities" in the early summer of 1876. Disraeli, always sceptical where any appeal to public emotion was concerned, was at first misled by the reports of the pro-Turkish ambassador at Constantinople, Sir Henry Elliot, into dismissing accounts of the atrocities as "coffee-house babble". His view on the Turkish hold on south-eastern Europe was the traditional one, which had been supported by Britain twenty years earlier in the Crimean War, namely, that Turkey was an invaluable bulwark for British interests in the Mediterranean against the encroachments of Russia, and that the Sultan's government of his Christian subjects could be improved by diplomatic pressure. In truth, long experience had suggested that in her present condition Turkey was incapable either of improvement, or of effective resistance to Russia, and it was Salisbury's first view of her at this time that finally led him to declare, in 1896, that Britain "had put her money on the wrong horse" in the Crimean War.

Gladstone, roused by the atrocities and by Disraeli's seeming indifference to them, produced early in September his famous pamphlet, *The Bulgarian Horrors and the Question of the East*, which sold more than 200,000 copies. There followed a great political campaign, which roused the country to a pitch of excitement, and culminated, after the crisis had passed, in the Midlothian speeches of 1879, the peak of Gladstone's achievements as an orator. Though he no longer held the leadership of the Liberal Party, which had passed to Lord Hartington (better known, perhaps, by his later title of Duke of Devonshire), Gladstone now became the leader and inspiration of popular opposition to Disraeli's policy. As J. L. Hammond has said, his career had ceased: it had become a mission.

K

From this time may be dated the beginning of the estrangement from Queen Victoria, which later caused him so much pain. By 1880 she had come to distrust him, partly because of his opposition to Disraeli (now created Earl of Beaconsfield), with whom she was on terms of personal friendship, but mainly because of the "democratic" tendencies of his campaign against the Government. To her he became "that half-mad *fire-brand*", and it was his intervention in foreign affairs that first earned him the title. Never before had an ex-Minister "stumped the country" on an issue of international politics which might well involve it in war, and both the Queen and Beaconsfield came to believe that, by his criticism of Turkey and the encouragement thereby rendered to Russia, Gladstone had assumed a good deal of responsibility for the war that broke out between the two in 1877.

## DISRAELI'S POLICY

It might be said of Beaconsfield that his strategy was sound, but that his tactics were poor. He had a clear view of the underlying principles of British foreign policy, but he did not appreciate the complexity of the situation with which he had to deal, and, in his anxiety to make British influence felt in Europe, he tried to force the situation into the mould of his preconceptions. Thus, he was acutely suspicious of Russia, and dismissed the grievances of the Balkan peoples as the creations of Russian intrigue. He was justly alive to the importance of the Mediterranean to Britain, especially after the opening of the Suez Canal, and his purchase of the Khedive of Egypt's shares in the Canal had been a stroke of high policy. But to the disappointment of many foreign observers, especially of Bismarck, he failed to draw the obvious conclusion that Britain must interest herself in Egyptian affairs. He resisted any idea of the partition of the Turkish Empire, but had no alternative policy, and bewildered Bismarck by his apparent willingness to risk a general war for the integrity of an Empire that seemed to be tottering to its collapse. Bismarck's own view was that the outlying parts of the Turkish Empire should be partitioned, with Britain occupying Egypt and Syria, but his chief concern was to avoid a war between Russia and Austria. For his part, Beaconsfield distrusted Bismarck's suggestions about Egypt, for he had always been an advocate of an understanding with France and had no desire to disturb French interests in the Levant. His aim, above all, was to disrupt the alliance of the Three Emperors, the close understanding that existed between Germany, Austria and Russia, and in this he claimed to have achieved some success. It is, indeed, true that after the Berlin Conference Russia did for a time draw away from her allies, who formed a secret understanding directed against her; while, later, the incompatibility of Russian and Austrian designs in the Balkans became apparent, and through clumsy handling led to war in 1914. But it was their Balkan designs, and not Disraeli's cunning, which created the tension between them.

A study of Beaconsfield's handling of the Eastern crisis confirms the view, which has been put forward by the leading authority on the period[15], that his policy was opportunist, as, indeed, so much of his career had been. When the opportunity presented itself he felt bound to exploit it in the general interests of British influence, but in so doing he brought the country to "the Dizzy brink of war" without adequately considering what interests were at stake. The end of the crisis found Britain in occupation of Cyprus, and saddled with responsibilities for the good government of Asiatic Turkey, the significance of which Beaconsfield himself clearly did not appreciate, and which were, indeed, soon allowed to lapse. Cynics, including Bismarck, welcomed the occupation of Cyprus as an indication that he had pursued a tortuous policy of British aggrandizement, but the "Big Bulgaria" whose creation he had so strenuously resisted came into existence seven years later as he, cynical in his turn, had indeed anticipated; his fears that it would prove a Russian tool were, however, unjustified. Despite his grasp of principles and his concern for Britain's position in Europe, his handling of foreign affairs was not effective, and served to confirm the ever-watchful observer, Bismarck, in the view that Britain was not a Power to be reckoned with on the Continent.

## Disraeli's Triumph—and Decline

The main strength of Gladstone's opposition to Beaconsfield's policy lay in the North, and the rivalry between the two men reached such a pitch that *Punch*, in a memorable cartoon, rebuked them for throwing mud at each other. In truth the dispute between them was less concerned with British interests than with the future of the Sultan's Balkan subjects in the face of Turkey's declining power. Neither wished to see the Russians at Constantinople, but while Beaconsfield wished as far as possible to bolster Turkey as a bar to a Russian advance towards the Mediterranean, Gladstone preferred to trust to the national spirit of free Balkan peoples. Hence his description of the Treaty of Berlin, with its arbitrary disregard for Balkan sentiments, as "an insane covenant": hence, too, his popularity from this time in the Balkan countries. Flushed, however, by his seeming success at Berlin, Beaconsfield flung back at Gladstone a phrase that has passed into the political vocabulary, taunting him as "a sophistical rhetorician, inebriated with the exuberance of his own verbosity", and in his triumph he had much of the country with him. Had he dissolved parliament in 1878 he might well have scored another electoral victory. As it was, 1879, with another bad harvest, the Isandhlwana disaster in South Africa, and the murder of Sir Louis Cavagnari at Kabul, went badly for the Government. When the elections were held in the following year the Conservatives were decisively defeated, and Gladstone characteristically ascribed the Liberal victory to "the great hand of God, so evidently displayed". The Queen tried to avoid sending for him, but he was in fact, if not in name, the leader of the party, and in April, 1880, he formed his second administration.

## Gladstone's Second Ministry

If the 1868–74 Ministry had suffered in reputation as the years passed, the decline in the fortunes of Gladstone's second government was even more marked. He saw his first task as "the gradual unravelling of the tangled knots" of "Beaconsfieldism", but, as G. M. Young has said, "a party which takes office with no programme except to reverse the course of history" invites history's ironies. In fact, the years from 1880 to 1885 are remembered for Majuba, the occupation of Egypt, Gordon's death at Khartoum, the Penjdeh incident, which brought war with Russia ominously near, and increasing tension in Ireland—a record even more unfortunate than the one Gladstone had sought to remedy. It may be convenient first to consider briefly the Government's domestic programme, and then to survey developments in Ireland, which at this time began to dominate the political scene.

## RADICALISM IN THE ASCENDANT: JOSEPH CHAMBERLAIN

This Government has well been described as "the bridge between two political worlds". With the entry of Joseph Chamberlain into the Cabinet the centre of gravity in the Liberal party began to shift towards the radical wing. Chamberlain (1836–1914) had been in Parliament only since 1876, but his leadership of advanced Liberalism in Birmingham had given him a national reputation, and from Birmingham he had directed the new National Liberal Federation. Based on the Birmingham "Caucus", the Federation had contributed largely to the Liberal victory of 1880, and won for Chamberlain the title of the new Carnot. Already he was coming to be regarded as the next in succession for the party leadership, and he himself was anxious to break with the Whiggish moderates in the party and lead a campaign for social reform on Radical lines. In 1883 his attack on the Conservative landowners as "the class who toil not neither do they spin", introducing as it did, a new and demagogic spirit into politics, electrified advanced opinion. Backed by his friend, Sir Charles Dilke (1843–1911), who entered the Cabinet in 1882, he was largely instrumental in shaping the extension of the franchise in 1884, which increased the electorate from two and a half to nearly four and a half millions. The measure very nearly caused a constitutional crisis, as it was resisted by the Lords, and, in a notable episode, the mediating influence of the Queen had to be used to secure its passage.

## THE THIRD REFORM ACT AND THE "UNAUTHORIZED" PROGRAMME

The Franchise Act of 1884 can now be seen as marking the end of Whiggism and the coming of Liberal Democracy. Logically it should have opened the way for a new programme of social reform, and Chamberlain prepared the ground with his "unauthorized programme" of 1885 (the phrase was

Goschen's, but Chamberlain delightedly adopted it). The *Radical Programme* which appeared in the summer of that year, with a preface from his pen, called for "the intervention of the State on behalf of the weak against the strong, in the interests of labour against capital, of want and suffering against luxury and ease", and sounded "the death knell of the *laissez-faire* system". This had an alarming ring, and Chamberlain reinforced it in August with a speech in which he called upon the newly enfranchised workers to overcome "the clamour of vested interests and class privileges". Already, earlier in the year, he had upset conservative opinion in both parties by demanding "what ransom will property pay for the security which it enjoys?". The agitated reaction that this drew caused Chamberlain to moderate "ransom" into "insurance", but the perturbation among right-wing Liberals, especially among such wealthy landowners as Hartington, foreshadowed the coming split in the Liberal party. This, when it appeared in the following year, was masked by the disagreement over Ireland, which threw Chamberlain into the same camp as his more conservative colleagues, but it would have come in any case, and Radical opinion throughout the country was looking to Chamberlain in 1885 as the future Prime Minister of a Radical administration which would attack social injustice and inequality. Chamberlain himself, as his election speeches in the last months of 1885 showed, was less thorough-going in practice than his earlier declarations had suggested: "it is not our duty . . . to pull down and abase the rich", he said on one occasion, "but . . . to raise the general condition of the people". This he proposed to do in the first place by graduated property taxes which would lighten the burden of indirect taxation upon the poor, and by compulsory land purchase to relieve the rural labourer ("three acres and a cow" would seem to have been a phrase of his own devising[16]). In addition, he wanted free education. This, in effect, was his "unauthorized programme". Other points, such as the reform of county administration, on which he insisted, were already in the Liberal programme, and others again—notably complete manhood suffrage and the payment of M.P.s—were not envisaged as immediate objectives. Whatever the precise details, the programme was, by modern standards, a moderate one, and most of it was achieved within the next thirty years; but it was regarded by many at the time as little short of revolutionary, though less on account of its contents than because of the challenging spirit in which it was presented. What would have happened had events moved on their normal course it is impossible to say. Social reforms that came only after 1906 might have been carried twenty years earlier, and the Labour movement have grown up in an entirely different atmosphere. But, as J. L. Garvin has said, "the Irish tempest was to sweep across the track of British social reform and stay its full march for decades". Ireland was to split the Liberal party, to divide Chamberlain both from Gladstone and from the Radicals, and to restore the Conservatives to office for twenty years of almost continuous power. Ironically enough, it was the Franchise Act of 1884, extending the principles of 1867 to the countryside, which made all this possible by strengthening the representation of the Nationalists of rural Ireland.

## IRELAND: THE AGRICULTURAL DEPRESSION

Ireland had been hit by bad harvests and the agricultural depression even more severely than England: in three years the loss in the value of crops amounted to £26,000,000, the equivalent of thirty months' rental for the whole country, and the harvest of 1879 was the worst since the Famine. Within a few more years the value of agricultural exports to England had fallen from £72,000,000 to only £54,000,000: the whole land problem took a turn for the worse. Increasing tension in Anglo-Irish relations was inevitable, and the need for drastic economic measures was becoming apparent. There was a recrudesence of agitation, which was further inflamed by a wave of evictions. The bad times prevented many peasants from paying their rents, and, as the Land Act of 1870 afforded them little protection under these conditions, a vast number of evictions took place, rising from nearly five hundred in 1877 to more than ten times that number by the end of 1880. The Act of 1870 had brought a certain improvement for a time, but distress had become general from 1878, and agrarian distress and agrarian crime now mounted together. A chain of murderous attacks on landowners and their agents started in 1878 and the number rose until in 1882 there were 26 murders and 58 attempted murders. The climax was reached in the Phoenix Park tragedy of that year, when a group of men, within sight of the Viceregal Lodge in Dublin, stabbed to death Burke, the chief permanent official of the Irish administration, and with him the new Chief Secretary, Lord Frederick Cavendish (younger brother of Lord Hartington and husband of a niece of Mrs. Gladstone), who had arrived from England only that day. The agitation which culminated in these crimes was roused by the Irish National Land League, founded in 1879 with the object of preventing excessive rents and of promoting the ownership of the land by the peasant occupiers, but the worst murders were the work of an extremist organization, the "Invincibles". The Land League was founded by two Fenians, Michael Davitt (1846–1906) and John Devoy (1842–1928), who had both served long prison sentences after the disturbances of the late 'sixties. It was Davitt who conceived the notion of combining agrarian and political agitation in one organization. Devoy, who had been released from prison on condition that he went to the United States, had there joined the American Fenian organization, *Clan na Gael*, and his rôle was to provide encouragement and funds. But what raised the movement to supreme importance was the association of agrarian revolt with parliamentary agitation: the Presidency of the League was accepted by Parnell.

## CHARLES STEWART PARNELL

Charles Stewart Parnell (1846–91) had entered the House of Commons in 1875, and had rapidly assumed the first place among the Irish members. Even before Isaac Butt's death in 1879 it was clear that his moderate policy had failed: already, in order to force Irish grievances upon England's attention, Parnell had taken up those methods of parliamentary obstruction which later assumed such proportions that serious alterations in the House's methods of business became necessary. The hold which Parnell acquired over the Irish party is one of the most extraordinary elements in an extraordinary and tragic situation. Cold, hard, reserved, aloof, and dictatorial, a landowner and a Protestant, he seemed the reverse of everything that was regarded as characteristically Irish. Of English descent, a member of the class that had long "garrisoned" Ireland, he has been described as "the most English Irishman ever seen", but he was filled with a burning hatred of England, instilled in him partly by his American mother. By the force of a commanding personality he imposed unity and confidence on a movement racked with divisions, and no Irish leader since has equalled him in power and influence. Yet, unlike the extremists, he aimed not at a separation of England and Ireland but at a new basis for their association: as a Protestant he might even have succeeded in conciliating Ulster, though he showed little understanding of the economic needs of industrial Belfast. His fall in 1890 was a major political disaster.

## CHAMBERLAIN'S ATTITUDE

The Land League rapidly became a national movement, and, as evictions increased, agrarian crime, the work of "Captain Moonlight", came to dominate the Irish scene. Gladstone, who had visited Ireland only in 1877, before the distress began, was slow to realize that he was confronted with a new situation. Relief was urgently needed, and the Land League proposed an emergency scheme for the suspension of rents, to be followed by a wholesale Land Purchase. Belatedly, the Government introduced in 1880 a Compensation for Disturbance Bill, to afford some relief to evicted tenants. It was rejected by the Lords. Chamberlain then proposed a programme of industrial development and land improvement, an application to Ireland of the spirit of his constructive work in Birmingham, but nothing was done. Chamberlain, now as later, sympathized with Ireland's practical grievances, but refused to consider a dissolution of the Union. The Irish, he wrote to Morley in 1881, "have great practical wrongs and grievances and one sentimental grievance—the Union. The latter is one on which we cannot and will not yield." He had already compared the resistance to Home Rule with the refusal of the Northern States to recognize a dissolution of the United States in the American Civil War, and four years later he set out his own position in an uncompromising speech:

> I cannot admit that five millions of Irishmen have any greater inherent right to govern themselves without regard to the rest of the United Kingdom than the five million inhabitants of the metropolis.

K*

In taking this line Chamberlain, as experience was to show, was reflecting a good deal of average English opinion. The agrarian outrages, now rising to their climax, shocked Englishmen, and determined many to refuse to violence the concessions that might have been offered to more moderate men. Parnell, with his utter disregard of English opinion and his insistence that he was responsible only to Ireland, forgot, as one authority has said, that there was an England behind the politicians.[17] Yet the English were no less indifferent to Irish national sentiment. As Chamberlain's remarks show, it was too readily assumed that the Union was sacrosanct, that there was something "inherently right" about it, despite the barriers of race and geography.

## THE "BOYCOTT": THE SECOND LAND ACT

At the end of 1880 a new movement started, and a new word was added to the language. In September Parnell proposed that anyone taking a farm from an evicted tenant should be sent to "a moral Coventry" by "isolating him from the rest of his kind as if he were the leper of old". The first victim was a Captain Boycott, and the method was applied with such effect that his name passed into the dictionary. The Government replied with a strong Coercion Bill which, impeded as it was by Irish obstruction in the House of Commons, took over five weeks to pass into law: one sitting lasted for forty-one continuous hours. But Gladstone had already realized that something more constructive was needed, and after long negotiations he introduced his second great Land Bill in April, 1881. This measure, "the most revolutionary measure that passed through Parliament in the nineteenth century", cleared the way for the later radical solution of the Irish land problem. It accepted the principles of the "three F's", for which Butt had long since pressed—Fixity of Tenure, Fair Rents, Free Sale—and it set up tribunals which both established fair rents and protected tenants against eviction. Through weeks of debate Gladstone pushed the Bill through the House, largely by his own exertions: it was probably his greatest achievement, and the physical effort alone was considerable for a man of seventy-one. The Bill did not go far enough, but it largely met the first demand of the Land League, and it spelt the ruin of the Irish landlords. Without it the later land settlement schemes, which bought the land for the peasant farmers, would scarcely have been possible.

## THE "TREATY OF KILMAINHAM"

For tactical reasons Parnell was irreconcilable, however. Organized agitation had proved too successful to be abandoned immediately, and it was important to do nothing which would dry up the flow of money from Irish extremists in America. The situation was not allowed to improve, and in October Gladstone, uttering the famous threat, "the resources of civilization are not yet exhausted", had Parnell arrested and the Land League itself proclaimed an illegal and criminal organization. Parnell had his own reasons for welcoming detention. In 1880 he had formed the association with Mrs. O'Shea that was eventually to ruin him; their first child was about to be born, and it suited him to be out of the way. But before he was arrested he had prophesied that "Captain Moonlight" would take his place in Ireland, and violence did, indeed, continue undiminished: the number of outrages actually increased by sixty per cent. One cause was the fact that some 100,000 Irish tenants who owed large arrears of rent could not, on that account, get the protection of the new Act. Through the instrumentality of Captain O'Shea, the husband of Parnell's mistress, a plan of co-operation was devised. Parnell was to be released and was to use his influence against the disorders. In return the Government would bring in a measure of relief for the arrears. Such was the "Treaty of Kilmainham" (1882), named after the prison where Parnell was confined. The main credit for it must go to Chamberlain, who hoped, by putting an end equally to coercion and agitation, to render possible Liberal reforms in both England and Ireland. The new policy was marked by the resignation of the Lord Lieutenant of Ireland, Lord Cowper, and the Chief Secretary, W. E. Forster. In their places were appointed Lord Spencer and, to the surprise of many who had expected to see Chamberlain as Chief Secretary, Lord Frederick Cavendish. The brutal murder of Lord Frederick which followed was an exposure of the limitations of the Irish police, who had been unaware even of the existence of the "Invincibles" who committed it.

PARNELL AT THE PEAK OF HIS INFLUENCE

Parnell, who had always been opposed to violence, was shocked by the crime into thoughts of abandoning politics and leading a peaceful life with Mrs. O'Shea. This was but a passing reaction, however, and he was soon at the height of his influence. An Arrears Act gave some relief to ruined tenants, and the energetic measures of Lord Spencer's administration, with George Otto Trevelyan as Chief Secretary, combined with the operation of the Land Act to quieten the disorders in Ireland. In the autumn of 1882 Parnell replaced the Land League by the National League, with Home Rule as its avowed object, but its activities were now kept by him on the right side of the law. Two years later the Government carried the Franchise Act, which, with its extension of the rural franchise, particularly affected Ireland. The result was seen in the election of 1885, when eighty-five Home Rulers followed Parnell to Westminster. He now held the balance between the English parties, and had become a major force in British politics. Few knew of the liaison with Mrs. O'Shea, and none could guess the ruinous effect it was to have.

The next stage in Irish developments passes beyond the limits of Gladstone's second administration, but it would be convenient to continue the story up to the end of the ascendancy of Parnell. It was to be several years before Ireland ceased to dominate the political scene.

THE FIRST HOME RULE BILL

In 1885 interest turned to Westminster, to Parnell's discussions with the party leaders and Gladstone's acceptance of the policy of Home Rule. It is impossible in a brief survey to do justice to the critical and complicated manœuvres of this period, but the main lines of development may be sketched. Gladstone's government had fallen, for a variety of reasons, in June, 1885, and Lord Salisbury took office, pending the general election which was shortly to take place. Coercion in Ireland was now dropped and the first tentative measure of land purchase passed. Parnell therefore pledged his support to the Conservatives at the election, in the hope of further favours to come. But the lapsing of coercive measures led to a great increase of boycotting, and the abrupt change of policy convinced many Liberals, including the late Lord Lieutenant, that a drastic decision must be made. There was clearly a risk that the parties would compete for Irish support, and that the Irish administration would become the sport of English political changes. Gladstone, foreseeing this and deprecating any "competition" over Ireland, remained silent until after the election, preferring not to intervene until Lord Salisbury had made his position clear. He had already reached his own decision, but, looking back through the century to 1829 (Catholic Emancipation), 1846 (Repeal of the Corn Laws) and 1867, he saw the historic advantages of having reform measures passed by a Tory Government. Salisbury, however, was opposed to Home Rule and would not accept the rôle of another Peel. When the election took place towards the end of the year there was a Liberal majority which was, however, exactly matched by the Irish Home Rule vote. Parnell was in touch with Gladstone through Mrs. O'Shea, but the Liberal leader continued to advise him to make his terms with Salisbury. Nevertheless, shortly after the election occurred the famous episode of what was generally but incorrectly regarded as an astute piece of "kite-flying" on Gladstone's part. His son, Herbert, let it be known that his father was a convert to Home Rule, and after that the issue was not long in doubt. Early in February, 1886, Gladstone took office for the third time, and in April his Home Rule Bill was submitted to Parliament. It provided for an Irish Parliament and Government in Dublin, subject in some "reserved" matters to the Imperial Parliament, where, however, no Irish representatives would sit. Lord Hartington had already refused to join the Government, and before the Bill was presented Chamberlain resigned. He had always favoured a measure of local control in Ireland, but was opposed to separation, as the remark already quoted has shown. He and Hartington now led a "Liberal-Unionist" group which was eventually to join with the Conservatives in a new, "Unionist", party. The Bill itself was defeated on its second reading, when nearly one hundred Liberals voted against the Government. Gladstone promptly appealed to the country, and suffered a decisive defeat, the Liberal majority of 86 over the Conservative being converted into a minority of 203 against the Conservatives and Liberal-

Unionists combined. The dissolution of Liberalism as a party creed had begun.

Gladstone was now well advanced in his seventy-seventh year, and the Liberal party had already lost the two most able men who might have succeeded him. Chamberlain had rebelled over Home Rule, and the political career of Dilke had been ruined, such was the temper of the times, by divorce proceedings in which he had been involved. "In ten years," G. M. Young has said, "Victorian history was twice deflected by divorce." Soon the second divorce case was to bring down Parnell.

## "PARNELLISM AND CRIME"

After the failure of the Home Rule Bill attention shifted back to Ireland, where there were further outbreaks of agrarian violence, stimulated by the "Plan of Campaign" against high rents of two new leaders, William O'Brien and John Dillon. In 1887 the Government brought in a new and drastic Crimes Act, having prepared the ground by changes in procedure to prevent Irish obstruction. During the passage of the Bill through the House there appeared in *The Times* a long and detailed attack on Parnell, in the form of a series of articles on "Parnellism and Crime", and the series led up to the publication, in April, of what purported to be the facsimile of a letter of 1882, in which Parnell condoned the Phoenix Park murders. *The Times* had bought the letter, with others, in good faith, but it was later discovered to be a forgery, and *The Times* had to bear the entire cost of the special commission eventually set up to investigate the matter. The enquiry lasted for six months in 1888–89, and was the sensation of the day. Fundamentally the charges of association with violence made against the Irish leaders were found to be justified, but Parnell himself was acquitted of complicity, and there was, in consequence, a revulsion of feeling in England in his favour. At the end of 1889, however, O'Shea at last began divorce proceedings against his wife, citing Parnell as co-respondent. The step might well have been taken years before, but O'Shea had been unwilling to sacrifice financial help and expectations from an elderly relative of his wife, who had eventually died in the summer of 1889. Parnell chose not to give evidence in the suit, thereby leaving it to be supposed that for nine years he had deceived O'Shea. It was this, even more than the adultery, that shocked opinion against him. Gladstone refused to set himself up as a judge of morals, but it was made clear to him that Liberal feeling was against Parnell: "home rule was not, in England, so popular a cause", a recent historian of Parnell's leadership has justly written, "that its advocates could insult popular emotions about sexual morality".[18]

## THE FALL OF PARNELL

Gladstone therefore let it be known that if Parnell continued to lead the Irish party his own leadership of the Liberals would be rendered "almost a nullity". With that, the Roman Catholic hierarchy in Ireland spoke out, and after bitter debate the majority of the Irish party broke with Parnell. He fought on, and in the summer of 1891 married Mrs. O'Shea, but in the autumn he was taken ill and died. He left his party rift with divisions, and a great opportunity had passed. Gladstone said in 1897 that if there had been no divorce proceedings there would by then have been an Irish Parliament, and it might well have been that, after the initial shocked reaction to Home Rule in 1886, Liberal opinion would have followed Gladstone's lead and rallied to his policy. If that had occurred, Parnell, as one commentator has said, might have proved the Botha of Ireland.[19] It is one of the most intriguing "ifs" of history.

## SECOND HOME RULE BILL, 1893

The General Election of 1892 returned Gladstone with a majority of forty, and in the following year he introduced the second Home Rule Bill, which differed from the first in some important particulars, particularly in the retention of Irish representation at Westminster. The Bill passed the Commons after an arduous session, but was rejected by the Lords, and Gladstone shortly afterwards retired from politics. He had been a Member of Parliament for nearly 62 years.

## THE PROBLEM OF ULSTER

Meanwhile, another aspect of Irish politics, to which, like Parnell, he had paid insufficient attention, now came rapidly to the fore. When planning the first Home Rule Bill Gladstone had endeavoured to make special provision for Ulster, that Protestant and intensely individualist part of northern Ireland, which had provided him with a model for his first Land Act. Yet it is doubtful whether he fully appreciated the opposition of Ulstermen to rule by southern Ireland—the resistance of industrial Belfast to the political dominance of Dublin. Parnell had lost much Ulster support by committing himself to a policy of protection for Ireland when she should have the control of her economic affairs in her own hands. He failed to recognize the special needs of Belfast, with its industry and commerce and its close links, both of sentiment and of interest, with England.[20] Chamberlain, however, had grasped the position. One of his objections to the Home Rule Bill had been its ignoring of the "great distinctions . . . of race and religion and politics" between the two Irelands, and he had demanded, prophetically as it proved, a "separate assembly" at Belfast.

## CONSERVATIVE POLICY IN IRELAND:
### (1) COERCION

After 1886 Irish policy rested largely in the hands of the Conservatives, and the Conservative answer to Home Rule was particularly associated with one man, Salisbury's nephew, Arthur James Balfour (1848–1930), who was Chief Secretary for Ireland from 1887 to 1891.

Salisbury had already expressed the view that what Ireland needed was twenty years of consistent government, free from the aberrations of party policy and the pressure of agitation at Westminster. "Apply that receipt honestly, consistently and resolutely for twenty years," he had said, "and at the end of that time you will find that Ireland will be fit to accept any gifts in the way of local government or repeal of coercion laws that you may wish to give her." It was this policy, usually summed-up in the popular phrase, "twenty years of resolute government", that Balfour began to apply at a time when disorder was at its height. The Land Act of 1881 had by no means solved the problem of Irish rents. Times were bad, and a Bill for a reduction of rents by one-half, which had been introduced by Parnell, had been rejected. The "Plan of

Campaign" was an organized attempt to force landlords to accept lower rents. Balfour, supported by the strong Crimes Act of 1887, declared it criminal, and used the harshest measures to put it down, and to reassert the Government's authority. A tragic episode at Mitchelstown, when police, in self-defence, fired on a crowd, was long remembered against him. Gladstone himself bade Ireland "remember Mitchelstown", and there were many who were roused by Balfour's stern measures to a more sympathetic appreciation of Irish difficulties. Gladstone was hopeful that the unpopularity of coercion would swing opinion over to his policy, but *The Times* articles on "Parnellism" and the controversy they roused served again to confuse the issue. The struggle between Balfour and the Irish Nationalists continued, and nothing would deter the Chief Secretary: some three thousand men and women were imprisoned, among them more than twenty M.P.s, and much bitterness was aroused by the treatment of political prisoners as common criminals.

## (2) LAND PURCHASE

Yet coercion alone was not the Government's policy. Already in 1885, during Salisbury's first Ministry, there had been passed the first modest measure for State-assisted purchase of land (Lord Ashbourne's Act). In 1890 Balfour introduced a Land Purchase Bill that pledged Government credit for loans to the extent of £33,000,000 to enable peasants to become the owners of their land. It was a courageous attempt to strike at the root of the unceasing conflict between landlord and tenant, and owed not a little to the inspiration of Chamberlain. Both men believed that by instituting "some rational system" of land tenure the sting would be removed from Nationalist agitation, that Home Rule would, indeed, be "killed by kindness". The Bill passed in 1891, and towards the end of his life Balfour was able to claim that he had made modern Ireland, with its prosperous smallholders and its ruined "great houses". His Act only began the process of Land Purchase: it was completed by the measure carried in 1903, when Balfour himself was Prime Minister, by George Wyndham, who had served him in Ireland as Private Secretary. The Act of 1903 in effect introduced a considerable measure of compulsory purchase of estates in the palatable form of Government loans and bonuses, and the repayments ("annuities") of the peasant proprietors continued to be paid to London regularly until 1932, when they were appropriated by the Free State Government. That Land Purchase should have been carried out by a Conservative administration is, indeed, "one of the great acts of retribution in history".[21]

## (3) LOCAL GOVERNMENT

Before Balfour left office he had the satisfaction of suspending the operation of the Crimes Act in almost every part of the country: Home Rule, he claimed, had become "a sleeping beauty". Something he owed to the split in the Home Rule party that followed the fall of Parnell, but his severity had produced results and had prepared the way for more enlightened measures of improvement. In 1892 he introduced a Bill for Local Government in Ireland, but it failed to pass. Six years later, when his brother Gerald was Chief Secretary for Ireland, a new system of local government was, however, set up, based on the reforms carried in England in 1888 and 1894. The Irish now began to take charge of their own affairs, and a new Ireland took shape. Patriots who had hitherto seen no outlet but agitation could gain experience of administration and devote themselves to local problems. It was, as an historian of the period has written, "one of the most beneficial pieces of legislation ever passed for Ireland by an English ministry".[22]

Another feature of this later period was the agricultural reorganization inspired by Horace Plunkett, which established a network of Agricultural Co-operative Societies, and gradually built up rural prosperity on a basis of peasant proprietorship. The old grievances were thus removed, and Ireland at long last began to revive. With a prosperous agriculture in the country and an almost unlimited market for her produce in industrial Britain, it seemed to many in England that after a century the Union was at last justifying itself. Yet bitterness remained. Social and economic reforms could not satisfy national aspirations: "good government could not be an alternative to national government". With the passing of the economic grievances which had long stimulated national agitation there arose a movement of cultural revival which finally produced *Sinn Fein*.

At bottom the Irish problem was a political one: not until too late was that wholly appreciated in England.

## ENGLAND FROM THE 'EIGHTIES: SOCIALISM AND LABOUR MOVEMENTS

But it is time to turn from Irish to English affairs, and to consider other aspects of the 'eighties and 'nineties. The twenty years from 1886 to 1905 were years of Conservative, or, as it came to be called when Conservatives and Liberal-Unionists coalesced, of "Unionist", ascendancy. The chief domestic interest of the 'eighties lies in the rise of new social forces which were eventually to take shape in the Labour Party. From the distress of the years of depression emerged the British Socialist movement, and Trade Unionism received a new impetus.

Three lines of development in left-wing politics can be traced from the 'eighties; theoretical Socialism, the "new Unionism" and the beginnings of a Labour Party. Each was distinct from the others, but each represented an aspect of the new movement, and all were stimulated both by the industrial distress of the times and by the impact, direct or indirect, of Marxist teaching.

## HYNDMAN AND SOCIAL-DEMOCRACY

Marx's work was long neglected in England: not until after 1881 was it widely studied. But already, in 1879, the appearance of the American Henry George's *Progress and Poverty* had excited discussion, coinciding as it did with growing depression and unrest. In the following year a wealthy stockbroker and amateur journalist, H. M. Hyndman (1842–1921), who had a lively sympathy with the oppressed of all nations, chanced upon a French translation of *Capital*, and, as he afterwards declared, it came to him "with the force of a revelation". He at once became an ardent propagandist for Marx's teaching, and in 1881 founded the Democratic Federation, with a programme, however, that went little further than Chamberlain's programme of 1885. Hyndman realized that the ground needed preparing, that few men in England, whether workers or intellectuals, would accept Marx's doctrines. In the Trade Union movement, particularly, the notion of the "class war" was long regarded with abhorrence, and it was not until the

Congress of 1899 that the idea of a Labour group in Parliament, independent of the Liberal Party, was accepted. Even in 1906 fourteen M.P.s representing the Miners' Federation were still members of the Liberal Party, though the Labour Party then had twenty-nine successful candidates of its own.

## THE FABIANS

Three years after he had taken the first step Hyndman adopted a genuinely socialist programme and renamed his organization the Social Democratic Federation. During 1884 a potential recruit to the Federation appeared in the person of a young Irish writer, George Bernard Shaw (1856–1950): after some hesitation he decided to attach himself to another group, the Fabian Society, and he soon became the most brilliant among the able men who led it. The Fabian Society had been founded early in 1884 with the vague object of "helping on" the reconstruction of society, but soon found itself turning to moderate Socialism, and through the work of four men—Shaw, Sidney Webb, Sydney Olivier and Graham Wallas—became a unique influence in shaping opinion. The aim of the Society, as it evolved, was by research and precept to teach "the inevitability of gradualness", to show how by collectivist stages the apparently eminently rational ideal of a reformed and reconstructed society could be achieved. It sought to attain the ultimate aims of Marx without the necessity either of passing through the unpleasant preliminary stages of revolution, or even, it has cynically been suggested, of wading through his writings. Hyndman dismissed the Fabians, contemptuously, as "the Micawber club",[23] and their direct achievements, to their disappointment, were slight. For purposes of practical politics they were soon pushed aside by the Labour Party, but their influence on many of its leaders was considerable. They saw, as Max Beer has said, that Socialism "needed light rather than heat",[24] and stressed, as in their *Report* of 1896, that "the difficulty in England is not to get more political power for the people, but to persuade them to make use of the political power they have". It was they who gave to the new municipal activity the name of "municipal socialism", and their teaching, backed by the pressure of events, prepared the way for the great extension of taxation later and the emergence of the "social service state". They became eventually "a bureau of information" rather than a political group,[25] but some dozen of their members were also members of the last pre-war parliament, and the proportion of "Fabians" among ministers in the Labour Governments of 1924, 1929, and 1945 was high. Among the most influential Fabian achievements three of enduring significance in different ways may be noted here: the founding of the London School of Economics in 1895 by Sidney Webb, then Chairman of the Technical Education Board of the L.C.C.; Beatrice Webb's membership of the Royal Commission on the Poor Law (1905–09), and the great series of books on Trade Unionism and Local Government which the two wrote together. In the words of G. M. Trevelyan, "the Fabians were intelligence officers without an army . . . but they influenced the strategy and even the direction of the great hosts moving under other banners".[26]

## John Burns and the "New Unionism"

The direct influence of the Fabians on working-class organization and opinion was slight, but they represented an intellectual aspect of a movement that was many-sided, and the 'eighties saw significant developments among workers and trade unionists. The years 1886 and 1887 were years of unrest throughout the western world, marked by strikes and riots. In England the Social Democratic Federation organized demonstrations by the unemployed, and its leaders now began to attract serious public attention. Foremost among them was John Burns (1858–1943), a young trade unionist who had been an early member of the Federation and was destined to become the first Labour leader to enter the Cabinet.

The older craft Unions took no part in the socialist agitation, and were, indeed, opposed to political action (as late as 1906 a member of one of them was returned as a Conservative M.P.). There arose, in consequence, a more active "new Unionism", and a demand for "Labour" representation in Parliament. Burns was the champion of the "new Unionism", and the dramatic event which gave the movement its impetus was the famous Dockers' Strike of 1889. This strike, led by

Ben Tillett (1860–1943), Tom Mann (1856–1941) and Burns himself, exposed the poverty of London's East End, which was already being revealed by Charles Booth's great survey of *The Life and Labour of the People of London*, begun in 1886 and completed, in seventeen volumes, in 1903. The strike aroused much public interest and support, and its success led to a rapid increase of the trade union movement on new lines, with unions organized by industries rather than by crafts, and including the hitherto neglected unskilled workers as well as the skilled. Burns now became the leading figure in the trade union world, but dropped his earlier Socialism and in 1892 entered Parliament as a Radical, supporting the Liberal Party. His aim was to consolidate the "new Unionism" and secure better conditions for the workers, without, however, committing them to specifically political action: in himself, in fact, he symbolized the culmination of "Lib.-Lab." co-operation. Gladstone had already made one trade union official a Junior Minister in 1886, when Henry Broadhurst, an ex-stonemason, had become Under-Secretary at the Home Office. Burns was the first to enter the Cabinet: in 1905 he was appointed President of the Local Government Board in Campbell-Bannerman's administration.

## KEIR HARDIE AND THE LABOUR PARTY

There were many, nevertheless, who felt that Burns had not carried his movement far enough. Among these was the Scottish ex-miner and Trade Union leader, James Keir Hardie (1856–1915), who also entered Parliament in 1892 (though, unlike Burns, he lost his seat in 1895). Keir Hardie is justly regarded as the founder of the Parliamentary Labour Party, for his was the leading spirit in the establishment in 1893 of the Independent Labour Party, out of which the Labour movement in Parliament was to develop. He realized that, great though the propagandist influence of the Social Democratic Federation had been, it had lacked roots in working men's organizations, and he therefore aimed at separating the Unions from the Liberals and getting their support for an independent political movement. Burns was not sympathetic to this policy, and the Parliamentary Committee of the T.U.C. also resisted it, but Hardie's supporters were in a majority at the Trades Union Congress of 1899, and in the following year the Labour Representation Committee (later to become the Parliamentary Labour Party) was established. It was with the support of this Committee that Hardie himself was elected to Parliament for the second time in 1900, and that in 1906 twenty-nine Labour M.P.s were returned. Thus was the historic association between the Liberals and the working-class movement, which Gladstone had inaugurated, brought to a close. Among the men who worked with Keir Hardie were many who later became leaders of the Labour Party and Ministers of the Crown—James Ramsay MacDonald, J. R. Clynes, George Barnes, and Philip Snowden.

## THE TAFF VALE CASE

The rapid success of the L.R.C. was due to a variety of causes, but particularly to one which could not have been foreseen. In 1900, the year in which the Committee was established, a strike took place on the Taff Vale railway in South Wales, and when the Railway Company claimed damages against the Union concerned, it was awarded £23,000 and costs. This "Taff Vale Judgment", which seemed to abrogate the protection given to the Unions by the Acts of 1871 and 1875, was a serious blow to them, but acted as a powerful stimulus in recruiting members for the L.R.C. Keir Hardies' case for political action now seemed proved, and membership rose within a year from some 350,000 to nearly 900,000. Feeling ran so high that in 1903 Balfour appointed a Royal Commission to look into the position of the Unions, but it was Campbell-Bannerman's administration in its first year, which, under pressure from them and from the L.R.C., passed the Trade Disputes Act (1906). This Act, a further milestone in Trade Union history, rendered impossible any repetition of the Taff Vale case, and put the Unions' funds, in Keir Hardie's graphic phrase, out of reach of their enemies' guns. Their position was still not altogether assured, as the Osborne case of 1910 was soon to show, and the Labour groups in Parliament numbered as yet no more than fifty-three. But it was clear that a new force had arrived in politics, and Labour influence was to be seen in the great legislative measures that filled the years from 1906 to 1914. Much was to happen, however, before the movement reached maturity. Twenty-five years of struggle and development separated the new Labour Party of 1906 from Hyndman's Democratic Federation of 1881: twenty-five years from 1906 were to bring 1931. Beatrice Webb recorded in her diary in 1906 a shrewd comment by Lees-Smith, Principal of Ruskin Hall (afterwards Ruskin College), which had been founded at Oxford in 1899 to provide working-class leaders with opportunities for residential education. His students, Lees-Smith said, were "perpetually discussing . . . not problems of administration but policy in its narrowest sense of getting your men *there*":

> Once there, the remedies for social ills would come of themselves
> —to them they seem almost *too* obvious to be discussed.[27]

By 1906 the Labour Party was beginning to "get its men *there*", but if any naïve hopes were entertained that the worst of the struggle was over they were soon to be shattered. The party's attitude was fundamentally reformist: unlike the Continental socialist movements it drew only part of its inspiration from the Marxist conception of the class war. Indeed, the choice of "Labour" rather than "Socialist" as a title was deliberate, and the party was not formally committed to Socialism until 1918. The early leaders realized, as an historian of the party's origins has written, "that the workers ought first to recognize their solidarity as a class, their common interest in economic reform, and the need to remove their existing social inferiority".[28] No party dedicated to revolution could have won the support of the realistic trade unions, whose first concern was with their members' economic betterment and their own legal position. Nor could a revolutionary group have attracted the solid strength of the rank and file, whose experience, as the early careers of so many later Labour leaders reveal, was rooted in the practical religious democracy of Nonconformity. In this important aspect alone, in fact, is to be found a clue to much of the difference between British and Continental socialist evolution.

## LORD SALISBURY AND FOREIGN AFFAIRS

Irish affairs, educational developments, the reform of Local Government and the rise of the Labour movement, together account for the greater part of the interest of the last fifteen years of Queen Victoria's reign in internal politics. Salisbury's long term of office ended soon after the beginning of the new reign, and he died in 1903. He had been Prime Minister for longer than anyone else during the Queen's reign, but had owed his position to the split in the Liberal party over Home Rule, and had had little of constructive value to offer the country, except in foreign relations. In that field he was long acknowledged a master, and from 1885 until a new situation developed about the turn of the century he largely personified British policy, while his outlook coloured Britain's dealings with other States.

Salisbury's personal leanings were towards France, the country for which he always felt a close affection and in which he spent his holidays. But in 1885 Anglo-French relations had already been badly strained by the occupation of Egypt, while colonial difficulties were to add to the strain throughout his years of office. Not until nearly twenty years later was it possible to see the colonial disagreements in their proper relation to the common interests of Britain and France in European peace. In 1885 the danger was becoming a real one that Britain, with her far-flung responsibilities, might find herself the victim of general European hostility. Salisbury was alarmed to find how isolated she had become since 1878. Between Britain and France there stood now the rivalry over Egypt: Russia, bitterly resentful of Beaconsfield's opposition to her Balkan projects, had been further angered by the resistance shown to her expansion in Central Asia, and the Penjdeh incident, early in 1885, had for a time seemed to threaten war. Turkey, disappointed at the failure of Britain to protect her from all territorial losses in the conflict with Russia, and apprehensive at Gladstone's ferocious criticism, had watched the occupation of Egypt with some alarm, while even the traditional friendship of Austria had cooled. Moreover, Anglo-German relations had also undergone a certain amount of strain. Bismarck, ever watchful for an opportunity of conciliating France, and now under pressure from the interests in Germany which wished to see the new Empire join in the scramble for colonies, had found it possible since 1883 to combine the two policies by

giving the British lion's tail a twist. His search for colonial
territory in Africa had eventually drawn a blessing from
Gladstone, but not before the dilatory methods of the British
Colonial Office had aroused in Germany the suspicion that
Britain was envious of her expansion. The wave of indignation
that followed was of temporary use to Bismarck in both
internal and external affairs, as is shown elsewhere, but it
represented a dangerous augury for the future. A leading
authority has said that "the year 1885 marks the end of
England's unquestioned pre-eminence in the colonial field.
She was no longer the one, real world power".[29] It must be left
for later chapters to describe in more detail the process of
colonial expansion which brought about this change, and the
diplomatic difficulties that flowed from it. It was some time
before Englishmen realized the implications, and it was
Salisbury who had to handle the complications of international
politics that arose. He took office at the moment when it first
became clear that Britain could hardly remain unaffected by the
great change which had taken place in the European balance
of power in 1870, that something more was needed in the
conduct of foreign affairs than the occasional use of a
"diplomatic boathook". It says much for his skill that in
a few years he had raised high the prestige of Britain and
that he became for a time, in the 'nineties, after Bismarck's
forced retirement, the predominant figure in international
diplomacy.

## SALISBURY'S POLICY

Salisbury's policy was as far as possible to remove causes of
friction without sacrificing real British interests, and at the
same time to avoid being too closely attached to any Continental Power lest that might involve hostility with others.
He always insisted on his dealings with foreign ministers that
responsibility to Parliament made it impossible for him to
commit Britain to any line of policy that depended on future
contingencies, but at the same time he was well aware that a
"neighbourly" attitude, combined with reserve towards any
limiting projects of alliance, was in the best interests of
Britain. "Isolation", whether "splendid" or otherwise, was
never his object. The phrase was used by him, it is true, in a

speech made in 1896, but it was thrown out ironically, and it was only a misunderstanding of his aims that caused it to be misinterpreted.

## ANGLO-GERMAN RELATIONS

Since, in the 'eighties, Germany appeared as a stabilizing influence on the Continent, he was particularly careful to establish good relations with Bismarck. With his characteristic realism he did not imagine that difficulties could never arise in Anglo-German relations, though for the present a clash seemed unlikely. To the British Ambassador in Berlin he had written in 1880 that "on the sound rule that you love those most whom you compete with least, Germany is clearly cut out to be our ally", but he had added significantly that this applied only "for the present":

> Matters will, of course, have changed if it should ever enter Germany's head to desire Copenhagen or Rotterdam.

The attack on Copenhagen and Rotterdam, though long foreshadowed in German nationalist propaganda, did not come for sixty years, but an equivalent menace was the development, from the turn of the century, of a powerful German battle fleet, ostensibly built for world-wide commercial protection but actually limited in cruising range to the North Sea. Salisbury did not live to deal with this challenge, but he was perturbed by the change in German foreign policy after Bismarck's fall, and on his guard, from the first, against any attempt to draw Britain into an exclusive alliance. In spite of the need for support for the British administration in Egypt against French opposition, he rejected Bismarck's offer of an alliance in 1889, and nine years later was telling the German Ambassador, "You ask too much for your friendship." However great his desire for a close understanding between Britain and Germany, he had no intention of allowing it to modify his policy of general "neighbourliness", and as time went on he became increasingly suspicious of German motives. From the middle of the 'nineties, and especially from January, 1896, when the "Kruger Telegram" shattered British illusions about German friendliness, Anglo-German relations steadily deteriorated. Something more positive than Salisbury's policy then became necessary, and a new line was being struck out even before he retired.

## BRITAIN'S ISOLATION AND THE NEW POLICY

The last years of the century found Britain, in spite of Salisbury's efforts, dangerously isolated. New problems throughout the world were straining the friendly relations he had endeavoured to establish, and the Boer War practically united Europe in hostility to Britain. Yet British naval power was not yet seriously challenged, and foreign intervention on behalf of the Boers was therefore impossible. Salisbury still preferred to rely on the Navy rather than on any limiting foreign alliance. To German warnings of the dangers of isolation he replied that "it would hardly be wise to incur novel and most onerous obligations in order to guard against *a danger in whose existence we have no historical reason for believing*". But circumstances were already beginning to tell against him. The rise of a powerful German fleet brought forward other "historical reasons" for a change of outlook, while the very refusal of a German alliance, *on Germany's terms*, intensified the hostility felt towards Britain. The *Entente* with France in 1904, though that might be regarded as typical of the policy of "neighbourliness", was by implication a reversal of Salisbury's avoidance of commitments, and was accepted in Germany as a challenge. Already, before Salisbury had retired, Chamberlain and Lansdowne, in turn, and in the face of his scepticism, had endeavoured without success to reach a limited agreement with Germany on outstanding issues. With his retirement an epoch ended. The framing of the Anglo-Japanese Alliance in the last months of his premiership was a significant comment on the change in the international scene.

## BALFOUR: THE LIBERAL LANDSLIDE, 1906

Salisbury was succeeded as Prime Minister by Balfour. The main legislative achievements of his administration were the Education Act of 1902, which introduced secondary education under the control of Local Authorities, and the Irish Land Purchase Act of the following year. These two measures alone would serve as a corrective to the popular view that the administration was a failure, but there were in addition two others which were of the first importance in view of the deteriorating international situation; the *Entente* with France and the establishment of the Committee of Imperial Defence in the same year, 1904. Balfour clung to office through all the difficulties of the previous year, when his Cabinet was split on the question of "tariff reform", because he was determined to carry these two measures, and with them the renewal of the Japanese alliance, to a successful conclusion. The Committee of Imperial Defence was essentially his creation, and proved to be a permanent and invaluable addition to the machinery of government. But the British public had little interest in problems of foreign relations, and was far more concerned at the revelations about the employment of Chinese labour on the Rand, to which Balfour had unthinkingly given his approval. At the end of 1905, realizing his weakness, and hoping to take advantage of divided views in the Liberal Party over Home Rule, he suddenly resigned. The Liberal leader, Campbell-Bannerman, though warned of the trap, felt it his duty to accept office, and the public, in the election of January, 1906, endorsed his decision. In the "landslide" Balfour himself was defeated, and when Parliament met his party found itself in a minority of well over three hundred. Balfour later declared that the Liberals had won the election on no policy at all, but the extent of the victory was an indication that the country wanted no more of him. As he considered the change that had taken place in the composition of Parliament with the sudden increase of Labour membership, Balfour realized well enough, however, that something of lasting significance had occurred:

> We have here to do with something much more important than the swing of the pendulum or all the squabbles about Free Trade and Fiscal Reform. We are face to face (no doubt in a milder form) with the Socialistic difficulties which loom so large on the Continent. Unless I am greatly mistaken the election of 1906 inaugurates a new era.

It was typical of this cool and aristocratic intellectual that the prospect of "a new era" revived an interest in politics which had been almost extinguished by the trials of recent years.

## THE "NEW ERA"

When, after his return to office during the First World War, Balfour had become an "elder statesman", he once contrasted the strenuous activity of international politics in the post-war period with his recollections of more leisurely days, and observed that "nothing ever really happened before 1914". The world of the 'twenties was, indeed, markedly different from the "flash" Edwardian world, which in retrospect appears inevitably as the sunset glow of the nineteenth century. Much had happened, for good and evil, which could never be undone, and institutions and standards had been swept away, which in 1914 had been regarded as largely immutable. The whole range of international affairs, in particular, had widened, and the subject had ceased to be one of the secret mysteries of statecraft. President Wilson's ideal of "open covenants openly arrived at" was still far from being realized, but the conditions of the late nineteenth century, when acute crises could be overcome with the public hardly aware that they existed, had passed away. In home affairs the war years had brought changes no less significant. The principle of full manhood suffrage had at last been accepted and women had also been admitted to the franchise. The Irish problem had flared out into civil war, and a temporary settlement, though no solution, had been found. Interest in social legislation was increasing, and the Labour movement had firmly established itself. Its part in the war had won for it a growing recognition, which had been amply reinforced by the influence of the Russian Revolution. Already some of its leaders had held office—had, in other words, "*got there*"—and the notion of a Labour Government could no longer be regarded merely as a subject for humour or panic.

Yet much that had happened would have happened in any case, though probably in a different manner, had there not been the profound disturbance of war. The war itself burst in 1914 upon a Britain that was largely unprepared for it and was rift with political divisions. Two bitter years of political conflict had preceded the passing of the Parliament Act of 1911, and had been succeeded by labour troubles, "suffragette" agitation and the threat of civil war in Ireland. The war imposed unity, but serious strains reappeared after 1918, and have still not worked themselves out. In fact, much had happened before 1914 that could certainly not be dismissed as a mere "nothing", and it is only the overwhelming shadow of the "Great War" that reduces the last ten years of peace before 1914 to apparent insignificance. With the documents exposed, and the pre-war negotiations and rivalries of the Powers revealed, it is inevitable that foreign affairs should tend to loom large in any study of the period. Yet it must be remembered that few took account of them at the time, and fewer still were informed on the issues involved. The Liberal Government itself, when it took office in 1905, was surprised at the seriousness of the international situation, and was to find its plans for peace and reform at home disturbed by the demands of the threatening conflict abroad.

## CAMPBELL-BANNERMAN

Campbell-Bannerman, when he formed his administration in 1905, had been recognized as leader of his party only since 1899, and had become widely unpopular since then because of his opposition to the South African War. His previous terms of office had lain mainly in the Service ministries, and the long Unionist supremacy had deprived him of opportunities of wider experience. His simple manner, homely personality and dry humour were not characteristics to strike the public imagination, and he had suffered while in Opposition from contrast with the brilliant Balfour. But all that was changed when he became Prime Minister: he at once acquired a new manner, revealing a quiet dignity and shrewd grasp of affairs that quite won over the "Liberal-Imperialists" of his own party who had disagreed with his Boer War policy. Balfour was worsted in his first encounter with his successor in debate, and took some time to adapt his manner to the new tone of the House, but "C.-B." proved an able leader of his mixed team. In the two short years before his death in 1908 he had set the new Liberalism on its course, and had rendered a service of the first importance to the whole British world.

## SELF-GOVERNMENT IN SOUTH AFRICA

His administration contained a team of brilliant men, with H. H. Asquith, Sir Edward Grey, R. B. Haldane, John

Morley, James Bryce, Augustine Birrell and the newcomer, David Lloyd George, in the Cabinet, while junior positions were held by such men as Reginald McKenna, Winston Churchill and Walter Runciman. All were destined to make their mark on events. But, apart from the skill he showed in leadership, Campbell-Bannerman's place in history is assured by his success in 1906 in carrying, against considerable opposition, the grant of self-government to the Transvaal and Orange River Colony, the Boer States which, only four years earlier, had been beaten into submission. The achievement was essentially the Prime Minister's own, for he had even to win over his reluctant colleagues to the step; but it made possible one of the most generous settlements in history and ensured that South Africa should be given every opportunity to achieve a real unity. The long-debated Union of the South African colonies followed in 1910, and when the unity of the Empire was tested four years later South Africans, with but few exceptions, stood by Britain. "It is indeed more than doubtful," G. M. Trevelyan has said, "whether Great Britain could have survived the two world wars if South Africa had not been previously reconciled."[30] That may well stand as an enduring tribute to Campbell-Bannerman's bold, imaginative, and, at the time, only doubtfully popular, measure in freeing his country's defeated opponents. Whether in the long run, the move—or, indeed, the Boer War itself—deflected the development of South Africa on Afrikaner lines may, however, half a century later, be doubted.

## THE HOUSE OF LORDS

The other measures of the administration's first years were, however, less fortunate. With their position in the Commons drastically weakened, the Unionists had decided to rely on their immense majority in the Lords to resist Government legislation. Balfour and Lord Lansdowne, the Unionist leader in the Lords, had agreed on "a common plan of campaign" to be followed by the party in both Houses, and the old issue of "the Lords v. the People", of which nothing had been heard during ten years of Unionist rule, now reappeared. The Government's programme for the first session of the new Parliament provided for no less than twenty-two measures, of which three—an Education Bill, the Trades Disputes Bill and a Plural Voting Bill—were of the first importance. For tactical reasons the Trades Disputes Bill, the outcome of the Taff Vale case, was allowed to pass the Lords, but the Education Bill, which attempted to satisfy Nonconformist grievances against the 1902 Act, was rejected, together with the measure aimed at suppressing "plural voting", that is, the right to vote in more than one constituency (which was not finally abolished until 1948). The Unionist argument was that the "landslide" of 1906 had been no more than a "swing of the pendulum", the inevitable outcome of nearly twenty years of Conservative rule, and that through its strength in the Lords the party should maintain its position until the recent defeat could be redressed at another election. But the election of 1906 had, in fact, seen something more than the normal mild reaction against the party in power. Radicals had been pressing for more than twenty years for a limitation of the authority of the Lords, and their influence was now strengthened by the new force which had appeared on the parliamentary scene, the Labour Party. By their tactics the Unionists, blind to the significance of the new movement, brought to a head a constitutional problem which but for the Liberal defeats over Home Rule would undoubtedly have called for attention much earlier. The rejection of the Education Bill was met by Campbell-Bannerman with challenging words:

> I say with conviction that a way must be found, a way will be found, by which the will of the people expressed through their electoral representatives in this House will be made to prevail.

Lloyd George summed up Liberal feeling in a brilliant flash when he said that the House of Lords had ceased to be "the watch-dog of the Constitution", and had become merely "Mr. Balfour's poodle".

In the summer of 1907 Campbell-Bannerman carried in the Commons a resolution stating that "the power of the other House to alter or reject Bills passed by this House must be so restricted by law as to secure that within the limits of a single Parliament the final decision of the Commons should prevail". Attempts, in which the King took an active and valuable part,

L

were made to smooth over differences and achieve a compromise, but no success was achieved. At a time when social problems and foreign affairs were demanding increasing attention, the country was about to be faced with a fundamental constitutional issue, an issue, moreover, which, as experience was to show, was capable of no simple solution, for it remains unsettled forty years later. The endeavour to introduce satisfactory *written* conditions into a constitutional system essentially based on custom and convention had to be made, but the experience showed that constitution-making is the most difficult of all the political arts, and one which is better avoided.

## HALDANE AND ARMY REFORM

In 1907 the Lords continued their wrecking tactics with attacks on various measures for Land Reform submitted by the Government, but the chief interest of the session lies in the considerable measure of Army reform carried by the Secretary for War, R. B. Haldane (1856–1928). Haldane was one of the few men in politics who had been trained in philosophy, and his deep knowledge of Germany and German institutions had shown him the need for a reorganization of the British Army. With a European war well within the bounds of probability it was clearly unwise to continue to rely on an army devised mainly for imperial policing, while efficient planning demanded the creation of a General Staff. Yet the interest of the Government's supporters was largely in economy: few saw the dangers of the foreign situation, or understood the part that Britain would be called on to play in it. Fortunately Haldane was able to combine efficiency with economy. At a time when the Naval Estimates were rising rapidly he was able to reduce the Army Estimates by some three millions, while reorganizing the home forces in two sections, an expeditionary force and the volunteer "Territorials", with a General Staff at their head. The whole system had exactly seven years in which to prepare itself, and when the testing time came it more than justified Haldane's hopes. Given the impossibility of applying conscription, and the necessity for speedy action, it proved, in all probability, as efficient an answer to the military problem as could have been devised.

## OLD AGE PENSIONS, 1908

Little had been achieved by 1908 in social legislation, but with typical caution Asquith was preparing a surplus for a measure which he had long since resolved to introduce, and in 1908, when he had already become Prime Minister on Campbell-Bannerman's death, he himself proposed the establishment of a system of Old Age Pensions. It had been clear for many years that some system of relief for the aged poor, other than the hated workhouse, was needed. Charles Booth, author of the great survey of London poverty, had advocated it in 1891, and Chamberlain had taken up the idea in the following year, while the German social insurance laws had inevitably exercised a good deal of influence. Several commissions of inquiry had looked into the matter during the 'nineties, and but for the Boer War, which made other expenditure necessary, some modest scheme might have been introduced. The main difficulty was to raise the money for pensions at a time when low taxation was regarded almost as a sacred principle. Chamberlain, when he began his campaign for "Tariff Reform", had hoped in that way to meet the cost without increasing direct taxation. Asquith, on taking office in 1906, had undertaken to bring forward a pension scheme as soon as he had made the necessary financial provision, and in 1908, with a budget surplus of some five millions anticipated, the time had come. The pension was a small one, allowing only 5s. at the age of seventy, or 7s. 6d. for a married couple living together, but it marked the first breach in the traditional view that poverty was a matter for charity, and recognized that the community had responsibilities towards its less fortunate members. It was, in fact, intended to be a first step towards the wider measures of social insurance that followed within a few years, though its ultimate significance lay rather in the tacit acceptance of an entirely new conception of the functions of the State as a constructive force for individual and social improvement, rather than merely for "police" purposes.

## NATIONAL INSURANCE, 1911

Old Age Pensions were non-contributory, but the next great measure of social policy was Lloyd George's vast insurance scheme for Sickness and Unemployment, based on compulsory contributions, which was introduced in 1911. The share of the cost to be borne by the Treasury added further to the demands on national taxation, and the strain was already being increased by other developments. Increasing international tension, and especially the growth of Anglo-German naval rivalry, were making heavy demands on the Service Estimates, and even before the additional burden was imposed in 1911 the effort to meet the needs both of defence and of social policy had brought a financial crisis, and with it the climax of the conflict between Commons and Lords.

## ASQUITH'S ADMINISTRATION

Campbell-Bannerman died in 1908, and was succeeded by Asquith, who had for some time been marked out as his obvious successor. A great administrator and parliamentarian, sound in leadership and unflurried in times of crisis, Asquith, for all his ability, lacked the qualities which draw devotion. A French historian has described him as "a man of sound judgment who lacked the flame of genius".[31] He lacked also the imaginative power that is demanded by true leadership, and failed during the war, it has been suggested, largely because he did not appreciate that in wartime a Prime Minister should not only be active, but should *appear* active. His portraits reveal clearly his solid strength and native shrewdness, together with a hint of his aversion from extremes. "If there could be such a thing as a Humour of Moderation," one writer has observed, "then Mr. Asquith was the perfect example of it." The contrast with the brilliant and ebullient Lloyd George, who eventually succeeded him in 1916, was marked.

## THE "PEOPLE'S BUDGET", 1909

Asquith chose Lloyd George as his Chancellor of the Exchequer (he also brought Winston Churchill into the Cabinet for the first time), but directed the Budget of 1908, which he had himself prepared. Lloyd George introduced his first Budget in the following year, and with it brought the constitutional crisis to a head. Hitherto the Liberals had been on the defensive: Lloyd George, true to his temperament, plunged into the counter-attack.

The first necessity was for additional expenditure on the

Navy. German building had reached such a pitch that the Admiralty demanded six of the new "Dreadnoughts", and after much public agitation it was decided to build eight ("We want eight, and we won't wait", ran the refrain). With provision for them, and for social legislation, Lloyd George had to find an additional fifteen millions. He did it by raising income-tax to 1s. 2d., and adding an extra tax, the "super-tax", on higher incomes. Death duties were increased, as were also the duties on tobacco, spirits and liquor licences. Above all, though their implications were political rather than fiscal, there were duties on Land Values, a direct blow at the land-owners. Out of the revenue to be raised, sums were set aside for road improvements, increasingly necessary with the coming of motor traffic, and for the establishment of a system of Labour Exchanges, which had been proposed by a brilliant economist, W. H. Beveridge, a name well known to later generations. One modification of the income-tax laws was proposed: there was to be a child allowance of £10, and the principle now modestly introduced was to become part of taxation policy.

Lloyd George's proposals astonish now only by their moderation, but the effect of this "People's Budget" on the Unionists was devastating. They opposed it less for what it did than for what it implied, rightly seeing in it the thin ends of many wedges. "This is a war budget," said Lloyd George in the peroration of the budget address, "it is for raising money to wage implacable war against poverty and squalidness"; and the implied challenge was taken up. Already the Cabinet had spent longer in consideration of the budget than had ever been done before, and in the face of Unionist opposition the delay in passing it through the Commons was without precedent. Meanwhile a campaign of agitation, opened by Lloyd George with his vituperative Limehouse speech, swept the country, and in November the Unionist peers, against the advice of their more moderate leaders, and even of the King, rejected the Finance Bill by 350 to 75.

## The Parliament Act, 1911

It was an unprecedented step, and called for unprecedented measures. An election was held in January, and the Liberals were returned, though with a reduced majority. The budget was again presented, and was now permitted to pass, just a year after its first introduction. But the question of the powers of the Lords to interfere with legislation was left to be settled. The details of the confused situation that followed, complicated as it was by the death of the King, need not detain us. Efforts at a compromise settlement failed, and eventually, after another election in November, 1910, the great Parliament Act of 1911 was passed. It was carried in the Lords only through the knowledge that the new King, George V, had undertaken, if it were rejected, to create enough peers to swamp the Unionist majority. The Act made it impossible for the Upper House to reject or amend Money Bills, and limited to three successive sessions their power to delay other legislation. There was also vaguely worded provision for the revision of the membership of the Upper House, which it proved impossible, over many years of discussion, to carry into effect.

The Parliament Act was the natural corollary of the Franchise Acts of 1867 and 1884. Its significance lay, however, rather in the acceptance of the primacy of the Commons than in the elaborate constitutional machinery for its enforcement. Indeed, by the irony of history the machinery has proved in practice of only limited value. It was invoked for two measures before 1914, the disestablishment of the Welsh Church and Irish Home Rule, but both were suspended "for the duration" before they could come into effect. The Welsh Church was finally disestablished in 1920, but by that time Home Rule was no more than a Victorian relic: Ireland was set on other paths. The only measure which has become law by the normal process of the 1911 Act, in fact, has been the further Parliament Act of 1947, which reduced the term of the Lords' power to suspend legislation from three sessions to one.[32] The Upper House itself continues in theory, though not altogether in practice, "unreformed" through continued failure to agree on its composition.

## PAYMENT OF M.P.s

Liberalism in 1911 still showed no lack of vigour, and was pressing forward to new measures. The National Insurance Act of 1911 has already been mentioned. In the same year was introduced the payment of M.P.s. Radicals had long advocated this, and it had figured in Chamberlain's "unauthorized programme" of 1885, but the immediate occasion of its passing was the "Osborne judgment" of 1910. In that case it had been laid down that it was illegal for trade unions to make a compulsory levy on their members for parliamentary purposes, and a number of M.P.s had at once found their trade union salaries cut off. An Act of 1913 established for unions the right of "political levy", to which, however, members were not bound to contribute, but the position of M.P.s was assured, though only moderately, by the payment of £400 a year from the Treasury.

## THE POOR LAW COMMISSION

One great failure of the Government must be recorded. Before its resignation the Balfour administration, disturbed by growing evidence of pauperism, had set up a Royal Commission to inquire into the working of the Poor Law. The Commission reported in 1909, presenting two great reports, a Majority and a Minority. Fabian influence was strong in the latter, which was written by Sidney Webb, but both advocated extensive reforms, in particular the abolition of the Boards of Guardians and the assumption of their responsibilities by Local Authorities, as had already occurred with other local Boards. John Burns at the Local Government Board proved incapable of giving a lead, however, and before any action was taken the war intervened. Beatrice Webb, as a member of the Royal Commission, with an eye to possible difficulties had expressed the hope that "the Liberals will adumbrate the scheme, but the Tories will carry it out".[33] The hope was tardily realized in 1929 when the first necessary reforms were carried by the second Baldwin administration: by that time the minority report itself had become a classic. By that time, also, unemployment insurance, first tentatively introduced as part of the National Insurance Act in 1911, had been extended and developed to meet the problems of post-war depression. But the failure of Asquith's government to grapple with the Poor Law was evidence of the lingering concern of the Victorians with public economy, which was soon to be rudely dispelled by the burdens of war.

## THIRD HOME RULE BILL AND IRISH DEVELOPMENTS

After 1911 the attention of the Government, under steady pressure from the eighty-four Irish M.P.s who held the balance of power in the Commons, turned to Ireland, and in 1912 the third Home Rule Bill was introduced. The developments in the Irish situation since the days of the two earlier Bills had been considerable. Both the face and the mind of Ireland had undergone striking changes. The poor, rack-rented peasants of the unhappy past were rapidly becoming a nation of small-holders: nine million acres had been acquired for them under the Land Purchase Act of 1903, against only some 1,500,000 affected by the previous Acts.[34] The more prosperous Ireland of today was taking shape. The political situation had not, how-ever, recovered from the tragedy of Parnell. Home Rule was still insisted on, and would not be killed by kindness, but the party was only a shadow of its former self, " a sheath without a sword", as an Irish historian has called it, sustained only by the "pale, proud, fierce ghost of Parnell".[35] The split between Parnellites and anti-Parnellites had been healed in 1900, when a united party had again been formed under the worthy leader-ship of John Redmond (1856–1918), but, although seemingly secure, it was losing its hold on the country: Home Rule had been too long delayed, and young Ireland was looking else-where for national self-expression. Most ominously, it was losing the confidence in parliamentary action which Butt and Parnell, in their different ways, had done so much to inculcate.[36] By 1914, it has been said, "the faith of Irishmen in English parties and English promises was dead".[37] Already the *Sinn Fein* movement was taking shape. The Fenian spirit of the 'sixties had lingered on, and after the violent digression of Parnell's career a number of local patriotic groups had gradually come together to form, in 1900, *Cumann na nGaedheal*, and eight years later *Sinn Fein*. The principal moving spirit was Arthur Griffith (1872–1922), who in the last year of his life was to become the Head of the first Irish Free State Government. Griffith defined *Sinn Fein's* aims in 1905 as national self-development through all Irish movements instinct with the national tradition "and not looking outside Ireland for the accomplishment of their aims",[38] the last being the decisive point. Arising as it did at this moment, *Sinn Fein* was inspired in part by the celebration of the centenary of the Irish rebellion of 1798, in part by the resistance of the Boers in the Boer War. It owed even more, perhaps, to the national cultural revival, which produced in 1893 the Gaelic League, founded to preserve and extend the use of the Irish language by a small group of men under the leadership of Douglas Hyde (1860-1949), the Protestant, Anglo-Irish classical scholar, the Parnell of the language movement,[39] who, many years later, was to crown his life's work with the Presidency of the Irish Republic (1938-45).

## ULSTER

The future was with this self-conscious, self-confident stirring: it is doubtful whether Home Rule would have meant much even if it had been carried. But the long delays gave an edge to nationalist feeling, which was still further embittered by growing tension in Ulster. The Irish leaders in Parliament were out of touch with the rising feeling in both South and North. In Ulster there was developing an ugly situation, in which resistance to the Government's measures was coming to be regarded as proof of loyalty to the British connexion. Under the forceful leadership of Sir Edward Carson (1854-1935), Balfour's late Solicitor-General, and with the active support of the Unionist leaders, a private army of "Ulster Volunteers" had come into existence, pledged to establish a Protestant Government in Belfast as soon as Home Rule became law. Balfour had been forced out of the Unionist leadership in 1911, and had been succeeded by Andrew Bonar Law (1858-1923), who did not hesitate to encourage Ulstermen in their threat of violent resistance. Violence inevitably begot violence, and the strong words of the North were matched by a similar readiness to fight in the South. Asquith, with his caution and moderation, was hardly the man to handle so delicate a situation. Trusting to a willingness to compromise which had long ensured the stability of British institutions, but which had suffered rude assaults in recent years, he let the situation slide. The passions which move men in politics were probably beyond his ken, and his handling of Ireland certainly does not show him at his best.

The Home Rule Bill was introduced in April, 1912, and

L*

passed the Commons in the following January after a long and stormy session. Rejected by the Lords, it was again sent up to them in 1913 and 1914, and would have become law but for the outbreak of war. It was finally placed on the Statute Book in September, 1914, but accompanied by a further Act suspending its operation until after the war.

## INCREASING TENSION AND NEW FORCES

Efforts were made by the King in 1913 and 1914 to bring the political leaders together for a compromise solution, but without success, and the Buckingham Palace Conference on the eve of the war failed to reach agreement. Meanwhile, guns were being "run" into Ireland by both sides, and the discipline of the Army had been shaken by the clumsy episode of the "Curragh mutiny" (March, 1914). The threat of civil war seemed real.

Whether, but for the outbreak of war with Germany, some solution might have been found, it is impossible now to say. With the diversion of attention to other matters, the Irish situation was left in suspense, and the drift to violence continued until the unhappy tragedy of the rebellions of 1916 and 1920. Despite all that had been done to remedy some of the worst evils of Irish life, much of the country remained irreconcilable: to the end the handling of Ireland proved the dismal failure of British politics. It may well have been that the problems of Ireland were insoluble: they were certainly insoluble by 1914 in the context of British politics. A charitable view has it that the failure was not due to any lack of good will:

> It was caused rather by an inability to understand the Irish political outlook, by confusion of mind as to the distinction between good government and national government. . . . (by a failure) when it was realized that a new order in Ireland was inevitable . . . to facilitate its emergence.[40]

We are brought back to the point made earlier, that Ireland was for too long regarded as no more than a remote and difficult annex of England; as, in fact, in the apt Shavian phrase, "John Bull's Other Island".

Apart from its effects in Ireland itself, this last stage of the Home Rule controversy is significant as an illustration of an increasing tendency to violent action in politics. The Lords' resistance to the Parliament Bill, the agitation stirred up throughout the country against the National Insurance scheme, the violence of the "militant suffragettes" in their struggle for votes for women, and the wave of strikes in 1910–12, all indicated the existence of a new and rougher spirit, and of a determination to use extra-parliamentary methods to force concessions. In truth there was a fundamental disillusionment. On the one side, Liberal reforms had not brought the millenium, and the entry of Labour representatives into Parliament had done little to improve economic conditions, which were showing signs of deteriorating. To the other side, educational advance and social and political reform had not brought social peace; property's "insurance", to return to Chamberlain's phrase of 1885, had not staved off further demands. New forces were at work, signalized by the development of a "syndicalist" movement in the trade union world, and the struggle with "capital" was becoming more open. A great period of reform, which had begun in 1867, had closed with the Parliament Act and the National Insurance Act, and the demand for more radical measures was rising. There was an impatience, too, with the compromises and slow march of parliamentary advance, and, among the more privileged, a fear of its inexorable pace. The very violence of the Unionists, for instance, was a measure of their helplessness in Parliament in the face of the combined voting strength of Liberals and Irish Home Rulers. The war transformed the situation, but great movements took place during its course, and there could be no return in 1918 even to the situation on the eve of the conflagration.

Yet for all its violence the period before 1914 was one of significant constructive achievement. The measures then carried enabled Britain to face the strains of the post-war world without serious danger of conflict or collapse. Many of the desperately fought issues now seem dim and cold, or too obviously beneficent or inevitable to have deserved such bitterness of opposition. By contrast with what was to come, the Edwardian era has since seemed at times almost a golden age. As we look back, we are struck, as one historian has said, by "the seething and teeming of this pre-war period, its immense ferment and its restless fertility".[41] Balfour's estimate, however euphemistic in intention, does not do justice to the achievement: much, in fact, had happened before 1914.

REFERENCES

This chapter has inevitably drawn heavily upon the wealth of material contained in the major biographies and histories of the period, notably the following, to which no detailed references are given:

| | |
|---|---|
| John Morley: | *Life of Gladstone.* |
| W. F. Monypenny & | |
|                          G. E. Buckle: | *Life of Disraeli.* |
| G. E. Buckle (ed.): | *Letters of Queen Victoria.* |
| J. L. Hammond: | *Gladstone and the Irish Nation.* |
| J. L. Garvin & J. Amery: | *Life of Joseph Chamberlain.* |
| Lady Gwendolen Cecil: | *Life of Lord Salisbury.* |
| Blanche Dugdale: | *Arthur James Balfour.* |

The brilliant interpretative study by G. M. Young, *Victorian England: Portrait of an Age*, has been a source of illumination as well as of telling phrases, and the help given to all students of the period by R. C. K. Ensor's authoritative survey, *England, 1870–1914*, is also acknowledged.

1. Ensor: p. 136.
2. G. M. Trevelyan: *British History in the Nineteenth Century*, p. 424.
3. *Great Contemporaries* (essay on John Morley), p. 69.
4. Cambridge University Local Lectures, Report for 1883.
5. S. O'Faolain: *The Irish*, p. 139.
6. *The Political Correspondence of Mr. Gladstone and Lord Granville, 1868–1876*: ed. Agatha Ramm, I, p. 87.
7. P. S. O'Hegarty: *A History of Ireland under the Union, 1801–1922*, p. 602.
8. ibid., p. 457.
9. T. de V. White: *The Road of Excess*, p. 322.
10. O'Hegarty: p. 477.
11. *The Queen and Mr. Gladstone:* ed. P. Guedalla, II, pp. 176–77.
12. Ensor: p. 35.
13. *The Letters of Disraeli to Lady Bradford and Lady Chesterfield, 1876–1881*, I, p. 260.
14. Monypenny and Buckle: *Life of Disraeli*, II, p. 1234.

15. R. W. Seton-Watson: *Disraeli, Gladstone and the Eastern Question*, passim.

16. C. H. D. Howard: "Joseph Chamberlain and the 'Unauthorized Programme' ", *English Historical Review*, Vol. 65; an article which this section owes much.

17. Ensor: p. 95.

18. C. C. O'Brien: *Parnell and His Party, 1880–90*, p. 294.

19. J. A. Spender: *Great Britain, Empire and Commonwealth, 1886–1935*, p. 40.

20. E. Strauss: *Irish Nationalism and British Democracy*, p. 179.

21. N. Mansergh: *Britain and Ireland*, p. 49.

22. F. S. L. Lyons: *The Irish Parliamentary Party, 1890–1910*, p. 68.

23. H. Pelling: *The Origins of the Labour Party, 1880–1900*, p. 231.

24. M. Beer: *A History of British Socialism*, II, p. 285.

25. Pelling: p. 194.

26. *British History in the Nineteenth Century.* p. 403.

27. *Our Partnership*, p. 353.

28. Pelling: p. 64.

29. W. Langer: *European Alliances and Alignments, 1871–90*, p. 318.

30. Quoted in *Manchester Guardian*, 9th July, 1948.

31. E. Halévy: *A History of the English People in the Nineteenth Century*, VI (1905–14), p. 235.

32. The whole story may be read in R. Jenkins's study, *Mr. Balfour's Poodle*.

33. *Our Partnership*, p. 418.

34. Strauss: p. 199.

35. O'Hegarty: p. 605.

36. Lyons: p. 264. See also *Parnell and His Party, 1880–90*: Epilogue.

37. N. Mansergh: *Ireland in the Age of Reform and Revolution*, p. 173.

38. O'Hegarty: p. 650.

39. ibid., p. 616.

40. Mansergh: pp. 117–18.

41. Ensor: p. 557.

# VII

## THE BRITISH EMPIRE, 1867-1914

### Trends in Imperial policy

#### Changing Attitudes

THE year 1870 marked a watershed in the imperial development of Britain no less than in her internal affairs. The creation of the Canadian federation in 1867, though it aroused little enough attention at the time, suggested that, as Lord Durham had foreseen nearly thirty years earlier, the British settlements overseas could achieve political maturity without necessarily desiring to sever the link with the home country, and within two years the coolness of Gladstone's government to New Zealand had aroused a storm of protest which can conveniently be regarded as marking the beginnings of the new imperialism. In the case of the dependent territories, valued for their commercial or strategic significance, or as sources of raw materials, even apart from the special problem of India the ''seventies and 'eighties were to reveal a new interest and an awareness of the advantages and responsibilities of continued control.

#### The Mid-Victorian Attitude

Yet only a few years earlier it had generally been assumed, almost without question, that all colonial settlements would eventually go the way of the United States, while the combined principles of free trade and national economy would lead to the abandonment of all but strategic posts necessary for the maintenance of order, the suppression of slavery and piracy or the protection of trade routes. After the loss of the American colonies there had remained a group of territories from which the future Dominion of Canada was to grow, and other settlements had been established in Australia, but more importance had been attached to the stations held for their commercial value in the West Indies and parts of Africa and India. Not until the eighteen-twenties, when the increase in the home population was causing concern, and the United States were attracting immigrants from Britain, was serious attention given to the Canadian and Australian settlements. Even then commerce remained the test: "colonies", it was argued in Parliament, "were preserved for the benefit of trading with them, and for the advantage of having a privileged trade with them".[1] When, therefore, a commercial revolution took place and "free trade" was adopted, while at the same time the settlement-colonies were being given control of their own local affairs (and even, by the early 'seventies, of their own tariff policies) there seemed no reason to suppose that the American precedent would not be repeated. Britain had more to gain by developing trade with other countries than by exploiting colonial territories, and economic interest seemed even to dictate a lessening of responsibilities in the name of economy, for colonies necessitated garrisons and garrisons were costly. Until their withdrawal by Gladstone's Secretary for War, Edward Cardwell, in 1870–71 as part of his programme of army reform, the colonial garrisons had, indeed, cost the British taxpayer more than three million pounds a year, and the cost was liable to increase in times of crisis, as when in 1862, during the American Civil War, a further sum of one million had to be spent on the reinforcement of the Canadian garrisons. To the average Englishman, unless he had relatives in the colonies, the Empire represented little more than this annual charge in the estimates, and the reluctance of the colonists themselves to bear more than a small part of the cost seemed to justify his indifference to colonial affairs. Disraeli, who was later to become the mouthpiece of the "new imperialism" of the 'seventies, was echoing a common view when he wrote, in 1852, "these wretched Colonies will all be independent in a few years, and are a millstone round our necks", and ten years later, when Canada had refused to contribute to the cost of the emergency measures rendered necessary by the American war, a prominent M.P. declared roundly that "we do not care one farthing about the adherence of Canada to England".[2]

Indifference to the more dependent territories was almost as great. The West Indies, long "the brightest jewel in the British crown", were now sinking into neglect. Their prosperity had depended on a constant supply of slave-labour from Africa and on the high protection afforded to their sugar production in the home market, but the slave-trade had been declared illegal in 1807 and slavery itself had been abolished in all British dominions in 1833. Twenty years later, despite all the efforts of the planter interest, the preference given to West Indian sugar had been removed. Rich colonies, which at the beginning of the century had accounted for one-third of British trade, now sank far below Canada and Australia in importance, for free trade demanded, and recognized, no preferences. Not until the end of the century, when Joseph Chamberlain was Colonial Secretary, was any effort made to remedy the decline of the Indies. Interest shifted to Africa, whence so many West Indians had originally been forcibly brought, but in the first place rather from a determination to see the slave-trade stamped out than from any desire to increase imperial responsibilities.

THE SLAVE TRADE—"PREVENTIVE" AND "POSITIVE" POLICIES

From 1807 the Navy had begun to patrol the African coasts to intercept slavers, and by the middle of the century some twenty-five ships were engaged upon this "preventive" work on the West African coast alone. Yet once the task had been undertaken complications arose. Ships afloat needed stations ashore, and from shore-stations steps might be taken to stop the slave-caravans even before they reached the coast, while missionary enterprise and the encouragement of legitimate commerce might succeed in checking slave-raiding at its source. Inevitably, therefore, the work had to be pressed into the heart of the continent, and a variety of motives—religious zeal, humanitarianism, commercial enterprise and a desire to penetrate Africa's mysteries—drew men into the interior, until the secrets of the "Dark Continent" were revealed. As early as 1798 Wilberforce had urged his countrymen to "make reparation to Africa as far as we can by establishing a trade upon true commercial principles", and this "positive policy" of striking at the root of the slave-trade by encouraging the African to develop the natural resources of his country was held up as a necessary corollary to the Navy's "preventive" measures. Foremost among the advocates of the "positive policy" was David Livingstone (1813–73), the intrepid missionary explorer, who sprang into fame for his journeys across Africa in 1853–55. Livingstone on his arduous marches had seen the horrors of the slave-gangs, and was determined to open a way into Africa for the commerce and civilizing influences that would check them. "The country must be opened up and commerce begun," his companion, John Kirk (1832–1922), wrote in 1860, "for until the natives can sell their produce, they cannot be expected to give up the Slave Trade."[3] Livingstone also wanted small British settlements, not colonies of the Canadian or Australian type, but settlements of men who could "take a leading part in managing the land, improving the quality, creating the quantity, and extending the varieties, of the productions of the soil".[4] To his ardent inspiration and gallant pioneer work British East Africa, in particular, owes much, and it is significant that his dramatic meeting with H. M. Stanley at Ujiji in 1871 and his lonely death near Lake Bangweolo two years later caught the public imagination. Nyasaland, which he was the first to explore, has well been called "the heritage of Livingstone", but apart from his contributions to the knowledge of African geography his most important achievement lay in drawing attention to the East African slave-trade based on Zanzibar. When Lincoln's emancipation of the American slaves in 1863 at last put an end to the west-coast trade, attention was directed, at Livingstone's instigation, to the east coast, and it was Kirk, now Consul at Zanzibar, who was mainly instrumental in inducing the Sultan of Zanzibar to abolish the trade throughout his territories (1873–76).

## AFRICAN POLICY—THE COMMITTEE OF 1865

It had always been assumed, however, that when once the dreadful traffic had been stopped, and Africa opened to ordinary commerce, the necessity for holding possessions in the great continent would pass. Trading posts, centres for the slave trade, had been held on the Gold Coast since the seventeenth century, and in 1787 a settlement of Negroes who had served in the British forces during the American War had been established at Sierra Leone. After the Napoleonic Wars, however, it had been decided, on grounds of economy, to abandon the posts, but pressure from missionaries and traders alike had prevented so drastic a move, and as "preventive" measures increased in scope the West African stations assumed greater importance. In 1850 the Danish trading posts were bought and in 1872 those of the Dutch, while in 1861 the island of Lagos had been annexed to check slave-smuggling. Yet there was every intention of withdrawing as soon as circumstances permitted, and in 1865 a Select Committee of the House of Commons was set up to examine the situation. Much against its will the Committee was compelled to recognize that the close relations which had been developed with native chiefs made an immediate withdrawal impossible, but it insisted that, with a view to economy, the government should be concentrated at Sierra Leone, and that, above all, there should be no further extensions of territory. "The object of our policy," the Committee's Report ran, "should be to encourage in the natives the exercise of those qualities which may render it possible for us more and more to transfer to them the administration of all the governments, with a view to our ultimate withdrawal from all, except, probably, Sierra Leone." Within ten years, however, the Ashanti war of 1874 was to show that these sweeping measures could not be applied without detriment to orderly development and peaceful commerce, and soon the economic rivalries of other Powers, later entrants upon the African scene, was to bring about a new forward policy. The "positive policy" was extended, but without official support and annexations of territory it could never have overcome the difficulties and rivalries of the African situation. The recommendations of 1865 rapidly became a dead letter.

## GROWTH OF A NEW ATTITUDE:
## (1) THE NEW ZEALAND DISPUTE

The change in the attitude to the settlement colonies came no less rapidly. In 1869 Lord Granville, as Colonial Secretary, refused a request by New Zealand for a loan for the organization of its own defence after the withdrawal of the British forces. The refusal was based on long-standing disagreements over New Zealand's handling of its Maori peoples, but it was interpreted by many in Britain as evidence that the Gladstone administration was endeavouring to drive the colonists into secession. Public agitation started, both on the platform and in the Press, and in the following year Granville modified his decision by approving a loan for civil, though not for military, purposes. From that moment, it may be said, the imperialist movement was launched, if anything so spontaneous and inchoate could be styled a movement. By 1872 Disraeli was criticizing the tendency to disintegration and calling on Britain to be " a great country, an Imperial country", and three years later, as recounted in the previous chapter, Forster could ask "Who talks now of casting off the colonies?" The change was abrupt and startling, but called for no serious readjustment. As no deliberate policy of imperial aggrandizement had ever been formulated, so there was no desire deliberately to cast the colonies loose; no more was called for than the acceptance of a changed situation.

## (2) FOREIGN DANGERS

A number of elements contributed to the new situation. With the withdrawal of the colonial garrisons a source of friction was being removed, and at the same time it was beginning to be realized that the British people did not lack strength and numbers in the face of the military power displayed both in the United States during their Civil War and on the continent of Europe in the series of wars that marked the rise of the German Empire. The self-governing colonies were no longer small and insignificant: their populations had reached such proportions that they could make an appreciable addition to Britain's man-power. "It seems to me of the greatest importance," wrote one well-informed observer in 1874, "that we should strengthen and evoke all the Nationalism and Imperialism left within us if we are to hold our own":[5] the growing colonial populations brought some consolation to many who were perturbed at the change that had taken place in the European balance of power. Canada's population, for example, had jumped in twenty years to more than 3,500,000, and despite the constant attraction of the United States was to reach five millions in the early 'nineties. Australia and New Zealand together accounted for nearly two millions more, and already there were optimists who prophesied a white population of eighty millions in the colonies by 1950. Some twenty million emigrants left the British Isles between 1812 and 1914, and although the greater part of these, some thirteen million, went to the United States, Canada received, in all, four million and Australia and New Zealand two. Already by the 'seventies many families in Britain had relations overseas, and improvements in communications were overcoming the barriers of distance. Steamships were ousting sails and speeding ocean crossings: 900,000 steamship tons on the British register in 1865 had become 1,900,000 ten years later and nearly four million tons by 1885, while the opening of the Suez Canal in 1869 greatly reduced the passage to India and the East. Closer contact was also assured by the development of the telegraph. The ten years from 1866 to 1875 saw the laying of most of the world network of submarine cables. After many failures a successful transatlantic cable was laid by the *Great Eastern* in 1866, while England was directly linked with India in 1870 and with Australia two years later. Widely scattered though they were the British communities gained in unity and self-consciousness.

## (3) ECONOMIC FACTORS

At home there were, in addition to the menacing political movements in Europe, disquieting economic disturbances to suggest that overseas territories which could provide men, markets and materials should not lightly be discarded. The late 'sixties was a period of some economic difficulty in Britain, as the rising figures for emigration suggest. Nearly one hundred thousand left the country in 1869, and there was agitation for state-aided emigration in 1870. That year is generally regarded as marking the peak of Britain's industrial supremacy: none, of course, could appreciate the position at the time, but it was sufficiently evident that, with the recovery of America and the rapid rise of Germany, Britain's lead could not be long maintained. Lord Carnarvon, who, as Colonial Secretary in 1866–67 and 1874–78, was associated with important imperial developments, expressed in an article in 1871 the gloomy feelings which were assailing thoughtful men:

Heavily weighted in the race of commercial competition; consuming with improvidence the resources on which much of our commerce depends . . . with enormous wealth to tempt, and with little power to defend . . . we talk as if Providence had ordained that our Government should always borrow at three per cent and that our trade should always come to us, because we live in a foggy island set in a boisterous sea.[6]

Although the alarm proved to be based on exaggerated fears, it was heightened by the international economic crisis which began in 1873 and by the increase of foreign tariffs from the end of the decade. Suggestions that Britain should find in the development of her colonies compensation for the loss of foreign markets were soon being made, and in the 'eighties there sprang up the "Fair Trade" movement, which proposed the restriction of free entry for foreign goods to countries which did not tax British exports, and combined with this the suggestion of a lowering of the duties still paid by some colonial products. The movement came to nothing, but the idea of "imperial preference" lingered on to receive new life from later developments. Meanwhile it seemed more than ever necessary to safeguard British economic interests throughout the world, and in the context of foreign tariff movements and imperial expansion this called for a more determined policy of annexation, especially in regions such as West and South Africa, where Britain already had responsibilities as well as interests. Within a few years the assumption that the British Empire could safely be left to break up had been abandoned, and the process had begun which by the end of Queen Victoria's reign had added to her dominions four million square miles of territory and some 140,000,000 people.

## TYPES OF IMPERIAL DEVELOPMENT

If Granville's dispute with New Zealand touched off the "new imperialism" as an emotional force, a number of events gave it formal recognition—the British North America Act of 1867, which established the Canadian "Dominion"; the proclamation of Queen Victoria as Empress of India on 1st January, 1877; the attempt, later in the same year, to set up a South African federation, inaugurated by the annexation of the Transvaal, and four measures of the year 1874, all of which were to prove the preliminary steps towards further extensions of colonial territory: the annexation of Fiji, the extension of British authority in Malaya, the Ashanti war and the proclamation of the Gold Coast Colony. To these might be added, as typical of the new era, the purchase of the Suez Canal shares in 1875, and the beginning of the occupation of Egypt seven years later. These events fall into several recognizable categories. There were, first, the movement of the settlement colonies towards maturity, from the "Dominion" of Canada in 1867 to the "Commonwealth" of Australia in 1900 and the "Union" of South Africa in 1910: with this went the more cautious development of British rule in India towards that "fulfilment" which has been realized in our own day. In the second place there was an extension of rule in such areas as West Africa and Malaya, where posts had hitherto been held for limited strategic and commercial ends: to these were now added further regions, notably in East Africa and the Pacific islands, where commercial interests and foreign rivalries encouraged expansion. South Africa also has a place in this category. Finally there was the increase of influence through trade and investment, especially in countries whose own systems of government were weak or decaying. China falls into this last category, but Egypt is the outstanding example, since it came under direct British control: the British administration of Egypt from 1882 is one of the most curious features of imperial history and in many respects the most revealing commentary on British policy.

## THE MISSION OF EMPIRE

Underlying these developments was an increasing pride in the Empire and faith in its mission. The stamping-out of the slave-trade, the development of peace and ordered government in so many dependent territories, the spread of civilization and Christianity and the steady advance of the settlement colonies, all combined to encourage the belief that the mission was a reality and a cause for legitimate pride. Not until much later did opinion become aware of the other side of the medal— the danger of exploitation, the break-up of tribal organization and tradition, the decay of colonies such as the West Indies which had served their purpose, the general dependence upon a western culture which was itself insecurely based. Nevertheless, the genuine sense of mission was present, and may not be decried: "it is an ignorant and false tradition", a South African historian has said, "that Great Britain undertook nothing that did not serve some profitable and material end".[7]

## Spokesmen of Imperialism: Dilke and Seeley

Two widely-read and influential works first drew attention, from different angles, to this aspect of imperialism, Sir Charles Dilke's *Greater Britain* (1868) and Sir J. R. Seeley's *Expansion of England* (1883). Dilke wrote as a widely-travelled man of affairs, after a tour of the world; Seeley, Professor of Modern History in the University of Cambridge, as a pioneer of imperial historical studies. To Dilke on his travels there had come a conception of "the grandeur of our race, already girdling the earth, which it is destined, perhaps, eventually to overspread". This conception provided him with the title of his book:

> In America, the peoples of the world are being fused together, but they are run into an English mould. . . . Through America England is speaking to the world. . . . If two small islands are by courtesy styled "Great", America, Australia, India must form a "Greater Britain".

It was the expansion of the British race and of British institutions that particularly inspired him:

> The possession of India offers to ourselves that element of vastness of dominion which, in this age, is needed to secure width of thought and nobility of purpose; but to the English race our possession of India, of the coasts of Africa and of parts of China offers the possibility of planting free institutions among the dark-skinned races of the world.

To this moral element, the responsibility of Britain for the extension of her political principles, Dilke returned constantly throughout the book, and to a confident, sober-minded generation its appeal was immediate. Seeley was equally intent upon a moral. He agreed with Dilke's interpretation of the significance of the expansion of British influence, and was concerned to show that it was no accidental development but something that had come about through the very growth of the British people themselves, something "profound, persistent, necessary to the national life". He examined the historical processes by which it had arisen, and chided the public for its indifference to the "prodigious greatness" of the achievement in a phrase which has become proverbial: "we seem to have conquered and peopled half the world in a fit of absence of mind". He therefore provided both explanation and justification for imperial expansion, and his realistic approach, with its acceptance of the inevitability of historical processes, chimed well with the prevailing mood. To the exhortations of Dilke he brought something akin to the now popular theories of "natural selection" to show why, when others had failed, Britain had come so far, and he urged his countrymen to see in imperial expansion the very essence of their history and their contribution.

## LORD CARNARVON

Soon there were many voices to take up the tale. When Colonial Secretary in 1877 Lord Carnarvon, in a speech in the Lords, had already described the Empire as "one of the most wonderful pieces of human administration the world has ever seen . . . both in what it does and in what it does not do. . . . We have discarded restrictions; we have looked to freedom of government as our ultimate object, and we have been rewarded by an almost immeasurable growth of freedom."[8] In the light of the development of responsible government in the settlement colonies, and of their obvious reluctance to sever the imperial connection, the claim was not unjustified. In the following year, in an address at Edinburgh, Carnarvon turned to the dependent peoples:

> there are obligations which we owe beyond these four seas. . . . We have races struggling to emerge into civilization to whom emancipation from servitude is but the foretaste of the far higher law of liberty and progress to which they may yet attain; and vast populations like those of India, sitting like children in the shadow of doubt, poverty and sorrow, yet looking up to us for guidance and help. To them it is our part to give wise laws, good government and a well-ordered finance . . . to provide them with a system where the humblest may enjoy freedom from oppression and wrong, equally with the greatest; where the light of morality and religion can penetrate into the darkest dwelling-places.[9]

## ANTHONY TROLLOPE

These views became general and found their way into the novels that reflected the sentiments and prejudices of the age. Anthony Trollope, one of the most widely read novelists of the day, was echoing prevailing opinion when he wrote of British rule in India, in one of his political novels, *Phineas Redux* (1870–71), as "the highest duty imposed upon us as a nation". He added, it is true, that a discussion of Indian affairs was as likely to empty the House of Commons as personal rivalry between Members of Parliament, the theme of his novel, was to fill it, but the very truth of his observation was a measure of the general acceptance of the responsibility for India as a high duty which could hardly be called in question. The strength of the sense of mission that prevailed was equally well revealed for the settlement colonies in Trollope's record of the lengthy tour he made in the Antipodes shortly after the completion of *Phineas Redux*, a record published in 1873 under the title *Australia and New Zealand*:

> To have founded such colonies is the greatest blessing which we have above other nations. . . . We may probably be justified in saying that our great increase of people has been given to us in order that we might populate such lands.

## RADICAL VIEWS

Trollope as a Liberal was at one with the Conservative Carnarvon, but there were others, more advanced in their political views, who also shared their opinions. There had always been Radical elements who in colonial policy were ardent to succour the coloured peoples. As the immensity of the task became apparent, and with it the advantages to be gained by the British and dependent peoples alike from the development of colonial resources, a strange amalgam of radicalism with imperialism emerged that found its greatest exponent in Joseph Chamberlain. A typical early expression of this doctrine is to be found in a Radical M.P.'s view of the occupation of Egypt in 1882:

> Our hands are to the plough and we cannot turn back. If we do, woe betide the hapless Fellaheen. Chaos would return. The finances would be fastened on by harpies, the taxes would be enforced by the curbash, justice would be bought and sold. . . . We voluntarily undertook the task, and duty, interest and humanity require us to stick to it. Cairo, too, is on the way to the Cape. Along it we will find sales for our goods, fields for our enterprise, scope for our philanthropy. There are roads to make, markets to open, lands to till, and slaves to emancipate. No grander outlet offers for colonizing genius.[10]

Only a few years earlier, under the shadow of the trade depression of the 'seventies, a Manchester merchant, James Bradshaw, in an address to the Trades Union Congress of 1879 had drawn attention to the importance of the "Cape-to-Cairo" route for British trade. Africa, he had claimed in the very title of his paper, was "the remedy for the trade depression of England", and the assembled trade union delegates had cheered his confident assertion that "centuries of commercial development could not exhaust the necessities of 350,000,000 of population" in the continent.[11]

Rhodes later spoke of the mixture of motives, somewhat cynically, as "philanthropy plus five per cent": the philanthropy was there, as in his own case, as well as the financial interest, though they were not always found in the same hands. Trade, civilization, philanthropy, the overthrow of corrupt and decaying systems of government, were all effective motives: no single, simple explanation will suffice. Out of the amalgam emerged the "far-flung", self-conscious Empire of the end of the century, sustained by a public opinion in an assertive, imperialist mood.

CASE-STUDIES:
(1) MALAYA

Some of the varied aspects of imperial development in the last quarter of the nineteenth century are touched on in the following chapters. Here two striking examples, Malaya and Egypt, may be briefly described. As manifestations of the new imperialism in practice they reveal the influences at work, the multitude of factors that had so recently put out of date the conception of limited responsibilities that had marked the mid-century years.

Malaya was to become the greatest of all centres of tin production, and tin provides a typical example of the process that lay behind industrial and imperial expansion. For centuries England had been the chief producer of the metal in Europe, but with the rise of industry Cornwall could not keep pace with the rapidly increasing demands for the metal. Tin was needed for the manufacture of brass, which was to be in even greater demand as the electrical industries sprang up, and had already acquired a new function as the result of the appearance of canned, or "tinned", foodstuffs. With the rapid growth of industrial populations, and the rise in standards of living, the import of foods had increased, and methods of preservation were sought. Refrigeration was not successfully applied until the early 'eighties, but experiments in canning had been made for some twenty years, and with the marked increase in the consumption of meat which took place in Britain between 1865 and 1875 the American and Australian canning industries developed. Every tin-plate they used was made in Britain, and the export increased during the 'seventies from about one-hundred-thousand to more than a quarter-of-a-million tons a year. Cornwall could provide raw materials for only one-sixth of this growing total. The rest came from the other side of the world, from the Malay archipelago, where Britain had long since built up important trading centres in the Straits Settlements (Singapore, Malacca and Penang). Tin was worked in Malaya by Chinese immigrants, and in the middle of the century rich finds in Perak had brought many thousands of Chinese into the country. The rule of the local sultans and rajas was already breaking down, and the anarchy and piracy which had long been endemic were stimulated by the irruption of the miners. Until 1873 the Government refused to intervene, but in that year the troubles in Perak had reached such a pitch that it was decided to extend a system already familiar in India by appointing British Residents to advise native rulers and assist in the establishment of law and order. Perak and Selangor received their first Residents in 1874, and the experiment of "indirect rule" was so successful that twenty years later it was possible to establish the Federated Malay States (Perak, Selangor, Negri Sembilan and Pahang). The peaceful settlement of the country attracted foreign capital to the tin-mines, which were beginning to call for costly equipment, but the bulk of the work in the mines was still performed by the Chinese, who continued to flow in until they equalled the native Malays in numbers and far surpassed them in activity and enterprise. By the end of the century Malaya was producing over forty thousand tons of tin a year, more than half of the world's total output. The prosperity of what rapidly became the richest of all colonial territories was thus bound up with a number of inter-related factors—

the pacification of a region long noted for its lawlessness; the encouragement of trade, especially that of the Chinese merchants in Singapore, through the suppression of piracy; the welfare of Chinese settlers; the provision of tin-plate for the canning factories of the West; the improved diet of European and American workers, and the prosperity of the cattle-raisers of Australia and the U.S.A. The whole episode, in fact, is an excellent illustration of the interdependence of modern economic developments, and of the truism that the Flag follows Trade (the later nineteenth century belief expressed in the slogan, "trade follows the flag", was based on the further development of trade that naturally flowed everywhere from the establishment of imperial authority). Nor was tin the only Malayan product of international significance. Efforts were made to find a crop of commercial value which could supplement tin and provide an alternative source of production if the ores should give out. Rubber was now coming into greater use, but the best type was gathered wild in Brazil, and the transplantation of seeds presented great difficulty. In 1876, however, a whole shipload of seed was successfully conveyed from Brazil to Kew Gardens and, although only a small proportion flourished, a dozen seedlings were sent to Perak in 1879. Out of these developed the great industry of plantation rubber. It was thirty years before production could get into its stride, but by that time the bicycle and automobile industries had caused a boom in rubber, and until the coming of synthetic products, aided by the tragic events of 1941, Malaya dominated the world rubber market. By 1914 the country's total trade had been increased very nearly a hundredfold since 1874, from less than £300,000 to more than £26,000,000, and the increase was still continuing.

The interdependence of Malaya and the new industrial civilization of the West through tin and rubber was matched in many parts of the world, particularly, as far as British possessions were concerned, by the vegetable oils and palm products of West Africa and the Pacific islands. But it provides a spectacular example of a development, itself dependent on industrial movements in the West, which contributed to the new approach to colonial problems after 1870. The history of Malaya, and of many other possessions, after 1874 reveals more purposeful action and less reluctance to incur responsibilities than had been shown even a few years earlier. There was still a very real desire to assist the peoples who were coming under British protection, but there was at the same time a growing realization of the contribution that those people could make to British prosperity, and a determination to encourage the development of the resources which their lands could offer and which western industry required. (Lugard was later to describe this dichotomy as the "Dual Mandate".) The external investment in Malayan rubber, for instance, eventually amounted to more than fifty million pounds, and in tin to some fourteen millions, In the period with which we are concerned, although the majority of British loans still went to foreign countries, the colonies provided an attractive field for investment, and governments became more responsive than they had hitherto been to the interests of investors.

## (2) EGYPT

Nowhere, perhaps was this more clearly seen than in Britain's dealings with Egypt. It had long been evident to foreign observers, as it had been to many Englishmen, that Britain's connexion with India would eventually compel her to intervene in the affairs of the region that formed the land bridge between the Mediterranean and the Indian Ocean. De Lesseps's great scheme for the construction of the Suez Canal, suspect as a French design for a short cut to India, was long resisted by Britain, but when, in 1869, the Canal was opened three-quarters of the shipping that used it flew the Red Ensign, and the great waterway became for Britain a vital economic and strategic link, reducing the journey to India by some four thousand miles.

A great part of the sixteen million pounds which the Canal had cost had been raised by de Lesseps in France, but a block of rather less than half the Company's shares had been allocated to the ruler of Egypt, Ismail, and these shares were to become historic. Ismail had succeeded in 1863 to a prosperous country and a full treasury, for Egypt was then benefiting from the American Civil War, which enhanced the value of its cotton, but he possessed extravagant notions for the future greatness of his country, and was ambitious to put it, at least in appearance, among the leading nations of the world. He inaugurated enormous and costly schemes, spent vast sums in purchasing from his overlord, the Sultan, the hereditary title of Khedive (Viceroy: literally, "Master"), and by 1876 had increased the Egyptian debt from the three millions which his predecessor left to something approaching ninety millions. For this a great deal of permanent value could be shown—the Suez Canal, railways, a great system of irrigation canals and harbour-works, together, it might be added, with the Cairo Opera House, scene of the first production of Verdi's *Aïda*, which in characteristic style the Khedive had commissioned to celebrate the opening of the Canal. But much had disappeared in extravagant display, and far more in ruinous rates of interest on borrowed money. Ismail in his attempts to emulate the rulers of Europe had learnt only too well how modern governments were financed, but had mortgaged the revenues of his country far beyond their capacity.

Already in 1870, hard pressed for money, he had offered his Suez Canal shares to the British Government, but Britain's earlier opposition to the Canal had been succeeded by doubts as to its commercial soundness, and the offer was refused. Five years later, however, it became known that the shares were in the market, and de Lesseps, anxious to have the whole control of the Canal in French hands, endeavoured to persuade the French Government to buy them. He was forestalled, however, by the celebrated dramatic coup by which Disraeli secured them for Britain, the most brilliant stroke of his romantic career. The price paid was something less than four million pounds, and in spite of contemporary doubts the bargain proved an excellent one: by 1914 the purchase price had been repaid eight times over in interest and dividends, and the shares themselves were worth forty millions. But the implications of the coup were to be more than financial. In announcing the purchase *The Times* justly remarked that "a new phase of Eastern policy" had opened, and that great realist, Bismarck, hailed the event as "the right thing at the right moment".[12] To him it appeared that Britain was at last taking action in Egypt, and that the time was coming when she would agree to a peaceful dismemberment of Turkey, with Egypt as her share. During the "Eastern Crisis" of the next few years Bismarck, in a characteristic attempt to appeal to the vanity of Disraeli and the Queen, repeatedly pressed the British Government to transfer "possession of the road to India through Egypt . . . from the suzerainty of the Sultan of Turkey to that of the Empress of India",[13] and the Khedive himself, at his wits' end for money, offered, for a consideration, to arrange the matter. Disraeli was deaf to all suggestions, however, and it is typical of the way in which events finally drove Britain into action in Egypt that, while he believed that Britain had achieved enough control for her purpose by the purchase of Ismail's shares, it was his successor, Gladstone, who had described that transaction as "tomfoolery", who reluctantly agreed in 1882 to the measures which brought Egypt under British control.

The purchase money soon disappeared down the drain of Ismail's indebtedness, and only a few months later, in 1876, repayment of all debts was suspended. There followed a long and painful struggle to introduce some order into the Egyptian finances and to reform the Khedive's administration. At first the British Government refused to intervene on behalf of British bondholders, and left them to take their own measures: only a few years earlier, in 1871, the Foreign Office had stated that in cases of default on private British loans to foreign governments, its policy was, and would continue to be, "limited to unofficial support and friendly remonstrance".[14] A Commission of the Public Debt was established in Egypt, and as the Government would appoint no official British representative the bondholding interests made their own appointment. Their choice was a fateful one, for it fell upon a young man, Evelyn Baring (1841-1917), who had recently achieved some distinction as private secretary to Lord Northbrook, Viceroy of India, from 1872 to 1876. Baring, better known by his later title of Earl of Cromer, was to become the architect of Egyptian reform and the creator of the British administration. After his arrival in Egypt in 1877, since the French Government was active in support of French bondholders, British policy was gradually modified. Lord Salisbury became Foreign Secretary in 1878, and, realizing the necessity for concerted action, proved less unwilling than his predecessor, Lord Derby, had been to bring pressure to bear at Cairo. "I should be glad to be free of the companionship of the bond-holders",[15] he wrote in 1879, but at the same time he was alive to the deeper issues involved. "When you have got a neighbour and faithful ally who is bent on meddling in a country in which you are deeply interested," he explained later, "you have three courses open to you. You may renounce—or monopolize—or share. Renouncing would have been to place the French across our road to India. Monopolizing would have been very near the risk of war. So we resolved to share."[16] "Sharing", in the interests equally of the bondholders, of the broader concerns of Britain and France in the Middle East, and, it can truly be said, of the oppressed people of Egypt, was the keynote of the policy of Salisbury and of the Gladstone administration that followed, until France withdrew in 1882, and Britain was left to deal with the situation alone.

The attempts made by the British and French repre-sentatives to set Egypt on its feet soon proved that no real reform was possible while Ismail remained Khedive, and after general pressure by the Powers at Constantinople the Sultan was persuaded to depose him in June, 1879. He passed into a gilded retirement at Naples, and was succeeded by his son, Tewfik, a man of mediocre attainments but far more stable character, who reigned until 1892. Baring had resigned his appointment in the last months of Ismail's reign, finding that, apart altogether from the difficulty of dealing with the Khedive, his task was too restricted in scope:

> I was interested in the work of Egyptian reform; but I had no wish to remain in Egypt as a mere receiver of money for the bond-holders. I was their representative; but my sympathies lay more with the wretched taxpayers of Egypt, who were ground to the earth by excessive fiscal burdens.[17]

After Ismail's fall Salisbury decided, in co-operation with the French Government, that there should be two Controllers-General of Revenue in Egypt, one French, one British, who should be in actual, but indirect, control of the country's finances, and the British appointment he now offered to Baring, who accordingly returned to Cairo. The Condominium at first worked successfully. Salisbury was anxious that the claims of the bondholders should not be regarded as the *first* claim on the Egyptian revenue, but with a naïveté characteristic of his approach to matters of high finance felt that the other Governments concerned took a much narrower view of the position:

> it is an unpleasant reflection that—as regards Egypt—France, Austria and Germany have all shaped their diplomatic action, and that with great perseverance, purely to satisfy the interests of certain bankers who were able to put pressure on their foreign offices. It is a new feature in diplomacy.[18]

German and Austrian interests were too limited to exercise any decisive influence, but it was certainly true that financial interests in France had done much to shape French policy. Nevertheless, Baring and his French colleague, de Blignières, successfully worked together: within a year of their return to Egypt certain necessary reforms of harsh taxation had been carried, the debt position had been stabilized and interest rates reduced. The Egyptian peoples were carrying a heavy burden of debt, for the creation of which they had been in no way responsible, but some of the worst excesses of the administration had been removed: on the other hand measures of reform would never have been undertaken but for the intervention of the European Powers, and many Egyptians, not unnaturally ignorant of the true facts of the situation, resented the subjection of their country to foreign influence. To add to their discontent there were the many privileges which Europeans had long enjoyed in Egypt under the system of "Capitulations". The general discontent would have smouldered ineffectively had there been nothing to bring it to a head, but the army had its own particular complaints, and it was the army which created the next disturbance, the first stirring of nationalist feeling in Egyptian history, and the immediate cause of the occupation of the country by Britain alone.

The army's grievances, as might be expected, were concerned with questions of pay and promotion. Pay was low and uncertain, and in 1878, as part of the campaign of economy, a large number of officers had been placed on half-pay. For long the higher ranks had been held mainly by Turkish officers, and native Egyptian officers now saw their countrymen ousted by foreigners in both civil and military employment, while many of their own number were placed in impoverished retirement. A movement of revolt began which was headed by

M

a native Egyptian Colonel of peasant origin, Ahmed Arabi (or, more properly, Orabi). The details of his movement need not concern us here. Suffice it to say that, further inflamed by the French occupation of Tunis in 1881, Arabi and his followers were in complete control of Egypt by the beginning of 1882, and that Tewfik was powerless to resist them. Under this test the Condominium broke down. Gladstone's Government was unwilling to intervene, except, as Granville, the Foreign Secretary, wrote, in case of "the existence of anarchy or some attack on the Canal", but France, under the resolute leadership of Gambetta, at first pressed for joint action. In January, 1882, however, Gambetta fell from power, and several months of confused counsels followed. In May, as a precaution against the disorders that threatened, British and French warships were sent to Alexandria, where, a month later, there broke out nationalist riots in which Europeans were killed. The disorders now increased, and it was clear that some action would have to be taken. At this critical moment, however, the French ships were withdrawn: faced with the prospect of a campaign in Egypt the French recoiled. Tunis had proved more troublesome than had been anticipated, and there was a disinclination to engage in further North African adventures, while in the background was the constant fear of Germany and of the surprises that Bismarck might spring in the event of a prolonged campaign in Egypt.

While the French hesitated, Arabi was increasing the fortifications of Alexandria, and on 11th July the British Fleet, now acting alone, opened fire, silenced the forts and bombarded the city. As there were no troops to land, the gesture, though impressive, was not particularly effective, though it had the result of driving Arabi himself from Alexandria. A month later, however, Wolseley arrived with an expeditionary force, and on 13th September Arabi was decisively defeated at Tel-el-Kebir. It seemed, wags said in London, "like Dizzy's days". Egypt was now in Britain's hands, and in September, 1883, Baring, who had been in charge of India's finances since 1880, returned as British Agent and Consul-General. He was to stay until 1907, and, in the course of twenty-three years as "Pharaoh in disguise",[19] was to remake the administration of Egypt. In 1883, however, the great

Cromer régime lay in the future: Gladstone's aim was to withdraw the British forces as soon as possible. Yet Egypt was too weak to stand alone after the collapse of Arabi, and while no other Power had been prepared to take action in 1882, Britain, on account of the Canal, could clearly not hand over her newly won authority to any other government. Annexation, or the proclamation of a Protectorate, would have been the logical course, but Gladstone would not consider such action, and it is doubtful whether it would have won approval in the country. Accordingly, although the Condominium was abolished, Baring was given a position of only indirect control, and, as events showed, this was to make the worst of all possible situations, for the other Powers, though without responsibility, were able to maintain their influence in Egypt and to add constantly to the British Agent's difficulties. France, in particular, jealous of the situation which she believed Britain had intended to create from the first, was persistently hostile: Egypt was a sore point in Anglo-French relations for twenty years, until the Entente of 1904. Gladstone and his colleagues, however, genuinely believed that in a few years Britain could withdraw, when, in the words of the Circular to the Great Powers of January, 1883, "the order of things to be established shall be of a satisfactory character and possess the elements of stablity and permanence". But even before Baring arrived in Egypt a religious leader, Muhammad Ahmad, the Mahdi, had raised the standard of rebellion in the Sudan, and it was soon clear that Egypt could not be safe while the Sudan remained unpacified. There followed the tragic, and mishandled, episode of the death of Gordon in 1885, and it was not until 1898 that order could at last be restored in the South. Not until then were "the elements of stability and permanence present." "I was sent to Egypt," Baring was later to write, "to tell the British Government what it was to do with a country which it had 'conquered in a fit of absence'. Before the question could be answered another fit of absence supervened, and the vast territory from the Southern Egyptian frontier to the equator was practically absorbed into the British dominions."[20] The quotation from Seeley is an apt comment on the situation which had emerged from the mixture of motives which had governed such policy as Britain had had in her dealings with Egypt, and no one was better qualified than Lord Cromer to use it. His own task, he wrote after his retirement, was,

> not indeed, to govern Egypt, but to assist in the government of the country without the appearance of doing so and without any legitimate authority over the agents with whom I had to deal.[21]

Something must be said later of the manner in which that task was carried out. Here it may be noted that it eventually won the commendation even of Arabi in the exile in Ceylon to which he had been sent.[22]

The affairs of Egypt have been dwelt on at some length because, as has already been suggested, they reveal, perhaps more clearly than any other aspect of British imperial policy, the varied motives and influences at work on that policy, and the frequent hesitancies and uncertainties that it reveals. There was, between developments in Malaya and Egypt, in particular, a marked similarity which reveals how British Governments were willy-nilly compelled to take action which resulted in an unwelcome extension of responsibilities. Nevertheless, there were very many who disliked even the appearance of support to financial interests that had been given. Thus, a month after Tel-el-Kebir, Chamberlain wrote in a memorandum to his colleagues in the Ministry:

> There is great anxiety, lest, after all, the bondholders should too evidently be the only persons who have profited by the war. . . . We have in Egypt interests and duties. The interests are a fair guarantee for the peace and order of the country, and the security of the Suez Canal and our route to India. The duty cast upon us, as the Liberal Government of a free nation, is to secure to the Egyptian people the greatest possible development of representative institutions.[23]

Chamberlain's purist views may be compared with those of another Radical M.P., already quoted. They represent the considerations that won public approval for the occupation of Egypt, despite general lack of sympathy for the woes of the bondholders.

## ATTEMPTS TO EVADE RESPONSIBILITY—CHARTERED COMPANIES

To avoid elsewhere the complications that had arisen through the wide extension of the interests of Great Powers, recourse was had during the 'eighties to an old policy, the creation of Chartered Companies. Thus, the British North Borneo Company received a charter in 1881, and three African Companies followed, the Royal Niger Company (1886), the Imperial British East Africa Company (1888) and the British South Africa Company, Rhodes's creation (1889). In each case the charter conferred the power to trade and administer territory, but no territory was formally annexed. By this means the rights of British traders in certain parts of the world were protected, at a time when other Great Powers were marking out territories for themselves, but annexation, with all its responsibilties, was avoided, though avoided only for the present, as events were to show.

North Borneo was declared a British Protectorate in 1888, though the Company continued to administer its territory, but the final stages in Africa did not come until later. Owing, mainly, to German pressure the East Africa Company proved unsuccessful, and its charter was abrogated in 1895, a Protectorate being established over its territory, which in 1920 became the Colony of Kenya. Further south the area administered by the South Africa Company received, in 1895, the name of Rhodesia: it was divided into two three years later, when Southern Rhodesia was granted a measure of self-government, but formal annexation did not come until 1923, when the Company's Charter finally expired. Southern Rhodesia then became a self-governing colony, while a Protectorate was established in Northern Rhodesia. In West Africa the Niger Company was relieved of all but its purely commercial functions in 1900, and reverted to the trading company which it had originally been. The two Protectorates of Northern and Southern Nigeria were then set up, their union, together with Lagos, in the Colony of Nigeria following in 1914. In each case, therefore, the creation of the chartered company proved to be no more than a temporary expedient: expansion followed in East and West Africa as irresistibly as in Egypt and Malaya. The conditions which made expansion unavoidable, however, must be considered at a later stage, when the pressure of international colonial rivalries in the 'eighties and 'nineties is examined.

## The Empire in the British Economy

Enough has now been said of the new elements in colonial policy, as they affected both the settlement colonies and the dependent territories, to indicate the character of the changes that were taking place from about 1870 onwards. Economic factors clearly played no small part, and, though they do not provide a full explanation of the rapid change in imperial policy from semi-indifference to enthusiasm, investment in particular clearly made its contribution to the new outlook. After 1850, it has been said, "the movement of capital became the primary economic relationship between the United Kingdom and the colonies",[24] and the sketch of colonial development which has been given will have indicated the significance of this definition. For the British capitalist, investment in the colonies had the advantage that the direction of colonial business enterprises tended to remain in British hands, while the money subscribed was usually spent either on British capital goods, such as railway equipment, or on the development of raw materials and foodstuffs for the British market. Moreover, colonial loans were generally regarded with favour by governments, and frequently received official backing. The advantages to the industrial worker in export demand, and in the assurance of cheap and plentiful foodstuffs and raw materials, were no less real, and contributed a good deal, it has been suggested, to the rise in real wages that took place between the 'fifties and the 'eighties.[25] Down to 1914, indeed, it was particularly on the opening up of new territories by railway development that the course of real wages ultimately depended.[26] Colonial development may therefore be said to have contributed to Britain's economic advancement at a period when new markets and sources of supply were being anxiously sought: "the Empire became in a new sense an integral part of the British economic system".[27] Yet the results must be seen in perspective. Inter-imperial trade accounted in 1913 for less than one-third of the total trade of the United Kingdom, and the corresponding figures for investment may be recorded. It was estimated in 1913 that although £1,779,498,000 of British money were invested in the Empire, the total for foreign countries was considerably higher—£1,934,666,000.[28] Of this latter figure the United

States accounted for no less than £754,617,000 and Argentina for £319,565,000, these being the largest foreign borrowers. Canada headed the Empire list, but with £514,870,000 of British money was far behind the U.S.A., while India and Ceylon at £378,776,000, South Africa at £370,000,000 and Australia at £332,112,000 were little above Argentina. For all her importance in British policy Egypt had attracted no more than £44,912,000, and therefore stood far below Brazil (£147,967,000), Mexico (£99,019,000), Russia (£66,627,000) and Chile (£61,019,000), though her total exceeded that of West Africa (£37,000,000) and Malaya (£27,293,000). In other words, the relations between economic and political empire were not always close, while even within the Empire itself the Dominions had absorbed nearly three times as much capital as India and the other dependent territories. Investment, a leading authority has said, "had undoubtedly helped to make (the) empire, but it had helped to make so much else".[29]

With the general situation described, and the new influences that were at work upon it indicated, the sections that follow will describe the development of various parts of the Empire, and especially the growth towards independent nationhood of the self-governing colonies. Canada, as the pioneer Dominion, is dealt with first, followed by Australia and New Zealand. An examination of the problems of the Pacific leads to a consideration of imperial defence and of the attempts made to foster a greater measure of formal imperial unity. The tangled history of South Africa is then surveyed, and the growth of the British Empire in India. Finally, the partition of the "Dark Continent" of Africa is examined, with particular reference to British policy.

## REFERENCES

1. R. L. Schuyler: *The Fall of the Old Colonial System*, p. 153.
2. C. P. Stacey: *Canada and the British Army, 1846–1871*, p. 141.
3. Sir R. Coupland: *Kirk on the Zambezi*, p. 183.
4. ibid., p. 271.
5. Sir R. Morier: *Memoirs and Letters*, II, p. 298.
6. Sir A. Hardinge: *Life of Lord Carnarvon*, II, p. 28.

7.   C. W. de Kiewiet: *The Imperial Factor in South Africa*, p. 6.

8.   *Life of Lord Carnarvon*, II, p. 323.

9.   ibid., III, p. 18.

10.  S. Maccoby: *English Radicalism, 1853–1886*, pp. 343–44.

11.  R. J. Harrison: *The Activity and Influence of the English Positivists upon Labour Movements, 1859–1885*: unpublished thesis accepted for the Degree of Doctor of Philosophy by the University of Oxford, 1955.

12.  W. Taffs: *Lord Odo Russell*, p. 112.

13.  ibid., p. 200.

14.  N. A. Pelcovits: *Old China Hands and the Foreign Office*, p. 135.

15.  Lady Gwendolen Cecil: *Life of Lord Salisbury*, II, p. 352.

16.  ibid., p. 331.

17.  Quoted in Lord Zetland: *Lord Cromer*, p. 72.

18.  *Life of Lord Salisbury*, II, p. 359.

19.  J. L. Garvin: *Life of Joseph Chamberlain*, I, p. 501.

20.  *Lord Cromer*, p. 92.

21.  Lord Cromer: *Modern Egypt*, II, p. 326.

22.  Sir V. Chirol: *Fifty Years in a Changing World*, p. 34.

23.  *Life of Joseph Chamberlain*, I, p. 451.

24.  H. J. Habakkuk: "Free Trade and Commercial Expansion, 1853–70" in *The Cambridge History of the British Empire*, II, p. 798.

25.  ibid., p. 804.

26.  A. K. Cairncross: *Home and Foreign Investment, 1870–1913*, p. 233.

27.  L. H. Jenks: *The Migration of British Capital to 1875*, p. 197.

28.  Quoted in W. K. Hancock: *Survey of British Commonwealth Affairs*, Vol. II, *Problems of Economic Policy*, Part I, p. 27 n.

29.  ibid., pp. 26–27.

# VIII

## CANADA

### The Growth of a Dominion

### The Lessons of Canadian Development

NOTHING in the modern history of that unique fusion of independence with unity which is the British Commonwealth of Nations—nothing, at least, before the changes of the years since 1945—has been more curious than the event with which that history opened in 1867: in all probability nothing has been more characteristic of the empiricism which has long marked the political evolution of the British peoples. The British North America Act of 1867, which, in the words of its preamble, "federally united into one Dominion" the Colonies of Canada, Nova Scotia and New Brunswick, not only created a new nation, but at the same time opened a new and striking chapter of the history of the British Empire. In fact it may be said to have introduced a fresh conception of that Empire, without which one of the most interesting experiments in political association ever undertaken, and possibly one of the most significant, would have been impossible. In the words used by John Coatman in his *Magna Britannia*,[1]

> the great new discovery of the British Commonwealth is that it is possible to have a political system resting on nothing but a free willingness to associate.

Such an arrangement, it can now be seen, was implicit in the establishment of the Canadian Dominion, and, though few at the time appreciated the fact, it was an inevitable corollary of the increasing self-reliance of the colonial peoples, and of the growing complexity of their problems. As other new nations arose, in Australia, New Zealand and South Africa, and as from 1887 a succession of Colonial Conferences revealed the fundamental community of interests that continued to bind them together, it began to be realized that freedom did not necessarily mean complete independence; that political maturity was not incompatible with a continuance of the imperial link.

The whole idea of Empire was gradually modified, and a new conception of free association eventually emerged.

The awakening in the United Kingdom from about 1870 of a sympathetic interest in the settlement-colonies has already been described. The first move towards a formal recognition of the new situation was the assumption by Edward VII, soon after his accession in 1901, of an enlarged royal title, which proclaimed him to be King "of the United Kingdom of Great Britain and Ireland and of the British Dominions beyond the Seas". Six years later the Colonial Conference of 1907 resolved that the self-governing Colonies should henceforth be known officially as Dominions, and the Canadian Premier, Sir Wilfrid Laurier, described them as "a galaxy of free nations under the British Crown". It was the war of 1914–19, however, which first revealed to the World that a group of new countries had grown to full nationhood, and the famous Declaration issued by the Imperial Conference of 1926 did no more than set the seal upon their achievement. Yet the very phrase, "the British Commonwealth of Nations", which then passed into general usage, had been foreshadowed by Lord Rosebery during a visit to Australia in 1883–84,[2] and with characteristic prescience Balfour, who was largely responsible for the happy phrasing of the Declaration of 1926, had long since seen whither developments were tending. "I believe, from a legal point of view," he said in 1911, "the British Parliament is supreme over the Parliaments of Canada, of Australasia, or the Cape, or South Africa. But in fact they are independent Parliaments, absolutely independent, and it is our business to recognize that, and to frame the Empire upon the co-operation of absolutely independent Parliaments."[3]

## THE NORTH AMERICA ACT, 1867

It is to the great Act of 1867, and to the creation of a united Canada, that we must look for the origin of these notions, and the coincidence which saw that Act appear in the same year as the extension of the franchise in Britain is a striking one. Yet, while the Franchise Act was the result of much discussion and agitation, both in Parliament and throughout the country, interest in the North America Act was slight. Canadians complained that it was treated as if it were no more than "a private bill uniting two or three English parishes", and it was reported that when the House of Commons passed to the next business, which concerned a tax on dogs, there was a perceptible brightening of interest.[4] As has already been shown, however, the general attitude towards the colonies was still one of indifference: not until 1869 were there signs of a revival of interest, and until then the new developments in Canada were regarded as the pre-liminaries to full independence, or to absorption into the United States. Yet this attitude had the paradoxical result of ensuring the continuance of the Canadian connexion with Britain as no other course could have done. As Lord Dufferin, Governor-General of Canada from 1872 to 1878, reported to the Colonial Secretary, Lord Carnarvon, in 1874:

> Nothing has more stimulated the passionate affection with which Canada now clings to England than the consciousness that the maintenance of the connection depends on her own free will.[5]

And it is precisely upon free-will that the later developments of the British Commonwealth have been based.

## ". . . IN DEFIANCE OF GEOGRAPHY. . . ."

Canada, it has well been said, "has been built in defiance of geography".[6] Its very existence might with equal truth be described as an accident of history, for few other countries can have owed their development so much to the moulding influences of historical events rather than of natural conditions. Canada was, in origin, a French colony, created on the St. Lawrence waterway, which opened a route into the interior of the North American continent from the north, even as the Mississippi provided a gateway to the south. In the seventeenth century the St. Lawrence proved the most practicable means of entry to the heart of the continent, and it was on the great river itself that Samuel de Champlain, founder of "New France", established the trading post and fort of Quebec in 1608. During the next hundred and fifty years the great struggle for North America was fought out between French and British, and, although the French controlled both the St. Lawrence and the Mississippi, the French settlers were heavily out-numbered, and France itself was too deeply involved with events in Europe to furnish adequate support. The Treaty of

Paris in 1763 left Britain supreme. But New France, or Canada as it came to be called, remained French, and remains French to this day. The expansion of the French population of some fifty-five thousand, over which Britain assumed control in 1763, by natural increase and without immigration, into the 1951 total of 4,319,167 (in a Dominion total of 14,009,429), has well been described as "one of the marvels of the world's history",[7] a tribute alike to French tenacity and British rule, which together have made Montreal, for instance, the second French city in the world. Dilke, in *Greater Britain* (1868), recorded his astonishment that British troops were employed in Canada "as guardians of the only true French colony in the world against the inroads of the English race", and the paradox explains much in Canadian history that is bewildering to the outside observer. Yet, but for two major events of the last quarter of the eighteenth century, the growth of the small and isolated French colony into the powerful Dominion of today could hardly have occurred. The first of these events was the revolt of the thirteen Colonies on the Atlantic coast, and the establishment of the United States of America, which left Britain with no secure hold upon North America; the second, the French Revolution, which snapped the last ties between Old and New France. French Canada remained essentially a creation of the *ancien régime*, opposed to the revolutionary and free-thinking character of Republican France. As late as 1914 the resistance of many *Canadiens* to Canada's entry into the war was inspired in part by a belief that the war itself was a divine judgment upon France for her sins against the Church, and it was a similar attitude which led the Dominion Government, in the Second World War, to maintain official relations with Pétain and the Vichy régime. But it was mainly in internal affairs, and in relations with Britain, that the individual outlook of the French Canadian made itself felt. Canada's existence as a nation, while it owes much to that outlook, and to the spirit of sturdy independence which sustained it, was largely a by-product of the American revolution.

## THE DURHAM REPORT, 1839

It was long after the separation of the American colonies, however, that British and French north of the United States began to draw together in a viable state. The process which led to the establishment of the self-governing Dominion of 1867 may be said to have begun with the mission of Lord Durham in 1838, which gave to the world the Durham Report, long acknowledged to be "the greatest state document in British imperial history".[8] Durham had been sent to inquire into the strained situation which existed in Canada, with acute tension between the French in Lower and the British in Upper Canada, and both peoples resentful of their political dependence. Durham found, as he reported in words which have become historic, "two nations warring in the bosom of a single state", and he recommended a union of the colonies, with responsible government in the management of their internal affairs. But he went farther. He looked beyond the immediate constitutional issue to the fundamental problems confronting the British colonies in North America at a time when an eventual severance of the imperial tie was generally regarded as inevitable, and when, as he showed in his Report, the United States were exercising increasing powers of attraction, and he argued that the attraction could be overcome only "by raising up for the North American colonist some nationality of his own: by elevating these small and unimportant communities into a society having some objects of a national importance; and by thus giving their inhabitants a country which they will be unwilling to see absorbed even into one more powerful". If this could be done, and responsible government granted, the bond with Britain, Durham maintained, would be strengthened; "the connexion would only become more durable and advantageous by having more of equality, of freedom, and of local independence".

Durham was in Canada only five months, but in that short time he had grasped the essentials not only of the government of a free Canada but also of the very continuance of the British Empire under changing world conditions. "The immense historical importance of the Durham Report," it has been said, "lies in the fact that it established the principles on which the British Commonwealth of Nations has been built."[9] Within little more than a quarter of a century of Durham's mission a new and greater Canada had come into existence, and with it the beginnings of a new conception of Empire.

## LORD ELGIN, 1847–54

Durham, however, had done no more than establish the principles. It was his son-in-law, Lord Elgin, who as Governor of Canada from 1847 to 1854 first began to put those principles into effect. No formal measure of transfer of power was proposed, but from the first days of his governorship Elgin made it clear that he would act as a constitutional ruler, and in this, despite appeals from Canadian "loyalists", he was upheld by Parliament in London. Gradually it came to be realized that responsible government was a reality, and the French, in particular, began to appreciate the protection which the British connexion afforded them. Unable to stand alone in a continent which was rapidly developing an Anglo-Saxon civilization of its own, they feared absorption into the United States, realizing, as Durham himself had pointed out, and as the example of Louisiana showed, that from that quarter assimilation would hardly come in any acceptable form. Under Britain their right to live their own life in their own way was increasingly acknowledged. Their best guarantee against interference, as Dilke noted with interest, was now the imperial connexion, provided that it left them to manage their local affairs in peace. The results of the following hundred years' experience were summed-up in a striking speech by M. Adelard Godbout, Premier of Quebec, in 1941:

> You will find very few people who do not realize that we (French-Canadians) are treated better under the British Crown than we would have been under our mother country, France. The people of this Province are more attached to the British Crown than any other element in Canada because we needed it. We are a minority and we have needed its protection.[10]

The combination of confidence in the British connexion and recognition of the value of its protection, which this statement reveals, began to make itself felt in Canadian political life from the time of Elgin's governorship. It rendered possible the union of 1867, and at the same time, as will be seen, dictated the conditions under which the union was effected: 1867 set the seal, but the process began under Elgin. "It was from that date," as Laurier said later, "that the British Empire started upon its triumphant march across the ages."[11]

## THE MOVEMENT FOR FEDERATION

The immediate results of the new policy which Elgin inaugurated were not, however, happy. Political stalemate between French and British followed, and both peoples began to look to a wider union for relief. A united State of British North America, mainly British in population but including in its constitution adequate guarantees for the French, was the obvious solution, and it was fortunate that on both sides leaders of outstanding ability appeared who were prepared to sink their differences in the common interest. Robert Baldwin (1804–58) and Louis Lafontaine (1807–64) prepared the way with their "Great Ministry" of 1848–51, and, although there were many setbacks, their work was continued by Sir John Macdonald (1815–91), Sir George Cartier (1814–73) and others. From this time onwards, in fact, the leaders of the great nation that Canada was to become were drawn from both races, as their names—Mackenzie, Laurier, Borden, Lapointe, Bennett, King, St. Laurent, to name only a selection— sufficiently testify. Mr. J. G. Diefenbaker, Dominion Premier in 1957, is no exception, for, although bearing a Dutch name, he is also of Scottish descent.

## THREAT OF U.S. EXPANSION: "MANIFEST DESTINY"

Many other factors also indicated after 1841 the desirability of a wider union. Among these were the hard facts of geography and economics, together with the rapid development of the great neighbour and exemplar to the south, the U.S.A., which was a striking feature of this period. The 'forties saw American settlement, with the acquisition of Oregon, California, and Texas, sweep right across the continent, from the Mississippi to the Pacific. By a treaty of 1818 the development of Oregon had been shared between the Hudson's Bay Company and American fur-trading interests, but with the arrival of settlers along the "Oregon trail" the Company was squeezed out, and in 1846 the "forty-ninth parallel" was agreed upon as the frontier. Within a few years, however, fresh pressure had emerged with the discovery of gold and the steady expansion of American settlement. It began to appear as if British interests on the prairies and the Pacific coast might be extinguished, and it was clear that the Company lacked the

means to offer adequate resistance. In 1858, therefore, a new
Colony of British Columbia was proclaimed on the Pacific
coast, though Vancouver Island was left under the Company's
jurisdiction until 1866. Yet the future of what are now the
Prairie and Pacific Provinces of the Dominion remained
uncertain. It had long seemed obvious that the natural forces of
geography and economics must eventually bring about the
union of the whole North American continent under a single
Power, and in the previous century, after the long struggle
that had culminated in the settlement of 1763, Britain had
gained the potential mastery of the whole vast area. But a
political quarrel had brought division, and had left the few
remaining British colonies clinging precariously to the north-
east fringe of the continent, controlling the St. Lawrence
waterway but little else. Was there room for two countries
in North America? It seemed unlikely. Yet the alternative
was obviously the reuniting of the whole region, this time under
the Stars and Stripes. With the absorption of much of the
interior of the continent by the U.S.A. this solution seemed
to many inevitable, for the frontier was no more than a line
drawn upon a map, and lay upon no natural barrier. Moreover,
the United States were in control of most of the routes by
which the produce of the interior could reach the Atlantic,
and, while the Republic's westward expansion was checked
by no natural obstacles, the colonies on the St. Lawrence
were separated from the rich prairies by the infertile wastelands
of the "Canadian Shield", extending from Hudson's Bay to
Lake Ontario. Hence the view that Canada was created "in
defiance of geography". Clearly, if Durham's hopes of "elevating these small and unimportant communities into a society
having some objects of national importance" were ever to be
realized, the colonists could not leave to the Americans the
settlement of the whole of the interior. Nor could they achieve
much while isolated from each other. The remedy was to be
found, as in the case of the United States themselves, in the
political ties of federation and the physical links of railway
development. Canada, a Canadian historian has said, "has
been a railway in search of a state",[12] for settlement and
development were in the main a consequence, and not, as in
the U.S.A., a cause, of railway construction.

## TRANSPORT ROUTES AND RAILWAYS

Before the coming of the railways water transport had moved the produce of the interior, at first chiefly furs and timber, but, later, grain and farm produce, from the Great Lakes to the Atlantic seaboard. But the St. Lawrence was frozen during five months of the year, and the most direct route was, in any case, by way of the Hudson River. With the construction in 1825 of the Erie Canal, linking the Hudson with Lakes Erie and Ontario, the supremacy of this route was assured, and with it the prosperity of New York, at the mouth of the river. Canals cut through the Appalachian barrier to the interior, and were followed within thirty years by railways. Canada was caught up in the commercial empire of the New England States, and Montreal, which was later to become the world's largest inland seaport, was linked by rail with Boston in 1851 in order to ensure an outlet to the sea throughout the year. The maritime colonies at the mouth of the St. Lawrence, connected by their seaborne traffic with the United States, but cut off from Canada by forest and wilderness, found in the American railways their most convenient link with their fellow-subjects of British North America: "we always cross the United States to shake hands", complained a Halifax newspaper in 1866.[13] By the 'fifties it was already apparent that if Canada and the other Colonies were to retain economic independence, and with it any share in the development of their vast hinterland, they must provide their own rail-routes and ice-free ports. American transport routes had cut across the traditional east-west pattern imposed by the Lakes and the St. Lawrence, but railways could restore it, and in so doing could open the prairies to settlement.

## THE U.S. CIVIL WAR AND FENIAN RAIDS

Railways, by linking the Colonies, could also buttress them against American political pressure. Americans had long been talking of "our manifest destiny to overspread the continent allotted by Providence for the free development of our yearly multiplying millions", and two attempts had already been made, during the Revolution and the war of 1812, to carry "manifest destiny" into effect by invading Canada. With the growth of the United States' population, outnumbering

British subjects by ten to one, and the revelation of their military power in the Civil War, the threat to the British colonies was immeasurably increased. The end of the Civil War, in particular, found the United States in a truculent, self-confident and expansionist mood. There was much hostility to Britain on account of the *Alabama* claims, and a not unnatural desire to complete the process of unification which the success of the Union States in war seemed to justify. The oustanding protagonist of this policy was the American Secretary of State, William H. Seward. It was he who in 1867 carried through the purchase of Alaska from Russia, and sought to buy out the Hudson's Bay Company's interests. In that same year, in a public address at Boston, he proclaimed his own faith in "manifest destiny":

> I know that Nature designs that this whole continent, not merely these thirty-six States, shall be, sooner or later, within the magic circle of the American Union.

Two years later Senator Sumner, Chairman of the Senate Foreign Affairs Committee, with the avowed support of President Grant, claimed Canada in settlement of the *Alabama* claims, and the seeming indifference of the British Government to the colonies lent colour to the American designs. Cardwell was now carrying through Parliament important Army reforms, which were intended to reduce the cost of defence largely by withdrawing the colonial garrisons, and this step, though, as has been shown, it had the paradoxical effect of reviving interest in the colonies in Britain, encouraged American expectations. Early in 1870 the American Secretary of State, Hamilton Fish, went so far as to suggest to the British Minister in Washington that a plebiscite on union with the United States should be taken in Canada,[14] and there were other American politicians who advocated more forcible measures.

The North American Colonies were, therefore, unavoidably caught up in the strained relations between Britain and the U.S.A. which followed the Civil War, and which were not smoothed over until the settlement of the *Alabama* dispute in 1872. Further, "manifest destiny" and the rapid expansion of American settlement into the West threatened not merely the development but the very existence of the colonies, while within the colonies themselves closer union seemed to be the only solution of political difficulties. To these factors was added the menace of Fenianism. The end of the American Civil War had left many Irish-American soldiers adrift, accustomed to the excitement of war, bitter in their opposition to Britain, and divided only in their views on action against her. In England the Fenian agitation led in 1867 to the unhappy episode of the "Manchester martyrs": in North America there were disturbances and threats of "invasion", which by the same year had caused the imperial garrison to be strengthened and more than thirty thousand volunteers to be embodied. The situation was not improved by American suggestions that the threat of Fenian incursions could be removed only by the withdrawal of British authority from North America, since Fenianism was "excited by the proximity of the British flag."[15] Inevitably the value of the British connexion was enhanced in colonial eyes, and closer union appeared increasingly to be the only defence against American pressure. Moreover, the colonists had their own disputes with the U.S.A., turning on the coastal fisheries and on the heated discussions over reciprocal tariff arrangements. With the denunciation by the Americans in 1866 of the Reciprocity Treaty of 1854 the colonies had to look for other markets, and the advantages of forming a great free-trade area in British North America were self-evident.

## THE GRAND TRUNK RAILWAY

Projects for union had begun to be mooted in the 'fifties. Political deadlock in the united Canadas had suggested a federal union as the only reasonable solution of the impasse between French and British, and similar unions had been proposed for the Maritime and Pacific Coast colonies. More ambitious projects had foreshadowed a great union of all the colonies, stretching from coast to coast and linked by railways. Considerations of trade and defence lent point to these wider plans, which were supported by railway interests and by the banking concerns behind them (in particular, by Glyn Mills and the Barings in London, and by the Bank of Montreal in Canada itself). Outstanding among railway projects was the Grand Trunk line, which, begun with Government backing in

1855 as a link between the Lakes and the sea, was extended in 1873 to Chicago, and eventually became one of Canada's three transcontinental lines. Faced as it was, however, by American competition, the Grand Trunk was in constant difficulties, and it was Sir Edward Watkin (1819–1901), the London financier and railway promoter (best known, perhaps, for his association with the Great Central Railway in England) who, after assuming the presidency of the Company in 1861, realized the possibilities of development that lay in it, and thereby made no small contribution to the evolution of the Canadian Dominion. Watkin saw that the railway could tap the markets it needed only by eastward and westward expansion. By connexions with the existing railway systems of New Brunswick and Nova Scotia it could ensure for Canada the ice-free ports that were needed to break American control; by striking westwards it could open the prairies to settlement and secure them for Canadian development. Watkin's hopes of economic returns were not to be altogether justified, for the Canadian railway system has always needed Government support and has accounted for a great part of the country's public debt, but without the railways the Dominion could hardly have come into existence. In particular, it was the promise of railway connexion which brought New Brunswick and Nova Scotia, and, later, British Columbia and Prince Edward Island, into federal union with Canada proper.

## THE ACHIEVEMENT OF FEDERATION

The first project for union was put forward in 1858 by Sir Alexander Galt (1817–93), a prominent Canadian politician and financier, who later became the first Dominion Minister of Finance and High Commissioner in London. By 1864 it was clear that only federation could ease the tense political situation in the Canadas, and at the same time the Maritime Colonies were drawing together. Financial influence was exerted in favour of the wider union, and political pressure was skilfully applied from London. Conferences were held in the colonies in 1864, and after considerable hesitation in the Maritime Colonies, which resulted in the abstention of Newfoundland and Prince Edward Island, representatives of the other three Colonies repaired to London. There, after further discussions, the British North America Act was passed at the end of March, 1867. Many Canadians had wished to have their country erected into a Kingdom, but the British Government, in deference to American feeling, refused its consent to the title, and on 1st July of the same year the "Dominion of Canada" formally came into existence.

The creation of the Dominion has been described by a Canadian historian as "one of the greatest acts of state-building in history",[16] for so it appears after the triumphs of recent years. But, as the same writer has recorded, the great nation to be was in 1867 "still a vision", and a vision which few, whether in North America or in Britain, had before their eyes. More than most countries Canada has had to win recognition in every generation, and it was not, perhaps, until "Canada's Hundred Days", from 4th August to 11th November, 1918, that the vision of 1867 became a splendid reality. It was then that the prophetic words used by the Prime Minister, Sir John Macdonald, in 1872, became justified:

> I hope to live to see the day, and if I do not that my son may be spared to see Canada the right arm of England, to see Canada a powerful auxiliary to the Empire, and not a cause of anxiety and a source of danger.[17]

The contrast between the weak and scattered colonies of the 'sixties, threatened by the economic and military power of the United States, and the victorious nation of 1918, is, indeed, an impressive one, which typifies the development through which the Dominion had passed in less than half a century.

In 1867, however, Canada's total population was still no more than 3,300,000. In *Greater Britain* Dilke quoted Canadians who maintained that with British help the number could be increased in ten years to as many millions, and that Canada could then stand alone. He was sceptical of the possibilities of such expansion, and events have justified his doubts, for it was not until the census of 1931 that a population of ten millions could be recorded. Had Canada kept pace with the United States, her population, it has been estimated, would by now have attained forty millions, but America was always a "benevolent vampire",[18] drawing Canadians and new settlers alike to the expanding and prosperous communities south of the border: American tariffs after 1866 excluded Canadian goods, but not Canadian men. By 1890, with the population of Canada still well below five millions, there were already nearly one million Canadian-born settled in the U.S.A., which had become for many, in the happy phrase of a character in one of Stephen Leacock's delightful scenes of Ontario life, "that goal from which no traveller returns".[19] It was only after 1890, with the passing of the "expanding frontier" in the Republic, that Canada was able to attract, and retain, a steady flow of immigrants. Hitherto the flow to the United States had more than balanced the intake from Europe, and had threatened Canada with a stationary population, but conditions changed during the 'nineties: of the three million immigrants who entered Canada between 1897 and 1914 Britain provided rather more than a third, but almost as many more came from the United States. By 1911 Canada's population had passed seven millions and was rising steadily: the danger of stagnation had passed.

### THE EXPANSION OF THE DOMINION

Meanwhile the Dominion had established itself territorially. The Act of 1867 had been welcomed in Canada proper, but had been received with open hostility in Nova Scotia, where on that notable first "Dominion Day", 1st July, 1867, the streets were draped in black. Nova Scotia's difficulties were mainly economic. It was feared that federation meant higher taxation, and higher taxation at a time when the shipping industry was in depression and trade with the United States had been diminished by the refusal to renew the Reciprocity Treaty. The colony had been hard hit by the change that was taking place from sailing-ship to steamers: the wealth of timber resources that had enabled the Maritime Colonies to assume the fourth place in the world for registered tonnage now counted for much less. The inter-colonial railway, promised before 1867, was completed in 1876, and did something to offset the losses, though it did not enable Halifax to oust Montreal, with all its winter disadvantages, from the position of Canada's chief port. Yet there was no happy alternative for the reluctant Province, and the position was gradually accepted. Elsewhere, the changes wrought by the

Act of 1867 were more impressive. Provision had been made in the Act for the purchase from the Hudson's Bay Company of the rights it exercised over the vast territories to the north-west, and in 1869 the deal was settled: Rupert's Land and the North-West Territory were formally absorbed into Canada in the following year. The step was not taken without opposition, for the fur-trappers on the Red River had long been resisting the approach of settlements, and in 1869 broke into rebellion under the French half-breed, Louis Riel (1844–85). With the help of British troops (under the leadership of Wolseley), who now served in Canada for the last time, the rising was suppressed, and the Red River settlements became the Province of Manitoba, a name destined before the century was out to win a leading place in the wheat markets of the world. In the following year, 1871, British Columbia agreed to enter the Dominion, on condition that a transcontinental railway should be constructed within ten years. The U.S.A., with its population of forty millions, had only recently (1869), completed its line across to San Francisco, and for Canada, with less than four millions, the decision must have seemed, as it has been described, "either magnificently bold or just plainly silly".[20] Nevertheless, the decision was made to construct a line which, unlike the Grand Trunk, would run only through Canadian territory. The decision was Macdonald's, a typically bold gesture of confidence in Canada's future, but the successful completion of the line owed as much to the imagination and drive of another doughty Canadian of Scottish origin, the financier, George Stephen, afterwards Lord Mount Stephen (1829–1921), who became president of the railway company in 1880. Construction was delayed by constant financial difficulties, aggravated by the hostility of the Grand Trunk, and Macdonald himself had to live down unsavoury revelations about the concessions for the line, which brought down his government in 1873. In 1886, however, the project was eventually completed as the Canadian Pacific Railway. Within the next twenty years two more trans-continental lines, the Canadian Northern and the Grand Trunk, were completed, and Canadians found themselves with more miles of railway for each thousand of the population than any other country in the world (though the figure is only slightly higher than that for Australia, where similar distances and obstacles had to be overcome). The total mileage, which had been little more than six thousand in 1878, had reached thirty-seven thousand by 1916 and was eventually to amount to forty-three thousand. The Atlantic and Pacific coasts were securely linked.

## THE RAILWAYS AND ECONOMIC DEVELOPMENT

Other Provinces were gradually added to the Dominion. In 1873 Prince Edward Island, the last remaining Colony, apart from Newfoundland, was admitted: for Newfoundland a decision was only taken reluctantly, and after many difficulties, seventy-six years later. To the west the construction of the railway gradually opened the prairies for settlement, and the Provinces of Alberta and Saskatchewan were created in 1905. Twenty years earlier, in 1885, the approach of the railway had caused the last trappers' rising in the North-West and for his part in this affair, and in the "Red River Rebellion" sixteen years before, Riel was executed. Yet, despite these two risings, the settlement of the North-West was undertaken with less violence, and with less harshness to the Indians, than had been the case further south, on the western plains of the United States. Canada had no "Wild West". The reason is to be found partly in the tradition of order established by the Hudson's Bay Company, which was maintained by the North-West Mounted Police (later, the Royal Canadian Mounted Police) established in 1873; but it is to be found mainly in the slow rate of settlement. It is significant that although the Canadian Pacific Railway passed through the regions which were to become Alberta and Saskatchewan in 1885, the Provinces themselves were not formed for another twenty years. During those years the tide of immigration from Europe began to flow to Canada as well as the United States, and, more important still, hard grains were cultivated, which would ripen in the short north-western summer. When, in the present century, greater immigration rendered possible a rapid increase of settlement, the preparatory work had been done, and wheat production, which had been 42,000,000 bushels in 1891, rose from 55,000,000 to 132,000,000 bushels in the first decade. At the same time the railways, which had been pushed across the inhospitable Canadian Shield to open a way to the fertile soil further to the west, called attention to the natural resources of the Shield itself, and turned it from a barrier into a national asset of increasing significance. Asbestos was discovered by railway builders in 1876, and nickel seven years later: in both Canada was soon to become the world's principal producer. Gold, silver, platinum, cobalt and copper followed in the early years of the new century, and in 1936 the most dramatic discovery of all revealed pitchblende, the source of radium and uranium. If by the time of the Second World War Canada, through her rich resources of foodstuffs and raw materials, and despite her comparatively small population, had become one of the major industrial powers of the world, it was the transcontinental railway system, in the first instance, which had placed her in that position. The founders of the Dominion had built better than they knew.

## THE CANADIAN CONSTITUTION

While the very existence of the United States has been a constant challenge to Canada and a stimulus to its development as an independent and viable nation, the lessons of American experience were taken to heart in the framing of the Canadian governmental system. To men discussing the framework of union in British North America, while a bitter fratricidal struggle was being waged to the south, the weaknesses of the American federal system were painfully apparent. In particular, the U.S.A. seemed to have suffered from an excessive deference to "States' rights", while the lack of strong central organs of government, with the sanction of tradition behind them, was manifest. To many Canadians "the American Civil War marked the final stage in the discredit, not merely of federation but also of democracy and republicanism".[21] These faults in the American system the founders of the Canadian constitution, and, in particular, Sir John Macdonald and Sir Alexander Galt, were determined to avoid. Macdonald, an astute political manager, who despite his shortcomings left an enduring mark on Canada's history, would have preferred a closer union, in a *kingdom* of Canada, but local patriotism, and especially the unyielding independence of the *Canadiens*, made a federal system unavoidable, and the British Government itself insisted on the title of "Dominion". Nevertheless, Macdonald was able to stress the retention of the Crown, and of much of British political practice. "We have desired in this measure," he explained to Queen Victoria in 1867, "to declare in the most solemn and emphatic manner our resolve to be under the Sovereignty of Your Majesty and your family for ever."[22]

With America's example before them, Macdonald and his colleagues endeavoured to limit the authority of the Provinces, and especially to ensure that residual powers should be vested in the central, Federal, Government, and not, as with the United States, in the States or the people (as provided in the Tenth Amendment to the American Constitution). Article 91 of the British North America Act expressly states that the Federal Parliament shall have power to make laws in all matters excepting those exclusively assigned to the Provinces, while the preamble to the Act, in significant contrast to the Constitutions of the United States and the Australian Commonwealth, cites the Provinces, and not "the people", as partners in the new enterprise. The contrast with the American system is also seen in the reference, in the preamble, to the constitution as "similar in principle to that of the United Kingdom", and this is interpreted in later sections of the Act as government by the "Crown in Parliament", with a House of Commons (bearing the very name of its English model) and a Senate which is no more than a modified version of the House of Lords. Yet the system established was federal. Without full protection for their rights the French would never have been induced to enter the Dominion, and, although their able and enlightened leader, Cartier, was able to carry them with him, the Act had to make formal provision for the protection of their language and schools.

The very care with which the Act was drafted, however, was to some extent its undoing. The attempt to enumerate the subjects on which the Federal Parliament should legislate inevitably suggested a limitation of its authority, and the division between Federal and Provincial matters was in any case difficult to draw, while the great expansion of the Dominion in its first thirty years raised a multitude of local issues with which Parliament was not best fitted to cope. As a result, while the general tendency has been towards a steady increase in the powers of government over wider fields of political and economic activity, and the United States have seen a gradual extension of Federal authority, in Canada the Provinces have tended to gain at the expense of the Federal government: the Act of 1867, in the words of a Canadian historian, has been "pretty well stood on its head".[23] The chief part in this curious process of historical inversion has been played by the Judicial Committee of the Privy Council, to which appeals under the Act of 1867 were directed. In the 'seventies and 'eighties the Committee's narrowly legalistic interpretation of the Act encouraged Sir Oliver Mowat (1820-1903), Premier of Ontario from 1872 to 1896, and a determined opponent of Macdonald, in his struggle for "Provincial rights". This is not the place for an examination of the long legal struggle over the Act, but it has to be noted that divergent interpretations have provided one of the bases of party division in Canada, and that the contest between "centralism" and "provincialism" has continued into our own day. Much has turned on the issue as to whether the Act was primarily a compact between the Provinces, or a grant of sovereignty, within certain limits, to the Dominion and its Provinces together. Legally and historically the compact theory has little validity, but it has had an important following in Canada, and has exercised considerable influence since the Statute of Westminster of 1931 upon the efforts made by Canadians to agree to the machinery for the amendment of their constitution. Provincial and Federal Governments have been at variance, and the French of Quebec Province, in particular, long resisted attempts to have the power of amendment transferred from the British Parliament to the Dominion, as in the case of Australia. The Statute of Westminster, at Canada's request, expressly reserved the Act of 1867 from the recognition of Dominion sovereignty, thereby assuring to the *Canadiens* the protection, while they felt it to be necessary, of powers of amendment and appeal outside Canada. The change was finally made, however, by the British North America Act, 1949, which nevertheless was careful to leave untouched Clause 133 of the Act of 1867, guaranteeing the equality of French with English as the medium of Parliament and the law-courts. In the same year the right of appeal to the Privy

Council in England disappeared. With a population of 4,300,000, as against 6,700,000 of British descent, the *Canadiens* may well feel that the precautions insisted on in 1867 may be relaxed.

The effect of the interpretations placed upon the Act has been to make the government of Canada in practice more federal in character than it was intended to be. In the words of a leading authority, "although Canada has not a federal constitution, it has a federal government".[24] Macdonald resisted the tendency, but economic difficulties in the early years of the new Dominion strained the new-found unity, and led many to question the very basis of the nation's existence. In 1887 an inter-provincial conference went so far as to make proposals for a considerable limitation of Federal authority. A serious factor in the situation was the execution, in 1885, of Louis Riel, which stirred up old racial and religious antagonisms, and shook the hold which Macdonald had long skilfully kept upon French opinion. The resultant stimulus to particularist feeling was further strengthend by the "Manitoba Schools Question", the dispute which arose in the early 'nineties over the rights of the French minority in Manitoba to a share in the provincial schools, a dispute which involved not only racial and religious issues, but also the fundamental question of Federal and Provincial powers. Macdonald had died before the matter came to a head, and, with four Prime Ministers in as many years to succeed him, the Conservative Party, which he had built up with such skill, blundered into the General Election of 1896, and went down before the resounding success of the Liberals, led by Sir Wilfrid Laurier (1841–1919). Provincial rights had been one of the main planks of the Liberal platform: henceforth it was to be practically an article of the constitution. The four Laurier administrations, continuous from 1896 to 1911, opened a new chapter in Canadian history.

ECONOMIC DIFFICULTIES

But, although traditional rivalries played their part in the early years, it was particularly in the economic field that the strain was felt. Here, as elsewhere, the hopes with which the Dominion had been inaugurated were not soon to be fulfilled.

It had been established at a time of rapid economic change, when the United States, their industrial development hastened in the forcing-house of the Civil War, were about to build up a great industrial empire behind the barrier of protective tariffs. The Reciprocity Treaty of 1854 had been dropped twelve years later, and the American tariffs, which had been raised during the war as an emergency measure, were not only maintained but pushed even higher, reaching their peaks in the McKinley and Dingley tariffs of 1890 and 1897. Canadian adjustment to this situation was painful, and was restrained both by the lack of an adequate home market and by the general economic depression which began in 1873. The twenty-five years following 1873, it has been said, "were probably the grimmest quarter century in the history of Canada".[25] The Maritime Provinces, in particular, were hit by the decline of wooden shipping, and it was not until improvements in ocean transport, and especially the invention of the steam-turbine, brought lower freight-rates that any considerable improvement in trade could begin. The Liberal remedy for the economic stagnation that threatened Canada was a "continental" policy of "unlimited reciprocity" with the United States, a hopeful gesture which, however, met with little response from the States themselves. From the Washington Treaty of 1871, which, while submitting the *Alabama* claims to arbitration, also sought to adjust Canadian-American fishing-rights, relations between the two countries were far from satisfactory. The Liberal administration of 1873-78, under Alexander Mackenzie (1822-92), attempted to negotiate a new reciprocity treaty in 1874, but met with a frigid reception in Washington, and later Liberal hankerings after a "continental" policy inevitably laid them open to the charge that they were preparing for the absorption of Canada by the United States. Macdonald preferred to rely sentimentally upon Britain and practically upon the development of Canada's own resources, behind the protection of tariffs. His "National Policy", with which he won the election of 1878, aimed at a fiscal policy which, he argued, would preserve the developing West as a market for the industrial produce of Eastern Canada and would therefore make the east-west railway system a paying proposition. In the end he was proved largely right.

The 'eighties saw an expansion of protected industry and the completion of the C.P.R., though it was not until several years after his death in 1891 that a real economic recovery began. By that time the closing of the "frontier" in the U.S.A., the opening of new goldfields, including Canada's own Klondike, and the first indications, in 1896, of a rise in the price of wheat, had contributed to an improvement of the situation, and had inaugurated a quarter-century of expansion such as Macdonald himself, with all his faith in Canada, could never have foreseen. Meanwhile freight charges for wheat were falling, and by 1902 were only one-quarter of their level in the 'seventies, while the pressure of American tariffs had caused Canada to turn increasingly to Britain, which by 1896 was taking little short of two-thirds of her exports. Macdonald had shown his astuteness by fighting his last election in 1891, at the age of seventy-six, with the slogan, "The Old Man, the Old Flag, the Old Policy", and the 'nineties saw the economic ties between Canada and Britain drawn ever closer, though it was Laurier who, in 1897, introduced the system of "Imperial Preference", with a reduction in the Canadian tariff for British goods.

## ECONOMIC EXPANSION

There followed a remarkable economic expansion, which was to a large extent financed by British capital, of which some £300,000,000 flowed into Canada in the first decade of the twentieth century. With capital came men, though here the British contribution was far outmatched by others. In the thirty-five years after 1896 some five million immigrants entered the Dominion, most of them from Northern, Eastern and Southern Europe, and, though only half of them became permanent settlers, they gave the West the extraordinary variety of population which provides Winnipeg, for instance, with newspapers in more than a dozen different languages. Today, in consequence, more than two and a half million Canadians are of other than British or French stock. Economic development more than matched this increase in population. The rise in the production of wheat from 42,000,000 to 132,000,000 bushels in the twenty years, 1891–1911, has already been referred to. After 1911 output was below 200,000,000 bushels only in 1914, 1918 and 1919. In 1915 the phenomenal total of 393,000,000 bushels was achieved, and by 1922 the 400,000,000 level was reached. In that year Canadian exports for the first time exceeded those of the United States.

## "THE CENTURY OF CANADA"

Meanwhile, in the industrial sphere Canada's wealth of water-power was harnessed for electricity, the lumber industry received a new lease of life through the manufacture of paper and newsprint from wood-pulp (which lowered the cost of newsprint by five-sixths between 1875 and 1897), and the uncovering of the mineral resources of the "Shield" was begun. In the first ten years of the new century the value of Canada's industrial output rose from 215,000,000 to 565,000,000 dollars, and it was as a result of the prevailing mood of optimism that the second and third transcontinental railway lines were constructed. Laurier's boast, soon after taking office, that "the twentieth century will be the century of Canada", seemed rapidly to be justified, and although the optimistic spirits who foretold a further increase of population to fifty millions, or more, were destined to be disappointed, Canada was clearly set on the path to industrial greatness, though she realized as little as did the United States, in their similar situation, the international responsibilities that would ensue.

## EXTERNAL POLICY
### (1) RELATIONS WITH BRITAIN

Caught as she was, however, between Britain and the United States, Canada's position as the residuary legatee of the British possessions in North America was one of peculiar difficulty. If it took more than half a century after 1867 to persuade the Americans that Canada was now something more than an outpost of British imperialism, the Dominion found her own interests sacrificed with unfailing regularity on the altar of Anglo-American friendship. Partly from need, and partly from unhappy experience, Canada found that she had to frame her own line of conduct. It has been said that her foreign policy has consisted "largely of a refusal to have any",[26] but until full national status and a substantial economy had been achieved a cautious reserve was unavoidable. History and geography have alike dictated that the fundamental factors in Canadian policy should be her relations with Britain and the United States, and strong elements in the Dominion have opposed too close a dependence on either. Macdonald resisted Liberal pressure for closer economic ties with the United States, but, although he was prepared to play on the sentiments of imperial loyalty for his own purpose, he equally opposed any attempt to establish an imperial Federation, even as Laurier after him resisted the ambitious projects of Joseph Chamberlain at the Colonial Conference of 1897. Macdonald had seen Canadian interests paid scant respect at the Washington Conference of 1871, and, at the risk of appearing provincial, had no intention merely of following a British lead in any part of the world. "The Suez Canal is nothing to us", he wrote in 1885, when a Canadian contingent for the Sudan campaign was suggested.[27] Indeed, Canada's task, as can be seen more clearly now, was to be herself, a nation in her own right, separate from Britain and the U.S.A. alike, and in view of her special position and difficulties the task was to absorb her energies for many years.   With a prescient grasp of the trend of events, Macdonald repeatedly declared that he wanted his country to be an auxiliary of Britain, not a dependency.

The most striking demonstration of the need for a purely Canadian policy was provided by the settlement of the Alaskan boundary dispute in 1903, when, under strong American pressure, the British representative on the judicial tribunal which considered the matter threw in his vote with the Americans. America's case was probably sound, but her methods were resented. In a significant, and angry, comment on the episode Laurier deplored both the "grasping actions" of the United States and the Canadians' lack of "the treaty-making power which would enable us to dispose of our own affairs". The affair rankled the more because British Canadian feeling had recently brought about Dominion participation in the Boer War. Laurier had justified this action, in 1900, in prophetic words:

> I am free to say that whilst I cannot admit that Canada should take part in all the wars of Great Britain, neither am I prepared to say that she should not take part in any war at all. I am prepared to look upon each case upon its merits as it arises. . . . What we have done we have done . . . in the plenitude, in the majesty of our colonial

legislative independence. I claim for Canada this, that, in future, Canada shall be at liberty to act or not act, to interfere or not interfere, to do just as she pleases, and that she shall reserve to herself the right to judge whether or not there is cause for her to act.[28]

At the same time he recognized that "every Canadian . . . would be ready to contribute our treasure and our blood . . . for the rescue of England, were she engaged in a life and death struggle", and the principles he enunciated were to guide Canada's action in two World Wars. The first was given formal recognition by the Imperial Conference of 1926 and the Statute of Westminster of 1931. Canada acted upon it in 1939 when the King, on the advice of his Canadian Ministers, declared a state of war to exist between Canada and Germany on 10th September, seven days later than for the United Kingdom. Canadian neutrality in a major conflict in which Britain was involved was out of the question, but it was for Canada, as Laurier insisted, to decide on the extent of her participation.

It was for Canada, also, to decide on the extent of her preparation. During the Boer War the small British garrison of the naval base at Halifax had been withdrawn, and in 1905, as part of the reorganization of the British fleet, the base itself was handed over to Canada. Four years later, when Britain, faced by the rising power of the German Navy, asked for naval contributions from the Dominions, Canada characteristically insisted on separate colonial navies rather than mere colonial additions to the Royal Navy. Laurier's Naval Service Bill of 1910 met with a storm of opposition, however: British Canadians opposed the notion of a separate navy, and the isolationist French were equally determined to have no navy at all. The conflict played a decisive part in Laurier's electoral defeat in 1911, to which a new turn in Canadian-American relations also contributed much.

## (2) RELATIONS WITH THE U.S.A.

Since the Alaskan dispute of 1903 relations had steadily improved, partly because the United States were beginning grudgingly to recognize that something of interest was happening north of the frontier, partly because they needed the markets and materials which Canada could obviously offer. In 1909 it at last proved possible to reach a decision on the

N

vexed question of fishing rights, which had plagued the relations of the two countries ever since the American Revolution. It was an indication of Canada's growth towards maturity as a nation, and was followed by a revival of the earlier attempts to frame a new Reciprocity agreement. Political conditions on both sides made it possible to reach an agreement in 1911, an especially influential factor on the American side being the demands of the Press for Canadian newsprint. Yet the agreement fell through, and fell through, significantly enough, because of Canadian opposition. Many Canadians felt that, having achieved so much in the teeth of American opposition, they could afford to stand alone, and their reaction helped to defeat Laurier in the election of 1911. Americans contributed to the failure through the last flickers of "manifest destiny". President Taft, the political heir of Roosevelt, who had wielded the "big stick" in 1903, was tactless enough to refer to Canada as at "the parting of the ways", and lesser men talked glibly of the Stars and Stripes floating "over every square foot of the British North American possessions clear to the North Pole". Americans, as an American diplomat has recorded, have always taken Canada for granted.[29] Now, through their very zeal for a reunited North America they again ensured its division.

## The Export of Newsprint

Nevertheless, one important agreement was salved from the wreck. The American tariff on Canadian newsprint was removed, and as a result Canadian exports, which had amounted in value to some two-and-a-half million dollars in 1910, had already reached more than fifty million dollars ten years later, and were still rising rapidly. Newsprint, indeed, became one of Canada's major exports: eventually the Dominion was to provide the newspapers of the world with three out of every five of their pages, and the United States, in particular, with four-fifths of their supplies. Moreover, although the favourable situation of 1910–11 did not recur, and it was not until 1935 that a tariff agreement could at last be reached, the newsprint concession had a broader significance. It contributed something towards a new conception of the relationship between the two countries, based upon their economic interdependence, and upon a recognition of the need to remove the politics from their economic contacts. In a shrewd comment on American policy the British Ambassador in Washington, Lord Bryce, claimed that "if there were no Canada, the United States would have to create one", though the full flavour of the remark could hardly be relished until after the war.

The election of 1911, which brought the Conservatives to power under Sir Robert Borden (1854–1937), was a brusque assertion of Canadian confidence, aimed at both Britain and the United States. It showed the country in the right mood for the testing-time that lay ahead. Borden abandoned Laurier's naval plans and offered to build three battleships for the Royal Navy, but was careful to demand in return a share in the framing of imperial defence policy. His scheme failed to pass the Senate and was quietly dropped, but war, in any case, was soon to render much of the recent debate unreal.

## THE WAR

The war, when it came, found Canada more nearly united than ever before. Its long-drawn agony imposed a strain on unity which was increased by a bitter dispute over conscription, but it advanced the one-time Colony the last stage towards recognition as an independent nation. This is not the place to record in detail the Dominion war effort, but the memory of Vimy Ridge, and other hard-fought actions, is never likely to fade while Britain and Canada survive. Canada contributed some 600,000 men to the Allied armies, and lost more than 62,000. With only about one-twelfth of the population of the United States, she suffered very nearly two-thirds of their casualties, and the award of no less than 65 Victoria Crosses bore witness to the spirit of her soldiers. Her industrial effort was no less significant: before the United States entered the war in 1917, for instance, Canada herself was providing between one-quarter and one-third of the shells fired by British artillery on the Western Front. The cumulative strain on a young, and comparatively small, country was considerable, and contributed much to the difficulties of the post-war years. Yet Canadian treasure and blood were freely expended, as Laurier had foretold, not only for Britain but for Canada, and for the way of life which was embodied in the imperial connexion, and the result could only be the removal of the last vestiges of dependent status. "Our recognition of this war as ours," said C. J. Doherty, Minister of Justice in Borden's administration, "our participation in it, spontaneous and voluntary as it is, determines absolutely once for all that we have passed from the status of the protected colony to that of the participating nation. The protected colony was rightly voiceless; the participating nation cannot continue so."

How Canada used her voice as a participating nation in the British Commonwealth cannot be considered here. Her Premier became a member of the newly constituted Imperial War Cabinet in 1917, she signed the Treaty of Versailles, and she became a member of the League of Nations from the first. Within a few years, as was shown by the Chanak episode of 1922, she was adopting a line of her own in the foreign relations of the British Empire. Already in 1907 the Dominion had independently reached a "gentlemen's agreement" with Japan over the problem of the admission of Japanese immigrants to Canada. In 1923, for the first time, an international treaty, the Halibut Treaty with the United States, was signed by the Canadian representative alone, without British participation. The Declaration of 1926, when it came, was, in fact, already overdue.

Laurier once said that Canada as a nation was "the most anomalous that has ever existed". This survey of her history will have shown how, created "in defiance of geography", she has asserted her right to individual existence, despite the divisions, both physical and moral, that exist within her. This study of her development up to the First World War may well conclude with the words of a Canadian historian:

> Canada has been created because there has existed, within the hearts of its people, a determination to build for themselves an enduring home. Canada is a supreme act of faith.[30]

## REFERENCES

1.  *Magna Britannia* (1936), p. 94.
2.  Lord Crewe: *Lord Rosebery*, I, p. 186.
3.  Blanche Dugdale: *Arthur James Balfour*, II, p. 378.

4.   R. M. Dawson: *The Government of Canada*, p. 45.

5.   Sir A Hardinge: *Life of Lord Carnarvon*, II, p. 114.

6.   A. R. M. Lower: *Colony to Nation: A History of Canada*, p. 560.

7.   B. K. Sandwell: *Canada*, p. 7.

8.   Sir R. Coupland: *The Durham Report*, Introduction, p. xlvi.

9.   ibid., p. vii.

10.  *The Times*, 16th July, 1941.

11.  *Robert Laird Borden: His Memoirs*, p. 274 n.

12.  *Colony to Nation*, p. 375.

13.  *The Government of Canada*, p. 30.

14.  C. P. Stacey: *Canada and the British Army, 1846-1871*, p. 231.

15.  J. B. Brebner: *North Atlantic Triangle: The Interplay of Canada, the United States and Great Britain*, p. 188.

16.  *Colony to Nation*, p. 560.

17.  *North Atlantic Triangle*, p. 197.

18.  J. McCormac: *Canada, America's Problem*, p. 176.

19.  *Sunshine Sketches of a Little Town* (first published, 1912), ch. XI.

20.  *Colony to Nation*, p. 355.

21.  D. Creighton: *John A. Macdonald: The Young Politician*, p. 320.*

22.  ibid., p. 463.

23.  *Colony to Nation*, p. 331.

24.  K. C. Wheare: *Federal Government*, p. 21.

25.  *North Atlantic Triangle*, p. 221.

26.  *Canada, America's Problem*, p. 61.

27.  D. Creighton: *Dominion of the North*, p. 374.

28.  R. M. Dawson: *The Development of Dominion Status, 1900-1936*, p. 135.

29.  W. Phillips: *Ventures in Diplomacy*, p. 70.

30.  *Colony to Nation*, p. 561.

* The second volume of Dr. Creighton's notable biography of Macdonald, *John A. Macdonald: The Old Chieftain*, appeared only after this chapter had been written.

# IX

## AUSTRALIA

### Colonies to Commonwealth

#### The Origins of Australia

THE history of Australia has much in common with that of Canada, for, although the great southern continent remained unknown to Europeans for two centuries after the penetration of North America had begun, its settlement as a British possession was essentially the consequence both of British sea-power and of the loss of the American colonies. Like Canada, indeed, Australia was "the child of the American Revolution": had the Thirteen Colonies not succeeded in their struggle for independence the development of both territories would have been markedly different, and the Canadian and Australian nations, if they had evolved at all, would probably have developed in quite different forms. Equally, as the retention of the Halifax naval base by Britain during the American war maintained a British hold upon the St. Lawrence waterway, and therefore upon the future Dominion, so British naval supremacy in the Indian Ocean and the South Seas, throughout the many years of conflict with France between the middle of the eighteenth century and 1815, ensured that the development of the newly discovered lands of Australia and New Zealand would rest with Britain. And when, after the Napoleonic Wars, the growth of population, with the accompanying expansion of industry and trade, brought about the establishment of new centres of settlement, and the exploitation of new markets and sources of supply, Australia, no less than Canada, proved to possess the resources, both actual and potential, which were increasingly required. Australian wool and foodstuffs matched Canadian timber and wheat in the British economy, while both Colonies became important centres of mineral production. In one particular alone did they differ considerably: the white population of Australia has always been almost entirely British in origin. The lateness of the continent's discovery, coupled with its rapid development by the foremost naval power, made it impossible for other countries to establish settlements, and the aborigines proved even less able than the Red Indians of North America to resist the white man's encroachments. While, therefore, Canada has evolved a dual civilization, both British and French in origin, Australia has preserved in its own development as an independent nation an exceptionally high proportion of the racial stock of the mother country, English, Welsh, Scottish and Irish. To this fact must be ascribed much of the difference of outlook that is apparent between Canada and Australia: the Irish, it is true, have provided an element of contrast, but, though considerable, it has been far less marked than in the case of the *Canadiens*.

In 1870, three years after Canada had started on its career as a united and self-governing Dominion, Australians celebrated the first centenary of the discovery of their land by Captain James Cook. Cook had been commissioned to seek evidence of a long-rumoured Antarctic continent, but his discovery of what he called "New South Wales" soon acquired an unexpected significance through the revolt of the American colonies. Hitherto, those colonies had provided, among other things, a place to which criminals sentenced to transportation could be sent, and after the outbreak of the American War a special committee was set up in 1779 with the task of finding another, and at least equally distant, penal settlement. The enthusiasm of Sir Joseph Banks, the naturalist who had accompanied Cook on his voyage, directed the committee's attention to "Botany Bay", where Cook had landed, and it was there that the first convicts were sent, under the newly appointed Governor, Captain Arthur Phillip, in 1787–88. Thus, inauspiciously, did Australia begin, and the anniversary of Phillip's landfall, 26th January, is still celebrated as the Commonwealth's " Foundation Day".

## Opening and Settlement of the Continent

The early years of the settlement were hard, but by 1870 the achievements had been striking, and although, as will be seen, the most startling development, the discovery of gold, had been made nearly twenty years earlier, in 1851, the 'seventies were a period of further expansion and consolidation. The unknown and almost deserted land of 1770, far distant from the centres of government, had by then been largely opened to settlement, and had attained a population of some 1,500,000. From the original colony of New South Wales three new colonies had been split off, Tasmania (Van Diemen's Land) in 1825, Victoria in 1850, and Queensland nine years later, in 1859; while two others had been created in distant parts of the continent, Western Australia in 1829, and South Australia in 1834. Of these, all but Western Australia had received responsible government by 1859, and Cardwell's reforms withdrew their British garrisons in 1870. The transportation of convicts, which the free settlers had come to regard as "moral vitriol-throwing", had long since ceased, except in Western Australia, where, for special reasons, it had been continued until 1867. Moreover, the free communities that were growing up were not only self-supporting but were making no small contribution to Britain's industrial and commercial prosperity. They had become one of the world's chief centres for the production of two important raw materials, wool and gold, and the main source of supply for Britain's woollen industry, while tallow, meat, and wheat were also being exported. In the phrase of an Australian historian, the "prison-yard and hunting-ground of savages" of 1788 had already become "a productive annexe to Europe and Asia",[1] and Dilke, on his visit in 1867, was struck by the fact that Australia had clearly "come of age".[2]

## ECONOMIC DEVELOPMENT:
### (1) SHEEP AND WOOL

The advance had come about through the efforts of free immigrants and the gradual revelation of Australia's variety of productive resources. Explorers, pressing inland from the coastal settlements, had pointed the way for pastoral settlers, who had later been followed by the mining prospectors who disclosed Australia's rich mineral wealth. Sheep had been introduced by Captain John Macarthur, the founder of Australian wool production, in 1797, and, thanks to his experiments in breeding, had soon produced wool for the

looms of England equal to the finest she could obtain in
Europe. Vast areas of Australia, inland from the coast, were
found to be ideal sheep-runs, and by 1850 Britain was
receiving from them more than half her total consumption
of raw wool. Production rose rapidly. In 1850 Australia sent to
Britain 39,000,000 lb. of wool, two-thirds by value of her total
exports, which were worth altogether, in that year, £2,400,000.
Twenty years later the wool clip of 1870 amounted to well
over 200,000,000 lb., and by 1879 it had increased by half
as much again, its value then being nearly £13,000,000.
Eventually Australia was to produce one-quarter of the world's
wool, and wool was to provide almost one-half of her own
exports. The small flock with which Macarthur had begun his
experiments had developed by 1879, with new imports of stock
and cross-breeding, into more than 50,000,000 sheep, and the
expansion continued until 1891, when a total of 106,000,000
was reached. Thereafter, the dry years from 1895 to the
"Great Drought" of 1902 halved the figure, and the
100,000,000 total was not reached again for nearly thirty
years, though improved breeding prevented a proportionate
decline in the clip. In figures such as these, which can be
matched in the case of gold and other ores, the very stuff of
Australia's history is displayed. Well might Dilke, with a
happy touch of inspiration, describe Australian statistics as
"figure-poems".

## (2) LIMITATIONS OF SETTLEMENT

The phenomenal development of wool production was due
to a variety of causes. England's commerce and industry had
first been founded upon wool, and it was to a large extent her
position as a mercantile, and therefore as a naval, power that
gave Australia into her keeping. "Free" settlers had followed
the convicts, and, although they had at first been confined by the
Blue Mountains to the eastern coastal plain, they had soon
broken through them to the open lands of the interior. There
the very extent of the plains, and the natural conditions of
geography and climate, had almost dictated the course of
events. Macarthur had had the genius to grasp the possibilities
early, but, as soon as a penetration to the interior had been
made, it was clear that Australia would develop by an extensive,

N*

and not by any intensive, natural economy. Agriculture was discouraged in favour of pastoralism, and food was actually imported to prevent labour being diverted to its production. Farming on an adequate scale was difficult, in any case, until scientific attention was given to its problems later in the century. Australia, though its area is six-sevenths of that of Canada, has less than half as much cultivatable land, and, while one-fifth of its area is desert, more than half is arid, and in the best years can do little more than support the flocks and herds that graze upon it. It was no accident that settlement was first made upon the east coast, and it is significant that it is on that coast, extending from Queensland south and south-west to Adelaide, that the great part of Australia's population, six-sevenths of the whole, lives today. Here is to be found most of that fifth of Australia's area which, it has been calculated, is alone capable, through its climate, of intensive development.

## (3) Gold and the "Diggers"

Yet, despite these natural limitations, Australia has escaped the dangers of over-specialization, and the reason is to be found in the exploitation of resources second, in point of time, to wool—the mineral wealth which first brought the country into dramatic prominence with the discovery of gold, the real turning-point in Australian history, in 1851. Within ten years gold to the value of £124,000,000 had been produced, and the lure of the precious metal had brought a sudden flow of immigrants which caused the population of the country to increase from less than half-a-million to 1,168,000. The first goldfields were in New South Wales and Victoria, but rich finds were later made throughout the continent, notably at the "hill of gold", Mount Morgan (Queensland), in 1882, and at Coolgardie and Kalgoorlie in Western Australia ten years later. By the end of the century Australia had contributed to the world's gold resources metal to the value of £400,000,000, and the discoveries, coming as they did so soon after the first "gold-rush" to California, had proved a powerful stimulus to international economic activity. For Australia itself they were no less significant. In the first place, they brought not only an increase of population but a change in the character of the people, and in their political and social outlook. Hitherto the pastoral "squatter", with his extensive sheep-runs, had dominated the Australian scene. Now there appeared, within a short space of time, a large and powerful class of industrial workers, individualist in their outlook and resentful of authority, destined to mould the Australian character and to provide, as industrial resources were discovered and industry began to develop, the core of a strong trade-union movement. Moreover, the immigrants who flocked to Australia in the early 'fifties were in very many cases Chartists from England or refugees from the Irish famine and the ill-fated European revolutions of 1848. To their influence must be ascribed much that is characteristic of Australian democracy. Before the end of the century most of the "six points" of the Chartists had passed into the Colonies' constitutions. The ballot was introduced generally in the 'fifties, and three of the Colonies, South Australia, Victoria and New South Wales, established manhood suffrage in the same period. Victoria led the way with the payment of M.P.s in 1870, and, although the Chartist claim for annual parliaments was rejected, triennial elections were general by the 'nineties, when South and Western Australia also extended the franchise to women. In short, Australia had established a democratic system, suited to the needs and views of its society, long before the mother country, though, as the "White Australia" agitation was particularly to show, it was a democracy only within limits, resting, in typically British fashion, not upon any philosophical basis but upon the facts of the Australian situation. "Democracy in the colonies is at present an accident, and nothing more", was Dilke's shrewd comment in 1867, but the discovery of gold was the "accident" that made possible its rapid advance.

## (4) Meat and Dairy Produce

In the economic life of Australia it was not merely the production of gold which brought rapid developments after 1851. Though at first the diggings threatened to ruin the sheep-farmers by depriving them of their labour, the increase of population and money brought a greater demand for meat, while the stimulus to trade and shipping lowered freight charges and made it possible to send more wool to Britain at lower cost. Agriculture, too, was encouraged: between 1851 and 1858 the land under cultivation in New South Wales was doubled, and by 1870 Australia had largely ceased to import wheat and was becoming an exporter. Ten years later the country was exporting more wheat to Britain than Canada was yet able to send, and with wheat went meat and dairy produce. Hitherto surplus sheep carcasses had had to be burnt or melted down for tallow: after 1851, as the population expanded, more meat was eaten, and the problem of getting exported meat safely through the tropics was tackled. Two Australian pioneers, James Harrison and Thomas Mort, came near to success with refrigerated cargoes in the 'seventies, but the first shipment to arrive in perfect condition was that of the *Strathleven* in 1880. This included mutton from New South Wales and beef from Queensland, and butter soon followed. By the end of the century meat to the value of £2,600,000 was being exported, and shipments of butter had risen from less than 2,000,000 lb. to rather more than 34,000,000 lb. "At the end of the century," an Australian historian has justly said, "it was easier to put Australian food on English tables in perfect preservation than it had been to put French or Irish produce there when Queen Victoria came to the throne."[3] Refrigeration had made this possible, as part of the process by which every branch of Australia's economic life adjusted itself to the stimulus of gold production. Closely linked as she was with the expanding industrial economy of Britain, Australia was able to play an increasingly important complementary rôle as a primary producer, and at the same time to supply a growing market for British manufactures. Hence the interest taken by British investors in the country from the 'fifties onwards, though by about 1870 Australia was already beginning to finance some of her own development. At that time the public debt of the various Colonies amounted to some £30,000,000: in the next decade £36,000,000 were borrowed, and by 1890 a further £90,000,000. Of all this the greater part, about three-quarters, was subscribed in Britain: by 1913 British investments in Australia totalled some £332,000,000, though this formed by then little more than one-half of the Commonwealth's debt.

## Development and Protection:
### (1) Land Settlement

Yet it was soon realized that primary production alone could not maintain the whole of the increased population that gold had attracted. As the gold diggings tailed off, or demanded expensive machinery for their development, many "diggers" were left stranded, and the Colonial Governments were faced with the problem of resettlement. Extensive programmes of land development were undertaken, to which much of the money borrowed in the 'seventies and 'eighties was devoted, but in addition labour was protected, partly by the imposition of tariffs and partly by the exclusion of coloured workers. Land settlement was an attempt to create a class of small farmers, but, until research into techniques and drought-resisting crops improved agricultural methods towards the end of the century, climatic conditions favoured a pastoral as against an agricultural economy, everywhere except in South Australia. Too often it was found that "the plough had out-stripped the rain-clouds", and a combination of climatic checks and evasions of the spirit of the law had the paradoxical result of bringing an increase of great land-holdings through the very methods that were intended to encourage small ones. By the 'eighties, for instance, while some 21,000 new settlers had been placed on the land in New South Wales, 8,000,000 acres had passed into the possession of only 96 "squatters" (the tradi-tional name of the sheep-farmers). Attempts were then made to redress the balance by taxation, but with only moderate success, and in any case Acts of Parliament alone could not overcome the natural difficulties that hampered Australian farming.

### (2) Tariffs and Public Works

Further assistance was given to the "digger" by the attempt to encourage local industries behind a tariff barrier. Victoria led the way in the 'sixties, under the powerful pressure of David Syme (1827–1908), editor and proprietor of the *Melbourne Age*, and when her tariff policy caused difficulties with the other colonies the Imperial Government formally ceded the right to levy differential tariffs in 1873. New South Wales remained loyal to free-trade principles, however, and the inevitable friction that followed was a powerful factor in the movement for federation. Nevertheless, Victoria prospered until the depression of the 'nineties, though the greater area and resources of New South Wales soon put her in the leading place which gold had for a time given to Victoria. The full significance of a tariff policy was not realized until after federation, however, when it became clear to the Labour Party that protection benefited the industrial worker no less than the manufacturer. By that time, for all their sturdy independence, Australians were accustomed to looking to Government for positive measures of national development, for only by State activity could land be opened for settlement, water-schemes and railways constructed, and "digger" unemployment relieved. Dilke recognized the need for this "State-socialism" in his *Problems of Greater Britain* (1890):

> in the rich young colonies the climate and soil offer wealth in return for population, but there are no people to construct the public works that are needed before the wealth can be won, and Government alone can do so.

## (3) The "White Australia" Policy

The era of public works began in the 'seventies, but before then another policy of lasting significance had been inaugurated, the decision to exclude the competition of cheap coloured labour by maintaining a "White Australia". This origindate in the diggers' resentment of Chinese competition when the gold-diggings began to fail, and was aggravated by the use of Chinese as strike-breakers and their employment on Australian merchant ships. The violence that broke out sporadically in the late 'fifties called for government intervention, and by 1886 all the Colonies had passed legislation against Chinese immigration. "Nothing will so rapidly bring together an Australian crowd," wrote Dilke, "as the rumour that Chinamen or rabbits are likely to be landed from a ship, and the one class of intruder is about as popular as the other." There was a lively fear of a "peaceful penetration" from "the nation of yesterday"(China) and other "servile nations of the world", a penetration by men whose demands on life were so much less as to be a standing menace to white Australians. If too many were admitted, it was felt, Australian civilization might be degraded, both by a lowering of standards and by the measures necessary to impose controls on peoples of different traditions. As a newspaper wrote of the Chinese immigrant in 1886,

> when he is simply vicious the vice is destructive; when criminal, a menace to the State; when industrious, he threatens revolution to the social system.[4]

Some years later Alfred Deakin (1856–1919), thrice Commonwealth Premier, put the objections frankly, though more charitably: it was not, he said, "the bad qualities but the good qualities of those alien races that make them dangerous to us; it is their inexhaustible energy . . . their endurance and their low standard of living that make them such competitors".[5] Anthony Trollope, who knew something of Australia at first hand, was reflecting the attitude he had encountered on his travels when in his Australian novel, *John Caldigate* (1877), he spoke of the patient labour of the Chinese, "who were contented to search for the specks of gold which more ambitious miners had allowed to slip through their fingers".

After the establishment of the Commonwealth the Immigration Restriction Act (1901) excluded coloured labour entirely from the whole country, though racial prejudice was veiled, partly at the instance of the Colonial Office, by the imposition of "dictation tests" at ports of entry. With the example of South Africa, with its Indian immigrants, before them, Australians did not lack reasons for a policy which, in the tropical north of the continent, was attended with economic disadvantages. The origins of the policy are to be found, however, in conditions on the goldfields and in Labour's call for protection, though the rise of Japan was soon to give it wider application, as a defence of the policy by W. M. Hughes (Commonwealth Premier, 1915–23) was later to show:

> We are a white island in a vast coloured sea. If we are not to be submerged we must follow the example of that indomitable people, the Dutch, and build dikes through which the merest trickle of the sea of colour cannot find its way.[6]

Only shortly before the outbreak in 1914 of that war which was to make Australia, like Canada, a factor in international affairs, and therefore to give a new significance to her policies, an Australian contribution to the *Round Table* presented a reasoned statement of the whole case for a "white Australia" at a time when the Japanese were replacing the Chinese as the principal cause of concern. The article recognized Japan's need for expansion, and expressed the fear that "other countries may by pressure of various kinds deprive Japan of her legitimate sphere of expansion and divert it to Australia". At the same time it claimed for Australia "freedom to develop a pure Western civilization unhampered by race difficulties", and argued that this could be secured only by "a policy of total exclusion":

> The settled policy of Australia is to exclude Asiatic races. . . . The political institutions developed under Western civilization can only be worked satisfactorily or at all in a homogeneous population . . . if the necessity of race separation began to appear, conflicts would begin at once. The people would have to choose between sacrificing the democratic form of their institutions and substituting a régime of force over the alien people or permitting the democratic institutions to be open to an alien race which did not understand them and would only use them to establish its dominance. . . . With an Eastern race the conflict of ideals and of civilization is fundamental, and the Imperial aspirations of Japan in the Pacific make it inevitable that any concession would be used as a stepping-stone to further advances.[7]

Such opinions, though widely held in Australia, were little understood elsewhere before the war. Within five years, however, they were to obtrude upon the idealism of President Wilson at the Paris Peace Conference, and they were to assume in the years to follow no small significance in the shaping of British policy and in the relations between Japan and the western world.

## (4) THE PUBLIC WORKS POLICY

From the first it was obvious that the best protection against the pressure of the coloured races was a well-filled "white" Australia. With the attempts to settle the "diggers" on the land, or to find them industrial employment, went the encouragement of further immigration and the extension of the farming areas by improvements in communications and water-supplies. From rather more than a million and a half in 1871 the population rose to two million and a quarter in 1881 and 3,174,000 in 1891. Men talked confidently of a population which by 1915 would outstrip that of the United Kingdom, and of an Australia that would eventually become greater and stronger than the United States. Sir Hercules Robinson, Governor of New South Wales from 1872 to 1879, urged that the land should be opened to settlement, and therefore inaugurated an active policy of railway construction which quadrupled the railway mileage during the 'seventies, and brought the total to 13,500 miles, practically all of it Government-owned, by 1901. A network of telegraph lines was created, including the Adelaide-Port Darwin line across the heart of the continent, and water supplies were assured by extensive irrigation works and the tapping of artesian resources. Port facilities were improved, and the general increase of prosperity was reflected in the volume of shipping cleared, which rose from 3,690,000 tons to 8,110,000 tons between 1871 and 1881. Well have the 'seventies been described as the era of "spirited public works". Loans were readily forthcoming, especially after the depression that struck Europe in 1873, and with the increase of settlement, and the improvement of facilities, the area under cultivation increased from 2,000,000 to considerably more than 4,000,000 acres. It seemed the age of *Australia Unlimited*: if the gold discoveries of the 'fifties had set the country on a new course, the constructive work of the 'seventies and 'eighties gave a depth and variety to its life that were fundamental to later development. The opening of the country through improved transport services was an especially notable feature of this period. Over-optimism, leading as it did to excessive investment, brought a sharp setback in the 'nineties, however, when drought combined with economic depression to check expansion and prevent the realization of the more extravagant hopes of the previous decades. Yet much sound work had been undertaken: "the generation to 1890", an Australian historian has said, was "the generation that built Australia".[8]

## (5) NEW MINERAL RESOURCES

The building was not done by intensive land-settlement, as had so often been hoped. The greater part of the population was absorbed not into the winning of wealth from the soil, but into industry, transport, the docks, and other secondary occupations. Fortunately gold proved to be by no means the only source of mineral wealth. Large deposits of silver, lead, copper, tin, zinc, coal and iron were discovered, and, while tin and silver production were important for a time, the twentieth century was to see Australia second only to the United States in her output of lead and zinc. Coal had been known from the time of the earliest settlements, and the discovery of iron-ore had soon followed. The first ironworks came into production in 1848, but the competition of imported metal checked this attempt at establishing heavy industry, and it was not until the early years of the twentieth century, when bounties and preferences were offered, that Australian steel-production became possible. The first steel was made in 1900, and the development of Lithgow and Newcastle, both in New South Wales, as steel centres followed within the next twenty years. Meanwhile, tin had been found in Tasmania and New South Wales, and for some years after 1870 the Mount Bischoff mines (Tasmania) were the richest single source in the world. Copper was also found in Tasmania, and when the great Mount Morgan mine in Queensland was opened in 1882 it produced copper as well as gold. In the following year, 1883, work was begun on a veritable hill of lead, zinc and silver at Broken Hill (N.S.W.), which has proved to be the largest lead-zinc deposit in the world: so far it has produced more than sixty million tons of ore, and its wealth is not yet exhausted. Mount Morgan was closed in 1925, by which time it had yielded more than 5,000,000 ounces of gold and 139,000 tons of copper, and had paid in dividends considerably more than £9,000,000, though this was only one-third of the sum paid in dividends during the same period by Broken Hill. Gold, in short, provided neither the only spectacular discoveries, nor the most enduring contributions to Australia's economy. In each Colony other metals were found, and if, as has been calculated, the total mineral production of the continent has reached some £2,000,000,000 in value, gold has accounted for less than half of this total, while of the gold output nearly as much has been produced by the more recent fields, those of Western Australia, and especially from the mines at Kalgoorlie and Coolgardie, opened in the 'nineties, as from the older centres of production in Victoria. Today gold stands second to lead among Australia's mineral exports, and both are far surpassed by wool, meat, wheat, and dairy-produce. Whether, in the long run, Australia has gained directly from the spectacular series of gold discoveries is a matter for some doubt, but it is at least certain that, indirectly, gold has given a succession of fillips to her development such as nothing else, in all probability, could have done. The original impetus of 1851 was matched by the discoveries of the 'eighties and 'nineties, and Western Australian production in the 'nineties, in particular, did much to offset the depression of those years. To the impetus given by gold succeeded the exploitation of other metals, of more direct significance for industrial development, but behind them all stood the steady growth of pastoral and agricultural production, which gave Australia her leading place in the world's economy.

## TRADE UNION DEVELOPMENT

With the extension of mining to less precious metals and the consequent development of industry there came into Australian life a new and powerful influence, that of the Trade Unions. Australian conditions were particularly well-suited to Union development. Pastoral and agricultural conditions did not favour the emergence of a class of small individual producers, and after the first exciting rush the gold-mines demanded capital and machinery which only well-organized companies could provide. Miners became wage-earners, and in Australia's major industry, that of wool production, were matched by the shearers: indeed, with shearing a seasonal occupation the same men were often miners and shearers by turns. Individualist and egalitarian ideas, combined with traditions of craft-unionism from England, led miners and shearers alike into organizations formed to protect their interests against both employers and cheap labour, especially that of the Chinese. Sir Henry Parkes (1815–96), an emigrant Birmingham foundry-worker who became five times Premier of New South Wales, expressed the representative view in an article in 1884:

> Every man (in Australia) is as good as, and no better than, his fellow citizen, except in so far as he may be greater than he in citizen virtue.[9]

Yet without a background of individual homesteads, such as

was characteristic of much of North America, this belief could not be effective unless labour were strongly organized: hence the differences between Australians and Americans, two peoples whose fundamental notions of equality and human dignity have much in common, but have been modified by differing environments.

Again, the development of industry and of extensive transport services, together with the difficulty of land-settlement, kept the majority of immigrants to the more closely settled urban areas of the south-east, where most of Australia's population still lives, and this fact also aided the growth of the Unions.

## THE LABOUR MOVEMENT

The first effective Unions appeared, characteristically enough, among gold and coal miners in the 'seventies, and in 1874 W. G. Spence (1846–1926), one of the first and greatest of Australia's Labour leaders, organized the inter-colonial Amalgamated Miners' Association. Twelve years later he founded the Amalgamated Shearers' Union, and in 1892 the Australian Workers' Union, a broadly based Union of the type that was beginning to emerge in England after the Dockers' Strike of 1889. The sense of Labour solidarity, on which Spence based his organizations, was revealed in the help which Australian workers subscribed for that strike: indeed, the sum of £30,000, which was sent from Australia, probably saved it from collapse. In the previous year the Unions had published a *History of Capital and Labour*, in which it was claimed that the working classes were making history, "especially in Australia", and the claim was justified by the solidarity of the Unions and by their success in making the "Eight Hours Day" general. But events soon showed that the strength of the Unions was based on the artificial prosperity of the 'eighties. In 1890 world prices began to fall. Wool, which had fetched about 1s. a pound during the 'eighties, had fallen to 7d. by 1893, and wheat reached the lowest price for centuries in the following year. Copper and silver prices fell almost as disastrously, and with the blow to investors' confidence that came from the failure of Barings in London in 1890 (an ominous consequence of over-confident investment in

South America) the stream of British money into Australia was suddenly checked. The consequences were serious, and reached their climax in the Bank failures of 1893, from which Australia was slow to recover. It was at this inauspicious moment, with employers calling for a lowering of wages, that the Unions determined to show their strength. The years from 1890 to 1892 were marked by industrial strife, which began on the docksides of Melbourne and Sydney and spread to the shearers of New South Wales and Queensland and the miners of Broken Hill. Economically the strikes were a disastrous failure. Faced by employers who were no less resolute to try conclusions, and who were inevitably able to appeal for governmental support, the Unions found that they lacked the resources for a sustained conflict. The gains they had made in the 'eighties were whittled down, and the inter-colonial solidarity of Labour suffered a severe setback, while Union membership fell heavily. Yet on balance the reverse was not without its advantages. The heady idealism of the 'eighties was checked, but in its place there arose a practical movement based on political rather than on industrial action. In 1891, encouraged by the newly introduced payment of M.P.s, the New South Wales Labour Party was formed, and immediately won thirty-six seats in Parliament, which enabled it to hold the balance between the rival Free-Trade and Protectionist groups. "Support in return for concessions" became the keynote of the Party's policy, and firm party discipline was developed to exploit the situation. Disillusioned by the results of direct action, the Labour Party in each Colony looked to governmental action for the protection of workers, advocating, in particular, the principle of compulsory arbitration, and the establishment of a standard minimum wage. Pioneer legislation in these directions was carried by South Australia and Victoria in 1894 and 1896, and the other Colonies soon followed their example. When the Commonwealth Constitution was framed it provided for Federal arbitration, and in 1904 a Commonwealth Conciliation and Arbitration Act was passed to cover disputes extending over more than one State: the Act also gave formal recognition to Trade Unions as a necessary part of the economic system. Three years later, in 1907, H. B. Higgins, one of the Presidents of the Court set up under the Act, proclaimed, in a case concerning McKay's harvester factory, the famous principle of the "fair and reasonable wage", which he defined as covering "the normal needs of the average employee, regarded as a human being living in a civilized community", and which he assessed, under existing conditions, at a minimum of 42*s.* a week. Thus, within fifteen years of the reverse they had suffered in 1890, the organized workers had achieved, through parliamentary machinery, a secure position, both economically and politically. From the first successes of 1891, indeed, the Labour Party was to play an active and constructive part in Australian political evolution: progress was steady until the party split on the issue of conscription during the First World War. Yet until after that war the party was in no strict sense "socialist". Its aims and achievements, in fact, were precisely those of the radical egalitarianism which had long been characteristic of Australian democracy: the Australian "cobber" has little in common with the Communist "comrade". An important corollary, however, was the conversion of the Labour movement to a policy of Protection. Only behind a tariff barrier could the "fair and reasonable wage" be guaranteed. "The unanswerable argument for Protection," Deakin claimed, "is that if you want to maintain a high standard among the workers of a community, so that these men may live the life of civilized beings, then you must impose duties to protect them against the underpaid labour . . . of foreign lands where less happy conditions prevail."[10] Thus, after Labour's recovery, were the conditions established for Australia's political maturity. The first Commonwealth tariff of 1902 (considerably extended in 1908–11) ranks with the Act of 1904 and Mr. Justice Higgins's "Harvester" judgment of 1907 as one of the fundamentals of the Commonwealth's development.

## Agricultural Improvements

Of fundamental significance also were the improvements in agricultural techniques which had been made by the end of the century. As early as the 'forties the need, under harsh climatic conditions, for speedy harvesting of wheat had led John Ridley in South Australia to devise his "stripper", the parent of modern harvesting machinery. Shortage of labour after the gold-rushes had encouraged its use, and it had spread to the other Colonies. With the settlement of more land in the 'seventies had come the "fire-rake", the "mallee (scrub) roller" and the "stump-jump plough" to make productive the scrub and stump-laden soil which were being developed, and the 'eighties saw the introduction of Hugh McKay's combine-harvester. All these were devices to economize in labour power and reduce costs while grappling with the natural difficulties of soil and climate: only through economy could wheat from distant Australian fields compete in European markets with the produce of America. There remained the problems of inadequate rainfall and impoverishment of the soil. To enrich the soil recourse was had to the recently discovered superphosphates. Government agricultural stations encouraged their use in the 'nineties, and the drill and combine drill-cultivator were devised to ensure proper application. Meanwhile the greatest of all the improvements were being made by an amateur botanist, William Farrer (1845-1906), whom poor health had driven to Australia from England in 1870 (much as it had sent Cecil Rhodes to South Africa in the same year), and who began to experiment with the breeding of wheat in the 'eighties. Farrer's object was to breed strains that would resist the heat and drought of Australian conditions, and although his "abstruse experiments in cross-fertilization" were criticized by "practical" men, he succeeded in producing many new strains, one of which, "Federation" (1902), revolutionized Australian wheat production. Its drought-resistant qualities were to prove as significant for Australian conditions as the breeding of hard grains were for the opening-up of the Canadian prairies in this same period. Wheat production, which had been 27,000,000 bushels in 1891, became 48,000,000 bushels in 1901, and had more than doubled by 1913, while the record harvest of 1915 produced no less than 179,000,000 bushels. The area under wheat increased from rather more than 5,000,000 acres in 1900 to an average of between 13,000,000 and 14,000,000 acres, while, years of severe drought apart, the average yield increased steadily. "The services rendered by Farrer to his adopted country," it has justly been said, "are second only to those rendered by Macarthur."[11]

## THE EVE OF FEDERATION

At the beginning of the new century, though the confident expectations of the 'eighties had been dashed by the drought and depression of the following decade, Australia was ready for the great step of Federation, which was taken in 1900, still just within the Victorian Age. The population was approaching 4,000,000, and exports had reached almost £50,000,000 in value. Drought had reduced wool production from 644,000,000 lb. in 1892 to only 391,000,000 lb. (the lowest figure since 1886), but meat exports had risen by 1,000,000 cwt. and butter had increased from 4,000,000 lb. to no less than 34,000,000 lb. The first Australian steel had been made, and engineering, leather and textile industries were developing: with the passing of inter-colonial tariffs through federation, and the establishment of a protective Commonwealth tariff, their expansion was to continue steadily. Within ten years, with population and production increasing, the ravages of drought repaired, and with a fresh stimulus given to public works, especially rail construction, trade had almost doubled, and the £13,000,000 wool clip of 1900-01 had become the £30,000,000 clip of 1910-11. Until the First World War dislocated world trade and compelled Australia, on strategic grounds, to intensify its policy of protection (a process further accentuated by the later depression and the Second World War), the Commonwealth was assuming an increasingly important rôle in the international economy, a rôle which was, moreover, out of all proportion to her population. She had come far since the first landfalls of 1770 and 1788, far even since the first centenary celebrations of 1870.

## QUEENSLAND AND "WHITE AUSTRALIA"

Before considering the federation movement and the establishment of the Commonwealth, it would be well to round off this sketch of colonial development with some account of the evolution of Queensland, which is of particular interest because there the difficulties of settlement had been increased by the need for adaptation to tropical conditions. Climatic conditions in northern Queensland have been compared to those of Bengal, and it was long believed that white settlement was impossible except on the basis of a "planter aristocracy" employing coloured labour. This notion has now been disproved, and Queensland has become the test-piece of the "White Australia" policy: its success, if success can be maintained, will be the justification of the hold of the comparatively small Australian population upon its vast homeland.

Queensland began its existence as a separate colony in 1859, when, with 28,000 colonists and only $7\frac{1}{2}d$. in its treasury, it was separated from New South Wales (and even the $7\frac{1}{2}d$. was lost when thieves broke into the "treasury"). It had developed, as the position of its capital, Brisbane, clearly shows, as a northern extension of the mother colony, and its history is the record of its extension inland and northward along the coast, the record, respectively, of the cattle and sugar industries. The opening of the country began in the 'sixties with increased immigration and the removal of "squatters" from further south to escape the land reforms of the older Colonies. Sheep stations developed, but greater heat and light rainfall made the land more suitable for cattle, and Queensland became Australia's great cattle-farm, with nearly one-half of the continent's herds. The Australian frozen and chilled beef that was exported to Britain from 1880 onwards was largely a Queensland product, and within seventy years from the successful voyage of the *Strathleven* events were to make Queensland's contribution to British standards of living an increasingly important one.

## SUGAR AND "BLACKBIRDING"

Sugar had been grown before separation, but its rapid development came in the 'sixties, with the failure of the attempt to grow cotton during the American Civil War, and was based upon the use of Kanaka labour from the Pacific Islands that had first been introduced for the experimental cotton plantations. By 1880 production along the coastal strip had increased so rapidly that sugar to the value of some £286,000 was exported, and as the plantations spread north into the fully tropical regions the demand for coloured labour grew. There developed in consequence the semi-slave trade known as "blackbirding", which, with all its unpleasant and tragic results for the islanders of the South Pacific, proved part of the "brown man's burden"[12] of European expansion into the Pacific. Public opinion in both Australia and Britain was moved to protest. In Britain a Polynesian Protection Act was passed in 1872, and, after the annexation of Fiji two years later, a High Commissioner for the Western Pacific was appointed. But while other Pacific Islands remained unannexed by European Powers these measures were inadequate, and Britain was reluctant, here as elsewhere, to assume further responsibilities, though Australian opinion was opposed to the appearance of other Powers in islands that were strategically vital to Australia's defence. This was particularly true of New Guinea, long claimed as "Australia's Isle of Wight".[13] Not until the end of the century were the rivalries of the various Powers satisfied, and the settlement then achieved was to be further disturbed by the two World Wars. Meanwhile, in the 'eighties Australians, like their fellow-subjects at the Cape, had been perturbed by Germany's colonial ambitions, and by Britain's failure resolutely to resist them. At one point in 1883, indeed, Queensland had gone so far as to attempt itself to annex part of New Guinea to the Crown, though the step had been immediately repudiated in London. Two years later, when Germany took possession of north-eastern New Guinea, Australian reactions were similar to those of the Cape when South-West Africa passed into Germany's hands: the territory became "almost an Alsace",[14] and bitterness was only partially assuaged by the occupation of British New Guinea (Papua) in 1888, and by the special responsibilities for its administration assumed by Australia in 1906.

## The end of "Blackbirding"

Naval patrols aimed at checking "blackbirding", and the gradual annexation of the Pacific Islands were, however, only part of the campaign against the employment of Kanaka labour on the Queensland sugar plantations. Feeling in the southern part of the Colony, especially among the workers, was strongly against the planters, and eventually measures were passed, first to ensure decent conditions of work for the Kanakas, and then to attempt to stop the traffic altogether. The reply of the planters was to petition for the creation of a new Colony of Northern Queensland, but this step the British Government refused to take. Eventually the problem was settled by a combination of developments. When the Commonwealth was established in 1901 the Federal Parliament was given powers with respect to "the people of any race, other than the aboriginal race in any State, for whom it is deemed necessary to make special laws" (Article 51, xxvi) and to "the relations of the Commonwealth with the islands of the Pacific" (51, xxx). Under the Pacific Island Labourers Act of 1901, which followed, the entrance of Kanakas was forbidden from 1st March, 1904, and in 1906 most of those that remained were returned to their home islands. The episode thus became not only a part of the far from happy story of the penetration of the Pacific Islands by Europeans, but an effective contribution to the evolution of the "White Australia" policy. Not merely racial discrimination, nor merely fear of the effect of coloured labour upon conditions of work, but an insistence upon Australia's individuality, was the driving force behind the policy. "A united race", declared Alfred Deakin, "implies . . . a people possessing the same general cast of character, tone of thought, the same constitutional training and traditions", and a united race was unthinkable except in a united Australia; "a continent for a nation, a nation for a continent", in the striking phrase of Sir Edmund Barton (1849–1920), first Commonwealth Premier. Hence the opposition not only to coloured labour but also, later, to the employment of Italians in Queensland.

Labour, jealous of its interests since the days of Chinese competition, took an active part in the final solution of the Kanaka question, but a solution would not have been so easy without the discovery both that Europeans could undertake manual work in northern Queensland without detriment to their health, and that the sugar industry could be operated by European labour alone. The industry was reorganized on the basis of small producers of cane, with central mills to handle the crop and produce the refined sugar, and the result was both an improved and an increased yield. The 15,000 acres of cane of the 'seventies, producing some 12,000 tons of sugar, had become 87,000 acres by 1901, with a production of 1,370,000 tons, most of it from Queensland. Protection was necessary against the importation of beet sugar, and this was increased during the First World War, after which the regulation of the sugar-refining industry passed largely into Government hands. The price of sugar in Australia was maintained at an artificially high level, but the necessity for this subsidizing of production was accepted by the non-sugar-producing States of the Commonwealth as the guarantee of the stability of the white settlement of tropical Australia, with its population of some 130,000. In short, the sugar subsidy was the economic equivalent of "a continent for a nation", and Australians accepted it as such.

The solution of Queensland's problems was essentially a federal one, and it is to the movement for federation, which culminated in the Commonwealth of Australia Constitution Act of 1900, that we must now turn.

## THE MOVEMENT FOR FEDERATION

"A continent for a nation, a nation for a continent" was a logical, if tardy, development. Although the five Colonies occupied one vast continental island, the settlements from which they had grown had all been established from the sea, and there are between them, even today, but two trans-continental links by land. The chief towns cling to the coast, or are easily accessible from it, and the sea long provided the readiest means of communication between them: there were no rich plains, as there were in Canada, to make an overland route a paying proposition. Each Colony developed separately, maintaining its individual relations with the United Kingdom, and for various reasons regarding the others with a jealous reserve. New South Wales and Victoria were for long economic rivals, while South Australia regarded both with some scorn as the home of convict settlements. Queensland was jealous of its rich and powerful parent, New South Wales, while Western Australia was despised for its reliance on convict labour, and, when that had passed, stood aloof as a poor relation until the gold discoveries of the 'nineties. Even then there were those in New South Wales who compared unfavourably the "three weeks' old" State, which gained responsible government only in 1890, with their own "great country".[15] As in the case of Canada, an external stimulus was needed to bring home the obvious advantages of unity. It came from the passing of political and geographical isolation, from the appearance in the Pacific of France and Germany as rivals to Britain's imperial position, and was strengthened by the economic strains of the 'nineties, by the evident desirability of an enlarged internal market, unhampered by internal barriers but protected by tariffs from external economic pressure. Already a modest beginning had been made in the 'sixties with a series of Intercolonial Conferences, but until the 'eighties there had been no sense of urgency. On the whole the attitude had been one of indifference to any but local affairs. The problems of the opening of a continent had absorbed all energies, while there were many who with typical radical individualism asked only to be left alone and sought no wider responsibilities; thus William Lane, the Utopian journalist and Labour leader, who left Australia in despair in 1893, after the failure of the great strikes, to found a New Australia in Paraguay:

> We want to be left alone. We don't care whether Canada loses her fishing monopoly or not; or whether Russian civil servants replace the British pauper aristocracy in Hindustan offices . . . or whether the sun sets on the British drum-beat or not—so long as the said drum-beat keeps away from our shores.[16]

## THE EXTERNAL STIMULUS—FRANCE AND GERMANY

Yet already in the 'eighties there were signs that the times were catching up with Australia as they had already caught up with Canada. The establishment of a French penal settlement in New Caledonia had been a shock, and in 1882 there were fears of French annexation of the New Hebrides. In the following year, as has already been mentioned, Queensland unsuccessfully endeavoured to forestall German designs on New Guinea, and when Germany occupied the island in 1885, and France took New Caledonia in 1886, without any British action to prevent these moves, it was felt that colonial interests had been sacrificed to the narrow demands of British policy in Europe. Australian reactions, in fact, were similar to those of Canadians in the face of British "conciliation" of the United States, and the demand for a strong and united country which could press its interests with more vigour and effect was stimulated. The Colonies, it was argued, should have "an acknowledged voice in the decision of questions deeply affecting their interests", and the status which this claim implied could clearly come only through union. Only a united Australia could impress upon the mother country the realities of a situation which was inevitably regarded from a different standpoint in London. There the Australian attempt to proclaim what Dilke in his *Problems of Greater Britain* described as "an Australasian Monroe doctrine" was regarded with scant sympathy, if not actual scorn. "I asked them whether they did not want another planet all to themselves," the Colonial Secretary, Lord Derby, reported to the Queen after an interview with an Australian deputation in 1883:

> The magnitude of their ideas is appalling to the English mind.... It is hardly too much to say that they consider the whole Southern Pacific theirs *de jure*; the French possession of New Caledonia they regard as an act of robbery committed on them. It certainly is hard for four millions of English settlers to have only a country as big as Europe to fill up.[17]

Thirty-six years later, at the Peace Conference of 1919, W. M. Hughes was equally to shock President Wilson by his insistence on Australian claims to the captured German colonies in New Guinea and the South Pacific. Then, as in the 'eighties, Australians were resentful of interference with their own strongly-felt, if somewhat narrow, conception of their best interests. If, as Lord Derby had suggested, they were too few to be considered seriously, they were at least "English settlers" (in which term he included, as was then customary, all the peoples of the United Kingdom) and carried with them the insular habits of thought of their original homeland. As a keen observer, Flora Shaw (later, Lady Lugard), who toured Australia for *The Times* in 1893, noted with interest:

> The inhabitants of Australia have only carried across the ocean the habit of mind which has characterized the people of England for generations.[18]

Canadians may have been affected by the insidious pressure of American culture, but Australia has no such near neighbour: in the words of an Australian historian, specialized though the type has become through the Australian environment, "for better or for worse, we are British—very British indeed",[19] a judgment with which sportsmen would unhesitatingly agree.

British the Australians certainly were in their empirical and unhurried approach to federation. There was no "Damas-

cus Road miracle" about the conversion,[20] and though Sir
Henry Parkes, then Premier of New South Wales for the
fifth time, impressed by the need for unity in defence, threw
out the first suggestions in 1889 and a draft constitution was
actually drawn up in 1891, the scheme was badly received.
Despite Parkes's advocacy, New South Wales, as the parent
colony, was still reluctant to see its junior partners admitted to
equality and to surrender its free-trade principles to their
protectionism. Already a Federal Council, though with
limited powers, had been formed by the British Parliament for
the Australian States in 1885, after the New Guinea scare, but
New South Wales had stood aloof and prevented it from
operating effectively. The strikes and economic difficulties of
the early 'nineties, however, caused a modification of attitude,
and isolationist opinion received a further shock from the
Japanese victory over China in 1894–95, which revealed
that new forces were on the move in the Pacific area. Meanwhile public opinion was gradually stirred into interest by the
oratorical campaigning of federationist societies. The appeals
generally offered a nicely calculated blend of sentiment and
self-interest, as in a typical specimen from a Tasmanian
campaign:

> if you vote for the bill you will found a great and glorious nation
> under the bright Southern Cross, and meat will be cheaper, and you
> will live to see the Australian race dominate the Southern Seas, and
> your sons will reach a grand heritage of nationhood, and you will have
> a market for potatoes and apples.[21]

## THE COMMONWEALTH ESTABLISHED, 1901

By such arguments as these was the ground prepared. In
1895 a Premiers' Conference agreed on a convention, to which
most of the States sent specially elected representatives in 1897.
A long tussle over details followed, with draft constitutions,
referenda and modifications. The final referendum of approval
was held in 1899, and with some modifications the necessary
Bill passed the British Parliament, under the guidance of
Chamberlain as Colonial Secretary, in the summer of 1900,
being signed by Queen Victoria in July (it was to prove, in
fact, one of the last of her major acts of State). The new
"Commonwealth of Australia" formally came into existence

on 1st January, 1901, just three weeks before the end of the reign which in little more than sixty years had seen the four scattered colonies of the Australian continent grow into a potentially powerful Federation of six States which were already rendering signal service to the Empire through their contribution of some sixteen thousand soldiers to the South African war. The Queen had, not unnaturally, been somewhat concerned at the choice of "Commonwealth" as a title, but had accepted Chamberlain's assurance that "it did not imply anything like a Republic, quite the reverse".[22] She would have preferred "Dominion", but the Australians were determined to avoid any comparison with Canada, and "Commonwealth" was, in fact, more in keeping with their radical and democratic background.

## FRAMING AND WORKING THE CONSTITUTION

The contrast with Canada was equally marked in other respects. The Dominion's constitution had been framed in London by British and Canadian ministers in consultation, and the people of the North American colonies had not been called upon to express any direct opinion upon it. The Commonwealth constitution, on the other hand, was essentially an Australian creation, on which, as Chamberlain said in his speech in the House on the introduction of the Bill, "the people of Australia, through their representatives, have worked alone, without either inviting or desiring any assistance from outside". Each of the two constitutions had to be formally passed as an Act of the Imperial Parliament, and Chamberlain had difficulty with the Australian leaders in the matter of appeals to the Privy Council, but, even allowing for the differing circumstances of Australia and Canada, it was evident that the Empire had taken a great step forward since 1867. "We have got to a point in our relations with our self-governing colonies," Chamberlain declared, "in which I think we recognize, once for all, that these relations depend entirely on their free will and absolute consent."

The actual form of the Australian federation was dictated by local conditions, though avowedly based on the model of the United States, with due regard, however, for British parliamentary forms and practice. Most of the constituent

Colonies of the Commonwealth had been viable States for many years, and were prepared to surrender only as much of their powers as was necessary to ensure an adequate handling of common problems. There was no reaction against "States' rights", as there had been in Canada, to encourage centralization. Indeed, the Commonwealth government was conceived by some on a very modest scale, calculated to cost each citizen literally "no more than a dog-licence". Yet an increasing measure of federal control has come. Under the terms of the constitution customs and excise duties became exclusively the concern of the Commonwealth government, which was to return to each State a proportion of what was collected within its borders. Taken together with the Commonwealth's general powers of taxation, the widening basis of social policy and the pressure of two world wars, this fiscal arrangement has inevitably tended to strengthen the federal government as against the States, as Deakin in 1902 foretold that it would. Despite the vast distances of Australia, therefore, and the pull of local issues, "the drama in parliamentary politics is now overwhelmingly centred in Canberra",[23] which since 1927 has been the specially created Commonwealth capital. Efforts have been made on occasion to increase federal powers by constitutional amendment through a referendum, as provided for in the constitution, but these have rarely been successful: the issues are usually complex, and the voter when he does not understand understandably does not approve. Nevertheless, the very tide of events has done much in itself, and the Commonwealth's financial powers are a potent weapon.

## Australia Takes Shape

The years between the establishment of the new Commonwealth and the First War saw the consolidation of Protection, the broadening of social and industrial policies and the formation of a strong Federal Labour Party, largely based on the trade unions and the centres of industry, with its opponents in the countryside dropping old labels and moving towards the later "Country Party" (no party could call itself "Conservative" in the Australian context). By 1914 trade union membership was higher in proportion to population in Australia than anywhere else in the world. Labour first held office in the

o

Commonwealth Parliament in 1904, and ruled for gradually increasing periods in 1908–09, 1910–13 and from September, 1914, until the split forced by Hughes over the conscription issue in 1916. The worker's position was increasingly protected by the recognition of trade unions, by minimum wage awards and by compulsory arbitration; industry was buttressed by tariffs and the farmer supported by bounties and loans. In a neat and revealing comment on the system that was taking shape, an Australian historian has said that, "the farmer always thought himself 'anti-socialist', but he believed in letting not his individualistic right hand know what his socialist left hand was doing (or taking)".[24] A new kind of society was, in fact, emerging, a vast structure of State-Socialism reared on the basis of Australian individualism and "mateyness", a logical development of the earlier tendencies that have already been described, a kind of co-operative—or, at least, collectivist—commonwealth, with "protection all round", which was eventually to reach such a pitch in the 'twenties that "everybody appeared to be paying a subsidy to everybody else".[25] The standard of living was rising and Australia seemed, indeed, "unlimited".

## THE WAR

When war came in 1914 support for Britain was immediately forthcoming. German New Guinea was seized in Australia's own interests, and a large volunteer force, which eventually reached a total of 417,000, was formed. If Canada won international recognition by her war effort, Australia no less made an imperishable mark on many fields, and nowhere more than at Gallipoli, for ever associated with the initial letters A.N.Z.A.C. (Australian and New Zealand Army Corps), which gave a new word to history. "Anzac Day" (25th April) has become for the two southern Dominions a day of solemn commemoration. But Australia's part in the Middle Eastern campaigns and in the great battles on the Western Front was no less magnificent, and her troops particularly distinguished themselves in the decisive retreat and advance of 1918: 60,000 men were lost in all, 10,000 more than the American total, as Hughes did not scruple to remind Wilson when they clashed at Paris in 1919. Australia fought unhesitatingly at Britain's side as a British nation, but she fought, no less than Canada did, for her own position in the world. In the words Hughes used in 1919 when presenting to the Commonwealth Parliament the Treaty of Versailles which he had signed as his country's representative at the Peace Conference:

> We went into this conflict for our own national safety, in order to ensure our national integrity, which was in dire peril, to safeguard our liberties, and those free institutions of government which, whatever may be our political opinions, are essential to our national life, and to maintain those ideals which we have nailed to the very topmast of our flagpole—White Australia, and those other aspirations of this young Democracy.[26]

The hard-fought conflict left Australia, as it left Canada, seemingly secure, fully conscious of her power in the world and recognized by all as a leading member of the British community. There was no need to press for more, for, as Hughes once commented, when "dominion status" was under discussion, "What is there that we cannot do?".[27] The challenge of the Commonwealth motto, *Advance Australia*, had been answered, even though cynics, in the dark days of disillusionment ahead, could ask pointedly, "Advance Australia—*Where?*"[28]

### REFERENCES

1. E. Shann: *An Economic History of Australia*, p. vii.
2. *Greater Britain*, II, p. 157.
3. *An Economic History of Australia*, p. 343.
4. V. Palmer: *The Legend of the 'Nineties*, p. 16.
5. A. G. L. Shaw: *The Story of Australia*, p. 198.
6. A. Brady: *Democracy in the Dominions*, p. 136.
7. *The Round Table*, June, 1914; quoted in R. M. Dawson: *The Development of Dominion Status, 1900–1936*, p. 143.
8. B. Fitzpatrick: *The Australian People, 1788–1945*, p. 216.
9. *Democracy in the Dominions*, p. 437.
10. *The Story of Australia*, pp. 198–99.
11. W. K. Hancock: *Australia*, p. 27.
12. Sir H. Luke: *Britain and the South Seas*, p. 19.

13. *Australia*, p. 66.
14. ibid., p. 243.
15. *The Legend of the 'Nineties*, p. 142.
16. ibid., pp. 81–82.
17. *Letters of Queen Victoria*, 2nd Series, III, pp. 432–33.
18. E. Moberly Bell: *Flora Shaw*, p. 147.
19. G. V. Portus: *Britain and Australia*, p. 67.
20. L. F. Crisp: *The Parliamentary Government of the Commonwealth of Australia*, p. 1.
21. *The Story of Australia*, p. 188.
22. From the Queen's *Journal*, June 27th, 1900: *Letters of Queen Victoria*, 3rd Series, III, p. 566.
23. *Parliamentary Government of Australia*, p. 279.
24. *The Story of Australia*, p. 206.
25. *Britain and Australia*, p. 42.
26. *The Development of Dominion Status*, p. 196.
27. *The Story of Australia*, p. 231.
28. The title of Brian Penton's critical survey, published in 1943.

# X

# NEW ZEALAND AND THE PACIFIC

## NEW ZEALAND AND THE COMMONWEALTH

THE Act constituting the Commonwealth of Australia
made provision for the entry into the federation of New
Zealand, which, though settled later than most of the
Australian colonies, had enjoyed responsible government since
1856, and was now, if small in population, a thriving outpost
of Empire. A commission was appointed in New Zealand in
1900 to examine the proposal, but could find no enthusiasm
for it. The twelve hundred miles of sea between the two
countries were, as the commission recognized, "a weighty
argument" against New Zealand's inclusion in the Commonwealth: in the well-known phrase of a leading politician of
the time, "twelve hundred obstacles to Federation will always
be found between Australia and New Zealand". Moreover,
even apart from the barrier of distance, New Zealand was
beginning to develop her own distinct national consciousness,
and did not in any way consider herself merely another
Australian colony. "New Zealand should be a country for
New Zealanders," a member of the colonial parliament had
said in a speech in 1890, "with the wings of Great Britain
over us we need look to no other country or colony for protection ... we are the pioneers of a great nation. ... I think we
shall become in every respect a country quite as great as
Australia, and with a nationality of our own."[1] New Zealand
therefore continued to go her own way, and in 1907 she was
raised to the status of a Dominion in her own right. Yet,
despite the resemblances that might have been expected, there
were significant differences of outlook and attitude between
her and her sister Dominions, Canada and Australia. All had
participated in the South African War, but while Australia
and Canada had sent their contingents as a gesture of national
consciousness, an assertion of their individual standing in the

439

world, as well as by way of a mark of imperial solidarity, in the
case of New Zealand, who had been the first to contribute her
quota, there had been far more of an instinctive rallying to
Britain. In her distant isolation and weakness New Zealand
was much more conscious of her dependence. Colonialism was
longer here than elsewhere the spirit of the new country, and
New Zealand has always retained a special bond with the
mother country. Thus, at the Colonial Conference of 1902,
when representatives of six colonies—Canada, Australia, New
Zealand, Newfoundland, Natal and the Cape—were brought
together on the occasion of the coronation of King Edward VII,
Sir Wilfrid Laurier, as the representative of Canada, characteristically spoke to Richard Seddon of New Zealand of "your
country" and Seddon no less characteristically referred in
reply to "our *Colony*".[2] And although participation in the South
African War did a great deal to strengthen local pride and
fortify national self-consciousness, there was still in 1907 a
feeling that to call so small and dependent an outpost a
Dominion was an act of pretentiousness.[3] The New Zealander,
indeed, long felt two loyalties, one to the local, national
home, the other to the imperial "Home",[4] and if before
1914, with the maturity of the second generation of local-
born New Zealanders, the notion of the imperial Home
was becoming clouded and remote, attitudes remained to a
greater or lesser extent ambivalent. However great their
control of their own affairs, however much their essentially
British characteristics might be modified by the new environment, the New Zealanders remained conscious of their ties.
A New Zealand writer, James Courage, has neatly hit
off the dual outlook in the description of the farmer,
Blakiston, in his short story *After the Earthquake*, set about
the turn of the century:[5]

> He had farmed in New Zealand for nearly twenty years but he
> still thought of England as home, his father's country, the original
> pattern. Colonial life was freer, less stiff, he liked it better, nevertheless
> something of the subtle flavour of the English way of living on which
> it had originally been founded was vanishing fast. The new climate
> was changing it, adapting its laws and forms to a younger society.
> And he himself had changed . . . he would never go back to England,
> as he had once intended to. He was a colonial farmer for life.

MAORI AND *Pakeha*

The establishment of New Zealand as a British nation dates only from 1840. The name was given by Tasman in the seventeenth century, in honour of his native State of the Netherlands, but it was Captain Cook, more than a century later, who first thoroughly surveyed the islands between 1769 and 1776. The Maori people, immigrants from Eastern Polynesia, had probably been settled some five hundred years in the islands, which they called, in a phrase of poetic beauty, *Ao Tea Roa*, "the long white cloud". Cook's discoveries opened the way for whalers, sealers, timber-cutters, and, in a different category, missionaries. A British Resident was appointed in 1832, and seven years later a "New Zealand Land Company", acting under the inspiration and direction of the ardent apostle of colonial settlement, Edward Gibbon Wakefield, sent its first batch of settlers. Annexation followed in 1840, just in time to forestall a similar move by the French. Other settlements were then established, self-government was granted in 1852, with responsible government only four years later, and an export trade in wool and grain begun. Gold was discovered in Otago (South Island) in 1861 and in other areas, though never in quantities comparable to the Australian fields. For thirty years clashes and misunderstandings with the Maoris over land led to a series of small-scale but tragic wars in the North Island, where the tribes were mainly concentrated, though the conflict was relieved, particularly in its later stages, by the loyal co-operation of many Maoris with the *Pakeha*. By 1871, when peace was finally restored, though the white population was more than a quarter of a million, the war had left a heavy burden of debt, while the destruction of property, the prevailing uncertainty and the cost of continued police precautions were for some years a drag on development. Eighteen-seventy was "one of New Zealand's dark hours".[6] Yet the South Island had not suffered. While the struggle had dragged on in the North, the South had achieved within thirty years a viable extension of British settlement. The Canterbury settlement, destined to make a famous name on the Englishman's dinner-table, had been successfully established, flocks had rapidly increased, and gold had been discovered, to stimulate settlement and render possible the

improvement of communications. Exports of wool, an index
of prosperity of greater significance and steadinesss than the
fluctuating output of gold, rose from £67,000 in value in 1853
to £2,702,000 twenty years later, and wool was largely a
South Island product. Flourishing exports guaranteed an
influx of immigrants more likely to settle than the restless,
treasure-hunting miners, for the ships that carried wool to
Britain brought back people, a point of significance in the
period of renewed development that lay ahead.

## The New Imperialism—and Public Works

The withdrawal of British troops at the end of the Maori
wars, as part of a calculated policy of leaving the colonists to
handle their own problems, and the refusal in 1869 of the
Colonial Secretary in London, Lord Granville, to guarantee a
New Zealand loan for war expenditure, proved at once a shock
to New Zealand, and, as has been shown elsewhere, the spark
that touched off late Victorian imperial enthusiasm. It seemed
as if, while Canada and the Australian colonies were expected
to achieve independence ere long, in the case of New Zealand
"the severance was being accomplished in very painful
circumstances".[7] Under the pressure of agitation both in the
colony and at home, Granville, while still withholding military
aid, agreed in 1870 to help New Zealand with a loan to be used
for the encouragement of immigration and the extension of
public works to open up the country. It was a turning point in
the history both of the Empire and of the Colony. Henceforth
less was to be heard of colonial separatism, more of imperial
unity. For New Zealand herself the loan opened a period
of striking development. If the difficulties of the North Island
were to be overcome, and the rapid progress of the South was
to be consolidated, vigorous development was called for. This
was impossible without greater financial resources than the
colony possessed and without a programme of public works.
With the home Government's encouragement the new policy
was inaugurated in 1870, and the following decade became, as
in Australia, an era of "spirited public works". The public
debt at the beginning of the period amounted to something
less than £8,000,000 (of which more than £2,000,000 had
been incurred through the Maori wars). By 1880 the total

was nearly £24,000,000 and ten years later it had reached almost £39,000,000. The money raised was spent largely on railways, roads, bridges, the encouragement of immigration and the purchase of land for settlement.

## Sir Julius Vogel

The driving spirit behind this forward economic policy was that of Julius Vogel, later Sir Julius (1835-99), an Englishman of Jewish descent who had been drawn to New Zealand during the gold rush of the 'sixties, had entered journalism, and from journalism politics, and was to become Colonial Treasurer in 1869 and Premier in 1873. Vogel has been variously described as another Disraeli—with the added qualification of a flair for finance—and, not inappropriately, as "a colonial Keynes".[8] His brilliant and imaginative personality and fine presence, his faith in New Zealand and in the wealth of its undeveloped resources, and his insistence on the need for public enterprise in the development of those resources, all made him one of the major figures in New Zealand history. Under his guidance the country took the first steps towards that "State Socialism" which was to characterize its later growth. His optimism overreached itself, it is true, and created a load of debt that proved a serious burden in the depression of the 'eighties, and contributed not a little towards it: "Vogelism" then became "a byword for wild schemes".[9] The merits of his policies have therefore been much debated. Yet it has to be remembered that those policies were sometimes pressed further than Vogel had intended, and that he was overruled in some of the precautionary measures he wished to adopt. Thus, he failed in his efforts to set aside six million acres in the Crown lands through which the new roads and railways were to run, in order to use the return on the sale of the developed lands for debt redemption. His policy here was a sound one, and its failure encouraged an orgy of private land speculation, on borrowed money at inflated prices, that was to prove an encumbrance in the depressed 'eighties and to bring to the verge of bankruptcy the principal lender, the Bank of New Zealand; a typical index of land values shows an increase from 17 to 128 in only eight years between 1870 and 1878.[10] Many railway lines were built, too, which have never made a return on their cost. A major difficulty

O*

was the pressure of local interests, and especially of the nine Provincial Governments with which, in addition to the central government, the country had been endowed in 1853. These had seemed necessary for the widely scattered settlements of earlier days, but were out of date by the 'seventies, and in 1876, despite strong opposition, Vogel was able to sweep them away. Yet he failed to carry a project for a central Public Works Board free of political ties. Through the local pressure for works and wealth he had, willy nilly, created a tradition of "logrolling" that was to prove an unfortunate feature of New Zealand political life (though by no means unknown in her sister colonies). The "roads and bridges" member of the House of Representatives (the New Zealand equivalent of the House of Commons) began to appear, and became so much accepted as part of the landscape that when he was Prime Minister Richard Seddon could openly say, with that transparent frankness that won him the sobriquet of "Downy Dick", that it was "unreasonable and unnatural to expect the Government to look with the same kindly eye on districts returning members opposed to the Government as on those which returned Government supporters".

Nevertheless, while Vogel's policy created debts, both public and private, in ominous profusion, it also brought in settlers: by 1880 the population had almost doubled, to 484,864.

## THE MAORI RECOVERY

Vogel also inaugurated the conservation of New Zealand's great forest resources, introduced the ballot and made the first attempt to carry women's suffrage, which eventually became law under Seddon's administration in 1893. Meanwhile his colleague, Donald McLean (1820–77), as Minister for Native Affairs from 1869 to 1876, had done much to reconcile the Maoris to the new conditions and to regain their confidence. The last serious disturbance, a deliberately pacific one on the part of Maoris led by the "prophet" Te Whiti, who had earlier fought against the *Pakeha* invaders, took place in 1880, the result of the long delay in guaranteeing land reserves for the Maoris. It was followed by the establishment of certain reserves, and the wars and skirmishes of the past soon became hardly more than an unhappy memory. Nevertheless, it was to be some years before the Maoris recovered confidence in their future. Their losses in inter-tribal warfare, as well as in the struggle with the British, had been serious. From an estimated total of 120,000 in 1849 their numbers had fallen by 1871 to some 37,000, and it was not until the new century that a slow expansion began. Today, including people of mixed race, the Maoris number in all more than 130,000, and having moved in less than a century from the New Stone Age they are making a significant contribution to New Zealand life—not least in the realm of sport. With increased white settlement from the 'seventies, however, much of their tribal land was alienated, often with compensation that was inadequate or too easily squandered, or which, through ignorance, paid too little regard to customary land tenure, the basis of tribal life. To many Maoris, with their devotion to the land, *Pakeha* peace seemed more to be dreaded than *Pakeha* war. Yet recent years have seen more understanding, and attempts were even made in the nineteen-twenties to redress some of the worst land grievances of the war period sixty years earlier. Of all the peoples shaken out of primitive isolation by white invasion and settlement the Maoris have suffered least. Much they owe to their own abilities and racial qualities; much also to the patient concern of such men as McLean, and to the increasing understanding of the whole New Zealand community of which they are now no insignificant part.

## An Unstable Economy

Vogel left New Zealand in 1876 to become the colony's Agent-General in London. Like other and later New Zealanders, he found the colonial stage too narrow for his abilities and energies. Yet although he returned in the 'eighties, and even held office again from 1884 to 1887, he never recovered his old hold, for soon after he had left in 1876 the boom had burst, and a depression had begun that was to last well into the 'nineties. Overburdened with debt New Zealand was hit by the general fall in prices that marked the period everywhere, and by the inevitable "instability of a dependent economy"[11] which had presumed too much upon the British market and upon British loans. Prices fell, and with them wages, salaries and imports; unemployment became rife, and mortgages on land were foreclosed, until the Bank of New Zealand was bankrupt, with a vast acreage on its hands of which it could not dispose until the Government came to its relief in the 'nineties. Thousands left the country in despair.

## THE ECONOMIC REVOLUTION

Part of the trouble lay in the excessive concentration of land in too few hands. As in Australia, the great demand for exports of wool and grain had led to the creation of large estates and runs, with but few people on them. Wool exports, which stood at £67,000 in 1853, had become £2,702,000 by 1873 and £3,014,000 ten years later, while grain exports in the same period had risen from £19,000 to £1,287,000, and the increases were largely the product of extensive farming and grazing over wide areas. A revolution, however, was at hand. In 1880, as recorded elsewhere, the first cargo of frozen meat from Australia had been landed in London from the *Strathleven*. A New Zealand agent had been quick to inspect and report upon it, and only two years later the *Dunedin* arrived from New Zealand with 4,410 sheep and 449 lamb carcasses in prime condition. It was indeed, as *The Times* commented, a "prodigious fact" for both Britain and New Zealand.[12] Hitherto, sheep had been little more than walking wool factories. Now their very carcasses could be used profitably: a new export industry, which was to make the name of New Zealand famous, had come into being. In the first year frozen meat to the value of £118,000 was exported. Ten years later this total had risen to over £1,000,000, and by 1913 it had reached £4,450,000. And it was not merely the meat-eater who benefited: refrigeration served the vegetarian equally well. Butter and cheese to the value of £42,000 and £7,000 respectively were exported in 1883, and within thirty years the figures were £2,062,000 and £1,770,000. Yet another valuable industry, that of dairy-farming for the distant export market, had arisen, based on the cream-separator that had begun to come into use about 1879. Meanwhile wool exports were increasing to over £8,000,000 in value, more than double the total for 1893, though grain exports, significantly enough, fell heavily: these had been at their peak in 1883, but had already fallen to £583,000 by 1893, and twenty years later, in 1913, they were only a quarter of even this figure. The world by this time was getting its wheat from Australia, Canada and the United States, and New Zealand was eating most of what she produced.

## The Development of North Island

Reflected in these figures of rise and fall is the revolution that had taken place in New Zealand life, a revolution that had its political counterpart in the election and the achievements of the Liberal-Labour governments of the 'nineties. Hitherto the chief benefits, both of positive development and of freedom from war, had gone to the South. Refrigeration and the cessation of the Maori wars opened the North to development, and opened it, not to large estates and sheep-runs, for which, with vast areas of uncleared bush, it was unsuited, but to closer settlement and the small farms which are the basis of the dairy industry. The first signs of the northward drift can be seen in the census of 1881.[13] In 1891 more than fifty-five per cent of the population of New Zealand was still living in the South Island, but the swing became rapidly more marked until ultimately the southern population has become less than one-third of the total. Experiments in the breeding of sheep and the cultivation of crops for their support, the fattening of lambs and the development of milking-herds, all tended to favour the small farmer, and the fall in wheat exports was a further blow to large-scale agriculture. Under Liberal-Labour control in the 'nineties the Government deliberately encouraged close settlement to relieve unemployment, and the produce of the farms came to be handled in co-operative dairies. Government grading of butter was introduced in 1894 to maintain standards and thereby retain markets. The agricultural community became, and to a very much larger extent than in Australia has remained, the basis of the population. Hence its political control of the country from 1912 until 1935. Hence, also, the differences between the two Dominions. Dilke saw the process beginning about 1890, and realized that, despite the gloom cast by the long depression, better times were ahead for New Zealand: indeed, he could see no reason why her population should not eventually reach thirty millions.

rather more than the population of England and Wales at the time he wrote. He gave in his *Problems of Greater Britain* an idyllic picture of the farming community after the first trials of bush clearance:

> the beautiful climate and the fertile soil make . . . the women and children of the settlers happy with a happiness that belongs to working women where the cows give plenty of milk and butter, the fowls give plenty of eggs, the land smiles upon them, and the children thrive.

## POLITICAL DEVELOPMENTS AND PERSONALITIES

Not until the mid-'nineties, however, did the recovery of international prices help to place all this development on a sound basis. The first ten years of refrigeration did little more than make good some of the losses of the depression,[14] and the 'eighties were a period of retrenchment and high taxation. From 1869 until 1891 politics were dominated, in the main, by the "Continuous Ministry", a shifting combination of political leaders who were largely land-owning oligarchs, and were led, in addition to Vogel, by McLean, Sir William Fox, and Sir Harry Atkinson (Premier 1876-77, 1883-84 and 1887-91). The Continuous Ministry was conservative in its land policy, and, being firmly attached to free trade and *laissez faire*, was disinclined to interfere directly with the economic ills of the period. It was not, however, unenlightened. Vogel had taught it the importance of public works, and it established, in 1877, New Zealand's advanced system of free and secular public education, while one of its leaders, Sir Joseph Hall, was a tireless advocate of women's suffrage. It fell, however, to another notable figure, a political opponent, to prepare the way for more advanced measures. This was the able and distinguished Sir George Grey (1812-98), who, having twice in earlier days (1845-53 and 1861-68) been Governor of New Zealand (and held the Governorship of the Cape from 1854 to 1859), had settled in New Zealand in 1871. Resistance to the abolition of the Provinces which, as Governor, he had helped to establish, drew him into politics in 1875, and from 1876 to 1890 he represented an Auckland constituency in the House of Representatives. Grey was a man of highly individual views and manner, an emotional Liberal whose opinions on matters of land tenure had been coloured by earlier experience of Irish conditions, but he was unfortunately a woolly and ineffectual speaker, and far from easy to work with. He became Premier from 1877 to 1879, but was worsted by the onset of the depression, and after his defeat his exasperated followers refused any longer to accept his leadership. He remains, nevertheless, a considerable figure in New Zealand history, and he appealed particularly to the growing class of poorer settlers who resented the domination of the landed oligarchy—and many of whom, in any case, brought with them unhappy recollections of rural poverty in England or of dispossession and eviction in Scotland and Ireland. Grey advocated a land policy which would restrict holdings, lease land rather than sell it outright and would impose taxes on it. With these proposals he combined demands for triennial parliaments, the abolition of plural voting and the election of Governors, good Radical—indeed, Chartist—measures, all of which but the last were later carried: to Grey must go much of the credit for bringing them to public attention. The abolition of plural voting, carried on a motion by Grey himself (then a private member) as an amendment to the Representation Act of 1889, was a blow to the political influence of landowners who had hitherto possessed voting rights based on land held in more than one constituency. Around Grey gathered a group of Liberals who carried on the party fight away from him after 1879. These included two future Premiers, Sir Robert Stout (1844–1930), one of the most notable parliamentarians of his day, who was Premier, with Vogel, in a joint Ministry from 1884 to 1887, and some years later became Chief Justice; and John Ballance (1839–93: Premier, 1891–93), the first Premier of the Liberal-Labour government of 1891 and a man whose views on the land question had been shaped by his Ulster origin. Among the few "Greyhounds" who remained faithful to the fallen leader was a third future Premier, destined to be the greatest of them all, Richard Seddon. To these men were added during the 'eighties other notable figures, including Joseph Ward, James Carroll, and William Pember Reeves. Sir James Carroll (1858–1926) was the son of an Irish settler and a Maori chieftainess, and was to become a notable Minister for Native Affairs. Sir Joseph Ward (1856–1930), a

"self-made man" who was highly successful in business as a
grain exporter, became Treasurer under Seddon and Premier,
after Seddon's death, from 1906 to 1912 (and again, late in life,
from 1928 to 1930): it was at his suggestion that New Zealand
was recognized as a Dominion in 1907. William Pember Reeves
(1857-1932) was one of the most distinguished of New
Zealand's first generation. Having by a happy chance been born
a few days after his parents' arrival in the colony in 1857, he was
born a New Zealander, and became the first of such to hold
political office. He was Minister of Education and afterwards of
Labour in the Ballance-Seddon Ministries of the 'nineties and
was responsible for some notable social legislation: indeed,
his was the brain behind the reforms then carried. In 1896
he went as Agent-General to London, where he became
prominent in Fabian circles, and he rounded off a remarkable
career as Director of the London School of Economics from
1908 to 1919. His best known book, *The Long White Cloud*,
remains one of the most readable accounts of his country's
development, and has contributed much to these pages.

## "LIB.-LAB."

With such men at its head a Liberal party took shape in the
'eighties and gathered to itself the first indications of a Labour
group, so that when Ballance formed his administration in
1891 it was a "Lib.-Lab." coalition. No independent Labour
members sat in Parliament until 1908. By the 'eighties, however, trade unions were being formed and were growing in
strength and consciousness in the face of the Government's
refusal to meddle in industrial questions. The London Dock
strike of 1899 and the bitter struggle in Australia that followed
had their repercussions in New Zealand. The franchise had
been widened in 1880, but to offset the influence of the towns
the rural representation was overweighted in the Act of 1889.
The result, however, was the overwhelming conservative defeat
of 1890, when trade unionists and small farmers combined in a
Liberal-Labour union behind Ballance to demand new policies.
The time had come to give political effect to the economic and
social changes already taking place in the country, and especially in the North Island, and to relieve the long strain of the
depression, though events were to show that the Liberal and

Labour elements in the electorate were not altogether at one in the remedies they sought.

## THE REFORMS OF THE 'NINETIES

There followed what Reeves has called the "eight years' tussle" (1890–98) between Liberal-Labour and conservative influences. The new government was put into power to carry further Vogel's pioneer work in public enterprise, and to make use of the resources of the State to correct the economic ills of the day. Its programme was loosely called "socialist", but it was socialism of an empirical and practical kind, the fruit of colonial conditions, and owed little or nothing to the theorizing of political philosophers. Apart from similar experiments in Australia it resembled most nearly the "municipal socialism" of the Fabians in Britain. The writings of the Fabians were, indeed, now being received from Britain, and exercised some influence, while Henry George had aroused interest in his views on land taxation as a remedy for social ills when he visited New Zealand in 1889. But Pember Reeves was almost the only politician who was concerned with the philosophical springs of political action. In the main, as Bernard Shaw wrote in a note published in the fourth edition of *The Long White Cloud*, through the need for public services on a scale beyond the scope of private means New Zealand was "forced into Fabian Socialism without dreaming of Socialism as such".[15] Reeves himself recorded of the Ballance Ministry that "most of its members did not know what Socialism was, and if they had studied it would not have agreed with it".[16] He himself was better informed, and the impelling force of the movement of protest which put the Government in power, together with the use of the State to carry social and economic reforms, gave a socialist colour to much that was done. In a series of newspaper articles on socialist utopias which he published in 1890, just before the decisive election, Reeves summed up the spirit of the Liberal-Labour movement, with its demand for a new deal after the buffetings of twelve years at the mercy of economic forces:

> The Socialist may be wrong; may be deluded; may be a blind leader of the blind. But at least he has something to offer, something to suggest. He does not mock us by bidding us be content with a society with which no thinking man can be content. There lies his strength.[17]

Ballance and his supporters were by no means content with society as they found it. Many of the remedies they adopted after 1890, notably Protection, land taxes and the settlement of smallholders, had been under discussion for some time, and a heavy programme of reforms was carried in only a few years. The Government's main concern was with conditions in agriculture and industry. On the land holdings were tending to increase in size, and too much Crown Land was passing as freehold into the hands of considerable holders. Between 1868 and 1893, for instance, while the number of landholders quadrupled, the acreage held increased thirteen times. Ballance had earlier tried to encourage closer settlement, and Sir John McKenzie (1838–1901), as Minister for Lands from 1893 to 1900, carried a number of measures to this end. The remaining Crown Lands were protected by a Land Act, land was leased in small settlements, instead of being sold freehold, certain private land was bought back and advances were made to small settlers. "From his childhood in the Scottish Highlands," it has been said, "McKenzie had brought one burning conviction: the right of a farming peasantry to have access to the soil."[18] The results of his work were already visible when he retired in 1900: the 45,000 landholders with ten million acres had become 65,000 with thirteen million acres. "New Zealand was well upon the road to becoming a nation of small farmers."[19]

## NEW PARTY GROUPINGS

Almost as soon as the new policy was put into operation its success was guaranteed by the turn in world prices. Between 1896 and 1914 the price of meat rose by 60 per cent, of butter by 36 per cent, of cheese by 72 per cent.[20] Taken together with the increase in demand these gains seemed to assure the prosperity of New Zealand farming: not until world prices fell again after the First War, and, more disastrously, from 1929, were there serious problems. The farming community had got what it wanted. After the first few years of reform it concentrated on consolidating its gains, and became a more conservative influence in the country. "Its members," Reeves has written, "had by 1898 had quite enough of change and experiment. . . . They did not want Socialism; they wanted better times, higher prices—even higher prices for land—

brisk trade, and more confidence."[21] Better times and higher prices the farmers had, but they tended in consequence to draw away from their Labour allies and to resist further social changes. It was, in fact, as much their attitude as a more independent Labour line that brought the Labour Party into existence in 1909. The change is apparent even as early as 1896, by which time the bulk of the reformist legislation had been carried: it is perhaps significant that Pember Reeves then left New Zealand for good. Moreover, by 1899 the older conservative group had been broken up by the continued success of the Liberal-Labour coalition, and the character of conservatism changed. Accommodating itself to the new balance of power in the agricultural interest, "it did not suffer a sea-change so much as a land-change",[22] and became the party of the small farmer, adopting as its name that of the "Reform Party". With the decline of Liberalism, and the growth of independent Labour, after Seddon's death in 1906, Reform gradually increased in strength and eventually in 1912, under the leadership of W. F. Massey, it took office and held it, in the main, until the sweeping Labour victory of 1935.

## THE RISE OF LABOUR

For Labour, also, much was done in the 'nineties. A Labour Department was established under Pember Reeves, with Labour Exchanges throughout the country; factory legislation was carried and an important Conciliation and Arbitration Act, the "Magna Carta" of New Zealand Labour, was also passed. New Zealand was for some years a pioneer in industrial arbitration, and the conditions of her workers the envy of many less fortunate. In the new century, however, the pace of reform was checked by the steadying influence of the farming interest. Arbitration tended to become narrow and stereotyped, and in 1908 an attempt to apply it to the wages of rural workers was defeated. A new and more militant Labour movement, inspired by Syndicalism and to some extent by Marxism, began to arise, and a wave of strikes that started as early as 1906 culminated in the bitter miners' and dockers' strikes of 1912-13, though it was to be many years before Labour was to rule.

Tariffs, which Atkinson had tried to carry in his last years of office—at the price of splitting his rather doctrinaire Free Trade party—were also imposed in the 'nineties, though New Zealand, unlike Australia, did not become a highly Protectionist country. Industry developed, but on a limited scale. New Zealand was essentially a primary producer, thriving on her export markets and owing more to the level of world prices than to Protection.

## "KING DICK"

The dominant figure of the Liberal-Labour Ministries was Richard Seddon (1845-1906), who held office from 1893 until his death, hastened by his exertions and restless activity, in 1906. An upstanding, dominating figure of a man, Lancashire-born and retaining much of the forthright quality of his native county, he had first come into politics, appropriately enough, as the representative of a mining community. He was a slogger, but capable and shrewd, and possessed a nice sense of the means necessary to political success in a colonial setting. Fortune favoured him, for Ballance left him a strong majority and it was not long before improving economic conditions played into his hands. He had no theoretical notions of government, but knew what improvements he wanted to make and by his speech-making tours kept himself closely in touch with the voters and their needs. "His sympathy with the people was undoubted," Reeves, who knew him well and worked closely with him, has said, "his ideas he picked up as he went along. . . . I never knew him read a Socialist book, though he did things that Socialists noted and admired, doing them as they came into his day's work."[23] His steadiness and solidity, his lack of any suspicious intellectual brilliance, which would have been out of place in the circumstances of his period and his environment, his lively interest in people and his ability to address them in terms they could understand, made him eventually the "King Dick" of New Zealand. "Colonial democracy," it has been said, "expects Ministers to take turns at firing the boilers and cleaning the brass, as well as navigating the ship."[24] Seddon could turn his hand to all three. He had a real zest for the chores of politics, and enjoyed his endless tours: he seemed, one observer said, to have obtained perpetual power by means of perpetual motion.[25] In any case New Zealand conditions demanded a general election every third year (Seddon fought five as Prime Minister), and elections are not to be won without speeches and tours. It was as well that he enjoyed them and as "the man for the masses" knew how to keep his grip on the electorate: "I played on them like a pianner," he once said with naïve satisfaction, indeed, after a lively meeting.

## OLD AGE PENSIONS

His greatest personal achievement was probably the carrying of the Old Age Pensions Act in 1898, after a three years' struggle. The pensions were to be paid from the national revenue, without contributions, a bold and unusual measure in which only Denmark (in 1891) had preceded New Zealand. The idea was not Seddon's own, for it had been discussed in the colony for some years, but it was he who pressed it through Parliament, in a notable unbroken session of nearly ninety hours, and it became the basis for much more recent welfare legislation. It was a gesture against pauperism and the depression years, which combined with other measures in defence of public health, and especially child health (in which Dr. Truby King in Dunedin was to become a notable pioneer), gave New Zealand some of the most advanced social legislation of the period throughout the whole world.

Much of the credit for what was done must go to Reeves, and it is worthy of note that Old Age Pensions were the only considerable measure of reform carried after his departure for England. No other Minister, least of all Seddon himself, had Reeves's power of intellectual grasp of problems and of finding legislative solutions for them. Seddon's approach was essentially empirical and practical: he could never have made an impression on political and intellectual circles in Britain as Reeves did—indeed, when in London for Colonial Conferences in 1897 and 1902 he caused some lifting of eyebrows. It is easy to understand, therefore, that after a few years of important achievement Reeves found Seddon an impossible leader, and longed, like Vogel before him, for greater scope. He was conscious of the narrowing of colonial life and interests as native-born generations grew to maturity and, like many others

of his countrymen, was not altogether happy in the inevitable
limitations of local life, which another New Zealand writer,
B. E. Baughan (born in 1870) has sympathetically described
in a vivid snapshot of pioneer conditions, *The Active Family*:[26]

> Oh dear! despite our soil and our sunshine, our independence
> and our labour laws, don't we some of us live really rather 'bad'?
> In our ardour for 'the land' are we not keeping our regard fixed
> rather too sedulously upon it? . . . unconscious that man really cannot
> ever live by bread alone; no, not even with the agreeable addition of
> roast mutton and butter!

## LATER REFORMS

The Liberal-Labour era came to an end, in any case, in
1906. By that time the foundations of what would now be
called a "welfare State" had been securely laid. In New
Zealand, as in Australia, democracy as it grew to maturity
turned its attention increasingly to the improvement of
standards of living: wealth of resources and limited population have made it possible to continue the process into our own
day. Other measures were carried at intervals after 1906,
notably widows' pensions in 1911 and family allowances in
1926, and when, in the 'thirties, New Zealand was again hard
hit by world conditions, it was to the example of the Liberal-
Labour governments, rather than to any alien ideology, that
she looked. In the important measures it carried after 1935
Labour, one authority has said, "merely moved further and
faster along the road chosen by the Liberals in the 'nineties".[27]
New Zealand rests on the foundations laid by Vogel, Grey,
Ballance, Reeves and Seddon.

After 1906 political ties were loosened, and the kaleido-
scope of politics was shaken, until eventually the Reform Party
took over in 1912. By that time the population, 626,000 in
1890, had, with natural increase and immigration, risen to over
a million. Immigration, which had reached a total of 197,000
in the 'nineties, rose to 347,000 in the first decade of the
twentieth century, and, apart from the interruption of war,
continued at something approaching this rate. Total production between 1890 and 1912 increased from £21,000,000
to some £60,000,000. Labour troubles apart, the country
seemed well set on the way to prosperity and strength.

## W. F. Massey and the Reform Party

The lead in the re-formed Opposition party from 1903 had been taken by W. F. Massey (1856–1925), an Ulsterman with something of Seddon's quality and stamp. He had been a farm-hand and a farmer, and was therefore an appropriate leader for a farmers' party: it was said of him that his first invitation to stand for Parliament had been handed to him on a pitchfork as he stood on a haystack. He was no match for Seddon, but he possessed the dour perseverance of the Irish Protestant and gradually won through, for himself and his party, to the leadership of the country. He has well been called "an animated straining post" in politics[28] and his qualities were perhaps those best suited, not only to the building up of a party among the farming community, in any country the element least susceptible of organization, but also to the mobilization of New Zealand's resources for the war that was so soon to come. Seddon had shown himself a devoted imperialist, though with a keen eye to New Zealand's interests, and, as will be seen, had played no small part in the discussions on the nature and organization of the Empire that marked the Colonial Conferences of 1897 and 1902. He had led the other Colonies in despatching troops to the South African War, for which New Zealand eventually provided some 6,500 officers and men, and had enjoyed the *éclat* of his stroke and the obvious approval of the electorate. In his crude way, it has been said, he gave his people a sense of importance: they could see that New Zealand was "cutting a figure in the world. It was a new experience and they loved it."[29] It fell to Massey, however—as an Ulsterman another good imperialist—to bring the country, united and unhesitating, into the more serious conflict of 1914. Nearly 120,000 New Zealanders (including 2,200 Maoris), more than ten per cent of the population and a higher proportion than in any other Dominion, then served overseas in the four years of struggle, and 16,700 did not return. The New Zealand Division distinguished itself in France, and shared with the Australians the enduring memory of Gallipoli. Massey could justly claim, when presenting the Treaty of Versailles to the New Zealand Parliament in 1919, that the war had turned a dependency into a partner:

The signing of the Peace Treaty, and the part the Dominions took in the Conference, was the most important event in their history. What has taken place has proved that their status is assured. They have ceased to be dependencies of the Empire. They have become partners.[30]

## NEW ZEALAND AND THE PACIFIC

Dilke, as has already been shown, found in Australia a desire to adopt an "Australasian Monroe Doctrine" with regard to the islands that lay to the north and east of her, and the Colonial Secretary of the day, Lord Derby, had been shocked in 1883 at the magnitude of Australian ambitions. By the time these views were expressed New Zealand also had staked her claims, which eventually brought under her control the Cook Islands, named after the famous navigator, and, as a Mandate from the League of Nations after the First World War, the ex-German western half of Samoa. Interest in these and others of the Pacific Islands had come early. The first Bishop of New Zealand, George Selwyn, had from 1847 supervised missionary activity among the islands, centred on St. John's Training College in Auckland, and notable work was done by missionaries, both before and after this date, in assisting the islanders to accommodate themselves to the unavoidable shock of European penetration. With the opening of the Pacific, commerce in sandalwood, coconut, sugar, and other tropical products had developed rapidly, and brought traders and the beginnings of British, French, German and American economic and political interest. The manpower of the islands also attracted "blackbirders", while the easy conditions of life only too often brought the scum of European society to exploit the primitive people. There came in consequence appeals from the islanders for official protection. Grey, when Governor of New Zealand in 1848, urged that Fiji and Tonga, which had recently petitioned for British protection, should be annexed, but the British Government, with more than enough colonial responsibilities to harass it, refused to move. New Zealand, however, did not let the matter drop. As the colony developed, the activities of French and German traders in the islands seemed to presage political control and therefore to threaten her security. Australia and New Zealand asked only to be left alone to develop their population and resources, but the Europe their people had left was creeping after them. They therefore wished to gain control, before it was too late, of strategic posts which in other hands might become a menace to them:

> they realized ... that it was necessary for them to remain, as far as possible, alone and without troublesome neighbours in the South Pacific. In this way the programme "Australasia for the Australasians" developed into "Oceania for the Anglo-Saxons".[31]

It seemed logical that, as British imperial power had turned Stone Age *Ao Tea Roa* into a modern colony, so from the colony the Empire could be extended among the Polynesian and Melanesian Stone Age settlements of the South Seas, from the latter of which, indeed, the Maoris themselves had come. Vogel, with his high-flown notions of New Zealand's growth, was an ardent advocate of this policy. "The ultimate object which I have in view," he wrote in 1874, "is the establishment of the Polynesian islands as a Dominion with New Zealand the centre of the Government, and the Dominion, like Canada, to be a British Dependency."[32] This seemed to the Colonial Office in London "foolish as well as impudent", and Vogel was branded as "the most audacious adventurer that perhaps has ever held power in a British Colony".[33] With the Maori wars only recently ended, and New Zealand's population still little more than a quarter of a million, the official view was not unreasonable, but Vogel was alive to the needs that must eventually arise. He was interested, too, in the possibilities of a fast mail steamer service across the Pacific, which would take advantage of the newly opened American transcontinental railway to hasten mails to Britain, and which would need the harbours which the islands provided. Some of the best and most conveniently placed harbours were in Samoa, with its three main islands of Savaii, Upolo, and Tutuila, and it was to Samoa especially that New Zealanders looked for an outpost, the more readily as the islands were one of the original homes of the Maoris. Their own experience with the Maoris encouraged them to feel that if the islanders needed protection against European intrusion they were qualified to provide it. Some settled order was required in any case to control the unruly white elements which had already installed themselves, and many of which were, as a New Zealand despatch of 1874 decorously put it, "the overflowings of Colonial Society".[34]

## SAMOA

But it was particularly the activities of the German traders, J. C. Godeffroy and Son, that stimulated New Zealand interest in Samoa. Under the energetic guidance of the firm's agent Theodore Weber, Samoa had become in the 'sixties the centre of a considerable German trade in coconut oil, much needed in Europe to meet the growing demand for fats for candles and soap. By 1875 copra, dried coconut flesh, to the value of £121,000 was being sent to Europe for processing, and with German plantations established Samoa had become the first German colonial venture, a point of some sentimental significance in later discussions of the island's fate. Fearing German annexation, New Zealand appealed to Britain to occupy Samoa, but this and other appeals in the 'seventies the Colonial Office contemptuously rejected. Nor was Bismarck at this time prepared to move. Yet, however much he and the British Government might dislike it, intervention was forced upon them. Samoan society was by tradition and temperament loosely organized, and such government as existed was therefore unstable, dynastic rivalries being a particularly fruitful cause of disputes. From 1869 until 1881 there was intermittent civil war in the islands between rival dynastic claimants, and its consequences were felt in the unsettlement of trade. Efforts were therefore made to restore peace and order. In these the United States, alive to her interests and "manifest destiny" in the Pacific which washed her western shores, also took a hand. Between 1873 and 1876, indeed, an American adventurer, "Colonel" Steinberger, acted as Prime Minister of the Samoan King, Malietoa Laupepa. Steinberger was disavowed by the United States and deported, but his removal brought Laupepa's downfall, and it was five years before the King was restored, in 1881, with British, German, and American support. His position was no easy one, however. The presence of so many foreigners, as he complained, made it impossible for his people to conduct their affairs in traditional manner, while they were not sufficiently advanced to establish a more civilized form of government. By 1884 it was clear that

Laupepa was losing control: foreign activity was, willy-nilly, breaking up Samoan society while putting nothing in its place.

## INTERNATIONAL RIVALRIES
### (1) GERMANY

Meanwhile, as recounted elsewhere, Australians had become perturbed at German policy in New Guinea and French moves in the New Hebrides. In 1883 an inter-colonial conference, at which New Zealand was represented, was held in Sydney to consider the situation. Samoa, 1,500 miles away, was ten times as far from New Zealand as New Guinea was from the north coast of Australia, but Vogel, now returned from Britain and again in office, still had earlier ambitions in mind, and even considered an official visit to Samoa to test local feeling on the subject of annexation. The Germans, however, were now receiving Bismarck's support, as part of his calculated policy of favouring colonial expansion, and they gradually pushed Laupepa aside until in 1887 they were able to deport him, replacing him with a rival, Tamasese, who now became their client and favoured candidate. Tamasese was opposed, in the best Samoan tradition, by a member of Laupepa's family, Mataafa, who received the support of Britain and the United States. Civil war between the rivals broke out in 1887, and led to strained relations between the local consular representatives of Germany on the one hand and Britain and the United States on the other. This *furor consularis*, to use the contemporary phrase, still further exacerbated the situation. Laupepa had unsuccessfully appealed to Britain in 1884 to annex Samoa—the last of a series of appeals that had been coming from the islands for some forty years—but in accordance with its attitude to German expansion elsewhere at this time the British Government would not have opposed German control. When he took office a few years later Lord Salisbury was critical of Germany's clumsy handling of the situation, but was too conscious of greater issues at stake elsewhere to stand in her way. "Samoa matters very little to us," he wrote to the British Ambassador in Berlin in 1889, "Prince Bismarck's Colonial undertakings are a great nuisance. . . . If they did Germany any good I should mind it less . . . but he has ruined everybody else's trade at Samoa . . . without in the least benefiting his own."[35] Samoa did in fact matter very little in so far as the volume and significance of its trade were concerned; as a German diplomat observed later, the islands were not worth the cost of the diplomatic telegrams that passed to and fro about them. Far more than trade was involved, however. For Germany Samoa, as her first colonial enterprise, had a sentimental appeal that was fortified by the obvious interest of the islands, in their distant isolation, for partisans of a strong navy: it was gratifying to national pride to be able to rival long-envied Britain in imperial enterprise. Robert Louis Stevenson, who, after several visits in search of health, settled in 1891 in Samoa, where he died three years later, wrote of the German traders and officials whom he saw there that, "they seem oppressed with greatness and the sense of empire".[36] It was a telling comment, both on their unconcealed pride in their achievement, and on their outlook and attitude, which contributed not a little to local difficulties.

## (2) The U.S.A.

For the United States the strategic importance of the islands was clear, and was soon to be reinforced by the cutting of a Central American canal. The need for outlying naval bases in the Pacific had been recognized for some time, and in the 'seventies a base had been established at Pago-Pago in Tutuila, the most easterly of the main Samoan group. Interest in the key position of Hawaii was of longer standing, and in 1887 the great natural base of Pearl Harbour, in the Hawaiian Islands, was acquired, the annexation of the whole group following eleven years later, in 1898. Pago-Pago remained, however, and even with Hawaii annexed the U.S.A. could not be indifferent to the fate of Samoa.

## Tripartite Control, 1889

Britain's interest in the islands was less keen, especially in view of her hold upon Fiji, but the anxious concern of Australia and New Zealand could no longer be ignored. In 1889, therefore, it was at length agreed by the three Powers, at a conference at Berlin, that a tripartite system of control should be established. Before this, however, the very elements had brought home to all parties the lack of proportion in the tense situation. On 16th March, 1889, an appalling hurricane struck the harbour of Apia, where lay seven warships, three German, three American and one British, brought together by the civil war and the local tension. All the German and American ships were wrecked, and the British vessel, the *Calliope*, escaped only by steaming out into the storm in a brilliant feat of seamanship that has become historic. The hurricane hastened the solution reached at Berlin, for it was recognized too late that, in Stevenson's words, "not the whole Samoan Archipelago was worth the loss in men and costly ships".[37]

## The Settlement of 1899—and Its Aftermath

Yet, as Lord Salisbury had foreseen, the tripartite system proved unworkable, and ten years later Germany took advantage of Britain's preoccupation with South African affairs to press for a final settlement. In 1899, therefore, as part of a general agreement on spheres of control in the Pacific, Germany took possession of the western islands of Samoa and the United States of the eastern. Britain received as her share recognition of her claims to Tonga and the Gilbert, Solomon, and Cook Islands. New Zealand had already laid claim to the Cook Islands as some compensation for her disappointment over Samoa, and in 1901 the islands, "a remote and worthless group" in the cynical Colonial Office view,[38] were duly placed under her control. Samoa, however, remained New Zealand's *irredenta*, as New Guinea was Australia's and when war broke out in 1914 the Dominion was quick to move. Before the end of August, 1914, German Samoa was occupied, and it was to New Zealand that the mandate for the islands was given in 1920. Vogel's "audacious" dream had at last been realized, though Samoa was no more to prove an easy sinecure to New Zealand than it had been to her predecessors.

### REFERENCES

1. K. Sinclair: *Imperial Federation. A Study of New Zealand Policy and Opinion, 1880–1914*, pp. 23–24.
2. J. Amery: *Life of Joseph Chamberlain*, IV, p. 416.
3. *Imperial Federation*, p. 21.
4. ibid., p. 49.
5. Reprinted in *New Zealand Short Stories* (*The World's Classics*, No. 534).

6.  W. P. Reeves: *The Long White Cloud* (4th edn., 1950), p. 224.
7.  Quoted from *Hansard* in J. E. Tyler: *The Struggle for Imperial Unity, 1868–1895*, p. 3.
8.  *Imperial Federation*, p. 9.
9.  S. Masterman: *The Origins of International Rivalry in Samoa, 1845–1884*, p. 89.
10. J. B. Condliffe: *New Zealand in the Making*, p. 489 n. 5.
11. The title of C. G. F. Simkin's historical study of the New Zealand economy, published in 1951.
12. Quoted in *New Zealand in the Making*, p. 134.
13. ibid., p. 208.
14. *Cambridge History of the British Empire*, Vol. VII, Part ii: *New Zealand*, p. 158.
15. *The Long White Cloud*, 4th edn., p. 13.
16. ibid., p. 282.
17. *New Zealand in the Making*, p. 164.
18. ibid., p. 190.
19. *Cambridge History of the British Empire: New Zealand*, p. 182.
20. *The Instability of a Dependent Economy.*
21. *The Long White Cloud*, p. 287.
22. ibid., p. 292.
23. ibid., p. 301.
24. A. W. Shrimpton and A. E. Mulgan: *Maori and Pakeha: A History of New Zealand*, p. 361.
25. Sir William Harcourt, quoted in *The Long White Cloud*, p. 302.
26. *New Zealand Short Stories.*
27. A. Brady: *Democracy in the Dominions*, p. 261.
28. *Maori and Pakeha*, p. 352.
29. *Imperial Federation*, p. 33.
30. *Cambridge History of the British Empire: New Zealand*, p. 221.
31. André Siegfried, quoted in *New Zealand in the Making*, p. 401.
32. *The Origins of International Rivalry in Samoa*, pp. 97–98.
33. ibid., p. 89.
34. ibid., p. 99.
35. *Life of Lord Salisbury*, IV, pp. 128 and 126.
36. *A Footnote to History* (1892), *Swanston* edn., p. 23.
37. ibid., p. 155.
38. *Imperial Federation*, p. 31.

Seddon's story can be read in R.M. Burdon's vivid study, *King Dick*.

# XI

# TOWARDS COMMONWEALTH

## PROBLEMS OF IMPERIAL UNITY AND UNION

SOME attention has been given to Samoa since it provides a case-study in imperialism, involving both the general problem of European (and American) expansion into fruitful primitive areas, and the particular concern of Britain with colonial administration and the problems of imperial and foreign relations. By the 'eighties most of the eligible portions of the globe had already been earmarked: the greater, therefore, the intensity of feeling about what was left, especially on the part of such newcomers as the German Empire. Britain herself might be prepared to give way to the newcomers in particular instances, but her colonies were rather more concerned at the strategic implications for their own future of the passing into other hands of such territories as South West Africa, New Guinea and Samoa. The whole question of imperial defence, in fact, began to take shape as so many hostages were given to fortune in distant seas, and the rise of the German navy, stimulated by such episodes as the Samoan disputes, soon gave real point to doubts and fears.

## SEA-POWER AND EMPIRE

The British Empire was the product of British sea-power, and would have been impossible without the almost unchallengeable supremacy which the island nation had held since 1713. Commerce and settlement alike took the supremacy for granted, and expanded behind the stout shield of the Navy without always being aware of its omnipresent influence. It was, indeed, "world power on the cheap", a degree of strength and security out of all proportion to its cost and, though envied, not wielded with a degree of disregard for others such as to excite resentment. In the smug words of Eyre Crowe's well-known Foreign Office memorandum of 1907:

It has been well said that every country, if it had the option, would, of course, prefer itself to hold the power of supremacy at sea, but that, this choice being excluded, it would rather see England hold that power than any other State.[1]

## THE SIGNIFICANCE OF THE RISE OF GERMANY

The rise of Germany altered the situation. For the first time in many years it became possible for another State to see herself as a rival to Britain in naval strength as much as in industry and commerce. Germany's will to world-power, backed by the resources and skill of her industries, soon made her not merely a competitor but a dangerous rival. This not only raised for Britain herself new questions of security; it posed problems of a new kind for the Dominions and Colonies. Hitherto imperial defence had been taken for granted. No great fleet existed in any but European waters, and at the most the colonies had before them, in the event of war between Britain and another Power, no more than the risk of armed raids. The rise of Germany, however, opened totally new possibilities for the very existence of the Dominions as self-governing nations.

## AN EARLIER THREAT—RUSSIA

In the 'seventies and 'eighties, before any colony but Canada had even begun to develop adequate strength and resources for defence, the chief danger had come from Russia. Had Britain and Russia gone to war—as seemed likely to happen on several occasions—sporadic raids on shipping routes and coastal towns might have been expected; as much so, indeed, as the threat to India through Afghanistan which has been discussed elsewhere. Thus, the Russian composer, Rimsky-Korsakoff, tells in his memoirs of the preparations for commerce-raiding in the Atlantic made earlier by Russia at the height of the differences with Britain over the Polish rising of 1863, at a time when he was a midshipman in the Tsar's navy.[2]

## MEASURES OF DEFENCE

Colonial defence was the subject of formal consideration during the "Eastern Crisis" in 1878, and a special committee was set up in 1879 to examine the problems involved. These were not studied with any degree of continuity, however, until 1885, when, as a result of the Penjdeh incident and the very real risk of war with Russia, an interdepartmental "Colonial Defence Committee" was established.[3] This, with the Joint Naval and Military Committee on Defence, set up in 1891, was the germ of the later "Committee of Imperial Defence", of which, indeed, it eventually became a sub-committee. The Colonial Defence Committee was, however, purely an affair of the home government, and contained only representatives of the Colonial Office, the War Office and the Admiralty. The responsibility for imperial defence rested solely on Britain's shoulders, and little effort was made to guide colonial opinion on strategic issues. As Robert Borden, when Prime Minister of Canada, told the Canadian House of Commons in 1912:

> For forty-five years as a confederation we have enjoyed the protection of the British Navy without the cost of a dollar.[4]

The cost of imperial defence went with the responsibility for its maintenance. Not until Britain was prepared to admit the Dominions to its counsels, and had devised the means of doing so; not until the Dominions themselves were willing to bear their share of the expenditure involved, was a joint Empire policy on defence a possibility. It was the German threat that hastened this process and helped to bring about the creation of the Committee of Imperial Defence, on which representatives of the Dominions sat almost from the first, and which was to evolve during the First World War into a true Imperial War Cabinet. Germany did more for imperial unity, it may be said, than the propaganda of all the sentimental imperialists, and imperial unity developed empirically, in typical British fashion, in response to real needs and problems.

## THE FIRST STEP—THE PROBLEM OF RESPONSIBILITY

In the 'eighties the Russian threat was taken sufficiently seriously for the Australian colonies, obvious targets for Russian raiders, to build port defences and press for the stationing of units of the Royal Navy in Australian waters. To the British Government's objection that the colonies should be prepared to share the cost, the answer was not infrequently

P

returned that the Navy was essential in any case for the protection of British trade and that colonial defence added nothing to the responsibility or the cost. John Ballance of New Zealand bluntly told the British Government, on one occasion, "you wish to make us pay towards what you are bound to do for your own interests".[5] The colonial view was, of course, a narrow one. It early came to accept the notion of paying for what it could see and of contributing towards the cost of ships in local waters, but for some time it failed to grasp that it was the presence of a battle-fleet in European waters that made any major attack on the colonies—as on the homeland—unthinkable. In the words used by the Secretary of the Colonial Defence Committee in 1887:

> The whole standard of defence of the Australian Colonies is based on the fact that the enemy could send small squadrons only into their waters. . . . But these limitations to an enemy's action . . . exist solely in consequence of the great ironclad fleet maintained by the Imperial Government in European waters, and based upon fortresses and coaling stations created and maintained without charge to Australian tax-payers.[6]

Winston Churchill, when First Lord of the Admiralty twenty-five years later, put the same view to the Canadian Government in 1912 in a memorandum on the naval defence of the Dominion:

> It is the general naval supremacy of Great Britain which is the primary safeguard of the security and interests of the great Dominions of the Crown, and which for all these years has been the deterrent upon any possible designs prejudicial to or inconsiderate of their policy and safety.[7]

At the same time the colonies could, and did, reply that they were involved in the danger of attack not from any acts of their own but through the general policy of Britain and its European rivalries. The possibility of their remaining neutral in the event of war was therefore mooted at intervals, and posed awkward niceties of international law. Until they had some share in the shaping of imperial policy they could hardly be expected to accept all its implications. As the New Zealand government put the matter in 1886:

> the wider question, relating to the expense of Imperial naval defences generally being shared by Great Britain and her several

colonies, involves that of the representation of the colonies in an Imperial Parliament—in short, leads to the consideration of the problem of 'Imperial Federation'."[8]

## THE FIRST COLONIAL CONFERENCE, 1887

In the following year the Golden Jubilee of Queen Victoria was made the occasion for the first Colonial Conference in London, and one of the Cape Colony representatives, J. H. Hofmeyr, raised in the same context of defence the need for a wider control of imperial policy. South Africa, in view of its geographical position and its considerable non-British white population, was perhaps rather more aware than Australia and New Zealand of its dependence for security upon the wise handling of British policy in Europe. Hofmeyr himself, as the Boer minister converting the pan-Boer and bitterly anti-British *Afrikander Bond* at the Cape into an instrument of co-operation between South Africa's two white peoples, was keenly alive to the advantages and protection of the British connexion. But he would follow no one's lead blindly. So long as the colonies were unrepresented in the imperial government, he argued at the Conference, "so long they cannot be expected in duty bound to defend themselves against the European enemies of England".[9]

## "FEDERATE OR DISINTEGRATE"

The imperial issues of the next half-century had now been set out. Problems of local defence called for immediate solution but were inextricably bound up with the defence of the Empire as a whole. Strategy dictated the concentration of the major part of the Fleet in European waters, where it could exert the greatest influence, but the colonies suspected that their interests were overlooked in Britain's obsession with European issues. The political direction of the Empire was therefore a matter of the first importance, and to this, as the colonies developed their own tariff policies, were soon to be added matters of economic moment. To many at the time it seemed that the Empire must either federate or disintegrate: the colonies must either be more closely associated in a formal partnership, which would allow them to influence policy, or they would break away. Politics are too easily seen, however, in this kind of dilemma. Its subtleties and complexities can rarely be resolved into but two stark alternatives, and the British nations were eventually to light upon a third course, shaped by their political traditions but responsive to the needs of the modern world. For many years, however, it was the issue of federation which dominated imperial discussions, and the whole problem of the formalization, in well-wrought principles, of the imperial unity that existed in practice, especially in critical times, has survived well into our own day. The loose bonds of Dominion Status and a Commonwealth of Nations could hardly have been foreseen.

RESULTS OF THE 1887 CONFERENCE

At the conference of 1887 the delicate situation in the Pacific kept defence issues to the fore, and it was decided that an Australian squadron of the Royal Navy should be established, to the cost of which the Australian colonies and New Zealand should make a contribution of £126,000 a year, and which should be used outside Australian waters only with their consent. Hofmeyr suggested a common tariff throughout the Empire, the proceeds of which, estimated at some £7,000,000 a year, should be devoted to defence purposes, and, although this proposal was coolly received by the home government, it was typical of the readiness of the colonial representatives to contribute in some way to the defence of the Empire provided that the burden were not too heavy. It was also a pointer to the greater scheme put forward later by Chamberlain. The success of the 1887 conference, modest though it was, was evidence of the value of joint discussions, and stimulated the propagandist organizations which were advocating closer unity in some form of imperial federation. On the whole schemes of this kind were regarded with suspicion in the colonies. They received some support in political circles, but the majority of the people, in the colonies themselves no less than in Britain, were apathetic. This was true even of New Zealand, which on account of its size and isolation tended to look to Britain more than others did.[10] There was concern everywhere lest closer union should increase the danger of entanglement in European squabbles, and even the establishment of the Australian squadron had to be presented in New South Wales as leaving "not a single loophole . . . for our being thrown into any quarrel outside our waters".[11]

## THE SECOND COLONIAL CONFERENCE, 1897

Eighteen ninety-seven saw the second Colonial Conference, a far more splendid gathering brought together to pay imperial homage to the old lady who had been "sixty years a Queen". The Diamond Jubilee was essentially a family and imperial occasion, and eleven Premiers, representing Canada, Newfoundland, New South Wales, Victoria, South Australia, Queensland, Western Australia, Tasmania, New Zealand, the Cape and Natal, sat down with Chamberlain, now Colonial Secretary, to discuss imperial problems. Again defence was considered. Australia and New Zealand renewed their contributions, and others were now added by the Cape and Natal. Chamberlain threw out suggestions about closer union, but they were not received with any enthusiasm. Such discussion as took place, both now and later, revealed much confusion of thought on the subject, and failed to reconcile the colonies' desire to make their own viewpoints felt with Britain's wider responsibilities and insistence on retaining the lead. Even if the oft-debated notion of an imperial parliament, with representatives from all the self-governing colonies, had been pursued, the size of Britain's population would have assured her a permanent majority. In fact, of course, the colonies were not greatly interested in any but their own local problems, and had no desire to be drawn into any degree of responsibility—or expense—for European issues, or even for the more general problems of empire. Thus, when Chamberlain, during the course of the conference, asked rhetorically whether the colonies were prepared for the burden of taxation which a closer union would entail, the genial, but shrewd, Premier of New South Wales, Sir George Reid, rapped back at him, with equal irony, "We are ready to manage the Empire for you at any time, so long as you pay the piper."[12]

## REID AND THE PROBLEM OF UNITY

It was Reid who, brushing aside the fears of those who maintained that not to federate was to disintegrate, put his finger on the very heart of the problem of imperial unity, and showed a sound—and, indeed, prophetic—insight into the realities of the situation:

> The great test of our relations, I submit, will be the next war in which England is engaged. She is not ever likely to be engaged in an unrighteous war or in an aggressive war. If engaged in a defensive war you would find that sentiment would determine everything. Our money would come; our men would come . . . but it is only in those moments that you can make the people one in the sense of sacrifice.[13]

This was, indeed, a realistic view. There might be much pride in the imperial association, especially at times of royal commemoration, but the colonies were not prepared, except in moments of real crisis, to assume additional burdens for any but their own local needs. When a crisis came only two years later, at the time of the South African war, the response also came, as Reid had foretold it would, and it continued to shape policy all through the years of uneasy relations with Germany up to the ultimate test of 1914. Then the people became one, and it was discovered that, even without formal constitutional machinery, the Empire could move as one, despite the growing independence of its parts. For the present, however, the colonies were, in the words addressed by Laurier to the conference, 'quite satisfied with the condition of things as they are".

## "Imperial Preference" and Chamberlain's Policy

The one direction in which the colonies were willing to make concessions was that of economics. The rise of German and American industry behind tariff barriers and the increasing competition which British exports had to face, even in the colonies, was causing serious concern, and there were alarmist reports of commercial decay and death. Chamberlain on taking office in 1895 had instituted inquiries into the competitive strength of British trade in the colonies. For their part most of the colonies were building up their own tariff systems, but a weakening of Britain through a decline in her trade, with a consequent reduction in her demand for colonial goods and in the resources available for investment, was not at all in their interests. In view of their own tariffs, "Empire Free Trade", as advocated by some enthusiasts in Britain, was an impossible aim, but it was hoped that free trade in Britain and protection in the colonies could be reconciled by a system of "imperial preference", by which British goods might receive a preferential reduction of colonial tariffs and thereby gain an advantage over their competitors. A colonial conference which met at Ottawa in 1894 first recommended this system of "preference", and it was adopted by Canada in 1897. It was discussed at the London colonial conference of that year, and, again, in 1902, when for a short time it seemed, through its enthusiastic acceptance by Chamberlain, to be on the verge of approval by the imperial government. Apart from adherence to free trade principles, a difficulty on the British side had been the lack of duties on colonial produce which could be reduced by way of reciprocity, but by 1902 a duty imposed on corn to help meet the cost of the South African war made a reciprocal arrangement possible, and Laurier came to the conference from Canada pledged to achieve it. Chamberlain's view, as he explained before the conference met, was that British trade was being restricted not only by tariffs but by the "great combinations" and "enormous trusts" that were developing with the industrial systems of its rivals, and he urged the drawing closer of imperial relations, "the ties of sentiment . . . and the ties of interest", in order to "keep British trade in British hands". In short, he advocated some kind of vast British Imperial Trust in the common interest of the whole Empire. His hope was, indeed, that imperial preference would, in the words of the final resolution of the conference, "by promoting the development of the resources and industries of the several parts, strengthen the Empire."

THE THIRD COLONIAL CONFERENCE, 1902

Though warmly advocated, the project fell, however, on the stony ground of the fanatical devotion of the Board of Trade and the Treasury to free trade. Yet it was the one proposal which promised well for imperial unity, and which, as Chamberlain and others hoped, might in time be developed into something greater. Despite the loyal support of the colonies during the South African war, which inevitably raised hopes of some permanent system of imperial unity; despite the

drawing together of the Australian colonies into a Commonwealth, an obvious pointer to some wider association; despite
the desire for a unification of the South African colonies which,
as many had hoped, proved to have been only delayed by the
unhappy episode of the war, the Colonial Conference of 1902
did little to encourage the advocates of closer association. In
the political sphere the colonies were unwilling to undertake
further responsibilities, and in the economic the Home
Government, despite Chamberlain's urgent advice, would not
modify its tariff policy to suit colonial requirements. Chamberlain himself presented to the conference a harrowing picture
of the burden on the mother-country of her imperial responsibilities in the graphic phrase, "the weary Titan staggers under
the too vast orb of its fate", and Australia, New Zealand and
the South African colonies duly increased their contributions
to the cost of the Navy, though not by any impressive amount.
Canada, however, announced her intention of creating her
own naval forces, and when the British Government proposed
the establishment of an Imperial Reserve for the army, to be
stationed in the colonies, it met with open opposition. Seddon
ingeniously argued that New Zealand's most effective contribution to imperial defence would be a preference of ten per cent
on British imports, which would represent, at the existing level
of trade, a sum equal to the interest on five million pounds, and
would therefore be "paying the interest on five battleships",[14]
but the "weary Titan" was not impressed. There was in fact a
divergence of views and understanding: Britain and the
colonies were each hoping to use the other to advance particular
interests. Moreover, if the colonies were unsympathetic to
Britain's needs, there was little real understanding in Britain
itself of their problems, or even of their conditions. Seddon had
had this driven home to him during his visit in 1897, when on
one occasion he had received an invitation to address a meeting
"in native attire",[15] a gesture which even "King Dick" could
hardly have made effective.

## CHAMBERLAIN: A NEW ATTITUDE

Chamberlain similarly was compelled to recognize the
existence of differing viewpoints. With his passionate faith in
the Empire and his zeal for its development, he had hoped that

the conference of 1902 would have come to some decision about not only defence and "imperial preference" but the formation of an "Imperial Council" as the constitutional expression of its unity in policy and action. His hopes had been dashed, both by the colonies themselves and by his own colleagues. Shortly after the conference he left for an extended tour of South Africa, and with his characteristic impressionability he began, under the influence of the South African scene, and with the disappointment of the conference fresh in his mind, to reshape his views. As he said at Bloemfontein of South Africa's problems, "somehow or other, in the atmosphere of London they appear to be different from what they are in the atmosphere of South Africa". Some kind of union of the self-governing colonies of the Empire had seemed practicable, and, indeed, necessary, from London, but the colonial atmosphere was hardly propitious. Chamberlain now therefore began to feel his way towards some different kind of association, "a group of free nations gathered round the motherland", as he told South African audiences, in which South Africa, "a free State and, at the same time, a member of the greatest Empire", would take her place.[16]

## A New Policy—"Tariff Reform"

Yet as a business man he was far from renouncing his belief in the need for commercial ties. The Empire called for development, and the colonies were prepared to make concessions to British trade. Britain must be persuaded to abandon its outworn faith in free trade and to adopt a system of Protection which could be modified for colonial products: through economic measures might come in time a strengthening of political association. Hence Chamberlain's wayward break with Balfour's government in 1903, and his indulgence, in his last years of political activity, in the "tariff reform" campaign, which soon, however, lost much of its imperial motivation and became an outright appeal for the protection of British industry against foreign competition. It was to be an unhappy descent from the high hopes of union with the colonies, and of development for the more backward dependencies, with which he had assumed office as Colonial Secretary in 1895: the frustrated, impatient imperial idealist became lost

P*

in the leader of protectionist industry. Notwithstanding the sparkling debate and polemical sallies with which, with all his accustomed oratorical skill, he conducted his campaign, he did not win over the country, which was in any case intent, during the period of Liberal government from 1905, on other issues. Yet the debate continued; long after he had had to abandon it, and, winning some curious allies by the way, it was eventually to make some at least of its points, under very different circumstances, in the years of post-war depression.

## THE END OF BRITAIN'S ISOLATION

The 1902 conference was not, therefore, without its results. It marked a significant stage in the development of the self-governing colonies and in their relations with the British homeland, a stage the more significant because of the changes that were taking place in the international situation and that were soon to exert a decisive influence upon imperial affairs. Relations with Germany were becoming strained, and Britain, perturbed at her international isolation during the period of the South African War, had taken the first step in a reorientation of her policy, six months before the conference, by making a treaty with Japan. This treaty of 1902, followed as it was within a few years by the defeat of Russia at the hands of the Japanese, and renewed and extended in 1905, fundamentally altered the balance of power in the Pacific and raised new problems for Australia and New Zealand, with their opposition to Asiatic immigration. The British Fleet was soon to be largely concentrated in home waters to face the German threat, and Japan to be left to consolidate the secure position in the Far East which she was to enjoy for so long. The nineteen-thirties were far away, but Japan was able now to begin to build up the security which she was to exploit with such disastrous effect from 1931. The treaty of 1902, unwelcome as it became to the Dominions who, with the United States, were instrumental in preventing its renewal after the First World War, in 1921, was in fact a portent of new developments in the Far East.

By the time of the next conference, in 1907, other changes had also taken place. Japan stood victorious in the Far East and, with Russian naval strength there destroyed, Britain was able to consider the shift in the balance of her own naval power to Europe that was demanded by the rivalry with Germany. She now had fifty-six battleships in commission or under construction, Germany thirty-three, and the German ships, unlike the British, were neither intended nor constructed for operation in distant seas. As Winston Churchill pointed out in 1912:

> this great fleet is not dispersed all over the world for duties of commerce protection or in discharge of Colonial responsibilities; nor are its composition and character adapted to those purposes. It is concentrated and kept concentrated in close proximity to the German and British coasts.[17]

This consideration was to prove decisive in the discussion of colonial naval contributions after 1907. Meanwhile, the *Entente* with France had been shaped, and had even undergone its first test at Germany's hands over Morocco. A new alignment of forces was taking place, and in 1907 an understanding became possible even with the old enemy, Russia.

## The Fourth Colonial Conference, 1907

The conference of 1907 was the first deliberately summoned without the excuse of a royal celebration, and marked in other ways a significant step forward. It was decided that meetings should in future be held regularly, every four years, and that in view of the standing of the self-governing Colonies the conferences should be styled "Imperial", while the British Prime Minister should preside over them, and no longer merely the Colonial Secretary. A permanent secretariat was also to be established, though only within the framework of the Colonial Office. Britain, in short, while paying a tribute of respect to her growing family, was not willing to spend much on its organization: it was not until 1925 that a Dominions Office was set up. Nevertheless, some regular means of discussion and consultation was being devised, though the fundamental problems of defence and unity still remained unsettled. Local defence and avoidance of European commitments were weighing heavily with the Dominions, as we can now begin to call them. Canada was planning the creation of her own navy, and had taken over the old Royal Navy dockyards at Halifax and Esquimault, while Australia, despite discouragement from the Committee of Imperial Defence, was also planning naval development. New Zealand for the present continued her subsidy to imperial defence funds which, indeed, she increased substantially, but within a few years she also was intent on building her local naval force. Attitudes were soon to change under the stimulus of growing tension with Germany, but for the present the danger was not imminent, and there was no agreement as to how the Dominions could steer clear of "continental troubles". Canada preferred not to be drawn into any discussion of Britain's problems of foreign policy, lest she be committed in some way: as Laurier argued at the 1911 conference:

> We may give advice if our advice is sought; but if your advice is sought, or if you tender it, I do not think the United Kingdom can undertake to carry out this advice unless you are prepared to back that advice with all your strength.[18]

Canada, Laurier then added, did not feel herself bound to take part in every war in which Britain might be involved, and therefore left the responsibility for major questions of policy to "the chief partner of the family, the one who has to bear the burden in part on some occasions, and the whole burden on perhaps other occasions".

## THE DEVELOPMENT OF DOMINION ATTITUDES

Canada, however, was conscious all the time of the additional security which she gained from her powerful neighbour. Australia and New Zealand took a somewhat different line. In 1906, following the course to which they had so often objected in the past, Britain had made an agreement with France about the New Hebrides without any consultation with the two Dominions, and there was concern lest this should continue to be the practice on even more serious issues. Australia and New Zealand both felt that they should be able to make representations when their local interests were involved—a point that Britain conceded in 1911—but, unlike Canada, both realized that they would have no freedom of choice if Britain were actually involved in war. Joseph Ward of New Zealand expressed their dilemma at the 1907 conference in the words, "We want a distinct line of demarcation between the responsibility we accept of our own free will and the responsibility which may be imposed on us without prior discussion."[19]

However great her unconscious reliance on the United States, Canada's was at the time the more realistic view, despite the legal anomaly that might have arisen had she endeavoured to take no active part in a British war. Whatever their opinion of the conduct of British foreign policy, none of the Dominions yet possessed the power and influence to justify participation in the shaping of policy. Their best hope lay in the spirit of British policy, in the expectation that if war came it would be over an issue which, as Reid had suggested in 1897, would "make the people one". So it was in 1914, when, although the responsibility for decisions rested solely with Britain, all the Dominions rallied immediately and unhesitatingly to her support. The dilemma resolved itself, and it was not until the post-war years that it had to be faced again. Britain then learnt not to move in any matter affecting peace and war without prior consultation. It was, however, the episodes of Chanak (1922), Locarno (1925) and Munich (1938) that then proved of greater moment than any conference of the pre-war period, at least before 1911. The policy finally worked out was a fusion of Laurier's approach with Ward's: in the main the Dominions continued to accept Britain's lead, but reserved judgment on matters that did not seem directly to affect them, and offered advice only when they could accept responsibility. That, however, is all part of another story.

## THE CONFERENCES OF 1909 AND 1911

Even before the first properly-styled Imperial Conference met in 1911 the international situation had deteriorated still further with the Bosnian crisis of 1908–09 and the "scare" over the suspected acceleration of Germany's naval building, intensified by the agitation for *Dreadnoughts* in Britain which is associated with the patriotic slogan of the hour, "We want eight and we won't wait". Anglo-German relations had now reached such a pitch that every argument used to justify increased naval construction in one country inevitably based itself on the similarly increased construction of the other, and served only to heighten the tension. The situation was sufficiently alarming for a special imperial conference on defence to be summoned in London in 1909, and the Dominion representatives who attended it were also present at a meeting of the Committee for Imperial Defence. Australia and New Zealand were torn between anxiety for their local defence position and concern for the maintenance of British naval superiority in home waters. Canada determined to push ahead with her own navy, though differences over policy and the change-over from Laurier's ministry to Borden's in 1911 made little progress possible before 1914. Australian ships were, however, laid down in Britain in 1910, and New Zealand spontaneously decided to present a battleship to the home country. The Australian ships were intended for service in Australian waters, though they were to be at the Admiralty's disposal in time of war. Nevertheless, it was beginning to be realized that the whole future of the Empire and of its constituent parts turned on the fortunes of the naval rivalry in the North Sea, and when the 1911 conference met it went into a joint session with the Committee for Imperial Defence at which the British Foreign Secretary, Sir Edward Grey, surveyed the whole field of foreign policy. It was the first occasion on which the Dominions had been admitted to the inner thoughts of the British Cabinet: the time had come, it has neatly been said, for the children to be told "the facts of life".[20] Nineteen-eleven saw also the last attempt to interest Britain and the Dominions in proposals for imperial federation. It fell flat, for the time for such proposals had long since passed: the international crisis was doing more for imperial unity than federation could ever have done.

There were to be many doubts and difficulties before 1914, but after 1911 it was clear that in essentials the Empire was one. Asquith, as British Prime Minister, admitted in 1912 that, in view of the share that the Dominions were taking in imperial defence, "they should be entitled to be heard in the determination of the policy and in the direction of Imperial affairs". For their part the Dominions, whatever their local preoccupations, accepted the blunt view of the situation which was put forward by Winston Churchill in 1914:

Two or three Australian and New Zealand Dreadnoughts, if brought into line in the decisive theatre, might turn the scale. . . . The same two or three Dreadnoughts in Australian waters would be useless the day after the defeat of the British Navy in home waters. Their existence would only serve to prolong the agony without altering the course of events.[21]

Borden, in presenting his own naval policy to the Canadian House of Commons two years before, had made a similar point, not improbably under Churchillian inspiration, though it was not one which his political opponents altogether accepted:

> it is the general naval supremacy of the Empire which primarily safeguards the Overseas Dominions. New Zealand's battleship is ranged in line with the other British battleships in the North Sea because there New Zealand's interests may be best guarded by protecting the very heart of the Empire.[22]

## UNITY IN DIVERSITY

Security and sentiment alike eventually dictated the course which the Dominions followed. Where every approach to imperial unity through reason, argument or principle had failed, the very logic of events was decisive: 1914 saw the British people, in Reid's fine phrase of 1897, "one in the sense of sacrifice". No machinery had been devised, or could be devised, however, to ensure unity of purpose while giving the Dominions scope for the expression of their own viewpoints as autonomous States: not until 1926, indeed, was the essence of the Commonwealth relationship summed up in a formula. Yet in practice unity in diversity was achieved, though achieved only when it was needed. If the British Empire before 1914 was an organization, it was an easy-going organization—until the time of need. In the face of the problems and dangers that confronted them the Dominions, while asserting their individuality and independence, had recognized the necessity for close, if informal, co-operation. Indeed, by a natural inversion, which few in Britain ever grasped, though they resented any suggestion of dependence, their very insistence on autonomy made it easier for them to seek, as *partners*, the co-operation which their security demanded. Britain for her part was slowly admitting them to a voice in her councils, and recognizing, in typical British style, that effective unity in action was to be preferred to a constitutional formula which would have been foreign to British political practice. There was after all no dilemma: the Empire need neither federate nor disintegrate, though none could say how the third course ultimately followed was to be described. The whole issue was finally evaded in the recognition of the existence—there was no "creation"—of a "Commonwealth", a Commonwealth, as a New Zealand historian much quoted in these pages has justly remarked, "whose precise nature belied the prophets as it defies the categories of traditional political theory".[23] But this in 1914 still lay in the future.

REFERENCES

1.  *British Documents on the Origins of the War, 1898–1914,* III, p. 403.
2.  *My Musical Life,* ch. V.
3.  See Professor N. H. Gibbs: *The Origins of Imperial Defence.*
4.  Ed. A. B. Keith: *Selected Speeches and Documents on British Colonial Policy, 1763–1917,* II, p. 333.
5.  K. Sinclair: *Imperial Federation,* p. 18.
6.  *The Origins of Imperial Defence,* p. 13.
7.  E. L. Woodward: *Great Britain and the German Navy,* p. 392.
8.  *Cambridge History of the British Empire: New Zealand,* p. 218.
9.  J. E. Tyler: *The Struggle for Imperial Unity, 1868–1895,* p. 126.
10. The New Zealand attitude is well described in Dr. Keith Sinclair's study, *Imperial Federation.*
11. *The Struggle for Imperial Unity,* p. 157.
12. *Imperial Federation,* p. 28.
13. *Life of Joseph Chamberlain,* Vol. III (J. L. Garvin), p. 191.
14. ibid., Vol. IV (J. Amery), p. 426.
15. *Imperial Federation,* p. 29.
16. The quotations from Chamberlain's speeches are taken from Vol. IV of his *Life,* pp. 339, 356 and 357.
17. *Great Britain and the German Navy,* p. 391.
18. R. M. Dawson: *The Development of Dominion Status, 1900–1936,* p. 11.
19. *Imperial Federation,* p. 40.
20. W. K. Hancock: *Survey of British Commonwealth Affairs,* I, p. 63.
21. *Speeches and Documents on British Colonial Policy,* II, p. 353.
22. ibid., p. 326.
23. *Imperial Federation,* p. 51.

# XII

## SOUTH AFRICA

### Briton, Boer and Bantu

#### Briton and Boer in History

SOUTH AFRICA, it has been said, is "more haunted by history than any other Dominion".[1] For considerably more than a century now it has been the battleground of two cultures, sundered by divergent loyalties—on two occasions to the point of war—and still uncertain of the outcome. And the struggle has been carried on amid a preponderance of coloured peoples, whose home South Africa equally is, but who, whatever their intellectual attainments and potentialities, are largely without the means of assisting to shape their own destinies and who, though they outnumber the white population by almost three to one, are hardly recognized as South Africans at all. Compared with South Africa's the history of Australia and New Zealand is almost an empty page, and even Canada can point to no more than the now unvexed issues of the rights of the *Canadiens* and of relations with the U.S.A. Overconsciousness of historical grievances, however understandable, is a dangerously narrowing influence, as the record of Ireland shows: the British people, one shrewd critic has argued, have owed much to their habit of forgetting the more recent past and assuming that "everything before that was a win for our side".[2] To Afrikaners, however, remote in all respects from the Europe from which they originally sprang, and intent, as they have always been, upon building up, amid the ocean of black, a white stronghold in which their culture could rest secure, relations with Britain over a century and a half have been the source of many painful memories to swell national pride and embitter relations. The Cape had been seized by Britain from the Dutch in the Napoleonic wars, to protect its communications with India, and had become formally British at the end of the war. Since then, from the "Slagtersnek rebellion" of 1815, with its unhappy sequel of hangings, through the Great Trek of the 'thirties and the loss of Natal to the British in the following decade, through the vacillating treatment of the Boer Orange River settlement by Britain, the annexation of Basutoland (1868), of the diamond fields (1871) and of the Transvaal (1877), the "First Boer War" of 1880-81 and the "Jameson Raid" (New Year, 1896), to the tragedy of the "Second Boer War" (1899–1902), the Afrikaners (Boers) had been presented with grievances enough, though rather, as will be seen, by blunders and stupidity than by sinister design. Chief among the grievances, and running like a thread through all the rest, was the fact that, try as they would, the Boers had been unable to put themselves beyond the reach of British interference. The Great Trek had been a desperate attempt to get far beyond the frontiers of government, for their independence of spirit made them both resentful of authority and unable effectively to combine against it. Of that spirit a South African writer, Stuart Cloete, himself of Afrikaner descent, has written in his vivid novel of the Trek, *Turning Wheels*, published in 1938:

> In this lay the great strength of this nation, their capacity for decentralization; in it lay also their weakness. For so competent were they as individuals that they hesitated to combine even when it was necessary to do so; acknowledging no man their master, each wished to lead and declined to follow.

The history of the most distant settlement of the Voortrekkers, the South African Republic (Transvaal), is a gloss on this judgment, yet there was no escape. British authority was unable to stay its hand, and frontiers pressed after the Boers until, with the discovery of diamonds and gold in the very territories in which they had taken refuge, not merely British influence but the economic interest of the whole western world broke in upon them. When, at the end of the century, the decisive struggle took place that brought the whole of South Africa under British sovereignty, the Afrikaner, compelled to accept the physical facts of defeat and absorption into the British system, again eluded control by returning to the spiritual and cultural springs of his life, and built up a new nationalism that was Afrikaner in its essentials and that was to make in time of his despised *taal*, Afrikaans, a State language. The unfolding South African nationalism and republicanism of recent years have been, indeed, the modern counterparts of the Great Trek and the resistance to British infiltration that followed it.

## BOER ATTITUDES

The Voortrekkers were an extreme expression of the Boer spirit. Many Boers there were who remained at the Cape, and, whatever their leanings towards republicanism and their indifference to British rule, accepted the necessity for co-operation if the colony were to flourish: Jan Hofmeyr (1845–1909) was their first great spokesman. But those beyond the frontiers who were engaged in subjecting the natives and carving out their own free Republics, represented the spirit and conscience of a hardy people, morally toughened by their narrow faith in Old Testament doctrines, untouched by widening contact and culture; Puritan survivals into new times and conditions. Their ties of blood with their kinsmen at the Cape were close, and the pull of blood and of creed was strong. The internal politics of the Cape and the relations between the British and the Boer Republics were therefore interlocked. There was in fact a fourfold problem for Britain. British troops and settlers had to be introduced to guarantee the colony's security, and Boer and British at the Cape had to learn to work together. The third problem was that of relations with the Republics: were they, could they, be left to their own devices, as agreed by the Conventions of 1852 and 1854? Above all, however—or rather, underlying all—was the dark shadow of the native races. Disagreement with the Afrikaner view of native policy was a constant source of conflict. To the Boer the problem was a simple one, for which he looked to the Old Testament for guidance: the natives were the children of Ham, "hewers of wood and drawers of water for the congregation, and for the altar of the Lord, even unto this day" (Joshua ix, 27). A major cause of the Great Trek had been resentment and fear at the equality between black and white which the British administration seemed to be encouraging under the pressure of missionary teaching in Africa and of liberalism at home. It was not, a Trekker complained, the freedom of the natives through the abolition of slavery that moved her people to their pilgrimage, but "their being placed on an equal footing with Christians, contrary to the laws of God and the natural distinction of race and religion". The attitude was embodied in the first constitution of the Transvaal (1856):

> The people desire to permit no equality between coloured people and the white inhabitants of the country, either in Church or State."

This denial of equality under all conditions represented to the Afrikaner the only certain means of ensuring not only white leadership but the very existence of a white society among the dark hordes, and was both buttressed and inspired by appeals to Scripture: where the New Testament was quoted, "in My Father's house are many mansions" was the favoured text.[3] Stiffened by insecurity and by the long struggle with Britain the inequality has persisted, with almost undiminished force, into our own day, to be given a new access of bitterness by the Second World War, when Afrikaner extremists openly approved of Nazism and its racial policy.

## British Policy: The Cape Tradition

It could not be pretended that British settlers were always and necessarily more liberal in their attitude, but the policy of the British government from the first favoured racial equality. At the Cape was passed in 1828, six years before the abolition of slavery, the famous "Ordinance 50", which gave to the coloured people in the colony almost the same legal status as whites. In 1853, when the colony received self-government, it was instructed that all the Queen's subjects, "without distinction of class or colour, should be united by one bond of loyalty and a common interest", and it carried Ordinance 50 to a logical conclusion by conferring the franchise upon all, white and coloured alike, who could satisfy the necessary modest qualifications of householding or salaried status. This measure particularly favoured the "Cape Coloured", the descendants of mixed marriages of European, African (Bantu or Hottentot) and Asiatic (Indian or Malay) of an earlier period, and an important element in Cape society, but it did not exclude such pure Bantu as could qualify. The qualification was raised in 1892, but the principle of equality for all men, of whatever race, of equal standing, and, from now on, of equal educational attainment, was preserved. There were hopes when the Union of 1910 was being framed that this long-established equality might be extended to the whole country, but Afrikaner principles eventually prevailed. The privileged equality of the Bantu ("Native") at the Cape disappeared in 1936, and steps have been taken more recently to lower also the status of the more strongly entrenched "Cape Coloured".

## THE ELEMENT OF FEAR

Opposing principles apart, equality between white and coloured was one thing at the Cape, where most coloured people were Europeanized and where the disproportion of numbers was not too marked. It seemed another matter in the interior of the country, where Boer and British alike were conscious of the masses of primitive people around them and still more so of the millions who lay beyond, to the north. The personal courage of the Afrikaners who pressed forward into the unknown was unquestionable, and in keeping with their hardiness and their unyielding Calvinist spirit: it was shown in many gallant actions, and has caused them to be regarded by Afrikaner nationalists of our own day as the true founders of a South African nation. Yet with their attitude to the peoples of the lands they occupied, an attitude inspired by the example of the Jews of old who fell upon Canaan, went a measure of insecurity, even of fear, to stiffen the traditional doctrine. Hence the unbending refusal to make concessions lest they end in the destruction or absorption of the white population. "Half the cruelty and injustice to a native race arises from fear" was the opinion of Lord Carnarvon in 1874, when, as Colonial Secretary, he pondered South Africa's problems.[4]

## POLICY IN NATAL

In Natal, which became the most purely British region of South Africa, policy was derived from British principles and the practice of the Cape, modified to suit the circumstances of a vast preponderance of black people, still in a primitive state of society, over white settlers. The colony had been annexed in 1843, when most of the Boers thereupon left, and was granted Crown Colony status, with an elected Legislative Council of limited powers, in 1856, when the white population was but 8,000. The earlier Bantu population had been largely destroyed or scattered by Zulu raids, but with peace and white settlement the broken tribes poured in in their tens of thousands, to outnumber the whites for some years by twenty to one, though the proportion settled eventually at about ten to one. Here was a new problem, far more difficult of solution than that at the Cape, and it was tackled in a way that took into account the primitive conditions of most of the Bantu people. The majority of the Bantu were left under native law, in large reservations governed by chiefs with the assistance of white magistrates and under the paternal eye of "Somtseu", the able and devoted Secretary for Native Affairs, Theophilus Shepstone (1817–93), and annual grants were made to be spent for the benefit of the native peoples. The whole policy was, in effect, one of racial differentiation, but it was not discrimination: a monogamous Bantu could claim exemption from tribal law, and the franchise qualification for the Legislative Council was low and not exclusive. Yet few natives ever could, or did, take advantage of the concessions open to them. Not a single Bantu had claimed exemption by 1876, and there were never more than two or three on the electoral roll.

## THE "IMPERIAL FACTOR"

Nevertheless, by contrast with the danger and insecurity of earlier years the native peoples gained from the settled order which had been established, no less, of course, by Boer than by Briton. Twenty years after her death, in consequence, "the great majority of Natives", a distinguished South African has written, "persisted in regarding Queen Victoria as the sole source of their meagre political blessings".[5] The native problem was not, however, solved: indeed, it remains to this pay unsolved. With so vast a coloured population to live with, and so varied a pattern of native policies, some uniform system was essential. Hence the intervention of the "imperial factor" into South African affairs, the policy of the imperial government which sought to impose its own liberal outlook and hoped to achieve it by a unification of the various States and colonies. Unification in some form, it was hoped, would both give security against the natives through the strength of unity, and, by the same token, reduce imperial charges and responsibilities for the maintenance of armed forces in South Africa, removing, as Carnarvon's Parliamentary Under-Secretary argued, "the liability under which we labour of spending our blood and our money upon these wretched Kaffir quarrels".[6] Much more of blood and money were in fact to be poured out before the liability was surrendered, but Carnarvon himself was hopeful of wider results. "The union of the States," he wrote in 1874, in a despatch already quoted, "would give a consciousness of strength which *might perhaps* go some way to make a humaner and kindlier (policy towards the natives) more likely." Native policy was therefore, as he realized only too well, "the key to South African politics". Others were, however, less certain of the results. Carnarvon's own Permanent Under-Secretary at the Colonial Office, Sir R. Herbert, took the view that "a strong South African Federation will be disposed to legislate unfairly and oppressively on Native Affairs", and feared that "we shall almost certainly come into collision with it on these subjects".[7] Time has justified his doubts. Yet the imperial government could not both grant autonomy and retain control over so vital a section of public policy. When Union was finally established the two Afrikaner Provinces, Transvaal and Orange Free State, retained unmodified their restrictions on native advancement, and it was the Cape policy that was put on the defensive. Since then, despite all the hopes and fears of many well-meaning men who have struggled with the racial issue, it has been the exclusive policy that has won the day: the steady whittling away of the Cape tradition has been "the most significant phenomenon in the history of race relations in South Africa".[8]

## THE ELEMENT OF ECONOMICS

There was, however, much more than insecurity and fear in the attitude of Afrikaners and of many European settlers to natives. The labour of the coloured people was essential to the settlers' prosperity. The Boer farmer, much as he might despise the Bantu among whom he lived, needed their menfolk, if not as hewers of wood and drawers of water, then as stock-men and tillers of the soil, and the women as servants in the house. When mineral wealth came to be exploited the need was even greater. Without such labour South Africa, with a white population only some half-million larger than that of New Zealand, in an area nearly five times as great, could not have developed its resources and achieved the standard of living which the majority of its citizens enjoy. There was, in fact, throughout most of the nineteenth century, little to attract settlers in large numbers to South Africa. Many realized that without extensive immigration from Britain the British hold could be maintained only with difficulty, but for the most part the emigrant ships, when they rounded the Cape, preferred to journey as far again, to Australia and New Zealand, where conditions of life were more congenial, the soil was, in the main, more fruitful and, after the 'seventies at least, there was no native problem to cause concern. As a result, South Africans of British stock today number less than the New Zealanders. South Africa's large-scale immigration came, however, from *within*: "her immigrants were black".[9] Racial superiority therefore combined with economic need to maintain the natives in a position of dependence. There was no exclusive "White South Africa" policy on the lines of "White Australia", for the coloured people were already present, in vast numbers, but their presence, vital though it was to the economy, could be otherwise ignored: socially and politically, ex-cept at the Cape, and to a lesser extent in Natal, they did not exist.

## "SEGREGATION" AND THE MIXED RACIAL ECONOMY

Yet "segregation", so much talked of in recent years, and long practised in Natal's "reserves", is unrealizable, for without Bantu labour South African industry, in particular, could hardly continue. It is, in fact, rather a state of mind than a policy. Earlier the problem was less to exclude the Bantu than to encourage him to take a place, albeit a humble one, in South African life. He might need, as in Natal and in the reservations later established by the Cape, careful handling in territory of his own, and protection against such evils as drink and guns, but it was believed that in time his level of culture could be raised and that contact with European standards of life would tend to elevate him. Shepstone's view of the problem was set out in a special Memorandum in 1850:[10]

> Whilst humanity and especially the injunctions of our religion compel us to recognize in the Natives the capability of being elevated to perfect equality, social and political, with the White Man, yet it is as untrue as it would be unwise to say that the Native is . . . in his present state, capable of enjoying or even understanding the civil and political rights of the White Man.

This "protective segregation" was inadequate both for the natives, as population pressure increased in the Natal reserves, and for the whites, who, controlling as they did most of the best land, needed labour to help them work it. But the Bantu exodus from the reserves was at first slow, and in the 'sixties the settlers began to introduce Indian workers, thereby laying up for themselves yet another vexed racial problem for future South Africans to tackle. Yet, unless far greater resources could be devoted to the educational advancement of the natives than the settlers were able, or willing, to spare, the natives could achieve little advancement while still within their reserves and maintaining traditional ways of life. The missionaries in the schools did much, but their means also were limited. Inevitably natives sought work, and settlers sought to attract them. "If Kaffirs only knew the advantages of serving under white masters," wrote a Cape farmer in the 'eighties, "they would gain more civilization in one year than they do from missionaries in fifty."[11] The problem was to arouse the desire for civilization and its advantages in a people with simple wants, accustomed to an extensive economy, to moving on to fresh land when grazing and other resources were exhausted, and kept down in numbers by inter-tribal warfare. The demands of taxation and the desire for European goods could do much, but with peace and the restriction of the land available the pressure of population did more. Numbers of natives were drawn first into the agricultural and then, with the mineral discoveries, into the industrial life of South Africa, until today more than half of the country's black population is living, not to itself in reserves, but in close contact with the white minority, and especially in and around the industrial centres. Without their help, indeed, the progress of the mines would have been seriously impeded, unless enough immigrant white labour could have been found. "What an abundance of rain and grass was to New Zealand mutton, what a plenty of cheap grazing land was to Australian wool, what the fertile prairie acres were to Canadian wheat, cheap native labour was to South African mining and industrial enterprise."[12] The reserves overspilled, and tribal life was broken. And in industry as elsewhere, the colour bar was applied, to ensure that the advantages which a prosperous industry might bring should be mainly reserved for Europeans. Hence the blunt statement of the General Secretary of the Miners' Union in 1914:[13]

> If Australia can keep out the Chinamen . . . can, on long lines of sound policy, build up a nation on a high standard of civilization, we have the same right here. . . . The Kaffir ousted the aboriginals . . . and we are now trying to oust the Kaffir from those spheres of industry which we maintain are the proper sphere of the white man.

Native wages were therefore lower than those for Europeans, for whom, in any case, the skilled occupations were reserved. The movement "from barbarism to pauperism"[14] had begun, and South Africa was before long to be faced with an *urban* coloured proletariat which has given to "segregation" a new significance in our own day. The result has been the formation of a "mixed" society, which yet does not mix, except on the plane of economics.

## *Apartheid*—AND ITS LIMITATIONS

Shepstone's aim has therefore been reversed. In the name of white security and supremacy, the "present state" of the native has been accepted as his permanent condition. He is to be helped to develop in his own communities and along his own lines—and South Africa in more recent times has not been ungenerous in the material help given, even if this has still failed to meet the immense need—but his position is to be one of permanent inferiority and dependence. Yet the past century has shown the indispensability of black labour to South Africa's advancement. In the forthright words of the 1948

Report of the South African Government's Native Laws
Commission:[15]

> It is a fact—and must be accepted as such, whether we think it
> desirable or not—that the economic structure of South Africa is based
> on the one hand on European initiative, organization and technical
> skill, on the other hand no less on the availability of a few million
> Native labourers.

Earlier observers did not err in seeing native policy as the key
to South African politics. In the long run—and modern South
Africa is a fairly recent creation—it is of greater significance
than the struggle between British and Boer which has for so
long dominated the scene.

### AFRIKANER NATIONALISM AND AFRIKAANS

Fundamental to Boer relations with British and Bantu alike
has been the conception of a purely South African nationalism,
Afrikaner in historical origin and recognizing no home but
South Africa. This conception had its origins in the long years
of Anglo-Boer suspicion and hostility, especially after the
annexation of the Transvaal in 1877, years that were succeeded,
despite the victory of 1881, by the defeat of 1902. The British,
secure in the satisfaction of victory, hastened after 1902 to
give the conquered Afrikaner an equal place in what was
nevertheless a British South Africa. Many Boer leaders, chief
among them Botha and Smuts, rose to the opportunity, and
made their distinguished mark, not only in South Africa but in
the Empire as a whole, contributing not a little to the growing
conception of Commonwealth. Others, however, nursed their
grievances and turned to past successes to nourish their
injured pride. Foremost among them was General J. B. M.
Hertzog (1866–1942), who regained for the Afrikaners their
pride and self-respect as a nation apart. For him and his
followers the Voortrekker "South African Republic" of the
Transvaal became the golden age of South African history.
Until the annexation of 1877 English had been freely used in
the Republic, but in the years that followed it had been
increasingly replaced by Dutch and Afrikaans, while at the
same time amendments to the Cape constitution had put Dutch
on an equal footing with English in politics, education and law.
After the South African war, and largely under the inspiration

of Hertzog, the Moses of his people, there was a reaction to the crude, simplified Dutch of the farmers, Afrikaans, once despised but increasingly adopted since the 'seventies, and now held in honour as the symbol of Boer hopes of freedom. Gradually Afrikaans was welded into a literary medium, and in 1925, with Hertzog now Prime Minister, it became an official language of the Union.

## THE BRITISH ATTITUDE TO THE BOER

Yet the British during the nineteenth century were often slow to appreciate the tenacity and essential qualities of the Boers, so different from their own. If the Cape Dutch towns-folk were a cultivated people, accepted as equals, there was often not a little scorn for the primitive Boer of the veld, scorn which found its most unfortunate—and most speedily avenged —expression among professional soldiers, who, as the two Boer wars showed, hopelessly misjudged their opponents' skill. The misjudgment was general between 1877 and 1881 among the British officials who administered the erstwhile Republic, and contributed not a little to the failure of annexation. The Transvaal leaders, among them the redoubtable Paul Kruger, "unprepossessing ordinary looking men whose services it did not seem important to win",[16] were seriously underestimated. The springs of South Africa's future lay in the Republic, but to the educated and liberal-minded politicians and administrators from London, and even from the Cape, it was in 1877 a miserable backwater, inhabited by uncouth and simple, if cantankerous, farmers.

How general this attitude was at the time is revealed by an episode of her childhood recounted by Olive Schreiner, the Anglo-German South African whose *Story of an African Farm*, first published in 1883, stands as one of the masterpieces of the literature not merely of South Africa but of the whole world. To her, when a child, a Boer child presented a handful of sugar, which, however, she threw away, fearing that it might contaminate her.[17]

## THE BRITISH DUAL LOYALTY

What, above all, has made a mutual understanding difficult has been the British conception of a double loyalty,

to Britain no less than to South Africa, which Afrikaners, with
no roots left in Europe, could hardly but resent. Sir James
Rose Innes (1855-1942), who, after a political career at the
Cape, was for many years a notable Chief Justice of the Union,
has described in his autobiography the differing traditions in
which he and young Boers of his age were brought up. To the
Boers the Great Trek was an event of historic significance:
James Innes's schooling largely ignored it, and concentrated
upon the history of Britain and the geography of Europe. By
the time the troubled 'seventies had arrived, "distinctions of
race had been accentuated by conflicting historical traditions".[18] South Africa had two streams of white origin, British
and Boer, but one of the streams rose in Britain, far from
South Africa, and increasingly there have been Afrikaners
who have held the view that to the British South Africa is
still not a true home but only the "Tavern of the Seas".[19]
The British in South Africa, the argument runs, must decide
where they belong, and, if they are to be regarded as South
African, must determinedly throw in their lot with the
Afrikaner. *"Die Afrikanerdom is vir ons die Volk van Suid-
Afrika"*, wrote an Afrikaner extremist in 1941 (it would seem
inappropriate to quote him in anything but the original
Afrikaans); *"en die res van die Suid-Afrikaners is, vir sover
hulle blank is, òf potensiële Afrikaners, òf vreemdelinge"* ("For us
Afrikanerdom is the People of South Africa, and the rest of the
South Africans are, as far as they are white, either potential
Afrikaners, or aliens").[20] This was an extreme view, but it
reflected the continuing division in South African life, the fruit
of many years of long past misunderstanding and mishandling
on both sides.

## The Contrast with Canada

The contrast with Canada, where, also, the British found
themselves associated with a virile people of another culture,
now equally divorced from their European origins, is an
instructive one, not merely to be explained by the differing
relative strengths. The *Canadiens* would seem at first sight to be
the Boers of Canada, the original settlers, now caught up by
force of circumstances in the British imperial system. But the
*Canadiens* were in a minority, concentrated largely in one

Province, Quebec, whereas the Boers were scattered throughout South Africa, apart from Natal, and outnumbered the
British by three to two. Natal, indeed, with its white population
almost entirely British, has tended to play in South African
affairs the part of Quebec in Canada, the dissident voice,
jealous of its distinctive character, though unable effectively
to control the course of events. Canada, however, has had no
colour problem to grapple with. If in South Africa Lord
Durham might again have found "two nations warring in the
bosom of a single state", it would have been in the presence of a
third. The imperial power intervened in Canada to lessen its
own responsibilities and to make possible an agreement for
union on which the Canadians themselves had already largely
decided. In South Africa, on the other hand, the presence of
millions of coloured folk made the "imperial factor" necessarily more potent and more active. From the 'seventies
onwards the imperial government sought South African
unity, believing that only through unity could be found
security for the British position and a liberal policy for the
coloured peoples. Yet, as in Canada, when union was finally
achieved, it took charge of the situation, obliterating the fact
of Boer defeat as effectively as earlier it had overlaid the events
which had left the *Canadiens* British subjects. From among the
defeated Boer leaders were to spring such men as Botha,
Smuts and Reitz, who made themselves imperial figures while
they remained good South Africans, and who saw all South
Africans as one. The analogy with such distinguished *Canadiens*
as Laurier, Lapointe, and St. Laurent is an obvious one. There,
however, the analogy ends. Botha and Smuts were men of
broad views who adjusted themselves to the new situation.
Other Afrikaners there were, such as Hertzog, no less able but
narrower in outlook and unwilling to merge Afrikanerdom
in a joint South Africa. For their part the British in South
Africa have never produced, since Rhodes, men of the stamp
of Macdonald, Borden and Mackenzie King in Canada.
They have been, in fact, as one among them has argued,
"laggards in politics, too preoccupied with business to challenge the solid front" of Afrikanerdom,[21] and they have
thereby given some handle to the accusation that their interest
in South Africa is a limited one.

## New Problems: the Basutos—Diamonds

It was the discovery of diamonds in 1868-69 that set South Africa on its modern phase of development, and presented Briton, Boer, and Bantu alike with fresh problems of adjustment. Taken together with the crisis in the affairs of the Basuto people which led to their being placed under British protection in 1868, the discoveries brought to an end the period of British abstention from affairs beyond the Orange River which had been opened by the Bloemfontein and Sand River Conventions (1852 and 1854). Abstention proved an impossible policy, for British interest and interests could not stop at the River, but its reversal inevitably caused suspicions to arise that were to prove unhappy auguries for future relations. The territories involved in the new moves lay to east and west of the Orange Free State—Basutoland to the east, between the Free State and Natal; the diamond-field territory, Griqualand West, to the west, north of the Cape's frontier and athwart its route to the interior, the famous "missionary road" along which Robert Moffatt (1795-1883), his even more famous son-in-law, David Livingstone, and many others had travelled. This was the route which Rhodes was later to follow in his grandiose imperial schemes, the "bottle-neck" between the Transvaal on the east and the Kalahari Desert on the west which was to be part of the "all-red route" from the Cape through Rhodesia to Cairo. It was also the route on which, when he was travelling along it in 1853, Livingtsone had had trouble with Boer frontiersmen over the treatment of natives, an episode which had but served to confirm British suspicions of Boer native policy.

## Basutoland

Basutoland was first in dispute. The Basutos were the relics of tribes shattered by Zulu and Matabele power, welded into a unity by a great leader, Moshesh, whose career and abilities challenged the view that the Bantu were an inferior people. Frontier warfare over land had been going on between them and the Boers of the Orange Free State for many years, and Moshesh had repeatedly called upon Britain for protection. In the 'sixties the Boers came near to breaking his power, and in 1868 Britain stepped in, though with little enthusiasm, to annex what was left of Basuto territory and preserve it for the tribe. Moshesh died at a great age in 1870, but had the satisfaction of seeing his people secure before he left them: "my country is your blanket", he wrote in graphic African style to Queen Victoria, "and my people the lice in it". The annexation came as a shock to the Boers, who had seen a solution to an old problem within their grasp. They kept the best of the Basuto land, but resented the loss of the rest, and the status of Basutoland has been a matter for dispute from 1868 to this day. The territory was handed over to the Cape in 1871, but the Basutos, preferring, as Moshesh had done, a more distant control, proved recalcitrant subjects, and in 1884 became once more an imperial Protectorate, a status which they retained, despite their position in the heart of the country, when South Africa became a Union in 1910, and one on which the British and South African Governments have for nearly half a century been unable to reach agreement. Whether, in the meantime, the British administration of Basutoland has been as effective as it might have been is another matter.

## GRIQUALAND AND DIAMONDS

More serious was the problem of Griqualand West. By the 'sixties Boer settlers, in their restless search for fresh land, were also moving into this region, which was part of the only considerable stretch of country still free for native occupation. A variety of treaties with native chieftains complicated such legal claims to the land as could be said to exist, though it was later discovered that, while Transvaal claims farther north were shaky, the Orange Free State case was in fact a good one. Into this complex situation burst from 1868 onwards a rush of diamond prospectors. Many of them were British subjects, and it seemed doubtful whether the Free State could cope with the situation, complicated as it was still further by the flow of migrant native labour to the diggings. Sir Henry Barkly, from 1870 to 1877 British High Commissioner in South Africa and Governor of the Cape, was resolved to set aside the limitations accepted in the agreements of 1852 and '54, and to intervene in Griqualand. A mixture of motives moved him, but he was not unmindful of the danger that with their new-won means of wealth the Republics might soon come to dominate the weak British settlements in the Cape and Natal, and like his predecessor, Sir Philip Wodehouse, who had annexed Basutoland, he was concerned lest all the land still unsettled should pass out of native occupation. He persuaded the Transvaal to submit its western frontier claims to arbitration, and when the decision went against the Republic he felt justified in taking a similar view of the Free State's frontier, and therefore annexed Griqualand (1871). It was an arbitrary move, for which he went beyond his instructions and which showed little appreciation of Boer claims and temper. Taken together with the annexation of Basutoland it marked an important reversal of British policy. The Free State eventually accepted £90,000 in compensation, but its confidence was shaken and it turned increasingly to its kinsmen across the Vaal. They in their turn began to cherish the notion of opening a back door for themselves, away from British interference. The opportunity presented itself in 1875 when the French President, arbitrating between British and Portuguese claims to disputed territory on the east coast, awarded Delagoa Bay to Portugal, though it was not until the means came with gold in the 'eighties that a railway to Lourenço Marques, on the Bay, could be built. Nevertheless, the diamond fields and the change in British policy had sown the seeds for much future trouble.

## CONSEQUENCES OF THE DIAMOND DISCOVERIES

The diggings had other consequences. They became the first basis of South Africa's modern prosperity, raising the means of what had been only modest settlements, and producing, to the present time, diamonds to the value of some £350,000,000. The whole economic life of South Africa was stimulated. Goods were imported in great quantities to meet the diggers' needs, and the import duties on them pushed up the revenues of the Cape and Natal to such an extent that rivalry for the lucrative trade, and the means of development which it would provide, became an additional argument for union. Moreover, the new traffic offset the losses in transit shipping occasioned by the opening of the Suez Canal and stimulated railway building, though the fluctuations in the world demand for diamonds, intensified by the world economic depression

Q

of the 'seventies, and the political troubles in South Africa in the late 'seventies, kept the Cape line from Kimberley until 1885. Meanwhile the difficulties and complexity of the diggings, as they penetrated deeper into the strange pipes of blue earth that bore the longed-for treasure, gradually removed the individual diggers and replaced them by powerful and competing corporations, led by men who were new phenomena not merely in South Africa but in the world at large—Rhodes, Alfred Beit, Barney Barnato, Julius Wernher, and the varied crowd of lesser lights who surrounded them—the supreme adventurers to date of capitalist enterprise. With the power and wealth which diamonds gave him Rhodes was to do strange things in the land of his adoption.

## THE "IMPERIAL FACTOR" AND NATAL: LANGALIBALELE

If the imperial government had intervened in Basutoland and Griqualand on behalf of the native peoples against the Boers, it was soon to show an impartial opposition to the treatment of natives by British settlers in Natal. There in 1873 a minor chieftain, Langalibalele ("Longbelly" to many Europeans), after a technical breach of the laws relating to the posession of firearms, fled into Basutoland and resisted capture, several Europeans being killed in the pursuit. He was surrendered by the Basuto, tried by a special tribunal and sentenced to life imprisonment, while his tribe was broken up and dispossessed of its lands. The severity of the sentence was evidence of the jumpiness of the Natal colonists, for ever conscious of the dark masses around them and of the unbroken power of the Zulus across the Tugela River on their northern frontier, but their action was endorsed by the Parliament of the Cape, self-governing since 1872, which passed a special Act permitting Langalibalele to be held on an island off Cape Town. The event caused an outcry in Britain, and was to have momentous consequences. Lord Carnarvon had just taken office as Colonial Secretary on the formation of Disraeli's Ministry in February, 1874, and the case was, significantly enough, one of the first with which he had to deal. It was complicated by the decision of the Cape Parliament, but after lengthy and careful consideration Carnarvon took the risk of overriding the decision of a self-governing colony, denounced the "illegality, unwisdom and injustice" of the Natal proceedings and ordered Langalibalele's removal to the mainland. The Cape then unwillingly repealed its Act. The conclusion which Carnarvon himself drew from the episode was the need for a more uniform and more liberal native policy throughout South Africa. This, as has already been shown, he believed could be achieved only by a union of the various white settlements, a union which by ensuring their security would remove the element of fear from native policy. "The most immediately urgent reason for general union," he wrote, "is the formidable character of the native question, and the importance of a uniform, wise and strong policy in dealing with it."22

## The "Imperial Factor" and Federation: Lord Carnarvon

It is unnecessary to detail the stages by which Carnarvon sought to carry his federation policy. His arguments were eminently reasonable, but he gave an impression of haste and treated with insufficient consideration the personalities and principles involved. And although he had been Colonial Secretary in 1866-67, when the Canadian federation had been under consideration, he failed to realize that in South Africa he was trying to impose union from without, whereas Canada had in effect been united from within (as Australia and South Africa itself were later to be) before receiving the legal blessing of the imperial parliament. Above all, he was attempting a wellnigh impossible task without an adequate appreciation of the complex background. From the first he took the view that an effective federation was impossible unless the Boer Republics formed part of it. Yet at the same time he considered that federation would render possible a liberalizing of native policy. The two aims were hardly compatible, and the conduct of the Cape in the affair of Langalibalele had already shown, as Carnarvon's own Permanent Under-Secretary had realized, that a self-governing federation would take its own line on native policy. Events in 1876 seemed, however, to be playing into Carnarvon's hands. In that year the magniloquently-styled South African Republic of the Transvaal was involved in the latest of a series of "native wars" which seriously overstrained its meagre resources: the moment seemed ripe for lending a hand to the bankrupt Republic and bringing it into a union with the rest of South Africa.

## THE CRISIS OF THE TRANSVAAL

The Transvaal Boers were the toughest and most narrow exponents of Afrikanerdom, resentful of interference and government control and concerned only with the spreading of their lands. The proud name of "South African Republic" which they had adopted was indicative of their lofty ambitions, but, as a South African historian has pointed out, their settlements had not yet developed into a state.[23] There was much disunity among them and their stern republican virtues did not include the ready payment of tax dues. The Republic's finances were therefore in a shaky condition, and it seemed on the verge of collapse. The population was in all some 45,000, settled amid native peoples to ten times that number, and supplies of land were running out. Pressure was therefore kept up at the frontiers, and native tribes complained, in the words of one old chieftain, that "in a little while the Boers will not leave me room enough in which to stretch my legs".[24] To the east of the Republic lay the Zulus, now led by a powerful and ambitious chieftain, Cetywayo (of whom more was to be heard), the Swazis, and the Bapedi under their chief, Sekukuni. Trouble broke out with the Bapedi in 1876, and the fighting that resulted led the Republic to the verge of bankruptcy. A Cape Bank which had made substantial advances tried to foreclose, and the State Postmaster was reduced to taking his salary in stamps: it was clear that drastic measures were needed. In view of the rising tension among the tribes, which was intensified by a serious drought, a unified native policy seemed more than ever essential, and there was widespread criticism of the Transvaal's treatment of the Bapedi. A Cape newspaper, indeed, went so far as to compare the Republic, in its treatment of subject peoples, with Turkey, then the target of much execration on account of the "Bulgarian atrocities" of this same year.[25] In these circumstances Carnarvon pressed forward. He had no doubt that, given the opportunity, the Boers would be relieved to be taken over by Britain, and towards the end of 1876 Shepstone, whom he had been consulting in London, was sent back to carry through annexation. A few months later Sir Bartle Frere, a seemingly happy choice on account of his brilliant administrative career in India, followed to succeed Barkly as High Commissioner and establish a South African Federation: meanwhile, the necessary legislation was passed through Parliament. Two things, however, ruined the project, the failure to win the approval of the Boers, either before or after annexation, and the disastrous and costly Zulu War.

## THE FAILURE OF ANNEXATION: (1) BLUNDERS IN TRANSVAAL

The Transvaal annexation, after what Shepstone believed to be adequate investigation of the situation on the spot, was proclaimed in April, 1877. It was acquiesced in, not altogether unwillingly, by many, if not most, of the Boers, who were bewildered at the breakdown of their own government. Almost from the start, however, the British administration failed to take the measure of the sturdy independence of the people, and especially of such leaders as the uncouth but shrewd and capable Paul Kruger (1825-1904), who was now beginning to loom large in South African affairs. The Transvaal administration needed to be set on a sound footing, but the semi-autocratic methods that were appropriate in a British Crown Colony were unsuited to the free conditions of a Boer Republic. Rhodes, who had his own quarrels with imperial authority, complained that the annexed territory was run "on the lines of a second-rate regiment". The worst blunder, though one committed in good faith, was the failure to summon the popular Assembly, the *Volksraad*, in the hope of receiving an endorsement of the annexation, which in the early stages might well have been given, if only on terms. This failure vitiated the British administration from the first. Boer resentment slowly grew, and, despite Carnarvon's hopes, the alarming prospect of war in Europe over the Eastern Question severely limited the assistance that Britain could give. A grant of £100,000 was made, but this was soon swallowed up, and although the revenue rose from 12s. 6d. to £174,000 between 1877 and 1880 it was only at the price of strict tax-collection and Whitehall measures of economy and control that were duly resented by the easy-going Boers. An attempt was being made, in short, to modernize overnight an archaic and semi-anarchic system with which, on the whole, the population was well content. It could not be done, certainly not by foreigners, until the country had the far greater revenues which gold-mining was soon to provide.

## (2) The Zulu War, 1879

For a time it seemed that salvation might be found in an active native policy. Cetywayo had been reconstructing Zulu power with an army of some 35,000 young warriors, and was a standing threat to both the Transvaal and Natal. If the Zulu threat could be broken, British authority throughout South Africa would be enhanced, and both a federation and a unified native policy might be imposed. Unrest was growing on the frontiers of Zululand, and Frere took advantage of the situation to issue an ultimatum. When it expired, in January, 1879, Zululand was invaded: an easy success was expected. The first result, however, came within ten days, the disastrous reverse of Isandhlwana, when nearly a thousand officers and men of the 24th Foot (South Wales Borderers), with as many native auxiliaries, were caught carelessly in camp and slaughtered almost to a man, only one or two escaping. The disaster was redeemed by the gallant defence of Rorke's Drift by a handful of men, and by the crushing victory of Ulundi in June, but the blow to British prestige in South Africa, and to the Government at home, was severe. It was not lightened by the death of the Prince Imperial, son of Napoleon III, who had volunteered for the campaign and was killed in a minor skirmish while on patrol. The intervention of the "imperial factor" was proving costly.

South Africa, it has been said, "has advanced politically by disasters and economically by windfalls".[26] The Zulu War marked one of the turning points in politics. The imperial government had burnt its fingers, and Carnarvon was, in any case, no longer Colonial Secretary, having parted from Disraeli over the Eastern crisis. South African unification had to be abandoned for the present, and was never again to be possible under such comparatively favourable circumstances. Conquered Zululand was not annexed, but was divided into thirteen chieftainships, a standing invitation to dispute. Boer settlers soon moved into the western region of the country and established a "New Republic". To save the rest of the country it was finally annexed in 1887 and attached to Natal. So, half-heartedly, was Frere's aim achieved, but the other policies that he had hoped to advance were left in the air.

## (3) The Boer Recovery: Majuba (1881) and its Consequences

The Zulu defeat eased the position of the Transvaal, and made British protection more than ever unnecessary in the Boer view. Then in 1880 came the Liberal victory in Britain. Gladstone, who had spoken strongly on the subject of the annexation, took office pledged to undo the evil effects of "Beaconsfieldism", but he was unwilling to undo the annexation without guarantees on native policy, and had, in any case, much else to consider. In December, 1880, the Boers, however, impatiently revolted and proclaimed the Republic. Troops sent against them were badly handled by the Commander, Sir George Colley, who proved a poor match for Boer tactics and marksmanship, and a body of 350 was out-manœuvred and defeated on Majuba Hill (February, 1881): 92 British soldiers, including Colley himself, were killed, but though far fewer lives were lost the defeat was immeasurably more significant, and more disastrous for Britain, than Isandhl-wana. Gladstone had already decided on retrocession, and insisted that Majuba should not be avenged. By the Convention of Pretoria (July, 1881) the Transvaal was restored to inde-pendence. It was a courageous gesture which proved to be largely wasted on the proud and self-righteous Afrikaners, who were now convinced that the whole annexation policy had been an act of imperial banditry which only their own courage had repelled. Had the great number of British troops available been used to hold the country until terms could be reached, Majuba might have taken its place as an episode and a signi-ficant warning of Boer skill. As it was, it became, in the illuminating phrase of a subaltern who was wounded in the battle, and who afterwards achieved fame as General Sir Ian Hamilton, "a sort of Bunker Hill in Afrikander history for all time".[27] The memory of Majuba sustained Boer pride in later years and encouraged contempt of the British. It therefore contributed not a little to the more serious conflict of twenty years later, and it remains to this day a nationalist watchword. In the words of an American commentator, "Mr. Gladstone did the right thing at the wrong time."[28]

## THE CONVENTION OF PRETORIA, 1881

Nor did the terms of the Convention tend to sweeten relations. The Transvaal was declared to be independent, "subject to the suzerainty of Her Majesty", a vague but elastic term which, though a sop to British pride, left ample room for disagreement: its immediately practical importance was that it limited the Republic's scope in foreign relations. In addition to this formula a British Resident had to be accepted, and Britain retained the right to veto native legislation: this was the limit to which the long-standing hopes of an ameliorization of native policy had been reduced. The whole policy of ten years had, in fact, collapsed in ruins, and the rift between Briton and Boer was wider than ever. Well might Gladstone say, in presenting the Pretoria Convention to Parliament, that South Africa presented "the one great unsolved, perhaps unsolvable, problem of our colonial system".[29]

## THE CONVENTION OF LONDON, 1884

Only three years elapsed before the Convention was revised. It had been accepted in the Transvaal merely because its rejection would have meant the resumption of war, and there was from the first a demand for its revision in the direction of greater independence. In 1883 Kruger, who was now attaining the outstanding position that he was to hold until his unhappy exile in 1900, was elected to the Presidency of the Republic, and went to London to open negotiations. The Convention of London (February, 1884) followed. The Transvaal was recognized as the "South African Republic" and no reference was made to the hated "suzerainty": the veto on native legislation, which was in any case ineffective, was also withdrawn. In return the Republic agreed to admit Europeans to civil rights and equal taxation, and to make no treaties either with native tribes or with other States (with the sole exception of the Orange Free State) without British approval. Circumstances were to make both of these clauses points of some importance; none could foresee in 1884 the dramatic changes in the Republic's position, still weak and uncertain, which the gold discoveries were soon to bring.

## THE APPEARANCE OF NEW POWERS: S.W. AFRICA

Meanwhile the situation was already changing in other respects. The "scramble for Africa" was beginning, and Anglo-Boer relations, which had for so long partaken of the nature of a family dispute, found themselves involved in international politics. It is explained elsewhere that by the beginning of the 'eighties Britain was compelled by the activities of other Powers to realize that, in the words used by Lord Salisbury in 1890, her people were no longer "masters of Africa without being put to the inconvenience of protectorates or anything of that sort". Others were seeking protectorates, especially in the wide frontier regions which had hitherto cut off South Africa from the rest of the world and made the approach to her possible only by sea. German interest in South West Africa, where German missionaries had been active for some time, was beginning to take shape, and, though the Portuguese claim to Delagoa Bay on the east coast had been recognized in 1875, there remained some two hundred miles of unclaimed coast between the Portuguese and Natal borders. Frere had hoped, as part of the policy of federation, to extend control along both coasts to the Portuguese frontiers, but neither the home government nor the Cape would accept the financial and political responsibilities of expansion along the west coast, though he was allowed to annex the best port on the coast, Walvis Bay. On the east any forward move was checked by the setbacks in the Zulu campaign. There followed, in 1884, the calculated colonial campaign by Bismarck which gave South West Africa to Germany. His inquiry about the British position in the area was so tardily handled, while the home government consulted the Cape, that German opinion, as explained elsewhere, was exasperated. The British Government failed to take the inquiry seriously and looked to the Cape for a lead. The Cape, for its part, was equally reluctant to see the territory pass into German hands or to bear the cost of administration itself. When it finally announced its interest it was too late. South

Q*

West Africa therefore became German, and, like New Guinea and Samoa, remained until 1914 a colonial *irredenta*.

## PRECAUTIONARY MOVES IN S.E. AFRICA

On the east coast more timely action was taken. The establishment of the "New Republic" in Zululand offered to the Transvaal Boers a way to the sea at St. Lucia Bay, where also German traders were active. At the end of 1884 the Bay was therefore annexed, the rest of Zululand being formally taken over three years later. In 1886 a protectorate was proclaimed over Pondoland, the one gap in the coastal line south of Natal: formal annexation to the Cape followed in 1894. There remained only Tongaland, immediately south of the Portuguese border, and with a possible port at Kosi Bay. A Transvaal railway here might have been possible with British agreement had not Kruger too obviously been looking for German co-operation. In 1895, after an indiscreet address by Kruger to Pretoria Germans, Tongaland also was annexed to Natal. The whole coast from the Orange River on the west to Mozambique on the east was now under British control, and Delagoa Bay provided the Transvaal's only independent opening to the sea. The "scramble for Africa", coinciding as it did with the Transvaal's attempts to assert an independent line of policy, had ended in the Republic's being shut in on all sides.

## RINGING THE TRANSVAAL: BECHUANALAND

Already the way to the west and the north had also been closed. Almost as soon as Germany took over the South West a railway eastwards from Angra Pequeña (Lüderitz), the only port on the coast apart from Walvis Bay, was projected. This could have been extended to the Transvaal through Bechuanaland, into which Boer settlers were already infiltrating. German Boer co-operation might then have closed the "missionary road", already becoming a "traders' road", and cut off the Cape from the interior. In 1885, therefore, British influence was extended into Bechuanaland, the southern part, between the Molopo River and the Cape frontier, becoming a Crown Colony and the more arid northern part a Protectorate. It was in return for the waiving of Boer claims to the "road" that all reference to "suzerainty" was omitted from the 1884 Convention, and it was control of the road, the "Suez Canal into the interior", as Rhodes called it, that was soon to make possible his ambitious plans for a British Central Africa that in effect completed the encirclement of the Transvaal. The eventual destinies of the two parts of Bechuanaland may here be noted. The Colony, like such other areas as Zululand which remained imperial responsibilities until the Cape or Natal had the resources to govern them, was held only until 1895, when, at Rhodes's request, it was attached to the Cape. Rhodes wished also to absorb the Protectorate, but the Bechuana, like the Basuto, preferred imperial rule, and their greatest chief, Khama of the Bamangwato (1828-1923), an even greater personality than Moshesh, led a delegation to London to press their case. The Protectorate remained an imperial responsibility, then and later, and with Basutoland is still a friendly issue between Britain and South Africa. The "imperial factor" (the phrase was Rhodes's own) here showed itself as doubtful of the native policy of British South Africans as elsewhere of the Afrikaners'.

When all these moves on the South African chess-board had been completed, by the middle years of the 'nineties, the moral that Briton and Boer must settle their difficulties together was still clear. Much though the South African Republic might have welcomed the nearer presence of another European Power to strengthen its own bargaining position, Britain's own presence in South Africa, her command of the sea approaches and her willingness, after a reluctant start in 1884, to take preventive measures in unannexed territory, kept other Powers at a distance. European opinion was alive to the Republic's problems, as its openly-expressed sympathies were to show in 1899, but it was powerless to intervene to solve them.

## DEVELOPMENTS IN CAPE COLONY: HOFMEYR AND DU TOIT

If the failure of the annexation of the Transvaal led to international complications, it became equally a cause of disturbed politics at the Cape. There the Dutch, long largely indifferent to political developments, had been moved to activity by the grant of self-government to the Colony, by the talk of federation and by the events in the Transvaal, which stirred their sympathies. As farmers, and especially as wine-farmers, they had been roused, too, by an increase in excise and import duties rendered necessary by the growing cost of government and defence. They began, in consequence, to assert their separateness. Their principal leaders were J. H. Hofmeyr and S. J. du Toit, the spokesmen of divergent tendencies that were destined to play an all-important part in South African political life. Du Toit, a Dutch minister of Huguenot descent, was one of the earliest advocates of the use of Afrikaans, and in 1875 founded an organization for the defence of "our Language, our Nation and our People". Four years later he established the *Afrikaner Bond*, a union of Afrikaners, avowedly anti-British in sentiment, which through its paper, *Di Patriot*, openly proclaimed that "there is just one hindrance to Confederation, and that is the English flag. Let them take that away . . . they must just have Simon's Town as a naval and military station on the road to India and give over all the rest of South Africa to the Afrikaners"[30]. After the retrocession of the Transvaal du Toit became responsible for education in the Republic, but was later disillusioned by the narrowness of Transvaal policy and became an ardent supporter of Rhodes's schemes. By his pioneer work in the 'seventies and 'eighties he had, however, given a new turn to South Africa's development and helped to make Afrikaners at the Cape as much aware of their national individuality as were their kinsmen in the Republics.

Hofmeyr, an able journalist and editor of the influential *Zuid Afrikaan*, stood for a less assertive Afrikanerdom. He loyally accepted the British connexion, and appreciated the advantages which accrued to South Africa from it: hence the active part he took in the Colonial Conferences at London in 1887 and Ottawa in 1894. Yet at the same time he was loyal to his own people and worked throughout his life to extend their part in South Africa's life. To them he became *Onse Jan* (Our John). He strove for their advancement, but, unlike du Toit, wished to see it come within a joint Boer and British South Africa. A conciliater by nature, he disliked the rough and tumble of political life and preferred to work behind the scenes,

refusing office but influencing events. Hence his nickname of
"The Mole". In his quiet way he was one of the greatest South
Africans of the eventful years which his career spanned.
Entering the Cape Parliament in 1879 he died in London
thirty years later while engaged in the negotiations that led to
the Union of 1910. It was typical of him that he was both a
friend of Rhodes and, in 1904, the leader of the committee
which received back to South Africa the body of President
Kruger after his death in exile. He knew, admired and
criticized both men, and was, in short, a true South African,
respecting equally the twin elements that were creating the
country's white civilization, while not one whit abandoning his
status as an Afrikaner. To du Toit's extreme demand that
there should be "no English shops, no English signboards,
no English advertisements, no English booksellers", he
opposed a broader view:

> I am a little bit of an Englishman as far as language is concerned.
> The Englishman loves his language and I mine. . . . The language
> question is a question of life and death. Despise the language and you
> despise your nationality; honour the language and you honour your
> nationality.[31]

## HOFMEYR AND THE BOND

Hofmeyr preferred Dutch to Afrikaans, and it was largely
his influence which secured for Dutch, in the early 'eighties, a
position of equality with English as an official language. With
this achievement to his credit he undertook the task of weaning
the Bond from its more extreme policies, and in 1883 he
became, in effect, the leader of the movement. This he was to
remain for the rest of his life. After the South African War
the Bond, in the hope of winning British South African
support, was renamed the South African Party, the name it
retained, despite changes in emphasis, after Hofmeyr's death
and under the leadership, first of Botha then of Smuts, until
merged in the "United Party" of Hertzog and Smuts in 1933.
It was therefore for more than half a century, and despite the
many storms it had to weather, a vehicle of Boer-British reconciliation. Hofmeyr himself always laid stress on this aspect of
its existence: "five Englishmen in the Bond", he said, "would
help South African unity more than a hundred Boers". But it

was not until after 1910 that Hofmeyr's aim was fully achieved, and even then the liberal native policy which he had always favoured, as part of his work of conciliation and unification, was running into difficulties.

## CECIL RHODES

Foremost among the Englishmen of earlier days who, though not members of the Bond, were most in sympathy with its aims for South Africa was Cecil Rhodes (1853-1902). As a young man of seventeen, threatened with consumption, Rhodes had come to South Africa in search of health. He was destined to become the most controversial figure of his day in the country and to leave an ineffaceable mark on its history. He had arrived late in 1870 and a year later was at the diamond fields. The next ten years he spent either there or at Oxford, where he graduated, after broken periods of residence, in 1881. Starting at the diamond workings at the age of only eighteen, he proved himself a patient, businesslike and far-seeing prospector. Luck was with him, but he early saw the need for the consolidation of holdings, the use of machinery and the limiting of output if overloading of the market was not to force prices too low. In 1880 he founded the de Beers Mining Company. He then went into financial organization on a big scale, and by 1887 was controller of the Company and ready to fight his most considerable rival at Kimberley, Barney Barnato, on his own ground. By skilful financial manipulations, backed by Rothschild resources, he forced Barnato to yield and combine, and in 1888 the de Beers Consolidated Mines came into existence, with assets valued at more than fourteen million pounds. A single cheque for £5,338,650 bought up the assets of the rival Company. Rhodes was now the dominant partner in a group which controlled nine-tenths of the world's diamond output. At the same time he was investing in the newly-discovered gold-mines of the Rand. Diamond production was deliberately limited to £4,000,000 a year, but there was an unlimited appetite for gold, and production had reached £15,000,000 before the South African War interrupted it. Rhodes's income in the 'nineties was probably in excess of £1,000,000 a year: as South Africa's mineral production was an international interest, so was he, in many respects its embodiment, an international figure.

## RHODES'S IDEALISM: "COMMERCE AND IMAGINATION"

When he went to the diamond fields in 1871 Rhodes had been but one of the many working there who hoped for great fortunes. By a combination of tenacity, daring, prescience and luck he forced himself to the front, and mastered all his competitors. He sought great wealth, but less for its own sake than for the power it gave him, and he had in him a strong streak of idealism, nurtured at Oxford by Ruskin, which won for him comparison with the hard-headed and religious-minded sea-captains of Elizabethan England. He was, as he admitted, a speculator, but a speculator on the grand scale, who gambled not merely in scrip and millions but in lands and men. "I have tried", he told General Gordon, "to combine the commercial with the imaginative", and he carried into business, as later into politics, an imaginative idealism which, though it eventually overreached itself, gave his name to a new country in Africa and to a great University Scholarship fund in England. In politics he aimed at a united South Africa, freed from imperial interference and stretching into the very heart of Africa. Such a consolidation of political interests was to him the corollary of the "Consolidated" diamond and gold-mining Companies, and he tried to use his power and his wealth as much for the one as for the other. Like a John D. Rockefeller, a William Lever or a Henry Ford, he was a man of great ability early in a field of business enterprise which offered, with the zest of bitter competition, almost unlimited scope for advancement. Like Julius Vogel, too, he looked with eager and ambitious eyes beyond the confines of the political bounds within which he had to act. He was fortunate in that a great field of endeavour lay within his reach: with the resources at his command he could "open up" a great country, a country which was, in fact, almost the last territory still awaiting development. Where Vogel had to look over the sea he had but to glance across a river: as African distances go, the Rhodesia which he created was on his doorstep. Yet he was conscious always of a race against time. His health was never good and by the 'nineties heart trouble compelled him to realize that his time was limited. Moreover, he had arrived on the scene at a time when the "scramble for Africa" was well under way: he had to move quickly to secure territories on which he had his eye. As an historian of South Africa has said, "it was Rhodes's tragedy that he must always work in a hurry in a continent where men of rival nationalities were also busy".[32] First in Bechuanaland, and then farther north, South Africa's way to the interior had to be kept open, and time was short. Time seemed short, too, in the management of affairs in the Transvaal. The very natural resources which gave Rhodes his wealth strengthened the hands of that other massive figure of South Africa, Paul Kruger, as he sat in his capital watching with shrewd, heavy-lidded eyes the manœuvres of the man who he had early realized would give him trouble. Gold provided nineteen-twentieths of the revenues of the Republic, which rose from a modest £178,000 in 1885 to more than £4,000,000 on the eve of the war. It was Rhodes's desire for quick results, before the Republic became too independent, or heart trouble carried off himself, that brought in 1895 the ill-considered design of the Jameson Raid.

## RHODES AND POLITICS

Rhodes first entered politics in 1880, when he was returned for a Griqualand constituency to the Cape Parliament. His political notions were, at 27, already largely formed. Three years earlier he had drawn up the first of the series of astonishing wills which were to dispose of his wealth, and had left his money to found a Society for "the extension of British rule throughout the world", the colonization of immense tracts, reunion with the United States and the establishment of a federated Empire which should give peace to the world for all time. But he had no desire to see the Anglo-Saxon predominance conducted from London. From his own observations he had already concluded that "the Dutch are the coming race in South Africa and they must have their share in running the country", and the war of 1881 taught him, as he told Hofmeyr, to respect them. He was moving towards the conception of "the government of South Africa by the people of South Africa with the Imperial Flag for defence", a formula which matched Hofmeyr's aims. "I believe in a United States of South Africa," he said in 1883, "but as a portion of the British Empire. I believe that confederated states in a colony under responsible government would each be practically an independent republic." Whatever the jumble of ideas he had absorbed, Rhodes was no narrow imperialist. Like many of his compeers in other self-governing colonies he believed passionately in the imperial connexion and desired to see it strengthened, but he believed no less in the independent strength and spirit of his own new country. Hence his consideration for Afrikaner feeling, which won him the confidence of Hofmeyr and du Toit, and caused the members of the Bond to regard him as "an Englishman after their own heart".[33] He had become, in short, a South African.

## The Gold Discoveries and their Consequences

The 'eighties, when Rhodes was beginning to concern himself with political issues, were a period of economic revolution for South Africa. The discovery of gold on the Rand in 1886 radically altered the balance of power, and poured undreamed-of, and to some extent unwanted, wealth into the laps of Kruger and his people. The centre of interest was suddenly drawn, as if by a magnet, and more than by the diamond discoveries, into the interior of the country. Soon the Transvaal Boers were outnumbered by the mining community, the *Uitlanders*, most of them British subjects, whose very existence raised new and difficult problems, which were to have a tragic outcome. For the present their needs strained South African trade and communications to new efforts. Already the Transvaal in its striving for a secure independence had raised tariff barriers against goods from the Cape and Natal, which had long derived not a little of their revenue from duties on imports destined to travel up-country. As late as 1885, indeed, Kruger, faced with the unending financial straits of the Republic, was willing to consider a customs union, though the gold discoveries soon caused him to draw back contentedly. Now, however, the tariff war was intensified. Not only did the Republic tax imports from the two Colonies, but they themselves struggled against each other, with differential rates, for the profits of the lucrative import trade. The case for some measure of federation seemed overwhelming, at the very time when the Transvaal was best able to resist it. It was to be still further reinforced by railway rivalries. The Cape railway reached Kimberley in 1885, and the obvious route for its extension lay across the Vaal to the Rand and Pretoria. Kruger, however, was already determined to exploit his back-door into Portuguese territory, and a survey of the projected line was made in 1887. Two years later the Transvaal border was connected with Delagoa Bay, but the difficulties of con-struction in the Republic itself were considerable, and it was only when money had been borrowed, with Rhodes's help, from the Rothschilds that the line could be finished. The first train from Pretoria to the Bay ran through in 1894. Meanwhile the Cape was running three lines, from Cape Town itself, from Port Elizabeth and from East London, while Natal was extending its line from Durban. Kruger firmly refused any link with Kimberley, and the approach to the Rand had therefore to be made across the Orange Free State. There President J. H. Brand was pursuing a moderate and conciliatory policy, and in 1888 formed a customs and railway union with the Cape. The Cape lines were thereupon linked with Bloemfontein and in 1892, in return for the timely help to the Delagoa line, were permitted to cross the Vaal. The first through train from Cape Town entered Pretoria in 1893; the first from Durban only two years later. Rivalries over lines were then succeeded, however, by a struggle over rates. The Transvaal railways were built and controlled by Dutch and German interests, the Netherlands South African Railway Company, and the lines from the south had to meet the competition of its strongly entrenched position. Its charges for running rights across its lines were heavy, and when, in 1895, the southern railways sought to avoid these by unloading goods on to ox-wagons at the frontier, Kruger promptly ordered the closing of the drifts (fords), which would have brought their traffic to a standstill. An ultimatum, drawing attention to the breach of the 1884 Convention, forced them open again, but the episode was an unpleasant revelation of the tenseness of the South African situation and of the extent to which economic considerations were adding to the strain. Kruger's policy had the result, however, of uniting Bond opinion at the Cape with British feeling against him—until the mad escapade of the Jameson Raid less than two months after the "drifts" crisis.

## THE SEARCH FOR GOLD—MATABELELAND

There remained after 1885 the problem of the advance from Kimberley. Until 1888 Rhodes was consolidating his diamond and gold interests. He was already, however, looking farther afield. There was no reason to suppose that a new Rand could not be found farther north, in the lands of the Matabele and Mashona peoples, dominated by the impressive figure of the Matabele leader, Lobengula, with his savage warriors trained on Zulu principles. If South Africa were ever to become a great and united country she must gain control of these lands before they were absorbed by others. Already restless Transvaal farmers were planning to move north, the one direction left open to them by the 1884 Convention, and German and Portuguese interests were also involved. Rhodes had determined earlier that the road to the north through Bechuanaland should pass into British hands, and had at first been shocked by the imperial government's handling of the situation into demanding that Bechuanaland should be left to the Cape. He now resolved to ensure that the right steps should be taken in Matabeleland and Mashonaland, the future Rhodesia, by taking them himself. He hoped, too, that, if gold could be found, the Transvaal might lose something of its pre-eminence, and, as but one of the producers of the wealth of a greater South Africa, be forced into a federal system. Matabeleland was for him, therefore, a means both for the acquisition of still greater wealth and power and for the achievement of lofty political ambitions. Given the situation and the period the aims were not incongruous. The days of Matabele and Mashona independence, for what it was worth, were in any case numbered, though none could foresee that within only a few years, in 1893, Lobengula was to die far from his royal kraal at Bulawayo, a broken man abandoned by his people, while Rhodes's name was to be given to his country.

## RHODES AND THE B.S.A.—"RHODESIA"

In 1888 Rhodes gained from Lobengula the exclusive right to prospect for metals and minerals in his territories. He then proceeded to buy out all other concessionaires and to win support, both at the Cape and in London, for a British South Africa Company, which was established by Royal Charter in October, 1889, and was granted wide powers for the development and government of the concession-lands. Some support Rhodes won over by his charm and personality, some by his enthusiastic idealism for African development. Others lent their aid in return for being let in on the ground floor of the new enterprise. Nothing dishonourable was done, but, Sir James Innes, a percipient contemporary observer, has recounted, the bait was often the tempting offer at par of shares standing at a premium: "it was delicately put; the idea was to interest the selected recipient in northern development".[34] The Prime Minister and the Colonial Office were won over by the prospect of securing for the British flag, at no cost to the Treasury, territory which was likely to become the subject of international dispute, together with the promise of a railway through Bechuanaland. The support of Parnell in the House of Commons was assured by a subscription to the funds of the Home Rule movement, in which Rhodes always took a lively interest, seeing in an independent Ireland linked with Britain an augury for the future status of South Africa. By these and other means Rhodes squared all interested parties, and in the South African winter of 1890 the first band of armed settlers, the "Pioneers", set out for Mashonaland. "Salisbury", named after the Prime Minister, was founded in September. Lobengula, uneasily aware that he had signed away his people's future, was held to his word by one of Rhodes's staunchest supporters, Dr. L. S. Jameson (1853-1917), who won the savage ruler's confidence by relieving the gout that afflicted him. In 1891 Jameson became administrator of the new territory. Yet Rhodes's high hopes were dashed. No new Rand was discovered, and the Company fell into debt. In 1893, however, the situation changed. The Matabele, in Zulu style, had long been accustomed to raiding neighbouring peoples, and despite the presence of Europeans continued to make the Mashona their victims. A clash was inevitable, and came in 1893. The Matabele power was broken, and Lobengula fled to his death. Some years later it was ruled that the Matabele War had automatically put an end to Lobengula's concession to Rhodes, which had thereupon reverted to the Crown. Meanwhile, however, the Chartered Territory was given in 1895 the name of Rhodesia, and Rhodes commented to a friend, with shy pride, that "to have a bit of country named after one is one of the things a man might be proud of". His position was not yet secure, for in the following year, when the unsuccessful raid into the Transvaal had put Jameson and many of his Police out of the way, the inevitable disagreements over land and cattle, exacerbated by one of South Africa's long droughts, and by an outbreak of cattle disease, caused both Matabele and Mashona to rise in revolt. Rhodes suppressed the revolts himself, as much by personal contact with the disaffected peoples as by force of arms, but the progress of the new territory was slow. No major gold finds were made, to oust the Transvaal Rand from its supremacy. It was some years before total production reached £1,000,000 and it now runs at something over £6,000,000 a year, about one-twenty-fifth of South African production. Tobacco, with an annual production approaching £20,000,000 in value, and with a protected market in Britain and South Africa, has proved, indeed, a more valuable product of the Rhodesias than the gold which Rhodes had hoped for. The most important mineral product has been copper, mined in the north of Northern Rhodesia, but copper could not be worked on any considerable scale until the nineteen-thirties, though with some half-million tons, valued at about £90,000,000, mined each year, it has now become Rhodesia's most important single product. It soon became clear, however, that Rhodesia was not the el Dorado which would provide the key to South Africa's problems. Rhodes's Company proved unable to pay any dividends, though when its Charter finally expired in 1923 it received £3,250,000 in compensation, a further £2,000,000 being added ten years later, when the Southern Rhodesian Government bought out its mineral rights. Nor did the territory become an extension of South Africa. When the Company's rule came to an end in 1923 the settlers, who numbered only 34,000 in the chief areas of settlement south of the Zambesi, preferred the status of a self-governing Colony to that of a Province of the Union. The Colony of Southern Rhodesia therefore came into existence, Northern Rhodesia remaining an imperial Protectorate:

the two were eventually merged with neighbouring Nyasaland in a Federation in 1953. Of the native policy pursued, which followed in the main the pattern of Natal's practice, something must be said when later periods are under consideration.

## RHODES AS PREMIER OF THE CAPE

To return to the South Africa of the 'nineties. Having consolidated his gold and diamond holdings and launched the B.S.A. Company, Rhodes turned his attention to Cape politics, and in July, 1890, shortly after the Pioneers had left on their long trek to Mashonaland, he became Premier of the Cape, deriving his support mainly from Hofmeyr and the Bond. In internal affairs he introduced two significant measures, the Franchise Act of 1892 and the "Glen Grey" Act of 1894, both of which closely touched native interests. Rhodes had long had close contact with natives, and, like so many Europeans similarly placed, had distinctly paternalistic notions on their treatment. His early solution of the problem of incompatible racial policies had been "a system of Indian despotism in our relations with the barbarians of South Africa", whereby "a United South Africa stretching to the Zambesi" might be created. Experience at the Cape, however, broadened his vision, and he also learnt much from the inspiration of Hofmeyr. By the time he became Premier the Bond members were becoming concerned at the implications of the Cape's low franchise qualification, and there were complaints that too many natives with the bare minimum of qualification were receiving the franchise. In 1892, therefore, Rhodes raised the qualification and introduced an educational test. It was the first step towards his eventual pronouncement of "equal rights for all civilized men, irrespective of races, south of the Zambesi", an aim still unrealized, and seemingly unrealizable half a century after his death. The measure drew him still nearer to the Bond, many of whose members, though opposed to education of the natives, were being steered into more liberal courses by Hofmeyr. Two years later there followed the policy of the development of land-owning and local government by natives in their reserves, which has received the name of Glen Grey, after the area in which it was first applied. This, though it was probably in part Hofmeyr's work, has well been described as "Rhodes's greatest legislative achievement",[35] "a bill for Africa", as he called it himself, offering to the Bantu a secure position and a measure of responsibility for local affairs to offset their depressed status, while preventing excessive pressure on the land by forcing natives without holdings to seek employment with Europeans. Early in 1895 Rhodes was sworn of the Queen's Privy Council, and in May of the same year came the proclamation of "Rhodesia". He was at the height of his fame and his power, and was beginning to show something of an impatience with others which was the effect at once of easy success and of despair at his prospects of health. Time was threatening to run out for him, and it was impatience, a desire for speed and a disregard for opposition, which suddenly brought him down, at the very beginning of the following year, in the crisis of the Raid.

## The Jameson Raid and its Results

The Jameson Raid marks yet another of the many turning points in South African history. The whole issue of the position of the Transvaal in a South Africa dominated by Britain, which had been dormant since 1881, now suddenly leapt into that place in the limelight which it was not soon to lose. Once again the Dutch at the Cape, who had been openly critical of the state of affairs in the Republic, were shocked into sympathy with their kinsmen. Rhodes's carefully nurtured relations with the Bond were destroyed at a blow, and Hofmeyr turned from him in disgust. Racial feelings reached a pitch unequalled save in the actual years of war that were to come. A farce in its execution, the Raid was a tragedy of the first order for South African development. Its results, with those of Majuba, are felt to this day. Its tangled history and consequences cannot be considered in any great detail here, and are, in any case, the subject of a considerable literature, in which the most recent work, and the one which has had the freest access to unpublished papers, is Dr. J. van der Poel's *The Jameson Raid*. But something must be said of the affair, of the events that led up to it and of its unhappy place in South African history. It repays attention as a case-study in imperialism and in the varied elements and personalities that made up the South African scene.

## UITLANDER GRIEVANCES IN THE TRANSVAAL

The Raid was an attempt to "rush" the Transvaal, to exploit the extensive footing which the Uitlanders concerned with gold-mining had gained in it, in order to break the obdurate independence of the Kruger régime and secure a united South Africa under British control. The chief grievance of the Uitlanders, who formed the majority of the population of the Transvaal and provided by far the greater part of its revenues, was that they were Uitlanders, that they did not belong. Kruger and those around him drew no distinction between the adventurer or the mining magnate, whose sole aim was to "get rich quick", and the steady engineer or mine-worker, often enough a South African by birth, who had come to settle on the Rand. Wherever gold or other rich resources had been found, in colonial territories throughout the world, men had been flocking for many years, and although some moved on, others stayed, to form local communities and eventually to achieve self-government as a colony. Thus it had been with the diamond fields in South Africa. What was to happen, however, when the discoveries were made not in unsettled lands but among the farms of a proud people whose one desire was to avoid contact with the "imperial factor"? Two entirely different ways of life developed side by side, but the government rested with the Boers, and they were determined not to be outvoted in their own country. Franchise rights were gradually narrowed until in the end, although the Boer had the vote at sixteen, the immigrant could get it only at the age of at least forty, after fourteen years in the Transvaal for twelve of which he had surrendered his previous nationality by taking a special oath of allegiance to the Republic. Yet during this time, while deprived of political rights, he was liable to military service. It was under these conditions that Smuts, for instance, who took service with the Republic in 1898, since he was born a British subject in Cape Colony, received citizen rights only by special grant when he became a general in the field in 1901.

## THE SITUATION IN THE TRANSVAAL

The conditions were made the more galling to many by the manner in which the affairs of the Republic were conducted.

Though Kruger himself was not interested in wealth, the administration was corrupt, many goods, especially the dynamite needed for the mines, were subject to costly monopolies and law was not above suspicion. Kruger's open flirtation with Germany also increased the distrust of the British on the Rand. Yet Kruger's party was not the whole Boer community. A more liberal opposition was arising, led by such men as Schalk Burger, Louis Botha and Piet Joubert, the last of whom came near to winning the presidential election from Kruger in 1893. The tough old Voortrekker hero might even be overthrown in his lifetime, but in any case he was seventy in 1895: his death could not be far off, and with that great changes must come. Time was needed, time in which Boer opinion might mellow, in which younger men with broader vision could come to the fore, in which Hofmeyr and his followers might bring their conciliatory influence to bear. Given the situation in the Transvaal and throughout South Africa as a whole, the Kruger régime was a disturbing influence, but, as has well been said, "its overthrow by peaceful means would have had very different results from its going down in a blaze of patriotic glory before superior force".[36] Moreover, it was not until 1894 that it was clear that the Uitlanders were on the Rand to stay. Not until then did it prove possible to follow the gold-bearing reefs to the depths. The early 'nineties were, on the whole, years of depression, and depression fans discontent. An Uitlander "National Union" was formed in 1892, and when the British High Commissioner, the sage Sir Henry Loch, visited Pretoria in his official capacity in 1893, and again in 1894, he felt that there was serious danger of an explosion, and made plans to intervene in case of need. But the beginning of work on the deeper levels, and the boom conditions that followed, radically altered the situation. There was much grumbling, and a good deal of wild talk but, when it came to the point, few men on the Rand had the time, or the inclination, to try to redress their position by force of arms.

## RHODES AND THE TRANSVAAL

Rhodes, however, seems to have made up his mind to take action during 1894. A tour he undertook in Matabeleland in that year made it clear that, whatever the mineral wealth there, it did not amount to another Rand. The Transvaal was still, therefore, the key to the position. On his way back to the Cape he called on Kruger, but failed to make any impression on him: indeed, they parted on bad terms. While on the Rand, however, Rhodes noted the bitterness of the Uitlanders—and their lack of arms. He felt that a rising was imminent, and that if it were not aided from outside it might lead merely to the establishment of another independent republic. Then, in January, 1895, came Kruger's famous speech to the German community in Pretoria, to which reference has already been made. This lost him his outlet to the sea, and was for Rhodes the last straw. He began to smuggle arms to Johannesburg. To ensure success a force must be held ready, somewhere near the Transvaal border, and ready to march at the decisive moment. Such a force Rhodes had ready to hand in the B.S.A. Police. As Chairman of the Company he therefore prepared a force under Jameson, while as a private individual, and a shareholder in the Rand mines, he bought arms for the Uitlanders. As Prime Minister of the Cape he was presumably aware of these activities of his *alter ego*, which it was his official duty to prevent, but he had by this time passed beyond the stage of distinguishing between the various capacities in which he acted. Already he had applied to the Liberal Government in London for the cession of British Bechuanaland to the Cape and for control by the B.S.A. Company over the Bechuanaland Protectorate. In June, 1895, the Government fell and Lord Salisbury formed his third Ministry, with Chamberlain as Colonial Secretary. British Bechuanaland was duly handed over, but Chamberlain, mindful of Khama's pleading, held on to the Protectorate. He did, however, agree, in return for financial concessions by the Company, to allow it a strip along the Transvaal border, where the railway north from Mafeking was to run. This was enough for Rhodes's purpose: in October the police went into camp on the border. Chamberlain knew of their existence, for talk of a Rand rising was in the air, and the new High Commissioner, Sir Hercules Robinson, an old friend whom Rhodes, with an eye to developments, had suggested for the position, had received formal instructions from Chamberlain, as from his Liberal predecessor, to be prepared to intervene if trouble should break out. That was understood to be the function also of the B.S.A. police. Then came the "drifts" crisis, and Chamberlain took a firm line, before which Kruger yielded. If the Uitlanders would but rise the battle would be won, Krugerism would pass away and a united South Africa come into existence. Jameson, to provide himself with an excuse for invading the Transvaal when the word was given, armed himself with the notorious, and bogus, "women and children" letter, which professed to call for help for the struggling rebels on the Rand, and waited hopefully.

## JAMESON'S RASHNESS—AND FAILURE

But no word came. When the leaders of the Rand movement sounded their fellows they found little enthusiasm, and could not even agree among themselves whether the rising should take place under the Union Jack or the Republic's *Vierkleur*. The whole affair was therefore called off. Jameson, however, with 500 men under his command, was not to be deterred. At the very end of December he set off for Johannesburg. Rhodes tried to stop him, but failed. A few days later his force was surrounded, and he was a prisoner of the Boers. The Uitlanders rose, but half-heartedly, and were soon persuaded to surrender. As *The Times* correspondent, who was deep in the affair, reported to his chief:

> They were not really game for the business and if he had not crossed the border would never have taken up arms. The great mistake made was trying to run races with cart horses.[37]

The "cart horses" paid dearly, for they were first imprisoned, and then heavily fined. More ominously, there was talk of bringing to Pretoria, for the execution of the ringleaders, the very beam on which the Slagtersnek rebels had been hanged eighty years since. That the suggestion should have been made is an indication of the depth of feeling that had been roused. No Boers would believe that the British Government was not heavily involved, and many efforts have been made, notably in Dr. van der Poel's recent book, to implicate Chamberlain. Jameson, whom Kruger wisely—and shrewdly—handed over to Britain for trial, believed that if he had won he would have been acclaimed as a hero. Without a rising, however, he could never have won. The tactics that he had adopted with success against the Matabele were of no avail against the skilled Boer fighters.

## THE CONSEQUENCES OF THE RAID

Jameson was tried in England and imprisoned, and a Parliamentary inquiry into the Raid followed. This was handled with such delicacy as to encourage suspicions that much was being covered up: the inquiry came to be cynically described as "the lying-in-state at Westminster". The equivocal part played by Sir Hercules Robinson was concealed, and Chamberlain's share in the affair was obscured. Yet, while Chamberlain was well aware that something was afoot *in the event of a rising*, he cannot be implicated in the mad venture of the Raid itself. Both Jameson and Rhodes were, however, acclaimed as popular heroes. The Boers, a Radical paper commented, "had goaded Englishmen past endurance by their refusal either to govern their country well or to permit Englishmen to take a share in mending matters".[38] Kruger, in fact, had long since forfeited all friendly feeling, and worse was to come. On 3rd January the German Emperor sent him a telegram of congratulation on his defeat of the invaders. This served but to confirm British suspicions of Germany's interest in the Transvaal, and to unite the country in patriotic denunciation of William II's rash act. It also diverted attention from Rhodes's misdemeanours, as Rhodes himself, on a visit to Germany, did not fail to tell the Emperor, with a smile. Anglo-German relations deteriorated from that moment, and cool judgment on South African issues was the less likely. For his part Kruger felt that he could never trust the British again: the Transvaal, the Orange Free State and many Cape Boers drew together against them. "South African politics started on a new course determined by ties of kinship and language that cut across the geographical and economic unity of the country."[39]

Even with Kruger out of the way a peaceful settlement would have been difficult after the Raid. When he stood for election again in 1898 he was, inevitably, re-elected with an overwhelming majority. Jameson's folly had but served to seat him still more firmly in power, and to unite behind him many who had had little sympathy with his policies. The stage was now set for the more tragic, though, apart from its scale, not necessarily more fateful, crisis of the war.

## The Coming of Milner

Rhodes resigned office on the morrow of the Raid, and with it, at Chamberlain's insistence, his place on the board of the B.S.A. He had, as he said, to start his career afresh. Later in the year, however, came his successful handling of the Matabele and Mashona rebellions, which won him the respect of the people among whom he chose to be buried in 1902. He was back in Cape politics in 1897, actively supporting the "Progressive" party which had developed in opposition to the embittered Bond. In that same year there entered upon the scene another forceful character who was destined to play a major part in South African affairs, Sir Alfred Milner (1854–1925), who was High Commissioner from 1897 to 1905, and simultaneously Governor of the Cape (1897-1901) and, later, of the conquered Transvaal and "Orange River Colony" (1901-05). Of mixed English and German descent, Milner had worked in Egypt under Baring and for five years been Chairman of the Board of Inland Revenue, where he had been largely responsible for Sir William Harcourt's introduction of death duties in 1894. His abilities had caught the eye of Chamberlain, who in 1897 was looking for a new High Commissioner. As his experience would suggest, Milner held social views in sympathy with the movements of the age, but he was above all else a great administrator, somewhat autocratic by temperament and lacking in appreciation of the points of view of those who disagreed with him. He was, therefore, not too well suited to understanding the Boer mentality, though he did his best by learning both Dutch and Afrikaans. His service in Egypt had made him a convinced imperialist, and he went to South Africa determined to uphold the British position there, which seemed to be threatened—and was increasingly to seem to be threatened—by the intransigent attitude of the South African Republic and by its contacts with foreign States. War came in 1899 because Britain felt that her position was endangered, while the Boers believed that until they had asserted themselves their whole way of life was at Britain's mercy. Yet, while after the Jameson Raid war seemed a possibility, there were few on either side who wished for it. Despite suspicions that have been entertained at times of their policies and attitudes, the records show that neither Chamberlain nor Milner sought war. They were resolved to press, more or less urgently, for changes in the Republic, but, as Milner wrote of the Boer leaders soon after his arrival in South Africa, "we should be very patient with them, very conciliatory, remembering how much excuse they have for regarding us with suspicion". "For the present at any rate", Chamberlain wrote to him in the following year, "our greatest interest in South Africa is peace", and the Colonial Secretary later agreed with the Prime Minister that their policy was "to keep the peace with Kruger unless he were very outrageous".

## THE DRIFT TO WAR

But outrageous from the British point of view Kruger was, and Milner was already writing home in 1898 that, "there is no ultimate way out of the political troubles of South Africa except reform in the Transvaal or war". Warned by the Raid, Kruger was spending heavily on military equipment, buying guns, including artillery from Krupps heavier than anything the British were to have at the Cape for some time, and building forts. There were many Afrikaners, not merely in the Republic, who felt that the future of Afrikanerdom lay in these defences against the pressure of Britain and of the unwelcome industrial capital interests which after 1894 had so clearly come to stay on the Rand. Olive Schreiner was by this time a fervent Afrikaner in sympathy: "ultimately we have nothing to fight the Capitalists with but the guns and forts of the Transvaal", she wrote,[40] and there were many who shared her views. Yet, if the Afrikaner way of life was protected in this manner, the constant pin-pricks inflicted on the Uitlanders, the refusal of concessions, the high-handedness of the police, the spectacle, as Milner was to put it in a famous despatch, "of thousands of British subjects kept permanently in the position of helots", was a reflection on Kruger and those around him, many of whom were Dutchmen or Germans who could not be expected to have any interest in the British connexion. Just before

Christmas, 1898, there occurred the case of the shooting by the police of a Rand boiler-maker, Tom Edgar, and the open encouragement of the police by the Transvaal judge in the trial that followed. This episode, in itself an epitome of the problems of the Rand, brought matters to a head for the Uitlanders, and in March, 1899, a petition was sent to the Queen appealing for intervention on their behalf. This, though there were counter-petitions on the Rand, could not be ignored without prejudice to the whole of the British position not only in South Africa but anywhere in the world where British people were settled. Chamberlain, fully alive to the stark alternatives, proceeded warily, and a meeting was arranged between Milner and Kruger at Bloemfontein in June. But for the suspicions that abounded, an agreement of some kind might have been reached, yet although Kruger went further in the promise of concessions than he had ever gone before Milner could feel no confidence that any agreement would be honoured,[41] for the Transvaalers, in the phrase of the then Chief Justice of the Cape, Sir Henry de Villiers, were too obviously "wriggling" out of any clear, simple decision. And the suspicions were mutual: "it is my country you want", Kruger cried out in bitterness, and with tears in his eyes, when the conference was broken off. In conditions such as these the breakdown of negotiations could only worsen the situation, and a steady drift to war began. It came in October, when the spring rains had refreshed the grass on the veld for the Boer horses, and the Orange Free State, linked for some years in sympathy with the Transvaal, though not always approving of its conduct of affairs, joined with its kinsmen across the Vaal. With some 50,000 highly-skilled fighters under arms, and the memory of Majuba still vivid, the Boers did not doubt for success. The British forces, even with some immediate reinforcements, were outnumbered by two to one, and, though more troops would soon be on the way, the Boers were hopeful of a speedy victory.

## Milner's Aims: "Leave the Rest to the Future"

The Boer War brought to a head the clash between two differing conceptions of South Africa's destiny. Rhodes in 1898 had summed up his own attitude in the original version of the well-known phrase "equal rights for every civilized man south of the Zambesi", which had read "*white man*" until, with an eye to the Cape-Coloured vote, he had altered "white" to "civilized".[42] Milner took the same view. He sought no more than political rights for settled non-Afrikaners in the Transvaal, and the recognition of British predominance in South Africa. The Boers, he wrote to Sir Edward Grey in 1899, wanted to preserve their "race oligarchy":

> I want a Republic in which both elements will have fair play, as in the Cape, as in Canada. And leave the rest to the future. One thing is clear to me—such a Republic . . . will not be that danger to British South Africa which a pure Afrikander State, armed to the teeth, and incessantly intriguing against us both in South Africa and in Europe, is.

"Leave the rest to the future": that was precisely Kruger's fear, the fear that on an equal footing, which with Britain's resources behind them could not be an equal footing, the Britons in South Africa would swamp Afrikanerdom and destroy "my country", which represented more than land or *Vierkleur*, for it enshrined a whole way of life. And his fears were not unjustified, for Milner was confident that "given *equality* all round, English must prevail". Yet Milner's aim was no ignoble one. "The *ultimate* end," he wrote very early in the war, " is a self-governing white Community, supported by *well-treated* and *justly governed* black labour from Cape Town to Zambesi. There must be one flag, the Union Jack, but under it equality of races and languages." Equality, he maintained, was what the British in South Africa were not permitted to enjoy. Self-government at the Cape gave equal rights to Boer and Briton, and the Boers were in the majority, but there was no reciprocal equality in the Transvaal, where the majority of people were British. The Boers "thus score all round and are masters of the situation". "Unless we had asserted ourselves," he wrote in a memorandum for the guidance of his successor, Lord Selborne, in 1905, "we should have lost South Africa." And with South Africa was involved the future of the Empire, on which the abandonment of the British position could not but have a serious effect: the war "involves the union or disruption of the Empire", he cabled in

October, 1899, to a New South Wales Minister, B. R. Wise, who was seeking arguments to justify the sending of Australian troops.[43]

## War Was Inevitable?

With all this Milner combined a characteristic lack of imaginative grasp of the Afrikaner position, whether in the Republics or at the Cape. If the Transvaal was unwilling to permit education in their own language for English-speaking children in its schools, Milner was impatient of the Cape Afrikaners' clinging to Dutch, when English was necessary if they "wanted to get on in life". And he distrusted their "radical duplicity":

> They are "British citizens", and fully prepared to take every advantage of that position, yet they are working against everything British.

In this attitude, and in the corresponding one on the Afrikaner side, is summed up so much of the essence of the struggle, and of the tragic misunderstanding over the years which had brought it about. Not until the war and the post-war settlement brought mutual respect and consideration was it possible to conceive of the dual loyalty, to a free and united South Africa and to the British connexion, which was eventually to emerge. Meanwhile there were those in the Transvaal who were spoiling for war. Their views were reflected in a much-quoted letter, written in September, 1899, which was captured in Pretoria in the following year:

> The only thing we are afraid of now is that Chamberlain, with his admitted fitfulness of temper, will cheat us out of the war, and consequently the opportunity of annexing the Cape Colony and Natal, and forming the Republican United States of South Africa.

Perhaps the war was, indeed, unavoidable. This was the view formed at the time by the Orange Free State citizen, and great South African of the future, Deneys Reitz, who, in exile in Madagascar after defeat, set down in *Commando* a brilliant record of what the conflict had meant to him:

> Looking back, I think that the war was inevitable. I have no doubt that the British Government had made up its mind to force the

R

issue, and was the chief culprit, but the Transvaalers were also spoiling for a fight, and from what I saw in Pretoria during the few weeks that preceded the ultimatum, I feel sure that the Boers would in any case have insisted on a rupture.[44]

## THE COURSE OF THE WAR

The war itself began badly for Britain. Had the Boers been better led they would not have dissipated their forces in watching British garrisons locked up in Kimberley, Mafeking or Ladysmith, but would have pressed on to the Cape and Durban before substantial reinforcements could arrive. When the British forces did arrive they, too, were badly led by generals who lacked knowledge of the South African terrain and were contemptuous of the warnings of such Intelligence staff as existed. Hence Sir Redvers Buller's costly and inept failures and the "Black Week" of 11th-15th December, 1899, when major battles were lost at Stormberg, Magersfontein and Colenso. These victories raised Boer hopes to expectations of a sudden peace, as after Majuba: "there were few of us", Reitz wrote, "who did not believe that peace would soon follow as it had . . . in 1881".[45] But there was no withdrawal this time. Buller was superseded by the aged Lord Roberts, with Kitchener as chief-of-staff, more troops arrived, and an appropriate plan of campaign was devised. At the end of February a Boer army under General Cronje was surrounded at Paardeberg, in March Roberts occupied Bloemfontein and, early in June, Pretoria. In February Kimberley, where Rhodes had been shut up, was relieved, in March, Ladysmith, and in May, Mafeking, which set off an hysterical outburst of excitement in London. The last Boer army was defeated in August and in October the Transvaal was formally annexed. It seemed the end of the war, but it was, in fact, only half over, for the Boer soldiers—marksmen, hunters, masters of veld-craft and strongly individualist as they were—now began the type of campaign for which they were best fitted, the commando raid, and it was not until March, 1902, that they finally sued for peace. Meanwhile the British had put into the field, in all, 448,000 men against some 80,000 on the Boer side, the British total including nearly 31,000 from Canada, Australia and New Zealand, and a further 30,000 British South Africans.

British losses had been nearly 6,000 in battle, but, significantly enough, more than 16,000 by disease, the Boer losses less than 4,000. "Probably no European army of the day," it has well been said, "faced, in a greater Spain, with all and more than all the difficulties that had harassed Napoleon in the Peninsula, would have done better than the British did."[46] Many in Europe and elsewhere exulted in the British defeats, but the lessons were learned. Military reforms, including the establishment of a General Staff, were among the results that flowed from a strict inquiry into the conduct of the war, though the fact that the war had been essentially one for cavalry was to have an unhappy effect when the military leaders were faced with totally different conditions in Europe in 1914. On the Boer side the conflict threw up some remarkable men, Louis Botha, Jan Smuts, Christiaan de Wet and Jan de la Rey, the heroes of memorable episodes, two of whom were destined in time to stand well before the world.

## THE "COMMANDO" WAR AND THE CONCENTRATION CAMPS

The late stages of the war, when Kitchener was striving to capture and wear down the elusive commandos, were marked by the institution of the "concentration camps" for non-combatants, which have left an unhappy stain on the British record in the war. Kitchener's policy was to destroy farmsteads which sheltered raiders who were at once soldiers and civilians and wore no distinguishing uniform. This left wives and families destitute, and the camps were opened to receive them. They were welcomed by the Boers, who were thus left free to continue campaigning, but were shockingly mismanaged and, in the primitive conditions prevailing, with inadequate sanitary and medical facilities, became death-traps for people accustomed to the space and clean air of the veld. "A war in which the British were feeding the Boer women and children while fighting the men was in itself fantastic",[47] but sixteen thousand children died, mostly from measles, and some four thousand women. It was not cruelty, but unpreparedness and military incompetence that caused the disaster, the same incompetence, and lack of sanitary care, that lost 16,000 British soldiers by disease. "The black spot—the one very black spot . . . a sad

fiasco . . . a bad business" were Milner's comments, and there
was an outcry in Britain which culminated in Campbell-
Bannerman's devastating phrase, "methods of barbarism",
welcomed by the Boers as an indication that they were not
alone in their struggle. These three words, as Botha was to say
later, "made peace and union in South Africa".[48] Improvements were soon made in the camps, and the tragically high
death-rate fell, but another had been added to the sorry tale of
Afrikaner grievances. The memory of the camps lay on
Afrikaner consciousness and British consciences, and when,
more than thirty years later, the evil Nazi camps were established under the same name, Hitler was able to deceive
not a few with propaganda based on the memory of earlier
tragedies.

## PEACE AND RECONSTRUCTION

Peace was eventually signed at Vereeniging in May, 1902,
and the work of reconstruction began. The terms of peace
were not severe: there was no humiliating reference to the loss
of cherished independence, and self-government was promised
as soon as possible, with £3,000,000 granted at once to aid
resettlement. Even the question of the native franchise was
left over until after self-government had been restored, a point
which Milner afterwards regretted, and which was to play its
part in shaping native policy in the future. Seventeen years
later, when he sat by Milner's side at Versailles at the end of
another and greater conflict, Botha, then Prime Minister of a
united South Africa, said, with feeling, "it was a generous peace
that the British people made with us, and that is why we stand
with them today side by side in the cause which has brought
us all together".

War and defeat, however, so far from reconciling the
Boers to their position, proved "a greater spiritual experience
even than the Great Trek" and made them as a people.[49]
Milner's policy was to stimulate the recovery of the mining
industry, and with the "overspill" thus created to "lift"
standards of life. This, with the aid of a loan of £35,000,000,
he did. Irrigation, forestry, roads, railways, education, public
buildings, all benefited, and the vexed question of a customs
union was at last solved. By the time he left, gold production

had reached more than £20,000,000, and South Africa was well set on the road to prosperity. This had not been achieved, however, without another questionable measure, the employment of Chinese workers to keep the mines going until the native labour, which had been cast off when war began, should drift back. Economically it was perhaps a necessary measure, but under the name of "Chinese slavery" the employment of these labourers, and the appalling conditions under which they were expected to live, shocked British opinion and contributed not a little to the "Liberal landslide" of 1906. The Australians and New Zealanders who had so recently fought in South Africa were perturbed, too, at the disregard for their susceptibilities. It was a typical example of Milner's inability to foresee the reactions of others to what seemed to him, at his desk, reasonable measures.

## THE COMING OF UNION

Education was reorganized in English on English lines: we must have time, Milner said, "to thoroughly anglicize the Transvaal". But the Boers countered by establishing their own schools, and it was now that the cult of Afrikaans began. What Milner hoped for, but never received, was a substantial immigration of British settlers. He hoped not only that the British on the Rand would return and qualify as voters before the promised self-government was given, but that there would be an "increase of the British population": "if, ten years hence, there are three men of British race to two of Dutch, the country will be safe and prosperous. If there are three of Dutch to two of British, we shall have perpetual difficulty". His thoughts, as always, were on a predominantly British South Africa, but that he was not to achieve, as he soon recognized. "It was evidently hopeless from the first," he said in 1907, "to try and make a good job of South Africa for the British people." Yet if the war had strengthened Afrikaner nationalism, it had made possible, at least for some years, the reconciliation of the two peoples and the creation of a wider South African nationalism within the framework of the British Empire, so soon to become, with the aid of South Africa's leading sons, a Commonwealth. And when Milner, years later, looked again at the work of reconstruction for which he had been responsible, "we have made this country for the Boers", was his comment, "they never could have done it for themselves". The reconstruction was, indeed, his greatest service to South Africa. In carrying it through he was assisted by the "Kindergarten", a team of notable young men, all destined to make their mark on affairs—Patrick Duncan, John Buchan, Geoffrey Robinson (Dawson), Lionel Curtis, W. L. Hichens, Fabian Ware, Basil Williams, R. H. Brand and Philip Kerr. By 1905 so much progress had been made that Milner could take his leave, and with the coming of the Liberal government in Britain a new chapter could be opened. Already in 1903, during his bold visit to South Africa, Chamberlain had said, in his last words to the annexed States, "I call upon you to help us to quench the embers of a strife that might never have arisen, and which is now happily over. And, if you do this, it will not be long before you will be again a free State and, at the same time, a member of the greatest Empire." Before he left two years later Milner had drafted a constitution which was to set the new colonies on the way to self-government, but the Liberal success swept it aside before it could be applied, and self-government was immediately granted. Nineteen hundred and seven saw Afrikaner governments in control in the Transvaal, where Botha ruled with Smuts, and in the Orange River Colony. At the Cape the "Progressives" had displaced the Bond during the war, and Jameson, his earlier transgressions forgotten, had become Prime Minister in 1904. Hofmeyr, however, had reconstituted the Bond as a reconciliatory "South African Party", and although Jameson renamed the Progressive Party "Unionist" the votes of reviving Afrikanerdom overthrew him: early in 1908 the Cape also had an Afrikaner Ministry. Natal remained alone as the Ulster of South Africa. Already closer union was under discussion, and towards the end of 1908 a National Convention, representing all four colonies, was brought together. Just a year later, in September 1909, the South Africa Act passed the Imperial Parliament and received the royal assent. It came into effect on 31st May 1910, "Union Day". South Africa was now a Dominion, and Botha became its first Prime Minister, almost exactly eight years after he had set his name to the terms of surrender at Vereeniging.

## United South Africa

If the establishment of the Union closed one long unhappy chapter, it opened another, only less difficult. Clause 137 of the South Africa Act recognized the dual character of the new State by prescribing that English and Dutch should be on an equal footing as official languages. Much past bitterness and suspicion was thereby removed, and it seemed that Boer and British aims, so long in conflict, had allowed themselves to be caught up in the greater ideal of a united South Africa. Milner's last speech in the country had looked forward to this, in a rare flight of imaginative understanding:

> The Dutch can never own a perfect allegiance merely to Great Britain. The British can never, without moral injury, accept allegiance to any body politic which excludes their motherland. But British and Dutch alike could . . . unite in loyal devotion to an Empire-State, in which Great Britain and South Africa would be partners.

It was in this spirit that Botha brought South Africa into war by Britain's side in 1914. Yet already the first indications of future political conflict had appeared. If there was to be equality, the Boers had numbers and tenacity on their side, and their memories were long. In 1912 Hertzog broke with Botha and founded the Nationalist Party, with an Afrikaner-dominated South Africa as its avowed aim. Soon after the entry into war in 1914 de Wet, de la Rey and other unreconciled Boers raised a rebellion, and although this was quickly put down, mostly with Afrikaner troops, by Botha, it added to the force of the nationalist tradition. At the end of the war Hertzog himself led an unofficial Nationalist deputation to Europe to plead for "a truly free South Africa". Moderate men of both races then drew together in politics, as they had stood together in war, and in 1920 the Unionist Party was absorbed into the South African Party led by Smuts as Botha's successor. The Nationalists remained the opposition until returned to power in 1924, but from 1912 a "renascent Krugerism"[50] was in the ascendant.

In the matter of native policy the South Africa Act made no attempt to liberalize the traditional policies of the Transvaal, the Orange Free State and Natal. The Cape franchise was left, "entrenched" in Clause 35 behind the provision that no amendment could be made without a two-thirds majority in a joint session of both Houses of Parliment, but this was no permanent protection, as events in the 'thirties and the 'fifties were to show. Nevertheless, it went as far as policy and opinon would permit. The "imperial factor", which in the past had been so often exercised by problems of native policy, was now withdrawn, and a united South Africa was free to work out its own solution. Part of the dreams of Carnarvon, Rhodes, Hofmeyr and so many others had been realized, but the "key to South African politics" remained. Mindful of this, still the greatest of all South Africa's problems, we can yet close this section with the noble words which Smuts addressed to Milner when he left in 1905:

> I am afraid you have not liked us; but I cherish the hope that, as our memories grow mellower and the nobler features of our respective ideals become clearer, we shall more and more appreciate the contribution of each to the formation of that happier South Africa which is surely coming.

Many difficult issues remained, and still remain nearly half a century later. Yet, by comparison with the stormy years which we have been surveying, it has been since 1910 a "happier South Africa"—at least, until more recent years.

## REFERENCES

The following indispensable works have been extensively drawn on for this chapter, but in view of the number of despatches, letters and speeches quoted from them no detailed references are given:

| | |
|---|---|
| Basil Williams: | *Cecil Rhodes.* |
| J. L. Garvin: | *Life of Joseph Chamberlain;* Vol. III, 1895–1900. |
| Julian Amery: | ibid., Vol. IV, 1901–03. |
| ed. C. Headlam: | *The Milner Papers.* |

1. A. Brady: *Democracy in the Dominions*, p. 403.
2. G. M. Young: *Daylight and Champaign* (1937).
3. R. F. A. Hoernlé: *South African Native Policy and the Liberal Spirit*, p. 62.

4. Sir A. Hardinge: *Life of Lord Carnarvon*, II, pp. 175–76.
5. Sir J. R. Innes: *Autobiography*, p. 280.
6. C. W. de Kiewiet: *The Imperial Factor in South Africa*, p. 67.
7. ibid., p. 68.
8. *South African Native Policy*, p. 146.
9. C. W. de Kiewiet: *History of South Africa, Social and Economic*, p. 87.
10. W. K. Hancock: *Survey of British Commonwealth Affairs*, Vol. II, Part 2, p. 9.
11. E. A. Walker: *A History of South Africa*, p. 438 n.
12. *History of South Africa, Social and Economic*, p. 96.
13. *Survey of British Commonwealth Affairs*, p. 42.
14. *History of South Africa, Social and Economic*, p. 85.
15. U.G. No. 28—1948, para. 25.
16. *Imperial Factor in South Africa*, p. 120.
17. V. Buchanan-Gould: *Not Without Honour. The Life and Writings of Olive Schreiner*, p. 130.
18. Innes: *Autobiography*, p. 16.
19. M. Roberts and A. E. G. Trollip: *The South African Opposition, 1939–45*, pp. 14 and 16.
20. ibid., p. 15.
21. J. P. R. Wallis: *Fitz. The Story of Sir Percy Fitzpatrick*, p. 166.
22. *History of South Africa, Social and Economic*, p. 101.
23. J. Agar-Hamilton: *The Native Policy of the Voortrekkers*, pp. 71 and 204–05.
24. *Imperial Factor in South Africa*, p. 218.
25. ibid., p. 103.
26. *History of South Africa, Social and Economic*, p. 89.
27. Sir Ian Hamilton: *Listening for the Drums*, p. 130.
28. R. I. Lovell: *The Struggle for South Africa, 1875–1899*, p. 35.
29. G. B. Pyrah: *Imperial Policy and South Africa, 1902–10*, p. 35.
30. Walker: *History of South Africa*, p. 393 n.
31. *Cecil Rhodes*, p. 60.
32. Walker: *History of South Africa*, p. 416.
33. Innes: *Autobiography*, p. 166.
34. ibid., p. 87.
35. ibid., p. 104.
36. A. Keppel-Jones: *South Africa: A Short History*, p. 132.

R*

37. *The History of The Times, 1884–1912*, p. 213 n.
38. S. Maccoby: *English Radicalism, 1886–1914*, p. 216 n.
39. *The Jameson Raid*, p. 261.
40. E. A. Walker: *Lord Milner and South Africa* (British Academy, 1942), p. 8.
41. Innes: *Autobiography*, p. 179.
42. ibid., p. 170.
43. H. H. Evatt: *Australian Labour Leader: The Story of W. A. Holman*, p. 88.
44. *Penguin* edition, p. 18.
45. ibid., p. 69.
46. Walker: *History of South Africa*, p. 488.
47. C. E. Carrington: *The British Overseas*, p. 705.
48. Wilson Harris: *J. A. Spender*, p. 146.
49. *Lord Milner and South Africa*, p. 24.
50. The phrase is L. S. Amery's: *My Political Life*, I, p. 170.

# XIII

## INDIA AND ITS NEIGHBOURS

### The Suez Canal and India

IF a new stage in the development of the settlement colonies
began with the creation of the Dominion of Canada in 1867,
the opening of the Suez Canal two years later was to prove as
significant for the history of modern India. Almost at a bound
India was brought into political and economic proximity to
Europe closer than ever before. Hitherto the voyage by sailing-
ship from Bombay to London via the Cape had taken three
months: now by steamer through the Canal it took little more
than as many weeks. Indian trade, not only with Britain but
with the whole of Europe, and especially with the Mediterranean countries, grew apace: in the 'sixties it had averaged
some £50,000,000 a year, but by 1875 it had reached
£90,000,000, and by the end of the century £200,000,000.
The Canal, it was said, had been extended to the foot of the
Himalayas, and the consequences for India were momentous.
Already the flow of cheap industrial products from the West
had crippled India's traditional manufactures, and village
economy had been upset. With the improvement of communications India became a major source of supply for the industrial
countries of Europe, and a great market for their products.
The development was the inevitable result of the industrial
revolution, but was aided by the fact that the pioneer of
industrialism was at the same time the predominant Power in
India and the leading commercial nation of the world. After
1869, as trade with Europe increased, the proportion of
India's total trade that was conducted with the Continent as a
whole rose to two-thirds, but of this considerably more than
half was with Britain. Indeed, until nearly the end of the century
India supplied the greater part of the important tropical
products imported into Britain from the Empire: cotton,
coffee, jute, hides, tea, rice and wheat were all exported in
increasing quantities. The export of fine cotton goods, which

first introduced cotton to England, has almost ceased, as Lancashire sent its products all over the world and captured much of the Indian home market, with unhappy results for many village weavers. But the export of raw cotton had grown, and had been stimulated by the American Civil War, rising in value from £5,000,000 to £35,000,000 between 1862 and 1866. The end of the war had brought a slump, but exports had settled at about £15,000,000, and the war-time demand had led to the creation of an Indian cotton industry, with the erection of the first mills at such important centres as Bombay, Ahmadabad, Cawnpore and Madras. A small-scale jute industry had also begun, but it was in foodstuffs that the most striking developments came at this time. The overseas market for Indian wheat was practically created by the Suez Canal, which obviated the necessity for a double journey through the tropics between India and Europe. By the early 'eighties exports of wheat were more than a million tons a year, much of it going to Britain, which at the end of the century was receiving from India, in good years, one-fifth of its total requirements.

## GROWTH OF THE TEA TRADE

Tea was also a considerable export. Originally of Chinese origin, it had been introduced into India in 1834, but had at first made little progress. In the 'fifties, however, the first reductions were made in the high duty on tea in Britain, and by 1865 it had been lowered, largely owing to Gladstone's achievements at the Treasury, from 2s. 2½d. a pound to only 6d. The tremendous rise in consumption that followed affected mainly Indian tea, which came to be preferred by the working-class consumer to the weaker and more expensive China tea, and it had important consequences for the social habits of the people. Hitherto a luxury consumed mainly by the well-to-do, tea now became the national beverage, with advantage to sober habits, and great plantations grew up in India to meet the demand. Production, which had been only 200,000 pounds in 1850, reached more than 6,000,000 pounds in 1870 and nearly 15,000,000 pounds only three years later. By the end of the 'eighties the total consumption in Britain was some 200,000,000 pounds, and of this the greater part was provided by India: imports from China were exceeded for the first time in 1888. Tea was then the seventh in value of Indian exports, and still further increases lay ahead. Ceylon, after the ruin of its coffee plantations by disease between 1868 and 1876, also turned to tea, but the chief centre of production was in Assam, a region of north-east India that was largely opened up by the new industry.

All this contributed directly to the well-being of Britain, but hardly less important was the indirect contribution of India's exports to Britain's balance of trade. Much of the total of exports was based on British capital invested in India, and therefore furthered the prosperity of British manufacturers, traders and investors. Without such returns on investment Britain's growing imports could not have been paid for, and India in this respect served as a "safety valve" for the British economy.[1]

## ECONOMIC GROWTH AND TARIFF POLICY

The tea plantations, and the export of tea, were mainly in European hands, but the steady increase of trade also strengthened and enriched the Indian merchant class, particularly at Bombay. From the wealth that now began to be created by shipping and cotton-mills the movement of national uprising, from its modest beginnings in the 'eighties, was soon to draw much of its support. The movement was encouraged among merchants and industrialists by the Government's tariff policy. At a time when the settlement colonies were beginning to control their own tariffs in defence of their nascent industries, Indian policy was dictated from London, and moved steadily towards free trade. After the Mutiny a general tariff of ten per cent was imposed for revenue purposes, but this was reduced in the 'sixties and 'seventies, and finally abolished in 1882. Twelve years later, however, the fall in the value of the rupee (due to the increased world output of gold—from South Africa and Australia in particular—and the consequent increase in the use of gold for currency, which depreciated the value of silver, India's traditional currency medium) necessitated a return to tariffs to raise revenue, and a five per cent duty was imposed. This was objected to in Lancashire as an unfair handicap to British cotton goods, and despite the

energetic protests of the Viceroy, Lord Elgin, the Indian
Government was compelled to lay an excise duty on cloth
produced in Indian mills. In 1896 the import duty was reduced
to 3½ per cent, and was balanced by an excise duty of the same
amount. "It was", a leading authority has said, "a short-
sighted policy, for it did more than anything else to strengthen
Indian distrust of British motives",[2] and it has long been quoted
by those who have sought to represent the British Empire in
India as a gigantic system of robbery. The advantages of the
"countervailing excise" to Lancashire were doubtful, as
British and Indian goods were very little in competition in the
same markets, while at the same time the growth of Indian
industry suggests that the duty was hardly a crippling burden,
but the moral effect was deplorable. For this reason, among
others, the middle-'nineties brought into Anglo-Indian relations a bitterness which was not to leave them until the
British *raj* itself was removed half a century later. India's
right to control her own tariff policy was recognized after
1919, and the excise finally disappeared in 1926, but it left an
unfortunate legacy of ill-will. Its effects were exacerbated by
the check to India's industrial expansion that was to some
extent set by British devotion to free-trade principles. Yet,
although India lacked the protection that was provided in other
newly-industrialized countries by tariff barriers, some of her
major industries did develop fairly rapidly. The cotton mills
established in the 'sixties numbered 58 in 1880, and by 1914
had increased to 264, employing 260,000 workers. Jute
mills in the same period rose in numbers from 22 to 64, and
coal output increased from something over 1,000,000 tons
to a figure little short of 16,000,000 tons. Moreover, the great
Tata steelworks, destined to become the largest in the British
Commonwealth, were established in 1912. The principal checks
to industrial growth, apart from natural difficulties, were the
comparatively low revenue and the lack of capital resources
adequate for the development of the vast area of a whole sub-
continent. In a society still bound by social and religious
conventions much capital, too, was locked up in unproductive
forms. When Disraeli described India as "the brightest jewel
in the British crown" his romantic imagination was inspired
by the glittering array of Indian princes who gathered to do

homage to the Queen-Empress's representative at the Imperial
Durbar of 1877, and an impression of jewelled pageantry
long formed the basis of such ideas of India as many Englishmen at home possessed. Few even of those on the spot could
yet grasp the significance of economic backwardness that lay
behind the famine that was raging at the very time that the
Durbar was being held.

## RAILWAY DEVELOPMENT

The immensity of the problem of development, and the
difficulty of acquiring capital on an appropriate scale were
well illustrated by the history of railway construction in India.
As in other great continental areas, the railway was the
indispensable pioneer of modernization, and it was the creation
of a railway system, in particular, which in effect extended the
Suez Canal to the foot of the Himalayas. Yet the raising of
capital for railway construction was a constant problem for
governments, and it was difficult for many years to interest
Indian capital, while the railways themselves did not pay until
the very end of the century. Under these circumstances, and in
view of the heavy cost of overcoming the great physical
difficulties involved, it was necessary for the Government to
take a more active part than would normally have been possible
in the heyday of *laissez faire*. Guarantees were given to
constructing companies, and between 1869 and 1877 the
Government itself actually undertook an extensive programme
of construction. Before this the urgent need for more lines had
been shown by the sudden demand for rapid troop movements
during the Mutiny, while in the years 1876–78 the need was
further illustrated by the terrible famine that assailed a great
part of the South. Railway development then became part of
the policy of famine relief. In 1880 the total mileage of track
had reached only 9,000 (though at this same time, it is true,
the rest of Asia possessed only some 800 miles). Within a
decade this figure had been doubled, and India finally acquired
a railway system extending over more than 40,000 miles.
Construction contantly lagged behind the needs of the country,
however, and during the last quarter of the nineteenth century
the difficulty of raising capital was increased by the fall in the
value of the rupee, which made governments chary of raising

sterling loans. Moreover, railway construction and the growth of trade necessitated a heavy and costly programme of harbour works. Yet the railways almost revolutionized Indian life, creating a hitherto unknown sense of unity, and encouraging the commercial and industrial development which was a necessary basis of national self-consciousness. If the original impulse in official railway policy was the easing of control and administration the results were a boomerang.

## FAMINE RELIEF

The benefits of railway development were shown most readily in the relief of famine, India's recurring scourge. The great famine of 1876-78, the result of the failure of two successive monsoons, has already been referred to. In the previous hundred years various parts of India had suffered no less than twenty famines, some of them extending over several years, and it has been estimated that during the whole nineteenth century more than 26,000,000 people perished through famine. Until the arrival of railways it was practically impossible to arrange adequate relief measures, or to move food in time over the great distances involved. Now, as an Indian historian has said, bad though the famine of 1876-78 was, it would have been even worse but for the 3,000,000 tons of grain carried by the railways.[3] Henceforth the problem became one less of providing food than of providing work, by means of which money could be earned for the purchase of food. During the famine years, 1876-78, the Viceroy, Lord Lytton, toured the distressed areas, and it was as a result of his experiences that a "Famine Code" was issued in 1883. More than £8,000,000 had been spent in relief during the famine years, yet of the 58,000,000 people involved more than 5,000,000 had died, and it was clear that some annual financial provision was needed to build up a reserve fund which could immediately be drawn on in case of need. The Code of 1883, while laying down regulations for the administration of relief, provided for the setting aside each year of a sum equivalent to £1,500,000 for "famine relief and insurance": in good years this was to be spent on irrigation schemes and the construction of railways and canals, all of which would serve as protective measures. The new system was not seriously tested until

1896-97, when one of the worst crop failures of which there was record involved nearly 70,000,000 people. Three-quarters of a million died, a proportion far smaller than on previous occasions, and a similar control of the disaster was shown two years later, when 60,000,000 people were affected and for weeks at a time more than 6,000,000 were in regular receipt of relief. Each famine (and there were more in 1907, 1911, 1913 and 1918) brought further knowledge and experience, and the general development of the country tended to diminish their ravages. Yet, as the terrible famine of 1943 was to show, the margin of protection was small. Under the stress of war and a changing political situation the precautions devised through the experience of sixty years broke down then in Bengal, and some million and a half people perished. It was a tragic reminder of an ancient threat that was assumed to have passed, but which had been under control for little more than a generation.

## POPULATION

To the protective measures of famine relief can be attributed, in part, the remarkable increase of population in India during the past three-quarters of a century. The first, incomplete, census of 1871 showed a population of some 200,000,000. Improved census methods in 1881 revealed a total of 253,000,000, and this had increased by 1901 to 294,000,000, by 1921 to 318,000,000, and twenty years later, in 1941, to 389,000,000. Though checked by epidemics, by the prevailing low standards of health, and by high rates of infant and maternal mortality, the surplus of births over deaths in recent years has been 5,000,000 a year: improvements in standards of living have been prevented, above all, by what has been described as "the devastating torrent of Indian babies".

## IRRIGATION SCHEMES: GOVERNMENT AND ECONOMICS

With railways and famine relief were associated great irrigation schemes and the establishment of "canal colonies", which relieved the pressure on over-populated districts by extending the area of cultivation. In a country where the rainfall varies from more than 400 inches a year in some parts to only 3 inches in others, and where the rain-bearing monsoon is liable to periodic failure, reservoirs ("tanks") and irrigation canals have been constructed from the earliest times. Government activity in this field began in the 'sixties, and has been particularly marked in Sind and the Punjab. Already by the end of the nineteenth century India possessed the greatest system of irrigation canals in the world, and before British rule came to an end more than 30,000,000 acres of cultivated land had been created from desert tracts by some 75,000 miles of canals. It is typical of the rapid increase of India's population, however, that some of these canal colonies, which were settled to relieve population pressure elsewhere, have themselves become over-populated. Thus, in one colony established in the 'nineties the average of population to the square mile had risen in forty years, without any immigration, from 15 to 357.[4] In itself this startling increase is symptomatic of the fundamental economic stresses of Indian life, which British rule, for all its activity, was unable to relieve. Given the economic doctrines which prevailed in official circles it is a matter of some interest, not that more was not done, but that so much was achieved by direct Government action. Moreover, economic conditions were closely linked with the social and religious beliefs of the people, which governments were bound not to disturb. A famous passage in Queen Victoria's proclamation of 1858, announcing the establishment of direct British rule, had declared that:

> Firmly relying ourselves on the truth of Christianity, and acknowledging with gratitude the solace of religion, we disclaim alike the right and desire to impose our convictions on any of our subjects.

In the course of time these liberal sentiments, which the Queen herself had intended as an expression not of neutrality but of tolerance, came to be interpreted as a cautious avoidance of anything likely to offend religious susceptibilities. Recollection of the Mutiny and fear of racial or religious disorders often delayed action in matters affecting the life of the people until there was ample evidence of the support of enlightened opinion. Yet if officials erred in the direction of caution they erred in the consciousness of the fact that a country almost as large as Europe, with a population of some 300,000,000, was held at peace by a garrison of only 60,000 white troops and

4,000 officials. Britain did much for India, but after 1858 it rarely ran risks or sought to probe too deeply into the causes of Indian backwardness. In the words used by a notable administrator and student of peasant problems, Sir Malcolm Darling, in the vivid survey he made of Indian conditions in 1946-47, on the eve of independence, "the aim was to give the peasant the kind of Government he trusted and respected—strong, just and accessible—rather than the kind he needed to face the modern world".[5] In fairness it has to be added that the demands of that world were less clear before 1914 than they afterwards became, while Victorian conceptions of government were not, in any case, concerned with the alteration of the bases of society. Lord Carnarvon's Edinburgh speech of 1878, which has already been quoted,[6] illustrates both the principles that inspired the British administration of India, and the limitations within which it operated.

## EMIGRATION

Railway and canal construction and famine relief have won for the second half of the nineteenth century in India the title of "the era of public works". Associated with these projects for economic improvement was the encouragement of emigration as a means of relieving the pressure of population. As in England at an earlier date, the growth of industry drew people from the countryside, while Assam was cleared, and its tea plantations were developed, by labour drawn from other areas. Burma and Malaya also attracted Indian workers, and under official regulation they were allowed to emigrate, as indentured labourers, to the West Indies, South and East Africa and Fiji. In these distant regions they have now formed considerable settlements, amounting in all to some two and a half million people, and though their presence has frequently complicated local problems (notably in South Africa), the recent development of these colonial areas has owed much to their efforts. With the flow of Chinese emigrants to Malaya this migration of Indians has well been described as the great Asiatic contribution to the colonizing movements of the nineteenth century, which are usually more closely associated with European developments. Together, the Indian and Chinese emigrants, one authority has said, "have created new colonial values, made whole regions of the British Tropics into paying assets, and created within the British Empire a new Indian Empire in the British West Indies and a new Chinese Empire in the British Straits Settlements".[7] What the long-term effects of these developments may be cannot yet be seen. At least one observer has foretold an eventual clash between India and China for the control of South East Asia.[8]

## GOVERNMENT AND POLITICAL ADVANCE

But although it is upon India's economic development that interest has tended to concentrate in more recent years, it was with the country's political position and evolution that official policy was chiefly concerned in the second half of the nineteenth century, and this was natural in an age which had narrowly restricted notions of the part to be played by the State in economic affairs. Moreover, the Mutiny had profoundly affected British opinions of India. Hitherto, while British control had gradually increased, and the British administrative system had expanded to cope with growing responsibilities, it had been readily assumed that British rule would eventually come to an end. Thus, Macaulay had said in the House of Commons in 1833:

It may be that the public mind of India may expand under our system till it has outgrown that system; that by good government we may educate our subjects into a capacity for better government; that, having become instructed in European knowledge, they may, in some future age, demand European institutions.[9]

It had been generally agreed that Indians needed a long period of education to prepare them for self-government, but that enlightenment would come under British guidance. "We should look upon India," Sir Thomas Munro, Governor of Madras, had written in 1824, "not as a temporary possession, but as one which is to be maintained permanently, until the natives in some future age have abandoned most of their superstitions and prejudices, and become sufficiently enlightened to frame a regular government for themselves."[10] These notions of progress had, however, received a rude shock from the Mutiny. It suddenly became evident that Indian "superstitions and prejudices" would not so easily be abandoned, that European ideas of moral and material progress were not necessarily acceptable to the people upon whom they were being imposed. Reformers who thought, with Bentham, that they could legislate for men dwelling by the Indus and Ganges as easily as for those by the Thames and Trent were confronted by intangible elements of Indian life and thought. As a result, the idea gained ground among many that Indians were in some peculiar way incomprehensible and unreliable. The British in India, few in numbers in comparison with the vast numbers they ruled and the gigantic nature of the tasks they had to perform, came to regard themselves, it has well been said, "as a garrison occupying a country which might always break out in a sudden rebellion".[11] From this attitude, itself the result of the fear and uncertainty of the Mutiny period, grew increased aloofness, which later drew from an eminent Indian the sarcastic comment that British officials were, "like tinned goods, untouched by hand".

## THE AFTERMATH OF THE "MUTINY"

On the Indian side the aftermath of the Mutiny brought a realization of the power and enduring nature of the British *raj*, with its modern notions and its new techniques. It is, as Seeley pointed out in *The Expansion of England*, a misnomer to speak of a British conquest of India: India, in his phrase, "has fallen to England", which, with its command of the sea, became the only power able to maintain peace and order in the country after the anarchy that followed the breakdown of Mogul rule. Yet without Indian co-operation British power could never have been established, and it was not until after the Mutiny, and the disappearance of the last remnants of "Company" rule, that the cleavage between Indians and Europeans became marked. Henceforth, for reasons both of security and of efficiency, British control of the machinery of government was strengthened. At the same time, improved communications, and a growing tendency for the wives of officials to join their husbands, increased the sense of solidarity among the British, and therefore their aloofness. There was as yet no opposition to British rule as being "foreign", for Indian nationalism was a later development, which was destined, in any case, to take strange forms, but, if British rule were accepted as readily—even as fatalistically—as any other would have been, by its very nature it laid itself open to greater criticism than any Indian government would have met, for it was both more efficient and more resolute to improve the lot of the people. And however cautiously improvements were attempted, in the last resort they could not fail to touch the "superstitions and prejudices" which it had earlier been hoped to remove by education and example. "The longer you stay in the country," wrote an enlightened official, Henry Beveridge (father of a famous figure of a later period) in 1873, "the more you will feel that at heart the natives fear and dislike us and that they look with suspicion on all our schemes even when they really are for their benefit."[12]

"Untouched by hand", the British ruling caste certainly was, the "White Brahmins" of India, efficient, incorrupt and incorruptible in an oriental society whose standards were in general more easy-going than those of the West. These "Men Who ruled India" were, in fact, as a modern historian of their achievement has justly styled them, the Platonic "Guardians" of a sub-continent:

> The Mutiny was over; things settled down. In the letters and biographies of the 'sixties and 'seventies, English administrators do not often betray a feeling of insecurity. In the whole of human history there can hardly have been another class of men so sure of themselves. . . . They belonged to a service which gave them an assured position and the right to be themselves. They were leaders of the official world, the rulers of India. They were doing work they knew was good.[13]

## INDIANS AND THE GOVERNMENT: (1) THE I.C.S.

Apart from its social aspects, which came to be resented by many Indians with increasing bitterness, British aloofness showed itself chiefly in a hesitation to admit Indians to any considerable share of political power. Queen Victoria's proclamation of 1858 had declared that "so far as may be, our subjects of whatever race or creed be freely and impartially admitted to offices in our service, the duties of which they may be qualified by their education, ability and integrity duly to discharge". Experienced British officials had long maintained that only by admitting Indians to high office would British rule be kept at peace or Indians themselves prepared for ultimate self-government, and resentment at exclusion from power had brought not a few Indian notables to support of the Mutiny. Yet the steps taken after 1858 were in fact calculated to limit to a minimum the entry of Indians into the Civil Service. Entry was by competitive examination, but as the examination was held in London few Indians could afford to compete, and as was shown by the case of Surendranath Banerjea, a successful candidate of 1871, success was no guarantee of acceptance into the official ranks. Banerjea, later Sir Surendranath (1848–1925), won a place which he had to take legal steps to enforce, and was dismissed after only a few years. He became, as founder and editor of the *Bengalee*, a notable journalist, took a leading, but moderate, part in the nationalist movement, and, by the irony of events, was appointed a Minister in the Bengal government after the Montague-Chelmsford reforms. He probably served India better in this way than if he had spent his life as an official, but his exclusion from the Service became an early nationalist grievance.

In 1878 entry to the Service by way of London was still more restricted by the lowering of the maximum age for candidates from 21 to 19. Lord Salisbury, then Secretary for India, justified this restrictive policy with the argument that the Indian educated class, as it then existed, "could not be any-thing else than opposition in quiet times, rebels in time of trouble".[14] "I can imagine no more terrible future for India," he wrote to the Viceroy in 1877, "than that of being governed by Competition-Baboos."[15] He was reflecting the common attitude of contempt for the worst type of Indian clerk, with his officiousness, his narrow pedantry, his literalness and his evasion of responsibility, and the attitude was not altogether unjustified, for there were then comparatively few Indians able to compete with British standards of efficiency. But little was done to remedy the deficiency, even when the development of higher education produced more promising material. By the end of the century the All-India and Provincial Civil Services numbered in all more than half a million officials. Of these by far the greater part was Indian, for India was never swamped, as French colonies have been, with hordes of Euro-pean minor officials, and only four thousand of the half million were British. Many Indians, indeed, hardly ever saw a British official in their lives: "the best thing that can be said of the British raj", an Indian writer has recorded, "is that a great number of Indians barely knew it existed".[16] Yet the four thousand held, in the I.C.S. and the I.P. (Indian Police), most of the key positions of the whole administration. Less than one-fifth of the posts in the I.C.S. were held by Indians, and the proportion was maintained until the recommendations of the Royal Commission of 1923 were put into effect. There was much to be said for maintaining the administration at the highest possible level of efficiency, but the price was paid in increasing discontent and pressure for reform. Lord Lytton (Viceroy 1876–80) saw the vicious circle in which the administration was caught. "We don't employ natives more largely because they are not well qualified," he wrote, "and they are not well qualified because we do not employ them enough."[17] But his own efforts to improve the situation by establishing a special Civil Service, which should not be recruited through examination in London, were frustrated, partly by the indifference of the type of Indian he wished to attract, and partly by official apathy and distrust.

## (2) LEGISLATION AND RESPONSIBILITY, 1861–1909

Similar caution was shown in the association of Indians with legislation. The Mutiny had taken the Government by surprise, and one of the most distinguished of British officials, Sir Bartle Frere (a brilliant administrator, better known, perhaps, for his unhappy failure later in South Africa), criticized in 1860 "the perilous experiment of continuing to legislate for millions of people with few means of knowing, except by rebellion, whether the laws suit them or not".[18] Frere's remedy was the institution of a council like the *durbar* of an Indian Prince, "the channel from which the ruler learns how his measures are likely to affect his subjects, and may hear of discontent before it becomes disaffection", and it was on this model that the Indian Councils Act of 1861 was based. The Act enlarged the Viceroy's Council by up to twelve additional legislative members, of whom not less than half were to be "non-officials", and gave legislative powers also to the Councils of the Provincial Governors, which were similarly increased by the addition of "non-official" members. From this first cautious step, intended to be no more than an empiric solution of the problems revealed by the Mutiny, developed not only the later measures, down to the Act of 1935, which increased Indian control over the government, but also the whole framework of Indian administration, with its division between Central and Provincial authority. Yet there was no intention of preparing India for representative government. Indeed, when he introduced the Bill in Parliament the Secretary for India, Sir Charles Wood (later Viscount Halifax, and grandfather of the Earl of Halifax, who was Viceroy, as Lord Irwin, in 1926-31), pointed out the impossibility of assembling "at any one place in India persons who shall be the real representatives of the Native population of that empire".[19] The notion of a united India, efficiently governed by a truly representative Assembly, seemed incapable of realization within any measurable period. Whatever the principles to which Britain paid lip-service, the more clearly India's fundamental backwardness and lack of homogeneity were realized, the less it seemed possible to extend to India the self-government that was granted to Canada, Australia, New Zealand and South Africa. "The longer, in fact, that the British Raj lasted," one authority has said, "the harder it seemed to contemplate its replacement by an Indian Raj."[20] The concessions of 1861 were enlarged in 1892 by a further Act, which increased the number of "non-official" members of the Councils, tacitly admitted the principle of their election, and granted them the right of discussing the budget and raising matters of general interest. Another step was taken in 1909. The Indian Councils Act of that year, known conveniently as the "Morley-Minto Reforms" from the names of the Secretary of State and the Viceroy, brought fresh developments which, though they claimed to introduce no new principle, were interpreted in India as doing so. By this measure the Councils were still further enlarged, and in the Provinces, though not at the Centre, were allowed "non-official" majorities. The principle of election was formally recognized, and the Councils were permitted to discuss and pass resolutions on any matter of public interest. In short, influence was conceded, but without responsibility, and it is significant that after 1909 the pace of reform was hurried. Yet Morley, Radical though he was, denied any intention of introducing representative government in India. "If it could be said", he told the Lords, "that this chapter of reforms led directly or necessarily to the establishment of a parliamentary system in India, I for one would have nothing at all to do with it", and in a phrase that has passed into history he dismissed any comparison between Canada and India as equivalent to the argument that because a fur-coat was needed in the Canadian winter it was needed in the Deccan. To Morley, as to all but the left-wing in Parliament, the peculiar conditions of India were a bar to developments on the British model, but he had nothing to offer in their place. When the moderate Indian leader, G. K. Gokhale, confessed to him that he hoped to see India "on the footing of a self-governing colony", Morley replied that "for many a day to come—long beyond the short span that may be left to us—this was a mere dream".[21] His meaning probably was that he could not see how such a dream could be realized, and more recent events have justified his doubts. To extend the moderate concessions of 1861, however, was no policy of political wisdom or foresight: the problem of Indian development demanded a fresh approach, as was realized when the next step, the "Montague-Chelmsford" reforms, was taken in 1919. Meanwhile, as will be shown later, every move that seemed to bring self-government nearer deepened the rifts in Indian life, especially those between Hindu and Moslem, and the results were seen in 1947. Yet there is, in retrospect, a touch of the irony of history in Morley's words to Gokhale, owing to a parallel in recent Russian history. In 1896 Nicholas II of Russia dismissed an appeal for a closer association of his people with the government as "senseless dreams", but the dreams were eventually realized, and realized in the most terrible manner. India's sufferings in the years between 1909 and 1947 were less than those of Russia, but in the end Gokhale's "mere dream" also became a reality, though the forms it took were far removed from his hopes.

## (3) THE BASES OF BRITISH RULE

In general, British policy in India may be said to have suffered from lack of imagination, a failing not unknown in other branches of British politics. Yet there were imaginative observers who could see clearly. Writing to Salisbury in 1877

Lytton criticized "the fundamental political mistake of able and experienced Indian officials . . . that we can hold India securely by what they call good government; that is to say, by improving the lot of the ryot (peasant), strictly administering justice, spending immense sums on irrigation works, etc."[22] Lytton, with his colourful literary background, had small hopes of winning popular support through sentiments of gratitude: far more was to be achieved, he maintained, by appealing through "sentiment" and "symbols" to the imagination of the chiefs and princes, to whom the peasantry still looked for leadership. This romantic view probably went to the other extreme, but the attitude which Lytton deplored, while it remained characteristic of the Indian administration at least until the First World War, created for itself a growing resentment. The sublime self-confidence of the "Guardians", their "almost patriarchal conception" of their functions (as was later said of Curzon, the supreme exponent of paternalism), their reliance on the Indian acceptance of government as *ma bap* (mother and father), their consciousness of the historic significance of the immense task they had undertaken, all combined to sustain them in an attitude that has been well described by an observer who saw its extension to Mesopotamia later after the expulsion of the Turks:

> as long as the material well-being of the subject peoples was being advanced, no other standard need be set up by which to judge the administration. As long as administrators spent the best of their bodily and mental vigour on the people, there was no need to justify the measures which kept them in authority. Political aspirations and the desire for self-government were to be dismissed as vagaries of ungrateful extremists or to be repressed as firmly as wayward thoughts in any adolescent youth.[23]

This heroic imperialism, which could be justified in the earlier period, but was outmoded by the development of India under its very guidance, had little enough in it to catch India's loyalty. In the words of a character created by another observer of the Indian scene, E. M. Forster, in his penetrating study *A Passage to India*, written in 1924:

> "Indians know whether they are liked or not—they cannot be fooled here. Justice never satisfies them, and that is why the British Empire rests on sand."

Flickerings of unease there were at times among the more sensitive, as Henry Beveridge's comment suggests, and Curzon himself asked, after he had left India for good, "what is in the heart of all these sombre millions?"[24] Close though relations frequently were, they were the relations of governor and governed: devoted though the administration unquestionably was, it was the work of foreigners.

## (4) THE POPULARITY OF LORD RIPON

How much opinion in India could be swayed by sentiments of gratitude was shown during the Viceroyalty of Lytton's successor, Lord Ripon (1880-84). Ripon's appointment followed the Liberal victory in the election of 1880, and was intended as a corrective to the colourful but costly imperialism of Lytton and the Disraeli administration. Ripon, though not a man of any outstanding ability, held advanced views and possessed great honesty of purpose. His rather doctrinaire Liberalism was perhaps not too well suited to the Indian scene, and he tended to judge all Indians, as one friendly critic pointed out, by the "educated and intelligent gentlemen whom the Viceroy sees in his Council or in his drawing-room", but his sympathetic interest in their well-being won for him an enduring reputation among Indians of all classes. His efforts to improve primary education and to encourage the participation of Indians in local government, though significant in their day, did not achieve any important results, but in a typically Liberal gesture he repealed the Act Lytton had passed to restrain the vernacular Press, and this step gained for him much popularity. This was afterwards increased by the vigorous opposition of many Europeans in India to the "Ilbert Bill", which Ripon supported, and which, as will be seen later, was to play a part in the establishment of the Indian National Congress. It was typical of the encouragement which he gave to Indian self-respect that among the Congress's aims was declared to be, "the fuller development and consolidation of those sentiments of national unity that had their origin in our beloved Lord Ripon's memorable reign". His Viceroyalty coincided, indeed, with new developments in Indian thought that must be described in their place, but in retrospect its significance probably lies in its revelation of the Indian's emotional response to the human touch in government. The contrast between the affection shown to Ripon and the dislike of Curzon, a far greater and abler man, with more positive achievements to his credit, but aloof and unbending in manner, is a revealing comment on Indian affairs.

## Ind. Imp., 1877–1948

It was in an attempt to establish closer personal links with India that an Act was passed by Parliament in 1876, during Lytton's Viceroyalty, to enable Queen Victoria to add to her titles that of Empress of India. The first proposal for such a step had been made in the 'forties,[25] and Disraeli had pressed for it in 1858, when the government of India had been transferred from the Company to the Crown. "You can only act upon the opinion of Eastern nations through their imagination", he had then told the Commons, and he had urged upon the Queen the necessity for a dramatic gesture to the peoples of India: "the name of your Majesty ought to be impressed upon their native life".[26] The morrow of the Mutiny was hardly a propitious moment, however, but Disraeli continued to maintain that the relations between the Queen and the peoples of India should be "drawn nearer", and, as the Queen was popularly credited with the title of Empress, she herself raised the matter in 1873, towards the close of Gladstone's first Ministry. Gladstone was unsympathetic, but when Disraeli became Prime Minister in 1874 action became possible. Disraeli's first step was to encourage the Prince of Wales to undertake the tour of India which he had planned for the cool season of 1875–76. The tour, the first made by a member of the Royal Family in India, was a marked success, and the decision to proclaim the addition to the Queen's title followed. It met with considerable opposition in Parliament and was regarded with suspicion by some sections of public opinion. There was a real concern lest the old and respected titles of King and Queen should be supplanted, and the very title of "Emperor", from its associations with Russian autocracy, the intrigues of Napoleon III and the recent fiasco of Maximilian in Mexico (1864–67), was viewed with distaste. Disraeli urged support of the measure as evidence "that the Parliament of England have resolved to uphold the Empire of

India" against the growing power of Imperial Russia in Central Asia, but although the Bill was carried it was opposed by Gladstone. The Queen was disturbed and puzzled at the opposition to a measure, which, she insisted, concerned India alone, and from this time can be dated the estrangement between her and Gladstone, which was so soon to be increased by his fierce resistance to Disraeli's handling of the Eastern Question. In India, however, the step was welcomed, and the Queen soon became the legendary figure of almost religious veneration, which she was becoming also in parts of British Africa. The sentiment of personal loyalty now encouraged was most strikingly manifested in 1911, when the only visit of a reigning King-Emperor was made by George V. Increasing political tension and the strain of the post-war period soon brought a change of feeling, however, and the reception of the Prince of Wales in 1921 was already markedly less enthusiastic. An imaginative gesture still suited to the conditions of the nineteenth century was rapidly outmoded as India progressed towards self-government, and the title of *Kaisar-i-Hind* was finally discarded, after 71 years, in 1948. Its chief significance throughout had probably lain in the special relations which it had helped to create between the Crown and the Princes of India, and it was to the "native aristocracy" that Lytton and Salisbury had looked for support for British rule when the royal title was under consideration.

## PRINCES AND "NATIVE STATES"

"British India", after the conquests and acquisitions of the first half of the nineteenth century, amounted to rather more than three-fifths of the total area of the sub-continent. The rest consisted of more than five hundred "Native States", many of them very small, but some of considerable size and significance: among these Hyderabad, Kashmir, Mysore, Travancore, Gwalior, Baroda and Indore were the most important. The patchwork that these States created upon the map of India is evidence in itself that the extension of the British *raj* was not the consequence of some great scheme of imperial policy. In the main the States continued to exist as the result of treaty engagements entered into with the East India Company, but, while these treaties were upheld after 1858, and it was decreed that no further annexations should take place, the assumption of authority by the Crown made it clear that Britain was now the Paramount Power in India, and this was recognized in the proclamation of 1877. Hitherto, misrule or a disputed succession in any State had almost invariably led to annexation. Now the Paramount Power intervened to reform or depose, but annexation was not resorted to. The removal of the Gaekwar of Baroda in 1875, the return of Mysore (under direct British rule since 1831) to a native ruler in 1881, and, in more recent years, intervention in the affairs of Hyderabad, Kashmir and Alwar, were evidence both of the sovereignty of the Crown, and of the determination that imperial rule should bring benefits to the peoples of British and Indian India alike. But it was long before the Princes were brought into any closer connexion with the imperial government. Lytton had urged that a council of Princes should be established to confer with the Viceroy on matters affecting all India, but memories of the Mutiny were still too recent, and it was feared in London that if the Princes were encouraged to act together they might take advantage of any conflict in which Britain was involved to lay their hands upon great parts of India which had been kept from them in the past only by British military power. With a Russian war as a very real possibility in the 'seventies and 'eighties, this was an understandable, though probably an excessive, measure of precaution. Thirty years later, when the revolutionary nationalist movement was in its stride, Lord Minto, Viceroy from 1905 to 1910, took up Lytton's suggestion, but, while the advantages of drawing together the conservative elements in India's political life were apparent, the difficulty of finding adequate scope for a Council of Princes caused the project again to be laid aside, though informal conferences were now held at intervals. The First World War, however, brought a complete change in the situation. The active support then given by the Princes won them much sympathy in Britain, and, for their part, the decision in 1919 to grant some measure of responsible government in British India indicated that a time would probably come when paramountcy would be exercised by a purely Indian government answerable to Indian opinion: it was clearly in the Princes' interests to draw together. As a result the "Montague-

Chelmsford" reforms of 1919 were followed two years later by the establishment of a Chamber of Princes, the first step, as events showed, towards the attempt made in 1935 to frame a Federal India.

## DEMOCRACY AND BUREAUCRACY

During the deliberations on the reforms of 1909 Morley once wrote to Minto of "the great riddle of how a Parliamentary Democracy is to govern India". "I say '*how*', not '*whether*' ", he added, "because the experiment has got to be tried somehow".[27] Whether, in fact, the British parliamentary democracy did succeed in governing India will be a matter for future consideration by historians, though none will be able to question the high seriousness of the debates upon Indian affairs that were held in Parliament before the great changes of 1909, 1919, 1935 and 1947. In effect, Indian policy was shaped at the India Office in London, and not only was parliamentary interest spasmodic in its operation, but the scope of the Viceroy himself was restricted.

Of necessity, too, the daily round of administration, within the "steel framework" (Lloyd George's later phrase) of the Service that sustained the whole imperial structure in India, went on largely regardless of the activities of the presiding functionaries, the Viceroys and Governors, who could often be little more than "ships that pass in the night".[28] The very extent of the duties to be performed with only a small European staff, the impossibility that every detail should be directed by Viceroy and Parliament, strengthened the tendency to bureaucracy. Curzon was to complain of the narrowness of "departmentalism" in the government, and Queen Victoria, when he was appointed in 1898, urged Lord Salisbury, then Prime Minister, to warn Curzon to keep clear of "red-tapist, narrow-minded" officials and to see and decide things for himself. The whole of her letter on this occasion deserves to be quoted as a typical expression of the mixture of sentiments felt by the average Englishman towards India. With its characteristic underlinings, it needs to be savoured to the full as a record of the attitude of a reasonably well-informed, warm-hearted woman, who took very seriously her responsibilities as sovereign of India (even to the extent of providing herself with Indian attendants, and trying to learn Hindustani), and who represented in her attitude a considerable class in Britain:

> The future Viceroy must really shake himself more and more free from his red-tapist, narrow-minded Council and entourage. He must be more independent, must *hear for himself* what the *feelings* of the Natives really are, and do what he thinks right, and not be guided by the *snobbish* and vulgar overbearing and offensive behaviour of many of our Civil and Political Agents, if we are to go on peacefully and happily in India, and to be liked and beloved by high and low, as well as respected as we ought to be, and not trying to trample on the people and continually reminding them and make them feel that they are a conquered people. They must of course *feel* that we are masters, but it should be done kindly and not offensively, which alas! is so often the case.[29]

Queen Victoria never saw India, but her grandson, George V, who resembled her in so many ways, when he visited the country as Prince of Wales in 1905–06 formed at first-hand a similar impression of the conduct of many Europeans: "I could not help noticing," he wrote, "that the general bearing of the European towards the Native was to say the least unsympathetic. In fact not the same as that of superiors to inferiors at home."[30] Yet despite narrowness and imperfections, what British rule, and the example of British constitutional government, manifestly did do were to create among Indians a sense of security and unity and a desire for self-government, all hitherto unknown. And, despite the doubts of Morley and others, with the example of Westminster before them Indians naturally wished to reproduce parliamentary government in India itself.

## THE RISE OF CONGRESS

The political history of modern India begins with the foundation in 1885 of the Indian National Congress, but the 'eighties were in general a period of reviving confidence and of adjustment to changing conditions, from which many later developments can be traced. The influence of the growth of trade has already been touched on. An even more potent influence was the spread of education and of the use of English among the educated classes: for the first time Indians had a single common language, and it is significant that from the

s

beginning Congress debates were conducted in English. Yet
there was a marked difference in the approach to Western
education of the two main religious communities, Hindu and
Moslem, and in the difference can be seen the first indications
of the division of India in 1947. Hinduism by its very nature
proved less of an obstacle to the training of its followers in
Western methods than did the more rigid tenets of
Mohammedanism, and as Indians were increasingly received
into government service as officials the Moslems found the
majority of official posts in Hindu hands. Moreover, the days
of Moslem rule were not long past, and tradition dies hard.
Outnumbered as they were by about three to one over the
country as a whole, Moslems resented the growing Hindu
ascendancy, for which there were many reasons, and communal riots, always endemic in some parts of India, tended to
increase. Moslems were to be found among the supporters of
Congress from the beginning, but at the end of the century
their numbers began to diminish in proportion to those of
Hindus, and although some continued their membership, and
thus preserved for Congress the semblance of All-India
representation, a new organization, the All-India Moslem
League, was founded in 1906. By that time passions had
increased and the problems of orderly development in India
been greatly magnified.

Congress had had its forerunners, notably an "India
Association" founded by Banerjea in 1876, but it owed its
immediate origins to the agitation of Europeans in India
against a Bill introduced in 1883 by Sir Courtenay Ilbert, the
legal member of the Viceroy's Council, to empower Indian
magistrates, some of whom had now reached senior positions,
to try European offenders. The Bill inevitably aroused racial
antipathies, and so bitter were the attacks on it from Europeans,
and especially from planters living isolated among Indians in
remote districts, that the Viceroy, Lord Ripon, was himself
openly insulted, and eventually the measure had to be modified.
It was an unhappy indication of racial feeling, "a bad example
to the elephant", as *Punch* called it,[31] which educated Indians
resented and never forgot. It provided them with an object
lesson in the value of organized agitation, and therefore proved,
in the words of an Indian historian, "one of the watersheds of

modern Indian history".[32] The Indian National Congress followed two years later, though when it held its first session in 1885 it showed no disloyalty to British rule, and received, indeed, some unofficial support. It was bound, however, to press for a closer association of Indians with the government, and therefore to adopt, in time, a more critical attitude. Its history is largely the record of its evolution from a small group of educated and westernized Indians, representing hardly anyone but themselves, into a mass revolutionary and nationalist movement, and is bound up with the careers of three remarkable men, G. K. Gokhale (1866-1915), B. G. Tilak (1856-1920) and M. K. Gandhi (1869-1948).

## SHAPERS OF INDIAN OPINION:
### (i) G. K. GOKHALE

The first session of the Congress, while it paid tribute to the achievements of British rule, saw itself as "the germ of a Native Parliament", which would "constitute in a few years an unanswerable reply to the assertion that India is still wholly unfit for any form of representative institutions". But its members represented, as the not unsympathetic Viceroy, Lord Dufferin, pointed out in 1888, a "microscopic minority", whose deliberations meant nothing to the vast mass of the Indian peasantry. Almost from the first the British attitude to the Congress expressed itself in the criticism that it was out of touch with the everyday realities of Indian life, with the needs and cares of the peasant, with which British officials were so constantly, and so closely, concerned. British critics argued also that the Congress was not sufficiently alive to the importance of the security, both internal and external, which British rule had established, and more was to be heard of this criticism when Congress methods became more violent. Until the First World War, however, although the Congress pressed repeatedly for greater political concessions to educated Indians, it remained moderate in its aims, demanding no more than self-government within the British Empire, and aiming at achieving this, in time, by strictly constitutional means. The chief exponent of this policy was the able and enlightened patriot, Gopal Krishna Gokhale, President of the Congress in 1905, who strove not only for the political advancement of India, but also for the moral, intellectual and economic progress of its peoples. He was the founder of the "Servants of India Society", an organization intended to train "national missionaries for the service of India, and to promote, by all constitutional means, the true interests of the Indian people".

## (2) S. D. SARASWATI

But, although Gokhale's moderating influence kept the Congress to constitutional paths until his death in 1915, it was challenged by more extreme influences, and was not long to survive him. The first element in these influences was that of orthodox Hinduism. Since the time of the great reformer, Rammohan Roy (1774-1833), attempts had been made to purify Hinduism of its worst abuses, and to adapt its teaching and practice to the changing conditions which Western influence was producing. These attempts to achieve a synthesis of all that was best in Hindu and Christian civilization inevitably brought a reaction in favour of orthodoxy, which received further stimulus from the growing "nationalist" agitation of many Hindu intellectuals against British domination. "Back to the *Vedas*" (the sacred books of the Hindus) became the watchword of both religious and political revival. The most significant aspect of the new movement was its influence not merely upon the educated minority but upon the mass of the people. It was Svami Dayananda Saraswati (1824-83), founder of the revivalist movement, *Arya Samaj*, who by his preaching first brought the people into contact with the growing intellectual ferment. He taught that all the developments of Western science had been foreshadowed in the *Vedas*, and it was from his time that the legend grew of a "golden age" of Hindu culture, which the British conquest of India had rudely shattered. At the same time he was strongly anti-Moslem, and founded the "Cow Protection Association" in 1882 in protest against the Moslem sacrifice of cattle, which were sacred to Hindus.

## (3) B. G. TILAK

It was Bal Gangadhar Tilak, however, who successfully fused the religious and political movements, and gave India's nascent nationalism a new and sinister twist. In contrast to

Gokhale's belief in constitutional progress, Tilak held that the British hold on India could only be relaxed by agitation and force. He inspired, though he did not altogether create, the spirit of violence that began to mark Indian politics from the end of the century. Tilak himself was a Maratha Brahmin, and belonged, therefore, both to the highest of Hindu castes and to the race of warriors whose power, founded by the great Sivaji in the seventeenth century, had long dominated western India and had been broken by the British only after a series of fierce struggles. Tilak revived the cult of Sivaji, and glorified the violence that had established the Maratha power. Had he done no more than this his appeal would have been limited, but he extended it by defending Hindu practices and stirring up religious and nationalist passions through his paper, *Kesari* ("The Lion"), which in his hands set the standards of political invective which were thenceforth to mark the Indian vernacular press.

Already in 1891 there had been an outburst of popular agitation against the Age of Consent Act, which had been passed, with the active support of enlightened opinion, in an attempt to check the worst evils of the Hindu practice of child marriage. Five years later there began, in Bombay, a serious outbreak of plague, and the Government's drastic measures for the segregation of suspected cases was denounced by Tilak as an outrage against religion. The result was the murder of two British officials, and Tilak was imprisoned for incitement. He had shown what could be achieved, however, and in particular had enlisted the support of students, who were to become the active agents of nationalist agitation throughout India. Within ten years the agitation had assumed a revolutionary character which it was never afterwards to lose. A variety of factors contributed to this development, but two which were external to India were particularly influential. Of these the first in time was the shock to British prestige caused by the Boer War, the other the stimulus to Eastern prestige which was administered by the Japanese victory over Russia in 1905. The success of Japan was greeted in India with delight, both as evidence that Europe was not invincible, and as an augury of India's own future: Indians had for so long been taught by the British to look upon Russia as the chief menace to their security that the Japanese victory was hailed as the opening of a new era in the history of Asia. Into this stirring of Indian feeling, further disturbed as it was by the famines of the late 'nineties and the steady spread of the plague, the Viceroy, Lord Curzon, now in his second term of office, flung, in 1905, the partition of Bengal. The division of so large a province had much to commend it, but as a measure passed without reference to Indian opinion it excited nationalist feeling at a difficult moment, and a group of secret societies, which owed much to Tilak's teaching and example, sprang into existence. There was a wave of political crime and assassination, culminating in the murder of a retired official in London in 1909. For complicity in that crime one of Tilak's pupils, V. D. Savarkar, was sentenced to transportation for life to the Andaman Islands, and it is worthy of note that after his release in 1924 he became the leader of the extreme Hindu organization, the *Mahasabha*, which was to play no small part in the confused politics of the next twenty years. The revolutionary agitation made itself felt throughout India, but its main centre was Bengal, and it found much support in the steadily increasing number of Indian students, too many of whom could find no acceptable occupation and inevitably contrasted conditions in India with the triumphant modernization of Japan. For the majority of students, it has been said, "higher education was proving an apprenticeship to discontent", and from 1905 the sense of frustration was a major factor in Indian development. Gokhale set himself against violence, denouncing those who regarded "disorder or misery, or even anarchy itself, as preferable to the presence of the foreigner in the land", and in 1907 he was able to retain the control of the Congress in moderate hands against a strenuous campaign by Tilak and his followers.

## (4) S. Banerjea

The moderates were not without their own means of expressing their discontent, and it was Banerjea who in 1905, in protest against the partition of Bengal, and encouraged by similar patriotic moves in Ireland and Hungary, introduced the *Swadeshi* movement for the use of home manufactures and the boycott of foreign goods. This was long to remain a characteristic expression of the nationalist spirit, at once a token of defiance, a reassertion of traditional Indian values against the all-pervading West and a gesture in keeping with the idealistic non-violence of Hinduism. It made a particular appeal to the Indian mind and was to acquire immense significance later under the inspiration of Gandhi. For the present it was the terrorist agitation that dominated the scene, and even as 1885 had seen the dawn of an Indian political revival, so 1905 marked a quickening of the national consciousness. The situation became markedly more difficult, the pace of agitation more hectic. The change has been recorded in an autobiographical study by an Indian who grew up into the new situation:

> the feeling . . . of there being a watching and protecting Government above us vanished at one stroke with the coming of the nationalist agitation in 1905. After that we thought of the Government . . . as an agency of oppression and usurpation.[33]

## (5) The Moslems: S. A. Khan

Meanwhile the Government was preparing the reforms of 1909, and had found it necessary to make a significant concession to Moslem feeling. The Hindu revival of the later nineteenth century had been matched by a Moslem reform movement, led by Sir Syed Ahmad Khan, founder of the Moslem College at Aligarh, which had brought about the establishment of the Moslem League in 1906. British official opinion, as has already been shown, denied any intention of introducing representative government on the British model, but this continued to be the aim of the Congress, as Gokhale always made clear. The prospect alarmed Moslem intellectuals, who saw their community, in spite of its size, as likely to be a permanent minority if the Congress's aims were realized, and the principle of communal electorates was therefore conceded in the 1909 Act. Henceforth Moslems would be represented by Moslems. Yet Moslem satisfaction was the measure of Hindu resentment, and from this time the British were faced with the charge that they were scheming to maintain their hold upon India by dividing its peoples. Not until 1947 was the full strength of the Moslem reaction appreciated by many Hindus.

## THE APPROACH TO RESPONSIBLE GOVERNMENT

The British denial of representative government in the face of Congress pressure speedily led to some disillusionment with the reforms of 1909. If those reforms were not intended to prepare the way for what Gokhale called the "long and weary step" towards "responsible administration", it was difficult for Indians to understand their intention. Representative members of Councils might exercise some influence over officials, but the position established in 1909 condemned them to the status of a permanent Opposition, with frustration and political irresponsibility as the inevitable results. With Tilak in prison for his contributions to the terrorist campaign, the Congress was soon pressing for further concessions, though continued British denials had the unhappy effect of arousing suspicions of Britain's intentions, which tended to weaken moderate influence and justify the actions of the extremists. What would have happened but for the outbreak of war in 1914 it is impossible to say. As it was, the war completely transformed the situation: the conditions of 1919 were totally different from those of 1914. In particular, many factors, among them the generosity of India's response to Britain's need, had caused a complete change in the British attitude. Early in the war Asquith had admitted that the Indian problem needed to be looked at "from a new angle of vision", and in 1917 E. S. Montagu, Secretary of State for India, made in Parliament the historic announcement which prepared the way for the "Montagu-Chelmsford Reforms" of 1919. "The gradual development of self-governing institutions with a view to the progressive realization of responsible government in India as an integral part of the British Empire" was declared to be the British aim. By a tragic irony Gokhale had then been dead for two years, and the new situation was to be dominated by a man who had little in common with him and little more with Tilak, Mohandas Karamchand Gandhi, "the Mahatma". But the events of the war and the years that followed lie for the present outside our scope.

## DEFENCE AND FOREIGN POLICY

There remain for consideration the important questions of foreign policy and defence, which, while the British connexion lasted, tended to be obscured by the military, and, more especially, by the naval, power of Britain. It was the possession of India which influenced the British attitude towards the Suez Canal project and brought about the occupation of Egypt. It was the protection of the Middle East, India's western defence zone, that caused British participation in the Crimean War and the resistance to Russian pressure that produced further crises in 1877–78 and 1885. Relations with Italy, Egypt and Turkey, the British attitude to the Berlin-Baghdad railway and the expansion of British territory in the Red Sea and on the East African coast, all these were governed eventually by the preoccupation with the defence of India. Indeed, it has often been suggested, especially by foreign critics, that in that preoccupation is to be found the key to British policy as a whole.

## (1) The North-West Frontier

It was in relations with the frontier States, Afghanistan and Burma, however, that the problem of defence most immediately influenced policy. India has frequently been invaded from the north-west, and after the annexation of the Punjab in 1849 Britain was faced with the twin tasks of maintaining order among the restless tribes on the frontier and of preventing the appearance of any military threat to India beyond it. The first presented problems of exceptional difficulty which were never fully solved. As the Punjab became settled, and increased in prosperity, the threat of raiding Pathan tribesmen became more serious, but at first no positive action was taken beyond the sending of punitive expeditions to punish depredations. Some twenty-six of these expeditions were organized, at great cost, between 1850 and 1870. A more active "forward" policy was then adopted, modelled on the successful relations which had been developed farther south, between British officials on the frontier of Sind and the Baluchi tribes. Frontier forts were built, and allowances were paid to the tribes in return for peaceful behaviour, but the policy was only intermittently successful, and the 'nineties, in particular, were a period of restlessness and disorder, culminating in the evtensive risings of 1897, which were put down only after serious fighting (including the famous Malakand campaign,

S*

about which Winston Churchill wrote his first book). Curzon, when he became Viceroy in 1899, then tackled the problem by setting-up a new Province of the North-West Frontier (1901), withdrawing and concentrating the British troops on the frontier, and improving their strategic communications with a network of roads and railways. The pacification which he established, though broken on several occasions, endured in the main until the unsettlement that followed the First World War. The special problems of the frontier peoples then became involved in the nationalist agitation throughout India, and have their place in the more recent history of the country. Fundamentally, the problems were those of the poverty and economic backwardness which are characteristic of so much of India, and, as the British administration was to some extent able to show after 1919, it is in economic rather than in military policy that a lasting settlement of frontier unrest is to be found.

## Afghanistan and the Russian Menace

Beyond the frontier, which, in any case, remained uncertain until in 1893 the missions of Sir Mortimer Durand marked out the "Durand Line", lay Afghanistan, and still further to the north the unsettled regions of Central Asia into which, during a great part of the nineteenth century, Russian power and influence were gradually percolating, much as British authority had already spread through India. The steady advance of Russia was marked by the establishment of a province of Russian Turkestan in 1867, the occupation of Samarkand in the following year and the formal absorption of Khiva and Bokhara in 1873. Salisbury was later to utter a warning that, to be seen in proper perspective, these advances should be plotted on large-scale maps, but at the time they appeared to many a dangerous threat to India. The potential threat was not necessarily one of invasion but of the stimulation of discontent in India. To recollections of the Mutiny were now being added the outpourings of an irresponsible vernacular press, reflecting the gossip of the bazaars and ripe, it seemed, for exploitation by Russian agents. It was partly to offset any attraction that might be exerted by the distant awesome figure of the Tsar that Queen Victoria was proclaimed Empress, but the suspicion of Russian intrigues remained. In a topical work, *England and Russia in the East*, which appeared in 1875, Sir Henry Rawlinson, an Indian official of long experience (who is better known as a pioneer of Assyriology), drew attention to the need for setting a limit to Russia's encroachments:

> India is a conquered country, where a certain amount of discontent must be ever smouldering which would be fanned into a chronic conflagration by the contiguity of a rival European power.[34]

There was in this attitude a genuine desire to keep India unspoiled and at peace, and to hold all possible rivals at arm's length, which was reflected in British policy towards both Afghanistan and Burma. India was secure from the sea while British naval power endured, but the garrison was too small to ensure internal peace and the safety of the wide-flung frontiers. *Punch*, so often the expression of public opinion and prejudice, on several occasions published warning cartoons of the Russian Bear's appearance through the passes of the North-West Frontier, and the general public interest in the Russian threat was shown by the success in 1876 of the gallant Colonel Burnaby's stirring record of his *Ride to Khiva*, which ran through eleven editions in twelve months.

## RUSSIAN PRESSURE

Russia had for some time been regarded with suspicion, and her first moves in Central Asia in the 'thirties had been the occasion of a British attempt, in the First Afghan War, to dominate Afghanistan as a defensive outpost of India. The fierce independence of the Afghan people had then brought disaster to the British forces in 1841, and although Kabul had been reoccupied in the following year the country had afterwards been left to itself. At the same time an informal agreement had been reached between the British and Russian governments to treat Afghanistan as neutral territory. The Russians had learnt, however, that by making threatening moves in Central Asia they could bring pressure to bear upon Britain in support of their policies in Europe, and from the time of the Crimean War a "forward" policy had again been pursued. Whether any real threat to India was ever intended, or even regarded as possible in Tsarist logistics, may be doubted: the physical difficulties of a campaign so far from adequate bases were almost insuperable. An explanation of Russian policy is to be found, in any case, in its "nuisance value": as late as 1899, at the time of the Boer War, the Tsar Nicholas II, whose sympathies were strongly with the Boers, was regretting that Turkestan lacked the railways which would have made it possible for him by an advance in force towards India to compel Britain to break off the war.[35]

## Crises of the 'Seventies: Second Afghan War

Whatever the true position, it was widely believed in Britain, and among soldiers in India, that an eventual attack was intended. Suspicion of Russia was particularly strong among the Conservatives, and when Disraeli took office in 1874 British policy assumed a distinctly anti-Russian tone. The moment was ripe for a re-examination of relations with Afghanistan, since the Amir, Sher Ali, who had succeeded his father, Dost Muhammad, in 1868, after four years of struggle with his numerous brothers, was anxious to ensure the succession for his own chosen heir. The Gladstone government, mindful of the ruinous policy of intervention pursued earlier, had refused to commit itself, and Sher Ali had therefore turned to Russia. This he had done the more readily since a pretender to the Amirate, his nephew, Abdur Rahman, was living in Turkestan under Russian protection. With the Conservatives in power it was decided to impose some restraint upon the Amir, and to insist upon the appointment of a British Resident in Afghanistan who could keep a watch on Russia's moves. "We cannot leave the keys of the gate," Salisbury wrote to the Viceroy, Lord Northbrook, in 1875, "in the hands of a warder of more doubtful integrity, who insists . . . that his movements shall not be observed."[36] Northbrook was unsympathetic to these views, and soon resigned, to be replaced by Lytton, who was sent out to apply a more active policy. Negotiations were opened with the Amir, and at the same time a long-pending move to occupy Quetta, across the Baluchi frontier, was carried out (1876). This brought Baluchistan under British control, and opened a way into Afghanistan from the

south. The great famine in India, and the threat of war over the
"Eastern Question", delayed further developments for some
time, but Russia took advantage of the threat of war to send a
representative to Kabul in 1878, and had war broken out there
would probably have been repercussions on the frontier.
A Russian envoy having been received by the Amir, Lytton
demanded that he should permit a British one to enter
Afghanistan. A distinguished soldier, General Sir Neville
Chamberlain (1820-1902), was sent, and on Russian advice
was stopped, but almost as soon as this had been done news
was received of the Treaty of Berlin, and the Russian attitude
changed immediately: the unfortunate Amir was told to make
the best terms he could with Britain. Meanwhile Lytton had
been pressing for action, against the advice of the Cabinet
in London, and at the end of 1878 he won their consent to an
invasion of Afghanistan. There followed the Second Afghan
War, the flight of Sher Ali, the succession of his son, Yakub
Khan, and the Treaty of Gandamak (May, 1879), which gave
Britain control of Afghanistan's foreign relations and established a British agent at Kabul. The representative selected,
Sir Louis Cavagnari, lacked, however, the tact necessary for
handling so difficult a people as the Afghans, and in September,
1879, there was a rising in which he and his staff were
murdered. The blow to the "forward" policy for which Lytton
had pressed was a serious one, but coming as it did so soon
after the disaster of Isandhlwana at the hands of the Zulus
(January, 1879), the blow to the Beaconsfield administration
itself was no less severe: Disraelian imperialism had suffered
a sharp setback.

## CRISES OF THE 'EIGHTIES: PENJDEH

Cavagnari's murder was speedily avenged by General
(afterwards Lord) Roberts (1832-1914), and Yakub Khan
went into retirement in India. Sher Ali had already died in
exile in Turkestan, and Abdur Rahman was allowed to return
to Afghanistan by the Russians, who, no doubt, hoped to
find in him a willing ally. Abdur Rahman, however, was a
shrewd and able man, with independent views. He realized
the advantages of standing well with Britain, and readily
responded to overtures from Lytton, who, for his part, was now

anxious to see a settled Afghanistan. Before negotiations had gone far Lytton was replaced by Ripon, who had instructions to withdraw the British troops from Afghanistan, and an agreement was soon reached whereby Abdur Rahman, in return for an annual subsidy, left the control of his foreign relations in the Viceroy's hands. So ended the second British intervention in Afghan affairs. The major problem of relations with Russia in Central Asia remained, however. In 1884, when the Russians captured Merv, the old fears revived, and there was an outbreak of what the Duke of Argyll called "Mervousness" in government circles. A boundary commission was proposed, but before it could investigate matters on the spot a further Russian move had led to the occupation of Penjdeh, dangerously near the key position of Herat in Western Afghanistan (March, 1885). A serious crisis followed, and war seemed near when Gladstone asked Parliament for a credit of £11,000,000. Russia had probably reckoned that the British Government's preoccupation with Ireland and the Sudan at this time would prevent so drastic a reaction, and had no intention of being involved in a European war for the sake of distant outposts. A settlement was therefore possible, and within a few months Russia's attention was, in any case, diverted by the reopening of the Bulgarian question. A frontier between her and Afghanistan was agreed, and with the transfer of Russian interest to the Far East a few years later Central Asia became more settled. Finally, the Anglo-Russian Entente of 1907 formally recognized that Afghanistan lay outside the Russian sphere of influence. By that time Abdur Rahman, and his son, Habibullah, who had succeeded him in 1901, had successfully established an ordered and independent country, and relations with India, though sometimes troubled, remained correct. The Third Afghan War of 1919, the invasion of India by Afghans, was a temporary aberration caused partly by the uncertainties in Afghanistan consequent upon the assassination of Habibullah early in the year, and partly by the unsettled conditions then prevailing in India. It had the effect, however, of bringing to an end both the subsidy to the Amir and the British control of his foreign policy, and therefore opened a new chapter in the relations between Britain, India, and Afghanistan.

## (2) THE EASTERN FRONTIER: BURMA

If Afghanistan has suffered from its geographical proximity to India and from being involved in the rivalries of two great European Powers, the same is no less true of Burma. Beyond Afghanistan the potential menace to India came from Russia; beyond Burma it came from France, which had begun the creation of the later colony of Indo-China with the acquisition of Cochin-China and Cambodia in 1862–63, and by 1885 had wrested from China the control of Annam. The aim of France was to open an overland trade-route into China from the south, but in aiming at this she opened the eastern flank of India's defences. Burma lay on that flank, and was no less a possible route to the interior of China. Hence the Third, and final, Anglo-Burmese War of 1885.

Already, long before 1885, Britain was in occupation of Burmese territory. From the reign of the Burmese King, Bo-daw-pa-ya (1782–1819), there had been frequent incursions across the eastern frontier of Bengal, and the First Burmese War (1823–26) was fought to secure the frontier: it left the government of India in control of the Burmese coastline. In the 'fifties, after disputes over trade, a second war led to the occupation of Lower Burma, the region round the delta of the Irrawaddy, and the two conquests were combined in 1862 in a province of British Burma.

### LOWER BURMA: ECONOMIC DEVELOPMENT AND PROBLEMS

At first the occupation of Lower Burma was not altogether successful, and it was not until about 1860 that the country was completely pacified. By then, however, the restoration of order and the increased opportunities for trade were drawing immigrants from Upper Burma, and the delta was soon being developed into one of the greatest rice-producing regions of the world. Hitherto, Burma's main export had been teak, which was widely used in ship-building, but with the growth of European demand, and the interruption to India's economy caused by the Mutiny, the export of rice began. Demand was variable, as it depended upon the quantity of the Indian and Chinese harvests, but the opening of the Suez Canal gave a great impetus to production. Before 1870 the export of rice had amounted to less than 400,000 tons a year, but in 1872 it increased to 720,000 tons and by the end of the century had reached 2,500,000 tons. During the same period the acreage under cultivation had more than trebled itself, and rice had come to account for three-quarters, in value, of Burma's total exports. Later experience was to reveal the dangers of this reliance upon one crop, but before the First World War, in Burma as elsewhere, they were not foreseen. Burma's chief customer for rice was India, where the rapidly increasing population led to increased imports of food. By 1914 India was Burma's best customer, taking as much of her total exports as Europe, Africa and America combined, and of the vast quantity which India imported rice formed a great part, amounting to about one-half of Burma's exportable surplus. Here again, a situation which had developed before 1914 was destined eventually to have tragic consequences: the terrible Bengal famine of 1943 was due in part to the loss of Burma, which cut off India's imports.

The increase in rice production had other consequences which were to exercise an unhappy influence upon the later development of Burma. The peasants who flocked into the delta to grow rice needed money to clear and prepare the land, and, there being no government scheme of credit or co-operative loan system, a class of moneylenders soon appeared. As usual in such cases, money was borrowed for unproductive as well as for more legitimate purposes, and many peasants were before long completely in the moneylenders' hands. Forced sales of land-holdings followed, but with the demand for rice still increasing it was always possible to find purchasers, and it continued to appear that the land was directly owned by the cultivators, though as early as 1895 an official commented that "land in Lower Burma was transferred as readily as shares on the London Stock Exchange".[37] Not until the world economic crisis of the nineteen-thirties was it apparent that the moneylenders were the real owners: the depression, with the resulting difficulty in finding purchasers for land, then revealed that in the main rice-producing areas more than two-thirds of the land was in the hands of non-agriculturalists. This economic development had its political consequences, for the majority of moneylenders were Indians, of the Madrasi *chettiar* caste, and the depression therefore did much to inflame the opposition of Burmans to Indians who had settled in their country.

## INDIA AND BURMA

Indians, indeed, had entered Burma in great numbers after the British occupation. The fundamental error in Britain's handling of Burma lay in the fact that the country was for long regarded as an outpost of India, and was governed from India on principles that had been evolved to suit the very different conditions of Indian life. Of the eighteen governors who held office in Burma from 1862 sixteen, it has been said, were members of the Indian Civil Service, and only four had served in Burma previously.[38] A number of the lesser officials had also received their training in the I.C.S. A legislative council, with appointed members, was established in 1897, and as Burma was regarded as a part of India this was enlarged after the Indian reforms of 1909 and 1919, while the 1919 system of "dyarchy" was set up in 1923. Not until 1937 was Burma formally separated from India, and, though the administration maintained the high standards which the I.C.S. had set, it naturally continued the traditions that had sustained it in India. The aloofness and neutrality which characterized the Indian administration were maintained among a people who, apart from the Karen and Shan tribesmen in the hills, were a homogeneous nation, conscious of past greatness, and only reluctantly acquiescing in foreign rule. With an administration shaped on the Indian model had come Indian officials, traders, moneylenders and workers. It was easier to employ Indians who were accustomed to European methods than to train Burmans, and Indian business men had experience and resources with which Burmans could not compete: eventually more than half of the foreign capital invested in Burma was Indian. It was characteristic of the situation which developed that as late as 1930, as one writer has said, "one could not use the telephone in Burma without a knowledge of Hindustani".[39] Indians tended to congregate in the large towns, and soon formed considerably more than half of their populations. The Burmans, in fact, became to some extent strangers in their own land. There were many reasons for this, but the situation was an artificial one, and it is not surprising that, as in India, nationalist agitation was fostered by the Russo-Japanese War, and that it reached such a pitch, in spite of political concessions, that when the testing time came in 1942 there were few in Burma, except among the Karens, who were not largely indifferent to the British connexion.

## THIRD BURMESE WAR, 1885: UPPER BURMA

Consideration of the developments that followed the annexation of Lower Burma in 1852 have carried us far beyond the point at which the British control of Burma became complete, but it was particularly in Lower Burma that the pressure from India was felt. In independent Burma the defeat of 1852 was followed by the accession of an able King, Mindon, who transferred the capital to the new city of Mandalay, which he founded in 1857. Mindon realized that his independence was precarious, and therefore resisted the attempts made by British merchants in Rangoon to open a new trade-route with China by way of the Irrawaddy and the mountain crossing that was later to become famous as the "Burma Road". He also cultivated relations with other Western nations, especially with France, and in view of French activities in Indo-China this move aroused some perturbation in London. Lord Lyons, British Ambassador in Paris, wrote to Salisbury later of his anxiety about "the condition of our Indian Empire, if it be in contact with a great European Power both on the north and on the east".[40] Mindon held his own until his death in 1878, but left a numerous family of sons, with no settled order of succession. A palace intrigue placed on the throne the semi-imbecile Thibaw, who promptly had all possible rivals destroyed, a step that accorded with ancient Burmese custom, but shocked European opinion. From India Lytton urged immediate annexation, and considerable pressure was brought to bear upon the Government from many quarters, but it was not until it became clear that Thibaw was establishing close relations with France that action was decided upon. Early in 1885 Jules Ferry, the imperially-minded French Premier, let it be known that a treaty had been arranged with Thibaw, and, through the pressure that was exerted upon a British company which had the right to work the teak forests of

Upper Burma, it became evident that British interests were to be extinguished in favour of French. Suddenly, as the result of reverses in Indo-China, Ferry fell from power, and Britain was free to move. An army marched "on the road to Mandalay", Thibaw was deposed, and on 1st January, 1886, the formal annexation of his kingdom was proclaimed.

## ANNEXATION AND ITS AFTERMATH

The annexation was not well received in Burma. Thibaw's troops dispersed, but continued a guerrilla resistance for five years, and a rising took place in Lower Burma. Not until 1890 was order fully restored, but the underlying stresses continued and made themselves apparent in the steady increase of serious crime. The annual incidence of murder per million of the population rose from 25 in the last years of the century to 39 on the eve of the First World War and nearly 60 by 1930. Continual strengthening and reform of the police failed to check the increase. The reasons cannot be analysed in detail here, but are to be found in the general unsettlement of Burmese life, and in the rise in the standard of living, which overthrew customary social restraints, no less than in the growth of a class of dispossessed cultivators which resulted from the operations of money-lending upon an unsophisticated people. Resentment of foreign rule, and especially of the incursion of Indians, was a further element, and something must be ascribed to the failure to recruit Burmans as soldiers. The army continued to be directed from India, and the military traditions of the Burmese, as of some Indian peoples who had proved particularly difficult to handle, were felt to be best forgotten. Later, recruitment was active among the hill tribes, especially the Karens, but this did not endear the army to Burmans.

Another factor in the situation which was overlooked, partly no doubt, because they were peculiar to Burma and had no precise parallel in India, were the numerous Buddhist clergy. Long revered and influential, they found no place in the new system and it is significant that when nationalist disturbances began after 1919 they were often led by monks. In short, however great the efforts made to rule Burma wisely and well, the peculiar problems of the country were not fully appreciated.

"What we gave Burma", an experienced official has said, "was not a government but an administration",[41] and the country suffered from being looked at for too long from Calcutta rather than from London. The consequences have been described by a leading authority on the affairs of South East Asia, in words which, while they have a significance for all colonial territory, are particularly applicable to Burma:

> Contact with the outer world should furnish new sources of inspiration and enrich native social life, art and religion. But the people are not brought into contact with the outer world except in the sphere of economics; they remain imprisoned in a dying civilization and their social life is impoverished and not enriched.[42]

This view is not unlike Sir Malcolm Darling's on Indian conditions, quoted earlier, that "the peasant was given the kind of government he trusted and respected . . . rather than the kind he needed to face the modern world", though it may be doubted whether the British administration ever won the confidence of the Burmese peasant as it did that of the Indian. In India as in Burma, it has often been said, the administration conceived its duty to be to "hold the ring". Much was done, especially in India, by way of railway, road and canal construction, famine relief, and the encouragement of village co-operatives, but if there was direct government intervention in economic matters rather earlier than was the case in the United Kingdom, the fundamental attitude of neutrality persisted longer.

## The Viceroyalty of Lord Curzon, 1899–1905

At the turn of the century Lord Curzon, with his exalted sense of duty and responsibility, undoubtedly exemplified in the most impressive manner the underlying preconceptions of British rule. To him, as he revealed in a phrase curiously reminiscent of the one used thirty years earlier by Anthony Trollope, that rule was "the highest touchstone of national duty",[43] but, as his biographer has recorded in a phrase already quoted, his conception of the relations between himself and "the India of his vision" was "almost Patriarchal".[44] His achievement was remarkable, and showed—as he intended it should—that a resolute, able, and, be it added, indefatigable, Viceroy could still make his impress upon India. Educational and agricultural development, the stimulation of further railway and canal construction, the establishment of co-operative credit societies and of an agricultural research institute, the encouragement of archaeology, care for India's historical monuments (including the Taj Mahal, which he restored), the creation of a North-West Frontier Province, the partition of Bengal and an active policy in Tibet, all flowed from his direct inspiration. Yet he won no affection or gratitude, for he resisted political concessions, and under-rated the influence of the growing educated minority, with its following in India's towns and cities. For him the patient masses of the peasantry were the real India, and when attacked, as he was so bitterly, by nationalists, he claimed to feel no resentment, "for I search my conscience and I ask myself who and what are the real Indian people?" Indeed, the whole problem of political advance was dismissed by him with the words, "more places on this or that Council for a few active or eloquent men will not benefit the raiyat". To him British rule was "the miracle of the world", and over-stated though this view is, he rightly sensed the magnitude and significance of the British achievement, though he signally failed in those personal relations which meant so much to a subject people at a critical period of their history. "His immense talents", a shrewd observer has said, "were directed to working for India rather than with India",[45] and therein lies the whole epitome of British rule. It was no accident that Curzon's Viceroyalty, for all its achievements, was followed by the rise of revolutionary nationalism.

## THE CORONATION DURBAR, 1911

Curzon was the last of the great imperial proconsuls. After him, an Indian writer has not unjustly said, "India had no Viceroy of genius".[46] In appearance British rule achieved its most spectacular success in 1911, six years after his resignation, with the Coronation Durbar held in honour of the visit of George V. But though the King-Emperor was then hailed with an almost religious devotion, the ferment of discontent was active beneath the surface: only a year later a bomb was thrown at the Viceroy, Lord Hardinge, as he entered Delhi in state on an elephant. The next thirty-five years were to prove a long and reluctant rearguard action.

## BRITAIN AND INDIA

Nineteen-fourteen is hardly the point at which to attempt to sum up the British achievement in India, but with the memory of the Durbar still fresh it marks the latest stage at which un-hesitating confidence could still be felt. The response of the peoples of India to the challenge of war showed, too, that there was still ample confidence on their side, though the long and weary struggle was soon to erode it. India could not have escaped the pressure of western development. Whether in the long run she gained or not by receiving it through British, rather than other, channels, can hardly yet be determined. That Britain, however, has set a mark on India cannot be doubted. It remains to be seen whether the mark will endure. For her part Britain gained from her association with India, gained in responsibility, in international status, in commerce.[47] India, while increasingly resenting her subjection, also gained much. This survey can best close with the words used by Nirad Chaudhuri, who grew up in India in the years before the First World War, in the dedication of his *Autobiography of an Unknown Indian*, published in 1951, which has already con-tributed to these pages:

> To the memory of the British Empire in India which conferred subjecthood on us but withheld citizenship; to which yet every one of us threw out the challenge *Civis Britannicus Sum* because all that was good and living within us was made, shaped, and quickened by the same British rule.

## REFERENCES

1.  S. B. Saul: "Britain and World Trade, 1870–1914"; *Economic History Review*, 2nd Series, VII, No. 1, pp. 64–65.
2.  Sir R. Coupland: *India: A Re-Statement*, p. 56.
3.  S. Gopal: *The Viceroyalty of Lord Ripon*, p. 179.
4.  Sir E. Blunt: *Social Service in India*, p. 37.
5.  Sir M. Darling: *At Freedom's Door*, p. 310.

6. See page 362 above.

7. L. C. A. Knowles: *The Economic Development of the British Overseas Empire*, I, p. 183.

8. A. Toynbee: *A Journey to China*, p. 259.

9. Quoted in *India: A Re-Statement*, p. 292.

10. ibid.

11. E. Thompson and G. T. Garratt: *The Rise and Fulfilment of British Rule in India*, p. 464.

12. Lord Beveridge: *India Called Them*, p. 96.

13. P. Woodruff: *The Men Who Ruled India:* Vol. II—*The Guardians*, p. 44.

14. Lady G. Cecil: *Life of Lord Salisbury*, II, p. 68.

15. ibid.

16. A. Menen: *Dead Men in the Silver Market*, p. 86.

17. Lady B. Balfour: *The History of Lord Lytton's Indian Administration* (1899), p. 532.

18. R. C. Majumdar, etc.: *An Advanced History of India*, p. 849.

19. *India: A Re-Statement*, p. 75.

20. ibid., p. 82.

21. Lord Morley: *Recollections*, II, p. 181.

22. *Lord Lytton's Indian Administration*, p. 109.

23. P. W. Ireland: *Iraq*, p. 141.

24. Lord Ronaldshay (Lord Zetland): *Life of Lord Curzon*, II, p. 419.

25. See the article by Vera Watson in the *Manchester Guardian*, 3rd September, 1952, based on unpublished papers in the Royal Archives at Windsor.

26. *Life of Disraeli*, I, pp. 1492 and 1566.

27. Lady Minto: *India, Minto and Morley*, p. 158.

28. The phrase is used by Sir S. Reed: *The India I Knew, 1897–1947*, as the heading of chapter V.

29. *The Letters of Queen Victoria*, Third Series, III, p. 251.

30. Quoted in H. Nicolson: *King George the Fifth*, p. 88.

31. Cartoon in *Punch*, 15th December, 1883.

32. *The Viceroyalty of Lord Ripon*, p. 166.

33. N. C. Chaudhuri: *The Autobiography of an Unknown Indian*, p. 48.

34. p. 147.

35. B. H. Sumner: *Tsardom and Imperialism in the Far East and Middle East, 1880–1914* (British Academy, 1940), p. 8.

36. *Life of Lord Salisbury*, II, p. 72.

37. J. S. Furnivall: *Colonial Policy and Practice. A Comparative Study of Burma and Netherlands India*, p. 87.
38. G. E. Harvey: *British Rule in Burma, 1824–1942*, p. 77.
39. *Colonial Policy and Practice*, p. 121.
40. Lord Newton: *Life of Lord Lyons*, II, p. 358.
41. *British Rule in Burma*, p. 30.
42. *Colonial Policy and Practice*, p. 299.
43. *Life of Lord Curzon*, II, p. 418: cf. the quotation from Trollope on p. 363 above.
44. ibid., p. 420.
45. *The India I Knew*, p. 51.
46. *Autobiography of an Unknown Indian*, p. 320.
47. *The India I Knew*, p. 70.

# XIV

# THE PARTITION OF AFRICA

### The New Situation in the 'Eighties

THE partition of Africa was one of the most striking features of the activities of the European nations in the second half of the nineteenth century. Within the space of little more than a single decade the greater part of a vast continent, hitherto hardly known, was divided among five of the Western European nations, and divided, be it noted, without war. Speaking in the House of Lords in 1890, Salisbury described how the pre-eminence which Britain had long exercised on the African coasts through her trade and her campaign against slavery had passed with the entry of other Powers upon the scene:

> Up to ten years ago we remained masters of Africa, practically or the greater part of it, without being put to the inconvenience of protectorates or anything of that sort, by the simple fact that we were masters of the sea and that we have had considerable experience in dealing with native races. So much was that the case that we left enormous stretches of coast to the native rulers in the full confidence that they would go on under native rulers and in the hope that they would gradually acquire their own proper civilization without any interference on our part.
>
> Then, suddenly we found out that that position, however convenient, had no foundation whatever in international law. We had no rights over all these vast stretches of coast, both on the West and the East coasts of Africa. We had no power of preventing any other nation from coming in and seizing a portion of them.[1]

The change had come about through a combination of the ambitions of the European States with the penetration of the African interior, and Salisbury's succinct account of it provides the key to the diplomatic and colonial activity during the 'eighties, when Africa became, as Salisbury himself acknowledged, "the subject which occupies the Foreign Office more than any other".

## CAUSES OF THE NEW SITUATION

Two major factors in the new situation were the changes in the balance of power brought about by the war of 1870-71, and the economic crisis of 1873, complicated as that shortly was by the pressure upon agricultural interests in Europe of the export of grain from Russia and America. From the war arose the weakened position of France, for which some of her political leaders, notably Ferry and Gambetta, sought compensation in expansion overseas. From the economic difficulties of the 'seventies sprang the tariff revival, in which Britain alone, still firm in her attachment to free trade, did not take part; and with the tariffs went the search for secure markets and sources of supply. French colonial policy still clung to the older principles of colonial economic dependence which Britain had abandoned with the coming of free trade. A later statement of French policy, issued in 1900, explained that "in a good colonial organization colonial production must be limited to furnishing to the metropolis raw materials or products which we do not produce",[2] and an historian of French policy has pointed out that France sought, not "a weakly knit congeries of self-sufficient entities, with the emphasis on an increasing devolution, but a great economic machine—a world within a world".[3]

## GERMANY AND SOUTH-WEST AFRICA

German aims were similar, but while in France colonial expansion was a matter of government policy, which received little public attention, in Germany there was a vociferous public agitation which was only spasmodically able to stir the government into activity in the colonial sphere. Earlier sections have referred to this public agitation and Bismarck's calculated response to it. A Bremen merchant, Adolf Lüderitz, had established himself in 1882 at Angra Pequeña (afterwards, Lüderitzbucht), on the south-west coast of Africa, some two hundred miles north of the Cape frontier. The only British post on the coast was at Walvis Bay, farther north, and when Bismarck inquired whether Britain claimed sovereignty in the region there was a delay of several months while the Cape government was consulted. Meanwhile, Bismarck lost patience. He could not understand the necessity for consulting the Cape, and affected to believe that an attempt was being made to forestall German action. In his view, either sovereignty was claimed or it was not, and in any case the British government should know the position. In short, he had exposed the weakness of British colonial rule, the lack of a policy until events made the framing of one unavoidable. With her widely scattered interests, more extensive than those of any other State, it was impossible for Britain to have in advance a clear-cut policy for every part of the world, and, as the quotation from Salisbury's speech of 1890 has shown, there was a naïve belief that the unregulated position in Africa could continue indefinitely. New elements in the situation made that impossible, however. Other countries were jealous of Britain's predominance, and had their own trading interests to encourage. Though, as far as trade was concerned, there might be no real case for annexation, as the British possessions were open to all, German opinion was affected rather by France's close economic policy in her colonies than by Britain's free trade practices. If lands hitherto unclaimed were to be occupied Germans were determined that France should not be permitted to snap up everything that the British, with their vast possessions, were not effectively holding. Moreover, prestige demanded that wherever possible trade should be conducted under the merchant's own flag, while with the return to tariffs there were advantages in having markets and resources within a national tariff area. Yet these factors would have weighed with Bismarck as little as they had ever done, had not political issues nearer home been involved, the attempted rapprochement with France and the quarrel picked with the German Radicals. It suited Bismarck to seem to be seeking a quarrel with Britain, and in April, 1884, he proclaimed a protectorate over the coast from Angra Pequeña to the Cape frontier. Shortly afterwards the zone was extended northwards to Angola, and German South West Africa came into existence.

## THE "SCRAMBLE FOR AFRICA" BEGINS

During the course of the negotiations with London Bismarck had angrily asked whether Britain intended to assert "a sort of Monroe doctrine" for Africa, and the exasperation of German opinion at what seemed to be a "dog-in-the-manger" attitude is easy to understand. Yet it was Bismarck's previous indifference to colonial agitation, frequently expressed, that had caused misunderstanding of his object in taking up the Angra Pequeña question. Gladstone's administration, pre-occupied with events in Ireland and Egypt, and with the Reform agitation at home, had underrated the effect that Bismarck's change of front would have upon feeling in Germany. Whatever the Chancellor's real purpose the dilatory conduct of the British Government made an unfortunate impression. Nevertheless, when the German protectorate was proclaimed Gladstone welcomed it in characteristic terms:

> If Germany is to become a colonizing Power, all I can say is, God speed her! She becomes our ally and partner in the execution of the great purpose of Providence for the advantage of mankind.

As Salisbury later acknowledged, "it was impossible that England should have the right to lock up the whole of Africa and say that nobody should be there except herself", but' difficulty arose from the very fact that Britain had been active for so long on the African coasts and had acquired numerous interests, together with not a little good will. Other German acquisitions, in East and West Africa, followed, and within the short space of a few months the greater part of the colonial empire which Germany was destined to hold only until the First World War had been built up. Roused by these activities, and by the corresponding advances which the French were making in West Africa, Britain hastened to mark out certain areas for herself: the "Scramble for Africa" had begun.

## THE OPENING OF AFRICA: STANLEY AND THE CONGO

The negotiations that followed centred upon the vast, and but recently explored, Congo basin, the heart of the continent, which was now being opened through the enterprise of the Belgian King, Leopold II, whose imagination and ambition had been fired by the work of Livingstone and other pioneers. The part played by Livingstone in the opening-up of Africa has already been touched on. When he died in 1873 he had been investigating the depredations of the slave-raiders in the region around Lake Tanganyika, and seeking for the sources

of the Nile and the Congo. Already in 1858 J. H. Speke
had seen, and named, Lake Victoria Nyanza, the main source
of the Nile, but although his discovery had been confirmed six
years later by Samuel Baker, who had also, in 1862, found
Lake Albert (named by him after the Prince Consort), it was
still not known whether the Nile flowed farther south from the
great lakes. Livingstone had died before he could penetrate
the mystery of the watershed, but Stanley resolved to carry
on this part of his work and in three years of travel, 1874–77,
he finally confirmed Speke's discovery, mapped the two lakes,
and then traced the Congo to the sea. He emerged fired with
enthusiasm for the possibilities of commercial development in
the Congo basin. The whole region, he wrote later, had been
left, owing to the physical difficulties of access, "to stew in its
own juice of fatness".[4] "Enormous" quantities of vegetable
produce awaited exploitation, and could be gathered by the
"most trifling labour" of the native peoples: £5,000,000 worth
of it could be collected within a year, and as much again of
elephant ivory, and these formed only a part of the region's
resources, which amounted in all to three times the natural
wealth of the better-known West Africa. "Forty million
native paupers" throughout the Congo could have their
standards of life raised, and could at the same time produce a
wealth of natural produce for Europe, if traders, the
"missionaries of commerce", would but settle among them in a
climate which was as favourable to Europeans as that of much
of India. This business-like anticipation of Lugard's "dual
mandate", designed to catch the interest of British merchants,
was Stanley's version of the plea for commerce to replace slave-
raiding which had been advanced by Livingstone and others.
It was indicative both of the difference of outlook between
him and Livingstone and of the new spirit that was beginning
to affect European enterprise in Africa.

## AFRICA'S LIMITATIONS AND PROBLEMS

In truth, the expectations which Stanley aroused were
seriously exaggerated. He both over-estimated the natural
resources of the Congo basin and minimized the difficulties,
of transport and of labour, that had to be overcome. It has well
been said that "there is little to be got out of Africa except

by those able and willing to put a great deal into it",[5] but there was little realization in Stanley's time of the serious limitations under which Africans laboured, and of the cataclysmic effects which the irruption of Europeans would have upon their society. The slave-traffic had already thrown many parts of the continent into confusion, and the greater convulsion of European penetration and enterprise was to come. Much had to be done before Central Africa could become a steady source of supply and at the same time provide the means for its own people's advancement. W. H. Lever (afterwards Lord Leverhulme: 1851–1925), when, in 1911, he received concessions in the Congo for raw materials for his vast soap interests, sharply criticized the relics of Stanley's optimistic impressions that still lingered in the popular mind:

> The word "Concession" conjures up in the mind of most people a "tom tiddler's" ground where the happy concessionaire merely has to stoop and pick up the sovereigns. . . . In fact we have to take great risks, use an enormous amount of capital, and tax our energy and strength to get this business on a sound, commercial footing.[6]

One of the major obstacles to development was the poor physical condition of so many Africans, especially in the tropical zones. Deficiency diseases were all too common, but such insect-spread scourges as malaria, yellow-fever, sleeping-sickness, and plague were endemic and widely spread, as were leprosy, yaws, and venereal disease. Trade and exploration only too often spread local epidemics over far wider areas. Sleeping-sickness, in particular, seems to have been spread from West Africa across the continent as it was opened up. Carried by the tsetse-fly it was endemic in the west but appeared in the east as communications were developed, and in 1901–02 killed some 200,000 people out of 300,000 in Uganda. A few years later it was killing millions in French Equatorial Africa and struck the southern Sudan: a British official of the Sudanese service has given in his recollections, *Sudan Days and Ways*, a grim picture of the effects of the epidemic.[7] Here was a terrible and unexpected consequence of "development". Stanley had described the "able-bodied warriors" whom he saw, but a modern authority has recorded the opinion that "the supposed healthy active vitality of the normal African is a myth",[8] and from the medical mission-post at Lambaréné in French

Equatorial Africa, where he started his work of healing in 1913, Albert Schweitzer has written compassionately of the ills of Africa and of Europe's duty to relieve them: "out here millions and millions live without help or hope of it".[9] The "laziness" of which the African has so often been accused is frequently the result of poor health and poor physique, though it also owes something to an approach to life markedly at variance with that of the restless European. African wants are limited, at least until close contact with European civilization has been achieved, and are generally satisfied without too much effort. "The African's standard", an experienced observer has said, "is repletion",[10] and repletion under African conditions is not always conducive to European standards of work, while it leaves the worker dangerously exposed to under-nourishment when supplies run short. "The fact is, the native has few wants", Lever noted in his diary when visiting the Congo in 1912, "a little salt and a little cloth are his indispensables", and he gave a graphic impression of the problems facing the white employer in the face of these limited requirements:

> Twelve months ago Chief Womba and his people were poor and few in number, and were keen to bring (palm) fruit. After twelve months or less of selling fruit he is rich and lazy, has ten wives, and his village is about four times the size it was, but he gathers little or no fruit. . . . The Palm tree is in these parts the Banking account of the native and he no more thinks of going to the Bank for fruit for money when his wants and ambitions are supplied than a civilized man would. His bank is always open when he wants to draw upon it.[11]

Poor health and limited requirements account for the difficulties experienced at times by all colonial peoples in inducing Africans to toil at the exploitation of the "Bank" of natural resources which Stanley and others had described in such glowing terms. Difficulty was also caused by the primitive shifting nature of the African agricultural economy, which appeared to leave large areas "empty" and available for white "development" or settlement. Only too often too little land was left to sustain the African at his modest standard of life. This had long been a familiar problem in pastoral South Africa and was to recur in East Africa, and even where, as in the Congo, white settlement was out of the question, "concessions" could be granted over areas so extensive that they left little space for native agriculture, or demands upon Africans for labour could be so heavy as to leave little time for the cultivation of their own "gardens". Yet complaints were frequent enough that "too much land" was being left to the African. Once Africa was penetrated its resources were bound to be developed, and it was inevitable that Africans should be looked to to provide the labour for the development. If the European, with his moral zeal for work, could not persuade the African to share his enthusiasm, he was bound to employ such inducements as he could command, money, taxes (which presupposed money for their payment), or restriction of native lands in order to compel men to work. The chief duty of governments, not often realized until much land had been alienated, was to preserve a balance, retaining enough land in native occupation to maintain a settled population, while safeguarding the interests of those who for one reason or another sought employment with Europeans. In this simple statement is summed-up much of the complex history of colonial policies in Africa. Rhodes's "Glen Grey" policy of 1894, referred to in an earlier section, was a successful attempt to ensure the native a secure place on the land, while compelling those whom the land would not support to seek a livelihood with white employers. Where, however, large-scale white settlement was out of the question, other incentives had to be found, and although more recent policies, especially in the industrial areas of the Congo, have achieved considerable success without damage to African interests, the exploitation of earlier years had disastrous results. Through the very attractiveness of the picture he drew Stanley must bear some share of responsibility for what was done in the name of economic development. The resources seemed so great to his uncritical mind, the labour requirements so "trifling". It was Stanley's account, above all, that fired the interest of the man who, through the accidents of history and his own ability and shrewd percipience, was to become the creator of the "Belgian Congo", Leopold II, King of the Belgians (reigned 1865–1909).

## LEOPOLD II AND THE BELGIAN CONGO

Leopold was a man of ability and imagination, whose talents demanded a wider outlet than his functions as constitutional ruler of Belgium could afford him. The mysteries of Africa had long appealed to him and in 1876, while Stanley was in Africa, he invited to Brussels the leading geographers of the world and founded an international association for the exploration and civilization of the continent, with himself as President. Expeditions to East Africa followed, under the association's auspices, but were unsuccessful, and Leopold was therefore the more impressed with Stanley's discoveries. On his return to Europe Stanley was invited to Brussels, and there in 1878 was established the "International Association of the Congo", from which was to emerge in time the "Congo Free State" and the Belgian colony. Stanley returned to the Congo in 1879, and acting in the Association's name, but supported by Leopold's funds, concluded treaties with chiefs and established posts. These moves alarmed Portugal and France, who had long been established in the area. France under Ferry was now seeking colonial expansion. Tunis was occupied in 1881, and in the same year an official expedition under the able explorer Savorgnan de Brazza struck inland from French posts on the west coast and established a foothold on the north bank of the Congo, on Stanley Pool (as it came to be called) where the river becomes navigable. Here was founded the settlement of Brazzaville, the capital of the French Congo, later French Equatorial Africa. De Brazza had served France well: when the frontiers of the new colony, with its extension northwards, were eventually defined, its area was almost as large as that of all the German African colonies put together.

## THE BERLIN AFRICAN CONFERENCE, 1884–85

Portugal had been nominally established on the African coasts since the fifteenth century, but with the decay of the home country her authority had become shadowy, and the claims she now began to put forward were sustained, as Salisbury once contemptuously said, by "archaeological arguments". Nevertheless, Stanley's reports of the potential wealth of the Congo region roused her interest, and she hastened to lay claim to both banks of the mouth of the great river. In February, 1884, Britain recognized this claim, though only in return for an undertaking that the Congo should be open to the commerce of all nations and that the

T

slave-trade should be suppressed. France and Germany, however, protested against the agreement, and in October jointly summoned a conference to Berlin to consider the situation. The decision of the conference was that the greater part of the Congo Basin (a region of nearly 900,000 square miles) should be left to the control of the Congo Association. No other solution would have avoided fierce rivalries between the countries concerned, and there was every determination to preserve the neutrality and international character of the huge region, though France had already taken her own precautions by securing the reversion of it. Leopold II now proclaimed himself sovereign of the "Congo Free State", and as time went on gradually lessened the international character of the territory, administering it increasingly through Belgians and exploiting its resources with scant regard for the obligations he had assumed.

Yet the conditions laid down by the conference, which were embodied in the General Act of Berlin of February, 1885, were not unimportant, and represented a significant development of international law. Throughout the "conventional basin of the Congo", which was defined as extending across Africa from west to east, free trade was established, monopolies were prohibited, and the slave-trade was declared illegal. The Powers bound themselves "to watch over the preservation of the native tribes, and to care for the improvement of the conditions of their moral and material well-being, and to help in suppressing slavery, and especially the Slave-Trade".[12] This pronouncement, the first of its kind, was followed five years later by the Brussels Act of 1890, which arose from an anti-slavery conference summoned at the suggestion of Lord Salisbury. This Act finally outlawed the slave-trade and laid down an international code of maritime law for its suppression: it was the last stage of the process which Britain had begun in 1807. The Brussels Conference recognized, however, that measures against the slave-trade were costly, and it was known that the Congo State, hitherto largely dependent upon the resources of Leopold II, was in financial difficulties. It was therefore agreed that the free-trade clauses of the Berlin Act should be modified, to permit of limited duties for purposes of revenue. This agreement, much abused by Leopold's administration, remained in force until after the First World War, when, as part of the peace settlement, the Convention of St. Germain-en-Laye, in 1919, removed the limitations on tariffs, though maintaining the principle of equality of treatment between the nationals of the signatory States which the Berlin Act had established.

## THE CONGO FREE STATE IN PRACTICE AND ITS EXPOSURE

Admirable though the principles laid down might seem, they lacked means of enforcement and were to be widely contravened during Leopold's rule in the Congo, while the obsession with the slave-trade was to blind many to the scarcely lesser dangers of European penetration. Yet, whatever the crimes and blunders committed, there was in Europe a public opinion to be roused, in case of need, to a sense of its responsibilities, and a body of international agreement to which it could appeal. Hence the critical scrutiny of colonial policy in Britain, Germany and Belgium, and the general outcry against Congo misgovernment from about 1896 which led, despite his evasive tactics, to the cession of the Congo to Belgium by King Leopold in 1908, the year before his death. Before this, however, much damage had been done. Leopold's first concern, when he gained control of the Congo, was to extend its frontiers to the widest possible extent. Slave-raiding was stamped out, but in pressing eastwards against the Arab slavers the Belgian forces found themselves confronted by no defined frontier. Before he was appointed by the British Government to his fatal mission to the Sudan General Gordon was invited by Leopold to lead the offensive against the Arabs on the upper waters of the Nile, but when the Sudan fell to the Mahdi there was nothing to prevent the Belgians from pressing into the Bahr el Ghazal (south-western Sudan) and establishing the Congo State's frontier on the left bank of the Nile. To this both Britain and France objected, and the frontier was eventually established in 1906 along the Congo-Nile watershed, though Leopold was permitted to hold the "Lado enclave" in the southern Sudan for the term of his life. Expeditions to suppress slave-raiding and delimit frontiers had proved costly, however, and, while it was soon apparent that the wealth of the Congo was not to be had merely for the asking, the tariffs permitted by the Brussels conference did not provide resources sufficient for the development of the country, and especially for the improvement of communications. As early as 1886 Leopold granted a large "concession" of land to a railway company, and the whole development of the Congo soon came to be based upon the policy of "concessions". Under free trade exports had risen from nearly 2,000,000 francs in 1887 to more than 8,000,000 francs in 1890, but this rate of progress was too slow, and rubber and ivory were declared State monopolies in 1891, vast concessions being granted to companies formed to gather them. By 1895, in consequence, exports rose to 11,000,000 francs, three years later to 22,000,000 francs, in 1901 to 50,000,000 francs and in 1903 to nearly 55,000,000 francs, though this was still less than half of the total of Stanley's optimistic forecasts. Considerably more than eighty per cent of the exports consisted of wild rubber, which by 1905 was becoming exhausted, and nearly ten per cent of ivory.[13] The labour necessary for this vast outpouring of the country's resources was far from being of the "trifling" nature which Stanley had foretold, and was brought together under the pressure of taxation which could be paid in work. The opportunities for the abuse of this system of forced labour, in regions distant from civilization, were immeasurably increased by the employment of supervisory officials on commission, and by the use of sentries to watch the workers. It is not likely that King Leopold was aware of all that was done in his name, but he never visited the Congo, and was interested solely in the wealth it could produce. Moreover, he ensured that the Congo State should be a considerable partner in the concessions granted, and the whole apparatus of the State was therefore involved in profit-making to the detriment of administration. Leopold amassed a great fortune, and also spent a great deal on African studies and on the embellishment of Belgium (together with not a little on less worthy objects), but it was at an alarming cost in human suffering. The perils of the concession system were only too obvious, and British colonial rule always rejected the system, while the French, though they adopted it in Equatorial Africa in 1899, largely at Leopold's persuasion, abandoned it ten years later. Leopold, however, remained to the last a defiant defender of the system. "The Congo was a personal work," he declared in 1906, in answer to widespread criticism, "and there is no more legitimate or respectable right than that of an author to the fruits of his labour. Not one of the Powers was called on to share in my efforts, and therefore not one of them has the right to intervene."[14] Ironically enough, the cover design of Stanley's book on the Congo State, published in 1886, showed an African figure crowning a bust of the King, to whom Stanley paid high tribute in the work, under the inspiring motto *Finis Coronat Opus*. By 1906 the true end of Leopold's rule had, however, been revealed, and was being greeted with a storm of international execration. Foremost among the critics was Lord Cromer in Egypt, who, after the reconquest of the Sudan in 1898, visited the territory, voyaging as far south as Lado, and was struck by the few signs of life on the left, Belgian, bank of the Nile, compared with the right, under British control. "The Belgians are disliked," he wrote, "the people fly from them . . . the (Congo) Government, so far as I can judge, is conducted almost exclusively on commercial principles."[15] The moving spirit in the criticism of the Congo régime was, however, that of the Liverpool shipping-clerk, E. D. Morel (1873–1924), who having discovered something of the truth during business trips to Belgium, resigned his post in 1897 and devoted himself to the exposure of Leopold's rule. He was supported by Chambers of Commerce, which protested against the Congo trade monopolies as violations of the Berlin Act, and after a debate in the House of Commons the British Government sent a formal protest in 1903. A consular official, Roger Casement, whose services in this connexion are less well-remembered than his unhappy fate as a German agent in Ireland in 1916, was then sent to investigate matters on the spot, and his revelations, presented to Leopold by the British Government, led to a commission of inquiry, and, in the end, to the promulgation of reforms. So strong was British feeling that the House of Commons debated the Congo nine times in five sessions, while the Belgian Socialist leader, Emile Vandervelde, pressed the matter in the Belgian Chamber. Eventually, in 1908, arrangements were made for the annexation of the Congo State by Belgium, though it was not until after Leopold's death that any programme of reforms could be inaugurated, while the existence of the monopolies and concessions was a bar to their effectiveness. It was not until 1913 that Britain felt able to give formal recognition to the annexation. The reforms then already begun were delayed by the war, but have succeeded in creating a colonial administration that is, in some respects, the best that Africa can show. The work of devoted Belgian public servants, of whom one of the first was Leopold's nephew and successor, the gallant King Albert, has now largely obliterated the unhappy memories of earlier days. The concessions policy has been maintained and extended, but has been subjected to limitations and safeguards. Two major concessions are those of the *Union Minière*, developing the mineral resources of the Katanga, in southeastern Congo, which include important deposits of copper and uranium, and the *Huileries du Congo Belge*, granted to Lever in 1911, and now a subsidiary of Unilever Limited. The Katanga is one with Northern Rhodesia, and was occupied by the Belgians in 1891, in time to set a limit to the northern extension of Rhodes's British South Africa Company. Its resources could not be developed until the railway from Beira, nearly one thousand miles away on the east coast, reached it, through Rhodesia, in 1910, but copper production began in 1911, and now runs at about a quarter of a million tons a year. About one-third of the world's known reserves of copper-ore are believed to lie in the Katanga and Northern Rhodesia, and the uranium mines are hardly less important.

Whatever the historical reasons, and the unhappy outcome, it remains an extraordinary fact that one of the most considerable beneficiaries of the partition of Africa should have been the able, but not over-scrupulous, King of the Belgians, who secured for himself an area almost as large as that of all the German colonies combined at a time when Italy, for instance, held nothing more than a base on the Red Sea. Had Bismarck been the *Kolonialmensch* that the German colonial societies would have had him be, he might have secured for his country a worthy empire.

## WEST AFRICAN DEVELOPMENTS

The Berlin Act of 1885 concerned itself also with the Niger, though in view of the British hold on the lower portions of the river, and of the French on the upper, it did no more than affirm the principle of freedom of navigation. Already, however, the division of West Africa had begun. In an earlier section reference has been made to the recommendation of the Select Committee of 1865 that the British occupation of positions on the West Coast should be brought to an end. With the final disappearance of the slave-trade, it seemed reasonable to hope, as Salisbury later argued in the speech already quoted, that the native peoples "would gradually acquire their own proper civilization without any interference on our part", and with legitimate trade and the missions as the only European contacts. Alternative articles of trade to replace slaves had been found in ivory and palm-oils, particularly in the oils as cleaner habits in Europe increased the demand for soap and the development of machinery called for lubricants. The export of palm-oil from West Africa, which had been little more than one hundred tons a year at the beginning of the nineteenth century, exceeded forty thousand tons by 1855, and considerable further increases were to come with the invention of margarine and the development of food-canning, the oil proving valuable as a flux in tin-plating:[16] within the next half-century, indeed, exports of palm-products increased seven-fold. It was on account of this flourishing trade that the delta of the Niger was long known as the Oil Rivers.

## TRADE AND HEALTH IN WEST AFRICA

After the abolition of the slave-traffic traders had established themselves on the coast to deal in these products, receiving their supplies from the coastal tribes, who served as middlemen and collected produce in the interior. These tribes naturally sought to prevent the traders from making their own contacts with the interior, lest the trade pass from their hands, and there was constant opposition, therefore, to explorers and merchants who tried to penetrate up the rivers. In many places traders were forbidden to land and had to conduct their business from moored hulks, while on the Gold Coast, although coastal "forts" were held, the way into the interior was barred by the fierce Ashanti people, who dominated the neighbouring tribes from their capital at Kumasi, and resisted the efforts that were being made to suppress the traffic in slaves.

On the Niger there was similar opposition, though it was less well-organized. The first Europeans to trace the course of this river, long a mystery to explorers, had been two Englishmen, Richard and John Lander, who had travelled downstream from the interior in 1830. Their success had led a Liverpool merchant, McGregor Laird, to try to establish steamers on the river, while an ill-fated Government expedition had followed in 1841. But, as had always happened on this deadly coast, disease proved an even greater menace than any native hostility: of the 145 European members of the expedition, for instance, 48 died in the course of only nine weeks. Not until the 'fifties, when the prophylactic qualities of quinine were understood, was it possible to send ships up the river without losing a great part of the crew, though forty years were still to pass before the researches of Sir Ronald Ross (1857-1932) at last, in 1897, solved the mystery of the transmission of the fatal malaria. Indeed, as late as 1896 an official report on Nigeria showed that 28 out of 150 Europeans had died within a few months, while on the Gold Coast in the same year the losses from fever in the second Ashanti campaign included Queen Victoria's son-in-law, Prince Henry of Battenberg, who had joined the expedition as a volunteer.

## THE GOLD COAST COLONY, 1874, AND THE ASHANTI WARS

The acquisition of Lagos in 1861, as part of the campaign against the slavers, has already been referred to. This proved for some years the limit of expansion of British authority, though the Danish and Dutch posts on the coast were bought in order to prevent the local tribes from playing off one nationality against another. The purchase of the Dutch stations, however, led to complications on the Gold Coast, where the Ashantis, under a bellicose new *Asantehene* (King), Kofi Karikari, resented measures which threatened their freedom of action. Several minor conflicts with them had already taken place, and, encouraged by earlier success, in 1873 they attacked the tribes under British protection. It was decided that the time had come to teach them a lesson, and early in the following year a skilfully conducted expedition under Wolseley penetrated to Kumasi, destroyed it and brought Kofi to terms.

At the same time the coastal territories, hitherto merely under British protection, and controlled since 1865 from Sierra Leone, were formally annexed to the Crown as the Colony of the Gold Coast (July, 1874). The expeditionary force withdrew from the Ashanti country, however, as soon as its immediate object had been achieved, and, although Kofi renounced the slave-trade and human sacrifice, experience soon showed that without occupation these undertakings could not be enforced. Continued unrest, combined with the increasing colonial activities of France and Germany, therefore led to a further expedition in 1896, when the ruling *Asantehene*, Kwaku Dua III, better known by his nickname of "Prempeh" ("Tubby"), was exiled to the Seychelles (whence he was not permitted to return until 1924), and a Protectorate was established. After a revolt in 1900 (caused by an ill-judged attempt to seize the sacred "Golden Stool" of the Ashantis) the territory was finally pacified and annexed to the Gold Coast in 1902, though it was not for twenty years that the Ashanti became reconciled to their position.

## "Annexation or Abandonment"

The Ashanti War of 1874 and the annexation of the Gold Coast in the same year were typical in that they revealed the necessity for effective government and the impossibility of carrying-out the recommendations of the Committee of 1865. Lord Carnarvon, as Colonial Secretary, deplored these "disagreeable duties", but a Colonial Office minute of 1874 reflected the growing opinion that "complete annexation or total abandonment are . . . the only alternatives", and events soon compelled the adoption of more positive policies. During the 'eighties it became evident that Britain must either consolidate her position on the West Coast or be excluded by France and Germany from the interior, and eventually, therefore, from the coast itself. Hence her increasing concern with developments up country in both the Gold Coast and Nigeria.

## French Expansion

With the activities of traders went the work of the explorers, who revealed the vastness of the areas that lay inland,

T*

and frequently brought back exaggerated accounts of the population and resources of the interior. Notable among the explorers was Dr. Gustav Nachtigal (1834–85), afterwards German Consul-General in Tunis, who in the four years 1869–73 travelled widely on the upper Benue River, the hinterland of the Cameroon coast, where the Duala people had for long firmly controlled the trade-routes and prohibited any Europeans to enter. When German control over the Cameroons was established in 1884 it was Nachtigal, significantly enough, who was selected to make the necessary treaties with the Dualas, and he carried with him on his mission instructions not only from the Imperial Government but also from the Hamburg firms who had been trading for some years on the Cameroon coast. German rivalry was a later development for Britain, however: it was chiefly from the French that competition was expected in the earlier period, and increasing French activity had not been without its influence on the decision to annex Lagos and, later, the Gold Coast. The French had long been established in Senegal, and under the inspiration of the brilliant and imperially-minded General Louis Faidherbe, Governor of Senegal from 1854 to 1865, had begun to press eastwards, towards the Upper Niger, while the important port of Dakar had been founded in 1862. At the same time they were feeling their way southwards from Algeria, claiming the whole Niger basin, cynics later declared, as the hinterland of their North African possessions, and a few years after the collapse of the Second Empire, in 1876, there began the long series of campaigns for the control of the Upper Niger which eventually brought them, in 1894, to Timbuktu. Already there were Frenchmen who were encouraged by the military qualities of the Senegalese to hope that in the manpower of the Sudan might be found some counterpoise to Germany's preponderance. But it was French economic activity and tariff policy that chiefly caused perturbation among other trading interests. British and German traders alike were disturbed by the establishment of a French post, to the west of Lagos, at Porto Novo (from which centre the colony of Dahomey later developed), and by the appearance on the coast of two trading companies, which, with the encouragement of Gambetta, tried to capture the Niger trade. This trade was now being conducted by several rival British firms, who were ill-equipped to face such powerful competition. The French aim was to gain complete control of the whole of the coast and interior of the great West African "bulge", and for a time it seemed that, with the British Government reluctant to acquire further territory in an area which had so evil a reputation, the French ambition would be realized. In 1877, however, there appeared on the Niger an able and forceful Englishman, who had an interest in one of the British companies and was quick to size up the situation. This was George Goldie Taubman, better known by his later name as Sir George Goldie (1846–1925), who was destined to become the true founder of British Nigeria.

## SIR GEORGE GOLDIE AND NIGERIA

Goldie's achievement was founded upon something akin to the "positive policy" which had lapsed since the disaster of 1841. His aim was to strengthen and develop British trade on the Niger and then to strike into the interior, opening up to legitimate commerce the great region of the Sudan, where, cut off from contact by deserts and forests, dwelt what he described as "this lost thirtieth of the human race". Every traveller who had penetrated the Sudan had reported on the prevalence of slave-raiding, and Goldie had seen something of it for himself. "The radical vice of the Sudan", he wrote, "the disease which, until cured, must arrest all intellectual and material progress, is . . . slave-*raiding*", and he believed that compared with it the numbers carried overseas by the slave-traders were "insignificant".[17] In the north, in the region which was later to become Northern Nigeria, great slave-raiding expeditions of ten to fifteen thousand men were sent out every year, and caravans of slaves were sent east to the Nile and north to the slave-markets of Tripoli, on the Mediterranean.[18] In the south, among the superstition-ridden people of the coast, there were the additional horrors of human sacrifice and cannibalism, especially at the "city of blood", Benin.

## THE ROYAL NIGER COMPANY: LUGARD

This was the country which was now to be opened. When Goldie arrived it was clear that only amalgamation could maintain the British firms in the face of French competition, and the United African Company was therefore formed in 1879. A hard commercial struggle followed, but in 1884 the French were bought out, and the Berlin Conference in the following year recognized the lower Niger as a British sphere of influence. A British protectorate was then proclaimed, and a year later Goldie received the Royal Charter for which he had been pressing for some time. The Royal Niger Company, as it was now called, was empowered by its charter to administer the Niger territories under certain conditions, which included the abolition of slavery. Some of the coastal tribes and chieftains not unnaturally resisted the breaking of their monopoly, and one chief, Jaja of Opobo (who owed his position not to any traditional rights but to his success as a trader) was removed in 1887 in circumstances which left a legacy of ill-feeling, while there was a serious rising at Brass in 1895. But the opening-up and pacification of the country on the whole proceeded steadily, though the Company lacked the resources to penetrate far inland. Typical of the tasks that fell to it was the expedition in 1897 against the slave-raiding Emirs of Nupe and Ilorin, which Goldie himself accompanied. Yet by the end of the century it was clear that the final settlement of the country was beyond the power of the Company, while the British government was already having to concern itself increasingly with its territories. Thus, in 1897 a punitive expedition had to be sent to Benin (even as a larger one had taken Kumasi in 1896), and in the same year the West African Frontier Force was constituted to check the increasing pressure of the French from Dahomey. In charge of this force was put a brilliant soldier and administrator, who had already distinguished himself in East Africa and seen some service with the Niger Company, Frederick (afterwards, Lord) Lugard (1858–1945). There then began that connexion with Nigeria which was to see Lugard as the first High Commissioner of Northern Nigeria (1900–06), as Governor of North and South Nigeria (1912), and finally as first Governor-General of the united Colony and Protectorate of Nigeria (1914–19). Yet it is doubtful whether the work which Lugard crowned with the establishment of united Nigeria could have been accomplished without the tenacity and vision of Goldie and his Company. "Goldie the capitalist," it has neatly been said, "abolished slavery throughout an area three times the size of Great Britain."[19]

## GERMANY IN THE CAMEROONS

If increasing French pressure affected developments in Nigeria from the time of Goldie's arrival there in 1877, it had no less an effect upon other parts of the coast. In the early 'eighties, as the result, in part, of de Brazza's activities, there were reports of French moves on the Cameroon coast, and Duala chiefs repeated requests which they had been making for nearly twenty years for the proclamation of a Protectorate which would exclude the French and also check rivalries between themselves. True to its customary view the Government hesitated to move in the matter, but instructions were eventually given in April, 1884. When, however, the local consul, Hewett, arrived at Duala, in the Cameroon estuary, on 19th July, he found that he had been forestalled. Bismarck had sent out Dr. Nachtigal in April, ostensibly to report on German trade, for which purpose he had received, at the Chancellor's request, the assistance of local British representatives. His real task, however, had been to annex the Cameroons and Togoland, and thus to secure for Germany some part of the territories which would otherwise have fallen entirely to France or Britain. There was in London a certain amount of resentment at this move, directed mainly at the secrecy which had been observed, but as no important British interests were involved and German support, as Bismarck was quick to point out, was needed to ease Britain's position in Egypt, the situation was accepted. It was to guard against further surprises of the kind, however, that the formal protectorate over the Lower Niger was proclaimed in 1885.

## THE CHARTERED COMPANIES

In only twenty years after the 1865 report, therefore, Britain's West African commitments, far from diminishing, were steadily increasing. Yet the principle of restricting commitments—and, decisive consideration from the Treasury point of view, the concomitant expense—to the minimum possible was still maintained. Chamberlain, as Colonial Secretary, was later to complain humorously that on behalf of the colonies he had had to go, "over and over again, to the Treasury to ask their assent to an expenditure of £5".[20] Low taxation and severe economy in public expenditure were still the stern principles of Treasury administration that they had been in Gladstone's heyday as Chancellor of the Exchequer. Except in matters of naval defence, which was beginning to assume serious importance, the days of inflated expenditure still lay well in the future: not until 1896 did the budget attain the £100,000,000 mark, and that was regarded by many contemporaries as "the knell of doom".[21] Colonial expenditure was not permitted to fall upon the British taxpayer. India and Egypt and the rest, all had to pay for their own services and officials. As typical instances one may cite the compensation paid to the Orange Free State for the loss of the diamond-fields, which was debited to the Griqualand budget, or the cost of the reconquest of the Sudan in 1898, two-thirds of which was met by Egypt, which also subsidized the recovered territory until its own budget balanced in 1913. Britain bore a share of purely military expenditure, but colonial development was limited by the resources of the colonies themselves, and it would manifestly have been impossible for Britain to have borne the financial burden which Germany, for instance, had to face in her limited colonial empire to justify holding it at all. Yet the humorous complaint made in 1904 by Sir Reginald Wingate (1861–1945), first Governor-General of the Sudan, that Britain's only contribution to the cost of the administration of the vast territory now under joint Anglo-Egyptian control was that she supplied the Union Jacks which flew side-by-side with the Egyptian flag throughout the Sudan, was not without point and justification.[22] Hence the reliance in the 'eighties upon Chartered Companies, which were a convenient device for safeguarding British interests without adding to the burden on the British taxpayer. The Companies could not, however, be more than a temporary device. Development and administration proved more costly than had optimistically been assumed, and hampered the economic functions which were the primary concern of the Companies. In every case, as already recorded, the charter had before long to be withdrawn and direct imperial administration substituted.

## BRITISH AND GERMAN RULE COMPARED

The charters themselves are, however, worthy of attention as evidence of British concern with standards of administration at a time when in the Congo and in the German colonies European rule was making a harsh impact upon native life. In every case the charters laid down that slavery was to be exterminated, native customs respected, the import of arms and liquor to be prevented and monopolies to be avoided. The safeguards were both more restrictive and more effective than any applied by Leopold II and the German Government. Moreover, the leading spirits in the British territories, men of the stamp of Rhodes, Goldie, Kirk and Lugard, though not all were of their calibre, were men of high principle, often enough with a touch of idealism, who were seriously concerned with the improvement of African conditions. Until the reforms of Dernburg, after the critical Reichstag elections of 1907, the German colonies could show few men as eminent. Karl Peters in East Africa and Leist and von Puttkamer in the Cameroons, with their harsh attitude to Africans, were no recommendation for German colonial expansion, though it was criticism of their actions by the Reichstag that caused the recall of Leist as Acting-Governor in 1894 and in 1907 that of Puttkamer, who had held the position of Governor since 1895. After 1907, as recorded elsewhere, the German colonial service was over-hauled by Dernburg, who was not above learning from British practice, and he and his successors, Lindequist and Solf, with the co-operationof such men as Theodore Seitz as Governor of the Cameroons, set German colonial rule, costly though it was, upon sound and not unenlightened lines. Yet the earlier experience of Germany's African colonies had on the whole been unfortunate, for they were treated too obviously as conquered territory. Not until 1907 did public and official policy come together in support of more enlightened measures, and, apart from the work of many German missionaries, there was no considerable public opinion, as there was in Britain, to concern itself over many years with the succouring of backward and oppressed peoples and the shaping of an enlightened official policy. There was, in short, nothing comparable to the long anti-slavery agitation in Britain, which, an historian of colonial development has argued, gave Britain a strong case for the

possession of additional African territories.[23] To say this is not
to claim that the Chartered Companies were always enlightened or disinterested in their handling of the territories
committed to their charge: the almost unavoidable tendency
towards monopoly, which should have been foreseen, was one
reason for the abrogation of the charters, while the grim
example of the Congo aroused fears of the depths to which
commercial exploitation, without an independent State administration, might descend. Yet, given that the work of development had to be done, it was probably done by the companies
as well as, under the circumstances, it could be done, and
consciences were active on the spot, as they were not always
in the Congo or the German colonies. This is, perhaps, the
point at which to add that despite all the criticism which
it had to undergo during the First World War, criticism which
was to be embodied in the Treaty of Versailles in 1919,
German colonial rule by 1914 had outgrown former abuses
and was showing signs of satisfactory development, though its
control of native peoples tended to be severe. Sir Donald
Cameron, who became Governor of Tanganyika, the former
German East Africa, in 1925, has expressed the opinion that
German rule was not, on the whole, so bad as to justify the
view that Germany had proved herself unfit to hold colonial
territory,[24] while an American investigator has said of the
Cameroons that "if Germany had been allowed to continue
as a colonial power after the war, her civil rule would have
compared favourably with the very best that the world knows
today".[25]

## THE POLICY OF "INDIRECT RULE"

In the 'eighties and 'nineties, however, all this lay in the
future. If the chartered companies proved in the end an
unsatisfactory means, and the necessity for economy remained
acute, there were other methods by which newly-won territories
might be governed without undue cost. Rule need not be direct,
and to soften the impact of Europe upon backward areas there
was, indeed, much to be said for "indirect" rule through native
authorities. Indirect rule became the feature of British
administration in Northern Nigeria and proved for a time a
significant development in colonial practice. Its origins were

to be found in India, where Native States had been left under their own rulers, and circumstances favoured its extension to Northern Nigeria, where the Mohammedan Fulani conquerors formed a feudal aristocracy dominating the subject peoples. To break their control was out of the question, and Goldie, after his first contacts with the North, maintained that "even an imperfect and tyrannical native African administration, if its extreme excesses were controlled by European supervision, would be, in the early stages, productive of far less discomfort to its subjects than well-intentioned but ill-directed efforts of European magistrates".[26] The significant points which Goldie kept in mind were that there should be European supervision and, a consideration that tended to be overlooked later, that indirect rule should be limited to the "early stages". It was Lugard, however, who adopted indirect rule throughout the northern territories as he brought them under submission between 1900 and 1906. He had been familiar with the principle in India, and had had the task of applying it in Uganda. Under his influence and guidance it now spread throughout Nigeria. He intended it, as he insisted, as a means towards better government, a means which avoided excessive demands either upon the British taxpayer, responsible for the size and cost of the colonial administration, or upon the adaptability of African society. It was thus a facet of his "dual mandate". It was not, however, a method of general applicability. Where, as in the coastal regions of West Africa, European influence and education were replacing native tribal authority, it was a conservative, if not actually a reactionary, influence, and Sir Donald Cameron, who was later to introduce the system to Tanganyika, has complained that it tended to become synonymous in Nigeria with the conception of sovereign rule by native chiefs,[27] a strange notion in African sight. Nevertheless, and especially by comparison with what was being done in other parts of Africa, it was a significant contribution to African development and colonial policy alike. A critic entitled to be heard, E. D. Morel, fresh from his Congo successes, praised it in 1911 as "an achievement, not of conquest, but of constructive and sober guidance",[28] a sound estimate. Lugard himself was alive to the dangers of the Indian system, and resolved to avoid them: in India, he has written, "the policy of the past rated administrative efficiency more highly than education in self-government".[29] The development of Nigeria since his day is perhaps the best comment that can be offered on the success of his broader policy, even when it was not always carried out as he would have wished, while through the men who worked with him his influence made itself felt throughout the African colonies: outstanding among his officials, apart from Cameron, who in addition to his service in Tanganyika was Governor of Nigeria from 1931 to 1935, were two later Governors of the Gold Coast, Sir Gordon Guggisberg (1919–27) and Sir Alan Burns (1941–48).

Lugard's aim was, essentially, to prepare the colonial peoples for self-government by adapting them gradually, and through their own institutions, to the urgent demands of the modern world, and, unlike many lesser men in the colonial service, he did not fail to foresee the growing pains that were to come:

> If there is unrest, and a desire for independence . . . it is because we have taught the value of liberty and freedom, which for centuries these peoples had not known. Their very discontent is a measure of their progress.[30]

## BRITISH AND FRENCH RULE COMPARED

Experience was to show that it was the educated West African who under "indirect rule" tended to be frustrated in his advancement. The situation was different in the French colonies. There the directing policy was that of "assimilation", by which educated Africans, or citizens from other French colonies, could become as Frenchmen, to whom no ambition was closed. Hence the career of such a man as Felix Eboué, born in French Guiana, who had a distinguished career in French Africa, and as Governor of Equatorial Africa in 1940 was the first colonial leader to rally to General de Gaulle. But "assimilation" had less than "indirect rule" to offer to the majority of Africans who could not be educated to European standards. Albert Sarraut, who as Colonial Minister in 1920–24 and 1932–33 largely shaped French colonial policy in the post-war period, and adapted "assimilation" to the needs of the more backward peoples, summed-up in an address in 1933 the differing aims of British and French in Africa:

> "You build day by day on what already exists. We dream of new and rectilinear architectures. ... You, in sum, wish the native races to place themselves in a condition to make their own happiness. We wish ourselves to make their happiness, urgently and with authority."[31]

At their best both methods have had much to offer to Africa, and, whatever the economic interests with which they have been entwined, neither lacked a touch of high idealism, the French the idealism of the principles of 1789, the British, at bottom, that of the Christian conscience and of faith in the individual's right to liberty in an ordered society.

In practice the difference in approach was most noticeable in educational policy. "Assimilation" brought the colonial peoples, however incongruously at times, into close contact with French education and culture. French was widely taught and widely spoken in French colonies and French political ideals remained the basis of government: one colonial governor, in Indo-China, ostentatiously began his rule by fixing to the walls of Hanoi a copy of the historic "Rights of Man", in a gesture that expressed both faith in the egalitarian principles of the Revolution and defiance to the ancient institutions of the territory. Lacking such ideological confidence, and less logical and more empirical in their approach, the British hoped eventually to encourage interest in the machinery of self-government, yet without altering native institutions too abruptly. Self-government, however distant as an ideal, was the British aim: assimilation into the life of France the French objective. British officials therefore learnt the native languages, while under the *Tricolore* the colonial peoples learnt French.

There were differences, too, in the very organization of control. French rule was sustained by a host of minor officials, poorly paid but in close touch with the dependent peoples. British rule was fundamentally more aloof. It tended to be exclusive and insular in outlook, and it was, in the main, in the hands of a small number of highly qualified, highly trained and highly paid officers, who formed a ruling caste, devoted and incorruptible, but essentially aloof from the people whose destinies it controlled. Aloofness at times had its merits, but it did not win hearts. In particular it was resented, and was increasingly to be resented, by the type of educated nationalist leader who found only limited scope for himself in a British colony, but who under French rule would have had all the advantages and opportunities of a citizen of the Republic. The differences in the two systems were therefore differences of ideology, of history and of national character and outlook. Experience was to show that, while each had certain advantages over the other, ultimately neither was able to provide full scope for the rising ambitions of the colonial peoples. But in the nineteenth century that development lay in the distant future.

## Economic Development in West Africa: Chamberlain's Policy

The extension of British rule in Nigeria, as in the Gold Coast, was to bring its own problems, but the establishment of an ordered government and the stamping-out of slave-raiding and inter-tribal warfare for some years gave the regions the best conditions they could ever have known. Their progress was seen in their economic advancement, and especially in the development of the Gold Coast into the principal source of cocoa, producing nearly one-half of the world's total needs. Cocoa was first introduced in 1879, and its development was rapid. From twelve tons a year in the early 'nineties exports had risen by the end of the century to over three hundred tons, by 1911 to twenty thousand tons and by the end of the war to over one hundred thousand. On the eve of the war the export value was some £2,500,000: forty years later it was well over £60,000,000. And cocoa is essentially a peasant crop, the produce of small farmers: on it, in many respects, are based the strength and prosperity of the colony. Nigeria has not been so fortunate, though her products are more varied, palm oil, groundnuts and tin being exported in addition to cocoa. Yet between 1900 and 1913 Nigerian exports rose from £1,887,000 to £7,097,000. A good deal of this expansion was made possible not only by pacification but by the opening-up of the country and the improvement of communications. It was Chamberlain who, as soon as he took office in 1895, stressed the need for harbours, roads and railways to give the access which would make development possible, and a good deal of railway building was then undertaken, Kano in Northern Nigeria being reached by rail from the coast in 1912. Chamberlain viewed the colonies as being, in a well-known phrase, "in the condition of undeveloped estates", awaiting development "for the benefit of their population and for the benefit of the greater population which is outside". He was not able to achieve much in the face of Treasury caution, and a plan he devised for using the dividends on the Government's Suez Canal shares as a colonial development fund was frustrated by the Chancellor of the Exchequer, but he stimulated interest in the dependent territories and by drawing attention to their needs initiated a more constructive policy. His encouragement of research into tropical diseases revolutionized, too, the conditions of life in West Africa and many other colonial territories. The malaria and sleeping-sickness investigations were carried to successful conclusions during his term of office, and the London and Liverpool Schools of Tropical Medicine, established in 1899, owed much to his inspiration and support: a new slogan was soon to be possible, "Health followed the Flag".[32] France, Belgium and Germany were quick to follow the lead which Chamberlain had given, and within a few years had established their own centres for the study of tropical disease.

## EAST AFRICA: BRITAIN AND GERMANY

If Chamberlain stimulated railway building in West Africa he did it no less in the East, where the railway from Mombasa on the coast to Kisumu on Lake Victoria was constructed between 1897 and 1902 and made possible the development of the colonies of Kenya and Uganda. The British interest in the slave-trade on the east coast, centred on Zanzibar, has already been referred to. After its formal suppression military operations against Arab slave-raiders in the interior had still to be continued, and Lugard began his career in this way in Nyasaland in 1889. Meanwhile German traders were establishing themselves in Zanzibar and on the mainland opposite, and in 1886 "spheres of influence" were delimited, the British gaining what was to become Kenya and the Germans the future Tanganyika. The British East Africa

Company was chartered in 1888, with power to administer the British sphere, and in the same year the Arabs in the German zone broke into revolt against Karl Peters's rule. German East Africa was then taken under the direct control of the German Government, but Peters, his ambitions unsatisfied, struck inland from Witu, north of the British area, with the ostensible object of relieving Emir Pasha in Equatorial Sudan, and reappeared in Uganda, where he obtained a treaty establishing a German protectorate. Meanwhile, however, Germany and Britain were drawing closer together after the crisis over Bulgaria, and Bismarck took the view that "Salisbury's friendship is worth more to us than the whole of East Africa". In 1890 an agreement was reached by which Britain received the protectorate over Zanzibar and the whole of the Kenya coast, including Witu, in return for the cession of Heligoland to Germany. In Stanley's exultant words, Britain had received a suit of clothes in exchange for a mere trouser-button. Moreover, Germany recognized that British controlled territory extended inland to Lake Victoria and the Congo frontier.

## UGANDA

In Uganda missionaries had been active since Stanley's enthusiastic reports of the Baganda people had appeared in 1875. From 1885, however, under the ferocious ruler, the *Kabaka* Mwanga, there had been attacks on missionaries and converts, and civil war had broken out. With Britain's prior claim now recognized Lugard entered Uganda in 1890 and pacified the country. A formal Protectorate was proclaimed in 1894, and the hostile and unreliable Mwanga was deposed in 1897. A definitive Agreement was made in 1900, and it was this which, under the general Protectorate, provided the basis for future relations between Britain and the Baganda.

## KENYA

East Africa, however, lacked the resources which had made the West, for all its discomforts, so enticing to European traders. "Central Africa is doubtless ready enough to take whatever England likes to send," a notable explorer, Joseph Thomson, who knew the country well, reported in 1884, "but she has nothing to give in return."[33] This was, perhaps, an

overstatement, but Thomson disapproved of Stanley's extravagant claims, and it was certainly the case that only in the
coastlands, where Zanzibar was soon to make from cloves
more than she had ever gained by the slave-trade, were there
exportable products. It was Thomson himself, however, who
had explored the Kenya highlands, and it was there that white
settlement was to begin. The main native peoples in Kenya
were the Kikuyu and the fierce pastoralists, the Masai, who
occupied the highland area. Cattle epidemics and inter-tribal
warfare had diminished the strength of the Masai by the
'nineties,[34] and in their lands, as in South Africa, the seeming
emptiness of grazing land over which cattle wandered gave the
impression of vast "unoccupied" areas open for settlement.
Moreover, the climate of the uplands was good, and the
territory seemed, therefore, ideally suited to become, in the now
famous phrase of its first High Commissioner, Sir Charles
Eliot, "white man's country". The East Africa Protectorate
was proclaimed in 1895, when the Company surrendered its
charter, and after taking legal advice in 1899 the Government
began to offer "unoccupied" land for settlement. An Ordinance
of 1902 required that regard should be had "to the rights and
requirements of the natives", but grazing rights were not easy
of definition, and already by 1904 it was agreed that land would
need to be set aside as native reserves. Masai and Kikuyu alike
were then beginning to feel the pressure of the claims of white
settlement, and disagreements over land policy, complicated
by the failure to define sufficiently early the limits of settlement,
have kept alive an element of bitterness in the relations between
Europeans and Africans that has had unhappy consequences:
this, despite the undoubted success of the settlers and their
interest in their new country.

In Uganda the density of the population ruled out the
possibility of settlement on any considerable scale, and
economic development was slow. After the coming of the
railway, however, missionary enterprise, by now an influential
element in Baganda life, introduced cotton, and Uganda was
soon to become one of the principal cotton-producing areas of
the Empire. By 1914 cotton to the value of more than
£300,000 was being exported, and Uganda's total exports
now amount to ten times this sum, considerably more than

those of Kenya: the greater part is cotton, most of which is exported to India. It was the railway which made this development possible, replacing backward conditions and the fear of slavery with a legitimate commerce; opening the country, also, to the ubiquitous Indian traders whose influence is strong upon it. British missionaries and explorers, and such government officials as Kirk, had long fought against slavery: whatever the future difficulties, the pacification and development of East Africa were a tribute to their untiring zeal. Yet to the debit side of development must be set the sleeping-sickness epidemic, which struck Uganda from 1901 and was only checked, after appalling mortality, when the surviving population was cleared from around Lake Victoria in 1906–09. Though the cause of the disease was now known, it was to be many years before a cure could be found: meanwhile the only remedy was to clear the population and destroy the bush in which the dread tsetse-fly flourished.

## ZIONISM: THE "UGANDA" OFFER, 1903

An unexpected result of the occupation of East Africa was the proposal to settle Jewish Zionists in the Kenya highlands. Something has been said in an earlier section of the pioneer work of the Zionist leader, Theodore Herzl. In the face of the Russian pogroms that took place at this time, and the consequent flight to the west of hundreds of thousands of Russian Jews, Herzl and his followers strove for the means to return to the Jewish homeland in Palestine. Negotiations with Turkey proved abortive, however, and a settlement at el Arish in Sinai was proposed. In view of the British occupation of Egypt this brought Herzl into touch with the British Government, and in 1902 he saw Chamberlain in London. Chamberlain expressed his interest, and asked only that Herzl should not use el Arish as a base for "a Jameson raid" upon Palestine,[35] an ironic comment on the misadventure of six years earlier. Later in the year, on his way to South Africa, Chamberlain travelled in East Africa on the Uganda railway, and saw the possibilities of settlement. On his return in 1903 he suggested that the Zionists should turn their attention to East Africa (Uganda was mentioned, but the area in question was actually in Kenya), and after the abandonment of the Arish site, which proved to be insufficiently well watered, Herzl accepted the proposal, only to have it rejected by his collaborators. The leading part in the opposition was taken by the Russian Jews, who, despite their sufferings, would not compromise on their desire for Palestine as the Jewish national home: "these people", Herzl angrily exclaimed, "have a rope around their necks, and still they refuse".[36] Such was the force of the longing for Zion, which has re-created Israel in our own day. Foremost among the Russian Jews was Chaim Weizmann, who was drawn to England by the interest shown in Jewish needs and settled here in 1903. In 1906, while lecturing at Manchester University, he met Balfour, who had been puzzled at the rejection of the "Uganda" offer, and was now impressed by Weizmann's ardour into an interest in Zionism that was to bear fruit in 1917 and produce the beginnings of a Jewish State. So did the Uganda railway, at one end of the great Rift Valley, come in time to influence events at the other end, two thousand five hundred miles to the north.

## EGYPT AND THE SUDAN

We have now said something of the development of Africa, South, Central, West and East. There remains the North, which, although geographically Africa, forms part of the Arab lands. And the north is particularly concerned with British rule in Egypt, dominated for so long by the proconsular figure of Lord Cromer. Between Egypt and the great mass of Africa to the south lies the Sudan, a great region extending from Nile valley and desert to equatorial forest, largely independent throughout its long and uneventful history until 1821, when it was conquered by Muhammad Ali and absorbed into the Egyptian dominions. If Egypt is not Africa the Sudan is its link with Africa, and it was Muhammad Ali who drew the link close. His interest in the Sudan had been principally in its human material, as soldiers and slaves, and in its rumoured gold resources. Slave-raiding and slave-selling were developed by government officials and slave-dealers alike, especially among the Central African peoples of the south, and after the death of Muhammad Ali himself in 1848 the misgovernment of the whole of the territory reached unhappy lengths. Samuel Baker, who travelled up the Nile in 1862 on the journey that brought him to Lake Albert, commented on the extortion and oppression that were rife: "the Soudan is worthless", he wrote, "but there is, nevertheless, a reason that first prompted its occupation by the Egyptians, and that is in force to the present day, *The Soudan supplies slaves*".[37] Indeed, by the time that it was finally settled and pacified by Britain and Egypt forty years later, after the conquest of 1898, the Sudan had become the last great haunt of slavers and slavery in Africa. Meanwhile, however, it was to suffer much tribulation.

So limited was the Egyptian control over the Sudan, so powerful were the leading slavers, that most of the South passed into their hands. And what was not theirs was misgoverned by rapacious Turkish and Egyptian officials. "The entire country," Baker wrote in disgust later, "was leased out to piratical slave-hunters, under the name of traders." Chief among these "traders" was the able Zubair Rahma, effective master of the Bahr el Ghazal, who was to achieve notoriety through his power and success and his relations with Gordon.

### KHEDIVE ISMAIL AND THE SUDAN: GORDON

From 1863 until he was deposed in 1879 Ismail ruled in Egypt. During the course of his extravagant attempt to ape the nations of Europe with the limited resources of his country, he was fired with the ambition to extinguish the slave-trade in the Sudan and to extend his control over the country, the frontiers of which were lost in the mystery of the sources of the Nile. Already slavers were pressing southwards into Uganda, and in 1870 Ismail, distrusting his own officials, appointed Baker to extend his authority to Lake Victoria. Baker campaigned vigorously but achieved little, and in 1874 Ismail invited a notable figure, Charles George Gordon (1833–85), to succeed him, with the title of Governor of "Equatoria". Gordon has remained to this day a figure to interest and fascinate succeeding generations. A powerful personality, able to inspire respect and devotion, an able soldier and military leader and a devout, if narrow, Christian, he had made a great name for himself in the suppression of the T'ai P'ing rebellion in China in 1863–65, and had therefore come to be known as "Chinese Gordon". He was, as Queen Victoria recorded, "a very strange man and very impulsive";[38] energetic and impetuous, but high-principled to the point of quixotry. The southern Sudan was an ideal field for his energy and idealism, but though he succeeded in establishing some order he despaired of achieving much in view of Egyptian misrule farther north. In 1877, however, Ismail made him Governor of the whole Sudan, and in a series of brilliant journeys by camel he impressed himself on the country, suppressing disorder and stamping-out the slave-trade, in which task he was supported by the joint Anglo-Egyptian "Slave-Trade Convention" (1877), which he had helped to frame. To assist him in his rule he gathered, in preference to Egyptians, a motley group of able men which included the German, Edward Schnitzer, better known as Emin Pasha, and the Austrian, Rudolph Slatin, both of whom were to become the heroes of strange exploits. Much was achieved, but it owed everything to Gordon's drive, and when he resigned in 1879, in sympathy with the unfortunate Ismail, to whom he felt he owed his loyalty, the Sudan fell to pieces again. A new movement was soon to stir, however. Already in Egypt there was serious discontent with the conditions to which the country had been reduced, and in 1881, as already recorded, Arabi Pasha led a nationalist revolt, Egypt's first nationalistic military revolt, led, significantly enough, by a Colonel.

## THE *Mahdiya*, 1881–98

Nationalism was an impossible phenomenon in the Sudan, but in the same year there arose there a devout religious leader, Muhammad Ahmad, who inspired a movement of puritanical religious protest against Egyptian misrule. Muhammad Ahmad (born about 1840) was a man of personality and charm, and a saintly character, but fanatical in his creed and able to inspire fanaticism in others. He proclaimed himself the long-awaited *Mahdi* ("Guide" and descendant of the Prophet) of the Mohammedan world, and summoned the faithful to a *Jihad*, a Holy War, against the unfaithful and unbelievers alike, a religious reformation which, like all such, was to have important political consequences. At his right hand was the able and ruthless Abd Allahi, the *Khalifa* ("Companion" or Lieutenant), who was to succeed him as leader of the movement on his death in 1885. The two dominate the whole period from 1881

to 1898 in the Sudan. Against them and their devoted following
the Egyptian troops garrisoning the Sudan were helpless:
unwilling conscripts, ill-trained and worse-led, they were at
the same time, as good Mohammedans, reluctant to resist a
holy cause.[39] The first armies sent to suppress the Madhi were
destroyed with ease, and in November, 1883, came the
crowning disaster, when a force of 10,000, under a retired
Indian Army Officer, Colonel W. Hicks, was wiped out in an
ambush near El Obeid. The Sudan was now practically in the
Mahdi's hands. Slatin, who was Governor of the distant western
province of Darfur, was compelled to surrender, and to
become a Mohammedan, for which Gordon, characteristically,
would not forgive him: he remained a prisoner for twelve
years until his dramatic escape in 1895. Emin Pasha, Governor
of yet more distant Equatoria, was able to hold out, but was
finally withdrawn, through Uganda, though only with great
reluctance, in 1889, after Stanley had mounted a much-
publicized relief expedition, his last African journey. It was in
ostensible search of his compatriot Emin that Karl Peters
made his mysterious journey into the interior from Witu in
this same year.

GORDON AND THE SUDAN, 1884–85

The position of Gladstone's government, in the face of
the events in the Sudan, was a most unhappy one. As recorded
elsewhere, Egypt had been occupied in 1882, but it was hoped
that British troops could soon be withdrawn. In September,
1883, shortly before the Hicks disaster, Sir Evelyn Baring
returned to Cairo with the title of Agent and Consul-General
and the task of setting Egypt on her feet. He was not to leave
for thirteen years, and it was the affairs of the Sudan, as much
as those of Egypt, which kept him in office. The "fit of
absence" which had left Britain in control of Egypt, left her
no less responsible for the Sudan. Baring had the ambition, as
he later recorded, "of leading the Egyptian people from
bankruptcy to solvency and then onward to affluence, from
Khedivial monstrosities to British justice, and from Oriental
methods veneered with a spurious European civilization
towards the true civilization of the West based on the principles
of the Christian moral code".[40] This lofty aim, so character-

istic of the man and the period, could not, he realized, be achieved if the means of pressure were withdrawn, but he was nevertheless prepared to recommend the withdrawal of troops as soon as possible. The Mahdi's successes, however, altered the situation. Until an effective Egyptian army could be trained the very security of the country depended on the presence of British forces. Gladstone was willy-nilly compelled to accept a greater degree of permanence for the occupation than he had desired. Yet by the same token the forces were lacking for a reconquest of the Sudan, and Egypt's resources were not in any case equal to such a task. It was therefore decided that such garrisons as remained in the south must be evacuated. In view of his recent experience of the Sudan Gordon had for some time been under consideration in official circles for a mission of investigation, but Baker seems to have been the first to raise the matter publicly, early in January, 1884.[41] After several weeks of discussion, with much journalistic agitation, Gordon was selected, and left with instructions which events were to show were woefully inadequate and vague. Gordon himself seriously under-estimated the Mahdi's power and influence. His earlier successes led him to believe that he could deal with the situation without difficulty, and with characteristic impetuosity and single-mindedness he planned, much to the indignation of anti-slavery opinion in Britain, to employ Zubair as a counter to the Mahdi. He assumed, in fact, that he had no more than a rebellious tribal chieftain to contend with: hence his offer to the Mahdi, when he arrived at Khartoum, of a provincial governorship. Those on the spot already knew better, however. "The holding of Khartoum", wrote Frank Power, *The Times* correspondent in the Sudanese capital, "is *bosh*",[42] and so the event proved. The whole complex story cannot be unravelled here. Suffice it to say that Gordon's Egyptian troops conducted themselves against the Mahdi no more successfully than had their unfortunate predecessors, and Gordon thereupon asked for a British force to cover his line of retreat, and pressed his proposal to use Zubair, while justly pointing out to Baring that if Egypt were to be safe the Mahdi would some time have to be "smashed". The British Government rejected both of Gordon's requests and long refused to believe that he was in any danger, though by April,

1884, he was already "hemmed in", and the Queen was expressing a good deal of the rising feeling in Britain when she wrote that, "if not only for humanity's sake, for the honour of the Government and the nation, he must not be abandoned".[43] Gladstone was preoccupied with the new Franchise Bill, however, and took the view that too much was being made of Gordon. Yet, as the months passed it was gradually borne in upon the Government that, however much they might wish to avoid an unpleasant duty which interfered with greater matters of internal politics, Britain alone was in a position to do anything. Preparations for a relief expedition, led by Wolseley, were therefore begun in August, though it did not actually start until October. Gordon hoped for a "flying column", which he thought would sufficiently impress the Mahdi, but Wolseley was taking no chances and progress was slow. It is doubtful, in any case, whether, in the face of Mahdist resistance, a small force could have achieved its purpose. When the first fierce battle of the campaign was fought, on 17th January, 1885, at Abu Klea (more properly, Abu Tlaih), where Burnaby, of Khiva fame, met his end when a British square broke, the Mahdi's followers proved themselves no mean warriors. They were defeated, but although contact was then made with Gordon's steamers, which had come up the river from Khartoum, the advance was not pressed hard, and when a steamer finally arrived before Khartoum on 28th January, it was to find that all was over. The city, its garrison worn out and starving, had been carried by assault on the morning of 26th, and Gordon was dead. "As a military achievement", it has well been said, "the defence of Khartoum will always rank among the great sieges of history",[44] but as everyone in Britain, from the Queen herself, exclaimed in horror, the relieving column had arrived "Too Late". Gordon had technically been serving the Egyptian Khedive, but the technicality deceived no one: British prestige had suffered a serious blow. The government was shaken, and a popular song of the day expressed the general feeling in the words:

> Too late, too late to save him;
> Too late, in vain we tried;
> Fighting for England's glory,
> A hero's death he died.

BARING AND EGYPT, 1883–1907

This dramatic episode was decisive for Britain's position in Egypt. A withdrawal was now for the present unthinkable, and Baring was therefore able to devote himself to his ambitions for Egypt and especially to placing her on a sound financial footing. He was not free to act as he would have wished, for the representatives of the other Powers in Cairo carefully watched the interests of their bondholders and ensured that any money that was available should be set to wiping off Egypt's debts. Yet by rigid economy, careful accounting and the repression of corruption he was able, by 1890, to achieve a surplus. Arrears of interest were paid off and the payment of interest henceforth made as it became due. Then, with balances in hand, taxation could be reduced and by 1896 plans could be laid for the construction of a great dam at Aswan, which would regulate the flow of Egypt's life-line, the Nile, and extend the area of cultivation. Meanwhile forced labour, the ancient curse of the peasant, was abolished, and with the help of experienced British officials, many of whom, like Baring himself, had seen service in the Indian administration, the departments of government were reformed and rendered efficient. Eventually 960 of Egypt's 11,000 civil servants were British, and although this did little to endear the administration to the more self-conscious or ambitious Egyptians, who naturally resented foreign control, it served to put the government of the country on a sound footing.

With the other reforms went a reshaping of the Army, and by 1889, when at length the Khalifa made a threatening move against Egypt, the Egyptian troops, carefully trained by British officers, were able to give a good account of themselves at the battle of Tushki. It can be said, in short, that by the 'nineties British control had already justified itself: by his firmness, his lightening of the burdens that had so long pressed on the *fellaheen* and his insistence on a high standard of justice, Lord Cromer, as he became in 1892, had earned the title which was accorded him of "The Friend of the Wearers of the Blue Robe",[45] the traditional garb of the Egyptian peasant. Yet success had been won in the face of bitter international rivalry. France and Russia were hostile, France the more so since despite her heavy financial commitments in Egypt, and her great work of creation in the Suez Canal, the control of Egypt rested in British hands. Not until the Entente in 1904 was the pressure relaxed. In the meantime her very position in Egypt kept Britain alive to the need for good relations with Germany. If, as Baring wrote to the Foreign Secretary in 1886, all the Powers with interests in Egypt were hostile, his position was a most difficult one. He impressed on the Government, therefore, "the necessity of working well with Germany", for "Berlin, and not Cairo, is the real centre of gravity of Egyptian affairs".[46] Any study of international relations in the 'eighties and 'nineties must keep this point in mind, for though not always obtruded it was an ever-present factor.

## THE RECONQUEST OF THE SUDAN, 1896–99

In 1896, when Cromer was at work on the Aswan project, the British Government suddenly determined that the reconquest of the Sudan should be taken in hand. The reason for this move was twofold. The recent defeat of the Italians by the Abyssinians at Adowa called for a digression to relieve the Khalifa's pressure against Eritrea. More significant than Italian difficulties, however, was the appearance in the southern Sudan of the French, who from their colony in Equatorial Africa were showing an interest in the unsettled conditions of the neighbouring region of the upper Nile, almost the last part of Africa to be still unclaimed by Europeans. Already the intrepid soldier-explorer, Major Marchand, had received instructions to penetrate to the White Nile, and the way was being opened for the fateful meeting between him and the victorious Kitchener at Fashoda in 1898. The condition of the Sudan undoubtedly invited intervention. The Khalifa was, by his own primitive standards, an efficient ruler,[47] but opposition was sternly repressed and the country was too tightly held down to flourish. The maintenance of large armies in the field, and the heavy casualties caused by the fanatical courage of the warriors, brought a decline in agriculture, and the famine of 1889, the result of a "poor Nile" in the previous year, caused great suffering. Nevertheless, the Khalifa's army, though it could not stand against disciplined troops and controlled fire, was a formidable fighting force, making up in courage what it lacked in training and equipment. In charge of the Anglo-Egyptian army was the legendary organizing figure of the *Sirdar*, Kitchener, a man after Cromer's own heart, and the campaigns by which the Sudan was recovered were essentially masterpieces of organization. The first advances were made in 1896, after which a railway was pushed forward in preparation for the major assault in 1898. The decisive battle was fought outside Omdurman in September, 1898, and the Khalifa's forces were destroyed, losing nearly eleven thousand killed to fewer than five hundred of Kitchener's army. The Khalifa himself escaped, but was finally brought to bay and killed in battle in November, 1899. At long last peace had come to the Sudan. Meanwhile, although Marchand had established himself on the White Nile and gallantly raised his country's flag, the French had decided, after a time of tension, with a real danger of war, that he should be withdrawn. The Sudan was then pacified, and, to avoid the difficulties experienced in Egypt from the nominal overlordship of Turkey, was placed under a Condominium, with joint British and Egyptian control.[48] This ingenious arrangement, though hardly to be explained in terms of international law, represented the facts of the situation: Britain maintained control, but the interests of Egypt were respected. Kitchener became the first Governor-General, but was shortly summoned to mend affairs in South Africa, and was succeeded by Sir Reginald Wingate, who created a notable Sudan Civil Service, mainly from Oxford and Cambridge graduates whose athletic prowess won for the Sudan the title of the "Land of the Blacks (the literal meaning of its name), governed by Blues".

After the years of war the growth of prosperity. The Sudan revenue in 1899 was £126,000, little more than half of the expenditure, and until 1913 subsidies had to be granted by Egypt. In that year, however, the budget balanced at £1,600,000, and progress in succeeding years was even more rapid. Egypt's advance, despite her heavy burden of debt, had been still more spectacular; population and trade were doubled, and revenue rose by one-half. But for the accumulated, and largely unproductive, debts of the past, progress would have been still greater.

ANGLO-EGYPTIAN RELATIONS:
(1) THE STATUS OF EGYPT

But whatever the progress in Egypt, foreign control, in its financial as much as in its political aspects, was a constant stimulus to xenophobia. Until 1914, when, on the outbreak of war with Turkey, a protectorate was proclaimed, the position of Britain in Egypt remained conveniently undefined. The situation was an anomalous one, for the country was governed in the Khedive's name by the Khedive's ministers. while the effective authority rested with the British Consul-General, who, on paper, was no more than the Consul-General of any other Power, and with the British advisers of the Egyptian ministers. An attempt was made in 1887 to regularize the position by agreement with Egypt's nominal overlord, the Sultan of Turkey, and it was even decided that 1890 should see the withdrawal of British troops. The agreement, which was negotiated in Constantinople by Sir Drummond Wolff, included, however, a clause permitting Britain to reoccupy the country in the case of renewed disorder, and under French and Russian pressure the Sultan refused to ratify it. Not until 1904 was France at last persuaded to accept the facts of the situation: her own interest in the crumbling Moroccan Empire then made it possible to strike a bargain that was rendered the more necessary by the growing power of Germany. The easing of the situation that followed, and the open recognition of the British position in Egypt, brought about new developments. Hitherto there had always been the possibility of an appeal by affronted Egypt to the other Powers, and especially to France. Now that last resource was lost, and Anglo-Egyptian relations entered upon a period of strain that was not soon to end.

(2) EGYPTIAN NATIONALISM

Egyptian nationalism had first roused itself in 1882. Thereafter, under Tewfik, who worked comfortably and quietly with his British advisers, it was quiescent, but on Tewfik's sudden death in 1892 it was stimulated and encouraged by his son and successor, the young Abbas II. The new Khedive had been educated in Europe, and was a young man of presence and charm. But he was autocratic by temperament, and while not unnaturally resenting his dependence, he lacked the ability either to make the best of the situation or to exploit it to the advantage of himself and his people. Cromer found himself surrounded by intrigue, and a serious crisis developed in 1894, when Abbas, on a visit of inspection to his army, publicly complained of its British officers to Kitchener, who promptly tendered his resignation. The crisis blew over, but relations between Cromer and the Khedive remained strained, while the old ruling class in Egypt increasingly resented the control of British officials. As in India, it came to be felt that despite all the declarations to the contrary, which were suspected of being hypocritical, the British had every intention of remaining in the country, and the agreement of 1904 served but to strengthen this view. Meanwhile, as Cromer commented, the British official and officer moved in a narrow, and predominantly British, circle. If he were respected, "he does not excite any lively sentiment of sympathy or friendship", whereas, "if a French army had been in Egypt, the officers . . . would have been sitting outside every café".[49] Cromer himself set the pattern of aloofness. If he was punningly styled "Over-Baring", the attitude indicated was probably too common among lesser men who were over-conscious of their superior position and too little mindful of the susceptibilities of those they controlled. Cromer won little but respect from the people he governed for so long: when he finally left Egypt in 1907 not a voice was raised in farewell as he drove through the streets of Cairo for the last time. What the British for their part felt of the people among whom they moved is amusingly indicated in Lord Edward Cecil's entertaining impressions of the eighteen years he spent in the Egyptian service, *The Leisure of an Egyptian Official.*

## (3) SAAD ZAGHLUL

Throughout Cromer's period of rule the emphasis was on material development: Egypt's financial straits were almost an obsession. Not until his last year did Cromer find it possible to spare money for education. His choice for the post of Minister of Education then fell upon a remarkable man who was to play a vital part in the development of Egypt and its relations with Britain, Saad Zaghlul (1860?–1927). Zaghlul was of peasant stock and had advanced himself through the law.

He was at this time a moderate nationalist, opposed to the intrigues and autocratic leanings of Abbas and a convinced supporter of the British connexion. A Nationalist party, *Hizb-el-Watan*, had come into existence under the leadership of a protégé of the Khedive, Mustafa Kami(1874–1908). In 1907 it was balanced by a more moderate organization, *Hizb-el-Umma*, the "Party of the People", of which Zaghlul was a member. It was not until the tense period of the war that he was to harden into a more strident nationalist and to create in the *Wafd* the political instrument of nationalist agitation. *Hizb-el-Watan* was closely associated with Mohammedan extremists and especially with the Mohammedan University of el Azhar, with its narrow fanatical curriculum and hostility to Egypt's dependence upon "infidel" Britain. To the general resentment had been added in 1899 the shock of the Sudan agreement. Instead of, as before, having the Sudan to govern, or misgovern, alone, the Egyptian official classes found themselves impotently associated with a British administration even more firmly entrenched in the Sudan than in Egypt. The Egyptian Minister who signed the agreement, Boutros Pasha, was a Christian Copt, and therefore suspect to Mohammedan Egyptians. His "betrayal" of the Sudan was to have tragic consequences.

## (4) THE DENSHAWAI TRAGEDY, 1906

In 1906 Boutros gave further offence to his critics. In June of that year some British officers on a shooting-trip to Dinshaway, a village in the Nile Delta, were involved in trouble with the local villagers and were set upon, one of them dying of his injuries. A special court was set up to try the case, with British and Egyptian judges, Boutros being appointed President. There was no doubt of the villagers' guilt, though its degree was uncertain, but the general concern at the incident was transformed into violent nationalist agitation when severe sentences of public hanging and flogging and penal servitude were passed. Cromer, who was absent on leave at the time, supported the sentences at first, but later criticized them as "unduly severe" and regretted them the more as they gave "a wholly false impression of the general spirit in which the administration of Egypt was being conducted".[50] They were, in fact, as unrepresentative of that spirit as the deplorable events at Amritsar in 1919 were of British rule in India, and can be ascribed only to a momentary access of panic, but they were equally seized on by outraged nationalist sentiment as indications of the true outlook of the British, obliterating the recollection of many services. Bernard Shaw, writing the preface to *John Bull's Other Island* early in 1907, denounced the unhappy episode, in sixteen bitter pages, as *The Denshawai Horror*, and Lord Lloyd, twenty-five years later, recorded the opinion that "Denshawai was, in fact, the opening of a new chapter in Egyptian history".[51] It was remembered only too well when, during and after the war, Britain, preoccupied with many cares, clumsily gave further offence. It was remembered, too, against Boutros, who added to the political charges against himself when four years later he agreed as Prime Minister to an extension of the Suez Canal Company's Concession from 1968 to 2008 in return for substantial financial aid to Egypt. Nationalist fury, ever sensitive to foreign control of so great an asset as the Canal, then compelled Boutros to withdraw the agreement, but feeling was so tense that on the same day he was assassinated (10th February, 1910). Henceforth a more fanatical spirit was abroad.

National feeling had been inflamed, too, by the Young Turk Revolution in Turkey in 1908, which in its reaction against the narrow tyranny of the Sultan Abdul Hamid seemed at first to offer the hope of a recovery of Turkish power, freed from foreign interference, and therefore to provide a hopeful augury for Egypt.

## (5) Gorst and Kitchener: the Gezira Scheme

Cromer was succeeded in 1907 by Sir Eldon Gorst (1861–1911), who adopted a more conciliatory attitude than his great predecessor, and was, in particular, more tactful in his handling of the Khedive, who reciprocated his friendliness by dashing incognito to Gorst's bedside when he lay dying in England in 1911. By this time, however, Gorst's policy seemed to have been discredited by the rising nationalist violence and Kitchener, with all the prestige of his re-creation of the Egyptian army still upon him, was appointed to succeed him and to tighten control. Kitchener's chief interest was the welfare of the peasant. He actively concerned himself with the opening of land colonies and the extension and regulation of water supplies, and established a long overdue Ministry of Agriculture. As an engineer he interested himself in the control of the Nile, and from the first supported the scheme for the irrigation of the Gezira district in the Sudan, between the two Niles. This project, inaugurated in 1913, was delayed for some years by the war, and did not come into operation until 1925. Its effects upon the economic life of the Sudan have, however, been revolutionary. It uses Nile water, without detriment to Egypt, to irrigate a rich region now extending over some 250,000 acres, and to make possible the development of cotton-growing. It was financed by a loan of £3,000,000, guaranteed by the British Government, which was eventually increased to £13,000,000, and has raised the cotton exports of the Sudan from 4,000 to 70,000 tons: the Sudan now rivals Uganda as a centre of cotton production.

For Egypt the Gezira scheme was a reminder of the joint dependence of the two countries upon the Nile, and British activity in the Sudan was therefore regarded with mixed feelings. Fears were not quieted by the development of Port Sudan, on the Red Sea, as an outlet for Sudanese produce and an alternative to the long route through Egypt.

## (6) PROCLAMATION OF THE PROTECTORATE, 1914

While the situation in Egypt and the Sudan was developing, international tension was increasing. Abdul Hamid in his later years had turned increasingly to Germany as a sympathetic friend, and Britain, having decided that in supporting Turkey for so long it had "put its money on the wrong horse", was concerned for the defence of the "land-bridge" of the Middle East and the route to India. Its hold on Egypt guaranteed the security of the Suez Canal, and in 1907, in place of the traditional policy of bolstering Turkey against Russia, an attempt was made to come to terms with Russia by the definition of "spheres of influence". The wartime promise of 1915, to permit a Russian advance to Constantinople, was the logical conclusion. The historic position in the Middle East was, therefore, already undergoing modification before 1914, but Egyptians could not fail to see in the diminished British interest in Turkey, and the increasing hold on the Sudan, a threat to their hopes of independence. The Khedive was openly pro-Turkish, and when war came in 1914 was paying his annual visit to Constantinople, whence he did not return. War was declared on Turkey at the end of October, and early in November he was deposed. He was replaced by his uncle, Hussein, who, since Egypt was now freed from Turkey and made a British protectorate, was accorded the title of Sultan. At the same time Britain gratuitously declared that she was in no need of Egyptian help. The declaration of the protectorate came as a blow to Egyptian aspirations, the rejection of help as a direct snub. The country was soon to become a British armed camp, and Egypt's equivocal position made many of her people more than ever resentful of their status. There was little direct opposition to the war, and the hatchet of nationalist agitation, it has been said, was for the present buried, though patriots did not fail to mark the spot.[52] But dependence rankled, and 1919 was to see the whole Egyptian problem, rendered more acute by wartime developments, urgently demanding consideration.

## THE DEVELOPMENT OF BRITISH RULE

Looking back over the course of British rule in Egypt to the eve of the declaration of Egyptian independence in 1922, Lord Lloyd has written of British policy in general:

> "We had undertaken—drifted into, or deliberately acquired—one fundamental responsibility, the welfare of the masses of the people. We envisaged always one ultimate goal, the political development of each country to a pitch where her own people could be trusted to take over that responsibility and discharge it fairly."[53]

Without denying that mistakes and miscalculations were made, that the agents of imperial rule were not always equal to the highest ideals sustaining that rule, this is not an unfair statement of a view of British responsibilities sincerely held by many who spent their lives in furthering the welfare of the people committed to their charge. The slave-trade and Egyptian misrule provided two manifestations of that concern for human welfare which was no small motive in the extension of British control in Africa. The desire to improve the government of Egypt and the Sudan was hardly less—and certainly no less sincere—than that of abolishing the traffic in slaves, and in the Sudan the two were closely connected. Though some responsibilities in the Dominions had been sloughed off, Britain by 1914 had assumed other responsibilities over considerable areas. As this survey will have shown, it would not be true to say that the responsibilities had been lightly assumed: they had been accepted, however, without a full appreciation of what they involved and of the difficulties and tensions which the attempt to establish enduring systems of ordered government would produce. The war was to prove a mighty catalyst. After 1919, though she had added still further to her responsibilities, Britain was forced on to the defensive. The development of the Dominions was not everywhere a matter for congratulation, and the problems of some other territories were to assume serious proportions, though there were not a few successes to record. In 1914, however, there was still little doubt of the beneficence of imperial rule. Cromer's attitude towards the Egyptian people has been quoted. It assumed too readily that the East had but to model itself on "the true civilization of the West" to achieve perfection, but the mistake was one which could hardly be avoided under the circumstances: the contrast between the well-ordered administration of Britain or of India and the chaos and corruption of Ismailian Egypt was too great. Yet, as in India, there was a confusion between the degree of tutelage that might be thought to be necessary and the degree which a proud people, taught to look forward to being eventually masters in their own house, might be prepared to submit to. Motives might be mixed, but to prefer self-government to foreign government, however beneficial, was not necessarily a mark of dishonesty or wrong-headedness. "One or more generations" in Cromer's view would have to pass before the withdrawal of foreign guidance could even be discussed.[54] He had hardly gone to his grave in 1917 before the demand for Egyptian freedom became explosive: five years later Egypt was an independent sovereign State.

The attitude of tutelage was similar in the case of Africans farther south. Lever objected to talk of the "lazy nigger": "he is a child and a willing child but he wants training and handling with patience". Above all, Africans "should be taught the value of regular habits and of working to time. Under such a régime, how could they fail to become both healthy and industrious, and how then could they fail to be happy?"[55] This view represented, in all its naïveté, the civilization of the West, in its nineteenth-century, industrialized form, but while we may now scorn such self-righteousness it is well to remember the many notable men who saw a mission in guiding and leading those who from the exalted height of European civilization, before its complacency was shattered by two World Wars, seemed, indeed, to be no more than children, if willing ones. The nineteenth century felt a confidence which we may sometimes envy today.

Yet, if, in bringing this broad survey of the British Empire in its heyday to a close, we seek a final word on the tangled story of Africa, we may find it in Arnold Toynbee's comment on Abyssinia:

> The spectacle presented by the one indigenous African state that has succeeded in retaining its complete independence is perhaps the best justification that can be found for the partition of the rest of Africa among the European Powers.[56]

It is a judgment worth pondering, despite the sinister use which Fascist Italy was to make of the argument in 1935.

## REFERENCES

No one writing on the problems of Africa could fail to pay tribute to Lord Hailey's monumental *African Survey*, first published in 1938 (revised edition, 1957).

1.  *Life of Lord Salisbury*, IV, pp. 225–26.
2.  S. H. Roberts: *History of French Colonial Policy*, I, p. 47.
3.  ibid., p. 63.
4.  This and the other quotations in the paragraph are from Stanley's *The Congo and the Founding of Its Free State* (1886).
5.  W. M. Macmillan: *Africa Emergent*, p. 134.
6.  C. Wilson: *The History of Unilever*, I, p. 170.
7.  H. C. Jackson: *Sudan Days and Ways*, ch. 13.
8.  *Africa Emergent*, p. 41.
9.  *On the Edge of the Primeval Forest*, p. 115.

10. G. Orde Browne: *The African Labourer*, p. 96.

11. *History of Unilever*, I, p. 176.

12. A. B. Keith: *The Belgian Congo and the Berlin Act*, p. 304.

13. The figures are quoted from Sir Alan Pim: *The Financial and Economic History of the African Tropical Territories*, pp. 95–97.

14. *Cambridge History of British Foreign Policy*, III, p. 372.

15. ibid., p. 368.

16. A. McPhee: *The Economic Revolution in British West Africa*, pp. 33-34.

17. D. V. Wellesley and S. Gwynn: *Sir George Goldie*, p. 167.

18. Lord Lugard: *The Dual Mandate in British Tropical Africa*, p. 618.

19. C. E. Carrington: *The British Overseas*, p. 827.

20. *Life of Joseph Chamberlain*, III, p. 107.

21. J. A. Spender: *Great Britain, Empire and Commonwealth*, p. 358.

22. Sir R. Wingate: *Wingate of the Sudan*, p. 130.

23. R. Coupland: *The Exploitation of East Africa, 1856–1890*, p. 392.

24. Sir D. Cameron: *My Tanganyika Service and Some Nigeria* p. 285.

25. H. R. Rudin: *Germans in the Cameroons, 1884–1914*, p. 419.

26. *Sir George Goldie*, p. 176.

27. *My Tanganyika Service*, p. 76.

28. W. K. Hancock: *Survey of British Commonwealth Affairs*, Volume II, Part 2, p. 172n.

29. *The Dual Mandate*, p. 226.

30. ibid., p. 618.

31. L. P. Mair: *Native Policies in Africa*, p. 189n.

32. *British Overseas*, p. 842.

33. *Exploitation of East Africa*, p. 371.

34. Lord Hailey: *An African Survey* (1938), p. 743.

35. *Life of Joseph Chamberlain*, IV, p. 262.

36. C. Weizmann: *Trial and Error*, p. 115.

37. A. B. Theobald: *The Mahdiya, 1881–99*, p. 13.

38. *Letters of Queen Victoria*, 2nd Series, III, p. 494.

39. M. Shibeika: *British Policy in the Sudan, 1882–1902*, p. 15.

40. Lord Zetland: *Lord Cromer*, p. 89.

41. *The History of The Times, 1884–1912*, p. 23.

42. ibid., p. 29.

43. *Letters of Queen Victoria*, 2nd Series, III, p. 488.

44. *The Mahdiya*, p. 119.

45. Amine Youssef Bey: *Independent Egypt*, p. 53.
46. *Lord Cromer*: p. 128.
47. See the account of his rule in *The Mahdiya*, ch. 10.
48. *British Policy in the Sudan*, p. 404.
49. Lord Cromer: *Modern Egypt*, II, p. 254.
50. Lord Cromer: *Abbas II*, p. x.
51. Lord Lloyd: *Egypt Since Cromer*, I, p. 48.
52. *Independent Egypt*, p. 56.
53. *Egypt since Cromer*, I, p. 358.
54. *Modern Egypt*, II, p. 567.
55. *History of Unilever*, I, pp. 169 and 167.
56. *A Study of History*, II, p. 365.

Two important studies appeared only after this chapter had been completed:

M. Perham: *Lugard: The Years of Adventure, 1858–98.*
R. Oliver: *Sir Harry Johnston and the Scramble for Africa.*

# RUSSIA TO 1917

THE sixty years between the end of the Crimean War and the outbreak of the World War in 1914 are particularly important for an understanding of contemporary Russia because in this period the modernization of the Russian Empire began, giving rise to new social, economic and political problems which led finally to the March and October Revolutions of 1917.

It is no coincidence that these upheavals occurred in the midst of military defeat. The 1905 Revolution had followed national defeat in the Far East and a similar defeat in the Crimean War, at the hands of Britain and France, preceded the Great Reforms of the eighteen-sixties, generally considered to mark the beginning of modern development in Russia. The Tsar Alexander II, known to history as the Tsar Liberator, ascended the throne in 1855 at a time when military defeat compelled an autocracy to embark upon extensive reforms. The Emancipation of the Serfs in 1861 is the most famous of these, not because of its immediate economic results but because the edict symbolized the end of an era in Russian history and made possible a radical discussion of the general structure of society.

## An Agrarian Society: the Peasantry

Russia in the mid-nineteenth century was an overwhelmingly agrarian society. Fifty of her sixty million inhabitants worked on the land, where they had been subject to feudal conditions for four centuries, with serfdom as the characteristic feature of the system. Twenty million peasants were bound to the persons of 250,000 noblemen, working on their estates, large and small, in the west and south of European Russia. Another twenty million, the so-called "state peasants", worked on state-owned land in the northern forests, and the remaining ten million were either free small-holders or minor serfs in various parts of Russia.

Conditions varied considerably. The lot of the state peasant was generally lighter than that of a bonded serf, but in the west many serfs had a fairly tolerable existence in places where money payment had replaced labour service or where they were free to work in factories. In the famous fertile Black Earth lands of South Russia, on the great estates dependent on serf labour for wheat cultivation, conditions were more unfavourable, but in the far south of the open steppes of New Russia the superior virtues of hired labour had been recognized and many independent farmers were to be found.

Generally the peasant, in all parts, was subject to two masters. He owed obedience to the landowner, whether nobleman or state farm official. The owner raised taxes from the peasant and secured recruits for the Imperial armies. In return he was allowed to exact from his peasants a monetary payment or labour service on the owner's land for at least three days a week. The landowner was lord of life and death for millions of Russians; he could send his serfs to Siberia, confiscate their goods, have them flogged, sent into the army, or even sold by families or villages as he pleased, and veto their marriages. Against misuse of these powers there was no appeal.

The peasant was also subject to the decisions of the commune or village, sometimes called *mir*, to which he belonged. As part of a family unit he cultivated a small piece of land given him by the landowner, nominally in return for the service or money paid to the latter. This land was cultivated under the direction of the heads of families in the commune. At their communal meeting they decided crop rotations under the prevailing three-field system, allotted shares of communally owned pasture land and could redistribute family holdings. The elders were responsible for the assessment and collection of taxes, under supervision, saw to the repair of roads and bridges, and settled minor disputes. As money payments replaced labour service the richer peasants began to exert greater influence at these meetings but, especially for poorer peasants, the commune remained an egalitarian institution long after the economic basis for this had departed.

The agrarian picture was depressing in the first half of the nineteenth century. There was little incentive to improve agricultural techniques because demand was strictly limited. Rationalization of farming necessitated a capital outlay which the small owners, who formed the bulk of the nobility, disposing of at most ten serfs, could not afford, heavily burdened with debt as most of them were. Only where the soil was rich, on some great estates in South Russia, and where capital was available, could intensive cultivation prove the superiority of hired labour. Most owners had no alternative but to try to improve their economic position in the first half of the century by more ruthless exploitation of their peasants, either by encroaching on their serfs' allotments to increase the area of land under their own direct control, or by turning serfs into landless labourers working exclusively on their land and disregarding the convention allowing only three days labour for the owner. But most owners derived little economic benefit from these measures. Their chief effect was to increase peasant discontent, for it is significant that the peasant always retained a belief that the land was God's and that the right to use it devolved on those who toiled on it. Serfdom was never accepted as a permanent or divinely ordained measure, but as a man-made imposition. "We are yours, but the land is ours", the serfs said to the noblemen. There was continual resistance to serfdom, and frequent local disturbances occurred, increasing considerably in the late eighteen-forties and throughout the eighteen-fifties as the owners exploited the peasants.

## THE LIBERATION OF THE SERFS

The Tsars were naturally reluctant to interfere with the agrarian system, recognizing its political advantages. Serfdom, remarked Count Uvarov, Minister of Education under Nicholas I, was "a tree which has taken deep root—it protects the Church and the throne and cannot be uprooted".[1] The landowner was the most reliable bulwark of Tsardom, keeping the peasants in order. It was the revelation of the weakness of a military machine based on serf conscripts, and fears that a peasant revolution might occur if no action was taken, which overcame Alexander's reluctance and made him promise to liberate the serfs in 1857, a promise fulfilled in the edict of 1861. "It is better," he remarked in a famous phrase, "to abolish serfdom from above than to wait for the time when it will begin to abolish itself spontaneously from below."

The edict which abolished legal serfdom represented a major advance. The peasant was no longer bound to his owner but able to acquire property, learn a trade, and marry freely. It was realized that millions of peasants could not be deprived of their means of subsistence without gravely endangering public order, and that land must be provided for them, but an independent peasantry of the French variety was not created for another forty years. On the contrary, the peasants' need for land was met within the framework of the commune. The open field allotments owned by the nobleman and tilled by the peasant were bought by the State and placed under the control of the communal authorities. The commune was preserved as an institution because it was felt that a strong authority was needed to keep the peasant in order and collect the taxes in place of the old owner.

The peasant remained a member of a segregated social group, subject to the fairly rigid control of the commune and tried by his own courts. Some semblance of self-government was introduced at the meeting of the heads of families and in the elected officials of the canton, a new unit composed of several communes. These officials collected taxes, found recruits for the army, collected the annual repayments for the land the peasant was buying—usually at inflated prices—saw to the road repairs, and issued passports. They could impose fines, confiscate property, order corporal punishment for offences and, as family needs altered, they were responsible for land repartition. They were disliked because their duties were unpopular and, as they lacked experience and were closely supervised by administrative and police officials, their powers were in practice considerably restricted.

## Peasant Dissatisfaction

There was, nevertheless, widespread disappointment and a wave of peasant disorders in 1861, for the peasants realized that their hopes had been too sanguine. The disorders were ruthlessly repressed, but a feeling of discontent grew with the passage of the years: many felt that the Tsar's good intentions had been frustrated by wicked bureaucrats. "Socialism without a doctrine", as Boris Nolde called it, grew in strength as the peasants awaited the day when the land remaining in the hands of noblemen and state officials would be theirs. The dissatisfied peasantry formed a most important and unstable element in Russian society which ensured that the settlement of 1861 would not last, and which enabled a revolutionary spirit to grow in the countryside, with profound results in the revolutionary years 1905 and 1917.

## THE GOVERNMENT: TSARIST AUTOCRACY

Russia in the mid-nineteenth century was an autocracy living in the age of Louis XIV. The Tsar was restricted by no constitution and was regarded as a semi-sacrosanct figure by the peasantry. Since the time of Peter the Great the nobility had possessed no effective political power and lacked a tradition of service to the crown. The Tsars ruled their vast empire with the assistance of a centralized bureaucratic machine with an unlimited range of action and constructed on German lines by Catherine the Great in the eighteenth century. It was a machine of mediocre quality, slow-moving, inefficient, riddled with corruption, suffering from excessive centralization and staffed by officials notorious for their arrogance to the people, although there were many well-meaning and hard-working administrators amongst them. An oppressive secret police system, based on the famous "Third Section" of Nicholas I, with a network of spies and informers, was used by successive Tsars to ensure that the people did not engage in subversive political activity. Imprisonment or exile to Siberia without trial on the arbitrary decision of the police was the fate of offenders. A loyal army, preventive censorship, and the support of the Greek Orthodox Church were equally important in preserving autocracy. The Church was closely associated with the régime and had a tradition of disengagement from public life differentiating it sharply from the Western Churches. Surrounded by the stiff ritual of the Imperial Court, intensely conscious of the sacred character of kingship, the Tsars were cut off from their subjects and inclined to consider all opposition as sin.

## REFORMS, THE *Zemstvos*

Although the power of the autocracy was preserved, there was an important reform of local government in 1864. In the provinces and districts into which Russia was divided, elected assemblies, the *zemstvos*, with powers in health, education, and roadmaking, were established. The franchise was limited, peasant members being elected indirectly, and forty to forty-five per cent of the seats were, at most times, held by landowners and officials. But despite considerable concessions to the landowning class the *zemstvos* gave the intelligentsia and enlightened members of the nobility the political training essential if they were to play an effective role in public affairs. In later years the *zemstvos* became centres of opposition to the régime, employing doctors, lawyers, engineers, and school-masters of radical views. The adoption of the elective principle was significant; the national assembly of 1905 lay implicit in the decree of 1864. By 1870 the principle was extended to the towns where elected municipal councils, or *dumas*, were set up. In all cases the central authorities retained control of vital police services.

## OTHER REFORMS

At the same time there were a number of legal, educational, and military reforms. A judicial system modelled on western lines was introduced, with trial by jury in criminal cases, publicity of proceedings, election of J.P.s in country districts and greatly accelerated judicial procedures. This replaced the old arbitrary eighteenth-century system and encouraged the growth of a considerable legal profession. Military reforms, including the introduction of conscription and the moderniza-tion of officers' training, laid the basis of a modern Russian army. Important educational reforms included a liberalization of university teaching and government in 1863, and during the conservative Count Dimitri Tolstoy's tenure of office as Minister of the Interior in the eighteen-seventies the curricula of secondary and primary schools were overhauled. Tolstoy was, however, bitterly attacked by the young intelligentsai for favouring the humanities as opposed to science which they regarded with superstitious reverence.

The Great Reforms of the eighteen-sixties, carried out by the progressive section of the bureaucracy, laid the foundations of modern Russia. It is significant that, despite a period of reaction between 1866 and 1905, no Tsar was able to turn the clock back completely to pre-Crimean War days: the reforms had undermined the basis of the old régime.

## EMERGENCE OF THE INTELLIGENTSIA

As a result of the reforms the Russian intelligentsia emerged as an active political force. The intelligentsia was an artificial growth which originated with the attempts of the enlightened despots Peter the Great, Catherine the Great, and Alexander I to modernize Russia. Consequently they lacked roots in the people, in contrast to their counterparts in Britain and France where social progress was a more uniform and organic process. But the intelligentsia were acutely conscious of the glaring contrast between their nineteenth-century education and the material progress of Western Europe, on the one hand, and the semi-medieval condition of the vast majority of the Russian people on the other. A restless spirit characterized them, for they were deeply imbued with a sense of social justice and anxious to bridge the wide gulf separating them from a people they could not understand. They were divorced from the state as well as the people, for most of them could find no congenial outlet for their abilities in the unprogressive bureaucratic machine they despised. Because they were not part of the ruling class, their thinking was restricted by no sense of responsibility to the State but ran along radical lines, giving expression to a mounting sense of frustration. Belinsky, a great radical of the eighteen-sixties, expressed these tensions in memorable words: "I do not want happiness, even as a gift, if I do not have peace of mind about each of my blood brothers, bone of my bone and flesh of my flesh."[2] Similar sentiments were expressed by Paklin, a character in Turgenev's novel *Virgin Soil*: "That's just our misfortune . . . that we know no one! We want to produce an effect, we want to turn the whole world upside down, but we live outside that world, we only have to do with two or three friends and go revolving in a narrow little circle."[3] A cataclysmic upheaval, creating a new social order, seemed the only solution capable of resolving the tension in their own souls.

The educational reforms under Alexander I at the beginning of the nineteenth century had stimulated the growth of the intelligentsia and, despite efforts made in the eighteen-forties and 'fifties by the heavy-handed autocrat Nicholas I to restrict the educational facilities offered to able pupils outside the ranks of the nobility, a considerable intellectual revival occurred in the University of Moscow, associated with the names of Alexander Herzen (1812–70), Michael Bakunin (1814–76), and Vissarion Belinsky (1810–48).

## THE INTELLIGENTSIA: EASTERNERS AND WESTERNERS

There were signs in the eighteen-forties of two schools of thought on social and political problems, the one western and broadly liberal in character, the other eastern and Slavophile. The differentiation between these schools was decisive for the future and interaction between them has remained a major theme in Russian development.

The Westerners, a collective term for heterogeneous elements sharing this viewpoint, believed that only by imitation of West European political and economic institutions could the gulf between the educated minority and the people be bridged. Western thought, particularly French, had always influenced the educated classes, appealing especially to those who had lost their faith in Greek Orthodoxy and were seeking a secular substitute for it. Herzen and Belinsky believed that Russia could fulfil her mission only by accepting political freedom and modernization on Western lines. This Western orientation worked itself out in the following century, leading to the formation of the liberal *Cadet* party and to the introduction of the opposed political philosophy of Marxian Socialism into Russia.

The Slavophile school, or Easterners, differed from the Westerners because, although equally conscious of the need for change, they believed that Russia must remain true to her past history. Not a continuation but a complete reversal of Peter the Great's western reforms would save Russia. The Easterners were hostile to the principles of individualism and rationalism, which eighteenth-century philosophers had emphasized as the basis of modern society, and they rejected the capitalist system with its attendant social evils. They believed that Russia had a unique contribution to make to civilization, although some thought the Orthodox religion, and others the spirit of her people, to be the basis of this contribution. They upheld autocracy and the Orthodox Church but criticized the German-style bureaucracy. They emphasized the communal sense of the Russian peasant, as opposed to the individualism of the West, and stressed the Russian mission to teach the West rather than learn from it. The Eastern orientation led to the foundation of the Panslav movement and Russian nationalism, and also to Populism, a variety of Socialism peculiar to Russia and associated with Bakunin. Thus both defenders and opponents of autocracy were to be found in this school.

The difference between Westerners and Easterners is important, but they were not mutually exclusive. Westerners like Herzen believed with the Slavophiles that Russia had a world mission to perform, while many Easterners, even when they emphasized the unique nature of Russian society, did not absolutely reject European culture. Nearly all the great intellectuals in the nineteenth century display in their lives the influences of both schools.

## THE INTELLIGENTSIA REBUFFED

The relaxation of the press censorship after the Crimean War enabled a Russian public opinion to form between 1857 and 1861. In numerous magazines Westerners and Easterners discussed the need for administrative and political reforms, including the establishment of a nationally elected parliament. But the high hopes of the intelligentsia were dashed when the decree of 1861 revealed the extent to which landed interests had protected themselves at the expense of the peasant. The cautious Tsar was not prepared for political change, but was soon alarmed by numerous peasant disorders and by the Polish Revolt of 1863. After an unsuccessful attempt on his life in 1866 a period of reaction set in. The *zemstvos* were subject in the early eighteen-seventies to increasing interference by the bureaucracy and provincial governors. The machinery of the new legal system was partially frustrated by the withdrawal of political cases from the courts' jurisdiction. The independence of the universities was again stifled and, despite the press regulations of 1865, books and papers were again closely censored in the late eighteen-sixties.

It was a turning point in Russian development for, had the

intelligentsia been given a limited constitutional framework within which to develop their views, the growing divorce between them and the Tsarist régime might have been bridged in the eighteen-sixties. By 1905 it was perhaps too late to remedy the omission.

## GROWTH OF OPPOSITION

The active section of the intelligentsia which had interested itself in political and social questions was not deterred by the unwillingness of the Tsar to concede all their demands, but became embittered opponents of the régime. It is significant that the non-noble members of the intelligentsia began to play a more prominent role in the agitation of the eighteen-sixties. While Herzen believed that the Tsar might still be converted to liberal ideas by the pleas of the "conscience-stricken gentry", as the enlightened lesser nobility has been called, radicals like N. G. Chernyshevsky (1828–89) felt that progress depended on their unaided efforts for nothing could be expected of the Tsar or nobility. The violence and bitterness of radical literature in the late eighteen-sixties reflects the fact that the non-noble intelligentsia had, unlike the nobility, personal experience of the sufferings of millions of Russians, giving them a more vivid awareness of the significance of failure to reform the Tsarist régime. It was a tragedy that the Tsars could only insist on blind obedience to autocracy, because the young radicals, with their sense of dedication and reverence for the working people, could have been captured by an imaginative appeal to use their talents to assist in the process of modernization initiated by the Great Reforms.

## THE RADICALS

Several features of radicalism in the eighteen-sixties and 'seventies are important. In the first place, interest had moved from political reform to questions concerning the material welfare of the people. Radicals agreed with Chernyshevsky that the liberalism of the educated classes, concerned only with constitutional liberties, could do little to alleviate the material hardship of the masses. "The road of history," wrote Chernyshevsky, "is not the pavement of the Nevsky Prospekt [the most famous street in St. Petersburg]. It passes over fields of dust or mud, over marshes, over rubbish. He who fears dirty boots must not occupy himself with public activity."[4] Radicals sought in some form of socialism an answer to material problems. They looked to the commune with its egalitarian tradition to form the basis of a new socialist Russia, hoping thereby to avoid the misery of capitalism. "Europe does not and cannot", said Mihailovsky, the most popular exponent of Populism, "understand our social aspirations. She is not our teacher in economic questions. We believe that we are called to contribute to history a new principle, to say a word of our own, and not to repeat the traces of Europe."[5] Peasant socialism, or Populism, played an important part in radical thinking, owing much to Slavophile influence, and even Marx, for a time in 1882, thought the commune the socialist path for Russia.

The radicals were all revolutionaries but they differed about the means for establishing the new socialist order. Most followed Peter Lavrov, who believed that patient propaganda would gradually convince the people of the need for revolutionary action. Others believed in the immediate use of physical violence: Michael Bakunin, founder of Anarchism and stormy petrel of revolution, who had taken part in the 1848 Revolution, believed conditions to favour a spontaneous mass rising destroying the régime and creating a free federation of peasant communes; Peter Tkachev, a lesser-known figure, conceived of revolution, in the Jacobin tradition, as the work of a determined minority seizing power by a *coup d'état*, a view admired by Lenin who followed it in 1917. The same method was advocated by Serge Nachaev, a fanatical and ruthless revolutionary, the first to formulate the principle of political terror, who emphasized the necessity for complete subordination of the member to the group. To effect this in a Moscow group which he commanded, he implicated all the members in the murder of a fellow student whom he denounced for the purpose.

## The *Narodniki*

Lavrov's views were in the asendancy when the famous *Narodniki* episode occurred between 1873 and 1875. Thousands of students went into the countryside, most of them convinced that Russia was on the verge of revolution, and urged the peasant to take the land that was his by right. A religious reverence for the people as an abstract entity and a strong apocalyptic strain characterized the *Narodniki* or adherents of "the Going to the People" movement. But many were soon disillusioned with the hardship of village life and could not understand the peasant, who either ignored them or allowed the police to round them up in hundreds.

## "People's Will" and Murder of Alexander II

The *Narodniki* failure caused the intelligentsia to lose faith in the people. In a mood of despair, and hunted relentlessly by secret police, the more ruthless radicals abandoned the idea that revolution should be made by the people, with the intellectuals merely arousing the popular conscience, in favour of action by radicals organized in secret societies and ready to use terrorist methods to overthrow Tsardom. At first *Land and Liberty*, founded in 1877, indulged only in reprisals against police and officials for their persecution of members, but *People's Will*, founded in 1879, pledged itself specifically to murder the Tsar. The terror campaign opened with the shot fired by Vera Zasulich, a member of the lesser nobility, at General Trepov, chief of police in St. Petersburg, for ordering the flogging of a revolutionary and ended with the successful attempt on the life of the Tsar in 1881.

The fantastic story of *People's Will* is worthy of a Phillips Oppenheim. The members were few in number, some twenty at first and only a few hundreds by 1881, and enjoyed little support from peasant or factory worker. But these fanatical revolutionaries finally penetrated the defences of the omniscient police and murdered the man who symbolized the upper class, which they confidently expected would capitulate after his "execution" and grant civil liberties facilitating their task of preparing for social revolution. In the *People's Will* were colourful figures like Alexander Mihailov, organizer responsible for printing illegal newspapers and producing false passports, who was adept at shaking off police agents set to shadow him, but eventually died in prison; and Stephen Khalturin, a St. Petersburg joiner, who founded the first trade union (then an illegal organization). In 1880 Khalturin planned to assassinate the Tsar and obtained employment at the Winter

Palace, where he hid the dynamite supplied by *People's Will* under his pillow and suffered excruciating headaches at night from the fumes. The Tsar escaped injury, however, when the room in which he was about to dine was shattered by an explosion, and Khalturin, like many professional revolutionaries, died on the gallows a few years later. There was also Sophie Perovskaya, daughter of a governor-general of St. Petersburg, who was in charge of the successful attempt on the Tsar's life in the next year. She was the mistress of Andrei Zhelyabov, son of a serf and leader of *People's Will*, who remarked in a phrase revealing the inner psychological tensions of revolutionary intelligentsia: *"History moves too slowly. It needs a push."*[6]

*People's Will* organized at least seven attempts on the Tsar's life with high explosives between 1879 and 1881. They were at the end of their resources, their leader in prison, when a bomb thrown at Alexander ended his life. But the dawn of a new Russia did not begin with his death. The executive committee of *People's Will*, naïvely optimistic, offered to cease their activities if an amnesty were granted and a representative assembly called. A favourable response could hardly be expected of the new Tsar, the police intensified their efforts and within a few years the committee ceased to function, the members being either imprisoned or forced into exile. Nevertheless, *People's Will* profoundly impressed the intelligentsia, for even those who abhorred the use of violence were so dissatisfied with the performance of the régime during the war of 1877 that they sympathized with the assassins. The terrorists were also beginning to obtain some popular support in the towns, where an industrial working class was growing up, support which the intelligentsia had lacked in the eighteen-sixties.

## PANSLAVISM

At the close of the eighteen-seventies a considerable Panslav movement emerged, stimulated by the active foreign policy the Tsar pursued in the Balkans. Russian foreign policy has been described elsewhere; it will suffice to say here that it was dictated largely by the need to control the Straits for strategic and economic reasons. These interests were reinforced by ideological factors. In the eighteenth century the defence of Greek Orthodoxy had interested Russia in her fellow Christians in the Balkans. In the nineteenth century the Panslav ideology played a similar rôle and during the Near Eastern Crisis of 1875–78 it played, for a time, a major rôle in the formulation of foreign policy.

Panslavism is difficult to define, for it was an attitude of mind rather than a precisely defined ideology. The early Slavophiles in the eighteen-forties believed that the Greek Orthodox religion would be the spiritual dynamic for an enlarged Russian Empire which would result from the liberation of the Slav peoples. It was in the later 'fifties and early 'sixties that an organized Panslav movement, properly so-called, grew up with the formation of Slavonic Benevolent Committees in many towns to propagate their views. It appealed to the upper classes, particularly in academic circles, and possessed in General Ignatiev its most flamboyant exponent, in the Tsarevitch, afterwards Alexander III, its most powerful protector. Danilevsky and Fadeev outlined the basic Panslav ideas in 1869; the community of Slav interest rather than Greek Orthodoxy was emphasized as justification for Russia's interest in South-East Europe which would be liberated from Habsburg and Turkish rule and associated in a federation under Russian protection. Fadeev expressed the Panslav belief in an ultimate conflict between Slavdom and the West to achieve these aims. Like the early Slavophiles, the Panslavs upheld the Tsarist system; though hostile to the bureaucracy, they wished to preserve the characteristic features of Russian society and believed in the historic mission of Russia. There was little practical basis for Panslavism, for although there is a similarity between the Slav languages there were great historical and religious differences between Catholic and Western orientated Poles and Greek Orthodox and Russophile Bulgarians. But Panslavism reinforced, and to some extent reflected, growing Russian national sentiment in the 'sixties and 'seventies and the desire for a national success after the disaster of 1856. The rising in Bosnia-Herzegovina gave a considerable impetus to the Slavonic Benevolent Committees which by 1877 had sent money and volunteers, mostly from the upper classes, to assist the Serbs and later the Bulgarians.

Their popularity was at its height when the Tsar, influenced by General Ignatiev and the Tsarevitch, declared war on Turkey. Russian armies advanced to within a few miles of Constantinople in the winter of 1877–78 and General Ignatiev negotiated the San Stefano treaty creating a Big Bulgaria.

Conservative professional diplomats, untouched by Slav enthusiasms, regained control of the situation in the spring of 1878, however, and, realizing Russian inability to wage war against Britain and Austria-Hungary, accepted a compromise settlement which took final shape at the Berlin Congress.

## ACCESSION OF ALEXANDER III

Foreign affairs were discussed in Russia in 1878–79 in a manner impossible during the Crimean War. Desp iterestrictions, a considerable Press had emerged in the 'sixties and 'seventies. The diplomatic defeat suffered at the Berlin Congress was criticized loudly by the Panslav press, and anti-German feeling was widespread. It is significant that the acute observer Bismarck wondered whether Russia was on the verge of collapse after a war which had revealed bureaucratic incompetence and resulted in financial chaos. Colour was lent to his doubts by the terrorist campaign already described. The Tsar began to consider making concessions to satisfy moderate opinion, as represented in the *zemstvos*. These had been hedged round with restrictions after 1866, but in 1878 some of them protested against the repressive measures used by the Government against terrorists and, encouraged by the granting of a constitution to Bulgaria, then under Russian protection, began to press for constitutional reforms. After the attempt on the Tsar's life in 1880 a popular war hero, General Loris-Melikov, was appointed to co-ordinate the anti-terrorist measures. Although ruthless with terrorists, the general was not unsympathetic to some of the demands of the *zemstvos*. As part of his "dictatorship of the heart" the reactionary Ministers of Education and Finance were replaced by liberals, and plans were prepared for the creation of a body elected by the *zemstvos* to advise on new legislation. The scheme was approved by Alexander II on the morning of 1st March, 1881. In the afternoon, on his way back from a military parade, he was assassinated. The scheme was, not unnaturally, shelved by his successor, the thirty-six-year-old Alexander III.

## THE REIGN OF ALEXANDER III:
### (1) PERSONALITIES

Alexander III mounted the throne, to quote a French historian, as a soldier mounts a breach.[7] "Our mistake in 1876 and 1877," he said, "was that we went with the masses and not with the governments. A Russian Emperor ought to deal only with the governments."[8]

An unimaginative conservative, Alexander regretted the Great Reforms and showed remarkable singleness of purpose in his attempts to return to the autocracy of his grandfather, Nicholas I, as far as that was possible in the eighteen-eighties. The characteristic features of his reign were the maintenance of the autocratic system of government, support of the Greek Orthodox Church, and the promotion of Russian national interest at home and abroad.

Alexander found his evil genius in the person of Konstantine Pobedonostsev (1827–1907), a distinguished jurist, tutor of the Tsar and his son, the future Nicholas II, and for twenty-five years chief procurator of the Orthodox Church. The most powerful man in Russia in the eighteen-eighties and 'nineties, Pobedonostsev exerted a decisive influence on policy. A sincere man of extremely narrow views, his bitter opposition to Western liberalism strengthened Alexander's determination to preserve autocracy. Constitutions were "the great lie of our time" for Pobedonostsev, who regarded even the *zemstvos* with great suspicion. His influence was decisive in securing the abandonment by Alexander of the Loris-Melikov scheme immediately after his father's assassination.

### (2) REACTION

The reign justifies the title of an era of counter-reforms, for determined efforts were made to restrict the Great Reforms. The power of the police was strengthened and political offences continued, as at the end of the previous reign, to be removed from the courts' jurisdiction. New prisons were built and conditions in penal settlements made harsher. The Press censorship was strengthened and the government reserved powers to suppress any periodical considered harmful. Universities found the freedom they had enjoyed since 1863 restricted and their autonomy weakened. Attempts were made to restrict the educational opportunities offered to able pupils from poor homes and to ensure that children received education appropriate to their social class. The Government, determined to preserve the position of the nobility, a declining class, abolished elected J.P.s and replaced them by nominated noblemen, called Land Captains, who were given extensive judicial and administrative powers over the peasants. An important modification of the *zemstvos'* regulations increased the powers of the nobility and reduced peasant representation, requiring them to elect their members indirectly. The powers of the courts were curtailed and the independence of the judiciary broken. The Orthodox Church was used to reinforce the régime; the clergy were given important functions in the supervision of the schools system and, as Pobedonostsev believed that church schools should predominate in the field of primary education, their number increased considerably.

## (3) INTOLERANT NATIONALISM

An intolerant nationalism characterized the treatment of the non-Russian subjects of the Tsar, important in an empire where 55,000,000 Great Russians formed less than half the total population. There were 22,000,000 Ukrainians acquired in the seventeenth and eighteenth centuries, 8,000,000 Poles annexed in the eighteenth-century partitions, 3,000,000 Finns acquired in 1809, 4,000,000 Lithuanians, Letts, and Esthonians along the Baltic coastline, Georgians and Armenians in Transcaucasia, annexed in the early nineteenth century, Tartars in central Asia and Jews in the towns, forming a racial medley as mixed as in Austria-Hungary. Since an emphasis on the Great Russian core of the empire, with hostility to non-Russian peoples and to all religions other than Greek Orthodoxy, characterized the reigns of Alexander III and Nicholas II up to 1905, it will be convenient to consider them together.

In Poland the Russification process was intensified after the revolt of 1863. The Russian legal system was introduced, Russian administrative officials replaced Polish and the Polish university of Warsaw was suppressed in 1869, being replaced by a purely Russian institution. Polish private schools were suppressed and a law of 1885 required the use of Russian in all primary schools, except for religious instruction. Russian social policy was more enlightened; the local government system was introduced and the serfs were liberated in 1864, a measure intended to earn the gratitude of the peasant and undermine the position of the nationalist leaders, the Polish nobility.

The Tsars were equally suspicious of the Ukrainian national movement, fearing the loss of the fertile south of Russia, and in 1876 an order forbade all publications in Ukrainian. In the Baltic provinces all schools were placed under the Russian Ministry of Education in 1886, with Russian as the language of instruction in all but the lowest classes, a measure which affected the Baltic Germans who had founded many secondary schools. The autonomy of Finland was not disturbed in Alexander III's reign, but in 1898 an attempt was made to place the Finnish army under Russian command, and in 1901 the Russian conscription system was introduced. In 1899 Imperial laws were declared to have precedence over Finnish, and the Finnish Diet was reduced to provincial status, measures which led to the growth of a passive resistance movement. Finally, the constitution was suspended and Russian introduced in the administration and schools.

## (4) RELIGIOUS INTOLERANCE

Religious intolerance was characteristic of relations with the non-Russian peoples, for Pobedonostsev was bitterly hostile to Catholics, Protestants, Jews, and dissenters. In Poland particular hostility was shown to the Catholic Church as the clergy sympathized with the Polish desire for independence. In the Baltic provinces loyal Protestants were subjected to interference and restrictions, while the Orthodox Church was allowed to carry on a vigorous campaign to convert the Balts and hindered the building of Protestant churches. In the Ukraine the Uniate Church, in communion with Rome, to which a minority of Ukrainians belonged, was suppressed in 1874. The 17,000,000 dissenters of the Orthodox Church—who had some civil and religious rights but were forbidden to proselytize—were persecuted, the leaders of some sects, such as the pacifist Dukhobors, being deported and punitive expeditions being sent to disperse their followers.

## (5) ANTI-SEMITISM

Anti-Semitism was characteristic of both reigns. Some five million Jews were scattered throughout the towns on the periphery of the empire from the Baltic to the Black Sea. There had been some relaxation of the old restrictions on them during Alexander II's reign, but his successors disliked them and the antipathy was shared by Pobedonostsev, Tolstoy, the chief of police Plehve, and by Katkov, the influential editor of the nationalist Press in the 'eighties and 'nineties. An impetus was given to anti-Semitism by the fact that a Jewess, Jessie Helfmann, was involved in Alexander II's assassination. In the spring and summer of 1881 occurred the first of the terrible pogroms, popular anti-Semitic outbursts which would not have succeeded without the connivance of police officials. New restrictions were placed on Jews in the eighteen-eighties; quotas were established for the number of Jews who might study at universities or be army doctors. "Jews need not apply" stated the notices of many *zemstvos* advertising for medical officers. A considerable Jewish exodus from Russia began in these years, those who remained being turned into opponents of the régime. The Russification policy added another unstable feature to the Russian scene and ensured that the non-Russian peoples would be hostile to the régime in 1905 and 1917.

## NEW FACTORS: INDUSTRIALIZATION

Alexander III succeeded in reducing the revolutionaries to order and even regained some of the power possessed by the régime under Nicholas I. But much more significant for Russia's future development was the industrialization which, beginning in the 'sixties, had by 1914 transformed a feudal country to one increasingly influenced by the western forces of large-scale industry, finance, and agriculture and closely tied to world markets. The introduction of twentieth-century industrial techniques began to alter the Russian social structure, and intensified the need for a modification of the outmoded police state to reflect these changes.

Industrialization did not recommend itself to conservative court circles, which feared that autocracy would be endangered if the agrarian basis of the Russian economy was undermined. It was the influential Serge Witte (1849–1915) who, with the support of the Tsars, did most to accelerate the industralization process. An able and ambitious man, originally a junior employee of the railway, he became Minister of Railways and between 1892 and 1903 Minister of Finance. A firm believer in autocracy, he considered that industrialization would strengthen it by increasing the national wealth and the military potential of the State.

## RAILWAY DEVELOPMENT

Russia possessed considerable supplies of the vital raw materials, coal, iron ore and petroleum necessary for industrialization; a cheap labour supply, replenished by an influx into the towns from the countryside; and, in a world of expanding trade, ready markets for her products. Serious disadvantages were poor communications—there were less than a thousand miles of railway in Russia in 1855—and a lack of capital. Railway construction began on a considerable scale in the eighteen-sixties because the Crimean War had shown the military importance of modern communications. It was stimulated enormously by Witte in the eighteen-nineties so that railway mileage was doubled between 1887 and 1902: by 1912 it totalled 63,500 miles.

The railway boom gave an impetus to the growth of heavy industries, especially metallurgy. In South Russia a great industrial area grew up based on the coal of the Donetz basin and the iron ore of Krivoirog, while in Transcaucasia a considerable oil industry sprang up around Baku. It is significant that the State played a major rôle in industrial expansion from the eighteen-eighties onwards. By 1902 the State owned sixty-two per cent of the railways and State contracts accounted for two-thirds of the metallurgy production, largely of armaments and railway materials. Without these contracts industrialization would have been much slower, because the low purchasing power of the Russian peasant prevented the growth of a large internal consumer market to absorb the products of industry. State contracts, subsidies, and tariff protection created close ties between officials and the new industrial classes. State intervention had been in the Russian tradition since Peter the Great, but manufacturers often complained of the stifling effects of too rigid control. Some writers consider that, because the State guaranteed the economic power of the industrialists, this section of the middle class was least interested in political change.

## FOREIGN CAPITAL

Russia had depended in the past upon the German money market, but German industrialization was now absorbing all available capital. In addition, for political reasons, Bismarck had forbidden the *Reichsbank* in 1887 to accept Russian securities as collateral for loans. Russia turned to France, obtaining her first loan in 1888. Increasing financial ties between the two countries paved the way for the Entente of 1891 and the alliance of 1894. Witte spared no effort to attract foreign investments; between 1894 and 1914 the number of foreign companies operating in Russia increased from 37, with a capital of 134,000,000 roubles, to 327, with a capital of 1,343,000,000 roubles.

## SOCIAL PROBLEMS

Industrialization inevitably created serious social problems in the towns. Men, women, and children toiling in the new factories, hours of work ranging from twelve to eighteen a day, extremely low wages, appalling housing, lack of safety precautions, excessive drinking, lack of adequate sanitation and heavy fines were characteristic of the conditions of the two to three million Russians who had left the countryside to work in textile mills, on railways, and in metallurgical establishments by the turn of the century.

There was considerable industrial unrest from the eighteen-seventies onwards. The first important strike occurred in 1879 in the St. Petersburg cotton mills, at a time of general unrest during the terrorist campaign, and in protest against wage cuts. It was at this time that Stephen Khalturin organized the first, though short-lived, union. Not until 1905 did the workers obtain the legal right to form unions. In the 'eighties and 'nineties industrial disturbances increased in frequency and extent. Great bitterness entered into labour disputes because the State intervened actively on the side of the employer, permitting the police to co-operate with him against strikers, exiling trouble-makers on the least provocation and using Cossacks against demonstrators. It is a tragic feature of the period that the Tsars did, relatively, so little to ameliorate conditions and acted as if they wished to substantiate the Marxist thesis that every state is a class state. The failure of the régime was the opportunity for the political agitator, whose task was facilitated by the fact that the workers were concentrated in a few concerns employing many thousands of hands.

It is only fair to add that some attempt was made to compel employers to improve working conditions. Nicholas Bunge, a former university professor of liberal views and an outstanding Minister of Finance between 1881 and 1886, was instrumental in securing the passage of a law in 1882 forbidding or limiting child labour, and obliging employers to allow children to attend school. But the inspectorate established to enforce the law was quite inadequate—it is said there were only two inspectors for 2,000 Moscow factories—and was bitterly opposed by employers exploiting a cheap labour force. In 1884 Bunge forbade night work for children and women, and in 1886 attempted to regulate conditions of employment. Thoroughly unpopular with the industrialists, he was replaced by a more conservative minister. Witte, conscious of the economic advantages of industrial peace, continued Bunge's policy and, after textile strikes in St. Petersburg in 1897, secured the passage of a law imposing a maximum working day of eleven-and-a-half hours for all workers, with a maximum of ten hours for night workers, and developing the factory inspection system. It was, however, a victory for labour in principle only; in practice there was widespread evasion and penalties were slight.

## Foreign Policy:
### (1) Central Asia

Industrialization had important effects on Russian foreign policy. Old expansionist tendencies in central Asia and the Far

v

East were reinforced by new economic motives, a development facilitated by the extension of the Russian railway system.

Russian interest in central Asia increased after the military defeat in the Near East in the eighteen-fifties. Transcaucasia was brought completely under Imperial control by the middle of the nineteenth century and during the eighteen-sixties and 'seventies the nomadic tribes of Turkestan were subjugated and Tashkent, Samarkand, and Bokhara occupied by Russian garrisons. In 1879 the Trans-Caspian railway was begun, a line facilitating the defence and consolidation of central Asia and enabling the cotton growing regions of Turkestan and coal and oil deposits to make a valuable contribution to industrialization. In the eighteen-nineties interest in central Asia led to the peaceful penetration of Northern Persia, for Witte realized that Persia provided a ready market for the Moscow textile industry and by 1914 over sixty per cent of Persian trade was with Russia.

## (2) THE FAR EAST

Russia never completely ignored the Near East even after her reverse in 1879. She maintained an interest in Bulgaria until the 1886-87 crisis and in 1896 there was a possibility that Nicholas II, much to Witte's alarm, would seize the Straits at the risk of beginning a major war. The danger passed, and by 1897 the Tsar had turned his attention exclusively to the Far East. Russian interests there dated back to the seventeenth century when Russian settlers reached the Sea of Okhotsk and entered the Amur Valley. Her first effective attempt to obtain a warm water port on the Pacific coast was made possible by the war waged by Britain and France against the Chinese Empire in the eighteen-sixties. Russia was able to extend her influence over Amur province and establish Vladivostok, but this port, like Montreal in roughly the same degree of latitude, is impeded by ice floes during part of the year. To obtain a completely ice-free port a foothold on the Yellow Sea was needed, implying control of the Chinese province of Manchuria.

Russia's interest in Manchuria was reinforced by the Trans-Siberian Railway project connecting the Far East with European Russia. The idea was discussed in the eighteen-

seventies but postponed as a result of the 1877 War. The
decision to build was taken in 1891 when it seemed as if
Britain were seeking to penetrate the markets of South
Manchuria. Witte was convinced of the importance of the line
and, writing to Alexander III in 1892, he maintained that the
line would revolutionize world trade, supersede the Suez
Canal as the leading trade route to China, enable Russia to
flood the Chinese markets with textiles and metal goods, and
give her political control of Northern China. Strategically the
line would strengthen the Russian Pacific Fleet and make
Russia dominant in Far Eastern waters.

The extension of the Russian railway system to the Persian
and Afghan frontiers caused a deterioration of relations with
Britain. Similarly, Russian ambitions in the Far East proved
incompatible with those of Japan because Russia desired to
build the line across Northern Manchuria to avoid the
engineering difficulties and prohibitive cost of constructing a
line along the Amur Valley to Vladivostok. Japan, however,
desired to obtain a foothold in Korea, a tributary Chinese
kingdom and ultimately extend her influence over Manchuria.

Japanese interference in Korea precipitated a conflict with
China in 1894 in the course of which Japan proved her
military capabilities. Russia realized that recognition of
Korean independence would encourage Japan to work for its
annexation because that would give her control of both sides
of the straits between Japan and Korea, endangering
Vladivostok's entry into the Yellow Sea. Russia posed as
China's friend, preventing Japan from obtaining Formosa
and the Liaotung peninsula. By the beginning of the
twentieth century Russia had made considerable advances in
Manchuria. Exploiting Chinese gratitude for her intervention
in 1895 she obtained permission to build the Chinese Eastern
railway across Northern Manchuria in 1896. In 1898 she
obtained a base on the Liaotung peninsula and built a
powerful naval base at Port Arthur. Japanese hostility to
Russia increased when in 1900 Russia occupied Manchuria
during the Boxer Rising, for Japan feared that in time a
Russian occupation of Korea would follow.

Witte had opposed the seizure of Port Arthur and the
occupation of Manchuria, for he feared that these actions would

antagonize Japan and might lead to the abandonment of the policy of peaceful penetration and to a disastrous war. Lamsdorff, the Foreign Minister, shared these fears and the Minister of War, General Kuropatkin, felt at least that Russia should not neglect the Balkans, her traditional sphere of influence, in favour of the Far East.

Unfortunately, the foreign policy of autocratic Russia depended ultimately on the Tsar's decisions and after 1901 Nicholas fell under the influence of a former cavalry officer, Bezobrazov, who favoured an adventurous policy in Asia and encouraged the Tsar in his fantastic dream of annexing Manchuria, Korea, Tibet, and Persia. Bezobrazov persuaded Nicholas to finance a company to exploit the timber resources of the Yalu river on the frontier between Manchuria and Korea in order to penetrate the latter. In the summer of 1903 the Tsar, by-passing the Foreign Ministry, appointed the inexperienced *bon vivant* and friend of Bezobrazov, Admiral Alexeiev, Regent of the Far East, with considerable power to conduct affairs. In the same month Witte was dismissed, a victory for his opponent Plehve who believed that Russia needed, "a little victorious war to stop the revolutionary tide".[9] Bezobrazov had been made an Imperial secretary and secretary of a special commission on Far Eastern affairs. "Russia has been made by bayonets not diplomacy," said a supporter of Bezobrazov, "and we must decide the questions at issue with China and Japan by bayonets and not diplomatic pens."[10]

The end was not long delayed. Attempts by Japan to secure Russian agreement to Japanese control of Korea in return for recognition of Russian influence in Manchuria failed. Russia wanted a free hand in Manchuria but had no intention of conceding the same to Japan in Korea. Nicholas was hesitating whether to declare for peace or war when, in February, 1904, the Japanese attacked Russian warships at Port Arthur and the Russo-Japanese War had begun.

The war, in which Russia was defeated, had extremely important results for Russian foreign policy and for her internal development. Dreams of easy expansion in the Far East ended and Witte, recalled from semi-retirement to act as Russian plenipotentiary at the Portsmouth Conference, had to exert considerable skill to limit Russian losses to the transfer to Japan of the Liaotung peninsula lease and railway concessions in Southern Manchuria, and the recognition of Japanese rights in Korea.

"The Japanese will not enter the Kremlin but the Russians will," remarked a Russian liberal to Sir Bernard Pares, a leading British authority on Russia.[11] The Tsar decided to end the war, not only because the military and administrative inefficiency of the State had been glaringly revealed and the best possible terms had to be obtained before worse befell Russia, but also because a loss of prestige in the Far East was preferable to the complete collapse of autocracy at home.

## ACCESSION OF NICHOLAS II

When Nicholas came to the throne in 1894, a youth of twenty-six tutored by Pobedonostsev and lacking experience of public affairs, he declared that he would "maintain the principle of autocracy just as firmly and unflinchingly as it was preserved by my unforgettable dead father". But he failed to stifle radical criticism of the régime as effectively as Alexander III. The opposition which Alexander had faced consisted in the eighteen-sixties of discontented intelligentsia lacking popular support. Only at the end of the eighteen-seventies were they beginning to obtain a very limited backing from the urban working class and little advance was possible under Alexander III. The intensification of industrialization in the eighteen-nineties, however, strengthened the growing middle class and the working class, enabling both to offer more effective resistance to the Tsar than their predecessors. Yet in a semi-industrialized society the intelligentsia, even with the support of urban workers, cannot overthrow the machinery of State without the mass support only to be found in the countryside. As long as conditions remained normal and the secret police operated effectively it was difficult for urban revolutionaries to establish contact with the peasantry. When the machinery of State was shaken by war in 1905, however, the intelligentsia was able to obtain the backing of the discontented peasants, although only for a few months because the régime was strong enough to recover power in 1906. The difference in similar circumstances in 1917, was that Nicholas was no longer strong enough to resist the united opposition and Tsardom was completely overthrown.

## POLITICAL DEVELOPMENT

Before the 1905 Revolution is examined the considerable political development at the turn of the century must be reviewed, for this formed an essential background to the revolution.

## POLITICAL PARTIES:
### (1) THE LIBERALS

A most significant development in the late eighteen-nineties and early nineteen-hundreds was the emergence of a considerable liberal party called the League of Liberators. It owed its formation to the work of the *zemstvos* which, despite the restrictions placed on them by Alexander III, had provided moderate liberal opinion with the opportunity to obtain valuable administrative experience. One of the most powerful stimuli to the growth of *zemstvo* liberalism was the agrarian crisis following the 1891–92 famine, since the magnitude of the relief problems arising from the famine and the ensuing cholera epidemic were beyond the ability of the central authorities to deal with adequately. The *zemstvos* were reluctantly allowed to tackle these problems at a local level, and were afterwards loath to return to the relative inactivity of former days. They had always interested themselves in the pressing educational and medical needs of the peasantry and, although frequently hindered by the Government, they won their confidence to a large extent. Hospitals and schools forged bonds between moderate liberal and peasant which the terrorist bombs had failed to create.

When Nicholas ascended the throne the liberals, reverting to the tradition of the late eighteen-seventies, were again demanding further reforms, including a central assembly to co-ordinate the work of the *zemstvos* and a popular elected representation to share in the work of government. Nicholas disappointed these optimists, rejecting as "senseless dreams" the requests of certain *zemstvos* for constitutional reforms. In 1896 the presidents of the *zemstvos* were assembled in St. Petersburg for the coronation of Nicholas II when Shipov, chairman of the executive board of the progressive Moscow *zemstvo*, suggested yearly meetings of the presidents to co-ordinate policy and discuss matters of general concern. But after the first conference, later in 1896, the Government forbade further meetings on the grounds of their "incompatibility with the constitutional order". The liberal revival could not, however, be checked so easily. The professional classes, especially those members employed by the *zemstvos*, were meeting in congresses in the late eighteen-nineties and discussing political as well as professional questions despite the caution of Shipov. The unrest at the turn of the century made the Government regard these developments with alarm and attempt to limit the powers of the *zemstvos*, but, as the political temperature rose, the basis of liberal opposition broadened. In 1901 Peter Struve, a Marxist converted to radical liberalism, attempted to found a newspaper to advocate the overthrow of autocracy. His initiative was welcomed by the *zemstvos*, more of whom were becoming convinced of the need for political action, and in 1902 *Liberation* began publication in Stuttgart, copies being smuggled into Russia. Finally, in the summer of 1903, *zemstvo* leaders and radical intellectuals met in Stuttgart and founded the League of Liberators, pledged to a programme of responsible government. The reactionary Plehve, appointed Minister of the Interior in 1902, was doing everything possible to strangle liberal activity, annulling the elections of the prominent *zemstvo* members and banishing the more radical of their employees. Nevertheless, the party succeeded in establishing a network of local branches in secret so that on the eve of the Japanese war liberalism had emerged as a considerable political force.

At the turn of the century the growing urban proletariat was beginning to assume a political shape. Wage rates and working conditions had improved somewhat during the boom years of the eighteen-nineties, but a slump between 1899 and 1903 caused prices and wages to fall and unemployment figures to rise to a peak in 1902. There was some improvement in 1903, but the war of 1904 caused a further deterioration.

The Government made several attempts to deal with the serious situation. The finance Ministry, under Witte's direction, secured in 1903 the passage of laws establishing the financial responsibility of the employer in industrial accidents and permitting the creation of a system of factory elders elected, with the employer's consent, to voice the workers' grievances. Neither law proved effective. Nor did the curious "police socialism" of the ex-revolutionary and chief of Moscow police, Zubatov, meet with much success. Zubatov argued that the workers' organization was very weak and that if a legal outlet was provided for the formulation of grievances, the influence of political agitators exploiting these would decline. The Government sponsored unions in several towns between 1901 and 1903 which attracted considerable support. When, however, the police found the unions involved in strike action the Government became alarmed and with the dismissal of Zubatov in 1903 the movement collapsed. Strikes were now assuming an increasingly political flavour, being accompanied by street demonstrations. The hostility of the workers to the employers increased, for the Government never ceased to expel political agitators from the factories or to use troops against strikers, as in 1903 when the first general strike in south Russia was called at the Baku oil fields.

## POLITICAL PARTIES:
## (2) THE SOCIAL DEMOCRATS

The Social Democratic Party was founded against this background of industrial unrest. Marxist groups had been formed in several towns in the eighteen-eighties, organized usually by students who led the workers in secret discussions of the ideas of Karl Marx. By the mid-eighteen-nineties the scattered Marxist groups realized the need for more contact with the working class, and supported strikes in order to turn the struggle for better living conditions into a political struggle to destroy the Tsarist régime. In 1898 an attempt was made to co-ordinate the activities of these groups at Minsk and the Russian Social Democratic Workers' party came into being.

The foundation of this party was a turning point in Russian development, for socialism had been hitherto conceived of in an exclusively agrarian context. Marxism, with its emphasis upon industrialization as an historically pre-ordained preliminary to the creation of a socialist society, broke completely with this tradition. Marxism had, at first, no appeal outside the towns, for it had nothing to offer the peasant whose commune was considered an anachronism which the operation of a capitalist economy would destroy. Nor did the party make an auspicious beginning; the members of its executive committee were soon arrested before they even had time to establish a party organization. Inside the party there were many shades of opinion. The so-called revisionists argued that Marxists should concern themselves with the workers' struggle for better living conditions, leaving the political struggle against Tsardom to the liberals. Others, like Georg Plekhanov (1857–1918), founder of the first Marxist socialist group in the eighteen-eighties, and Vladimir Ulianov, better known as Lenin (1870–1924), insisted on the primacy of political considerations, denouncing the "trade unionism" of their opponents as defeatism. The latter founded *Iskra* (Spark) in Munich in 1902, smuggling the paper back to Russia and distributing it to members through an underground network which acted as a substitute for a party organization.

## MENSHEVIK AND BOLSHEVIK

At the second conference of the party, held in Brussels in 1903 and adjourned to rooms in Tottenham Court Road in London, important differences of opinion resulted in the formation of two groups, Mensheviks and Bolsheviks. The names originated when the followers of Lenin, a minority in the party, temporarily obtained a majority at one session of the conference and succeeded in electing a majority to the editorial board of *Iskra*. From this time onward the followers of Lenin referred to themselves as Bolsheviks or men of the majority, and to their opponents as Mensheviks, or men of the minority. The groups remained inside the party, co-operating very uneasily, until in 1912 the Bolsheviks founded the famous daily paper *Pravda* (Truth), and held a separate party conference at Prague, claiming to be the only orthodoxist Marxist party. Their opponents, the Mensheviks, held their conference at Vienna.

The debate on the constitution of the party at the second conference revealed for the first time the fundamental differences between Bolshevik and Menshevik. Although Lenin's point of view did not prevail in 1903 he argued in favour of a

v*

highly centralized party machine, the members of which must be wholehearted Marxists prepared to sacrifice themselves for the cause. This concept of party as the vanguard of revolution, a fanatical minority of dedicated class-conscious revolutionaries, working for political change and leading the masses, who would remain outside its ranks, was French rather than Russian in origin, although there are clear signs of this concept in Bakunin, Tkachev, and Nechaev. The Menshevik concept was much less rigid. They conceived of party as a federation of all those interested in the party programme, whether active workers or passive members, all enjoying the democratic right to share in policy making. This concept was approved by the 1903 Conference. But it was Lenin's monolithic concept which triumphed in 1917 and has become familiar as the pattern of the Communist Party in the Soviet Union.

## INTERPRETERS OF MARX: (1) PLEKHANOV

This difference of opinion was partly the result of a different interpretation of Marxism. Revolution for Marxists was a two-phase development. The feudal order is superseded by the capitalist, or bourgeois democratic order, which, in its turn, is inevitably replaced by the socialist order. Russia, in the Marxist view, was an agrarian-feudal society, for the working class was still only a minority of the population. The Mensheviks maintained that the middle class would play the leading rôle in the bourgeois revolution, which would give Russia the parliamentary institutions characteristic of this social order and allow the capitalist economy to develop freely. In the bourgeois revolution the working class was doomed by history to play a subordinate rôle. Mensheviks like Plekhanov thought that a considerable time must elapse between the bourgeois and socialist revolutions, because until industrialization was well advanced conditions for the transition to socialism would be absent. During the interim period the working class would grow in numbers and strength until it formed a majority of the population. In time a socialist revolution might be achieved by parliamentary majorities, as social democrats in Western Europe believed.

## (2) LENIN

But Lenin, the leading Bolshevik, thought that the Russian middle class was too weak to play the rôle cast for it by history and would betray the bourgeois revolution if allowed to take the lead. The working class must, therefore, assume the initiative and carry out the bourgeois revolution for the bourgeoisie and since, by their leading rôle in establishing the so-called "revolutionary dictatorship of the proletariat and peasantry", the working class would derive most benefit from this stage, it would be possible to advance more quickly to the socialist phase: the two revolutions would be "concertinaed" into each other. In addition, while Mensheviks conceived of revolution vaguely as a spontaneous uprising of the people, Lenin, with French models in mind, saw revolution as the work of the determined spearhead of the proletariat and insisted upon the need for military training and knowledge of conspiratorial techniques as a preparation for the seizure of power when the time came.

The Bolshevik interpretation of Marxism was partly a reflection of Lenin's temperament. Obstinate, quarrelsome, convinced of his own infallibility, he favoured an interpretation justifying his desire for action, realizing that Menshevism made revolution too remote a possibility. Yet, as the social structure of Russia altered under the impact of industrialization, the Menshevik view of a relatively peaceful evolution seemed more realistic than Lenin's concept of minority dictatorship based on the seizure of power. With the growth of mass movements in the more relaxed atmosphere after 1907 conspiratorial organization seemed anachronistic. Before 1914 Lenin was the impractical dreamer and Plekhanov the realist. Only in the famine and chaos of 1917, when the machinery of State collapsed, was Lenin given an opportunity to apply his tactics.

For the Marxist the factory worker was the chosen vessel for achieving a socialist society. The peasant, however, was a counter-revolutionary at heart, clinging to his land and opposed to socialism. Socialists, like early nineteenth-century liberals, regarded the peasant as the bulwark of conservative order. Universal suffrage in an agrarian society was more likely to favour political reaction than either liberalism or socialism.

It is significant that until 1936 the franchise in the Soviet Union was weighted in favour of urban centres where the Marxists had a firmer hold on the population.

Although Marxism, with its emphasis on collectivization, must ultimately run contrary to the peasant desire for individual land ownership, Lenin, as an outstanding tactician, recognized, especially after the 1905 Revolution, that the peasantry was a revolutionary class. Conscious that the Emancipation Edict had made them only half free, the peasantry desired further change to complete the process. Lenin understood that in a semi-industrialized country an alliance between worker and peasant was essential to enable the former to seize power and establish the "revolutionary democratic dictatorship of the proletariat and peasantry". The peasantry would co-operate in effecting the bourgeois revolution if offered a redistribution of land as their reward. To satisfy their land hunger Lenin adopted the Socialist Revolutionary Party's programme for surrender of the land to the peasantry for redistribution, with eventual nationalization when a democratic republic was established. Tactical reasons predominated with Lenin. He hoped that land redistribution would accelerate the differentiation into classes in the countryside, creating a considerable rural proletariat, the natural allies of the urban proletariat. Then, provided that a socialist revolution occurred in an advanced West European country, it would be possible for the workers, with the aid of the landless rural proletariat, to seize power and begin the socialist revolution directed against the bourgeoisie and rich peasantry. The Mensheviks, however, remained hostile to the peasantry and opposed land redistribution, fearing a dislocation of the economy prejudicial to working-class development. Their view prevailed at the fourth conference, held at Stockholm in 1906, but in the summer of 1917 Lenin's slogan "Land for the peasant" proved the usefulness of his modification of orthodox Marxism.

POLITICAL PARTIES:
(3) THE SOCIALIST REVOLUTIONARIES

The Social Democrats did not obtain much support in the countryside and had only limited support in the towns. The

party which made the greatest impression on the rural areas
was the Socialist Revolutionary Party (S.R.). In the closing
years of Alexander II's reign most of the agrarian socialists
had been arrested and exiled. In the eighteen-nineties many of
them returned and renewed their contacts with the peasants
during the famine of 1891–92. In 1902 the leaders of several
populist groups succeeded in co-ordinating their activities
and founded the Socialist Revolutionary Party. A newspaper,
*Revolutionary Russia*, was printed abroad and smuggled into the
country. A typical Russian radical party, the S.R. demanded
civil liberties and universal suffrage. Its members considered the essence of socialism to lie in land redistribution.
Land in the possession of the nobility or State would be
socialized, administered by elected peasant committees, and
finally redistributed to individual peasants within the framework of the commune. Their leader, Victor Chernov (1876-
1952), afterwards Minister of Agriculture in the Provisional
Government of 1917, envisaged similar communal groups in
industry to be loosely federated with the rural communes, and
self-determination for the non-Russian peoples. Members
of the Socialist Revolutionary Party shared with the anarchists
a mistrust of State centralization—an essential of Marxism—
and like the anarchists favoured a policy of violence. They
believed that attacks on property owners would interest the
peasants in the party while assassination of leading officials
was in keeping with the old popular belief that, once the upper
crust of Russian society was removed, it would be easy to
create a socialist society without enduring the miseries of
capitalism. The Marxists, however, although they applauded
the terrorism of the S.R., rejected acts of individual terrorism
as futile and relied more upon the strength of their party
organization to make progress.

The terrorist organization of the Socialist Revolutionary
Party consisted of a small group of men and women drawn
from all social classes, including Tatiana Leontev, daughter
of a vice-governor of Yakutsk, who volunteered to murder the
Tsar at a ball which, in fact, was cancelled, and Boris Savinkov,
a revolutionary of exceptional daring and resource. Between
1901 and 1907 this group was responsible for many armed
robberies, or "expropriations", and for the assassination of

many officials, including two Ministers of the Interior, Sipiagin in 1902 and Plehve in 1904, and a Minister of Education, Bogolepov, in 1901. The terrorists' activity did much to increase the background of unrest at the turn of the century.

The S.R. was also gaining considerable support in the countryside at this time, owing to the deterioration of rural conditions after the famine of 1891–92 and the crop failures in 1897, 1898, and 1901. These disasters intensified the difficulties under which the peasant lived after the Emancipation. The basic problem lay in the increase of the population of the fifty provinces of European Russia from fifty to seventy-nine millions between 1860 and 1897, despite the malnutrition and epidemics which caused the death of ninety-five per cent of all peasants before the age of sixty. Although the average holding in the eighteen-eighties was sixteen acres, compared with nine in France, the peasant was unable to support the rapidly growing population. The technical backwardness of the wasteful open field system, the conservative control of the commune and lack of capital made intensive cultivation impossible. As prices fell in the 'seventies and 'eighties conditions grew worse.

Despite the growth of huge grain exports, only a small minority of peasants, the so-called *kulaks*, could be considered prosperous. The vast majority lived a marginal existence in great poverty and squalor, heavily taxed by the commune, *zemstvo*, and State, suffering from a perennial shortage of bread, and consoled only by the ministrations of the village priest. The establishment of the Peasants' Bank in 1883 enabled them to acquire more land but, to eke out a living, a third of their number rented land from the old owners or worked on the great estates as hired labourers, practices which restored the atmosphere of pre-Emancipation days in many areas. The Government, disturbed by signs of unrest, made renewed efforts to improve the peasant's lot at the turn of the century. Interest rates on loans from the Peasant's Bank were reduced, the repayment of arrears of redemption postponed, and various commissions of investigation established. Nevertheless, mounting dissatisfaction was revealed in the hundreds of disturbances between 1879 and 1904, the most serious being in the provinces of Kharkov and Poltava in the spring of 1902, when peasants seized the landowners' grain to feed themselves and their animals. Far from directing such outbreaks the S.R. was itself swept along for, as one peasant remarked to a magistrate after that of 1902, "I think that if we lived better the little books would not be important, no matter what was written in them. What's terrible is not the little books but this: that there isn't anything to eat."[12]

## The Revolution of 1905

Thus, on the eve of the Japanese War, opposition to the régime was growing on all sides. The outbreak and subsequent course of the war increased the discontent, bringing it to a head in the famous Revolution of 1905, a turning point in the period, which resulted in the establishment of constitutional monarchy in Russia.

The declaration of war at first evoked patriotic demonstrations, and liberals in particular felt that the time was inopportune to press for political change. In the spring and early summer news of disasters and defeats arrived and this mood altered. Old tensions rose quickly to the surface when an expelled student and S.R. terrorist hurled a bomb at Plehve, Minister of the Interior, in July, 1904. His assassination led to a revival of political activity, for his successor, Prince Sviatopolk-Mirsky, was a nobleman of enlightened views who promised some relaxation of the repressive policy pursued by his predecessors for over twenty years. The partial amnesties and relaxation of police regulations during the "political spring" did not, however, satisfy the opposition facing Nicholas II as it might have satisfied the intelligentsia of the 'sixties.

## Liberal Activity

Political agitation came out into the open in November at the conference of *zemstvo* presidents held in St. Petersburg with the tacit approval of Prince Mirsky. An eleven point resolution was unanimously adopted, calling for civil liberties, the equality of all before the law, a political amnesty, and the summoning of a representative assembly. Only on the last point was there disagreement between those, like Shipov, who favoured a consultative assembly and the majority who requested a legislative one. The resolutions were adopted by *zemstvos* and *dumas* all over Russia in November and December, and were embodied in addresses sent by these bodies to the Minister of the Interior. Lawyers, doctors and journalists began to organize themselves in professional unions and adopted a political programme similar to that of the *zemstvos*, while even the Marshal of the Chernigov Nobility tele-graphed a similar resolution to the Tsar. At first the Tsar approved Prince Mirsky's suggestion for a moderate reform, adding some elected *zemstvo* and *duma* members to the State Council, but under pressure from Pobedonostsev, the Empress, and Witte, who feared any diminution of the powers of autocracy, he rejected Mirsky's draft at the last moment, promising instead some rather vague reforms to be prepared by the bureaucracy.

## "RED SUNDAY"

At this point the urban proletariat played, for the first time, a considerable political rôle. A strike had broken out in St. Petersburg early in January, 1905, spreading to a number of factories and involving several thousand workers. The strike was organized by the so-called "Assembly of Russian Workingmen", a trade union founded by the Orthodox priest Father Gapon, an associate of Zaburov. Gapon had police approval for his union, intended to be patriotic and anti-revolutionary, but he decided to mobilize the workers in support of the demand for political change with, however, special emphasis on workers' needs. On 22nd January thousands of workers singing patriotic songs and bearing petitions demanding an amelioration of working conditions took part in the celebrated procession to the Winter Palace. The revolutionary element amongst the strikers was probably slight, and the demonstration was conducted in an orderly fashion. Yet troops barred their way at several points and, probably on the orders of the Tsar's uncle, the Grand Duke Vladimir, opened fire on the procession, killing and wounding several hundred people. This, the massacre of Red Sunday, is generally regarded as the beginning of the 1905 Revolution.

The news of the massacre produced an epidemic of strikes in St. Petersburg and other cities. In Poland, the Baltic provinces and Transcaucasia general strikes were called which soon developed into civil war when the Government used troops against the strikers. A frightened Government attempted to revert to repressive policies to break the threat to Russian industrial life and by implication to autocracy itself. Prince Mirsky was dismissed, being replaced by the reactionary Bulygin. General Trepov, son of the man whom Vera Zasulich shot at in 1878 and famous for his motto "not to spare the cartridges", which the Tsar approved, was appointed governor of St. Petersburg with dictatorial powers.

Nevertheless, the disorders continued and news arrived of the murder of innumerable police officials all over Russia, shot down by unknown assailants. On 4th February the Tsar's uncle, the harsh and arrogant Grand Duke Serge Aleksandrovitch, commanding officer of the Moscow region, was killed in the Kremlin by a student and S.R. terrorist. Influenced by the enlightened Minister of Finance, Count Kokovtsev, and by the head of a group of French bankers visiting Russia, the Tsar decided to grant a consultative assembly to the people. It was too late, however, for liberal opinion now favoured a constituent assembly elected by universal suffrage and empowered to establish a legislative assembly. This demand was supported by the League of Liberators, by the Union of Unions, a central organization formed to co-ordinate the views of fourteen newly founded professional unions, and later in the summer by the *zemstvos* and *dumas*. The liberals were strengthened in their opposition to a consultative assembly by the publication of "Bulygin's constitution" in August, which revealed that the limited franchise arranged by the Tsar's bureaucratic advisers would give little representation to the intelligentsia or proletariat.

## THE REVOLUTION SPREADS

In the summer of 1905 the whole of Russia was in a ferment following the news of the annihilation of the Russian fleet in the Tsushima Straits in May. The number of agrarian disturbances increased, particularly in the Baltic provinces, where the Latvian and Estonian peasantry attacked their German landowners, and culminated in a large-scale revolt in the Volga region in September. "For three hundred years," remarked one peasant, "the Romanovs have done nothing for the peasant and the grand dukes do nothing but drink . . . as for us, we have no one to set our hopes on, but we must take all by force."[13] Under the leadership of the S.R. the peasants expelled landowners, burnt their houses, and established rudimentary peasant republics. These actions were approved by the Peasant Union, an embryonic agrarian party, founded in May by members of the Socialist Revolutionary Party. At its first congress in Moscow it demanded the transfer of all land to the peasants, the calling of a constituent assembly and, significantly, a political alliance with all opponents of the régime; at last the isolation of the peasantry from other classes was breaking down. The unrest spread to the armed forces and, although most soldiers remained loyal, there were many disturbances in the navy, including the mutiny on the battleship *Prince Potemkin* in which the crew seized control, raised the red flag, attempted to shell Odessa, and finally surrendered a few days later to the Roumanian authorities.

## THE GENERAL STRIKE

In the towns industrial strife continued. At the end of September the Moscow printers and bakers went on strike and fellow workers in St. Petersburg struck in sympathy. A hesitant Government ordered the arrest of a Railwaymen's Congress meeting in Moscow, and the local union declared a general strike in retaliation on 7th October. It was a decisive action, for within a few days the strike spread rapidly in the towns, engulfing the telegraph and telephone services, paralysing industry and threatening food supplies. The strikers, primarily interested in political change, demanded an eight-hour day, civil liberties, a constituent assembly, and the establishment of a democratic republic. It is significant that this programme was endorsed by the professional unions and that the Cadet party at its first congress, declared "complete solidarity with the strike movement" and its readiness "to support the conquest of freedom by force". Even the Moscow industrialists believed that factory workers should be given a restricted franchise. Shops, banks, and municipal offices closed down, barricades appeared in some cities and the economic life of Russia came to a standstill.

## THE FIRST SOVIETS

In some places strike committees of factory workers, called *soviets*, had appeared to represent the working class. Around these nuclei grew trade unions, for there was a general desire for permanent machinery to safeguard their interests. During the general strike the St. Petersburg *Soviet* was founded on 13th October and began publication of the journal *Izvestia* (News) a few days later. The *soviet* consisted of over five hundred delegates elected by the workers to co-ordinate the activities of all strike committees in the city. It rapidly assumed a position of authority and prestige, having as its president the Menshevik lawyer Nosar, and as vice-president another Menshevik, Leon Trotsky (1877–1940). Recognized by the professional unions, the *soviet* pledged itself to secure an eight-hour day and a democratic republic. Theoretically non-party, it was strongly influenced by the Mensheviks, who were more interested in the creation of strong unions than their Bolshevik opponents, although on the central executive committee of the *soviet* both factions had equal representation. Lenin, a comparatively unknown figure, returned to Russia from exile in November, and soon recognized the possibilities of *soviets* as popular institutions capable of replacing the existing government in the event of the successful insurrection which he constantly demanded. The *soviets*, controlled by the Mensheviks, were opposed to insurrectionary tactics and more interested in the economic welfare of their members than in the overthrow of the régime, a task for liberals in their opinion.

## THE OCTOBER MANIFESTO

The peasant disturbances, reinforced by the effect of the strikes, compelled the Tsar to issue his "October Manifesto" granting Russia a constitution. Witte returned to St. Petersburg from the United States, where he had concluded peace with Japan in August, and used his new-found fame as a peacemaker to advise Nicholas in favour of constitutional monarchy as opposed to the military dictatorship which the Tsar wanted. Witte believed autocracy to be the best form of government but only if the Tsar was a capable man, as Alexander III had been. Nicholas, Witte considered, was not the ideal autocrat. Reluctantly the Tsar gave way when his choice for dictator, his uncle, the excitable Grand Duke Nicholas, threatened to shoot himself in the Tsar's presence if he refused to accept Witte's draft manifesto. "I had nobody to rely on except honest Trepov," wrote the Tsar, "there was no other way out than to cross myself and give what everyone was asking for."[14]

The manifesto, published on 17th October without reference to the committee of ministers, guaranteed fundamental civil liberties and promised to enfranchise those groups excluded from the *Duma* in the August constitution. Although the Tsar still asserted that supreme power belonged to him, the consent of the *Duma* to all legislation would be necessary and it would possess supervisory powers over the bureaucracy. Shortly afterwards the Tsar promised the cancellation of all redemption payments by the peasantry after 1906 and increased assistance from the Peasants' Bank for the purchase of land.

The manifesto was greeted with great excitement throughout Russia. At first it gave added momentum to the revolutionary wave, for freedom of the Press ended censorship and freedom of association deprived the police of their powers over meetings. The police stood aside whilst the pogroms were carried out, the administrative machine was in a state of chaos, and in the Far East the Trans-Siberian Railway was in the hands of restless soldiers. In the countryside disturbances increased, for the peasants understood the freedom of the manifesto as permission to act as they pleased. "We shall work," declared the peasants looting and burning a manor house, "while there is freedom. After New Year's there won't be any freedom any more."[15]

## THE LIBERALS DIVIDED

The manifesto had a disintegrating effect upon the temporarily united opposition facing the Tsar in October. The liberals were divided in their attitude. Those of moderate views, led by Shipov, formed the "League of October" and became known as "Octobrists" because they accepted the Manifesto. They consisted of liberal noblemen, right wing *zemstvo* members and the new industrial magnates, who wanted a check on, but not a substitute for, autocratic government. They favoured a restricted franchise to the consultative assembly, opposed concessions to the non-Russian peoples and were vague in their views about land reform and civil liberties. The more radical liberals, mostly from the professional classes and intelligentsia, regarded the Manifesto only as a beginning. They founded, under the chairmanship of the leading radical, Professor P. N. Milyukov (1859–1943), the Constitutional Democratic Party, or "Cadets", and worked for full civil rights, a progressive income tax, radical land reform with compensation, and health insurance for workers. They wished to ensure the permanence of the new *Duma* by drafting a constitution making the Tsar titular ruler, but giving real power to a responsible ministry. Thus the Manifesto separated moderate and radical liberals. Even the latter, after the peasant disorders and the Moscow rising, declared that they regarded the *Duma* as their field for activities and repudiated the idea of participation in an armed rising which they had once supported.

## THE ST. PETERSBURG SOVIET

In the towns the St. Petersburg *Soviet* remained the centre of revolutionary activity. The general strike was called off when the Manifesto appeared because many strikers returned to work. Social Democratic opinion of the constitution was, however, expressed by Trotsky who wrote, "Witte has come, but Trepov remains" and rejected "the police whip wrapped in the parchment of a constitution", demanding as before a democratic republic. There was less support for the *soviet* because many believed that a real constitution had been granted and public opinion was alienated by the inconvenience caused by the general strikes. When the *soviet* ordered a general strike on 1st November in protest against the declaration of martial law in Poland, they failed to achieve their object and called off the strike a few days later. This failure encouraged Witte to declare martial law in the capital, forbid public meetings, and arrest Nosar, president of the *soviet*. In retaliation the *soviet* urged citizens to refuse payment of taxes and soldiers to refuse to obey orders. Next day the members of the *soviet* were arrested and the general strike they called in protest failed miserably.

## RISING IN MOSCOW

Leadership now passed to the Moscow *Soviet* where the Bolshevik section, against Menshevik advice, attempted an armed uprising in December. They lacked support and soldiers from St. Petersburg crushed it after fierce street fighting. "The abscess was growing gradually, causing much pain and suffering, and now it has burst," wrote the Tsar with satisfaction.[16] For Lenin the abortive rising was the most significant event in 1905 and "the signpost to future victory". The Revolution had ended because the loyalty of the army was assured and the middle class was alienated by the futility of the Moscow rising.

## COUNTER REVOLUTION

An important feature in the closing months of 1905 was the support given to the Tsar by opponents of constitutional change. Many conservative landowners rallied round the Tsar, co-operating with Russian nationalists, army officers, and officials in the "Union of the Russian People", founded in St. Petersburg in October by Dr. Dubrovin to uphold Orthodoxy, autocracy, and Russian nationalism. Exploitation of the Tsar's popularity, and hostility towards Jews and non-Russian peoples, characterized the Union. The Tsar, who shared these sentiments, accepted honorary badges of the Union for himself and his son, and many high officials, including Pobedonostsev and Goremykin, a future Prime Minister, were supporters of it. Partly through official patronage the Union succeded in establishing a network of local agencies enjoying support from the lower middle class and the clergy. The activities were reinforced by the notorious "Black Hundred", recruited from the lower middle class, perennial supporters of counter-revolutionary movements, as later of Fascism, and from unskilled workers. With the connivance of the police and of many officials, these hooligans were responsible for the murder of many radicals and particularly Jews. Hundreds of pogroms were directed against the latter in the spring and summer of 1905, the worst being at Kishenev, in Bessarabia, which resulted in seven hundred deaths. These bands were generally discredited in the eyes of the public, but they helped to strengthen the Tsar's position at the end of 1905.

## SIGNIFICANCE OF THE REVOLUTION

The Revolution of 1905 is often regarded as a "failure" because the Tsar had succeeded in regaining the essentials of his authority in the spring of 1906, but the process of transforming autocracy into a modern monarchy had begun and the *Duma*, in a modified form, had important political results to be discussed later. The inferior legal and social status of the peasants and their liability to arbitrary treatment and harsh punishment was only partly removed, but after 1906 they undoubtedly benefited considerably from the cancellation of redemption payments. The ablest among them also took advantage of later reforms allowing them entry to higher educational institutions and to certain official posts from which they had previously been debarred.

Despite the guarantee of civil liberties, Russian citizens were as liable after the Revolution as before to arbitrary interference at the hands of the police, whose powers remained unlimited. Large areas of Russia were frequently under special régimes after 1906, correspondence was examined by the police, and freedom of assembly often existed only on paper. Yet the relaxation of Press censorship remained: *Pravda*, for example, was often suspended but was able to appear openly until 1914. Universities also enjoyed a more liberal atmosphere until 1911. Industrial workers derived some slight benefit from the Revolution because trade unions, which expanded suddenly in the towns in 1905, were given legal recognition. By strike action a ten-hour day was secured for metal workers and an eight-and-a-half hour day for textile workers. Co-operatives were recognized and the success of the co-operative principle can be judged from the fact that in 1914 12,000,000 peasants were members of 33,000 co-operatives.

There had been a temporary relaxation of the racial and religious persecution of non-Russian peoples during the Revolution. Russians were permitted to leave Orthodoxy without incurring penalties, Russification measures in Poland were relaxed, Finland regained her autonomy, becoming for a time a refuge for political offenders from Russia, and non-Russian peoples obtained generous representation in the first two *Dumas*. But most of these gains were lost when the Tsar reverted to the old Russification policy.

## THE CONSTITUTION

The hastily drafted October Manifesto provided a basis upon which sound constitutional government could have been built, but the task of transforming an autocracy with a largely illiterate population, lacking experience of self-government and established political traditions, into an effective constitutional monarchy required that the framing of the new institutions should be in the hands of convinced parliamentarians. Neither Nicholas nor his wife believed in constitutional government and Witte, President of the Council of Ministers since October, 1905, had accepted the innovation only for tactical reasons. Speaking to Sir Bernard Pares in 1908, Witte remarked, "I have a constitution in my head; but as to my heart . . ." and spat on the floor.[17] Witte's influence and that of his bureaucratic colleagues ensured that the Manifesto would be narrowly interpreted and that liberal opinion would not be consulted. In fairness to Witte it must be admitted that he approached Cadets and Octobrists and attempted to include certain *zemstvo* leaders in the Council of Ministers. He met with no success, however, for no one trusted him and he could not accept liberal demands for a constituent assembly.

Mistrust of constitutional government permeated the structure of the new legislature of two chambers, the State *Duma* and the State Council, and yet another opportunity of rallying the intelligentsia round the Crown was lost. The *Duma* was elected indirectly through electoral colleges based on social classes, the franchise being given to those owning property or paying house tax. Particularly generous representation was given to the peasantry because conservative bureaucrats supposed, erroneously, that they would be a conservative political force. The powers of the *Duma* were, however, strictly limited, and there was no ministerial responsibility to the legislative body, for ministers were appointed by the Tsar and remained in office as long as they possessed his confidence, regardless of any votes of censure passed by the *Duma*. Witte remarked with satisfaction that it was "a constitution, but a conservative constitution without parliamentarism".

## The First *Duma*

Elections for the first *Duma* were held in March, 1906, when the balance of power was turning decisively in favour of the Government. Since the suppression of the Moscow rising the Tsar had regained his confidence and took vigorous action to repress further disorders. He was enabled to do this by the return of soldiers from the Far East, upon whose loyalty he could rely, and particularly by a very large loan secured by Witte from France, which made him independent of the *Duma*. Socialists bitterly denounced France for this and vowed that such loans would not be repaid—a promise kept by Lenin twelve years later. Civil liberties were restricted, and the punitive expeditions sent to restore order in the countryside by Durnovo, the reactionary Minister of the Interior, were encouraged to act without mercy. Floggings and wholesale executions crushed spasmodic peasant resistance, sixty of eighty-seven provinces were placed under martial law, and many officials of liberal views were dismissed.

The elections did not, however, produce the results expected by the Government. The Cadets, who alone had carried on an organized electoral campaign under the slogan "Political freedom and social justice," secured 179 of the 524 seats and were the largest party in the *Duma*. The S.R. decided at its congress in January that, as an armed uprising to secure a constituent assembly still seemed possible, the elections should be boycotted, but the peasants used their votes and ninety-four seats were secured by members of S.R. views known as the Labour group. The Social Democrats did not take part in the elections; the Bolsheviks had opposed participation in the belief that an insurrection was still possible, and the Mensheviks had been undecided. Some eighteen members, mostly Mensheviks, were elected by the workers and eventually approved by the party. The moderate liberals were represented by seventeen Octobrists and fifteen from other groups. There were sixty to seventy members of national groups, including Poles, Ukrainians and Estonians, who favoured autonomy and had radical views. The Government was particularly disappointed at the attitude of the 200 peasant members who voted for the most radical solutions of the land problem.

GOVERNMENT AND *Duma*, 1906

It was inevitable that a government which regarded the present position of the *Duma* as the maximum concession, should clash violently with the Cadets who dominated it and believed that they could transform it into a body with the powers of the British Parliament by constant reiteration of their case. In an address to the throne they demanded parliamentary government, abolition of the State Council, an amnesty, and land reform based on expropriation of large estates. The Tsar refused to accept the address and Goremykin, who had replaced Witte as President of the Council in May, rejected all the demands. In the stormy session which followed the *Duma* called in vain for the resignation of the Government. Surprisingly enough there was, for some weeks, a possibility that a government including Cadets and Octobrists might be formed, a proposal supported by Isvolsky, Minister of Foreign Affairs, and Stolypin (1863–1911), Minister of the Interior. Court circles finally decided the Tsar against it, and when the *Duma* issued a proclamation promising agrarian reform with expropriations as opposed to the less drastic government proposals, the Tsar acted. On Sunday, 9th July, troops occupied the Taurida Palace, meeting place of the *Duma* and the former residence of Catherine the Great's favourite, Potemkin, and in his decree the Tsar declared the *Duma* incapable of discharging its duties and accused it of exceeding its powers.

The Cadet and Labour members replied by meeting at nearby Viborg in Finland a few days later and issuing a manifesto appealing to the people to refuse to pay taxes or serve in the army and to withdraw all savings from banks until the *Duma* was restored, "for no power can resist the united, inflexible will of the people". This appeal to moral force failed. The authors and signatories of the Viborg Manifesto were disfranchised, tried, and sentenced to three months imprisonment. Lacking organization in the country, the Cadets failed to prepare the public for this manifesto and, although public opinion, as the elections indicated, was left wing in sympathy, the revolutionary enthusiasm of the previous autumn had evaporated.

## THE OPPOSITION BROKEN

The Government was taking strong action against a recrudescence of disorders in the countryside in the spring and summer of 1906, for which the S.R. was partly responsible and which resulted in the murder of 1,600 officials. In August terrorists blew up the summer residence of Peter Stolypin, killing thirty-two people and wounding twenty-two, including his son and daughter. Stolypin quickly established his reputation as a strong man, declaring a state of emergency which lasted until the spring of 1907. Military courts, "Stolypin's neckties" as they were called, were established to try and execute within forty-eight hours those found guilty of violence and brigandage. Between September, 1906 and April, 1907 hundreds of people were sentenced by these courts, particularly in the Baltic provinces, and many more shot without trial. Civil liberties were suspended with the full approval of the Tsar and house searches, arrests, and thousands of deportations to Siberia without court warrants became the order of the day. Even Witte wrote his memoirs abroad, fearing examination of his correspondence in Russia.

NEW ELECTIONS

Despite reactionary suggestions that the *Duma* be abolished the Tsar, to his credit, ordered elections to the second *Duma* in February, 1907. He was strongly supported in this by Stolypin, now Prime Minister, who, despite his ruthless but necessary suppression of disorders, declared that he was "fighting on two fronts—against revolution but for reform" and wished Russians to realize that "we have parted company for ever with the old police order of things". The Government showed considerable interest in the elections, giving financial support to the Union of Russian People and other Right-wing groups through the funds of the Ministry of the Interior. Civil servants were forbidden to join opposition parties, several groups of electors were disfranchised by the courts, election meetings of Cadets were broken up by the police and their clubs closed.

The Cadets suffered from Government interference and the disfranchisement of the Viborg signatories, on the one hand, and from denunciations by Social Democrats and the S.R. on the other. The latter parties decided, significantly, to take part in the elections because the marked decline in strikes and peasant disorders in the closing months of 1906 made them abandon hope of a popular rising. Only 92 Cadets were returned, but the extremes had been strengthened. On the Right wing Octobrists and moderate conservatives secured 32 seats and extreme conservatives, with police assistance,

22 seats. On the Left wing were 65 Social Democrats, 34 S.R. members, and 101 from the Labour group. The remaining 160 members belonged mostly to national groups, Poles, Moslems, or Cossacks. It was an important election for, as the franchise was still fairly wide and representative, the results indicated that opinion was moving from the moderate to the more revolutionary parties in protest against the dissolution of the first *Duma*. The Government could rely upon little more than ninety votes in the assembly.

## THE SECOND *Duma*

It was hardly surprising that the Second *Duma* soon followed the first into oblivion. There were frequent clashes between the Government and the opposition who demanded the abolition of field courts martial and rejected Stolypin's agrarian legislation as inadequate. The Cadets, lacking able leaders, tried to avoid dissolution but there were provocative attacks from the extreme Right who were trying to discredit the *Duma* as an institution, and revolutionary outbursts from the Left wing whose extremists, especially the Bolsheviks, wished to prove that the people's interests could be served only by an insurrection and not through the *Duma*. The Tsar's sympathy for extremist parties on the Right wing was growing and, infuriated by an S.R. remark that Russian armies only won victories when fighting the Russian people, he encouraged Stolypin to dissolve the *Duma*. Curiously enough, Stolypin had believed an agreement possible, and on the day before had discussed with Cadet members ways of avoiding dissolution, but the discovery of an alleged plot to assassinate the Tsar led him to ask that the *Duma* should waive the immunity of the Social Democrat members said to be involved, in order to facilitate their arrest. While the *Duma* temporized, Stolypin acted. The members returning the following day found a dissolution order affixed to the gates of the Taurida Palace.

## A NEW ELECTORAL LAW

The Government was determined to secure the election of a *Duma* subservient to its wishes and altered the electoral law, violating thereby the Tsar's promise that constitutional amendments required the *Duma's* consent. The framework of indirect election was retained but, by reducing the number of members elected by the peasants, workers, and non-Russian peoples, and increasing considerably the number elected by the larger landowners, the composition of the electoral colleges was altered decisively in favour of landed interests. The alliance between the Crown and the landed nobility had been renewed because the radicalism of peasant members had destroyed the bureaucratic theory of the innate conservatism of the peasantry. The number of members was reduced to 442 and the representation altered so that one member was elected by 230 landowners, 60,000 peasants, or 125,000 workers. The people of Central Asia were deprived of all representation, the Polish seats were reduced from thirty-six to fourteen and in border districts the Russian population was favoured. The law amounted to a *coup d'état* and was applauded by the Right wing extremists as "Russian in spirit". It is significant that on the day he dissolved the *Duma* the Tsar sent a telegram to the Union of Russian People approving their activities and promising them support.

## THE THIRD *Duma*

The Electoral Law served its purpose. The Third *Duma*, which lasted until 1912, was dominated by conservatives. The Octobrists, many of whom held high official positions, secured 154 seats and other Right-wing parties 127 seats. The Cadets secured only 54 seats and the Social Democrats a mere 17, while national groups were greatly reduced in size. The conservative character of the *Duma* was emphasized even more in the Fourth and last *Duma* between 1912 and 1917, in which Right-wing parties secured 185 seats, including 88 nationalists, a group sponsored by Stolypin in the Third *Duma*. The Octobrists declined to 97, the Cadets secured 58 seats, and the Social Democrats 14: the S.R. boycotted the elections and had no representation in either *Duma*.

## CONSTITUTIONAL DEVELOPMENT 1907–14

Although by the summer of 1907 the revolutionary movement had been defeated, as the continued decline in the number of strikes and agrarian disturbances proved, and the Tsar had secured a *Duma* to his liking, it is arguable that the period between 1907 and 1914 was most important for constitutional development. The Octobrists under the able leadership of Alexander Guchkov (1861-1936), grandson of a serf and son of a Moscow merchant, and of Nicholas Homyakov, were prepared to use the limited powers of the *Duma* to engage in an intelligent and informed, if restrained, criticism of government legislation, rather than raise questions certain to lead to deadlock and dissolution. By using their power of annual examination of the budget and working through commissions set up on various aspects of the administration, the *Duma* was able to influence ministerial policy. Ministers often came in person to give information to these commissions and listened to their informed criticism in order to secure acceptance of their measures by the *Duma*. Stolypin and Kokovtsev, the Minister of Finance, were especially ready to co-operate with enlightened conservatives who placed their administrative ability at the disposal of the State. The Tsar had these *Dumas* in mind when he remarked in 1912 that, "The *Duma* tried to start too fast, but now it is slower and better."[18] This phase in constitutional development is often dull, but always essential if the techniques of constitutional government and the art of political compromise are to be acquired.

## ORDER RESTORED

To a certain extent the *Duma*'s change of attitude was a reflection of the desire for order and "normalcy" in Russia. The dissolution of the Second *Duma* and the electoral law had met with only slight resistance and by the autumn of 1907 agrarian disorders had come almost completely to an end. A decline in the strength of revolutionary parties characterized the period between 1907 and 1912. The terrorist groups had been broken up in 1907 and the S.R. suffered an eclipse. The Social Democrats broke up into unco-ordinated groups torn by inner conflicts, depleted in numbers by mass arrests, and enjoying little support from the workers. Trotsky and Lenin left Russia in December, 1907, admitting that a revolutionary situation no longer existed. Neither returned until 1917. By the spring of 1908 nearly all the revolutionary leaders were in prison or in exile. The traditional liberal stronghold, the *zemstvos*, declined in importance and passed under conservative control. Only on the extreme Right was there much political activity. The Union of Russian People was regarded by the Tsar as "the mainstay of the throne" and as "a standard bearer of legality and order", although its criminal activity was notorious; Dubrovin and his associates murdered two Cadet members in 1906 and 1907 and twice attempted Witte's life, but remained unpunished.

## AGRARIAN REFORM

One of the most important measures adopted by the Government in this period was the agrarian reform of November, 1906, completed by further laws in 1910, 1911, and 1912. Before the 1905 Revolution a growing body of official opinion was opposed to the preservation of the commune, basis of the 1861 reform. Witte, for example, once a firm defender of it had become its opponent in the eighteen-nineties. The abundant evidence of the radical temper of the peasantry during the Revolution finally swept away the conservative distaste for change. Far from being the bulwark of order in the countryside, it seemed to be, as the *Narodniki* had maintained, a potential basis of socialism.

The reform of 1906 is associated with Stolypin who, although a determined opponent of Revolution, was as a landowner fully aware of the need for change. Firmly opposed to land expropriations, as demanded by the Second *Duma*, he nevertheless showed exceptional, almost revolutionary, boldness in his treatment of the agrarian problem. "The Government," he said, "has placed its wager not on the needy and the drunken, but on the sturdy and the strong—on the strong individual proprietor who is called upon to play a part in the reconstruction of our Tsardom on strong monarchical foundations."[19] He hoped that a landowning peasantry would become a conservative force, respecting property rights and preserving the régime. The idea, as an eminent authority has expressed it, was not to give the peasants land but to teach them not to try to take it.[20]

Stolypin aimed at the abolition of communal land tenure, enclosure of scattered strips into compact holdings and the establishment of independent owner farmers living outside the commune. To achieve this all the remaining legal disabilities

on the peasant were removed, the powers of the commune over
him were curtailed and the land captains lost their jurisdiction.
The heart of the reform was the provision made for the peasant
to withdraw from the commune and obtain permanent title
to his land. Liberalization of the financial procedure of the
Peasant's Bank was intended to assist the peasant in buying
more land to consolidate his holdings.

## EFFECTS OF THE REFORMS

It is difficult to assess accurately the effect of Stolypin's
reforms. The formidable task of transforming thirteen to
fourteen million householders into small owners required many
years to effect and within a decade the Tsarist régime had been
swept away. The reforms were the continuation of a process
already under way in the communes, where a third of the land
was owned by ten per cent of the population. The destruction
of the commune which had impeded technical progress was
ultimately in the interests of all social groups, although it
brought immediate hardship to the poorer peasants. No doubt
the reform resulted in some slight improvement in agrarian
conditions before 1914, as the increase in acreage under
cultivation and the increased yield of certain crops suggested.
The efficiency of Russian agriculture improved particularly
on the big estates in the south and on many peasant holdings,
especially in Northern Caucasia, where a class of prosperous
small farmers, the *kulaks*, emerged. The *kulaks*, however,
accounted for only fifteen per cent of the rural population and
for the vast majority, who remained revolutionary in spirit,
the reforms meant little. The growing population, general
technical backwardness, and prevalence of the three-year crop
cycle made the peasants' demand for more land increasingly
acute with the passage of time. It is true that the number of
families owning land increased from 3,000,000 before the
reforms to 7,000,000 by 1915, half the total households,
but ninety per cent of these failed to consolidate their holdings
or remove themselves completely from the communal economy
after securing the title deeds to their land. Most consolidation
occurred in South Russia where wheat cultivation for export
was extensive, but farther north fewer peasants left the
commune; many sold their holdings, either because they were

too small to be economic or because the wages as hired labourers proved more attractive. In 1917 the trends encouraged by Stolypin were reversed; when the peasant seized the land he divided it up into strips, a testimony to the strength of the egalitarian tradition of the commune. Under the "New Economic Programme" in the 'twenties the consolidation of holdings was encouraged in order to raise production, but the pattern was radically modified by the agrarian revolution of 1929-30, which introduced collectivization and produced the present-day collective and State farms.

## OTHER ASPECTS OF THE *Duma's* Work

The Third *Duma* assisted greatly in the implementation of Stolypin's reforms. In other fields the work of this, and the succeeding *Duma*, was important. Progress was made in elementary education, especially under the best *zemstvos*, and a law of 1908 provided for the gradual enforcement by 1922 of compulsory free education for all children between eight and eleven. The advances were substantial, but in 1914 only half the children in this age group were attending school. Illiteracy was one of the most pressing problems bequeathed to subsequent régimes. Good work was achieved in the reorganization of the finances with the full co-operation of Kokovtsev. The *Dumas* showed particular interest in military affairs. Guchkov's revelations of military and naval incompetence during the War of 1905 aroused considerable interest and through the Commission of Imperial Defence much was done to reform and reorganize the army. It was, for example, due largely to the *Duma* that Russia possessed at least some machine-guns in 1914. In this field the *Duma* was eager not only to accept but to increase the estimates, given assurances that they would be spent wisely.

## WEAKNESSES OF RUSSIAN SOCIETY

By 1914 Russia was, as Sir Bernard Pares has expressed it, drifting imperceptibly towards greater liberty. The *Duma* was establishing itself as an indispensable institution for the ventilation of grievances, new classes were growing up, the barriers between town and country were breaking down, and more education and civil liberty was narrowing the gap between the

w

educated minority and the majority of the people. Kokovtsev believed, with the characteristic over-optimism of the bureaucrat, that, given ten years of sensible government, Russia would have been at the summit of her prosperity.[21] There were, however, some serious weaknesses in Russian society. The balanced social structure, characteristic of West European countries, where society and the State machine are interlocked at all levels, was absent in Russia. No group, except perhaps the bureaucracy, felt any sense of responsibility towards a State machine imposed from above. Particularly after 1912 the Government failed to give a positive lead to the people, but drifted aimlessly along while the bureaucracy clung to its traditional conservatism. Some part of the responsibility for this inertia rests with the Tsar, who failed to see the need for further political change to correspond with the changing social and economic pattern.

## THE TSAR AND TSARITSA

Nicholas was a charming and intelligent landowner, a conscientious worker and sincerely religious, but narrow in his views and lacking any profound understanding of the affairs of State. He was deeply convinced that he must not allow his autocratic powers to be impaired and was strengthened in this belief by his wife, the Tsaritsa, a former German princess and grand-daughter of Queen Victoria. Basically the Tsar was a weak character lacking the iron will and determination of Alexander III. He was easily influenced, and neither he nor his wife was a good judge of character. They failed to appreciate the value of good ministers and did not consistently follow their advice. Nicholas allowed court reactionaries to prejudice him against Stolypin on the grounds that as Prime Minister he was becoming too powerful a figure. It was also characteristic of Nicholas that when Stolypin was assassinated in 1911 he did not disturb his arrangements to attend the funeral. "He is gone," remarked the Tsaritsa coldly, "let us hear no more of him."[22] Appointments to high office after Stolypin's death were generally ill-made. Kokovtsev, the new Prime Minister, for example, was an able financier aware of the need for change, but lacking in the drive and vigour needed to deal with growing reactionary influences in the Council of Ministers. Maklakov, the new Minister of the Interior, had as his only qualification the fact that, as provincial governor, he had once entertained the Tsar's children by imitating a panther.

## RASPUTIN

Most serious of all was the ascendancy which an illiterate Siberian peasant, Gregory Rasputin, exerted over the Imperial couple—and by implication over the State machine—by 1911. The Tsar and Tsaritsa were first introduced to Rasputin in 1905 and, because he undoubtedly possessed a strange power to cure their young son and heir, Alexis, of haemophilia, he became a firm favourite with them. They opposed all criticism of Rasputin and of his scandalous conduct in private life. Rasputin unfortunately encouraged the Tsar to believe that nothing but his will mattered, and confirmed the growing reaction in his attitude. Thus in 1912 the Tsar forbade the Press to mention Rasputin, and by 1914 a recommendation by "our friend" was sufficient to secure promotion. In this way the aged and incompetent Goremykin became Prime Minister when Kokovtsev, a critic of Rasputin, was suddenly dismissed in 1914. It is not without significance that Nicholas toyed with the idea of reducing the powers of the *Duma* at a meeting of his ministers held in July, 1914.

## ECONOMIC PROSPERITY

A wave of prosperity, the so-called "Stolypin Boom", characterized the Russian economy between 1908 and 1914. Production doubled between 1905 and 1914 and foreign capital played an increasingly important rôle in industrial expansion attracted by the growing stability of Russia and the publicity given to finance by *Duma* debates. By 1914 1,200,000,000 roubles were invested in Russian industry, thirty-two per cent from France, twenty-five per cent from Britain, and five per cent from America. One third of the total share capital in Russia was foreign, over half invested in the metallurgical and mining industries. But it was a basically unbalanced economy since only export markets flourished. Home consumption remained low, and the industrial combinations which grew up in this period kept internal prices high and maintained pressure for high tariffs to exclude cheap foreign imports. It was the rich owner in the Black Earth lands and not the peasant who benefited from the massive grain exports which enabled Russian industry to expand.

Between 1907 and 1912 strikes had declined in number because the workers had tired of revolutionary slogans and were concentrating on practical issues. Unions were now legal, but severely restricted in their activities, and strikes remained illegal. Unionism was a weak force in Russia, partly because of these restrictions, and partly because the peasant background of the workers made organization difficult. The number of unions declined, reaching a very low ebb in 1909–10.

## Renewed Industrial Unrest

In 1912, however, there was a revival of industrial unrest, which continued into the summer of 1914, and which began with the Lena goldfield strike in April, 1912, when the police fired without warning on the strikers, killing and wounding over one hundred. The failure of the Government to ameliorate working conditions gave an impetus to the labour revival, for measures such as the Accidents Insurance Act of 1912 were too limited to satisfy the workers. The number of strikes rose from 200 in 1910, affecting 47,000 workers, to 4,000, affecting 1,500,000 workers in the first half of 1914. When Poincaré visited St. Petersburg in July barricades were going up in the workers' quarters, the Social Democrats (especially the Bolsheviks) were again active, the *Duma* was sharply critical of the Government, and the Octobrist leader Guchkov declared that there had never been a time when Russia was so deeply permeated by the revolutionary spirit. The war saved the régime, for a wave of patriotism swept through the country. When the Tsar stood on a balcony of the Winter Palace on 2nd August and declared, in the words of Alexander I in 1812, that he would not make peace until the last foreign soldier had left Russian soil, the great crowds knelt down and sang "God save the Tsar" in the square where, on Red Sunday nine years before, their brothers had been shot down by the Tsar's soldiers. In the *Duma*, when the war credits were voted, only the Labour group and the Social Democrats abstained, and even they agreed to co-operate in what they considered a defensive war. It was left to the Bolsheviks to urge that the workers should turn the imperialist war into a civil war to overturn the régime.

## FOREIGN POLICY, 1905–14

Russian foreign policy has been described in the chapter on international affairs. Reference must, however, be made to the growth of a new nationalism in the decade before 1914 when Russia, after her defeat in Asia, turned once more to her traditional sphere of influence in the Balkans.

As the *Duma* established itself after 1907 the members showed increasing interest in foreign affairs—a field reserved to the Tsar—and were encouraged by the fact that the support of conservative opinion in the Third and Fourth *Dumas* was welcome to the Government; Sazonov, appointed Foreign Minister in 1910, made frequent speeches on foreign policy in the *Duma*. At first the Neoslav ideology enjoyed a certain popularity. It emphasized the need for friendship among all Slavs, insisted on the cessation of anti-Polish and anti-Jewish measures to facilitate a reconciliation with these peoples, and sought French and British support against Austria-Hungary and Germany, the enemies of the Slavs. Both Stolypin and Isvolsky were friends of Britain and the Anglo-Russian agreement of 1907 was applauded by the Neoslavs. They also held a series of conferences in 1908, 1909, and 1910, emphasizing the cultural and economic ties between Slav peoples and attracting some Polish and Czech support.

## RENEWAL OF PANSLAVISM

By 1910 this Neoslavism was superseded by a revival of the narrow Panslavism of the eighteen-seventies in the form of a Russian imperialism which favoured the Serbs and Bulgars as instruments for expansion in the Balkans, and which led to a renewed persecution of non-Russian peoples in the Russian Empire.

Stolypin's concept of "Great Russia" was easily reconcilable with the imperialist spirit shared by conservatives such as Rodzianko, president of the *Duma*, and by radical liberals such as Struve who urged Stolypin, in 1909, to make Russia a great power and defend the Slav cause. As an admirer of British colonial administration, Stolypin opposed the federal tendencies of non-Russian peoples, and in the Electoral Law of 1907 drastically reduced their representation in the *Duma*. In 1910 he considerably cut the powers of the Finnish Diet, and by 1914 Russification had proceeded so far that the Finns were ripe for revolt. The Ukrainians and Jews were subjected to further restrictions and in 1911 Stolypin's municipal government bill for western Poland secured the predominance of Russian minorities in these bodies, and ordered the exclusive use of Russian in them. The renewal of the Russification policy caused a deterioration in relations between the non-Russian and Russian peoples, preparing the way for the separatist movements in 1918.

## THE BALKANS AND THE COMING OF WAR

In the Balkans the conflict between Austria-Hungary and Russia was the main feature after 1908. The imperialist thesis of inevitable conflict between Slav and Teuton was strengthened enormously by the Bosnian Crisis, for there was great resentment at the German ultimatum and a growing feeling that Germany would challenge Russia in the future. For this reason the *Duma* showed great interest in Russian rearmament. Court circles and Right-wing extremists continued to defend the traditional policy of an understanding with Germany, but the Tsar and his wife were pro-English and Sazonov was eager to strengthen ties with Britain. The Balkan Wars in 1912–13 aroused great interest in Russia; the *Duma* applauded the Bulgarian victories, Rodzianko urged the Tsar to seize the Straits and raise the Government's prestige by a popular war and the nationalist Press bitterly denounced Sazonov's failure to support the Slavs. By 1913 many Russians believed a conflict inevitable, and when Kokovtsev warned the Tsar of this, after the Liman von Sanders affair in 1914, he said, looking out over the Black Sea, "In all the will of God".[23] The Tsar strove hard to avoid a conflict during the Sarajevo Crisis, but the German declaration that the dispute concerned only Austria-Hungary and Serbia raised an issue of prestige which Russia could not ignore. The enemy, commented Sazonov, "were determined to increase their power by enslaving our natural allies in the Balkans, destroying our influence there and reducing Russia to a pitiful dependence upon the arbitrary will of the Central Powers".[24] With a heavy heart the Tsar agreed and ordered general mobilization which, as described elsewhere, set up a chain-reaction ending with the outbreak of a general war.

## " . . . THE END OF RUSSIA AND YOURSELVES . . ."

The war, unlike that of 1904, was popular with many Russians, but there were observers who recognized the gravity of the situation. Witte pointed out to Paléologue, French ambassador in St. Petersburg, that Russia had territory enough at home to develop without seeking more. The closure of her markets would be fatal and even if she won, the end of German domination meant the proclamation of republics in central Europe and, by implication, the end of Tsardom. "I prefer to remain silent," he said, "as to what we may expect on the hypothesis of our defeat . . . my practical conclusion is that we must liquidate this stupid adventure as soon as possible."[25] Rasputin, who had counselled against war in 1909 and 1912 on the grounds that the Balkans were not worth fighting about, was equally alarmed. In a prophetic telegram to the Tsar he warned, "Let Papa not plan war, for with war will come the end of Russia and yourselves, and you will lose to the last man."[26] Within four years the grim prophecy was fulfilled, almost to the letter.

### REFERENCES

The following standard works have been used extensively:
B. Pares, *History of Russia*; B. H. Sumner, *Survey of Russian History*; H. Seton-Watson, *The Decline of Imperial Russia, 1855–1914*; M. Florinsky, *Russia: A History and an Interpretation*, Vol. II; and a stimulating work by J. Maynard, *Russia in Flux*.

1. Quoted in *Russia: A History and an Interpretation*, p. 777.
2. Quoted in *Survey of Russian History*, p. 321.
3. Turgenev: *Virgin Soil*, Vol. I, chapter IV.
4. Quoted in *Russia in Flux*, p. 183.
5. Quoted in *The Decline of Imperial Russia*, p. 61.
6. Quoted in D. Footman, *Red Prelude: A life of A. I. Zhelyabov* p. 87.

7. Rambaud: *Histoire de Russie*, p. 756.
8. Quoted in B. H. Sumner: *Russia and the Balkans, 1870–1880*, pp. 575–76.
9. Quoted in *The Decline of Imperial Russia*, p. 213.
10. Quoted in *Survey of Russian History*, p. 304.
11. B. Pares: *My Russian Memoirs*, p. 59.
12. Quoted in G. T. Robinson: *Rural Russia under the Old Régime* p. 144.
13. Quoted in *Survey of Russian History*, p. 133.
14. *My Russian Memoirs*, p. 90.
15. Quoted in *Rural Russia*, p. 174.
16. B. Pares: *The Fall of the Russian Monarchy*, p. 91.
17. *My Russian Memoirs*, p. 86.
18. ibid., p. 236.
19. Quoted in *Rural Russia*, p. 194.
20. ibid., p. 189.
21. *Out of My Past: Memoirs of Count Kokovtsov* (sic), p. 388.
22. *Russia in Flux*, p. 92.
23. *The Fall of the Russian Monarchy*, p. 179.
24. ibid., p. 125.
25. M. Paléologue: *An Ambassador's Memoirs*, Vol. I, pp. 122–23.
26. *The Fall of the Russian Monarchy*, p. 188.

# XVI

# THE UNITED STATES:

## From Civil War to World War

### (1) The Background: a Survey of Fifty Years

THE dramatic and moving scene in Appomattox Court House on 9th April, 1865, when Lee surrendered to Grant, and the murder in Washington only five days later of President Abraham Lincoln, mark a watershed in American history. The surrender of Lee's remnant of 9,000 Confederate soldiers to Grant's powerful Union army of 118,000 was the close of a struggle decisive for America's future; the death of Lincoln an event of sinister significance for the immediate years of peace and reconstruction. Appomattox has passed into legend as one of those moments of high drama in the history of a nation which simplify complex issues and come to embody a host of national ideals and aspirations, giving them a form and a name which succeeding generations even of the simplest can recall with pride and satisfaction. It was the vindication of the United Republic: the Civil War which there ended its tragic course saw the rebirth of a nation and of the ideals for which it stood—"a new birth of freedom" in the proud phrase used by Lincoln at Gettysburg in 1863. The simple faith expressed by the characters in W. D. Howells's novel *A Hazard of New Fortunes* (1890) in the Bunker Hill of 1775 and the Appomattox of 1865 as "the beginning and end of all possible progress in human rights" lies at the bottom of much that foreigners find difficult to understand in the American outlook. These were among the political myths that cemented the rapidly growing society of the New World.

### The Civil War

The Civil War has well been called the Second American Revolution[1], the harsh, abrupt break which divided the United States as originally conceived from the bustling, vigorous

w*                             699

giant of the industrial era. Seen in historical perspective it is a watershed more startling, more dramatic and still more significant than the change that took place in Great Britain in the following decade. Before 1860, though mighty forces were already stirring, the country largely preserved the pattern laid down in the original Federal Republic, with the agricultural interests, and especially "King Cotton", dominating the scene, and "States' rights" jealously guarded. The war, and the disastrous collapse of the South, established the primacy of the urban and industrialized North-East, which was rapidly to stamp the whole continent with its pattern, and replaced the earlier decentralization with a system which, while still far from unitary, recognized the primacy of the Federal Government. The generation that grew up after the war saw such changes that by 1900, in the words of a close and penetrating observer, "the world of 1860 stood already on a distant horizon somewhere on the same plane with the republic of Brutus and Cato, while schoolboys read of Abraham Lincoln as they did of Julius Caesar". While Queen Victoria still lived, indeed, Lincoln had already become an heroic memory, and the bitter struggle which he had carried through to victory had faded to little more than the occasion for jubilant reunions and political wire-pulling on behalf of "veteran" pensioners. Yet, although many of its scars healed quickly, the struggle had been a bitter one. In all, the Federal States, with their 22,000,000 population, had called-up between 1861 and 1865, for varying periods of service, nearly 3,000,000 men, of whom some 360,000 had died, 110,000 in action. The dissident Confederates, with 9,000,000 of people, had mobilized some 1,300,000 and lost more than a quarter of a million, 75,000 of them in battle. The direct cost of the war, apart from the desolation of the South, had amounted to six billion dollars; its total cost has been estimated at some twenty billion. It had been, in all respects, one of the costliest and most fiercely fought contests in history.

## THE AFTERMATH OF THE WAR: "RECONSTRUCTION"

As to its main cause the war had been decisive; the Union had been preserved. But for that fact the triumphant expansion of the years that followed would hardly have been possible, or would have come only slowly and disjointedly, and probably with outbreaks of renewed strife. Yet the high idealism of the war years, expressed for the North in simple, imperishable language by Lincoln as the inspired mouthpiece of all that was finest in its cause, rapidly disappeared with his passing from the scene, to be replaced by the bitterness and narrowness of "Reconstruction", the sharp practices of industrial expansion and the crudities of corrupt politics. In the severe judgment of two leading American historians, "the material problems of the war could be solved and the material devastation repaired; the moral devastation was never wholly repaired". The victory was complete, and the cause of the South was stamped with the brand of failure and moral obloquy. The success of the North seemed, in the simple conditions of American life, a triumph of Right and Justice, and encouraged the "holier than thou" attitude so characteristic of political immaturity. The great moral issue of slavery underlay the conflict, but, as Lincoln constantly insisted, the war was waged by the North for the preservation of the Union, not for the abolition of slavery. Nevertheless, much of the driving-force that sustained the Union in the grim years of war came from religious and moral opposition to slavery. Lincoln expressed it with characteristic mildness in his second Inaugural, delivered only a few weeks before his assassination: "it may seem strange that any men should dare to ask a just God's assistance in wringing the bread from the sweat of another man's face, but let us judge not that we be not judged".

There were few, however, who could rise to these heights of charitableness. Feelings had been deeply stirred by the war and it took time for passions to cool. More than this, there were substantial political reasons for keeping hatred alive. The South was mainly Democrat in its party allegiance, the North largely, though by no means wholly, Republican, and in the critical election of 1860 more votes had been cast against the Republicans than for them. American parties are fortuitous combinations of varied interests, not easily definable or recognizable in terms of British party differences. It was an obvious political gambit after 1865 to denounce the Democrats as the party of treason, and for many years Republicans were urged to "vote as they shot" and, later, "the way their fathers shot". Lincoln had closed his second Inaugural on a note of reconciliation, appealing, in well-known words, for "malice towards none . . . charity for all" in order to achieve "a just and lasting peace". Grant, the victorious Commander-in-Chief of the Union forces, found, soon after the war ended, that the South was no less willing to forget the unhappy past and to work for peace and reconciliation. The majority of men there, he told Andrew Johnson, Lincoln's successor as President, had already accepted the verdict of the war on slavery and states' rights as "settled for ever by the highest tribunal—arms—that man can resort to". Yet reconciliation was not for long achieved, and unhappy memories remained to embitter American politics. Whether, in the face of all the opposition to his often forceful enlargement of the President's influence, Lincoln could have stemmed the desire for revenge, it is impossible to say. There were not a few who were relieved at the removal of his firm, just hand. But, with Lincoln gone, the South, already desolated by the war, was subjected to the blunders and malice of "Reconstruction", and Johnson, who sought to stay the process, was impeached for his pains. The result was an enduring division in American life, which is felt to this day.

The South had fought, less to protect the institution of slavery, than to resist what were felt to be Northern encroachments upon the preservation and development of Southern ways of life. It was not their self-proclaimed humanity that inspired the leaders of the North, declared the Confederate President, Jefferson Davis: "it is that you may have a majority in the Congress of the United States and convert the government into an empire of northern aggrandizement". Economic and political forces were, in fact, working in this direction, and the collapse of the economic supremacy of the old planter aristocracy may, therefore, be styled, as some historians have argued, America's first, rather than her second, revolution. Yet, however great the destructiveness of the war, more might have been done to revive the defeated South and to bring it back on equal terms within the circle of the Federal Union, as Lincoln had planned. In the post-war reaction the triumph lay with the worst and bitterest elements of the North, which were resolved to exclude the Southern States for as long as possible, in order to secure the political dominance of the North and the Republican Party. Inevitably this attitude opened the way to political opportunism and corruption, aggravated by the war profits which created the crude plutocracy of the "Gilded Age" that was to follow. The devotion to principle which the war had inspired, and which Lincoln had sustained, had, as in most wars, its less savoury counterpart. The reaction and disillusionment that followed, the intrigues of the lesser men who traded on victory and on the opportunities for personal enrichment provided by the rapid economic development of the country in the flush of a reborn confidence in the American future, all conspired to put the game for a time into the hands of the Goulds and Fisks and other caterpillars of the commonwealth, and left a stigma of disgrace even on the figure of Grant, who, able and inspired as he showed himself in war, appeared as one of the most pathetic figures in American history during his two terms as President, from 1869 to 1877.

## THE CONDITIONS OF DEVELOPMENT

The very triumph of the principles for which the war had been fought, coupled with the diversion afterwards of so much energy into the development of the West, left the more ruthless unrestrained. The South was the first to feel their unhappy influence, but the rest of America was to experience it in turn. Economic development, and the vast wealth it brought, was to set the pace, and politics to come dangerously near to submitting to economic control. There were many reasons for this, first among them the very political and social conditions of North America and the wealth of resources on, and in, its soil. The United States were, above all else, an egalitarian Republic, with no limit to the positions its citizens could hope to achieve, and no restraints in social tradition or class structure to serve as a check. Even so slight an aristocracy of blood and wealth as had existed in the South had had its power broken in the Civil War. The "unalienable Rights" to "Life, Liberty and the pursuit of Happiness", so confidently proclaimed in the Declaration of Independence of 1776, and the concomitant limitation of the powers of government in the Constitution of 1787, opened the way to an individualism that was to attain monstrous proportions of ruggedness. And if social and political restraints were lacking, the situation was aggravated by the very conception of the Republic as a federation of States, each jealous of the powers of the Federal Government, each with the recognized right to run its affairs in its own way. From the eighteenth century, indeed, the United States inherited, and has largely carried forward into our own day, a suspicion of government that was derived partly from contractual theories of the origins of the State, partly from resentment at the practice of British rule. Restraint not only of personal liberty but of the individual enterprise that was presumably concerned with the pursuit of happiness was therefore anathema, and the Fourteenth Amendment to the Constitution, passed in 1868, which forbade any State to "deprive any person of life, liberty, or property, without due process of law", was to become for many years the bulwark of unrestrained free enterprise.

## THE PACE OF DEVELOPMENT

Restraint was in any case unthinkable if America's vast spaces and wealth of resources were to be adequately developed. It was a far greater, far more self-conscious Republic that emerged from the Civil War, and the war itself had served as a forcing-ground of development. Industry had had to be rapidly expanded to meet military needs, and within the decade 1859–1869 the number of industrial establishments rose by eighty per cent, that of workers by half, while industrial output came little short of being doubled. As W. D. Howells's paint manufacturer and quondam Union Colonel, Silas Lapham, was made to complain regretfully in 1875, he had found on returning from the war that he had come back to another world:

> the day of small things was past, and I don't suppose it will ever come again in this country.[2]

## TARIFFS AND DEVELOPMENT

The expansion took place behind a tariff barrier that marked a revolution in American economic policy and firmly set the country on the path of high protection. Tariffs had always been the principal source of federal revenue and the Republicans were determined to raise them, both to increase revenue and to protect industry. Indeed, a fundamental difference of opinion over tariff policy had been a contributory

factor in the origins of the Civil War, for the South, with its
dependence on exports, was by tradition and interest a low-
tariff area. The new policy began after the Secession with the
Morrill Tariff of 1861, but rates were doubled by 1864 to
protect the new industries which had been stimulated by the
war. Henceforth America was highly protectionist, Republicans
and Democrats differing only, though considerably, as to the
degree of protection required. From 1861 the way was clear
to the Republican Tariff Acts of 1890 (McKinley), 1897
(Dingley), 1922 (Fordney-McCumber) and 1930 (Hawley-
Smoot): a system that began as Protection soon became,
through the pressure of special interests, the stay of monopoly,
and eventually a threat to international economic stability.
Behind the tariff wall that grew higher from 1861 industry
developed rapidly. By 1899 the three billion dollars of
industrial output of 1869 had become thirteen billion and the
number of workers had risen from two million to more than
five million. It was the natural resources of the country,
however, that made this expansion possible. The land was
filled, and its wealth exploited. The original Thirteen States
had by the eve of the Civil War increased to thirty-four. Thirty
years later, in 1890, they numbered forty-four, and by 1912
the last four of the continental land mass had been added.
Population during the same period rose from thirty-one to
ninety-two million, immigration accounting for no less than
twenty-three million.

## RESOURCES AND DEVELOPMENT:
## (1) IRON AND COAL

Meanwhile the earth yielded up its treasures. The output
of both coal and iron ore increased twentyfold between 1870
and 1913, and as early as the 'eighties American steel production surpassed that of Britain, while within less than twenty
years it was greater than the total for Britain and Germany
combined. By 1913 it had attained thirty-one million tons
against a German total of seventeen million and a British of
seven million. This striking advance was largely made possible
by the richness of the ore resources of the Lake Superior
region, especially the easily-worked ores of the Mesabi Range,
together with the vastness of the coal reserves of the

Appalachians. These were brought together by a number of able and ruthless organizers, outstanding among them the Scottish immigrant Andrew Carnegie (1835–1919), who was eventually to sell his holdings in 1901 for $225,000,000. By this time mechanical handling of the rich resources had brought the American output of ore per worker to double the British and German figures.

## (2) OIL

The rise of oil, one of the most significant of all American products, was still more striking. Its discovery dates only from 1859, but by 1865 2,500,000 barrels were being produced, and $16,000,000 worth exported: "a commodity that had been a curiosity when Lincoln was nominated had become a necessity of civilization before he was murdered".[3] Taking into account all its consequences and implications it was the most momentous economic development of the century, a striking and characteristic expression of the resources and enterprise of the expanding Republic. "I have seen America spread out fr'm th' Atlantic to th' Pacific", said F. P. Dunne's creation, the immortal "Mr. Dooley", in 1897, "with a branch office iv the Standard Ile Company in ivry hamlet",[4] and in his accustomed cheerfully cynical way thereby set both developments in perspective. Within a few years of the completion in 1869 of the transcontinental railway, indeed, Rockefeller's Standard Oil Company, founded in the following year, had become literally a household word throughout not only America but the whole world. Before the end of the century oil production had reached 100,000,000 barrels and exports $60,000,000, while still greater days lay ahead with the coming of the internal-combustion engine, whose insatiable demands caused production to be multiplied fivefold by 1917.

## (3) ELECTRICITY

Another, and no less significant, source of light and power, in which America's needs and opportunities, rather than her resources, made her a pioneer, was that of electricity. The last quarter of the century saw the rise of a new industry, associated with the experimental and developmental work of such men as Thomas Edison, Charles Brush, Elihu Thomson and Edwin

Houston, Edward Weston and George Westinghouse, whose names, like Rockefeller's, were to become household words throughout the world. The pioneer arc lights were rapidly replaced by the incandescent bulb, invented by Edison in 1879, of which 250,000 were in use in 1885, 18,000,000 in 1902 and 90,000,000 in 1912. Edison himself opened the world's first electric plant in New York in 1882, and the first hydro-electric plant was built in Colorado in 1890. Meanwhile the use of electricity in industry developed apace. In this field only Germany could be compared with the United States, Britain being slow to realize its potentialities. The whole mighty process, of which electricity, with oil and steel, formed part, is summed up in the fact that by the early years of the twentieth century America's industrial production had already surpassed that of Britain and Germany together, at a time when her population was little more than two-thirds of their combined total.

## THE "GREAT GAME"

A large, expanding and protected market, matched by huge resources, and exploited by adventurous men confident in their country's future and lacking many of the restraints of the Old World, set the pace for American development. "The national resources", Lincoln had said during the Civil War, "are unexhausted, and, as we believe, inexhaustible", yet he had little notion of the possibilities that lay ahead. In the words of a distinguished American historian, F. J. Turner, "since the days when the fleet of Columbus sailed into the waters of the New World, America has been another name for opportunity",[5] and however true this may be it was never so true as during the generation after the Civil War. The principles and practices of American life accounted for much, but the resources that lay to hand gave them full scope:

the United States was endowed in a fashion which seemed grotesque to the European visitors who came to enquire into the sources of her strength. Somehow, rich iron ore, base metals and soft coal, which could be mined from open pits by steam shovels, were the last straw to foreign competitors.[6]

It was the seeming inexhaustibility of this natural wealth, whether the land itself, what grew on it, or what lay within it, that gave to American life its expansiveness, that "frontier" quality, of which Americans are still so proud, that concern with economic development—in short, with "business"— rather than with politics, as the principal preoccupation of civilized man. And it was in the years that followed the Civil War that American life took this characteristic tone. In the words used by an eminent historian in a study of an outstanding figure of the period, John D. Rockefeller (1839–1937), which bears the sub-title *The Heroic Age of American Enterprise*:

> Business—the development of the resources of the half-explored country—was then America's principal challenge to her young men. . . . It was much more than the road to wealth; it was the field to which the great majority of Americans looked for distinction, power, and the joys of self-expression. . . . It was the central field of usefulness; it was the Great Game . . . the immediate necessity of the time.[7]

As Rockefeller himself said, in later years, "That's the thing— accomplishment, playing the game". It was a hard game in which many went to the wall, and its very tempo, with the great stakes involved, put a premium upon tenacity and unscrupulousness. Even the less fortunate gloried in the accomplishment, and dreamed of having a hand in the game. Success was the test, and the task was too great, the stakes were too high, to permit of much indulgence in caution, scruples or half-heartedness. In the words used of a slightly later period by an American novelist, "they're too busy to listen to anyone who isn't making something besides criticisms".[8]

## THE WASTAGE OF RESOURCES

The vigour with which the great enterprise was conducted was matched by an appalling wastage of resources that was part of a sublimely unconscious indifference to the price to be paid. Kipling in 1889 was horrified at the casual destruction of natural wealth, especially of virgin forest:

> the great American Nation . . . very seldom attempts to put back anything that it has taken from Nature's shelves. It grabs all it can and moves on.[9]

Not until the time of Theodore Roosevelt, in the early years of the new century, was serious attention given to problems of conservation, and the results of extravagance were soon to be seen in the "dust-bowls" and eroded lands that aroused the public conscience in the years between the two World Wars.

## RAILWAY DEVELOPMENT AND ITS RESULTS

It was the railways, however, with the scandals that only too often accompanied their construction, that became the supreme expression of a confidence that attained sublimity and a casualness that degenerated into improvidence. Railways, and especially transcontinental lines, were essential for the development of the country, and in the prevailing optimism almost no price was considered too great to pay for their construction. Hence the railway boom in the years immediately following the Civil War, and especially the wilful extravagance of the first transcontinental line, the Union Pacific, with all the unsavoury financial manipulation that accompanied it.

On the eve of the war there had been some thirty thousand miles of railway in operation in the United States, and an East-West system was already beginning to take shape, though few lines yet reached farther than the Great Lakes. The iron roads were, however, one of the essential links between the North and the West in their struggle with the South, and in the early stages of the war the Union Government gave charters to two groups of financiers for the construction of a transcontinental line in two sections, one running east, the other west. The charters were backed by construction loans and immense grants of public land, and although the work was not really pressed forward until after the war, the railway was completed, amid universal enthusiasm, in 1869. It had then cost, in all, $94,000,000, but the profits made by the contractors were enormous: they had in all probability raised and spent —or diverted to their own pockets—up to $50,000,000 more than the actual cost, and much of the work had been done so hastily that considerable reconstruction was necessary. A great part of the inflated profits had gone to the contractors as shareholders in the Crédit Mobilier construction company, which they had themselves created, and it was the revelation in 1872 of the bribery of Congressmen by the company to secure its activities from investigation that first showed the public what was going on. Meanwhile towns along the railway's route had been blackmailed by threats of by-passing into contributing funds for work that was already covered by Federal financial guarantees, and where outright bribery was unnecessary or undesirable interest was purchased by such decorous devices as the issue of free passes. Similar practices were followed in the construction of other lines, and by the 'eighties it was estimated that more than a quarter of the nominal value of the railways of America existed only on paper. In the words of a later railroad president, "the system was indeed, fairly honey-combed with jobbery and corruption".

The need was so great, however, the advantages so obvious and the resources so rich, that often enough little objection was taken to the means employed. James Garfield, who was implicated in the Crédit Mobilier scandal of 1873, found himself, eight years later, President of the United States, and was described in one newspaper as "exceptionally clean for a man who has been engaged for twenty years in active politics", while a notable figure of a slightly later period, the mid-Western editor and Liberal Republican, William Allen White (1868–1944), has recorded in his autobiography his gradual awakening to the corrupting influence of the free-pass system to which he had for many years owed his holiday journeys.[10] Able and ruthless men competed for the gigantic tasks of spinning a web of iron rails over a growing continent, and the machinery to restrain their worst excesses did not exist, while members of State Legislatures, and even of Congress itself, had it in their power to bestow privileges upon which the very fact of competition put a measurable value. Not all railway financiers and builders were corrupt, a notable exception, perhaps, being the Canadian James Hill (1838–1916), who built the Great Northern, one of the last of the transcontinental lines, which was completed in 1893. Many of them, however, were interested in building not railroads but secure financial positions for themselves. As one of the most successful of railway-stock manipulators, William H. Vanderbilt, worthy son of his tough father, "the Commodore", is alleged to have said when a question of the public interest arose, "The public be damned. I am working for my stockholders"—the greater part of the stock concerned being his own. Not until the railways were running, and new devices for creating excessive profits through the control of rates were being put into effect, did a movement for control begin. The period from the 'seventies until the end of the century was then dominated in the West by the agitation of the farmers, organized in their "Granges", against railroad exploitation, an agitation which contributed to the later anti-trust legislation. Meanwhile the race for an adequate railway system had set a deplorable example of corruption, and had contributed much to the wastage of national resources through the enormous grants of land made to the builders of the lines.

## Developing the Land: "Homesteads" and Railway Grants

Land grants were an essential condition of railway construction, but they were a condition which cut across much that was traditional in American values. The railways encouraged, and, indeed, almost forced, settlement of the great spaces of the West, but the pattern of society that emerged was not always what strict American democrats had hoped to see, or what they had hoped to achieve from the Civil War. Lincoln, with his profound insight into the inner reality of movements, had realized that the destiny of the whole North American continent was at stake in the war. The States could not remain "half slave and half free", and upon the outcome of the struggle depended whether "government of the people, by the people, and for the people", in its American context, should endure. This was a great matter, for in a largely undemocratic world the American experiment was still on trial, and the war itself suggested to many European observers that democracy was but another name for chaos. In a more limited sense, however, the future of the West, of the still undeveloped half, or more, of the continent, was closely concerned in the conflict. By 1860 the frontier of settlement had moved westwards until it was approaching the 98th meridian, the significant dividing-line between adequate and sparse rainfall. Sixty years earlier the view had been that in the vast lands west of the Mississippi the United States had scope for a thousand years of expansion. Development had proceeded apace, however, and by the middle of the century some half-dozen frontier States had been created, and further new

"Territories" marked out for future statehood. It was over the possible expansion of slavery into the Kansas and Nebraska Territories in particular, that the passions which found their vent in the Civil War first made themselves felt, and it was the dispute over these Territories which brought about the establishment, in the 'fifties, of the new "Republican" Party, which Lincoln was soon to lead. The dispute turned on more than slavery, for the conservative South wished to see settlement proceeding on the basis of land-purchase, while the more radical North added to its insistence upon "Free Labour and Free Men" a demand for "Free Soil", for the establishment of small homesteads, the ideal—and idealized—basis for an agrarian democracy. It was the combination of the agitation against the spread of slavery with the demand for free land, of North with West, that broke the power of the South. The interests of North and West were not, in the long run, identical, as later events were to show, but the alliance stood fast during the war, and in 1862, during Lincoln's first term as President, the West's demands for land were met by the passage of the Homestead Act, which granted 160 acres free to a settler of five years' standing, or allowed him to commute his claim by payment at $1.25 an acre after six months' settlement. It was this Act, passed in the early stages of the Civil War, that stimulated the settlement of the Great Plains and created the American Mid-West: even during the years of war no fewer than 15,000 homestead grants were made. Combined with the gold and silver discoveries farther west, the land grants made to homesteaders and, still more significantly, perhaps, to the railways, populated, with varying degrees of density, the remaining two-thirds of the continent, until in 1890 it was possible for the Superintendent of the Census to announce that a frontier of settlement could no longer be said to exist. Settlement continued for a further generation, the peak of Homestead development being reached only in 1913, but the farming depression of the 'nineties showed that a new situation was already emerging. It is significant that the very year, 1890, which saw the announcement of the virtual closing of the frontier, saw also the sudden uprising of the radical "Populist" Party into politics, the outward form of the West's resentment of Eastern domination.

## "Go West, Young Man . . ."

In all, nearly a quarter of a billion acres were eventually allocated in Homestead grants, and, while during the Civil War nearly one million immigrants from the Eastern States and from Europe settled in the mid-West, in the expansive twenty years after 1870 the population was to increase by ten millions more. "Go West, young man, go West and grow up with the country", had been the words, later almost proverbial, used in 1854 by the Republican publicist Horace Greeley (1811–72), long an advocate of the Homestead system as a barrier to the spread of slavery, and it was with the flood of immigration that the country grew up. The tragedy for so many was that the new country stretched into the less well-watered regions beyond the 98th meridian, and presented serious farming problems. Yet it was a mighty impulse of hope and freedom that drew the immigrants on. If there was idealism in the bloody struggle of the war there was no less in what William Allen White, himself a mid-Westerner, called "the heroic adventure that came when men poured pell-mell, helter-skelter over the Alleghanies into the Mississippi Valley and up the slopes of the Rockies, dragging railroads, cities, colleges, factories, farmhouses and equipment behind them".[11]

## Greeley's Aims—and Achievements

Greeley's aim had been as much to maintain prosperity for the industrial workers of the East as to develop prosperous communities of free farmers in the West. He believed that the level of industrial wages could be maintained only if surplus labour moved West, and the empty plains were for a time, indeed, something of a safety-valve against industrial unrest, giving the American Labour movement a special character. America was the land of opportunity, and it was in the undeveloped West that opportunity was to be found. Fortified by the colourful activities of the miners and ranchers and railwaymen who opened up the West, and ignoring the substantial assistance given to railway speculators by State and Federal governments, the legend of individualism arose, glorifying the lone homesteader who "broke the plains", and seeing in him the quintessential American. This was the ideal of Greeley, as of so many others, and has exerted great influence, even into our own day. Theodore Roosevelt summed it up, with characteristic pugnacity, when in 1886 he contrasted the men on his ranch with the strikers of the industrial East:

> My men work longer hours for no greater wages than most of the strikers, *but they are Americans through and through.*[12]

"Opportunity" and the realities of homesteading never, in practice, quite realized the hopes of the idealists, but they were an effective argument for industrialists and contributed not a little to the outlook of American Labour. Moreover, when the frontier of settlement eventually disappeared, a new frontier of industrial expansion took its place. Not until the great slump that began in 1929 were the ideals questioned by more than a section of the American economy. Meanwhile, however, Greeley's policy had been stood on its head. Homestead settlement, and the intensive efforts made to attract immigrants to take advantage of it, drew from Europe not only skilled workers but great numbers of the unskilled, who, landing in the industrial East and eagerly seeking employment there, tended to depreciate wages. Homesteads were not usually for men without means or skill.

## THE LAND GRANTS

In other respects, also, Greeley's hopes were not realized. The right to commute homesteads for purchase played into the hands of speculators, and made possible the concentration of holdings which was opposed to the very principle of the grants. More serious still were the block-grants to railways and the companies' exploitation of their privileged position. Land grants had for some years been made to railway promoters by the States, but it was in 1862, the very year of the Homestead Act, that the principle was first adopted by the Federal Government, to make possible a transcontinental line. The Union Pacific received nearly fourteen million acres of land along its track, and other lines were still better endowed. Much of the land was sold at a handsome profit, but by the time that the abuses were recognized and further grants stopped, in 1871, no less than 116,000,000 acres of public land had been disposed of. The railways had had their costs of construction handsomely covered, and although speedy construction could probably not have been guaranteed in any other way, the price paid was, in all respects, a heavy one, morally no less than materially. In the end, with all adjustments made, the land-grants to railways, whether directly from the Federal Government, or through the States, amounted to more than 132,000,000 acres, Homestead grants to 285,000,000 acres, though much of this latter total had been commuted into larger holdings. In addition, under the Morrill Act of that same year of significant legislative achievement, 1862, grants of land were made for the establishment of agricultural colleges and State universities, which have since received 182,000,000 acres as endowment (the famous Massachusetts Institute of Technology was founded on grants under this Act). How much homesteading genuinely contributed to the development of the West, which was continuing by purchase in any case, it is impossible to say: much of what might have been gained was lost in speculation, and by the end of the century fewer than half of American farmers owned their land. The advantage to education through land-grants was clear enough, but no less evident were the substantial gains of the railway interests.

## The Railways and Immigration

Nevertheless, the rapid spread of the railways was a major American achievement of the post-war period, and with the railways came the flood of settlers from the Eastern States and overseas. By 1870 the total railway mileage had reached 53,000 but in the next two decades it leapt ahead to 93,000 and 163,000, reaching its maximum of 250,000 miles by the time of the First World War. In the same period the number of immigrants exceeded 25,000,000, and many of these were attracted by the propaganda of the railway companies, which sold their land-grants in lots and provided the transportation which alone made the land a workable proposition. By no means all of the immigrants went far beyond the eastern seaboard, however. Between 1870 and 1910 the total population of the United States rose from 38,000,000 to 92,000,000, that of all the States to the west of the Mississippi only from 6,000,000 to 26,000,000, and much of the increase in these States was due to the westward movement of easterners. Means, skill, and character to withstand loneliness were needed to make a homestead flourish in what was at times a howling wilderness, and very many immigrants, lacking these attributes, became no more than cheap labour for Eastern industry. More than 13,000,000 of the 92,000,000 of America's population in 1910 were foreign-born, but two-thirds of them were town- and city-dwellers. The bait of smiling farm-land in the "land of opportunity" was often enough the lure that drew the immigrants over the sea, but it was the transport agent who dangled the bait. The famous Statue of Liberty, presented by France to her sister Republic in 1886, offered a welcome to "your tired, your poor, your huddled masses yearning to breathe free", but the appeal of the railway and shipping agents, offering cheap passages and glowing prospects, was probably still more effective. In the words of a leading authority, "the desire to get cheap labor, to take in passenger fares, and to sell land have probably brought more immigrants than the hard conditions of Europe, Asia and Africa have sent", though it was to the centres of over-population and agricultural depression that the railway and shipping agents looked:[13] hence their activity in Ireland, Austria-Hungary, Italy and parts of Germany. Like the slave-ships of earlier years, the Atlantic steamers brought human cargoes in return for American exports of food and raw materials.

## "ASSIMILATION"

The rapid creation of this vast "melting-pot" of humanity inevitably affected the development of American conditions, political and economic no less than social. The remarkable thing was that the assimilation proceeded so steadily. Part of the success was due to the no less rapid physical development of the country. America *was* the land of opportunity, if not for all, then for many; if not for the immigrants themselves, then for the next generation. And education, political rights, all were there, in contrast to conditions in so many of the lands of origin. A member of a Russian-Jewish immigrant family has told how her father took her to school for the first time "as if it were an act of consecration" whereby "he took possession of America":[14] to many of the newcomers, indeed, education was the supreme opportunity. With education went political assimilation. The task of fitting the unceasing flow of the politically immature into an established system, with its rigid party organization; of preparing them for the exercise, when citizenship had at length been granted, of their rights as voters; of ensuring that they voted on the correct party ticket, all served to bring out what was at once both best and worst in American political organization, and made of the new citizens so much political cannon-fodder. The party-system interested itself in them, but made them only too often the tool of the local political "boss", while powerful local groups arose, particularly among the Irish and the Germans, to dominate local affairs and ensure—and, if necessary, enforce—conformity. Conformity was, indeed, part of the price that America had to pay for the success of assimilation, and it was reinforced by the radical notions as to property rights which some of the immigrants brought with them. When Theodore Roosevelt praised his ranchers as "Americans through and through" he was contrasting them with Anarchist "agitators" from abroad who were the first to be branded as guilty of "un-American activities".

## THE SOURCES—AND RESULTS—OF IMMIGRATION

The principal sources of immigrants were the United Kingdom, with Ireland accounting for considerably more than half of the British total, together with Germany, Austria-Hungary, Russia and Italy. Britain sent 1,000,000 people during each decade from the 'forties until nearly the end of the century, Germany half as many again during the 'eighties, Austria-Hungary and Italy 2,000,000 each in the decade 1901–10, and Russia 1,500,000 in the same period. The focus of emigration to America, which was first, and for a long period, in North-Western Europe, swung rapidly through Central Europe to Russia and south to the Mediterranean lands. The census returns have shown that the peak figure of American residents born in Britain or Germany was reached in 1890, that of Central Europeans in 1910, of Russians in 1920, but of Italians only in 1930, though the Italian total was already high in 1910. Without the unskilled labour of many of these hopeful invaders, these Polacks, Hunkies, Kikes and Dagos, as they were contemptuously called, the Great Game could not have been played so fast: even the longed-for Union Pacific line was largely built by Irish and Chinese. At the same time the immigrants provided a constantly renewed pool of cheap labour which could undersell the native-born, and serve as strike-breakers in times of industrial dispute: it is against this background that the history of labour relations in America must be studied. It is against this background, too, that the movements for social reform must be considered. The constant crowding in of hundreds of thousands of poverty-stricken immigrants meant not only industrial exploitation but miserable social conditions and wretched housing. The proportion of town-dwellers in the total population of the country rose from twenty per cent in 1860 to forty per cent in 1900 without any improvement in local government to cope with the resulting problems, but, as in Britain at the same period, there began in the 'nineties a campaign of exposure, led by writers and sociologists whom Theodore Roosevelt later characterized as the "Muckrakers", which gradually brought improvements. The miserable conditions of the poor of the great cities was, however, both a result of, and a standing invitation to, the exploitation and corruption to which American conditions were prone.

## POWER, POLITICS AND "SPOILS"

Power, as we have so often been reminded, tends to corrupt, and power, especially social and financial power, came in America so swiftly that the individualism and freedom from government control which were part of the national heritage led, in fact, to a severe restraint of the liberty of the many in favour of the few. America was by no means alone in possessing a host of what Roosevelt was to call "malefactors of great wealth", who deliberately or otherwise rode roughshod over so many of their fellow-countrymen, but nowhere else were their power and influence so untrammelled, their riches so vast. Political and social restraints were practically non-existent, and the very conditions of politics gave full play to the not over-scrupulous. The political parties were conducted on a "spoils system", by which practically every public office went to the supporters of the party in power, and, as there was little difference of fundamental principle between Republican and Democrat, party allegiance and personal interest were closely allied. Politics was at times little more than a battle of the ins and outs, but since there were not, as in Britain, many men of independent means prepared to give their time to local and national affairs, the spoils were an important consideration. Nor was there room for more than two parties: there were, as Theodore Roosevelt ruefully confessed after his failure to carry a new and "Progressive" Republican movement in 1912, "no loaves and fishes" for a third. Hence the petering-out of the "Populist" and "Progressive" movements, and the impossibility of forming a "Labour" Party. Moreover, with the Civil War ended politics were not taken seriously, except during the pleasant turmoil of elections. The business of America, as was said later, was business, the "great game" which held out such vast prizes. It was for business, as W. D. Howells wrote in a novel in 1890, that "the good timber" was wanted, not for marginal pursuits; and it was business, not political success, as in Britain, that carried prestige. Add to this that sovereignty in America is in each State, political authority divided by strict constitutional procedure. The Representative, whether in State or in Federal Legislature, was measured by his ability to get things done for those who had sent him, and if powerful financial interests gave their help with the expenses of election, and with other favours, they expected in return the concessions which Legislatures had it in their power to grant. It was said of Standard Oil by one of the "Muckrakers" that at one stage of its career it had done everything to a certain State Legislature except to refine it, and in this it was no more than typical of the financial powers of its day. Politics, in fact, became "largely a Punch and Judy show", with business interests working the puppets.

The rewards of the exploitation of America's resources were so great that competition was ruthless, and there were few legal restraints. If legal authority were needed there were ways and means of gaining favourable decisions in a system where, in the sacred name of democracy, judicial office was elective, and State Legislatures were often ready enough to grant wide powers: New Jersey, in particular, proved so accommodating to monopolies as to earn the title of the "trust factory". In short, the strictly limited conception of government with which the country had been endowed in an earlier age was rapidly outgrown. As Henry Adams wrote when the system had come under criticism at the beginning of the new century, "the fathers had intended to neutralize the energy of government and had succeeded, but their machine was never meant to do the work of a twenty-million horse-power society". The result was the prostitution of law and justice to narrow and selfish ends. Law fell into disrepute and the police became the tools of corrupt political control. America was faced with the problem not so much of purifying public life in the spirit of an established ethos as of creating social controls which would cope with a situation that had far outgrown the ideas that had coloured its origins. If the men who dominated—and profited by—economic developments were personally honest, as many of them were, the freedom to act in their own interest, without regard for the public, that was generously accorded to them, was too wide in scope to permit the scruples which would in any case have hampered them in their dealings with competitors. In the words of Lincoln Steffens (1866–1936), greatest of the "muckrakers", "the prizes we offer for successful stealing from the public, the riches, honors, prestige, are too much for strong men".[15]

## Speculation and the Rise of "Business"

Yet it was less in direct production that the greatest prizes were to be found than in the successful manipulation of finance. After the Civil War, as, later, after the First World War, the country fell into an orgy of speculation. It was in the raising and manipulation of the funds that fed the economic life of the country that real power was to be tasted. A young British diplomat commented of the lives of the American rich in the 'eighties that "as the chief enjoyment derived from money seems to be power, they have to go to Wall Street to find a field for ambition".[16] With little scope in politics and public life to tempt them, and few opportunities for wide social and cultural contacts except in Europe, when they had made enough to visit there, the business men of America sought the springs of power in high finance. Clarence Day hit them off in his brilliant and sympathetic portrait of his stockbroking *Father*, in the last quarter of the century, with his air and feeling ' of enormous authority", and his fierce resentment of governmental interference that later caused him, in President Wilson's

time, to lose control of his dental plate, "when I read my
paper in the morning, and say what I think of that man
Wilson".[17] It was the pioneer American sociologist Thorstein
Veblen (1847–1929) who first drew a distinction between
direct production and "business", and it was as the relative
importance of primary producers and the rural population in
the American economy declined that a new type of American
came into being and the cult of the "business man" arose:

> The ideal of the sturdy, self-sufficient, independent farmer, so
> seldom realized, in fact, has been supplanted by the ideal of the middle-
> class city-dweller, drawing a good salary and making money on the
> stock market.

## THE ACHIEVEMENT OF FIFTY YEARS, 1861–1911

Yet, whatever its limitations and its excesses, the ideal of
opportunity, of enterprise, of individualism, rugged or
otherwise, lived on, and given the circumstances it is by no
means certain that the great growth of the Republic—"the
most marvellous movement in the history of mankind", as it has
been called by two leading historians in a moment of patriotic
enthusiasm—could have been achieved in any other way.
If the progress of the U.S.A. in the second half of the nineteenth century can in any way be compared with that of the
U.S.S.R. in the first half of the twentieth, the advantage of the
comparison is by no means necessarily with Russia. The record
of the advancement of thirty-one million people, on the eve of
their Civil War, with a million-and-a-third wage-earners and a
total foreign trade of some three-quarters of a million dollars,
to the ninety-two million of fifty years later, with seven million
wage-earners and a foreign trade of three-and-a-half million
dollars, together with a school population that had risen from
less than seven to more than seventeen million, can justly be
called the most remarkable movement in history to its time.
Much was owed to the happy chance of America's wealth of
natural resources, much to her geographical isolation, which
allowed her to concentrate upon development the resources and
energies which others had to devote to defence. Not a little was
due also to the close friendship of Britain, however much that
may have been taken for granted on both sides: British naval
power was the sure defence of that great "liquid asset" of

America, the Atlantic, and kept the country free from foreign intervention, while British investments, which eventually reached a total of some £754,000,000 and were greater than those for any other single country, were indispensable at first for the exploitation of America's natural wealth and the development of her communications. Yet, when all this has been said, the achievement remains an impressive one, the more remarkable because not restricted to material growth. Despite many dangers freedom was preserved, and not merely preserved but enlarged. When greater responsibilities came they found the United States with unmatched resources, sustained by a liberal ideology, which, if naïve and inexperienced, was ardent and deeply felt. Few can have foreseen in the dark days of civil war that a nation rent by so terrible a conflict would, in only half a century, become a decisive influence in world affairs. How this came about, against the background that has been sketched, must now be considered.

### (2) The Growth of a Nation—Political, Social, Economic

#### The Legacy of War and "Reconstruction"

The very ferocity of the Civil War, and the vigour with which development proceeded even during its course, were evidence of the vitality that was to achieve such spectacular results. Afterwards development continued at such a pace that in detail the conflict could be largely forgotten. Fundamental differences of outlook continued between North and South, but it was the political game that exploited them, and "Reconstruction" accounted for more bitterness in Southern memories than the fact of defeat. Only ten years after the end of the war W. D. Howells's Silas Lapham could be made to say that it was "time to let those old issues go", while in the 'nineties Woodrow Wilson argued that neither side would have fought so hard had it not felt that it had "a legal right to do so".[18] Wilson, however, was not then in politics: more characteristic of the political approach was the unsubtle Theodore Roosevelt's robust view of the South in 1904 as "wrong with a folly that amounted to madness, and with a perversity that amounted to wickedness".[19] Chameleon-like, opinion on the merits of the rival causes has tended to vary according to the political conditions of the hour, and it has taken the present age to see the cause of the South, with the grievances of the post-war years, as issues fundamentally no less serious now than then:

the role of the Negro in American life; the interrelationship between majority will . . . and the 'minority rights' of geographical sections; and the question of how to secure peaceful settlement of intersectional and international disputes.[20]

If these were the issues the war did little or nothing to solve them. The place of the Negro, in particular, was made, if any-thing, more rather than less difficult, and a legacy of racial conflict was left which has begun to disappear only in our own day. At the same time the victorious majority, or those who governed in its name, paid too little regard to the minority rights of either white or black in the defeated States. Hence, in contrast to the flaunting extravagance of the dominant triumphant elements of the North, the long depression of the South and the unhappy state of the Negroes, no longer slave but neither wholly free. Such was the immediate, and only too patent, outcome of the victory of the Union:

The most striking products of (the Yankee) crusade were the shoddy aristocracy of the North and the ragged children of the South. Among the masses of Americans there were no victors, only the vanquished.[21]

To say this is to take a pessimistic view of the situation, but for all their expansiveness in so many fields of American endeavour the first years of peace were years of tension and uncertainty, which left the South unreconciled to the passing of its domination, and created in the North economic powers as great and as influential as the old slave-owning interest had been, and still more dangerous to democracy. Much of what happened would, perhaps, have come in any case, but, when all allowance has been made for the limitations of the American system, it remains true that, after Lincoln's skilful steering, the country fell into the hands of men, too many of whom when they were not merely inept were dishonest. Lincoln had held firmly, and through many discouragements, to the course that ultimately brought victory, and had framed, even before that victory came, the policy that should bring peace and reconciliation and ensure a restored unity. Almost before the

x

first steps could be taken he was struck down, and his successor, well-intentioned though he was, lamentably failed to restrain the influences and jealousies which were liberated by the restoration of peace.

## Lincoln's Peace Plans—and their Frustration

The restoration of the normal balance of government when it has been disturbed by the rule of a strong President, and particularly when the conduct of a war has made doubly necessary a strengthening of the President's hands, is by now a familiar problem in American history. Lincoln, for all the cult that has grown up around him as the "supreme American", was not only a dominating President but a most astute politician. His Vice-President and successor, Andrew Johnson (1808–75), though more capable than is often believed, was neither. As early as 1863 Lincoln had formulated his plan for the reconstruction of the Union, by which an amnesty would be given to all secessionists who would take an oath of loyalty, and a State government could be restored as soon as the oath had been taken by one-tenth of the voters. In his view, secession being *ipso facto* invalid, the Confederate States had never been more than out of their proper relation with the Union, and should be brought back as soon as possible, only certain groups of rebel leaders being excluded from the general amnesty. The prevailing view in Congress, however, was very different. There Lincoln's extension of the Executive authority during the war—of doubtful constitutionality, as the President himself admitted—was keenly resented, and his reconstruction policy came in for particularly severe criticism. The more extreme Republicans held that the Southern States had forfeited their privileges, and must be treated as conquered territory, to be remade in the Northern image. This was an understandable attitude, though it had more to it than mere bellicosity or concern for the liberated slaves. Good Republicans had no desire to see Southern Democrats too soon back in Congress, resisting the measures by which the North-East was shaping the future of the continent. In the words of one of the most bitter opponents of the Southern States, Thaddeus Stevens, they should never be readmitted to the Union "until the Constitution shall have been so amended . . . as to secure perpetual ascendancy to the party of the Union", which, as he was soon to show, could be achieved only by the enfranchisement of the Negro. To ensure the Negro the vote would be to realize the principle of Lincoln's Gettysburg address, that the United States were "dedicated to the proposition that all men are created equal". Given that the freed men, the liberated slaves, voted with their Republican liberators, and not with their Democratic former masters, it would achieve more; it would ensure that the Republican conception of a continent-wide nation, more nearly a united nation than a mere federation of States, with free land for homesteads, linked by privileged railway systems, with a rapidly-rising industrial strength protected by tariffs and with economic and financial power firmly in the hands of the North-East, would suffer no legislative checks. Hence the Congressional insistence, soon to be buttressed by the Fourteenth and Fifteenth Amendments to the Constitution, that the defeated States should accept the new order of things before they could be readmitted to equality with their conquerors. Foremost among those who strove to enforce this policy were the two Republican leaders in the Congress of 1864, the forceful and savage Thaddeus Stevens (1782–1868) and the more intellectual, but no less intolerant and self-righteous, Senator Charles Sumner (1811–74), later notorious as the would-be invader of Canada. Their aim was as much to restore the balance of the Constitution in favour of Congress as to reshape the South, and it was the death of Lincoln that gave them their opportunity.

## PRESIDENT ANDREW JOHNSON, 1865–69

Lincoln himself had rejoiced that when the war ended Congress was not in session, since that left him free to follow his own reconciliatory line. His assassination, however, removed the only man with the authority, ability and standing in the country to resist the Congressional leaders. The new President was an anti-secessionist Southerner, a Democrat from Tennessee, who had been chosen to run with Lincoln in the election of 1864 in order to demonstrate that the Union cause represented more than merely the Republican party. His origins had been as simple, and his upbringing as hard, as Lincoln's, and although he lacked his predecessor's intellectual and moral stature, he was known as a staunch democrat with an inveterate, and often tactlessly expressed, hostility to wealth and privilege. As Representative and Senator he had laboured for years to put the Homestead Act on the statute book, and, significantly enough in view of his later career, it had been his resolution proclaiming the war as one not for conquest but for the preservation of the Union that had been carried by the Senate in 1861. He was lacking, however, in political nous and in skill in the handling of men, and as President was easily outmanœuvred by his opponents, failing to realize that with the coming of peace the President's actions would be more narrowly watched and circumscribed than during the war. Hence the difficulties that led in 1868 to the extraordinary, and quite unwarrantable, spectacle of his impeachment by the men whose vengeance he had sought to restrain.

As soon as he had settled in office Johnson reconstituted the governments of the Southern States on the lines laid down by Lincoln, and in little more than a year proclaimed the restoration of peace and order throughout the Union. It was a barren success, for his work was speedily undone by Congress, he himself was denounced by Sumner as "an insolent drunken brute in comparison with which Caligula's horse was respectable", and finally he was impeached for "high crimes and misdemeanours". Johnson's failure was not merely a disaster for himself and the South, however; it imperilled the very basis of constitutional government in the United States, threatening the replacement of presidential by congressional government. The solitary decisive vote in May, 1868, which dismissed the extravagant charges against him, was significant for America's constitutional development, even if for some years Congress were still to dominate the political scene.

## CONGRESS TAKES CONTROL: CONSTITUTIONAL AMENDMENTS AND "RECONSTRUCTIONS"

Congress joined issue with the President when it assembled in December, 1865. The Southern governments were now at work, and had accepted the Thirteenth Amendment to the Constitution abolishing slavery. At the same time they had passed various laws discriminating against the freedmen, laws which had inevitably roused Northern wrath and cast doubts on the wisdom of the Lincoln-Johnson policy of conciliation. Congress therefore refused to admit Southern representatives and passed a Civil Rights Bill to protect the freedman. Johnson, with his Southern concern for the rights of the States against Federal interference, vetoed the Bill, but was overrruled, and to make assurance doubly sure Congress in the summer of 1868 embodied the Act in the Fourteenth Amendment to the Constitution, acceptance of which was made a condition of readmission to the Union. The Fourteenth Amendment, despite the seemingly unexceptionable nature of the sentiments it expressed, was one of the most momentous ever passed. It was both the last blow of the Civil War and an attempt to strengthen the Federal Government, in certain directions, against the States. By its 4th and 3rd clauses all Confederate debts were repudiated, and no secessionist who had held office before the war was for the time being eligible for State or Federal office. This exclusion was a drastic step which had the intended effect of shutting out the greater part of the governmental experience of the South, giving control into the hands of the freedmen, the rare whites who had been Unionist, and those others, generally "poor whites", who had held no office in the past. The whites who took office under the congressional régime were known by their compatriots as "scalawags", and were widely regarded as traitors who had lent themselves to Northern dominance less to raise the Negro than to degrade the white. They were joined by Northern "carpet-baggers", who settled temporarily in the South, some with a sincere desire to help the freedmen, others for what they could make out of the despoiling of the defeated. Not until the 'seventies, in most cases, were political privileges restored to the ex-confederates, and their final disabilities were not removed for another twenty years (there was an outcry in the mid-'eighties when Cleveland, the first Democrat President since the war, wished to return their captured standards). Meanwhile congressional policy stultified the political development of the Southern States, unified them far more solidly behind the Democrat Party than ever before, and taught them to see in Negro rights only white degradation. The consequences are felt to this day.

The 1st and 2nd clauses of the Fourteenth Amendment

were no less significant. By the 1st no State could limit the privileges of a citizen or "deprive any person of life, liberty or property without due process of law" (a condition of which much was to be heard later in unexpected contexts); by the 2nd a State's representation in Congress was to be limited if any of its citizens were denied the franchise, and this clause was later amplified by Amendment Fifteen of the Constitution (1870), which forbade any denial of the right to vote "on account of race, color, or previous condition of servitude". On paper little more could have been done for the political rights of the freedmen: in practice it amounted to little enough. To secure respect for its wishes and obedience to the conditions of the Amendment, Congress in March, 1867, passed a Reconstruction Act, which, nearly two years after the end of the war, placed the Southern States under military rule until such time as elections could be held under conditions of full manhood suffrage, with equality for white and black, and the Fourteenth Amendment had been ratified by governments so established. Thus did Congress attempt to remake the South by the rule of Negroes, scalawags, and carpetbaggers. Between 1868 and 1870 new "black and tan" governments were set up, and though the results could have been worse, and much useful legislation was passed, there was a great deal of waste, not a little corruption, and a fearful piling-up of debt, much of which was later repudiated. Above all, however, there was a rising tide of bitterness among the disfranchised, who were hardly to be persuaded by this means to pay more regard to Negro rights. Meanwhile Congress continued to do all that solemn resolutions could do in defence of those rights, even going so far as to pass in 1875, in deference to the memory of the lately dead Sumner, an Act guaranteeing social equality to the freedmen in such places as hotels and theatres. By this time, however, Republican rule and Negro rights in the South were utterly dependent on the support of the Federal troops who had been sent in 1867. As the troops were withdrawn, between 1869 and 1877, from the various States, so, despite all the resolutions that had been passed, did strictly conservative Democrat rule become restored. Already organizations such as the Ku Klux Klan had terrorized Negro voters. With the removal of the troops, and of the carpetbaggers whom they had sustained, social pressure and political discrimination against freedmen rapidly increased. They were reinforced by the actions of the Supreme Court, which, after a dishonourable period of acquiescence in Congress's flouting of the constitution by interference in the internal affairs of States, ruled in a series of cases between 1875 and 1883 that the Fourteenth and Fifteenth Amendments protected the Negro only against indiscriminatory State legislation aimed at *civil* rights and based on tests of *race* or *colour*. In short, the whole basis of Southern discrimination, which was now essentially social in character, was placed, in strict accordance with the principles of the Constitution, beyond the reach of the Federal courts, and left to the individual States, which soon found other means of discrimination in educational and property tests which were not explicitly inspired by race or colour prejudice, but were none the less effective. Of clause two of the Fourteenth Amendment, however, nothing was heard: after its acquiescence in "carpetbag" election methods Congress could not look too closely at Southern election returns.

## THE FAILURE OF CONGRESS

Congress, in fact, had failed. Indeed, it had made the situation worse. The Lincoln-Johnson policy might have encouraged the more liberal elements in the South to find means of reconciling white and black interests, at least in the States where freedmen were in a minority. "Reconstruction", however, condemned the South to two generations of political catalepsy. In the words of the biographer of President Hayes, who withdrew the last of the Federal garrisons in 1877, "in 1865 the South was singularly lacking in ill feeling; in 1876, the land was consumed with hatred". The Negro was held down, and was to remain so for many years, "the chief sufferer from the curse that Thaddeus Stevens laid upon the South".

## THE ECONOMIC STATUS OF THE NEGROES

More serious in the long run than the failure to ensure political and social rights for the freedman, was the lack of realization of the need to secure his economic position. Having been technically freed he was left without resources, to make for himself a new place in a social order ruined by war and expropriation. At a time when empty lands in the West were being divided for homesteads, or for the enrichment of railroad promoters, and when great ruined estates were going begging in the South, not a cent was forthcoming to help to establish him on the land and give him something more than a merely legal status. In consequence, few of the four million liberated slaves ever became landowners, even on a small scale: most of them had to be content with the position of a tenant or share-cropper, with severely limited opportunities for educational or social advancement. The task of liberation, in fact, had been only half done, and what had been done had been too hurried, both for the bewildered Negro, hustled in only a few short years from servitude to the full weight of political responsi-bility, and for his resentful erstwhile master. Both were the victims of an unhappy amalgam of idealism and political jobbery. Among the freedmen the best-off, at first, were those who remained with their old masters: for the rest, in the words of the Negro leader Frederick Douglass (1817–95), the freedman was "free from the individual master, but a slave of society"; possessing neither money, property, nor friends, "he was free from the old plantation, but he had nothing but the dusty road under his feet". As had become apparent in Russia in the same period, legal freedom was little without effective political rights and economic opportunity.

## President and Congress

While Congress forced on President Johnson a recon-struction policy at variance with his own intentions, it endeavoured as much in other respects to bend the executive, and even the judicial, authority to its will. By the Command of the Army Act and the Tenure of Office Act it sought to prevent the President from controlling the Army and the Executive officials, even those in his own "cabinet": it was his defiance of the latter act as unconstitutional, an opinion in which posterity has upheld him, that was the ostensible reason for his impeachment. The Supreme Court similarly had its hands tied by legislation denying its jurisdiction in matters affecting the military control of the South, legislation which the Court, in the face of the prevailing temper of Congress, pusillanimously failed to criticize. The Court reasserted itself in the 'seventies, and the Tenure of Office Act was first modified in 1869, when Grant took office, and finally repealed in 1886. Nevertheless, by these means Congress was able to impose its reconstruction policy without immediate check, and when Grant succeeded Johnson he proved so malleable a tool that further pressure was unnecessary. It was left for Presidents Hayes (1877–81) and Cleveland (1885–89 and 1893–97) to continue Johnson's resistance to congressional domination, though it was not until the unexpected appearance of Theodore Roosevelt in 1901, on the assassination of McKinley, that, for the first time since the end of the Civil War, a powerful personality occupied the presidential office. Even then it was another twelve years before, in the person of Woodrow Wilson, a man became President who could be named in the same breath as Lincoln.

## THE PRESIDENTIAL OFFICE

It is one object of the United States Constitution to preserve a division and balance of powers in the government, but experience of its working has long since shown that unless the President is able and willing to give a lead the country flounders. Congress is less a reflection of the country's unity than a sum of parts; the Congressman less a representative of the whole nation, like the British M.P., than the delegate of a locality whose interests he must serve. Without presidential leadership strange aberrations are possible, and policy can be dictated by such narrow or selfish interests as can, by devious means, attract to themselves a sufficient majority of votes: Sumner and Stevens were among the more reputable representatives of a not uncommon type. Johnson knew his duty, though he performed it in the clumsiest possible manner. Grant, however, had not the slightest conception of it, and few of his successors before T. Roosevelt added much to the dignity or prestige of their office, or gave anything but a limited lead. Among the many elements that go to the choice of a candidate for the Presidency is the ability to make few political enemies, an ability rarely joined with political genius or a commanding personality. As a penetrating Irish observer has written, "from Abraham Lincoln's re-election in 1864 down to the end of the nineteenth century there had not been a single presidential

x*

candidate (always excepting General Grant) of whom his friends could say that he had done anything to command the gratitude of the nation".[22] Nor was it easy to unite the widely different sections and interests of the country in a common policy. Once the effort of reconstruction was over, therefore, and the war crisis brought to an end, normal conditions reasserted themselves, and it was only when abuses forced themselves on the public attention that a new movement of reconstruction in politics began. Americans, like the good democrats that they are, are slow to move in unity except in a crusade. The Civil War had been for both sides nothing if not a crusade, but until fresh crusading opportunities arose, as in time they did, there was more scope for energy and enthusiasm in the development of American resources than in political life.

## PRESIDENT U. S. GRANT, 1869-77

It was in these conditions that Grant became President in 1869. Ulysses S. Grant (1822-85) is one of the mysteries of American history. A lonely, moody, unimpressive man, with a taste for hard drinking—"inarticulate, uncertain, distrustful of himself", in Henry Adams's phrase—a failure in most things that he had attempted before the war, with no liking for military life and no understanding of politics, he had yet made himself during the war, by sheer tenacity and tactical insight, the leading soldier of the Union forces, loyally sustained by Lincoln, in the darkest days, for his dogged willingness to do battle and his confidence in the outcome. A simple, honest spirit, who had impressed the world at Appomattox with the dignity and compassion with which he had treated Lee and his army, he was unskilled in the subtleties of politics and inept in his judgement of the *genus* politician. Impatient of opposition, he was childishly susceptible to flattery and easily awed by wealth and display. Above all, he saw the executive branch of the government as but the tool of the legislative, and took from Congress his detailed instructions in peace as, in a subordinate capacity, he had taken a general directive in war. He was, therefore, an easy tool of ambitious Congressmen and the representatives of special interests, and, much though his régime came to be distrusted, his personal reputation and appeal long served as a cloak to their more unpleasant machinations. Having no policy and little conception of his office, he was content to let things drift at a time when skilful direction and a sharp eye to the interests of the American people were more than ever needed. In the scathing words of Henry Adams, "the progress of evolution from President Washington to President Grant was alone evidence enough to upset Darwin".

## PARTY WARFARE

Grant began well. The noble words of his letter accepting nomination as presidential candidate, "Let us have peace", made a happy impression, and he did at first attempt to introduce a policy of conciliation. Faced as he was, however, with congressional determination, and with the rising tide of resentment in the South, which found a vent in the Ku Klux Klan and other terrorist activities, he allowed himself to be persuaded, and agreed to a determined effort to suppress terrorism and buttress the freedman's position by law. There was the more reason for this since, even with a negro vote of some 700,000 in his favour, his majority in the election of 1868 had been only 300,000. It was larger in 1872, when he stood for re-election, but the Republican attempt to secure permanent control was frustrated by popular reaction against "reconstruction" and the corruption of the Grant régime. In the mid-term elections of 1874 the Democrats gained the control of the House of Representatives which they were not to lose for any considerable period until 1894, and in 1876 their candidate for the Presidency, Samuel Tilden, actually had a majority of the votes, though eventually, after a long wrangle, his Republican rival, Rutherford B. Hayes, was declared elected, having won the acquiescence of Southern Democrats by promising to withdraw the federal troops from their States. Two years later the Democrats for a time won control of the Senate, and in 1884 they gained, with Grover Cleveland, their first Presidential success since the Civil War. By this time, of course, the South, with the Negroes firmly in their place, was actively united behind the Democrat Party: the "solid South" had come into existence, and was to show few cracks until the middle of the following century.

For too long the Republicans "waved the bloody shirt" and

strove to brand all Democrats as traitors, glossing over the real problems of the country in order to emphasize the one issue of defence of the Union which would provide a simple election-cry and preserve party unity. Since, by the terms of the Constitution, elections have to be held in the United States at regular intervals, and as voters can rarely be polled on cold intellectual issues, a cry has to be found. War memories were a convenient cement for the Republican party, a cement that concealed, until the 'nineties, the divisions within the party, especially the growing split between West and East. Hence the struggle to win the votes of the ex-soldiers organized in the "Grand Army of the Republic" (G.A.R.), which, beginning with the Democrat successes of 1874, when every source of Republican strength had to be tapped, reached its climax in the presidential campaign of 1888—after which the price of support had to be paid in the form of the over-generous Disability Pension Act of 1890, "which cost the federal government more than one-fifth of its total revenue".[23]

## THE RESULTS OF PARTY STRIFE

The result of these manœuvres—apart from the cost of pensions, which eventually amounted in all to some eight billion dollars—together with the influence of the too solid South upon the Democrats, was a sterility in American politics which was not broken until new issues and new forces appeared with the rise of the Populist movement in the 'nineties. It is significant that after 1894 the Democrats did not regain control of the House of Representatives until 1910, while, although the split in the Republican ranks gave their candidate, Woodrow Wilson, the Presidency in 1912, there was no Democratic majority in a Presidential election between 1892 and 1916. From the 'nineties, indeed, American politics began to take new forms, the full significance of which did not appear until the days of Franklin D. Roosevelt and the "New Deal".

## ECONOMIC STRESSES AND POLITICAL UNREST

It was under Grant that the stresses first appeared which were eventually to produce "Populism", Theodore Roosevelt's "Square Deal" and "Progressive" Party, Woodrow Wilson's "New Freedom", and the "New Deal" of later years. They were to be found, in the first place, in the strained economic and financial conditions which resulted from the Civil War, and in the serious division of opinion between the Western and the North-Eastern States (the "North" of the war period) as to the policies to be pursued. The years of war, as always, had been years of inflation and high production. Paper money to the value of $450,000,000 had been issued in the form of dollar-bills, popularly known as "greenbacks", and prices had risen steeply. Industry had expanded rapidly, but the Army's needs and the growing population, and the stimulus of the Home-stead Act, had brought about a correspondingly rapid expansion of agricultural production, much of it on land purchased or equipped through loans contracted at the inflated price-level. With the coming of peace, despite a great increase of exports, both demand and prices fell, and farmers were faced with lower incomes but with no decrease of indebtedness. The paper currency was seriously depreciated, and financial interests were anxious to return to a policy of "sound" money, based on gold, with, in the meantime, a deliberate deflation (to reduce the greenback issue) and the payment of dues to bondholders in gold. This policy was adopted by the Republicans: in 1869 gold payment of government debts was promised, and ten years later the gold standard was restored. Strenuous efforts were made to reduce the number of greenbacks, but this led to such an outcry that it was eventually stabilized at $350,000,000. Financial policy and overproduction, however, caused the price-level to fall by more than half between 1865 and 1880, and it was not until after the mid-'nineties that the decline was checked. By that time the price of wheat, for instance, had fallen to one-third of its 1866 level. Meanwhile the agricultural States had been in a ferment of discontent that culminated in Bryan's "Populist" bid for the Presidency in 1896.

## THE MONEY ISSUE

In 1876 an "Independent National", or "Greenback", Party was formed, which made an impressive showing at least at Congressional elections. When, three years later, the gold standard was restored, interest turned to the possibility of cheapening money by increasing the coinage of silver. Owing to the scarcity of this metal the minting of silver dollars had been suspended in 1873, but almost immediately the discovery of new deposits, and the extension of the gold standard in Europe, lowered the price of silver and led to criticism of the "crime of '73". There followed a long and bitter wrangle between the bi-metallists and the advocates of a single, gold, standard, which culminated in the great scene at the Democrat Convention at Chicago in July, 1896, when Bryan denounced the attempt to "crucify mankind upon a cross of gold". In the presidential election that followed Bryan, however, polled 6,500,000 votes to the Republican McKinley's 7,000,000, and the single, gold, standard was finally established four years later.

## THE FARMER'S PROBLEMS:
## (1) THE NEED FOR CREDIT

One reason for the farmer's need for cheap money was the impossibility of cultivating the great regions of the Mid- and Far-West without agricultural equipment: on the treeless plains great quantitities even of metal fencing had to be bought. Loans and mortgages were unavoidable: "the Great West was the least self-sufficient rural community in the world". Few rural communities are completely self-sufficient, and the moneylender, be he banker, *kulak* or *banya*, has always been a necessary part of the agricultural community. The American farmer, however, tackled virgin land which produced great quantities of crops, which were needed by growing communities on the Atlantic seaboard and across the ocean. Rapid development promised him a prosperous livelihood, but labour was scarce and costly equipment was needed which had to be paid for at high rates of interest. The situation was rendered the more difficult because of the comparative scarcity of banking facilities outside the North-East, a deficiency which, apart from some concessions in the Currency Act of 1900, was not to be remedied until Woodrow Wilson's creation of the Federal Reserve System in 1913. The farmer was therefore at the mercy of economic forces which he could neither comprehend nor control: hence his long agitation for banking as well as currency reform. The industrialist who produced the farmer's equipment, on the other hand, was working in a market protected by high tariffs, which not only kept prices artificially high but also encouraged monopolies, against which the farmer struggled in vain: "the towers of New York", one historian has said, were built "upon southern and western backs".

## (2) THE RAILWAY MONOPOLY

For the disposal of his crop the farmer was utterly dependent on the railways, which also controlled, in many cases, all the storage facilities he required. For this monopolistic service, too, he had to pay dearly, and it was the railways' abuse of their power that not only brought him actively into politics, but eventually, when evidence of discriminating practices in industrial haulage, also, was forced upon its attention, stirred the Federal Government into its first intervention against monopoly power with the Interstate Commerce Act of 1887, ineffective though the measure proved to be.

### SCANDALS OF THE GRANT RÉGIME

Grant, mindful of the interests of Western Republicans, was not opposed to a continuance of the greenback issue, but with his influential supporters to sustain him favoured in general a "sound money" policy and a high tariff, a tariff that tended to be framed to suit special interests rather than the general economic advancement of the country. From this time, indeed, dates the intensive lobbying of Congress which led Wilson to complain, in 1913, when he was shaping his own tariff legislation, that it was impossible to throw a brick anywhere near the Senate Chamber without hitting a representative of a special interest. Grant, pulled this way and that by influences he did not understand, was particularly vulnerable, and though honest and incorruptible himself, was surrounded by men who did not hesitate to take advantage of his gullibility and of the cover his office afforded them. Hence the squalid scandals of his two administrations.

### "BLACK FRIDAY"

The first scandal, an attempt to exploit the currency situation by cornering gold, broke within six months of Grant's Inauguration. The protagonists were Jay Gould and Jim Fisk, a pair of precious rascals, typical products of the opportunities and opportunism of the times, whose names have become a byword for flaunting venality, and who contributed much to the brash opulence that caused Mark Twain to style the Grant era "the gilded age". By financial jugglery Gould and Fisk had earlier gained control of the Erie railroad, an important line from New York to Buffalo, which they so crippled by the manipulation and "watering" of its stock from seventeen to seventy-eight million dollars that for many years it paid no dividends, and, having no funds for improvements, gained an unenviable reputation for the unreliability of its services and the lack of security for its passengers. This unfortunate line they ran from an Opera House in New York. Gould's aim was to crown his financial activities by cornering gold, which he could do provided that the U.S. Treasury did not intervene by selling its own stocks. Through the President's brother-in-law, who was amenable to appropriate methods of persuasion, he was introduced to Grant, whom he entertained at the Opera House. Grant declined to be drawn on financial policy, but gave no sign of objecting to being questioned, and allowed Gould to foist on him, as Assistant Secretary of the Treasury, an old comrade-in-arms, General Butterfield. There followed a drive on gold, which, on "Black Friday", 24th September, 1869, forced its price up to 162 before Grant intervened and ordered the Treasury to sell. Gould, warned by Butterfield, wriggled out in time, but the shock to trade and to public confidence was a serious one. A Congressional investigation brought the scandal uncomfortably close to the White House, but Fisk, cynically distorting the comment of an earlier adventurer, gaily proclaimed that nothing was lost save honour, while Gould lived to control the Union Pacific, among other things, and to build up a fortune of more than seventy millions before his death in 1892 (the Union Pacific, significantly enough, went into liquidation in the following year).

OTHER SCANDALS

The Erie Railroad and the gold corner were typical, though extreme, illustrations of what financial manipulation could, and did, do. Three years after "Black Friday" came the Crédit Mobilier revelations, and between 1874 and 1876 a whole series of exposures: the Secretary of the Treasury was found to be in collusion with collectors of overdue taxes, Grant's private secretary was involved in a "Whiskey Ring" to defraud the revenue, and both his brother, Orvil Grant, and the Secretary of War were shown to be making money out of licensing Indian trading-posts. Grant was not himself involved, but he excited suspicion through his generous refusal to distrust a friend. Later came evidence that James G. Blaine, Speaker of the House of Representatives, and a man with presidential ambitions (he became the Republican candidate in 1884), had accepted considerations from a railway company for legislative favours received, and that there had been serious fraud in the Post Office over contracts for the carriage of mails on certain important roads popularly known as the "Star Routes". Such, unhappily for the reputation of the hero of Appomattox, were the conditions of "Grantism". The Republicans, however, had no monopoly of crooked dealings. The opportunities of the Democrats, since they were out of the federal government, were more limited, but they were not unaffected by Congressional scandals, and had scope in State and city administration.

## THE "TWEED RING"

The most spectacular example of Democrat corruption was the "Tweed Ring" in New York. New York had long been dominated by the Democratic "Tammany Hall" organization, formed at the end of the eighteenth century for social and charitable purposes. This was the organization which cared, among other things, for the welfare of immigrants and guided them into the intricacies of American politics. It thus came to command votes, and, therefore, power, and, through the default of those citizens whose normal avocations kept them from giving close attention to political matters, the professional politicians who controlled it became the masters of the city and of its resources, at a time when rapid development, with a population increasing from three to eight hundred thousand in the twenty years from 1840 to 1860, offered great opportunities to men on the make. The man who came to control Tammany at this period, and therefore to dominate New York, was "Boss" William M. Tweed (1823–76), whose flagrant dishonesty cost the city $100,000,000. Among his cronies was the egregious Fisk, and it was judges in Tweed's pay who aided Fisk and Gould in their raids on the Erie railroad. Only when the members of the "Ring" began to quarrel among themselves in 1871 did exposure begin. Then there was, as in other places under similar conditions, a cleaning-up process that lasted until the reformers relaxed, when, only too often, the process had in time to be repeated. After 1871 the "Tweed Ring" was broken, and Tweed himself died in prison in 1876, but Tammany remained, with other bosses, such as "Honest John" Kelly and Richard Croker, to exercise Tweed's sway, if with less evil intent and consequences and in pursuit only of what was euphemistically styled "honest graft". The need for further reforms survived even Theodore Roosevelt's onslaught as Police Commissioner in the 'nineties.

## THE MOVEMENT FOR REFORM

Tammany's power had come about partly through the "spoils" system of appointment to public offices, which had actually originated in New York State, and the system had led to such abuses by the time of Grant that there was a movement for Civil Service reform, to take some government posts out of politics and thereby diminish, if not actually remove, the scope for corrupt dealings, by which, for instance, government officials were expected to subscribe to the funds of the party that gave them their posts. It was one of the counts against Grant that he showed no interest in this important reform.

## THE CRISIS OF 1873

When Grant stood for re-election in 1872 Civil Service reformers were among those who broke away from the Party and formed a Liberal Republican movement of protest which put forward Horace Greeley as its candidate. Grant's position was too strong, however, and he was too well supported by entrenched interests: Greeley failed by 750,000 votes. Yet within six months of Grant's second Inauguration something of a day of reckoning arrived when, in September, 1873, the failure of Jay Cooke's banking house exploded the inflated prosperity of the post-war years, and introduced a long period of depression. Cooke had made a large fortune through dealings in government bonds during the Civil War, and had since plunged into railroad development with the Northern Pacific, a line which, generously subsidized in the accustomed manner by land-grants, eventually made some seventy million dollars on its land-sales. Cooke had overreached himself, however, and his collapse not only shook the stock market but brought much of America's industry to a standstill and threw thousands out of work. Moreover, coinciding as it did with a similar crisis of too rapid development in Germany, it opened a long period of depression on both sides of the Atlantic.

The years that followed are of special significance in American history, for they saw the nation beginning the slow process of adjustment to changing conditions. A detailed analysis would be out of place in this study, but four aspects may be considered; civil service reform, the rise of Labour movements, agrarian revolt and the attack on monopolies and trusts.

## THE REFORM MOVEMENT: (1) THE CIVIL SERVICE

Of particular significance in the development of American governmental practice was the campaign for civil service reform and the encouragement of appointment to the public service on merit and not merely as a reward for party services. Under the conditions of American political life a certain amount of presidential patronage is essential, if the work of local organization is to proceed at all (between 1953 and 1955, for instance, Dwight D. Eisenhower, as the first Republican President for twenty years, was responsible for nearly seventy thousand appointments[24]). All Presidents have complained of the burden of patronage, and the story is well known of Lincoln's concern, at a critical period of the Civil War, less with the military situation than with the difficulty of deciding on an appointment to a minor position in the Post Office, the branch of the federal service which, through the many openings it offers, is traditionally one of the principal sources of federal patronage. The limitation of patronage in the interests of efficiency, and as a check to corruption, was an issue in Grant's first term, and an Act establishing a system of competitive examinations, on the British model, was passed in 1871, though vested interests rendered it ineffective. Grant's successor, Hayes, pledged his support to reform, but his scope was limited by the peculiar conditions of the disputed election which returned him, and which left him a number of eager supporters to reward. He cleared up the administration, however, and asserted an independence of Congress, to which Grant had never aspired, by refusing to acquiesce in all the appointments Senators and Congressmen required him to make for their followers. In particular, he fought hard, and in the end successfully, against the abuse by Senator Roscow Conkling, boss of New York State, of the New York Customs House as a comfortable and profitable berth for his party henchmen. Since Sumner's resignation, after the failure to impeach Johnson, Conkling had been the most powerful figure in the Senate, which he had led in its efforts to keep Presidents in their place. He was, however, worsted in his struggle with Hayes, who knew his powers and exercised them, dismissing from the Customs House Conkling's nominees, Alonzo Cornell and Chester Arthur, and resolutely refusing to reinstate them. Conkling now became something of a personification of the spoils system. In the 1880 election he campaigned for a third term for the more obliging Grant, but James A. Garfield, a Congressman of long standing, with a good record as a Civil War soldier, was chosen as Republican candidate, and was duly elected, though in an attempt to placate the Conkling faction Chester Arthur was associated with him as Vice-President. Garfield soon showed that he was as determined as Hayes to make his own appointments to the Customs House. Conkling, to test his strength, resigned from the Senate with his friend Tom Platt, and stood for re-election, only to be badly defeated, to the general surprise and delight. He had to retire into the practice of the law, where he shortly distinguished himself before the Supreme Court by arguing, significantly as it proved, that the famous clause of the 14th Amendment which forbade any State to "deprive any person of life, liberty *or property* without due process of law" protected business against interference by State legislatures. Meanwhile, another event had occurred, even more decisive in its effect on corrupt spoilsmen than the fall of Conkling. Only a few months after his inauguration Garfield, the second of the three Presidents to be assassinated in office, was mortally wounded by a disappointed place-seeker. Arthur succeeded him (1881–85), but to the chagrin of the spoilsmen rose above his past, and proved a better President than could have been expected. In 1883, by the Pendleton Act, a Civil Service Commission was established, which put a proportion of the posts in government offices beyond political control and empowered the President to extend the list. Arthur chose his Commission well, and later Presidents, especially Wilson and the two Roosevelts, greatly extended the list of non-partisan appointments, though it was not until the Hatch Act of 1939, passed to prevent New Deal appointments from becoming party rewards, that federal employees were finally forbidden to take any part in political activity. Even then, as the practice of more recent Presidents has shown, a Civil Service on the British model is not necessarily the most appropriate answer to the government's requirements under the conditions of American political life. The Pendleton Act did a good deal, however, to check some of the worst abuses of the spoils system: its moral effect probably counted for more than its immediate practical results.

THE REFORM MOVEMENT:
(2) RECONSIDERATION OF "SEPARATION OF POWERS"

This first civil service reform is associated with the name of Senator George Pendleton of Ohio, who steered the necessary measure through the Senate. Pendleton also had views on wider sesues of governmental reform. He realized the weakness of the system that rigidly separated Executive and Legislature, and favoured a modified version of the British practice which would permit members of the President's Cabinet to take part in Congress debates on legislation. At about the same time a student of politics in his late twenties named Woodrow Wilson was working on a Ph.D. thesis on Congressional Government, which was published in 1885. Like Pendleton, Wilson deplored the weakness that flowed from the separation of powers, and from the increasing supremacy of the legislative over the executive branch since 1865, and looked to some adaptation of the British system as a remedy. He was to change his views when Theodore Roosevelt's example revealed to him what presidential leadership, effectively exercised, could achieve, but his study of the American system in these critical years of the Grant era and after was fundamental to his later achievement. For long the Presidential function was to watch legislation in the general interest, and to try to prevent an irresponsible Congress, or sectional interests, from paying too little regard to that interest. The function was, in fact, something of a negative, rather than a positive one, and President and Congress seemed at times to operate in different spheres. Hence the desire to establish formal links. Grant's conception of his office had been a doubly negative one, but his immediate successors were more active, and Grover Cleveland, in particular, while rarely taking a positive line, became noted for the firmness with which he resisted Congressional and sectional pressure. It was left to Theodore Roosevelt and Wilson in the new century, however, to develop the constructive rôle of which the Presidential office was capable, but which remains a matter of personality, opportunity and political skill, rather than of strict constitutional precedent.

## THE REFORM MOVEMENT:
## (3) THE RISE OF LABOUR

If the growing complexity of American life raised problems of the scope and functions of the executive power in the administration, it posed, no less, serious questions of the relations of industry to the community, and of the relationship within the industrial sphere of capital and labour. As elsewhere under modern industrial conditions the scales were long weighted against labour, but trade union organization, and growing social awareness of the inadequacy of *laissez faire*, gradually brought improved conditions, economically, socially and legally, though the United States in the main lagged behind Britain, and it was not until the days of the "New Deal" in the nineteen-thirties that an adequate code of reforms was finally secured. Meanwhile labour's share of the national wealth failed to keep pace with the expansion of American riches. In the forty years from 1874 to 1914 the national income doubled, but real wages rose by less than one-fifth.[25] A well-known estimate of 1890 calculated that one per cent of the families of the country owned more than the remaining ninety-nine per cent, and a generation later, in 1920, nearly twelve per cent of the national income went to less than one per cent of those in receipt of incomes. Within the world of labour itself trade unionism was, inevitably, the product of American conditions and attitudes, and though similar in many of its manifestations to British trade-unionism, with which, indeed, it had at times close links, it has in the main developed along different lines. In particular, while, as in Britain, the more easily organized craft unions of the skilled workers were formed first, the industrial unions, embracing all workers in a particular industry, which were characteristic of the "New Unionism" of Britain in the 'nineties, were not generally formed in the United States until the nineteen-thirties, with the appearance of the Congress of Industrial Organizations (C.I.O.). In the mid-nineteenth century the tendency, as in Britain, was to devise wide and all-embracing unions, with broad political and social aims of a utopian nature. These largely failed, and it was through more limited objectives that a well-organized labour movement eventually emerged.

## THE NATIONAL LABOR UNION: IMMIGRATION CONTROL

The first attempt at a general union was made in 1866, when the National Labor Union was formed. Though this lasted only six years, it built up a large membership and was able to persuade Congress to pass some significant legislation. During the Civil War employers had been empowered to bring workers to America on contract, and in addition to Europeans many Chinese had been introduced. Contract labour was bitterly resented by American workers, and there now began that resistance to uncontrolled immigration on the part of organized labour which was eventually to contribute much to the severe restrictions imposed after the First World War. A restrictive Bill, imposing a literacy test, was first passed by Congress in 1897, and, after four presidential vetoes, was carried over Wilson's veto in 1917: the far more drastic "quota" laws were to follow in 1921, 1924 and 1929. America ceased to be an open door for immigrants in 1921, but as early as the 'sixties American workers, through the National Labor Union, were calling for restrictions on contract labour and

Chinese immigration. Contract labour was forbidden by law in 1885, though it was some years before the ban became effective. Three years earlier, in 1882, the first formal restriction on immigration had been imposed by the exclusion of Chinese. Chinese had settled in California in large numbers since the 1849 gold rush, and had been widely employed in railroad construction. As in Australia and New Zealand, however, they were felt to be an alien, inassimilable element, and their presence was a source of conflict with white labour. Their exclusion, at first temporary, became permanent in 1902. By that time Japanese immigration was also causing concern in California. Discriminatory State legislation led to President Roosevelt's "Gentlemen's Agreement" with the Japanese Government in 1907, but the problem was not solved until the Immigration Act of 1924 completely barred Chinese and Japanese alike.

The National Labor Union had opposed contract labour and Chinese immigration, seeing in them devices by which employers sought to undercut American labour. It had also called for an eight-hour day in industry and a Federal Department of Labour, and given its support to the "greenback" movement. The eight-hour day was imposed by Congress on public works in 1868, and was extended to all federal employees in 1892, while a Bureau of Labor Statistics was established in 1894: this became a Government Department jointly with Commerce in 1903, and a separate Department of Labor ten years later.

## DIFFICULTIES OF THE LABOUR MOVEMENT

There were, however, many difficulties in the way of the improvement of labour conditions. The constant flow of immigrants created an unending reservoir of mainly unskilled labour, which tended to keep wages down and hampered union activity through the babel of languages it introduced and the cheap strike-breakers it provided. American society was, in any case, highly fluid, and in the "land of opportunity" it was many years before there was any general understanding of what Theodore Roosevelt was to describe in his *Autobiography* as "the crass inequality in the bargaining relation between the employer and the individual employee standing alone". It is significant that it was in the industries controlled by the largest and wealthiest organizations, in coal, iron and steel and oil, that union organization faced its greatest difficulties, being frustrated by "iron-clad oaths" and "yellow-dog" contracts, and, later, by company unions and welfare schemes. It was in these industries, too, that unskilled labour could most readily be employed. So much labour was required, indeed, as these great and vital industries expanded, that the employment of unskilled men was unavoidable, and contributed to the development of mechanization to overcome lack of skill. This in turn had its effect on immigration, encouraging the "new immigration" from Central and Southern Europe. In the words of the report of the Immigration Commission, published in 1911–12, "recent immigrants who, before immigrating to the United States, had never seen a coal mine" were ready to work in one "after a few days' apprenticeship".[26] (The automobile industry, with its mass production techniques, was to be built up on this rationalization of the diminished importance of industrial skill.)

## LEGAL DIFFICULTIES: THE INJUNCTION

There were also serious legal bars to the improvement of labour conditions and the development of union organization. Numerous Acts, both State and Federal, were declared by the Courts to be unconstitutional for interfering with personal liberties or property rights which were guaranteed, or seemed to be guaranteed, by the Constitution, while the Federal Government had the power of making regulations only in the case of its own employees or, under Article 1 of the Constitution, in matters affecting interstate commerce (hence the comparatively early passage of legislation on behalf of railway workers). The most powerful weapon against unions was the injunction against striking, first invoked in the bitter conflict of the Pullman strike of 1894, and nominally invoked then because interference with the railways meant the interruption of interstate commerce and the federal mails. The "injunction" came to be widely used, and was eventually regarded as being based on the celebrated Sherman Anti-Trust Law of 1890, which had declared illegal any "combination or conspiracy in restraint of trade among the several states". A Supreme Court decision of 1908 formally recognized a labour organization as coming under this ban, though Senator Sherman, when he introduced his Bill in 1890, had not conceived it as restricting labour in any way, and had, indeed, considered this to be so obvious as not to call for mention in the text. Wilson's "New Freedom" attempted to reverse the Court's ruling, but the Clayton Act of 1914 left so many loopholes that the Courts interpreted away what had seemed to be gained. Not until 1932, when the Norris-La Guardia Act was passed, was the use of the injunction prohibited in disputes not affecting the national well-being.

## ATTITUDES TO STRIKES

In all industrial societies, until recent years, labour organization and its weapon, the strike, have tended to be regarded with suspicion. Through its very national ethos America was, perhaps, particularly prone to this view. To strike in the land of freedom and opportunity, where no rigid class structure existed, was considered by many as at least a contradiction in terms, at most an act of rebellion comparable to that of 1861.[27] This outlook was reflected, partly from conviction, partly from experience, in the attitude of the labour organizations themselves. The National Labor Union, idealistic in outlook, was prepared to support strikes in the last resort, but hoped to achieve its aims by negotiation and education. In particular, it sought a general eight-hour day, arguing that increased leisure would swell the requirements, and therefore the purchases, of the workers, and thereby expand the internal market for industry's products, so that manufacturers and workers alike would become more prosperous and the status of the workers would be raised "until the capitalist and the laborer are one". This shrewd grasp of the interdependence of the prosperity of worker and owner was eventually to become the basis of America's industrial fortunes, though not explicitly until the nineteen-twenties, when Herbert Hoover (President 1929–33) could foresee "the final triumph over poverty". In the 'sixties the National Labor Union was too utopian in outlook. Capital and labour were to drift apart, and American capital to be distinguished by its paternalistic attitude, and its opposition to workers' organizations: the sublime comment of an extreme representative of narrow capitalism, at the time of the great anthracite strike of 1902, is well known:

> The rights and interests of the laboring man will be protected and cared for—not by the labor agitators, but by the Christian men to whom God in his infinite wisdom has given the control of the property interests of this country.

## THE "KNIGHTS OF LABOR"

The National Labor Union represented an attempt to combine all workers in a vast, national union. The next great effort at labour unity, the "Knights of Labor", founded in 1869, was hardly less idealistic in its aims, but was organized as a federation of essentially local Assemblies, both "trade" and "mixed", with a General Assembly under a "Grand Master Workman". The emphasis upon the locality was an obstacle to the broad craft organization, on which, in America as in Britain, trade-unionism was to grow, and was to prove a factor in the eventual decline of the Knights. In their day, however, they were a large and vigorous organization, with, at their height, a membership of some 700,000. Local and District Assemblies were established throughout the United States, and extended even to Europe, one British union at least, that of the Stove-Grate Workers, owing its origins to the Order.[28] The aim of the Knights was "agitation, education and organization' to bring to an end "that curse of modern civilization—wage slavery", but strikes were discouraged as "deplorable in their effects", a reflection of the disastrous failures of the 'seventies. It was under Terence V. Powderly (1849–1924), Grand Master Workman from 1879 to 1893, that the Order achieved its greatest successes. The boycott was preferred to the strike as a weapon, but it was a series of strikes in the 'eighties that built up the Order's prestige and raised its membership from 1,000 to 700,000, creating administrative problems which Powderly had neither the means nor the ability to tackle. The greatest triumph was the successful strike in 1885 against a group of South-Western railroads controlled by Jay Gould, but the very rapidity of the Order's rise alarmed moderate opinion, and in the following year Gould returned to the attack. Another series of strikes then failed, while all labour organizations were discredited, however unjustly, by the unhappy Haymarket Square bomb outrage in Chicago. The Knights now declined almost as rapidly as they had risen. Powderly was no powerful labour leader to dominate a vast union in a period of tension. Essentially an idealist, and preferring to deal with lofty principles, he was harassed by practical difficulties. "Opposing strikes and always striking", he complained on one occasion, "the trade element in our Order has always kept me busy at the base of the breast-works."[29] It was precisely there, in the trade element and at the base of the breastworks, that the next, and most enduring, development in American labour history was to come, in the shape of the American Federation of Labor. As in Great Britain, effective trade-unionism was to succeed through the attainment of limited, practical objectives after the discrediting of its earlier utopianism.

## THE A.F. OF L.—THE ACHIEVEMENT OF GOMPERS

The American Federation of Labor (A.F. of L.) arose as an association of unions which preferred organization in *national* craft unions, with limited practical aims, to the mixed *local* assemblies, embracing all types of labour, of the Knights. Its foundation dates from 1886, though its origins in a fundamental difference of opinion with the Knights can be traced back to 1881. Its leadership, to which it owed much, was provided by the Cigar Makers' Union under two remarkable immigrants from Europe, the Hungarian Adolph Strasser and the Dutch Jew from the East End of London, Samuel Gompers (1850–1924). It was Strasser who, even before 1886, defined the aims for which the Federation was to stand: "we are going on from day to day. We fight only for immediate objects—objects that can be realized in a few years". It was Gompers, however, who was to be the dominant figure of the Federation between its establishment and his death in 1924. This shrewd, practical and tough man, "all machinery", like a New York tugboat, as a friend once described him, devoted his life to the movement, and saw its membership develop under his Presidency from some 150,000 in 1886 to more than 4,000,000 in 1920. His approach was essentially a patient, steady one: he worked intuitively, and sought, in the face of countless disappointments and distractions for the industrial workers, to make collective action, in his own phrase, "a habit". The Knights of Labor, of which he had been a member, he condemned as "an organization with high ideals but purely sentimental", and, dramatic though his appearance and actions could be, there was nothing sentimental about his hard-headed approach. Yet his zeal knew no limits, and the driving force of his attachment to the cause of labour was a deeply felt idealism and longing for justice and opportunity for his fellows. "Though we labor men usually try to express the labor movement in practical terms," he wrote in his autobiography, "still it is fundamentally spiritual—a cause which inspires dedication as completely as any religious movement."[30] For long years he was, to all intents and purposes, the A.F. of L., and when he died it was a similar, though less colourful, character, William Green, who continued his work. If he made the Federation, he kept it, in the main, within the narrow limits of craft organization, and the establishment by the dramatic and passionate John L. Lewis in 1935 of the rival Congress of Industrial Organizations was a reflection on his achievement, or at least on the failure to adapt it to new conditions. Nevertheless, he was as much a pioneer at the base of the breastwork of modern America as any who broke the soil or dug for minerals.

## THE ANTHRACITE STRIKE, 1902

The A.F. of L. was not entirely opposed to industrial unionism, for it included within its ranks unions of miners and textile workers organized on an industrial rather than a craft basis. The unions were its constituent members, and they were left free to follow their own line. Thus, it was as a member of the Federation that the United Mine Workers, under the brilliant leadership of their able President, John Mitchell (1870–1919), scored the dramatic success in the Pennsylvania anthracite strike of 1902 which Gompers, who stood behind Mitchell throughout, regarded as "the most important single incident in the labor movement of the United States".[31]

## THE "WOBBLIES"—EUGENE DEBS

It was soon after this episode, however, that an independent industrial movement was founded, the Industrial Workers of the World (I.W.W.), based largely on unorganized, unskilled labour, for which the A.F. of L. had little attraction. The "Wobblies", as they came to be called, regarded the Federation as a conservative influence, and drew their inspiration from Socialism of various kinds. Their aim was through the class war to sweep away capitalism and establish "One Big Industrial Union", and their most distinguished figure was Eugene V. Debs (1855–1926), notable for his leadership of the railway workers in the Pullman strike of 1894, and five times Socialist candidate for the Presidency of the United States between 1900 and 1920. The greatest success of the I.W.W. was the organization of the Lawrence, Mass., textile strike of 1912, but its doctrinaire radicalism prevented it from winning much support and was to lead it into strange courses during the war, when many members suffered for their pacifist convictions. Though it revealed the need for industrial organization, public revulsion against some of the I.W.W.'s wilder activities kept the A.F. of L. on its moderate course. Gompers was always for trade-unionism "pure and simple" (a phrase of his of which much was made by critics), and rejected all political moves, refusing to allow the Federation to be dragged into what he called "the quagmire of Socialism". The American Socialist movement never developed, therefore, the intimate association with the trade unions which has characterized the British movement during the past half century.

## CRITICAL YEARS, 1877, 1886, 1892, 1894

Gompers's opposition to political action was due in part to disposition, in part to his experience in New York in 1874, when he was involved in a police charge against unemployed. He realized then how easily sympathy with the worker in distress could be lost through agitation, and the forces of government turned against anything that seemed to threaten the social order. The twenty years that followed 1874 saw the lesson driven home. If they were the years that saw the change-over from the idealistic to the practical in American labour organization, they were no less years of many bitter industrial conflicts. When depression came the tendency was to maintain interest payments to stockholders, even when much of the stock was watered, and to seek compensation for lowered earnings in lower wages. Hence the first great strike in American history, that of 1877, when railway workers were beaten by the intervention of federal troops, though only after fierce rioting and destruction at Pittsburgh. It was the fear that a strike situation might get out of hand, together with the knowledge that *agents provocateurs* were freely used by employers, that contributed to the cautious policies of both Powderly and Gompers. Nearly a decade later came the Chicago bomb explosion. Chicago was a centre for revolutionary elements from Europe, both Marxists and anarchists, among immigrant workers. A strike for the eight-hour day led in 1886 to a clash with police at the McCormick Harvester Plant, and a protest meeting was held in Haymarket Square. This would have passed off peacefully, apart from some impassioned oratory, but as it was dispersing a bomb was thrown at the police, killing, in all, a dozen people, and injuring more than a hundred. In a fit of public panic eight known anarchists were at once arrested, and, though nothing could be proved against them, five were hanged. The whole episode was a blow to the labour movement throughout the country. Still more serious was the failure of the stand against wage-cuts made in 1892 by steelworkers at Homestead, Pennsylvania, which led to an open battle with strike-breakers protected by a private army of the notorious Pinkerton detectives hired by Henry Frick, manager of the Carnegie Steel Plant. Frick's aim was to break the steel union, and this, aided by an anarchist attempt on his life, he achieved. After 1892, despite attempts in 1901, 1910 and 1919, no independent unionism was permitted at Homestead, or at other steel centres, until the C.I.O. took up the struggle in 1936. As late as 1933, indeed, F. D. Roosevelt's Secretary of Labor, Frances Perkins, was prevented from addressing steelworkers in the streets of Homestead, and had to adjourn to federal property in the Post Office.[32]

## DEBS AND THE A.R.U.

Within a year of the Homestead strike came the severe depression of 1893, like that of twenty years earlier the result of over-rapid expansion and overmuch speculation: 600 banks and 74 railroads failed, and 3,000,000 men were unemployed. Many strikes occurred, but the most serious was that at

Pullman, Illinois, where George Pullman manufactured his "palace cars". This was the situation that made Eugene Debs a national figure—and a Socialist. Debs had been Secretary of one of the independent railway unions, but aimed at uniting railway workers in a great industrial union. This, the American Railway Union, he formed in 1893, and when Pullman refused even to consider the many grievances of his workers, the Union for a time paralysed the northern railway system. President Cleveland, appealed to by the railway magnates, sent in federal troops; but not until an injunction was resorted to, and Debs was sent to prison, was the strike broken. The Union collapsed, though the A.F. of L., which had characteristically remained neutral, later organized much of its membership in separate craft unions. Debs, in prison, seeking to rationalize his protest against the economic order, read, and was converted to, Socialism. In the words of one who knew him well, "he became a Socialist because no worthier cause was available":[33] he was, in fact, an intellectual radical of the type that grasped Socialism as a remedy and was later to be disillusioned by the Soviet dictatorship. Apart from him, the man who came best out of the tense situation was the reforming Governor of Illinois, John P. Altgeld, who had recently pardoned the survivors of the Haymarket Square trial, and who now resisted the President's despatch of federal troops, maintaining that he had the situation well in hand with local militia. Altgeld, however, wished only to hold the ring: other, and more powerful, influences were determined to break the strike, and much public opinion was with them. Debs could not but be regarded as a dangerous firebrand, and Altgeld's resistance to federal intervention was denounced as "the same States Rights rot that was the cause of the rebellion".[34] To many good Republicans and conservative northern Democrats Altgeld and Debs seemed for a moment almost as great a menace to the Union as Jefferson Davis had been.

Had the trade-union movement been stronger, and the A.F. of L. prepared to intervene in politics, this period of the mid-'nineties, with the growing appeal of Populism, might have seen the coming together of industrial and agrarian unrest in a great movement of reform. Hence the suggestion that the presidential election of 1896 was "the most fateful . . . since

1860". The campaign for silver, however, with its prospect of inflation, a more doubtful blessing to the industrial worker than to his farming brother, offered little to bring industrial and agricultural workers together, and the fear of inflation was skilfully exploited by the Republican supporters of gold. After President McKinley's Inauguration the protest movements were obscured by rising prosperity and the patriotic emotion of the war with Spain, but they remained to inspire Theodore Roosevelt's Progressivism and the reforms of Wilson.

## The Reform Movement:
### (4) Agrarian Protests: The Farmers' Achievement

The origins of agrarian protest in the financial difficulties of the years after the Civil War have already been touched on. The labours of the farmer may not lend themselves as readily to celluloid entertainment as the more dashing exploits of the trapper and cowboy whom the cinema has ennobled as the first American heroes, but it was above all the farmer who first made the United States. Without the vast expansion of food production, and, no less important, of food exports, which the farmer made possible, the population of the country could not have grown as it did, or received from abroad, in return for exports of food, the resources that went to build up American industry. In 1866 the production of wheat was 152,000,000 bushels. By 1897 it had topped 600,000,000, and apart from poor harvests in 1900 and 1904 it was not to fall below this figure until the tragic years of depression in the nineteen-thirties. Exports of wheat, some 140,000,000 bushels in 1866, reached a peak of nearly 240,000,000 bushels in 1901, and during the same period exports of corn rose to 200,000,000 bushels and those of meat to some 700,000,000 pounds. All this reflected the increase in the number of farms, which was 2,000,000 in 1860 and 6,000,000 fifty years later; yet the farming population expanded only slowly, and relatively to the rest of the population actually declined. Apart from the richness of the virgin land, it was, in fact, mechanization that made this vast outpouring possible. Faced with a shortage of labour on the land from the Civil War years onwards, America made herself the pioneer of agricultural mechanization, even as she

Y

was stimulated to the development of mechanized processes in industry by the pressure of immigration.

## MECHANIZATION IN AGRICULTURE

The very physical conditions of the newly-opened areas dictated the use of mechanical contrivances. As settlement moved out on to the great plains beyond the 98th meridian it struck a dry, treeless waste that could not be cultivated until the hard, though rich, soil had been broken, water had been raised from underground, and farms had been protected by fencing. The tough soil was dealt with by the steel plough, invented by James Oliver of Indiana in 1869, the water problem by the use of windmills, and the lack of timber for fencing overcome by the use of barbed-wire, invented by two Illinois farmers, Joseph Glidden and Jacob Haish, in 1874. Without barbed-wire and the windmill settlement must have come more slowly, but the pace of agricultural development was determined no less by the speed with which a ripening crop could be harvested. Cyrus McCormick's famous reaper had been invented in 1834, but did not come into general use until the farmer was hit by the labour shortage of the Civil War. The decisive invention, however, was that of the twine-binder, devised by John Appleby in 1873, which made the modern harvester possible. The twine-binder increased eight-fold the speed of harvesting, and did more than any other machine to raise the output of American farms. Threshing-machines followed, and before the end of the century the combine-harvester. Great teams of up to twenty-four, or even thirty, horses were used to draw the machines, preparing the way for the further revolution that was to come later with the petrol-driven tractor. The labour time needed to produce a bushel of wheat had fallen by the end of the century from three hours to ten minutes, and the value of farm machinery in use risen nearly fourfold to $750,000,000. The great crops produced were easily disposed of. The development of railway and steamship routes made it possible to ship overseas what was not consumed at home, and the low cost ensured sales. It was the cheapness and sheer bulk of the exports, indeed, that shook the economy of Europe as nothing had done since the influx of another New World export, silver, in the sixteenth century.

The effects in agricultural depression in Britain, and the raising of tariffs elsewhere, have been touched on in other chapters. They were summed-up in the estimate made by an American in 1889, that, although American agricultural wages were four times those of the Rhineland, the cost of production of wheat in the U.S.A. was only one-half the European figure.[35]

## The Farmers "farmed"

Large quantities and low prices did not necessarily benefit the farmer overmuch, especially when costs tended to be dictated by efficient, well-equipped farms on good land, and the indispensable machinery had to be paid for on a falling income or at high rates of interest. Hence the increasing tendency for farmers to become tenants rather than owners, the rapid increase in the number of agricultural labourers, and the high proportion of mortgages in certain rural States. Apart from the extravagant grants to railways, much land was monopolized by mining and lumber interests, which took advantage of the possibilities of commutation provided by the Homestead Act, and there was also much speculation by syndicates: by 1886, for instance, some 27,000,000 acres of land were owned by foreign syndicates alone.[36] The ideal of a land covered with the prosperous settlements of a property-owning democracy of independent small farmers was far from being realized. Farmers complained bitterly of being "farmed" by the railways, the banks and the stockbrokers. In addition to predatory humans, of course, they had to face such natural hazards as flood, drought, blizzard, prairie fire and grasshopper plague, and in certain regions they had to develop special techniques of "dry farming" to overcome the scarcity of water. And always, until the coming of the automobile revolutionized rural life, there was the problem of loneliness. Many farmers moved on when the first richness of a settlement had been exhausted, hoping for better conditions elsewhere. Until the end of the century, at least, American agriculture was still largely extensive: the area under cultivation increased between 1866 and 1899 from 15,000,000 to 44,000,000 acres. Hence the tragic erosion that followed much pioneer settlement, especially in regions of light soil and low rainfall: enormous quantities of good earth are now carried away every year by American rivers, much of it the result of the prodigal misuse of the soil.

## THE "FARM PROBLEM"

With all these difficulties to contend with, and lacking the means of bringing pressure to bear upon the law-makers in distant Washington as readily as the industrial interests could do, the farmers have hardly ceased since 1865 to present a serious issue: the "farm problem" is, indeed, endemic in American politics. With the creation of new States in the West, and the consequent addition of senatorial seats, farmers have at least been able to make themselves heard in the Senate, but for long years after the Civil War they felt that their interests were being neglected. Much help has been given, however, since the Homestead Act was passed in 1862. The Morrill Act has already been referred to, and 1862 saw also the establishment of a Federal Department of Agriculture, which was raised to Cabinet rank in 1889. In 1887 the Hatch Act was passed, providing for agricultural experimental stations in each State, and much experimental work has been done on such problems as pest control and the improvement of strains, and especially on drought-resisting grains. At the end of the century, with the realization that the available land was fast being allocated, a movement arose for the reclamation of dry land through federal development of irrigation. In 1902 was passed the Reclamation (Newlands) Act, under which great irrigation and water-conservation schemes have been developed. Later was to come a similar demand for the federal exploitation of hydro-electric resources, which was to be given particular significance by New Deal developments in the Tennessee Valley. Meanwhile credit facilities were provided for farmers by two great measures of the Wilson administration, the establishment of the Federal Reserve System in 1913 and the Farm Loan Act of 1916.

## THE FARMERS' REMEDY—ORGANIZATION: THE "GRANGES"

If Federal legislation advantageous to farmers was longer in coming than measures that benefited industry and commerce, it was in the Legislatures of the predominantly agricultural States that local remedies, at least, could be sought.

The first necessity was organization, and this was provided by the "Patrons of Husbandry", founded in 1867 by a government clerk, Oliver Kelley, who had been sent by President Johnson on a tour of the South, and had seen something of the depressed state of the rural areas. Kelley realized the need for educational and social organization among the farmers, and his movement, organized in local "Granges", spread rapidly throughout the country: in less than ten years there were 20,000 Granges, with a total membership of some 800,000. This Granger movement gave the farmer not only social unity but the opportunity to organize for political and economic ends. Co-operative societies were formed, and although they achieved only limited success, the Granges inspired a significant new feature in American life, the mail order business, first devised by Montgomery, Ward and Co. of Chicago in 1872 to deal with them. (A parcel-post was a long desired federal service which was established by a Congress majority of reforming Democrats and Republicans only in 1913.) In politics the Granges were chiefly concerned with the exploitation by the railways of their transport monopoly. In 1869, under Grange pressure, Illinois passed the first Act limiting railway rates, and within the next few years a number of States followed suit. The railways maintained that the regulation of rates involved interstate commerce and therefore lay outside the power of the States, and that it was, in any case a violation of the property rights specifically guaranteed against State intervention in the Fourteenth Amendment. Throughout the 'seventies the Supreme Court resisted this interpretation, but under constant pressure from business interests it changed its mind in several cases between 1886 and 1889, when it argued that the reasonableness of rates was a matter for the courts, not the legislatures, to decide. The issue then became a federal one. Already in 1887 the Interstate Commerce Act had been passed to check some of the worst abuses, but the Commission set up by the Act had only limited powers, which were whittled down by judicial interpretation. It was not until the Hepburn Act of 1906 that effective control of abuses in railway charges became possible. The immediate political results of Grangerism were, therefore, limited, and the movement lost some of its hold in the early 'eighties, which were years of mild recovery in agriculture. In 1887, however, began a succession of bad years of drought and depression, which were soon to be aggravated by the general financial depression of the early 'nineties. Under these circumstances arose a new, and more aggressively political, movement, the "Farmers' Alliances", the object of which, in the words of one fiery leader, was to "raise less corn and more Hell". Out of the Alliances was to develop the Populist movement of 1890–96.

## OTHER REMEDIES: "POPULISM"

Already, in 1879, Henry George, seeing the source of American difficulties in the abuse of her land resources, had pointed to the "single tax" on land values as the panacea for the paradox of *Progress and Poverty*, and more than two million copies of this famous book were sold, to stir up opinion in Britain, Ireland, Australia and elsewhere, no less than in the United States. Others saw panaceas in greenbackism or the free coinage of silver, and behind all the agitation was the deep religious emotionalism of simple people close to nature. This was the force which was later to inspire Prohibition, and it preserves a "Bible belt" in the United States to this day. Bryan, the Populist, who became the Democratic candidate of 1896, was its greatest spokesman, and naturally chose a biblical image when he made his "cross of gold" speech in that year: significantly enough, the last act of his career was the defence of Fundamentalism against the doctrines of evolution in the Scopes trial at Dayton, Tennessee, in 1925. It was out of the depression and agitation of 1887 onwards that Populism was to arise under the leadership of such men as Bryan, and the movement was nothing if not revivalist. Its defeat in 1896 can be ascribed to the double fact that its appeal was rather to the agricultural than to the industrial worker, at a time when America was clearly in process of becoming a predominantly urban and industrial country, and that, while many traditionally Republican farmers in the Middle West were Populists, they did not favour the movement's absorption into the Democratic party. The fact that the "new immigrants", now swarming into Eastern industry, were mainly Roman Catholic, and allergic to Protestant revivalism, may also have played its part.

## The Aims of Populism

Nevertheless, Populism represented a powerful movement: it brought to a head nearly thirty years of farmers' discontent, and presented for remedy a formidable list of grievances. It indicted the existing situation for breeding only two classes, "tramps and millionaires", and demanded reforms to check corruption, to increase popular political control and to improve the conditions of the people. Public ownership of the railways was insisted on since "the time has come when the railroad corporations will either own the people or the people will own the railroads", and other specific measures demanded were— a freer currency, based on both gold and silver; a graduated income tax; the protection of labour by the introduction of the eight-hour day and the restriction of immigration; the recovery of excessive railway land grants, and greater popular control in politics through the initiative and referendum (for bringing forward new measures and testing public reaction to them), the secret ballot and the popular election of Senators (who were still nominated by State Legislatures, as originally ordained by the Constitution). Populism was to go down to defeat, but most of the programme it advocated was before long to be adopted. The movement was to play, in fact, the conventional Third Party rôle in American politics by introducing proposals which the firmly established major parties could regard as tested, and adopt. True, the railways were not taken over, and the silver battle was lost, but the Acts of 1900, 1913 and 1916 eased the farmer's credit problem; an income tax, passed in 1894 and declared unconstitutional by the Supreme Court in the following year, was adopted by the Sixteenth Amendment to the Constitution in 1913; an eight-hour day was laid down for all workers on interstate railways in 1916, and the first major bar to immigration was set up in the following year. A Railroad Subsidy Forfeiture Act in 1890 declared forfeited any railway land grants not in actual use (though legal wrangles over interpretation reduced the effectiveness of the measure), and the General Revision Act of 1891 at last checked the waste of public lands. Many States discovered means of associating electors with the appointment of Senators, and in 1913 popular election was legalized by the Seventeenth Amendment. Meanwhile, other aspects of the Populist programme had been adopted by the States. The secret ballot became general and the initiative and referendum were eventually adopted by about half of the States, South Dakota leading the way in 1898. In the industrial field most States had passed before the First World War laws protecting women and children in industry, and many others had limited the hours of work for men in the interests of public health and safety (the limits beyond which the courts would not permit legislation to pass), and had adopted schemes of workmen's compensation. True to its creed, the A.F. of L. took little part in these developments, preferring that unions should negotiate with employers direct. The Clayton Act, passed under Wilson's administration, formed part, however, of the general reform movement which the Populists had inaugurated. With the acceptance of so many of its policies, indeed, Populism, in William Allen White's words, had "shaved its whiskers, washed its shirt, put on a derby and moved up into the middle of the class".[37] Yet if reform became respectable and established, the task was still far from complete. The Populists had sought protection for the farmer and industrial worker against economic insecurity and political weakness. If conditions in America improved from the 'nineties, the next great depression, which began for the farmers in the 'twenties and hit the rest of the country a stunning blow in 1929, revealed the need for further measures. The Agricultural Adjustment Act of 1938 completed for the farmers, as the Fair Labor Standards Act of the same year achieved for the industrial workers, what had been sought fifty years earlier by Populism and other movements of protest against injustice and inequality.

## Populism Defeated, 1896: William Jennings Bryan

Standing on its own in 1892 Populism suffered the usual fate of third parties in American politics. It put forward as candidate for the presidency a Civil War veteran and reformer, James Weaver, and polled one million votes in a total of some twelve million. William Jennings Bryan (1860–1925), who had already distinguished himself in the movement in his adopted State of Nebraska, set himself the task of increasing its strength by winning the Democrats to its side and thereby reconstituting the old alliance of agricultural West and South which the Civil War had broken. Bryan was a profoundly honest man of high principle, a great preacher and orator and an impressive figure, a perfect example of all that was best of the simple middle-class West of his day; "the Great Commoner", throughout his long public career, to millions of Americans. The tide, however, was running against what he stood for. He brought Populists and Democrats together, but even in the year of the fateful election of 1896 the agricultural depression at last lifted, and with the Klondike and other gold discoveries of the next few years the economic position eased. The half million votes in thirteen million that defeated Bryan indicated the new America that was coming into existence. The divergence of interest between the industrial and the agricultural worker was too great, despite all Bryan's attempts to attract the labour vote, and the last attempt of the farming interest to control the destinies of the United States was foiled. Henceforth, reform, not a change in the balance of political power, was the hope of the ordinary American: the verdict of Appomattox was underlined.

## THE WAY OF THE FUTURE—MCKINLEY

It was, in fact, with the America of industry, big business and the trusts that the future lay, and this America was embodied in the victor of 1896, the Republican William McKinley and his backer, the able, but not over-scrupulous, mine-owner, Marcus Alonzo Hanna, who, though he believed in the leadership of business, had been for twenty years an advocate of labour arbitration and the first mine-owner to recognize the miners' union. Both Hanna and McKinley believed that the best interests of America demanded vigorous business expansion, through which all, owners and workers alike, would benefit, and Hanna had denounced George Pullman for refusing to negotiate in the grim days of 1894. Their campaign in 1896 was for "the full dinner pail", and one of the first acts of the new administration was to pass a tariff law, behind which American industry could feel more than ever secure.

## PRESIDENT GROVER CLEVELAND AND REFORM

Industry and production were now assuming something of their modern form, and the Democratic administrations of

Y*

Grover Cleveland (1885-89 and 1893-97) had failed to check the steady rise of the tariff. Cleveland, the first Democratic President since the Civil War, and probably the only President of any distinction between the unexpected assumption of office by Vice-President Johnson in 1865 and Vice-President Roosevelt in 1901, did something in his first term to check the drift in American affairs that Grant had encouraged. He recovered much public land that had been fraudulently acquired, resisted sentimental appeals for pensions for all ex-soldiers (thereby jeopardizing his chances of re-election), supported the Interstate Commerce Act to check railway abuses, and courageously demanded a lowering of the tariff, which stood so high as every year to bring embarrassingly large surpluses to the federal revenues. He had little to offer the country but honest administration, and showed in his use of federal troops against the strikers in 1894, as well as in his steady support of gold during the depression of his second term, that he had no conception of the social and economic problems stirring the country. Under Benjamin Harrison, who succeeded him in 1889, the tariff issue was settled by an Act introduced by McKinley which raised some rates and devised new ones. To ensure the passage of this measure a political deal gave support to the Sherman Silver Purchase Act, the price of the support of Republicans from the Western silver-producing States, under which the Treasury guaranteed regular purchases of silver. When Cleveland returned to office in 1893 it was to meet the full force of the depression. Once again he acted with stubborn courage, calling a special session of Congress to repeal the Sherman Silver Act in the interests of "sound" money, and endeavouring, though with little success, to reduce tariffs. He had little else to offer to overcome the crisis, and his conservative financial policies, with the benefit they brought to financial interests in New York, lost him his Democratic supporters to the Populists.

## THE REFORM MOVEMENT:
## (5) THE TRUSTS

Towards the end of his first term Cleveland had drawn attention to the danger that business corporations were becoming "the people's masters". Already a number of States had passed anti-trust legislation, and the concern of the country was becoming evident at the growing power of monopolies and near-monopolies to control resources and production. Both political parties pledged themselves to reform in the election of 1888, and in 1890 the Sherman Anti-Trust Law passed Congress with but one dissentient voice. It was by the irony of circumstances—and judicial interpretation—that the Act was at first more effective against labour than against capital. It was Cleveland who, in effect, invoked it against the railway strikers in 1894. Not until 1905, when the Supreme Court reversed a decision of 1895, and recognized manufacturing as involved in interstate commerce—and therefore subject to federal legislation—did the Act begin to be really effective.

## The Rise of Trusts: John D. Rockefeller and Standard Oil

The combination and concentration of business enterprises was a result of the conditions of rapid expansion after the Civil War, of the fierce competition engendered and of the shock to confidence of the panic of 1873. The advantage lay with sheer size, as not a few ruthless men were quick to realize. The market could be controlled by apportioning business in a "pool", but more could be achieved by vertical combination, that is, by concentrating every stage of production and distribution into a few hands and using every means to squeeze out competitors. This was the method adopted by Standard Oil, which under the direction of John D. Rockefeller to a large extent set the pattern. The rapid rise of oil production has been referred to earlier. Rockefeller's advantage lay in his position at Cleveland, Ohio, well served by transport systems, and by his early, shrewd realization that the secret of the oil business was less in production than in refining and distribution. Having seen the wasteful competition and irregularity of supplies of the early days of oil production, he believed firmly in the merits of combination, in which, as he said in later years, he saw "the origin of the whole system of modern economic administration".[38] Though personally honest, he was ruthless in his search for business efficiency, and did not inquire too closely into the methods by which his subordinates got their results. Thus, he accepted the customary rebates from railways (which were not to be declared illegal until 1903), and merely made more of them because of his far-sightedness, his bargaining skill and his notable concern for detail. Thus, too, the variety in Standard Oil prices in different parts of the country, according to the degree of competition; the ruthless cutting of prices when a competitor was to be driven out of business; the greasing of legislative and legal wheels. Vast profits were made, for both supply and demand in oil seemed unlimited: earnings rose, for instance, from eleven to eighty-one million dollars between 1883 and 1903, and dividends in the same period from four million dollars to more than forty. Rockefeller was seriously concerned to market a cheap product, but it was never made as cheap as it might have been, for, as Rockefeller dryly observed, "the Standard Oil Company did not claim that they were a benevolent missionary institution".[39] His greatest success was in the creation in 1882 of the first "trust", a device by which a group of "trustees" consolidated and controlled a whole group of companies, and in effect established a monopoly. The trust had great advantages over the loose "pool", and Standard's example was widely followed, but the monopoly aspect aroused hostility. As early as 1881 Henry D. Lloyd published the first attack on Standard Oil, which he was to develop in 1894 in the influential *Wealth Against Commonwealth*, and in 1892 the trust was dissolved by the Ohio courts. By this time the Sherman Act had been passed, but in 1895 the Supreme Court declared that it could not apply to manufacture, and, to make the monopoly less obvious, Rockefeller then hit on the device of a "holding company", a finance company controlling part of the stock of other companies. In this guise Standard Oil was reconstituted under the accommodating laws of New Jersey in 1899, and the holding company then became the main instrument of consolidation throughout industry: the United States Steel Corporation, the "billion dollar corporation", took the same pattern when it was formed by J. P. Morgan in 1902 to combine his steel interests with those of Andrew Carnegie. It was as Standard Oil of New Jersey that Rockefeller's creation was eventually, in 1911, declared a monopoly by the Supreme Court and ordered to be separated into its thirty-eight components. By this time, however, the development of industry had gone too far for combination, in some form, to be avoided. The first passionate reactions, in the 'eighties and 'nineties, had been, in the sacred name of individualism, against monopoly as such. By the time the twentieth century arrived it was clear that the eggs could not be unscrambled; small individual enterprises or genuinely independent companies in the various States were an anachronism and an impossibility in major business. When finally the anti-trust laws were strictly applied it was the method rather than the aim of combination that came under attack: it was *undue* restraint of trade that was condemned. The problem, as Henry Adams saw it, was "not so much to control the Trusts as to create a society that could manage the Trusts", and for all Theodore Roosevelt's characteristically violent endorsement of "trust-busting", the shrewd comment of his indulgent critic, "Mr. Dooley", on these "neefaryous but magnificent entherprises" neatly sums up the ambivalent attitude of many observers after the worst abuses had been corrected or exposed:

> Th' thrusts are heejous monsthers built up by th' inlightened interprise ov th' men that have done so much to advance progress in our beloved counthry. On wan hand I wud stamp them undher fut; on th' other hand, not so fast.

## The Significance of Theodore Roosevelt

It was under Theodore Roosevelt that an attempt was at last made to check the more flagrant abuses of monopoly and call to order the "malefactors of great wealth", and it was McKinley's assassination at the hands of an anarchist in September, 1901, only a few months after the beginning of his second term, that made Roosevelt President and opened a new era in American history. "The adjustment of capital to democratic ends", to which he was to direct the nation's attention, was to become, as has well been said, "*the* American story of the first half of the twentieth century."[40]

McKinley, born in 1843, was the last Civil War soldier to become President. He had had a quiet, successful career as lawyer and politician, and, with his faith in business expansion, was content to preside over the vigorous America that soon recovered its confidence after the economic shocks of 1893, and even began to turn its attention to events abroad. William

Allen White described him, with his reserve and cool aloofness, as "the statue in the park speaking",[41] and the contrast between him and his successor was the greatest in the line of American Presidents. Theodore Roosevelt (1858–1919), a member of an old New York family, was the most vivid personality that has ever held the Presidency. A young man of moderately wealthy family, he had deliberately chosen to enter politics, but had also spent several years ranching after the death of his first wife in 1884, and had gained a broader knowledge of America than it was given to most politicians to acquire. Under President Harrison he had been a Civil Service Commissioner, and the stand he had then made against the spoils system had kept him in office under Cleveland. In 1895 he became a Police Commissioner in New York, and for a time dramatized reform and cleaner politics in a notoriously corrupt service. Under McKinley he had been made Assistant Secretary for the Navy. His great opportunity, which he seized with both hands, came in 1898, during the war with Spain, when, with his Western experience in mind, he formed a cavalry regiment of "Rough Riders" and took it to Cuba, where he led the famous uphill charge at San Juan. It was this that made him. He returned from Cuba, one observer has written, "as Lindbergh later came back from Paris: a hero . . . he could have been elected to anything".[42] In fact, he was elected Governor of New York. There his zeal for reform caused him to fall foul of the State boss, Tom Platt, who had left the Senate with Conkling in the far-off days of President Garfield, and had succeeded his old chief as the dominant influence in New York State. In 1900, when McKinley stood for a second term, Platt, anxious for a more pliable Governor, so arranged matters in the party that Roosevelt was nominated for the Vice-Presidency, that last resort of the unwanted. A few months later "that damned cowboy", as Mark Hanna called him in baffled fury, was President of the United States.

## ROOSEVELT AND REFORM

Little was known of Roosevelt in 1901 but his vigour and that ability to dramatize himself and the issues which concerned him, which caused "Mr. Dooley" to maintain, with sly humour, that the account he published of the Cuban campaign should have been entitled *Alone in Cubia* [*sic*]. He was to hold the stage as no President since Lincoln had been able to do, and with his immense gusto for life and office was to enjoy the Presidency as few men but his distant cousin Franklin have ever done. He was not without intellectual gifts, but it was in vigorous decision that he excelled, for his reactions to the questions of the hour were emotional, and he had no theory of government. He was, in fact, as Henry Adams wrote of him, "pure act". William Allen White, who knew him intimately, recording an occasion when Roosevelt's daughter jumped into a swimming-pool with her clothes on, commented that her father was constantly doing precisely the same thing in politics.[43] It was his emotional response to abuses, and his warm human sympathies, that made him a reformer, though it was what he said, rather than what he did, that was significant. For all his impetuosity and boyishness he was by long training a shrewd politician, and, although he made an immense pother about reform at a time when the country was beginning to feel concern at what was happening, he was careful not to alienate completely any powerful interests. This was particularly true during his first term, when he was President by accident, and did not want to prejudice his chances of becoming President in his own right. His aim was not to limit wealth, but to check its abuse: it was the *malefactors* of great wealth at whom he struck with such vigour in his speeches. He insisted that wealth should be used "for and not against the interests of the people as a whole", but this was no revolutionary doctrine, and he could therefore place himself at the head of the progressive Republicans, while denouncing Bryan as a dangerous demagogue and warning the Democrats that Populist policies would split the country. "He was not a reformer in the White House," wrote another who knew him well, Lincoln Steffens, "he was a careerist on the people's side, but working to wangle some concessions from the powers that be and make them do some things for the country at large."[44] This was not the approach of a crusader, but it was sound politically, under existing conditions, and Roosevelt did what Bryan could never do, he made reform respectable and therefore acceptable —while, as his later career was to show, acquiring most of the Populist aims for himself in the process.

## ROOSEVELT AND THE PRESIDENCY: A NEW CONCEPTION

His greatest service was his reversal of the largely negative and unconstructive interpretation of the Executive power that had obtained since 1865. He showed that the country could be given vigorous leadership, and that the President had all the powers he needed for the purpose: in his own words, "I did and caused to be done many things not previously done by the President. . . . I did not usurp power, but I did greatly broaden the use of executive power." Gompers, who was often in touch with him, summed up his achievement in the words:

> he captured the imaginations of the American people and became their great Evangelist in a demand that the government should serve the people.[45]

Much of what he was able to achieve was, of course, won with the help of Democrats in Congress. Wilson, when his turn came in 1913, had learnt much from Roosevelt's example, and found opinion prepared for what he wished to do. Had Roosevelt lived—and he was only sixty when he died in 1919 —he might well have been the Republican candidate in 1920, and would then have continued his and Wilson's work: the sorry tragedy of Warren Harding might then never have been.

## ROOSEVELT AND THE NORTHERN SECURITIES COMPANY

In the year in which Roosevelt took office the United States Steel Corporation was formed, and there was wide concern at this further evidence of the concentration of wealth and power. In 1902 J. P. Morgan went forward with plans for a great railway merger in the North-West, a fusion of his own interest with those of James Hill and others. Already, in his first message to Congress, Roosevelt had stressed the need to "do away with any evil" in the trusts, and like many people in the country he was concerned to discover whether the Government had any power at all to control them. He now, therefore, invoked the Sherman Act against Morgan's new merger, the Northern Securities Company. Morgan, shocked at such ungentlemanly behaviour, and relying on the Supreme Court verdict of 1895, tried to deal with him as between one potentate and another, but failed, and the Supreme Court eventually decided against Northern Securities. Roosevelt took particular pleasure in this reversal of the earlier decision, and initiated twenty-five anti-trust suits under the Sherman law before he ceased to be President, while his friend and successor, Taft, initiated nearly twice as many. Roosevelt could never persuade Congress to give him power to regulate, rather than merely to punish, the trusts, but a Department of Commerce was set up in 1903, and much information about their activities then became available, supplemented by the revelations which the "muckrakers" were now putting out.

## Roosevelt and the 1902 Strike

A step in Roosevelt's education in social problems came with the Pennsylvania anthracite strike of 1902, in which he intervened to break an *impasse* caused by the refusal of the owners to negotiate. The leading figure among the owners was George Baer, whose sublime confidence in the divine concern for private property has already been quoted. Roosevelt was impressed by the responsible attitude of the miners' leader, John Mitchell, and learnt how narrow and irresponsible the worst of employers could be. His intervention, for which there was no legal warrant, caught the public imagination, and indicated a new conception of the presidential office, together with more sympathy for labour than Cleveland had shown in 1894. To many industrialists, of course, Roosevelt's action smacked of "intrusion", and it was precisely their disavowal of wider responsibility that he came to resent and resist.

## Other Reforms

Having enforced the Sherman Act Roosevelt turned to the railways, tightened the long neglected Interstate Commerce Act of 1887 and encouraged the Elkins Act of 1903, which stopped the undesirable practice of paying rebates to favoured customers. In 1906 came the Hepburn Act, which for the first time empowered the Government to regulate, though not yet to fix, rates. Among other measures of this year were laws enforcing the inspection of slaughterhouses and checking the adulteration of food. Roosevelt was moved to act in both cases by information brought to him by others; in the case of the meat packers by Upton Sinclair, whose famous muckraking revelations of Chicago slaughterhouses in *The Jungle* appeared in 1906. For the nation as a whole, and especially for the West, which he knew and loved, Roosevelt introduced a vigorous policy of conservation and reclamation of resources, and created national parks and game reserves, which stand, perhaps, as his greatest monument. Above all, however, he gave the American people, it has well been said, "a new sense of pride and confidence in their government".[46]

## President Taft, 1909–13

When Roosevelt left office in 1909 he was succeeded by the genial burly figure of William Howard Taft (1857–1930), whom he himself had recommended to the Republican party as the favoured candidate. Taft, however, proved a disappointment to him. An attempt to improve the tariff led, through the pressure of interests upon Senate, to the Payne-Aldrich Act of 1909, which raised most tariffs and thereby contributed to the Republican defeats in the mid-term elections of 1910, and there were signs of some reversal of Roosevelt's conservation policies. Taft was well-intentioned, and sympathetic to reform, but weak and dominated by the "Old Guard" of the party, and cautious in his dealings with Congress. He admitted himself that when first addressed as "Mr. President" he looked round for Roosevelt, and he was well described as "an amiable island entirely surrounded by men who know exactly what they want". He had promised to carry out Roosevelt's policies, and did so, as one critic complained, "on a shutter". Hence the split in the Republican party between progressive and conservative elements which put Wilson in the White House in 1913.

## Roosevelt and "Progressivism"

Roosevelt left America for a year in 1909–10, and when he returned, at the age of only fifty-two, he was inevitably drawn back into politics. His own thinking had proceeded farther in the direction of social reform, and he now came out for what he called "the square deal", "more substantial equality of opportunity and reward", together with restrictions on the power of special interests to influence government. This was suprisingly near to Populism, and put him at the head of all

Progressive Republicans. In 1911 was formed the Progressive Republican League, and after much manœuvring the League split from the main body of the party and put Roosevelt forward as its candidate for the presidential election of 1912. Roosevelt agreed to stand, feeling, as he put it in a phrase that became famous, "like a bull moose", and hoping to change the balance of power in the Republican party. In the event he received four million votes to Taft's three million, but Wilson, with six million, was returned.

## The Coming of Woodrow Wilson

Roosevelt's programme in the election he had styled "The New Nationalism"; Wilson had countered with "The New Freedom". The difference between the two programmes was indicated in the title. The Republicans were, by tradition and the verdict of 1865, the Nationalist party, opposed to separatism on the part of the States, and Roosevelt had learnt the power of the federal government, and wished to use it to control wealth in the interests of all. This was in time to become accepted Democratic doctrine, when, under Franklin Roosevelt, the traditional rôles of Republican and Democrat were to be reversed. Theodore Roosevelt realized after the election that he had made the mistake of leaving the Republican party to the more conservative elements, who, however, controlled the local organizations and therefore the hopes of future "loaves and fishes". As he ruefully admitted, the Progressives could only repent and return to the fold. It was to be left for Eisenhower, many years later, to reshape Republican thinking, and the "New Nationalism" was to fade out.

Wilson in 1912 wished to return to an earlier tradition, to liberate Americans from organized wealth, to break up the trusts (not merely to regulate them) and to restore free competition. This was the "New Freedom" with a vengeance, and showed little understanding of the economic forces at work. He and Roosevelt, were at one, however, in wishing to extend the executive power in order to carry out their aims. Their only difference, otherwise, was over the tariff, which Democrats traditionally wished to lower, Republicans to maintain.

## President Woodrow Wilson, 1913–21

If Roosevelt had been educated within politics, Woodrow Wilson (1856–1924) had been educated into them. A native of Virginia, son of a Presbyterian minister, he was of mixed Scots and Irish descent, and grew up in the defeated South. He went to Princeton, where he later became a Professor in 1890 and President of the College in 1902. From Princeton he was to enter politics in 1910 as Governor of New Jersey, and within three years after that he was to be in the White House. He came to office, therefore, with little political background. At Princeton he had shown the same inspired and capable leadership that he was to show in Washington, and the same intellectual arrogance and intolerance of opposition which were later to handicap him so seriously. The practice of government had always been a favourite study, as his earlier writings had shown, and while at Princeton he made something of a name for himself as a conservative Democrat: he was, it has well been said, "a politician among scholars".[47] As early as 1906 his name was put forward as a Democratic candidate for the Presidency more acceptable to conservative elements than Bryan. (George Harvey, the New York editor who proposed him, was later to leave the party in disgust at Wilson's policies, and to have the doubtful privilege, at the Republican convention of 1920, of proposing another strange candidate, Warren Harding.) In 1910 Wilson was invited by the Democrats of New Jersey to stand for the Governorship of the State. New Jersey was a notoriously boss-run State, but the winds of reform were blowing and the Democrats wanted a respectable candidate. Wilson stood and was elected—and then rounded on the corrupt gang which had put him in. He made himself the leader of the party in the legislature, supported an extensive programme of reforms, and in a few months had made himself known throughout the country. It was a trial run which gave him the nomination for the Presidency in 1912.

### Wilson—Strength and Weakness

When in 1913 Wilson took office, he showed from the first that he meant to lead by appearing before Congress to deliver an inaugural message, a step that no President had taken for more than a century. Until his last unhappy years, when he was preoccupied with Europe, he used all his talents for leadership to get what he wanted from Congress, not hesitating at times to appeal over its head to the electorate, as he was to appeal to the people of Europe over their governments' heads with disastrous effect in 1919. There were those who called him "a cold fish", and he could be stiff and unbending—and, as Europe was to see, self-righteous with all the righteousness of his Calvinist ancestry. Yet he had a great natural dignity, and was moved by a high idealism. Gompers came to feel for him a reverential admiration, and in his autobiography accords him the rare title of a President "for whom we did not have to make excuses".[48] He could be rigid and unshakable in what he felt to be right, and this was in time to prove a serious drawback. He felt that he knew what the people of America wanted done, but his estimate of the situation was his own, and, although he was mainly right in his early days, he had lost touch by 1919. He was, moreover, too much the party leader, and made little attempt to put himself at the head of all progressive feeling in the country. The Democrats had been out of power since 1897, and he showed himself a good party manager. His first three Congresses had Democratic majorities, but Wilson failed to grasp the significance of the change that took place in the mid-term elections of 1918, and his final failure was due in no small part to his partisan attitude. Nevertheless, there was true greatness in him, and the achievements of his two administrations, before war engrossed all his attention, were impressive, even if the Republicans afterwards allowed much to lapse. He owes not a little of his place in history to the fact that he reconciled the traditionally "States' rights" party of the Democrats to confidence in the use of federal power: on this conversion Franklin Roosevelt was later to build much.

## WILSON AND REFORM

The programme of reform which Wilson put before the country in his brief Inaugural address was achieved in less than two years. The aim, he had previously declared, lay in "setting the government free and the business of the country free". Nineteen-thirteen saw carried a lowering of the tariff by the Underwood Act, and the establishment of the Federal

Reserve; 1914 the setting up of the Federal Trade Commission, to investigate trusts and unfair competition, and the passage of the Clayton Anti-Trust Law, which sought to supplement the operation of the Sherman Act. In 1915 came the Seamen's Act to improve conditions in the merchant marine, and in 1916 a Workmen's Compensation Act for federal employees, an Act restricting child labour in interstate commerce (later to be declared unconstitutional), and another establishing the eight-hour day for railway workers. In addition, loans and credits were made available for farmers, and agricultural education encouraged. The effect of all these measures was seen in 1916, when, with no separate Progressive candidate in the field, Wilson stood for a second term, and received nine million votes, as against the six million of 1912. He had clearly won over many Progressives. Yet by this time other preoccupations were uppermost in men's minds. As war drew near "the bell tolled for social reform in the United States",[49] and war was to bring a radical change in the situation. Wilson, however, had achieved much. Building on Theodore Roosevelt's example, he had shown how the Federal Government could give a lead in positive policies of reform and reconstruction, while his aid to agriculture (as also to road construction) had revealed what the Federal Government could achieve with the greater resources made available by the now constitutional income-tax. Whatever may be said of his intellectual inflexibility, Wilson's own thinking had broadened under the experience of responsi-bility, and, like Gladstone, whom he somewhat resembled, he had passed from the right towards the left wing of his party. He was a conservative reformer, but stirred by the clear evidence of the need and desire for reform he "distilled the best and sanest of the radical thinking of his time into law".[50] The government of the United States could never be the same after his achievements and those of Theodore Roosevelt. It was a new and positive conception of government, and especially of presidential leader-ship, that these two distinguished, though so very different, Americans left as their legacy to the people of the United States.

## (III) THE UNITED STATES AND THE WORLD

The conditions that led up to America's entry into war in 1917 must be considered in another context. Here something has still to be said of American relations with the rest of the world before the outbreak of the conflagration of 1914, and of the growth of policies to match her expanding wealth and power.

## A "CONTINENTAL" POLICY

The foreign policy of the United States has been no less a reflection of their internal development than that of any other Power. Policy at home was to round off the continent, and it is not entirely a coincidence that war with Spain in 1898 followed so soon after the closing of the frontier. The disputes that had led earlier to the incorporation of Texas, New Mexico and California were equally matters of home and foreign politics, and much the same can be said of relations with Canada, long the outstanding problem of the continent. This "continental" policy, with its corollary, the Monroe doctrine, to keep interlopers away, was the reflection of American understanding of the magnitude of the task that had been undertaken in developing a vast territory and building up a democratic republic in a hostile world, and it underlay the "too proud to fight" attitude of the early years of the First World War.

## THE UNITED STATES, CANADA AND BRITAIN

The independence of Canada was long a sore point, both a reminder of the ancient wrongs of colonialism, and, with so many Irish settled in the United States, a standing temptation to anti-British demonstrations. Alaska, Secretary of State Seward's "snow-farm", was bought from Russia in 1867, and it was not until the 'eighties that Canada came to be accepted. It was the wise T. F. Bayard, in President Cleveland's first administration, who was the first Secretary of State to urge his countrymen to accept the fact of Canadian autonomy.[51] The feeling about Canada, however, was typical of the American approach to foreign problems when they came to be presented. America was bitterly divided on party issues, but a specious unity could be manufactured in abuse of the foreigner, and the British were *the* foreigners, the only members of the species of whom many Americans had any knowledge. Hence the long-honoured custom of twisting the lion's tail, which made it impossible for Joseph Chamberlain in 1888, for instance, to announce his engagement to the daughter of Cleveland's Secretary of War, W. C. Endicott, until after the presidential election of that year, lest the administration be associated too closely with an Englishman—and an Englishman, at that, who had so recently rejected Home Rule for Ireland. Chamberlain's reticence did not, as it happened, help Cleveland, as the British Ambassador, Sackville-West, was trapped into expressing his preference for him. When Cleveland did his own twisting of the lion's tail in 1895, over the Venezuelan frontier question, this stupid, but unfortunate, episode may still have rankled.

## The Conditions of Policy Making: Ideals and Disillusionment

True to her traditions and her preoccupations, America wished to keep out of the world, in isolation. "The Secretary of State," wrote Henry Adams, "exists only to recognize the existence of a world which Congress would rather ignore." If an issue of foreign policy had to be publicly debated, it was presented simply and vigorously, with no subtlety or finesse, but with some warmth of feeling and moral force thrown in, for it had to be understood over some three thousand miles of territory. That the great distances "can only be overcome by shouting"[52] is one of the disadvantages under which American foreign policy constantly laboured, and still labours. Unity could most easily be achieved in criticism or denunciation, and an appeal to principle was more likely to be effective than one to interest, which varied so much between the different parts of the great republic and between the peoples who composed it. Yet there is a distinction between words and deeds. In 1917, and again in 1941, the country responded to a challenge thrown down, as the North and South had responded to the challenges of 1861. Only in this way could America, with all the checks that its constitution provides, be brought into major conflicts. When a choice is possible the decision is far more difficult: it was the blowing up of the *Maine* that touched off the spark of war in 1898, and it was the sinking of ships that was similarly decisive in 1917 and 1941. Nevertheless, the idealism of the American people, the idealism that created the Republic and sustained it through the stresses of the Civil War, is ever-present. It has been said that every American election is a revolution, and to the American people every war that has brought them into contact with the wider world has been a revolution from which they expected to achieve better conditions. Hence the disillusionment after 1919, enhanced as it inevitably was by the fact that the United States could achieve security—or so it seemed—in her geographical isolation and the plenitude of her resources. To Wilson by 1917 it was evident that America could not remain at peace with a powerful nation which denied the idealistic basis of American thought and action. Her security was at stake with that of the other democratic nations, and "the world must be safe for democracy". Only idealism can sustain a great people through a long conflict, and the very magnitude of the struggle with Germany, and their distance from it, persuaded many Americans that they had disinterestedly intervened to save democracy elsewhere from destruction. Wilson's fine language could be quoted to lend colour to the notion, and there was the undoubted fact of victory, which seemed as clear an indication of the justice of the cause as it had done in 1865 (let it be remembered, too, that the United States knew no defeat between 1812 and 1941). As an American student of public reactions to foreign affairs has written, "we began to project our newly born conviction back into the days before April, 1917, and to believe that we had plunged into the holocaust, not to battle for our basic rights, but to make the world safe for democracy".[53] The disillusionment and reaction when they came were all the greater: that their basis was emotional is clear enough from the fact that the two-thirds, who, according to Gallup poll calculations, believed in 1937 that the intervention of twenty years earlier had been a mistake, had by 1944 dropped to less than one-fifth.[54] Between the wars, however, the country could sink back into isolation and preoccupation with everyday local affairs. "It isn't very easy for a country to have world sense," a notable American observer has written, "when it hardly knows its own."[55] If Congress preferred to ignore the existence of a world outside, that was, with even more reason, the attitude of the majority of the people. Typical of the mid-Western, middle-town, attitude, at least before 1914, was William Allen White's comment in his paper, the *Emporia Gazette*, on the dispute over Venezuelan debts in 1902:

> Everyone in this town is busy and earning money and saving it. Everyone is engaged in honest work and is looking after his own family. The Gazette contends that that is better than bothering with Venezuela.[56]

Distance, preoccupation and the Monroe doctrine all played their part in shaping such an attitude, together, it might be added, with reliance on the friendly power of Britain, much though that was taken for granted.

## THE PACIFIC, THE CARIBBEAN AND THE CANAL

The Federal Government could hardly be so indifferent to events. Something has been said elsewhere of relations with Canada and Britain and with the Far East, and the story of the United States' dealings with most of Latin America can best be treated in another context. The main developments in American foreign relations before 1917 turned on the Pacific and the Caribbean, and on the project for a canal to link them.

### (1) CHINA AND JAPAN

It had been America that had opened Japan to Western trade, and Sumner acquired Alaska to strengthen the country's position in the Pacific, while trade and the need for coaling-stations brought Hawaii and Samoa within the American orbit (after many years of debate Hawaii was finally absorbed in 1898, and Samoa, as explained elsewhere, was divided with Germany in 1900). In 1899 and 1900 Secretary of State John Hay, who as Ambassador to Britain had been familiar with the British view, issued his "Open Door" notes on China. With the imperialist expansion which was taking place, and from which China, in particular, seemed likely to suffer, the United States could not stand aside and see markets and strategic positions divided up by others. Exports were increasing, and had reached a value of $1,500,000,000 by 1900, with manufactures a rapidly increasing proportion of the total. China was too important a market to lose: hence the acquisition of the Philippines as a potential Hong-Kong. "We have pretty much everything in the country to make it happy," said President McKinley, with customary *insouciance*, in 1900, "but what we want is new markets, and as trade follows the flag, it looks very much as if we were going to have new markets."[57]

In the event Japan was to prove a much more valuable customer than China, and McKinley himself before his tragic end was to suggest that the way for trade expansion lay through tariff reciprocity, a doctrine that the Senate was to boggle at for another ten years. If the Open Door were effective in China, it was mainly Britain's power and economic stake that kept it so, though on Japan, at least, the United States was able to exercise some influence. Before long the Philippines were seen to be the "Achilles heel" of the American position in the Pacific, the legacy of what has been called "The Great Aberration of 1898".[58] They represented, however, America's determination not to be shut out of the Western Pacific, and by such means as she could command to prevent the partitition of China. Yet this was essentially a government policy, and, the acquisition of the Philippines apart, was never submitted to Congressional consideration. It was, nevertheless, a policy which emphasized the primacy of the Pacific and Asia in American thought on foreign affairs. In addition to markets the Pacific contained potential menaces to American security. Concern with Europe had long seemed to offer nothing but the danger of entanglements, and the Monroe doctrine, while warning European States against any active interference in the affairs of any part of the American continent, eschewed any United States entanglement in Europe. It was not until 1917, indeed, that it began to be realized that what happened there could be a matter of vital concern.

(2) THE IMPERIALIST URGE, 1898

The acquisition of the Philippines arose out of American concern at events in Cuba, raised eventually to the pitch of war by a mood of jingoism. With so much talk of war and imperialism in the air it was difficult not to assert the American position, and the rapid growth at this time of a popular Press, shaped by such men as Joseph Pulitzer and William Randolph

Hearst, made Americans more alive not only to what was going on in the world, but to their own national identity. As part of its pension agitation the G.A.R., at the peak of its influence in 1890, had been pressing for "loyal" history books and the raising of the U.S. flag over every school, and the general adoption of the "flag ceremony" followed.[59] The teaching of Captain A. T. Mahan (1840–1915) on naval affairs, principally embodied in his *Influence of Sea Power upon History, 1660–1789*, published in 1890, made a great impression on a nation vulnerable through its long seaboard and growing commerce, and emphasized the need for a connecting link between the two seas. If, however, there were to be a canal, its defence would require bases in some of the West Indian islands. Hence the interest in Cuba, which in addition had become a major producer of sugar for the American market, though the Danish West Indies (Virgin Islands), acquired by purchase in 1917, were to provide a better base.

## (3) War with Spain: Cuba and the Philippines

Cuba had long been in revolt against Spain, notably in 1868–78. In 1895 a fresh revolt occurred, stirred up in part by the 1894 changes in the American tariff on sugar. Spanish measures of repression roused opinion in the American press, and there was a general demand for intervention. President Cleveland had already given public opinion its head by taking, in 1895, a strong line against Britain in connexion with a British frontier dispute with Venezuela, and his successor, McKinley, was gradually pushed into war. In February, 1898, the battleship *Maine* was mysteriously blown up at Havana, and McKinley sent an ultimatum to Madrid. The ultimatum was accepted, but McKinley yielded to the clamour, and in April war began. By July the "splendid little war" was over, the Spanish Empire was no more, and the United States found herself with Cuba, Puerto Rico and the Philippines on her hands. It was, indeed, an aberration, if a triumphant one, but McKinley's re-election in 1900, against Bryan's denunciation of "imperialism", showed that a great part of the country approved. From Rudyard Kipling, long resident in the United States, until he left in disgust at the criticism of Britain over

Venezuela, came the warning that the "White Man's Burden" was not an easy one to bear, and this the years of struggle with the Filipinos from 1899 to 1902 were to confirm. A sound administration was established, but the Filipinos demanded independence, and this was eventually promised by President Wilson, who first conceded a considerable measure of local government. Arrangements to grant independence were not, however, finally made until 1934, to come into effect in ten years, and the Philippine Republic was at last established in 1946. Cuba became formally independent, but with an over-sight of her affairs by the United States, though this also was brought to an end by President F. D. Roosevelt in 1934. Even more than the Philippines, however, Cuba has been closely linked with the United States economically, Much valuable and constructive work has been done in both countries, but the problems they have raised are evidence of the light-heartedness with which the war of '98 was undertaken. As usual, "Mr. Dooley" had the apt comment: speaking of the Philippines to his friend Hennessy he said;

> 'tis not more thin two months since ye larned whether they were islands or canned goods. . . . There are eight thousan' iv thim islands, with a population iv wan hundherd millyon naked savages, an' me bedroom's crowded now with me an' th' bed.

## (4) ROOSEVELT AND THE CANAL: "I TOOK PANAMA . . ."

During the Spanish war the U.S. Battleship *Oregon* had made a dramatic dash, in record time, from San Francisco to Florida, but it had taken seventy-one days. Here was the strongest possible argument for an Isthmian canal, and it was President Roosevelt who achieved it. There had been since 1850 an understanding with Britain for a joint canal, but in 1900, with the Boer war on her hands and in her concern for American co-operation in the Far East, Britain, by the Hay-Pauncefote treaty, agreed to recognize America's exclusive rights. A company had been founded by de Lesseps in the 'seventies to build a canal across Panama, but had gone bankrupt. After it had been decided that this was the best route, the company was bought out by the United States, and when the Government of Colombia, in whose territory Panama lay, delayed its consent to the project, a revolt, with President

Roosevelt's knowledge, if not actual connivance, established an independent Republic of Panama which leased the canal zone to the United States in perpetuity. "I took Panama," wrote Roosevelt later, "without consulting the Cabinet." It is by no means certain that his highhandedness was justified, or even necessary, and there have been ugly stories about the compensation paid to the bankrupt company. It was not one of the more pleasant episodes in Roosevelt's career, and it is perhaps significant that he was ever afterwards touchy about it. Colombia insisted on compensation, and it was one of Roosevelt's later counts against Wilson that in 1914 Wilson agreed to pay $25,000,000, though Roosevelt's friends in the Senate held off the payment until 1921. The canal itself was opened in 1914, but the memory of Roosevelt's action was for long a hindrance to good relations between the United States and the Latin American countries.

## The Impact of Foreign Affairs

Roosevelt regarded many of these countries as "bandit nests", and argued that the Monroe doctrine gave the United States the right to intervene in their often disorderly affairs. Wilson and his Secretary of State, Bryan, were anxious to adopt more conciliatory policies, but took the hardly less objectionable view that they must "teach the South American republics to elect good men". The result was intervention in the Caribbean and war with Mexico, all of which was also to take time to live down. Yet Bryan as Secretary of State earnestly hoped to consolidate peace, throughout the world, and negotiated treaties of conciliation with thirty countries. Germany, however, was one that declined. When he became President, Wilson had expressed the hope that he would not be compelled to deal chiefly with foreign affairs. In the event he was to be more closely concerned with them than any of his predecessors had ever been. The war was to cause immense changes in America, and to place her, at a bound, among the first nations of the world, with the potential strength of the leading Great Power. True to tradition she was to sink back into isolation again, cynically regarding the war, since it had not achieved all her hopes, as yet another aberration. By 1917 the world could not do without America, but the disputes over Wilson's policy were still being fought in 1941. America had to be forced into two struggles before she accepted the responsibilities which her strength, her principles and her needs alike imposed upon her.

## REFERENCES

Certain works are indispensable to any general understanding of the American background, and to these no detailed references are given:

> S. E. Morison and H. S. Commager: *The Growth of the American Republic.*
>
> H. Agar: *The United States: The Presidents, the Parties and the Constitution.*
>
> H. U. Faulkner: *American Economic History.*
>
> H. U. Faulkner: *American Political and Social History.*
>
> *The Education of Henry Adams* (first published 1907).

1.  In C. A. and M. R. Beard: *The Rise of American Civilization.*
2.  *The Rise of Silas Lapham* (1885).
3.  A. Nevins: *John D. Rockefeller*, I, p. 207.
4.  *Mr. Dooley in Peace and War*, p. 172.
5.  *The Significance of the Frontier in American History* (1893), p. 37.
6.  J. B. Brebner: *North Atlantic Triangle: The Interplay of Canada, the United States and Great Britain*, p. 232.
7.  *John D. Rockefeller*, I, p. 99.
8.  Booth Tarkington: *The Midlander* (first published in 1923, but dealing with the period some thirty years earlier).
9.  *From Sea to Sea*, p. 169.
10. *The Autobiography of William Allen White*, p. 365.
11. ibid., p. 359.
12. H. F. Pringle: *Theodore Roosevelt*, p. 110.
13. For a statistical examination see B. Thomas: *Migration and Economic Growth.*
14. Mary Antin: *The Promised Land* (1912).
15. *The Autobiography of Lincoln Steffens*, II, p. 831.
16. Ed. S. Gwynn: *The Letters and Friendships of Sir Cecil Spring-Rice*, I, p. 65.

17. Clarence Day: *Life with Father*.

18. T. J. Pressly: *Americans Interpret Their Civil War*, p. 322.

19. J. B. Bishop: *Theodore Roosevelt and His Times*, I, p. 349.

20. *Americans Interpret Their Civil War*, p. 171.

21. ibid., p. 29, quoting K. M. Stampp.

22. Lord Bryce: *The American Commonwealth* (2nd edition, 1910), II, p. 226.

23. M. R. Dearny: *Veterans in Politics. The Story of the G.A.R.*, p. vii.

24. R. J. Donovan: *Eisenhower: The Inside Story*, p. 101.

25. B. Weber and S. J. Handfield-Jones: "Variations in the Rate of Economic Growth in the U.S.A., 1869–1939"; *Oxford Economic Papers*, 1954, p. 127.

26. Quoted in *Migration and Economic Growth*, p. 171.

27. *Veterans in Politics*, p. 443.

28. H. Pelling: "The Knights of Labor in Britain, 1880–1901"; *Economic History Review*, December, 1956, p. 323.

29. F. R. Dulles: *Labor in America*, p. 138.

30. S. Gompers: *Seventy Years of Life and Labor*, I, p. 335.

31. ibid., II, p. 126.

32. Frances Perkins: *The Roosevelt I Knew*, pp. 177–78.

33. R. Chaplin: *Wobbly*, p. 343.

34. *Veterans in Politics*, p. 442.

35. *Migration and Economic Growth*, p. 169.

36. R. M. Robbins: *Our Landed Heritage*, p. 274.

37. W. Johnson: *William Allen White's America*, p. 55.

38. *John D. Rockefeller*, I, p. 622.

39. ibid., I, p. 671.

40. F. L. Allen: *The Big Change: America Transforms Itself, 1900–1950*, p. ix.

41. *The Autobiography of William Allen White*, p. 333.

42. *The Autobiography of Lincoln Steffens*, I, p. 345.

43. *The Autobiography of William Allen White*, p. 342.

44. *The Autobiography of Lincoln Steffens*, II, p. 514.

45. *Seventy Years of Life and Labor*, I, p. 529.

46. A. H. Hansen: *The American Economy*, p. 183.

47. H. Hale Bellot: *Woodrow Wilson*, p. 5.

48. *Seventy Years of Life and Labor*, I, p. 551.

49. *The Autobiography of William Allen White*, p. 516.

50. *The American Economy*, p. 180.

51. *North Atlantic Triangle*, p. 247.

52. W. W. Rostow: *The American Diplomatic Revolution*, p. 9.

53. T. A. Bailey: *The Man in the Street. The Impact of American Public Opinion on Foreign Policy*, p. 171.

54. ibid., p. 172.

55. J. Gunther: *Inside U.S.A.*, p. 917.

56. *William Allen White's America*, p. 251.

57. E. H. Zabriskie: *American Russian Rivalry in the Far East, 1895–1914*, p. 51 n.

58. S. F. Bemis: *A Diplomatic History of the United States;* the title of chapter XXVI.

59. *Veterans in Politics*, chapters 11 and 12.

# XVII

# CHINA, JAPAN AND THE WEST

## THE ADVANCE OF JAPAN

OF all the dramatic events of the last quarter of the nineteenth century none was more striking in itself, or of greater significance for the future, than the crumbling of the ancient civilization of China before the steady pressure of the West, and the adjustment of Japan's less inflexible system to the new conditions. Precisely in this period are to be found the springs of many later actions. In the case of Japan the "Restoration" of 1867, and the subsequent embellishment of native forms with the appearance of western styles and institutions, pointed the way towards the wars with China (1894) and Russia (1904) and ultimately to the terrible events of the years from 1931 to 1945. The internal stresses and fanatical ambitions that were responsible for the attrition of China by Japan which began in 1931, and for the desperate onslaught upon the Western Powers ten years later, were already present not only in the war of 1894 but in the earlier crisis over Korea and Formosa in 1873–74. Nor were the very methods of 1941 without earlier precedent: attack preceded the formal declaration of war in 1894 and 1904 no less than at Pearl Harbour. Yet for Japan herself the years between 1867 and the outbreak of war in 1914 were years of rapid advance in both internal development and international prestige. Only the most percipient of foreign observers could have been aware of the dangers implicit in the country's rapid growth, of the militaristic tendencies that were masked by the semblance of constitutional forms, of the ambitions for the domination of Asia that were stimulated by the easy victories over China and Russia and by the growing preoccupation of the other Powers with their European rivalries. By the time that the First World War withdrew for a period the restraining influence of some of Japan's potential rivals in the Far East, and broke the power of others, the island

Empire had established its position as one of the leading nations of the world. Privileged positions of extra-territoriality for the nationals of other States, everywhere the hallmark of backwardness and dependence, had been abolished since 1899, and an alliance as of equals with Britain had existed for more than a decade. Population and national wealth were increasing apace, and trade was expanding at a rate twice as fast as that of Britain during the nineteenth century.[1] The country had come far in less than fifty years.

## THE DECLINE OF CHINA

For China, on the other hand, the unwilling recipient of western favours and attentions since first her gates had been forced in 1842, the later years of the nineteenth century were years of decline and decay, marked by the loss of outlying territories and the growing threat of partition. With the majority of her people no less ignorant of the world outside than indifferent to affairs beyond their limited concern, with a skilfully balanced system of administration, nicely calculated from ages past to preserve an archaic system in its ossified forms, with an effete dynasty and corrupt officials, China seemed to be tottering to collapse. A land and people, above all a civilization, but rarely a unity in governmental control, and never until more recent times anything which westerners could recognize as a nation, China was a prey to conflicting forces, lacking for more than a century from 1842 the ordered adjustment to western influences which Japan had initiated in 1867, only thirteen years after Commodore Perry had compelled her to accept contact with the West in 1854. A brief flicker of reform in China in 1898, following the disastrous war of 1894, had been smothered in the xenophobia of the Boxer rising in 1900, but re-emerged, to prepare the way for the fresh start of the Republic of 1911. The first tentative beginnings of an effective central control had already made their appearance, though they were to be checked by the internecine strife of rival warlords and were to disappear later in the welter of the Japanese attack and in the ineptitude of *Kuomintang* rule, until in the end a power arose in the land in the nineteen-forties that proved able to unite a long-suffering people as never before, converting "an inchoate mass into a united nation, capable of organizing and bringing into use the immense resources of China".[2] The process had taken more than a century, but its origins are to be found in the Anglo-Chinese war of 1840–42 and the first opening of the Celestial Empire to outside influence. Not for some fifty years after that event, perhaps, did many Chinese become aware of the insidious pressure that was closing in on them from the distant West, from Russia in the north and even from Japan, and which their own imperial system was powerless to avert. Meanwhile the pseudo-Christian T'ai P'ing Rebellion (1850–66), which in another age might have swept away the ruling dynasty, as had happened so often in the past, had itself been suppressed after a long and bitter struggle, and other risings had also been put down. The effort had exhausted the dynasty, however, and its traditional resistance to change had been encouraged.

## THE REVOLT AGAINST THE WEST

In the 'nineties China looked like being the next victim of the rival imperialisms which had already, in the previous decade, disposed of Africa. Public-spirited Chinese who were alive to developments around them began to despair, and among others a blind resentment developed that found its first vent in the Boxer rising. Japan in the meantime had been robbed by the other Powers of the fruits of her victory of 1894, only to see them indulging in a scramble for Chinese territory that was as bitter to her as the victor as it was to the vanquished Chinese. Hence the thrill which the Japanese triumph over Tsarism in 1904–05 sent throughout all Asia, touching off the spark of violent nationalism even in distant India. Underlying all the events of these years must be seen the growing resentment at Western intervention, despite all it had to offer, which has at times taken terrible forms, and seems likely to remain for some time a powerful influence in Asian, and no less in world, affairs.

## THE CONDITION OF CHINA

China in the nineteenth century was no Africa, undeveloped, sparsely populated and backward, to be divided as the prize of imperial expansion. The inheritor of an ancient civilization, with an orderly and well-regulated social pattern, sustained by long-established religious and philosophical doctrines, and especially by the cult of reverence for ancestors, this vast country, with a population of more than three hundred millions, regarded itself as the leading nation of the world, to which all others were tributary. Throughout its history it had been surrounded by lesser peoples. Its civilization, modified but basically unchanged during some two thousand years, had been evolved without the inspiration or challenge of foreign contact. Mountains, desert and the sea made of the country a world within a world, sufficient to itself and sublimely confident that the peoples beyond its frontiers were barbarians who either owed allegiance and tribute or were too remote to be considered. The Sublime Emperor, the Son of Heaven, was supreme on earth, and all others, rulers and people alike, must prostrate themselves before him. In the words put by prescribed etiquette into a letter from the King of Burma shortly before that country was finally absorbed into the British Empire, "as the sunflower bows before the sun, so does all mankind turn with adoration towards the Imperial person".[3] It mattered not if the Emperor were weak or dissolute or imbecile: it was enough that he existed, and little more was required of him. He presided over the pyramid of Chinese society, preserving the balance of the social order, and, as the descendant of the priest-kings of old, ensured the protection of the gods and their benevolent concern for the welfare of the Chinese people by performing at prescribed intervals the customary sacrifices and making the customary offerings to the shades of his ancestors. Government in the western sense was not his concern. His function was, through the virtue of his conduct and his strict adherence to traditional forms and ceremonies, to spread a benevolent influence over his people: if he fell short, the sufferings would be theirs, but the "Mandate of Heaven" would eventually be withdrawn and a new Emperor and dynasty would take his place. The order remained unchanged: the Emperor was its minister as much as his subjects.

The actual government of China was largely a local concern, a matter for the village and the province. Yet its functions were limited. "Govern a great state as you would cook a small fish . . . the more the rules the poorer the people . . . the more laws the more law-breakers" were among the precepts associated with the uncertain figure of the philosopher Lao-Tzŭ (third century B.C.?) and respected through two thousand years. The vast mass of the people were peasants, devoted to the land and to the gods who made it fruitful, and to their families, the object and source of their principal loyalties. Sun Yat-sen, the founder of the Chinese Republic, spoke of his countrymen, in a well-known phrase, as "a plate of sand". Social order was not lacking, but there was little social or civic sense. The family was the centre of each man's world, respect for the elderly and for ancestors the cement of the family group. The enormous power and prestige exercised by the Dowager-Empress Tzŭ Hsi in the last years of the Empire she owed, like any other matriarch in China, to her position as the revered senior member of the ruling family: even an Emperor prostrated himself before a venerable grandmother or aunt. The principles of family life and conduct had remained unchanged throughout the centuries, and were, indeed, unchangeable except under the impact, unthinkable to the Chinese, of some more powerful external force. Invasions there had been before, some of them, such as that of the Mongols in the thirteenth century, successful through China's military weakness, but the western "invasion"—for such it was—of the nineteenth century was effective as no invasion had been before, since it allied overwhelming force and technical skill with a new conception of society and the individual. Hitherto the peoples with whom the Chinese had come into contact had been either, like the Mongols, Manchus and Tibetans, of inferior standing, or, like the Japanese, Koreans and Annamese, eager to assimilate Chinese culture. Until the appearance of the Western barbarians from over the seas nothing had occurred to shake China's complacent confidence in her system as supreme, the divinely-ordained exemplar for all.

## China from Ch'in to Ch'ing

The good order of China, and a high standard of material civilization, had been maintained, periods of invasion and civil war apart, since the short-lived Ch'in dynasty of the third century B.C. which gave the Empire its true beginning and its name. The other great constructive dynasties were those of Han (206 B.C.–A.D. 221) and T'ang (A.D. 618–907). The ideas and practices laid down in these early periods remained the bases of Chinese society under the Sung (960–1279), the Mongol conquerors (Yüan dynasty, 1280–1368), the Ming (1368–1644) and finally the Manchu invaders, who under the dynastic name of Ch'ing ruled the Empire from 1644 until their collapse in 1911. "No other people," it has well been said, "has had a record of bringing together under one régime and set of institutions so large a population and so wide a territory over so long a period of time."[4] Through all the vicissitudes of history—and the country has not lacked its share of invasions and conquests—Chinese society remained largely static, essentially traditionalist and bound by ancestral precedent. The social and political ideals upheld were those of the famous K'ung Fu-tse (551–479 B.C.), known to the West under the Latinized form of his name, Confucius, which with modifications at various periods remained the basis of such political philosophy as China possessed until the twentieth century. Confucius, living at a time of political disunity and social laxity, taught respect for the ideal simplicity of an earlier golden-age and inculcated the principles of loyalty to rulers and filial piety. Above all, he stressed the importance of education in right principles. Through his influence, and that of his followers and later disciples, the scholars, trained in the study of the Confucian classics, became the arbiters of Chinese society: from their ranks were chosen all the members of the government and administration. Dynasties came and went, but while they respected the power and privileges of the scholarly class they were safe from all but foreign invasion or their own decay. Hence the long-drawn decline of the Ch'ing dynasty of Manchu conquerors from the north, who after the reigns of the great Emperors K'ang Hsi (1661–1723) and Ch'ien Lung (1736–1795), sank into a state of degeneracy and corruption which endured until 1911. The wheels of administration turned, the scholar rulers went through their accustomed motions, the Empire stood seemingly four-square even while it rotted at the heart. Stifled in the rarefied atmosphere of the Imperial quarter of Peking, the "Forbidden

City", and dominated by the eunuch-ridden court which they had inherited with all else, the last Ch'ing Emperors, Hsien-Feng (1851–61), T'ung-Chih (1862–74), and Kuang-Hsü (1875–1908), were, in Disraeli's phrase concerning another ineffectual political figure, "transient and embarrassed phantoms", unable to do more than perform the rigid ceremonial prescribed by immemorial precedent for the well-being of the Empire. Yet the system endured. Foreign conquerors as they were, never popular in many parts of China, the Manchus maintained themselves by carrying almost to excess their uncritical deference to the Confucian system as, in the popular phrase, "for the Chinese what water is for fish". In the words of a leading authority:

> The real cause of the rapid decline of the Manchu Empire in the nineteenth century was intellectual stagnation, brought about by the domination of a small alien ruling class, itself dominated by a petrified cultural tradition. To the end the Manchus clung to this tradition as their sheet-anchor.[5]

The unfortunate Kuang-Hsü had a glimmering of what was needed to save China, but his was no forceful personality, and his efforts during the "Hundred Days" of reform in 1898 were speedily stultified by the reactionary Court system in which he was permanently imprisoned, a system personified in the dominating figure of the Empress-Dowager, Tzǔ Hsi, widow of Hsien-Feng and mother of Kuang-Hsü's predecessor T'ung-Chih—the very person, indeed, to whom Kuang-Hsü owed his place on the throne. Emperor and imperial system alike existed, in fact, in what a penetrating English observer, George Curzon (afterwards the celebrated Lord Curzon) described in 1894 as "this colossal Imperial nightmare", from which it was impossible to liberate them.

## THE ORGANIZATION OF GOVERNMENT

Under the Confucian system, thus long preserved, the way to political office was through examinations which tested the candidate's knowledge of the classics and skill in writing. The written word was traditionally regarded with an almost religious veneration, and skill in handling the Chinese brush-pen was essential to success. Otherwise little was required but parrot-learning and an ability to point a moral with an appropriate Confucian tag or epigram—"prehistoric platitudes concerning the art of government . . . wise quips and saws of the ancients applied to social economy and ceremonial precedents". The men who stood highest in China, the mandarins, as they were known to the West, were those who could recite and quote the classics without error, and write essays and reports that were models of classical style and calligraphic artistry. Some there were who even mastered the classics to the extent of reciting them backwards. Having won his way into the inner circle of the élite in a country where learning was honoured above military or financial skill, the scholar was a member of a hierarchy with roots far in the past which reached up to the foot of the imperial throne. Something of the religious veneration that attached to the Emperor himself therefore clung to all his officials. They represented no permanent vested class interest, for they were essentially civil servants, men who had advanced themselves in the first place by their intellectual gifts, not members of an hereditary ruling caste. Many, indeed, were of peasant stock. The system had much in theory to commend it, were it not that the training had long since become stereotyped and hopelessly out of date. A purely literary training in the classics, which was hardly worthy of the name of education, could not fit a man to grapple with the variety of problems that faced Manchu China in decay. Many men of genuine ability did come forward, for, as Tzŭ Hsi proclaimed in an expostulatory decree restoring the traditional system of examinations after Kuang-Hsü's abortive changes, "if the candidate is really a man of ability, the fact that he has been made to compose verses in accordance with time-honoured methods . . . will never prevent him from making his way in the world". The method of selection which the Dowager-Empress thus backhandedly commended did not, indeed, prove a bar to the advancement of men of mark. Outstanding among the senior officials of their day were such men as the astute Li Hung-chang, on whom Tzŭ Hsi herself leaned so long and so heavily; the able military leaders Tso Tsung-t'ang and Tseng Kuo-fan, who suppressed the T'ai P'ing and other rebellions; Tseng Chi-tse, son of Tseng Kuo-fan, who was China's first Ambassador in Europe; the provincial viceroys Liu K'un-i and Chang Chih-t'ung, who did

z*

much to prevent the Boxer rising of 1900 from spreading south; and, most significant of all for the future, Weng T'ung-ho, Tutor to the Emperor Kuang-Hsü, and K'ang Yu-wei, the Cantonese reformer, who together inspired the Emperor to the abortive programme of reform in 1898. Yet, as Tzŭ Hsi was driven to recognize after the failure of the Boxer tragi-comedy, traditional methods were not equal to China's needs. "China's great and increasing danger today", ran a decree of 1906, "is largely due to her unwise adherence to antiquated methods", though, with typical respect for the venerated past, reform was advocated on the grounds that, if the methods of government were not modified to suit changing conditions, "we shall be violating the spirit which animated our Imperial ancestors".

## THE "VENERABLE IMPOSTURE"

Something more than a change in the educational system was, however, required. China was, as another English observer, Valentine Chirol, noted in the 'nineties, nothing less than a "venerable imposture". Nowhere was the contrast more marked between the theory that sustained the State and the practice that animated it; nowhere was the appearance of unity and strength more blatantly a façade. There was, indeed, something symbolic in the wooden boards painted with cannon that filled the embrasures of the walls of Peking. For one thing, the deference paid to literacy and the impossibility of turning out by literary examinations enough men trained for practical affairs, led to a confusion between the word and the deed. If the right decree were issued, a necessary measure was as good as carried out, a conclusion which Gilbert amusingly parodied in the final scene of The Mikado (1885), composed at a time when the quaint manners of the East were first becoming widely known in sophisticated Britain. "The belief that to write words on paper is to perform an act," wrote an acute observer nearly fifty years later, "seems to be almost ineradicable. The result is that politics too often end where they should begin, with the assertion of intentions."[6] This theme could well be developed as a comment on the tragic decline of China in the century before the Communists seized control in 1949. One illuminating example must suffice:

when she assumed control from Kuang Hsü in 1898 Tzŭ Hsi, to impress the people with the vigour of which the unreformed system was still capable, ordered that attention should be given to the flood-defences on the Yellow River, long known as "China's Sorrow", where yet another of the recurrent disastrous floods had recently occurred. Her remedy was not, however, calculated to gain her credit for anything but the good intentions which were the stock-in-trade of Chinese government: she instructed the Ministries concerned to consult together, and sent Li Hung-chang to report on the amount likely to be needed to create effective defences—and there the matter rested.

Flood control had always been a vital function of government in China, and money was sent every year from all over the Empire for the containment of the terrible Yellow River. The necessary orders were given, and appointments made, but it was no less characteristic of the "venerable imposture" that the money largely disappeared into the sleeves of the ill-paid officials who had the task of administering it. So it was with many of the institutions upon which the life of the country depended. Lord Charles Beresford, touring China in 1898, noted with concern that one section of the important Grand Canal was silted up, though an official was "paid a large sum of money annually to keep the canal clear". By the same token, soldiers, for whose equipment with modern weapons money had been granted, could be seen shooting with bows and arrows—and giving more attention to the elegance of their posture in shooting than to the accuracy of their aim.

While, therefore, Confucius was revered and the loftiest principles of statecrat were daily enunciated, the realities of administration were far more crude. The public examinations always produced more qualified candidates than there were places to fill. Appointment and advancement, while by no means regardless of ability, depended, in consequence, to no small extent upon interest, family devotion—always of fundamental importance in China—and the greasing of palms. The system had not long since been familiar enough in the West, but rarely to such an extreme. Moreover, with salaries miserably inadequate, and no system of accounting to check peculation, bribery, graft and "squeeze" were rife. "A magistrate, had he got nothing but his regular pay, would have had to support himself by begging gratuities from the prisoners before him in the dock", an unhappy possibility evaded by retaining some portion of the revenues which passed through his hands. Taxation was, on the whole, not high, but though estimates of the losses to the Imperial Treasury necessarily vary greatly, it seems certain that at least three times as much remained in the officials' hands as reached Peking. Nor did the graft stop at the officials. Tzŭ Hsi spent on an elegant palace money raised for a Navy that might have turned the scales in the disastrous war with Japan in 1894, and little could be done at Court without heavy bribes to officials and eunuchs. Tzŭ Hsi's Chief Eunuch, Li Lien-ying, was notorious for the vast fortune he accumulated from Chinese and foreigners alike, and his takings were almost certainly shared with his mistress and with Li Hung-chang, who also profited from his contacts with foreign Powers. As had so often happened before in Chinese history, the influence of the Chief Eunuch at a time when the Emperor was a nonentity was nothing short of disastrous.

Essential to the dignity of the venerable imposture was the preservation of form and prestige. The long-established courtesies of Chinese society, the restraint and reserve of social intercourse, the elegance of manners and the polished forms of speech, were all contrived to gloss over harsh reality. Tzŭ Hsi after the Boxer rising ordered all record of the event to be expunged from the annals, "for purposes of historical accuracy". "Face" must be maintained if the divinely-ordained system were not to be swept away in chaos. Throughout the troubled years of contact and conflict with the West, therefore, the Imperial Court refused concessions until they were extorted by force. If the barbarian intruders could not be repelled, fair words must be offered and the invaders bought off, after which the Empire could sink back into its accustomed tranquillity, seemingly undisturbed by what had occurred. Thus, after the humiliation of the first Anglo-Chinese war, which ended with the cession of Hong-Kong and the opening of the country to European trade, an edict of 1843 sublimely recorded that,

> these foreigners having but newly been brought back to peace, a border quarrel must not be suffered again to break out.

It was clear thus early that only force would move the Imperial government, which lacked none of the arts for indefinitely spinning-out negotiations to an uncertain conclusion, and was soon to learn to play off one rival Power against another. "Nothing but the conclusive evidence of irresistible force will ever fully satisfy the Imperial Government", reported Admiral Seymour from the China Station in 1858, but it was not until after the failure of the Boxers in 1900 that there was any evidence that the lessons so sharply taught had been learnt, and little enough was then actually carried out by way of reform. Meanwhile, the great structure of imperial China, while preserving its "face", the outward semblance of undisturbed antique calm, was crumbling from within. For sixty years the West banged at the door, until the illusion could be sustained no longer: "to the amazement of all, within and without, the great structure, riddled by white ants, suddenly collapsed, leaving the surprised Europeans still holding the door handle".[7]

## ADMINISTRATIVE WEAKNESS

In truth the position was largely misunderstood, and both China's strength and her weakness were under-estimated. The fundamental error in which the West persisted lay in regarding the central government of the Empire as comparable in authority and power to their own, able by its own acts and decrees to change the course of Chinese history. "It required an effort to believe that a nation of four hundred millions *could* be so weak as China sometimes seemed", and many were the hopeful prophecies of impending recovery. Britain in particular sought from the first by treating with the Imperial Government direct to strengthen its authority. An effectively united China was likely to prove a better market for British goods than a weak and disunited country, a standing invitation to partition. Decentralization was, however, the very essence of Chinese administration: it is significant that Li Hung-chang, for instance, with whom the European Powers had so many dealings, except on the occasions when he was appointed to lead a special mission, owed his power and influence to his position as a Provincial Governor, not as a Minister of the Court. Nevertheless, the constant pressure upon Peking was not without its effect. Gradually it was borne in upon the leaders of China that a greater degree of centralization was essential to the survival of the Empire, and Li Hung-chang himself contributed not a little to the process. Communist rule in China has been seen by a close observer from India as "the fulfilment of a hundred years of evolution—the movement towards a strong central government which the great mandarins of the later Manchu period had themselves initiated".[8] Neither the Ch'ing dynasty nor the Kuomintang which succeeded it proved, however, to have the vigour, the honesty and the freshness of outlook which were needed to break the cramping bonds of the past: hence, in great part, the ultimate victory of Mao Tse-tung.

## ECONOMIC WEAKNESS

What, in particular, was not understood in the nineteenth century was the economic crisis through which China was passing, and which, despite the efforts made from within, and much help from outside, only the Communists have proved able to grapple with effectively. China, like Russia and India, was a land of peasants, with but little industrial development to absorb the surplus of rural population. Census returns have been made for purposes of taxation since the Han period, infinitely longer than in any other country, but with the great increase of population in modern times exact returns have been difficult to obtain. It would seem, however, that while from T'ang until Ming times, except in periods of disorder, the population numbered between fifty and sixty millions, it rose rapidly under the early Ch'ing Emperors to more than two hundred million and stood during the nineteenth century at something between three and four hundred million. The first census of the Communist régime, carried out in 1953-54, has shown a total of well over 550,000,000. The main centres of population have always been the basins of the great rivers, the Yangtze and Hwang (Yellow), and European travellers in the nineteenth century constantly noted with astonishment the dense settlement and cultivation of the rich earth in these areas, which made the land appear one vast market-garden. Agriculture, however, could support so great a population only at a level of bare subsistence: the poverty of the Chinese peasant was notorious. The rural economy was almost self-sufficient, but much of the population was chronically under-employed as well as under-nourished. As much as one-fifth of the people, it has often been suggested, has been engaged in transport, since "there is nothing which is cheaper":[9] from China have come, significantly enough, both the wheel-barrow and the sedan-chair. The vast distances involved (some two thousand miles from north to south and from east to west), and the many natural barriers, were as much an obstacle to economic integration as to effective administration. As in India, therefore, famine and flood took constant toll of densely populated localities, with little prospect of relief from more fortunate areas. During the Ch'ing period (1644–1908) 8,600 localities were affected by flood, it has been estimated, and 4,600 by drought.[10] The famine of 1849 probably destroyed more than 13,000,000 people, that of 1878–79 almost as many. To these figures must be added the terrible results of civil disorder: some 20,000,000 are believed to have perished during the T'ai P'ing rebellion. Pressure on the land, the need for some ready money for necessities such as salt which the local community could not produce, together with the customary celebration of marriage and other festivals, inevitably produced, as in all peasant societies, the ubiquitous —and too often iniquitous—money-lender and the hard-fisted wealthier peasant (the *kulak* of Russia), while the tax-farmer, the corrupt official, and the indispensable but leech-like middleman were a further prey upon the peasant producer. Land-owning and renting were, perhaps, less of a problem than elsewhere, for something like half the peasantry consisted of small proprietors, but the problem was serious enough. Under these conditions of extreme rural poverty famine was endemic, and rioting, banditry and civil war, the ultimate gestures of hopelessness, hardly less so.

EMIGRATION:
(1) OVERSEAS

Many Chinese, despite imperial prohibitions, took refuge in emigration. From South China, in particular, they spread into South-East Asia, making of Malaya, for instance, a new country, and penetrating to America and Australia, where special immigration laws were soon devised to shut them out. Dilke, in *Greater Britain*, reflected the common attitude of the time by shrewdly styling them "the Irish of Asia", but although poverty and over-population at home drove many overseas from China, as from Ireland, the analogy is not a close one. The Chinese emigrants were but a minute proportion of the whole, and bore little resemblance to the large-scale movement of Irish to America and Australia. Moreover, with their strong sense of ancestry and family unity comparatively few Chinese at first chose to cut themselves off from the homeland, though it was the fear of the hordes which might follow that was in part responsible for the policies of exclusion adopted by the white peoples of the Pacific.

## (2) MANCHURIA

The movement overseas was, nevertheless, a significant one, with important consequences for the economic life of the areas concerned, through Chinese skill in trading, and for China's own balance of payments, through the remittances sent home by emigrants. It was also a means by which new ideas were absorbed and disseminated in China. The main object of Chinese emigration, however, was not overseas but in Manchuria, hitherto, except in the south, a sparsely populated region from which Chinese were excluded until the last years of the Ch'ing dynasty, which had wished to preserve its homeland for the Manchu people. When emigration to Manchuria was finally permitted, a seepage which had already begun quickly became a flood, reaching in the early years of the Republic, and in the nineteen-twenties, proportions which have won for it the description of "perhaps . . . the greatest peaceful migration in history".[11] Despite Russian and Japanese ambitions the Chinese have, indeed, been the true conquerors of Manchuria. The three "Eastern Provinces" of Heilunkiang, Jehol and Kirin, to which the West gave the convenient, but non-Chinese, name of "Manchuria", have now, according to the census of 1953, a population of some twenty-eight millions, of which fewer than three millions are separately classified as Manchu. Manchuria, regarded by the Chinese, at least since Ming times, as part of their historic Empire, is now irrevocably theirs.

## THE WEST AND CHINA:
## (1) THE TREATY PORTS

Poor though the mass of people in China was, especially after the rapid increase of population, the fabled wealth of the Empire was immense, and was enhanced by the artistic treasures in which Chinese culture had long been so rich. With the development of Western commerce in the East in early modern times these artistic treasures, and with them the luxury products of tea and silk, became much in demand in Europe. British traders from India sought them and a considerable trade grew up, handicapped only by the fact that the West did not yet produce anything which China wanted and therefore had to send specie in exchange. The lofty reply of Ch'ien Lung to George III in 1793, declining the gifts which had been sent to the Emperor to impress him with the desirability of a truer commerce, is well-known:

As your Ambassador can see for himself, we possess all things. I set no value on objects strange and ingenious and have no use for your country's manufactures.

It was, indeed, little enough that European traders could offer until there sprang up, in the early years of the nineteenth century, a brisk trade in Indian opium. Opium, though prohibited by the Imperial Government, was in great demand in China, offering, when not used to excess, the same narcotic comfort that tobacco was increasingly bringing to Europe. Its importation was, therefore, openly connived at by officials. The only port of entry was Canton, to which European traders had long been restricted, and a clumsy attempt to enforce the law there led in 1840 to the fateful war which brought about the cession of Hong-Kong to Britain and the opening of five ports, including Canton and Shanghai, to foreign trade and settlement. This was the first breach in the "Chinese Wall" of exclusion, and was soon followed by similar treaties with other Powers. By the early years of the twentieth century nearly fifty "treaty ports" had been opened to trade. Moreover, the principle of extra-territoriality, by which foreigners in China were to be subject only to their own laws and consular officials, was formally accepted and embodied in

treaties, while customs dues were limited to five per cent and
Christian missionary activity was permitted.

## (2) CUSTOMS CONTROL

Extra-territoriality, abolished in Japan as early as 1899,
was to endure in China until the Second World War, a
constant, and in later years a bitter, reminder of the country's
inferior status. The limitation of tariffs lasted almost as long,
until 1928, and, while its effects were not felt for some time,
it restricted both China's revenue and her industrial development, even if for many years there was no effective central
government to use the one intelligently to encourage the other.
The sole advantage, though no small one, was that, under the
guidance of the notable Ulsterman, Sir Robert Hart (1835–
1911) as Inspector-General from 1863 until 1911, the Customs
Service became a powerful instrument for reorganization and
reform in China, and made no small contribution to the
country's general economic development.

## (3) MISSIONARY ACTIVITY

Missionary activity made an even more immediate impact
on Chinese life, for within a few years it became a part, albeit
an unconscious one, of the inspiration of the T'ai P'ing
("Great Peace") rebellion against Manchu rule. The Chinese,
in general an easy-going and tolerant people, were not at first
averse to Christian teaching, but the association with the
rebellion stirred up prejudice, which was increased by the
missionaries' discouragement of ancestor-worship, the basis
of Chinese society, and by distorted accounts of Christian
practices. As missionary activity increased there were, therefore, sporadic outbreaks of violence, which culminated in the
Boxer rising, when many missionaries were brutally murdered
with thousands of their converts.

## WESTERN OVERESTIMATES OF CHINESE TRADE

The main interest of Europeans lay in the development of
trade, the magnet which had drawn them to China. From the
first, however, extravagant notions prevailed as to the possibilities of commercial development, notions that almost
parodied themselves in the enthusiastic despatch to China,

in the years immediately following the British victory, of cargoes of such highly unsuitable articles as pianos and table-cutlery.[12] The area and population of China were so vast that the possibilities seemed without limit, and, although expectations were constantly being disappointed, good reasons were always found in the lack of sufficient ports of entry or of access to the interior, in bad communications or heavy transit dues, or in the obstructionism of the mandarins. If remedies for these could but be found, the West would prove to be, as Curzon reported in the 'nineties, "only standing on the threshold of Chinese commercial expansion". Hence the constant pressure on the British Government to make of China either one vast Treaty Port or another India, a pressure to which successive governments as constantly refused to submit. Only by such direct means, the commercial interests felt, could China's economic potentialities be realized. The view which British Governments steadily held to was first expressed, however, by a Board of Trade official in 1869: it had taken three wars to open a way for trade into China, he wrote, and a naval squadron had to be maintained in the Far East for its protection:

> it is a great question on which side of the national ledger the balance will be found to stand.

Despite constant appeals, particularly from the "China Association" of merchants after it was formed in 1889, the British Government never wavered in the view that the China trade was not worth a major war or the costly responsibility of a second Indian Empire. Much of the explanation of British policy is to be found in the fact that, while exports of United Kingdom products to India amounted in 1875, for instance, to some £24,000,000, China took British goods to the value of only £8,000,000. Nor did there seem to be great scope for development: ten years later, in 1885, exports to China were at much the same level, while those to India had increased by £5,000,000. Yet Britain for long controlled three-quarters of China's total trade.

The China merchants for their part maintained that the development of trade was impossible without political reforms, and saw in every difficulty the hand of some hostile mandarin. Later developments confirmed their view, but the official

British opinion was that China must find her own means of reforming: pressure might achieve only the collapse of the imperial régime, with unhappy consequences for trade. Lord Elgin, who was sent out by the British Government to bring the Imperial Government to terms in the Second Chinese War of 1856–60, explained sharply to the merchant community that they were faced "not with barbarism but with an ancient civilization in many respects effete and imperfect, but in others not without claims on our sympathy and respect". To the British Government he pointed out in 1859 that British manufactures had to compete in China with the cheap goods produced at home "at intervals of rest from agricultural labour, by this industrious, frugal and sober population", and he added the tart comment:

> it is a pleasing but pernicious fallacy to imagine that the influence of an intriguing Mandarin is to be presumed whenever a buyer shows a preference for native over foreign calico.

Some years later Sir Robert Hart, unconsciously echoing Ch'ien Lung, put the whole matter in a nutshell:

> Chinese have the best food in the world, rice; the best drink, tea; and the best clothing, cotton, silk, and fur . . . they do not need to buy a penny's worth elsewhere.

## CHINESE RECOVERY AND COMMERCIAL DEVELOPMENT

A gradual increase of trade did, nevertheless, begin in the 'eighties, in response to a number of factors. Under the terms of the treaty which had been negotiated by Lord Elgin at Tientsin in 1858, the interior of China had been opened to Europeans for the first time, and merchant shipping had been permitted well up the Yangtze River, Hankow being opened as a treaty port. Eighteen years later the Chefoo Convention of 1876 opened Ichang, higher up the river, and in 1890 Chungking, twelve hundred miles from the sea. The Chefoo Convention followed the murder in 1875 of a British consular official, A. R. Margary, while investigating a possible trade-route between Burma and China (the route of the celebrated "Burma Road" of a later period), and marked a determined effort by Britain, with the jealous concurrence of the other Powers, to force open more of the interior to commerce. The policy was the more practicable because of the re-establishment of the authority of the Imperial government after the quarter-century of rebellions that had opened in 1850 and had seemed to herald the downfall of the Ch'ing. The most considerable menace, the T'ai Ping movement, was finally crushed in 1866, but was immediately followed by a successful rising among the Chinese Mohammedans in distant Sinkiang, led by the able and powerful Yakoub Beg. This in turn was suppressed between 1867 and 1878 by the mandarin turned soldier, Tso Tsung-t'ang, and another Mohammedan rebellion, in Yunnan, was also stamped out in 1873. The reconquest of the revolted provinces, followed as it was in the 'eighties by a good showing against the French in Indo-China, not only opened the way for trade but increased interest in China and respect for the Imperial régime: there was even talk of a Chinese "steam-roller",[13] a notion that was to play its part in later estimates of China's powers of recovery. There was, it seemed, a clear case for pressing upon China as much of the equipment of a modern industrial society as she could be persuaded to take. Hence, for instance, a British firm's offer of a railway to the dissolute young Emperor T'ung-Chih in 1873 as a wedding-gift. Railways and steamboats on the great rivers, were regarded, in characteristic nineteenth-century style, as the necessary precursors of civilization no less than of increasing trade. This was clear enough, however, to the Chinese them-selves. The first railway in the country, built by foreign merchants in Shanghai in 1876, was, indeed, bought from them and torn up in the following year, but it was not long before the Chinese began to interest themselves in strategic railways to increase their powers of resistance to the West.

To the strengthening of the internal position that followed the restoration of order must be added the economic advantage derived by China from the 'eighties onwards from the remit-tances of emigrants abroad. In general, however, the terms of trade were turning against China, for, like India, she was affected by the steady decline in the value of silver, the staple of her currency, as the gold standard became general at this time. In the fifty years between 1860 and 1910 the sterling value of the *tael* fell from 7s. to little more than 2s. 6d.: increased exports therefore brought little relative advantage.

It was not, in any case, until after the Boxer rising, with its evidence of the hopelessness of further resistance to western penetration and industrial development, that the pace of commercial development markedly quickened with the increase of concessions and loans. China's foreign trade in the 'seventies amounted to some £40,000,000 and barely exceeded £50,000,000 in the 'nineties, but before 1914 the totals of the 'nineties had already been doubled, and still further increases lay ahead.

## CHINESE EXPORTS

The principal items of export for China were at first tea and silk, which even at the end of the century still accounted for nearly two-thirds of the total of goods sent abroad. Exports of silk increased fourfold between 1880 and 1910, though apart from brick-tea, which went overland to Russia, tea exports fell steeply as Britain drew on expanding production in India and Ceylon. Between 1886 and 1905, indeed, British imports of tea from China fell from 127,000,000 lb. to 22,000,000 lb., while supplies from India increased from 90,000,000 lb. to 264,000,000. The change was due partly to taste, but owed even more to the superior organization of the Indian tea plantations under European direction. In the primitive conditions of the Chinese economy production was variable in quality, and with tea, as with other commodities, an increased demand led to adulteration. It was partly on this account that the preparation and processing of much of China's produce for export passed under European control, though, owing to language and other difficulties, Chinese middlemen, *compradores*, long continued to act as purchasing agents. Typical of the commerce that developed in this way was the trade in hides and skins and in pigs' bristles, both of them products of the upper basin of the Yangtze, which became available as the interior was opened. In bristles, in particular, China became a principal source of world supply until the invention of nylon.

## CHINESE LABOUR

A further attraction for the European producer was, of course, the cheapness of Chinese labour. An extreme example of the way in which this was exploited was the manufacture of hair-nets. These were made in China from hair originally bought in China but shipped to Europe or America for bleaching and dyeing before being returned to be made up by Chinese domestic workers.[14] In China could be found the raw material, and the cheap labour for its manufacture, but not the industrial skill necessary for its preparation: the double journey was therefore worth while. It was conditions such as these that caused Dilke to exclaim in *Greater Britain*, that "Nature seems to intend the English for a race of officers, to direct and guide the cheap labour of the Eastern peoples."

BRITISH EXPORTS TO CHINA:
(1) COTTON

The English were, above all, traders, and their Eastern trade was largely in cotton goods. The complaint was often heard that if the Chinese would but wear their shirts a few inches longer—and, of necessity, pay more for them—the fortune of everyone in the industry would be made. As in India, but to a much lesser extent, foreign imports discouraged village industry, though the Chinese peasant on the whole preferred his own coarse but strong cloth, with its quilting for winter warmth, to foreign material which he could, in any case, rarely afford. Nevertheless, cotton piece goods remained the most important single item of British exports to China, accounting for more than half of the total until the First World War, when Japan was able to capture the market. For handloom weaving in China large quantities of yarn were imported from India, but Japan early captured this market also, and held it until displaced by Chinese production. Not until the nineteen-thirties, however, was China able to meet her own needs in cotton production on an industrial scale.

(2) THE OPIUM TRAFFIC, AND ITS SUPPRESSION

From India came also opium, from which the Indian Government garnered a considerable revenue in excise, and there were also imports from Persia and Turkey. With the abandonment by the Chinese Government, however, of any attempt to interfere with the habit, there was a rapid increase of local production, and imports fell from £6,500,000 to £4,750,000 between 1880 and 1900. After the Boxer episode westernized Chinese, alive to the fact that even the despised Japanese had long since suppressed the traffic in the drug, insisted that it should be banned, and in 1908 and 1911 international agreements were made for the parallel reduction of both imports and home production. Legitimate imports finally ceased altogether in 1917, a significant moment in China's history in view of the part played by opium in the opening of the country to Western influence. This was not by any means, however, the end of home production. Opium continued to be grown, particularly in Manchuria, where it proved a lure to settlement as effective as gold in California or Australia,[15] and where it was later to be deliberately encouraged by the Japanese.

## (3) The "Open Door"

If the total of British trade continued to be smaller than merchants hoped for, it was never insignificant, and in the expansive years after 1900 it more than doubled, reaching nearly £20,000,000 by 1913. Throughout, British policy was essentially that of the "open door", not from motives of altruism but because it was confidently felt that given free entry and fair competition British goods would always hold their own. Thus, Valentine Chirol, after a tour in the Far East on behalf of *The Times* in 1894–95, was convinced that Britian could look forward with confidence, provided that her trade had "the fair play which alone it requires". The doctrine of the "Open Door" is associated with the name of the American Secretary of State, John Hay, who formally enunciated it in a circular to the Powers in 1899, but he was, in fact, expressing the traditional British viewpoint, which had been put before him by a distinguished British officer in the Chinese Customs service, A. E. Hippisley (1848–1939), at a time when, under the stress of the international rivalries that arose from the revelation of China's weakness in her war with Japan (1894–95), the door, open since 1842, seemed in danger of being slammed shut.

## (4) Hong-Kong

Before the 'nineties Britain, France and Russia had all taken advantage of China's weakness to add to their territories,

Britain in Hong-Kong, France in Indo-China and Russia, exploiting the opportunities presented by Yakoub Beg's rebellion, in Central Asia. The interests of Britain and France, however, had been largely commercial. Hong-Kong had been taken in 1842 to serve both as a trading-centre and as a base from which further pressure could, if necessary, be brought to bear upon China. It had considerable advantages over nearby Canton as a port, however, and rapidly developed a vigorous life of its own, attracting a large Chinese population under the peace and security offered by the British flag. Much of Britain's exports to China were transhipped in the port, and until the end of the century, as a free-trade port open to all, it handled little short of one-half of China's total trade. A thriving city created on a bare and rocky island, it was one of the first and most striking of Western creations in China. It was far from the centre of government at Peking, but while no other Power was established nearer Britain sought no further territorial concessions. When, in 1897, however, Kiaochow (Tsingtao) in Shantung was ceded to Germany, Britain promptly established herself at Weihaiwei in the same peninsula.

## THE WEST IN CHINA:
### (1) SHANGHAI

Hong-Kong, which remained a British possession, was an impressive achievement, but the greatest of all Western enterprises in China was the creation, amid the mud-flats of the Yangtze delta, of Shanghai, today the second city of the East and the fourth of the whole world, with a population of more than five millions. European settlement on leased land at Shanghai began in 1843, but it was only after 1862, when the Yangtze was effectively opened to foreign shipping, that the true significance of the site became apparent. Situated as it was at the mouth of the river which drained the largest and most productive area of China, extending westwards as far as Szechwan, Shanghai rapidly became the chief centre of Chinese trade, controlling two-thirds of the total trade from Chinese ports in the 'seventies and still one-half in 1914. A great modern city and port were built on the leased land, which was divided into an International Settlement (British and American and, later, Japanese) and a French Settlement, and both the

importance and the population of the city were further increased
after 1895, when, by the Treaty of Shimonoseki, the Japanese
gained the right to establish industry at the treaty-ports, a
right shortly shared, through the "most favoured nation"
clause of all Chinese treaties, with the other Powers. Hence the
great increase of China's trade in the early years of the present
century. As industry developed Shanghai became the centre
for about one-half of China's modern industrial production,
and attracted a vast number of Chinese industrial workers.
There, it has been well said, "modern China was born".[16]
Shanghai felt the full impact of western industrial civilization
as did no other centre (by 1931 it had absorbed more than one-
third of the total of foreign investment in China), but the
territory of the city remained (nominally) Chinese, and very
many Chinese—capitalists, merchants, *compradores*, peasants
and industrial workers—contributed to its growth and its
prosperity. Shanghai has been, indeed, a leading agent in the
momentous economic and political changes which have at last,
after a century of uneasy adjustment, broken with China's
material backwardness. Communism, it can reasonably be
argued, "is merely the present vehicle, not the creator, of the
revolution which has carried it to success",[17] and that revolution had no small part of its beginnings in Shanghai. This may
be remembered when the "longest bar in the world", the far-
famed symbol of Western hedonism in the International
Settlement, is but a fading recollection of the oldest of old
China hands.

## (2) The Customs Service: Sir Robert Hart

Shanghai was essentially an open door into China, but
the "sign and symbol of the 'Open Door' " was the Chinese
Customs Service, directed by an international team, which was
originally created at Shanghai in 1854 by the joint action of the
Chinese Government and the foreign Powers in order to check
abuses in the collection of customs dues by Chinese officials,
but later became the instrument which saved China, for all her
weakness, from the fate of Egypt, and which, after the
Revolution of 1911, preserved administrative continuity
amid the chaos of rival aspirants to government. Already in
1860, when China had to pay a war indemnity to Britain and

France, the Customs Service had become both a means of raising the money and a security for its payment. The indemnity was, indeed, paid off by 1866, but the Customs revenue then became, within the limits set by treaty to the rates of duty, not only a source of reliable income but security for loans and further indemnities, especially after the Japanese war and the Boxer rising: it long stood between the government and bankruptcy. It did more than that, for it advised the government, especially on foreign affairs, financed its diplomatic service, charted and lighted China's coasts and navigable rivers and built up a modern postal service, all in addition to easing by its honest efficiency the passage of commerce between China and the world. As the great Inspector-General, Robert Hart, wrote to Lord Salisbury in 1885, when declining appointment as British Minister in China:

> The Service which I direct is called the Customs Service, but its scope is wider and its aim is to do good work for China in every possible direction.

"We have helped to keep China quiet and the dynasty on its legs, and I hope this is something", Hart wrote to a friend, in characteristic self-depreciation, nearly ten years later. It was typical of the anomalous position he held that it was not until 1902, when he had been Inspector-General for forty years—and the dynasty was barely on its legs—that he was received in audience by the Dowager-Empress who owed so much to his loyal service.

## The Beginnings of Partition:
### (1) Russian Policy

But for the Customs Service, indeed, it is difficult to see how China could have escaped the fate of Egypt, or, rather, in view of its size, how it could have avoided being carved into a number of Egypts. Partition did come, however, and it is usual to mark its beginnings in the war of 1894–95, followed as it was by the entry first of Japan and then of Russia into Manchuria and Korea, by the French acquisition of railway concessions in South China and by the loss of Kiaochow and Weihaiwei to Germany and Britain. The process of partition began, in fact, in the 'eighties, with the French conquest of

Tonkin. Hitherto the chief concern of the Powers had been to open China to their trade. Now a combination of circumstances began to make of China, in succession to Africa, a field for rival imperialisms. China proper was still left under its own government—or misgovernment—though commercial, and, later, railway, concessions were sought, and there was in time to be talk of partition into regions of commercial preponderance. Outlying provinces, however, were whittled away, partly for the sake of their own resources, partly to serve as bases for the better commercial exploitation of China itself. The process might even be said to have begun as early as the 'fifties. Then Russia, checked in the West by the Crimean War, had taken advantage of China's weakness to establish herself across the Amur River, in the long-disputed Maritime Provinces, where, near the Korean border, Count Nicholas Muraviev, whose successes won for him the addition of "Amurski" to his title, founded in 1860 the port of Vladivostok. Later, during Yakoub Beg's rebellion, Russia occupied Chinese territory in Central Asia, though most of this she returned in 1880, being too much exhausted by the Turkish war of 1877–78 to undertake a further distant campaign. The Turkish war, however, caused one of those swings of Russian opinion away from Europe which were a recurrent feature of Tsarist policy. Alarmed by the signs of an Austro-German understanding, Russia drew nearer to France, and there began that financing of Russian development by French capital which made possible, in 1890, the beginning of the Trans-Siberian railway, with Vladivostok as its Asiatic terminus. With French money to support her, and the great transcontinental line to link her widely-divided territories, Russia by the 'nineties was in a position to force her attentions upon China. Her policy then was not to partition but to dominate, both militarily and economically. Given the economic control of Korea and Manchuria, which she gained in effect in 1896, given military control of the vital short cut for the Trans-Siberian railway across Manchuria, and concessions for connected lines into China itself, it suited Russia to see China remain united and governed from Peking, conveniently placed as the imperial city was within reach of Russian bases. Manchuria was vital to Russia's Far Eastern position, and with

Port Arthur (Lü Shun K'ou) in her hands her dominant position in North China was assured.

## (2) FRANCE AND INDO-CHINA

It was not until the 'nineties, however, that Russian pressure made itself felt, and it was France in the previous decade which introduced new moves on the Chinese chessboard. Though the Upper Yangtze was opened to trade after 1876, the route was long and slow, and both Britain and France sought alternatives. The most direct route to Yunnan Province was that by the Yuan (Red) River from Tonkin, though if the mountain barrier could be penetrated there was another route from Burma. Exploration of the Burma route had led to the murder of Margary in 1875, but although a railway was planned later the physical difficulties proved too great. The Red River, however, was another matter. In the words of a distinguished French explorer, France sought there "a box for the French sentinel . . . at the head of the line leading directly to the most populous and one of the most productive empires in the world". She found it in Tonkin, which was conquered from China in 1885 and linked with Cochin China, Cambodia and Annam in 1887 to form the colony of *Indochine français*. The step was dictated by a variety of motives, the need for new outlets for trade and capital, especially after the depression of the 'seventies, and a desire both to maintain France's position in the world as a great imperial Power and to offset Britain's commanding position in India. There was also the shock of the British occupation of Egypt to be avenged. Eventually Indo-China became a great and prosperous colony, second only to Burma as an exporter of rice, but the campaign in Tonkin proved difficult, and in 1885 cost Jules Ferry, *le Tonkinois*, his Premiership. Nor was it until 1896 that the pacification of the country, associated with the distinguished names of Galliéni and Lyautey, was complete. In that same year, however, taking advantage of the Sino-Japanese war, France realized the promise of her position by winning consent for the extension of her Tonkin railways into South China and securing certain privileges for the exploitation of the mineral wealth of the region. Britain objected, and France eventually arranged to share any mining privileges with her, but with both France and Russia advancing their interests there seemed to contemporary observers a real possibility that Britain might be squeezed out of Central China. Hence Lord Salisbury's famous suggestion to Russia in 1898 of a partition not of territory but of preponderance, which, although it seemed an abandonment of Britain's traditional policy in China, was in fact a transparent (and abortive) attempt to impose some restraint upon the political, as opposed to the economic, domination of North China by Russia.

## (3) Chinese Reactions

Despite the gallant resistance of guerrilla troops in 1885 in the difficult country of the Red River basin, associated particularly with the strongpoint of Langson, the Dienbienphu of its day, China was powerless to check the French advance in Tonkin. The war, and some transient successes of the Chinese forces, did something, however, to stir up a new spirit in the Chinese people. There were anti-foreign riots at Canton in 1883, and it was noted by close observers that the ever-willing coolies of South China, who had played an indispensable part in helping the British and French forces in their attack on Peking in 1860, would not now load French ships at Hong-Kong. It was something more than a local reaction against foreigners and their ways, such as had burst out in terrible destructiveness at Tientsin, for instance, in 1870: it was the first manifestation of resentment both at the humiliations that were being imposed upon China and at her helplessness, resentment that was to flare up in the Boxer rising and to continue as a bitter undercurrent in Chinese life. It was to be true for many years that while, for various reasons, the Chinese proved unable to do much for themselves, they could actively resent much that was done to them, as was to be shown by the series of trade-boycotts that began in 1905 with a protest against America's immigration policy. Yet the spirit which was, perhaps, first revealed in the 'eighties drew little response from the victorious West, confident that its activities in China were ultimately in the best interests of all, Chinese and foreigners alike. In the words of a leading authority:

> The Celestial Empire was simply a great market to be exploited to the full, a rich territory to be carved up like a sirloin steak.

Nevertheless, while the Imperial Government could be over-awed, the spirit of many of its leaders was never broken, and there were already indications of the existence of another China, unorganized but as independent in spirit as Japan, and conscious of its country's proud history and present shame. Within a few years of the French successes Hart was writing that Chinese despair "may find expression in the wildest rage", as was to happen in 1900.

### (4) THE KOREAN PROBLEM AND JAPAN

If Tonkin was a portent in the south it was from the affairs of Korea that China was to suffer her most shattering blows. Korea, the incongruously named *Chosen*, "Land of the Morning Calm", was an ancient and decrepit kingdom which throughout its long history had been a tributary of either China or Japan. Geography had given it an important strategic position, and it has often been compared in its relation to Japan with the Netherlands in relation to Britain. For China it was a defensive shield for the Eastern Provinces of Manchuria. It was the last of the Far Eastern States to be opened to foreign trade (hence its name of the "Hermit Kingdom") and was opened, significantly enough, by Japan, which in 1876 punished an attack on one of its ships by forcing Korea to accept precisely the kind of treaty which the West had thrust upon China and herself. Japan thus gained in Korea the extra-territorial and other rights which she was not to acquire in China until 1895.

There followed nearly twenty years of intrigue and unrest, which the ineffective rulers of Korea were powerless to control. Japan soon came to dominate the economic life of the country, which both now and later she treated in the worst spirit of colonialism, and built up a party in her own favour. The Korean Court clung to the connexion with China, which, after an anti-Japanese outbreak in 1882, appointed a Resident, Yüan Shih-k'ai (1859–1916) (afterwards famous as a leader of the ill-fated Chinese Republic of 1912), to guard her interests. A further outbreak two years later, when China was pre-occupied with France, led to the Convention of Tientsin, by which China and Japan agreed that neither should garrison Korea without due notification to the other. Ten years later came the final crisis. Again there were outbreaks of violence, and when the King of Korea appealed to China for military aid Japan sent troops in even greater numbers. The moment was a critical one for Japan. As will be seen shortly, her internal politics had reached an impasse which only the patriotic stimulus of foreign adventure could break. Moreover, with the Trans-Siberian Railway under construction, it was necessary for her to forestall the moves which increased strength and mobility would enable Russia to make. Japan therefore insisted upon reforms in Korea, and when the King proved recalcitrant, seized him and compelled him to declare war upon China.

## THE SINO-JAPANESE WAR, 1894–95

The war with China that followed opened the world's eyes to the nature of the "venerable imposture" that was the Celestial Empire. Even so close an observer as Robert Hart had thought that "if the war lasts long enough we must win: Chinese grit, physique, and numbers will beat Japanese dash, drill and leadership". There were individual acts of gallantry on both land and sea, but neither for the first time nor for the last the spirit of the Chinese people was stultified by lack of organization, equipment, leadership and honest administration. It was typical of the state of affairs that the gallant Admiral Ting, commanding several ironclads, found himself, through peculation in the dockyards, engaging the Japanese fleet with but three rounds to serve his impressive-looking ten-inch guns. It was typical, too, of all that was best in the spirit of ancient China that Ting committed suicide rather than surrender. But, whatever Hart might think, there was no time to mobilize Chinese grit, even had the means and will to do it been present. As in 1941, Japan had laid her plans too well. Her Intelligence had long been active, and many Chinese, even among Ting's staff, were in her pay. The result was a promenade rather than a war. Fighting began with the sinking of a Chinese transport towards the end of July, 1894, and war was formally declared a few days later, on 1st August. Within six months Port Arthur was captured and Japanese troops were advancing through South Manchuria upon Peking. Peace was made at Shimonoseki in April, 1895. China agreed to recognize the independence of Korea and to extend to Japan the privileges enjoyed by the Western Powers in China. In addition she ceded Formosa and the Liaotung peninsula, on which stood Port Arthur, and undertook to pay a large indemnity.

China's catastrophic defeat opened a new phase in Far Eastern affairs. Japan was now a force to be reckoned with, and during the next few years was admitted as an equal among the Powers. The hopes long held of a Chinese recovery had, however, been shown to be illusory. China seemed to be incapable of putting her house in order. If she could not govern herself, the English *North China Herald* said ominously in 1895, there were others who could and would do it for her. This was only too well understood by many Chinese, and was to prove a factor both in the desperate attempts at reform in 1898 and in the Boxer troubles two years later. Chinese everywhere, as travellers testified, were stunned by the disasters of the war, and were quick to resent the new attitude of contempt which foreigners now developed. "Since the disgraceful defeat of our eastern forces," ran a memorial to the Emperor in 1898, "the Western Powers despise us and treat us like barbarians. Now that the partition of Africa is finished they are talking of dividing up China. The newspapers discuss the matter . . . with detailed plans and no concealment."[18]

## THE WEST INTERVENES, 1895

The first reaction of the other Powers to China's collapse was to exclude Japan at once from any significant share of the spoils. Now that the Trans-Siberian railway was progressing, Russia sought an easier and shorter line to Vladivostok than the Amur valley afforded, and the obvious route lay across Manchuria. Vladivostok itself was blocked by ice for three months in the year, and an ice-free port farther south was therefore needed. Port Arthur in Japanese hands would check both these desirable developments. Already, before the treaty of Shimonoseki was signed, Russia therefore intimated to China that she would not permit Port Arthur to be lost. France, though more concerned with European than with Far Eastern developments, did not fail to support her ally, and it suited Germany to see Russia involved far from Europe. Britain alone was unconcerned at Japan's success. The clauses of the peace treaty which opened China to Japanese trade were, indeed, advantageous

2A

to Britain, since for the first time they permitted industrial development which would automatically be possible for all other countries with treaty rights in China. It was not foreseen, on the other hand, that Japan could be for many years in a position to endanger Britain's strategic and economic position in the Far East, while, although the full significance of the transcontinental railway for Russia was not yet appreciated, it was felt that Japan might prove a useful check on Russian policy. Britain's cool attitude, consistent as it was with her traditional policy of strictly commercial development in China, came as a shock to Chinese opinion, and influenced the swing towards Russia which was soon to characterize Chinese policy.

Russia, indeed, made a great impression with her seemingly disinterested friendship. No sooner was the treaty of Shimono-seki signed than with French and German support she compelled Japan to return the Liaotung peninsula, at the price of an increased indemnity. The indemnity was met by the raising of three international loans in 1895, 1896 and 1898, all of them secured on the indispensable Customs revenue. They were China's first considerable international loans, and brought her £43,000,000, for which she ultimately paid no less than £102,000,000. They brought far more, for they gave to the Powers a more direct interest in China's affairs than any had previously possessed. In particular, the loans ensured that the declining Ch'ing dynasty would be bolstered, lest China fall into a ruinous anarchy. Hence the continued acceptance of Tzŭ Hsi's hold on the country after 1900, which was to prove disastrous to China. More loans followed, until by 1914 the governmental debt of China, which had stood at less than £7,000,000 in 1895, had reached £105,000,000, though this was only one-third of the total of foreign money invested in the country.

## RUSSIA'S PRICE, AND ITS CONSEQUENCES

When Japan had withdrawn from Liao-tung Russia presented her bill. Both Russia and China were in need of guarantees against a revival of Japanese power on the mainland, and Russia therefore offered herself as a disinterested protector. To the concern of many Chinese she offered a treaty of alliance in return for the right to conduct a railway across Manchuria, together with, in time, access to a port on the Yellow Sea. There was nothing for it but for China to accept the bear's hug: in 1896 the treaty was signed, and the way was prepared for the "Chinese Eastern Railway" across Manchuria. In the following year Germany in turn presented her first demand. With nine per cent of China's trade in her hands she was second only to Britain (fifty-eight per cent) among foreign trading nations; yet she possessed no port or base, and had to depend on Hong-Kong. For some time her eyes had been fixed upon the bay of Kiaochow in Shantung Province, and in 1897 the murder of two German missionaries in Shantung provided convenient justification for a naval descent upon the bay. In March, 1898, she secured the lease of it, and Russia then took advantage of the opportunity to press a claim to Port Arthur. Resistance was great, but was overcome by heavy bribery at the Imperial Court, and the 1896 agreement was duly completed: Port Arthur became a Russian "concession". Not to be outdone, Britain and France presented their claims and leased Weihaiwei and Kwangchow-wan, respectively. Russia, meanwhile, had also been extending her influence in "independent" Korea. Only three years after she had been rescued from Japan China seemed completely at the mercy of her rescuers, and powerless to prevent their encamping on her soil.

## THE RESHAPING OF BRITISH POLICY

The "leases" at the ports were followed by pressure for railway and mining concessions which were to "open up" China still further, and provide the Western Powers with spheres of economic influence, France in the South, Russia in the North, Germany in Shantung and Britain in the Yangtze Valley. This carving up of the "sirloin steak" Lord Salisbury characterized in his famous "Dying Nations" speech in May, 1898, in all sincerity, as the removal of "desolation and sterility". Provided that the "open door" were preserved, Britain, whose economic stake in China continued to be the most considerable, had no objection to the participation of others in this humane task, in regions to which, as Salisbury explained, "our arms cannot extend". Hence the suggestion to Russia of a "partition of preponderance", which must be seen in conjunction with the approval, in 1899, of the American

"Open Door" Circular, itself an expression of traditional British policy. The occupation of Port Arthur, however, introduced a new, and more forceful, element. Suspicion of Russia's designs was one of the factors which led to Britain's abandonment of "isolation" in her foreign policy. The first indications of a new line were to be found in Chamberlain's approaches to Germany in 1898. Germany, however, had no intention of disturbing Russia's preoccupation with the Far East, and when, after the exposure of Britain's dangerous isolation during the Boer War, the first ally had to be found, it was found, significantly enough, in Japan, who had no less reason to seek support against Russia. And without the British alliance Japan would hardly have ventured upon war with Russia in 1904. The German move in Kiaochow in 1898, from which these other events flowed, was in itself, therefore, an event of no small importance.

## CHINESE ATTEMPTS AT REFORM: (1) CHANG CHIH-T'UNG AND WENG T'UNG-HO

In 1899 Hart drew an ominous picture of the reactions of the Chinese people to the imperialistic attrition that was taking place:

> The Chinaman is very philosophical and matter of fact . . . but there are lots of rowdies among every thousand men, and the proof that their own Government is weak, as shown by the inroads of foreigners, will encourage their natural rowdyism; while, instead of seeing superior civilization in the foreigner, they will regard him as simply another rowdy, and chip in for their share of what disorder can wring from weakness.

It was, indeed, resentment at the pressure of foreigners, and at the weakness and corruption of the Government, which, aided and abetted by reactionary influences, flared out in 1900. Yet already there were scholars and officials who realized that China's only hope lay in reform on Japanese lines. Foremost among these were the Viceroy of Hukuang, Chang Chih-t'ung, and the Imperial Tutor, Weng T'ung-ho. Both were distinguished examples of the best type of Chinese official, conservative in their outlook, but aware after 1894 that changes were necessary. Weng brought influence to bear upon the willingly-persuaded Emperor Kuang-Hsü; Chang wrote a tract for the times, significantly entitled *Ch'uan Hsüeh Pien* ("Exhortation to Learn"), which achieved a circulation of one million. Neither, however, sought any fundamental change in the pattern of Chinese life. Each assumed that China might free herself of Western domination if she would but adopt some of the trappings of Western life, in particular, railways and efficient armed forces. Chang appealed for popular education, but did not consider what was to be taught and how it should be reconciled with Confucian precepts. Indeed, he urged his countrymen to cling to Confucianism. Now and later, as a close observer has pointed out, "Chinese statesmen of great ability have . . . handled the question of 'Western power' not as if it were subject to rational analysis but as if it were some kind of knack or trick, which could be used without having to be understood".[19] The Japanese had caught the trick, and it seemed that it only remained for China to pick it up.

## (2) K'ANG YU-WEI

More advanced in his views than Chang or Weng was the Cantonese thinker and reformer K'ang Yu-wei, who, introduced at Court by Weng, became the Emperor's inspiration in the reform edicts of 1898. K'ang was a native of Kwangtung (Canton) Province, the region of China which had had the longest contact with the outside world, and was traditionally a centre of opposition to the Manchus. K'ang had read the histories of other nations, and published studies of their reform movements. He was an idealist who saw in a reformed Confucianism, combined with the best principles of the West, a hope not only for China but for the world, and contemporaries ironically styled him the "modern Confucius". He longed for an Emperor who, like Peter the Great in Russia, would abruptly set his country on the path of reform, and had his chance in 1898. Kuang-Hsü was no Peter, however, and from 1898 K'ang spent his life in exile.

## (3) SUN YAT-SEN

Of greater significance for the future than any of these was another Cantonese, Sun Yat-sen (1866–1925). Sun was a new portent in China. Many students were now going abroad and missionaries were spreading Western ideas of education in

China itself. Sun had no background of Chinese education. He had been brought up by a brother in Honolulu, and trained as a doctor in missionary hospitals in Canton and Hong-Kong. In 1894 he was involved in preparations for a revolt and had to flee into exile. For years he travelled widely. Like all the best revolutionaries he worked for a time in the British Museum, and in 1896 he made a dramatic escape when imprisoned in the Chinese Legation in London. True to his American training he was a republican, and he sought to introduce in China a parliamentary system based on Western models. Through the *Kuomintang* (Nationalist) movement which he founded in Tokyo in 1907 as the *T'ung Meng Hui* (League of Unity) he gave a lead to the growing number of Chinese who, especially after 1900, wished to break with the past, and became the "Father of the Revolution". In some respects he was the Lenin of China, though he lacked Lenin's ruthless grasp of affairs: he might, perhaps, better be compared with Mazzini. For a time, in 1911–12, he was the first President of the new Republic. Later, disillusioned with developments in China and with the Western world at war, he turned to Soviet Russia for inspiration, and before he died had become, through his *San Min Chu I* (Three Principles of Democracy) of 1924, the driving force in the revived *Kuomintang* of the 'twenties. Associated with him was a representative of the small group of Chinese who were completely westernized, C. J. Soong, who had been brought up in the United States and had returned to China to work, first as a Methodist missionary and then as a successful merchant. Soong's son and three daughters, through their connexion with Sun, were later to play a prominent part in the new China: Sun eventually married one daughter, Chin-ling, as a second wife and his disciple, Chiang Kai-shek, another, Mei-ling. Both were remarkable women, and a time was to come when the "Soong dynasty" would be a major influence in Chinese affairs.

## (4) THE EMPEROR KUANG-HSÜ

Reform was in the air in the 'nineties. The turning-point towards revolution, as Sun Yat-sen later recorded, came with the catastrophe of 1900 and the final discrediting of the dynasty. For a short time before this, however, hopes turned on the young Emperor. Kuang-Hsü (1870–1908) was a young man of intelligence and charm, by no means uninformed or unconscious of his responsibilities, but nervous and of a melancholy turn of mind, easily dominated, and handicapped by ill health that was to bring him to an early death. Unlike many of those around him he had as lively an interest in Western civilization as his enforced seclusion permitted. A miniature railway had been installed in his Palace grounds, and he was a keen student of English: when Queen Victoria sent him Martin's *Life of the Prince Consort*, he was eager to have it translated so that he might study its precepts. His position on the "Dragon Throne" was an irregular one, which he owed to the masterful personality of his aunt, the Empress-Dowager Tzǔ Hsi, for as a cousin of the previous Emperor Tung-Chih, Tzǔ Hsi's son, he was, by Chinese custom, precluded from succeeding. Tzǔ Hsi, however, having been *de facto* ruler of China from 1861 to 1873, during the long minority of her son, had ensured on his early death in 1875 that a mere child should succeed him, and had again kept the imperial authority in her hands until 1889. Tzǔ Hsi (1835–1908)—the name means "Motherly and Auspicious" and was the first of the many titles she acquired during her long life—owed her position in the first place to the accident which had made her in 1861 the mother of the only child of the dissolute Emperor Hsien-Feng, and afterwards to her own personality and force of character. In an inept and hidebound Court she was the only one who knew her mind and had the strength of purpose to carry out her aims, though she owed much to the loyal support of her chief eunuch, Li Lien-ying, and of her shrewd and able kinsman (and, it was widely rumoured, lover) the military commander Jung Lu. For the greater part of the period 1861 to 1908 hers was the controlling influence in the Empire. Even after Kuang-Hsü attained his majority in 1889 her control was hardly relaxed, and it was her authority which reversed his reform edicts in 1898 and thereafter set him aside as little more than a State prisoner.

## KUANG-HSÜ'S "HUNDRED DAYS", 1898

The imperial reforms of 1898 were something more than an expression of the widespread desire for an improvement of

China's desperate situation. K'ang Yu-wei represented the ancient opposition of the South to Manchu domination, embittered as it was by corrupt and inefficient Manchu rule. He wished to see China set on the path so successfully followed by Japan, and resented the influence so obviously exercised at Peking by the reactionary power of Russia. The reform movement was, therefore, something of a reflection of the rival pulls that were afflicting China. The movement began in the summer of 1898 when Kuang-Hsü, summoning K'ang to advise him, issued a series of decrees which summarily swept away, on paper, many of the antiquated institutions and abuses of the Empire. The old examination system was abolished, educational reforms were undertaken, foreign technical books were ordered to be translated, the army and navy were reorganized and a vast number of sinecures was struck out. Far too much was attempted, however, within only a few months. China lacked the centralized administration and the obedient and efficient officials to establish the new régime, and neither the Emperor nor K'ang himself had any idea of the practical problems involved. It was a gallant but hopeless effort which K'ang carried too far. Realizing that the position was insecure while Tzǔ Hsi was at large, he persuaded the Emperor, in September, 1898, to order her arrest, and as a precautionary measure to have Jung Lu executed. The official commissioned with these delicate tasks was, however, Yüan Shih-k'ai, a loyal follower of both victims, to whom the plot was immediately betrayed. Tzǔ Hsi promptly took charge of the situation and resumed the regency. K'ang was able to escape to Hong-Kong, but a number of reformers were executed and the unhappy Emperor, who was saved only by the intervention of the foreign envoys, became his aunt's prisoner for the rest of his days.

## Tzǔ Hsi and Reaction: the "Boxers"

The *coup d'état* was soon followed by the last desperate attempt to rid China of all foreigners, in which Tzǔ Hsi took an active part. Immediately on resuming control she sought to raise funds for the strengthening of the army under Jung Lu, and adopted a higher tone towards the Western Powers, refusing, for instance, a belated Italian request for a "concession". The attempt to increase revenue coincided, however, with serious floods in Shantung, where the population was already excited and resentful of the German incursion. A dangerous situation developed which was only too easily steered in an anti-foreign direction. Throughout China secret societies, the last resort of the oppressed against an unheeding system of rule, had always been active, particularly in periods of dynastic decline. There now arose in Shantung a society styled *I Ho Ch'uan* (Righteous Harmony Fists), which from its name, and the peculiar magical exercises practised by its members, became known to Europeans as the "Boxers". The motto of the Boxers was "Cherish the dynasty and exterminate the foreigners," but the movement was a wild protest against the distresses of China, "the blind lashing out of a people tortured beyond endurance", which if frustrated might easily have directed itself against the dynasty. Such, at least, was Tzŭ Hsi's conclusion, and the movement therefore received her support. Others took a longer view. When the Boxers advanced on Peking in the summer of 1900, Yüan Shih-k'ai, now in control of Shantung, prevented any further outbreaks in the province, while Li Hung-chang in Kwangtung, Chang Chih-t'ung in Hankow and Liu K'un-i in Nanking preserved peace and order in the south. Jung Lu tried to exercise a moderating influence at Peking, but was overruled by the reactionary Princes at Court, and in wide areas of North China foreigners and Chinese Christians were slaughtered. In June, 1900, the Boxers entered Peking and began there the massacre and destruction which were intended to rid China of all "foreign devils" and their works: even the lowly but useful match was forbidden. On 20th June the German Minister, Baron von Ketteler, was murdered in the street, and the foreign Legations, which had hastily gathered together a small force of guards, were besieged. The siege lasted until 15th August, when relief forces arrived, but owing to Jung Lu's influence was never pressed home (firing was also suspended at times, in characteristic Chinese style, when Tzŭ Hsi wished for quiet). Jung Lu realized, as he telegraphed to Liu K'un-i in July, that "if we can save the foreign ministers, it will be good for the future".[20] Patriotic fanatics in Peking, and even Tzŭ Hsi herself, felt, however, that, if the Transvaal could

2A*

hold out against Britain, China should be able to beat off the foreigner, and in default of news there were wild rumours in Europe in July that the Legations had been stormed and their inhabitants slaughtered. The whole tragic episode was misunderstood, and a dreadful vengeance was taken by the relieving troops when they arrived. William II's exhortation to his contingent (which arrived too late) to behave like Huns is well-known, and no discrimination was shown: good friends of the West, who had taken no part in the disturbances, were treated as cruelly as the rest. A Dutch diplomat has recorded the tragic story of his Chinese tutor, whose confidence in European decency was betrayed, and who therefore committed suicide with his whole family, in classic Chinese style.[21]

## THE RESULTS OF THE BOXER RISING

When the relief columns approached, Tzŭ Hsi fled from Peking in disguise, dragging with her the unwilling but help-less Emperor. In view of his long record of association with the West Li Hung-chang had already been appointed to get from the Powers the best terms he could, but the days when his charm and skill could win concessions were past. An agreement on the terms of a settlement was not reached until December, 1900, and not actually signed until the following September. The chief gainers from the whole affair were the Russians, who took advantage of Boxer activities in Manchuria to over-run the provinces, and then endeavoured through Li to gain Chinese agreement to a continued occupation, or at least to considerable economic concessions. In Peking the Russians stood aloof from the other Powers, hoping by not exacting harsh terms to gain a free hand in Manchuria. The terms imposed on China were, however, sufficiently onerous. Leading officials had to be punished (though Russia protected Li Lien-ying), foreign guards were to be stationed in Peking, a properly constituted Foreign Office was to be created in place of the *Tsungli Yamen*, the Board which had hitherto conducted—or, rather, protracted—relations with foreign States, and more shipping, including even protective gunboats, was to be permitted on China's rivers. Above all, an indemnity of some £67,000,000 was imposed, secured on the indispensable Customs. Later this indemnity was converted to China's advantage by being used for educational purposes and for the purchase of industrial equipment, a policy that was inaugurated by the United States in 1908. In general, however, the result of the Boxer rising was to complete China's dependence on the West: "from now on . . . Westerners in China behaved as though the Empire was a conquered occupied country".[22]

## LI HUNG-CHANG: HIS AIMS AND ACHIEVEMENTS

Within two months of the signing of the settlement Li Hung-chang died at the age of seventy-eight. His death symbolized the passing of the old China which had sought to come to terms with the West without fundamental changes. He had first achieved distinction during the T'ai P'ing rebellion, and had then learnt, particularly from General Gordon, something of the qualities of the West. Later, as a provincial Viceroy, while feathering his own nest in accustomed style, he had interested himself in commercial development, establishing the China Merchants Steam Navigation Company, which waxed fat under his official protection, and constructing a profitable railway to bring coal to his ships at Tientsin. He was no lover of the West, but he had no prejudice against the material advantages it had to offer. By the late 'eighties he was an ardent advocate of railway development for both economic and strategic reasons, and his project for a line into Manchuria was a factor in hastening Russia's decision to build the Trans-Siberian. In addition he had textile factories at Shanghai, together with considerable interests in opium-growing in his home province of Anhui. As Viceroy of the key Province of Chihli and Assistant Director of the Board of Admiralty, he was largely responsible for the defences of China which crumbled so pitiably in the war with Japan, and corrupt though his administration was he learnt the need for a more centralized control of affairs—and gave sufficient contracts for Krupp's to erect a statue of him after his death. For some thirty years he was, in addition, largely entrusted, from his headquarters at Tientsin, with the conduct of China's foreign relations, and won some note from his dealings with foreign Powers. His policy was, while recognizing China's limited powers of resistance, to play for time, to concede what was unavoidable, to play off one Power against another and in every possible way to spare China as long as possible the shock of intimate contact with the West so that she might be better prepared to receive it. The tasks he sought to achieve were beyond the powers of any one man, however honest and disinterested he might have been, in the conditions that prevailed in China. In the end, aided by substantial *douceurs*, he had to accept reliance on Russia and to take at their face value Russian assurances of respect for China's integrity. It was his known dependence upon Russia, and the exasperation of the Powers with any policy of patience with China, that made him less effective than hitherto in his dealings after the Boxer rising. Before that he had redeemed the disgrace of the defeats of 1894–95 by his courageous dealings with the Japanese at the Shimonoseki peace conference (where his life was attempted by a patriotic Japanese fanatic) and by the tour of Europe he had undertaken in 1896. Had he wished he could almost certainly have made himself Emperor: it was his loyalty to Tzŭ Hsi that helped to keep the Ch'ing dynasty on the throne. Hart called him "a common-place man", remarkable only for his elevation. For all his faults, however, he remained an interesting figure through his tortuous grapplings with the problems of the relations between a declining China and the rising power of the West. He was called in his day the Bismarck of the East, and Bismarck he himself admired. Had he adopted a motto, however, it would have been "Blood and Silver", not "Blood and Iron". He was no Bismarck, but he was not lacking in a shrewd appreciation of his country's needs and interests.

## Tzŭ Hsi's Change of Heart

Li lay dying as Tzŭ Hsi and the Imperial Court made their way back to Peking after the Boxer settlement, travelling by train as an earnest of a change of heart. Great were the changes that the Dowager Empress was to try to carry through in her final years of power, but a new China was taking shape in which the Ch'ing had no place. An almost religious veneration surrounded the "Old Buddha", as she was widely known, in her last years, but with Li dead and K'ang in exile there were few to rally to the dynasty. Tzŭ herself was ageing, and the Emperor was a dying man with no hopes of an heir. It was the beginning of "twilight in the Forbidden City".[23]

## CONTRASTS BETWEEN CHINA AND JAPAN

The contrast in development between China and Japan, which was dramatically revealed to the world in the war of 1894–95, was the result of differences not merely in the reactions of the two countries to the impact of the West, but in fundamentals of national life and social organization. The very size of China, the nature of her government and the lack of an hereditary aristocracy accustomed to give a lead, all rendered a change of system difficult to achieve. In addition, as has been shown, the Chinese were taught to regard their ancient civilization as perfect: the very notion of improvement at the instance of outsiders was almost inconceivable. Through all the dynastic upheavals of more than two thousand years the social system and ideology of Chinese life had changed but little. Changes of government had come from outside by invasion or from below through revolt: rarely had any change been dictated from above, except to remedy abuses in traditional practices. Hence China's helplessness in the face of Western pressure. Though such men as Li Hung-chang saw the necessity for alterations, they sought them as a means of holding off the West rather than of coming to terms with it.

The response of the Japanese to the Western challenge was fundamentally different, and early brought a position of relative power and prosperity which, while it proved a menace to China, also stimulated such men as Sun Yat-sen to a radical questioning of the Chinese system. The Japanese, as has so often been explained, have always been less of innovators than of imitators. Though of different racial stock and language from the Chinese, their culture and their script had been adopted from China more than a thousand years since, and Buddhism and Confucianism had been taken over with the Chinese pattern of administration. They had, however, been superimposed upon an older pattern of culture, which was to exist side by side with them through the centuries and eventually to gain an enhanced significance as an essentially Japanese element in a system which had borrowed so much from the West. There was, therefore, a tradition of receptivity in Japan, in contrast to the intellectual self-sufficiency of the Chinese. Above all, however, there was a tradition of discipline, of obedience to inherited authority, and of centralized control, which was quite unlike the semi-anarchic system of China. Changes in Japan had always come from above, and adaptation to Western ideas therefore presented far fewer difficulties. There was no scholarly caste to oppose to new doctrines the ideals of an earlier age, for the basis of the Japanese system was not the scholar practising the precepts of an ancient seer, but the feudal warrior who dutifully followed his lord: the able young men who started Japan on her new path in the 'sixties were all members of the military caste. Hence the rapidity with which Japan adapted herself to new conditions, so that, while the peasantry in the fields, the craftsmen in their little workshops— and, indeed, all classes in their homes—continued the traditional ways of life, a whole new industrial civilization was created and the government of the country brought to such a pitch that within forty years a modernized Japanese army and navy could beat a Western State at its own game. While Western traders and agents were creating a Shanghai in China, Japan was creating for herself a whole series of Shanghais, at first with technical help from the West but soon from her own developing resources. And where Shanghai existed in the first place for Western enterprise, such industrial centres as Tokyo, Osaka, Kobe and Yokohama, though owing much in origin to the West, existed essentially for Japan.

## THE BACKGROUND OF JAPAN'S ADAPTATION TO THE WEST: THE SHOGUNATE

Japan, like China, boasts a long history, and her Imperial House claims descent from the Sun-Goddess through the first Emperor, Jimmu, who is traditionally regarded as having reigned in the seventh century B.C. The person and authority of the Emperor (*Tenno*) were therefore divine emanations: even more confidently than the Emperor of China could the *Tenno* claim the overlordship of the world. The basis of Japanese society was, however, the patriarchal unit, or clan, and much of the country's history is the record of the struggles of clans for domination. It was from these struggles that there developed the long seclusion of the Emperors, shut away in their palace at Kyoto on the pretext that the affairs of government were beneath their august notice, their authority exercised by the Shogunate. This extraordinary system, so effective that when Commodore Perry paid his first visit to Japan in 1853 it was to the *Shogun* that he presented a letter from the President of the United States, had its origins in the period from the seventh to the ninth centuries A.D. Contact with China had always been close, but it was at the pinnacles of Chinese culture in the Han, T'ang and Sung dynasties that Japan learnt most from her great neighbour, and of these the T'ang exerted the greatest influence. In the seventh century, at the height of T'ang influence, and to avoid the dangers of clan separatism, Japan was reorganized on Chinese lines, with the free people of the Empire divided into governing and supporting classes, both with their share of rice-lands nominally held from the Emperor, but with the official class paying no taxes. This class, however, was not recruited by examination, as in China; entry to it was restricted, in practice, to members of the existing ruling class. Hence the rapid development of military feudalism and the setting-aside of the actual person of the Emperor. Clan rivalries continued and were exacerbated by disputes over unallocated land, while peasant rice-holdings passed into the hands of nobles in return for military protection. The Emperors, their revenues diminished by land-alienation, became mere ciphers, and the country was controlled by the most powerful of the feudatories as Regent until, in 1192, after a fierce struggle for control between the Taira and Minamoto clans the victorious Minamoto Yoritomo was named by his protégé, the young Emperor Go Toba, *Sei-i-tai-Shogun* (Foreign-Barbarian-Repressing Great General). Henceforth the government of Japan was a dyarchy, with all effective authority in the hands of the Shoguns at their own Court, known from its origins as the *Bakufu* (literally, "tent government"), while the Emperors, to whom all outward forms of veneration continued to be paid, were pale and cloistered shadows, not infrequently in actual want. The Shogunate itself was not always effectively exercised, however, and clan warfare continued at intervals until the sixteenth century, when a succession of three able men, Oda Nobunaga (1534–82), Toyotomi Hideyoshi (1536–98) and Tokugawa Ieyasu (1542–1616) restored unity and order, Ieyasu founding the Tokugawa Shogunate, which was to endure until 1867.

EARLY RELATIONS WITH THE WEST: SECLUSION

By the time of the Tokugawas Japan was already confronted with the problem of relations with the West, for missionaries and traders had become active in the country during the sixteenth century and Christianity, despite sporadic persecution, had made great headway. Having with difficulty suppressed their internal opponents, the Tokugawa were not, however, inclined to risk their being revived by contact with rival European forces, and they feared the possible political consequences of missionary enterprise. Hence the banning of Christianity in 1614, which was followed in 1640 by the extraordinary measure which closed Japan to foreigners and forbade any Japanese to travel abroad. But for this the European Powers, when they appeared in the Far East in strength in the nineteenth century, might well have found much of it already in Japanese hands. After 1640, though a trickle of trade continued, Japan was largely cut off. "With the exception of medicines", wrote a Japanese economist in 1708, "we can dispense with everything that is brought to us from abroad",[24] a statement reminiscent of Ch'ien Lung's later message to George III, though reflecting a totally different outlook.

THE CONDITIONS OF THE "RESTORATION" OF
IMPERIAL RULE

Contact was not completely lacking, for the Dutch were permitted a small degree of trade, and through them inquiring Japanese were kept informed of developments in the West, and especially of scientific and technical advances. Early in the nineteenth century foreign shipping was occasionally seen in Japanese waters, and the Anglo-Chinese War of 1840, with its revelation of the armed strength of the West, made a great impression. By the time that Perry appeared in 1853, with his demand for the opening of Japanese ports to American ships, the *Bakufu* realized that Japan lacked the power to resist, and there followed the treaties of 1854–55 and 1858, which gave the Western Powers privileges similar to those already enjoyed in China. Part of the driving force of the "restoration" movement of the next decade arose from a determination to place Japan upon an equal footing with the Powers, so that these "unequal treaties" might be revised, and the privileges of the foreigners withdrawn.

## DECLINE OF THE SHOGUNATE

Quite apart from the pressure from outside, by the middle of the nineteenth century Tokugawa rule was in decline. The rigid system of control established by Ieyasu and his immediate successors was breaking down, rival clans, still unreconciled to Tokugawa domination, were stirring, and there were grave economic difficulties. The restoration of direct imperial rule seemed essential, both to ensure a more effective system of government and to unite the country in the face of the growing pressure from outside, which might aim at exploiting internal divisions. The Restoration must be seen, however, as something more than a defensive response to an outside stimulus. It marked another round, and that not the last, in the long history of clan rivalries, and carried over into the new period, disguised though they were by Western forms, many of the characteristics and influences of earlier centuries. Above all, it was a move effected from above, owing little to any stirrings of popular forces. Time was to show that by exalting the Emperor as the symbol and focus of national loyalty, and reviving, in deliberate contrast to the ideology of *Bakufu* times, the ancient principles of pre-feudal *Shinto*, with its emphasis upon the divinity of the Emperor, the way was being opened for dangerous developments. It is important to remember that between 1598 and 1945 Japan did not suffer a defeat in war. The long seclusion of the Tokugawa period, followed as it was by the rapid rise to Great Power status, with the comparatively easy triumphs of 1894–95 and 1904–05, seemed to justify traditional notions, and induced a spirit of arrogant jingoism which was to have disturbing consequences.

## FEUDAL ORGANIZATIONS: (I) THE CLANS

Under the Tokugawa Japan was divided into feudal fiefs, with loyal feudatories, *daimyo*, in control in key positions throughout the country. Hostile clans were known as "outside lords", *tozama* (a notion that was to be carried over into the battles of ins and outs in parliamentary politics), and the most powerful and least easily controlled of these were the *Satsuma* in Southern Kyushu, with their neighbours the *Choshu, Hizen* and *Tosa*. These were the clans that brought about the Restoration: their geographical position and distance from the capital had long made it possible for them to maintain trade with China and the West and to learn something, in particular, of the improvements in the military sciences which the West had introduced. With the Restoration the *Satsuma* and *Choshu* were to dominate Japanese politics for several decades.

Below the *daimyo*, and owing allegiance to them, were the sword-bearing warriors, the *samurai*, a privileged caste which had no functions but military service, and which had become parasitical in the long peace maintained by the Tokugawa. Unattached *samurai* were the *ronin* (wandering men), a class tending to increase in times of peace when occupation was gone and many *daimyo* found themselves unable to maintain their feudal levies. Many *samurai* and *ronin* settled in the cities and turned to foreign studies, becoming champions of the Restoration and afterwards its chief supports, filling most of the civil and military posts under the new régime. Numbering as they did, with their families, more than one million, they were an important element in the new Japan as in the old.

It was the military prowess of the West that inevitably attracted the attention of these classes. Observing the fate of China, they realized that without modern armies and armaments Japan would soon suffer the same fate. The Restoration was for them a re-assertion of Japan's place in the world, and their control of the movement gave it from the first a militaristic bias. "The Japanese," it has well been said by an Indian historian, "were not interested in Western humanism or in the liberalization of thought, but in penetrating the secrets of Western power."[25] The *samurai* were confident that given those secrets they could save the Empire.

## (2) THE PEASANTRY

Below the feudal classes were the peasantry, upon whose labours all else rested. Heavily taxed, and subject, like peasants everywhere, to the exactions of the village moneylender, their situation under Tokugawa rule, rigidly controlled as it was, led to repeated risings. The limits of subsistence within the deliberately closed economy seem to have been reached early in the eighteenth century, when the population of Japan became stationary at some thirty millions, a total greater than in any comparable area of Europe at this time. It remained at this figure for more than a century, restricted not only by natural calamities but by the deliberate practice of infanticide, *mabiki* (literally, "thinning"). With the margin so narrow poor harvests meant much suffering, and the peasants had no remedy but to desert the land or hit out wildly at their over-lords. With the Restoration their burdens actually increased for a time, for it was ultimately the peasantry, as in Italy, that had to pay at first for the creation of a modern State before the growth of the industries that could provide the means to support it. The land-tax was long a bitterly contested issue in Japanese politics, and the early post-restoration years were some of the worst for peasant unrest. The pressure of taxation was eventually lessened in 1873, and with the development of new resources the population of Japan rose by twelve millions during the next thirty years. The rapid increase that followed, which gave the country by 1940 a population of 73,000,000, more than double that of 1873, created further economic pressure which contributed to the militaristic ambitions of 1931–41.

## (3) MERCHANTS AND FINANCIERS

Of increasing importance during the Tokugawa period had been the merchants and financiers, *chonin*, upon whom the economic organization of the régime had come to depend. In particular there were the great merchant houses which handled, and advanced money on, the tribute rice of *Bakufu* and *daimyo* alike, and through usury gained control of much land. With the growth of trade the towns developed, attracting unsettled peasants from the countryside and poverty-stricken *samurai* and *ronin*, until Yedo (the later Tokyo) had a popula-tion of one million, and Osaka, in which some four hundred thousand people and nearly three-quarters of the wealth of the country were said to be concentrated, was called "the city of merchants". Foremost among the *chonin* were the Mitsui, the financial mainstays of the Tokugawa, who transferred their allegiance to the Emperor at the Restoration and largely

financed the new administration, receiving in return opportunities for financial control on an enormous scale. Already
before the Restoration Mitsui had widely varied interests,
including banking, mining and Yedo department stores, and as
one of the group of great financial houses, the *zaibatsu*
(plutocracy) it was to play a major part in Japan's later economic
development. Government patronage, privileges and monopolies were the perquisites of the *zaibatsu*, as the providers of
ready funds, in Tokugawa times, and the practice inevitably
continued under the new dispensation. It was the more readily
followed since the aim of the new rulers was speedily to build
up Japan's military power, a policy succinctly expressed in the
popular slogan *Fukoku Kyohei* ("Rich nation, strong army").
Hence the emphasis upon heavy industry, which only the
*zaibatsu* could finance, and their close connexion with government policy. By the end of the century it was being said that if
Japan ever became a republic a Mitsui would be the first
president.

## THE END OF THE SHOGUNATE: THE RESTORATION AND THE *Tozama*

Mitsui was an old-established house, dating from the
seventeenth century. A later creation was Mitsubishi, founded
by the *samurai* Iwasaki Yataro in the early years of the
Restoration, and the recipient of many imperial privileges
which enabled it to build its dominating position in shipping,
engineering and arms manufacture. Commanding though the
position of these financial magnates was to be, their origins
are to be seen in the Tokugawa era. By the end of that period the
merchants had created great fortunes and were closely bound
by interest to the *daimyo*, but hampered by the restrictive
policies of the *Bakufu*, which was in financial difficulties and
dependent upon their support. With the peasantry restless
and the *tozama* unreconciled, with numbers of the *samurai*
anxious to play a more effective part, and many Japanese of all
classes alive to the dangers and possibilities presented by the
approach of Western power, the days of the Tokugawa were
numbered. Already, before the end of the eighteenth century,
a reaction had set in among intellectuals to the Chinese
influences favoured by the *Bakufu*, with its encouragement of

Buddhism and Confucianism. The early records of Japanese history were studied, with the result that the Tokugawa were denounced as usurpers, and the restoration of *Shinto* and direct imperial rule was demanded. With the later incursions from the West this movement came to be crystallized in the slogan *Sonno Joi* ("Revere the Emperor: expel the barbarian"), the battle-cry of the Restoration. The barbarians showed no sign of going, however, and on several occasions displayed the power of their "black ships" to disastrous effect, while in 1865 they insisted upon direct contact with the Emperor. The movement for change now came to a head. In February, 1867, died the Emperor Komei, to be succeeded by his fifteen-year-old son, Mutsuhito, who took the reign-name of Meiji ("Enlightened Peace"). The new Emperor was no powerful personality, but a man of charm, open to advice from the able group of young men which formed around him, and willing to play a more active part. In November of the same year the last *Shogun*, Yoshinobu, resigned under pressure from the *tozama*. A brief interlude of civil war followed, but in January, 1868, the new Meiji era began, with a government formed, significantly enough, largely of *samurai* of the anti-Tokugawa clans, and including such notable figures as the *Choshu* Ito Hirobumi (1841–1909), Yamagata Aritomo (1839–1922), Inouye Kaoru (1835–1915) and Kido Junichoro (1834–77); the *Satsuma* Saigo Takamori (1827–77) and Okubu Toshimichi (1832–78); the *Tosa* Goto Shojiro (1837–97) and Itagaki Taisuke (1837–1919) and the *Hizen* Okuma Shigenobu (1838–1922). These were the men who made the new Japan, and they owed their position in the first place to their skill as warriors. Thus, when a British envoy (who had suffered at the hands of Chinese patriots only eight years earlier) was attacked by xenophobe *ronin* in his presence in 1868, Goto immediately leapt from his horse and sliced off the head of one of the assailants. Yet it was characteristic of the new economic forces stirring in Japan that Ito, the greatest of the Restoration leaders, was not a *samurai* by long descent: his father, a prosperous farmer, had bought *samurai* status.

In the main the *daimyo* played but a small part in the changes of the 'sixties. Associated with the leading *samurai*, however, was a group of Court nobles (*kuge*) from ancient families long connected with the imperial household. Outstanding among these were Iwakura Tomomi (1835–83), who played a leading part in the earlier years, and Saionji Kimmochi who, born in 1849, survived until 1940, and in his later years was the revered "elder statesman" of Japanese politics. Another notable *kuge* family which had a prominent place in the political life of a later period was that of Konoe.

## THE END OF FEUDALISM

In less able hands, and without the menace of the West, the restoration might have led to little more than a change of clan government, with the *tozama* in control in place of the Tokugawa. It was speedily followed, however, by the abolition in 1871 of the clan system and the buying-out, with *chonin* help, of the *daimyo*, who became financial magnates in the new Japan. At the same time the *samurai* were replaced by an army on a new basis of conscription (1873). This was the creation of the able Yamagata (later Field-Marshal and Prince), who visited Europe at a decisive moment in 1870 and studied the Prussian model. A navy was also founded, on British lines, by Inouye. Many *samurai* were absorbed into the new Services, though others resented the loss of feudal privileges. Serious disagreement arose in 1873 over foreign relations, some of the more ardent of the *samurai* wishing to use Japan's new-found vigour to revive ancient claims upon Korea. The government leaders, who were by no means reluctant to see Japan asserting her place in the world, insisted, however, that the country's internal strength must first be built up. The result was a split which was only partially healed when in the following year an expeditionary force was sent to Formosa to let off some patriotic emotion and, by agreement with China, to punish attacks on Japanese fishermen. Sporadic *samurai* revolts now broke out, and in 1877 the most serious of them was launched by Saigo, one of the earliest supporters of the Restoration, who now claimed that the imperial authority was being used improperly. Saigo was defeated after a six months' campaign and met on the battlefield a traditionally Japanese heroic end, which has become legendary. He was defeated by the new regular troops, and their victory at Kagoshima, aided as it was by their use of the newly-introduced telegraph, marked the real end of feudalism.

## UNCHANGED CONDITIONS

Not every feature of feudalism died with Saigo, however. Although the clans had been broken up, the administration tended to be concentrated in the hands of clan groups. Thus, *Choshu* long tended to dominate the Civil Service and the Army, *Satsuma* the Navy, while the high proportion of *samurai* in the police force—together with the necessity for the firm maintenance of order in these bewildering years—gave the police something of a sinister character which only recent events have checked. Later, in the 'eighties, a peerage was established, on the best Western models, and many *daimyo* and *kuge* nobles became peers, while the Constitution of 1889 gave the House of Peers equal rights in legislation with the House of Representatives. Despite the disappearance of feudalism, therefore, social stratification remained rigid, though many of the restoration leaders, exploiting the opportunities presented to them, made vast fortunes and entered the ranks of the peerage.

## THE EXALTATION OF THE EMPEROR . . .

Police and army were the mainstays of the new régime, and took their inspiration from the exaltation of the Emperor which was encouraged after 1877 to ensure unity and conformity. The Emperor himself rarely intervened in politics, but as he was held to be of divine origin and the hopes for Japan's future were concentrated in his newly-won authority, opposition was stamped not merely as treasonable but as sacrilegious. Neither now nor later did the notion of a "loyal Opposition" emerge, and in the sacred name of the Emperor much was done that was strange and terrible in Western eyes. Assassination from patriotic motives became a feature of Japanese political life, and was to claim many victims, from Okubo in 1878 to the moderate statesmen who were murdered in the strained conditions of the nineteen-thirties. Such was the hold of traditional doctrine that in political assassination the motive counted for more than the deed, and assassins were excused their crimes on account of the devotion of their principles. Respect was similarly given to those who, in traditional style, enforced their views by suicide. The most notable of these in the Meiji era was General Nogi, the victor of Port Arthur, who on the death of the Emperor in 1912 committed suicide with his wife in protest against the westernization of Japanese life.

## ... ITS CONSEQUENCES:
## (1) THE CONSTITUTION

Two most significant consequences followed from the exaltation of the Emperor. The first concerned the basis of the Japanese Constitution, the second the place of the Services in the State. The constitution was drawn up by Ito, after a close study in the 'eighties of European models, and was largely based upon the constitution of Imperial Germany. It was presented in 1889 as an act of grace by the Emperor, in order, in the words of the proclamation, "that, on the one hand, Our Imperial posterity will possess an express guide for the course they are to follow, and that, on the other, Our subjects shall thereby be enabled to enjoy a wider range of action in giving Us their support". The wording was significant. The constitution was an imperial gift, with no hint about it of any theories of contract or of political rights, for who could bind a divine ruler? The Emperor was the personification of Japan, and indicated, through the constitution, how his subjects could assist him in the governing of the Empire. Ministers were appointed by him and were responsible only to him, responsible only individually so that no Cabinet was possible. A House of Representatives was established on a narrow franchise, but had no control over Ministers and could exercise only a limited check on government finance.

Even more remote than the Ministers from anything that smacked of popular control was the Privy Council, nominated by the Emperor to advise him, and the still more influential body of elder statesmen, the *genro*, which though, unlike the Privy Council, it had no place in the constitution, during the life-time of such men as Yamagato and Saionji exerted an all-powerful influence and was constantly consulted by the Emperor.

## (2) The Services and Government

The Emperor was supreme commander of the armed forces, and the independence of the forces from any parliamentary control, which was, in effect, guaranteed by the constitution, was jealously preserved. In view of the difficulty encountered in the working of the constitution, and of the need from 1894 for national unity in the face of foreign dangers, trusted Service leaders were frequently called upon to lead governments. Yamagata was one of the first, and it was he who, taking advantage of the war-fever of 1894–95, instituted a practice that was to have serious consequences. It was then decreed that the Service Ministries should always be in the hands of officers on the active list, which meant that no government could be formed or maintained without the approval and support of the Services. Given that the Service chiefs had access to the Emperor at all times, it followed that the military traditions of the *samurai* and the needs of national defence combined to encourage the Services to maintain the divine status of the Emperor and almost guaranteed them the freedom of action that was to be seen in its most extreme expression in Manchuria in 1931. Hence, too, the activities of the young officers in the nineteen-thirties, who murdered the ministers responsible for the naval treaty of London of 1930, regarded as treasonable since it limited Japan's power, and in 1935 brought about the suppression of the teaching of the distinguished constitutional lawyer Dr. Minobe Tatsukichi, who had evolved a doctrine of the Emperor as *kikan* (organ of state), which was regarded by traditional minds as suggestive of parliamentarism and responsible government.

## (3) Education: the Imperial Rescript, 1890

Education reflected no less the supremacy of the Emperor. State control of schools was established in 1880, and a far-reaching Education Law passed in 1886 by the Minister Mori Arinori (1847–89) (who, such was the temper of the times, was to be assassinated in 1889 for an accidental violation of an historic shrine). It was realized that the secret of Western success was to be found in education no less than in technical advances, and though the burden of taxation imposed by the educational system was a heavy one it was borne willingly.

Between 1886 and 1906 the percentage of children attending school rose from forty-six to ninety-five, and in these figures is to be found part of the explanation of Japan's rapid rise as an industrial and commercial nation. Underlying the provision of educational services, however, was the ideal of the supremacy of the State. "What is done", Mori said, "is not for the sake of the pupils, but for the sake of the country", a pregnant comment. In the same spirit Tokyo University became, in effect, a branch of the Civil Service, responsible for the training of officials. In 1890 was issued the famous Imperial Rescript on education, which was ordered to be read and studied in all schools. It was addressed in the Emperor's name to "Our subjects ever united in loyalty and filial piety" and laid down the unexceptionable maxims which should help them to "guard and maintain the prosperity of Our Imperial Throne coeval with heaven and earth". It remained the "bible" of Japanese education until 1945, and still retained after then much of its appeal, even under the changed conditions of the post-war era.[26]

## The End of Western Influence

The Imperial Rescript was a deliberate restatement of traditional doctrines and can be regarded, perhaps, as marking the end of the period of intoxication with Western ideas which had begun in the 'sixties. In the 'seventies and 'eighties English political novels were popular in translation, Disraeli's *Coningsby*, for instance, being translated as *Spring Warblings: A Tale of Political Parties*, while *Robinson Crusoe* was studied as a guide to the development of an island's resources. By 1890, however, Japan had her own constitution and was conscious of being less dependent upon the West for advice. The change of attitude is reflected in the number of foreign experts employed, which fell from 500 to 200, and in the rejoicings at the launching, in 1891, of the first warship to be built in Japanese yards. A new period opened with the 'nineties and before the end of the decade Japan had already become a force to be reckoned with in world politics.

## Constitutional Problems: the Parties and the Services

The introduction of the constitution quickly led to a political impasse from which a way of escape was deliberately sought in 1894 through the war with China. The provisions of the constitution had been copied from Germany, but they were applied in a Japanese spirit, and the domination of the *Sat-Cho*, the combination of *Satsuma* and *Choshu* clans, accompanied as it was by all the pressure that traditional forces could bring to bear, and by the limitations set to the powers of the Diet, created conditions in which, as was intended, responsible government could not grow. Financial economy and ministerial responsibility were, however, matters on which the members of the House of Representatives, at least, had strong views, particularly if they were outside the charmed circle of the *Sat-Cho*, and the first ten years of constitutional government were years of political turmoil. Four times between 1890 and 1894 did the Government appeal to the country in the hope of getting a complaisant majority, and both bribery and violence were resorted to. In 1893 so strong was the opposition to an increase of taxes for naval expenditure that the Emperor ordered a ten per cent reduction in all official salaries—including those of members of the Diet —to make good the amount required, a device which even the resourceful Bismarck had never contemplated. Parties of sorts had already come into existence, the *Jiyuto* (Liberal) party representing agricultural interests and led by such men as Goto and Itagaki, and the *Kaishinto* (Reform) party, led by Okuma, with Mitsubishi backing, and representing the new forces of commerce and industry. The strength of both parties lay in their *Tosa* and *Hizen* membership, opposed to *Sat-Cho* predominance, but they were factions rather than true parties, groupings of individuals rather than associations deriving their strength from political principle, and their opposition could often be turned by bribes and places, or, in the last resort, by a word of Imperial reproof. Party government was rendered impossible in any case by the individual responsibility of Ministers to the Emperor, while to make assurance doubly sure Yamagata in 1894 was able to issue a decree preventing anyone without administrative experience (that is, anyone relying on party support in the House) from holding office. Yamagata's power was steadily increasing with the proof which the China war afforded of Japan's military efficiency, and a personal feud developed between him and Ito. In 1898, in an

attempt to check Yamagata, Ito persuaded the Emperor to
allow Okuma and Itagaki to form a joint party administration,
but the two groups failed to work together and an incautious
reference by the Minister of Education, Ozaki, to the notion
of a Japanese Republic with a Mitsui President brought down
the Ministry. Ito then formed from the relics of the Liberal
groups the powerful *Seiyukai* ("Constitutional") party, based
on landed and business interests, which, after his retirement,
Saionji was to lead from 1903 until 1915. After the war with
Russia the *Seiyukai* worked closely with the military leaders
and bought off opposition in the Diet by sharing the spoils of
office. Political peace was largely preserved, in contrast to the
turbulent 'nineties, but at a price: in the words of a contemporary observer, "the complete domination of Japan's political
system by a military oligarchy is the most significant fact in
the history of the later years of Meiji".[27] The *Seiyukai* became
the Conservative party of Japan, largely *Choshu* in its leadership
and supporting the Army in its ambitions for conquest on the
mainland. More Liberal groups formed themselves in the
circles of "big business", favouring commerical expansion
overseas and naval rather than military development, and
tending to be *Satsuma* in leadership, though associated with
Okuma until his death in 1922. From these groups was to be
formed in the nineteen-twenties the *Minseito* party.

## Constitutional Problems and War: China, Korea and Russia, 1894-1904

The parliamentary difficulties of the 'nineties were the
immediate cause of the war with China. Public agitation for the
repeal of the "unequal treaties" and for an assertion of Japanese
supremacy in Korea had long been vigorous, and war over
Korea was therefore popular, rallying the House of Representatives to loyal co-operation with the Government as nothing
else could do. After the war, and the shock of the enforced
retrocession of the Liaotung peninsula, there were many
Japanese who wished to see their country asserting herself in
China. Japan's immediate interests, however, were limited to
Korea, which was strategically vital to her defence, and
attempts were made to reach an understanding with Russia
which would leave Korea as a buffer-state. This was the policy

of Ito, in particular, but although the more far-seeing of Russian leaders, such as Witte, would have welcomed a limiting of Russian interest in the Far East in favour of activity in more rewarding areas, there were irresponsible financial interests at work in both Manchuria and Korea which had the Tsar's ear. The possibility of defeat at Japan's hands was scoffed at, despite the fact that the Trans-Siberian railway was still not quite complete, and Japan's attempts at an understanding were therefore ignored. Hence the Japanese agreement with Britain in 1902. Both countries had difficulties with Russia, but while Japan feared lest if she were involved in war with Russia France might join in against her, Britain for her part was more concerned to prevent any Russo-Japanese understanding which might jeopardize her position in the Far East. Her rôle after the agreement was, in effect, "to keep the ring whilst Japan attacked Russia".[28] The attack came in February, 1904, when it was clear that Russia had no intention of coming to terms. Japan struck without warning, at the very moment when the first loosening of the ice enabled her to move her troops, and speedily outflanked Korea, gained command of the sea and invested Port Arthur. The Russians fought with their accustomed stubborn gallantry, but were outnumbered and badly led. Port Arthur surrendered, after bitter fighting, in January, 1905, and the decisive battle of the war was fought around Mukden in March. In May the Russian Baltic fleet, which had been crawling round the world since October (and been involved *en route* in the despicable Dogger Bank incident), was caught and destroyed off Tsushima, the Trafalgar of the war. So long had this fleet been on the way that its destruction sent a thrill of pride throughout the East. China and India were stirred, and even in distant French-controlled Annam peasants planted in their fields the Japanese lotus. It was, in fact, a victory of a westernized Japan over a frankly oriental Russian régime in the Far East, but to the peoples of Asia, long taught to regard the West with awe, it brought a message of encouragement and hope.

## JAPAN'S GAINS, 1905-10

In the West also the Japanese victory was received with acclaim. Japan, said the American President, Theodore

Roosevelt, through whose mediation peace was eventually made, "is playing our game", and it was not until later that it became clear that the West had as much to lose by Japanese domination in the Far East as by Russian. By the peace made at Portsmouth, U.S.A., Japan gained much. Russia surrendered her lease of Port Arthur and her control of the railway through south Manchuria, and recognized Japan's supremacy in Korea. Japan, conscious of her 120,000 war losses, stood out for a large indemnity, but this was refused, and America let it be known that if the demand were pressed no further loans would be forthcoming. The abandonment of the demand and the failure to stake a claim to Manchuria, which had now been overrun by Japanese troops twice in ten years, led to riots in Tokyo, but Japan was exhausted and the peace had to be signed. The greater, however, was Japanese determination to consolidate her position in Korea and South Manchuria. In 1906 the South Manchurian Railway Company was formed, the counterpart of the Russian-controlled Chinese Eastern Railway, and became the instrument of Japanese economic penetration of Manchuria. Korea, which gave little indication of welcoming Japanese control, was formally annexed in 1910, after the assassination of Ito by a Korean fanatic (not unassisted, perhaps, by rival political circles in Tokyo).

## JAPAN AND BRITAIN

Meanwhile agreements of the greatest significance for Japan's future development had been arranged with Britain, France and defeated Russia. In 1905, before the end of the war, the Anglo-Japanese agreement had become a formal treaty, pledging each party to assist the other in the case of aggression. Japan was thereby guaranteed against Russian revenge, while Britain was able to concentrate her attention on the growing "naval race" with Germany. Japan's position was becoming progressively stronger, and with Britain's naval power in the Far East diminished she was on the way to that naval supremacy in the north-western Pacific region which was ultimately to receive recognition by the Washington Treaty of 1922.

## JAPAN AND RUSSIA, 1907–10

Russia also was turning her attention to Europe, and an agreement with Japan was at length possible. In July, 1907, the two Powers agreed to respect each other's interests in China, and, by a secret clause, to divide Manchuria into spheres of influence, with Russia paramount in the north and Japan in the south. A similar agreement with France recognized this situation together with France's special interests in Yunnan. The one people whose interests were given no consideration were the Chinese: it was, indeed, in part a determination to exclude Chinese control from Manchuria that brought Japan and Russia together, and it was the later threat of a revived China to reoccupy Manchuria which in 1931 launched Japan on her fatal course of aggression.

## JAPAN AND THE U.S.A.

Still more significant than the agreements was the action of the British Government in 1907 in preventing a British company from building, at Chinese request, a line to compete with the South Manchurian railway. American railway interests were also concerned with Manchuria, but were excluded in 1910 by still closer agreement between Japan and Russia, who made clear their determination to monopolize Manchuria. This was the first indication of the disagreement between Japan and America over China which was eventually to have terrible consequences. For the present Britain's support of Japan caused some coolness in relations with the United States, though when the Anglo-Japanese alliance was renewed in 1911 Britain insisted that it could not be invoked in the case of a dispute between Japan and America.

## JAPAN IN KOREA

The annexation of Korea was in part a result of the disclosure of America's interest in Manchuria, in part an attempt to overcome Korean hostility. The Japanese wished to make of Korea another India, with themselves as the new *sahibs*, but with no tradition of civil administration to sustain them they tended to behave aggressively, and to rely, as at home, on strong military and police measures. As a close observer later commented, "the Tokyo Government was anxious that Koreans should be loyal and contented, but had very little idea how such an aim was to be achieved",[29] and the Japanese diplomat who had been responsible for the first agreement with Britain, Hayashi Tadasu, recorded in his *Secret Memoirs* that the troops on the mainland had behaved badly. To the Chinese, he noted sadly, Japan must appear as "the wolf that follows the tiger", and the disillusionment in Korea was no less. After the annexation Korean national sentiment was maintained by a colony of exiles in the United States, prominent among them the notable figure of a later period, Syngman Rhee.

## JAPAN AND CHINA, 1915

In Manchuria Japan bided her time, building up an economic system which was the precursor of the régime that took the bit between its teeth in 1931. The great opportunity came when the outbreak of war in 1914 left Japan supreme in the Far East. Such an opportunity, said patriotic extremists, would not occur again in a thousand years. In January, 1915, having overrun the German concession at Kiaochow, Japan presented to China her notorious "Twenty-one Demands", to most of which China was compelled to agree, under pressure, in May. Japan succeeded Germany in Shantung and was accorded greatly increased rights of trade and settlement in South Manchuria, which enabled her to exploit the important coal and iron resources of the region.

## THE JAPANESE ACHIEVEMENT

It was an unhappy precedent. Alone of the Oriental nations Japan had raised herself to terms of equality with the West. Her achievement had been remarkable, but it had also been rapid, so rapid as to leave unaffected many elements in her national life. In 1894 a revival of ancient ambitions had been deliberately undertaken to divert attention from the stresses of internal politics, in which new forms and old traditions were struggling together for control. The militaristic tone of Japanese life, a tone strikingly in contrast to that of China, had therefore been reinforced. A growing population and industrial capacity called for wider resources and outlets, and such resources as the rice of Korea and the raw materials of Manchuria, were, indeed, to prove of value to the Japanese economy. Militarism, however, knew only one way of securing resources and at the same time of controlling the social tensions which the increasing complexity of the national life was producing. Ito had feared the growth of militarism, but had died at the assassin's hand in 1909. Yamagata lived on until 1922, the most influential of the *genro*, and no friend of parliamentarism or civilian rule. Meanwhile disordered China was a standing invitation to the execution of Japan's "divine mission". The tragedy for the whole world, no less than for China, was that the mission and the methods used to promote it were so little in accord. Nevertheless, what was done must be seen against the background of Japanese history and tradition. The dichotomy between feudal methods and Western constitutionalism, between the simple pleasures of traditional life and the complex civilization shaped on Western lines, between the charm of Japanese manners and the arrogance of the soldiery abroad, is summed up in the simple fact that when a Japanese civil code was devised, on Western lines, a new word, *kenri*, had to be coined to express the notion of civil rights, a notion foreign to Japanese feudal tradition. Apart from a brief, hopeful period in the nineteen-twenties, it was not until 1945 that an attempt was to be made to resolve the dichotomy.

## ECONOMIC DEVELOPMENT

The strength which Japan was to use so ruthlessly was based on the impressive economic developments of the Meiji era, and especially of the years after the Russian war. Between 1900 and 1914 Japan's industrial output increased fourfold, and it was to be doubled again in the next ten years.[30] Much of the increase went into military preparations and the industries needed to sustain them, as is clear from the growth of government expenditure, which, starting at only some £2,000,000 at the Restoration, had reached £8,500,000 by the time of the Chinese war, but had risen to £25,000,000 by 1904 and was little short of £60,000,000 in 1914.[31] In this process, of course, Japan was but adopting yet another Western practice of the time.

## FOREIGN AID

Early industrial development was largely financed by the *zaibatsu*, but after 1895 Japan's credit stood high and foreign money could be borrowed. British money was readily forthcoming, as British technical advice had been available earlier. Half of the experts who helped to modernize Japan were British: "more than all the other Western States", a French historian has observed, "Britain helped Japan to become a Great Power",[32] and it was particularly after the agreement of 1902, of course, that help was made available. The Russian war was largely financed by British and American money, and by 1914 Japan's foreign debt stood at some £200,000,000, considerably more than the total of investment, on all counts, in China. Japan's trade had increased correspondingly. Exports had grown from a mere £1,600,000 in 1868 to £63,000,000 in 1913, and were to be stimulated still further by the lack of foreign competition between 1914 and 1919. They were, however, dangerously limited in range. Two-thirds of the goods exported consisted of raw silk to America and cotton-goods to China, and the post-war depressions were to show that Japan had too many eggs in too few baskets.

## POLITICS AND FINANCE

Much of Japan's life, especially in the countryside, remained untouched by these economic developments, but, although the majority of the people still lived poor and simple lives, there was, despite the steady growth of population, a modest increase in the average standard of living: food production doubled under Meiji and the output of raw materials increased sevenfold. Most of the new wealth was concentrated, however, in the hands of the *zaibatsu*, the Mitsui and Mitsubishi and, with them, the Sumitomo and Yasuda. These great houses dominated the economic life of the country, and owed much to their connexion with political leaders, Mitsui's with Ito and Inouye, Mitsubishi's with Okuma. This connexion between political and financial power, resented as it was by the Army, was to prove a factor of the greatest significance in the uncertain conditions of the post-war world.

## CHINA: THE END OF THE CH'ING

If Japan's record in the ten years before 1914 is one of rapid advance, China's is less happy. It was early in 1902 that Tzŭ Hsi returned to Peking, resolved, on Jung Lu's advice, to make herself agreeable to foreigners and to carry a programme of reform similar to that attempted by the Emperor in 1898. The lesson had been learnt, but there were few men of ability to carry out the reform edicts. Jung Lu himself died in 1903, and the Empress-Dowager then relied upon Yüan Shi-k'ai, who became Viceroy of Chihli and was given the task of building up an efficient army. The ancient examination system was abolished in 1905 and a reform of the government and administration undertaken. In 1908 a constitution was outlined and a parliament was promised ten years hence. Schools were opened on Western lines, and many students went abroad to study, a great number to Japan, though the remission by the United States of her share of the Boxer indemnity made it possible for others to study in America, or in the American University which was established near Peking. After 1905 Japan was looked to in particular, as the exemplar of successful westernization, and it was in Tokyo in 1907 that Sun Yat-sen founded among students and Chinese expatriates the *T'ung Meng Hui*. The League had many supporters among Chinese merchants in Canton and Shanghai and in the Chinese trading communities overseas, who saw no hope for their country while the dead hand of the Ch'ing lay upon it, and it was from them that the funds for revolutionary agitation were supplied. Little action could be expected from North China, where Manchu influence had always been stronger, and where Yüan Shi-k'ai's army kept a firm hold on the country, but the South had always been only moderately loyal. The split between the two, which was to prove decisive for the future, now began to be apparent.

## RAILWAY DEVELOPMENT AND THE "DOUBLE TENTH" (1911)

Patriotic and revolutionary feeling was also stirred by the activities of foreigners in China after the Boxer failure. Railway interests were particularly active, and were, indeed, the immediate cause of the outbreak of the Revolution in 1911.

Now that China had finally capitulated to the West, railway projects were pressed forward to open the country and tap its long-fabled wealth. Elsewhere railway development was a matter of economics and finance; in China, owing to the futility of the Government and the economic rivalries of the interlopers, it was also a matter of politics, of concessions and spheres of influence. Thus, France constructed a line into Yunnan, Germany built railways in Shantung, and a Manchurian system was developed by Russia and Japan. With these railways went rights of economic development which eventually made the South Manchurian Railway, for instance, "the greatest single enterprise on the continent of Asia",[33] and its port, Dairen, second only to Shanghai in the volume of its trade. In 1911, when an important section of the North-South railway was to be constructed, the Chinese government, seeking financial assistance, was faced with a "Consortium" of international Banks which wished to share in the enterprise. It was faced also with opposition from Chinese financial interests, which had already begun the construction of a line, and provincial opposition to control from Peking, combined with suspicion of foreign activities, led to the rising at Wuchang on 10th October, 1911 (the famous "double tenth" of the Chinese Revolution), which unexpectedly brought to a head all the rising resentment against the Manchus and raised the cry for a republic.

## THE REPUBLIC PROCLAIMED

Tzŭ Hsi and Kuang-Hsü had died in 1908, and the Dowager-Empress's last equivocal service to her country had been the choice of a child, P'u Yi, to succeed. In the following year provincial assemblies, which had been one of the reforms promised by Tzŭ Hsi, met for the first time and demanded the speedy summoning of a parliament. The ineffective Regent, who had dismissed Yüan Shi-k'ai, whom he disliked, was incapable of giving a lead, and the Wuchang revolt took the Government by surprise. The revolt soon ran through the South, uniting the disaffected of all schools, and Sun Yat-sen returned to China in December to be proclaimed at Nanking on 1st January, 1912, provisional President of the Republic.

## Yüan Shi-k'ai President: the Coming of Disorder

Unhappily the risings were accompanied in many cases by the slaughter of the hated Manchu, a presage of the terrible happenings of the civil war into which China was so soon to sink. Yüan Shi-k'ai was now recalled, and, commanding as he did an efficient army, began to reconquer some of the lost territory. However, an armistice was arranged and in February, 1912, the Ch'ing dynasty at last abdicated. Sun then resigned, so that Yüan could become President, and undertook the task of organizing the various revolutionary groups into the *Kuomintang*. A National Assembly was elected in 1913, but Yüan soon showed that he recognized no limits to his authority. A revolt of southern provinces was crushed, and Sun had to flee to Japan once more. In 1915, however, when Yüan made preparations to have himself proclaimed Emperor, there was a more successful revolt in Yunnan. Yüan hastily changed his mind, but opposition to him grew steadily, and chagrin hastened his death in June, 1916. China was now left with no effective central authority, and speedily fell apart. The *Kuomintang*, which Yüan had tried to suppress, set up an administration in Canton, and in the North rival commanders struggled for power, one of them even endeavouring for a time in 1917 to restore the boy Emperor, P'u Yi. In Manchuria Chang Tso-lin, an ex-brigand of whom much was to be heard in the years ahead, was making himself master of the country. The future lay, however, with the *Kuomintang* at Canton, though it was to be some years before that became apparent.

## "China's Sorrow"

The vast mass of the people of China remained unaffected by these disturbances, except when, as was to happen with increasing frequency, the troops of the various "war-lords" fell upon them. The struggle raged over their heads, and at their expense. A modern system of government and civilization had been introduced in India under British rule, and in Japan under the firm, traditional control of the Emperor. In China it came only through years of war and suffering, and in an unexpected form. The seventy years from 1842 to 1912 had been years of change and adjustment, with, in the later stages, an ever-increasing pace. The next forty years, however, were to be some of the worst in the history of a country which has known much suffering.

## REFERENCES

Several indispensable works have been heavily drawn on for this chapter, and no detailed references are given to them. They are:

E. V. G. Kiernan: *British Diplomacy in China, 1880–1885.*
W. L. Langer: *The Diplomacy of Imperialism, 1890–1902.*
E. H. Norman: *Japan's Emergence as a Modern State.*
N. A. Pelcovits: *Old China Hands and the Foreign Office.*
G. B. Sansom: *The Western World and Japan.*
S. F. Wright: *Hart and the Chinese Customs.*

Among older works which have contributed much the following should be acknowledged:

Lord Charles Beresford: *The Break-Up of China* (1899).
J. O. P. Bland: *Li Hung-Chang* (1919).
J. O. P. Bland and E. Backhouse: *China Under the Empress Dowager* (1914 edn.).
V. Chirol: *The Far Eastern Question* (1896).
N. Curzon: *Problems of the Far East* (1896 edn.).

1.  W. W. Lockwood: *The Economic Development of Japan, 1868–1938*, p. 102.
2.  K. M. Pannikar: *In Two Chinas*, p. 177.
3.  V. Purcell: *The Chinese in Southeast Asia*, p. 83.
4.  K. S. Latourette: *A History of Modern China (Pelican History of the World)*, p. 51.
5.  C. P. Fitzgerald: *China: A Short Cultural History*, p. 543.
6.  R. H. Tawney: *Land and Labour in China*, p. 174.
7.  C. P. Fitzgerald: *Revolution in China*, p. 18.
8.  *In Two Chinas*, p. 176.
9.  *Land and Labour in China*, p. 120.
10. G. B. Cressey: *Land of the 500 Million*, p. 93.
11. O. Lattimore: *Manchuria, Cradle of Conflict* (revised edn. 1935), p. 3.

12. G. C. Allen and A. G. Donnithorne: *Western Enterprise in Far Eastern Economic Development*, pp. 17–18.

13. V. G. Kiernan: "Kashgar and Central Asia, 1868–78"; *Cambridge Historical Journal*, XI, 3, pp. 341–42.

14. *Western Enterprise*, pp. 88–89.

15. *Manchuria*, p. 188.

16. R. Murphey: *Shanghai: Key to Modern China*, p. 3.

17. ibid., p. 4.

18. E. R. Hughes: *The Invasion of China by the Western World*, pp. 110–11.

19. *Manchuria*, p. 90.

20. C. C. Tan: *The Boxer Catastrophe*, p. 113.

21. W. J. Oudendyk: *Ways and By-ways in Diplomacy*, p. 109.

22. *History of Modern China*, p. 96.

23. The title of the study by Sir R. Johnstone, tutor to P'u Yi, of the last years of the Ch'ing.

24. *The Economic Development of Japan*, p. 305 n.

25. K. M. Pannikar: *Asia and Western Dominance*, p. 341.

26. J. Stoetzel: *Without the Chrysanthemum and the Sword. A Study of the Attitudes of Youth in Post-War Japan*, p. 162.

27. W. W. McLaren: *A Political History of Japan, 1867–1912*, p. 352.

28. Ed. A. M. Pooley: *The Secret Memoirs of Count Hayashi*, p. 64.

29. A. Morgan Young: *Japan under Taisho Tenno, 1912–26*, p. 200.

30. *The Economic Development of Japan*, p. 117.

31. G. C. Allen: *A Short Economic History of Modern Japan, 1867–1937*, p. 186.

32. P. Renouvin: *La Question d'Extrême-Orient, 1840–1940*, p. 97.

33. *Western Enterprise*, p. 137.

XVIII

INTERNATIONAL RELATIONS TO 1914

THE DOMINANCE OF THE GREAT POWERS

THE characteristic feature of the Europe of 1870–1914 is its domination by half a dozen Great Powers of roughly equal strength or pretensions: France, Germany, Russia, Austria-Hungary, Italy, and Britain. The importance of their rôle had been emphasized by changes in the technique of warfare at the beginning of the nineteenth century. As they alone possessed the material force necessary to wage war on the scale which became general during the Napoleonic era, their responsibility for the preservation of peace was correspondingly increased. Small powers tacitly, if unwillingly, accepted the implications of this inequality between sovereign states, and at every international conference from the Congress of Vienna in 1815 to the London Conference in 1913 it was the Great Powers who exerted decisive influence on the course of the deliberations. Where questions of power politics were at stake little attention was paid to the opinions and needs of small states: the affairs of the Balkans and North Africa, for example, concerned the Great Powers only because their own strategic interests were involved in these areas, or because the international repercussions of local conflicts could threaten the peace which they had an interest in preserving.

But criticism of the dominant rôle played by the Great Powers in this period must be qualified by the reflection that they play a considerable part in international affairs at all times, whether international organizations like the League of Nations or United Nations exist or not. It is clear, for instance, that the mistaken policy of the Great Powers, Britain and France, in the nineteen-thirties was decisive for the future of the League of Nations. In the same way, the effectiveness of the United Nations Organization has been dependent, in more recent years, upon the state of the cold war between America and Russia. In short, it will always be a major problem in international politics to regulate relations between sovereign states so that all, great and small, may have a voice in the councils of the nations, whilst recognizing the prime responsibility of Great Powers in the preservation of peace.

## NATIONAL INTEREST AND "BALANCE OF POWER"

Before 1914 Great Powers did not disguise the fact that they were engaged in the legitimate pursuit of their national interests within the framework of the existing social order. These interests, rooted in geography and economics, were ultimately reducible to questions of national defence. The tensions of 1914 were, in part, the result of conflict between these interests. The Anglo-German naval race, for example was caused by British fears that the possible domination of the North Sea coastline by Germany would endanger home defence, and by Germany's belief that it was essential for her prestige that she should have naval parity. Similarly the rivalry between Britain and Russia in Persia, Tibet, and Afghanistan in the later nineteenth century was motivated on the British side by the need to secure her strategic links with the Indian Empire and on the Russian by an expansion due to a combination of strategic and economic factors. Issues of the same kind arose between Russia and Austria-Hungary in the Balkans. In addition, the Great Powers were concerned to prevent any one of their number becoming so strong as seriously to endanger the independence of the rest. They were, therefore, constantly engaged in manœuvres to maintain a certain balance of power, while at the same time trying to place themselves in a position to tilt the balance decisively in their own favour, or—and this was particularly the case between 1907 and 1914—in favour of the alliance to which they belonged.

## MORAL RESTRAINTS

The basic instability of the system was, to some extent, offset by the fact that governments accepted a common pattern of behaviour between states and at least some of the moral restraints imposed on men and states by the Natural Law; agreements were held to be binding, unless very good reasons existed for breaking them; good faith and honesty counted,

on the whole, for more than force and fraud; and if war could
not be avoided it was to be localized, carried on as decently and
dispassionately as possible and terminated at the earliest
opportunity. Moreover, no state felt any urge to undertake
ideological crusades against its neighbours from the time
Russian troops crossed the Carpathians to put down the
Hungarian Revolution in 1849 until the Red Army entered
Poland in 1920.

## BALANCE OF POWER A PERMANENT FACTOR

It is necessary to qualify the popular denunciations of the
Balance of Power system and of the pursuit of national interest
heard so frequently in 1919. These are permanent features of
international politics and, although their existence does not
mean that other consideration go altogether unheeded, it would
be unrealistic to suppose that Great Powers do not pursue these
ends as keenly as ever within the framework of the international
organizations, such as the League of Nations and the United
Nations. Enlightened self-interest, and at times some sense of
moral obligation to the community of nations, may exercise
some restraint, but when vital questions of national security
arise disagreement will always ensue. That has been true of
America and Russia since 1945 and this preoccupation has
affected their attitude to all major international problems, both
in Europe and Asia. It applied also between the wars. Britain
and France used the League of Nations to preserve the Balance
of Power in their favour against Germany in the nineteen-
twenties just as America and Russia sought in the nineteen-
forties to weaken each others' military potential and win
majority support for their respective policies in the General
Assembly of the United Nations.

## WEAKNESS OF THE PRE-WAR SYSTEM

In spite of these arguments, however, popular criticism of
the pre-war system still has much force. The peoples of Europe
have paid a very heavy price for the creation of national
states. In the forty years before 1914 the centralized national
state added considerably to its power: its citizens were
subjected to military service and national systems of education,
and heavy direct and indirect taxes were imposed on them to

pay for national defence. There was a constantly increasing burden of armaments: between 1870 and 1914 France and Britain doubled their army estimates, Russia trebled, and Germany quadrupled, hers, and with the elaboration of military techniques and the addition of more destructive weapons the military establishments of the powers played an increasingly important part in their policies. Proposals for disarmament at the Hague Conferences of 1899 and 1907 failed, for no power was prepared to endanger its security by implementing them. Particularly after 1907, when the rival alliance systems were in being, their mutual distrust was reflected in armament increases, which in turn aggravated existing suspicions. Much of the tension in Europe in the summer of 1914, for example, was due to the increase in armaments which followed the Balkan Wars. The vast military machines geared for action and staffed by officers who expected a conflict every spring, and whose influence during the final stages of the 1914 crisis was decisive, were factors of incalculable importance in heightening the atmosphere. The popular demand for some measure of disarmament after the war represented a sound reaction against this dangerous state of affairs.

## War an Instrument of Policy

Moreover, though it is true that no Great Power wanted to precipitate a general war during these years, war was nevertheless regarded as a legitimate instrument for furthering national interest and upholding prestige. The Russian war against Turkey in 1877, the British war against the Boers in 1899, and the American war against the Spanish in 1898; the Japanese attack on China in 1894 and on Russia in 1904, and that of Italy on Tripoli in 1911, not to mention the Balkan Wars of 1912 and 1913, are all examples of this use of war. The mere threat of force became increasingly important after 1904 as the need arose to maintain the prestige of the systems of alliance which were coming into being. The conduct of Germany and Austria-Hungary in 1905, 1909, 1911 and 1913 reveals them as skilful exponents of "prestige politics", but in the end their threatening diplomacy brought a major conflagration appreciably nearer.

## LACK OF A SUPREME AUTHORITY

This use, or threatened use, of force to promote national interest reveals a fundamental weakness in the pre-war international structure. Since the breakdown of medieval society in the sixteenth century this has been based on the theory that national states possess absolute sovereignty, have no obligations to the community of nations, and are subject only to such restraints as they may voluntarily accept. No final authority existed to which appeals might be made in a crisis, and though the Hague Court (established in 1907) performed valuable work in a limited field, it was inadequate as a preserver of the peace. When a conflict of national interests occurred, whether real or apparent, the threat of war was considered perfectly legitimate. Popular instinct was justified in welcoming the creation of the League of Nations in 1919, which would provide the permanent ordered framework for the community of nations that had always been the aim of the best Christian tradition. It is true that the Great Powers were as reluctant after 1919 as before to submit questions of power politics to peaceful settlement, but the chances of avoiding future conflict were much greater when the machinery of the League of Nations was available. It was the supreme tragedy of the nineteen-thirties that the League was not used effectively.

## THREE PERIODS OF DEVELOPMENT

In tracing the interaction and cumulative effect of the friction between the Powers in Europe and overseas, and the growth and consolidation of their rival alignments, it is convenient to regard the period between 1870 and 1914 as divided into three. First is the twenty-year period of German dominance after the defeat of France in 1870 which is associated with the name of Bismarck. France and Austria-Hungary were preoccupied with the problems arising out of defeat, and Britain was, on the whole, satisfied with the relief of her fear that France might dominate Belgium and at being enabled to concentrate once more on colonial expansion. Russia was at least as interested in extending her control over Central Asia as in the affairs of Western Europe and Italy, united in 1870, hardly counted as a Great Power by material standards.

## BISMARCK'S POLICY

The chief threats to the stability of the new order were a possible French attempt to reverse the decision of 1871, and the complications which might arise from the Near Eastern question. It is debatable whether Bismarck ever expected France to be reconciled to the loss of Alsace and Lorraine: he may have thought the resultant tension convenient in playing on German fears in order to retain control at home. But even without the annexation of Alsace-Lorraine, France's resentment at the loss of the dominant position she had enjoyed in Europe for two hundred years would have compelled her to seek a favourable opportunity for redressing the balance. Bismarck was concerned, therefore, to isolate France and deprive her of the allies without whom a war of revenge was impossible. In the Balkans Bismarck was not directly affected by the conflict of interests between Russia and Austria-Hungary, but he was troubled by the consequences for Germany if she were compelled to choose between the two. France would probably find in the rejected power an ally in a war of revenge, and it was therefore essential for Germany to prevent hostilities between Austria-Hungary and Russia which would spread into a general conflict involving her. The danger, as a German historian has pointed out, was that an electric current would be set up between the two centres of unrest, a current which some would regard as being set up in 1894 when the Franco-Russian Entente came into being.[1]

Germany, as Bismarck realized, was a satiated power needing a long period of peace in which to acquire internal stability. To maintain the peace and keep France isolated he relied on the friendship of both Russia and Austria-Hungary.

## THE "LINE TO ST. PETERSBURG"

Friendship with Russia had always been of cardinal importance in Bismarck's diplomacy. Russian neutrality had been extremely useful to Prussia when she attacked Austria in 1866 and France in 1870. To the end of his life Bismarck insisted on the necessity of keeping the line to St. Petersburg open because Germany, lying in the centre of Europe, could never afford to be on bad terms with both Russia and France: a war on two fronts would be disastrous for her—as two world wars have proved. In this, Bismarck has not lacked imitators, for in the Weimar Republic and in the post-war West German Federal Republic influential industrialists seeking markets in Eastern Europe and politicians seeking to raise German prestige—or, as in the nineteen-fifties, to reunite Germany—have realized the possibilities inherent in an understanding with Russia.

## Austria-Hungary

Despite the war of 1866 Bismarck was able to retain the friendship of Austria-Hungary. This was the result partly of Bismarck's moderate attitude in the hour of victory, and partly of Austria-Hungary's acceptance after 1870 of the decisive nature of her defeat in central Europe, which caused her to concentrate instead on the Balkans. Encountering Russian enmity there, she looked to Germany for assistance.

## The Three Emperors' League

The new alliance, the Three Emperors' League, was established after meetings between William I, Francis Joseph and Alexander II, in 1871–73. Throughout the eighteen-seventies it remained in being, providing for consultation between the three powers in the event of a threat of war in Europe, and upholding the principle of monarchical solidarity. It was intended to constitute a silent warning to Republican France that these monarchical powers would not tolerate any attempt by her to redress the Balance of Power, and also to obscure the differences arising between Austria-Hungary and Russia in the Balkans. But there were limits to the extent to which Bismarck succeeded in these basic aims of German policy, even during this period. There was a point beyond which Germany dare not go in her efforts to isolate France, as the events of 1875 revealed, and the Near Eastern Crisis of 1875–78 intensified the antagonism of Austria-Hungary and Russia, splitting the Three Emperors' League and necessitating a certain reorientation of German policy in 1879.

## The War Scare of 1875

France had made a rapid recovery after her defeat. By September 1873 the war indemnity, imposed on her by

Germany in 1871, had been paid off and the occupation troops had been withdrawn. In the same year the monarchist Marshal Macmahon had become French President and the new Foreign Minister, the Duc de Decazes, strove to draw attention to himself by suggesting to Britain, Russia, and Austria-Hungary that France was in danger of a German attack. Some justification was provided by Bismarck's tactics but on the whole the fears were exaggerated.

But it was not until 1875 that Decazes met with any marked success in his attempts. In March of that year certain French military measures became the subject of discussion in the German press. The German Government banned the export of horses and a series of articles, including the famous "Is War in sight?", appeared during April in the *Berlin Post*. Later in the month Decazes received a report from Gontaut Biron, French ambassador in Berlin, describing the after-dinner indiscretions of Radowitz, the German diplomat and friend of Bismarck, who had mentioned certain German circles as favouring a preventive war against France. Decazes immediately informed the Great Powers of the report, allowing it to be published in *The Times*, and found, to his immense satisfaction, that Britain and Russia were at last prepared to treat French fears seriously.

Britain had already begun to suspect Bismarck of designs on Belgium, largely as a result of a sharp German note to the Belgian Government protesting against criticism by the Belgian clergy of Bismarck's anti-Catholic measures in Germany; and Disraeli, now Prime Minister, while no friend of the Three Emperors' League, disliked Bismarck. Russia was more guarded in her attitude, as befitted a friend of Germany, but Gorchakov, Foreign Minister since 1856, wished to seize this opportunity to put Bismarck in his place. The result was that Britain and Russia co-operated at Berlin in May, 1875, to warn Germany of the dangers attendant on a breach of the peace.

This joint démarche brought the so-called "War Scare" of 1875 to an end, but it was in any case a false alarm. Bismarck, nervous and irritated as he was by his comparative failure to check growing French confidence, had no intention of going to war, and even if France had wished to do so she was militarily

unprepared. Nevertheless, it was a diplomatic defeat for
Germany: Decazes was elated with his success and Gorchakov was satisfied with Bismarck's humiliation. Britain and
Russia were not willing to help France redress the Balance of
Power in her own favour, but their united action had made
it plain, exaggerated though their fears of war might be, that
Great Powers were not prepared to see one of their number
completely annihilated. In 1875 the three powers were only
drawn temporarily together by fear of Germany, since they
had little else in common, but by 1907 they had other mutual
interests and the ensuing alignment became a permanent
international feature.

## BALKAN CONFLICTS

The conflict between Austria-Hungary and Russia in the
Balkans could not be charmed away by the mere creation of the
Three Emperors' League, as the events of the late eighteen-
seventies indicated, and Bismarck could only hope that the
cause of monarchical solidarity would prove more important.
The rising of the Christian population of Herzegovina in
July, 1875, which drew the attention of the Great Powers
once more to the Near Eastern Question, marked the end of
this hope, and within a very few years the relations between the
two interested powers had deteriorated so seriously that the
Three Emperors' League practically ceased to exist.

There had been risings before in Bosnia and Herzegovina,
the two provinces at the extremity of the Ottoman dominions
peopled by Serbian and Croatian peasants, but the rising of
1875 was more serious because both Serbia and Montenegro
were deeply involved in it. Serbian aspirations found a
sympathetic hearing in Panslav circles in Russia and at the
same time the military advisers of Francis Joseph were hopefully encouraging a rising which, as they believed, would
facilitate the early annexation of Bosnia-Herzegovina by
Austria-Hungary.

But the Austrian militarists eager for Balkan adventures
and Russian Panslavs rendering assistance to Serbs and
Bulgars did not exert decisive influence on the foreign policies
of their respective empires in 1875. Had they done so an
Austro-Russian war might well have occurred. In fact the

Foreign Ministers, Andrássy and Gorchakov, realized that there was more to be said for the preservation of the Ottoman Empire than for its dissolution.

## RUSSIAN INTERESTS

The Empire controlled the Straits of the Dardanelles and Bosphorus which were Russia's major interest in the Near East during the nineteenth century, for vital strategic and commerical reasons, as well as for considerations of prestige. In the middle of the nineteenth century Russia had not been allowed to send warships through into the Mediterranean in time of peace, but since other powers were debarred at the same time from sending warships into the Black Sea Russia had at least been secured against attack. This position was altered by the declaration of the London Conference in 1871 that the Sultan had the right to allow foreign warships to use the Straits in time of peace, and by Britain's insistence that the Sultan alone must decide whether foreign powers could use them in time of war. Turkey, traditionally hostile to Russia, would clearly allow Britain to use the Straits in order to attack her. At this time Britain was Russia's greatest enemy, for the interests of the two expanding empires conflicted in the Near East, in Persia, Tibet, Afghanistan, and in the Far East. In the Near East Britain feared the threat to her link with India, and Russia the severing of her vital economic artery of the Straits and an attack on her weakest point in the Ukraine, the agrarian heart of Russia.

This Anglo-Russian antagonism was of international importance until 1907, and caused successive British governments to defend the Ottoman Empire as a barrier against Russian expansion. It was because she feared that liberated Balkan peoples would quickly fall a prey to Russia that she opposed their national aspirations. Only at the beginning of the twentieth century when relations with Turkey became less friendly and when the Ottoman Empire had become less useful as a defensive barrier did Britain considerably modify her policy admitting in a famous phrase of Salisbury's, that she "had backed the wrong horse in the Eastern Question". Russia's interests lay in keeping the Straits closed to foreign warships while her own were privileged to pass at will and once she had obtained this favoured nation treatment, she had no desire—most of the time—to dissolve the Ottoman Empire to facilitate the seizure of Constantinople and of the Straits; she had rather a positive inducement to preserve it as a barrier against Bulgaria, which in 1912 was casting greedy eyes on Constantinople. To these strategic reasons were added the growing economic importance of her export of wheat and imports of machinery through the Straits as the century advanced, and the prestige consideration that all Great Powers had access to the Mediterranean.

## RUSSIA, AUSTRIA AND TURKEY

The Panslav ideology, referred to in the chapter on Russia, and later Russian nationalist propaganda did reinforce the defence of these national or imperial interests but these ideological elements, which were anti-Turkish as well as anti-Austrian exerted much less influence on official circles in St. Petersburg than is often realized. General Ignatiev, ambassador to Turkey and an influential and ardent Panslav was the exception and not the rule amongst diplomats. Only on occasions, as in 1877, did Russia abandon the pursuit of her national interest in favour of an ambitious Panslav policy, so that it is probably correct, on balance, to suppose that responsible Russian statesmen saw more benefit than harm in the continued existence of the Ottoman Empire. Austria-Hungary was equally interested in its preservation: pre-occupied with the threat to the stability of her own empire which arose from the national aspirations of the Slav peoples both inside and outside its borders, she could not fail to welcome Turkey's resistance to national movements in her dominions. Moreover, it was realized in Vienna that the collapse of the Ottoman Empire would provide Russia with an opportunity to strengthen her position in the Balkans. Austria-Hungary certainly desired to extend her influence in the Western Balkans to check Serbian aspirations and there were active military groups advocating expansion in Bosnia-Herzegovina at Turkey's expense, but influential Magyars, on the other hand, remained adamantly opposed to the inclusion of more Slavs in the Empire, and liberal and German elements were concentrating on economic expansion southwards which was facilitated by the unified political control of the area under Ottoman rule.

Andrássy and Gorchakov realized that the rising in Bosnia and Herzegovina threatened the peace which they desired to preserve in the Balkans, and they attempted in 1875 and 1876 to persuade the Sultan to carry out reforms in the affected provinces. Bismarck, anxious to maintain good relations between Austria-Hungary and Russia, gave eager approval, but the negotiations failed: the Bosnian insurgents wanted at least local autonomy, the Sultan had no intention of implementing any promises he made, and Britain was reluctant to agree to any joint action by the Great Powers because, in her obsession with suspicions of Russia, she feared it would only afford an opportunity for Turkey's destruction.

The situation deteriorated rapidly in 1876. In June the pressure of national feeling forced Serbia and Montenegro to declare war on Turkey, Serbia openly declaring her mission to be the liberation of the Southern Slavs and receiving aid in money and volunteers from Russian Panslavs.

## A New Turn in Russian Policy

Most serious of all was the change in Russian policy in the autumn when it became clear that the Serbs could not hold out alone against Turkey. Tsar Alexander II, conscious of the growing clamour of the small but active Panslav circles in Russia, decided to pursue a more forward Balkan policy designed to fulfil "our sacred mission", as he described it at Moscow in November. In this he was strengthened by a turn of events which had paralysed the British Government. In the summer of 1876 the Turks had suppressed a Bulgarian revolt with particular ferocity, and when news of this Bulgarian Massacre arrived in Britain there was a revulsion of feeling against the Turk. Russian public opinion was compelling the autocratic Tsar to pursue a more adventurous policy at a time when British public opinion was compelling the Government to abandon any hope of immediate action in support of Turkey— much to Disraeli's dismay.

As Russia had no Black Sea fleet her armies required free passage through Roumania in the event of war with Turkey,

and this in turn necessitated Austrian neutrality if Russia
was to avoid the humiliation of the Crimean War when an
Austrian ultimatum had forced her to withdraw from this area.
Since Andrássy wished to limit Russian expansion by agreement as much as possible, Russia was able to come to an
understanding with Austria-Hungary in 1877, but she paid a
heavy price for the guarantee of Austrian neutrality. She was to
regain Bessarabia, lost after her defeat in the Crimean War in
1856, but in return she had to recognize Austria-Hungary's
right to occupy Bosnia-Herzegovina, and had to promise that
no large Slav state would be created in the Balkans in the
likely event of Turkish defeat. Assured now of Austrian
neutrality, and convinced that Britain would be unable to
intervene, Russia declared war on Turkey in April, taking as
her pretext the refusal of the Sultan to carry out certain reforms
pressed on him by the Great Powers.

## BRITISH REACTIONS

As the Russian armies advanced slowly but surely towards
Constantinople opinion in Britain began to change: dislike
of the Turk was replaced by renewed fear of the Russian, much
to the satisfaction of the Queen and of Disraeli, now Earl of
Beaconsfield. When Russian troops occupied the town of
San Stefano, a few miles south of Constantinople, in January,
1878, Beaconsfield obtained the Cabinet's permission to send
the Fleet to the Straits. It passed through them, despite
Turkish fears of the Russian reaction, and anchored forty miles
south of Constantinople. For the next ten weeks the situation
was most tense, for in Britain a Russian occupation of
Constantinople was considered imminent, while in Russia
Britain was feared to be planning an attack. The fears of both
sides were exaggerated but war seemed inevitable.

## THE SAN STEFANO CRISIS

The tension increased when news of the peace of San
Stefano, concluded between Russia and Turkey in March,
reached London and Vienna. The treaty, negotiated by the
victorious Panslav General Ignatiev, secured her pre-Crimean
War frontiers for Russia and provided for territorial gains for
Serbia and Montenegro. There was no mention of Austria-

Hungary's right to occupy Bosnia-Herzegovina. The most sensational feature was undoubtedly the proposal to create a large autonomous Bulgaria, including most of Macedonia and extending southwards to the Aegean Sea, a proposal which contradicted Russia's promise to Austria-Hungary that a large Slav state would not be created. There was an immediate deterioration of relations between Russia and Austria-Hungary, for Andrássy realized that Russia had decided to pursue a Panslav policy at the expense of their agreement. Determined not to give way, he looked to his defences, and called for a meeting of the Great Powers to prevent unilateral Russian action in the Balkans. Beaconsfield was equally alarmed by the treaty, agreeing with Andrássy that the creation of an independent Bulgaria, to be occupied by Russian troops for two years, would give Russia enormous influence in the area. Supported by a rising tide of anti-Russian feeling, expressed in Jingoist songs, he adopted the vigorous measures he had always favoured; the reserves were called out and seven thousand Indian troops were brought to Malta.

## PEACE PRESERVED

But war did not break out. The Russian General Staff realized that Russia was militarily incapable of fighting Britain, who would probably be supported by Austria-Hungary, and that there was no hope of German support against the latter, since Bismarck had refused to choose between his two friends. He had declined to consider Andrássy's proposals for an Austro-German alliance, and when the Tsar had asked the German plenipotentiary whether Russia could count on German neutrality in an Austro-Russian conflict he had replied that it was not in German interests to see either empire seriously defeated.[2] By this time moderate elements had regained their former ascendancy in Russia, and Ignatiev's Panslavism was no longer in favour. His rival Schuvalov, who was ambassador to Britain, denounced the San Stefano treaty as an "act of stupidity"[3] and came to a secret understanding with Salisbury, the British Foreign Secretary, about the extent of the territorial changes which they would permit in the Near East. Russia agreed to abandon the Big Bulgaria, accepting British views about its future, whilst Britain agreed that Russia should regain Bessarabia and make some territorial gains from Asiatic Turkey.

## THE BERLIN CONFERENCE

This compromise agreement formed the basis of the settlement of the Near Eastern Question drawn up by the Great Powers meeting in Congress at Berlin in June, 1878, under the chairmanship of Bismarck, who was playing the rôle of "honest broker". It was agreed that an independent Bulgaria should be created north of the Balkan mountains, whilst "Eastern Roumelia", south of the mountains, received only administrative autonomy. The Macedonian parts of the San Stefano Bulgaria remained under Turkish rule. Russia regained Bessarabia, and obtained Batum and Kars in Asiatic Turkey. Andrássy's request for the right to occupy Bosnia-Herzegovina was granted and the British occupation of Cyprus was approved. The independence of Serbia, Montenegro, and Roumania was formally recognized, territorial compensation being given to the first two states and Roumania receiving the Dobruja in return for her cession of Bessarabia to Russia.

The Treaty of Berlin which gave expression to these territorial changes represented a severe diplomatic setback for Russia. The Panslav policy which had carried Alexander into war had been abandoned and, because Russia had been exhausted by the war, Britain and Austria-Hungary were able to gain most from the weakening of Turkey. Russia remained thoroughly dissatisfied with the treaty. The Tsar denounced Bismarck as the leader of an anti-Russian conspiracy, Gorchakov attacked his old rival and a bitter Press campaign was waged against the Germans in 1879.

## THE POWERS AND THE SETTLEMENT

Britain gained much at little cost. Russia had been checked, the Ottoman Empire had been preserved in a modified form and a new naval base had been acquired at Cyprus. The British Cabinet had decided to secure a strategic point in the Eastern Mediterranean nearer Constantinople than Malta in order to defend Turkey in the event of future Russian aggression. They chose Cyprus and in June, before the Berlin Congress met, a secret Anglo-Turkish Convention was signed by which if Russia gained Batum and Kars (as Britain had agreed she would) Britain was to occupy Cyprus to defend Turkey against aggression. When Russia was confirmed in her possession of Batum and Kars by the Congress, the Convention was revealed, approved by the Congress and accepted by a reluctant Sultan, peremptorily warned by Salisbury that Britain would occupy Cyprus with or without his permission. The British strategic position was further strengthened by Salisbury's declaration to the Congress concerning the Straits. He said that Britain considered that the Sultan had the right to call the British Fleet into the Black Sea at will and even if he refused under pressure, Britain reserved the right to force her way in. Not unnaturally, the declaration caused alarm to Russia, concerned to keep Britain out of the Black Sea. Thus the British gains were considerable and Beaconsfield spoke in London of "peace with honour", although Gladstone denounced the Cyprus Convention as "an act of duplicity not surpassed and rarely equalled in the history of nations".[4]

Austria-Hungary made considerable gains. Russia had been checked and Bosnia-Herzegovina had been occupied. Andrássy took advantage of British opposition to Russia to destroy the most objectionable features of the San Stefano treaty; in particular the proposal to divide the Sandjak of Novibazar between Serbia and Montenegro had been rejected and Austria-Hungary obtained the right to garrison this vital strategic area, control of which guaranteed economic penetration of the Western Balkans and prevented a union between Serbia and Montenegro at a later date. Andrássy did not desire to acquire Bosnia-Herzegovina but had regretfully given way to the pressure of the Emperor and his military advisers. However, Andrássy had ensured that the provinces were occupied and not annexed in order to conciliate Magyar opinion opposed to the inclusion of more Slavs in the Empire.

Such was the settlement of the Near Eastern Question in 1878 of which the Italian representative said that, "everybody was telling everybody else to take something which belonged to somebody else".[5] The Great Powers had dominated the Congress, considering the interests of the Balkan states solely in the light of their effect on their own rivalries. The settlement has been criticized for its failure to re-create the Balkans along national lines, but it must be remembered that the strength of the Ottoman Empire, as displayed in the war, would in any case have prevented the application of principles of self-determination. The Powers certainly underestimated the strength of Balkan nationalism and paid scant regard to Turkish feelings. Yet major warfare was averted in the Balkans for thirty years. It would have taxed the ingenuity of any diplomatic gathering at the best of times to have satisfied the conflicting ambitions of the Balkan peoples.

## BISMARCK'S ALLIANCE SYSTEM

The main interest of the twelve years between the Congress of Berlin in 1878 and the dismissal of Bismarck in 1890 lies in the alliance system with which his name is associated. In the eighteen-seventies Bismarck had been an important figure in Europe; after 1878 he dominated the scene, constructing his system from four main alignments: the Austro-German Alliance of 1879, the Three Emperors' Alliance of 1881, the Triple Alliance of 1882, and the Reinsurance Treaty of 1887. The 1879 and 1882 agreements are particularly important for they constitute the first of the rival alliances characteristic of the period between 1907 and 1914. In these twelve years Bismarck was still preoccupied, as before, with the problems arising from Franco-German tension and Austro-Russian rivalry in the Balkans.

## THE AUSTRO-GERMAN ALLIANCE

The Austro-German alliance was negotiated by Bismarck in 1879 to meet the situation created by the intensified hostility between Austria-Hungary and Russia which had destroyed the Three Emperors' League. As a conservative, he wanted to re-establish the understanding between the three Empires which he considered the obvious and most sure guarantee of the stability of the order established in 1871.

But the task was difficult, for Austria-Hungary had found that Britain and France were willing to co-operate with her in opposing Russia. Bismarck recognized, therefore, that an understanding with Austria-Hungary must precede one with Russia, for if he came to terms with Russia first Germany might find herself faced with an alliance between Austria-

Hungary, Britain, and France—all of whom opposed Russia to a greater or lesser extent. But more than pious phrases about monarchical solidarity were needed to secure an alliance, and some attempt had to be made to assuage Austro-Hungarian fears of Russia.

Probably Bismarck did not believe in the danger of a Russian attack, and at that time it was unlikely, but he found it a useful argument in overcoming the natural and serious opposition of Emperor William I to these negotiations. The old ruler, a rigid conservative for whom good relations with autocratic Russia were axiomatic, feared the alliance would send Russia into the arms of France. He only abandoned his opposition when Bismarck threatened resignation: "Bismarck is more necessary to Germany than I am", he remarked.[6] Thus in October, 1879, Andrássy and Bismarck signed the Austro-German Alliance, the first to be concluded formally for the preservation of peace in the nineteenth century. This secret pact, which remained in force until 1918, was the cornerstone of German foreign policy throughout the period. It simply provided that if either partner were to be involved in war with another power, France or Italy for example, the other would remain neutral. Andrássy had shown no desire to be dragged into a Franco-German conflict which did not concern Austria-Hungary, and Bismarck made no real effort to secure Austrian assistance against France, believing Germany capable of dealing with this problem on her own.

## THE DECISIVE CHOICE OF 1879

Russia might dislike the new alliance, but there seemed little fear of her finding allies elsewhere in Britain and France. Nevertheless, the old German Emperor had been right; the Alliance led eventually to a Franco-Russian understanding in 1891, and to a war on two fronts which ended in German defeat. It has been said in Bismarck's defence that the tension between France and Germany and between Austria-Hungary and Russia made a Franco-Russian alliance a possibility at all times, and that he did at least succeed in restraining Austria in the Balkans and in minimizing the Austro-Russian conflict by this pact of 1879. There is, also, much truth in the contention of some German historians that German foreign policy

ended in disaster after Bismarck's dismissal in 1890 because
his successors, lacking the touch of the master, could no longer
restrain Austria-Hungary.[7] Yet Bismarck, as the originator of
the alliance cannot escape some share of responsibility for the
ultimate failure of German policy, because Austria-Hungary
was a liability to Germany whose interests did not conflict with
those of Russia at that time. Salisbury showed shrewd insight
when he welcomed the arrangement, for it implied that
Germany would now give Austria-Hungary the same support
against Russia which Britain had given her in the past. In
effect Bismarck made his choice between Austria-Hungary and
Russia in 1879, and the next thirty years led logically to the
summer of 1914 and German support for aggressive Austrian
action against Serbia.

## THE THREE EMPERORS' ALLIANCE, 1881

Bismarck did not look so far ahead, and the alliance
certainly served its immediate purpose, probably its only
purpose, for in the spring of 1880 negotiations for an alliance
between Germany and Russia were under way. These negotiations prepared the ground for the second major alignment of
these years, the Three Emperors' Alliance which came into
being in 1881 when Austria-Hungary decided to come to terms
with Russia.

Bismarck's approach to Russia was simple. The Austrian
alliance he explained away to Saburov, the new Russian
ambassador in Berlin, as a defensive measure against a friend
who had suddenly gone mad. Reassured, Germany was now
prepared to continue her walk with that friend "in the same
amicable fashion but in a more comfortable state of mind".
Perhaps he was nearer the truth when he remarked that he
had worked to "dig a ditch between [Austria] and the
Western Powers".[8]

In any case, Saburov wanted an understanding with
Germany: uninterested in Panslav ideas, he intended to place
Russian national interest at the Straits first. After Salisbury's
declaration at the Berlin Congress of the new British attitude to
the Straits Question, he felt obliged to seek allies to defend
Russia against British attack in the area, especially as she had no
Black Sea Fleet, and in the event of war German neutrality

would be valuable, as would an understanding with Austria-Hungary and Turkey about the Straits.

Difficulties arose in Vienna for Haymerle, the new Austro-Hungarian Foreign Minister, bitterly anti-Russian, was suspicious of the negotiations between Russia and Germany, and looked to Britain for assistance against Russia. His position was undermined by the defeat of the Conservatives at the British elections in 1880 since Gladstone, the Liberal Prime Minister, was hostile to Austria-Hungary and disinclined to pursue a forward policy against Russia. Disillusioned, Haymerle was ready for the negotiations with Germany and Russia which led to the Three Emperors' Alliance of 1881. The three powers promised to remain neutral if one of them was involved in war with a fourth, and that they would work for a mutual understanding in the Near East and to ensure that the Straits remained closed to foreign warships. They agreed also not to object to the union of East Roumelia and Bulgaria, and to recognize the right of Austria-Hungary to annex Bosnia-Herzegovina at will.

This alliance represented the maximum Bismarck could do to veil the hostility between Austria-Hungary and Russia. By recognizing Bulgaria to be in the Russian sphere of influence and Bosnia-Herzegovina in the Austrian, he hoped to avoid friction. For Russia the gains were considerable: she was assured that Germany and Austria-Hungary would not assist Britain against her, and that they would help her to keep the British out of the Black Sea. Austria-Hungary was less fortunate. It is true that the edge of the Austro-Russian antagonism was dulled, and that she was able to consolidate her position in the Western Balkans, but she had long recognized Russian predominance in the remaining half, was restrained in her anti-Russian policies by Germany, and had been manœuvred into hostility towards her old friend Britain. For Bismarck it was the conservative alliance of his dreams. But the difficulty was that although he could satisfy Austrian and Russian claims separately he could never square the circle. In the eighteen-eighties increased tension between Austria-Hungary and Russia destroyed the Three Emperors' Alliance as it had destroyed the Three Emperors' League in the eighteen-seventies.

## THE TRIPLE ALLIANCE, 1882

The third major alignment for which Bismarck was responsible was the Triple Alliance of 1882, between Germany, Austria-Hungary, and Italy. This alliance, which remained in being until 1915 when Italy entered the World War on the side of the Allied Powers, represents the first of the rival alignments whose antagonism characterizes the period between 1907 and 1914.

Competition in the colonial field partly underlay the Italian decision to seek an understanding with Germany and Austria-Hungary. In the last quarter of the nineteenth century all the Great Powers began to show an interest in the acquisition of extra-European territory which they placed under their direct political control. The stabilization of the political order in Europe enabled them to turn their attentions to Africa, particularly to the North African coastline, and project their European rivalries on to a larger screen.

Italy and France had been competitors in Tunis since the principality was opened up by the economic penetration of the Powers in the 'sixties, but in 1881 France had occupied it, largely to forestall Italian action. Italian public opinion was roused by the indifference of the Powers to Italian protests and it demanded a more active foreign policy from the Government. The latter was also afraid that Pope Leo XIII, still unreconciled to the loss of the Temporal Power in 1870, might leave Italy as a result of recent anti-clerical demonstrations and might find certain Powers interested in intervening in Italy on his behalf. Austria-Hungary was approached in an attempt to guard against this but, as Italy had nothing to offer in return, the negotiations were unsuccessful. Only when Bismarck, alarmed by signs of a Franco-Russian rapprochement in 1882, decided that an understanding with Italy might be useful (if only to give Austria-Hungary additional protection in the event of a war with Russia) were these reopened. General Skobelev, a leading Panslav, had made a fiery speech in Paris which suggested that Panslav circles surrounding the new Tsar, Alexander III, might influence him in favour of a French alliance. Bismarck now encouraged Austria-Hungary to come to terms with Italy, and when Germany adhered to this agreement the Triple Alliance was created.

The partners were to aid each other if attacked by France and Russia. Should Austria-Hungary and Russia be at war, Italy and Germany would remain neutral. In the event of a Franco-German conflict only Italy would come to Germany's aid, but if Italy were attacked by France both Austria-Hungary and Germany would assist her. In a protocol to the treaty Italy expressed the hope that the alliance would not affect her traditional friendship with Britain.

In practice the alliance did not amount to much. Italian neutrality during a war between Austria-Hungary and Russia merely meant that Austrian troops need not be tied down on the Italian border. Germany, too, gained little, for although Bismarck succeeded in restraining Italy in North Africa (just as he had restrained Austria-Hungary in the Balkans) he had allied his country with a restless power whose basic hostility to her old Austrian enemy had merely been obscured by desire for an African Empire. Italy did gain the status of a Great Power, even if her Allies treated her as a poor relation, and was also assured against foreign interference on behalf of the Pope, but by 1900 her improved relations with France had destroyed the *raison d'être* of the alliance and she was beginning to break away.

## THE REINSURANCE TREATY, 1887

The fourth important alliance, the Reinsurance Treaty of 1887, was in effect a confession of failure by Bismarck who, for all his skill, was never able to resolve the tension between France and Germany or between Austria-Hungary and Russia. After the British occupation of Egypt he had shown interest in co-operation with France in the colonial field: "I want you to forgive Sedan as after 1815 you forgave Waterloo", he remarked to the French ambassador Courcel. He may have been sincere in his desire for reconciliation and willingness to help France, provided that she accepted the loss of Alsace-Lorraine, but effective joint action continued only for two years. It ended in 1885 with the fall of the Jules Ferry ministry because France was not prepared to forget the past and become completely dependent on Germany for assistance against her British colonial rival.

Developments in the late 'eighties also showed clearly his

inability to compose the differences of Austria-Hungary and Russia in the Balkans. Both powers had extended their influence there since the Berlin Congress. Serbia, ruled by the pro-Austrian Prince Milan, allied herself with Austria-Hungary in 1881, and Roumania allied herself with Austria-Hungary and Germany in 1883. For her part Russia had been less successful. Opposition was growing in Bulgaria to the autocratic police methods of Russian officials and officers, and she disapproved of the bloodless revolution of 1885 which had united Bulgaria and Eastern Roumelia under Prince Alexander of Battenberg.

In 1886 a more serious crisis occurred when Alexander of Battenberg was kidnapped by Russian officers and agreed to abdicate at the command of his uncle, the Russian Tsar, who had opposed the union of the two Bulgarias in 1885. His subjects, however, were not prepared to accept such dictation, and by November had severed relations with Russia. There seemed every possibility of Russian intervention in Bulgaria and consequent war between Russia and Austria-Hungary for the latter power had now lost interest in schemes to divide the Balkans into spheres of influence and had begun to dream of a railway network to extend her commercial influence into the Eastern as well as the Western half.

These circumstances rendered a renewal of the Three Emperors' Alliance impossible in 1887, but in view of the deterioration of relations between France and Germany Bismarck was particularly anxious to maintain the link with St. Petersburg. The growing strength of French nationalism, symbolized by General Boulanger, and the nationalist pressure in Russia, suggested that there was at least a possibility of a Franco-Russian alliance. In the event of a Balkan war this might mean that Germany would be faced with the two-front struggle which was Bismarck's constant dread. Fortunately for him, the conservative diplomats in Russia desired an understanding as much as he did, and negotiations began in the summer of 1887.

The Reinsurance Treaty which resulted, regarded by some as the cornerstone of the alliance system, was modest in scope. Hampered by the implications of the Austrian alliance, Bismarck could not give Russia a free hand against Austria-

Hungary, and was inevitably refused a free hand against France. The treaty provided only for Russian neutrality if France were the aggressor against Germany, and for German neutrality if Austria-Hungary were the aggressor against Russia. If Russia attacked Austria-Hungary Germany could not be neutral, and if Germany attacked France then Russia refused to promise neutrality. A Franco-Russian agreement was not excluded by these terms, and the alliance of 1894 was compatible with them. In both cases Russia promised to aid France only if Germany were the aggressor.

The treaty was useful to Russia in that Germany was pledged once more to resist the opening of the Straits to foreign warships, and had acknowledged Bulgaria to be in the Russian sphere of influence. No doubt it was also of some immediate use to Bismarck in securing the German position in 1887, and the promise to aid Russia at the Straits was neutralized by the Second Mediterranean Agreement between Britain, Italy, and Austria-Hungary which pledged these powers to resist Russian ambitions at the Straits and in Bulgaria. It was inescapable, however, that Germany could not remain neutral in the event of a Balkan conflict, whatever the cause, if the prestige of Austria-Hungary as a Great Power were at stake.

## THE "MASTER TOUCH" FAILING

The alliance system was making heavy weather after 1888 despite Bismarck's complicated diplomatic manœuvres. Economic and financial ties were already drawing France and Russia together, and the accession of William II worsened Russo-German relations further. Unlike the old emperor, William II was a flamboyant young monarch not prepared to do Bismarck's bidding. He shared the anti-Russian sentiments of his military friends, favoured close links with Austria-Hungary and Britain, and placed far less reliance on the Russian connexion than his Chancellor. His declaration to the Austrian chief of staff, in the presence of Francis Joseph, that Germany would support Austria-Hungary against Russia, whatever the cause of conflict, was the negation of Bismarck's plan for a dual friendship. Faced with this and with a hostile majority in the Reichstag, Bismarck reluctantly tendered his resignation: the Pilot was dropped and an era was ended.

It would be an exaggeration to suppose that Bismarck's alliance system alone maintained peace in Europe for twenty years. The fact that no Great Power wished to be engaged in major warfare, seeking an outlet rather in colonial expansion, was equally important. More serious than the criticism that Bismarck failed finally to balance the conflicting interests of the Great Powers satisfactorily, is the charge that for him there was nothing outside Germany. As representative of the dominant Power, he gave international relations between 1870 and 1890 a most unfortunate character, since he sought security exclusively in increased armaments and secretiveness in diplomacy, lacking completely that wider vision of a community of nations bound by the moral law beyond the narrow conceptions of national self-interest. When others, lacking his sense of restraint, controlled Germany's destiny his methods proved a disastrous heritage.

## France and Russia

The fourteen years between his resignation and the Anglo-French Entente of 1904 constitute a formative period of the utmost importance. The first significant development of this period was the Franco-Russian alliance of 1894. Bismarck later maintained that it was the result of his successor's failure to renew the Reinsurance Treaty on its expiration in 1890, but that was the over-simplification of a frustrated and unsuccessful old man. It is true that the new Chancellor, General von Caprivi, influenced by Baron Holstein, the anti-Russian head of the political section of the Foreign Office, refused to renew the treaty on the ground of its incompatibility with the 1879 alliance. He felt that Bismarck's complex diplomacy was liable to misfire in his inexperienced hands, and feared that, if Russia chose to reveal the secret treaty, Britain and Austria-Hungary might be alienated. But in any case France and Russia had been moving closer since 1887, when Germany made it clear that Russia could not have a free hand in the Balkans. The first of many French loans to Russia was made in 1888, and was followed by Russian orders for French armaments in 1889, and when the conservative Foreign Minister, Giers, failed to maintain the traditional understanding with Germany in 1890 nationalist circles in Russia rejoiced.

Russia had valued the understanding with Germany because it had given her some protection against Britain at the Straits and had precluded any alliance between Britain and Austria-Hungary as long as the latter was restrained by Germany. Russian concern deepened as there were signs of a rapprochement between Britain and Germany. Relations between the two Powers were more cordial than at any time in the previous twenty years. William II visiting his grandmother, Queen Victoria, in 1890 spoke in public of the British Fleet forcing its way through the Dardanelles, and his visit to the Sultan gave added cause for alarm to Russia by displaying a new German interest in the Near East. These fears were increased in 1891 at the time of the renewal of the Triple Alliance, for it appeared as if Britain had joined the alliance. Actually Italian boasts of British adherence were intended to secure more British support for Italian adventures in North Africa and were repudiated by Salisbury. Nevertheless, the apparent formation of a formidable hostile coalition to check France in North Africa and Russia at the Straits drove the two powers into each others' arms.

## LIMITED AGREEMENT, 1891

Even so, the Franco-Russian Entente of August, 1891, was a very limited understanding, because their interests were by no means compatible. They could agree only to joint consultations if the peace were disturbed or if one were threatened by an aggressor. Russia's greatest enemy was Britain and, having as yet no quarrel with Germany herself, she had no interest in going to war to recover Alsace-Lorraine for France. France, on the other hand, was certainly an opponent of Britain, but not in the same geographical areas as Russia. North Africa was outside Russian interests, and France not only had no direct interest in the Balkans but traditionally supported Britain and Austria-Hungary against Russia at the Straits. Thus, France sought to give the Entente an anti-German bias and Russia sought to give it an anti-British bias: France thought in terms of joint mobilization if a Triple Alliance power mobilized, and Russia wanted a general agreement so that France would give her cover in Europe whilst she fought Britain in Central Asia. The 1891 Entente was a

2C

victory for the Russian viewpoint, for Russia had promised no military aid against Germany, but she had involved France diplomatically in the Balkans.

However, France was not satisfied until Russia agreed to a military convention in 1892 which provided that if France were attacked by Germany, or by Germany and Italy, Russia would come to her defence, and if Russia were attacked by Germany, or by Germany and Austria-Hungary, France would do the same. Under another provision France and Russia were to mobilize if any member of the Triple Alliance did so. At last Russia was committed to offensive action against Germany, and following the exchange of diplomatic notes between the French and Russian Governments in December, 1893, and January, 1894, the convention came into effect and the Franco-Russian alliance was established.

It was a major event, although both parties continued to place their own interpretation on the agreement. France was reluctant to push opposition to Britain too far and never proved accommodating to her ally in the Balkans, and Russia did little to prepare for action against Germany if need arose, but at least the days of Bismarck's alliance system were shown to be over. Later, when Britain and Russia were reconciled in 1907 and when Russo-German enmity had developed, this alliance provided the basis of the most powerful alignment in Europe. In the meantime, France gained a certain moral authority and prestige with the end of her isolation, but it is arguable that she gained little besides, for she ultimately became deeply involved in the Balkans and lost most of the vast sums of money she lent to Russia. This money was indispensable for Russian industrialization, and the eastern partner also gained the certainty that France and Germany would neutralize each other while she concentrated on Asia.

## GERMAN MISCALCULATIONS

The changes in German foreign policy in the 'nineties, another important development of the period, were of decisive significance for Europe. Superficially, Germany was in a strong diplomatic position between 1890 and 1904: Austria-Hungary and Italy were her allies, relations with Russia were much improved after 1894, those with France were tolerable—at times even cordial—and Britain was seeking her friendship at the turn of the century. Her error lay in assuming that the bad relations between Britain and France, and between Britain and Russia, on which her arbitral position in Europe depended, were necessarily permanent, and that she could continue to pursue the policy of the "Free Hand", remaining on good terms with all Powers and profiting by their dissensions.

The triple understanding between Britain, France, and Russia in 1907 ended this situation at once, but the event had actually been long in preparation. From the time of the Austro-German alliance, friendship with Russia was in continual jeopardy: there might be an improvement when Nicholas II ascended the throne in 1894, as he did not share the Panslav sympathies of his father, but personal friendship between him and William II could not counterbalance the Franco-Russian alliance. Similarly, German relations with France might improve, but full reconciliation was impossible even at the time of the Fashoda incident; Italy had ceased to be a reliable ally by 1900, and a German understanding with Britain was never really feasible. In practice, only Austria-Hungary could be relied upon at all times, though this was not apparent until 1907.

## GERMAN *Weltpolitik*

In addition Germany committed grave mistakes in these years during which she abandoned the Bismarck tradition of restricting German interest to Europe in favour of *Weltpolitik*. The young generation, conscious only of the material strength of the new Empire, sought tangible signs of German greatness overseas; but this interest in colonial possessions and the creation of a navy at the beginning of the twentieth century alienated Britain. In the same way, Germany's forward policy in the Near East alienated Russia, and brought into being in 1907 the triple alignment against her which she most had reason to fear.

Her colonial policy was aimless and vague rather than sinister, for her scattered colonial possessions in the Pacific and in Africa did not provide a suitable nucelus for an empire. She did not wish to be ignored in the partition of Africa and Asia, and wanted to use her arbitral position in Europe to extort colonial compensation from Britain, or at least impress the need for Anglo-German understanding. The dangers of such a policy are illustrated by the incident of the Kruger telegram at the time of the Jameson Raid: the ostentatious telegram of congratulation to the Boer President aroused intense popular feeling in Britain, where it was regarded as unjustifiable meddling by a hitherto friendly monarch in matters of vital concern to the Empire.

Simultaneously, the growth of German economic interest in Asia Minor began to alarm Russia. Bismarck had maintained that the Near East was not worth the bones of a Pomeranian grenadier, but the German attitude changed in the 'nineties when markets were being sought for her expanding industries, and the Pan-German League was enthusiastically supporting the Berlin to Baghdad railway project. In 1898 William II made the Damascus speech, in which he assured the Sultan and the three hundred million Moslems that they had a friend in Germany, and though Chancellor von Bülow assured Russia that German interest in the Near East was non-political, it was not surprising that Russia refused to regard with complacency the stabilization of the Ottoman Empire. She did not want to destroy it, but she had no desire to see Germany acting as its protector and threatening her own interests in the Straits. For the first time the interests of the two powers were in direct conflict.

## The End of "Splendid Isolation"

Another significant feature of the period was Britain's attempt to end her own isolation. During the nineteenth century her naval supremacy had guaranteed her commercial interests abroad and made it unnecessary for her to seek allies except on those rare occasions, such as the Napoleonic Wars, when she had been compelled to intervene in Europe. But in the 'eighties and 'nineties doubts were being cast on the validity of a policy of "Splendid Isolation", now that colonial expansion in Africa and the Far East had led to disputes with France, Germany, and Russia, making it clear that she no longer enjoyed a monopoly in this field. Franco-German co-operation in 1883 and 1884 had enabled those powers to lay the foundations of African empires without asking British consent, and there was a fear that her rivals might settle their differences and combine to form a Continental League. Having isolated her, they would be able to bring pressure to bear in South Africa and Egypt, compelling her to pay even greater attention to their colonial policies.

In 1898 Britain was on the verge of war with the Boer Republics, and she faced a serious situation in North East Africa, for the question of the control of the upper reaches of the Nile had caused Franco-British relations to deteriorate since 1894. Britain considered this control to be essential in order to preserve a link between Egypt and British East Africa, but France was trying to extend her political control eastwards across the Sahara towards the same area. As Kitchener advanced into the Sudan and Captain Marchand, leader of the French expedition, advanced eastwards a clash seemed imminent in 1898. Britain was also alarmed by Russian advances in the Far East, particularly the leasing of Port Arthur in 1898. The combined effect of these events suggested that the time had come for a modification of policy. Salisbury was reluctant to accept the necessity because, fascinated by the glorious traditions of the Royal Navy, he felt that major crises could still be survived without outside aid. The initiative was left to the Colonial Secretary, Joseph Chamberlain, who argued that since Britain could never build up an army to supplement her navy she must seek continental allies immediately.

It was the Russian advances in the Far East which alarmed him most. At the turn of the century the Chinese Empire seemed on the verge of collapse, a fact which encouraged the Great Powers to obtain economic privileges from the Chinese and establish spheres of influence in the country. Germany first signified her interest in *Weltpolitik* by seizing Kiaochow, for which she obtained a lease in November, 1897. Russia followed this up by leasing Port Arthur in 1898, thus securing a warm water port on the Yellow Sea, and a vantage point of immense strategic importance for later extension of her control. British commercial interests, in charge of eighty per cent of China's trade, resented the Russian action, and to placate them Salisbury reluctantly acquired the lease of Wei-hai-wei a few days later. Chamberlain sought American and Japanese assistance against the Russian advances in vain, and in March,

1898 approached Germany with a proposal for the partition of the Chinese Empire into spheres of influence and a defensive alliance against further Russian expansion.

## BRITAIN AND GERMANY

Britain made three approaches to Germany: in 1898, in 1899 when William II visited the country during the Boer War, and finally in 1901; but each time the German attitude was the same. Germany realized that Britain was interested in Europe only because she wanted a cheap form of insurance against the effects of her colonial rivalry with Russia. In the event of hostilities, Germany would have to bear the brunt of land warfare against Russia and France (for since 1894 German strategy had been based on the assumption of a two-front war in which Germany would attempt to deal a "knockout" blow at France before proceeding to deal with Russia at her leisure), but Britain would always confine her action to naval warfare in defence of her colonial possessions. Geography could not be altered and it mattered in a pre-atomic age. German security in Europe necessitated good relations with Russia, and the fact that Russia was preoccupied with the Far East and had arranged a truce with Austria-Hungary in the Balkans in 1897 encouraged Germany to believe that this state of affairs would continue. There was no real basis for an Anglo-German alliance, because it was not in German interests to assist Britain against Russia. Only in 1955, when Britain had an equal interest in the defence of Europe was an alliance possible when the German Federal Republic entered N.A.T.O.

Yet, although Germany did not want an alliance, she wanted to appear to do so, believing that if she only waited long enough an Anglo-Russian conflict was inevitable and, in some unspecified way, she would secure better terms from Britain. In any case a forward German colonial policy would be more difficult if relations with Britain were bad. The naval programme just being launched by Admiral von Tirpitz was also an important consideration for it was believed that, if not handled with care, Britain might attack the new fleet before it could challenge her naval supremacy. Germany, therefore, continued her policy of the Free Hand, ignoring Chamberlain's warning that if she rejected British advances an understanding might be reached with France and Russia.

## THE WEAKNESSES OF GERMAN POLICY

The fundamental weakness of the German attempt to remain on good terms with both Russia and Britain was revealed by events in China in 1901. In the last resort Germany was reluctant to offend Russia for the sake of Britain, for the German need for Russian friendship to guarantee her security in Europe was greater than her need for British friendship to facilitate her colonial expansion. The Great Powers had co-operated in 1900 to put down the anti-European Boxer Rebellion which had threatened their economic and political interests in China. Using this as a pretext Russia had occupied Manchuria, arousing British suspicions as to her intentions. To safeguard her interests in Central China Britain had signed the Yangtse Agreement with Germany, which guaranteed commercial equality for all and maintained the integrity of the Chinese Empire. Then in 1901 it became known that Russia was insisting on political control of Manchuria as a *sine qua non* for the withdrawal of her occupation forces. Japan was alarmed by this development, a threat to her own designs there, and was prepared to resist it, provided that France would not aid Russia. Britain, eager to encourage Japan, asked Germany to ensure that France did remain neutral, but Germany was not prepared to risk war in Europe for British interests in China and declared that the Yangtse Agreement had not been intended to cover the case of Manchuria (as Britain knew) and, furthermore, that Russian advances in that area did not concern Germany.

## THE ANGLO-JAPANESE ALLIANCE

The lesson was not lost on Britain. She looked elsewhere for an ally and found one in Japan who, unlike Germany, had a positive interest in resisting Russian expansion in the Far East. Following the occupation of Manchuria, Korea too, an area of vital strategic importance to Japan, might soon come under Russian influence, and Japan approached both Russia and Britain in an attempt to safeguard her interests. Little progress was made in St. Petersburg, but in London there was a receptive audience.

Britain was prepared to recognize Japan's special interests in Korea, and Japan to resist further Russian advances in that area, and so the Anglo-Japanese Alliance of 1902, the fourth important development in these years, came into being. For Britain the price was not heavy, since she was obliged to support Japan only if France intervened. That was unlikely, for the France who had not dared to resist Britain in the Sudan in 1898 would hardly do so in Korea.

At last Britain was emerging from Splendid Isolation. France and Russia naturally disliked the increased chance of a Russo-Japanese conflict, but Germany welcomed it as strengthening her own arbitral position in Europe. This was a complete miscalculation, for within five years the international scene was transformed: the estrangement between Britain and France ended in 1904, and when Britain and France came to an understanding in 1907 the last assumption underlying German foreign policy was destroyed.

## THE ENTENTE, 1904

The Anglo-French Entente of 1904, another major development of the period, also ended British isolation in Europe. The initiative was taken by France, partly in a desire to avoid being involved in a Far Eastern war and partly because an understanding with Britain was necessitated by her growing interest in Morocco.

At the beginning of the twentieth century several Great Powers were turning their attention to the future of this nominally Turkish principality. Continual internal unrest, a weak Sultan, and the appearance of pretenders to the throne provided ideal conditions for foreign interference, and the country's position in the north-western corner of Africa with both a Mediterranean and Atlantic littoral raised vital strategic issues for Britain and France. By her conquest of Algeria and her advances across the Sahara, France had become Morocco's neighbour, and the constant threat of raids across the frontier by the unruly tribes over whom the Sultan exercised scant authority increased the possibility that she would occupy the territory, ostensibly to restore order, but primarily to consolidate the French North African Empire. For Britain the domination of the coastline by a hostile power would menace

Gibraltar, key to the Mediterranean and the Suez link with India, and in addition it was her agents who had the largest share of Moroccan trade, competing with the French for influence at the Sultan's court. A third and smaller power, Spain, also had important Moroccan interests, including a number of coastal settlements dating from the sixteenth century and, although quite unable to obtain control of the hinterland, she concerned herself increasingly with these last vestiges of a colonial empire after the loss of the Philippines in 1898.

## THE POLICY OF DELCASSÉ

Delcassé, French Foreign Minister from 1898 to 1905, was determined to advance his country's influence in Morocco, and to prepare the way for eventual occupation by making the Sultan a dependant of France. Realizing the need for prior agreement with the other interested powers, he approached Italy, Spain and Britain between 1898 and 1904.

He had considerable success in his negotiations with Italy, with whom France had been on extremely bad terms since the occupation of Tunis, for there was a growing Italian conviction that the Triple Alliance was much less useful to them than it had been twenty years before. In 1898 the tariff war between the two ended, and in December, 1900, Delcassé reached a secret agreement with Prinetti, the Italian Foreign Minister, under which France declared her disinterestedness in Tripoli and Italy in Morocco, and it was arranged that Italy should take action in Tripoli as soon as France moved in Morocco.

Delcassé followed up his triumph in 1902 when, in effect, he detached Italy from the Triple Alliance. Italy renewed her alliance with Austria-Hungary and Germany in 1902, but in an exchange of letters a few days later Prinetti assured the French ambassador that Italy was not committed by it to take part in a war against France. Neutrality was promised if France were attacked and by exploiting to the full the ambiguous phrase "without due provocation"—the condition which had to be fulfilled before Italy aided her allies against France—Italy established a footing in both camps. Delcassé's declaration later in 1902 that Italy would never join in an attack on France, followed in 1903 by King Victor Emmanuel's visit to Paris and by the French President's visit to Rome in

2C*

1904, made it evident that a decisive change had taken place. The significance of the Franco-Italian rapprochement was minimized by von Bülow, who remarked that, "In a happy marriage the husband must not be jealous if his wife for once has an innocent dance with another man. The main thing is that she should not elope, which she will not do if she is best off where she is."[9] It was an unduly optimistic view, for the flirtation with France was not an "extra dance" but a last waltz. The façade of the Triple Alliance was maintained but Italy could be considered only an unreliable ally after 1902.

Having secured Italian friendship, and a German assurance that she had no interests to defend in Morocco, Delcassé turned to Spain with a proposal for partition. Spain was attracted by the offer, but she knew that Britain was opposed to any alteration in the *status quo* and that Britain's naval supremacy would enable her to enforce her views. She refused, therefore, to agree to the proposals unless Britain were a party to the agreement.

Delcassé's negotiations with Britain in 1903 were facilitated by the gradual improvement of relations between them as memories of the Fashoda crisis dimmed, and by the anxiety of both not to be involved against each other in the Russo-Japanese war which broke out in February, 1904. All the colonial differences between them from Siam to Newfoundland came under review, but the Egyptian and Moroccan questions were the crux of the understanding. Finally, after protracted talks, France agreed not to obstruct British action in Egypt and accepted financial reforms in that country, while Britain recognized the French right to restore order in Morocco and introduce reforms. France further conceded that she would preserve the political *status quo*, respect Spanish rights, and leave the coast unfortified. Both powers promised each other diplomatic support in implementing the agreement.

As far as the British Government was concerned the Entente was a purely colonial agreement which gave her the free hand she needed in Egypt and which reduced her opponents by one. In the Far East a new ally had been found against the old enemy Russia, whilst in Europe the quarrel with an old enemy, France, had been ended. Britain need no longer fear isolation by combined French, German, and Russian pressure.

But although there was much popular anti-German feeling in Britain between 1901 and 1903, as a result of German colonial and naval policy, Lansdowne (British Foreign Secretary from 1900 to 1905) had no intention of giving the Entente an anti-German bias.

For Delcassé the Entente primarily ensured that France would not be involved in a Far Eastern war and that Britain would not interfere with French activities in Morocco. Yet, although the radicals then in the ascendancy in France were in favour of good relations with Germany as well as Britain, there is no doubt that Delcassé did envisage a triple understanding between Britain, France, and Russia, and that he realized that an understanding with Britain, unlike one with Germany, did not preclude the possibility of the eventual recovery of Alsace-Lorraine.[10]

In the decade between 1904 and 1914 which forms the last period of this survey, the main trends of the previous fourteen years were confirmed. There was a deterioration of relations between Britain and Germany after 1906 as a result of naval rivalry, continued alienation of Russia from Germany which reached a peak in 1913–14, an intensification of the friction between Austria-Hungary and Russia in the Balkans after 1906, and a renewal of that between France and Germany in the west. Against this background of mounting tension between the opposing alliances existing by 1907, a number of crises occurred.

## THE FIRST MOROCCAN CRISIS, 1905–06

The first Moroccan Crisis of 1905–06 was caused by Germany's realization of the shift of the Balance of Power in France's favour since the eighteen-nineties. At first von Bülow and William II had thought that the impending Russo-Japanese war would soon destroy the Entente by involving Britain and France on opposite sides. When war broke out Germany worked hard to worsen relations between Britain and Russia at the time of the Dogger Bank Incident, when Russian warships on their way to the Far East fired in panic on British fishing trawlers off the Dogger Bank. But the "inevitable" Anglo-Russian outbreak did not come, for Britain did not want war and the protagonists of a forward policy in Russia were already losing favour. By the spring of 1905 the heavy and unexpected defeats sustained by Russia in the Far East, and the revolutionary situation at home, had temporarily eliminated her as a factor in international affairs, and offered Germany a unique opportunity for redressing the Balance of Power in her own favour. On the advice of Baron Holstein, William II and von Bülow resolved to exploit the Moroccan situation to achieve a diplomatic success which would weaken the Entente and compel France, isolated in Europe, to come to terms.

A pretext for intervention was soon provided when France sent a mission to Fez, the Moroccan capital, to press a comprehensive reform plan on the Sultan which would give her financial and military control. In March, at von Bülow's request, William II landed at Tangier and during his visit declared to the Sultan that he recognized the latter's independence and that Germany, who had previously shown little interest in Morocco, would oppose French attempts to establish a protectorate there. This was followed up by a German proposal for a conference of interested powers to discuss the whole question, for von Bülow believed that at the conference table French designs would be opposed by a majority of the others, and that this severe diplomatic defeat would correspondingly increase German prestige.

Von Bülow benefited from his knowledge of the difference of opinion in the French Council of Ministers at this time. The nationalist-minded Delcassé opposed the German attempts to internationalize the Moroccan Question and thereby frustrate unilateral French action. Germany was bluffing, he argued, when she spoke of crossing the French frontier if France tried to establish a protectorate in Morocco. He wanted France to rely on Britain whom he believed, perhaps erroneously, had offered France a firm alliance to resist German bluff. On the other hand the radical Prime Minister, Rouvier, reflected public feeling in opposing this course of action, for he believed it would lead to war, and like most radicals he desired an understanding with Germany. His view prevailed and Delcassé resigned. His resignation was hailed with delight in Berlin, von Bülow was made a prince by his grateful master, whilst in Britain faith in the usefulness of the Entente was shaken.

## THE ALGECIRAS CONFERENCE

But the Germans were not satisfied with their diplomatic victory. Rouvier soon discovered that they were not prepared for a bilateral agreement on Morocco, but still insisted on holding a conference at which France might be publicly humiliated. Disillusioned on German intentions, Rouvier reluctantly consented and the conference met at Algeciras, near Gibraltar, early in 1906.

It proved a Pyrrhic victory for Germany. The Powers certainly agreed to preserve the territorial integrity of Morocco and guaranteed commercial equality for all, but France, who had recovered her nerve by this time, made the practical gains, obtaining in particular control of the police force. Germany tried in vain to win support for a genuine internationalization of this vital service, but she was outvoted and could ensure only that the Diplomatic Corps at Tangier should exercise some nominal control over the French and Spanish police instructors. At best, the Conference was a drawn battle for Germany; the alignment of the Powers against her indicated that she had lost the arbitral position she had enjoyed in the 'nineties and that Austria-Hungary was her only constant supporter. It was significant that Baron Holstein, whose unofficial advice had influenced German policy for the last sixteen years, resigned in 1906 after his Moroccan plan had been discredited.

## BRITISH OBLIGATIONS TOWARDS FRANCE

Nor had Germany shaken the Anglo-French Entente. It emerged strengthened from its baptism of fire, for in both countries there had been resentment of German policy. In Britain the German attitude was regarded as a challenge to the Entente, and Lansdowne, believing erroneously that she wanted a Moroccan port, promised France full diplomatic support. Rouvier had at first wanted to appease rather than resist Germany, but after she had refused to come to terms on the fall of Delcassé he asked Britain for military support in the event of Germany's being frustrated in her plans at the impending conference and deciding to attack. Grey, Foreign Secretary in the new Liberal Government, was no more prepared to enter into binding commitments than Lansdowne.

He could only warn Germany that Britain would fight if war should break out, and inform France that he considered British public opinion would favour intervention. Yet, because he feared that Britain might find herself facing an alliance of France, Germany, and Russia if she did not stand by France, he took the momentous step of approving secret conversations between the French and British military authorities. These were defended on the ground that Britain would not otherwise be able to help France in an emergency,[11] but once the strategic dispositions adopted by a country are based on the participation of another in a war, a moral obligation can in time arise even where no formal alliance exists. Perhaps the French did not attach much importance to British military assistance, but Grey's impression of retaining freedom of choice in an emergency was illusory. He was bound down by slender threads, as Gulliver had been in Lilliput. A real Entente Cordiale now existed, and, despite all Grey's qualifications France heard only "Yes".

In her search for diplomatic triumphs on the cheap Germany had never intended to go to war for the sake of Morocco, but she had, nevertheless, driven Britain and France into each other's arms, and when the Anglo-Russian understanding was concluded in 1907, her diplomatic isolation was further emphasized.

## THE ANGLO-RUSSIAN ENTENTE, 1907

Lansdowne had been as interested as Grey in bringing to an end the traditional hostility between Britain and Russia, if only to strengthen the Entente by improving relations with France's ally and to prevent the conclusion of a Russo-German alliance detrimental to British interests. The task was made easier because the edge of their mutual hostility had been blunted both in the Far and the Near East. The Japanese victory had checked Russia's forward policy in the former, and British control of Egypt, guaranteeing her domination of the Eastern Mediterranean, had diminished the value of the Straits as a barrier to Russian expansion in the latter. Russian activities in Northern Persia, however, were still a cause of alarm, suggesting a desire for a base on the Persian Gulf which would threaten communications with India, and a direct menace to India itself was seen in Russian interest in Tibet and Afghanistan.

An understanding was at length rendered possible by the appointment in 1906 of a new Russian Foreign Minister, Izvolsky, who recognized the need for a reorientation of his country's policy. Japanese resistance made further advances in the Far East impossible and in any case Japan, exhausted by the war, was ready for a moderate settlement which confirmed Russian predominance in Outer Mongolia, established her own in Korea, and divided Manchuria into spheres of influence. Forward action in Central Asia was equally impossible, because the renewed Anglo-Japanese alliance extended the obligations of the signatories to cover India, and provided for joint action whether France aided Russia or not. A compromise settlement was, therefore, also desirable here, so that Russia would be freed in the Near East where British concern to prevent her advance to the Straits was decreasing. This momentous decision meant the end of the 1897 truce in the Balkans and led not only to worsened relations between Austria-Hungary and Russia but, owing to the growing interests of Germany in Asia Minor, between Germany and Russia.

The Anglo-Russian agreement reflected the desire of both sides for a compromise. Both agreed to respect the independence of Tibet and to refrain from intervention in its internal affairs, while Afghanistan was recognized as in the British sphere of influence. Persia, the crux of the negotiations, was divided into three spheres of influence: the richest area, in the north round Tehran, went to Russia; Britain secured control of the south-east, guarding the roads to Afghanistan; and in the neutral zone between the two it was agreed to seek economic concessions only by joint arrangement.

Certainly the preconditions for independence hardly existed, but in making this division Britain and Russia showed Persia scant respect and did little to prepare her for membership of the community of nations. Here, as in North Africa and China, the expansion of the Great Powers was achieved at the expense of the smaller, for by the beginning of the twentieth century the liberal theory of a natural harmony of interests among nations had been modified by the biological idea of the "survival of the fittest", and the new harmony rested on the subordination of the weak to the strong.

The new agreement was not, however, directed against Germany. Russia might view her activities in Asia Minor with uneasiness, but as yet there was no outright clash of interests, and Britain, for all her determination to support France over Morocco, did not wish to create an anti-German alignment in 1907 any more than in 1904. In spite of this, within two years the Triple Entente, as the new alignment of France, Britain, and Russia was called, had begun to assume an anti-German complexion.

## THE BALKANS AGAIN: THE BOSNIAN CRISIS

Influential in this change was the Bosnian Crisis of 1908–09. Izvolsky was seeking to increase Russian prestige after the Far Eastern defeat by some dramatic stroke of policy which would secure free passage through the Straits for her warships, and at the same time Austria-Hungary was forced to pay increased attention to the Balkans by the entry of the Southern Slav problem into a new and critical phase with the accession of the Karageorgović dynasty in Serbia in 1903. Relations between Serbia and Austria-Hungary, uniformly good during the reign of Prince Milan, began to deteriorate, for Peter Karageorgović and Pašić, the Radical Prime Minister, were determined to shake off Austrian control and secure for Serbia her irredenta in Bosnia and Herzegovina. When Serbia refused to buy her armaments from the Skoda works in 1906, Austria-Hungary broke off commercial relations, closing her frontiers to the import of Serbian livestock. The "Pig War" did not bring Serbia to heel, for she found new markets and remained as determined as ever to secure her irredenta: a new and important element in the 1914 crisis had been created. The chance of war was increased by the appointment of Baron Aehrenthal as Foreign Minister of Austria-Hungary in 1906, for this impatient and arrogant diplomat was determined to raise the prestige of the monarchy by some master stroke of policy directed against Serbia, whom he and the new chief of staff, Conrad, regarded as a permanent threat to Austro-Hungarian security. In particular, they desired to annex Bosnia-Herzegovina and end Serbian hopes for their irredenta.

At first it seemed as if Izvolsky and Aehrenthal would come to an understanding. Knowing that Russia was militarily weak and that he could only obtain a settlement of the Straits Question in Russia's favour by agreement with Aehrenthal, Izvolsky approached him with a proposal for a reciprocal arrangement on both this and the Bosnian Question. Aehrenthal was willing as he had been frightened by the Young Turk Revolution in the summer of 1908 which, since these young radical reformers wished to strengthen the Ottoman Empire, might lead to a repudiation of Austrian occupation rights in Bosnia, and he had lost no time in obtaining the consent of the Emperor to the annexation of Bosnia-Herzegovina. In September at Buchlau Castle Aehrenthal and Izvolsky agreed on terms. Izvolsky was to support annexation in return for Austrian support for a revision of the Straits Convention, but Isvolski seems to have thought that these changes would be the subject of a conference of the interested powers, as they clearly constituted a breach of the Berlin Treaty. Aehrenthal deliberately concealed from him the fact that the annexation was imminent, and that he was determined to act before Izvolsky had time to secure British and French approval of changes at the Straits and to arrange a conference. On 5th October, when Izvolsky was in Paris, Ferdinand of Bulgaria, encouraged by Aehrenthal, assumed the title of Tsar (thereby ending Turkish sovereignty over his country) and twenty-four hours later Francis Joseph proclaimed the annexation of Bosnia-Herzegovina. Simultaneously the Austrian garrison was withdrawn from the Sandjak of Novibazar, partly to conciliate the Great Powers, for this wedge of territory separating Serbia and Montenegro had been occupied by Austria-Hungary in 1878.

## GERMANY SUPPORTS AUSTRIA-HUNGARY

It is significant that Austria-Hungary was able to rely on German support in this crisis. William II was annoyed by news of the annexation which might endanger German economic policy in Asia Minor by antagonizing Turkish opinion, but he finally agreed with von Bülow that Germany must accept the situation, for her diplomatic isolation was becoming apparent. At Algeciras Germany had been opposed by a majority of the Powers and in 1907 Britain and Russia had settled their differences, contrary to her expectations. It was a clear demonstration of the failure of the policy of the Free Hand, pursued so confidently in the 'nineties, that in 1908 there was talk in Germany of Encirclement by the Triple Entente. "Our position," remarked von Bülow, "would indeed be dangerous if Austria lost confidence in us and turned away. . . . In Eastern questions above all we cannot place ourselves in opposition to Austria, who has nearer and greater interests in the Balkan peninsula than ourselves. A refusal or a grudging attitude in the question of the annexation of Bosnia and Herzegovina would not be forgiven."[12] When, on 30th October, he informed Aehrenthal that Germany would accept whatever measures Austria-Hungary decided to take against Serbia, the Bismarckian tradition in the Balkans was ended; Germany had assented to the logical conclusion of the 1879 alliance and had handed to Aehrenthal a blank cheque which his successor presented for payment in 1914.

The annexation brought a storm of protests from the Young Turks, who naturally objected to losing even nominal authority over Bosnia-Herzegovina, and from the Serbs, whose hopes of recovering the irredenta were now indefinitely postponed. Serbia waged a bitterly anti-Austrian press campaign, attempted to secure Russian support for her cause, and mobilized her army along the Austrian frontier in the hope of compensating herself by sharing with Montenegro in the partition of the Sandjak of Novibazar. Britain and France denounced the annexation of Bosnia-Herzegovina as a breach of the Berlin Treaty whilst Izvolsky, infuriated by Aehrenthal's duplicity, strove desperately to retrieve his own position.

## IZVOLSKY IN DIFFICULTIES

But Austria-Hungary had the advantage, for neither Britain nor France intended to go to war to preserve the Balkan *status quo*, and Russia, as Izvolsky knew, dared not risk war. At first Izvolsky attempted to secure British and French agreement to changes at the Straits in Russia's favour, but Grey was displeased with Russian behaviour in Persia, where friction had continued despite the 1907 agreement, and he was unwilling to embarrass the Young Turks whom he hailed as fellow liberals. He was not opposed in principle to a modification of the Straits Convention, but he considered the moment inopportune for unilateral Russian action. British opposition and French indifference compelled Izvolsky to abandon all attempts to obtain his share of the Buchlau bargain.

His failure in London and Paris and his realization that many Russian ministers were bitterly opposed to the Austrian annexation of Bosnia, made him determined to humiliate Austria-Hungary by bringing the question before an international conference. At the same time he began to support Serbian demands for compensation, a striking development, for previously Russia had regarded the Western Balkans as an Austrian sphere of influence. Britain and France were prepared to support demands for a conference but Austria-Hungary flatly refused to attend unless the annexation was accepted in advance for, like France in 1905, she had no desire for public humiliation. Germany, too, was unwilling to persuade her ally to modify her attitude, for von Bülow hoped to humiliate Russia and weaken the Triple Entente. The year 1908 closed on an ominous note, with the diplomatic deadlock virtually unresolved and with increasing tension between Austria-Hungary and Serbia threatening peace in the Balkans.

The tension slackened in the spring of 1909. Aehrenthal's position was strengthened when the Young Turks abandoned their claims to Bosnia in return for a cash payment. Meanwhile the game was going against Izvolsky: France informed Russia that she did not consider any vital Russian interests to be at stake and refused to see a *casus belli* in the dispute. Britain was not now prepared to support Serbian claims for compensation and finally, in March, the Russian Government decided formally that intervention in an Austro-Serbian dispute was impossible.

## THE GERMAN ULTIMATUM

But the crisis was not quite over. On 17th March Germany had suggested to Russia that, with Austria-Hungary's approval, they jointly propose to the other Powers that the annexation be recognized and the matter settled. Izvolsky was agreeable but reluctant to abandon all hope of a conference. On 21st March von Bülow repeated the suggestion, adding that Izvolsky must give a definite answer and that, "an evasive, involved, or vague answer would have to be regarded by us as a refusal. We would then withdraw and let things take their course; the responsibility for all further eventualities would fall entirely on M. Izvolsky." In substance this was an ultimatum and was intended as such. Izvolsky was left with no alternative but to accept and the Bosnian Crisis ended.

A few days later Serbia reached an understanding with Austria-Hungary. Aehrenthal had decided that internal opposition in the Empire as well as the financial burden of a war against Serbia made such a campaign inadvisable in 1909, although it is significant that he should have believed that ultimately only war could end the Pan-Serbian dream; that policy, inherited by Berchtold, led to the fatal ultimatum in 1914. Conrad, angry but powerless, had to accept the decision for peace. The Serbs, abandoned by Russia, were ready to accept the Austrian terms which included a declaration by Serbia that she gave up her claims for compensation, would live henceforth on good terms with Austria-Hungary, and would demobilize her army at once.

## A HOLLOW TRIUMPH

The diplomatic triumph of Austria-Hungary and Germany was a hollow one. Aehrenthal had emphasized the importance of Austria-Hungary in the 1879 alliance, but he had not solved the Southern Slav problem. Indeed, Conrad argued that the last chance had been lost when Aehrenthal rejected war against Serbia in 1909. Antagonism between Serbia and Austria-Hungary was now a permanent feature of the Balkan scene. Despite the 1909 declaration the secret society *Narodna obrana* continued its anti-Austrian activities, for Serbia dreamt of revenge to be achieved with Russian assistance. The ties between Serbia and Russia were drawn closer in the years which followed, for Russia was equally determined to avoid a second humiliation at the hands of Austria-Hungary.

Germany gained little by her part in the crisis. The ultimatum in March did irreparable damage to Russo-German relations. Von Bülow was no more able to resist the temptation to play prestige politics in 1909 than he had been in 1905, and paid dearly both times. Berchtold, Austrian ambassador to Russia, observed that the lion's share in promoting the crisis was attributed to Germany and that, "my German colleague . . . has become overnight a terrifying and sinister Nibelung figure, the cruel Hagen of Tronge after he slew the unsuspecting Siegfried". It was assumed at a popular level in France and Britain that deep-laid aggressive designs must lie behind the irresponsible use of the "mailed fist" in diplomacy.

## German Military Plans

In his eagerness to revive German prestige and break the chain of encirclement von Bülow committed Germany deeply to the defence of Austria-Hungary. In the spring of 1909 Conrad and Moltke, Chief of the German General Staff, agreed that an attack by Austria-Hungary on Serbia would involve Germany against Russia if the latter mobilized. In the event of war Germany agreed to attack France, leaving thirteen divisions in Prussia to hold the Eastern front whilst Austria-Hungary attacked in Galicia. The strategic plans for 1914 were ready, for at last the military implications of the 1879 alliance were being accepted in Germany.

The crisis profoundly affected the Triple Entente. Russia embarked upon a radical reorganization of her army in a determination to avoid a second public exposure of the weakness of the Entente. Germany and Austria-Hungary had gained their victories without bloodshed. Similarly, wrote Nelidov, Russian ambassador to France, once the Entente Powers were militarily strong the balance of power could be redressed in their favour without the risk of war.[13] Their alliance had been strengthened rather than weakened by the episode, for the estrangement between Germany and Russia had provided a single common enemy who seemed to be attempting to dominate Europe.

It was a dress rehearsal for 1914, all the elements of the later crisis being already present. War was avoided because Russia was too weak to fight, France more interested in Morocco than Serbia, and Britain unwilling to take up arms in support of Serbian compensation claims. Germany had never intended to do more than score diplomatic victories, and

Austria-Hungary had shrunk from extreme measures against Serbia at the last moment, but the shadow of a general war had taken shape and the mutual suspicions of the rival alignments had deepened.

## THE NAVAL RACE

In particular, the naval race consequent on the foundation of a German navy by William II and Admiral Tirpitz between 1898 and 1900 had begun to affect Anglo-German relations seriously by this time. The German navy was built primarily to provide a tangible sign of her equality with other Powers which, as a new nation state, she was anxious to emphasize. Far from leading to war Tirpitz had argued that the new navy would result in an understanding with Britain, for Germany would be so strong at sea within a few years that her rival would not dare to attack as she would be unable to face the combined French and Russian fleets afterwards. This Risk Theory assumed Britain, France, and Russia would be permanently on bad terms, and was rendered futile by the Triple Entente, and by the defeat of the Russian fleet in the Far East in 1905 which enabled Britain to concentrate on the German challenge to her maritime supremacy, which she considered vital to maintain in the interests of Imperial defence.

In Germany it was not yet apparent, however, that a fleet comparable to that of Britain could only be built at great financial sacrifice and with the permanent loss of British friendship. The launching of the first Dreadnought in 1906 seemed to mark Germany's opportunity to build on equal terms, for the new ship rendered all existing battleships obsolete. At the same time it was noted that the new Liberal Government in Britain was anxious to divert money from such armaments to social services, and had actually reduced naval expenditure in 1907. It was forgotten that Liberals and Conservatives alike believed it vital to maintain Britain's naval supremacy, even though the former might favour naval reductions so long as a relative superiority to other Powers remained. Moreover, particularly in the Foreign Office and Diplomatic Service, influential circles considered the very creation of a German navy as adequate proof of future aggressive intentions. Not unnaturally, Germany refused to recognize

Britain's position as sacrosanct, and when in 1908 Sir Charles Hardinge, Permanent Under-Secretary at the British Foreign Office, insisted that Germany should either stop or retard her naval programme William II informed him bluntly that she would rather fight for a question of national honour than accept such terms. By the summer of 1908 a considerable anti-German campaign was being waged in Britain and William II's assertions that no sinister designs were entertained were regarded as crude attempts to create a false sense of security, for the Emperor was now also talking excitedly of "Encirclement" as German diplomatic isolation became more pronounced. Thus, the meeting of Edward VII and the Tsar at Revel in 1908 was interpreted in Berlin as evidence of the Triple Entente's intention to destroy Germany by this means, and the impression was confirmed by the British refusal to negotiate with Germany about the Baghdad railway unless France and Russia were in agreement. As in our own day the disputes between Russia and America, supported by their respective allies, have created a vicious circle of mistrust and misunderstanding almost impossible to break, so between 1907 and 1914 the rival alliances attributed aggressive intentions to each other.

## ANGLO-GERMAN CRISIS

In the spring of 1909 a further deterioration in Anglo-German relations coincided with the adverse effect on the relations between Austria-Hungary and Russia caused by the Bosnian Crisis. McKenna, First Lord of the Admiralty, announced in the House of Commons that considerable increases in the British naval programme were required to ensure the safety of the Empire. The country was greatly alarmed by his suggestion that the German Dreadnought construction would almost equal that of Britain by 1911, and the Unionist opposition was able to raise the cry "We want eight and we won't wait", demanding an accelerated programme to which the Liberals agreed later in the year. Until now the naval race had not significantly affected the British public's attitude, but after this scare popular feeling remained anti-German for a generation.

No understanding was possible on this question after 1909

because, even when Germany was willing on occasion to retard, though not to reduce, her programme, her willingness was made dependent on an assurance of Britain's benevolent neutrality if Germany were attacked by other Powers. Determined to maintain her supremacy, Britain considered retardation of German building as no concession at all, and Grey and the Foreign Office regarded the demand for neutrality with grave suspicion as an attempt to divide the Entente and prepare the way for a German domination of Europe. Much as Grey, in deference to his Liberal colleagues' opinion, wanted to retain freedom of choice and avoid binding commitments, he realized that neutrality could not be promised if France or Russia were at war with Germany.

## THE SECOND MOROCCAN CRISIS, 1911

In 1911 came a second Moroccan Crisis which arose, as did the first, from a German belief that the situation in Europe favoured an attempt to redress the Balance of Power in favour of the Triple Alliance. The increasing helplessness of the Chinese Empire and the revolutionary situation in Persia had aroused Russian expectations, and Sazonov, who had become Russian Foreign Minister in 1910, was ready to exploit the position in Persia in the certainty that Anglo-German naval rivalry had weakened the possibility of effective British resistance—whatever Grey might say. He was equally willing to take a similar advantage of Germany to negotiate an agreement by which Germany recognized the Russian railway monopoly in Northern Persia in return for Russian abandonment of opposition to the Baghdad railway. Sazonov was careful to evade German attempts to extract from him a promise of neutrality in the event of a European war, but Britain and France were, nevertheless, displeased.

This apparent weakness of the Triple Entente convinced Kiderlin, appointed Secretary of State for Foreign Affairs in 1910, that Germany could secure a diplomatic victory by intervention in Morocco in the spring of 1911. France had continued her forward policy there after the Algeciras Conference, and it became increasingly obvious that the concepts of the preservation of Moroccan independence and commercial equality for all powers there, which had been upheld in 1905, no longer corresponded with reality. Early in 1911 a revolt at Fez compelled France to send troops to occupy the city to protect French nationals, restore order, and defend the Sultan, who was sheltering in the French consulate from his subjects. Grey saw that this was a violation of the spirit, if not of the letter, of the Algeciras Act. "We are," he observed, "already skating on very thin ice in maintaining that the Act of Algeciras is not affected by all that has happened."[14]

Kiderlin calculated that France would find withdrawal difficult, and that Germany would then be able to use her own release from the legal obligations of the Algeciras Act to obtain increased prestige and a compensating addition of territory elsewhere in Africa in return for recognition of the changed situation in the north of the continent. Although he neither desired nor expected war to result, he was not satisfied when France, whose Radical Government earnestly wished to settle the problem, approached Germany at the end of June, but thought that a show of force would make her more amenable and demonstrate German strength. "Bring us back something from Paris", he remarked to Paul Cambon, the French ambassador, when the latter took leave of him on 21st June.[15] But he did not wait for a reply. With the consent of William II and of the Chancellor, Bethmann-Hollweg, he sent the gunboat *Panther* to Agadir on 1st July. Simultaneously he sent a note to the Powers claiming the defence of German nationals as his justification, and declaring that, since French action had invalidated the Algeciras Act, Germany was ready to solve the Moroccan question with the interested parties.

Surprise and some alarm followed this flamboyant German gesture, not least in France, where it was considered both unnecessary and provocative. Germany had been informed in advance of the decision to occupy Fez, and France's inability to see why the courtesy had failed to be returned made negotiations difficult and embarrassing. Yet, even if Caillaux, the new French Prime Minister, had not been a firm believer in Franco-German friendship, there was no alternative to coming to an understanding with Germany on the question. Russia would not consider a colonial dispute a cause for war, and little assistance was to be expected from Britain if Caillaux had wanted to resist.

When negotiations with Germany were renewed on 9th July, Kiderlin remained intransigent, demanding the entire French Congo to compensate Germany for unilateral French action in Morocco, a demand which France at once rejected. Kiderlin, believing that great concessions could be won if he were bellicose enough, was, as has well been said, "a man who considered that the only proper and successful way of conducting politics was with a pistol in your hand or at least bulging in your coat pocket".[16] Fortunately, William II, annoyed at the growing reaction to the "Panther Spring" told him that war could not be waged for the sake of Morocco, and enforced a more moderate attitude. Even so, there was still deadlock at the end of July, although Kiderlin rephrased his demand to allow for a return to the *status quo* in Morocco as an alternative to the surrender of the Congo.

## BRITISH CONCERN

The episode caused some agitation in Britain. Grey warned Germany that her action violated the Algeciras Act and that Britain would honour her obligations to France and defend her interests in Morocco. Not without justification, Germany pointed out that France had been responsible for the initial change in the situation. But, basically, Britain feared that Germany wanted a Moroccan port, probably Agadir, whereas Kiderlin actually intended to use the *Panther's* visit only as a lever to extract concessions from France. In spite of this misconception, Grey recognized the need for care: "We are bound and prepared," he said, "to give France diplomatic support, but we cannot go to war to set aside the Algeciras Act and put France in virtual possession of Morocco. If she can get that for herself we are bound not to stand in her way . . . but if we go to war it must be in defence of British interests. An attempt by Germany to humiliate France might affect British interests so seriously that we should have to resist it, but there is no case for that at present . . . the best solution would be a deal between France and Germany based upon some concession in the French Congo."

At this point Grey and the Prime Minister, Asquith, with

the enthusiastic support of Winston Churchill, approved the famous speech delivered by Lloyd George at the Mansion House dinner on 21st July, in the course of which the Radical Chancellor of the Exchequer declared that "if a situation were to be forced upon us in which peace could only be preserved by the surrender of the great and beneficent position Britain has won by centuries of heroism and achievement, by allowing Britain to be treated where her interests were vitally affected as if she were of no account in the cabinet of nations, then I say emphatically that peace at that price would be a humiliation intolerable for a great country like ours to endure".

## THE SHADOW OF WAR

The speech, probably intended to force Germany to clarify her position, had as profound an effect on German public opinion as had the Tangier speech on opinion in Britain and France in 1905. It seemed to the indignant Germans that Britain was trying to interfere with Franco-German negotiations, and to thwart their legitimate colonial ambitions by threatening war. The German ambassador informed Grey that a return to the *status quo* in Morocco would be insisted on by force of arms if negotiations with France failed. War between Britain and Germany was suddenly very close. Grey warned McKenna that the British fleet might be attacked at any moment, and General Wilson arranged with his French colleague the details of an expeditionary force to be sent to Europe if war broke out.[17]

It is true that Germany did, as a result of the Mansion House speech, hasten to inform Britain that she had no intention of securing a Moroccan port, and consequently British fears subsided. But the speech was political dynamite, for it needlessly antagonized German public opinion when normal diplomatic channels could have been used to ascertain this fact. If Kiderlin had intended to retain Agadir such a speech would have made it difficult for him to give way.

## A SETTLEMENT REACHED

The conversations between France and Germany had been renewed by Caillaux, anxious for a settlement and embarrassed by the British attitude, and under pressure from William II

Kiderlin modified his intransigence. On 4th November an agreement was signed in which Germany recognized a French protectorate in Morocco and received part of the French Congo, with other territories, as compensation. The Moroccan question had been settled and did not, until after the Second World War, trouble the peace of Europe again, but it had served to reveal once more the danger of irresponsible diplomacy. Kiderlin, like von Bülow before him, made the serious mistake of supposing that threats would accomplish more than patient, confidential negotiation, and it is significant of the situation inside Germany that Bethmann-Hollweg, despite his misgivings, kept silent until the damage had been done. The Triple Entente was strengthened, not weakened, by the new threat from Germany. Britain had been nearer war than at any time since 1877. It did not come because Germany had never intended to take the final step for the sake of Morocco, while the desire of Caillaux for peace had been decisive in the French cabinet, and Russia had had the satisfaction of reminding France of her negative attitude during the Bosnian Crisis.

Public opinion in Germany was severely critical of the weakness of Kiderlin and Bethmann-Hollweg in signing the agreement with France, and on the French side Press comment and the speeches of the politicians became increasingly strident as German threats intensified the revival of national feeling which had started in 1905. Caillaux was forced from office in 1912 and replaced by the nationalist Poincaré, who made it his mission to strengthen the Triple Entente as a safeguard against further humiliation of France and in the hope of turning the Balance of Power once more in her favour.

## THE NAVAL PROBLEM AGAIN

The interval between the Moroccan Crisis and the outbreak of the Balkan Wars in the autumn of 1912 was dominated by the naval problem. Though relations between Britain and Germany had deteriorated so badly in 1911, an attempt to reduce the tension by ending their naval race was made in 1912. Britain wished to be set free to concentrate on growing Russian penetration in Persia, and in Germany, even if Admiral Tirpitz was demanding the introduction of a new

Navy Bill to raise German prestige after the bitter internal criticism of the Moroccan agreement, there was still an influential political group, including Bethmann-Hollweg, which desired to improve Germany's diplomatic position by an understanding with Britain. For her part, Britain was willing to accept the existing level of German building, provided that there were no increases, and most Liberals were also in favour of a political agreement calculated to preserve Britain's freedom of action.

## THE HALDANE MISSION

Nevertheless, the negotiations carried on in Berlin by Haldane, the Minister of War, in the spring of 1912 were a failure. William II and Tirpitz insisted that their new Navy Bill be counted as part of existing German naval strength, whereas Britain considered that its provisions were so substantial as to necessitate further British increases; any remaining hope of political agreement was wrecked by the continued German demand for British neutrality. The result was that Tirpitz passed his Bill through the Reichstag, and Britain went on outbuilding the Germans. It was a major German blunder for, although the naval race was not the cause of the First World War, it ensured that Britain would be on the opposite side in a crisis. The new navy did not even serve the purpose for which it was created, as Tirpitz himself admitted to William II in 1910, when he wrote that "if the English fleet is permanently and fundamentally made and maintained so strong as to make it safe to attack Germany, then German naval development from an historical standpoint was a mistake and Your Majesty's Fleet policy an historical fiasco".[18]

The failure of the Haldane negotiations led to closer ties between Britain and France. The passage of the new German Navy Bill made inevitable British increases, which were announced by Churchill, as First Lord of the Admiralty, in the spring of 1912, and the Fleet was ordered to withdraw from the Mediterranean to the North Sea. In the autumn France moved her fleet from the North Sea to the Mediterranean, and used the opportunity to press for a formal alliance such as Britain had always avoided in the past. Britain was still only prepared to promise that, in the event of a threat to peace, she would discuss whether joint action should be taken and in what form: she insisted that military and naval talks did not automatically commit her to support France. Yet the new naval dispositions appeared to make the strategy of the two countries interdependent, and even if Britain retained theoretical freedom of choice her moral obligation to aid a France attacked by Germany had been correspondingly increased.

## RENEWAL OF BALKAN UNREST

In September, 1911, when war broke out between Italy and Turkey, the centre of interest began to shift once more to the Balkans. Italy had for many years sought to expand in North Africa, and when France obtained virtual control of Morocco in 1911 she decided that the moment had arrived to demand a protectorate over Tripolitania and Cyrenaica. On Turkey's refusal war broke out, and Italy was confident of success for, although the Powers disapproved, they were not prepared to lose her friendship by opposition. Thus, when Conrad urged Aehrenthal to attack Italy, whose Balkan ambitions conflicted with those of Austria-Hungary, his advice was ignored, for even formal Italian adherence to the Triple Alliance was better than nothing. In the same way, Grey, who had denounced the Bosnian annexation, did not condemn Italy, because his desire not to alienate her from the Triple Entente overcame his distaste for a violation of international law.

As the war went on into the summer of 1912 unrest in the Balkans increased. Nationalist sentiment was stimulated, for as the Sultan's difficulties increased with the outbreak of guerrilla warfare in Albania and Macedonia, the Balkan states perceived an opportunity for their own territorial aggrandizement. Russia, too, was alive to the possibilities of the situation. In the autumn of 1911 Izvolsky, ambassador in Paris since the previous year, had persuaded the acting Russian Foreign Minister, in Sazonov's absence, to try to obtain from Turkey free passage through the Straits for Russian warships in return for a guarantee of the *status quo*. The attempt failed, for Britain's displeasure with Russia in Persia led her to oppose the suggestion, and France was still unwilling to interest herself in the Balkans.

## THE BALKAN LEAGUE

Sazonov had more success when he attempted to create a Balkan League in 1912. He feared that Austria-Hungary and Germany might profit by the dissensions of the Balkan states to pursue a forward policy while Russia was still too weak to offer opposition. To prevent this he urged Serbia and Bulgaria to sink their differences and form a defensive league. In March, 1912, these two signed a treaty ostensibly pledging them to joint military action to preserve the existing position in the Balkans in face of aggression by a Great Power. In reality they were planning an attack on Turkey, and in secret clauses to the treaty they agreed to partition Macedonia and award Northern Albania to Serbia. In the summer Greece joined the alliance and Montenegro was attached to it by verbal agreement with Serbia.

It was a considerable achievement to have persuaded the Balkan States to resist aggression by a league under Russian protection, with the Tsar appointed as arbiter in the event of disputes between the members, but Sazonov was deceived in imagining that the states could be restrained from war with Turkey. Tension mounted in the late summer of 1912. Yet no Great Power, least of all Russia and Austria-Hungary, wanted to be involved in a major war for such a cause. Sazonov began to feel apprehensive about the League's intentions, and the headstrong and incapable Berchtold, now Foreign Minister of Austria-Hungary since Aehrenthal's death early in 1912, lacked a coherent policy and was prepared to co-operate with others in maintaining the *status quo*. The Powers suggested reforms in Macedonia and asked Austria-Hungary and Russia to approach the Balkan States, admonishing them to keep the peace and warning them that territorial changes would not be tolerated. The note arrived too late. On 8th October Montenegro declared war on Turkey and the "First Balkan War" had begun.

## THE FIRST BALKAN WAR, 1912

It was widely believed that the Turks would be able to hold their own, but within a few weeks the Serbian, Bulgarian, and Greek armies had torn the Ottoman Empire in Europe to shreds. The Turkish defeat in 1912 signified, as had the

French defeat in 1870, that the national idea had at last obtained full recognition. Europe had to recognize radical alterations in the Balkan political map.

At first Austria-Hungary and Russia stood aside slightly bewildered at the speed of events. First to recover was Russia, for the rapid advance of Bulgarian troops towards Constantinople threatened her interests at the Straits, and she was quite prepared for war to prevent the city being occupied. In the event it was unnecessary for her to move since stiffening Turkish resistance checked the Bulgarian advance, and no Great Power was prepared to support Bulgarian claims to Constantinople at a conference.

## AUSTRIA'S VACILLATION

Austria, unconcerned about the Straits, was roused by Serbia's success in occupying the Sandjak of Novibazar, which gave her at last a common frontier with Montenegro, and part of Northern Albania, where she claimed a port on the Adriatic. The hesitant and illogical policy of Berchtold served Austria-Hungary ill at this crucial moment. From the narrow viewpoint of self-interest, Austria-Hungary should either have crushed Serbia militarily, or else have attempted to conciliate her and solve the Southern Slav problem peacefully. Berchtold did neither. He did not even oppose the Serbian occupation of the Sandjak, a key point for the domination of the Western Balkans. Later attempts to pretend that he lacked German consent for military action were without foundation for Kiderlin had promised unconditional support, nor could Russia have intervened, for Sazonov had made it clear that he would not fight for Serbian interests. On the other hand, the offer of a customs union to Serbia was neutralized by Austrian opposition to the Serbian demand for an Adriatic port at Durazzo. Berchtold opposed the Serbian case for prestige reasons, and also because possession of Durazzo would enable Serbia and her allies to blockade Austrian ports in time of war.

There was a certain amount of tension between Austria-Hungary and Russia over the Serbian question at the close of 1912. Some troops were mobilized in Austria-Hungary and Russia had cancelled orders releasing conscripts from her armies for, although he had no intention of going to war for the sake of Serbia, Sazonov was prepared to support Serbian claims for an Adriatic port and had been encouraged by Poincaré to do so.

## FRENCH SUPPORT FOR RUSSIA

An important change in the French attitude to Russian policy in the Balkans had occurred since Poincaré had come to power in 1912, for he had realized that failure to co-ordinate their aims in this region had been the greatest weakness of the 1894 alliance. During his visit to St. Petersburg in August, 1912, he admitted to Sazonov that France could never fight for purely Balkan issues, unless Germany intervened, but he was prepared to offer Russia more assistance than before. The military agreement of 1892 had provided for French assistance only if Austria-Hungary or Germany attacked Russia: Poincaré now promised support if Germany intervened to assist Austria-Hungary against a Russian attack arising out of Balkan rivalries, and there can be no doubt that this modified the defensive nature of the alliance. It was a dangerous policy, but it was not intended to precipitate a conflict. Poincaré sought to ensure the solidarity of the three Entente Powers and believed that by giving the maximum support to Russia he would encourage her to avoid a repetition of the humiliation of 1909 and in the process uphold the prestige of France and Britain as well.

In November, therefore, Poincaré encouraged Sazonov to stand by Serbia, for if Russia went to war France would support her, "as we know that in this question Germany is behind Austria", and it is not surprising that this has been stigmatized as warmongering. Perhaps Poincaré was only concerned to prevent a rapprochement between Austria-Hungary and Russia detrimental to the Triple Entente. He was certainly determined that Russia should not be able to say that her failure to support Serbia was due to lack of French backing. Just as Germany had in 1909 been ready to aid Austria-Hungary against Russia at all costs for the sake of the Triple Alliance, so now France was going beyond the obligations of the 1892 agreement for the sake of the prestige of the Triple Entente. That war was averted in 1912 was due more to the desire of Austria-Hungary and Russia to avoid it, than to France, who feared that a passive Russian attitude would endanger the Entente's prestige.

## THE LONDON CONFERENCE, 1912-13

In December, 1912, an armistice was arranged between the belligerents, and a conference of the Great Powers met in London to give formal recognition to the territorial changes which had occurred and to settle the question of a Serbian outlet to the sea. The ambassadors of the Six Powers held over sixty meetings, but their deliberations were interrupted by Enver Bey's military *coup d'état* at Constantinople which led to a resumption of hostilities in February, 1913. April saw the renewal of the armistice and in May the Treaty of London was signed by the Powers.

Austria-Hungary succeeded in her attempt to prevent Serbia from obtaining Durazzo. Grey, who strove earnestly to treat the problem impartially, considered that the desire for a commercial outlet could be met by the use of an Adriatic port and control of a railway to it rather than by territorial cession. Russia agreed, and when Serbia finally consented the matter was ended.

The most important work of the conference was the recognition of an independent Albania, whose tribesmen had already shaken off Turkish rule. The step pleased Austria-Hungary because the new state excluded Serbia from the Adriatic and might in time prove strong enough to check Serbian expansion southwards, while Italy was gratified by the opening of a likely field for economic expansion, a process which was to culminate in Mussolini's occupation of the country in 1939.

## THE SECOND BALKAN WAR, 1913

It was not long before the victorious Balkan States quarrelled. Serbia considered that she should retain the Bulgarian part of Macedonia, occupied during the fighting, because her ambitions in the Adriatic had not been satisfied. Bulgaria disagreed and, confident that she could defeat Serbia and Greece combined, attacked the Serbs on 29th June. Within a very few weeks Greek, Serbian, and Roumanian armies had forced Bulgaria to sign an armistice and later the Peace of Bucharest, by which she lost territory to all her opponents and had even to surrender Adrianople to Turkey. The peace was not submitted to the Great Powers for their approval; the Balkan states had at last come of age and were able to arrange their own settlements, and the frontiers established in 1913 after the Second Balkan War have remained substantially unaltered ever since.

Although the two Balkan Wars passed without involving Europe in a major conflict they had profound effects upon the situation in the remaining months before the Sarajevo Crisis of 1914. General unrest had increased in the Balkans themselves, because no one there was satisfied with the new settlement. Bulgaria was seeking revenge on her former allies, Greece was quarrelling with Turkey, Italy and Greece were planning to occupy unstable Albania, and Serbia's ambitions had grown with her territorial gains. Nearly doubled in size and with a population increased by fifty per cent, Serbia remained unswervingly hostile to Austria-Hungary and ever-hopeful of soon recovering Bosnia. "The first round is won," remarked the Serb Prime Minister, Pašić, "now we must prepare for the second against Austria."[19]

## BERCHTOLD'S POLICY

The wars also laid bare the inconsistency and bankruptcy of Austro-Hungarian policy in the Balkans. Berchtold had only succeeded in preventing Serbia securing an Adriatic port in 1912, because Russia was not quite ready to challenge him on the issue. Had he wished to crush the Serbs by force the Second Balkan War offered him an ideal opportunity, but there was no crisis because, despite some blustering threats, the vacillating Berchtold had no intention of going to war: later attempts to suggest that Germany had restrained Austria-Hungary were an excuse for inaction rather than an explanation.[20] That there were substantial differences between the two countries on Balkan issues was shown by the Kavala incident in the summer of 1913. Austria-Hungary wished to restore this coastal town, taken by the Greeks from the Bulgars during the war, to Bulgaria because great importance was attached to her potentialities as an ally against Serbia in a future war. But Germany insisted that Kavala remain in Greek hands because the Queen of Greece was William II's sister, and Germany considered Greece of more importance than Bulgaria. Berchtold disagreed strongly, arguing that it had always been tacitly conceded that Germany should follow Austria-Hungary's lead, but Kavala was still not restored to Bulgaria.[21]

## THE ULTIMATUM TO SERBIA, 1913

Deeply offended by what he regarded as the German failure to aid her ally, Berchtold made a bold and significant attempt to revive Austria-Hungary's prestige in the autumn of 1913. Serbian troops still remained on what the London Conference had decided was Albanian territory, and had actually advanced further into Albania on the pretext of suppressing a revolt on the frontier. Berchtold feared that the Serbs were attempting to gain an Adriatic port, and with the sudden determination of the weak he decided to bring the Serbs to heel. Conrad urged preventive war, but, though sympathetic, Berchtold was hesitant. He feared the intervention of the Powers in the interval between mobilization and the beginning of hostilities, and he expected that the Serbs would in any case comply with an ultimatum. It is worthy of note that he secured prior German agreement. William II was eager for action and when Berchtold spoke of a Serbian surrender said: "That would be most deplorable. Now or never! Some time or other peace and order must be established down there." The ultimatum of October, 1913, was complied with by the Serbs, but it drew protests from the Triple Entente and still further increased the tension between Serbia and Austria-Hungary. The parallel with 1914 is obvious. The difference was that Serbia and Russia then resisted the Austrian ultimatum and general war ensued.

## INCREASING TENSION

The Balkan Wars were responsible, too, for a period of mounting uneasiness in Europe generally because the swift victories of the Balkan States caused an overhaul of military resources everywhere so that comparable triumphs might be achieved when war, which many feared was inevitable, should at last break out. The renewed armaments race began in January, 1913, when the Germans introduced a Bill to add three army corps to their forces and raised the peacetime footing from 663,000 to 761,000 men. In August France followed suit, extending her period of service to three years to compensate for her lack of manpower, so that by January, 1914 she had 790,000 men under arms. Finally, in December, 1913, Russia adopted a vast military programme calculated to add 500,000 men to her peacetime army, which was already 1,300,000 strong. These increases were usually accompanied by government campaigns to convince the various peoples of the need for defensive preparations, and to stimulate their ardent defence of national honour if the need should arise. There can be little doubt that the armaments race and the exaggerated nationalism which it produced in Europe did much to prepare the way for the Sarajevo crisis. Colonel House, visiting Europe in May, 1914, wrote to President Wilson that, "the situation is extraordinary. It is militarism run mad. Unless someone acting for you can bring about a different understanding there is some day to be an awful cataclysm. No one in Europe can do it. There is too much hatred, too many jealousies."[22]

## Germany and Turkey

The deterioration in Russo-German relations in the autumn of 1913 and spring of 1914 had a considerable bearing on the events of the following summer, and was caused by the German acceptance of a Turkish request in May, 1913, for assistance in reforming their army after the defeats of the first Balkan War. In November General Liman von Sanders and forty-two officers were sent on a five-year mission to Constantinople, von Sanders being given powers over all training in Turkey, a seat on the War Council, control of all army promotion, and command of the first Army Corps stationed at Constantinople. The decision to aid Turkey was to some extent the logical outcome of German economic interest in Asia Minor in the preceding thirty years. In the past Germany had relied on British and French opposition to Russia operating in Turkey's favour, but Britain was now no longer interested in defending the Straits and after the weakening Balkan War Turkey could not be relied on to defend herself, so that some military assistance was necessary to protect German interests.

Despite the crisis of 1909, Russia had until now no desire for a serious quarrel with Germany, because the mutual hostility between Germany, Britain and France had enabled her to pursue a forward policy in Persia without danger to her position in Europe, but the challenge presented by the Liman von Sanders mission could not be ignored. By placing Turkey under German protection, it seemed to strike at the basic consideration of Russian foreign policy that no Great Power must be allowed to control the Straits so vital to the economic well-being and military security of Southern Russia.

Sazonov protested at once and sought French and British approval for his action. The French response was satisfactory but Grey was hesitant at first, feeling that as a British admiral, Limpus, had been in charge of the Turkish navy for some time it was somewhat difficult to object to a German citizen performing a similar service for the Turkish army. Sazonov was bitterly critical of this hesitancy, remarking that "this lack of homogeneity and solidarity between the three Entente Powers arouses our serious apprehension for its constitutes an organic fault of the Triple Entente which will always place it at a disadvantage in face of the solid bloc of the Triple Alliance".[23] However, Germany sincerely desired a peaceful settlement and Russia was still militarily incapable of waging war. In January, 1914, a solution was found when General Sanders was given a Field-Marshal's baton, which made him relinquish command of the troops stationed at the Straits, the point to which Russia had taken exception. But Russia had been alarmed by the incident and sought security both in increased armaments and in attempts to transform the Triple Entente into an alliance so strong that there would be no need to fear Germany. As far as Germany was concerned William II not unjustly commented in February, 1914, that, "Russo-Prussian relations are dead once and for all. We have become enemies."

By the summer of 1914 the major factors, whose development has been traced in this chapter, had combined to produce an explosive situation in Europe. In the Balkans Russian confidence in her ability to avoid another diplomatic defeat was growing as she worked diligently to recreate a Balkan League. She had already detached Roumania from the Triple Alliance and continued to encourage Serbia to expect the "liberation" of Bosnia at an early date. But in Austria-Hungary there was a mounting feeling of desperation, and a realization that only bold action could preserve the Empire during the next crisis. Behind Austria-Hungary stood an isolated Germany, on bad terms with France and Russia, and ready to aid her ally in upholding the prestige of the Triple Alliance, just as France was eager to back Russia and the Triple Entente. Everywhere the general staffs were becoming more and more restive, the armament burdens heavier, and the sense of the inevitability of war greater. Seen in the light of these circumstances it is not surprising that the murder on 28th June by a Serb of the Archduke Francis Ferdinand, heir to the throne of Austria-Hungary, should have caused another Balkan Crisis.

## The Root of War

Yet it is deceptively easy to think of the Sarajevo Crisis and of the World War which followed as the last and inevitable links in a chain of reactions started a few decades before. There is no clear-cut formula to fit a tragedy of this magnitude. It is too mechanistic an explanation to suppose that a number of distinct factors such as the piling-up of armaments, the undue influence of military advisers and extreme nationalism, combine to produce a situation which can only end in war. Human beings are not puppets driven on by blind forces to final destruction as if they were characters in a Hardy novel. They are reasonable and responsible individuals, conditioned by their environment but in turn conditioning it. Their choice is a limited one, but is nevertheless very real, so that in the last resort, as St. Augustine observed, bad times are due to bad men. The underlying causes of the war certainly set limits to the freedom of action of William II, Berchtold, Sazonov, Poincaré and Grey, and guard one against the error of restricting responsibility to a few men in the European capitals, but it is equally important to remember that its outbreak cannot be ascribed exclusively to impersonal forces.

## Austria Seeks a Prestige Victory

Berchtold was determined to use the assassination as a pretext for war against Serbia at last. The assassination itself was no doubt planned by the "Black Hand", a terrorist organization operating in Bosnia and working for the union of all Southern Slavs, which had Colonel Dimitrievič, chief of Serbian military intelligence, as its head. Pašić, the Serbian Prime Minister, probably knew something of the plot and only warned Vienna of it in a roundabout and uncertain manner because he feared reprisals, but the Austrian decision did not depend on evidence of the Serbian Government's complicity. Francis Joseph thoroughly agreed with Berchtold that the Serbs must be taught a sharp lesson.

## GERMAN SUPPORT FOR AUSTRIA

Germany endorsed this decision as the logical outcome of the 1879 alliance. Austria-Hungary was not only assured of a completely free hand, but was given positive encouragement to be stern. The German Foreign Office and the Emperor certainly did not deliberately engineer a world war in 1914, but while they were inclined to consider intervention by the Entente unlikely, they were fully prepared to take the risk because it seemed essential to maintain the prestige of the Triple Alliance and of Austria-Hungary as a Great Power. If a general war must come, they preferred to face it while Germany had a military advantage—as she was supposed to have in trained reserves until 1917—rather than wait until the balance should have altered in favour of the Triple Entente.

Assured of full German support Berchtold was able to overcome the reluctance of the Hungarian Prime Minister, Tisza, who feared that war would expose Hungary to Russian attack. By 14th July it had been decided to send an ultimatum to Serbia framed in such terms that it would be rejected and Austria-Hungary would be afforded an opportunity of dealing swiftly with her, thus prolonging the life of the dual monarchy, if only for a few years. The ultimatum was not presented until 23rd July, because Berchtold feared that if it were delivered before or during Poincaré's visit to St. Petersburg (arranged for 20th to 23rd July), France and Russia would have an ideal opportunity to plan concerted action. In the meantime, Sazonov was alarmed by rumours of an impending Austrian move and no doubt Poincaré and the French Foreign Secretary, Viviani, encouraged him to stand firm. There is no evidence that they wished to precipitate war, but they must certainly have strengthened Sazonov's belief that Russia could not allow Serbia to be humbled if the Triple Entente were to count for anything in international affairs.

## THE ULTIMATUM

On the evening of 23rd July Austria-Hungary formally presented the ultimatum, which contained a number of onerous demands. Serbia was required to dissociate herself publicly from anti-Austrian propaganda, to suppress hostile newspapers and secret societies, to remove teachers and officials considered undesirable by Austria-Hungary, and to allow Austrian policemen to co-operate with their Serbian counterparts on Serbian soil in tracking down terrorists. Grey described it as the "most formidable document I had ever seen addressed by one state to another that was independent". It was timed to expire in forty-eight hours.

"This is a European war", exclaimed Sazonov when he read the terms.[24] He was determined not to stand by and allow Serbia to be attacked, and that this was Austria-Hungary's intention seemed evident from the ultimatum and the circular note sent by Germany to the Powers, in which she pointed out that the affair concerned only Austria-Hungary and Serbia and implied that there should be no intervention. Sazonov informed Serbia that he considered the ultimatum unacceptable and would defend her legitimate interests. This advice, and news that Sazonov had obtained the Tsar's consent for partial mobilization when necessary, decided Serbia in favour of rejection, though she had seriously been considering acceptance in view of her own military unpreparedness and fear of being abandoned by Russia as in 1912. Before sending her reply Serbia ordered mobilization, thinking that only unconditional surrender would have satisfied Vienna, and this belief was confirmed by the behaviour of the Austrian ambassador, Giesl. He received the Serbian reply at 5.55 p.m., glanced through it, signed a prepared note breaking off diplomatic relations, caught the 6.30 train from Belgrade and was on Austrian soil a few minutes later.

The diplomatic activity of the Powers started in earnest when the terms of the ultimatum were known on 23rd July.

Russia hoped for a peaceful solution and urged Serbia to be cautious. Britain attempted to intervene on 26th July, proposing that France, Britain, Germany, and Italy should meet in conference, while Serbia, Austria-Hungary, and Russia (as interested parties) should give a promise not to begin military operations during the talks. Grey considered the Serbian reply reasonable enough to form a basis for discussion, and France and Italy were agreeable, but Germany declined to take part. After having urged Austria-Hungary to strike swiftly at Serbia, Bethmann-Hollweg could hardly advise her to appear before a Four Power arbitration court to suffer a diplomatic defeat. The proposal was passed to Vienna without comment and no attempt was made to prevent the declaration of war. This followed on 28th July, for Berchtold was determined to frustrate all attempts at mediation in the belief that the last chance for settling accounts with Serbia must not be allowed to pass.

### GERMANY APPLIES THE BRAKE IN VAIN

Not until 29th July when news of the repercussions of the declaration reached Bethmann-Hollweg did he begin to realize the danger of Germany's position. He still hoped for a brilliant diplomatic victory, but as he heard of the Russian order for partial mobilization and of British naval preparations he realized that localization of an Austro-Serbian war was impossible. Only then did he urge Vienna to resume direct conversations with St. Petersburg, conversations from which he had previously dissuaded her, and commended to Berchtold a British proposal that only Belgrade be occupied as a pledge of good Serbian behaviour. Austria-Hungary, accustomed to German support, did not take the proposals seriously; for the sake of appearances she resumed conversations with Russia, but she insisted that military operations against Serbia continue and that Russian mobilization be cancelled before serious discussions began.

On 30th July Russia ordered general mobilization. No doubt Sazonov hoped to avoid war by indicating to Germany and Austria-Hungary that Russia was in earnest this time, but he does not appear to have realized fully, that Russian and French military experts regarded mobilization as, in effect, a

declaration of war, and that his action had made German and
Austro-Hungarian mobilization a certainty. Russian mobilization, for which the bombardment of Belgrade was offered as
justification, made nonsense of the Austro-Russian conversations and ensured the failure of Bethmann-Hollweg's belated
attempts to restrain Austria-Hungary.

## THE GENERALS TAKE OVER

Events were now in the hands of the generals. In Germany
they were now only concerned to ensure the smooth working
of the Schlieffen Plan which depended upon the rapid elimination of France before Russia was defeated at leisure. At
Moltke's bidding, Germany sent an ultimatum to Russia on
31st July demanding the cessation of all Russian war measures
within twelve hours, for Bethmann-Hollweg agreed that
Russia must not be allowed a long lead in the mobilization of
her gigantic war machine. The German declaration of war
followed on her refusal to comply and, though no formal
response was made to this, Russian armies invaded East
Prussia before the expiration of the time limit. Thus by
1st August the line to St. Petersburg had been severed and the
two countries were at war.

## BRITAIN HESITATES

Britain was still most reluctant to commit herself for Grey,
conscious of the disunity in the Liberal Party and of the
remoteness of Serbian affairs from the public mind, attempted
to maintain an artificial impartiality. On 31st July he was still
able to inform Paul Cambon, the French ambassador, that
". . . we had come to the conclusion in the Cabinet today that
we could not give any pledge at the present time . . . up to
the present we did not feel that any treaties or obligations were
involved". When Germany had attempted on 29th July to
ascertain upon what terms British neutrality might be secured
Grey had avoided a direct answer. Germany had been prepared
to forgo annexations of French territory and to respect
Belgian neutrality after the war, but Grey replied that Britain
must keep her hands free.

When news of the Russian mobilization and of the
proclamation of a state of emergency in Germany arrived in

London Grey had to ascertain whether France and Germany would respect Belgian neutrality. France, whose strategic plans did not involve the violation of Belgium, agreed at once, but Germany, whose Schlieffen Plan depended on it, replied that an answer would reveal her campaign strategy. Germany was now preparing the way for action in the west. She asked France what her attitude would be in the event of a Russo-German conflict. France replied on 1st August that she would consult her interests, and began to mobilize.

Britain felt compelled to clarify her position, and on 2nd August Grey obtained Cabinet approval for his declaration that the British Navy would aid France if the German fleet attacked her coastline. Although Grey maintained that this did not imply automatic intervention in a Franco-German war, it did in fact do so. There was at least a moral obligation to assist the country whose naval dispositions had been based, in some degree, on the assumption of British friendship. Furthermore, as Grey declared on 3rd August in the House of Commons, it was plainly not in British interests to see France defeated and Belgium, Holland, and Denmark under the control of one Power. The British expeditionary force had already been mobilized when in the evening Grey confirmed the rumours that Germany had sent an ultimatum to Belgium the previous day, and on that same evening of 3rd August Germany declared war on France.

The next morning, when news of the invasion of Belgium by German troops arrived in London, the Cabinet approved an ultimatum to Germany demanding her withdrawal. By midnight no reply had been received, and the British Empire was at war. Two days later Austria-Hungary declared war on Russia, and Britain and France declared war on Austria-Hungary.

## The Unwanted War

Lloyd George was right in thinking that no one at the head of affairs quite wanted war in 1914.[25] Austria-Hungary, for example, after years of indecision and unable to solve her own internal troubles, desired only to raise her prestige by a victorious local war against Serbia. From that everything else followed. Germany had to pay the price of the 1879 alliance by supporting, perhaps lightheartedly, her one remaining ally. If this support led to a general war, then Germany preferred it in 1914 rather than when Russia and France had had more time to gain strength, but a bloodless victory did not seem completely impossible, though her own blundering diplomacy had actually made it so by playing on the fears of the members of the Triple Entente. Russia had now recovered from the weakness of 1909 and was resolutely determined to maintain her prestige, which she regarded as inseparable from that of Serbia, and if she were resolute enough a peaceful outcome seemed not improbable. France had no desire for a general war, but stood by the alliance which was the guarantee of her security. It would have mattered little had Grey made Britain's position clear earlier. France and Russia were determined to resist Austria-Hungary in any case and, had Britain refused them her assistance, she would have suffered a most crushing diplomatic defeat. Belgian neutrality was merely the occasion, not the basic reason, for her intervention, since whatever the British attitude the Schlieffen Plan could hardly have been altered. Germany was interested in British neutrality not for military reasons but because, at an earlier stage, it might have disheartened France and Russia. Italy, as expected, stood aside; since 1876 she had been moving away from the Triple Alliance and the process ended with her adherence to Triple Entente in 1915. No one had realized how little room for manœuvre remained as a result of the history of the preceding decade. So, in the summer of 1914, the Great Powers entered upon the first of the total wars of the twentieth century during which four empires disappeared, millions of lives were lost, and the economic basis of the prosperity of the nineteenth century was completely undermined.

## REFERENCES

The literature on International Relations between 1870 and 1914 is vast. A number of works have been used throughout this section, and to them no detailed references are given: they include W. Langer's detailed studies, *European Alliances and Alignments, 1871–1890* and *The Diplomacy of Imperialism, 1890–1902*, and A. J. P. Taylor's stimulating study, *The Struggle for Mastery in Europe, 1848–1918*, together with the following invaluable collections of diplomatic documents:

> *British Documents on the Origins of the War, 1898–1914*,
> *Documents diplomatiques français*,
> *Die Grosse Politik der europäischen Kabinette, 1871–1914* (German documents),
> *Österreich-Ungarns Aussenpolitik, 1908–1914* (Austro-Hungarian documents).

1. E. Brandenburg: *From Bismarck to the World War*, p. 37.
2. O. *von Bismarck, the Man and the Statesman*, II, p. 234.
3. E. Corti: *Alexander of Battenberg*, p. 43.
4. Quoted in R. W. Seton-Watson: *Britain in Europe, 1789–1914*, pp. 540-41.
5. Sir C. Dilke: *Europe in 1887*, p. 27.
6. General von Schweinitz: *Denkwürdigkeiten*, II, pp. 76–77.
7. cf. *From Bismarck to the World War*.
8. J. Y. Simpson: *The Saburov Memoirs*, p. 74.
9. G. P. Gooch: *Before the War. Studies in Diplomacy*, I, p. 240.
10. ibid., p. 157.
11. Lord Grey of Fallodon: *Twenty-Five Years, 1892–1916*, I, p. 75.
12. *Before the War*, I, p. 276.
13. L. Albertini: *The Origins of the War of 1914*, I, p. 293.
14. *Before the War*, II, p. 70.
15. ibid., p. 219.
16. *From Bismarck to the World War*, p. 384.
17. W. Churchill: *The World Crisis*, I, pp. 47–48.
18. *From Bismarck to the World War*, p. 299 n.
19. S. B. Fay: *The Origins of the World War*, I, pp. 445–46.
20. *Origins of the War of 1914*, I, pp. 466–70.
21. ibid., p. 464.
22. C. Seymour: *The Intimate Papers of Colonel House*, I, p. 255.
23. B. von Siebert: *Entente Diplomacy and the World War*, p. 798.
24. *Origins of the War of 1914*, II, p. 290.
25. Quoted in G. P. Gooch: *History of Modern Europe, 1878–1919*, p. 559.

# PRINCIPAL FIGURES

## HEADS OF STATE

GREAT BRITAIN AND EMPIRE
Queen Victoria, 1837–1901
King Edward VII, 1901–10
King George V, 1910–36

### SOUTH AFRICA
ORANGE FREE STATE
*Presidents*
Sir J. H. Brand, 1864–88
F. W. Reitz, 1889–95
M. T. Steyn, 1896–1902

SOUTH AFRICAN REPUBLIC
(TRANSVAAL)
*President*
S. J. P. Kruger, 1883–1902

### EGYPT
*Khedives*
Ismail, 1863–79
Tewfik, 1879–92
Abbas Hilmi II, 1892–1914
Hussein, 1914–17
(*Sultan*)

### FRANCE
*Presidents*
L. A. Thiers, 1871–73
M. de MacMahon, 1873–79
J. Grévy, 1879–87
S. Carnot, 1887–94 (ass.)
J. Casimir-Périer, 1894–95
E. F. Faure, 1895–99
E. Loubet, 1899–1906
A. Fallières, 1906–13
R. Poincaré, 1913–20

### GERMANY
*Emperors*
William I, 1871–88
Frederick III, 1888
William II, 1888–1918

### AUSTRIA–HUNGARY
(Dual Monarchy from 1867)
*Emperor — King*
Francis Joseph, 1848–1916

### SERBIA
*Kings*
Milan Obrenović (*Prince* from 1868),
1882–89
Alexander Obrenović, 1889–1903
(ass.)
Peter Karageorgević, 1903–21
(Regency under son, Alexander,
afterwards King of Yugoslavia,
from 1914)

### RUSSIA
*Emperors*
Alexander II, 1855–81 (ass.)
Alexander III, 1881–94
Nicholas II, 1894–1917 (ass.)

### ITALY
*Kings*
Victor Emmanuel II, 1849–78
Humbert, 1878–1900 (ass.)
Victor Emmanuel III, 1900–44

*The Papacy*
Pope Pius IX, 1846–78
Pope Leo XIII, 1878–1903
Pope Pius X, 1903–14
Pope Benedict XIV, 1914–22

### UNITED STATES OF AMERICA
*Presidents*
A. Lincoln (R), 1861–65; 1865 (ass.)
A. Johnson (R), 1865–69
U. S. Grant (R), 1869–73; 1873–77
R. B. Hayes (R), 1877–81
J. A. Garfield (R), 1881 (ass.)
C. A. Arthur (R), 1881–85
G. Cleveland (D), 1885–89
B. Harrison (R), 1889–93
G. Cleveland (D), 1893–97
W. McKinley (R), 1897–1901; 1901
(ass.)
T. Roosevelt (R), 1901–05; 1905–09
W. H. Taft (R), 1909–13
W. Wilson (D), 1913–17; 1917–21

## HEADS OF STATE (*continued*)

### CHINA

*Emperors*
T'ung Chih, 1862–75
Kuang Hsü, 1875–1908
Tzǔ Hsi, Empress-Dowager: Regent, 1862–73, 1875–89, 1898–1908
Hsüan T'ung, 1908–12

*President of the Republic*
Yüan Shih-k'ai, 1912–16

### JAPAN

*Emperors*
Komei, 1846–67
Mutsuhito (Meiji), 1867–1912
Yoshihito (Taisho), 1912–26

## VICEROYS, GOVERNORS, etc.

### IRELAND

*Lords Lieutenant of Ireland*
Earl Spencer, 1868–74
Duke of Abercorn, 1874–76
Duke of Marlborough, 1876–80
Earl Cowper, 1880–82
Earl Spencer, 1882–85
Earl of Carnarvon, 1885–86
Earl of Aberdeen, 1886
Marquis of Londonderry, 1886–89
Earl of Zetland, 1889–92
Lord Houghton, 1892–95
Earl Cadogan, 1895–1902
Earl of Dudley, 1902–05
Earl of Aberdeen, 1905–15

### CANADA

Lord Monck, 1867–69
Lord Lisgar, 1869–72
Earl of Dufferin, 1872–78
Marquess of Lorne, 1878–83
Marquess of Lansdowne, 1883–88
Lord Stanley, 1888–93
Earl of Aberdeen, 1893–98
Earl of Minto, 1898–1904
Earl Grey, 1904–11
Duke of Connaught, 1911–16

### AUSTRALIA

*Governors-General of the Commonwealth*
Earl of Hopetoun, 1901–03
Lord Tennyson, 1903
Lord Northcote, 1904–08
Earl of Dudley, 1908–11
Lord Denman, 1911–14
Lord Novar, 1914–20

### NEW ZEALAND

*Governors*
Marquis of Normanby, 1874–79
Sir H. Robinson, 1879–80
Sir A. Gordon, 1880–83
Sir W. Jervois, 1883–89
Earl of Onslow, 1889–91
Earl of Glasgow, 1891–97
Earl of Ranfurly, 1897–1904
Lord Plunket, 1904–10
Lord Islington, 1910–12
Earl of Liverpool, 1912–20
    (*Governor-General*, 1917)

### INDIA

*Viceroys*
Lord Northbrook, 1872–76
Lord Lytton, 1876–80
Marquess of Ripon, 1880–84
Earl of Dufferin, 1884–88
Marquess of Lansdowne, 1888–94
Earl of Elgin, 1894–99
Lord Curzon, 1899–1905
Earl of Minto, 1905–10
Lord Hardinge, 1910–16

### SOUTH AFRICA

*High Commissioners and Governors of Cape Colony*
Sir P. Wodehouse, 1862–70
Sir H. Barkly, 1870–77
Sir B. Frere, 1877–80
Sir H. Robinson, 1881–89
Sir H. Loch, 1889–95
Sir H. Robinson, 1895–97
    (Lord Rosmead, 1896)
Sir A. Milner, 1897–1901

## VICEROYS, GOVERNORS, ETC. *(continued)*

SOUTH AFRICA *(continued)*
*High Commissioners for South Africa*
Lord Milner, 1901–05
Earl of Selborne, 1905–10

*Governors-General of the Union*
Lord Gladstone, 1910–14
Lord Buxton, 1914–20

### EGYPT
*British Agents and Consuls-General*
Lord Cromer, 1883–1907
Sir E. Gorst, 1907–11
Lord Kitchener, 1911–14
Sir H. MacMahon, 1914–16
  (High Commissioner)

*Governors-General of the Sudan*
Lord Kitchener, 1896–99
Sir R. Wingate, 1899–1916

### JAPAN
*Last Shoguns*
Iyemochi, 1858–66
Yoshinobu, 1867–68

### HUNGARY
*Ban of Croatia*
I. Mažuranič, 1873–80
Count C. Khuen-Héderváry, 1880–
  1903
Baron T. Pejačevič, 1903–08
Baron P. Rauch, 1908–10
N. Tomásič, 1910–12
V. von Cuvaj, 1912–13
Baron I. Skerlecz, 1913–

### SERBIA
Council of Regency headed by
  J. Ristič during minority of King
  Alexander, 1889–93

### CHINA
*Viceroys of Chih-li*
Tseng Kuo-fan, 1868–70
Li Hung-chang, 1870–95
Wang Wen-shao, 1895–98
Jung-lu, 1898
Yü-lu, 1898–1900
Li Hung-chang, 1900–01
Yüan Shih-k'ai, 1901–07

# FIRST MINISTERS

### GREAT BRITAIN
W. E. Gladstone, 1868–74
B. Disraeli, 1874–80
  (Earl of Beaconsfield, 1876)
W. E. Gladstone, 1880–85
Marquis of Salisbury, 1885–86
W. E. Gladstone, 1886
Marquis of Salisbury, 1886–92
W. E. Gladstone, 1892–94
Earl of Rosebery, 1894–95
Marquis of Salisbury, 1895–1902
A. J. Balfour, 1902–05
Sir H. Campbell-Bannerman,
  1905–08
H. H. Asquith, 1908–16

### CANADA
Sir J. Macdonald, 1867–73
A. Mackenzie, 1873–78
Sir J. Macdonald, 1878–91
Sir J. Abbot, 1891–92
Sir J. Thompson, 1892–94
Sir M. Bowell, 1894–96
Sir C. Tupper, 1896
Sir W. Laurier, 1896–1911
Sir R. Borden, 1911–20

FIRST MINISTERS *(continued)*

## AUSTRALIA
Sir E. Barton, 1901–03
A. Deakin, 1903–04
J. C. Watson, 1904
Sir G. Reid and A. Maclean (joint),
1904–05
A. Deakin, 1905–08
A. Fisher, 1908–09
A. Deakin, 1909–10
A. Fisher, 1910–13
Sir J. Cook, 1913–14
A. Fisher, 1914–15
W. M. Hughes, 1915–23

## SOUTH AFRICA *(continued)*
ORANGE RIVER COLONY
A. Fischer, 1907–10

TRANSVAAL
L. Botha, 1907–10

UNION
L. Botha, 1910–19

## NEW ZEALAND
W. Fox, 1869–72
G. M. Waterhouse, 1872–73
J. Vogel, 1873–75
D. Pollen, 1875–76
Sir J. Vogel, 1876
H. A. Atkinson, 1876–77
Sir G. Grey, 1877–79
J. Hall, 1879–82
F. Whitaker, 1882–83
H. A. Atkinson, 1883–84
R. Stout and Sir J. Vogel (joint),
1884–87
Sir H. A. Atkinson, 1887–91
J. Ballance, 1891–93
R. J. Seddon, 1893–1906
Sir J. G. Ward, 1906–12
W. F. Massey, 1912–25

## EGYPT
Nubar Pasha, 1878–79
Sherif Pasha, 1879
Riaz Pasha, 1879–81
Sherif Pasha, 1881–82
Mahmud Sami, 1882
(Ahmed Arabi Minister of War)
Riaz Pasha, 1882
Sherif Pasha, 1882–84
Nubar Pasha, 1884–88
Riaz Pasha, 1888–91
Mustafa Pasha Fehmy, 1891–93
Riaz Pasha, 1893–94
Nubar Pasha, 1894–95
Mustafa Pasha Fehmy, 1895–1907
Boutros Pasha Ghali, 1907–10 (ass.)
Mohamed Said Pasha, 1910–14
Hussein Rushdi Pasha, 1914–18

## SOUTH AFRICA
CAPE COLONY
J. C. Molteno, 1872–78
J. G. Sprigg, 1878–81
T. C. Scanlen, 1881–84
T. Upington, 1884–86
J. G. Sprigg, 1886–90
C. J. Rhodes, 1890–96
J. G. Sprigg, 1896–98
W. P. Schreiner, 1898–1900
J. G. Sprigg, 1900–04
L. S. Jameson, 1904–08
J. X. Merriman, 1908–10

## GERMANY
*Imperial Chancellors*
Prince O. von Bismarck, 1871–90
L. von Caprivi, 1890–94
Prince C. zu Hohenlohe-Schillings-
fürst, 1894–1900
B. von Bülow, 1900–09
(Prince, 1906)
T. von Bethmann-Hollweg, 1909–17

## FIRST MINISTERS (*continued*)

### FRANCE
Duc de Broglie, 1873–75
L. J. Buffet, 1875–76
J. A. S. Dufaure, 1876
J. Simon, 1876
Duc de Broglie, 1877
J. A. S. Dufaure, 1877–79
W. H. Waddington, 1879
C. L. de Freycinet, 1879–80
J. Ferry, 1880–81
L. Gambetta, 1881–82
C. L. de Freycinet, 1882
C. J. E. Duclerc, 1882
J. Ferry, 1883–85
E. H. Brisson, 1885
C. L. de Freycinet, 1885–86
R. Goblet, 1886–87
M. Rouvier, 1887
P. E. Tirard, 1887–88
C. T. Floquet, 1888–89
P. E. Tirard, 1889–90
C. L. de Freycinet, 1890–92
E. Loubet, 1892
A. F. J. Ribot, 1892–93
C. A. Dupuy, 1893
J. Casimir-Périer, 1893–94
C. A. Dupuy, 1894–95
A. F. J. Ribot, 1895
L. Bourgeois, 1895–96
F. J. Méline, 1896–98
E. H. Brisson, 1898–99
P. Waldeck-Rousseau, 1899–1902
J. L. E. Combes, 1902–05
M. Rouvier, 1905–06
G. Clemenceau, 1906–09
A. Briand, 1909–11
J. M. Caillaux, 1911–12
R. Poincaré, 1912–13
A. Briand, 1913
J. L. Barthou, 1913
G. Doumergue, 1913–14
R. Viviani, 1914–15

### RUSSIA
(From the 1st *Duma*)
Count S. Y. Witte, 1905–06
I. L. Goremýkin, 1906
P. A. Stolypin, 1906–11 (ass.)
Count V. N. Kokóvtsev, 1911–14
I. L. Goremýkin, 1914–16

### AUSTRIA
Count F. Beust, 1867
Count A. Auersperg, 1867–70
Count C. Hohenwart, 1870
Count A. Auersperg, 1870–79
Count E. Taaffe, 1879–93
Prince A. Windischgrätz, 1893–95
Count E. Badeni, 1895–97
Baron P. von Gautsch, 1897–98
Count F. Thun, 1898–99
Count M. Clary, 1899–1900
E. von Körber, 1900–04
Baron P. von Gautsch, 1904–06
Baron M. von Beck, 1906–08
Baron R. von Bienerth, 1908–11
Baron P. von Gautsch, 1911
Count K. Stürgkh, 1911–16 (ass.)

### HUNGARY
Count J. Andrássy, 1867–71
K. Tisza, 1875–90
Count J. Szapáry, 1890–92
A. Wekerle, 1892–95
Baron D. Bánffy, 1895–99
K. Széll, 1899–1903
Count C. Khuen-Héderváry, 1903
Count S. Tisza, 1903–05
Baron G. Féjerváry, 1905–06
A. Wekerle, 1906–10
Count C. Khuen-Héderváry, 1910–12
L. Lukács, 1912–13
Count S. Tisza, 1913–18 (ass.)

### SERBIA
*Principal Ministers*
J. Ristić, 1872–73
     ,,   1876–80
General A. Gruić, 1887–91
N. Pašić, 1891–92
General S. Gruić, 1893–94
S. Novaković, 1895–96
N. Pašić, 1903
General S. Gruić, 1903–04
N. Pašić, 1906–10
M. Milovanović, 1911–12
N. Pašić, 1912–19

## FIRST MINISTERS (*continued*)

### ITALY
M. Minghetti, 1873–76
A. Depretis, 1876–78
B. Cairoli, 1878–81
A. Depretis, 1881–87
F. Crispi, 1887–91
Marquis A. di Rudini, 1891–92
G. Giolitti, 1892–93
F. Crispi, 1893–96
Marquis A. di Rudini, 1896–98
L. Pelloux, 1898–1900
G. Saracco, 1900–01
G. Zanardelli, 1901–03
G. Giolitti, 1903–05
A. Fortis, 1905–06
G. Giolitti, 1906–09
S. Sonnino, 1909–10
L. Luzzatti, 1910–11
G. Giolitti, 1911–14
A. Salandra, 1914–16

### JAPAN
Marquis H. Ito, 1885–88
Gen. Prince A. Yamagata, 1889–90
Prince M. Matsukata, 1890–93
Marquis Ito, 1893–96
Prince Matsukata, 1896–98
Marquis Ito, 1898
Marquis S. Okuma, 1898–99
Prince Yamagata, 1899–1900
Marquis Ito, 1900–01
Gen. Prince T. Katsura, 1901–06
Marquis K. Saionji, 1906–08
Prince Katsura, 1908–11
Marquis Saionji, 1911–12
Prince Katsura, 1912–13
Adm. Count G. Yamamoto, 1913–14
Marquis Okuma, 1914–16

## FOREIGN MINISTERS

### GREAT BRITAIN
Earl of Clarendon, 1868–70
Earl Granville, 1870–74
Earl of Derby, 1874–78
Marquis of Salisbury, 1878–80
Earl Granville, 1880–85
Marquis of Salisbury, 1885–86
Earl of Rosebery, 1886
Earl of Iddesleigh, 1886–87
Marquis of Salisbury, 1887–92
Earl of Rosebery, 1892–94
Earl of Kimberley, 1894–95
Marquis of Salisbury, 1895–1900
Marquess of Lansdowne, 1900–05
Sir E. Grey, 1905–16

### FRANCE
(Usually held by First Minister when no name given)
Duc Decazes, 1873–77
W. H. Waddington, 1877–79
L. Gambetta, 1881
L. E. Flourens, 1886–88
R. Goblet, 1888–89
A. F. J. Ribot, 1890–93
G. Hanotaux, 1894–95
,, 1896–98
T. Delcassé, 1898–1905
L. Bourgeois, 1906
S. J. M. Pichon, 1906–11
J. de Selves, 1911–12
C. Jonnart, 1913
S. J. M. Pichon, 1913
G. Doumergue, 1914
T. Delcassé, 1914–15

### GERMANY
H. von Bismarck, 1886–90
Baron A. Marschall von Bieberstein, 1890–97
B. von Bülow, 1897–1900
Baron O. von Richthofen, 1900–06
H. von Tschirschky, 1906–07
Baron W. von Schoen, 1907–10
A. von Kiderlen-Wächter, 1910–12
G. von Jagow, 1913–17

### AUSTRIA-HUNGARY
Count F. Beust, 1866–71
Count J. Andrássy, 1871–79
Baron H. Haymerle, 1879–81
Count G. von Kálnoky, 1881–95
Count A. Goluchowski, 1895–1906
Count A. von Aehrenthal, 1906–12
Count L. von Berchtold, 1912–15

FOREIGN MINISTERS (*continued*)

## SERBIA
(When not held by First Minister)
N. Pašić, 1904–06
M. Milovanovic, 1908–11

## RUSSIA
Prince A. Gorchakóv, 1856–82
N. de Giers, 1882–95
Prince A. Lobánov, 1895–96
Count M. Muraviev, 1897–1900
Count V. N. Lamsdorf, 1900–06
A. P. Izvolsky, 1906–10
S. Sazónov, 1910–16

## ITALY
(Usually held by First Minister when no name given)
Marquis E. Visconti-Venosta, 1869–76
Count L. Corti, 1878
P. S. Mancini, 1881–85
Count N. di Robilant, 1885–87
B. Brin, 1892–93
Baron A. Blanc, 1893–96
Marquis E. Visconti-Venosta, 1896–1901
J. Prinetti, 1901–03
T. Tittoni, 1903–05
Marquis A. di San Giuliano, 1905–06
T. Tittoni, 1906–09
F. Giucciardini, 1909–10
Marquis A. di San Giuliano, 1910–14
S. Sonnino, 1914–19

## UNITED STATES OF AMERICA
*Secretaries of State*
W. H. Seward, 1861–69
H. Fish, 1869–77
W. M. Evarts, 1877–81
F. T. Frelinghuysen, 1881–85
T. F. Bayard, 1885–89
J. G. Blaine, 1889–92
J. W. Foster, 1892–93
W. Q. Gresham, 1893–95
R. Olney, 1895–97
J. Hay, 1898–1905
E. Root, 1905–09
P. C. Knox, 1909–13
W. J. Bryan, 1913–15
R. Lansing, 1915–20

## JAPAN
Count K. Inouye, 1881–88
Marquis S. Okuma, 1888–89
Viscount S. Aoki, 1889–91
Count M. Mutsu, 1892–95
Marquis K. Saionji, 1895–96
Marquis Okuma, 1896–97
Viscount Aoki, 1898–1900
Baron T. Kato, 1900–01
Marquis J. Komura, 1901–06
Count T. Hayashi, 1906–08
Marquis Komura, 1908–11
Viscount Y. Uchida, 1911–12
Baron Kato, 1912–13
Viscount Uchida, 1913–14
Baron Kato, 1914–15

## COLONIAL MINISTERS

### GREAT BRITAIN

Earl Granville, 1868–70
Earl of Kimberley, 1870–74
Earl of Carnarvon, 1874–78
Sir M. Hicks Beach, 1878–80
Earl of Kimberley, 1880–82
Earl of Derby, 1882–85
Sir F. Stanley, 1885–86
Earl Granville, 1886

E. Stanhope, 1886–87
Lord Knutsford, 1887–92
Marquess of Ripon, 1892–95
J. Chamberlain, 1895–1903
A. Lyttelton, 1903–05
(9th) Earl of Elgin, 1905–08
Earl of Crewe, 1908–10
L. Harcourt, 1910–15

## COLONIAL MINISTERS

### IRELAND

*Chief Secretaries for Ireland*
Lord Hartington, 1870–74
Sir M. Hicks Beach, 1874–78
J. Lowther, 1878–80
W. E. Forster, 1880–82
Lord F. Cavendish, 1882 (ass.)
G. O. Trevelyan, 1882–84
H. Campbell-Bannerman, 1884–85
Sir W. Hart Dyke, 1885–86
J. Morley, 1886
Sir M. Hicks Beach, 1886–87
A. J. Balfour, 1887–91
J. Morley, 1892–95
G. W. Balfour, 1895–1900
G. Wyndham, 1900–05
J. Bryce, 1905–07
A. Birrell, 1907–16

### INDIA

*Secretaries of State (in Britain)*
Duke of Argyll, 1868–74
Marquis of Salisbury, 1874–78
Lord Cranbrook, 1878–80
Lord Hartington, 1880–82
Earl of Kimberley, 1882–85
Lord R. Churchill, 1885–86
Earl of Kimberley, 1886
Lord Cross, 1886–92
Earl of Kimberley, 1892–94
Sir H. Fowler, 1894–95
Lord G. Hamilton, 1895–1903
St. John Brodrick, 1903–05
J. (Lord) Morley, 1905–10
Earl of Crewe, 1910–15

### FRANCE
(Separate Ministry, 1894)
T. Delcassé, 1894–95
André Lebon, 1896–98
P. Decrais, 1899–1902
G. Doumergue, 1902–05
R. Milliès-Lacroix, 1906–09
G. Trouillot, 1909–10
A. Messimy, 1911
A. Lebrun, 1911–14
G. Doumergue, 1914–17

### GERMANY
(Separate administration, 1906)
B. von Dernburg, 1906–10
F. von Lindequist, 1910–11
W. H. Solf, 1911–18

# INDEX

In the main, the names of persons have been entered in the form by which the individuals concerned are best known, e.g. *Disraeli*, not *Beaconsfield*; *Hartington*, not *Devonshire*.

*Great Britain* appears as *Britain, Great*, in order that the various British references may be kept together.

The cross-references provided should prevent any confusion or difficulty

937